D1307635

UNIVERSITY OF WINNIPEG
LIBRARY
515 Portage Avenue
Winnipeg, Manitoba R3B 2E9

Ref.
Z
2234
.T7M8
1965

A Critical Bibliography of

GERMAN LITERATURE IN ENGLISH TRANSLATION

1481-1927

By

BAYARD QUINCY MORGAN

Professor of German, Stanford University

SECOND EDITION

Completely Revised and Greatly Augmented

The Scarecrow Press, Inc.

New York and London 1965

COPYRIGHT 1938 BY THE BOARD OF TRUSTEES
OF THE LELAND STANFORD JUNIOR UNIVERSITY

Reprinted 1965 by permission.

L. C. Card No. 65-13549

TO MY WIFE JOHANNA

MY MOST CONSTANT CRITIC

AND

SOMETIME COLLABORATOR

TABLE OF CONTENTS

INTRODUCTION

The present volume is the culmination of studies which have extended over more than twenty years and which have already borne fruit in print ("Bibliography of German Literature in English Translation," University of Wisconsin Studies, 1922). It was in 1916 that the writer, reaching out for new scholarly worlds to conquer, asked Professor A. R. Hohlfeld to suggest some line of investigation which might be consonant with his powers and his predilections. As all scholars who follow such matters know, Professor Hohlfeld had long been deeply interested in the literature of translation as one phase of the general subject of Anglo-German literary relations and under his direction a number of ambitious bibliographical investigations have been undertaken and completed (M. H. Haertel, "German Literature in American Magazines 1846-1880"; S. H. Goodnight, "German Literature in American Magazines Prior to 1846"; Lucretia V. T. Simmons, "English Translations of Goethe's Lyrics Prior to 1850"; Stella M. Hinz, "English Translations of Goethe's Lyrics after 1860"; Lillie V. Hathaway, "German Literature of the Mid-nineteenth Century in England and America as Reflected in the Journals 1840-1914"). Studies tracing the echoes of German literature in British magazines are now approaching completion and still other studies are under way. Mention might also be made, in this connection, of the published investigations of Professor Lawrence M. Price, who has been studying for years the influence of English literature in Germany--upon the suggestion, and partly under the guidance, of Professor Hohlfeld. Knowing my deep interest in the theory and practice of translation (I am the first, I think, to have offered a university course in the subject), Professor Hohlfeld suggested that I undertake a study of the English translations from German literature published in book form, from the beginning of printing down to the present day. Neither of us, I am confident, had any clear conception of the great magnitude of the task involved. It seems doubtful to me now, viewing the weary road that has led to this point, whether I should have thought it possible that a single worker, virtually unaided, could travel it to the end.

The basic character of the bibliography was clearly visualized from the start. It was not to be a mere aggregation of titles, important as such a compilation would certainly be: the critical evaluation of the translations was to be one of the principal features of my work, and the one which I thought might be more widely appreciated than any other. My thought was to assist the scholar, the reader, the book-buyer, and the librarian to make intelligent selections from the mass of published translations. It was my hope that publishers intending to issue inexpensive series of foreign works in translation would find valuable hints in my pages; and I thought it possible that translators would consult them to find out what had not yet been translated into English, or at any rate not adequately. My lists, I am assured, have been diligently consulted by colleagues who conduct college courses in which students are assigned collateral reading in English and for whom it is extremely important to know whether or not a given translation is satisfactory. But aside from such practical considerations, I confess that I was much influenced by a purely theoretical one. It seems to me that there is something anomalous about an uncritical bibliography of any kind, i.e., one which should merely list names or titles without any scrutiny whatever; but the anomaly is even greater in the case of a list of translations. One hardly takes a translation in his hands without wishing to know something of its relation to the original; and yet it is impossible for the average person to obtain such information by himself.

My critical procedure in the present edition follows in general the lines laid down in the first. What I endeavored to ascertain, by an intensive if sometimes very brief examination of each translation for which an original could be found, was (1) if the translator was honestly striving for completeness and accuracy, and (2) how far he succeeded in achieving them. The first point was not infrequently settled by consultation of preface or introduction, in which the translator so often takes his readers into his confidence. There always followed, however, a careful comparison of some portion of the translation with the corresponding passage of the original. Experience showed that such a procedure rarely failed to reveal both the translator's competence and also what I may term his "will to accuracy." If a translator plays fast and loose with his original in the first paragraph, he is likely to do so in the last one; and, conversely, if he has the ability to render a single complex sentence into correct and idiomatic English, he is not likely to lapse into slovenly procedure at any time. An expert musician can tell by the opening chords of a composition whether or not it shows promise; long practice has given me something like a similar facility for apprehending the fundamental quality of a translator. At the same time, I should not wish to assign any absolute value to the judgments rendered here. All grading, as good teachers everywhere are well aware, is not only subjective, and hence liable to error, but also highly responsive to mood, fatigue, and other extraneous factors. In many cases I rendered judgment on the same translation at different times with identical result; but I must in candor confess that sometimes my judgment varied. On the other hand, I not infrequently found myself in disagreement with some critics whose judgments I had accepted for my first edition (in the case of works which I had not had a chance to examine myself), and so I came to the conclusion that errors could occur even when the critic took time for extended study of the translation in question. Some of the critical judgments which I took from others for the first edition (e.g., Baumann's of "Faust") I have retained; many others I have been able to replace by my own, thanks to my long sojourn at the British Museum. I was the more ready to do this in that the examination of the actual books necessitated in making critical evaluations proved to be the most interesting phase of the work--indeed, at times it even had an element of excitement, as when I made some "discovery" or other--and the one which chiefly enlivened the entire undertaking. Then these dead titles and names suddenly came to life and put on flesh and blood; and in the communion with their authors I felt the pulse of humanity.

The system of diacritical marks adopted for the first edition has proved to be both practical and useful, and has been retained in the present edition, with a reversion to the plan which I had originally set up but which the former printer could not follow. The asterisk (*) indicates excellence; it does not mean perfection, which is no more often attained in translation than in other fields of human endeavor, but implies that a reader may safely take a version so marked as a reasonably satisfactory rendering of the original. In many cases a word of comment appended to the bibliographical entry gives the sign a more specific meaning. Occasionally the double asterisk (**) is used to indicate unusually high quality. The section mark (§) is somewhat more negative in character; it says in effect: I have examined this translation and find it neither wholly good nor wholly bad. Expressed in terms of examination grades, it represents the rank between B and C. In a collection of lyrics, such a mark means that you may find a very good or even excellent version here and there but you cannot be sure of doing so consistently, for the bulk of them are in some way or other defective.

The dagger (†) is comparable to the inverted thumb in the ancient Coliseum, and its interpretation leads to a brief consideration of those qualities that constitute merit in a translation. Every work of literary art has two component elements: substance and form. By substance I mean the entire subject matter in its fullest extent, including shades of meaning, connotations, imagery, and the like. The true appreciation of the entire substance of a piece of writing calls for an intimate knowledge of the foreign tongue as well as a thorough acquaintance with the life and customs and literature of the people who speak it. Strangely enough, it is weakness in substance that most often betrays the otherwise skilled translator and that necessitates adverse criticism of such talented men as Bowring, Lytton, and Mangan. Is the modern world growing more modest? Or is it only a passing fashion that dictates the restrictions on translators' license? At all events, it is perhaps not too much to say that Pope's "Iliad" would be unthinkable in our day, both in its inception and its popularity: people would say, if such a work actually found a publisher, "It's a fine poem, but not Homer." -- Cf. my comment on Rossetti's "translation" of Bürger's "Lenore." It is the writer's conviction that nothing but the consciousness of innate genius can justify the translator in altering the substance of his original (except in the way of expurgation, which demands a chapter all its own), and few versions are commended in this book which are known to tamper with the substance of their sources.

On the stylistic side, I am particularly impatient with translators who insist on "improving" their author, at least if he is a writer of real distinction and of individuality. On the other hand, I concede that there may be justification in pruning a verbose original or in reducing bulk to suit a different taste; and I also make a distinction between works of purely literary appeal and those in which an informational purpose is much to the fore. In all cases known to me, I have indicated in my appended comments the extent to which the translation aims to reproduce the original work. The question mark (?) prefixed to a German title indicates that the "translation" bears little or no relation to the supposed original.

That mere dictionary "faithfulness" will not turn the trick, to be sure, is amusingly illustrated by the following choice example from a little work by L. W. Schaufuss on Correggio's "Träumende Magdalena," and evidently translated by a perspiring German with the most literal help of such dictionary as he may have had:

> "The slightly sensual features still impressed upon their charming appearance and admixed to their penance -- combined with the deep excitement of the mind, which mark the aspect of the Magdalene's, generally speaking, bestows to them a surpassing picturesque character, and no master did succeed more perfectly to express the same, as Correggio."

The quality of form is much less tangible, but for that very reason is not seldom caught unconsciously. It includes not only meter, of course, but all those imponderable elements of word choice and sentence arrangement that we conveniently call style. A writer's style can be, for example, ponderous without being heavy, light without being insipid, fluent without being verbose, archaic without being crabbed. It is the translator's highest function to apprehend such qualities in the original and pass them on to the reader of his version. In general, I believe, such a result is best attained by an intelligent fidelity to the outward form of the original work. This opinion is strikingly confirmed by the injunctions written by Count Hermann Keyserling to the translator of his celebrated "Reisetagebuch eines Philosophen" (which I make bold to translate!):

> "I worked for seven long years on my travel-diary, and there is not a word and not a comma in it whose meaning and position have not been carefully considered. No one will pardon the translator who does not achieve his task with the unconditional reverence for his original, and with the absolute devotion to a great cause, that Carlyle showed with respect to Goethe....[Translate] with strict literalness, word for word, and comma for comma.... Under no circumstances whatever put in an 'and' that is not in the original (every 'and' you inserted I have had to strike out); adhere closely to my commas, semicolons, and periods; do not under any circumstances connect sentences which I separated; and remember in all cases that in me you have to do with a severe, dynamic, concentrated essence which will not suffer the slightest dilution or slackening in style.... Consider further that the transfer of a German melody to an English one, which we once discussed orally, can only be understood in this sense, that my exact cadence, my rhythm, my melody should be set to English words, not that anything else should be put in its place."[1]

[1]For the benefit of those who read German readily, I quote the philosopher's own words: "An meinem Reisetagebuch habe ich volle sieben Jahre gearbeitet, und es steht kein Wort und kein Komma darin, dessen Sinn und Ort nicht genau bedacht wären. Niemand wird dem Uebersetzer je verzeihen, der seine Arbeit nicht mit der unbedingten Ehrfurcht vor dem Originaltext und mit der absoluten Hingebung an eine grosse Sache geleistet hätte, welche Carlyle Goethe gegenüber bewies...[Uebersetzen Sie] strikt wörtlich, Wort für Wort, und Komma für Komma...Bringen Sie unter garkeinen Umständen ein 'und' an, das nicht im Originaltext stände (jedes von Ihnen gesetzte 'und' habe ich ausstreichen müssen), halten Sie sich peinlich genau an meine Kommata, Semikolons und Punkte, ziehen Sie unter garkeinen Umständen Sätze zusammen, die ich getrennt habe und bedenken Sie überall, dass Sie es in mir mit einem strengen, dynamischen, konzentrierten Geist

Granted that there is more than a trace of affectation here, and that Keyserling's injunctions cannot safely be followed in toto in all cases (e.g., as to punctuation and "word-for-word" rendering), the basic doctrine is sound and should be taken to heart by every young translator.

The dagger (†), then -- to revert to our diacritical marks -- indicates a gross violation of one of these principles (commonly both), and may be succinctly interpreted as "negligible," or "highly unreliable."

In passing I may remark that there are certain fields in which a high excellence is almost uniformly attained. They are those in which the translator has some other than a purely commercial interest in his work, or is moved by other forces than publication vanity, for instance. Thus I find that the philosophers, in general, have been very competently rendered, of course with variations; that sectarian publications are usually translated with great care and seriousness; that many writings of the socialist leaders have been almost flawlessly done; and that the psychoanalysts and the theosophists, in our own day, have enjoyed similar benefits. In all these cases, to be sure, it was more a question of substance than of style; and Nietzsche, the stylist, has suffered more than some other philosophers in translation; but it is clear to me that we could have better translations if we cared to demand them.

A further distinguishing characteristic of this bibliography, in addition to the critical one, has only gradually emerged in my thinking about it, partly as a result of certain friendly criticisms of the first edition. For the first time, I believe, an entire national literature is here seen through the distorting medium of another language; and the resulting picture, as has been clearly realized by students everywhere, is totally different from that given by the histories of literature or indeed any other critical source. For this reason I have insisted on retaining in the second edition all the material that my chosen field could possibly embrace. This not only applies to separate titles but extends to reissues or reprintings of a given book as an index to its popularity. It has been objected that it is not possible to achieve absolute completeness in this matter and hence that the data given by me are, if not valueless, at least much reduced in importance. In spite of the actual limitations of my lists, which I concede, I still think the principle a correct one, and believe that my listing of all the editions I could trace may come to have some little value in the future. For I conceive of the possibility that at some time there will be studies made of the history of literature from a new angle. Investigators will endeavor to draw a picture of the progress of writing as reflected by the popularity of authors and their works, seeking thus to secure an image of the soul of the people who had read or at least bought these books. A similar consideration seems to me to hold good with respect to this bibliography. Is there no significance in the abnormal popularity of Luise Mühlbach's novels, for instance, in America and not in England? Does not the course of the vogue of Bogatzky's "Golden Treasury," or "Münchhausen's adventures," or the "Swiss family Robinson," as shown by the dates of their

---

zu tun haben, der nicht die leiseste Verdünnung und Entspannung des Styls verträgt...Bedenken Sie weiter, dass die Uebersetzung der deutschen Musik in englische, von der wir damals mündlich sprachen, doch nur so zu verstehen sein kann, dass mein genauer Takt, mein Rhythmus, meine Melòdie nun englisch erklänge, nicht dass irgent etwas anderes an seine Stelle gesetzt werden dürfte."

reissues, suggest interesting speculation with regard to the buyers and potential readers of these works at different periods of time? I cherish the hope that the very completeness of my lists (not fully realized, I am quite aware) will be one of their chief contributions to future investigations in this field. The following pages fairly bristle with suggestions for interesting socio-literary studies, and might well be taken as a starting point for some of them. Certainly I have the distinct feeling that the principle of indiscriminate inclusion was vital in a work which aimed not so much to present conclusions as to furnish source material on which further study could be based. As it stands, then, the book takes its place among those fundamental compilations out of which, in course of time, a complete and accurate picture of Germany as seen through English eyes can be drawn.

This leads me to a consideration of one problem which arose at the very outset of the work, and which continued to clamor for a solution up to the very end--the definition of the term "literature" as used in my title. It seemed proper to interpret it liberally; but the question of the place to draw the line was never satisfactorily answered, and it is not improbable that some titles have been lost beyond recall as a result of a restricted plan which gave way to a more liberal one a week later--for consistency is surely one of the most elusive virtues. Gradually something like a defensible scheme evolved, and "literature" became defined as "humane letters." The book now aims to include the following: essays, travel and description, German history and biography, history of German literature, history of Greece and Rome, history and theory of art and music, aesthetics, philosophy, and personal letters. In general, the idea was to list those books which are most likely to be consulted, not for professional advantage or information, but for their cultural value and the aesthetic pleasure they may afford. For this reason, historical monographs of a highly technical nature were generally excluded, as well as all technical works dealing with the natural sciences--though here it was not always easy to distinguish between technical treatises and popular treatments intended for the lay reader. On other grounds, sermons and other purely edifying literature were not systematically listed, the citations from Luther, for example, being almost exclusively biographical--his table-talk, his letters. An exception, however, was made in favor of hymns, which so often conform to the highest standards of literary art. It should also be said that the principle of exclusion was less rigidly applied with respect to the eighteenth century and earlier periods, where the historical interest of the entry might outweigh other considerations.

A further problem of inclusion or exclusion grew out of the fact that Germans have not always used their mother tongue. The German nun Hrotsuitha composed her plays in Latin; the Prussian king Frederick II wrote his voluminous works in French. On the other hand, a perfectly good German like Holbach became practically a Frenchman and like Frederick wrote in French. Should one include Holbach as racially German? or should one exclude Hrotsuitha and Frederick as linguistically non-German? My decision was to consider Latin or French as without weight if they were the medium of expression of a writer whose environment and racial adherence were German, and my lists contain not a few items translated from those languages. Holbach, on the other hand, I considered to have lost his claim to be regarded as a German author.

The titles contained in the following pages are derived in the main from four great catalogs: (1) British Museum (consulted on the spot for the second edition; see my Preface, and including the special Catalog of Music). (2) Library of Congress (examined for the most part on the spot, and including the so-called Old Catalog--see below--and the special catalog of the Music Division). (3) The American (Publishers') Catalog, including the earlier bibliographies of Roorbach and Kelly. And (4) the English (Publishers') Catalog. For a list of special bibliographies consulted, see List B, p.574 The method of search was a simple if very time-consuming one: I went through each list from beginning to end, stopping at each name that looked German, and examining the titles under it to see if any were translations. In preparing the first edition, I had some help on the BM catalog; for the second edition, my wife read the entire BM catalog; all the rest of this search was done by myself. Such a method has at least three disadvantages: first, it makes the compilation of anonymous works largely a matter of chance; second, it loses sight of MS material almost entirely; and, third, it is open to serious error due to fatigue or wandering attention of the reader. But there is no other method to be pursued, and the disadvantages are in part counteracted, in part unimportant. Anonymous and MS material is rarely of high value, so that its loss could be viewed with resignation. Gaps, on the other hand, had a fair chance of being detected in the process of going over the same ground in another catalog. Special bibliographies did their share in eliminating error and furnishing additional information. I regret in this connection the fact that Charles Evans's monumental bibliography of early Americana has not advanced further toward completion, since the volumes now in print gave me a number of new entries. In general, the field of periodical literature is not covered here, and completeness was attempted only as far as books and pamphlets are concerned. However, I have not hesitated to include translations of entire plays, short stories, and other substantial items, if they came to my attention.

In the preface to my first edition I wrote: "Probably few persons will pick up this volume without a feeling of amazement at the extent of its contents...." I feel in duty bound to caution the student who may casually compare the second edition with the first against the assumption that the surplus of over 4000 entries shown by the former represents so many accessions to the original compilation. While a very large number of new titles have been added, plus a considerable number of later editions of works already listed, a great many of the new numbers are due to a different method of arranging successive issues of the same work. Thus the actual growth of the bibliography is perhaps nearer 50 than 75 per cent -- which is, however, a very substantial figure, after all, and might well justify the preparation of the new edition. Part of the accretion, of course, is due to the publications of the years 1918-1927; another considerable number resulted from the inclusion of certain works not taken into the first edition: e.g., Bogatzky's "Golden Treasury," the "Adventures of Münchhausen," and Caxton's translation of "Reynard the Fox."

It will be of interest to pass in brief review the chronology of my findings, which forms the basis of Chart I p. 8 The earliest translation listed in the first edition was dated 1509; my decision to include Caxton's translation of "Reynard the Fox" (see my note to "Reineke Fuchs," List A) carries us almost thirty years

CHART OF TRANSLATIONS OF GERMAN BOOKS INTO ENGLISH, 1500-1927

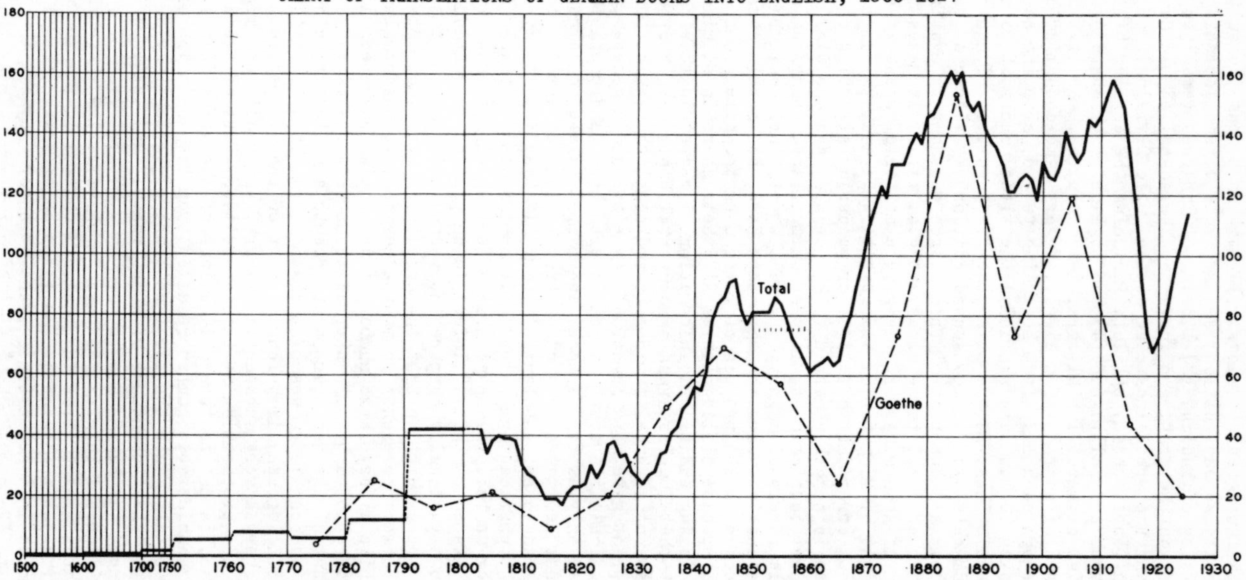

NOTES ON CHART OF TRANSLATIONS OF GERMAN BOOKS INTO ENGLISH, 1500-1927

Data for "Total" are on an annual basis, considerably compressed for the years 1500 to 1750. The total given for any period--i.e., 1501-1600, 1601-1700, 1701-1750, 1751-1760, and up to 1791-1800--has been divided by the number of years involved. From 1801, when annual data became available, five-year moving averages (averages of five-year periods shifting one year at a time) were made to smooth out the extreme annual fluctuations.

Data for "Goethe" are totals for the decade in the center of which each point is plotted. In the original data the last point was a total for the period 1921-1927; this figure was divided by seven and multiplied by ten, making it comparable with preceding data. Leaving the Goethe data as ten-year totals is equivalent to plotting average yearly figures on a scale expanded ten times, and facilitates comparison with the "Total" line.

farther back toward the beginnings of printing, for the famous English version of Reynard's escapades and adventures, which forms the basis for the great majority of all treatments of that beast-epic in English, was printed by William Caxton in 1481. But the real stream of translations, flowing rather thinly to begin with, sets in only with the sixteenth century; and here the earliest item is Barclay's celebrated version in 1509 -- really a very able adaptation -- of Sebastian Brant's "Narrenschiff," in both languages one of the most interesting documents of its day and age. Another translation, done by Thomas Watson and published as a second edition in 1517, may possibly be the same as that noted by Goedeke as having been done from the French in 1507 (I have no bibliographical data for this work). Barclay's translation, by the way, achieved reprints, according to Goedeke, in 1570 and 1590; but I have not seen them. The next earliest publication is Hieronymus Braunschweig's treatise on surgery, in 1525; and I have also included in the present edition the following works by the same author: "The vertuous boke of Distyllacyon...of herbes," published in two different editions in 1527, and the "Homish apothecarye," published in 1561. The pranks of Eulenspiegel begin their march through English lands with two editions of the same translation, probably antedated by BM as 1528 and 1530, after which there is no record of another issue for more than a century. In 1537 there is a theological disputation by one Alexander Alesius, "professor of theology at Leipzig," the first of a great number of writings of similar character. Something like a "best seller" among sixteenth-century translations is "A comparison betweene the Olde learnynge and the Newe" by Urbanus Rhegius, translated by Wyliam Turner, Dean of Wells, and published in 1537, with a reissue in the following year and a corrected and augmented edition ten years later.

The next item in chronological order is by Heinrich Bullinger, who has no less than eleven numbers to his credit, four of them being issues of his discussion of "The Christen state of matrimony, wherein housbandes and wyfes maye lerne to kepe house together with loue" (perhaps no easier to do in that day than at present); these came out in 1541, 1543, and 1552. Of Bullinger's more theological treatises, particular interest attaches to his "Confutation of the Pope's bull...against Elizabeth...queene of England," 1574, also to his "Most necessary and fruitfull Dialogue, betwene the seditious Libertin or rebel Anabaptist (Simon), and the true obedient Christiã (Ioiada)," published in 1551. The first echoes of the German Reformation come into my list in connection with Philipp Melanchthon, whose "Very godly defense...defending the mariage of preistes... sent unto the Kyng of Englond, Henry the aight," was published in 1541. Another communication to King Henry, possibly containing the same matter, appeared in 1547.

Two writings dealing with Luther may also be mentioned: Melanchthon's funeral oration, published in 1546, and his "History of the lyfe and actes of M. Luther," published in 1561. A sort of political manifesto, urging concerted action on the part of Christendom against the Turks, written by T. Bibliander, came out in 1542. The year 1545 brings out the first translation from Agrippa von Nettesheim, a writer who had much more vogue in the seventeenth century than in his own; this is his "Commendation of matrimony." His work "On the vanitie and uncertaintie of artes and sciences" appeared in 1569, with a reissue in 1575, and was retranslated in 1676 to be again reissued in 1694. Two of his other works appealed especially to the seventeenth century, one achieving three, the other four, editions. One was his occult philosophy, first issued in 1651 and then, in a different translation, in 1655 and 1665; the other was his "Glory of women...declaring the excellency and preheminence of Women above Men," which saw four editions from 1652 to 1683, and was, oddly enough, revived once more in a fresh rendering in 1873. Justus Jonas's "True hystorye of the Christen departynge of...D. Martyne Luther," including Melanchthon's oration, came out in 1546. Another writer on matrimony was Wolfgang Meuslin, called Musculus, whose treatise was published in 1548 and reissued in 1550. His "Common places of Christian religion" also went through two editions, 1563 and 1578. Martin Bucer's "Gratulation...unto the churche of England for the restitution of Christes religion" was published in 1549, and his treatise on the distribution of alms in 1557. His death at the stake is narrated in a treatise published in 1562. It is of interest that Bucer's "Judgement...concerning divorce, written to Edward the Sixt," was "Englisht" by John Milton in 1644.

An early German chronicler is Johann Carion, whose "Three bokes of chronicles" were issued in English in 1550, with an appendix, by Johann Funcke of Nuremborough, covering world events from 1532 to 1550. This begins the long and honorable line of German historians whose works have been translated into English. Another pioneer is Sebastian Muenster, who inaugurates in English translation the field of travel, exploration, and geography which evidently had a perennial appeal for English readers; a selection from Muenster's "Cosmography" entitled "A treatyse of the newe India" came out in 1553, and a collection of extracts from that work appeared in 1572 and was reissued in 1574. Myconius's life of Zwingli, another echo of the Reformation on the Continent, appeared in 1561.

The celebrated Bishop of Ratisbon, Albertus Magnus, was not to find a translator until the seventeenth century; but a spurious work assigned to him, "The boke of secretes of Albartus Magnus," evidently a treatise on magic, came out in 1565. Two interesting Latin poems by Thomas Kirchmeyer, called Naogeorgus, were translated by B. Googe and published in 1570, or thereabouts; one is entitled "Spiritual husbandrie," the other is "The popish kingdom or reigne of Antichrist," which was reprinted in 1880. Ludwig Lavater's treatise "Of ghostes and spirites walking by nyght... " was published in 1572 and reissued in 1596. Another traveler found an English public in 1575, when the (Latin) accounts of Hieronymus Turlerus were published as "The traveiler of Jerome Turler." Two years later we have "A Christian confession taken from the last will and testament of Friedrich III," Kurfürst von der Pfalz, called der Fromme. A further oddity is the "Declaration made by the archbishop of Collen [i.e., Gebhard, Truchsess von Waldburg] upon the deede of his marriage," published in 1583.

The year 1592 marks the first appearance in English of the story of Faust -- a narrative which was to prove the most lastingly popular of all the early German "Volksbücher." Possibly the same B. Googe who translated Kirchmeyer's poems also turned his hand to popular science (i.e., magic?) in his translation of a treatise by one Anton Bertholdus on "The wonderful and strange effect of a new Terra Sigillata lately found out in Germanie," published in 1587. New to this edition is "A breife and learned treatise...of the Antichrist" by G: Sohn, "professor at Heidelberg," published in 1592.

The celebrated Paracelsus, from whose works the seventeenth century witnessed a considerable number of English translations, barely comes in at the end of this period with a couple of items. The entertaining story of "Fortunatus," which bulks large among the old English chapbooks, makes its first appearance in English dress in Thomas Dekker's comedy of "Olde Fortunatus" (see A161) in the year 1600. The same year very probably saw another odd anonymous publication, entitled "The vertuous Scholehous of ungracious women (see A513).

The seventeenth century furnishes us in the new edition with nearly twice as many entries as the sixteenth (108 as against 50), some of which merely continue names or works which we have already encountered. Thus I have versions of "Faust" (11), "Fortunatus" (4), "Reineke Fuchs" (11), and additional translations from Agrippa von Nettesheim (9) and Paracelsus (9), whose work was clearly regarded in the light rather of magic than of science. We may take a somewhat similar view of the translations (5) from Basilius Valentinus, who sought to find the "philosopher's stone." To the speculative tendency of the seventeenth century the mystical works of Jakob Boehme evidently appealed strongly, for we have no less than 25 items under his name in the space of about fifty years. Of Albertus Magnus there are three genuine and two spurious works in this century. The excitement of travel is vicariously afforded by the writings of Martin Baumgarten, Adam Brand, Bernhard von Breydenbach, Hermann Kirchner, Johann von Mandelslo, Adam Olearius, Leonhard Rauwolff, and Johannes Scheffer. Alchemy and magic are further represented by Johann Andreae, with his "Hermetick romance, or the chymical wedding," and by Johann Glauber -- whose name is incidentally used as cover for a sharply satirical attack upon the whole field of alchemy (see #2336). Religious and mystic speculation is found in the writings of Johann Gerhard, Philipp Nicolai ("Prophesie of Doomesday"), and G. Pictorius ("The nature of spirits"). Natural "science" of a popular character is represented by Konrad von Gesner's "Historie of foure-footed beastes;" a truly delightful work. Contemporary history of a kind figures in "Lachrymae Germaniae" (A202), in Georg Weckherlin's description of the "Triumphall shewes set forth lately at Stutgart," 1616, and in "The relation of the death of (Wallenstein)," 1634. Additional items of more or less interest are a commemorative oration by Henricus Alting; the "Living librarie" of Philipp Camerarius, which had two editions; Friedrich Dedekind's "Grobianus," tr. in 1605 as "The schoole of slovenrie, or Cato turned wrong side out," and over a hundred years later as "Grobianus, or the compleat booby"; two letters from the Great Elector in the interest of political affairs; the first English edition of Martin Luther's "Table-talk," a really admirable rendering, which came into existence in an almost miraculous manner; and a "Goodly disputacyon" by Hans Sachs, who by the way has found very little echo in English-speaking countries until recently. At the end of the century there are three translations from Samuel Pufendorf, one of the first important writers on what we should now call political science.

The first three decades of the eighteenth century show no advance over the seventeenth: they furnish only 30 entries in all, or somewhat less, on the average, than the previous century; nor is this surprising, for there was little in the German literature of that time that was likely to appeal to English readers. Nine of the 30 entries are due to Pufendorf and two to Leibniz, while some of the others derive from reissues of "Eulenspiegel," "Faust," and "Reineke Fuchs." Only with the fourth decade does the tide set in more strongly: we have 23 entries between 1730 and 1741, and 42 in the following decade. After that the general course of translation can be followed in Chart I, on which I comment below. Up to 1750 there is little of significance. There are new editions of "Faust," "Fortunatus," and "Reineke Fuchs," and the names of Baumgarten, Dedekind, Leibniz, Mandelslo, Pufendorf, and Rauwolff recur. German hymnology begins to loom up, with 9 entries before 1750. New in this edition is the name of Baron von Poellnitz, whose memoirs give us 13 numbers in this period -- they mark the beginning of the scandal-mongering which the 18th century loved. Not far removed from this field are the Memoirs of Marie Countess Königsmarck, which also come in here. The name of Francis Baron Trenck reminds us of that more celebrated personage whose history will come to our attention in the next half-century. Frederick II, King of Prussia, also makes his first very modest appearance in this period. Other names which I need not dwell upon, but which may be mentioned for completeness' sake, are: August Francke, Peter Kolb, Lorenz Lange, Johann Mascov, J. J. Rambach, Philipp von Reck, Philipp Stralenberg, and Zacharias Wagener. Two oddities, finally, may be noted as belonging to the fifth decade of the century: an anonymous pamphlet called "The groans of Germany" (A202), which ran through six editions in the year 1741 and did not appear again; and a curious little work by "Baron Huffumbourghausen," called "The congress of the beasts" (#4626), satirizing the congress at Aix-la-Chapelle, which also had six editions (counting two American reprints) in 1748.

With the year 1751 we enter upon the pre-classical period of German literature, which goes over into the classical period before the eighth decade is over. The first translation from Gellert comes in 1752, and Rabener's "Satirical letters" appear in 1757, while Bodmer's "Noah" is translated in 1767, Gessner's "Death of Abel" in 1761, his "Pastorals" ("Idyllen") in 1762, Klopstock's "Messiah" in 1763, also his "Death of Adam," Lavater's "Secret journal of a self-observer" in 1770, Lessing's "Laokoön" as early as 1767 (according to Goedeke), Wieland's "Trial of Abraham" in 1764, and Winckelmann's "Reflections on Greek art" in 1765-66. Of other names which bulk somewhat large in these two decades, we might mention that of Bogatzky, with his enormously popular "Golden treasury," also of course Frederick the Great, who remains in the foreground for four decades, and never entirely fades out of our picture (assuming that the ascription to him of the "Matinées royales," see #1996, is correct). The first recorded translation from Goethe is that of "Werther" in 1779. Haller's "Usong" comes out in 1772, the first translation from J: G: Zimmermann, the author of the once passionately admired work on "Solitude," in the same year. The latter work is not issued in English until 1791. The next decade witnesses the first translation from Herder, who remains rather a stepchild in this field; it is his "Tribute to the memory of Ulrich von Hutten," falsely ascribed to Goethe, and published in 1789. Lavater's popular "Aphorisms on man" also appear for the first time in this decade, in 1788. Another work of immense vogue makes its first English appearance at this time: "Munchausen's adventures," first published in 1786. Still another favorite is the autobiography of Frederick Baron Trenck, the German Casanova, which first appeared in 1788. Important new names which appear for the first time in the last decade of the eighteenth century are Gf. August Bürger, whose "Lenore" vies with Schiller's "Lied von der Glocke" as one of the most frequently translated poems (as far as English is concerned) in German literature; Iffland and Kotzebue, once popular dramatists, who took not only their own country but also England by storm; Immanuel Kant; August Lafontaine, the favorite novelist of his day; Friedrich von Schiller; and Heinrich Zschokke, another widely read romancer.

Further analysis of this kind is rendered superfluous by Chart II, which shows at a glance the vogue of a large number of German authors from 1751 down to the present. The method of selecting the data for this chart was a purely empiric one: the compiler merely noted the names of those authors who had at least five items in each of at least two decades. In making this tabulation, each volume of a given work was counted as a unit, and if a number of editions appeared in the same year or decade (e.g., Kotzebue's "Spanier in Peru" in Sheridan's version), each edition was counted as a unit.

It may be of interest to append here the total figures distributed in this chart, in order to see how individual writers compare in the number of publications devoted to them; students with a penchant for statistics may wish to compare these findings with the tabulation given in my prefatory note to List C, where of course the basis for the computation is a totally different one. In both cases, however, Goethe and Schiller head the line, and Goethe so far outstrips the rest as almost to be in a class by himself. I give the first fifty names from Chart II: Goethe (770), Schiller (377), Grimms Märchen (308), Wagner (281), Kotzebue (255), Wyss (181), Heine (144), Fouqué (135), Schmid (131), Muehlbach (121), Humboldt (108), Ebers (106), Werner (101), Zschokke (94), Lessing (90), Spyri (83), Gessner (81), Fz. Hoffmann (78), Nietzsche (75), Marlitt (71), Bogatzky (70), Muenchhausen (69), Gerstaecker (66), Kant (66), Lafontaine (66), Nieritz (65), Steiner (63), Auerbach (56), Schopenhauer (55), Hauptmann (54), Luther (51), Richter (49), Zimmermann (49), Klopstock (48), Marx (48), Friedrich II (46), Hauff (46), Heyse (45), Sudermann (45), Wieland (45), Barth (44), Schnitzler (44), Heimburg (43), Niebuhr (43), Freytag (42), E.T.A. Hoffmann (40), Buerger (39), Mommsen (39), and Trenck (38).

In the survey of the earlier periods of my total range which I gave above, the starting point was the publication date of the particular work, the tacit assumption always being that the translation followed fairly closely on the original. While this mostly holds true it is after 1800, to be observed less regularly with respect to earlier centuries, and does not apply at all, of course, to the ages that precede the invention of printing. Consequently I felt moved to look into the appearance in my lists of literary figures who lived prior to the fifteenth century, and ultimately I set up the following rather interesting little table. Column A enumerates those persons who have already been cited in the chronological analysis; column B includes authors who appear only in "Collections," whether in List C or elsewhere; column C embraces only hymn writers, as a special group that might have been included with B; and column D tabulates authors (and some works) that have been found worthy of separate or extended publication in the nineteenth or twentieth century. I shall comment on these names below. The rather surprising number of names in the twelfth and thirteenth centuries is due, of course, to the fact that most of the _Minnesingers_ are represented in the various collections devoted to the

CHART II

Name From / To	1751 1760	1761 1770	1771 1780	1781 1790	1791 1800	1801 1810	1811 1820	1821 1830	1831 1840	1841 1850	1851 1860	1861 1870	1871 1880	1881 1890	1891 1900	1901 1910	1911 1920	1921 1927
Auerbach, Bd.										5	5	18	23	10	5	5	3	
Barth, C. G.									12	6	12	8	8					
Baur, W.												9	5					
Bogatzky, K:					5	6	5				11	11	10	7	3	5	5	1
Buerger, G. A.					11	3	1	1	1	4	3	6	6	1	1	1		
Busch, W:												1	18	4	1	2	1	
Campe, J. H.				9	12	2	5	7			1							
Carmen, Sylva														5	6	4	7	
Chamisso, Adt. v.								3	1	6	1	2	4	3	4	3	3	2
Curtius, E.												6	10		5			
Ebers, G:												2	17	43	24	4	16	
Eckstein, E.													1	11	4	4		
Eucken, Rd.												1	1			5	16	5
Fichte, I. H.										10	2	7	1	5	1	1		2
Fouqué, de La M.							3	13	1	25	8	8	17	24	10	18	7	1
Freytag, G.											8	7	6	10	6	2	3	
Freud, S.																2	18	10
Friedrich II	9	8	3	17	2		1	1				1			1	1	1	1
Froebel, F.											1		1	8	3	5	1	
Gerstaecker, F:										2	23	11	21	4	2	1	2	
Gessner, S.		12	3	3	13	22	11	3	1	2	1			1				
Goethe			4	25	16	21	9	20	49	69	57	24	73	153	73	119	44	14
Grimm								3	1	4	8	21	33	29	33	77	61	38
Hackländer, F:										1	9	1	6	5	2			
Hahn-Hahn, Ida										10	4	3	3		2	1	1	
Hauff, W:									3	5	2	3	4	12	6	6	3	2
Hauptmann, G.															8	11	27	8
Heeren, A.								6	5	9								

CHART II (Continued)

Name	From To	1751 1760	1761 1770	1771 1780	1781 1790	1791 1800	1801 1810	1811 1820	1821 1830	1831 1840	1841 1850	1851 1860	1861 1870	1871 1880	1881 1890	1891 1900	1901 1910	1911 1920	1921 1927
Heimburg, W.														2	20	21			
Heine, H:										1		4	9	12	21	34	35	19	9
Heyse, Pl.												1	6	5	18	8	6	1	
Hillern, W. v.													1	14	8	2	1	1	
Hoffmann, E.									3		1	4		4	15	3	5	3	2
Hoffmann, Fz.												3	25	27	18		3		2
Hoffmann, H.											1	3		2	1	5	9	3	2
Humboldt, A. v.								28	4	3	27	16	2	22	4	2			
Janssen, J:s.																17			
Jung-Stilling, H:								1		3	6								
Kant, I.						6		2		4	2	1	1	5	13	12	8	11	3
Klopstock, F.			7		1	1	12	15	8	1	2		1						
Kohl, J. G.											11	2	4	7	3	1			
Kotzebue, A. v.						119	77	18	16	7	8	2	2	2	1		3		
Kugler, F.											4	5	2						
Lafontaine, A.						11	45	10											
Lavater, K.			2		7	9	2		1	2	2			1	1				
Lessing, G. E.			1	1	4	4	6		2	2	2	5	9	13	8	15	7	8	3
Lotze, Hm.															16	6			
Luebke, W.												1	3	9	2		2		1
Luther, M.						1		2	2	3	7	6	3	2	10	4	4	6	1
Marlitt, E.													6	24	26	10	3	2	
Marx, K:											3				9	8	13	6	9
Moltke, H.														2	2	12		1	
Mommsen, Td.												1	12		5	1	18	2	
Moser, G.														4	17	5	1		1
Muehlbach, L.												2	35	3	11	46		22	
Muenchhausen					6	6	6	3	5	1	2	2	6	9	5	6	6	2	5

CHART II (Continued)

Name	From	1751	1761	1771	1781	1791	1801	1811	1821	1831	1841	1851	1861	1871	1881	1891	1901	1911	1921
	To	1760	1770	1780	1790	1800	1810	1820	1830	1840	1850	1860	1870	1880	1890	1900	1910	1920	1927
Musaeus, J.						2	6		4		5	1	7	1		1			
Niebuhr, B.										3	19	14	1	3		1	2		
Nieritz, G.											2	14	12	16	12	7	2		
Nietzsche, F:																2	28	14	31
Nordau, M.															2	20	7	2	2
Pfeiffer, Ida												20	5	1		1			
Pueckler-M.										7	5								
Richter, J. P.										1	13	4	13	3	10	2	2	1	
Schiller, F.						35	12	4	29	40	69	35	20	32	41	24	25	11	
Schlegels								4		4	12	3	2	3	9		1		
Schmid, C.									1	7	34	24	16	22	11	7	6	3	
Schnitzler, A.																	6	23	15
Schopenhauer, A.											2	1		1	5	22	12	6	6
Schubin, O.															4	11	2		
Sealsfield, C.									1	1	17	6		1					
Spielhagen, F:													4	9	9	1	2	1	
Spillmann, Js.															1	8	8	7	2
Spyri, J.															13	1	10	19	40
Steiner, Rd.																	5	20	38
Strauss, D. F.											9	3	4	8	2	3	1		
Sudermann, H.															1	7	19	14	4
Trenck, F:					6	15	3	2	1	1	1	4		1	3				1
Ueberweg, F:														7		2			
Wagner, R:												3	1	34	36	57	68	65	17
Werner, E.														31	43	24	2	1	
Wieland, C. M.		1	9	1	11	7	1	5	1	1		2					1		
Wildermuth, O.													8	12					
Wyss								4	2		7	7	15	36	22	26	27	20	15
Zell, F.														5	25		2		
Zimmermann, J. G.				2		22	15	6	4		1	1		1					
Zschokke, H:						1	13	3	3	7	23	11	11	6	12	1	1	2	

early period (cf. C27, C310, C416, C427, C532). Anonymous works of the medieval period which have been reproduced either wholly or in part in modern times, such as "Gudrun," "die Klage," "Nibelungenlied," etc., have been listed in column D, and each is assigned to the century which would correspond to the probable dates of its author.

TABLE OF EARLY GERMAN WRITERS

Born before	A	B	C	D	Totals
700		1		1	2
800		2		2	4
900				3	3
1000				1	1
1100		4			4
1200		36		8	44
1300	1	46	1	8	56
1400		5	1		6
1500	11	1	10	8	30
1600	21	9	32	7	69
Totals	33	104	44	38	219

Column D, of course, interests us most: here are 38 writers of an earlier day who have been "discovered," so to speak, in our age and once more brought to public attention. In a good many cases, to be sure, it is not a predominantly literary interest which has brought about such revivals; but I think it may fairly be said that in the large majority of the cases their appeal is not solely due to their subject matter (what the Germans would call "stoffliches Interesse") but derives at least in part from some sort of literary merit. The names fall rather naturally into four main categories, with one homeless waif left over: Tritheim's "Book of secret things." The writings of early travelers: Megiser, Schweinichen, B. Springer, Hans Staden, L. v. Wedel, were doubtless brought out in response to antiquarian and historical values attaching to them, and something similar might be said of the following, who can be regarded as furnishing in the main historical source material: Berlichingen's autobiography (A214; Goethe's "Götz" was very likely a motivating force), Dürer's journals and other writings (interest in a great personality enters in here), Ebo's and Herbord's lives of Otto of Pomerania, Eginhardus's and Notker's lives of Charlemagne (the figure of Charlemagne is of course the drawing card in these cases), Joannes de Hildesheim's "Three kings of Cologne" (historical and literary antiquarianism are both involved), Thomas Platter's autobiography (combines religious interest with the personal touch), and B. Sastrow's "Memoirs," which throw light on the Germany of Luther's day. It is primarily on religious grounds that the next group comes to be translated and published for modern readers, though literary values are by no means lacking, and antiquarian historical interests also are served by numbers of them: we have early mystics and ecstatics -- such as Eckhart and Tauler, Mechtild and Gertrud von Hellfde and Mechtild von Magdeburg -- the earliest account of a holy man in Germany, Willibald's life of St. Boniface, poets of religious inspiration, Heinrich von Meissem ("Frauenlob") and Otfried von Weissenburg, and three prophets of the Reformation -- Wessel Gansfort, Martin Luther, and Ulrich Zwingli. Almost at the end of our self-chosen period comes J. Drexel with his "Considerations on eternity." Lastly I cite a group in which literary interest (sometimes with a historical or antiquarian slant) is clearly predominant: "Hildebrandslied" and "Ludwigslied," "Nibelungenlied" and "Klage" belong here, and Pfaffe Lamprecht's "Alexander," the celebrated epics of Gottfried von Strassburg, and Hartmann von Aue, and Wolfram von Eschenbach, the lyrics and aphoristic poems of Walther von der Vogelweide, the Latin dramas of the nun Hrotsuitha, and, as a final literary curiosity, Jakob Ayrer's "Comedy of the beautiful Sidea."

The relative hiatus in translations from the middle period of the nineteenth century, involving such names as Fontane, Grillparzer, Hebbel, Keller, Ludwig, C. F. Meyer, and Storm, and paralleled to a certain extent by the fact that Goethe's death in 1832 was taken as terminal point for a number of the older histories of German literature, was commented on in my first edition and remains similarly obvious in the present one. The tide of translation continued to swell through those years, as my graph shows, but a good deal of its bulk was supplied by mediocre writers or by works outside the field of pure literature. When the naturalistic movement set in on German soil, translations again began to reflect both contemporary interest and literary value, and this trend continues in the main down to the present day. There are few names which are highly regarded in Germany today that do not appear in my lists; and I have the impression that our age will not repeat the passion for popular but essentially ephemeral novels which accounts for the extraordinary vogue of such writers as Ebers, Heimburg, Marlitt, Mühlbach, and Werner -- to name only those numerically most outstanding.

It may be of interest to note the names which occur most frequently in the postwar lists of translations: Freud (the entire psychoanalytical school enjoys great popularity just now); Goethe (reduced in vogue but still alive as a literary figure, whereas I have not found a single new item or reissue from Schiller in the years 1921-1927); "Grimms Märchen" (their hold seems unshakable); Hauptmann (still to the fore, although the bulk of his important work had been translated before the War); Heine (his popularity apparently not greatly reduced); Hofmannsthal (largely through his operatic texts); Kautsky and Marx (socialistic discussion is of course much in evidence); T: Mann; Nietzsche (the fascination of his much-controverted philosophy strikingly evidenced in the continued publication of his writings in English); Schnitzler (the Viennese cynic and exponent of sex psychology allures even those whom he horrifies); Spyri (the authoress of "Heidi" has been "discovered" as a children's classic and enjoys a popularity similar to that of Barth, Franz Hoffmann, and Nieritz in the nineteenth century); Steiner (the zeal of the sectarian is reflected in the English sale of his works); Wagner (while German opera holds the field Wagner cannot be lost to sight); Wassermann (his ultimate rating may be in dispute, but there can be no doubt of his immediate importance); Werfel (certainly not a "popular" writer, his prominence in my list seems to me quite significant); Wyss (the "Swiss family Robinson" has also become a juvenile classic); Zweig (suggesting somewhat the same comment as in the case of Werfel).

The general trend of translations from the German during the nineteenth and the twentieth centuries is graphically displayed in Chart I, which not only shows, as in my first edition, the cumulative figure for each decade but also enables the interested reader to follow the progress from 1800 to 1927 by single years. I have also prefixed to the decade-graph a line which shows the enormous advance in the number of translations after 1750. Analyzing the nineteenth century by years, we note the peaks in 1845, 1882 and 1884, 1891, 1902, and 1910; these peaks fall in with those of the decade-graph and indicate the likelihood that an explanation for this greater intensity of publication at certain times might be found in general political or social conditions.

Generalization on such matters is always hazardous, and the following suggestions are thrown out for what they may be worth: As for the peak at the end of the eighteenth century, which still holds over into the year 1801, it was due to a variety of causes. There was a marked interest in German literature, partly owing to the connections between English romanticism and German Storm and Stress, partly to dawning recognition of the greatness of Goethe and Schiller; Benjamin Thompson in his German Theatre bears witness to British concern with German drama; and it is not impossible that we have here one result of England's rejection of the French Revolution, which might have encouraged an interest in German life and letters. The largest single factor in this peak, of course, is the extraordinary vogue of Kotzebue.

The sudden leap from the thirties to the forties of the nineteenth century suggests a number of considerations. On the one hand, we note a marked slump in the first two decades of the nineteenth century, which perhaps reflects the economic depression that followed the Napoleonic wars, coupled with some suspicion of German literature as "revolutionary." The subsequent rise may be partly due to the economic recovery and the expansive tendency of the new industrial epoch. Perhaps more important is the new wave of interest in German literature, promoted in England by Carlyle and in America by Emerson and the Transcendentalists. The factors affecting the American situation are carefully studied by Goodnight (B10), who shows that German letters and philosophy enjoyed a marked popularity in this country around 1840, and, what is possibly even more important, were quite as violently attacked in some quarters as they were zealously praised in others.

The peak in the 'eighties almost surely resulted from the phenomenal rise of united Germany to the rank of a great world power, and the consequent focusing of the eyes of the world on her affairs. Here enters in also the insatiable appetite of the American public for narrative literature: witness the vogue of Auerbach, Ebers, Fouqué, Gerstäcker, Hackländer, Hauff, Heimburg, Heyse, Marlitt, Mühlbach, Werner, Zschokke, not to mention such writers as Barth, Franz Hoffmann, Nieritz, and Schmid, or those juvenile favorites, Grimms' fairy tales and the "Swiss family Robinson." Note that interest in Goethe reached its peak in this period, if these figures are a valid measure of it, and shows a downward tendency since then. It may be remarked in this connection that the translations from Goethe -- multiplied by ten for purposes of comparison and represented on Chart I by the dotted line -- follow the main line decade by decade, with only one exception, the final decade of the eighteenth century. Thus Goethe appears to be something like a barometer for the whole field of German literature in translation.

The decline which set in after 1890 may reflect the growing political tension which was to lead eventually to war. It may also be said that the publication activity of the two previous decades had probably been somewhat abnormal, so that a reaction was almost certain to occur. The rise from 1901-1910, as compared with the preceding decade, was doubtless due in part to interest in Germany's younger and promising writers, perhaps also to determined fostering of friendly relations between Germany and the United States. Before the next decade ended, the war had involved not only the British Empire but also the American republic, so that it is impossible to tell whether the upward trend of the years 1901-1910 would have continued or not. Even now the figures are not entirely self-explanatory. The year-line shows that 1919 marked the bottom of the downward sweep, reaching a figure which we have to go back to the 'thirties to equal, after which the recovery is fairly steady if not very rapid. Should that trend continue -- and there are indications that it is doing so -- then the figure for 1921-1930 forecasts a return to the average level of the half-century preceding the World War, with a possibility that the next following decade will carry the line still higher.

In closing, I wish to reiterate the hope expressed in my first edition that this volume not only may have its own intrinsic value but may stimulate the activity of others along cognate lines: to prepare careful critical bibliographies of special areas in the general field of translation, to fill gaps in the translation literature by making new and acceptable versions of hitherto untranslated or badly translated works, and to aid the literary historian in carrying out studies in comparative literature. If it should also encourage publishers to issue, and readers and librarians to purchase, none but meritorious translations, it will have gone far to justify itself.

MAIN LIST

MAIN LIST

EXPLANATORY NOTE. In the main, the practice of the LC has been followed in these lists, and it was my aim to give pages and formats wherever they were accessible; during my last extended stay at the British Museum I measured hundreds of books with a centimeter rule in order to increase the accuracy of my data. (However, I did not carry this out in the case of books which I had already seen on previous flying visits to the BM, so that complete consistency was not attained in this respect.) It is to be noted that each of the four main lists referred to in the Introduction has its own system of giving the format -- and one of them differs in giving the paging -- of a book. The LC measures the height of the page in centimeters, adding the width if it is at all unusual. The BM and EC (in earlier periods) employ a series of Latin abbreviations -- fol., 4to, 8vo, 16mo, 18mo, 24mo, 32mo, 64mo -- sometimes adding a further qualification, as Ryl. (royal) 8vo, sq. (square) 12 mo, obl. (oblong) 4to, sm. (small) 4to, and the like. These terms originally signified the number of folds made in a standard sheet of paper to secure the page used in a particular book, but are now more commonly read as indicating the approximate size of the volume; this has led to some confusion, and it not infrequently happens that the same book is given by BM as 8vo and by EC as 12mo and vice versa. (For this reason I advocate the adoption of LC practice.) In recent issues, EC has taken to giving, besides the conventional 8vo or 12mo, the size of the page in inches; I have taken these figures with regard to recent books which I have not seen. The AC, which in earlier issues used the conventional abbreviations, subsequently adopted its own system, whereby the book sizes are designated by a series of letters: D, O, T, etc. I have perforce taken these symbols when AC was my only source of information. As to paging, LC and AC (now) give preface or introduction in small Roman figures, whereas EC adds such a figure to that of the Arabic paging of the book; this has frequently been a considerable disadvantage to me, as it made it impossible to identify with certainty a given edition. I must also plead guilty to inconsistency with respect to paging: In my first edition, I ignored prefaces, and gave merely the Arabic figures; in preparing my second edition, realizing that such figures are often quite valuable and in some cases indispensable, I began to put them in. But since I did not make this decision until part of the material had been assembled it was no longer possible to carry the scheme through without gaps. My failure to list a preface in a particular case is therefore not absolute proof that the book has none. On the other hand, I hope to earn the gratitude of co-workers for supplying the publisher and paging in the cases of hundreds of books listed in the BM catalog without specification of either one. In the cases of works which appeared in many editions, e.g., Goethe's "Werther," Gessner's "Death of Abel," etc., I have given data also regarding illustrations, comparative paging, and the like which may facilitate the identification of editions in other libraries. With regard to the dating of books, there are certain discrepancies which can probably not be avoided. One type of divergence grows out of the practice of announcing publication in advance of the actual appearance of the book; this leads to the listing of a certain book for 1848, for instance, although it did not actually come into the market until 1849 and bears that date on the title page. More perplexing to me were a number of cases in which the EC lists a certain book as of 1849 let us say, whereas the copy in BM is dated 1848; I have found no explanation of this. In general, I have assumed identity in such cases, usually indicating the divergence in a note. In the listing of undated books carried in earlier issues of the AC (Roorbach and Kelly), I have adopted a different plan in the new edition: instead of referring to the particular volume of AC, I have given the date-range, which is usually not very great; the information thus afforded for the first period, 1820-1852, is, however, not at all satisfactory, and the best I could do was to state that the book must have come out "before 1852."

The use of serial numbers in the following lists is a purely practical device, indispensable in making up the index of translators, as also in the cross-referencing which I have carried out rather extensively. Nowhere has the fallibility of the human mind been more painfully impressed upon me than in my desperate but vain struggles to keep the sequence of these numbers straight; here, as in the first edition, I have been repeatedly forced to have recourse to the device of appended letters, since the correction of a slip in any other way would have involved an inordinate amount of renumbering, with risk of probable errors of a different kind.

A special note is in order with regard to LCO. In the spring of 1917, when I did the bulk of my work on the first edition at the LC, there were still upwards of 200,000 handwritten cards in the so-called Old Catalog, representing volumes that had not yet been recatalogued and so did not appear among the printed cards. Many of these cards, however, stood for books that had been lost in the meantime and that therefore never will appear in the printed catalog. To a considerable extent this still held true in 1927, when I again spent several weeks in the LC; such titles bear the designation LCO.

The following library and catalog abbreviations are used, indicating in most cases that I obtained my information directly from and in that library: ABP, American Books in Print (1912, in some cases 1876); AC, American (Publishers') Catalog; BM, British Museum (refers to the catalog there), BMM, Music Catalog of the British Museum; BPL, Boston Public Library; CU, Columbia University Library; EC, English (Publishers') Catalog, including earlier issues back to 1800; HCL, Harvard College Library; LC, Library of Congress, LCO, see above, LCM, Music Division of the Library of Congress; NL, Newberry Library (not visited); NY, New York Public Library; SU, Stanford University, UCal, University of California (not visited); UW, University of Wisconsin. In listing some references from Evans (B6a) I have taken over his notation as to where the book can be found but have given this information in a note. If my only source of information is a bibliography (see list B, page 574), then the reference is given thus: (B6a). In the same way I have handled information gleaned from LC cards, which sometimes say, for example, "first

[1]At the very end of this study, after the revised MS had been typed, I stumbled quite by accident upon a special Appendix to the EC for 1835-1862 -- English books printed on the Continent. It is the only volume of the EC, I believe, which contains such a supplement. From it I gleaned several new titles and a considerable number of new editions.

edition 1876." In a few instances I bought some of the Little Blue Books (Haldeman-Julius) to get the detail on them; such entries are followed by: (BQM). In the new edition I have always assigned a book to both LC and BM if I was certain of its being housed there; but since I have not visited the LC since my work at the BM was done, the absence of the LC notation after a book is not definite proof that LC does not have it.

Other abbreviations frequently used are:

abr., abridged
ad., adapted, adaptation
ca., circa
corr., corrected
d., died
ed., edition, edited
ff., folios (used in case of older books or unpaged modern books)
fl., flourished
front., frontispiece
il., illustrated, illustration(s)
l., leave(s)
libr., libretto
L., London
n.d., no date
n.i., no imprint
p., pages
pl., plate(s)
port., portrait
pt., part
rev., revised
s.sh., single sheet
sel., selected, selection
seq., and following page(s)
t.p., title page
tr., translated by, translation, translator
tw., typewritten
unb., unbound
unp., unpaged
v., volume(s)

The symbol do. (ditto) normally signifies identity of the German original, while "same" refers to the translation, or even, if no other information is given, to the edition, with publisher, paging, etc. In a number of instances, however, do. refers to the translator or editor just named, and in other cases to the identity of German and English title. In listing the numbers of books given in List C which contain selections from a given author, I have starred those which contain a considerable amount of the writer's work, usually setting the line at 10 poems (or pages), but sometimes in special cases going below that figure.

Abbreviations of German given names are listed below; for abbreviations of English given names see the explanatory note to the index of translators, page 631

ABBREVIATIONS OF GIVEN NAMES

The following abbreviations refer only to German given names; as far as possible, those of women's names were made to end in a vowel. For abbreviations of English given names, see the introductory note to the index of translators, p.631

A:	August	Bms.	Bartholomäus	Ech.	Emerich
A:e	Auguste	Bn.	Benedikt	Ed.	Edmund
A:n	Augustin	Bna.	Bettina	Edme.	Erdmuthe
Ab.	Albert	Bne.	Benedikte	Eg.	Eugen
Abh.	Abraham	Bp.	Baptist	Ege.	Eugenie
Abr.	Albrecht	Bpa.	Baptista	Egs.	Eligius
Acs.	Achatius	Br.	Bruno	Ehd.	Ehrhard
Ad.	Adolf	Bs.	Basilius	Ehe.	Ehrengarte
Ade.	Adelheid	Bta.	Bertha	Ehf.	Ehrenfried
Adle.	Adeline	Bte.	Babette	El.	Emil
Adn.	Adrian	Bts.	Bombastus	Ela.	Elena
Ads.	Amandus			Ele.	Elise
Adt.	Adelbert	C:	Carl	Eli.	Elisabeth
Af.	Alfred	C:e	Caroline	Elre.	Eleonore
Ag.	Agnes	Ca.	Clara	Els.	Elias
Als.	Aloys	Cb.	Christlieb	Em.	Emanuel
Am.	Adam	Cd.	Conrad	Eme.	Emilie
Ama.	Amalia	Cde.	Clotilde	En.	Engelbert
Amb.	Ambrosius	Ce.	Claire	Ep.	Ephraim
Amds.	Amadeus	Cf.	Christof	Er.	Erich
Ame.	Amalie	Cfl.	Christoffel	Ern.	Ernst
An.	Anton	Cg.	Chlodwig	Erne.	Ernestine
And.	Andreas	Cks.	Cyriakus	Erw.	Erwin
Ane.	Antonie	Cl.	Clemens	Es.	Erasmus
Anete.	Antoinette	Cle.	Clementine	Esb.	Eusebius
Anga.	Angelika	Clr.	Colmar	Ew.	Edwin
Ans.	Anselm	Clt.	Clement	Ewd.	Ewald
Anst.	Anastasius	Cms.	Chrysostomus		
Ant.	Antoninus	Cn.	Christian	F:	Friedrich
Ante.	Annette	Cne.	Christiane	F:e	Friederike
Ap.	Apelles	Cph.	Christoph	Fce.	Felicie
Arn.	Arnold	Cphe.	Christophe	Fd.	Ferdinand
Art.	Arthur	Crn.	Cornelius	Fde.	Ferdinande
Au.	Aurora	Cs.	Cäsar	Fdr.	Feodor
Aue.	Aurelie	Cst.	Constantin	Fgt.	Fürchtegott
Aus.	Aureolus	Cte.	Charlotte	Fri.	Fritz
Ax.	Alexander			Fs.	Fridericus
Axe.	Alexandrine	D:	David	Fx.	Felix
		Dc.	Dominic	Fz.	Franz
B:	Benjamin	Dd.	Diedrich	Fza.	Franziska
Bba.	Barbara	Dms.	Dominicus		
Bd.	Berthold	Dn.	Daniel	G:	Georg
Bee.	Beatrice	Do.	Dorothea	Gb.	Gottlieb
Bh.	Bernhard	Dt.	Dietrich	Gbd.	Gebhard
Bhe.	Bernhardine	Dv.	Detlev	Gbe.	Gottliebe
Bkd.	Burckard			Gf.	Gottfried
Bl.	Bogumil	E:	Eduard	Gg.	Gregor
Bld.	Balduin	Ea.	Emma	Ghd.	Gotthold
Blr.	Balthasar	Eb.	Eberhard	Ghf.	Gotthelf

Gl.	Gabriel
Glb.	Gottlob
Gle.	Gabriele
Glf.	Gotthilf
Gr.	Günther
Grd.	Gerhard
Grt.	Gerhart
Gst.	Gustav
Gsta.	Gustava
Gtd.	Gotthard
Gtg.	Gottgetreu
H:	Heinrich
Hb.	Herbert
Hbt.	Hubert
He.	Hedwig
Hg.	Hugo
Hle.	Helene
Hlm.	Helmuth
Hm.	Hermann
Hn.	Hilarin
Hna.	Helmina
Hne.	Hermine
Hr.	Harro
Hrns.	Hieronimus
Hs.	Hans
Hz.	Heinz
I:	Isaak
Ig.	Ignaz
Igs.	Ignatius
Im.	Immanuel
Ire.	Irene
Is.	Israel
Iso.	Isolde
Iz.	Innozenz
J:	Johann
J:a	Johanna
J:e	Johanne
J:s	Johannes
Jc.	Jacob
Jg.	Jürgen
Jk.	Jakob
Jl.	Julius
Jle.	Julie
Jm.	Joachim
Jne.	Juliane
Jns.	Joannes
Jr.	Jeremias
Js.	Joseph
Jse.	Josephine
Jt.	Justus
Jth.	Jonathan
Jts.	Justinus
K:	Karl
K:e	Karoline
Ka.	Klara
Kb.	Kunibert
Kd.	Konrad
Kl.	Klemens
Kle.	Klementine
Kn.	Kuno
Kp.	Kaspar
Ks.	Klaus
Kst.	Konstantin
Kta.	Katharina
L:	Ludwig
La.	Laura
Las.	Laurentius
Lbt.	Leberecht
Ld.	Ludolf
Lgt.	Lobegott
Lh.	Leonhard
Lp.	Leopold
Lpe.	Leopoldine
Lr.	Lazar
Ls.	Lazarus
Lt.	Lothar
Lu.	Luise
Lz.	Lorenz
M:	Markus
Ma.	Maria
Mae.	Mariane
Md.	Manfred
Mde.	Mathilde
Me.	Marie
Mel.	Melchior
Mg.	Magnus
Mge.	Margarete
Ml.	Michael
Mlse.	Melusine
Mn.	Martin
Ms.	Marius
Mt.	Matthias
Mta.	Martha
Mts.	Matthäus
Mx.	Maximilian
Mxe.	Maximiliane
Mz.	Moritz
N:	Nikolaus
Na.	Natalie
Nk.	Nepomuk
Nl.	Nathaniel
Ny.	Nataly
O:	Otto
O:r	Ottokar
Oa.	Olga
Od.	Otfrid
Ok.	Oskar
Or.	Ottocar
Os.	Oswald
Ote.	Ottilie
P:	Peter
Ph.	Philipp
Phe.	Philippine
Pl.	Paul
Ple.	Pauline
R:	Richard
R:a	Ricarda
Ra.	Rosa
Rb.	Robert
Rd.	Rudolf
Rh.	Reinhard
Rl.	Raphael
Rld.	Reinhold
Rle.	Rosalie
Rn.	Ruleman
Rod.	Roderich
Rp.	Ralph
Rs.	Renatus
S:	Samuel
Sb.	Sebastian
Sbl.	Sebaldus
Sf.	Siegfried
Sg.	Sigmund
Sgd.	Siegmund
Sgs.	Sigismund
Sl.	Salomon
Slm.	Salomo
Sm.	Simon
So.	Sophie
Sr.	Salvator
St.	Stephan
T:	Thomas
Ta.	Thekla
Tb.	Theobald
Td.	Theodor
Tds.	Theodorus
Te.	Therese
Tps.	Theophrastus
Ts.	Tobias
Tt.	Traugott
U:	Ulrich
Ua.	Ursula
Ud.	Udalricus
Ula.	Ulrica

V:	Viktor
Va.	Valeska
Vl.	Valentin
Vlr.	Valerius
W:	Wilhelm
W:e	Wilhelmine
Wb.	Willibald
Wcs.	Wenceslaus
Wf.	Wolf
Wfg.	Wolfgang
Wl.	Walther
Wlr.	Waldemar
Wol.	Woldemar
Wr.	Werner
Wz.	Wenzel
Wzs.	Wenzeslaus
X:	Xaver
Z:	Zacharias
Zb.	Zenobius

MAIN LIST

ABBELEN, P: M.
1. Golden grains of true piety; or, the eight beatitudes applied to the Christian's daily life. Tr. and arr. anon. NY: Riffarth 1889. 615p. 24. [LC]
2. Venerable mother M. Caro. Friess. St. L: Herder 1893. 12. [AC]
3. do. 1917. [same] 2d ed. Herder. O. [AC]

ABEKEN, Bh. Rd. 1780-1866.
4. An account of the life and letters of Cicero. Ed. [and tr.] G: C: Merivale. L: Longman 1854. 484p. 19cm. [BM.LC]

ABEKEN, He. See #5, which she ed. and also wrote in part.

ABEKEN, H: (J: W: Rd.) 1809-72.
*5. (Ein schlichtes Leben in bewegter Zeit.) Bismarck's pen: the life of H: A--, ed. from his letters and journals [and partly written] by his wife. Tr. Mrs. Barrett-Lennard and M. W. Hoper. L: Allen 1911. 376p. il. 22cm. [BM.LC]
[Good despite questionable liberties taken.]

ABEKEN, Hm.
*6. (Babylon und Jerusalem.) B-- and J--: a letter to Ida, countess of Hahn-Hahn. Tr. anon. L: Parker 1851. xii;116p. 17cm. [BM.LC]
[Translator's pref. is signed W.]

ABELE, Hyacinth.
7. (Die Violine, ihre Geschichte und ihr Bau.) The violin; its hist. and its construction il. and descr...from many sources,... Tr. J: Broadhouse. L: W. Reeves 1907. viii;207p. 8. [BM]

ABRAHAM A SANTA CLARA, 1644-1709. Sel. in C194;219;373.

ABRAHAM, K: 1877-1925.
8. Dreams and myths: a study in race psychology. Tr. W: A. White. NY: Journal of mental and nervous disease pub. 1913. 74p. 8. [BM]
9. Selected papers [psychoanalysis]. Tr. D. Bryan and Alix Strachey. L: Woolf 1927. 527p. 23cm. [BM.LC]

ABT, Fz. 1819-95. Cantatas: Briar-rose. Cinderella. Little red riding-hood. Little snow-white. The seven ravens. See Francke, Hm. Christmas. See A43.

ACHENWALL, Gf. 1719-72.
†10. (Einige Anmerkungen über Nord-Amerika und über dasige grosbrittanische Colonien.) A--'s observations on North America, 1767. Tr. J. G. Rosengarten. Phil: "Penn. Mag. of hist. and biog." Reprint. 1903. 19p. 25cm. [LC]
[Inexcusable treatment of a histor. document; whole sentences omitted, and tr. is very careless.]

ACKERE, Ma. v. Sel. in C90.

ACKERMANN, G: Cn. Bn. 1763-1833.
*11. (Das Christliche im Plato...) Christian element in P-- and the platonic philos. Tr. S: R. Asbury. Ed: Clark 1861. 280p. 22cm. [BM.LC]
*12. do. 187-. [same] NY: Scribners. [AC]

ADALBERT [i.e., H: W: A--], prince of Prussia, 1811-73.
**13. (Reise seiner königlichen Hoheit des Prinzen A-- v. Preussen nach Brasilien.) Travels...in the south of Europe and in Brazil ...up the Amazon and the Xingu. Tr. Sir R. H. Schomburgk and J: E: Taylor. L: Bogue 1849. 2v. 22cm. [BM.LC]
[Excellent; some differences in text from the copy before me.]

ADALBERT, C:
14. (Das Buch mit sieben Siegeln.) The book with seven seals: a novel. Tr. Miss Whyte. L: Remington 1879. 2v. 307;280p. 18cm. [BM]

ADELUNG, J: Cph. 1732-1806.
15. (Leben und Charakter des...Grafen v. Brühl in vertraulichen Briefen entworfen.) The life and character...of Count Bruhl [sic]... Carefully tr. anon. L: Cooper & Seyffert 1765? viii;215p. 17cm. [BM]

ADLER, Af. 1870-1937.
16. Marriage as a task. Tr. 1926. In C308.
17. The practice and theory of individual psychology. Tr. P. Radin. L: Paul 1924. viii;352p. 8. [BM]
*18. (Ueber den nervösen Charakter.) The neurotic constitution. Tr. B. Glueck and J: E. Lind. L: Paul 1921. xxii;222p. 8. [BM]
18a. Understanding human nature. Tr. Walter Beran Wolfe. Greenberg 1927. xii;286p. O. [AC]

ADLER, Fx. Sel. in C469.

ADLER, F: 1857- .Sel. in C28.

ADLERJUNG, J: L:
19. A series of tales from a preceptor to his pupils. Tr. W: Wennington. L: Chapple 1811. 168p. front. 12. [BM]

ADOLF, F: (Abr. H:) duke of Mecklenburg-Schwerin, 1873- .
*20. (Ins innerste Afrika.) In the heart of Africa. Tr. G E. Maberly-Oppler. L;NY: Cassell 1910. 295p. il. 26cm. [BM.LC]
§21. (Vom Kongo zum Niger und Nil.) From the Congo to the Niger and the Nile...1910-11. Tr. anon. L: Duckworth 1913. 2v. 526; 524p. il. 23cm. [BM.LC]
[Tr. cuts quite freely, without warning or apology.]

AEMILIA Jle., Gräfin. Sel. in C244.

AGRICOLA, G: And.
22. The artificial gardener: being a discovery of a new invention for the sudden growth of all sorts of trees and plants. Tr. anon. from the High-Dutch. L: E. Curll 1717. 36p. 12. [BM]
[Something like an advertisement: each of 160 persons willing to subscribe 25 guilders would receive a copy of his "secrets."]
§23. (Neu- und nie erhörter Versuch der Universal-Vermehrung aller Bäume....) A philosophical treatise of husbandry and gardening. Tr. from the High-Dutch [by H. G.]. Rev. by R: Bradley. L: P. Vaillant 1721. 300p. large 4. [BM]
[Evidently the exposition of the methods advertised in #22. Tr. seems to be quite faithful for that time.]

AGRIPPA VON NETTESHEIM, H: Crn. 1486?-1535.
24. Sel. in "Raphael," the art of talismanic magic. L: author 1879. 105p. 24cm. [BM]
[Lithographed on one side of the paper. Little Agrippa.]
25. The commendation of matrimony made by C. A. and tr. into englishe by D: Clapam. Londini: T. Berthelet 1545. ff. a-c.8.[BM]
[Dedicated to Lord Cromwell.]
26. (De incertitudine et vanitate scientiarum.) Of the vanitie and uncertaintie of artes and sciences: Englished by Jas. San(ford) (or Sandford), Gent. Imprinted at London by H: Wykes dwelling in Fleete streat, at the signe of the blacke Elephant. Anno. 1569. ff.187. 17cm. [BM.LC]
27. do. 1575. [same] Imprinted at London by Henrie Bynneman, dwelling in Knightryder streete, at the signe of the Mermayde. Anno. 1575. ff.187. 18cm. [BM.LC]

AGRIPPA VON NETTESHEIM
28. do. 1676. [another tr.] The vanity of arts and sciences. L: Prt. for Speed. 368p. 18cm. [BM.LC]
29. do. 1694. [same] L: R. Bentley. 368p. 18cm. [BM]
30. (De nobilitate et praecellentia foeminei sexus.) The glory of women; or, a Treatise declaring the excellency and preheminence of Women above Men... Tr...for the Vertuous and Beautiful Female Sex of the Commonwealth of England by E: Fleetwood. L: Rb. Ibbitson 1652. 32p. 18cm. [BM]
[T.p. has 1651 in handwriting.]
31. do. 1652. The glory of women; or, a looking-glass for ladies ...now turned into heroicall verse [from the foregoing] by H. C[are], Gent. L: Frances Coles. 47p. 14cm. [BM]
32. do. 1670. Female pre-eminence; or, the dignity and excellency of that sex, above the male. An ingenious discourse,... Done into English, with additional advantages, by H. C[are]. L: Prtd. by T. R. and M. D. And are to be sold by H. Million. 22;83p. 15cm. [BM.LC]
33. do. 1683. [same] In "The wonders of the female world." L. 14cm. [BM.LC]
34. do. 1873. On the superiority of woman over man,... Tr. into French by Amaudin, 1713...Tr. into English, 1873, in New York. NY: Am. news. 24p. 18cm. [LC]
35. (De occulta philosophia.) Three books of occult philos. tr. out of the Latin tongue by J. F. L: Gregory Moule 1651. 583p. 18cm. [T.p. has 1650 in handwriting.] [BM]
36. do. 1655. Fourth book of occult philos. Tr. Rb. Turner. L: Harrison. 217p. il. 17cm. [BM.LC]
37. do. 1665. [same] L: T. Rooks. 206p. 4. [BM]
[Agrippa's treatise takes up pp. 1-68.]
38. do. 1783. [same] L: 16. [LC]
39. do. 1898. Three books of occult philos. or magic... Book one. Natural magic. Ed. [from #35] by W. F. Whitehead. Chic: Hahn & Whitehead. 288p. il. 25cm. [LC.BM]

AGTE, Cphe. Sel. in C229.

AHLBORN, Frau Lu. See "Haidheim, L."

AKUNIAN, Frau Ilse (Lévien), 1852-1908. See "Frapan, Ilse."

ALBER, Es. d.1553. Sel. in C271.

ALBERT, prince consort of Queen Victoria of England, 1819-61. Sel. in C499.

ALBERT, king of Saxony, 1828-1902. See Harden, M. #3701.

ALBERT, H: 1604-68. Sel. in C269;271;276;412.

ALBERTI, Frau So. (Mödinger), 1826-92. See "Verena, So."

ALBERTINI, J: Bp. v. 1769-1831. Sel. in C276;570.

ALBERTUS MAGNUS, bishop of Ratisbon, 1205?-1280.
40. (De adhaerendo Deo.) A treatise of adhering to God. Tr. Sir K. Digby. L: H: Herringman 1654. 15cm. [BM]
[T.p. has 1653 in handwriting.]
41. do. 1850. The treatise of A-- M--...of adhering to God. Tr. from the Latin. anon. L: C: Gilpin. 65p. 14cm. [BM]
42. do. 1912. On union with God. With notes. Tr. by a Benedictine. L: Washbourne. 110p. 14cm. [BM]
[Much freer than earlier versions.]
43. (Tractatus...de veris & perfectis virtutibus,...) The paradise of the soule; or, a treatise of vertues... (Also) Of the union with God. [Tr. T: Everard.] St. Omer: 1617. 372p. 12cm. [BM]

ALBERTUS MAGNUS
44. do. 1682. The paradise of the soul,... Tr...N. N. L: W: Brooks. 240p. 14cm. [BM]

"ALBERTUS MAGNUS," pseud.
45. (De virtutis herbarum.) The boke of secretes of Albartus M--, of the vertues of Herbes, stones and certaine beastes...L: Wyllyam Copland 1565? ff. a-liii. 12cm.[T.p. prints: MDxxV.] [BM]
46. do. 1617. [same] The secrets of A-- M-- of the vertues of hearbs, stones and certaine beastes,... L: W. Iaggard. ff. a-Iiv. 13cm. [BM]
47. do. 1626. [same] L: Isaac Iaggard. 14cm. [BM]
[Newly printed, with orthographic revision.]
48. A-- M--: being the approved, verified, sympathetic and natural Egyptian secrets; or, white and black art for man and beast. NY: no pub. 1880? 3v. 160p. 17cm. [BM]
[Continuous pagination. No apparent relation to the foregoing.]

[De secretis mulierum. False ascription; see Henricus de Saxonia.]

ALBINUS, J: G: 1624-79. Sel. in C233;244;271;276;287.

ALBRECHT, Markgraf v. Brandenburg-Baireuth, 1522-57. Sel. in C287; 570.

ALBRECHT, Markgraf v. Brandenburg-Culmbach. Sel. in C489.

ALBRECHT v. JOHANNSDORF, fl. 1185-1209. Sel. in C27;427.

ALBRECHT v. RAPPERSCHWYL, early 14th cent. Sel. in C27;416;427;532.

ALESIUS, Ax. 'professor of theology at Leipzig.'
49. Of the auctorite of the word of God agaynst the bisshop of London, wherein are conteyned certen disputacyons had in the parlament howse betwene the bisshops abowt the nomber of the Sacraments... Leipsic: 1537. 46 leaves. 8. [BM]

ALEXANDER, DER WILDE, 13th cent. Sel. in C27;416;427.

ALEXANDER VON BATTENBERG, prince. See Koch, Ad. Prince A-- of B--; reminiscences of his reign... #5096.

ALEXANDER, J.
50. Con amore: poetical introd. to musical instruction. Tr. into Engl. verse by Hugh Jones. L: Augener 1897. viii;39p. 8. [BM]

ALEXANDER, L., Ig. Beissel, and -- Thissen.
51. Aix-La-Chapelle (Aachen) as a health resort. Tr. J. Donelan. L: Churchill 1892. viii;323p. 8. [BM]

"ALEXIS, Wb." [Häring, W: 1797-1871.] Sel. in C41;106;295;372.
52. (Der Roland von Berlin.) The burgomaster of Berlin. Tr. W. A. G. L: Saunders & Otley 1843. 3v. 12. [BM]
53. Hans Preller: a legend of the Rhine falls. Tr. C: L. Lewes. In "Tales from Blackwood," 3d ser., V. 3, 1889, pp. 90-116.[BM.LC]
*54. (Walladmor.) Walladmor, freely tr. from...Walter Scott [really by Alexis], tr. from the German. anon. L: Taylor & Hessey 1825. 2v. 16. [BM]
[Delightful pref. explains the tr.'s alterations, corrections, and reductions -- from 3 vols. to 2 -- of the original.]

ALKUIN, ca. 735-801. See Lorentz, F:, Life of A--. #5865.

ALLENDORF, J: L: Kd. 1693-1773. Sel. in C223;244;276.

ALLMERS, Hm. 1821-1902. Sel. in C571.

ALTENBURG, J: Ml. 1583-1640. Sel. in C45-6;269;276.

ALTING, Henricus.
55. A votive oration for the auspicial government of the most high and mightie prince and lord, Lord Fredericke the v. Palatine of Rhene...made the last day of September...1614...in the Vniuersity of Heidelberge...and tr. by W: Walker. L: J. Hodgets 1615. 24p. 4. [BM]

ALTMANN, A. The rose maid. Operetta. See Dörmann, Fx. #1255.

ALVENSLEBEN, Frau Anna Gbe. Lu. W:e (v. Loë) v. 1771- . Sel. from her diary, 1793-1803. Tr. Jessie Haynes. In Mz. Kaisenberg, 'Memoirs of Baroness Cécile de Courtot...' L: Heinemann 1900. [BM]

AMALIE Me. F:e A:e, princess of Saxony, 1794-1870.
56. Social life in Germany, il. in the acted dramas of the princess A-- of Saxony. Tr. Mrs. Anna Jameson. L: Saunders & Otley 1840. 2v. 8. [BM]
57. do. 1848. Six dramas il. of Ger. life. L: Parker. 350p. 12. [BM]

AMBROS, A: W: 1816-76.
58. (Die Grenzen der Musik und Poesie.) The boundaries of music and poetry: a study in musical aesthetics. Tr. J: H: Cornell. NY: Schirmer 1893. 187p. 19cm. [LC]
59. do. 1900. [same] New issue. 16. [AC]

AMBROSIUS, J:a. See Voigt, J:a A., 1854-

ANDREAE, J: Vl. 1586-1654. Sel. in C570.
*60. (Chymische Hochzeit des Christiani Rosenkreuz.) The hermetick romance; or, the chymical wedding. Tr. E. Foxcroft. L: A. Sowle 1690. 226p. 15cm. [BM.LC]
[BM and LC both ascribe to Cn. Rosencreutz.]
61. (Reipublicae christianopolitanae descriptio.) Christianopolis, an ideal state of the 17th cent. Tr. F. E. Held. NY: Oxford. 1916. 287p. il. 19cm. [LC.BM]
[EC has: L: Milford 1917. -- Ph.D. thesis, Univ. of Ill.]

ANDRIAN-WERBURG, Lp. zu. Sel. in C39.

"ANGELUS SILESIUS" [J: Scheffler, 1624-77.] Sel. in C166;229; 230-5;240;244;269;271;273;276;287;398-9;400;423;489;570.
*62. (Der Cherubinische Wandersmann.) Angelus Silesius: a sel. from the rhymes of a Ger. mystic. Tr. Pl. Carus. Chic: Open Court; L: Paul 1909. xxviii;174p. il. 16cm. [LC.BM]
§63. do. 1914. The spiritual maxims of A-- S--. Tr. w. introd. by H: Bett. L: C. H. Kelly. 72p. unb. 12. [BM]
[Smaller sel. than the foregoing, grouped under subject headings. Form is uneven, sense not always fully rendered.]

ANNA, Gräfin Stolberg. See Wellmer, Arn. #10003.

ANNEKE, Mda. Fza. Sel. in C32.

ANTON U: duke of Braunschweig-Wolfenbüttel, 1633-1714. Sel. in C231-2;276;486;489;570.

ANZENGRUBER, L: 1839-89.
64. (Das vierte Gebot.) The fourth commandment: drama in 4 acts [prose]. Tr. and ad. A. Sigmann. Pittsburg: 1912. Tw. [LC]
*65. (Der Meineidbauer.) The farmer forsworn: drama in 3 acts [prose]. Tr. A. Busse. 1913-15. In C154(16).
65a. (Der Schandfleck.) The blot of shame. Tr. B. Q. Morgan. 28p. 26cm. Tw. [Chaps. VI, XI, XVII, XVIII.] [SU]
65b. (Die Kreuzelschreiber.) The Cross-Makers. A comedy of rustic life. Tr. substituting an Irish for the original Bavarian setting by B. Q. Morgan. 70 leaves. 25cm. Tw. [SU]

APEL, J: A: 1771-1816.
§66. (Der Freischütz.) The fatal marksman. Tr. anon. 1823. In C456.
67. do. 1824. [same title] Tr. "Globus, Septimus." L: Baldwyn. 25cm. pp. 49-68. [BM]
68. do. 1825. The Freischütz; or, the magic balls. Tr. W: S. Hayward. In "Tales of the wild and wonderful." L: Prt. for Hurst, Robinson. [BM.LC]
*69. do. 1833. The orig. legend of the F--; or, the free shot. Tr. anon. L: Schloss. 56p. 14cm. [BM]
70. do. 1848. [same title] Hayward's tr? In C484.
71. do. 1855. Der Freischutz [sic]. Tr. G: G. Cunningham. In C82.
[For the opera, cf. Kind, F:]
72. The piper of Neisse. Tr. G: G. Cunningham. 1829. In C80-82.

APPENZELLER, J: Kd.
73. Gertrude de Wart; or, fidelity until death. (Hist. novel, based on authentic traditions, of the 13th and 14th cent. in Switzerland.) Tr. anon. L: Longman... 1826. 167p. 12. [BM]
["I have taken the liberty both to curtail and to amplify; but, I hope, never without a sufficient reason."]

APPUHN, A. W.
74. Memoir of the Rev. H: Moewes, late pastor of Altenhausen and Ivenrode, Prussia. Tr. anon. L: Hatchard 1840. 209p. 8. [BM]
[Introd. by Rev. J. Davies. Based in part on Bonnet's "Archives du christianisme," but most of it tr. from A--.]

ARCHENHOLTZ, J: W: v. 1741-1812.
75. (England und Italien.) A pict. of England. Tr. anon. L: 1789.. (B36.) [Tr. from the French.]
*76. do. 1797. A pict. of England. A new tr. anon. L: Pub. for the booksellers. 12. [Rather free but good.] [BM]
*77. do. 1791. A pict. of Italy. Tr. Js. Trapp. L: Robinson. 2v. 12. [Very good.] [BM]
*78. (Geschichte des siebenjährigen Krieges in Deutschland, 1756-63.) Hist. of the seven years' war in Germany. Tr. F. A. Catty from the 5th ed. Frankfort o. M. C: Jugel 1843. 542p. 18. [BM]
79. Hist. of the pirates, free-booters, or buccaneers of America. Tr. G. Mason. L: Stratford, also Hughes, 1807. 240p. 12. [BM]
[Based largely on French journals of Ravenneau de Lussan, Charlevoix, du Tertre, and Labat. Tr. says: "Some passages... expunged that seemed to breathe too much of party-spirit and party-virulence against a neighboring nation."]

ARENDS, W: Es. d.1721.
80. Early piety recommended in the life and death of C. L. von Exter. Rendered from the High-Dutch. anon. L: J. Downing 1710? 51p. 12. [BM]

ARITHMAEUS, Vl. 17th cent. Sel. in C483.

ARLBERG, Max
81. (Joseph Freifeld. Ein Sozialroman aus dem deutschamerikanischen Leben.) J-- F--. Tr. anon. Milwaukee: Caspar 1887. 12. [AC]

ARNDT, Ern. Mz. 1769-1860. Sel. in C12;17*;29;44;67;88;97;106;132; 149;166;169;171;178;215;218-9;229;231-2;273;276;287;296;309;317; 366;372-3;380;387-8;391;393;423;461;467;469;486.
§82. (Erinnerungen aus dem äusseren Leben.) Life and advent. Tr. J: R: Seeley. L: Seeley, J. & H. 1879. 450p. 19cm. [BM.LC]
[Arndt's autobiog., abr., with extracts from letters and writings. Some sel. from his "Wanderungen und Wandelungen mit dem Reichsfreiherrn...v. Stein," esp. on his life in Russia and the period of the "Befreiungskriege." Tr. is not by Seeley; only two poems by him.]

ARNDT, Ern. Mz.
†83. (Geist der Zeit.) Ardnt's [sic] spirit of the times. [Spain and Portugal. Turkey.] Being the work for the pub. of which the unfortunate Palm, of Erlangen, was sacrificed by Napoleon, the destroyer... Tr. P[eter] W[ill]. L: Thiselton 1808. 116p. 8. [BM] [Tr.'s pref. declares that he thought the first part without interest. He conceals his identity for fear of Napoleon's vengeance. Very free translation.]
84. (Märchen.) The three towers; The gnome's cap; Paiwai and Paiwuzzo; The seven piebald mice. Tr. Jas. S. Laurie. 1861. In C315.
*85. do. 1896. Fairy tales from the Isle of Rügen. Sel. and tr. Anna Dabis. L: Nutt. 237p. il. 8. [BM]
[18 tales. Not closely faithful, but excellently done. Tr. had access to some other than the 1842 edition.]

ARNDT (or Arnd), J: 1555-1621. See Wildenhahn, A:, J: A--, a historical life-picture, #10202.

ARNHEIM, Me. v.
86. Memoirs; written by herself. Tr. from the orig. [German] MS. anon. L: Longmans, Brown 1848. 313p. 12. [BM]

ARNIM, Bna. (Brentano) v. 1785-1859. Sel. in C142.
87. (Goethes Briefwechsel mit einem Kinde.) Goethe's corr. with a child. Tr. by herself and Mrs. Austin. L: Longman 1837. 540p. [LC card]
88. do. 1837-9. L;Berlin: Longman. 3v. 390;347;325p. 8. [BM]
[Vols. I and II say "in two vols." Vol. II has subtitle "Diary."]
89. do. 1838. The diary of a child. Berlin. 325p. 12. [BM]
[Really vol. III of foregoing.]
90. do. 1840. [same] L: Longman. 8. [EC]
91. do. 1841. First Amer. from Lond. ed. Lowell, Mass: Bixby. 2v. 8. [UW]
92. do. 1859. Bost: Ticknor & F. 504p. 18cm. [LC]
[Reprinted from Lond. ed.]
93. do. 1868. [same] [LC]
*94. do. 1913-15. [extracts] Tr. W. S. Murray. In C154(7).
**95. (Die Günderode.) Günderode. Bost: Peabody 1842. xii;106p. 19cm. [LC]
[LC card says: "First number of Marg. Fuller's tr. of the fictitious corr. between Bettina Brentano and Caro. Günderode, preceded by tr.'s pref. and an extract from her article in the "Dial," entitled "Bettina B-- and her friend G--." The tr. was later completed by Mrs. Wesselhoeft in her anonymous ed...1861."]
**96. do. 1861. Corr. of Fräulein Günderode and Bettina von Arnim. Bost: Burnham. xii;344p. 19cm. [LC.BM]
[In two parts, paged continuously. Pp. 1-86 are by M. Fuller, the remainder by Mrs. Minna Wesselhoeft. The work of both is excellent.] See Grimm, Hm., "Literature." #3132.

ARNIM, Harry Kurd E: K: v. 1824-81.
*97. (Brief an den Fürsten v. Bismarck. Entgegnung...) Reply to the charges contained in a letter from Prince B-- to the Emperor of Germany, April 14th, 1873. Tr. by permission. anon. L: Hardwicke & Bogue 1877. 151p. 8. [BM]
*98. (Pro nihilo. Vorgeschichte des Arnim'schen Prozesses.) Pro nihilo. The prelude to the Arnim trial. Tr. anon. 1st pt. L: Chapman & Hall 1876. 233p. 8. [BM]

ARNIM, L: (Jo)Achim v. 1781-1831. Sel. in C12;17;311;460-1.
99. (Des Knaben Wunderhorn.) Sel. tr. by M. Münsterberg. 1913-15. In C154(5).

ARNIM, L:
100. (Isabella v. Aegypten, Kaiser Karls V. erste Jugendliebe.) Isabella of Egypt. Tr. [abr.] C. F. Schreiber. 1927. In C452.

ARNIM, R. v.
101. (Aus dem Tagebuche eines Kompagniechefs.) Extract from an infantry captain's journal. Tr. C. J. East. Kansas City, Mo: Hudson-Kimberley 1897. 12. [AC]

ARNOLD, Fz. and G: Okonkowski.
102. (Das Fräulein vom Amt.) "Hello central." Operetta by "Jean Gilbert." Ad. by Lorenz M. Hart. Libr. 1917. 35;38;20p. Tw. [LCM] [Very free adaptation.]

ARNOLD, Gf. 1666-1714. Sel. in C223;233;244;269;276;287;570.
103. (Vitae patrum.) Life of Taulerus cont. in a coll. called "The honey comb." Tr. [and abr.] by P: Lossing. York: Alexander 1831. 90p. 11cm. [Phraseology "improved" by editor. Tr. states that he is not a master of English.] [BM]

"ARNOLD, Hs." [Bte. v. Bülow, 1850- . Sel. in C422.

ARSENIEW, Nicolas, 1888- .
103a. (Ostkirche und Mystik.) Mysticism and the eastern church. Tr. Art. Chambers. Pref. Friedrich Heiler. Introd. Evelyn Underhill. S.C.M. 1926. 173p. 8. [EC]

ARX, Adn. 1817-89. Sel. in C438.

ASSCHENFELD, K: Jl. 1792-1856. Sel. in C273;489.

ASSING, Ra. Ma. Anete. Ple. (Varnhagen v. Ense) 1783-1840. Sel. in C90.

ASSMANN, Cn. Gf.
104. Life of C-- G-- A-- written by himself. Pref. C. B. Tayler. L: Rel. tract soc. 1838. 122p. 8. [BM]
[Really rewritten and much abr. from the orig. of 350p.]

"AUER, Ade. v." [Cosel, Cte. v. 1818- .]
105. It is the fashion. By the translator of "Over yonder," "Magdalena," etc. Phil: Lippincott 1872. 293p. 19cm. [LC]
[Tr. is probably Mrs. Elgard. Cf. #6074; 6077.]
106. do. 1879. [same] 16cm. [LC]

AUERBACH, Bd. 1812-82. Sel. in C366*;469;574.
*107. [Coll.] (Schwarzwälder Dorfgeschichten.) Village tales from the Black Forest. Tr. Meta Taylor. L: Bogue 1846-7. 2v. 16. [BM]
[Tr. is not ideal, but very good. -- Vol. 1. Tolpatsch ("Der T--"); Hansjörg and his pipe ("Die Kriegspfeife"); Vefele ("Des Schlossbauers Vefele"); Sepper and Tonele ("Tonele mit der gebissenen Wange"); Village law: The may-tree, the axe ("Befehlerles"); The brothers ("Die feindlichen Brüder"). Vol. 2. Ivo ("Ivo, der Hajrle").--Each vol. has sep. t.p., but paging is continuous. Vol. 2. reprints the pref. with slight alterations.]
*108. [Coll.] 1858. Christian Gellert, and other sketches. L: S. Low. 186p. 8. [BM]
[Christian Gellert's last Christmas; The stepmother; Notes from the memorandum-book of the pastor of the mountain.]
*109. [Coll.] 1869. German tales. Introd. C: C. Shackford (probably the translator, Cf. #126). Bost: Roberts. 352p. 17cm.[LC.BM]
[Christian Gellert's last Christmas; The stepmother; Benigna; Rudolph and Elizabeth; *Erdmutha ("Erdmuthe"). -- Seems to be very competent and in good style. First two stories taken almost unchanged from foregoing.]

UNIVERSITY OF WINNIPEG
LIBRARY
515 Portage Avenue
Winnipeg, Manitoba R3B 2E9

AUERBACH, Bd.

*110. [Coll.] 1869. Black Forest village stories. Tr. C: Goepp. NY: Holt 1869. 377p. il. 17cm. [BM]
[The gawk ("Der Tolpatsch"); The pipe of war ("Die Kriegspfeife"); Manor-house farmer's Vefela ("Des Schlossbauers Vefele"); Nip-cheeked Toney ("Tonele mit der gebissenen Wange"); Good government ("Befehlerles"); The hostile brothers ("Die feindlichen Brüder"); Ivo, the gentleman ("Ivo, der Hajrle"); Florian and Crescence ("Florian u. Creszens"); The Lauterbacher ("Der Lauterbacher").]

*111. [Coll.] 1874. [same as foregoing.] NY: Holt. [LC]

*112. [Coll.] 1883. Two stories. Christian Gellert; The stepmother. L: Sonnenschein. 250p. 8. [Same tr. as #108.] [BM]

113. [Coll.] 1890. Tales. Tr. A. H. Fox. L: Longman. (B13)

114. [Coll.] n.d. Stories of the Black Forest. Tr. anon. L: Longman. (B13)

*115. Aloys. Tr. C: T. Brooks. NY: Holt 1877. 263p. 17cm. [LC]

115a. do. 1877. [same] Young Aloys; or, the gawk from America. Lippincott's Mag. 19(1877):240, etc. (B15a)

*116. (Auf der Höhe.) On the heights. Tr. F. E. Bunnett. Lpz: Tauchnitz; NY: Leypoldt & Holt 1867. 3v. 16cm. [LC]

*117. do. 1868. [same] 3d ed. Bost: Roberts. 544p. 8. [BM]
[Prt. in double columns.]

*118. do. 1869. [same] Rev. ed. Bost: Roberts. 544p. 18cm. [LC]

§119. do. 1875. Tr. S. A. Stern. NY: Holt. 624p. 19cm. [LC]
[Too free.]

120. do. 1891. Tr. anon. Chic: Rand, McNally. (B13)

121. do. 1896. Tr. anon. Bost: Caldwell. 12. [AC]

§122. do. 1899. [Stern's tr.] NY: Holt. 2v. 821p. 17cm. [LC]

*123. do. 190-. [Bunnett's tr.] NY: Burt. 692p. 19cm. [LC]

124. do. 1902. Tr. anon. Winston. (B13)

125. do. 1910. [Sel.] On the height. Tr. anon. In C574.

§126. do. 1912. [Stern's tr.] NY: Holt. One v. 19cm. [LC]

127. do. [n.d.] Tr. anon. Phil: Porter & Coates. (B13)

§128. (Barfüssele.) The barefooted maiden. Tr. anon. Il. by E: H. Wehnert. L: Low 1857. 211p. 8. [BM]

§129. do. 1858? Tr. anon. Bost: Munroe. 12. [AC]
[Tr. by Eliza B. Lee; see "Harper's Mag." 21:696.]

130. do. 1861. [abr.] Cinderella of the Black Forest. Tr. G. Gordon. In C170.

§131. do. 1867. The little barefoot. Tr. E. B. Lee. Bost: Fuller. 275p. il. 18cm. [LC]

131a. do. 1869. Little barefoot. Tr. anon. "New Eclectic Mag." 4(1869):301, etc.

132. do. 1872. Tr. anon. L: Routledge. il. 8. [EC]

*133. do. 1873. Little barefoot; or, strive and trust. Tr. H: W: Dulcken. Il. by B. Vautier. L: Routledge. 195p. 4. [BM]

*134. do. 1913-15. [abr.] Tr. H: W: Dulcken and P. B. Thomas. In C154(8).

134a. A battle for life or death. Tr. Mrs. St. Simon. "Amer. Whig Rev." 9(1849):265. (B15a)

135. (Befehlerles.) The axe. Tr. Zimmern. 1880. In C575-7.

*136. (Brigitta.) Brigitta. Tr. Ca. Bell. Lpz: Tauchnitz; L: Low 1880. 286p. 16cm. [Good, competent tr.] [LC.BM]

*137. do. 1880. [same] NY: Munro. Seaside lib. 22p. 32cm. [LCO]

†138. do. 1902. Tr. J. A. McBrayer, Sr. Louisville, Ky: Carothers. 97p. 19cm. [LC]

139. Christian Gellert's last Christmas. Tr. anon. 1898. In C509. [Taken from #108.]

140. The convicts and their children. Tr. C: T. Brooks. NY: Holt 1877. 281p. 17cm. [LC]

AUERBACH, Bd.

141. do. 1877. [same] L: Dulau. 8. [EC]

§142. (Das Landhaus am Rhein.) The villa on the Rhine. Tr. Jas. Davis. NY: Leypoldt & Holt 1869. 2v. 17cm. [LC]

142a. do. 1868. The country house on the Rhine. Tr. anon. "Littell's Liv. Age" 99(1868):490, etc.

§143. do. 1869. Villa Eden: the country-house on the Rhine. Tr. C: C. Shackford. Bost: Roberts. 549p. 22cm. [LC]
[Tr. lacks the will to faithfulness and accuracy.]

*144. do. 1870. The country house on the Rhine. Tr. anon. L: Bentley. 3v. 8. [Seems to be good and accurate.] [BM]

§145. do. 1911. [Davis's tr.] NY: Holt. 990p. 19cm. [LC]

§146. (Deutsche Abende.) German evenings (with other tales by G. v. Heeringen, A. v. Imhof, afterwards Helwig, and F. Kruse). Tr. J. L. Lowdell. L: Chapman & H. 1869. 325p. 20cm. [BM.LC]

*147. (Dichter und Kaufmann.) Poet and merchant: a picture of life from the time of Moses Mendelssohn. Tr. C: T. Brooks. NY: Holt 1877. 460p. 8. [LC]

147a. (Die feindlichen Brüder.) The hostile brothers. Tr. Mrs. St. Simon. "Christ. Parlor Mag." 4(1848):118. (B15a)

148. (Die Frau Professorin.) The professor's lady. Tr. Ma. Howitt. NY: Harper 1850. 8. [Cf. #150.] [AC]

†149. do. 1851. The professor's wife. Tr. anon. L: Parker. 196p. 8. [Quite inaccurate, though in good style.] [BM]

150. do. 187-. Tr. Ma. Howitt. NY: Harper. [AC]

151. do. 1882. [same] NY: Munro. Seaside lib. 20p. 32cm. [LCO]

§152. do. 1903. The professor's wife. Tr. F. E. Hynan. L: Drane. 232p. 8. [Rather free and not wholly accurate.] [BM]

§153. (Edelweiss.) Edelweiss. Tr. Ellen Frothingham. Bost: Roberts 1869. 345p. 17cm. [LC]

*154. do. 1877. Tr. C: T. Brooks. L: Dulau. (B8)

155. (Florian und Creszenz.) Florian and Crescence. Tr. Meta Taylor. L: Chapman & H. 1853. 95p. 12. [Cf. #107.] [BM]

156. (Der Forstmeister.) The foresters. Tr. anon. NY: Appleton 1880. 191p. 17cm. [LC]

157. (Ivo, der Hajrle.) Ivo, a village tale. Tr. anon. L: Bogue 1847. 16. [Probably by Meta Taylor (cf. #107), and see "Athenaeum" 20(1847):91. Review says: il. by J: Absolon.] [EC]

§158. (Joseph im Schnee.) Joseph in the snow. Tr. anon. L: Lovell 1867. Bost: Fuller 1868. 196p. 18cm. [LC]

§159. do. and, The clockmaker. Tr. Lady Wallace. L: Saunders & O. 1861. 3v. 12. [Fair, rather free tr.] [BM]

§160. (Landolin von Reutershofen.) Landolin. Tr. Annie B. Irish. NY: Holt 1878. 265p. 17cm. [Undistinguished, careless.] [LC]

161. Lorley and Reinhard. Tr. C: T. Brooks. NY: Holt 1877. 377p. 17cm. [LC]

162. do. 1877. [same] L: Dulau. 8. [EC]

163. Master Bieland and his workmen. Tr. E. Hancock. NY: Holt 1883. 266p. 17cm. [LC]

163a. The rock of the legion of honor. Tr. anon. "Harper's Mag." 41(1870):912. (B15a)

§164. (Spinoza.) Spinoza. Tr. E. Nicholson. Lpz: Tauchnitz; L: Low 1882. 2v. 16cm. [LC.BM]

§165. do. 1882. [same] NY: Holt. 444p. 17cm. [LC]

§166. do. 1882. [same] NY: Munro. Seaside lib. 47p. 32cm. [AC]

**167. (Tagebuch aus Wien.) Narr. of events in Vienna, from Latour to Windischgrätz. Tr. J: E: Taylor. L: Bogue 1849. 252p. 18cm. [Excellent tr.] [BM.LC]

§168. (Waldfried.) Waldfried. Tr. anon. L: Sampson Low 1874. 3v. 8. [BM]
[Very freely handled. Sentences rearranged and "normalized."]

AUERBACH, Bd.
169. do. 1874. Tr. S. A. Stern. NY: Lovell. NY: Holt. 514p. 18cm. [Cf. Stern's tr. of Auf der Höhe, #119.] [LC]
*170. (Zur guten Stunde.) The good hour; or, evening holiday. Tr. H: W: Dulcken. L: Routledge 1876. 632p. 8. [BM.BPL] [Collection of stories and sketches, mostly quite short.]

AUERSPERG, An. Ax. Graf v. 1806-76. See "Grün, Anastasius."

AUGUSTA, grand duchess of Mecklenburg-Schwerin. See Jahn, K., A--, a biog. sketch, #4731.

AYRENHOFF, Crn. Hm. 1733-1819.
171. (Der Postzug.) The set of horses, by Emdorff (Ayrenhoff). Tr. H: Mackenzie. 1792. In C386.

AYRER, Jk. d. ältere, d.1605.
*172. The comedy of the beautiful Sidea...the only drama extant which points to the plot of Shakespeare's "Tempest"; and, the comedy of the beautiful Phaenicia [abr.]...containing the plot of Shakespeare's "Much ado about nothing." Tr. T: Solly. 1865. In C70.

BABO, Fz. Js. Ms. 1756-1822. Sel. in C12.
173. (Dagobert der Frankenkönig.) Dagobert, king of the Franks: tragedy. Tr. B: Thompson. 1801. In C535. [See C535 for judgment on Thompson as translator.]
174. do. 1903. [same] In C18.
175. (Otto von Wittelsbach.) O: of W--; or, the choleric count. Tragedy in 5 acts. Tr. B: Thompson. 1801. In C535.
176. (Die Strelitzen.) The Strelitzes: drama in 5 acts. Tr. anon. 1800? In C157(1).

BACH, J: Sb. 1685-1750.
See Bitter, K:, Life of J. S. Bach, #472.
See Forkel, J:, Life of J: Sb. Bach, #1654.
See Schweitzer, Alb., J. S. Bach, #8720.
See Spitta, Jl., J. S. Bach, #8898.
See Ziemssen, L:, J: Sb. Bach, #10617.

BACH, K: Ph. Em. 1714-88. Letters. In C429.

BAECK, Leo, 1873- .
177. Marriage as mystery and command. Tr. 1926. In C308.

BAEDEKER, K: [The English guide-books published by this firm are not included here, for various reasons. Strictly speaking, of course, they are not really translations anyway.]

BAEHR, Jl.
178. Naughty boys and girls. Tr. Mme. de Chatelain. L: Addey 1852. il. 4. [BM]

BAHNMAIER, Jth. F: 1774-1841. Sel. in C269;287;489.

BAHR, Hm. 1873- .
179. (Das Konzert.) The concert. Ad. Leo Ditrichstein. 1910. (B38)
180. do. 1921. Tr. B. Q. Morgan. In C100a.
181. (Der Meister.) The master. Auth. tr. B: F. Glazer. Brown 1918. 89p. D. [B38 says this is an adaptation.] [AC]
§182. (Expressionismus.) Expressionism. Tr. R. T. Gribble. L: Henderson 1925. 116p. 8. [BM] [Correct, but style seriously altered.]

BAHR-MILDENBURG, Anna, 1872- . and Hm. Bahr.
§183. Bayreuth and the Wagner theatre. Tr. T. W. Makepeace. L: Unwin 1912. 95p. 19cm. [Not close enough.] [LCM]

BAHRDT, K: F: 1741-92.
184. (Alvaro und Ximenes.) All's well that ends well; or, A-- and X--. A Spanish tale. 2v. [See "Gentleman's Mag." 67(1797):1:410.] (B26)

BAIERLEIN, E. R.
185. The land of the Tamulians and its missions. Tr. J. D. B. Gribble. Madras: Higginbotham 1875. 242p. 8. [BM]

BAKONYI, K: v. and Rb. Bodansky.
186. (Ein Herbstmanoever.) The gay hussars: milit. operetta in three acts by E. Kálmán. Ad. by M. B. Kirby. Vocal score. Engl. NY: Stern 1909. 105p. 28cm. [BMM]
187. do. 1912. Autumn manoeuvres: a mus. play. Ad. H: Hamilton. Lyrics by Percy Greenbank. Vocal score. Engl. L: Enoch. 105p. 28cm. [BMM]

BALL, Hm.
188. (Thierza oder die Anziehungskraft des Kreuzes.) Thirza; or, the attractive power of the cross. Tr. E. M. Lloyd. L: Wertheim 1842. 12. [BM]
189. do. 1877. [same] 72nd thous. L: Elliot Stock. 16. [BM]

BALL, K: J:s.
**190. (Jerusalem wie es war und wie es ist.) Jerusalem. Tr. Sophia Taylor. Pref. by A. McCaul. L: Wertheim 1843. 180p. 12. [Excellent tr.] [BM]

BAMBERGER, L: 1823-79.
*191. (Herr von Bismarck.) Count Bismarck: a polit. biog. Tr. C: Lee Lewes. Breslau. Günther; L: Trübner 1869. 229p. 18cm. [BM.LC] [Orig. pub. in French, then tr. (by K. A.) under the author's supervision into German, 3 new chapters being added, and some slight alterations made. The Engl. tr. made from the proof-sheets and pub. simultaneously. Though good, the tr. is not as close as it could be made.]

BANDELIN, J: N: 1741-1824. Sel. in C169.

BARBAROSSA [F: I of Hohenstaufen, 1123?-90.] See Kühn, Fz. B--. #5488.

BARTH, Cn. Glb. 1799-1862. Sel. in C244.
192. [Coll.] Winter evening stories. Tr. anon. L: Darton 1838. 16. [EC]
193. [Coll.] 1841. Examples and warnings. Tr. anon. L: Darton. 16. [BM]
194. [Coll.] 1845. Bible stories for the young. Tr. from 30th Ger. ed. anon. L: Rel. tract soc. 280p. il. 12. [BM]
195. [Coll.] 1872-6. do. Tr. anon. Phil: Presb. bd. n.d. 2v. 18. [AC]
196. Benoni; or, the triumph of Christianity over Judaism. Tr. S: Jackson. L: Wertheim 1856. 140p. 12. [BM]
197. The child of the rock. Tr. anon. Phil: Presb. bd. 1869. 192p. 18. [LCO]
*198. Cuff, the negro boy. 3d ed. Tr. anon. Ed: Paton & R. 1851. 108p. 24. [Same as #214.] [BM]
199. do. 1868. [same] L: Houlston. 18. [EC]
*200. (Der arme Heinrich oder die Pilgerhütte am Weissenstein.) Poor Henry. Tr. anon. L: W: Foster 1840? 103p. 32. [BM]
§201. do. 1851. New tr. by S: Jackson. L: 128p. il. 8. [BM] [Very freely tr.]
§202. do. 1854. Poor H--; or, the pilgrim hut of Weisenstein [sic]. Tr. S. A. M. L: Wertheim. 97p. il. 18. [BM] [Tr. doesn't understand or ignores the orig.]

BARTH, Cn. Glb.
§203. do. 1854. [same] L: Darton. 16. [EC]
204. do. 1872-6. Tr. anon. Phil: Presb. bd. n.d. 18. [AC]
205. do. 1876. Tr. anon. NY: Am. S. S. U. 96p. 18. [LCO]
§206. (Der Fensterladen.) The juvenile artist. Tr. S: Jackson. L: Darton 1838. 92p. 16. [BM]
[Humor of the orig. mostly dulled.]
*207. do. 1850. Gregory Krau; or, the window-shutter. Tr. Rb. Menzies. Ed: Paton & R. 104p. il. 24. [Same as #214.] [BM]
208. do. 1868. [same?] Gregory Viran [i.e., Krau]. L: Houlston. 18. [EC]
209. (Der Weihnachtsmorgen oder das Tintenfässchen.) Christmas morning; or, the little ink cask. Tr. anon. Ed: Paton & R. 1851. 92p. 12. [Same as #215.] [BM]
210. do. 1857. [same] L: Hamilton. 18. [EC]
211. do. 1868. [same] L: Houlston. 18. [EC]
212. (Die Rabenfeder.) The raven's feather. Tr. anon. NY: Am. S. S. U. n.d. [1872-6.] 18. [AC]
*213. do. 1878. Tr. anon. L: Rel. tract soc. 64p. il. 16. [BM]
*214. (Erzählungen für Christenkinder.) Stories for Christian children. Tr. Rb. Menzies. Stuttgart. J: B. Müller 1850-1. 3 pts. paged sep. 87;77;91p. 12. [BM]
[Mick and Nick, or the power of conscience; Gregory Krau, or the window-shutter; Cuff, the negro boy.]
§215. do. 2d series. Tr. J. E. Ryland. Ed: Paton & R; L: Hamilton 1854. 356p. il. 12. [BM]
[Christmas morning, or the little ink cask; The weaver of Quellbrunn, or the roll of cloth; Natalie, or the broken spring; Setma, the Turkish maiden. -- Tr. is not close and has no style.]
§216. do. 1857. [same] L: Hamilton. 18. [EC]
217. General hist. briefly told. Tr. anon. L: Rel. tract soc. 1840. 18. [EC]
218. Huguenot galley-slaves. Phil: Presb. bd. n.d. [1872-6.] 18. [AC]
219. J: G: Schmidgall: a true tale. Tr. S: Jackson. L: Lingham 1838. 98p. il. 12. [BM]
220. do. 1838. J: G: Schinidgall [i.e., Schmidgall]. L: Darton. [EC]
221. Mick and Nick; or, the power of conscience. Tr. Rb. Menzies. Ed: Paton & R. 1849. 98p. il. 12. [Same as #214.] [BM]
222. do. 1868. [same] L: Houlston. 18. [EC]
223. Moravians. Tr. anon. L: Darton 1838. 16. [EC]
224. Natalie; or, the broken spring. Tr. anon. L: Hamilton 1849. 18. [Probably same as #215.] [EC]
225. do. 1868. [same] L: Houlston. 18. [EC]
§226. do. and, Setma, the Turkish maiden. (Setma, das türkische Mädchen). Ed: Paton & R. 1853. 133p. 12. [Same as #215.] [BM]
227. René, the young crusader. Tr. anon. L: Darton 1839. 16. [EC]
228. (Setma, das türkische Mädchen.) Setma, the Turkish girl. Tr. anon. Phil: Presb. bd. 1869. 120p. 18. [LCO]
*229. do. and, Woodroof, the Swedish boy. L: Darton & H. 1838. 184p. 8. [BM]
230. do. 1876. Setma, the Turkish maiden. Tr. anon. NY: Am. S. S. U. 88p. 18. [LCO]
230a. do. 1876. [same?] Setma, the Turkish captive. Tr. E. J. Whately. L: Rel. tract soc. 18. [EC]
*231. (T: Platters merkwürdige Lebensgeschichte.) Autobiog. of T: Platter, a schoolmaster of the 16th cent. Tr. by E. A. McCaul, afterwards Finn. L: Wertheim 1839. 106p. il. 12. [BM]
[Edited by Barth. Cf. #7203.]
232. The wanderer. Tr. anon. L: Darton 1838. 16. [EC]

BARTH, Cn. Glb.
§233. The weaver of Quellbrunn; or, the roll of cloth. Tr. T. E. Ryland. Ed: Paton & R. 1851. 127p. il. 24. [Same as #215.] [BM]
§234. do. 1851. [same] The weaver of Quilbrum. L: Hamilton. [EC]
§235. do. 1868. [same] L: Houlston. [EC]
236. The young Tyrolese. Tr. anon. L: Darton 1838. 16. [EC]

BARTH, H: 1821-65. Sel. in C469.
237. (Reisen und Entdeckungen in Nord- und Zentral-Afrika.) Travels and discoveries in North and Central Africa, 1849-55. L: Longmans 1857-8. 5v. 8. [BM]
[No tr. named. German pref. dated March, Engl. one May, 1857. German pref. much longer and more detailed. Probably author supervised the tr. and wrote a new pref. for the Engl. ed. Engl. text shows considerable omissions.]
238. do. 1857-8. 2d ed. Vol. 1-3 only. [BM]
239. do. 1890. [First half of #237.] In Minerva lib. xxxii;608p. 8. [BM]
240. do. 1890. [Second half of #237.] In Minerva lib. xvii; 548p. 8. [BM]

BARTSCH, Rd. Hs. 1873- .
241. (Der steirische Weinfuhrmann.) The Styrian wine-carter. Tr. B. Q. Morgan. 1913-15. In C154(19).
§242. (Die kleine Blanchefleure.) Song of the cowherd: opera (Der Kuhreigen) by W: Kienzl. Text by R: Batka after R. H. B--. Tr. anon. Libr. Fr;Engl. NY: 1913. [Not very good.] [LCM]
*243. (Elisabeth Koett.) E-- K--. Tr. L. Lewisohn. NY: Fitzgerald 1910. 265p. 19cm. [Questionable liberties.] [LC]
244. (Schwammerl.) Lilac-time: operetta by A. M. Willner and H. Reichert, partly based on Bartsch. See Willner.

BASEDOW, J: Bh. [properly J: Berend Bassedau] 1723-90. See Raumer, K., Ratich, Comenius, and B--. #7354.

BATKA, R: 1868-1922.
§245. (Der Kuhreigen.) Song of the cowherd: opera by W: Kienzl. Text after "Die kleine Blanchefleure," a story by R. H. Bartsch. Tr. anon. Libr. Fr;Engl. NY: 1913. [Not very good.] [LCM]

BATKA, R: and Ax. S. Pordes-Milo.
§246. (Versiegelt.) Attached: opera bouffe in one act by Leo Blech. Tr. anon. Libr. Ger;Engl. NY: Rullman 1911. 39p. 8. [LCM]
[Prose, correct. Orig. is in rhyme.]

BAUDISSIN, Wf. [Er. Hg. El.] Graf v. 1867-1926.
247. (Erstklassige Menschen.) First-class men: novel of Ger. army life, by "Freiherr von Schlicht." Tr. anon. NY: Schnitzer 1904. 285p. 18cm. [LC]
248. do. 1904. Life in a crack regiment: novel of German military manners and morals. Tr. anon. L: Unwin. 368p. 8. [BM]
249. do. 1908. [same] [EC]
250. do. 1914. [same] 4th ed. L: Unwin. 320p. 8. [EC]
251. do. 1914. 6th ed. L: Unwin. [LC card]
252. do. 1915. [same] NY: Dodd, Mead. 320p. 19cm. [LC]

BAUER, Bh. A.
253. (Weib und Liebe.) Woman and love. Tr. Eden and Cedar Paul. L: Heinemann 1927. 360p. 8. [BM]
254. (Wie bist du Weib?) Woman: treatise on anat., physiol., psychol., and sexual life of woman. With app. on prostitution. Tr. E. S. Jerdan and N. Haire. Introd. N. Haire. L: Cape 1927. 413p. 8. [BM]

BAUER, Bh. A.
255. do. 1927. Woman and love. NY: Boni. 2v. O. [AC]
[Vol. 1 = #254, vol. 2 = #253.]

BAUER, K:e [Phe. A:e] 1807-77.
256. (Nachgelassene Memoiren von K-- B--.) Posthumous memoirs. Tr. anon. L: Remington 1884. 2v. 8. [EC]
257. do. 1885. [same] 2d ed. [EC]
258. do. 1885. [same] 3d ed. L: Remington. 4v. 23cm. [BM.LC]
259. do. 1885. [same] NY: Scribner & W; Bost: Roberts. 644p. 19cm. [LC]
260. do. 1885. [sel.] C. B-- and the Coburgs. Tr. C: Nisbet. L: Vizetelly. 404p. 16. [BM.LCO]

BAUER, Ka. 1836-76. See "Detlev, Carl."

BAUER, L: Ads. 1803-46. Sel. in C448.

BAUER, O: 1881- .
261. (Die österreichische Revolution.) The Austrian revol. Tr. [abr.] H. J. Stenning. L: Parsons 1925. 287p. 8. [BM]

BAUERNFELD, E: v. 1802-90. Sel. in C178;571.

BAUM, P: 1869- . Sel. in C28.

BAUMANN, J.
262. The rose of Jericho; or, Christmas eve. Tr. G: G. Cunningham. 1829. In C80, cf. C81-2.

BAUMBACH, Rd. 1840-1905.
§263. (Erzählungen und Märchen. Sommermärchen.) Summer legends. Tr. Helen B. Dole. NY: Crowell 1888. 287p. 18cm. [LC]
[Inaccurate; style very good.]
§264. do. 1889. [same] L: Scott. 8. [EC]
§265. do. 1890. [same] Tales from wonderland. L: Scott. 287p. [LC]
§266. do. 1891. [same] L: Scott. Camelot classics. 287p. 8. [BM]
267. do. 1903. [abr.] Ad. W: Silber. NY: Lovell. 122p. 19cm. [LC]
[Less than half.]
268. do. 1903. [same] Wonderful wonderland tales. L: Simmons. (B13)
269. do. 1903. [same] Ed. by J. M. Stradling. NY: Stradling. 146p. [From London ed.] [LC]
§270. do. 1913. Heart's-ease and Christmas roses. Tr. Jean E. Kennedy. Felling-on-Tyne: Scott. 25p. 12. [BM]
[Not very faithful; almost rewritten.]
271. do. [n.d.] Tales. NY: Crowell. (B13)
§272. (Das Wasser der Jugend.) The fountain of youth. Tr. Minnie B. Hudson. 1907. In C447.
§273. do. 1913. The water of youth. Tr. Jean E. Kennedy. L: Scott. 33p. 16. [Cf. #270; same comment.] [BM]
§274. do. 1915. [Same as #272.] In C179.
§275. The Egyptian fire-eater. Tr. Helen B. Dole. 1898. In C509. [From #263.]
276. The forgotten well. Tr. White. Lord 1901. (B13)
277. The meadow sprite and other tales... See "Leander, R:" #5624.

BAUMGAERTEL, Max.
278. Prelim. to the restoration of the Wartburg; The restoration of the Wartburg. Tr. G. A. Greene. 1907. In C555.

BAUMGAERTNER, Ax.
279. Namameha and Watonilka. Tr. Helena Long. 1897. In C370a.

BAUMGART, Hm.
280. Goethe's "Märchen." A politico-national confession of faith. Tr. I. N. Judson. 1892. In C300(22).

BAUMGARTEN zu Braitenbach, Mn. v. 1573-1641.
281. Sel. from the journals. In Purchas, S: "Purchas his pilgrimes," pt. 2. L: W. Stansby for H. Fetherstone 1625. fol. [BM]
282. Travels...through Egypt, Arabia, Palestine, and Syria, with the author's life done out of Latin [by Cph. Donauer]. In Churchill, A. & J., "Coll. of voyages and travels," 1:381-452. L: for J. Walthoe, T: Wotton, etc. 1732. fol. [BM]
283. do. 1744. [same] In Churchill... L: Lintot & Osborn. 1:313-384. [BM]
284. do. 1752. [same as foregoing] [BM]
285. do. 1785? Travels into the east [compiled by C. Donauer, without the biog.] In Moore, J. H. "New coll. of voyages," vol. 2. fol. [BM]
[A wholly new tr., much abr., and seemingly fused with accounts of other travelers.]

BAUMGARTEN, Sgd. Jk. 1706-57.
286. A supplement to the universal history, from the German. Tr. anon. L: Lynde. See "Scot's Mag." 16(1754):206. (B26)

BAUR, W: 1826-97.
287. Religious life in Germany during the wars of independence. Tr. Jane Sturge. L: Strahan 1870. 5v. 8. [BM]
288. do. 1870. L: Strahan. 2v. 362;330p. 12. [LCO]
289. do. 1870. NY;L: Routledge. 2v. 8. [AC]
290. do. 1872. [same as #287] [BM]

BAYER, [K:] Rb. [Emmerich] v. See "Byr, Rb."

BEBEL, Fd. A: 1840-1913.
291. Assassination and socialism. From a speech...Nov. 2, 1898. Tr. Boris Reinstein. NY: Labor news. 31p. 17cm. [LC]
*292. (Aus meinem Leben.) B--'s reminiscences. Tr. from 1st Ger. ed. E. Untermann. NY: Socialist lit. co. 1911- . 20 cm. [LC]
§293. do. 1912. My life. Tr. anon. L: Unwin. 344p. 23cm. [BM.LC]
[Cut severely; otherwise excellent.]
*294. (Die Frau in der Vergangenheit, Gegenwart und Zukunft.) Woman in the past, present, and future. Tr. H. B. Adams Walther. L: Internat. lib. of soc. science 1885. 264p. 8. [BM]
*295. do. 1886. [same] NY: Lovell. 268p. 18cm. [LC]
*296. do. 1886. [same] Brooklyn, NY: Bordollo. S. [AC]
*297. do. 1891. [same as #295] [LC]
*298. do. 1893. [same as #294] Bellamy's lib. 8. [BM]
*299. do. 1915. [same] L: Reeves. 264p. 8. [BM]
300. (Die Frau und der Sozialismus.) Woman under socialism. Tr. from 33d ed. by D. De Leon. NY: Labor news 1904. 379p. 19cm. [LC]
*301. do. 1910. Woman and socialism. Jubilee 50th ed. Tr. Meta L. Stern. NY: Socialist lit. co. 521p. 20cm. [LC]
*302. do. 1918. [same] Woman past, present, and future. NY: Boni & L. 512p. D. [AC]
See also Richter, Eg. Pictures of the socialistic future, freely ad. from B--. #7429.
See also Vollmar, G., for speech by B--. #9567.

BECHER, J:s R. 1891- . Sel. in C95.

BECHSTEIN, L: 1801-60. Sel. in C169.
§303. (Deutsches Märchenbuch.) The old story teller: popular Ger. tales. Coll. by L: B--. Tr. anon. L: Addey 1854. 287p. 8. [56 stories. Tr. not very acc.; Ger. apparently not understood.] [BM]

BECHSTEIN, L:
304. do. 1861. The dog's distress; Strong Godfrey, or the Christmas-box; Lilly and Bessy. Tr. Jas. S. Laurie. In C315.
§305. do. 1872. As pretty as seven, and other pop. Ger. tales coll. by L: B. Tr. anon. L: Hotten. 367p. il. by Richter. 8. [BM] [Adds to B--'s 56 tales 9 stories from "Grimms' Märchen"; not the same tr. as #303.]

BECK, Jk. Sg.
306. (Grundriss der kritischen Philosophie.) The principles of crit. philos. sel. from...Emmanuel [sic] Kant...and expounded... Tr. anon. L: J. Johnson, W. Richardson 1797. lxxx; 454p. 22cm. [The tr. is A. F. M. Willich, cf. #4787. Chiefly exposition; rather freely tr.] [BM]

BEÇK, K: 1817-79. Sel. in C17;67;311;317;448.

BECK, K: Is. 1801-79. Sel. in C301.

BECK, W:e, Baronin v. der, d.1851.
?307. (Memoiren einer Dame während des letzten Unabhängigkeitskrieges in Ungarn.) Personal adventures in Hungary. Tr. M. A. Garvey. L: Bentley 1850. 2v. 19cm. [BM.LC] [Engl. ed. pub. Oct. 1850. German ed. Dec. 1850. Text is not the same, esp. at the beginning. Chapter summaries totally different. Baroness perhaps wrote both herself, assisted by Garvey in the Engl. ed.?]

BECKER, A: 1828-91.
?308. (Des Rabbi Vermächtnis.) Tempted of the devil: passages in the life of a cabbalist. Retold by M. W. Macdowall. Bost: Cupples & H; Paisley: Gardner 1888. xvi;330p. 19cm. [LC.BM] [No immediately apparent relation in form or substance.]

BECKER, H: Crn. Sel. in C233.

BECKER, J: Ph. 1808-87. Sel. in C301.

BECKER, K: F: 1777-1806. Sel. in C563.
309. Achilles. Tr. and abr. G: P. Upton. [Life stories for young people.] Chic: McClurg 1912. 154p. il. 17cm. [LC] [From his Erzählungen aus der alten welt für die Jugend.]
310. Ulysses of Ithaca. Tr. G: P. Upton. [Life stories for young people.] Chic: McClurg 1912. 164p. il. 17cm. [same source] [LC] See also Schmidt, F., joint author. Gods and heroes.

BECKER, N: 1809-45. Sel. in C29;67;123;142;153;166;372;443.

BECKER, W: Ad. 1796-1846.
**311. (Charicles, Bilder altgriechischer Sitte.) Charicles; or, illustrations of the private life of the ancient Greeks. Tr. by Rev. F: Metcalfe. L: Parker 1845. 371p. 8. [BM] [See note to #313.]
**312. do. 1854. [same] New ed. Collated and enl., with notes and excursuses from the German [by I. T.]. L: Parker. 512p. 8. [BM]
**313. do. 1866. [same] 3d ed. NY: Appleton. 512p. 19cm. [LC] [Admirably done, with loving care. Alterations explained in pref.]
**314. do. 1874. [same] 4th ed. L: Longmans. [LC]
**315. do. 1889. [same] 8th ed. L;NY: Longmans. [LC]
**316. do. 1899. [same] New impression. 512p. [LC]
**317. (Gallus: oder römische Szenen aus der Zeit Augusts.) Gallus; or, Roman scenes of the time of Augustus. Tr. F: Metcalfe. L: Parker 1844. 421p. 8. [See note to #313.] [BM]
**318. do. 1849. [same] Enl. ed. L: Parker. 535p. 20cm. [LC.BM]
**319. do. 1866. [same] 3d ed. NY: Appleton. [LC.BM]

BECKER, W: Ad.
**320. do. 1876. [same] 5th ed. L: Longmans. [LC.BM]
**321. do. 1888. [same] 9th ed. L: Longmans. [LC.BM]
**322. do. 1898. [same] New ed. L: Longmans. 535p. [LC]

BECKER, W: Gb. 1753-1813 Sel. in C106.

BEER, A. Sel. in C466. ["A. T. Beer" was pseudonym of A: Binzer.]

BEER, Max
*323. (Allgemeine Geschichte des Sozialismus und der sozialen Kämpfe. 1. Teil.) Social struggles in antiquity. Tr. H. J. Stenning, rev. by author. L: Parsons 1922. 222p. 19cm. [BM.LC]
*324. do. 1924. (2. Teil.) Social struggles in the Middle Ages. Tr. H. J. Stenning. NY: Small. 215p. 19cm. [BM.LC]
*325. do. 1925. (3. Teil.) Social struggles and socialist forerunners. Tr. H. J. Stenning, rev. by author. NY: Small. 224p. 19cm. [LC.BM]
*326. do. 1925. (4. Teil.) Social struggles and thought (1750-1860). Tr. H. J. Stenning, rev. by author. NY: Small; L: Parsons. 218p. 19cm. [LC.BM]
*327. do. 1925. (5. Teil.) Social struggles and modern socialism. Tr. H. J. Stenning, rev. by author. NY: Small; L: Parsons. 224p. 19cm. [LC.BM]
328. (Karl Marx, eine Monographie.) Life and teachings of K: M--. Tr. T. C. Partington and H. J. Stenning, rev. by author. L: Nat. Labour Press 1921, also Parsons 1921. xxxii;132p. 19cm. [BM.LC]
329. do. 1924. [same] NY: Small. 132p. 19cm. [LC.BM]

BEER, Ml. 1800-33.
§330. (Der Paria.) The paria: a tragedy. Tr. Earl of Ellesmere. L: Sams 1836. 30p. 8. [Good blank verse, not very close to the original. Stage directions reduced or omitted.] [BM]

BEETHOVEN, L: van, 1770-1827. Sel. in C366.
331. Impressions of contemporaries. Compiled, annotated, and in part tr. by O. G. Sonneck. NY: Schirmer 1926. vii;231p. il. 22cm. [A few tr. by Theodore Baker, the majority by F. H. Martens.] [LC.BM]
332. do. 1927. [same] L: Milford. [BM]
*333. Letters, 1790-1826. Tr. Lady Wallace. L: Longmans 1866. 2v. 19cm. [BM.LC]
*334. Letters; critical ed. with notes by A. C. Kalischer. Tr. J: S. Shedlock. L: Dent; NY: Dutton 1909. 2v. 23cm. [BM.LC] [Section sampled made excellent impression.]
§335. do. 1913-15. Letters, tr. by Shedlock. In C154(6). [This section showed inaccuracies, also liberties with style.]
§336. do. 1926. [same] Sel. and ed. by A. Eaglefield-Hull. L: Dent; NY: Dutton. xvi;410p. il. 22cm. [LC]
*337. Life. Beethoven, the man and the artist, as revealed in his own words. Comp. by F. Kerst, tr. H: E: Krehbiel. NY: Huebsch 1905. 110p. 20cm. [This copy examined.] [LC]
*338. do. 1906. [same] L: Gay & Bird. [BM]
*339. do. 1926. Reissue w. diff. title-page. L: G. Bles. 8. [BM]
See Bekker, Pl., Beethoven, #343.
See Elterlein, E., Beethoven's pianoforte sonatas explained. Beethoven's symphonies in their ideal significance, #1445-8.
See Hiller, Fd., On the hundredth anniversary of B--'s birth, #4329.
See Hoffmann, Fz., L: v. B--, #4476.
See Marx, A., B--'s F minor sonata, #6088.
See Mueller, Hg., A dramatized episode from B--'s life, #6509.

BEETHOVEN, L: van
See Nohl, L:, B-- depicted by his contemporaries. Life of B--, #6901-2.
See Rau, H., B--, a biographical romance, #7337.
See Reinecke, K:, The B-- pianoforte sonatas, #7381.
See Schindler, A., Life of B--, #8250.
See Tenger, M., Recoll. of Countess Teresa, #9341.
See Wagner, R:, B-- etc., #9621 seq.
See Wegeler, Fz., Furioso; or, passages from the life of B--, #9970.

[Opera Fidelio. See Sonnleithner, Js.]

BEHEMB, Mn. 1557-1622. Sel. in C271,287.

BEHRENS, Bta. 1850-1912. See "Heimburg, W."

BEHRENS, G: Henning, 1662-1712.
§340. (Hercynia curiosa, i.e., Curiöser Hartz-wald.) The natural history of Hartz-Forest, in his majesty King George's German dominions. Tr. J: Andree. L: Osborne 1730. 164p. 20cm. [BM.LC] [Tr. cuts very substantially; knowledge of German seems adequate.]

BEILIS, Mendel, 1874- .
340a. The story of my sufferings. Tr. Harrison Goldberg. Introd. Herman Bernstein and A. D. Margolin. Author 1926. 264p. il. [AC]

BEISSEL, Ig. See Alexander, L., joint author.

BEISSEL, J: Cd. 1690-1768.
341. A dissertation on mans fall. Prtd. Ephrata, anno 1765. Sold at Phil. by Messrs. C. Marshall & W: Dunlap. 37p. 8. (B6a)
342. (Mystische Sprüche.) A unique MS by Rev. P: Miller...written for B: Franklin...with a tr. of B--'s mystical proverbs, orig. prt. by B: Franklin in 1730. Lancaster, Pa: The Penn. Ger. Soc. 1912. 44p. 24cm. [LC]

BEKKER, Pl. 1882- .
*343. Beethoven. Tr. and ad. M. M. Bozman. L: Dent 1925. 401p. 22cm. [Not close in form, but well done; the essential spirit is caught.] [BM.LC]
*344. (Musikgeschichte als Geschichte der musikalischen Formwandlungen.) The story of music. Tr. M. D. Herter-Norton and A. Kortschak. L: Dent 1927. 277p. 8. [BM]

BENATZKY, Rp. 1884- and I. M. WELLEMINSKY.
†345. (Apachen.) The Apache: operetta in 3 acts by R. Benatzky. Tr. (freely ad.) Dion Titheradge. Libr. n. i. 1926. Tw. 29cm. [Really rewritten.] [LCM]

BENCKENDORFF, Graf Paul.
345a. Last days at Tsarskoe Selo: personal notes and memories of the last sojourn of the Emperor and the Empress of Russia... Mar. 1 to Aug. 1, 1917. Tr. M. Boring. Heinemann 1927. 176p. 8. [EC]

BENEDIX, Jl. Rod. 1811-73.
*346. (Das Lügen.) Is lying easy? A comedy. Tr. and ad. Annie Wall. St. Louis: Jones 1877. 72p. 12. [BPL]
†347. (Der Dritte.) Mabel's manoeuvre; or, a third party. Tr. Sydney Rosenfeld. NY: De Witt 1876. 10p. 19cm. [Very free.] [LC]
†348. do. 1915. The third man. Tr. B. H. Clark. NY: French. 20p. 19cm. [LC.BM]
†349. (Der Prozess.) The law-suit: a comedy in one act. Tr. B. H. Clark. NY: French 1915. 23p. 19cm. [Too free.] [LC.BM]

BENEDIX, Jl. Rod.
§350. (Der Weiberfeind.) The woman-hater. Tr. H. B. Sonneborn. Chic: Denison 1890. 16p. 12. [LC]
351. (Die Eifersüchtigen.) Married bachelors; or, pleasant surprises. Ad. Sydney Rosenfeld. NY: De Witt 1876. 11p. 19cm. [LC]
§352. (Die Hochzeitsreise.) The wedding trip. Tr. H. B. Sonneborn. Chic: Denison 1890. 33p. 12. [LC]
353. (Die Lügnerin.) Who told the lie? Tr. H. B. Sonneborn. Chic: Denison 1890. 33p. 12. [LC]
354. (Eigensinn.) Obstinacy; or, who shall yield? Tr. anon. Phil: Leypoldt 1865. 16. [AC]
†355. do. 1876. The obstinate family. A farce in one act. Tr. and ad. In "NY. Drama," 2:27-32. [BPL]
*356. do. 1882. Obstinacy. Tr. anon. Harrow: Wilbee. 18p. 8. [BM]
357. do. 1886. The obstinate family. Tr. anon. Chic: Dram. pub. D. [AC]
358. do. 1888. The table is set. Ad. Welland Hendrick. Syracuse, NY: Bardeen. 26p. 19cm. [LC]
359. do. 1903. Tr. W. H. H. Chambers. In C18, vol. 11.
§360. (Ein Lustspiel.) The three bachelors; an amusing play. Tr. by a young lady. L: Chard 1862. 98p. 8. [BM]
[Good, but not good enough.]
361. do. 1862. Three bachelors: play in 4 acts. L: Hamilton. 12. [EC]
362. do. 1878. Mrs. Walthrop's bachelors. Tr. and ad. G: M. Baker and Willard Small. Bost: Baker. 67p. 12. [LCO]

BENGER, G.
*363. (Rumänien im Jahre 1900.) Rumania in 1900. Tr. A: H: Keane. L: Asher 1900. 286p. il. 28cm. [BM.LC]

BENN, Gf. 1886- . Sel. in C95.

BENZMANN, Hs. 1869- . Sel. in C28.

BERG, Leo, 1862-1908.
§364. (Der Übermensch in der modernen Literatur.) The superman in mod. lit. Tr. anon. L: Jarrold 1916. 258p. 19cm. [BM.LC]
[Not complete, and not wholly accurate.]

BERGER, J: Nk. 1816-70.
365. The life of the right Rev. J: N. Neumann. Tr. Rev. E. Grimm. NY: Benziger 1884. 457p. 12. [LCO]

"BERKOW, K:" [i.e., Wolfersdorff, Ele. Cte., freiin v. 1849-1921.]
366. ("Vae victis!") "Woe to the conquered!" A romance of the Moors in Spain. Tr. H. E. M(iller?) Chic: Rand, McNally 1892. 218p. il. 21cm. [Pseudonym is Beskow, according to Kosch.] [LC]

BERLEPSCH, Hm. Ax. v. 1883- .
*367. (Die Alpen in Natur- und Lebensbildern.) The Alps; or, sketches of life and nature in the mountains. Tr. Sir Leslie Stephen. Il. by Emil Rittmeyer. L: Longmans 1861. 407p. 22cm. [Not entirely accurate, but very good.] [BM.LC]
368. The Lucerne-Rigi rail at Vitznau. Tr. anon. 1884. 40p. il. In C294.

BERLICHINGEN [Götz Gst.] Ad. Frhr. v. 1840- .
369. Maron, the Christian youth of the Lebanon. Tr. Helena Long. St. Francis, Wis: St. Aemilianus Orph. Asylum 1895. 76p. il. 17cm. [LC]
370. do. 1916. [same] 4th ed. St.L: Herder. 107p. D. [AC]
371. Prince Arumugam, the steadfast Indian convert. Tr. Helena Long. St. Francis, Wis: etc. 1895. 86p. il. 16cm. [LC]
372. do. 1914. [same] St.L: Herder. 115p. [AC]

BERLICHINGEN, Gf. [Götz] v. 1480-1562. See "Gottfried of the iron hand," A216.

BERNARD, A. Hm.
373. Legends of the Rhine. Tr. Fr. Arnold. 8th ed. Mayence: Halenza 187-. 316p. il. 16cm. [First Engl. ed. 1862. LC card.][LC]
374. do. 1900. [same] 11th rev. ed. Wiesbaden: G. Quiel. viii;306p. 8. [BM]

BERNARD, F:
375. Garcia Moreno: trag. in 3 acts. Adapted. anon. St.L: Herder 1916. 29p. unp. O. [AC]

BERNARD, Js. C: 1780-1850.
376. Faust, a lyric play: opera in 3 acts by L: Spohr. Tr. anon. Libr. Ger;Engl. L: Schloss 1842. 85p. 17cm. [BM]
[Prose, line for line without rhyme or meter. Sense well given. No relation to Goethe's "Faust."]
§377. do. 1852. Tr. anon. Libr. Ital. [by Manfredo Maggioni];Engl. L: Brettell. 84p. 17cm. [BM.LCM]
[English in rhythmic prose, apparently taken from the Italian, which is fairly close to the German.]
*378. do. 1852. Faust: a lyric tragedy. Tr. J. W. Mould. Music ed. W. S. Rockstro. Vocal score, Ger;Engl. L: Boosey. 284p.25cm.[BMM]

BERNAUER, Rd. 1880- and Lp. Jacobson.
379. (Der tapfere Soldat.) The chocolate soldier: operetta in 3 acts by Oscar Straus. Tr. Stanislaus Stange. Score. NY: Remick 1909. 201p. fol. [Heavily adapted. No dialog given.] [LCM]
*380. do. 1925. Tr. G. I. Colbron. Libr. Engl. NY: Bartsch. 24;31;14p. Tw. 30cm. [LCM]
[Text based on Shaw: "Arms and the man." Dialog excellent. No lyrics.]

BERNAUER, Rd. and SCHANZER, Rd.
381. (Filmzauber.) Girl on the film: musical farce by Walter Kollo, Willy Bredschneider, and Albert Sirmay. Tr. Jas. T. Tanner. Libr. Engl. L: Chappell 1913. 28p. [LCM]
382. do. 1913. [same] Vocal score. Engl. L: Chappell. 147p. 28cm. [BMM.LCM]

BERNAUER, Rd., Ern. WELISCH, and Eg. SPERO.
383. (Der liebe Augustin.) Princess caprice: operetta by Leo Fall. Tr. Ax. M. Thompson w. orig. Engl. lyrics. Vocal score. Engl. L: Chappell 1912. 228p. 4. [LCM]
384. do. 1912. [same] 244p. 27cm. [BMM]
384a. do. 1912. [same] Libr. L: Chappell. 38p. 21cm. [BM]

BERNGER VON HORHEIM. 12th cent. Minnesinger. Sel. in C427.

BERNHARD, Me.
385. The household idol. Tr. Elise L. Lathrop. NY: Worthington 1892. 327p. il. 19cm. [LC]
386. The pearl. Tr. Ma. S. Smith. L;NY: Internat. News 1894. 307p. 19cm. [LC]
387. The rector of St. Luke's. Tr. E. L. Lathrop. NY: Worthington 1891. 19cm. [AC]
388. (Um meinetwillen.) For my own sake. Tr. Ma. S. Smith. L: Internat. News 1893. 258p. 12. [LC]

BERNHARDI, F: Am. Jl. v. 1849- . Sel. in C161.
389. [Sel.] B-- converted; a comparative study of the effect of "drastic medicine" on the expressed opinions of Gen. v. B--. L: Darling 1915. 15p. 25cm. [Eclectic.] [LC]

BERNHARDI, F: Am. Jl. v.
390. [Sel.] 1915. The new B--: "World power or downfall." Tr. anon. L: Pearson. [Eclectic. Chaps. I-IV = #395.] [LC]
*391. (Deutschland und der nächste Krieg.) Germany and the next war. Tr. A. H. Powles. L: Arnold 1912. 300p. 22cm. [LC.BM]
*392. do. 1914. [same] Popular ed. NY: Longmans; L: Arnold. 288p. 19cm. [LC.BM]
*393. do. 1918. [same] 25th impression. [EC]
§394. (Unsere Zukunft.) Britain as Germany's vassal; together with "Kriegsbrauch," The customs of war. Tr. J. Ellis Barker. L: Dawson; NY: Doran 1914. 255p. 19cm. [Loose and careless.][LC.BM]
395. do. 1915. Germany and England. Tr. anon. NY: Dillingham. 93p. 19cm. [LC]
*396. (Vom heutigen Kriege.) On war of today. Tr. K: von Donat. L: Rees 1912-13. 2v. 22cm. [LC.BM]
*397. do. 1914. [same] NY: Dodd, Mead. 2v. maps. O. [AC]
*398. do. 1914. [same, abr.] How Germany makes war. NY: Doran. xiv;248p. 8. [Excellent as far as it goes. Edits slightly the text of the foregoing, but is essentially the same.] [LC.BM]
*399. (Vom Kriege der Zukunft, nach den Erfahrungen des Weltkrieges.) The war of the future in the light of the lessons of the world war. Tr. F. A. Holt. L: Hutchinson 1920. 271p. 22cm. [On the whole, excellent. He takes some needless liberties.] [LC]
*400. do. 1921. [same] NY: Appleton. xix;310p. 22cm. [LC]

BERNHART, Josef, 1881- .
401. Marriage as a sacrament. 1926. In C308.

BERNSTEIN, Cn. An. d.1699. Sel. in C229;269.

BERNSTEIN, E: 1850- .
402. American opinions of the world war as seen by a German. Tr. J: Mez. NY: Am. assoc. for internat. concil. 1916. 28p.19cm. [LC]
§403. (Die Voraussetzungen des Sozialismus....) Evolutionary socialism. Tr. Edith C. Harvey. L: Ind. labour party 1909. xxiii;224p. 19cm. [Tr. not wholly adequate to the task.] [BM.LC]
404. (Erinnerungen eines Sozialisten.) My years of exile; reminisc. of a socialist. Tr. Bernard Miall. NY: Harcourt; L: Parsons 1921. 287p. 22cm. [LC.BM]
405. Fd. Lassalle as a social reformer. Tr. Eleanor M. Aveling. NY: Scribner; L: Sonnenschein 1893. xiv;192p. 19cm. [LC.BM]

BERNSTEIN, Elsa Porges, 1866- . See "Rosmer, Ernst."

BERNSTORFF, A. v., Graf. See Ringhoffer, K: The B-- papers, etc. #7504.

BEROLZHEIMER, Fr. 1869-1920.
406. (System der Rechts- und Wirtschaftsphilosophie.) The world's legal philosophies. Tr. Rachel S. Jastrow. Introd. by Sir J. MacDonnell and Albert Kocourek. Boston book co. 1912. liv;490p. 21cm. [LC]
407. do. 1921. [same] Macmillan. lv;490p. O. [AC]

BERTHOLDUS, An., of Oschatz.
408. (Terrae Sigillatae, nuper in Germania repertae....) The wonderful and strange effect and virtues of a new Terra Sigillata lately found out in Germanie... Tr. B(arnabe) G(ooge?) L: R. Robinson for R: Watkins 1587. 39p. 13cm. [BM]

BERTHOLET, Af.
409. The transmigration of souls. Tr. J. H. Chaytor. NY: Harper 1909. viii;132p. 8. [BM]

BETHGE, Hs. 1876- . Sel. in C28.

BETHMANN-HOLLWEG, Tb. v. 1856-1921. Sel. in C161.
*410. (Betrachtungen zum Weltkriege.) Reflections on the world war. Tr. G: Young. Pt. 1. L: Butterworth 1920. 180p. 23cm. [LC.BM]
NY: Harper 1920. il. O. [On the whole, excellent.] [AC]
*411. (Reden.) Seven war speeches, 1914-1916. Tr. anon. Zürich. Füssli 1916. 87p. 8. [Excellent in the main.] [BM]
412. do. ... Despatch from his majesty's ambassador at Berlin, transmitting the tr. of a speech delivered in the Reichstag by the imperial German chancellor on the subject of the events preceding the Franco-German-Morocco agreement on Dec. 5, 1911. [LC]
413. do. 1914. Speeches. (Session of August the fourth, 1914.) Germanistic soc. of Chicago. pa. [AC]
414. Speech before the Reichstag on April 5, 1916. Tr. furnished through German embassy. Am. assoc. for internat. concil. 1916. 21p. pa. D. [AC]

BETHUSY-HUC, Va. R. See "Reichenbach, Mz. v."

BETTAUER, Hg. 1877-1925.
§415. (Die Stadt ohne Juden.) City without Jews; a novel of our time (i.e., of the future). Tr. Salomea N. Brainin. NY: Bloch 1926. viii;189p. 19cm. [Good but not wholly accurate.] [LC]

BETTEX, Frédéric, 1837-1915.
416. (Das erste Blatt der Bibel.) The first page of the Bible. Tr. W.R. Burlington, Ia: Ger. lit. bd. 1903. 71p. 17cm. [LC]
417. (Die Bibel Gottes Wort.) The Bible the word of God. Tr. from 3d enl. Ger. ed. anon. Cincin: Jennings & P; NY: Eaton & Mains 1904. 314p. 21cm. [LC]
418. Glory of the triune God. Tr. Andreas Bard. Burlington, Ia: Ger. lit. bd. 1914. 78p. 19cm. [LC]
419. (Israels Hunger.) The hunger of Israel. Tr. Andreas Bard. Burlington, Ia: Ger. lit. bd. 1915. 37p. 19cm. [LC]
420. Miracle. Tr. H(enry) M(ueller?) 2d ed. Burlington, Ia: Lutheran lit. bd. 1918. 121p. 20cm. [LC]
[H: Mueller, Defiance, O., took out copyright in 1900. Hand-book press. 78p. 8.]
421. (Naturstudium und Christentum.) Science and Christianity. Tr. anon. Cincin: Jennings & Pye; NY: Eaton & Mains 1901. 326p. 21cm. [LC]
422. do. 1903. Modern science and Christianity. Tr. w. add. and notes by Edmund K. Simpson. L: Marshall bros. xvi;354p. 8. [BM]
423. Six days of creation in the light of modern science. Tr. D: Heagle. Introd. by L. Franklin Gruber. Burlington, Ia: Ger. lit. bd. 1924. 64p. 20cm. [LC]
424. (Was dünkt dich von Christo?) What think ye of Christ? Tr. J: F. Krueger. Burlington, Ia: Ger. lit. bd. 1907. 102p.21cm.[LC]
425. The word of God. Tr. Andreas Bard. Burlington, Ia: Ger. lit. bd. 1914. 113p. 19cm. [LC]

BEUST, F: Fd. Graf v. 1809-86.
*426. (Aus drei Viertel-Jahrhunderten. Erinnerungen und Aufzeichnungen.) Memoirs...written by himself. Tr. anon. L: Remington 1887. 2d. ed. 2v. 398;391p. 8. [BM.LCO]

BEUVIUS, Am.
427. (Henriette oder der Husarenraub.) Henrietta of Gerstenfield (or --feld; also: Gerstend): a German story. Tr. anon. L: Lane 1787-8. 2v. 8. See["Crit. R." 63(1787):389.](B26)
[Ascribed to Wieland. See Goedeke IV^3, i.e. 3d ed., 1, 595.]

BEYERLEIN, Fz. Am. 1871- .
§428. (Jena oder Sedan?) Jena or Sedan? A novel...somewhat abbrev. by W: Thompson. L: Heinemann 1904. 361p. 8. [BM]
[Tr. in good style, but has many bad errors.]
§429. do. 1913. [same] Bost: Priv. print. 387p. 21cm. [LC]
§430. do. 1914. [same] [BM]
§431. do. 1916. [same] L: Heinemann. 361p. 8. [EC]
432. (Zapfenstreich.) Taps: a play of Ger. military life. Ad. A. I. du P. Coleman. NY: Herman 1904. (B38)
*433. do. 1905. Lights out: a play in four acts. Tr. H. Havelock. L: Heinemann. 130p. 12. [BM]
434. do. 1915. Taps. Tr. C: Swickard. Bost: Luce. 119p. 19cm. [LC]

BEYRICK, Frau Cle. (Helm). See "Helm, Cle."

BIANOVSKY, W. v. Sel. in C229.

BIBLIANDER, Tds. 1504-64.
435. (Ad nominis christiani socios consultatio, qua nam ratione Turcarum dira potentia...) A Godly Consultation...by what meanes the cruell Power of the Turkes bothe may and ought for to be repelled of the Christen people... Tr. anon. Basill: H. Bonifante 1542. clii ff. 8. [BM]

BIE, Ok. 1864- .
436. (Das Klavier.) History of the pianoforte and pianoforte players. Tr. and rev. Ern. E: Kellett and E: W. Naylor. NY: Dutton; L: Dent 1899. xi;336p. il. 24cm. ["This work does not profess to be so much a literal tr. as a somewhat free version." [LC.BM]

BIELSCHOWSKY, Ab. 1847-1902.
*437. (Goethe, sein Leben und seine Werke.) Life of Goethe. Tr. W: A. Cooper. NY; L: Putnam 1905-8. 3v. il. 24cm. [AC]
*438. do. [n.d.] NY: Stechert (1912-17). 2v. [AC]

BIENEMANN, Kp. 1540-91. Sel. in C271.

BIERBAUM, O: Jl. 1865-1910. Sel. in C28;423.
*439. (Lobetanz.) Merrydance: opera in 3 acts by L: Thuille. Tr. M. T. E. Sandwith. Libr. Ger;Engl. NY: Schirmer 1911. 26p. 8. [On the whole, very good.] [LCM]

BIERMANN, (K: W:) G: 1880- .
440. (Florenz und seine Kunst.) Florence and her art. Tr. F. F. Cox. L: Siegle, Hill 1912. 83p. il. 16cm. [LC.BM]
--McKay 1912. 83p. il. S. [AC]
441. do. 1921. [same] NY: Stokes. 83p. il. S. [AC]
442. Venice. (Art monographs.) Stokes 1921. [AC]

BIERNATZKI, J: Cph. 1795-1840. Sel. in C92-3.
*443. (Die Hallig.) The maid of the hallig; or, the unfortunate islanders. A narr. founded on fact. Tr. S: Jackson. L: Cradock 1843. 228p. 8. [Good style, not wholly correct.] [BM]
*444. do. 1857. The hallig; or, the sheepfold in the waters. A tale of humble life on the coast of Schleswig. Tr. Mrs. C. P. Marsh. Bost: Gould & Lincoln. 298p. 8. [BM]
[A better tr. than the foregoing.]

BIESE, Af. 1856- .
§445. (Die Entwicklung des Naturgefühls....) The development of the feeling for nature in the middle ages and modern times. Tr. anon. L: Routledge; NY: Dutton 1905. 376p. 19cm. [BM.LC]
[Neither close nor accurate.]

BIESENTHAL, Jm. H: Rl.
446. "Aus dem Cheder." Pictures of Jewish life. Tr. Mrs. Baron. L: Morgan & Scott 1903. 58p. 8. [BM]
[Reprinted from "The scattered nation."]

BILLER, Ea.
447. Ulli: the story of a neglected girl. Tr. A. B. D. Rost. L: Trübner 1888. viii;304p. 8. [BM]

BILSE, Os. Fr. 1878- .
*448. (Aus einer kleinen Garnison: ein militärisches Zeitbild.) Life in a German garrison town: the military novel suppressed by the Ger. govt. Tr. anon. Introd. by Arnold White. NY; L: Lane 1904. 301p. 19cm. [LC]
*449. do. 1904. [same] 3d ed. [BM]
450. do. 1904. A little garrison. By "Fritz v. d. Kyrburg." Tr. and ed. Wolf von Schierbrand. NY: Stokes. 307p. 19cm. [LC]
451. do. 1914. [same as #448] [LC]
§452. (Lieb Vaterland.) Dear fatherland. Tr. anon. L; NY: Lane 1905. 257p. 8. [AC has: 1904. Inaccurate.] [BM]

BINZER, A: Dl. Frhr. v. 1793-1868. Sel. in C215;317.

BIRKEN, Sg. v. 1626-81. Sel. in C271;530.

BISCHOFF, Js. E: Kd. 1828-1920. See "Bolanden, Kd. v."

BISMARCK, J: A. See Harden, M., Word portraits. #3699.

BISMARCK[-SCHOENHAUSEN], O: [E: Lp.] Fürst v. 1815-98. Sel. in C320, 366*;469.
453.[Sel.] Bismarck calendar: a quotation from the writings and sayings of Prince B-- for every day in the year. Sel. by J. M. Kennedy. L: Palmer 1913. 133p. 8. [BM]
*454. (Briefe.) Letters, 1844-70. Tr. F. Maxse. L: Chapman & Hall 1878. 8. [This copy examined.] [HCL]
*455. do. 1879. [same] 2d ed. 259p. [HCL]
*456. do. 1901. Love-letters, 1846-89. Tr. under supervision of C. T: Lewis. NY; L: Harpers. 427p. 21cm. [LC]
[Letters, see also Wilhelm I. The correspondence of W-- I and B--. #10231.]
*457. do. 1903. Letters to his wife...1870-1. Tr. C. A. Harder. NY: Appleton. 145p. 20cm. [LC.BM]
§458. do. 1915. Letters to his wife. Newly tr. anon. L: Jarrold. 118p. 22cm. [Foregoing tr. is much better.] [LC]
*459. (Gedanken und Erinnerungen.) B-- the man and the statesman: being the reflections and reminiscences written and dictated by himself. Tr. under supervision of A. J: Butler. L: Smith, Elder 1898. 2v. 8. [This copy examined.] [BM]
*460. do. 1899. [same] NY; L: Harpers. 2v. 22cm. [LC]
*461. do. 1920. Kaiser vs. B--: suppressed letters by the Kaiser and new chapters from the autobiog. of the Iron Chancellor; with an histor. introd. by C: D. Hazen. Tr. B. Miall. NY; L: Harpers. xii;196p. il. 20cm. [LC.BM]
[The third vol., orig. to be withheld from publication until the death of W: II. Tr. is not faultless, but very good.]
*462. do. 1921. [same] New chapters of B--'s autobiography. L: Hodder & S. 343p. 8. [BM]
463. Life. B-- intime. By a fellow student. Tr. H: Hayward. L: Dean; NY: Appleton 1890. 286p. il. 8. [BM.HCL.BPL]
464. do. 1898. [same] B-- and all about him. Tr. H: Hayward. L: Dean. 264p. 8. [Another ed. The wording is slightly revised.][BM]
465.(Reden.) Speeches...Jan. 29 and Feb. 13, 1869. Berlin; L: 1869. 95p. 22cm. [LC.BM]

BISMARCK, O: v.
466. do. 1888. Speech...before the Ger. Reichstag Feb. 6, 1888. Tr. Sa. Zimmermann. In Lord, J: "Two Ger. Giants." NY: Fords, H. & H. 12. [LCO]
467. (Tischgespräche.) B--'s table-talk. Ed. C: Lowe. L: Grevel 1895. 387p. 8. [Based on Poschinger's "Tischgespräche," but not strictly a translation of it.] [BPL]
468. do. 1898. [same] New ed. 396p. [EC]
469. do. 1900. Conversations with Prince B--. By H: Ritter v. Poschinger. Ed. Sidney Whitman. NY; L: Harpers. 299p. 20cm. [LC]
See Bamberger, L:, Count B--. A political biography, #191.
See Busch, Jl., B-- in the Franco-German war. B--, some secret pages. Our chancellor, etc., #943-7.
See Garlepp, Br., B-- memorial, etc. Germany's iron chancellor, etc., #2121-2.
See Görlach, W., Prince B--. A biographical sketch, #2350.
See Harden, Mx., word portraits, #3699 seq.
See Hesekiel, J., The life of B--, #4241-2.
See Sonnenburg, Fd., B--, his life and times, #8791.

BISSING, Mz. Fd. Frhr. v. 1844-1917.
470. Bissing's testament: a study in German ideals. Tr. anon. L: Unwin 1917. 36p. 21cm. [BM.LC]
471. do. 1918. [same] NY: Harper. 31p. 19cm. [LC]

BITTER, K: Hm. 1813-85.
472. Life (abr. from 381 to 103p.) of J. S. Bach. Tr. Janet E. Kay-Shuttleworth. L: Houlston 1873. 153p (with list of works). 8. [BM]

BITZIUS, Ab. 1797-1854. See "Gotthelf, Jr."

BLAUL, F: 1809-63. Sel. in C169.
473. True to their faith: a tale of the Walloons in the Palatinate. Tr. R. H. Schively. 1890. In C491.

BLAURER (or Blarer), Amb. 1492-1564. Sel. in C570.

BLEI, Fz. 1871- .
*474. (Die Puderquaste. Ein Damenbrevier.) The powder-puff: a ladies' breviary. Tr. anon. L: Chatto & Windus 1909. NY: Duffield 1910. 218p. 18cm. [Style well caught.] [BM.LC]

BLENNERHASSETT, Cte. Jla. (v. Leyden), lady, 1843-1917.
§475. (Streiflichter.) Sidelights. Author. tr. Edith Gülcher. L: Constable 1913. 245p. 23cm. [Many finesses lost.] [BM.LC]

BLIGGER VON STEINACH, fl. 1165-1209. Sel. in C27;427.

BLOBEL, O.
476. Little Herta's Christmas dream: a Christmas fairy tale of the mountains. Tr. anon. Il. by H. Grimm. L: Low 1911. 4. [EC]

BLOCH, Iwan, 1872-1922.
477. (Das Sexualleben unserer Zeit in seinen Beziehungen zur modernen Kultur.) The sexual life of our time in its relation to modern civilization. Tr. from the 6th ed. by M. Eden Paul. L: Rebman 1910? xvi;790p. 25cm. [LC]

BLOEM, Wl. S. 1868- .
§478. (Das eiserne Jahr.) The iron year. Tr. Stella Bloch. L; NY: Lane 1914. 400p. 19cm. [Rather poor; inaccurate.] [BM.LC]
479. The soul of the moving picture. Auth. tr. Allen W. Porterfield. NY: Dutton 1924. xx;168p. il. 20cm. [LC]

BLOMBERG, Hg. Frhr. v. 1820-71. Sel. in C450;501.

BLUEMNER, Hg. 1844-1919.
*480. (Leben und Sitten der Griechen.) The home life of the ancient Greeks. Tr. Alice Zimmern. L: Cassell 1893. xv;548p. il. 19cm. [Very good.] [LC.BM]
*481. do. 1895. [same] New and rev. ed. xxiii;548p. il.19cm.[LC.BM]
*482. do. 1910. [same] 3d ed. Cassell. [BM]
*483. do. 1914. [same] Funk 1914. 571p. il. D. [AC]

BLUM, G: (Strand und See.) Sel. Tr. Mrs. A. L. Wister. 1864. In C572.

BLUMAUER, Als. 1755-98. Sel. in C419.
484. (Abenteuer des frommen Helden Aeneas.) The death of Dido. Tr. W: Taylor. 1829. In C533.

BLUMENHAGEN, Ph. W: G: A: 1781-1839.
§485. (Eva von Troth.) Eva von Troth; a chronicle of the 16th cent. ...Tr. Louisa Addison. With other tales from the Ger. (i.e., Othello, and The word of honour, by J. F. Weigl. L: Thomas 1841. 2v. 12. [Really rewritten.] [BM]

BLUMENTHAL, K: Kst. Ab. Lh. Graf v. 1810-1900.
§486. (Tagebücher...) Journals, 1886 and 1870-1. Tr. Maj. A. D. Gillespie-Addison. L: Arnold 1903. 347p. 23cm. [LC] [Inadequate command of German.]

BLUMENTHAL, Lu. J:e. Lpe. (v. Platen) v. 1742-1808.
*487. (Lebensbeschreibung Hans Joachims von Zieten.) The life of Gen. de Zieten...Tr. by Rev. B: Beresford. Berl: Prt. for auth. and sold by R. Philips in Lond. 1803. 2v. 22cm. [BM.LC] [Not faithful in the modern sense, and still very good.]
*487a. do. 1810. [same] 2d ed. 2v. Berlin. 8. [EC]

BLUMENTHAL, Ok. 1852-1917.
488. After business hours: a comedy in 4 acts. Tr. Augustin Daly. NY: 1886. (B38)
**489. (Die grosse Glocke.) The big bell: a comedy in four acts. Tr. anon. Berlin? 1884. 17;16;12;13p. fol. Tw. [Admirable.] [BM]
490. A drop of poison: play in four acts. Auth. tr. anon. Berlin? 1885? 17;15;15;12p. Tw. [BM]
491. Dynamite: a comedy in three acts. Tr. and ad. G: Arthur and R. A. Weil (i.e., Weill). NY: 1893. (B38)
492. Little Miss Million: a comedy in four acts. Tr. A. Daly 1890. (B38)

BLUMENTHAL, Ok. and Gst. Kadelburg.
493. (Die Orientreise.) The orient express: a comedy in three acts. Ad. F. C. Burnand and A. Daly. NY: 1913. Tw. [LC]
§494. (Im weissen Röss'l.) At the white horse tavern: comedy in three acts. Ad. Sydney Rosenfeld. NY: Kauser 1907. 63p. 18cm.[LC] [Much adapted. The German MS was printed by Cherouny in 1898.]
495. Is marriage a failure? A comedy in four acts. Tr. and ad. L. Ditrichstein. NY:1909.(B38)
496. The last spark: a comedy in three acts. Ad. Cte. Thompson. NY: 1913. Tw. [LC]
497. Number nine; or, the lady of Ostend. A comedy in three acts. Tr. F. C. Burnand and A. Daly. NY: 1897. (B38)
498. A test case; or, grass versus granite. Tr. A. Daly. NY: 1893. (B38)

BLUMENTRITT, Fd. 1853-1913.
*499. (Die Philippinen. Eine übersichtliche Darstellung...) The Philippines; a summary account. Tr. D: J. Doherty. Chic: Donohue 1900. 69p. 22cm. [LC]

BLUMLER, Mn. F:
500. A history of amulets. Tr. [from the Latin] by S. H., Gent. Ed: Priv. prt. 1887. 47p. 22cm. [BM]

BLUNTSCHLI, J: Kp. 1808-81.
*501. (Lehre vom modernen Staat.) The theory of the state. Auth. tr. from 6th Ger. ed. by D: G: Ritchie (bks. I, IV, VII), P. E. Matheson (bks. II,III), and R: Lodge (bks. V, VI). Oxford: Clarendon 1885. xx;518p. 8. [BM]
*502. do. 1893. [same] 2d ed? Frowde. [EC]
*503. do. 1898. [same] 3d ed. [reprint of 2d.] Clarendon. xxv;550p. 8. [LC.BM]
*504. do. 1901. [same] Clarendon. [LC]

BODANZKY, Rb., joint author. See Bakonyi, K: v.; Willner, A. M.

BODANZKY, Rb. and Fr. GRUENBAUM.
505. (Der Liebeswalzer.) The kiss waltz: operetta in two acts by C. M. Ziehrer and Jerome Kern. Tr. Edgar Smith. Vocal score. Engl. NY: Harms & Francis 1911. 115p. 4. [LCM]

BODANZKY, Rb. and Br. HARDT-WARDEN.
506. "Whirled into happiness." Mus. farce in three acts. Ad. by Harry Graham. Vocal score. Engl. L: Ascherberg 1922. 115p. 28cm. [BMM]
*507. (Der Tanz ins Glück.) Sky high: operetta in three acts by R. Stolz. Libr. n.i. 1925. 75 numb. leaves. Tw. 29cm. [LCM] [Dialog excellent.]

BODDIEN, -- v. Sel. in C506.

BODE, W: v. 1845-1929.
508. (Botticelli.) Sandro B--. Tr. F. Renfield and F. L. R. Brown. L: Methuen; NY: Scribner 1925. xii;183p. il. 26cm. [BM.LC]
509. (Die italienischen Bronzestatuetten der Renaissance.) Italian bronze statuettes of the R--. Tr. W: Grétor. Berl: Cassirer 1907-12; L: Grevel 1908-12. 3v. il. 50cm. [BM.LC] [Assisted by Murray Marks.]
§510. (Die italienischen Hausmöbel der Renaissance.) Italian R-- furniture. Tr. Ma. E. Herrick. NY: Helburn 1921. 48p. 71pl. 25cm. [Inadequate knowledge of German.] [LC.BM]
*511. (Florentiner Bildhauer der Renaissance.) Florentine sculptors of the R--. Tr. Jessie Haynes. L: Methuen 1908. xii;240p. il. 8. [LC has: 26cm.] [BM.LC]
512. (Rembrandt.) The complete work of R--, with a study of his life and art. Text by W: v. B-- assisted by C. H. de Groot. Tr. F. Simmonds. Paris: 1897-1906. 8v. fol. [BM]
§513. (Rembrandt und seine Zeitgenossen.) Great masters of Dutch and Flemish painting. Tr. from 2d rev. ed. by Marg. L. Clarke. L: Duckworth; NY: Scribner 1909. ix;358p. il. 20cm. [BM.LC] [Annoying lapses from strict accuracy.]
§514. do. 1911. [same] [LC]
515. (Vorderasiatische Knüpfteppiche aus älterer Zeit.) Antique rugs from the Near East. 3d rev. ed. with contributions by Ernst Kühnel. Tr. R. M. Riefstahl. NY: Weyhe 1922. 65p. il. 26cm. [LC]

BODENSTEDT, F: M: 1819-1882. ("Mirza Schaffy") Sel. in C65;112; 169;180;196;309;366*;423;448;450;469;470;497;504;566.
**516. (Gedichte.) The songs of Mirza Schaffy. Tr. Elsa d'E. Keeling. Hamburg: Grädener 1880. 228p. 8. [BM] [Very creditable; sense is well caught and verse is good.]
**517. do. 1887. The songs of Mirza Schaffy. Tr. Jas. Y. Gibson. Also, The Cid ballads and other poems and tr...Ed. Mary D. Gibson. L: K.Paul. 2v. 19cm. [BM] [Tr. very good.--Vol. 2, pp.221-307. Also, Schiller, Sehnsucht.]

BODENSTEDT, F:
§518. do. 1894. The mountain lake, and other poems. Tr. J. Preston. L: Roxburghe. 126p. 8. [Introd. Einkehr und Umschau (13-46); [BM] Mirza Schaffy (47-92); From orig. MSS (93-102); Funeral ceremony and orations (103-118); Bibliography. Tr's skill does not match her zeal and industry.]
*519. (Tausend und ein Tag im Orient.) The morning land; or, a thousand and one days in the East. Tr. R: Waddington. L: Bentley 1851. 2v. 12. [BM]
*520. do. 1853. [same] 2d series. [BM]
*521. (Völker des Kaukasus.) Schamyl. Tr. from F. Wagner's "Schamyl," with extracts from B--. In "The traveller's lib." vol. 14. L: 1856. 8. [BM]
[Rather close and good tr. of sections dealing with Schamyl.]

BODENSTEIN, -- v. See Seyppel, C. M., joint author. My book: an odd Egyptian MS.,etc. #8776.

BODMANN, Em. Frhr. v. 1874- . Sel. in C28.

BODMER, J: Jk. 1698-1783. Sel. in C366;373;469.
†522. (Noah.) Noah. Attempted from the Ger. by Js. Collyer. L: Prt. for Collyer, Dodsley, Durham, and Newbery 1767. 2v. 16cm. [Takes great liberties.] [BM.LC]
†523. do. 1767. [same] Dublin: for Murphy, Potts, etc. 2v. 12. [BM]
[Paging is quite different from L. ed.]
†524. do. 1770. 2d ed. Collyer. 2v. 12. [BM]
[Has additional title-pages and frontispieces engraved.]

BOECKH, Ph. A: 1785-1867.
§525. (Die Staatshaushaltung der Athener.) The public economy of Athens. Tr. Sir G: C. Lewis. L: J:Murray 1828. 2v. 8. [BM.LC]
§526. do. 1842. [same] 2d ed. [BM]
*527. do. 1857. The public economy of the Athenians. Tr. from 2d Ger. ed. by A. Lamb. Bost: Little, Brown; L: Sampson Low. xxxi;826p. 23cm. [LC.BM]

BOECKLIN, Arn. 1827-1901. See Harden, M. Word portraits. #3699.

BOEHLAU, Hle. 1859- .
528. (Die Kristallkugel.) The ball of crystal. Tr. A. I. du P. Coleman. 1913-15. In C154(19).

BOEHME, D: 1605-57. Sel. in C287.

BOEHME, Jk. 1575-1624. Sel. in C194;469.
529. [Coll.] The works of J-- Behmen...with figs., il. his principles, left by the Rev. W: Law. With a portrait. L: M. Richardson 1764-81. 4v. 4. [BM]
["Ed. by G. Ward and T. Langcake. The translations, except in the case of the 'Weg zu Christo,' where the 1775 ed. has been used, are those by J: Sparrow, J: Ellistone, and H. Blunden, with the phraseology occasionally slightly altered." BM cat.]
530. [Coll.] 1661. Several treatises of J. B--. Tr. J: Sparrow. 8 pts. L: L.Lloyd. 4. [BM]
[1. A book of the great six points: as also a small book of other six points. 2. The 177 theosophick questions: the first thirteen, answered. 3. Of the earthly and of the heavenly mystery. 4. The Holy Week, or a Prayer-book. 5. Of divine vision. To which are annexed the Exposition of the table of three principles; also an Epistle of the Knowledge of God, and of all things. Each pt. has sep. t.p.]

BOEHME, Jk.

531. [Coll.] 1661-2. The remainder of books written by J-- B--. Tr. J: Sparrow. L: G.Calvert. 490p. 4. [BM.LC] [The apologia against Richter, Stiefel, Meth, and Tilken, together with the Four Complexions, a number of the Epistles, and C. Weissner's "Relation." 7 pts. Each pt. has separate t.p., and all but the first are dated 1661.]

532. [Coll.] 1919. Six theosophic points and other writings, newly tr. J: R. Earle. L: Constable; NY: Knopf. vii;208p. (220p.) 21cm. [Six theosophic points; six mystical points; On the earthly and heavenly mystery; On the divine intuition.] [BM.LC]

SELECTIONS

533. 1649. Mercurius teutonicus: or, Christian information concerning the last times...gathered out of the mystical writings. Tr. anon. L: H.Blunden. 52p. 4. [BM]

534. 1656. [same] New t.p. L: Lodowick Lloyd. [BM]

535. 1691. J. Behmen's theosophick philosophy unfolded. Also the principal treatises of the said author abridged. And answers given to the remainder of the 177 theosophick questions...left unanswered by him... Tr. by E. Taylor. L: Tho. Salusbury. 434p. 4. [BM]

536. 1770. A compendious view of the grounds of the teutonick philosophy, with considerations by way of inquiry into the... writings of J. Behmen...also several extracts from his writings... A treatise of eternal nature. By J. P(ordage), M.D. L: Bathurst, Baker, etc. 3 pts. 12. [BM.LC]

537. 1795. Extracts from mercurius teutonicus...being divers prophetical passages of the fall of Babel and the new building in Zion. In Brothers, R. "Prophetical passages concerning the present times..." 8. [BM]

538. 1891. Fz. Hartmann, Life and doctrines of J. B--. L: Paul, T. & T. 338p. 21cm. [Contains many extracts from B--'s writings.] [BM]

539. 1896. Thoughts on the spiritual life. Tr. Cte. A. Rainy. Pref. by Ax. W(hyte). Ed: Oliphant. 87p. 8. [BM]

540. 1908. J-- B--. Ed. by Cte. A. Rainy. Pref. by Hugh Black. L; Ed: Jack. 112p. 16. [BM]

541. 1920. Confessions. Compiled and ed. by "W. Scott Palmer." Introd. by Evelyn Underhill. L: Methuen; NY: Knopf. xxxv;153p. 17cm. [BM.LC]

542. 1921. From darkness to true illumination; and, Of heaven and hell. Tr. anon. Akron, O: Sun pub. 60p. pa. T. [AC]

543. (Bedencken über Esaiae Stiefels Büchlein...) A consideration upon the book of E. Stiefel of the threefold state of man, and his new birth. Tr. anon. L: J.Macock 1653. 158p. 16. [BM]

544. (Beschreibung der drei Prinzipien göttlichen Wesens.) The second booke. Concerning the three principles of the divine essence of the eternall, dark, light, and temporary world... Tr. J: Sparrow. L: H.Blunden 1648. 396p. 4. [BM]

545. do. 1910. [same] Reissued by C: J: B(arker). Introd. by Pl. Deussen. L: J.M.Watkins. lxiv;809p. 8. [BM]

546. (De signatura rerum.) S-- r--; or, the Signature of all things, shewing the Sign and Signification of the severall Forr and Shapes in the Creation... (The 177 Theosophick Questions. Tr. J: Ellistone, with pref. and postscript by the translato L: Gyles Calvert 1651. 224p. 4.

BOEHME, Jk.

547. do. 1912. Signature of all things, and other writings. (Also: Of the Supersensual Life. The Way from Darkness to True Illumination.) Tr. of J: Ellistone. Introd. by Clifford Bax. L: Dent; NY: Dutton. (Everyman.) xiv;295p. 17cm. [BM.LC]

548. (Morgenröte im Aufgange.) Aurora. That is, the day-spring... That is the root...of philosophie, astrologie and theologie from the true ground... Tr. J: Sparrow. L: Gyles Calvert 1656. 643p. 4. [BM]

549. do. 1914. [same] Ed. C: J: B(arker) and D. S. H(ehner). L: Watkins. xlvii;723p. 8. [BM]

550. (Mysterium magnum.) M-- m--; or, an exposition of the first book of Moses. Tr. J: Ellistone and J: Sparrow. Also his four tables of divine revelation, tr. H. Blunden. L: H.Blunden 1654. 3 pts. fol. [BM]

551. do. 1924. [same] Ed. C: J: B(arker). L: Watkins. xxxii;981p. 8. [BM]

552. do. 1924. [same] Reprint of 1654 ed. 2v. il. 24cm. [LC]

553. Personal Christianity a science: the doctrines of J-- B--, the God-taught philosopher. Tr. anon. Introd. and notes by Franz Hartmann. NY: Macoy 1919. 336p. 21cm. [LC]

554. (Tafeln von den drei Prinzipien göttlicher Offenbarung.) Four tables of divine revelation. Tr. H. B(lunden). Also, a tr. of the original "Tafeln" from B--'s 47th epistle. L: Blunden 1654. fol. [Also with "Mysterium magnum," #547.] [BM]

555. (Theosophische Send-Schreiben.) Two theosophical epistles, wherein the life of a true Christian is described...Whereunto is added, a dialogue between an enlightened and a distressed soul... Tr. anon. L: B.Allen 1645. 84p. 12. [BM]

556. do. 1649. 35 epistles; also, a reall and unfeigned testimonie concerning J. Beme. Tr. J: Ellistone. A warning from J. Beem... to such as reade his writings. L: M. Simmons for Gyles Calvert. 3 pts. 4. [BM]

557. do. 1886. [same] reprint. The works of J-- B-- with an introd. by a graduate of Glasgow University (F. F.). Vol. 1. The epistles. Glasgow: D.Bryce. xi;216p. 4. [BM]

558. do. 1886. [same] Glasgow. J. Thomson. 216p. 8. [BM] [Duplicate with different t.p. and without introd.]

559. (Trost-schrift von vier Complexionen.) A consolatory treatise of the four complexions; that is an instruction in the time of temptation for a sad and assaulted heart,... Tr. C. Hotham. L: Blunden 1654. viii;51p. 12. [BM]

560. do. 1661. Of the four complexions. Tr. J: Sparrow. L: Calvert. 30p. sm. 4. [LC]

561. do. 1688. Philosophically divine, treating of the being of all Beeings... Also, a treatise of the four complexions. (By J-- B--.) Part one of The temple of wisdom, ed. by Dan. Leeds. Phil: W.Bradford. Pt. 1, 125p. 8. (B6a)

562. do. 1730? The four complexions; or, a treatise of consolatory instruction,... Tr. anon. L: J.Scott. viii;51p. 12. [BM]

563. do. 1775. A treatise of the four complexions,... (Sparrow's tr. revised.) [With the way to Christ, #584.]

564. True spiritual illumination. Tr. anon. NY: Dodd 185-. 32. [AC]

565. (Vierzig Fragen von der Seele.) XL. questions concerning the soule, propounded by Dr. Balthasar Walter and answered by J. Behmen... Also, The clavis, or key; or, an exposition of some principall matters, and words in the writings of J. B--. Both tr. J: Sparrow. L: M.Simmons 1647. 2 pts. 4. [BM]

566. do. 1665. Answered in the year 1620 by J-- Behme...Engl. by J: Sparrow. Also, a brief account of the life and conversation... by A. van Franckenberg. L: L.Lloyd. 425 p. 8. [BM]

BOEHME, Jk. -- Vierzig Fragen von der Seele.
567. do. 1911.[same] The forty questions of the soul and of the clavis... Reissued (with pref.) by C: J: B(arker). With emendations by D. S. Hehner. L: Watkins. 2 pts. 8. [BM]
568. (Vom dreifachen Leben des Menschen.) The high and deep searching out of the threefold life of man through or according to the three principles. Tr. J: Sparrow. Reissued by C: J: B(arker), with an introd. by G. W. Allen. L: Watkins 1909. xlvii;628p. 8. [BM]
569. (Vom übersinnlichen Leben.) The supersensual life; or, the life which is above sense. Tr. anon. NY: Dodd 1850. 32. [AC]
570. do. 1870? The higher Christian life; in a dialogue. (Tr. and paraphrased.) Reprinted by H.D. L: Hamilton, Adams; Wakefield: A. W. Stanfield. 36p. 12. [BM]
[Tr. abr. from that pub. in the "Works," 1764-81. #529.]
571. do. 1901. Dialogues on the supersensual life. Ed. by B. Holland (from the "Works," #529). L: Methuen. xxxviii;144p. 8. [LC says: "First three dialogues tr. by W: Law." This seems to be an error; see note to #529.] [BM.LC]
572. do. 1907. The supersensual life. Allenson. 12. [EC]
573. do. 1908. The supersensual life; or, the life which is above sense. Tr. W: Law. L: (Heart and life booklets.) 60p. 8. [BM]
[Wrong attribution; the tr. is from the "Works," #529.]
574. do. 1921. Supersensual life. Tr. anon. Akron, O: Sun pub. 57p. pa. T. [AC]
575. (Von Christi Testamenten.) Of Christ's testaments, viz:- Baptism and the Supper... Tr. J: Sparrow. L: M.Simmons 1652. 75p. 4. [BM]
576. do. 1656. [same] Lodowick Lloyd. [BM]
577. (Von der Gnaden Wahl.) Concerning the election of grace; or... predestination. Tr. J: Sparrow. L: G:Calvert and J:Allen 1655. 3 pts. 204p. 4. [With appendix...the key to the understanding of the divine mysteries concerning repentance. J. B--'s table of the divine manifestation, or an exposition of the threefold world.] [BM]
578. (Von der Menschwerdung Jesu Christi.) The tree of Christian faith: being a true information how a man may be one spirit with God,... Tr. anon. L: J:Macock 1654. 56p. 4. [BM]
[The tr. closely resembles that of J: Sparrow, 1659.]
579. do. 1659. The fifth book of the authour, in three parts. The first, of the incarnation of Jesus Christ,... Tr. J: Sparrow, with a preface. L: Lodowick Lloyd 1659. 239p. 4. [BM]
580. (Weg zu Christo.) The way to Christ discovered,... (A letter... from J. Behmen...20. April, 1624, tr. by J: Ellistone. An explication of some words in the writing of J. Behmen.) Tr. anon. L: H.Blunden 1648. 5 pts. 12. [BM]
581. do. 1656. [same] L: Lodowick Lloyd. [BM]
582. do. 1752. [same] Manchester: Js. Harrap. 360p. 8. [BM]
[The tr. of the epistle of April 20, 1624, is by Ellistone.]
583. do. 1769. Treatises...of the mixed world...Dialogue between an enlightened...and an unenlightened soul...A compendium of repentance. Of true resignation,... In "Important truths relating to Christianity,..." Pub. by a gentleman retired from business. 120p. 17cm. [The tr. is that of the 1648 ed.] [BM]
584. do. 1775. To which are added some other pieces...also a treatise on the four complexions. Bath: Hazard, for Mills in Bristol. xvii;433p. 8. [Tr. of 1648, with alterations and the marginal explanations incorporated in the text.] [BM]
585. do. 1850. NY: Dodd. 32. [AC]
586. do. 1894. With il. memoir by G. Moreton. Canterbury: Moreton. xiv;115p. 8. [The trs. are those of the "Works," exc. that [BM]

BOEHME, Jk.
of "The supersensual life," taken from the 1648 ed.]
587. do. 1911. Reprint of 1775 ed. by C: J: B(arker). L: Watkins. 302p. 8. [BM]
588. (Leben.) Memoirs of the life, death, burial, and wonderful writings of J-- Behmen (i.e., the life by A. v. Frankenberg, with the narrative by C. Weissner); now first done at large into English, with pref. by F. Okely. Northampton: Tho. Dicey 1780. xvi;153p. 12. Cf. #566. [BM]
See Hegel, G:, On J-- B--. #3992.

BOEHME, Mge. 1869- .
§589. (Das Tagebuch einer Verlorenen.) The diary of a lost one. Tr. anon. L: Sisley; NY: Hudson press 1908. 318p. 19cm. [LC.BM]
[Errors or wilful alterations. Style is good.]
§590. do. 1908. [same] 5th ed. [EC]
§591. do. 1913. [same] Pop. ed. L: Gardner. [BM]
*592. (W.A.G.M.U.S.) The department store. Tr. Ethel C. Mayne. NY; L: Appleton 1912. 466p. 19cm. [LC]
[On the whole, excellent, despite little slips.]

BOEHMER, (Art.) H: 1869-1927.
593. Coming of the friars minor to England and Germany; being the chronicles of Brother Thomas of Eccleston and Brother Jordan of Giano. Tr. from the critical eds. of A. G. Little and H. Boehmer by Emma Salter. NY: Dutton 1926. xxxvi;198p. il. D. [AC]
594. Life of Luther. NY: Quadricentenary com. 1917. [AC]
595. Luther in the light of recent research. Tr. Carl F: Huth, Jr. NY: Christ. Herald 1916. 318; 89p. il. 23cm. [LC]
596. do. 1916. [same] 323p. [AC]

BOEHMER, Jt. Henning, 1674-1749. Sel. in C273;287;489.

BOEHN, Max U: v. 1860- .
*597. (Miniaturen und Silhouetten: ein Kapitel aus Kulturgeschichte und Kunst.) Miniatures and silhouettes. Tr. E. K. Walker. L: Dent 1926. viii;214p. 200 il., 40 col. pl., 8. [BM]
*598. (Die Mode. Menschen und Moden im 19. Jahrhundert, etc.) Modes and manners of the 19th cent., as represented in the pict. and engr. of the time. Tr. M. Edwardes. Introd. by Grace Rhys. 1790-1817. L: Dent; NY: Dutton 1909. 3v. 8. [BM]
*599. do. 1927. Rev. and enl. with chapters by Grace Thompson. L: Dent. 4v. 8. [BM]

BOELSCHE, W: 1861- .
600. (Das Liebesleben in der Natur.) Love-life in nature: the story of the evolution of love. Tr. Cyril Brown. NY: Boni 1926. 2v. 504;726p. 24cm. [LC]
601. (Der Sieg des Lebens.) The triumph of life. Tr. May W. Simons. Chic: Kerr 1906. 157p. 17cm. [LC]
**602. (Die Abstammung des Menschen.) The descent of man. Tr. anon. L: Simpkin 1926. 92p. il. 8. [Excellent tr.] [BM]
603. do? 1905. The evolution of man. Tr. Ernest Untermann. Chic: Kerr. 160p. il. 17cm. [LC]
604. (Ernst Haeckel, ein Lebensbild.) Haeckel, his life and work. Tr. Js. McCabe. L: Unwin 1906. 336p. il. 23cm. [BM.LC]
§605. do. 1909. [same] New and rev. ed. L: Watts. 128p. 8. [BM]
[Alters form and sometimes sense.]
606. do. 1912-17. Truth seeker co. n.d. pa. [AC]

BOELTE, Amely (i.e., Ame. Cte. Ele. Mae.) 1811-91.
607. (Frau von Staël.) Mme. de Stael: an histor. novel. Tr. Td. Johnson. NY: Putnam 1869. iv;487p. 18cm. [LC.BM]

BOELTE, Amely -- Frau von Staël.
608. do. 1883. [same] [LC]

BOERNE, L: [really Löb Baruch] 1786-1837.
609. Goethe as a patriot. Tr. J. D. Haas. 1839. In C183, pp. 381-2.
See Heine, H: Recoll. of a revolutionary.

BOERSCH, Js.
610. (Wieland der Schmied.) Wayland the smith: drama in 5 acts. Tr. A. Comyn. L: K.Paul 1898. viii;128p. 8. [BM]

BOERSCHMANN, Ern. 1873- .
611. (Baukunst und Landschaft in China.) Picturesque China, architecture and landscape: a journey through twelve provinces. Tr. by L: Hamilton. NY: Brentano's 1923. xxvi;288p. il. 31cm. [LC]

BOETTCHER, G:
612. Wiesbaden and her thermal springs. Tr. L. J. Allen. Wiesbaden: J. F. Bergmann 1910. vii;99p. 8. [BM]

BOETTGER, Ad. 1816-70. Sel. in C497;571.

BOETTIGER, K: A: 1760-1835.
613. (Sabina, oder Morgenszenen im Putzzimmer einer reichen Römerin.) Sabina; or, morning scenes at a toilette of a Roman lady of fashion. Tr. anon. In "New Monthly Mag." 10(1818-9): 416 etc. (B26)

BOGATZKY, K: H: v. 1690-1774. Sel. in C229;269;276;486;570.
614. (C. H. v. B. güldenes Schatz-Kästlein der Kinder Gottes...in auserlesenen Sprüchen der heiligen Schrift, samt beigefügten erbaulichen Anmerkungen und Reimen.) A golden treasury[1] for the children of God,... Tr. from 19th ed. of the German. L: A.Linde 1754. 12;366p. obl. 16. [BM]
[Only the prose is translated: hymns of Watts are -- mostly -- substituted for the verses, except that a few of B--'s poems are paraphrased in prose. There is one page for each day, with Bible text, prose commentary, and appropriate verses. This arrangement was followed in many subsequent editions. The translations themselves are close and good.]
615. do. 1754. L: obl. 12. [Printed on one side only.] [BM]
616. do. 1762. L: obl. 12. [BM]
617. do. 1774. L: obl. 16. [BM]
618. do. 1775. L: xvi;384p. obl. 8. [This ed. has a different preface, and made other changes; see note to #678.] [BM]
619. do. 1780? L: obl. 8. [BM]
620. do. 1784. L: obl. 16. [BM]
621. do. 1787. York: 8. [BM]
622. do. 1793. Phil: H:Willis. x;374p. obl. 32. (B6a)
623. do. 1796. Bost: S. Hall. 366p. obl. 16. [LC]
624. do. 1797. NY: Wilson & Kirk. xvi;376p. obl. 32. (B6a)
[Available: AAS.JCB.NYPL.]
625. do. 1799. York. obl. 12. [BM]
626. do. 1803. York. 12. [BM]
627. do. 1803. A new and genuine ed. L: Williams. 316p. 12. [BM]
[Some stanzas omitted; but apparently little other change.]
628. do. 1804. Brackley. obl. 8. [BM]
629. do. 1810. York. obl. 12. [BM]
630. do. 1810. L: 12. [BM]

[1] The "Golden Treasury" bears but a tenuous relation to German literature, for which reason I excluded it from my first edition. It now seems to me that that was an error; but I have not thought it necessary to examine all the editions; only about a dozen have been through my hands.

BOGATZKY, K: --Golden Treasury

631. do. 1811. Phil: G. W. Mentz. 365p. obl. 48. [LC]
632. do. 1812. L: 12. [BM]
633. do. 1820. A new ed. L: Seeley. xii;382p. 8. [BM]
[Carefully revised and corrected.]
634. do. 1820. Stereotype ed. (Vol. II...A new ed. rev...with a life of the author by...C. F. Steinkopff.) L: Burton, Smith. 2v. 12. [This seems to be the only edition in which B--'s supplementary G. T. was published in English.] [BM]
635. do. 1820-52. NY: Carter & Bros. n.d. [AC]
636. do. 1821. Ed: obl. 8. [BM]
637. do. 1824. L: 8. [BM]
638. do. 1827. L: Hamilton. 32. [EC]
639. do. 1829. L: obl. 8. [BM]
640. do. 1830. Dublin: Tims. xiv;386p. 8. [BM]
641. do. 185-? NY: Amer. tract soc. 479p. 13 x 8cm. [LC]
642. do. 1851. L: Aylott. 32. [EC]
643. do. 1851. L: Simpkin. 32. [EC]
644. do. 1854. L: Rel. tract soc. 12. [EC]
645. do. 1855? Birmingham. 16. [BM]
646. do. 1856. L: Rel. tract soc. 32. [EC]
647. do. 1856. L; Ed; NY: Nelson. Ed. and enl. by Rev. J. Smith. 16. [BM]
648. do. 1858. Phil: Luth.bd. 480p. 17cm. [LC]
649. do. 1858-60. [same?] Phil: Luth. bd. 18. [AC]
650. do. 1861. L: Hamilton. 12. [EC]
651. do. 1862. A new ed...rev... Halifax: Milner & Sowerby. 397p. 8. [BM]
652. do. 1863. L: Rel. tract soc. 12. [EC]
653. do. 1864. New ed. L: Tegg. 368p. 8. [BM]
654. do. 1865. L: Routledge. 12. [EC]
655. do. 1866. L: Warne. 12. [EC]
656. do. 1867. L: 16. [BM]
657. do. 1867. NY: Carters. 24. [AC]
658. do. 1868. L. 16. [BM]
659. do. 1869. L: Nelson. 12. [EC]
660. do. 1870. New ed. L: Tegg. 8. [EC]
661. do. 1876 (in print). NY: Nelson. 32. [AC]
662. do. 1876 (in print). NY: Amer. tract soc. 32. [AC]
663. do. 1876 (in print). NY: Carter. 24. [AC]
664. do. 1876 (in print). NY: Routledge. 16. [AC]
665. do. 1876 (in print). NY: Routledge. 32. [AC]
666. do. 1876 (in print). Tr. C. W. Schäffer. Phil: Luth.pub.16. [AC]
667. do. 1878. L: Tegg. Cr. 8. [EC]
668. do. 1878. L: Warne. 32. [EC]
669. do. 1879. Red line ed. L: Nisbet. 16. [BM]
670. do. 1879. New ed. L: Routledge. 8. [BM]
NY: Routledge. [AC]
671. do. 1881. L: Morgan. Cr. 8. [EC]
672. do. 1882. L: Griffith & Farran. xv;368p. 16. [BM]
673. do. 1883. W. biog. sketch by J. Kelly. L: Rel. tract soc. 8. [Kelly's knowledge of the Engl. eds. is quite limited.] [BM]
674. do. 1883. L: Suttaby. 367p. 16. [BM]
675. do. 1885. L: Routledge. xvi;368p. 8. [BM]
[A sort of standard edition.]
676. do. 1888. L; NY: Scott. 367p. 24. [LC]
677. do. 1889. New ed. L: Routledge. 8. [EC]
678. do. 1891. A reprint of Mr. J: Thornton's ed. of 1775, together with crit. notes, hitherto unpub., by J. Berridge, and important corr. by the same hand. Ed. C. P. Phinn, w. introd.

BOGATZKY, K: -- Golden Treasury
by J. C. G. Moule. L: E.Stock. xxiv;26ff. unp. plus index. 8.[BM]
[The pref. contains a valuable crit. discussion of the hist. of the G. T. in Engl., indispensable to the student.]
679. do. 1895. NY: Christ.Herald. 373p. 15cm. [LC]
680. do. 1899. L: J.Blackwood. Cr. 8. [EC]
681. do. 1903. L; Ed: Nelson. 32. [BM]
682. do. 1906. [same] [BM]
683. do. 1907. New ed. L: Rel. tract soc. Cr. 8. [EC]
684. do. 1910. New ed. L: Morgan & Scott. 372p. Cr. 8. [EC]
685. do. 1912 (in print). NY: Amer. tract soc. [AC]
686. do. 1912 (in print). Phil: Luth. pub. [AC]
687. do. 1912 (in print). NY: Simmons. [AC]
688. do. 1912 (in print). NY: Whittaker. [AC]
689. do. 1920. L: Morgan & Scott. 366p. 8. [BM]
690. do. 1925. Re-issue. L: Warne. Cr. 8. [EC]
*691. (C. H. v. B.'s Lebenslauf, von ihm selbst beschrieben.) The life of B--, written by himself. Tr. (and somewhat abr.) S: Jackson. L: Seeley 1856. 8. [BM]
[The tr's omissions seem sensible and desirable.]
§692. (Der vertraute Umgang einer gläubigen Seele mit Gott, etc.) The first step of a close walk with God. Tr. H. D. L: Wertheim & Macintosh 1855. 8. [BM]
693. Edifying thoughts on God's paternal heart. L: Linde 1759. 250p. 18 x 11cm. [BM]
694. do. 1762? Richardson. See "Monthly R." 26(1762):159. (B26)
695. do. 1903. Corr. and ed. J. Laidlaw. L; Ed: Oliphant. 250p. 8. [BM]
696. God's thoughts of war in peace. NY: Prtd. by Jas. Rivington 1780. (B6a)
697. (Was fehlt mir noch?) The important question: what do I lack? In "Monthly R." 32(1765):149. (B26)

BOHRMANN-RIEGEN, H: and Fz. GENÉE.
*698. (Das Spitzentuch der Königin.) The queen's lace handkerchief: opera by J: Strauss. Versified tr. of the songs, choruses, and mus. dialogs...by Jas. D. Trevor. Libr. Engl. NY: Pond 1882. 29p. 8. [LCM]
*699. do. 1882. Tr. and ed. L: C. Elson. Vocal score. Bost: White, Smith. 197p. 4. [LCM]
†700. do. n.d. NY: Brentano. Libr. with music. 31p. 8. [LCM]
[Very little relation.]

"BOLANDEN, Kd. v." (i.e., Bischoff, Js. E: Kd. 1828-1911).
701. (Barbarossa.) Barbarossa; an histor. novel of the 12th cent. Tr. anon. Phil: Cummiskey 1867. 486p. 19cm. [LC]
702. do. 1899. New issue. Phil: McVey. D. [AC]
703. (Der neue Gott.) The new God: a tale for the people. Tr. Rev. Td. Noethen. NY: Pustet 1872. 113p. 18. [LCO]
†704. do. 1873. Tr. anon. L: Richardson. 78p. 16. [BM]
[Tr. doesn't understand, or alters at will.]
705. (Fortschrittlich.) The progressionists; and, Angela. Tr. anon. NY: Catholic pub. soc. 1873. 211p. 24cm. [LC]
706. (Kelle oder Kreuz.) The trowel and the cross, and other stories. Tr. anon. Catholic pub. soc. 1878. [AC]
707. King Ratbodo. Tr. anon. 1902. In C481.
708. (Königin Bertha.) Bertha: an histor. romance of the time of H: IV. Tr. S. B. A. Harper. NY: Sadlier 1876. 396p. 19cm. [LC]

BOLDT, Ern. 1880- .
§709. (Von Luther bis Steiner.) From L-- to S--. Tr. Agnes Blake. NY: Dutton; L: Methuen 1923. xx;213p. il. 19cm. [LC]
[Tr. seems unable to handle author's thought, and abandons him.]

BOMBAST VON HOHENHEIM, Ph. Aus. Tps. 1493-1541. See Paracelsus.

BONAR, La Baronne de. Sel. in C90.

BONAWITZ, J: H: 1839-1917. Ostrolenka. Grand opera in 4 acts. See Haimbach, Ph.

BONE, H: 1813-93. Sel. in C459.

BONER, U: fl. 1324-49. Sel. in C56;373.

BONITZ, Hm.
*710. (Über den Ursprung der homerischen Gedichte.) The origin of the Homeric poems: a lecture. Tr. L. R. Packard. NY: Harper 1880. 119p. 16. [BM]

BONSELS, Wlr. 1881- .
*711. (Das Anjekind.) Angel-child. Tr. Cte. Remfry-Kidd. L: Stockwell 1926. 110p. 8. [BM]
[Deliberate alteration of original is annoying. Good style.]
§712. (Die Biene Maja und ihre Abenteuer.) Adventures of Maya, the bee. Tr. Adèle Seltzer; poems tr. Arthur Guiterman. Il. by Homer Boss. NY: Seltzer; L: Hutchinson 1922. 224p. 23cm. [LC]
[Prose rather poorly done; no feeling for style. Good verse, but inaccurate.]
*713. do. 1922. Maya: the adventures of a little bee. Tr. Cte. Remfry-Kidd. L: Hutchinson. 259p. 8. [Same comment as on #711][BM]
714. (Himmelsvolk.) Heaven folk. Tr. Adèle Seltzer; poems tr. Arthur Guiterman. NY: Seltzer 1924. 257p. O. [AC]
[See comment on #712.]

BOOS, Mn. 1762-1825.
715. (Martin Boos der Prediger...sein Selbstbiograph.) The life and persecutions of M-- B--, an evangelical preacher of the Romish church. Chiefly written by himself and ed. by J. Gossner. Tr. C. Bridges. L: Seeley & Burnside 1836. xlvii; 461p. 18cm. [BM]
716. do. 1847. Life of M-- B-- (abr.), a Roman Catholic clergyman in Germany. Tr. anon. L: Rel. tract soc. x;192p. 12. [BM]

BOPPE, Master, fl. 1270-87. Sel. in C427.

BORA, Kta. v. 1499-1552. See Stein, A., K-- v. B--, a picture from life. #9028.

BORCHARDT, G: Hermann, 1871- . See "G: Hermann."

BORNEMANN, W: 1776-1851. Sel. in C33.

BOSSERT, Hlm. Td. 1889- .
717. Ornament. [LC has: Ornament in applied art.] Two thousand decorative motifs in color, forming a survey of the applied art of all ages and all countries. Tr. anon. Introd. and catalog by H. T. B--. L: Benn; NY: Weyhe 1924. ix;35p. cxx pl. 38cm. [BM.LC]
[Tr. L: Hamilton. Very little text; mostly plates and catalog.]
718. Peasant art in Europe... Plates...sel. and arr. by H. T. B--. L: Benn 1927. xii;44p. cxxxii pl. 38cm. [BM]
[Companion pub. to foregoing.]

BOUTERWEK, F: 1765-1828. Sel. in C543.
719. (Graf Donamar, eine Sammlung von Briefen.) Count Donamar; or, the errors of sensibility. A series of letters written in the time of the thirty years' war. 1797. 3v. (B43)

BOYKOW, H.
719a. Geographical value of the (airplane photographs). In Mittelholzer, Wl. #6252.

BRACHMANN, K:e. Lu. 1777-1822. Sel. in C90;97;123;173; #6209a.

BRACHMANN, K:e. Lu.
720. The three sons. Tr. anon. (Cf. C528.) 1827. In C436.

BRACHVOGEL, Ab. El. 1824-78.
721. Beaumarchais; an historical novel. Tr. Thérèse J. Radford. NY: Appleton 1868. 295p. il. 23cm. [LC.BM]
722. do. 187-. NY: Appleton. il. 8. [AC]
?723. (Friedemann Bach.) F-- B--; or, the fortunes of an idealist. Tr. and ad. by "Grapheus." L: Tinsley 1875. viii;303p. 19cm. [BM] [Text very freely treated, rewritten. Chaps. 26, 32, 34, partly new; Chaps. 6, 10, 36 wholly new.]
?724. (Narciss.) Narcisse, the vagrant: a trag. in five acts. Ad. by Jas. Schönberg. L; NY: French 1869? 48p. 18cm. [BM] [Follows action, but treats text quite freely.]
725. do. 1875. Narciss; or, the last days of the Pompadour. A romantic histor. drama in 5 acts. Tr. C: F. Buck. New Orl. (B38)
726. Rizzio: an histor. tale of Scotland. Tr. anon. NY: Appleton. ca. 1868. [Publisher's advt.]
727. Schubart and his friends. Tr. anon. NY: Appleton. ca. 1868. [Publisher's advt.]

BRACKEL, Fde. Freiin v. 1835-1905.
728. (Die Tochter des Kunstreiters.) Nora: a novel. Tr. Princess Marie Liechtenstein. L: Burns & Oates 1877. viii;358p. 20cm. [BM]
729. do. 1896. The circus-rider's daughter. Tr. Ma. A. Mitchell. NY; Cincin: Benziger. 317p. 19cm. [LC]
730. do. 1913. [same] Benziger. [AC]
731. The fatal beacon. NY; Cincin: Benziger 1904. 201p. 20cm. [LC]
732. Just a simple story. Tr. anon. 1902. In C481.

BRAHMS, J:s, 1833-97.
§733. (Briefe.) The Herzogenberg correspondence. Tr. Ha. Bryant. NY: Dutton 1909. 429p. 23cm. [LC]
L: Murray 1909. xix;425p. 23cm. [BM]
733a. do. Letters of Clara Schumann and J-- B--. See Schumann, K.
See Deiters, Hm., Biog. Sketch of J-- B--, #1184.
See Dietrich, Ab. and Widmann, J., Recoll. of J-- B--, #1228.

BRAMMER, Jl. and Af. GRUENWALD.
§734. (Eine vom Ballet.) The dancing Viennese: operetta in 2 acts by Oscar Straus. Libr. L: 1912. 29p. Tw. [Close, unmetrical tr.] [LCM]
§735. do. 1912. Tr. C. H. Bovill. Libr. 42p. Tw. [LCM] [Clever verse, but remote from original. No dialog.]
736. (Gräfin Mariza.) Countess Maritza: operetta in 3 acts by E. Kálmán. Tr. Grace I. Colbron. Libr. Engl. n.i. 1926. 30;27;19p. unp. Tw. 30cm. [Only dialog.] [LCM]
737. do. 1926. Mariza. Ad. by H. B. Smith. Libr. Engl. n.i. 1926. 48;50;24p. Tw. 28cm. [LCM]
738. Wanda: operetta in 3 acts by Leo Ascher and Emil Gerstenberger Ad. by W: C. Duncan. Libr. Engl. n.i. 1926. Tw. 29cm. [LCM]

BRAMMER, Jl., Af. GRUENWALD, and Eg. SPERO.
739. (Der lachende Ehemann.) The laughing husband: comic opera in 3 acts by Edmund Eysler. Tr. and ad. by A. Wimperis. Libr. L: Enoch 1913. 23p. 8. [Without dialog.] [BM.LCM]
740. do. 1913. Vocal score. L: Enoch; NY: W. Karczas. 156p. 28cm. [Prints both Grünbaum and Grünwald. Very free adaptation. No dialog.] [BMM.LCM]

BRAND, Am., 17th cent.
741. (Beschreibung der chinesischen Reise.) A journal of the embassy from...J: and P: Alexievitz Emperors of Muscovy over land into China...to Pekin...by E. Isbrand...1693-5. Written by A--

BRAND, Am.
B--. Tr. from the High Dutch. L: Brown & Goodwin 1698. 134p. 18cm. [To which is added, Curious observations concerning the products of Russia (pp. 121-34, sep. t.p.) by H.W.Ludolf.] [BM]

BRAND, W: F.
742. (Londoner Streifzüge.) London life seen with German eyes. Tr. anon. L: Field & T. 1887. 257p. 8. [BM]
743. do. 1902. [same] New and rev. ed. L: Siegle. 211p. 8. [BM]

BRANDENBURG, Er. 1868- .
*744. (Von Bismarck zum Weltkriege.) From Bismarck to the world war: a hist. of Ger. foreign policy, 1870-1914. Tr. Annie E. Adams. L; NY: Oxford univ. press 1927. xiii;542p. 23cm. [BM.LC]

BRANDENBURG, G. Sel. in C570.

BRANDENBURG, Lu. Hte. Kurfürstin v. 1627-67. See Luise Hte.

BRANDENBURG-ANSPACH, -- Markgraf v. See Gros, K: Funeral oration ...in honour of etc. #3516.

BRANDES, J: Cn. 1735-99.
§745. (Der Gasthof; oder Trau! schau' wem!) The German hotel: a comedy (in five acts and in prose). Tr. "Marshall" (i.e., T: Holcroft). L: Robinson 1790. 72p. 21cm. [BM.LC]
[Very free, to the disadvantage of the play.]
§746. do. 1790. [same] 2d ed. [BM]

BRANDIS, Cn. A: 1790-1867. Sel. in C12.
747. On the character of Niebuhr.
See Niebuhr, B., Life and letters, #6732.

BRANDSTAETTER, Hm.
748. Eric's vacation; or, taking God into one's work. Tr. Ma. E. Ireland. Elgin; Chic: Cook 1899. 96p. il. sq. 8. [LC]

BRANT, Sb. 1458-1521. Sel. in C190;366;469.
*749. (Das narrẽ Schyeff, etc.) This present Boke named the Shyp of folys of the worlde was translated in the College of saynt Mary Otery in the counte of Devonshyre: out of Laten, Frenche, and Doche into Englysshe tonge by Alexander Barclay Preste... the yere...MCCCCCVIII.[1] L: R.Pynson 1509. Register: †, a-z, &. A-Y. Pagination is irregular. fol. [Barclay really writes a "Ship of fools" of 16th cent. England, in simple and facile verse.] [BM]
†750. do. 1517. The shyppe of fooles. Tr. T: Watson. 2d ed. L: Wynkyn de Worde. unp. ff. A-V, Aa-Gg. il. 4. [BM]
[Rough prose paraphrase, with a few verses to head each section. Gives no idea of Brant's fluent style.]
*751. do. 1874. [same as #749] Repr. Ed; L: Sotheran; NY: Appleton. 2v. il. 24cm. [BM.LC]
[A valuable introd. discusses the tr.; gives a biog. of Barclay.]

BRATUSCHEK, Ern. 1837-83.
752. Philosophy in Europe. Tr. A. Amson. 1877. In C300(7).

BRAUN, Ax.
753. (Die Eiszeit der Erde.) The glacial epoch of our globe. 1879. In Estes, D., Half-hour recreations in popular science. Bost: Estes 1874. xvi;498p. 8. [BM]

BRAUN, A: El. 1809-56.
*754. (Die Ruinen und Museen Roms.) The ruins and museums of Rome. Tr. anon. Brunswick: Vieweg 1854. 515p. 8. [BM]
[Not entirely accurate. -- EC says: xli;516p. 12.]

[1] There were reprints in 1570 and 1590 and there was a tr. from the French in 1507, but I have no bibliographical details of these editions.

BRAUN, A: El.
§755. (Vorschule der Kunstmythologie.) Introd. to the study of art-mythology. Tr. J: Grant. Gotha: Perthes 1856. 56p. il. 32cm. [Unnecessary liberties. Several entire opening paragraphs omitted.] [LC.BM]

BRAUN, J: K: Ritter v. Braunthal, "Jean Charles," 1802-66.
§756. (Das Nachtlager in Granada.) A night in G--: grand opera in two acts after F. Kind's drama by K. Kreutzer. Tr. anon. Libr. Engl;Ger. L: Schloss 1842. 47p. 17cm. [BM]
§757. do. 1845. [same] 2d ed. rev. and corr. [BM]
§758. do. 1864? Tr. anon. Libr. Engl;Ger. NY: Acad. of mus. 17p. [Prose, good.] [LCM]

BRAUN, J. P.
759. Outpouring of thankfulness to Hofrath Dr. De Leuw. Tr. by Rev. F. C. Blackstone. L: Williams & N. 1856. 15p. 8. [BM]
[Verses on several birthdays, tr. into good verse.]

BRAUN, O: 1897-1918.
**760. (Nachgelassene Schriften eines Unvollendeten.) Diary w. sel. from his letters and poems. Ed. Julie Vogelstein. Tr. F. W. Stella Browne; introd. by Havelock Ellis. NY: Knopf; L: Heinemann 1924. 362p. 20cm. [Poetry by Browne; prose by Ella Winter. Prose very admirable; poetry less successful.] [LC.BM]

BRAUNSCHWEIG, Hrns. 15th-16th cent.
761. (Hantwerck der Cyrurgien.) The noble experience of the virtuous handywarke of Surgeri practysyd and compyled by...Jherome of Brunswycke...tr. out of the speche of hye Almayne into lowe Duche, and afterward into our mothers tongue of Englyss...P. Treveris, at London, in Southwarke. 1525. unp. fol. [BM]
762. (New vollkommen Distillierbuch.) The vertuouse boke of Distyllacyon of the waters of all maner of herbes...now newly translated out of Duyche into Englysshe (by Laurence Andrewes). Imprinted at London by me Laurens Andrewe, the xvii. day of Apryll, 1427 [i.e., 1527] fol. [BM]
763. do. 1527. The vertuous boke, etc. L: L. Andrew, the xviii. day of Apryll, 1527. fol. [BM]
[This ed. varies considerably from the foregoing.]
764. (Thesaurus pauperum, Hauss apoteck.) A most excellent... homish apothecarye, or homely physick booke for all the grefes and diseases of the bodye. Tr. out of the Almaine speche by J. Hollybush. Collen: A. Birckman 1561. ff. 45. fol. [BM]

BREDOW, Gf. Gl. 1773-1814.
765. Compendious view of universal history and literature. Tr. from the 4th Ger. ed. w. consid. additions by Maj. Jas. Bell. L: Baldwin, Cradock & Joy 1820. vii p. 40 leaves. 50cm. [BM.LC]
[Pref., 14 tables of history, 5 of literature, one of painters. First pub. by J: G: Büsch, brought down to 1796 in 2d ed. Bredow continued it to 1810.]
766. do. 1824. [same] 2d ed. enl. and improved. L: fol. [Same no. of tables; pref. xvi p.] [BM]
767. do. 1833. [same] 4th ed. L: Baldwin & Cradock. Enl. col. and improved. fol. xxi p., ff. A-Y. [BM]
768. do. 1842. [same] 5th enl. ed. L: R.Baldwin. fol. [BM]
[No apparent improvement over 4th ed. 15 p., ff. A-Y.]
769. Elements of universal history. Tr. B.S. L: Treuttel & Würtz, etc. 1827. 270p. 18cm. [BM]
770. do. 1850. Compendium of universal history. Tr. C: T. Stafford. L: Longmans 204p. 17cm. [BM]

BREDOW, Gf.
771. do. 1851. [same] 2d ed. L: Longmans. xii;226p. 17cm. [BM]
772. do. 1860. [same] 4th ed. rev. cor., and enl. Ed. Mrs. P. Sinnett. L: Longmans. xxiv; 283p. [BM]
773. do. 1861. [same] 5th ed. [BM]

BREDSCHNEIDER, Willy. Girl on the film: musical farce. See Bernauer, R.

BREHM, Af. Ed. 1829-94.
*774. (Vom Nordpol zum Aequator.) From North Pole to equator: studies of wild life and scenes in many lands. Tr. Marg. R. Thomson (Thompson?) L; Glasgow; Dubl: Blackie 1896. 592p. il. 25cm. [cf. #7008;9995.] [BM.LC]

BREITHAUPT, Jm. Jt. 1658-1732. Sel. in C240;486.

BREITZMAN, Ag. 1841- . See "Halden, Eli."

BRENNENBERGER, der, See Reinmar V. Brennenburg.

BRENTANO, Eli. See Arnim, Bna.

BRENTANO, Fr. Sel. in C422.

BRENTANO, Fz.
*775. (Vom Ursprung sittlicher Erkenntnis.) The origin of the knowledge of right and wrong. Tr. C. Hague. Westminster: Constable 1902. xiv; 125p. 8. [BM]

BRENTANO, Kl. 1778-1842. Sel. in C17;38;151;187;309;366;372;380; 469;537;571.
*776. (Das Märchen von dem Witzenspitzel.) Wittysplinter. Tr. anon. 1897. In C126. [Verse turned into prose; otherwise very clever.]
777. (Des Knaben Wunderhorn.) Sel. tr. by M. Münsterberg. In C154(5).
§778. (Geschichte vom braven Kasperl und dem schönen Annerl.) Honor; or, the story of the brave Casper and the fair Annerl. Tr. w. introd. by T. W. Appell. L: Chapman 1847. 74p. 16. [BM] [Not accurate.]
§779. do. 1849. [same] L: Chapman. 12. [EC]
780. do. 1927. The story of the just Casper and fair Annie. Tr. C: F. Schreiber. In C452.
†781. (Gockel, Hinkel, Gackeleja.) The wondrous tale of Cocky, Clucky, and Cackle. Freely tr. by C: W: Heckethorn. Il. by H.W. Petherick. L: Hogg 1889. 188p. 8. [BM]
[Much abridged, and much of the humor and most of the poetry gone. Apparently for children.]
782. do. 1914. Gockel, Hinkel and Gackeleia. Tr. Mrs. N. H. Dole. NY: Silver. 200p. il. D. [AC]
783. Life of Anne K. Emmerich. Tr., very freely, in #1454.
*784. (Märchen.) Fairy tales told by Kate F. Kroeker. Il. by F. Carruthers Gould. L: Unwin 1885. xxiii;252p. 8. [BM]
[Dear-my-soul; The story of Sir Skip-and-a-jump; The story of Ninny Noddy; The story of Wackemhard and of his five sons.]
*785. do. 1888. New fairy tales. Tr. Kroeker. L: Unwin. 261p. il. 21cm. [Gockel, Hinkel, and Gackeleia; Frisky Wisky; Myrtle maiden; Brokerina; Old father Rhine and the miller.] [BM]
786. do. 1890. [same as #784?] Fairy tales in English. New ed. [EC]
787. do. 1902. [same as #785?] New fairy tales. New ed. Il. by Gould. L: Unwin. 261p. 8. [BM]
*788. do. 1925. Kroeker's tr. Fairy tales from Brentano... L: Unwin; NY: Stokes. 326p. 20cm. [BM.LC]
[Stories edited and abbreviated. Much poetry omitted.--The story of old father Rhine and the miller; The story of Frisky Wisky;

BRENTANO, Kl.--Märchen
The story of the myrtle maiden; The story of Brokerina; Dear-my-soul; The story of Sir Skip-and-a-jump; The story of Ninny Noddy.]

BRENTANO, Lujo, 1844-1931.
*789. (Das Arbeitsverhältnis gemäss dem heutigen Recht.) The relation of labor to the law of today. Tr. P. Sherman. NY: Putnam 1891. viii;305p. 8. [BM]
790. Hours and wages in relation to production. Tr. Mrs. W. Arnold. L: Sonnenschein 1894. viii;143p. 8. [BM]

BRETSCHNEIDER, K: Gb. 1776-1848.
791. Apology for the modern theology of protestant Germany; or, a review of..."The state of the protestant religion in Germany" by H. J. Rose. Tr. W: A. Evanson. L: E.Palmer 1827. 88p. 21cm. [BM]
792. do. 1828. Reply to H. J. Rose's work on the state of protestantism in Germany. Tr. F. Haywood. L: Whittaker. viii; 44p., notes. 8. [BM]
*793. (Heinrich und Antonio; oder die Proselyten der römischen und evangelischen Kirchen.) Henry and Antonio. Tr. from the 3d ed. by Rev. M. Morgan. L: Rivington 1829. 260p. 12. [BM]
794. do. 1834. or, the proselytes of the romish and evangelical churches. Tr. J: G. Morris. Balto: Lucas & Deaver. 254p. 20cm. [LC]
795. do. 1856. To Rome and back again; or, the two proselytes. Largely rewritten with new characters, and the scene transferred to this country. Tr. anon. Balto: Kurtz. 238p. 19cm. [LC]

BRETZNER, Cph. F: 1748-1807.
†796. (Belmont und Constanze; oder, die Entführung aus dem Serail.) The seraglio: the celebrated opera by Mozart, as performed... Piano score, Engl. only. Ed. C. Kramer. L: Clementi & Chappell n.d. 219p. 35cm. [Little relation to the orig. text.] [BMM]
§797. do. 1854. Libr. Ger;Engl. and the music of the principal airs. L: Davidson. 25p. 24cm. [Prtd. in double cols.] [BMM]
*798. do. 1874. Il Seraglio. Text arr. by G. Stephanie. Tr. J. Troutbeck. Score, ed. B. Tours. L: Novello. 165p. 26cm. [BMM]
*799. do. 1910. Dialog. arr. by P. Greenbank. Lyrics tr. J. Troutbeck. Libr. L: Novello. 27p. 21cm. [BM]

BREUR, Isaac.
799a. The Jewish national home. Tr. by M. Aumann. Agudas Israel world organ. 1926. 105p. 9 x 6. [EC]

BREYDENBACH, Bh. v.
800. Mt. Sinai, Oreb, and adjoining parts of Arabia descr. out of... journals of Breydenbach, Baumgarten.... In Purchas his pilgrimes, ... pt. 2. L: W.Stansby for H. Fetherstone 1625. fol. [BM]

BRINCKMEYER, Hm.
801. Hugo Stinnes. Tr. A. B. Kuttner. NY: Huebsch 1921. 150p. 19cm. [LC]

BROCKHAUS, Ab. 1855-1921.
*802. (Netsuke. Versuch einer Geschichte der japanischen Schnitzkunst.) Netsukes. By A. Brockhous [sic]. Tr. (and abr.) Miss Ma. W. Watty (i.e., Wathy). NY: Duffield; L: Unwin 1924. xviii;175p. il. 22cm.[Tr. leaves a good deal to be desired.] [LC.BM]

BROCKMANN, Jl. H:
803. (Christian und Ernst.) Oddfellowship: its doctrine and practice... in the light of God's word. Tr. anon. Milwaukee: 1874. 4. [BM]

BROD, Max, 1884- . Sel. in C95.

BRODBECK, Ad.
*804. (Das Ideal der Hochschulen.) The ideal of universities. Tr. with "various additions" by the author (with the aid of H. F. L. Mayer). NY: Metaphys. pub. 1896. 103p. 8. [BM]

BRONIKOWSKI, Ax. A: Fd. v. Oppeln, 1788-1834.
805. Court of Sigismund Augustus; or, Poland in the 16th cent. Tr. W. S. Krasinski. L: Longmans 1834. 3v. 12. [BM]

BRUCK, ----- Sel. in C105.

BRUECKE, Ern.
*806. (Schönheit und Fehler der menschlichen Gestalt.) The human figure, its beauties and defects. Pref. [and prob. tr.] W: Anderson. Auth. tr. rev. by author. L: Grevel 1891. 188p. il. 8. [BM]
*807. do. 1900. [same] New and cheaper rev. ed. [BM]

BRUEGGE-VALLON, Wl.
808. That strange affair. Tr. G. A. Page. L: S.Paul 1914. 307p. 8. [BM]

BRUEGGEN, Ern. Frhr. v. d. 1840-1903.
*809. (Das heutige Russland, Kulturstudien.) Russia of today. Tr. M. Sandwith. L: Digby, Long 1904. viii;306p. 19cm. [BM.LC]

BRUEHL, H: Graf v. 1700-73. See Adelung, J., The life of, etc.,#15.

BRUHN, D: 1782- . Sel. in C272.

BRUHNS, K: Cn. 1830-81.
*810. (Ax. v. Humboldt.) Life of Ax. v. H--. Compiled in honor of the centenary of his birth by Jl. Löwenberg, Rb. Avé-Lallemant, and Af. Dove. Ed. K: C. B--. Tr. Jane and Caro. Lassell. L: Longmans, Green; Bost: Lee & Shepard 1873. 2v. 23cm. [BM.LC]
[Not perfect; slight deviations from sense of original.]

"BRUNECK, O: v." (i.e., O: Elster)
811. (Der kleine Midshipman.) The little midshipman: operetta in 3 acts. Ad. Af. H. Quaritch and M. Raye. Synopsis. L: Quaritch 1911. ff.6. Tw. 33cm. [BM]
812. (Klaus Erichsen.) Prince Henry's sailor boy. Freely ad. Ma. J. Safford. Il. by G: Af. Williams. NY: Holt 1904. 293p. 19cm. [LC]

BRUNN, ----- Sel. in C44. [Perhaps F:e Brun, 1765-1835.]

BUBE, Ad. 1802-73. Sel. in C195.

BUCER, Mn. 1491-1551.
813. (De regno Christi.) A treatise, how by the worde of God, Christian men's Almose ought to be distributed. n.i. 1557? 29p. 15cm. [BM]
814. The gratulation of the mooste famous clerke M. M-- B--... unto the churche of England for the restitucion of Christes religion. Tr. out of Latin by Sir T: Toby. L: R:Iugge 1549. n.p. 8. [BM]
815. The judgement of M-- B-- concerning divorce, writt'n to E: the Sixt, in his second book of the kingdom of Christ, and now Englisht (by J: Milton)...L: Simmons 1644. 24p. 4. [BM]
[Also in J: Milton, Works, 1753; vol. 1; Works, 1806, vol. 2.]
816. (Leben.) A briefe Treatise concerning the burning of B-- and Phagius at Cambrydge...Tr. A. Goldyng. L: T:Marshe 1562. 8. [BM]

BUCH, Cn. Lp. v. Frhr. v. Gelmersdorf, etc. 1774-1853.
§817. (Reise durch Norwegen und Lappland.) Travels through Norway and Lapland, 1806-8. Tr. J: Black. L: Colburn 1813. xviii;460 (i.e.,440)p. 27cm. [BM.LC]
[Not very good; text not fully understood.]

BUCHBINDER, Bh.
*818. (Die Förster-Christel.) The girl and the Kaiser: operetta in 3 acts by G: Jarno. Tr. L. Liebling. Vocal score. NY: Harms & Francis 1908,1910. 163p. 4. [LCM]

BUCHER, Br. and K: WEIS of Vienna.
§819. (Wiener Baedeker.) Handy-guide to Vienna. Tr. Griffin. Vienna: Faesy & Frick; L: Longmans 1873. 378p. 13cm. [BM]
[Inadequate knowledge of German.]

BUCHER, F. Sel. in C67.

BUCHFELDER, E. W. Sel. in C269.

BUCHFELNER, Sm.
820. Authentic accounts of Dominica Lazzari, the Addolorata, and Maria von Mörl, the Ecstatica, now living in the Tyrol. Tr. F. C. Husenbeth. Norwich: Bacon, Kinnebrook & Bacon 1841. 24p. 12. [BM]

BUCHHEIM, A. Sel. in C111; 149.

BUCHMANN, J. N.
821. My first communion; or, the happiest day of my life. Tr. R: Brennan. Cincin: Benziger 1881. il. 16. [AC]

BUECHER, K:
822. Industrial evolution. Tr. from 3d ed. S. M. Wickett. L: Bell 1901. xi;393p. 8. [BM]

BUECHNER, Ax. 1827-1904.
822a. Life of L: Büchner. Tr. Js. McCabe. 1901. In #826.

BUECHNER, (F: K: Cn.) L: 1824-1899.
*823. (Aus dem Geistesleben der Tiere.) Mind in animals. Tr. from 3d rev. ed. by Annie Besant. L: Freethought pub. 1880. xii;359p. 8. [BM]
*824. (Die Stellung des Menschen in der Natur.) Man in the past, present, and future. Tr. W: S. Dallas. L: Asher 1872. xv;363 (i.e.,379)p. 22cm. [BM.LC]
*825. do. 1894. [same] Phil: Lippincott. 349p. il. 21cm. [LC]
*826. (Im Dienste der Wahrheit.) Last words on materialism and kindred subjects. Life...by his brother, Ax. B--. Tr. J. McCabe. L: Watts 1901. xxxiv; 343p. 8. [BM]
[Essays sel. from the orig. Tr. seems to be very good.]
*827. do. 1902. [same] 2d ed. [EC]
*828. do. 1901. [same][Sel.] Christianity and Buddhism. L: Watts. 14p 8. [Reprinted from foregoing.] [BM]
829. The influence of heredity on free will. Tr. Annie Besant. L: Freethought pub. 1880. 14p. 8. [BM]
*830. (Kraft und Stoff.) Force and matter. Tr. J. F: Collingwood. L: Trübner 1864. lxvi; 258p. 19cm. [BM.LC]
[Tr. not wholly satisfactory.]
*831. do. 1870. [same] 2d ed. compl. from 10th Ger. ed. L: Trübner. ciii;271p. [BM]
*832. do. 1891. [same] Tr. fr. 15th Ger. ed. enl. and rev. by the author. NY: Eckler 1891. D. [AC]
833. Materialism: its history and influence on society. Tr. Ax. Loos. NY: Butts 1873. 28p. 8. [LCO.BM]

BUECHNER, G: 1813-37.
*834. Plays. Tr. w. introd. by G. Dunlop. L: Howe; NY: Viking 1927. 274p. 19cm. [BM.LC]
[Regrettable that tr. is not more accurate; tone and style are excellent. Leonce and Lena ("Leonce und Lena"); Danton's death ("Dantons Tod"); Wozzeck ("Woczek," properly "Woyzeck").]

BUECHSEL, K:
*835. (Erinnerungen aus dem Leben eines Landgeistlichen.) My ministerial experiences. Tr. anon. Ed; L: Strahan 1863. 290p. 8. [Tr. by the author?] [BM.LCO]

BUECKLER (Bickler), J: called "Schinderhannes," fl. 1783-1803.
836. Schinderhannes, the robber of the Rhine. Tr. anon. 1852-5. Phil: Perry n.d. [See Schinderhannes, #8249a.] [AC]

BUEHLMANN, Josef, 1844-
836a. Classic and renaissance architecture (with an English text translation). Helburn 1916. 75 pl. F. [AC]

BUELOW, Frau Bte. v. see "Arnold, Hs."

BUELOW, Bh. H: Mn. K: Fürst v. 1849- . Sel. in C161.
*837. (Deutsche Politik.) Imperial Germany. Tr. Marie A. Lewenz. NY: Dodd, Mead 1914. 290p. 25cm. L: Cassell 1914. 283p. 4th impression 1914. [LC.BM]
*838. do. 1916. [same] New and rev. ed. Foreword by J. W. Headlam. L: Cassell. xliv; 334p. 8. [BM]
*839. do. 1917. [same] NY: Dodd. 335p. O. [AC]

BUELOW, Gle. v. 1791-1887.
**840. (G. v. Buelow, Tochter W: v. Humboldts. Ein Lebensbild. Aus den Familienpapieren W: v. H--s und seiner Kinder.) The daughter of W: v. Humboldt. Tr. Ca. Nordlinger. L: Smith, Elder 1897. 447p. 8. [Some omissions; mostly excellent] [BM]

BUELOW, Hs. Guido v. 1830-94.
**841. (Briefe und Schriften.) The early correspondence. Ed. Marie v. B--. Sel. and tr. Constance Bache. L: Unwin 1896. xiv;266p. 23cm. [Tr. seems to be excellent.] [LCO]
*842. do. 1897. [same] NY: Appleton. 266p. 8. [BPL]

BUELOW, Ma. He. Gräfin v.
843. The tale of the swallow. From the German of H(edwig) von B(uelow?) by C(hristopher) B(enson?) Wiesbaden. Schellenberg 1884. 47(i.e., 24)p. 12. [Printed on one side of the paper. [BM] Names as above written on the title page.]

BUELOW-WENDHAUSEN, Bta. Freiin v. 1848- .
844. Life of the Baroness v. Marenholtz-Bülow, by her niece. Tr. with the aid of the authoress. Extracts from the "Gedankenbücher" tr. by Susan Blow. NY: Harrison 1901. 2v. 22cm. [LC]
845. Greeting to America: reminiscences and impressions. Tr. Mrs. Lena Eisler. NY: Harrison 1900. 147p. il. 21 x 16 cm. [LC]

BUERDE, S: Gb. 1753-94. Sel. in C231-2;244;287.

BUERGER, Gf. A: 1747-94. Sel. in C2;7;10;17;22;25-6;31;34;43-4;50; 54*;66-7;69;75;84;88;92;97;106;120-1;123;132*;133;142;149;152-3; 166-7;177;190;196;198;219;309;357;366*;372-3;378;391;393;410-1; 428;448;461;467;469;499;500;507;533;562;564,#2720.
†846. [Coll.] The chase (Der wilde Jäger) and William and Helen (Lenore); two ballads (adapted) by Sir Wl. Scott. Ed: for Manner & Miller 1796. 41p. 26 x 21cm. [BM.LC]
[Also pub. by Cadell & Davies in London. "The chase" appears as

BUERGER, Gf. A:
"The wild huntsman" in Scott's works. Earl Walther is now The Wildgrave, and a few alterations are made.]
847. [Coll.] 1840. Ballads. Outlines by M. Retzsch to Lenora (tr. by Beresford); Song of the brave man, and The parson's daughter of Taubenhayn. Lpz: Fleischer; L: Black & A. obl. fol. [BM]
[Ger. and Engl. Each ballad paged sep. Commentary by C. B. v. Miltitz also printed in both languages, and very well tr. by F: Shoberl.]
*848. [Coll.] 1870. The wild huntsman; i.e., the ballads of Bürger. Tr. and imitated in the rhythm and rhyme of the original by C: J. Lukens. Phil: Prtd. by Collins. 22p. 25cm. [LC]
["Fifty complimentary copies printed in advance of publication."]
849. [Coll.] 1872. [same] Retzsch's outlines. (Lytton's tr.? Doubtful.) Bost: Roberts. obl. fol. [AC]
850. do. 1875. [same] L: S. Low. 16p. plus plates. [BM]
[A different tr. No German, different and much briefer commentary, also introd. on "M. Retzsch and Bürger."]
†851. (Der Raubgraf.) The freebooter. Tr. anon. Glasgow: Brash & Reid 1810? 8p. 15cm. [LC]
§852. (Der wilde Jäger.) The wild huntsman's chase. (Tr. of Sir W. Scott.) L: Low 1798. 15p. 4. [BM]
853. do. 1797. A poem from the Ger. of B--. Tr. anon. Mudie & Constable. See "Scots Mag." 59(1797):266. (B26)
854. do. 1801. [same] The wild huntsman. In C357.
855. do. 1801? The wild hunter. Tr. J. C. In C157(3).
†856. (Des Pfarrers Tochter von Taubenhain.) The lass of fair wone; or, the parson's daughter betrayed. A ballad. Tr. anon. Glasgow: Brash & Reid 18--. 18p. 18. [LCO]

LENORE[1]

857. ANON. Miss Kitty; a parody on Lenora. Tr. from the German by several hands. Ed: Reid 1797. 29p. 8. [BM]
[Parody printed opp. Taylor's tr. "Tr...by several hands" probably alludes to various versions of Lenore which had appeared before this date.]
§858. ANON. Leonore. Lenora. Two verse translations. Cambridge: Macmillan 1858. 39p. 17cm. [BM]
[One tr. is by W: Whewell; cf. #903.]
§859. BASKERVILLE, Af. 1853. In C8.
†860. BERESFORD, B: Leonora. 1798. In C22; cf. C23-6.
§861. BORROW, G: 1823. In "Monthly Mag." 56(1823):334. (B26)
[Also in his works, 1923, vol. 8. Tr. is good, though rhyme-scheme is altered.]
**862. BRINTON, W. L: Priv. print. 1850. 12. [BM.UW]
["The most successful version," says Bll.]
863. BROMEHEAD, W. C. Macmillan 1885? (Bll)
[This item from publisher's catalog.]
*864. BROOKS, C: T. 1838. In C44.
†865. CAMERON, Julia M. Leonora. Il. by D. Maclise. L: Longmans 1847. 38p. 23cm. [BM.LC]
†866. CAMPBELL, J: J. 1836. In C54.
[Bll: "This is quite the most puerile of all the versions... The tr. knows neither Ger. nor Engl., and has the most rudimentary notions of verse."]
§867. CHARLTON, W. H. Lenoré. 1868. In C66.
§868. CHAWNER, E: 1879. In C67.
§869. CHRISTIAN, J. Rb. In Leonora: a trans. And minor poems. L: Priv. print. 1870. 21cm. [LC]

[1] Some critical judgments furnished by Bll.

BUERGER, Gf. A:--Lenore
§870. COLOMB, Col. G. H. Lenora. L: Chapman & Hall 1877. 13p. 16. [NY]
871. do. 2d ed. 1878. 16. [NY]
[With Schiller's "Song of the bell," cf. #7875.]
872. CORBIN, Royal? Plattsburgh, NY? 1904. 12p. 17 x 10cm. [LC]
§873. CRAIGMYLE, Eliz. 1892. In C75.
§874. EVERETT, A. H. 1845. In C121.
†875. FLUEGEL, J. G. 1835. In C133.
†876. GOODFELLOW, J: Lenôré. 1904. In C167.
†877. GRANT, J. W. L: Murray. 1865. 12. [EC]
*878. HEDLEY, F. H. Lenore. 1876. In C196.
†879. HERSCHEL, J. W. F. In his Essays, etc. L: 1857. 8. [BM]
§880. LEWIS, M. G. 1801. In C357.
[Changes meter, making two quatrains. Otherwise not bad.]
881. LUKENS, H: C. (Parody.) Lean'nora: a supernatural though sub-pathetic ballad...after the German of G. A. B--. By Heinrich Yalc Snekul. (i.e., H: Clay Lukens.) Phil: 1870. 4. [BM]
882. do. 1878. [same] Reprint of the foregoing. (A good long way--almost 97 years--after...Bürger.) NY: Clarke. 17cm. [LC]
883. MANGAN, J. C.? In "Dublin Univ. Mag." 28(1846):656. (B27)
†884. MAURER, G: P. 1840. In C410.
885. M., S. and H. T. 1845. In C153.
†886. OXENFORD, J. In Birmingham musical festival. 1855. 4. [BM]
[B11: "Quite worthless." I query this judgment, as O. is usually competent.]
†887. PYE, H. J. Lenore: a tale. L: Low 1796. 4. [BM]
†888. ROSSETTI, D. G. L: Ellis & Elvey. 1900. 15p. ff. 19-35. 4. [Good poem, but not Bürger.] [BM.NY]
§889. SMITH, Ab. Lenora. In "Wild oats and dead leaves." L: Chapman & Hall 1870. 359p. 19cm. [BM]
§890. do. 1880. [same] 2d ed. 359p. [LCO]
†891. SPENCER, W: R. Leonora. L: Edwards 1796. il. fol. [BM]
892. do. 1799. [same] Pref. by Spencer. Designs by Lady Diana Beauclerc. To which are annexed, two other translations, by Stanley (#896) and Pye (#887), with a version after the manner of the old English ballad (i.e., Ellenore by W: Taylor, #898-9), and the original German. Dublin: Archer. 12. [BM]
[Paged separately, and each tr. has sep. t.p.]
893. do. 1809. [same] 2d. ed. L: Prtd. for Edwards & Harding. 35p. fol. [BM]
894. do. 1820. [same] In Kaleidoscope 1(1820):132. (B26)
895. do. 1797. [same?] Lenore...in drei englischen Übersetzungen. Göttingen. (B11)
†896. STANLEY, J: T. Leonora. Freely tr. L: Miller (Feb.) 1796. viii;13p. 8. [BM]
†897. (Apr.) 1796. [same] Tr. and altered. New ed. Il. W: Blake. L: Miller. xi; 16p. 4. [BM]
§898. TAYLOR, W: Ellenore. In C156, reprinted from "Monthly Mag." 1796. Also in "Annual Register" 38:2:496, as Lenora. Also in "Ed. Mag." (II) 7(1796):465. [BM]
[Rewritten as old English ballad; good verse, general sense correct.]
§899. 1796. [same] Revised. Norwich: March; L: Johnson 1796. [LC]
§900. 1810? [same] In Poetry: original and selected. Glasgow: Brash & Reid. 8p. 14cm. [LC]
[Reprinted in C31(1836); C166(1869); C533(1829).]
§901. TROTTER and COLTMAN. 1870. In C132.

BUERGER, Gf. A:--Lenore
†902. TYNDALE, W. W. in The Bürger and Brighton Leonora; or, romance versus railway. L: 1849. il. obl. 4. [BM]
[German, translation, and parody.]
†903. WHEWELL, W: 1847. In C562; also, 1858, in #858.
§904. WHITMAN, Sa. Lenora. 1853. In C564.
[No feminine rhyme; otherwise good.]
§905. WIREMAN, H: D. Phil: Kohler 1870. 16. [AC]
[Also in C309(1885); C571(1869).]
§906. (Männerkeuschheit.) Man's chastity. Tr. J: King. ca. 1800. In C157(2).
[Münchhausen. For Bürger's probable share in the creation of the Baron's marvelous adventures, see my note to Münchhausen.]

BUERSTENBINDER, Eli. 1838-1918. See "Werner, E."

BUESCH, J: G: 1728-1800. See Bredow, Gf., compendious view of... hist... #765.

BUESCHING, J: Gst. Gb. 1783-1829. Sel. from his "Popular traditions..." Lpz: 1820. In C82; 477; 537.

BUETTNER, H: of Berlin.
907. Sketches from the diary of Queen Natalie of Servia. Tr. Ma. C. Howse in 1900. L: Priv. prt. 1902. 69p. 8. [BM]
[Pref.: "Tr...from a Ger. book...purports to be from the diary of Queen Natalie..."

BUETTNER, J: K:
908. (Buettner der Amerikaner. Eine Selbstbiographie.) Narr. of J. C. B-- in the Amer. revol. NY: Prtd. for Heartman 1914. 69p. 8. [Probably tr. by C: F: Heartman. Only Amer. advent.] [BM]

BULLINGER, An.
909. (Hegels Lehre vom Widerspruch.) Hegel's doctrine of contradiction. Tr. Alice A. Graves. 1892. In C300 (22).

BULLINGER, H: 1504-75.
910. (Compendium Christianae religionis.) Commonplaces of Christian relig. Tr. by Rev. J: Stockwood. L: T.East and H.Middleton for G: Byshop 1572. ff. 252. 8. [BM]
911. A confutation of the Pope's (Pius V) bull...against Elizabeth ...queene of England...together with a defence of the sayd... queene, etc. Tr. anon. L: J:Day 1574. ff. 86. 4. [BM]
912. (De sacro sancta coena.) The Christen state of matrimonye, wherin housbandes and wyfes maye lerne to kepe house together with loue. Tr. Myles Coverdale. n.i. 1541. ff. lxxviii, plus table. 8. [BM]
913. do. 1543. [same] n.i. ff. 92. 16. [BM]
914. do. 1543. [same] L: J:Mayle for J:Gough 1546 (i.e., 1543). 8. [This ed. contains pref. of 15 leaves by T: Becon. Orthography is slightly altered. Title page prints 1546 for 1543.] [BM]
915. do. 1552. [same] Set forthe (i.e., tr.) by M. Coverdale. L: Nycholas Hyll for Abraham Wele 1552. ff. xci. 16. [BM]
[Omits pref. Adds four chapters on divorce.]
916. (De Scripturae Sanctae auctoritate, ...) A most Godly and learned discourse of the woorthynesse, authoritie, and sufficiencie of the holy Scripture; also of the cleerenesse, and plainness of the same...wherein is discussed...whether the Canonical Scriptures have authoritie from the Church, or rather the Church receive authoritie from the Scriptures. Tr. J: Tomkyns. L: W:Ponnsonby 1579. 119p. 12. [BM]
917. A most necessary and fruitfull Dialogue, betwene the seditious Libertin or rebel Anabaptist (Simon), and the true obedient

BULLINGER, H:
Christiã (Ioiada), wherin...ye shal se the excellencie and worthynesse of a christiã magistrate. Tr. Ihõ Veron Senonoys. Worcester: Jhon Oswen 1551. ff. a-fiiii. 12. [BM]
918. Questions of religion cast abroad in Helvetia by...adversaries ...and answered by H. B. reduced into 17 common places. Tr. J: Coxe. L: Henrie Bynneman 1572. ff. 145 and conclusion. 8. [BM]
919. Resolution...concernyng thapparel of ministers. Tr. anon. n.i. 1566? pp. 27-46. 8. [BM]
920. A treatise of the cohabitation of the faithfull with the unfaithfull, etc. Tr. anon. n.i. 1555. ff. 1-65. 8. [BM]

BUND, L:
921. Puck's nightly pranks. Tr. C: T. Brooks. Bost: Roberts 1871. 10 leaves. Il. by P. Konewka. sq. 8.[9 stanzas.] [NY.BM]

BUNGE, Rd.
**922. (Der Trompeter von Säkkingen.) The trumpeter of Sackingen [sic]: opera by V: Nessler. Text based on Scheffel's poem (#7705) with some of the original lyrics. Tr. J: P. Jackson. Libr. Ger;Engl. Metropolitan opera house 1887. xiv;24; 25p. 8. [LCM]
*923. do. 1889. Trumpeter of Sakkingen. Tr. Helen D. Tretbar. NY: Tretbar. Libr. Engl. 36p. 8. [LCM]
[Not as good as the foregoing, but very good.]

BUNSEN, Cn. K: Josias, Frhr. v. 1791-1860. Sel. in C469.
924.(Briefe.) Letters from B-- to Max Müller, 1848-59. Tr. by G(eorgina) A. M(üller?) In Müller, F. Max, Chips from a German workshop. L: Longmans 1870. [BM.LCO]
*925. (Die Zeichen der Zeit.) Signs of the times: Letters to E. M. Arndt on the dangers to religious liberty in the present state of the world. Tr. Susannah Winkworth. L: Smith, Elder 1856. 519p. 8. [BM.LCO]
**926. (Gott in der Geschichte.) God in history; or, the progress of man's faith in the moral order of the world. Tr. by Susannah Winkworth. Pref. by A. P. Stanley. L: Longmans 1868-70. 3v. 8. [Excellent tr.] [BM.LCO]
Lyra germanica. See C276 seq.
927. Niebuhr as a diplomatist in Rome. In Niebuhr, B. G. "Life and letters," vol. 2. Niebuhr's political opinions and character. ibid. vol. 3. L: Chapman & Hall 1852. 8. [BM.LCO]
928. Preface to Freytag's Debit and Credit. Tr. anon. In #1944, vol. 1.

BUNSEN, Mie. v.
*929. (Gegen den Strom.) A winter in Berlin. Tr. Mrs. Dugdale. L: Arnold 1899. 219p. 8. [Rather free but essentially faithful.] [BM]

BURCKHARDT, Jk. 1818-1897.
*930.(Der Cicerone. III. Malerei.)The cicerone: an art guide to painting in Italy for use of travellers and students. Ed. by Dr. A. v. Zahn, editor of 2d ed. of "Der Cicerone". L: Murray 1873. 297p. 18cm. [BM.LC]
[Tr. Mrs. A. H. Clough. Zahn rev. Engl. tr. and made additions which appeared soon after in 3d ed.]
*931. do. 1879. [same] Re-ed., rev., and corr. by J. A. Crowe. 304p. [BM.LC]
*932. do. 1908. [same] New and il. impression, pref. by P. G. Konody. L: Laurie; NY: Scribner. 303p. pl. 19cm. [BM.LC]
*933. do. 1918. [same] New imp. L: Batsford. il. Cr.8. [LC]
*934. (Die Kultur der Renaissance in Italien.) The civilization of the period of the renaissance in Italy. With add. by L. Geiger.

BURCKHARDT, Jk. 1818-1897.
Tr. S. G. C. Middlemore. L: Paul; NY: Scribner & W. 1878. 2v. 22cm. [BM.LC]
*935. do. 1890. [same] Macmillan. 8. [AC]
*936. do. 1890. [same] L: Sonnenschein. xvi;559p. 8. [BM]
*937. do. 1898. [same] L: Sonnenschein. [EC]

BURCKHARDT, J: Gb.
938. The life and character of...Luther. In "Colloquia mensalia; or the familiar discourses of...M. L." Tr. anon. L: Heptinstal 1791. pp.iii-xix. fol. [BM]
939. do. 1818. [same] pp.xv-xxxviii. 8. [BM]
940. Meditations (i.e.,prayers). Tr. J. Snow. L: Hatchard 1832. 144p. 18. [BM]

BURG, Ma.
941. The inquisitive boy. Tr. "Trauermantel." 1859. In C548.

BURGGRAF VON LUENZ. See Heinrich, Burggraf v. L--.

BURGGRAF VON REGENSBURG, 12th cent. Sel. in C27.

BURGGRAF VON RIETENBURG, 12th cent. Sel. in C27;427.

BURIÁN VON RAJECZ, St., Graf, 1851-1922.
§942. (Drei Jahre aus der Zeit meiner Amtsführung im Kriege.) Austria in dissolution: personal recoll. Tr. Brian Lunn. L: Benn; NY: Doran 1925. 455p. 8. [BM]

BURKART VON HOHENFELS, 13th cent. Sel. in C27;416;427;532.

BURMANN, Glb. W: 1737-1805. Sel. in C133.

BUROW, Jle. 1806-68. Sel. in C309;571.

BUSCH, Jl. Hm. Mz. 1821-99.
*943. (Graf Bismarck...während des Krieges mit Frankreich.) Bismarck in the Franco-German war. Authorized tr. anon. NY; L: Scribner 1879. 2v. 20cm. [LC.BM]
§944. (Tagebuchblätter.) Bismarck, some secret pages of his history: being a diary kept during 25 years' official and private intercourse. Tr. anon. L; NY: Macmillan 1898. 2v. 23cm. [BM] [Some deviations from the original.]
§945. do. 1898. [same] L; NY: Macmillan. 3v. 8. [LC.BM]
§946. do. 1899. [same] Condensed ed. ix;576p. 8. [BM]
**947. (Unser Reichskanzler.) Our chancellor: sketches for a histor. pict. Tr. W: Beatty-Kingston. L: Macmillan 1884. 2v. 19cm. [Very competent.] [BM.LC]

BUSCH, P: 1682-1744. Sel. in C244.

BUSCH, W: 1832-1908. Sel. in C405a.
?948. [Coll.] A bushel of merry-thoughts. Tr. (or rather written) by W. Harry Rogers. L: Low 1868. 14;16;16; 16p. il. obl. 16. [BM] [The naughty boys of Corinth; Cat and Mouse; Sugar-bread; Ice-Peter. Sep. paged. Verses are by Rogers, with suggestions from Busch's pictures.]
949. [Coll.] 1878. Hookey-beak, the raven, and other tales. Tr. H: W: Dulcken. L: Routledge. 87p. 18cm. [BM] [The pea-shooter, or the tragedy in a country garden; The story of the worrying bluebottle, and of the gentleman who lost his temper; The riddle, a mysterious story; Tom Tippety's troubles, or the triumph of perseverance; The Christmas goose, or the reward of duplicity, a moral story; Sam Shirkit's day's work, or the model labourer, a lay of the present day; Gymnastics, and the lessons they teach.]

BUSCH, W:
?950. [Coll.] 1883. The fool's paradise...as seen in the strange, surpassing peep-show of Prof. Wolley Gobble. Tr. from "Münchener Bilderbogen" by H. Llewellyn Williams. L: Griffith & Farran. 72p. 4. [BM]
[The music master; The woeful panorama of the toothache; The three young rooks and the bird-nesters; The troublesome boys and Diogenes the wise; The giant bear hunter and the bruin who nearly caught him; The bad black hunter and the ponderous elephant; The goat and the swing; The jolly angler and the monstrous fish; The merry sledge party and their marvellous slide; The joking miller and the farmer; The angry doctor; The greedy, greedy ducks and the persecuted frog. Selection from two series pub. by J: C. Hotten in 1871 and 1873. Nothing of Busch but the pictures. Flat prose descriptions.]
§951. (Die fromme Helene.) Naughty Jemima: a doleful tale. Tr. J: Mac Lush [pseud?] L: Nimmo 1872. 119p. il. 8. [BM]
§952. do. 1874. [same] 16. [BM]
?953. (Diogenes oder die bösen Buben von Korinth.) Diogenes and the two naughty young Corinthians. By A. B. Westmacott. L: Hays 1879. il. 4. [Not much of Busch but the pictures.] [BM]
§954. (Eduards Traum.) Edward's dream: the philosophy of a humorist. Tr. and ed. Pl. Carus. Chic: Open court 1909. 74p. 16. [LC]
[Tr. selects and omits, and is not seldom in error.]
955. (Hans Huckebein, der Unglücksrabe.) The amusing story of Jack Hook-a-bone. Tr. anon. NY: Inger 1872. 8p. il. 16cm. [LC]
956. do. 1872-6. Jack Huckaback, the scapegrace raven. Tr. J. S. S. Rockwell. NY: Stroefer & Kirchner. 24p. il. 8. [AC]
957. do. 1877. Hookey-beak, the raven. Tr. anon. Routledge 1877. il. 4. [AC]
958. do. 1878. Dick Dimple, and the wicked crow. Tr. anon. NY: Sneider. 1 folded sheet. il. 11cm. [LC]
959. Hurdy gurdy: woodcuts, with stories in rhymes. Tr. anon. NY: Stroefer & Kirchner n.d. (1872-6) 8. [AC]
**960. (Max und Moritz.) Max and Maurice: a juvenile history in seven tricks. Tr. C: T. Brooks. Bost: Roberts 1871. il. 56p. 20cm. [LC]
*961. do. 1874. Tr. anon. Munich. Braun & Schneider; L: Myers 1874. 53p. il. 8. [BM]
962. do. 1886? [same] Tr. anon. Myers. 8. [BM]
963. do. 1899. [same as #960?] New issue. NY: Little, Brown. il. sq. D. [AC]
964. do. 1906? [same as #961] Siegle & H. 100 il. in color. 54p. [BM]
§965. do. 1913. Freely tr. Arundell Esdaile. L: Routledge. 27p. 8. [BM]
[Printed on one side of the paper. Expansion dilutes the humor as well as the test.]
966. Mischief book. Tr. A. L. Alger. NY: Worthington 1879. il. obl. 12. [AC]
**967. (Plisch und Plum.) Plish and Plum. Tr. C: T. Brooks. Bost: Roberts 1883. 67p. 8. [LCO]
968. do. 1899. [same?] New issue. NY: Little, Brown. il. sq. O. [AC]
?969. The power of sound. By A. B. Westmacott. L: Hays 1879. 8p. il. 4.[Cf. comment on #953.] [BM]
§970. (Schnurrdiburr oder die Bienen.) Buzz a buzz; or, the bees. Tr. W. C. Cotton. L: 1872. il. 8. [BM]
§971. do. 1873. Tr. Hezekiah Watkins. NY: Holt. 80p. il. 8. [LC]
?972. The siege of Troy. By A. B. Westmacott. L: Hays 1879. 7p. 4. [Cf. comment on #953.] [BM]

BUSCH, W:
973. The tall student. Tr. C: T. Brooks. Bost: 1873. il. ff.17[HCL]
?974. (Vetter Franz auf dem Esel.) Cousin Freddy's first and last donkey-ride. By A. B. Westmacott. L: Hays 1879. 7p. il. 4. [BM]
[Cf. comment on #953.]

BUSS, Ern.
975. Canton Glarus and the lake of Wallenstadt. Tr. anon. 143p. il. In C294.

BUSCHOR, Ern. 1886-.
*976. (Griechische Vasenmalerei.) Greek vase-painting. Tr. G: C. Richards. Pref. by Percy Gardner. NY: Dutton; L: Chatto 1922. xii; 179p. il. 25cm. [LC.BM]

BUSSE, K: 1872-1918. Sel. in C28.

BUSSE-PALMA, G: 1876-1915. Sel. in C28.

BUSSON, Pl. 1873-1924.
977. (Die Wiedergeburt des Melchior Dronte. Roman einer Seelenwanderung.) The man who was born again. Tr. Prince Mirski and T: Moult. L: Heinemann; NY: Day 1927. ix;302p. 8. [BM]

BUTZ, Kp. 1825-88. Sel. in C40.

BUWENBURG, -- v. Sel. in C532.

"BYR, Rb." (i.e.,K: Rb. Emmerich v. Bayer, 1835-1902.)
978. The cipher dispatch. Tr. E. L. Lathrop. NY: Worthington 1893. 308p. (B29)
979. (Sphinx.) Sphinx; or, striving with destiny. Tr. "Auber Forestier." Phil; NY: Maclean 1871. 400p. 19cm. [LC]

CALISIUS, J: H: 1633-1698. Sel. in C244.

CAMENISCH, Nina. Sel. in C438.

CAMERARIUS, Ph. 1537-1624.
980. (Operae horarum subcisivarum sive meditationes historicae. Centura I.) The living librarie; or, meditations and observations historical, natural, moral, political, and poetical. Ed. by R. Baddeley. Tr. J: Molle (from the French tr. by S. Goulart). L: Islip 1621. 403p. fol. [BM]
[Another copy of the same year has "The walking librarie."]
981. do. 1625. [same] 2d ed. With some additions by H: Molle (i.e. parts of Centura II). L: Islip. 428p. 29cm. [LCO]

CAMMERHOFF, J: Cph. F: 1721-51. Sel. in C19.

CAMPE, Jm. H: v. 1746-1818.
§982. (Kleine Seelenlehre für Kinder.) (14) Elementary dialogues for the improvement of youth. Tr. Mrs. Seymour. L: Hookham & Carpenter 1792. 192p. 17cm. [BM]
[Quite free, though not unfaithful to general sense.]
*983. (Kolumbus.) The discovery of America for the use of children. Tr. anon. L: J.Johnson 1799. 282p. 17cm. [BM]
[Pt. I of Die Entdeckung von Amerika. No mention of Cortes or Pizarro in this ed. This tr. is closer and better than Helme's, but not excellent.]
§984. do. 1799. Columbus; or, the discovery of America. Tr. Eliz. Helme. L: Low. 2v. in one. See "Brit. Crit." 15(1800):194. (B26)
§985. do. 1811. [same] ...as related by a father to his children. New ed. with the tr.'s last corrections and improvements. L: Cradock & Joy. 271p. 17cm. [BM]
§986. do. 1828. [same] New ed. L: Baldwin & Cradock. viii;270p. 18cm. [BM]

CAMPE, Jm.
987. (Kortes.) Cortes; or, the discovery of Mexico. Tr. anon. Birmingham: J. Belcher; L: Johnson 1800. 272p. 18cm. [BM]
[Same series as #983, part II.]
988. do. 1799. Cortez; or, the conquest of Mexico. Tr. Eliz. Helme. L: Low. 2v. in one. See "Brit. Crit." 15(1800):194. (B26)
989. do. 1800. [same] Pub. by Hurst in 1800. 2v. See "Crit. R." (II) 31(1801):346. (B26)
990. do. 1811. [same] ...as related... New ed. L: Cradock & Joy. 259p. 18cm. [BM]
991. do. 1826. [same] New ed. with the tr.'s last corrections and text improvements. L: Baldwin, Cradock & Joy. 259p. 18cm. [BM]
992. (Pizarro.) Pizarro; or, the conquest of Peru. Being a continuation of the discovery of America. Tr. anon. Birmingham: J. Belcher; L: Johnson 1800. 243p. 17cm. [BM]
[Same series as #983, part III.]
993. do. 1799. Tr. Eliz. Helme. L: Low. 2v. in one. See "Brit. Crit." 15(1800):194. (B26)
994. do. 1811. [same] ... as related... L: Cradock & Joy. New ed. with corrections, etc. 237p. 18cm. [BM]
995. do. 1819. [same] New ed., etc. Baldwin, Cradock & Joy. 237p. 17cm. [BM]
996. Polar scenes, exhibited in the voyages of Heemskirk and Barenz to the northern regions, and in the adventures of four Russian sailors at the island of Spitzbergen. Tr. anon. 2d ed. L: for J. Harris 1822. 138p. il. 17cm. [LC]
997. (Robinson der jüngere.) Robinson the younger. Tr. anon. Hamburg. Print. for C. E. Bohn 1781-2. 2v. 8. (B45)
§998. do. 1788. The new Robinson Crusoe: an instructive and entertaining hist. for the use of children. Tr. from the French. Embellished with 32 beautiful cuts (by J. Bewick). L: J:Stockdale. 4v. 173;156;137;177p. 18cm. [BM]
§999. do. 1789. [same] Stockdale. 265p. [BM]
[Same cuts. Much finer type.]
1000. do. 1789. Il. by German notes for the use of those which are learning the English. Tr. anon. (by F. C. Mertens). Francfort upon the Main. Prtd. for J. J. Kessler. 678 p. [See #1002.](B45)
1001. do. 1790. reprint?(of #998?)Bost: Thomas & Andres. 270p. 18cm. [LC]
1002. do. 1800. [same as #1000] A new ed. rev. and corr. Bremen: Prtd. for F. Wilmans. Tr. F. C. Mertens, Bremen. 8. (B45)
1003. do. 1800. Robinson the younger. Tr. J: Timäus. Braunschweig: Schulbuchhandlung. 8. (B45)
1004. do. 1803. Phil. 12. (B48)
§1005. do. 1809. [same as #998] Cork. Evory & Odell. 287p. 16cm[BM]
1006. do. 1811. An abridgment of the new R-- C--. NY: (B48)
1007. do. 1823. The new R-- C-- . Tr. anon. NY: Morgan. 147p. il. [B12]
1008. do. 1824. An abridgment, etc. (From #998.) Phil: Bioren. 182p. il. 18cm. [LC]
1009. do. 1827. The new R-- C-- . (Abridged.) Tr. anon. Dublin: Smith. 180p. il. 14cm. [BM]
1010. do. 1830. [same] Dublin. P. Dixon Hardy. 180p. [BM]
**1011. do. 1855. R-- the younger; or, the new Crusoe. Tr. R. Hick. L: Routledge. 240p. 17cm. [A real translation.] [BM]
1012. do. 1870. The new R-- C--. (Abridged.) Tr. Ma. Howitt. in C212, p. 43-96.

CANITZ, F: Rd. Frhr. v. 1654-99. Sel. in C276;486.

CARION, J:
1013. The three bokes of Chronicles...appendix, conteyning all... notable thinges...mentyoned in cronicles to have chaunced in sundry partes of the worlde from...1532 to...1550. Gathered by J: Funcke of Nuremborough. Imprynted at London for Gwalter Lynne, dwellynge on Somers Keye, by Byllinges gate. In the yeare of our Lord M.D.L. And they are to be solde in Paules church yarde, nexte to the great Schole, at the sygne of the Sprede Egle. ff. cclxxxix, 12 leaves of table. 18cm. [BM]

CARL Ax. of Saxe-Weimar-Eisenach.
1015. Reminisc. of the restoration of the Wartburg. Tr. G. A. Greene 1907. In C555.

CARLÉ, Erw. 1876- See "Rosen, Erw."

"CARMEN SYLVA" (i.e., Eli. Queen of Roumania, 1843-1916). Sel. in C366.
1016. The dreamer of dreams. Tr. anon. Il. by Edmund Dulac. L; NY: Hodder & S. 1915. 181p. 25cm. [LC]
1017. (Durch die Jahrhunderte. Pelesch Märchen.) Legends from river and mountain. By C-- S-- and Alma Strettell (afterwards Harrison). Il. by T. H. Robinson. L: G. Allen 1896 (1895). xi;328p. 20cm. [First 10 stories from above-named; remaining 9 from German "Märchen," expanded and edited.] [BM.LC]
1018. Edleen Vaughan; or, paths of peril. Tr. anon. NY: Cassell 1891. 412p. 19cm. [LC]
1019. (Gedichte.) Poems. Tr. A. H. Exner. L: Jarrold 1912. 122p. 18cm. [Includes some selections from Vom Amboss.] [BM.LC]
**1020. (Handwerkerlieder.) Songs of toil. Tr. J: E. Bowen. NY: Stokes 1887. 143p. 16cm. [LC]
[31 poems, Ger. and Engl. Tr. very good]
*1021. do. 1888. [same] [LC]
*1022. do. 1892. [same] [LC]
1023. A heart regained. Tr. Mrs. Ma. A. Mitchell. Bost: Cupples & H. 1888. 129p. 17cm. [LC]
1024. How I spent my sixtieth birthday. Tr. H. E. Delf. NY: Scribner 1904. [AC]
1025. (Leidens Erdengang.) Suffering's journey on the earth. Tr. Marg. A. Nash. Il. by Percy A. Nash. 2d ed. L: Jarrold 1906? 139p. 19cm. [LC]
1026. (Märchen einer Königin.) A real queen's fairy tales. Tr. Edith Hopkirk. Il. by H. Nelson and A. G. Jones. Chic: Davis 1901. 229p. 8. [LC]
[LC card: "Tales based upon old Rumanian legends, published... Bonn (1901). The present ed. contains...8 stories...from the original collection and six additional tales...from the MS."]
†1027. (Mein Penatenwinkel.) From memory's shrine: the reminisc. of C-- S-- . Tr. Edith Hopkirk. Phil; L: Lippincott 1911. 270p. il. 21cm. [Tr. pads and alters unmercifully. Simple, pleasing style is wholly lost.] [LC]
†1028. do. 1911. [same] 265p. 8. [BM]
†1029. do. 1912. [same] New and cheaper ed. L: Low. 274p. [EC]
†1030. do. 1914. [same] New ed. L: Low. 272p. il. 8. [EC]
1031. Pilgrim sorrow. A cycle of (12) tales. Tr. Helen Zimmern. L; NY: Holt 1884. 13; 262p. 17cm. [BM]
1032. A royal story book. Tr. anon. L: Digby, Long 1911. 192p. il. 8. [BM]
1033. Shadows on life's (or love's) dial. Tr. anon. Downey 1895-6. 8. [EC]

"CARMEN SYLVA"
1034. Tales. The mother-in-law; In fetters. In Roosevelt, Blanche. "Elizabeth of Roumania: a study." With two tales. pp. 193-374. Tr. anon. L: Chapman & H. 1891. 22cm. [BM]
1035. (Vom Amboss. Also, Les pensées d'une reine.) Thoughts of a queen. Tr. H. S. Edwards. L: Eden 1890. 139p. 17cm. [BM]
[Short aphorisms, grouped under subject headings.]
1036. do. 1895. Tr. anon. New ed. Macqueen. 12. [EC]
1037. do. 1910. [same as #1035] Golden thoughts of C-- S--. L: Lane. xvi;80p. 15cm. [BM]
1038. do. 1912. Sparks from the anvil; or, thoughts of a queen. Tr. A. H. Exner. From French and German. L: Jarrold. 108p. 16cm. [BM]
See Stackelberg, Na., Life of C-- S--. #9009.

CAROVÉ, F: W: 1789-1852.
§1039. (Das Märchen ohne Ende.) The story without an end. Tr. Sa. Austin. With a pref. to her little daughter. Il. W: Harvey. L: E. Wilson 1834. 123p. 13cm. [Tr. is not wholly satisfying.] [BM]
§1040. do. 1836. [same] Bost: Francis. 123p. il. sm. 4. [LCO]
§1041. do. 1856. [same] In C83, pp. 237-66.
§1042. do. 1864 (1863). [same] New and impr. ed. L: Virtue Bros. 130p. 13cm. [BM]
§1043. do. 1868. [same] Il. (in col.) Mrs. E. V. Boyle. L: Low. 40p. 25cm. [BM]
§1044. do. 1872. [same] Il. Boyle. L: Low. 16. [EC]
§1045. do. 1874. [same] Il. Boyle. L: Low. 8. [EC]
1046. do. 1885. Tr. J. C. Pickard. Chic: Winchell. 33p. 16. [LCO]
1047. do. 1886-1887. [same] With the palace of vanity; from the French. Bost; Chic· Interstate. S. [AC]
§1048. do. 1889. Tr. Sa. Austin. In Chamisso, Peter Schlemihl, C492.
§1049. do. 1897. [same] Il. Boyle. Portland, Me: Mosher. 58p. 13cm. [Printed on vellum] [LC]
§1050. do. 1899. [same] Bost: Estes. 74p. il. 12. [LC]
§1051. do. 1899. [same] Il. Aimée G. Clifford. L: Gardner. 108p. 7cm. [No preface.] [BM]
§1052. do. 1900. [same] Mosher. 61p. [LC]
§1053. do. 1902. 1903. [same] Bost: Heath. Pref. T. W. Higginson. Il. Boyle. 57p. 19cm. [LC]
§1054. do. 1904. [same] NY: Putnam. il. 12. [AC]
§1055. do. 1904. [same] Introd. C. Wager-Smith. Phil: Altemus. 110p. il. 19cm. [LC]
§1056. do. 1904. [same] Il. Pl. Henry. L: Duckworth. vii;77p. 14cm. [BM]
§1057. do. 1912. [same] Il. Frank C. Papé. L: Duckworth. xv;165p. 22cm. [Prtd. on one side of the paper.] [BM]
§1058. do. 1913. [same] NY: Duffield. il. [AC]
1059. The story of Gottfried and Beata. Tr. A. Moline. Il. H: Newman. L: Harvey & Darton 1844. 96(i.e.,76)p. 19cm. [BM]

CARRIERE, Mz. 1817-95.
1060. Sculpture and painting. Ad. as "Ancient Art" by Allan Marquand in the "Iconographic encyclopedia." Phil: 1887. vol. 3. [LCO]

CARSTEN, H:
1061. (Aschenbrödel.) Cinderella: cantata by Carl Reinecke. Tr. Lewis Novra. Libr. Engl. L: Augener; NY: Schirmer 1879. 20p. 18cm. [BM]
1062. do. 1879. Tr. anon. Vocal score. Engl. L: Augener; NY: Schirmer. 57p. 27cm. [BMM]

CARSTEN, H:
1063. (Dornröschen.) Little rosebud; or, the sleeping beauty. Cantata by Reinecke. Tr. L. Novra. Libr. Engl. L: Augener; NY: Schirmer 1878. 20p. 18cm. [BM]

CARUS, K: Gst. 1789-1869.
*1064. (England und Schottland im Jahre 1844.) The king of Saxony's journey through England and Scotland...1844. Tr. S. C. Davidson. L: Chapman & H. 1846. 391p. 21cm. [BM]

CASPARI, K: H: 1815-61.
1065. (Der Schulmeister und sein Sohn.) The schoolmaster and his son: a narr. (founded on a MS of U. Gast) of...the thirty years' war. Tr. from the 3d ed. Phil: Luth. board 1861. 216p. il. 16cm. [BM]
1066. do. 1863. [another tr.] L: Morgan. 209p. il. 16cm. [BM]
1067. do. 1888. [same as #1066] New ed. L: Gardner. 12. [EC]
1068. do. 1916. [same as #1065] Il. Jessie Gillespie. Phil: Luth. pub. soc. 216p. 18cm. [LC]
1069. ("Zu Strassburg auf der Schanz.") Frank's friend; or, the rampart of Strasburg. Tr. anon. Phil: Luth. bd. 1862. 82p. 18. [LCO]

CASPARY, --- . Sel. in #7717.

CASTELLI, Ig. Fz. 1781-1862. Sel. in C53;137a;394:
1070. The castle of Cleves; or, the witness-hand. Tr. J. D. Haas. 1839. In C183, pp. 345-356.
*1071. (Der häusliche Krieg.) The conspirators; or, the household war. (Substantially a tr. of Aristophanes' "Lysistrata.") Ed. and tr. G: L. Osgood. Vocal score. Engl. Bost: Ditson 1883. 134p. 4. [LCO]
†1072. (Die Schweizerfamilie.) The Swiss family: lyric opera in 3 acts (founded on "La famille Suisse" by de Saint Just). Tr. C. B. Burkhardt. Libr. NY: Herald 1845. 10p. 8. [LCO]

CATHREIN, V:
§1073. (Der Sozialismus.) Socialism exposed and refuted...a chapter from the author's moral philosophy. Tr. (chiefly from the 4th Ger. ed.) Rev. Jas. Conway. NY: Benziger 1892. 164p. 19cm. [BM] [Tr. omits freely and is otherwise unfaithful.]

CHALYBAEUS, H: Mz. 1796-1862.
**1074. (Historische Entwicklung der spekulativen Philosophie von Kant bis Hegel.) Histor. survey of speculative philos. from Kant to Hegel. Tr. from 4th ed. Af. Tulk. L: Longmans 1854. xvi;397p. 18cm. [Excellent translation.] [BM.LC]
*1075. do. 1854. Histor. dev., etc. Tr. Rev. A. Edersheim. Ed: Clark. 443p. 22cm. [Not quite as good as the foregoing.] [BM]
1076. do. 185-. [same?] Andover, Mass: Draper. 12. [AC]

CHAMBERLAIN, Houston Stewart, 1856-1927.
*1077. (Das Drama R: Wagners: eine Anregung.) Wagnerian drama: an attempt to inspire a better apprec. of Wagner as a dram. poet. Tr. anon. L: Lane 1915. 240p. 19cm. [LC]
§1078. (Die Grundlagen des 19 Jahrhunderts.) The foundations of the 19th cent. Tr. J: Lees. L; NY: Lane 1911. 2v. il. 22cm. [LC.BM] [Tr. is correct, but rather bungling and awkward.]
§1079. do. 1912. [same] 20cm. [LC]
*1080. (Immanuel Kant. Die Persönlichkeit als Einführung in das Werk.) I-- K-- ; a study and a comparison with Goethe, Leonardo, Bruno, Plato, and Descartes. Tr. A. B. Freeman-Mitford. L; NY: Lane 1914. 2v. 456;530p. 23cm. [BM.LC]

CHAMBERLAIN, Houston Stewart
*1081. (Kriegsaufsätze.) The ravings of a renegade: being the war-essays of H. S. C-- . Tr. Ç: H. Clarke. L: Jarrold 1915. 207p. 19cm. [BM.LC]
§1082. (R: Wagner.) R: W-- . Tr. G: A. Hight and rev. by the author. Munich: Bruckmann; Phil: Lippincott; L: Dent 1897. xvii;402p. il. 31cm. [BM.LC]
§1083. do. 1900. [same] [BM]

CHAMISSO, Adt. v. 1781-1838. Sel. in C3;17*;40-1;47;77;88-9;99;106;123;129;142;144;146*;152-3;166;172-3;178;184;192;194*;195-6;219;296;309*;311;313;318;366*;372-3;380;412;414-5;422-3;448;452;459;460;469;470;499;531;539;554;571;574.
1084. (Bemerkungen und Ansichten vom dem Naturforscher der Expedition.) Remarks and opinions of the naturalist of the expedition. In O: v. Kotzebue's voyage of discovery into the south sea, etc. Vols. 2 & 3. Tr. H. E. Lloyd. L: Longmans 1821. 3v. il. 21cm. [LC.BM]
1085. (Frauen-Liebe und Leben.) Woman's love and life: a cycle of song. Tr. F. V. McDonald. Cambridge, Mass: Wilson 1881. ff.9. 8. [HCL]
*1086. (Faust; ein Versuch.) Faust: a dramatic sketch. Tr. H: Phillips, Jr. Phil: Priv. print. 1861. 23p. 19cm. [LC]
*1087. (Peter Schlemihls wundersame Geschichte.) P-- S-- , from the Ger. of Lamotte Fouqué [sic]. Tr. Sir J: Bowring. Pl. G: Cruikshank. L: Whittaker 1824. 165p. 18cm. [BM]
[Very good style; not quite correct.]
*1088. do. 1824. [same] Il. Cruikshank. Bost: Wells & L. 139p. 16. (B48)
1089. do. 1838. Tr. Emilie de Rouillon. L: Lane. 18. [EC]
§1090. do. 1843. The wonderful history of P-- S-- . Tr. W: Howitt. Ger. and Engl. Nürnberg; Lpz; L: Longmans. 281p. 16cm. [BM.HCL]
§1091. do. 1843. P-- S--, the shadowless man. Tr. Jas. Burns? In C473.
§1092. do. 1843? [same as #1090] NY: Burgess & Stringer 1844. 42p. 24cm. [Cover title gives date 1843.] [LC]
1093. do. 1845. Tr. Burns? The shadowless man; or, the wonderful history of P-- S--. L: Burns (or Lumley). 75p. il. 16cm. [BM.LC]
1094. do. 1845. The shadowless man. Tr. anon. In C494.
**1095. do. 1849. The wonderful history of P-- S--. Tr. F: H: Hedge. In C194.
§1096. do. 1860. Howitt's tr. L: Longmans. [HCL]
1097. do. 1861. Bowring's tr. Il. by Cruikshank. 3d ed. L: Hardwicke & Bogue. 122p. 19cm. [BM.LC]
*1098. do. 1874. [same] NY: Denman, Alexander. [AC]
1099. do. 1877. [same as #1093.] L: Routledge. 75p. 19cm. [BM]
*1100. do. 1878. Bowring's tr. L: Hardwicke & Bogue. 122p. 25cm [LC]
1101. do. 1879. Burns's tr? L: Routledge. Cf. #1099. [EC]
1102. do. 1882. The shadowless man. Tr. anon. With the new Paul and Virginia, by W. H. Mallock. NY: Am. news; Nashville, Tenn: Setliff. [AC]
1103. do. 1889. [same tr. as #1093] In C492.
1104. do. 1893. [same as #1088] Bost: Knight. il. [AC]
1105. do. 1898. Tr. anon. P-- S-- . In C509.
1106. do. 1898? P-- S--, the shadowless man. Tr. anon. Il. Burne-Jones. Introd. J. Jacobs. L: G. Allen 1899. xxxi;147p. 19cm. [BM.BPL]
[Slightly revised from #1093.]
*1107. do. 1899. Hedge's tr. The wonderful history of P-- S--, the man who lost his shadow. Bost: Ginn. 118p. 18cm. [LC]
*1108. do. 1903. Bowring's tr. Il. Cruikshank. NY: Putnam. 32. [AC]
*1109. do. 1910. [same] NY: Warne. 106p. il. (B12)
*1110. do. 1910. [same] The shadowless man, P-- S--. Il. Gordon

CHAMISSO, Adt. v. - Peter Schlemihl.
Browne. L: Chatto & Windus. xxiv;106p. 20cm. [BM]
1111. do. 1913. [same tr. as #1093] The marvellous history of the shadowless man. In C493.
*1112. do. 1913-15. Hedge's tr. In C154(5).
1113. do. 1915. Tr. anon. Allen & U. 18. [EC]
*1114. do. 1923. The wonderful history of P-- S--. Tr. and il. by Theo. Bolton. NY: Huebsch. 113p. 20cm. [LC]
[Not without error, but very good.]
1115. do. 1924. The shadowless man. Ed. J: Drinkwater (from Bowring's tr.) for schools. L; Glasgow: Collins. 96p. 19cm. [BM]

CHARLEMAGNE (i.e.,K: I, der Grosse, 742-814). Sel. in C230.
See Eginhardus, Life of the emperor K: the great, #1424 seq.
See Kohlrausch, H: The character of C--, #5168.
See Prutz, Hs., The age of C--, #7248.
See Schmidt, Fd., C--, #8439.

CHARLES of Hesse-Cassel, prince. Letters to H: Jung-Stilling. Tr. 1836. In #4767.

CHARLOTTE Eli. v. Baiern, duchesse d'Orléans, 1652-1721.
*1116. Secret memoirs of the court of Louis XIV and of the Regency. Extracted from the...corr. Preceded by a notice of this princess, etc. Tr. anon. L: Whittaker 1824. viii;472p. 21cm. [BM]
[Extracts relating to particular persons grouped. Tr. appears to be good.]
*1117. do. 1889. Life and letters...Compiled, tr. and gathered from various...sources, etc. anon. L: Chapman & H. 1889. viii;341p. 22cm. [Extracts from her letters virtually constitute the biography. Tr. seems to be very good.] [BM]
*1118. do. 1895. Secret memoirs, etc...and accomp. with notes. Tr. anon. L: Nichols. xii;360p. 22cm.[Re-issue of 1824 ed.] [BM]
†1119. do. 1899. Corr...with that of Marie-Adelaide de Savoie, and Mme. de Maintenon. Sel. and tr. Kath. P. Wormeley. (pp. 39-181.) L: Heinemann. 326p. 22cm. [BM]
[Sel. tr. from a French ed. which was abridged.]
*1120. do. 1904 [same as #1116] Secret memoirs, etc. L: Grolier soc. 403p. il. 22cm.[Reprints 1824 ed. without acknowledgment.] [BM]
*1121. do. 1924. The letters of madame. The corr...Tr. and ed. G. S. Stevenson. L: Chapman & Dodd. 2v. 21cm. [BM]
[Vol. 1. 1661-1708; vol. 2. 1709-22. Taken from a German ed. of the Lit. Verein in Stuttgart, and a French ed. by E. Jaegle in 1880. Tr. seems to be faithful and good.]

CHEMNITZ, Mts. F: 1815-70. Sel. in C317.

CHEZY, Hna. Cne. v. 1783-1856. Sel in C90.
§1122. (Euryanthe.) Euryanthe: romantic opera in 3 acts by C. M. v. Weber. Tr. anon. New ed. rev. and corr. Libr. Ger;Engl. L: Millar 1841. 41p. 18cm.[Prose; not very good.] [BM]
*1123. do. 1842? Tr. anon. Libr. Ger;Engl. L: Schloss. 51p. 17cm. [Tr. is close, unrhymed, but mostly in same meter.] [BM]
*1124. do. 1842? [same] 2d ed. rev. and corr. L: Schloss. 48p. 17cm. [BM]
*1125. do. 1843. [same] 3d ed. 48p. [BM]
*1126. do. 1882. Ed. by B. Tours. Tr. W: Thornthwaite. Vocal score. Ger;Engl. L: Novello. 196p. 26cm. [LCM.BMM]
*1127. do. 1887. Tr. F: A. Schwab. Libr. Ger;Engl. NY. 12. [LCO]

"CHRISTEN, Ada" (i.e.,Cne.(Friderik)Breden, 1844-1901). Sel. in C450; 501.

CHRISTIAN VON HAMLE, 13th cent. Sel. in C27;310;416;427;532.

CHRISTIAN VON LUPIN, fl. 1292-1312. Sel. in C27;427;532.

CHRISTOFFEL, Raget, 1810-75.
*1128. (H: Zwingli.) Zwingli; or, the rise of the reformation in Switzerland. Tr. J: Cochran. Ed: Clark 1858. 462p. 22cm. [BM]
*1129. do. 1860. [same] L: Hamilton. [EC]

"CLAUDIUS, Mn." (i.e., Rosa Petzel)
1130. (Das Häuschen am See.) The cottage by the lake. Tr. Rebecca H. Schively. Phil: Luth. bd. 1869. 160p. 17cm. [LC]

CLAUDIUS, Mt. 1740-1815. Sel. in C17;22;25-6;29;41;44;46;86;106; 111;129;132-3;137a;166;169;185;194;215;235;269;273;276;309;366; 372-3;380;383;385;387-8;405a;410;423;501;504-5;533;538.
1131. Essays, letters, and fragments from his works. See Herbst, J., Claudius, #4203.

"CLAUREN, H:" (i.e., C: Gb. S: Heun, 1771-1854.)
§1132. (Liesli.) Liesli: a Swiss tale. Tr. J. D. Haas. L: Whittaker 1826. 144p. 18cm. [Inadequate command of German.] [BM]
§1133. do. 1839. [same] Liesli, the maid of Solothurn; or, the cemetery of Schwytz. In C183, pp. 2-48.
§1134. do. 1845. [same] Liesli: a Swiss tale, etc. With Aeinrich (Heinrich) and Blanca; or, the three brothers. L: Burns. pp. 1-46. 16cm. [The second story is by Cph. v. Schmid; cf. #8304.] [BM]
§1135. do. 1845. [same] In C494.

CLAUSEWITZ, K: v. 1780-1831. Sel. in C161.

CLAUSNITZER, Ts. C. 1618-1684. Sel. in C269; 271; 287.

COHN, Ca (Viebig). See "Viebig, Ca."

COHN, Mn. d. 1894. See "Mels, A."

COHN, Pl. 1872- .
1136. (Briefe einer Wienerin.) Betty: letters of a Viennese. By "Paul v. Hohenau." Tr. Vivia de Varenne. Berlin: Continental times 1914. 54p. 21cm. [LC]

COLLIN, H: Js. v. 1772-1811. Sel. in C44.

COLLIN, Mts. v. 1779-1824. Sel. in C137a.

CONRAD VON QUEINFURT. Sel. in C570.

CONRAD, A: 1842- .
*1137. (Schatten und Lichtblicke aus dem amerikanischen Leben während des Sezessions-Krieges.) The destruction of Columbia, S. C. Tr. W: H. Pleasants. Roanoke, Va: Stone print. 1902. 31p. 23cm. [From chaps. 19-22.] [LC.BM]

CONTESSA, W: Salice, 1777-1825.
*1138. (Ich bin mein Bruder.) I am my brother: a comedy. Tr. anon. In "Scots Mag." (II) 6(1820): 225. [BM]
1138a. The alchemist's daughter. Tr. Mrs. Bushby. In "Colburn's new monthly mag." 106(1856):17, etc. (B27)

CORNELIUS, P: 1824-74.
§1139. (Der Barbier von Bagdad.) The barber of B--: a comic opera in two acts. Words and music by C--. Libr. Ger;Engl. NY: Metropolitan opera house 1890. 15; 15p. 24cm. [LCM]
[Tr. close to sense but would not go with music.]
§1140. do. 1905. Tr. M. E. Browne. Score. Ger;Engl. Lpz: Breitkopf & H. 234p. 4. [LCM]
[Not very close but follows music. Struggle with rhymes.]
§1141. do. 1906. [same]. Libr. Ger;Engl. Breitkopf. 28p. 24cm. [BM]
**1142. do. 1925. Tr. F: H. Martens. Libr. Engl. 39p. 21cm. [LCM]
[Very good, both rhymes and verse.]

CORRÉE, COMTESSE de la. Sel. in C448.

CORVIN-WIERSBITZKI, O: Jl. Bh. v. 1812-86.
1143. (Aus dem Leben eines Volkskämpfers.) A life of advent.: an autobiog. Tr. anon. L: Bentley 1871. 3v. 21cm. [BM.LC] [Much abridged and somewhat bowdlerized; virtually a new work.]
1144. (Illustrierte Weltgeschichte für das Volk.) Yorston's pop. hist. of the world. Tr. H: W: Dulcken. NY; Cinc: Yorston 1884-6. 8v.il. 25cm. [LC]

COSEL, Cte. v. 1818- . See "Auer, Ade. v."

COUDENHOVE-CALERGI, R: N: 1894- .
1144a. (Pan-Europa) Pan-Europe. Introd. by N: M. Butler. Knopf '26. xix;215p. D. [AC]

CRAMER, Jns. Fs.
1145. The funeral elogy and character of...the late princess Sophia. Tr. (from the Latin) by Mr. Toland. L: B.Lintott & J.Roberts [BM] 1714. 14p. 17cm. [Another copy has: elegy.]

CRAMER, J: And. 1723-88. See Gellert. The life of professor G-- etc. #2143.

CRAMER, K: Glb. 1758-1817. Sel. in C570.
1146. (Der deutsche Alcibiades; and, Hermann v. Nordenschild.) Albert de Nordenshild; or, the modern A--. Tr. anon. L: Robinsons 1794. 2v. See "Analyt. R." 24(1796): 404. (B26)
Hermann of Unna. [False ascription; see Naubert, Cne.]

CRASSELIUS, Bms. 1677-1724. Sel. in C240;269;276.

CREMER, Hm.
§1147. (Ueber den Zustand nach dem Tode...) Beyond the grave. Tr. Rev. S: T. Lowrie. Pref. by Rev. A. A. Hodge. NY: Harper 1886. xxxviii;153p. 17cm. [BM]
[Style much altered, but sense and substance mostly retained.]

CRESCENTIUS. Sel. in C318.

CREUZNACH, Td. Sel. in C450. [Perhaps Td. Creizenach, 1818-77.]

CROJAN, J. Sel. in C169.

CRONEGK, J: F: Frhr. v. 1731-58. Sel. in C111.

CUBASCH, W.
1148. The Bürgenstock. Tr. anon. 40p. il. In C294.

CURTI, Fz. 1854-98. Lili-Tsé. Operetta. See "Kirchbach, W."

CURTIUS, Ern. 1814-96. Sel. in C196;366.
*1149. (Griechische Geschichte.) The hist. of Greece. Tr. Sir A. W. Ward. L: Bentley 1868-73. 5v. 22cm. [BM.LC]
*1150. do. 1870-4. [same] Rev. by W: A. Packard. NY: Scribner. 20cm. [LC]
*1151. do. 1871-4. [same] Scribner. 19cm. [LC]
*1152. do. 1892. [same] Scribner. 21cm. [LC]

CURTMANN, W: Jk. G: 1802-71.
1153. Short stories for children. Tr. Ida Curtman. St.L: 1909. 81p. 23cm. [LC]

CUVILLIER, Chas. The lilac domino: operetta. See Gatti, Ech., and Bela Jenbach.

CZERNIN VON UND ZU CHUDENITZ, O:r Tb. O: Ma., Graf v. 1872- .
**1154. (Im Weltkriege.) In the world war. Tr. anon. L: Cassell 1919. 352p. [Seems to be excellent.] [BM]

CZERNIN VON UND ZU CHUDENITZ
*1155. do. 1920. [same] NY: Harper. 387p. 8. [LC]

DACH, Sm. 1605-59. Sel. in C166;190;229;231;244;276;309;316;371-3; 486;489;530;570-1.

DAEUBLER, Td. 1876- . Sel. in C95.

DAHLKE, Pl. 1865- .
1156. Marriage as a fetter. Tr. anon. 1926. In C308.

DAHLMANN, Js. 1861- .
1157. Great Tokyo earthquake...1923. Experiences and impressions. Tr. and ad. V: F. Gettelman. NY: America press 1924. xiv;130p. 19cm. [LC]

DAHN, Fx. L: Sophus, 1834-1912. Sel. in C309;311;366*;448;450;469; 501;571.
1158. (Attila.) Attila the hun: a novel. Tr. anon. NY: Minerva 1891. 253p. 18cm. [LC]
*1159. (Bissula.) A captive of the Roman eagles. Tr. Ma. J. Safford. Chic: McClurg 1902. 434p. 20cm. [LC]
*1160. (Ein Kampf um Rom.) A struggle for Rome. Tr. Lily Wolffsohn. L: Bentley 1878. 3v. 18cm. [BM]
*1161. (Felicitas. Historischer Roman.) Felicitas: a tale of the German migrations, A. D. 476...Tr. by M. A. C. E. L: Macmillan 1883. 223p. 19cm. [BM]
*1162. do. 1883. Tr. Ma. J. Safford. NY: Gottsberger. 208p. 16cm. [LC]
1163. do. 1890. abr. L: Longmans. (B13)
1164. do. 1893. Macmillan. (B13)
*1165. do. 1903. Safford's tr. Chic: McClurg. 341p. [LC]
*1166. do. 1903. Tr. Ma. G. Lansdale. Washington, D. C.: Neale. 160p. 20cm. [LC]
1167. do. 1903. Tr. anon. Industrial pub. (B13)
*1168. (Gelimer.) The scarlet banner. Tr. Ma. J. Safford. Chic: McClurg 1903. 418p. 20cm. [LC]
1169. do? n.d. [same?] The fall of the Vandal dragon. Tr. anon. McClurg. (B13)
*1170. (Sind Götter? Die Halfred Sigskaldsaga...) Saga of Halfred the Sigskald: a northern tale of the tenth cent. Tr. Sophie F. E. (or rather F.) Veitch. Paisley. Gardner 1886. 184p. 18cm. [BM]

DALEI, Bn. Sel. in C213;373.

DAMBERGER, Cn. F:
1171. Travels through the interior of Africa...1781-97. Tr. by "Zacharias Taurinius"? L: R.Phillips 1801. 544p. col. pl. 21cm. [Fictitious voyage. BM takes Z.T. to be the author's real name, Damberger a pseudonym. See my note to "Taurinius, Z:"] [BM]
1172. do. 1801. Tr. anon. L: J.Lee. 360p. col. pl. 18cm. [BM]
1173. do. 1801. NY: Durrell. 2v. 18cm. [LC]
[Reprint of Phillips ed? LC says printed by Longmans.]
1174. do. 1801. [same?] Bost: Larkin. 523p. 21cm. [LC]

DAREWSKI, Max. See Granichstaedten, Br., joint author.

DARMSTAEDTER, Pl. Sel. in C563.

DAUMER, G: F: 1800-75. Sel. in C505.

DAUT, J: Max. 18th cent.
1175. The approaching judgment of God upon the Roman empire...Tr. B. Furly. L: Prtd. for the booksellers...1711. 108p. 18cm. [BM]

DAUT, J: Max. 18th cent.
1176. do. 1804? Reprtd. by G. Terry. 127p. 21cm. [BM]

DAUTHENDEY, Max, 1867-1918. Sel. in C28;95.
1177. (Die Spielereien einer Kaiserin.) The caprices of an empress: dramatic comp. in four acts. Tr. Mie. M. MacDonald. NY: 1912. Tw. [LC]

DECIUS, (i.e., von Hofe), N: fl. 1500-29. Sel. in C230;269;273;423.

DEDEKIND, F: 1525?-98.
*1178. (Grobianus; de morum simplicitate.) The schoole of slovenrie; or, Cato turned wrong side outward. Tr. out of Latine into Engl. verse, to the use of all Engl. Cristendome, except court and cities. By R. F., Gent. L: V.Simmes 1605. 20+136. 18cm. [BM.BPL]
†1179. do. 1739. G--; or, the compleat booby. An ironical poem. Tr. R. Bull. L: T.Cooper. 276p. 8. [Paraphrase.] [BM.NY]
*1180. do. 1904. Reprint of #1178. Berlin. "Palaestra" XXXVIII.

DEECKE, W: 1831-97.
*1181. (Italien.) Italy: a popular account. Tr. H. A. Nesbit. L: Sonnenschein; NY: Macmillan 1904. 485p. il. 26cm. [BM.LC]

DEEG, J. G. Sel. in C173.

DEHMEL, R: 1863-1920. Sel. in C28*;95;366;423.
*1182. (Gedichte.) Selected verse, 48 poems. Tr. E. H. Zeydel. In "Poet-Lore" 31(1920):401. [Very good.]

DEINHARDSTEIN, J: L: Fz. 1794-1859.
§1183. (Das Bild der Danae.) Salvator Rosa; or, the portrait of Danae. A comedy (in two acts and in verse). Tr. J. D. Haas. 1839. In C183, pp. 291-320. [Good verse, but not very close to original.]

DEISSMANN, Gst. Ad. 1866- .
1183a. (Licht vom Osten. Das neue Testament und die neuentdeckten Texte d. hellenistisch-römischen Welt.) Light from the ancient east; the New Test. il. by recently disc. texts of the Graeco-Roman world. Tr. L. R. M. Strachan. Scribner 1907. [AC]
1183b. do. 1910. [same] Doran. [AC]
1183c. do. 1927. New and completely rev. ed. with 85 il. from the latest Ger. ed. Harper;Doran;Hodder. xxxii;535p. O. [AC]
1183d. (Paulus. Eine kultur- und religionsgeschichtliche Skizze.) St. Paul, a study in social and relig. hist. Tr. Lionel R. M. Strachan. Doran 1912. xix;316p. il. O. [AC]
1183e. do. 1927. Tr. by W: E. Wilson. 2d ed. rev. and enl. with 6 pl. and 7 diagrams. Harper; Doran. xv;323p. O. [AC]
1183f. The relig. of Jesus and the faith of Paul. Tr. W: E. Wilson. Doran 1923. 287p. D. [AC]
1183g. do. 1926. [same] 2d rev. ed. Doran; Harper. 284p. O. [AC]

DEITERS, Hm. 1833- .
*1184. (J:s Brahms.) J-- B--. Tr. Rosa Newmarch. L: Unwin 1888. 160p. 18cm. [BM.LC]

DELBRUECK, Hs. G. L. 1848-1929. Sel. in C563.
*1185. (Regierung und Volkswille.) Government and the will of the people. Tr. R. S: MacElwee. NY: Oxford 1923. xiii;192p. 23cm. [LC.BM]
1186. How to improve Anglo-German relations. Tr. anon. NY: Dutton 1912. 4p. 19cm. [LC]

DELFF, H: K: Hg. Sel. in C300(17).

DELITZSCH, Fz. 1813-90.
*1187. (Ein Tag in Capernaum.) A day in Capernaum. Tr. from 3d Ger. ed. by Rev. G: H. Schodde. NY: Funk & W. 1887. 166p. 19cm.[LCOBM]
*1188. (Iris. Farbenstudien und Blumenstücke.) Iris: studies in color and talks about flowers. Tr. A. Cusin. Ed: Clark 1889. 227p. 21cm. [Twelve lectures on religious subjects.] [BM]
1189. José and Benjamin: a tale of Jerusalem in the time of the Herods. Tr. J. G. Smieton. L: Hodder 1882. 232p. 8. [BM]
1190. The oaks of A La Ronde. Tr. A. F. O. I. L: Adams 1880. 15p. 8. [Reprinted from "Hebrew Christian Witness."] [BM]

DEMME, Hm. Cph. Gf. 1760-1822. Sel. in C125.

DENGLER, P.
1191. The baths of Reinerz. Tr. anon. 32p. il. In C294.

DENICKE, D: 1603-80. Sel. in C231.

DENIFLE, H: Seuse, 1844-1905.
1192. Humanity, its destiny and the means to attain it: a series of discourses. Tr. Very Rev. Fd. Brossart. Ratisbon; NY: Pustet 1909. 257p. 20cm. [LC]
*1193. (Luther und Luthertum.) Luther and Lutherdom, in the first development. Tr. from 2d rev. ed. by R. Volz. NY: Bu. of the holy name soc. 1917. li;465p. O. [LC says: Somerset, O: Torch press 1917-. Vol. 1, Pt. 1. 24 cm. (In progress.)] [AC]

DENK, V: Mn. O: 1853-1918. See "Schaching, O: v."

DE NOEL, M. T. (i.e. J.)
1193a. (Der Dom zu Köln.) An histor. description of the cathedral of Cologne. Tr. Marian Bayley. Cologne. 1838. 12. [Not in Heinsius.] [EC]

DERWINUS, L. Sel. in C301.

DESSLER, Wfg. Cph. 1660-1722. Sel. in C269;271;273;276;287;489; 570;#8904.

DETJEN, ---. Sel. in C497.

"DETLEF, C:" (i.e., Ka. Bauer, 1836-76).
1194. (Auf Capri.) At Capri: a story of Italian life. Tr. by MS. Phil: Porter & C. 1875. 353p. 19cm. [LC]
1195. (Bis in die steppe.) Clemence d'Orville; or, from the palace to the steppe. A novel of Russian high life. Also, Clelia, from family papers, by "A. Mels." Tr. T. H. Fairfax. Bost: Littell & Gay 1870. 112p. 23cm. [LC]
*1196. (Das einsame Herrenhaus.) A Russian country house. Tr. Mrs. J. W. Davis. NY: Worthington 1890. 311p. il. 20cm. [BM]
1197. do? 1882. Irene; or, the lonely manor. Tr. anon. NY: Lovell. 209p. 18cm. [LC]
1198. (Musste es sein?) Must it be? A romance. Tr. by M. S. Phil: Lippincott 1873. 134p. il. 23cm. [LC]
1199. (Nora.) Nora. Tr. Marian Ford. NY: Munro 1888. 239p. 19cm[LC]
1199a. (Schuld und Sühne.) Dead to the world; or, sin and atonement. Tr. by M. S. Bost: Gill n.d. See "Lit. World" 6(1875):16. (B15a)
1200. (Zwischen Vater und Sohn.) Valentine, the countess; or, between father and son. Tr. by M. S. Phil: Porter & C. 1874. 377p. 19cm. [LC]
1201. do. 1885. [same] [LC]

DEUSSEN, Pl. 1845-1919.
1202. (Allgemeine Geschichte der Philosophie. Zweiter Teil.) The philos. of the Upanishads. Tr. Af. S. Geden. Ed: Clark 1906. 220p. 23cm. [LC]

DEUSSEN, Pl.--Allgemeine Geschichte der Philosophie.
1203. do. 1906. [same] Ed: Clark. xiv;429p. 8. [BM]
1204. do. 1908. [same] 429p. [LC]
1205. do. 1912. The system of the Vedânta...Tr. C: Johnston. L; Luzac; Chic: Open ct. 513p. [LC]
1206. do. 1913. [same] [AC]
1207. The elements of metaphysics...tr. from 2d Ger. ed. C. M. Duff. With appendix...on the philos. of the Vedânta...L: Macmillan 1894. xxiv;337p. 18cm. [First ed. pub. 1877.] [BM]
*1208. (Erinnerungen an Indien.) My Indian reminisc. Tr. A. King. Madras: G. A. Nateson 1912. vi;262;ix p. 18cm. [BM]
1209. Outlines of Indian philos. Tr. anon. Berlin. Curtius; L: Probsthain 1907. vi;70p. 5 x 8 in. [BM]
1210. Outlines of the Vedânta system of philos. according to Shankara. Tr. J. H. Woods and Cath. B. Runkle. NY: Grafton pr. 1906. L: Luzac 1907. 45p. 20cm. [LC.BM]
[Appendix to "System of the Vedânta." #1205.]
1211. do. 1915. [same] 2d ed. Harv. univ. pr. 75p. 12. [BM]
1212. The philos. of the Vedânta in its relation to occidental metaphysics...Tr. anon. Bombay: 1893. 15p. 20cm. [BM]
[An address. A summary of the author's views.]
1213. do. 1903. [same] Bombay: Rajaram Tukaram. 33p. 13cm. [BM]

"DEUTSCH. Cn." See J:s H: A: Ebrard, 1818-88.

DEVRIENT, E: 1801-77.
*1214. (Meine Erinnerungen an F. Mendelssohn-Bartholdy und seine Briefe an mich.) My recoll. of Fx. Mendelssohn-Bartholdy, and his letters to me. Tr. Natalia Macfarren. L: Bentley 1869. 307p. 20cm. [BM.LC]

"DEWALL, J:s van" (i.e., A: Kühne, 1829-83).
1215. Dear Elsie: a novel. Tr. Ma. J. Safford. Il. W. B. Davis. NY: Bonner 1892. 345p. 19cm. [LC]
1216. (Der Ulan.) The hussar: a romance of the Franco-Prussian war. Tr. Hettie E. Miller. Chic: Donohue, Henneberry 1891. 263p. 19cm. [LC]
1217. Far from home. By "J. van Derval." Tr. Kath. Hamilton. Bost: Lothrop 1884. 250p. 19cm. [LC]
1218. do. 1886. [same] [LC]
1219. A great lady: a romance. Tr. M. S. Phil: Lippincott 1874. 125p. il. 23cm. [LC]
1220. do. 1879. Tr. Mrs. M. B. Harrison. L: Tinsley. 313p. 8. [BM]
*1221. (Der gordische Knoten.) The marriage tie. Tr. K. E. Stantial. L: Rivingtons 1879. 2v. 228; 256p. 18cm. [BM]

DE WETTE, W: Mn. Lbt. 1780-1849. See Wette.

DIEDE, Cte. (Hildebrand), Frau, 1769-1846. Letters of W: v. Humboldt to a female friend (i.e., Cte. Diede, by whom the letters were edited). See Humboldt, #4688 seq.

DIEFENBACH, ---. Sel. in C89.

DIEHL, L: 1880- .
§1222. (Ahasuerus.) The sardonic smile. ("The romantic life of H: Heine.") Auth. tr. Louise C. Willcox. Bost; NY: Houghton Mifflin 1926. 299p. il. 19cm. [Needless liberties. Prose full of minor inaccuracies; verse inadequate.] [LC]

DIEL, J:s Bpa., 1843-76.
1223. The stone cutter of Cologne: an histor. narr. of the 14th cent. Tr. Rose Dulzo. Il. by Fr. Bergen. Soc. of divine word 1915. 120p. 12. [AC]

DIELITZ, Td. 1810-69.
1224. The hunters of the world; or, wild sports and advent. in encounters with wild animals in every part of the world. Tr. by a lady. Il. on stone. Phil: Hazard 1856. 159p. 18cm. [BM]

DIEMER, Hne. (v. Hillern), 1859-
*1225. (Oberammergau und seine Passionsspiele.) O-- and its passion play: a retrospect...description of the country, etc. Text tr. Wl. S. Manning. Il. from drawings and photos. Munich; Oberammergau: Seyfried 1900. 264p. 30cm. [BM]

DIEPOLD VON VOHBURG, fl. 1212-25. See Markgraf v. Hohenburg.

DIETERICH, J. S. d. 1797. Sel. in C244;272.

DIETERICH, (J. F. A.)K: 1869- .
*1226. Hellenism in Asia Minor. Tr. C. N. Brown; with introd. pref. by Td. P. Ion and article...by D. H. Oeconomides. Am.-Hellenic soc. 1918. 70p. 24cm. [LC]

DIETMAR VON AIST, fl. 1143-70. Sel. in C27;309;421;427;530-2.

DIETRICH, Dr.
1227. The German emigrants; or, F: Wolgemuth's voyage to California. Tr. "Leopold Wray." Guben: F. Fechner 185-? 39p. 8 il. 17cm. [LC]

DIETRICH, Ab. Hm. 1829- . and J. V. WIDMANN.
*1228. (Erinnerungen an J:s Brahms.) Recoll. of J:s B--. Tr. Dora E. Hecht. L: Seeley 1899. 211p. 21cm. [BM.LC]
[Some errors, and some liberties taken.]

DIETZ, J: 1665-1738.
1229. Master J: D--, surgeon in the army of the great elector and barber to the royal court; from the old MS (autobiog.) in the royal lib. of Berlin. Tr. B. Miall; first pub. by Ernst Consentius. NY: Dutton; L: Allen & U. 1923. 315p. il. 23cm. [LC.BM]

DIETZGEN, Js. 1828-88.
1230. (Das Acquisit der Philosophie.) The positive outcome of philosophy. Tr. E. Untermann. Chic: Kerr 1909. 444p. 20cm. [LC]
1231. Some of the philosophical essays on socialism, etc. Tr. M. Beer and Th. Rothstein. Chic: Kerr 1906. 362p. 20cm. [LC]

DIEZEL, Gst.
*1232. (Russland, Deutschland und die östliche Frage.) Russia, Germany, and the eastern question. Tr. Frederica M. Rowan. L: Ridgway 1854. 131pp 21cm. [BM.LC]

DINCKLAGE-CAMPE, Ame Ehe. So. W:e v. 1825-91.
1233. (Das Comtessel.) The little countess. Tr. Sa. E. Boggs. Il. by W. B. Davis. NY: Bonner 1891. 319p. 19cm. [LC]

DINGELSTEDT, Fz. Frhr. v. 1814-81. Sel. in C17;50;69;309;366;372-3; 395;448;469.
**1234. (Die Amazone.) The Amazon. Tr. Jas. M. Hart. NY: Putnam 1868. 315p. 18cm. [LC.BM]
*1235. do. 1869. [same] Ed: Edmonston & Douglas. 322p. 19cm. [BM]
[Edits the phraseology of the foregoing, without marked improvement, to my thinking.]
1236. do. 1872. [same?] New ed. NY: Putnam. [AC]
§1237. (Meister Gutenbergs Tod.) J: Gutenberg, first master printer, his acts and most remarkable discourses, and his death. Tr. C(aroline) O. W(intour). L: Philobiblon soc. 1858. 141p. 21cm. [BM]
[Poor tr., careless or incompetent.]
§1238. do. 1860. [same] L: Trübner. 141p. 21cm. [BM.LC]
[Title page has: C. W. Only 100 copies printed.]

DINGER, Hg. 1865- .
1240. (Die Meistersinger von Nürnberg.) (R: Wagner's) The mastersingers of N--. Tr. J: Bernhoff. Lpz: Wild; NY: Breitkopf & H. 1892. 96p. 20cm. [LC]

DINTER, Gst. F: Sel. in C461.

DITTERSDORF, C: Ditters v. 1739-99.
?1241. (Doktor und Apotheker.) The doctor and the apothecary. Music ad. from D-- and comp. by S. Storace. (Text from the French.) L: Birchard & Andrews 1788. 34p. obl. 8. [LCM]
[No apparent relation to the original.]
1242. do. n.d. [same] Another ed. L: Longmans. 34p. obl. 8. [LCM]
*1243. (Lebensbeschreibung, seinem Sohne in die Feder diktirt.) Autobiography, dictated to his son. Tr. A. D. Coleridge. L: Bentley 1896. xx;316p. 20cm. [LC.BM]

DOBER, Anne Schindler. Sel. in C269.

DOCK, Cph. d. 1771.
1244. The life and works of C. D--, America's pioneer writer on education, with a tr. of his works...by M. G. Brumbaugh, 1862. Phil: Lippincott 1908. 372p. 25cm. [LC]

DODEL, afterwards Dodel-Port, Arn.
1245. (Moses oder Darwin? Eine Schulfrage.) Moses or Darwin: a school problem for all friends of truth and progress. Tr. from 3d Ger. ed. w. pref. by F: W. Dodel. NY: Truth seeker co. 1891. 326p. 19cm. [BM]

DOELLINGER, J: Js. Ig. v. 1799-1890.
*1246. (Akademische Vorträge.) Studies in European hist. Tr. Marg. Warre. L: Murray 1890. 6+426p. 22cm. [BM.LC]
*1247. do. 1894. Addresses on hist. and lit. subjects. Tr. Marg. Warre. L: Murray. 10;300p. 22cm. [BM.LC]
[Continuation of the foregoing.]
1248. Conversations of Dr. D--. Tr. Kath. Gould. L: Bentley. 1892. 264p. 19cm. [LC]
*1249. (Die Universitäten sonst und jetzt.) Universities past and present: a lecture (from the "Akademische Vorträge")...1866. Tr. C. E. C. B. Appleton. Oxford: Rivingtons 1867. 49p. 21cm. [BM]
1250. Luther: a succinct view of his life and writings (from an encyclopedia article). Pref. signed C. A. S. L: Richardson 1853. 102p. 12cm. [BM]

DOERING, J: Ml. H: 1789-1862.
1251. Life and character of Beethoven. Tr. anon. 1841. In Schindler, An. Life of B--. #8250.
1252. The rescue. Tr. Corbett. 1828. In C528., vol. 1, pp.221-352.
1253. Aloyse. From the German of D-- and the Danish of Elmquist. Tr. Corbett. 1828. In C528, vol. 2, pp. 81-137.

DOERLE, A.
1254. Little Joseph; or, the young Savoyard. Tr. A. M. S. Dublin: Jas. Duffy 1850. 73p. 13cm. [BM]

DOERMANN, Fx. and A. ALTMANN.
?1255. (Bub oder Mädel.) The rose maid: operetta in 2 acts by B. Granichstaedten. Tr. Harry B. and Rb. B. Smith. Vocal score. NY: Stern 1912. 130p. 4. [LCM]
[Very marked revision of music to suit altered words.]

DOERMANN, Fx. and Lp. JACOBSON.
*1256. (Ein Waltzertraum.) Waltz dream: operetta in 3 acts by O. Straus. Tr. Grace I. Colbron. Vocal score. NY: Continental 1908. 131p. 4. [LCM]

DOERMANN, Fx. and Lp. JACOBSON.
1257. do. 1908. Adapted. Lyrics by A. Ross. Vocal score. L: Metzler; Chappell. 179p. 28cm. [BMM]
§1258. do. 1908. Tr. Js. Herbert. Vocal score. NY: Stern. 152p. 4. [Very free and easy.] [LCM]

DOLMETSCH, H.
1259. (Der Ornamentenschatz.) The historic styles of ornament... Hist. and desc. text from the German. Tr. anon. L: Batsford 1898. 90pl. (partly with text, very much reduced from the original). 33cm. [BM]
1260. do. 1912. [same] 2d rev. ed. 100 pl. mostly in color. 34cm. [BM.LC]

"DOLOROSA," 1879- . Sel. in C28.

DOMANIG, K: 1851-1913.
1261. The postilion of Schoenberg. Tr. anon. 1902. In C481.

DOVSKY, Bce.
§1262. (Mona Lisa.) M-- L--: opera in 2 acts by Max Schillings. Tr. F: H. Martens. Libr. Ger;Engl. NY: Rullman 1923. 57p. 25cm. [LCM] [Good; prosy, not absolutely correct.]

DRAEXLER(-MANFRED), K: Fd. 1806-1879. Sel. in C152;375;571.

DRESE, Am. 1620-1701. Sel. in C269.

DRESSLER, F: A:
§1263. (Moltke in seiner Häuslichkeit.) Moltke in his home. Tr. Mrs. C: E: Barrett-Lennard. L: Murray 1907. 163p. 22cm. [BM.LC] [Style is altered, and there are errors.]

DREWES, J: F: L: 1762- . Sel. in C275.

DREWES, Lbt. 1816-70. Sel. in C276.

DREWS, Art.
*1264. (Die Christusmythe. 1. Teil.) The Christ myth. Tr. from 3d rev. ed. C. D. Burns. L: Unwin 1910. 304p. 21cm. [BM]

DREXEL, Jr. 1581-1638.
1265. Considerations on eternity. Tr. Sister Marie J. Byrne (from the Latin). Ed. by Rev. Fd. E: Bogner. NY: Pustet 1920. xi;208p. 19cm. [LC]

DREYER, Max, 1862- .
*1266. (Der Probekandidat.) On probation. Tr. Ma. Harned. In "Poet-Lore" 14(1902).

DRIESCH, Hs. 1867- .
1267. The history and theory of vitalism. Tr. C. K. Ogden. Rev. and in part rewritten for the Engl. ed. L: Macmillan 1914. viii;239p. il. 19cm. [BM.LC]
**1268. (Leib und Seele.) Mind and body: a criticism of psycho-physical parallelism. Auth. tr. from 3d ed. by Td. Besterman (w. rev. and some add. passages by the author). L: Methuen 1927. 183p. 19cm. [BM]
1268a. The science and philosophy of the organism. L: Black 1908. 2v. 344;398p. [EC]

DROBEGG, W:
*1269. (Der Pietist.) The ring of fate: tragic opera in one act by Hg. Kaun. Tr. W: O: Sonbronn. Vocal score. Ger;Engl. Lpz. Breitkopf 1895. 175p. 4. [LCM]

DROSTE-HUELSHOFF, Ante. V. 1797-1848. Sel. in C17;90;311;380;423; 448.

DROSTE-HUELSHOFF, Ante. V.
*1270. (Die Judenbuche.) The Jew's beech-tree. Tr. Lillie Winter. 1913-15. In C154(7).

DROYSEN, J: Gst. 1808-84. Sel. in C538.

DUECKERSHOFF, Ern.
1271. How the English workingman lives. Tr. C. H. d'E. Leppington, w. pref. by Dr. Boehmert. L: King 1899. viii;97p. 18cm. [BM]
[Tr. from a series of newspaper articles.]

DUENTZER, J: H: Js. 1813-1910.
*1272. (Goethes Leben.) Life of G--. W. authentic il. and facsimiles. Tr. T: W: Lyster. L: Macmillan 1883. 2v. xxii;462;525p. il. 19cm. [To some extent a reworking of D--.] [BM.LC]
*1273. do. 1908. [same] Popular ed. L: Unwin. 810p. 8. [EC]
*1274. (Schillers Leben.) Life of S--. Tr. P. E. Pinkerton. W. il. and facsimiles. L; Ed: Macmillan 1883. x;455p. 19cm. [BM.LC]
*1275. do. 1902. [same] De luxe ed. Bost: Nicolls. 492p. 23cm. [Included also in Schiller's "Works," 1902: See #7780.] [LC]

DUERER, Abr. 1471-1528.
**1276. Briefe, Tagebuch. Tr. by Mrs. C: Heaton in her "Hist. of the life of A-- D--." L: Macmillan 1870. xv;340p. 25cm. [BM]
[Contains his "Tagebuch der Reise in die Niederlande," many of his letters, and his verses. Very carefully and competently translated.]
**1277. do. 1881. [same] 2d. enl. ed. L: Seeley. xiv;373p. [BM]
*1278. do. 1889. Literary remains of A-- D--. Ed. (and tr.) W: M: Conway. W. transcriptions from Brit. Mus. MSS and notes...by Lina Eckenstein. Cambridge: Univ. press. x;288p. il. 26cm. [BM]
--NY: Oxford press 1889. x;288p. il. 28cm. [LC]
["Tagebuch" tr. from 1884 ed. Letters and other documents paraphrased by Thausing. Verse tr. taken from Mrs. Heaton. His trs. seem to me not quite as exact as hers.]
§1279. (Tagebuch, etc.) Records of journeys to Venice and the Low Countries. Tr. Rud. Tombo, Jr. Bost: Merrymount 1913. 117p. 25cm. [Too free.] [LC.BM]
See Grimm, Hm., A-- D--, #3125; Literature, #3132.
See Knackfuss, Hm., D-- (life and work), #5084.
See Nüchter, F:, A-- D--, his life, etc. #6972.
See Schefer, Lp., The artist's married life, #7695.
See Scherer, Vl., The work of D--, #7731.
See Thausing, M., A-- D--, his life and works. #9349.

DUERNER (or Düring), der, late 13th cent. Sel. in C27;310;532.

DUNCKER, Mx. Wfg. 1811-86.
*1280. (Geschichte des Altertums.) The hist. of antiquity. Tr. Evelyn Abbott. L: Bentley 1877-82. 6v. 22cm. [BM.LC]
**1281. do. 1883-86. The hist. of Greece, to the end of the Persian war. Tr. Sa. F. Alleyne and Evelyn Abbott. L: Bentley. 2v. 22cm. [BM.LC]--NY: Scribner & W. [AC]
[All but 100p. of vol. 2 by Miss Alleyne.]

DUNKER, Blr. An. 1750?-1807. Sel. in C391.

DU PREL, K: L: A: F: Mx. Af. Frhr. v. 1839-99.
*1282. (Die Philosophie der Mystik.) The philos. of mysticism. Tr. C. C. Massey. L: Redway 1889. 2v. 332, 316p. 23cm. [BM.LC]
[Fair to very good; on the whole, good.]

EBELING, Ad. 1827-97.
*1283. (Lebende Bilder aus dem modernen Paris.) Sketches of mod. Paris. Tr. Fes. Locock. L: Bentley 1870. x;323p. 19cm. [BM.LC]
[Very good tr.]

EBER, Pl. 1511-69. Sel. in C234-5;276;287;570.

EBERHARD, Cn. A: Glb. 1769-1845. Sel. in C106.
1284. (Hannchen und die Küchlein.) Hannah and her chickens. Tr. Jas. Cochrane. Ed: Johnstone & Hunter 1854. 145p. 19cm. [LC]

EBERHARDT, P. Sel. from the popular traditions coll. and narr. by him. Tr. T: Roscoe. 1826. In C477.

EBERS[1], G: Mz. 1837-98. Sel. in C163;366;469;574.
§1285. [Coll.] The elixir, and other tales. Tr. Mrs. E: H. Bell. L: K. Paul; NY: Gottsberger 1890. 261p. 17cm. [BM.LC] [The elixir ("Das Elixir"); The greylock, a fairy tale ("Die graue Locke"); The nuts, a Christmas story ("Die Nüsse, ein Weihnachtsmärchen.") Inadequate command of German.]
*1286. (Aegypten in Wort und Bild.) Egypt; descriptive, historical, and picturesque. Tr. Ca. Bell. W. introd. and notes by S. Birch. L; NY: Cassell 1881-2. 2v. xxiv;314; xxii;388p. 37cm. [BM.LC]
*1287. do. 1887. [same] Cassell. 2v. il. 33cm. [BM.LC]
*1288. do. 1898. [same] New ed. Introd. and notes by S. Birch. Cassell. 2v. 33cm. [BM]
*1289. (Arachne: historischer Roman.) A--. Tr. Ma. J. Safford. L: Low; NY: Appleton 1898. 2v. 288; 310p. 17cm. [LC.BM] [Some errors.]
*1290. (Barbara Blomberg.) B-- B--. Tr. Ma. J. Safford. NY: Appleton 1897. 2v. 402; 333p. 16cm. [LC.BM]
1291. (Der Kaiser.) The emperor. Tr. Ca. Bell. Rev. and cor. NY: Gottsberger 1881. 2v. 16cm.
1292. do. 1881. [same?] NY: Munro. Seaside lib. 32cm. [AC]
1293. do. 1888. Tr. C. H. Storrs. NY: Munro. 12. [AC]
1294. do. 1915. Bell's tr. NY; L: Appleton. 2v. in 1. 20cm. [LC]
§1295. (Die Frau Bürgermeisterin.) The burgomaster's wife: a tale of the siege of Leyden. Tr. Ca. Bell. L: Macmillan 1882. 365p. 8. [BM]
1296. do. 1882. [same?] NY: Munro. Seaside lib. 32cm. [AC]
§1297. do. 1882. Tr. Ma. J. Safford. NY: Gottsberger. 351p. 16cm. [Fair tr., marred by inaccuracy.] [LC]
1298. do. 1888. NY: Munro. 12. [AC]
1299. do. 1896. Tr. Annie W. Ayer and Helen T. Slate. NY: Burt. 347p. 19cm. [LC]
§1300. do. 1915. Safford's tr. NY; L: Appleton. 351p. 20cm. [LC] [With "A word only a word."]
*1301. (Die Geschichte meines Lebens.) The story of my life from childhood to manhood. Tr. Ma. J. Safford. NY: Appleton; L: Hirschfeld 1893. 382p. 19cm. [LC.BM]
*1302. (Die Gred. Roman aus dem alten Nürnberg.) Margery: a tale of old Nuremberg. Tr. Ca. Bell. Auth. ed., rev. NY: Gottsberger 1889. 2v. vi;279;300p. 16cm. [BM]
§1303. do. 1889. Gred of Nuremberg: a romance of the 15th cent. Tr. E. V. Conder. NY: Munro. 299p. 19cm. [LC] [Tr. loses quaintness of archaic style.]
1304. (Die Nilbraut.) The bride of the Nile. Tr. Ca. Bell. Auth. ed. rev. NY: Gottsberger 1887. 2v. 16cm. [LC.BM]
1305. do. 1887. Tr. anon. NY: Harper. 4. [AC]
1306. do. 1888. Tr. anon. NY: Munro. 2 pts. 12. [AC]
1307. do. 1905. 1910. Sel: On the barge. Tr. anon. In C163.

[1] D. Appleton got out Historical Romances of G: E-- in a popular uniform ed. 1915. 20cm. LC has: The burgomaster's wife; An Egyptian princess; The emperor; Homo sum and Serapis; The sisters and Joshua; Uarda; A word, only a word.

EBERS, G:.- Die Nilbraut
1308. do. 1915. Tr. anon. NY; L: Appleton. 2v. in 1. 20cm. [LC]
1309. do. n.d. Bell's tr. NY: Burt. (B12.)
*1310. (Die Schwestern.) The sisters. Tr. Ca. Bell. Lpz: Tauchnitz; L: Low 1880. 2v. 311; 295p. 15cm. [Several errors noted.] [BM]
*1311. do. 1880. [same] NY: Gottsberger. 16. [AC]
*1312. do. 1880. [same] NY: Munro. Seaside lib. 47p. 32cm. [LC]
*1313. do. 1888. [same] NY: Munro. 236p. 19cm. [LC]
*1314. do. 1895. [same] NY: Appleton. (B12.)
*1315. do. 1915. [same] NY; L: Appleton. 352p. 20cm. [LC] [Includes "Joshua".]
1316. (Die Unersetzlichen.) The king and queen of Mollebusch; or, the indispensables. Tr. Ma. J. Safford. Bost: Brown 1899. 124p. il. 19cm. [LC]
*1317. (Ein Wort.) A word, only a word. Tr. Ma. J. Safford. NY: Gottsberger 1883. 348p. 16cm. [LC.BM]
*1318. do. 1883. Only a word. Tr. Ca. Bell. L: Macmillan. 350p. 19cm. [Safford's tr. is better.] [BM]
1319. do. 1883. [same] NY: Munro. Seaside lib. 46p. 32cm. [LC]
1320. do. 1888. [same] NY: Munro. 238p. 19cm. [LC]
*1321. do. 1915. Tr. Safford? NY; L: Appleton 1915. [LC] [With "The burgomaster's wife."]
*1322. do. n.d. Safford's tr. NY: Burt. 348p. (B12.)
†1323. (Eine aegyptische Königstochter.) An Egyptian princess. Tr. Eleanor Grove. Lpz: Tauchnitz; L: Low 1870-71. 2v. xx;330;375p. 16cm. [LC.BM] [Tr. turns sentences upside down, and is not accurate.]
1324. do. 1871. The daughter of an Egyptian king. Tr. H: Reed. Phil: Lippincott. 368p. 19cm. [LC]
1325. do. 1877-84. Grove's tr.? NY: Munro. Seaside lib. 32cm. [AC]
§1326. do. 1880. Grove's tr. rev. and cor. NY: Gottsberger. 2v. 16cm. [LC]
*1327. do. 1887. Tr. Emma S. Buchheim. L: Bell. xiv;466p. 8. [BM]
1328. do. 1888. Grove's tr.? NY: Munro. 2v. 12. [AC]
*1329. do. 1895. Buchheim's tr. L: Bell 1895. 466p. 18cm. [LC]
§1330. do. 1901. Grove's tr. NY: Appleton. 2v. [LC]
*1331. do. 1907. Buchheim's tr. L: Bell. xiv;466p. [BM]
1332. do. 1910. Sel. Tr. anon. In C574.
*1333. do. 1913. Buchheim's tr. L: Bell. [EC]
§1334. do. 1915. Grove's tr. NY; L: Appleton. 2v. in 1. [LC]
1335. (Eine Frage.) A question: the idyl of a picture by his friend Alma Tadema. Tr. Ma. J. Safford. NY: Gottsberger 1881. 125p. 16cm. [LC.BM]
1335a. do. 1881. [same?] A question. Tr. anon. "Appleton's Journal" 25(1881): 385.
1336. do. 1893. [same] NY: Appleton. (B12.)
1337. (Elifên, ein Wüstentraum.) In the desert. Tr. Ma. J. Safford. NY: Dodd, Mead 1900. 329p. 19cm. [LC]
*1338. (Homo sum.) Homo sum: a romance of the anchorites of Mt. Sinai. Tr. Ca. Bell. Lpz: Tauchnitz 1878. 2v. 270; 248p. 16cm. L: Low. 19cm. [BM]
*1339. do. 1880. [same] NY: Gottsberger. 299p. 16cm. [LC]
1340. do. 1877-84. [same?] NY: Munro. Seaside lib. 32cm. [AC]
1341. do. 1888. [same?] NY: Munro. 12. [AC]
*1342. do. 1900. [same] 299p. [LC]
1343. do. 190-? [same?] NY: Burt. n.d. [UW]
*1344. do. 1915. [same] NY; L: Appleton. 2v. in 1. 20cm. [LC] [Including "Serapis."]
1345. (Im blauen Hecht.) In the blue pike: a romance of German civilization at the commencement of the 16th cent. Tr. from 5th

EBERS, G:
Ger. ed. by Ma. J. Safford. NY: Appleton 1896. 230p. 16cm. [LC]
--L: Low 1896. 230p. 17cm. [BM]
1346. (Im Schmiedefeuer.) In the fire of the forge: a romance of old Nuremberg. Tr. Ma. J. Safford. NY: Appleton 1895. 2v. 16cm. [LC]
1347. do. 1896. [same] L: Low. 2v. 320;346p. 17cm. [BM]
*1348. (Josua.) Joshua: a biblical picture...only authorized ed. Tr. Ca. and Marg. Bell. NY: Lovell 1889. 269p. 8. [BM]
*1349. do. 1890. [same] Joshua: a story of biblical life. Lpz: Tauchnitz; L: Low. 2v. 270; 263p. [BM.LC]
1350. do. 1890. [same?] NY: Munro. 12. [AC]
1351. do. 1890. A story of biblical times. Tr. Ma. J. Safford. NY: Gottsberger. 371p. 16cm. [LC]
1352. do. 190-? [same?] NY: Burt. n.d. (B12)
1353. do. 1915. [same] NY: Appleton. 371p. 20cm. [LC]
*1354. (Kleopatra.) Cleopatra. Tr. Ma. J. Safford. NY; L: Appleton 1894. 2v. 302; 296p. 17cm. [LC.BM]
1355. Lorenz Alma Tadema: his life and works. Tr. Ma. J. Safford. NY: Gottsberger 1886. il. 16cm. [LC.BM]
*1356. (Per aspera.) Per aspera. (A thorny path.) Tr. Ca. Bell. Lpz: Tauchnitz 1892. 256(i.e., 356); 348p. 16cm. --L: Low 1892. 19cm. [Some slight errors.] [LC.BM]
*1357. do. 1893. [same] A thorny path. NY: Appleton. 2v. 16cm. [LC]
1358. (R: Lepsius. Ein Lebensbild.) R: L--: a biography. Tr. Mrs. Zoe D. Underhill. NY: Gottsberger 1887. 347p. 19cm. [LC]
§1359. (Serapis.) Serapis. Tr. Ca. Bell. Rev. and cor. NY: Gottsberger 1885. 387p. 16cm. [LC]--BM has only pp. 1-176.
*1360. do. 1885. Tr. Ma. S. Smith. NY: Munro. Seaside lib. 57p. 32cm. [Better tr. than foregoing: closer and more accurate.] [LC]
*1361. do. 1885. [same] NY: Munro. 210p. 18cm. [LC]
§1362. do. 1915. Bell's tr. NY: Appleton. 20cm. [LC]
[Bound with "Homo sum."]
*1363. (Uarda.) Uarda: a romance of ancient Egypt. Tr. Ca. Bell. Lpz: Tauchnitz; L: Low 1877. 2v. 333; 320p. 15cm. [BM]
*1364. do. 1880. [same] NY: Gottsberger. 2v. 16cm. [LC]
1365. do. 1880. [same?] NY: Munro. Seaside lib. 32cm. 4. [AC]
1366. do. 1881. [same?] NY: Amer. book exch. 16. [AC]
1367. do. 1882. [same?] S. W. Green. sq.16. [AC]
1368. do. 1887. [same?] NY: Munro. 12. [AC]
*1369. do. 1901. [same] NY: Appleton. [LC]
*1370. do. 1915. [same] NY; L: Appleton. 2v. in 1. 20cm. [LC]

EBERSWEILER, F:
1371. (Die heiligen drei Könige.) The three holy kings: an histor. drama in five acts (and in verse). Tr. by a member of the S. J. St.L: Herder 1904. 103p. 20cm. [Some music given.] [LC]

EBERT, K: Egon, 1801-82. Sel. in C178;391;393;497;531;543; #8001.

EBERTY, Fr.
*1372. (Die Gestirne und die Weltgeschichte.) The stars and the earth; or, thoughts upon space, time, and eternity. Tr. anon. L: Bailliere 1846. 48p. 14cm. [BM]
*1373. do. 1847. Part II. L: Bailliere. 59p. 14cm. [BM]
*1374. do. 1874. 4th Amer. from 3d Engl. ed. Bost: Noyes, Holmes. 88p. 15cm. [BM]
*1375. do. 1880. Rev. and enl. with notes. 13th thous. L: Bailliere, Tundall & Cox. 60p. 16cm. [BM]
*1376. do. 1882? 5th Amer. ed. Bost: Lee & Shepard. 88p. 15cm. [BM]
*1377. do. 1895. 16th thous. L: Bailliere, etc. 60p. 16cm. [BM]
[Tr. is the same throughout.]

EBNER-ESCHENBACH, Me. v. Freifrau, 1830-1916.
**1378. (Aphorismen.) Aphorisms. Tr. Mrs. A. L. Wister. Phil: Lippincott 1883. 159p. 16 x 12cm. [LC.BM]
[Tr. of the first three Hunderte, two to a page. BM copy unpaged.]
*1379. (Comtesse Muschi, Comtesse Paula.) The two countesses. (Two tales.) Tr. Mrs. Ellen Waugh. NY: Cassell 1893. 176p. 18x9cm. [LC]
*1380. do. 1893. [same] L: Unwin. 190p. 17 x 9 cm. [BM]
§1381. (Das Gemeindekind.) The child of the parish. Tr. Ma. A. Robinson. NY: Bonner 1893. [Tr. is only fair.] [LCO]
*1382. (Der Kreisphysikus.) The district doctor. Tr. Julia Franklin. 1913-15. In C154(13).
*1383. (Krambambuli.) Krambambuli. Tr. A. Coleman. 1913-15. In C154(13).
1384. A man of the world. Tr. R. T. House in "Poet-Lore," vol. 22. --Also pub. sep. by Badger, 1912.
1385. (Unsühnbar.) Beyond atonement. Tr. Ma. A. Robinson. NY: Worthington 1892. il. 12. [BPL]
1386. do. n.d. [same?] NY: Bonner. NY: Hurst. (B12)

EBO, d. 1163.
1387. (Ottonis vita.) The life of Otto, apostle of Pomerania, 1060-1139, by Ebo and Herbordus. Tr. C: H. Robinson. L: S.P.C.K.;NY: Macmillan 1920. 193p. 18cm. [BM.LC]
[Introd. to p. 15 summarizes present knowledge. Book I of Ebo is summarized, books II and III tr. with additions from Herbord.]

EBRARD, J: H: A: 1818-88. ("Cn. Deutsch," "Gf. Flammberg"). Sel. ("Deutsch") in C151.
1388. Bilihild: a tale of the Irish missionaries in Germany, A. D: 703. Tr. Julie Sutter. L: Rel. tract soc. 1883. 153p. 8. [BM]
1389. The siege of a Huguenot town. Tr. C. G. Zipf. 1890. In C491.

ECKARDSTEIN, Hm. Freiherr v. 1864- .
§1390. (Lebenserinnerungen, etc.) Ten years at the court of St. James, 1895-1905. Tr. and ed. G: Young. L: Butterworth; NY: Dutton 1922. 255p. il. 22cm. [BM.LC]
[Tr. good with consid. liberties. 760p. reduced to 252.]

ECKARDT, Jl. v. 1836-1908.
1391. Modern Russia: comprising Russia under Ax. II, Russian communism, The Greek orthodox church, and The Baltic provinces. Tr. anon. L: Smith, Elder 1870. 388p. 22cm. [BM.LC]
§1392. (Russland vor und nach dem Kriege.) R-- before and after the war. Tr. E: F. Taylor, w. later additions by the author. L: Longmans 1880. xiv;436p. 22cm. [BM.LC]
[Not wholly faithful to original.]

ECKARTSHAUSEN, K: v. 1752-1803.
1393. The cloud upon the sanctuary. Tr. and notes by Isabelle de Steiger. Pref. by J. W. Brodie-Innes. L: Redway 1896. x;131p. 19cm. [BM]
1394. do. 1909. [same] Introd. by Art. E: Waite. 3d issue, rev. and enl. L: Rider. xxxix;143p. 18cm. [BM]

ECKELMANN, --- . Sel. in C450.

ECKER, Ax.
*1395. (Lorenz Oken.) Lorenz Oken: a biog. sketch. Tr. Af. Tulk. L: K. Paul 1883. xxiv;183p. 19cm. [BM]

ECKERMANN, J: P: 1792-1854. See Goethe, Conversations with E--, #3039 seq.

ECKHART, Brother, 1260?-1327.
1396. After supper in the refectory: a series of instructions...to ...the friends of God, about...1300. Tr. N. Leeson. Pref. by Jesse Brett. L: Mowbray 1917. vii;122p. [16 moral preachments] [BM]
**1397. Meister Eckhart (i.e., works, ed.) by Fz. Pfeiffer. Tr. w. some omissions and additions by C. de B. Evans. L: Watkins 1924. xx;483p. 21cm. [Section sampled is excellent.] [BM]
§1398. Meister E--'s sermons. First tr...Claud Field. L: Allenson 1909. 60p. 16cm. [7 sermons; not very well done.] [BM]

ECKSTEIN, Ern. 1845-1900. Sel. in C422;501.
1399. Against the stream. Tr. anon. 1885. 1890. In #4578 and C404. [This is perhaps Heyse's "Gegen den Strom."]
1400. do. 1886. [same?] Chic: Schick. 29p. 12. [LCO]
1401. (Aphrodite.) A--: a romance of ancient Hellas. Tr. Ma. J. Safford. NY: Gottsberger 1886. 289p. 16cm. [LC]
1402. The boarding-school girls. Tr. anon. 1890. In C404.
1403. (Das Vermächtnis.) The will. Tr. Ca. Bell. Rev. and cor. NY: Gottsberger 1885. 2v. 352;358p. 16cm. [LC.BM]
1404. do. 1891. A sealed inheritance: a melodrama in 5 acts (ad. and very materially altered from "Das Vermächtnis"). By A. S. Bost: 31 leaves. Tw. [LCO]
*1405. (Der Besuch im Karzer.) The visit to the cells: a humorous tale. Tr. Sophie F. J. Veitch. L: Provost; Lpz: Hartknoch 1876. 52p. il. 17cm. [BM]
*1406. do. 1895. The visit to the lockup. Tr. anon. 1890. In C404.
1407. do. 1909. The incarceration of the Herr Professor. Tr. Müller-Casenov. In C422.
*1408. (Der chaldäische Zauberer.) The Chaldaean magician: an adventure in Rome, in the reign of the emperor Diocletian. Tr. Ma. J. Safford. NY: Gottsberger 1886. 112p. 16. [LC]
1409. (Der Mönch vom Aventin.) A monk of the Aventine. Tr. Helen H. Johnson. Bost: Roberts 1894. 196p. 19cm. [LC]
1410. The eternal laws of morality. Tr. and ad. from the German of E. E--. In #7708, pp. 25-39.
1411. (Hertha.) Hertha. Tr. Mrs. E: H. Bell. NY: Peck 1892. 360p. 16cm. [LC.BM]
1412. (Kyparissos.) Cyparissus: a romance of the isles of Greece. Tr. Ma. J. Safford. NY: Peck 1897. 348p. 16cm. [LC]
1413. (Nero.) Nero. Tr. Ca. Bell and Ma. J. Safford. NY: Gottsberger; L: Trübner 1889. 2v. 244;284p. 17cm. [LC.BM]
*1414. (Prusias.) Prusias. Tr. Ca. Bell. Rev. and cor. NY: Gottsberger; L: Trübner 1884. 2v. 16cm. [LC]
1415. do. 1905. Tr. anon. NY: Peck. 2v. (B12)
§1416. (Quintus Claudius.) Q-- C--: a romance of imperial Rome. Tr. Ca. Bell. Rev. and cor. NY: Gottsberger; L: Trübner 1882. 2v. 16cm. [LC]
1417. do. 1905. Tr. anon. NY: Peck. 2v. (B12)

EDELING, Cn. L: d. 1742. Sel. in C231; 489.

EDERSHEIM, Af. 1825-89. Sel. in C469.

EDLER, K: Erdmann, 1844- .
§1418. Baldine and other tales. Tr. E: Lord Lytton. L: Bentley 1886. 2v. xliv;289;291p. 19cm. [BM]
[Vol. 1: Baldine ("Baldine"). Vol. 2: "Notre dame des flots" (same); A journey to the Grossglockner mountain ("Eine Glocknerfahrt"). Tr. is too free.]
§1419. do. 1887. [same] NY: Harper. 302p. 17cm. [LC]

EDWARD, G: Sel. in C39.

EELKING, Max v. 1813-73.
§1420. (Die deutschen Hülfstruppen...) The Ger. allied troops in the North Amer. war of independence. Tr. and abr. J. G. Rosengarten. Albany, NY: Munsell 1893. 360p. 23cm. [LC.BM]
[Neither close nor accurate.]
**1421. (Leben und Wirken des...F: Ad. Riedesel.) Memoirs, and letters and journals of Maj. Gen. R--, during his residence in America. Tr. W: L. Stone. Albany, NY: Munsell 1868. 2v. 22cm. [LC.BM]
[On the whole, excellent. Carefully done, though much abridged.]

EGINHARDUS, abbot of Seligenstadt, 770-840. Sel. in C469.
1422. (Briefe.) Letters of Einhard. Tr. H. Preble. Annotated by Jos. C. Ayer, Jr. NY: Amer. soc. of church hist. Papers, vol. 1. 1913. 22cm. [pp. 109-58.] [BM]
1423. do. 1913. [same] Reprint. [BM]
1424. Life of the emperor K: the great. Tr. W: Glaister. L: Bell and S. 1877. 100p. 19cm. [BM]
1425. do. 1880. Life of Charlemagne. Tr. S: E. Turner. NY: Harper. 82p. 12cm. [LC]
1426. do. 189-? NY; Cinc: Am. book co. 82p. 13cm. [LC]
1427. do. 1922. Early lives of Charlemagne, by E--and the monk of St. Gall. Tr. and ed. A. J. Grant. NY: Oxford; L: Chatto & Windus. xxv;179p. il. 17cm. [Eginhard's "Life" is pp. 4-57.] [LC.BM]

EHLERT, Louis, 1825-84.
1428. (Aus der Tonwelt.) From the tone world. Tr. Helen D. Tretbar. NY: Tretbar 1885. D. [AC]
*1429. (Briefe über Musik an eine Freundin.) Letters on music, to a lady. Tr. Fanny R. Ritter. Bost: Ditson 1870. 216p. 17cm[LC.BM]
*1430. do. 1877. [same] L: Reeves. 167p. 19cm. [BM]
1431. Rb. Schumann and his school. Tr. Helen D. Tretbar. NY: Tretbar 1885. D. [AC]

EHRENSTEIN, Ab. 1886- . Sel. in C95.

"EHRLICH, A." (i.e., Ab. Payne, 1842-1921).
*1432. (Berühmte Geiger.) Celebrated violinists. Ed. (i.e., tr.) R. H. Legge. L: Strad lib. 1897. 281p. il. 19cm. [BM.LC]
1433. (Berühmte Klavierspieler.) Celebrated pianists of the past and present time. Tr. A. L. Manchester. L: Grevel 1894. 367p. il. 19cm. [BM]
1434. do. 1894. [same] Enl. Amer. ed. Phil: Presser. 423p. 20cm[LC]
1435. do. 1921. [same] L: Reeves. [EC has: 1920.] [BM]

EICHENDORFF, Js. K: Bn. Frhr. v. 1788-1857. Sel. in C17;38;67;73; 92-3;97;106;111-2;129;149;152;171;173;178;180;187;195;309;311; 317;366*;372;375;380;393;399;400;423;448;469;470;501;531;571.
?1436. (Aus dem Leben eines Taugenichts.) The love frolics of a young scamp. Related by himself and ed. by C: Marvel. L: Vickers 1864. 316p. 16cm. [BM]
[Chapters 1-8, 25, 26 retell Eichendorff's story.]
*1437. do. 1866. Memoirs of a good-for-nothing. Tr. C: G. Leland. Il. E. B. Bensell. NY: Leypoldt & Holt. 192p. 17cm. [LC.BM]
**1438. do. 1889. The happy-go-lucky; or, leaves from the life of a good-for-nothing. Tr. Mrs. A. L. Wister. Il. P. G. Johann, E. Kanold, and Eva N. Wolff. Phil; L: Lippincott. 114p. 23cm. [LC]
*1439. do. 1906. [same] 22cm. [LC]
*1440. do. 1913-15. [same] Sel. in C154(5).
1441. do. 1916? [same as #1438?] [Handy literal tr.] Tr. pub. 15cm. [AC]
1442. (Das Marmorbild.) The marble statue. Tr. F. E. Pierce. 1927. In C452.

EICHENDORFF, Js. K: Bn. Frhr. v.
§1443. (Gedichte.) Happy wanderer and other poems. Tr. Marjorie Rossy. Bost: Badger 1925. 38p. 19cm. [LC]
[38 poems. Poor verse, and not wholly correct.]

EICHHOLZ, ---. Sel. in C44.

EICHRODT, L: 1827-92. Sel. in C450.

EIFFER, P. T. Sel. in C169.

EINSTEIN, Ab. 1879- .
1443a. Relativity: the special and the general theory. Auth. tr. by Robt. M. Lawson. NY: Holt 1920. xiii;168p. il. O. [AC]
Methuen 1920. 151p. 8. [EC]
1443b. Sidelights on relativity; 1, Ether and relativity; 2, Geometry and experience. Tr. by G. B. Jeffery and W. Perett. NY: Dutton 1923. 56p. D. [AC]

EISENMANN, Ok.
1444. The brothers van Eyck; Quentin Matsys. Tr. A: H. Keane. 1880. In C102.

EKKEHARD I von St. Gallen, d. 973.
1444a. (Waltharius manu fortis.) Waltharilied. Sel. Tr. Mme. Davésiès de Pontès. 1858. In C88.
1444b. do. Sel. 1906. Tr. anon. In C190.

ELISABETH, Consort of Fis. Js. I, 1837-98. See "Küchler, C: Eli. empress of Austria, etc." #5486.

ELISABETH Ple. Ote. Lu., queen of Rumania, 1843-1916. See "Carmen Sylva."

ELSTER, O: 1852- . See "Bruneck, O: v."

"ELTERLEIN, Ern. v." (i.e., Ern. Gottschald, 1826-).
*1445. (Beethovens Klaviersonaten...erläutert.) B--'s pianoforte sonatas explained for lovers of musical art. Tr. Emily Hill. Pref. E. Pauer. L: Reeves 1875. v;120p. 17cm. [BM]
[Good but with needless liberties.]
*1446. do. 1879. [same] 2d ed. vii;120p. 19cm. [BM]
*1447. do. 1898. [same] Rev. tr., 5th ed. 141p. il. 19cm. [BM.LC]
§1448. (Beethovens Symphonien nach ihrem idealen Gehalt.) B--'s symphonies in their ideal significance. Tr. Fis. Weber. With an account of...B--'s 9th symph. by L: Nohl. L: Reeves 1893. xvi;118p. 19cm. [Much too free.] [LCM]

ELTZBACHER, Pl. 1868- .
*1449. (Der Anarchismus.) Anarchism. Tr. St. T. Byington. NY: Tucker; L: Fifield 1908. xxi;309p. ports. 18cm. [LC]
1450. Germany's food: can it last?...A study by German experts, ed. P. E--. Tr. ed. S. Russell Wells. Crit. introd. A. D. Waller. L: Univ. press 1915. xxxi;232p. 21cm. [BM]

ELZE, K: 1821-89. Sel. in C195.

EMBDEN, L: v., Graf.
1451. (Heinrich Heines Familienleben.) The family life of H: Heine. Tr. C: de Kay. NY: Cassell 1892. xviii;356p. 4 port. 19cm. [LC]
*1452. do. 1893. Tr. C: G. Leland. L: Heinemann. xviii;276p. Il. by 122...letters...to him. 21cm. [BM]

EMILIE Jne. Gräfin v. Schwarzburg-Rudolstadt, d. 1706. Sel. in C244;287.

"EMIN PASCHA" (i.e., E: Schnitzer, 1840-92).
*1453. (Emin Pascha.) E-- Pasha in central Africa: being a coll. of

"EMIN PASCHA"
his letters and journals. Introd. Rb. W: Felkin. Tr. Mrs. Felkin. L: Philip 1888. xviii; 547p. 23cm. [BM.LC]
See Peters, K:, New light on dark Africa. #7089.
See Plehn, M. C., E-- P--. #7205.
See Schweitzer, G:, E-- P--. #8726.

EMMERICH, Anna Kta. 1774-1824.
1454. The dolorous passion of our Lord Jesus Christ. From the meditations of Anne C. E--. With pref. by Abbé de Cazalés. Tr. anon. L: Burns & Lambert 1862. 354p. 16cm. [BM]
[The "meditations" were dictated to Klemens Brentano, who published them with a sketch of her life, pp. 11-59. Tr. of this biog. is extremely free.]
1455. do. 1914. The passion of our Lord...according to the revelations...Preceded by a brief biog. Tr. anon. Clyde, Mo: Benedictine convent. 381p. 20cm. [LC]
See Schmöger, K:, Life of A-- C-- E--. #8457.
See Wegener, T:, Sister A-- K-- E--, etc. #9973.

ENGEL, Ax. 1869-. and Jl. HORST.
1456. The blue mouse: comedy in 3 acts. Ad...Clyde Fitch. (B38)
1457. The gentleman from the secession: a farce in one act. Tr. anon. NY: 1915. Tw. [LC]
1458. (Glück bei Frauen.) The florist's shop. Tr. and ad. Oliver Herford. NY: 1909. Tw. [LC]

ENGEL, E: 1851- .
1459. I and it, and other stories. Tr. C. B. L: Norgate 1893. 75p. 17cm. [The tramp; Sunshine; The fiery ordeal.] [BM]

ENGEL, F:
1460. (Versuch einer Theorie von dem Menschen und dessen Erziehung.) A new theory of human nature with a correspondent system of educ. Tr. anon. L: Linde 1755. xii;280p. 17 x 10cm. [BM]

ENGEL, G: 1866- .
§1461. (Hann Klüth der Philosoph.) The philosopher and the foundling. Tr. Eliz. Lee. L: Hodder & S. 1906. viii;374p. 19cm. [BM]
[Needless deviations.]

ENGEL, J: Jk. 1741-1802. Sel. in C461.
†1462. (Der dankbare Sohn.) The affectionate son: a comedy in one act (and in prose). Tr. T: Holcroft. L: Theatrical recorder 1805. vol. 2. pp. 163-180. 8. [BM]
†1463. Essays and tales, moral, literary, and philosophical. Tr. T: Horne. L; Coxhead 1808. 336p. 17cm. [BM.LC]
[Tr. pads in a flowery style. Fragments of a journey to Mt. Etna; Enraptured trance of Las Casas; The goddesses, an allegory; Epistle of Maecenas to Augustus Caesar; Speech of a physician at a convivial repast; Dissertation upon death, in two dialogues; Dialogue on the probable relapse into superstition; The oak and the acorn; Remarks on the moral excellence of poetry; Jos. Timm; Toby Witt; Eliz. Hill; Vision of Galileo; The hawk; The receptacle for lunatics.--Erroneously ascribed by BM to M. E. Engel.]
1464. The goddesses. Tr. (B:?) Beresford. Berlin: Hayn 1800. 48p. [Cited in C157.]
*1465. (Herr Lorenz Stark.) Lorenz Stark: a characteristic pict. of a German family. Tr. J. Gans. L: Treuttel 1826. 2v. 207;204p. 18cm. [BM]
*1466. do. 1843. Laurence Stark: a family picture. Tr. T. Gaspey. Heidelberg: Ch. Groos. 241p. 19cm. [BM]
*1467. do. 1881. Herr Lorenz S--: a sketch. Tr. F. and R. Storr. In C510, pp. 49-194.

ENGEL, J: Jk.
1468. The page. Tr. anon. 1801. In C302.
1469. Tales: The anti-speculator; Toby Witt; Lady Eliz. Hill. Tr. T: Roscoe. 1826. In C477.

ENGELMANN, Géza, 1887- .
1470. Polit. philos. from Plato to Jeremy Bentham. Tr. K: F: Geiser. Introd. by Oc. Jaszi. NY: Harper 1927. xxiv;398p. il. 8. [AC]

ENGELMANN, R: 1844-1909.
*1471. (Pompeii.) P--. Tr. T. Ely. L: Grevel;NY: Scribner 1904 (1903). 112p. il. 24cm. [Not wholly satisfactory.] [BM.LC]

ENGELS, F: 1820-95.
*1472. (Der deutsche Bauernkrieg.) Peasant war in Germany. Tr. M. J. Olgin. Introd. D. Rianazov. NY: Internat. pub. 1926. L: Allen & U. 1927. 190p. 19cm. [LC.BM]
1473. (Die Entwicklung des Sozialismus von der Utopie zur Wissenschaft.) The development of socialism from utopia to science. Tr. E: Aveling. Ed: Socialist labour party 1908? 29p. 18cm. [BM] [The same as the following, without preface.]
*1474. (Herrn E. Dührings Umwälzung der Wissenschaft.) Socialism, utopian, and scientific. Tr. E: Aveling...with a special introd. by the author. L: Sonnenschein; NY: Scribner 1892. xxxix;117p. 19cm. [BM]
*1475. (L: Feuerbach und der Ausgang der klassischen deutschen Philosophie.) Feuerbach, the roots of the socialist philos. Tr. Austin Lewis. Chic: Kerr 1903. 133p. 17cm. [LC] [Tr. is good, but not excellent.]
1476. Principles of communism. [Engel's orig. draft of the communist manifesto.] Tr. Max Bedacht. NY: Daily worker 1925. 32p. T. [AC]
[See Kautsky, K:, F: E--, his life, his work, and his writings. #4882.]

ENGELS, P. J.
1477. King Salomo: grand hist. mus. spectacle in 3 acts and one introd. scene. Libr. and mus. by P. J. E--. Tr. Anna L. v. Raven. n. i. 1927. 35p. Tw. 28cm. [LCM]

ENNEMOSER, Js.
*1478. (Geschichte des tierischen Magnetismus. Teil 1. Gesch. der Magie.) The hist. of magic. Tr. W: Howitt. Appendix of...stories of apparitions...witchcraft...table-turning and spirit rapping, sel. by Ma. Howitt. L: Bohn 1854. 2v. xvi;471;518p. 18cm. [BM]

ENSLIN, R. Sel. in C51; 169.

EPPINGHOVEN, Ursula, countess v. [pseud?] [In 1904, H: W. H. Fischer published "William II and his consort: a secret history of the court of Berlin. From the papers and diaries...of a lady-in-waiting on her majesty..."The same text appeared in the same year in 2 vols. as "Private lives of W: II and his consort." In 1909 it was issued in 3 vols. under the same title; and also in a "shilling series" as "The secret history of the court of Berlin." The name Eppinghoven did not appear in the first issue. The whole thing is probably fabricated.]

ERBACH-SCHOENBERG, Me. C:e, Fürstin zu, 1852-1923.
1479. (Erlebnisse und Erkenntnisse.) Reminiscences. Tr. anon. NY: Brentano; L: Allen & Unwin 1925. xi;383p. il. 21cm. [LC]

ERDMANN, J: E: 1805-92.
*1480. (Grundriss der Geschichte der Philosophie.) A hist. of philos. Tr. ed. by W. S. Hough. L: Sonnenschein; NY: Macmillan 1892-7. 3v. 8. [BM.LC]

ERDMANN, J: E:- Grundriss...
*1481. do. 1893. [same] 3d ed. [BM]
*1482. (Grundriss der Logik und Metaphysik.) Outlines of logic and metaphysics. Tr. from 4th rev. ed. w. pref. by B. C. Burt. L: Sonnenschein; NY: Macmillan 1896. 253p. 19cm. [BM.LC]

ERHARD, El.
1483. Uncle Herman. Tr. M. Tyson. L: Stock 1886. 110p. 19cm. [BM]

ERMAN, Ad. 1854- .
*1484. (Aegypten und aegyptisches Leben im Altertum.) Life in ancient Egypt. Tr. H. M. Tirard. L; NY: Macmillan 1894. xii;570p. il. 24cm. [BM.LC]

ERMAN, G: Ad. 1806-77.
*1485. (Reise um die Erde durch Nord-Asien, etc.) Travels in Siberia. Tr. W: D. Cooley. L: Longmans 1848. 2v. 495; 536p. 20cm. ["In the earlier portion of this work...we have ventured to abridge the original."] [BM.LC]
*1486. do. 1850. [same] Phil: Lea & B. 2v. 19cm. [LC]

ERNDTEL, Ch. H:
1487. (C. H. E. D. de itinere suo anglicano et batavo...) The relation of a journey to England...1706-7, by a Saxon physician. Tr. anon. L: J: Morphew 1711. 140p. 19cm. [BM]

ERNST II, duke of Saxe-Coburg-Gotha, 1818-93.
1488. The duke of Coburg's pamphlet on Russia. ("The despots as revolutionists.") Tr. F. Marx. L: Hardwicke 1859. 27p. 21cm. [BM]
1489. Memoirs. Tr. Percy Andreae. L: Remington 1888-90. 4v. 22cm. [Vols. 1,2: 1888. Vols. 3,4: 1890.] [BM.LC]

ERNST, O: (i.e. O: Ern. Schmidt, 1862-1926.) Sel. in C571.
*1490. (Asmus Sempers Jugendland.) Asmus Semper: the story of a boyhood. Tr. Aletheia Caton. L: Griffiths 1909. xii;304p. 19cm. [Very good; not ideal.] [BM]
1491. Dolls, dead and alive. Tr. A. C. Caton. L: Caton 1911. 42p. 15cm. [BM]
†1492. (Flachsmann als Erzieher.) Master Flachsman: a comedy. Tr. H. M. Beatty. L: Unwin 1909. 155p. 19cm. [BM] [Tr. knows too little German.]
†1493. do. 1912. [same] NY: Duffield. 155p. 19cm. [LC]
1494. Roswitha: being leaves from the life of my little daughter. Tr. A. C. Caton. L: Caton 1913. 322p. 19cm. [BM]
1495. do. 1913 [same?] 2d ed. L: Simpkin. 66p. 8. [EC]
1496. do. 1913. [same?] Tr. anon. L: Caton. 65p. 19cm. [LC]
1497. do. 1914 ...or philosophy. Part 2 of R--. New and rev. ed. L: Caton. 8. [EC]

ERNST, Pl. 1866-1933.
1498. Marriage and proletarianism. Tr. anon. 1926. In C308.

ERTINGEN, Ad. Sel. in C450.

ERZBERGER, Mt. 1875-1921.
*1499. (Der Völkerbund, der Weg zum Weltfrieden.) The league of nations: the way to the world's peace. Tr. B. Miall. L; NY: Hodder & S. 1919. vii;328p. 22cm. [BM.LC]
*1500. do. 1919. [same] NY: Holt. 331p. D. [AC]

ESCHE, Lu.
1501. Grandmother and granddaughter. Tr. Caro. R. Corson. 1863. In #9181.

ESCHENBACH, Oa.
1502. The pearls. Tr. "Trauermantel". 1857. In C547.

ESCHSTRUTH, Ny. v. 1860- .
1503. (Comödie.) A priestess of comedy. Tr. Elise L. Lathrop. Il. W. B. Davis. NY: Bonner 1893. 307p. 19cm. [LC]
1504. do? 1894. A princess of the stage. Tr. E. L. Lathrop. Il. J. Fagan. NY: Bonner. 300p. 19cm. [LC]
1505. (Erlkönigin.) The erl queen. Tr. Emily S. Howard. NY: Worthington 1892. 291p. il. 19cm. [LC]
1506. The gray nun. Tr. Lionel Strachey. 1915. In C179.
1507. Her little highness. Tr. Elise L. Lathrop. Il. J. Fagan. NY: Bonner 1894. 303p. 19cm. [LC]
1508. The opposite house. Tr. Ma. J. Safford. Il. H. M. Eaton. NY: Bonner 1894. 282p. 20cm. [LC]
1509. (Polnisch Blut.) Polish blood. Tr. Cora L. Turner. NY: Alden 1889. 367p. 19cm. [LC]
1510. do. 1894. Countess Dynar; or, Polish blood. Tr. anon. NY: Bonner. 367p. 19cm. [LC]
1511. The wild rose of Gross-Stauffen. Tr. Elise L. Lathrop. NY: Worthington 1892. 282p. il. 19cm. [LC]

EUCKEN, Rd. Cf. 1846-1926.
*1512. [Coll.] Coll. essays. Tr. M. Booth. NY: Scribner; L: Unwin 1914. 354p. 23cm. [19 essays, largely from periodicals.] [LC.BM]
1513. Back to religion. Tr. anon. Bost; NY: Pilgrim press 1912. 31p. 18cm. [LC]
§1514. (Der Sinn und Wert des Lebens.) The meaning and value of life. Tr. Lucy J. Gibson and W: R. B. Gibson. L: Black 1909. xi; 157p. 19cm. [Considerably rewritten, simplified.] [BM.LC]
1515. (Der Sozialismus und seine Lebensgestaltung.) Socialism: an analysis. Tr. Js. McCabe. L: Unwin 1921. NY: Scribner 1922. 188p. 23cm. [BM.LC]
*1516. (Der Wahrheitsgehalt der Religion.) The truth of relig. Tr. W: T. Jones. L: Williams & N; NY: Putnam 1911. xiv;622p. 22cm. [BM.LC]
*1517. do. 1913. [same] 2d ed. from 3d rev. ed. xvi;600p. 22cm. [Not quite adequate.] [BM]
§1518. (Die Lebensanschauungen der grossen Denker.) The problem of human life as viewed by the great thinkers from Plato to the present time. Tr. W. S. Hough and W: R. B. Gibson. NY: Scribner 1909. L: Unwin 1910. xxv;582p. 23cm. [LC.BM]
§1519. do. 1914. [same] Rev. enl. ed. NY: Scribner. xxv;614p. 21cm. [LC]
1520. (Einführung in eine Philosophie.) The life of the spirit: an introd. to philos. Tr. F. L. Pogson. 2d ed. L: Williams & N. 1909. ix;403p. NY: Putnam. ix;406p. 19cm. [BM.LC]
§1521. (Erkennen und Leben.) Knowledge and life. Tr. W: T. Jones. L: Williams & N; NY: Putnam 1913. xvi;307p. 19cm. [BM.LC]
1522. Ethics and modern thought: a theory of their relations. The Deem lectures, delivered in 1913 at N. Y. U. Tr. from Ger. MS by Marg. v. Seydewitz. NY; L: Putnam 1913.127p. 19cm. [LC]
1523. do? 1913. [same?] Present-day ethics in their relations to the spiritual life, being the Deem lectures. Ed. W: T. Jones. Tr. Marg. v. Legdewitz. L: Williams & N; NY: Putnam. 141p. 18cm. [Tr.'s name evidently misprinted in this ed.] [LC.BM]
§1524. (Geistige Strömungen der Gegenwart.) Main currents of modern thought: a study of the spiritual and intel. movements of the present day. Tr. M. Booth. L: Unwin 1912. 488p. 22cm. [LC.BM] [Excessive liberties.]
1525. (Geschichte und Kritik der Grundbegriffe der Gegenwart.) The fundamental concepts of mod. philos. thought, crit. and histor. considered...with additions...by the author. Introd. N. Porter. Tr. M. S. Phelps. NY: Appleton 1880. xii;304p. 20cm. [LC.BM]

EUCKEN, Rd.
*1526. (Grundlinien einer neuen Lebensanschauung.) Life's basis and life's ideal: the fundamentals of a new philos. of life. Tr. A. G. Widgery. L: Black 1912. xxii;377p. 22cm. [BM]
*1527. do. 1912. [same] 2d. rev. ed. L: Black. xxi;377p. 23cm. [LC]
*1528. do. 1918. [same] New ed. L: Black. 399p. 8. [EC]
*1529. (Hauptprobleme der Religionsphilosophie der Gegenwart.) Christianity and the new idealism. Tr. from 3d ed. Lucy J. and W: R. B. Gibson. L; NY: Harper 1909. xvi;162p. 17cm. [LC.BM]
*1530. do. 1912. [same] [LC]
1531. The individual and society. Tr. W. R. V. Brade. L: Faith 1923. xii;58p. 18cm. [BM]
*1532. (Können wir noch Christen sein?) Can we still be Christians? Tr. Lucy J. Gibson. NY: Macmillan; L: Black 1914. 218p. 20cm. [LC.BM]
1533. (Lebenserinnerungen.) R-- E--, his life, work, and travels, by himself. Tr. Js. McCabe. L: Unwin 1921. NY: Scribner 1922. 216p. port. 23cm. [BM.LC]
1534. Naturalism or idealism? The Nobel lecture...1909. L: Heffer 1912. 44p. 8. [EC]
1535. Religion and life. (Lect. deliv. at Essex Hall, L:) Tr. G. F. Beckh. L: Brit...unitarian assoc. 1911. 50p. 17cm. [BM.LC]
1536. The spiritual outlook of Europe today. Tr. W. R. V. B(rade). Ed. Hakluyt Egerton. L: Faith; NY: Morehouse 1922. 96p. 8.[BM.LC] ["Not yet...published in Germany."]
1537. The transient and the permanent in Christianity. Tr. W: T. Jones. L: Lindsey 1914. 16p. 16cm. [BM]

EVERS, Jm. Lz. Sel. in C375.

EWALD, F: 1730- . Sel. in C461; 560.

EWALD, G; H: A: v.
*1538. (Geschichte des Volkes Israel. Bd. 5.) The life of Jesus Christ. Tr. and ed. O. Glover. Cambridge: Deighton Bell 1865. xvi;364p. 19cm. [BM]

EWERS, Hs. Hz. 1871- .
1539. Ant people. Tr. C. H. Levy. NY: Dodd; L: Lane 1927. ix;323p. il. 18cm. [BM]
1540. (Der Zauberlehrling.) The sorcerer's apprentice. Tr. L. Lewisohn. Il. Mahlon Blaine. NY: Day 1927. 337p. 23cm. [BM]

EYE, J: Ld. A: v. 1825-96.
1541. Hist. of culture. In "Iconographic encyclopedia." Phil: vol. 2. [LCO]

EYLER, Emile. See "Osten, Mary."

EYLERT, Rn.F: 1770-1852.
*1542. (Charakter-Züge und historische Fragmente aus dem Leben... F: W: III.) The religious life and opinions of F: W: III, king of Prussia. Tr. J. Birch. L: Hatchard 1844. 126p. 21cm. [BM.LC]
*1543. do. 1845. [same] Characteristic traits, personal, moral, domestic, and religious, of F: W: III, king of Prussia. Tr. J. Birch. L: Bell 1845. 176p. 22cm. [BM.LC]

EYSLER, Ed. C. 1874- . Operettas: The laughing husband. See Brammer and Grünwald. The love-cure. See Stein and Lindau.

FABER, Ernst.
1544. (Eine Staatslehre...oder Lehrbegriff des Mencius.) The mind of Mencius: polit. econ. founded upon moral philos. Tr. A. B. Hutchinson. Bost: Houghton, Mifflin 1882. 8. [AC]

FABRICIUS, F: 1642-1703. Sel. in C233.

FABRICIUS, Jk. 1598-1654. Sel. in C489.

FALCKENBERG, R: F: O: 1851-1920.
1545. (Geschichte der neueren Philosophie.) Hist. of mod. philos. from Nicolas of Cusa to the present time. First Amer. from 2d Ger. Ed. Tr. A. C. Armstrong. NY: Holt 1893. xv;655p. 22cm. [LC]
1546. do. 1895. [same] L: Bell. xv;655p. 8. [BM]

FALCKNER, Jt. 1672-1724. Sel. in C223;269.

FALK, J: Dn. 1768-1826. Sel. in C42.

FALKE, Gst. 1853-1916. Sel. in C28;423.

FALKE, Jk. v. 1825-97.
*1547. (Die Kunst im Hause.) Art in the house: hist. and aesth. studies. Tr. from 3d Ger. ed. w. notes by C: C. Perkins. Bost: Prang 1879. xxx;356p. il. 27cm. [BM]
*1548. (Hellas und Rom.) Greece and Rome, their life and art. Tr. W: H. Browne. NY: Holt 1882. xii;351p. il. 40 x 30cm. [LC.BM]

FALKENHORST, C. (i.e.,K:)
1549. (Aus der Zeit der Entdeckung Amerikas.) With Columbus in America. Ad. Elise L. Lathrop. NY: Worthington 1892. 302p. il. 19cm. [LC.BM]

FALKLAND, H: Sel. in C501.

FALL, Leo. Operettas: Princess caprice. See Bernauer, Rd. The dollar princess. See Willner, A. M. The girl in the train. See Leon, V: The siren. See Stein, Leo.

FAUST, Bh. Cph. 1755-1842.
1549a. The catechism of health; sel. from the diary of Dr. Faust (by J. H. Basse) and consid. impr. by Dr. Gregory, of Ed. NY: R. Wilson for S: Campbell 1798. xli;iv;146p. 12. [NYPL]

FECHNER, Gst. Td. 1801-87. Sel. in C375.

FEIL, Js.
1550. (Die Schweden in Oesterreich 1645-6.) Torstenson before Vienna. Tr. J. W. de Peyster. NY: Ludwig 1885. 68p. 23cm. [BM] [Tr. picks out passages here and there, including some of Feil's footnotes, thus rearranging and also abridging the original. Tr. appears to be competent.]

FELD, H: Sel. in C240.

FELD, Leo, 1869- . and V: LEON.
1551. The great name. Tr. anon. Ad. Jas. C. Harvey. NY: 1911. (B38)
1551a. do. 1910 [same] Libr. Engl. n.i. 43;47;31p. Tw. [LCM]

FELDER, Hn. 1867- .
1552. Christ and the critics. Tr. J: L. Stoddard. L: Burns, Oates 1924. 2v. 425; 457p. 21cm. [BM]
1553. The ideals of St. Francis of Assisi. Tr. B. Bittle. NY; Cincin: Benziger; L: Burns, Oates 1925. xvi;518p. 23cm. [LC.BM]

FELL, G:
*1554. (Die Unsterblichkeit der menschlichen Seele philosophisch beleuchtet.) The immortality of the human soul philosophically explained. Tr. L. Villing. L; Ed: Sands; St.L: Herder 1906. xxiii;267p. 18cm. [BM]

FELS, Gsell. See "Gsell-Fels."

FERBER, J: Jk. 1743-90.
*1555. (...Briefe aus Wälschland.) Travels through Italy, in the

FERBER, J: Jk.-Briefe aus Wälschland
years 1771 and 1772, in a series of letters...Tr. R. E. Raspe. L: Davis 1776. xxxiii;377p. 21cm. [LC.BM]

FERNAU, Hm. 1883- .
*1556. (Durch! Zur Demokratie!) The coming democracy. Tr. anon. NY: Dutton 1917. viii;321p. 19cm. [LC]
*1557. do. 1917. [same] L: Constable. 320p. 21cm. [BM]
*1558. (Gerade weil ich ein Deutscher bin.) Because I am a German. Ed. w. intro. by T. W. Rolleston. NY: Dutton 1916. 159p. 19cm[LC]
*1559. do. 1916. [same] L: Constable. 154p. 18cm. [BM]

FERNHAIN, Ele. v.
1560. Erna Stark: a story of conscience. Tr. Ma. E. Ireland. Phil: Am. baptist pub. soc. 1892. 192p. il. 18cm. [LC]

"FERRAND, E:" (i.e., E: Schulz, 1813-42.) Sel. in C3;97;152;178;571

FESCHER, F: A.
1560a. Travels in Spain, 1797-8. Tr. anon. L: Longmans 1803. 8.[EC]

FEUCHTERSLEBEN, Ern. Frhr. v. 1806-49. Sel. in C67;178;380;423;448.
§1561. (Zur Diätetik der Seele.) The dietetics of the soul. Ed. from the 7th ed. and tr. H: A. Ouvry. L: Churchill 1852. ix;202p. 16cm. [BM.LC]
1562. do. 1852-5. [same?] NY: Francis. [AC]
1563. do. 1856. [same?] NY: Francis. 12. [AC]
§1564. do. 1873. [same] or, true mental discipline. Rev. from the 32d Ger. ed. anon. L: Kerby & Endean. vi;224p. 16cm. [BM]
*1565. do. 1910. Health and suggestion: the dietetics of the mind. Tr. and ed. L. Lewisohn. NY: Huebsch. 168p. 19cm. [LC]

FEUCHTWANGER, Lion, 1884- .
*1566. (Die hässliche Herzogin, Margarete Maultasch.) The ugly duchess: an historical romance. Tr. Willa and E. Muir. L: Secker 1927. 312p. 19cm. [BM.LC]
*1567. (Jud Süss.) Jew Süss. Tr. Willa and E. Muir. L: Secker 1926. 424p. 20cm. [BM]
*1568. do. 1926. [same] Power. Tr. W. and E. Muir. NY: Viking press 1926. 424p. 21cm. [LC]
*1569. do. 1927. [same] Ltd. signed ed. Secker. 536p. 9 x 6in. [EC]

FEUERBACH, L: And. 1804-72. Sel. in C5;6;469.
*1570. (Das Wesen des Christentums.) The essence of Christianity. Tr. from 2d Ger. ed. Marian Evans. L: Chapman 1854. xx;340p. 20cm. [BM]

FEUERBACH, Pl. J: Ans. Ritter v. 1775-1833. Sel. in C5.
*1571. (Kaspar Hauser.) Caspar H--. Tr. H. G. Linberg. Bost: Allen & Ticknor 1832. 178p. 16cm. [LC]
*1572. do. 1833. [same] 2d ed. Bost. [LC]
*1573. do. 1834. [same] 2d ed. With a memoir of the author. To which are added further details, by G. F. Daumer and Schmidt von Lübeck. L: Simpkin & M. xiv; 173p. 18cm.[This copy examined.][BM]
*1574. do. 1834. [same] 3d ed. Addenda on his assassination and "a clue to the mystery of his birth." xix;212p. 16cm. [BM]
1575. Narratives of (14) remarkable trials. Tr. Lady Duff Gordon. L: Murray 1846. xi;368p. 22cm. [Abridged about one-half.] [BM.LC]
1576. do. ca. 1846. Tr. anon. NY: Harper n.d. [AC]
1577. The trial of the Rev. Fis. Riembauer...for the murder of Anna Eichstaedter. Phil: Barrett & J. 1846. 27p. 19cm. [LC]

FEY, Mother Clare, 1815-94.
1578. Lenten meditations. St.L: Herder; L: Burns, Oates 1924. xii; 244p. 18cm. [BM]

FEY, Mother Clare
1579. Meditations for advent and Christmas. Tr. by a member of the congregation. L: Burns, Oates 1925. x;277p. 19cm. [BM]
1580. do. 1927. [same] NY; Cinc: Benziger. [AC]
1581. The practice of Mother C-- F--. Tr. anon. L: Burns, Oates 1925. vii;77p. 19cm. [BM]
1582. do. 1925-6. [same] St.L: Herder. [AC]
1583. Thoughts for meditation with practical resolutions for the different seasons of the year. Tr. by a member of the congregation. L: Burns, Oates 1927. xv; 304p. 19cm. [BM]

FICHTE, J: Gb. 1762-1814. Sel. in C12;56;158;194*;366*;461;469.
*1584. [Coll.] The popular works. Tr. W: Smith. With a memoir of the author. L: Chapman 1848-9. 2v. 19cm. [BM.LC]
[Vol. 1, 554p. The vocation of the scholar; The nature of the scholar; The vocation of man. Vol. 2, 529p. The character of the present age; The way towards the blessed life, or the doctrine of religion; Outlines of the doctrine of knowledge.]
1585. [Coll.] 1862. [same?] 2d ed? Tr. anon. 2v. [EC]
*1586. do. 1873. [same] 3d rev. ed. L: Trübner. 564p. 22cm. [BM]
[EC has 1874. Memoir; the vocation of the scholar; The vocation of man; The doctrine of relig.]
*1587. do. 1889. [same as #1584] 4th ed. L: Trübner. 2v. 478;517p. 21cm. [BM.LC]
1588. [Sel.] 1860. Contributions to mental philos. Tr. and ed. J: D. Morell. L: Longmans. 159p. 18cm. [BM.LC]
1589. [Sel.] 1926. The educational theory of...F--...with tr. (of the educ. writings except the <u>Reden an die deutsche Nation.</u>) by G: H: Turnbull (pp. 119-283.) L: Hodder & S. 283p. 21cm. [BM]
1590. (<u>Anweisung zum seligen Leben, oder auch die Religionslehre.</u>) The way towards the blessed life. (Probably tr. W: Smith; cf. #1584.) L: Chapman 1844. xvi;221p. 19cm. [BM]
1591. do. 1849. [same] Criticism of philos. systems. Tr. A. E. Kroeger. 1871. In C300(1).
1592. Criticism of Schelling. Tr. A. E. Kroeger. 1882-3. In C300 (12,13).
1593. (<u>Das System der Sittenlehre nach den Prinzipien der Wissenschaftslehre.</u>) The science of ethics, as based on the science of knowledge. Tr. A. E. Kroeger. Ed. W: T. Harris. L: Paul 1897. x;399p. 21cm. [BM]
1594. (<u>...die Bestimmung des Gelehrten.</u>) The vocation of the scholar. L: Chapman 1847. 72p. 20cm. [Also in #1584.] [BM.LC]
§1595. (<u>Die Bestimmung des Menschen.</u>) The destination of man. Tr. Jane Sinnett. L: Chapman 1846. 128p. 19cm. [LC]
*1596. do. 1848. The vocation of man. Tr. W: Smith. L: Chapman. xii;178p. 20cm. [Also in #1584.] [BM.LC]
*1597. do. 1906. Re-issue of #1596. L: Paul; Chic: Open court. [BM.LC]
1598. do. 1849. Tr. F: H: Hedge? In C194.
1599. do. 1913-15. Tr. F: H: Hedge. In C154(5)
1600. (<u>Die Grundzüge des gegenwärtigen Zeitalters.</u>) The characteristics of the present age. Tr. W: Smith. L: Chapman 1844. xi;271p. 19cm. [BM]
1601. do. 1847. [same] [Also in #1584.] [BM.LC]
1602. do. 1852. [same?] L: Trübner. 8. [EC]
1603. (<u>Die Wissenschaftslehre...</u>) The science of knowledge. Tr. A. E. Kroeger. Phil: Lippincott 1868. 377p. 18cm. [BM]
[In the pref. to #1604, K. says that he both added and omitted freely, making almost an independent work "much superior to the German original."]
*1604. do. 1869. New exposition of the science of knowledge. Tr. A.

FICHTE, J: Gb. - Die Wissenschaftslehre...
E. Kroeger. St.L. 155p. 22cm. [LC]
[Lauding himself for accuracy, he begins with a bad blunder.]
1605. do. 1870. [same as #1603?] L: Trübner. 8. [EC]
1606. do. 1889. [same as #1603?] L: Trübner. xxiii;377p. 21cm [BM.LC]
1607. do. sel. Tr. A. E. Kroeger. 1871,3. In C300(1,3).
1608. Facts of consciousness. Tr. A. E. Kroeger. 1875 etc. In C300 (5,6,7,17,18).
*1609. (Grundlage des Naturrechts...) The science of rights. Tr. A. E. Kroeger. Phil: Lippincott 1869. x;505p. 19cm. [LC]
1610. do. 1883. [same?] L: Trübner. 8. [EC]
*1611. do. 1889. [same] L: Trübner. x;505p. 21cm. [BM.LC]
*1612. (Reden an die deutsche Nation.) Addresses to the German nation. Tr. L: H. Gray. 1913-15. C154(5).
**1613. do. 1922. Tr. R. F. Jones and G: H: Turnbull. Chic; L; Ed: Open court 1922 (i.e., 1923). xxiii;269p. 21cm. [LC.BM]
[Admirable, on the whole; very faithful. Some awkward English.]
1614. (Sonnenklarer Bericht über das...Wesen der neuesten Philosophie.) Sun clear statement...concerning...the newest philos. Tr. A. E. Kroeger. 1872. In C300(2).
*1615. (Ueber das Wesen des Gelehrten.) On the nature of the scholar, and its manifestations. Tr...w. a memoir of the author, by W: Smith. L: Chapman 1845. 220p. 19cm. [BM]
*1616. do. 1848. [same] 2d ed. Chapman. 131p. 20cm. [LC.BM]
[Also in #1584.]

FICK, Hm.
1617. Life and deeds...Luther. Tr. M. Loy. Columbus, O: Schultze & Gassm'n 1869. 181p. 16. [LC]

FINK, Gf. W: 1783-1846. Sel. in C67;106.

FISCHEL, Ok. 1870- . joint author with Max v. Boehn. See #598.

FISCHER, C., M. D. zu Cöthen.
1618. A biog. monument to the mem. of S. Hahnemann. Tr. w. alterations and add. L: Jas. Leath 1852. 130p. 22cm. [BM]

FISCHER, Cn. A: 1771-1829.
*1619. (Gemälde von Madrid.) A pict. of Madrid: taken on the spot. Tr. anon. L: Mawman 1808. vii;306p. 19cm. [BM.LC]
1620. (Gemälde von Valencia.) A pict. of Valencia: taken on the spot. Tr. F: Shoberl. L: H:Colburn 1808. 309p. 21cm. [BM]
§1621. (Reise nach Hyères.) Travels to Hyères, in the south of France. Tr. anon. In "A coll.of mod. voyages," vol. 5. L: 1805. R:Phillips 1807. 76p. 21cm. [BM.LC]
[Gen. t.p. 1807; special t.p. 1805. Tr. is curtailed and not wholly faithful.]
*1622. (Reise nach Montpellier.) Letters written during a journey to Montpellier in 1804. In "A coll. of mod. voyages," Vol. 3. L: R:Phillips 1806. 87p. 22cm. [BM.LC]

FISCHER, Hm. 1867- .
1623. Life of Arnold Janssen, founder of the Soc. of the divine word and of the missionary congregation of the Servants of the Holy Ghost. Tr. F: M. Lynk. NY: Mission press 1925. 520p. il. O. [AC]

FISCHER, J: G: 1816-97. Sel. in C32;97;108;149;195;309;448;501;571.

FISCHER, Kn. 1824-1907. Sel. in 366;469.
*1624. (Benedikt Spinozas Leben und Charakter.) Life and character of Baruch S--: a lecture. Tr. Frida Schmidt. In W: Knight, "Spinoza." L: Williams & N. 1882. pp. 77-127. 23cm. [BM]
1625. Centennial of the critique of pure reason. Tr. B: Rand. 1871. In C300(17).

FISCHER, Kn.
§1626. (Franz Bacon von Verulam.) Fis. Bacon of V--. Realistic philos. and its age. Tr. J: Oxenford. L: Longmans 1857. xxiii; 508p. 19cm. [Tr. seems to me to carry his rewording so far as to alter the exact course of the argument.] [BM.LC]
*1627. (Geschichte der neueren Philos.) A commentary on Kant's critick of the pure reason: tr. from the hist. of mod. philos. by J: P. Mahaffy. L: Longmans 1866. lxxx;374p. 19cm. [BM.LC]
*1628. do. 1887. Hist. of mod. philos: Descartes and his school. Tr. 3d rev. Ger. ed. by J: P. Gordy. NY: Scribner; L: Unwin. xvi; 589p. 22cm. [LC.BM]
*1629. do. 1888. A critique of Kant. Tr. W. S. Hough. L: Sonnenschein. xi;188p. 22cm.[Tr.of Chaps.1-5 in vol.5 of 2d ed.][BM.LC]
*1630. (Goethes Faust.) Goethe's Faust. Tr. H. R. Wolcott. Manchester, Ia: H. R. Wolcott 1895. 218p. 20cm.[Vol.1 only.] [LC]
1631. (Kritik der Kantischen Philosophie.) A critique on Kantian philos. Tr. W. S. Hough. 1889-90. In C300(20,21).
§1632. (Lessings Nathan der Weise.) Essay on Nathan the wise. (Condensed.) In #5775. [Tr. hardly does him justice.]

FISCHER, Max A.
*1633. (Das Heidelberger Schloss in 14 Ansichten.) The castle of H-- in 14 views. Text tr. R. H. Whitelocke. Carlsruhe: Wagner 1842? 66p. 12 x 10cm. [BM]

FISCHER, W: See Wagner, R., Letters to his Dresden friends. #9897.

FITGER, Art. 1840-1909. Sel. in C28.

FLAISCHLEN, Cs. 1864-1920. Sel. in C28.

"FLAMMBERG, Gf." (i.e.,Ebrard, J: H: A: 1818-88). See #1389 and C491.

"FLAMMENBERG, Lz." (i.e., K. F. Kahlert).
1634. (Der Geisterbanner.) The necromancer; or, a tale of the Black Forest. Tr. P: Teuthold. L: Lane 1794. 2v. See "Analyt. R." 20 (1794):52. (B26)
1635. do. 1927. [same] L: Holden. xv;232p. 8. [BM]

FLATHE, H: Td. 1827-1900.
1636. The reconstruction of Europe. Tr. anon. 1902. Vol. 19 of C201, 450p.
1637. Restoration and revolution. Tr. anon. 1902. Vol. 18 of C201, 434p.

FLESCH, K: 1873- .
1637a. (Die Kunst des Violinspiels.) The art of violin playing. Tr. F: H. Martens. Fischer 1924. Vol. 1. 171p. F. [AC]

FLEMMING (or Fleming), Pl. 1609-40. Sel. in C244;271;287;366;461; 487;530-1;570.

FLESSA, J: Am. 1694-1775. Sel. in C244.

FLETTNER, An.
*1638. (Mein Weg zum Rotor.) The story of the rotor. Tr. anon. L: Crosby Lockwood 1927. NY: Willhoft 1926. xxx;110p. 106 il. 23cm. [BM]

FLIEDNER, Td. 1800-64.
1639. The German pastor; or, sketches of the life of T-- F--. Ed: Oliphant; L: Hamilton Adams 1866. 48p. 14cm. [BM]
1640. do? 1867. Life of pastor Fliedner of Kaiserswerth. Auth. tr. Cath. Winkworth. L: Longmans. xxvi;155p. front. 17cm. [BM.LC]

FLOTOW, F: Freiherr v. 1812-83. Operas. Martha. Alessandro Stradella. See "Friedrich, W:"

FLUE, N: v. der (properly Löwenbrugger), 1417-87. Sel. in C224. See Goerres, G., The blessed Nicholas v. d. F--. #2356.

FLUGI, A. v. Sel. in C438.

FOERSTER, F: W: 1869- .
1641. Franco-German reconciliation; text of an address...July 6, 1923, at Paris. Tr. anon. NY: Am. ass'n for internat. concil. 1923. 12p. 19cm. [LC]
1642. Indispensability of the ascetic ideal. NY: Amer. press 1914. [AC]
1643. (Jugendlehre.) The art of living: sources and il. for moral lessons. Tr. Ethel Peck. L: Dent; NY: Dutton 1910. ix;217p. 18cm. [Selected portions of the original work.] [BM]
*1644. (Sexualethik und Sexualpädagogik.) Marriage and the sex problem. Tr. M. Booth. L: Wells Gardner; NY: Stokes 1912. xx; 228p. 18cm. [BM]
1645. Voice from Germany; why German peace declarations fail to convince, and Austria's peace proposals: the letter to Prince Sixtus. Tr. anon. NY: Am. ass'n for internat. concil. 23p. 20cm. [LC]

FOERSTER-NIETZSCHE, Frau Eli. 1846-1935.
1646. Biog. of F: Nietzsche, as introd. to #6816.
§1647. (Das Leben F: Nietzsches.) The life of N--. Tr. A. M. Ludovici. NY: Sturgis & W. 1912-15. 2v. il. 25cm. [LC] [Vol. 2. tr. Pl. V: Cohn; better than L.]
*1648. (Der einsame N--.) The lonely N--. Tr. Pl. V: Cohn. L: Heinemann 1915. xii;415p. 23cm. [BM]
1649. (Der junge N--.) The young N--. Tr. A. M. Ludovici. L: Heinemann 1912. x;399p. il. 24cm. [BM.LC]

FOERTZSCH, Bs. d.1619. Sel. in C276.

FOLLEN, A:, afterwards Ad. L: 1794-1855. Sel. in C29;44;373;391; 393;438;#6209a.

FOLLEN, K: 1795-1840. Sel. in C317.

FOLLENIUS, Em. F: W: Ern. 1773-1809.
1650. (Continuation of Schiller's Geisterseher: The Armenian, etc.) Tr. W: Render. In #7967, vol. 1, pp. 106-63; vol 2. pp. 1-176.

FONTANE, Td. 1819-98. Sel. in 395;423;450.
**1651. (Effi Briest.) E-- B-- (abr.) Also, extract from "My childhood days." Tr. W: A. Cooper. 1913-15. In C154(12).
**1652. (Irrungen, Wirrungen.) Trials and tribulations. Tr. Kath. Royce. 1917. In C186.

FORBES-MOSSE, Ire. 1864- Sel. in C28.
1653. The little death: a novel. Tr. Mrs. H: Head. L: Unwin 1921. 216p. 18cm. [BM]

FORKEL, J. N. 1749-1818.
**1654. (J: Sb. Bach.) Life of J: S. Bach. L: Prtd. for Boosey 1820. xi;116p. 21cm. [BM.LC]
*1655. do. 1920. J: Sb. Bach: his life, art, and work. Tr. w. notes and appendices by C: S. Terry. Rev. ed. L: Constable; NY: Harcourt. xxxii;321p. il. 23cm. [BM.LC] [Not as good and close as the foregoing.]

FORSTER, J: G: Am. 1754-94. Sel. in C461*.

FORSTER, J: Rld. 1729-98.
1656. Hist. of the voyages and discov. made in the north. L: Prtd. for J. Robinson 1786. xvi;489p. 28cm. [BM.LC]

FORSTNER, (Ax. F: P: Rb.) G: Gr, Frhr. v. 1882-.
1657. Journal of submarine commander v. Forstner. Tr. Mrs. Russell

FORSTNER
Codman. Introd. by J: Hays Hammond, Jr. NY: Houghton 1917. 136p. 18cm. [LC]

FOUQUÉ, F: H: K: Frhr. de La Motte-, 1777-1843. Sel. in C9;12;31; 88;106;133;140;142;153;158;163;166;190;195;229;231-2;276;287;318; 366*;391;393;428;448;469;489;501.
1658. [Coll.] §Wild love (Wilde Liebe) and other tales. L: Lumley (BM has: Burns) 1844. 215; 51; 22; 20p. il. 17cm. [LC.BM]
[Contains also: *Rosaura and her kinsfolk ("R-- und ihre Verwandten"); *The oak of the idols ("Die Götzeneiche"); The field of terror ("Das Schauerfeld"). The first rather poorly done, the next two very well.]
1659. (Adler und Löwe.) The eagle and the lion. Tr. anon. 1843. In C473, cf. 474-6.
1660. (Aslaugas Ritter.) Aslauga's knight. Tr. T: Carlyle. 1827. In C58. Cf. C59-62. Also in his works.
1661. do. 1843. A-- and her knight: an allegory. New tr. anon. L: Hamilton, Adams. 84p. 16. [NY]
*1662. do. 1845? (So EC.) A--'s knight: a romance. L: Lumley 1846? 42p. il. 17cm. [LC]
[Really one part of 1694-7, probably tr. Jas. Burns.]
*1663. do. 1867. Tr. F. E. Bunnett. In #1696.
1664. The cypress crown: a tale. Tr. anon. about 1820. In C117, pp. 1-48.
1665. do. 1888. [same] In Morley, H:, A miscellany. L: Routledge. 272p. 20cm.
[Said to be tr. by a Dutchman.] [BM.LC]
1666. (Das Galgenmännlein.) The bottle-imp. Tr. anon. 1823. In C456.
*1667. do. 1841. The vial-genie and mad farthing. Tr. T: Tracy. In C542.
1668. do. 1912. The crazy half-heller. Tr. C. J. T. In C518.
1669. do. Ad. R: Brinsley Peake. The bottle imp: a melodramatic romance in two acts (and in prose). L. 1838? 29pp. 12. [BM]
1670. (Das Gelübde.) The vow. Tr. The Misses Corbett. 1826. In C435.
1671. do. 185- . Tr. anon. In C474.
1672. (Das Schauerfeld.) The field of terror. Tr. R. P. Gillies. 1820. In "Blackwoods" 8(1820):131. (B26)
1673. do. 1826. The field of terror; or, the haunted field. Tr. T: Roscoe. In C477.
1674. (Das Schwert des Fürsten.) The prince's sword. Tr. anon. 1843. In C473.
1675. (Der Geheimrat.) The privy councillor. Tr. anon. 1842. In C473.
1676. (Der neue Regulus.) The modern Regulus. Tr. G: G. Cunningham. 1829. In C80.
1677. (Der Siegeskranz.) The crown of victory. Tr. anon. 1824. In "New Monthly Mag." 10(1824):235. (B26)
1678. do. 1843. The victor's wreath. Tr. anon. In C473.
1679. do. 1848. The crown of victory. Tr. anon. In C376.
1680. (Der unbekannte Kranke.) The mysterious invalid. Tr. The Misses Corbett. 1826. In C435.
1681. do. 1843. The unknown patient. Tr. anon. In C473.
1682. (Der Zauberring.) The magic ring: a romance. Tr. anon. Ed: Oliver & Boyd 1825. 3v. 17cm. [BM.LC]--L: Whittaker 1825. [EC]
*1683. do. 1846. A knightly romance. New tr. by Ax. Platt. L: Burns. viii;328p. 19cm. [BM]
1684. do. 1875. 1882. L: Routledge. 12. [EC]
§1685. (Die beiden Hauptleute.) The two captains: a romance. Tr. anon. L: Lumley 1846? (EC has Burns 1845.) 52p. il. 17cm. [LC]
[Bound with "Aslauga's knight." Really parts of #1694-5.]

FOUQUÉ, F: H: K: Frhr. de La Motte- .
†1686. (Die Fahrten Thiodolfs des Isländers.) Thiodolf, the Icelander. Tr. anon. L: Burns 1845. 2v. in 1. il. 16cm. [BM.LC]
†1687. do. 1845. [same] NY: Wiley & Putnam. 349p. 12. [NY]
[With "Aslauga's knight" in tr. of #1694.]
†1688. do. 1862? 1867? [same] NY: Miller. 308p. 19cm. [LC]
1689. do. 1876. New ed. L: Routledge. 12. [EC]
1690. do. 1885. New issue. Knox. il. D. [AC]
1691. do. 1887. NY: Routledge. 16. [AC]
1692. do. 1889. NY: Pollard. 12. [AC]
1693. (Die Geschichten von Rübezahl.) A story of Number Nip. Tr. G: G. Cunningham. 1829. In C80.
§1694. (Die Jahreszeiten.) The seasons. Four romances from the German. Undine (spring). The two captains (summer). Aslauga's knight (autumn). Sintram and his companions (winter). Tr. anon. L: Burns 1843. 4 pts. 98;52;42;120p. 8. [BM]
[Undine ed. from #1751; The two captains a fair tr. Aslauga's knight well tr. Sintram, by Jas. Burns, fair. -- All four also issued sep.]
§1695. do. 1846. [same] L: Lumley. 18. [LCO]
**1696. do. 1867. Tr. F. E. Bunnett. Lpz: Tauchnitz; L: Low. 361p. 8. [BM]
§1697. do. 1867. Undine and other tales. Il. H. W. Herrick. Bost; NY: Houghton. 146p. 17cm. [LC]
[Undine in tr. of #1765; rest in tr. of #1694.]
§1698. do. 1871. [same] NY: Hurd & Houghton. 16. [NY]
§1699. do. 1875. [same as #1694?] The four seasons. New ed. L: Routledge. 12. [EC]
§1700. do. 1889. [same as #1697] Houghton. [LC]
**1701. do. 1901? Undine and other tales. Tr. Fanny E. Bunnett. NY: Burt. 320p. 19cm. [LC]
§1702. do. 191- . Undine (i.e., the four seasons). Tr. anon. NY: Crowell. 313p. 12. [NY]
[Slightly revised from #1697; Undine is different tr.]
1703. (Die Köhlerfamilie.) The collier's family. Tr. anon. 1823. In C456.
*1704. do. 1841. The collier-family; or, red-mantle and the merchant. Tr. T: Tracy. In C542.
1705. do. 1844. Red mantle. Tr. anon. In C457.
1706. do. 185- . Berthold. Tr. anon. In C474.
1707. (Die Laterne im Schlosshofe.) The lantern in the castle yard. Tr. The Misses Corbett. 1826. In C435.
1708. do. 185- . Tr. anon. In C474.
1709. (Eugenie.) Eugenia. Tr. anon. (Jas. Burns?) In Twelve nights' entertainments. L: Jas. Burns 1845. 29p. 16cm. [BM]
1710. do. 185- . [same?] In C474.
1711. Head master Rhenfried and his family. Tr. T: Roscoe. 1826. In C477.
1712. do. 1843. Tr. anon. In C473.
1713. Kibitz. Tr. anon. 1823. In C456.
1714. The magic dollar. Tr. anon. 1823. In C456.
1715. The mandrake. Tr. T: Roscoe. 1826. In C477.
1716. The pilgrimage: a drama. (Scenes from it.) Tr. J: Anster. 1837. In C9 (47p.).
1717. (Rose.) Rose. Tr. anon. 1843. In C473.
**1718. (Sängerliebe.) Minstrel-love. Tr. G: Soane. L: Simpkin 1821. 2v. lx;256; 380p. 18cm. [BM]
[Interesting discussion of literal and idiomatic tr.]
*1719. do. 1822. reprint. NY. (B48)
*1720. do. 1845. A romance. New tr. anon. with orig. designs. L: Lumley (BM: Burns). 333p. 16cm. [BM.LC]

FOUQUÉ, F: H: K: Frhr. de La Motte-
1721. do. 1876. Tr. anon. 12. [EC]
1722. The siege of Algiers. Tr. 185- . In C474.
§1723. (Sintram und seine Gefährten.) Sintram and his companions. Tr. J. C. Hare. L: Ollier 1820. xiv;267p. 12. [BM]
[Soane, #1718, makes much fun of the "translator's English" in this version; but Hare's tr. is not bad.]
*1724. do. 1844. A tale of the north. Tr. anon. L: W:Smith. 39p. 23cm. [In double columns.] [BM]
§1725. do. 1848. Tr. Jas. Burns. Il. by H. C. Selous. L: Lumley (BM: Burns). 120p. 16cm. [BM.LC]
1726. do. 1875. 1876. Tr. anon. L: Routledge. 12. [EC]
[With "Aslauga's knight."]
§1727. do. 1877. Burns' tr. Bost: Osgood. 156p. il. 12cm. [BM]
1728. do. 1881. Tr. anon. NY: Munro. Seaside lib. 28p. 32cm. [LC]
§1729. do. 1883. A romance. Tr. anon. Il. Heywood Sumner. L: Seeley. vii;124p. 21 x 16cm. [BM]
[Founded on Hare's tr., #1723, which is pruned considerably.]
§1730. do. 1883. [same] Il. Sumner. NY: Scribner & W. 4. [AC]
§1731. do. 1887. Burns's tr. L; NY: Cassell. 192p. 14cm. [BM]
[With "Aslauga's knight."]
1732. do. 1890. Cf. #1735. Tr. anon. Il. C: Robinson. L: Dent. 222p. 12. [With "Aslauga's knight."] [EC]
§1733. do. 1896. Burns's tr. Introd. Cte. M. Yonge. Il. Gordon Browne. L: Gardner & D. xix;279p. 20cm. [BM]
[With "Undine" in Tracy's tr., ed. as in #1694.]
1734. do. 1900. Tr. anon. Macmillan. il. 16. [AC]
[With "Aslauga's knight."]
§1735. do. 1900. Burns's tr. (#1725). 12 il. C: Robinson. L: Dent. 218p. 15cm. [With "Aslauga's knight" in tr. of #1694, prob. by Jas. Burns. Cf. #1732.] [BM]
§1736. do. 1900. New tr. A. M. Richards. Il. Anna Richards. L: Freemantle. 188p. 18cm. [BM]
1737. do. 1901. Tr. anon. Phil: Lippincott. (B13)
1738. do. 1901. [ad.] Sintram, a drama by Helen Leslie, founded on F--'s story. L: Chapman & H. vii;258p. 19cm. [BM]
["The play is...in parts a faithful tr. of the story."]
1739. do. 1902. Tr. anon. L: Constable. 12. [EC]
1740. do. 1904. Tr. anon. NY: Putnam. 32. [AC]
1741. do. 1905. Tr. anon. L: Blackie. 48p. 8. [EC]
1742. do. 1905. Tr. anon. L: Blackie. 140p. 17cm. [BM]
[Edited by Rouse.]
§1743. do. 1908. Tr. A. C. Farquharson. Il. E. H. Sullivan. L: Methuen. viii;193p. 23cm. [BM.NY]
§1744. do. 1909. [same as #1733] Il. Browne. NY: Stokes. 279p. 21cm. [With "Aslauga's knight."] [LC]
1745. do. 1911. The story of Sintram, etc. Ed. Ma. Macleod (from Burns's tr.) Il. G. Browne. L: Wells Gardner. lx;129p. 16cm. [BM]
1746. do. 1922. [ad.] Sintram: a drama in blank verse in 4 acts from the story...by...Fouqué, by Flor. E. De Cerkez. Bost: Badger. 205p. 19cm. [LC]
1747. Sir Elidoc: an old Breton legend. L: Mozley 1849. viii;448p. 17cm. [BM]
§1748. (Undine.) U--: a romance. Tr. G: Soane. Ed: Bell & B; L: Simpkin and M. 1818. 205p. 19cm. [BM]
["I have taken neither few nor trifling liberties with the original: I have added, expunged, or substituted, on many occasions."]
1749. do. 1824. A tale. Tr. anon. Bost; Phil: Littell. (B48)
[Probably reprint of foregoing.]

FOUQUÉ, F: H: K: -- Undine
§1750. do. 1830. Tr. anon. L: Simpkin & M. 250p. 19cm. [BM]
[Rather poor.]
*1751. do. 1839. Tr. T: Tracy. NY: Colman. 157p. [LC card]
**1752. do. 1841. [same] U-- or the spirit of the waters. L: Clements. (The romancist and novelist's lib.) 49p. 21cm. [BM.LC]
*1753. do. 1841. [same] In C542.
*1764. do. 1844. [same] A miniature romance. L: Clarke. x;138p. 13cm. [BM]
§1765. do. 1844. Tr. Lady C. L. Lyttelton. In #10348, 126p.
[Easy but too free.]
*1766. do. 1845. Tracy's tr. L: Burns. xxiv;98p. 16cm. [BM]
§1767. do. 1845. Lyttelton's tr. L: Bell & D. 12. [EC]
§1768. do. 1845. New tr. Il. J: Tenniel. L: Burns. xxiv;96p. 16cm. [BM]
1769. do. 1845. Tr. anon. In C494.
*1770. do. 1845. Tracy's tr. NY: Wiley & Putnam. xiv;238p. 19cm. [With "Aslauga's knight" in Burns's tr., and "Sintram".] [LC]
*1771. do. 1852. [same] New ed. 238p. 18cm. [LC]
1772. do. 1852. Tr. anon. L: Chapman. (Il. lit. of all nations.) 23p. 28cm. [Based on Tracy's tr.] [BM]
1773. do. 1854. Tr. anon. Phil: Hazard. 12. [AC]
[With "Aslauga's knight."]
1774. do. 1856. Tr. anon. NY: Francis. 16. [AC]
§1775. do. 1858. Newly tr. by the author of "Night." L: Smith, Elder. xv;107p. 17cm. [BM]
§1776. do. 1859. Lyttelton's tr. L: Bell & D. 122p. il. 16cm. [BM]
§1777. do. 1860. New tr. NY: Phinney, Blakeman & Mason. 154p. il. 16. [Stilted language.] [NY]
1778. do. 1861. U--, or, the water-spirit. Tr. anon. NY: Jas. Miller. 16. [AC]
§1779. do. 1868. A tale. Tr. anon. Il. H. W. Herrick. NY: Hurd & H. 116p. 17cm. [LC]
§1780. do. 1868. Lyttelton's tr. [Reissue of #1767.] Bell & D. [EC]
1781. do. 1872-6. Tr. anon. NY: Miller. il. 12. [AC]
[With "Aslauga's knight."]
1782. do. 1872-6. Tr. anon. NY: Scribner, W. & A. [AC]
[With "The two captains."]
*1783. do. 1873. Tracy's tr. NY: Ford. (Lib. of famous fiction, embracing the [9] standard masterpieces of imaginative lit.) 1065p. 23cm. [NY.BM]
1784. do. 1875. 1876. Tr. anon. L: Routledge. il. 12. [EC]
[With "The two captains."]
*1785. do. 1875. Bunnett's tr. (Cf. #1696.) L: Low. 162p. 12. [BM]
[With "The two captains."]
1786. do. 1876. Tr. anon. Loves of Undine and Sintram. World pub. il. 12. [With "Paul and Virginia," by J. H. de Saint Pierre.][AC]
§1787. do. 1877. Lyttelton's tr. Chic: Donnelley, Lloyd. Lakeside lib. pp. 897-927. il. 32cm. [LC]
[With "Solomon Isaacs" by B. L. Farjeon.]
§1788. do. 1877. Lyttelton's tr. Bost: Osgood. 110p. 16. [BM]
§1789. do. 1879. [same] Rochester, NY: Fitch. 43p. 8. [NY.LC]
1790. do. 1881. Tr. anon. NY: Munro. Seaside lib. 32cm. [AC]
1791. do. 1883. Tr. anon. L: Seeley. 18. [EC]
[With "The two captains."]
§1792. do. 1884. 2d ed. of #1775. Pub. L: by the tr. 104p. 18cm[BM]
*1793. do. 1885. A legend. Bunnett's tr. Il. Jl. Höppner. L: Griffith & Farran. unp. 35 leaves. 48cm. [Very beautiful ed.] [BM]
1794. do. 1885. Tr. anon. NY: White & S. S. [AC]
1795. do. 1885. New issue. Tr. anon. Knox. il. D. [AC]
[With "Aslauga's knight."]

FOUQUÉ, F: H: K: -- Undine.
*1796. do. 1886. Bunnett's tr. NY: Lovell. 94p. 18cm. [LC]
[With "The two captains" in tr. of #1702.]
1797. do. 1886. Tr. anon. L: Cassell. 192p. 13cm. [BM]
["Undine" based on Tracy's tr. "The two captains" in tr. of #1694]
1798. do. 1886. [ad.] The spirit of the waters. A poem containing a version of the narrative, etc. By W: Hipsley. L: Stock. xiii; 184p. 19cm. [BM]
1799. do. 1888. Reissue of #1777. NY; Miller. [NY]
*1800. do. 1888. [same as #1768] Introd. by Julia Cartwright. Il. H. Sumner. L: Chapman & H. 174p. 8. [BM]
1801. do. 1888. Tr. anon. NY: Putnam. il. T. [AC]
1802. do. 1889. or, the naiad queen. Tr. anon. Pollard. 12. [AC]
*1803. do. 1895. Bunnett's tr. Phil: Altemus. 174p. 16. [NY]
**1804. do. 1896. Tr. (with a crit. study of F--) by Edmund Gosse. Il. W. E. F. Britten. L: Lawrence & Bullen. 189p. 8. [BPL]
*1805. do. 1897. [same] Il. F. M. Rudland. L: Lawrence & B. 286p. 19cm. [BM.BPL]
*1806. do. 1897. A tale. Tr. Abby L. Alger. Bost; L: Ginn. 106p. 18cm. [LC]
*1807. do. 1897. Bunnett's tr. Il. Rosie M. M. Pitman. L: Macmillan. xxiii;293p. 20cm. [BM.BPL]
*1808. do. 1899. Tracy's tr. U--, or, the water-spirit. Sintram, etc. NY: Appleton. 243p. il. 8. [LC]
1809. do. 1901-1902. Tr. anon. NY: Scribner. il. 16. [AC]
[With "Aslauga's knight."]
*1810. do. 1901. Tracy's tr. ed. Il. Harold Nelson. L: Newnes. xiii;192p. 20cm. [BM]
[With "Aslauga's knight," very well tr.]
*1811. do. 1902. [same] L: Newnes. [EC]
*1812. do. 1902. Bunnett's tr. A romantic fairy tale. Il. Jl. Höppner. Bost: Heath. 149p. 19cm. [LC]
1813. do. 1904. Tr. anon. NY: Putnam. (B13)
1814. do. 1905. Tr. anon. NY: Caldwell. (B13)
1815. do. 1905. sel. In C163.
*1816. do. 1908. A romance. Tr. G: P. Upton. Chic: McClurg. 138p. 17cm. [LC]
1817. do. 1908. Told to the children by Ma. Macgregor. Il. Kath. Cameron. L: Jack; NY: Dutton. xi;115p. 15cm. [LC.BM]
[Not a tr., but well done.]
§1818. do. 1909. Ad. W: L. Courtney. Il. A. Rackham. L: Heinemann; NY: Doubleday. 136p. 25cm. [BM.LC]
1819. do. 1909. [Ad.] U-- and Huldbrand. Founded on, etc. By T. R. N. Crofts. L; Methuen. 12. [EC]
*1820. do. 1911. Bunnett's tr.Il. F. B. Comstock. NY: McLoughlin. 126p. 24cm. [LC]
§1821. do. 1912. [reissue of #1818.] NY: Doubleday; L: Heinemann. [LC]
*1822. do. 1912. Gosse's tr. New ed. L: Sidgwick & J. 207p. 19cm. [BM]
1823. do. 1912. The story of U--. Ed. by Ma. Macleod (from #1775). Il. Gordon Browne. L: Wells Gardner. 133p. 16cm. [BM]
1824. do. 1913-15. Sel. Bunnett's tr. In C154.
1825. do. 1914. [Ad.] A poem ad. in part, etc. By Mrs. Antoinette Patterson. Fisher. 34p. O. [AC]
1826. The victim of priestcraft. Tr. anon. 1823. In C456.
1827. Violina: a miniature romance. Tr. anon. L: Clarke 1845. 134p. 12. [NY]
1828. (Wilde Liebe.) Wild love: a romance. Tr. anon. Phil: Ferrett 1845. 112p. 23cm. [LC]
1829. do. 1877. Tr. anon. NY: Routledge. 16. [AC]

FOUQUÉ, K:e A:e (v. Briest), Baronin de La Motte-, 1773-1831.
Sel. in C469.
1830. The castle on the beach: a tale. Tr. G: G. Cunningham. 1829. In C80.
§1831. (Die Vertriebenen.) The outcasts: a romance. Tr. G: Soane. L: Whittaker 1824. 2v. xv;258;287p. 18cm. [BM]
["I have allowed myself many deviations from the original...to render (it) generally acceptable."]
1832. (Die Verwünschung.) The curse. Freely tr. N. Stenhouse. Ed: Priv. prt. 1825. 15p. 21cm. [LC]
1833. The physician of Marseilles, (and three other) tales. Tr. anon. L: Burns 1845. 72;16;20;23p. 16cm. [BM.LC]
[Also: The Christmas tree; The revolutionists; Valerie.]
1834. do. 1854. [reissue] Sophie Ariele; or, the physician, etc. L: Lumley. [BM]
1835. Scharfenstein castle. Tr. R. P. Gillies. 1826. In C164.
1836. The turn coat, a vision, etc., in the night of the 7st [sic] of August 1814. Tr. anon. 1820. In C117,pp. 49-83.

FRAAS, Ok. 1824-97, G. H. v. SCHUBERT, and I. ROTH.
1837. Palästina. New album of the Holy Land, 50 views of important places...by I. M. Bernats...with...notes by (the above). 2d ed. Stuttgart. Steinkopf 1868. ff. 15. unp. 27 x 21cm. [BM]
[German, English, and French in parallel columns. Fraas supervised this ed. and commented on the last pictures on the death of the others.]

FRANCK, J: 1618-77. Sel. in C235;271;273;276;287;489;570;#8904.

FRANCK, S. 18th Cent. Sel. in C271;276;287.

FRANCKE, A: Hm. 1663-1727. Sel. in C240;244;276;287;486.
1838. Nicodemus; or, a treatise against the fear of man. Tr. from the High Dutch. 3d ed. Bost: Rogers & Fowle 1744. xxiv;180p. 16. (B6a)
1839. do. 1795. Tr. J: Wesley, M. A. late fellow of...Oxford. Phil: Prtd. by H: Tuckniss 1795. 50p. 12. (B6a) [Available: AAS. JCB]

FRANCKE, Hm.
1840. (Aschenbrödel.) Cinderella: cantata by F. Abt. Tr. Lewis Novra. Libr. Engl. L: Augener; NY: Schirmer 1879. 22p. 18cm. [BM]
1841. do. 1879. Vocal score. Engl. L: Augener; NY: Schirmer. 57p. 27cm. [Same tr.] [BMM]
*1842. (Das Märchen von den sieben Raben.) The seven ravens: a series of seven vocal pieces (by F. Abt.) connected by recitation. Tr. Ma. A. Robinson. Libr. NY: Schubert 1882. 14p. 12. [LCO]
*1843. do. 1882. Cantata by F. Abt. Tr. Ma. A. Robinson. Vocal score, Ger;Engl. Offenbach a. M. André. 46p. 33cm. [BMM]
*1844. do. 1900. Tr. E: Oxenford. Vocal score. L: Augener. 53p. 28cm. [BMM]
*1845. do. 1900. [same tr.] Libr. L: Augener; NY: Schirmer. 16p. 19cm. [BM]
1846. (Dornröschen.) Briar-rose: cantata by Fz. Abt. Tr. E: Oxenford. Libr. Engl. L: Augener; NY: Schirmer 1900. 16p. 18cm. [BM]
1847. do. 1900. [same tr.] Vocal score. Engl. L: Augener. 55p. col. t.p. 28cm. [BMM]
*1848. (Rotkäppchen.) Little red riding-hood: cantata by Fz. Abt. Tr. Eliz. M. Traquair. Libr. L: Augener 1878. 17p. 18cm. [BM]
*1849. do. 1879. [same tr.] Vocal score. L: Augener. 51p. col. t.p. 27cm. [BMM]
1850. (Schneeweisschen und Rosenrot.) Snowdrop and rosebud: cantata by C: Reinecke. Libr. Engl. NY: Schirmer 1890. 19p. 19cm. [BM]

FRANCKE, Hm.
1851. (Sneewittchen.) Little snow-white: cantata by Fz. Abt. Tr. E. M. Traquair. Libr. Engl. L: Augener; NY: Schirmer 1880. 19p. 18cm. [BM]
1852. do. 1880. [same tr.] Vocal score. Engl. L: Augener; NY: Schirmer. 47p. col. t.p. 27cm. [BMM]
1852a. do. 1915. [same?] Text ed. Sylvia Child. Bost: Birchard. [AC]

FRANCKE, O: Sel. in C563.

FRANCKENBERG, Abh. v.
1853. (Gründlicher und wahrhafter Bericht von dem Leben...J. Böhmens.) Memoirs of...J. Behmen. Tr. Fis. Okely. Northampton, Eng. For the translator 1780. 153p. 12. [LCO]

FRANÇOIS, Lu. v. 1817-93.
*1854. (Die letzte Reckenburgerin.) The last von Reckenburg. Tr. "J. M. Percival." 1st Amer. from 3d Ger. ed. Bost: Cupples & H. 1887. ix;370p. 19cm. [LC]
*1855. do. 1888. [same] L: Gardner. 370p. [BM]

FRANK, Bruno, 1887- .
1855a. The days of the king. Tr. by H. T. Lowe-Porter. NY: Knopf; L: Allen 1927. 165p. il. O. [AC]

FRANK, K: S. J.
*1856. (Die Entwicklungstheorie im Lichte der Tatsachen.) The theory of evolution in the light of facts...With a chapter on ant guests and termite guests by P. E. Wasmann. Tr. C: T. Druery. 48 il. L: K. Paul; St.L: Herder 1913 (1912). xii;241p. 21cm. [BM]

"FRANK, U:" (i.e., Frau Ulla (Hirschfeld) Wolff, 1850- .)
1857. Simon Eichelkatz; The patriarch. Two stories of Jewish life. Tr. anon. Phil: Jewish pub. soc. of Amer. 1907. 431p.19cm.[LC.BM]

FRANKE, O: Sel. in C563.

FRANKE, Wb.
1858. Voices from another world: the waking dreams and metaphysical phantasies of a non-spiritualist. Edited (i.e., written) by "F. Gurtis" (i.e., Wb. Franke). Tr. Lillian A. Clare. L: Unwin 1923. 244p. 21cm. [BM]

FRANKL, L: A: 1810-94. Sel. in C375;501.

FRANZ Js. I. K: emperor of Austria, 1830-1916.
**1859. (Fz. Js. I. in seinen Briefen.) Fz. Joseph as revealed in his letters. Ed. by O: Ernst. Tr. Ag. Blake. L: Methuen 1927. xi;304p. il. 22cm. [On the whole, excellent.] [BM]
[See Harden, M., Monarchs and men. #3701.]

FRANZ, Ag. 1794-1843. Sel. in C543.
1860. The best dowry; The friends; The rivals. Tr. "Trauermantel." 1857. In C547.

FRANZL, L. A. Sel. in C317.

FRANZOS, K: El. 1848-1904. Sel. in C501.
1861. (Der Präsident.) The chief justice. Tr. Miles Corbet. L: Heinemann; NY: Lovell 1890. 272p. 19cm. [BM.LC]
1862. do. 1915. The judge: a play in four acts. Tr. T: J. Block. Bost: Badger. 119p. 19cm. [Founded on the German.] [LC]
*1863. (Die Juden von Barnow.) The Jews of B--. (Stories.) Tr. M. W. Macdowall. Ed; L: Blackwood 1882. 341p. 19cm. [BM.LC]
[Not without error.]
1864. do. 1882. [same?] NY: Munro. Seaside lib. 33p. 32cm. [[illegible]]

FRANZOS, K: El. - Die Juden von Barnow
*1865. do. 1883. [same] NY: Appleton. 334p. 18cm. [LC]
*1866. (Ein Kampf ums Recht.) For the right. Tr. Julie Sutter. Pref. by G: Macdonald. L: Clarke 1887. x;531p. 19cm. [BM]
*1867. do. 1888. [same] NY: Harper. 198p. 21cm. [LC]
*1868. do. 1889. [same] New ed. L: Clarke. vii;278p. 19cm. [BM]
§1869. (Judith Trachtenberg.) J-- T--. Tr. Mrs. L. P. Lewis and C. T. Lewis. NY: Harper 1891. 221p. 21cm. [LC.BM]
[Good, but careless here and there.]
1869a. A Podolian sketch. Tr. G: C. Eyrick. "Lippincott's Mag." 21(1878): 365. (B15a)

"FRAPAN, Ilse" (i.e., Frau Ilse (Lévien) Akunian, 1852-1908.)
*1870. (Die Last). Heavy laden; and "Old fashioned folk." (Altmodische Leute.) Tr. Helen A. MacDonell. L: Unwin 1892. 216p. 18 x 9cm. [BM]
1871. God's will, and other stories. Tr. Helen A. MacDonell. L; NY: Cassell 1893. 214p. 18 x 9cm. [Also: Our Jenny; The old bookkeeper; A Christmas story; The first; The scorcher.] [LC]

FRAUENLOB. See Heinrich v. Meissen.

FREDERICH, Bta. (Heyn) 1825-82. See "Raimund, Golo"

FREIDANK, 13th cent. Sel. in C27.

"FREIER, Gst." See Lafontaine, A:

FREILIGRATH, Fd. 1810-76. Sel. in C3;5;17;37;40-1;43;45-6;50;67;75; 77;86;89;90;97;111-2;116;123;142;149;151;153;166;171;173*;180; 195-6;208;210;213;219;296;299;301*;309;311*;317;366;372*;373*; 374;382;391*;393*;395;397;423;428;448;460;467;469;489;497;499; 501;504-5;531;554;571; #4082.
**1872. (Gedichte.) Poems. Ed. by his daughter, Käthe Freiligrath Kroeker. Lpz: Tauchnitz; L: Low 1869. xviii;241p. 16cm. [BM]
[75 poems, mostly eclectic; 16 very well done by the editor.]
**1873. do. 1871. [same] 2d enl. ed. 260p. 16cm. [LC]
1874. Ireland's calamity. Tr. C. Peter. Detroit? 1880. 3p.23cm. [LC]

FRENSSEN, Gst. 1863- . Sel. in C366*.
§1875. (Die drei Getreuen.) The three comrades. Tr. L. Winstanley. L: Constable; Bost: Estes 1907. 362p. 20cm. [LC]
1876. do. 1907. [same?] L: Constable. 372p. 19cm. [BM]
§1877. (Hilligenlei.) Holyland. Tr. Ma. Ag. Hamilton. L: Constable; Bost: Estes 1906. 375p. 19cm. [LC]
§1878. (Jörn Uhl.) Tr. F. S. Delmer. Bost: Estes; L: Constable 1905. 416p. 19cm. [LC]
[Uses some Scotch expressions to give effect of dialect.]
§1879. do. 1913. [same] Introd. L: Lewisohn. NY: Boni & L. 17cm [LC]
§1880. do. 1922. [same] 416p. [LC]
§1881. (Klaus Hinrich Baas.) K-- H-- B--: the story of a self-made man. Tr. Esther E. Lape and Eliz. F. Read. NY: Macmillan 1911. 440p. 20cm. [LC.BM]
*1882. (Peter Moors Fahrt nach Südwest.) P-- M--'s journey to southwest Africa: a narr. of the Ger. campaign. Tr. Marg. M. Ward. Bost; NY: Houghton, Mifflin 1908. 244p. 19cm. [LC.BM]
*1883. do. 1914. [same] L: Constable. vii;247p. 18cm. [BM]

FREUD[1], Sg. 1856- .
1884. [Coll.] (Sammlung kleiner Schriften zur Neurosenlehre.) Coll. papers...Auth. tr. under the supervision of Joan Riviere. Vol. 1.

[1]While much of Freud's writing is technical, the widespread interest in psychoanalysis--witness the blackened and dog's-eared copies of his books in every library--has led me to include him here.

FREUD, Sg.
L: Internat. psycho-anal. press 1924. Early papers on the hist. of the psycho-anal. movement. Vol. 2. L: Woolf 1924. Clinical papers. Papers on technique. Vol. 3. L: Woolf 1925. Case histories. Tr. Alix and Jas. Strachey. 24cm. [BM]
[Papers regrouped in consultation with Freud.]
1885. [Coll.] 1909. Selected papers on hysteria and other psychoneuroses. Auth. tr. A. A. Brill. NY: Journal of nervous & mental disease pub. 200p. 25cm. [LC.BM]
[Brill's translations are mostly very good.]
1886. do. 1912. [same] 2d ed. ix;215p. [LC.BM]
1887. do. 1920. [same] 3d enl. ed. vi;225p. [LC.BM]
*1888. [Coll.] Three contrib. to the sexual theory. Auth. tr. A. A. Brill. NY: Journal of nervous and mental disease pub. 1910. 91p. 25cm. [LC.BM]
*1889. do. 1916. [same] 2d rev. & enl. ed. 117p. 24cm. [LC.BM]
*1890. do. 1918. [same] 3d rev. ed. NY; Washington. xii;117p. 24cm. [LC.BM]
**1891. (Das Ich und das Es.) The ego and the id (5 essays). Tr. Joan Riviere. L: Woolf 1927. 88p. 24cm. [Excellent tr.] [BM]
*1892. (Der Wahn und die Träume in W. Jensens "Gradiva.") Delusion and dream: an interpretation...of Gradiva, etc. Tr. Helen M. Downey. Introd. by G. Stanley Hall. NY: Moffat Yard 1917. 243p. 21cm. [Tr. of "Gradiva" is not quite so good.] [LC]
*1893. do. 1921. [same] L: Allen & Unwin. 213p. 22cm. [BM]
1893a. do. 1927. [same] NY: New Republic. 268p. D. [AC]
*1894. (Der Witz u. seine Beziehungen zum Unbewussten.) Wit and its relation to the unconscious. Auth. tr. A. A. Brill. NY: Moffat Yard 1916. vii;388p. 21cm. [Tr. is not wholly satisfying.][LC.BM]
*1895. do. 1922. [same] Reissue with diff. t.p. L: K. Paul. [BM]
§1896. (Die Frage der Laienanalyse.) Problem of lay-analyses. Introd. by S. Ferenczi. NY: Brentano 1927. 316p. 19cm. [BM]
[The "Problem" is rather poorly tr. by A. P. Märker-Branden. Follows an excellent tr.: "An autobiographical study" ("Selbstdarstellung") by Jas. Strachey.]
*1897. (Die Traumdeutung.) The interpretation of dreams. Auth. tr. from 3d ed. by A. A. Brill. L: Allen 1913. xiii;510p. 22cm[BM.LC]
[Not flawless, but very good.]
*1898. do. 1915. [same] 4th ed. L: Allen & U; NY: Macmillan. [LC]
*1899. do. 1923. [same] New ed. Tr. anon. NY: Macmillan. [LC]
1900. (Eine Kindheitserinnerung des Leonardo da Vinci.) L-- da V--: a psychosexual study of an infantile reminisc. Tr. A. A. Brill. NY: Moffat Yard 1916. 130p. il. 19cm. [LC.BM]
1901. do. 1922. [same] Reprint w. pref. by Ernest Jones. L: K.Paul. 130p. 23cm. [BM]
1901a. Inhibition, symptom and anxiety. Auth. tr. supv. L. Pierce Clark. NY: L.P.Clark 1927. 103p. O. [AC]
*1902. (Jenseits des Lustprinzips.) Beyond the pleasure principle. Auth. tr. from 2d Ger. ed. by Miss C. J. M. Hubback. Ed. by Ernest Jones. L; Vienna: Internat. psycho-anal. press 1922. 90p. 24cm. [BM.LC]
*1903. do. 1924. [same] NY: Boni & L. 90p. 23cm. [LC]
*1904. (Massenpsychologie und Ichanalyse.) Group psychology and the analysis of the ego. Auth. tr. Jas. Strachey. Ed. Ernest Jones. L; Vienna: Internat. psycho-anal. press 1922. 134p. 24cm. [BM.LC]
*1904a. do. 1924. [same] Ballou. 134p. O. [AC]
*1905. (Psychopathologie des Alltagslebens.) Psychopathology of everyday life. Auth. tr. from 4th Ger. ed. A. A. Brill. NY: Macmillan; L: Unwin 1914. vi;341 (BM: 342)p. 22cm. [LC.BM]
[Some of the cases modified or replaced by others.]
*1906. do. 1917. [same] [LC]

FREUD, Sg.
*1906a. do. 1926. [same] L: Unwin. 10th impr. 350p. 8. [EC]
1907. (Totem und Tabu.) Totem and taboo: resemblances between the psychic lives of savages and neurotics. Auth. tr. A. A. Brill. NY: Moffat Yard 1918. 265p. 21cm. [LC]
1908. do. 1919. [same] L; NY: Routledge. xii;268p. 22cm. [BM.LC]
1908a. do. 1927. [same] NY. New Republic. 297p. D. [AC]
*1909. (Über den Traum.) Dream psychology: psychoanalysis for beginners. Auth. tr. from 2d Ger. ed. M. D. Eder. Introd. W. Leslie Mackenzie. L: Heinemann 1914. xxxii;110p. 19cm. [BM] [One bad error on the first page.]
*1910. do. 1920. [same] Introd. André Tridon. NY: McCann. 237p. 22cm. [LC]
*1911. do. 1924. [same] NY: Mulligan. 237p. [AC]
§1912. (Vorlesungen zur Einführung in die Psychoanalyse.) General introd. to psychoanalysis. Auth. tr. anon. Introd. by G. Stanley Hall. NY: Boni & L. 1920. x;406p. 21cm. [LC.BM]
*1913. do. 1922. Introd. lectures on psycho-analysis. Auth. tr. Mrs. Joan Riviere. Pref. by Ernest Jones. L: Allen & U. 395p. 22cm. [BM.LC]
§1913a. do. 1927. [same as #1912] 17th ed. NY: Liveright. [AC]
*1914. (Zeitgemässes über Krieg und Tod.) Reflections on war and death. Auth. tr. A. A. Brill and Af. B. Kuttner. NY: Moffat Yard 1918. 72p. 18cm. [LC]
*1915. do. 1922. [same] 71p. [BM]
1916. (Zur Geschichte der psychoanalytischen Bewegung.) Hist. of the psychoanalytic movement. Auth. tr. A. A. Brill. NY: Nervous & mental disease pub. 1917. 58p. 25cm. [LC.BM]

FREUND, Jl. See Okonkowski, G:, joint author.

FREY, Andrew
1917. A true and authentic account of A. F...the occasion of his coming among the...Moravians, his observations on them...and the reasons for which he left them. Tr. anon. L: J.Robinson et al. 1753. 72p. 19cm. [Autobiographical.] [BM]

FREY, Henry. Sel. in C19.

FREY, L: Sel. in C63.

FREYLINGHAUSEN, J: Anst. 1670-1739. Sel. in C222-3;229;231-3;244; 269;271;276;570; #8904.

FREYTAG, Gst. 1816-95. Sel. in C366*;469.
*1918. (Bilder aus der deutschen Vergangenheit.) Pict. of Ger. life in the 15th, 16th, and 17th cent. Tr. Mrs. Malcolm. L: Chapman & H. 1862. 2v. 19cm. [LC]
1919. do. 1863. 2d ser...18th and 19th cent. Tr. Mrs. Malcolm. L: Chapman & H. 2v. 19cm. [LC]
*1920. (Der Kronprinz und die deutsche Kaiserkrone.) The crown prince and the Ger. imper. crown: reminisc. Tr. G: Duncan. L: Bell 1890. 130p. 19cm. [BM.BPL]
§1921. (Die Journalisten.) The journalists. Tr. anon. Cambridge. Sever 1888. 100p. 20cm. [Literally tr. Fair to good.] [LC]
§1922. do. 1888. Comedy in 4 acts. Tr. anon. Cambridge, Mass: Waterman & Amee. 100p. 20cm. [A critical tr.] [LC]
†1923. do. 1904. literally tr. Herb. Leslie. NY: Hinds, N. & E. 140p. 15cm. [LC]
*1924. do. 1913. Tr. R. T. House. In "The drama," no. 9(1913). [Not quite excellent.]
§1925. do. 1913-15. Tr. E. F. Henderson. In C154.
1926. do. 1916. Literal tr. Vivian E. Lyon. NY: Tr. pub. 159p. 15cm. [LC]

FREYTAG, Gst.
*1927. (Die Technik des Dramas.) The technique of the drama: an exposition of dram. comp. and art. Tr. from 6th Ger. ed. by E. J. MacEwan. Chic: Griggs 1895. 366p. 20cm. [LC]
*1928. (Die verlorene Handschrift.) The lost manuscript. Tr. Mrs. Malcolm. L: Chapman & H. 1865. 3v. 19cm. [BM.LC]
*1929. do. 1869. [same] NY: Appleton. 8. [AC]
*1930. do. 1880. [sel.] The Ger. professor. Tr. Zimmern. In C575-7.
1931. do. 1887. Tr. from 16th Ger. ed. anon. Chic: Open ct; L: Arnold. 2pt. 8. [BM]
1931a. do. 1888. [same] Tr. anon. "Open court," 1(1888):646,etc.
1932. do. 1890. [same] Open ct. 2v. [LC card]
1933. do. 1891. Tr. anon. NY: Appleton. 259p. 24cm. [LC]
[In double columns.]
1934. do. 1892. [same as #1931] Chic; L: Open court. 2pt. in 1 vol. 20cm. [LC]
1935. do. 1898. [same] Open court. 544p. [NY]
†1936. (Erinnerungen aus meinem Leben.) Reminisc. of my life. Tr. Kath. Chetwynd. L: White 1890. 2v. 12. [LC]
1937. Frederick the great. Tr. E. H. Babbitt. 1913-15. In C154(12).
*1938. (Ingo.) Ingo: the first novel of..."Our forefathers." Tr. Mrs. Malcolm. NY: Holt & W. 1873. 327p. 17cm. [LC]
*1939. (Ingraban.) Ingraban: the second novel, etc. Tr. Mrs. Malcolm. NY: Holt & W. 1873. 304p. 17cm. [LC]
*1940. do. 1873. [same as two foregoing.] L: Asher. 2v. 327;304p. 19cm. [BM]
*1941. (Dr. Luther.) Mn. L--. Tr. H: E. O. Heinemann. Chic: Open court 1897. 130p. il. 8. [LCO.BM]
*1942. do. 1913-15. Doctor L--. Tr. E. H. Babbitt. In C154(12).
*1943. do. 1916. Tr. G. C. L. Riemer. Phil: Lutheran pub. 203p. il. 19cm. [LC]
*1944. (Soll und Haben.) Debit and credit. Pref. Bunsen. Tr. Mrs. Malcolm. L: Smith Elder 1856. xii;519p. 22cm. [BM]
*1945. do. 1857. [same] L: Hamilton. 2v. 8. [BM]
†1946. do. 1857. Tr. L. C. C(umming). Ed: Constable. 2v. 17cm. [LC]
[Tr. cuts ruthlessly.]
§1947. do. 1857. Debtor and creditor: a romance. Tr. W: J. Stewart. L: Blackwood. viii;315p. 17cm. [BM]
[On cover: "Speculation or debtor and creditor." Rather poorly done; not overly particular.]
*1948. do. 1857. Malcolm's tr. L: Bentley. 500p. 19cm. [BM.LC]
[LC has: 1858.]
†1949. do. 1858. Cumming's tr. NY: Harper. 564p. D. [AC]
*1950. do. 1873? Malcolm's tr. L: Ward, Lock. 503p. 17cm. [BM]
1951. do. 1876. [same?] New ed. L: Ward & L. 12. [EC]
*1952. do. 1882. Malcolm's tr. NY: Munro. Seaside lib. 2v. 32cm [LC]
†1953. do. 1893. Cumming's tr. NY: Harper. 564p. 20cm. [LC]
†1954. do. 1909. [same] NY: Abbatt. 564p. 20cm. [LC]

FRICKER, Barth.
1955. Baden in Switzerland. Tr. anon. 40p. il. In C294.

FRICKER, K:
*1956. (Antarktis.) The antarctic regions...with maps, pl. and il. Tr. A. Sonnenschein. L: Swan Sonnenschein 1900. xii;292p. 23cm. [BM]

FRIED, Af. Hm. 1864- .
1957. A brief outline of the nature and aims of pacifism. Tr. J: Mez. NY: Amer. ass'n for internat. concil. 1915. 19p. 19cm. [LC]
§1958. (Das Tagebuch eines zum Tode Verurteilten.) The diary of a condemned man. Tr. S. van Straalen. L: Heinemann 1899. viii;177p. 18cm. [BM]

FRIED, Af. Hm.
†1959. (Der Kaiser und der Weltfrieden.) The Ger. emperor and the peace of the world. Tr. anon. L; NY: Hodder & S. 1912. xx;214p. 21cm. [Careless; alters at will.] [BM.LC]
1960. A dozen truths about pacifism. Tr. J: Mez. NY: Amer. ass'n for internat. concil. 1915. 7p. 19cm. [LC]
§1961. (Europäische Wiederherstellung.) The restoration of Europe. Tr. L. S. Gannett. NY: Macmillan 1916. xiv;157p. 19cm. [LC.BM] [Tr. makes the style rather childish, and alters the sense.]
1962. Fundamental causes of the world war. NY: Amer. ass'n for internat. concil. 1915. 14p. 19cm. [LC]
1963. Internat. co-operation. Tr. anon. Newcastle-on-Tyne: Richardson 1918. 16p. 21cm. [LC]

FRIEDERICHS, K: 1831-71.
§1964. (Bausteine.) Greek sculpture: selections, etc. Tr. and ed. D. C. Eaton. New Haven, Ct: Tuttle, M.& T. 1881-3. 5v. 19cm. [LC] -- BM has: Pt. 3. Period of the highest devel. 107p. [Text is treated quite freely.]
1965. Handbook of Greek and Roman sculpture. 2d rev. and enl. ed. Tr. anon. Bost: Osgood 1884. 415p. 19cm. [LC.BM]

FRIEDERIKE So. W:e, Markgräfin v. Bayreuth, 1709-58. Sel. in C366. ("W:e v. Bayreuth.")
§1966. (Memoiren der Prinzessin..1709-42.) Memoirs...written by herself. Tr. from the French (which is a garbled and often incorrect tr. of the German). anon. L: Colburn 1812. 2v. 21cm. [BM]
§1967. do. 1828. [same] L: Hunt & Clarke. 2v. 15cm. [BM.LC]
§1968. do. 1877. [same] With an essay by W: D. Howells. Bost: Osgood. 2v. 15cm. [Probably a reprint of the foregoing]
*1969. do. 1887. Tr. Princess Christian of Schleswig Holstein. L: Stott. 458p. 23cm. [BM.LC] [Not wholly satisfactory; not closely faithful.]
§1970. do. 1905. [Reissue of #1968.] Bost: Houghton Mifflin. [LC]
See "Horn, G:," The margravine of Bayreuth and Voltaire, #4581.

FRIEDHEIM, M. Sel. in C466.

FRIEDLAENDER, L: 1824-1909.
**1971. (Darstellungen aus der Sittengeschichte Roms.) Roman life and manners under the early empire. L: Routledge; NY: Dutton 1908-13. 4v. 20cm. Vol. 1. tr. L. A. Magnus; vol. 2. tr. Magnus and J: H: Freese; vol. 3. tr. Freese; vol. 4. tr. A. B. Gough. [The work of all three tr. seems excellent.] [LC.BM]
1972. (Städtewesen in Italien im ersten Jahrhundert.) Town life in ancient Italy. Tr. W: E. Waters. Bost: Sanborn 1902. 62p. 20cm. [LC]

FRIEDLAENDER, L: Hm.
§1973. (Ansichten von Italien.) Views in Italy during a journey... 1815-16. In New voyages and travels. L: R:Phillips 1821. 124p. 21cm. [BM] [General title page has: 1820. Orig. is much pruned, but I observed no errors.]

FRIEDMANN, Af.? 1845- . Sel. in C501.

FRIEDRICH I, called Barbarossa, d. 1190. See Kühn, Fz., Barbarossa, #5488.

FRIEDRICH, Herzog v. Württemberg, 1554-93. Sel. in C483.

FRIEDRICH II, called the Great, king of Prussia, 1712-86. Sel. in C12;63.

FRIEDRICH II

*1974. Posthumous works. Tr. T: Holcroft. L: Robinson 1789. 13v. 21cm. [BM.LC]
[Vol. 1. xxvii,241;301p. The hist. of my own times ("L'histoire de mon temps.") Vols. 2,3. xv;313;376p. Hist. of the 7 years' war ("Hist. de la guerre de sept ans"). Vol. 4. viii;386p. Memoirs from the peace of Hubertusberg to the partition of Poland, and of the Bavarian war ("Mémoires depuis la paix de H-- jusqu' à la paix de Teschen"). Vol. 5. 393p. Polit., philosoph. and satyrical miscellanies. Vols. 6-13. 544;521;562;440;499;463;512;520p. Corr. with Voltaire, Marchioness du Chatelet, M. Jordan, M. de Fontenelle, M. Rollin, Count Algarotti, Marquis d'Argens, M. d'Alembert, M. de Condorcet, M. Grimm, M. d'Arget, Gen. Fouquet. Miscellanies.- Mostly prose works; poetic items, e.g., "Dialogues of the dead," are done into prose.]

1975.[Sel.] 1786. In Johnson, S:, Memoirs of C: F: To which are added tr. of select poems, written by the king of Prussia. L: Harrison. 20cm. [BM]
[Contains: Ode to courage; Epistle to Voltaire, tr. J: Gilbert Cooper; Ode to death, Tr. Dr. Hawkesworth.]

§1976.[Sel.] 1788. Characteristic anecdotes, etc. (Chiefly from Anekdoten und Charakterzüge aus dem Leben F:s II.) Notes and pref. [and probably tr.] B. H. Latrobe. L: J:Stockdale. xxii;342p. 21cm. [Includes 19 misc. letters. Very freely handled.] [BM]

†1977. (Anzeige der Ursachen...) A view of the motives which have obliged the king...to grant auxil. unto his imperial majesty. Tr. anon. L: Mary Cooper 1744. 24p. 19cm. [BM]
[Pp. 16-21. Tr. is anything but accurate.]

1978. do. 1756. Motives which have obliged his majesty...to prevent the designs of the court of Vienna. Tr. anon. Berl; L: Fr. and Eng. 4. [BM]

§1979. (Avant-propos sur la "Henriade" de M. Voltaire.) The king of Prussia's criticism on the Henriad of M. de V--. Tr. anon. L: Rivington 1758. 34p. (pp. 1-16.) 20cm. [Tr. is not very good][BM]

*1980. (Correspondance de Voltaire avec le roi de Prusse.) Letters of V -- and F: the Gt. Sel. and tr. w. introd. R: Aldington. L: Routledge 1927. xviii;395p. 22cm. [BM]
[223 of the orig. 654 letters are tr. wholly or in part.]

*1981. (Correspondance familière et amicale...) Familiar and friendly corr...w. M. F. de Suhm. Tr. anon. L: Robson & Clarke etc. 1787. xv;371p. 21cm. [BM]

§1982. (Eloge de Voltaire.) The panegyric of V--. Tr. anon. L: Murray 1779. viii;56p. 19cm. [Very free and not adequate][BM.LCO]

*1983. (Eloge du prince Henri.) Elogy on Prince H: of Prussia. Tr. anon. L: P.Elmsly 1768. 48p. 17cm. [BM]

*1984. (Epître à Maupertuis.) The 7th epistle attempted in Eng... Tr. anon. L: T. Osborne and W. Owen 1761. 14p. 33cm. [BM]
[Tr. cuts down the orig., but without essential loss.]

§1985. (Epître...à M. Voltaire.) An epistle...to M. V--. Tr. anon. L: Dodsley 1758. Fr. and Engl. 11p. 24cm. [BM]

§1986. do. 1758. [same] 2d ed. [BM]

*1987. (Examen du prince de Machiavel.) Anti-Machiavel. In "The works of N: Machiavel." Tr. Ellis Farneworth. L: Davies 1762. 2v. 26cm. Vol. 1, pp. 467-703. [BM.LC]

*1988. do. 1775. [same] 2d ed. [BM.LC]
["Examen" is in vol. 2. of this ed.]

*1989. (Instruction militaire du roi de Prusse pour ses généraux.) Mil. instructions...written by the king of Prussia to the generals of his army. Il. w. copper-plates. Tr. by an officer (from the French). L: Becket & De Hondt 1762. xv;246p. 20cm. [BM]

FRIEDRICH II - Instruction
["Dictée en allemand par le roi, et traduite en Français par M. Faesch, lieutenant colonel dans les troupes saxonnes."]
1990. do. 1797. (also) Particular instruction to the officers of his army. Tr. Lieut. T. Foster. Sherborne. W: Cruttwell. 2 pts. 176;112p. 19cm. [BM]
1991. do. 1818. [same] 5th ed. Sherborne. Cruttwell. 150; 102p. 23cm. [LC]
§1992. (L'art de la guerre.) The art of war: a poem in 6 books. Tr. Sa. Hamilton. L: Mawman 1826. 131p. 30cm. [BM]
*1993. (Le delassement de la guerre.) The relaxation of war...a poem...written by his majesty, etc. Tr. anon. L: W. Prat 1758. 11p. 24cm. [BM]
1994. do. 1758. The relaxation of war; or, the hero's philosophy. A poem. Tr. anon. Phil: Prtd. by W. Dunlap. Also, NY: Prtd. by Hugh Gaine. (B6a)
§1995. (L'école du monde.) The school of the world: a comedy. Tr. anon. In "Lady's Mag." 20(1789):476, etc. (B26) [Not very good.]
†1996. (Les Matinées du roi de Prusse.) [1]Royal matins; or, Prussia's public confession in five mornings. From the French. By a gentlemen of the U. of Cambridge. Cambridge: J:Archdeacon 1768. 58p. 21cm. [BM]
[Quite garbled and unreliable.--Only one 18th cent. ed. had six mornings, the 6th dealing with the army.]
*1997. do. 1770? Royal mornings. Tr. anon. n.i. (London?) 82p. 12cm. [5 mornings, like the foregoing.] [BM]
*1998. do. 1798. [same] Royal mornings: Frederic loquitur. L: D:Steel. 78p. 16cm. [5 mornings.] [BM.LC]
§1999. do. 1870. Tr. anon. Mornings with F: the Gt. Glasgow. 8.[BM]
[Clippings from the "Glasgow Herald" pasted in a notebook. Tr. from "La Politique prussienne d'après F: II," pub. 1870 in Paris. Tr. is not sure of his French, or is indifferent.]
§2000. do. 1870. Origin of the Bismarck policy; or, the Hohenzollern doctrine and maxims described and defined by F: the Gt. Tr. M. C. L(eadreyt?) Bost: Crosby & Damrell. 52p. 19cm. [BM]
[5 mornings.]
§2001. do. 1897. The 5 mornings of the king of Prussia. Tr. Col. S. H. S. Inglefield. L: Gibbings. 96p. 17cm. [BM]
[Quite free; seems to be somewhat paraphrased.]
*2002. do. 1901. F: the gt. on kingcraft. W. reminisc. and Turkish stories. By Sir W: Whittall. L: Longmans. viii;236p. 22cm.[BM.LC]
[Contains the (6) "Matinées" in a copy of an original MS, pp. 67-116, and literal Engl. tr., pp. 15-66. Pref. gives interesting account of the source of the MS.]
*2003. do. 1914. Confessions of the F: the gt; and, The life of F:...by H: v. Treitschke. Ed. w. introd. by Douglas Sladen. L: Hutchinson. 191p. pa. 18cm. [BM]
[On cover: The origin of v. Bernhardi's gospel of inhumanity. Has 7 mornings, the last one probably spurious; see note to #1996]
*2004. do. 1915. same. Foreword by G: Haven Putnam. L; NY: Putnam's. xxv;208p. 19cm. [LC]
*2004a. (Lettres au public.) (Three) letters to the public. Tr. anon. L: W. Owen 1753. 29p. 18cm. [BM]
*2005. (Lettre sur l'éducation.) Letter upon education. 2d ed. Tr. anon. L: Nourse 1777. 130p. 15cm. [BM]
§2006. (Louis XV aux Champs Elysées: drame en vers.) Louis (the Bourbon) in the Elysian Fields: a dialogue or drama. In Charon, Sermons from Styx (by Hargrave Jennings). L: W.H.Allen 1886. 80p. 18cm. [BM]
[Pp. 1-20. Prose from verse, but sense well rendered. Taken from #1974.]

[1]For a careful and probably definitive study of the authorship of this curious document, see an article by Lionel Giles in "The Library," April 1902, p. 148 seq. Giles comes to the conclusion that Frederick actually was the author, and that there are six "Matinées" in the original, which has been lost. A seventh "Matinee" on finance, which crept in around 1800, is probably a forgery; and one on manners and gallantry, which made its first appearance in a French ed. of 1871, is clearly invented.

FRIEDRICH II
*2007. (Mémoires...pour servir à l'histoire de Brandebourg.) Memoirs of the house of Brandenburg. Tr. anon. L: Dodsley 1748. 56p. 20cm. [Goes as far as F: W: der grosse Kurfürst.] [BM]
*2008. do. 1751. A different tr. L: Nourse. 286p. 16cm. [BM] [To the death of F: I, with two "dissertations" added.]
*2009. do. 1757. [same tr.] L: Nourse. 286p. 16cm. [BM] [Identical with foregoing. Bound with it are A preliminary discourse to the whole work and two further dissertations, 66p. with a sep. t.p.]
*2010. do. 1758. [same] Nourse. 340p. [BM] [All the matter of the foregoing freshly prt. in one vol.]
*2011. do. 1758. [same] 3d ed. Dublin: Wilson & Exshaw. 2 pts. 162; 35p. front. maps. 21cm. [LC]
*2012. do. 1768. Vol. II. Tr. anon. L: Nourse. 242p. [BM] [Continues from the death of F: III (i.e., F: I) to death of F: W:, the father of F: II.]
§2013. An Ode...after the victory at Rosbach. Tr. anon. L: J. Staples 1758. Fr. and Engl. 7p. 24cm. [BM]
§2014. (Sylla.) Sylla: a dram. entertainment presented...27th March 1753. Tr. S: Derrick (in verse from the orig. prose, which he follows closely.) L: P.Vaillant et al. 1753. vii;39p. 21cm. [BM]
See Freytag, G., F: the Gt. #1937.
See Grimm, Hm., Literature, #3132.
See Kugler, Fz., Life of F: the Gt, #5507.
See Mühlbach, Lu., #6385; #6390; #6408; #6409; #6413.
See Raumer, F:, Contributions to mod. hist., #7343.
See Schrader, Fd., F: the Gt. and the 7 years' war, #8616.
See Zimmermann, J:, Select views of...F: the Gt., #10625. Also his Conversations with (Frederick), #10660.

FRIEDRICH III, called der Fromme, Kurfürst v. d. Pfalz, 1515-74.
2015. (Christliche Konfession...) A Christ. confession of the late ...Prince Friderich...taken word for word out of his last will and testament. Tr. anon. L: C.Barkar 1577. ff.A-F. 13cm. [BM]

FRIEDRICH III, deutscher Kaiser, 1831-88.
2016. (Das Tagebuch des Kronprinzen. Aussprüche, Briefe u. andere Kundgebungen.) The crown prince of Germany: a diary. Tr. and comp. anon. L: Low 1886. 275p. 19cm. [BM] [Many of the prince's letters and speeches are in part tr., also other German documents, with extracts from his diary.]
2017. do. 1888. New and cheaper ed. Tr. anon. L: Low. 275p. 21cm. [BM]
2018. (Kaiser F:s Tagebuch.) The suppressed diary of the late emperor F-- The only complete and unabridged ed. Tr. anon. L: Pall Mall Gazette 1888. 16p. [BM] [Prob. from a French tr. of parts of article in the "Deutsche Rundschau."]
2019. do. 1888. The emperor's diary of the Austro-German war 1866 and the Franco-German war 1870-71. To which is added, Prince Bismarck's rejoinder. Ed. by H. W. Lucy. L: Routledge. 144p. 16cm. [Not from the same text as the foregoing, but probably [BM] also via the French.]
*2020. do. 1902. Diaries...also journeys to the east and to Spain. Ed. by Mge. v. Poschinger. Tr. Fes. A. Welby. L: Chapman & H. xiii;368p. 22cm. [Includes, pp. 192-262, the famous [BM.LC] 'Tagebuch' as pub. in the "Rundschau," being excerpts from the orig. by H: Geffcken.]
**2021. do. 1927. The war diary of the emperor F: III, 1870-71. Tr. and ed. A. R. Allinson. L: S.Paul. xi;355p. il. 21cm. [BM]

FRIEDRICH III
[Valuable Foreword gives hist. of 4 successive recensions of the celebrated diary, of which the fullest is here tr.]

FRIEDRICH H: L: called Prinz H: 1726-1802. See Friedrich II, Elogy on Prince H: #1983.

FRIEDRICH W: der grosse Kurfürst, 1620-88.
2022. A letter...to the king of France, declaring the reasons...to take up arms against the king of Sweden. Tr. from the Latin. L: J:Crooke. 6p. 18cm. [BM]
2023. A letter...to Richard lord protector...on the protecting and defending of the reformed protestant cause. Tr. from the Latin. L: 1659. 4. [BM]
See Mühlbach, Lu., The reign of the great elector, #6398. Also, The youth of the great elector, #6400.

FRIEDRICH W:, König von Preussen, 1770-1840.
2024. A letter...to...the...duchess of Coethens, on...her conversion to...the church of Rome. Tr. anon. L: Hatchard 1826. 8p. 21cm. [BM]
See Eylert, R., The religious life and opinions..., #1542.

FRIEDRICH W: Kronprinz, see Wilhelm, Kronprinz von Preussen.

FRIEDRICH VON HAUSEN, 1140?-1190. Sel. in C27;427.

FRIEDRICH VON LEININGEN, fl. 1214-39. Sel. in C27.

FRIEDRICH, F: 1828-90.
2025. (Die Frau des Arbeiters.) The workingman's wife. Tr. Hettie E. Miller. Chic: Weeks 1894. 264p. 20cm. [LC]
2026. (Die verschwundene Depesche.) The lost despatch. Tr. L. A. Williams. Bost: Osgood 1871. 107p. 24cm. [LC]--Estes 1871. [AC]
2027. Gone: a drama in three acts. Ad. by "Ryam Notlag" (Ma. Galton.) 1871. (B38)

"FRIEDRICH, W:" (i.e., F: W: Riese)
§2028. (Alessandro Stradella.) Stradella: romantic opera in three acts by Flotow. Tr. anon. Libr. Ger. and Engl. NY: Acad. of music n.d. 19p. 25cm. [Rather poor] [LCM]
§2029. do. 1863. [same] Libr. Ger;Engl. NY: Acad. of music. 19p. 25cm. [LCM]
*2030. do. 1867. Tr. E. H. Hesse and G. G. Gibson. St.L: 1867. [Engl. text without dialog. Good tr.] [LCM]
§2031. (Martha.) Martha: opera in 4 acts by Flotow. Libr. Ital;Engl. Tr. anon. NY: 1857. 15p. 4. [LC]
[Italian poor. English fair to good, but poor rhymes or none.]
§2032. do. 1857. Engl. version and the music of the principal airs. Tr. anon. Ital. and Engl. L: Davidson. 31p. 24cm. [BMM]
[Engl. is line for line from the Ital.]
†2033. do. 1860. Libr. Ital;Engl. Tr. anon. Bost: Ditson. 31p. 8. [LC]
†2034. do. 1860. [same] Vocal score. Ital;Ger;Engl. Bost: Ditson. 230p. 4. [LC]
†2035. do. n.d. [same] Libr. Ed. by G: W. Tryon, Jr. Phil: Lee & Walker. 15p. 28cm. [Verse identical with that in foregoing.] [LCM]
§2036. do. 1863. [same as #2031.] Libr. Ger;Engl. NY: Acad. of mus. 29p. 4. [LC]
†2037. do. 1865. Libr. Ital;Engl. Tr. anon. NY: Acad. of mus. 43p. 23cm. [Poor Eng. from poor Ital.] [LCM]
†2038. do. 1867. [same as #2033.] Ad. C. M. Richings. As performed by the Richings opera co. Libr. Eng. Phil: Ledger prt. 27p. 23cm. [LCM]

"FRIEDRICH, W:"--Martha.
†2039. do. 1871. [same as #2037] Libr. Ital;Engl. Tr. anon. NY: Bryant. 43p. 23cm. [LC]
2040. do. 1871. Tr. anon. Ed. Art. Sullivan. Libr? L: Boosey. 8.[EC]
†2041. do. 1871. [same as #2037] Libr. Engl. NY: Theatre ticket office. 43p. 23cm. [LCM]
2042. do. 1871. Tr. anon. Vocal score. Ital;Engl. L; NY: Boosey. 248p. 25cm. [BMM]
†2043. do. 1872. [same as #2037] Libr. NY: Nesbitt. 43p. 8. [LCM]
†2044. do. n.d. [same] Libr. Ital;Engl. NY: Acad. of mus. 23p. 6p. music. 8. [LCM]
2045. do. 1874. Opera in 5 acts. Ad. and rev. Ca. L. Kellogg (from #2033). Libr. Engl. Balto: Sun prt. 32p. 22cm. [LCM]
2046. do. 1874. The fair at Richmond: comic romantic opera. Tr. anon. L: Novello. 8. [EC]
2047. do. 1874. Tr. N. Macfarren. Vocal score. Ger;Engl. L: Novello; NY: Peters. 247p. 28cm. [BMM]
[Cf. paging of #2042.]
2048. do. 1875. Arr. and ad. (i.e., shortened from #2033) by E: S. Payson for Redpath opera co. Libr. Bost. 12p. 4. [LC]
†2049. do. 188-. [same as #2034] Libr. Ital;Engl. NY: Rullman. 27p. 8. [5p. music.] [LCM]
†2050. do. 188-. [same] Libr. Engl. 26p. 8. [6p. music.] [LCM]
†2051. do. 1888. [same as #2033] Vocal score. Bost: Ditson. 4.[LCM]
§2052. do. 1891. Libr. Engl. Tr. anon. L: Turner's opera co. 30p. 17cm. [BM]
†2053. do. 1902. [same as #2047] Vocal score. Ger;Engl. NY: Schirmer. 246p. 4. [LCM]
†2054. do. 1913. Engl. ed. by M. Louise Baum. Libr. Engl. Bost: Burchard. 42p. 8. [LC]
2055. do. 1916. or, the market at Richmond. Arr. and ed. El. Kreuz. Tr. N. Macfarren. Vocal score. Ger;Engl. L: Novello; NY: Gray. 154p. 26cm. ["The usual cuts have been adopted."] [BMM]
2056. do. 1925. [ad] Story retold by J. W. McSpadden. In C390.

FRIEDRICH-FRIEDRICH, Emmy. See "Rhoden, Emma v."

FRIES, Jg. N: 1823-94.
2057. (<u>Bilderbuch zum heiligen Vater Unser.</u>) Homes in Schafhausen: stories from the seven petitions of the Lord's prayer. Tr. from 10th Ger. ed. by Ma. E. Ireland. Burlington, Ia: Ger. lit. bd. 1913. 183p. 18cm. [LC]
2058. The emigrants. Tr. Ma. E. Ireland. Columbus, O: Luth. bk. concern 1918. 94p. pl. 19cm. [LC]
2059. Twilight and dawn. Rock I., Ill: Augustana bk. concern 1926. 124p. il. 17cm. [LC]

FRIES, R.
2060. Gretchen; or, the day-laborer's daughter. Tr. anon. Amer. tract soc. 1873. il. 16. [AC]
2061. The uhlan's wife. Tr. anon. Amer. tract soc. 1874. il. 16[AC]

FROBENIUS, Hm. 1841-1916.
*2062. (<u>Des Deutschen Reiches Schicksalsstunde.</u>) The German empire's hour of destiny. Pref. by Sir Valentine Chirol. Tr. W. H. B. L: Longmans 1914. 137p. 18cm. [Some errors noted.] [BM]
*2063. do. 1914. [same] Germany's hour of destiny. Pref. by W: R. Shepherd. Fatherland 1914. 64p. unb. O. [AC]

FROBENIUS, Leo, 1873- .
2064. (<u>Aus den Flegeljahren der Menschheit.</u>) The childhood of man: a pop. account of the lives, customs, and thoughts of the primitive races. Tr. A: H: Keane. L: Seeley 1909. xviii;504p. 415 il. 23cm. [BM.LC]

FROBENIUS, Leo
2065. Marriage and matriarchy. Tr. anon. 1926. In C308.
*2066. (Und Afrika sprach.) The voice of A--...exploration 1910-12. Tr. Rd. Blind. L: Hutchinson 1913. 2v.714p. il. 25cm. [LC] [BM has: xxiii;349;682p.--Vols. 1 and 2 of the German, adding and omitting one chapter.]

FROEBEL, F: W: A: 1782-1852. Sel. in C366*;469.
*2067. (Autobiographisches.) Autobiog. Tr. and annotated by E. Michaelis and H: K. Moore. L: Sonnenschein 1886. 144p. 8. [BM] [Two letters, one to the Duke of Meiningen, the other to K: Cph. F: Krause.]
*2068. do. 1886. [same] NY: Kellogg. [LC]
*2069. do. 1887. [same] NY: Kellogg. S. [AC]
*2070. do. 1889. [same] Syracuse, NY: Bardeen. 167p.21cm. [LC]
*2071. do. 1899. [same] 7th ed. L: Sonnenschein. 168p. 18cm. [BM]
*2072. do. 1901. [same] New ed. 172p. [EC]
*2073. do. 1903. [same] 9th ed. L: Sonnenschein. 168p. [BM]
*2074. do. 1906. [same] New ed. 172p. Sonnenschein. [EC]
*2075. do. 1908. [same] 11th ed. 174p. Sonnenschein. [EC]
*2076. do. 1916. [same] 12th ed. L: Allen & U. [EC]
2077. (Mutter- und Koselieder.) Mother-play and nursery songs, with notes to mothers. Tr. anon. Lee & S. 1879. il. 4. [AC]
§2078. do. 1885. Mother's songs, games, and stories. Tr. Fes. and Emily Lord. L: Rice. xxxi;212; 75p. (music). 22cm. [BM]
§2079. do. 1888. [same] New. rev. ed. L: Rice. 2 pts. xxxvi;212; 75p. (music). 22cm, [BM]
§2080. do. 1890. [same] L: Rice. 212; 75p. [LC]
?2081. do. 1895. The mottoes and commentaries of...mother play... rendered into Engl. verse by Mrs. Henrietta R. Eliot. Prose commentaries tr. Susan E. Blow. NY: Appleton; L: Arnold. xxii; 316p. il. 18cm. [Very freely adapted.] [LC.BM]
?2082. do. 1896. Songs and music of...mother play. Songs newly tr. and furnished with new music. Prep. and arr. by S. E. Blow. NY: Appleton; L: Arnold. xv;272p. il. 18cm. [LC] [Supposedly tr. by various hands; really new rhymes.]
2083. do. 1906. Poetry, music and pictures for the noble culture of child life. Tr. Fannie E. Dwight and J. Jarvis. Ed. by Eliz. P. Peabody. Bost: Lothrop, L. & S. 192p. 30 x 23cm. [LC]

FROEBEL, Jl. 1805-93.
2084. Seven years' travel in Central Amer., Northern Mexico, and the far west of the U. S. Rev. and tr. by the auth. from Aus Amerika, bks. 2, 4, 5. L: Bentley 1859. 586p. il. 22cm. [BM.LC]

FROEHLICH, Abh. Em. 1796-1865. Sel. in C438; #6209a.

FROEHLICH, K: Hm.
2085. K: F--'s frolicks with scissars [sic] and pen. The rhymes tr. and ad...Mme. de Chatelain. L: Joseph, Myers 1860. viii;25p. 8. [Prt. on one side of the paper.] [BM]
2086. do. 1863. [same] L: Myers. [EC]
2087. do. 1879. [same?] NY: Worthington. 8. [AC]

FROEHLICH-BUM, Lili.
2088. Ingres: his life and art. Tr. Maude V. White. L: Heinemann 1926. viii;66p. 79pl. 31cm. [Name misprinted: Bume.] [BM]

FROSCHAMMER, Jk. 1821-93.
2089. The romance of Romanism. Tr. W. H. Ed: D: Douglas 1878. 86p. 21cm. [BM]

FROMMANN, I. U. Sel. in C244.

FROMMEL, El. 1828-96.
2090. Heinerle von Lindelbronn. Tr. anon. Phil: Luth. pub. 1886[AC]

FUCHS, Rld.
2091. Helga: a tale in verse. Tr. K. I. Priv. prt. Lerwick. Johnson & Greig 1897. 47p. 16cm. [BM]

FUELÖP-MILLER, René Js. Gg. 1891- .
*2092. (Geist und Gesicht des Bolschewismus.) The mind and face of Bolshevism. Tr. F. S. Flint and D. F. Tait. L; NY: Putnam 1927. xvi;308p. 26cm. [BM]
*2093. (Lenin u. Gandhi.) L-- and G--. Tr. F. S. Flint and D. F. Tait. L; NY: Putnam 1927. xi;343p. 22cm. [BM]

FUETER, E: 1876- .
*2094. (Weltgeschichte.) World history, 1815-1920. Tr. S. B. Fay. NY: Harcourt; L: Methuen 1922. 490p. 21cm. [LC.BM]

FUGGER news letters. See Klarvill, V: v., ed., #5009.

FULDA, L: 1862- . Sel. in C405a; 423.
2095. (Das verlorene Paradies.) The lost paradise. Tr. anon. Ad. H: C. De Mille. NY: Goldmann, printer, 1897. 77p. 19cm. [LC] [No apparent relation to original.]
2096. do. 1898. or, work and wages. Ad. J: A. Fraser. Chic. Tw.[LC]
2097. (Der Dummkopf.) The blockhead: a comedy in 5 acts. Tr. J. L. Jones. Chic: 1908. (B38)
2098. (Die Jugendfreunde.) Friends of youth: comedy in 4 acts. Tr. Mn. Schuetze. Phil: Avil print. co. (B38)
2099. do. 1911. Our wives: farce comedy. Tr. Helen Krafft and F. Mandel. Tw. [LC]
2100. (Die Zwillingsschwester.) Twin sisters: a play in 4 acts. Tr. L. N. Parker. L: 1902. (B38)
2101. The fur coat. Tr. Mrs. J. M. Lancaster. 1907. In C447.
2102. Moonbeams: satire in 3 acts. Tr. A. H. Schwartz. NY: 1914. Tw. [LC]
2103. (Unter vier Augen.) By ourselves. Tr. Oc. Leonard. St.L: 1907. (B38).
*2104. do. 1912. Tr. Haya Wally. "Poet Lore" 23(1912): 1-24. [Very good.]
§2105. do. 1913-15. Tête-à-tête. Tr. E. L. Townsend. In C154(17). [Needless deviations.]

FUNCKE, O:
§2106. (Christliche Fragezeichen.) Self will and God's will. Tr. from 9th ed. Eliz. Stirling. Introd. Ax. Whyte. L: Hodder & Stoughton 1887. xx;172p. 18cm. [BM]
2107. A home abroad. In Schimmelmann, Adeline, Countess, Glimpses of my life, etc. L: Hodder & S. 1896. pp. 33-69.
2108. How to be happy and make others happy. Tr. So. Taylor. L: Hodder & S. 1896. xii;286p. 19cm. [BM]
2109. The world of faith and the everyday world, as displayed in the footsteps of Abraham. Tr. from 6th Ger. ed. So. Taylor. Ed: Clark 1891. xvi;353p. 21cm. [BM]

FUNK, Gf. Bn. d. 1814. Sel. in C244.

FURTWAENGLER, Ad. 1853-1907.
**2110. (Denkmäler griechischer und römischer Skulptur.) Greek and Roman sculpture. Tr. H. Taylor. L: Dent; NY: Dutton 1914. xii; 241p. il. 23cm. [Excellent tr.] [BM.LC]
*2111. (Meisterwerke der griechischen Plastik.) Masterpieces of Greek sculpture: a series of essays on the hist. of art. Tr. anon. Ed. Eugénie Sellers. L: Heinemann 1895. xxiii;487p. 18pl. 186 il. 4. [Too freely handled.] [LC.BM]
*2112. do. 1895. [same] In two vols., ltd. ed. xxiii;487p. [BM]

FUSS, Jns. Dms. 1781?-1860.
2113. (Antiquitates romanae.) Roman antiquities. Tr. Revs. A. W. and B. Street. Oxford: Talboys 1840. 608p. 22cm. [BM]

GAETSCHENBERGER, St.
2114. (Die Nachbarpussten.) Love is lord of all; or, neighboring steppes. Ad. Ma. J. Safford. Il. W. B. Davis. NY: Bonner 1892. 351p. 19cm. [LC]

"GALEN, Ph." (i.e., Ern. Ph. K: Lange, 1813-99.)
§2115. (Der Irre v. St. James.) The madman of St. James: a narr. from the journal of a physician. Tr. T. H. L: Hope 1860. 3v. 19cm. [Tr. with great freedom.] [BM]
§2116. do. 1861. [same] L: Clarke. Parlour lib. 380p. 16cm. [BM]

GANS, Gst. H: See Putlitz, Gst. H:

GANSFORT, Jn. Wessel, 1420?-1489.
2117. Life and writings by E: W. Miller; principal works, tr. J. W. Scudder. NY: Putnam 1917. 2v. 333;369p. il. 23cm. [LC]

GANZ, Hg. 1862- .
2118. (Vor der Katastrophe.) The land of riddles (Russia of today). Tr. and ed. by H. Rosenthal. NY;L: Harper 1904. 330p. 21cm. [LC]
2119. do. 1904. [same?] The downfall of R--. Behind the scenes in the realm of the Czar. L: Hodder & S. 320p. 19cm. [BM]
2120. do. 1905. [same?] The downfall of R--; under the surface in the land of riddles. 3d ed. L: Hodder & S. 320p. 20cm. [LC]

GARLEPP, Br. 1845-
2121. (Unseres Bismarck Heimgang.) B-- memorial. The passing of Germany's great chancellor: a narr. etc. with an elegiac poem by F. Dahn. Akron, O; Chic: Werner 1898. 69p. il. [LC]
2122. Germany's iron chancellor. Tr. and ed. S. Whitman. Akron, O; NY: Werner 1897. 403p. il. 38cm. [LC]

GARVE, K: Bh. 1763-1841. Sel. in C229;269;275.

GAST, Ud. See Caspari, K:, for a story founded on a MS of U. G--. #1065.

GASTEIGER (Khan), Ab.
*2123. (Vom Teheran nach Beludschistan.) From T-- to B--...in 1881. Tr. Jl. J. Königs. Simla: Govt. central branch press 1884. 48p. 25cm. [Not excellent.] [BM]

GATTI, Ech. v. and Bela Jenbach.
2124. (Der lila Domino.) The lilac domino: operetta in 3 acts by C: Cuvillier. Engl. book by Harry B. Smith. Lyrics by R. B. Smith. Vocal score. Engl. NY: Stern 1911. 172p. 28cm. [BMM]

GAUDY, Fz. v. 1800-50. Sel. in C17;97;309;378;394.

GEBHARD, Truchsess v. Waldburg, Kurfürst, Erzbischof v. Köln, 1547-1601.
§2125. A declaration made by the archbishop of Collen, upon the deede of his marriage, etc. Tr. acc. to the coppie imprinted at Collen, 1583. By T: Deloney. L: J:Wolfe 1583. ff. A-C. 14cm. [BM]

GEDIKE, F: 1754-1803. Sel. in C157(2).

GEDIKE, L: F: Glb. Ern. 1760-1838. Sel. in C244.

GEHE, E: H: 1793-1850.
*2126. (Jessonda.) J--: opera in 3 acts by L: Spohr. Tr. W. Bartholomew. Vocal score. Ger;Engl. L;NY: Novello n.d. 179p. 35cm. [BMM.LCM]

GEIBEL, Fz. Em. A: 1815-84. Sel. in C3;17;41;52*;65;67;69*;73;97; 105;112;149;152;166;173*;180;195-6;207;218;296;309;311;317;366; 372;375;380;391;393;395;417;423;428*;446;448;450;469;497;501*; 517;531;538-9.

*2127. (Brunhild; eine Tragödie...) Brunhild: a tragedy from the Nibelungen saga. Tr. G: T. Dippold. Bost: Ginn & Heath 1879. 116p. 16cm. [LC]

2128. (Gedichte.) Poems. Tr. Lucy H. Hooper. Phil: Leypoldt 1864. 96p. 16. [LCO]

†2129. do. 1879. Adaptations...by H: J: D. Stowe. L: Bowden, Hudson. 72p. 18cm. [41 poems; very mediocre.] [LC]

2130. (Loreley.) Loreley: an unfin. opera by Mendelssohn. Tr. W. Bartholomew. Bost: Ditson n.d. (1872-76) 8. [AC]

§2131. The wooing of King Sigurd, and, The ballad of the page and the king's daughter. Tr. Ellen Cook. L: Bell & D. 1864. il. 18 leaves. [BM.NY]

GEIGER, Ab. 1866-1915. Sel. in C28.

GEIGER, Hm.

2132. Lydia: a tale of the 2d cent. Tr. anon. L: Washbourne 1866. 8. [EC]

2133. do. 1867. [same?] Tr. anon. Phil: E. Cummiskey. 275p. 19cm. [LC]

GEIGER, Ls.

*2134. (Zur Entwicklungsgeschichte der Menschheit.) Contributions to the hist. of the devel. of the human race. Tr. from 2d Ger. ed. by D: Asher. L: Trübner 1880. viii;156p. 21cm. [BM]

GEIGER, L: 1848-1919. See Burckhardt, Jk., #934.

GELLERT, Cn. Fgt. 1717-69. Sel. in C17;41-2;44;88;122-3;125;129; 166;190;193;229;231-3;241;244;269;271;273;287;295;373;423;434; 443;461;469;470;486;489;533;560;570; #5963.

§2135. (Die zärtlichen Schwestern.) The tender sisters: a comedy. Tr. T: Holcroft. L: Theatrical recorder 1805. Vol. 1, 3-50. [Not bad.] [BM]

§2136. Fabeln. Free tr. from Ger. of G-- and other poets. By J: A. Nuske. L: Whittaker 1850 (date of pref.). 64p. 24cm. [Seems to be chiefly from Gellert's fables. Rather good, not close.] [BM]

2137. Gellert; or, the loving care of our heavenly father. Ad. by M. M. Campbell. L: S. P. C. K. 1879. 128p. 17cm. [Facts of Gellert's life woven into a story.] [BM]

2138. Instructions from a father to his son. Tr. anon. 32p. 12. Pmph. [LCO]

2139. (Leben der schwedischen Gräfin von G***.) Hist. of the Swedish countess of Guildenstern. Tr. anon. L: Dodsley 1752. 12. (B47).

†2140. do. 1757. Tr. anon. L: Scott. 2pts. xi;112; 156p. 17cm. [Expanded.] [BM]

§2141. do. 1776. The life of the countess of G. Tr. by a lady. L: Low. 2v. 8. [Tr. seems to have known and followed the foregoing.] [BM]

2142. do. 1776. The life of the Swedish countess de G*. Tr. by Rev. Mr. N--. L: J:Donaldson. 272p. 17cm. [This is a real translation.] [BM]

§2143. (Moralische Vorlesungen.) The life of Prof. G-- by J: An. Cramer; w. a course of moral lessons...by him. Taken from a French tr. (by Mie. Eli. (Bouée) de Fite) of the orig. by Mrs. M. Douglas. Kelso. Ballantyne for Hatchard in L. and Manners & M. in Ed. 1805. 3v. 21cm. [LC.BM]

GELLERT, Cn. Fgt.- Moralische Vorlesungen
[Life fills pp. 1-192 of vol. 1. Tr. is not accurate.]
§2144. do. 1810. [same] 2d ed. 16cm. [LC]
2145. do. 1832. Considerations on religion. Tr. anon. L: Rivingtons. 24p. 17cm. [Taken from his Moral. Vorles.]
2146. The sick wife. Tr. B. H. Clark. 1926. In C68.
[See Horn, W., Three days in the life of G--. #4586 seq.]

GELLERT, Pl. Sel. in C229.

GELTAR, 13th cent. Sel. in C27.

GELZER, H: 1813-89.
§2147. (Dr. Mn: Luther, der deutsche Reformator.) The life of M. L--, in 50...designs by Gst. König. To which is added a sketch of the rise and progress of the Ref. in Germany. Tr. anon. L: N. Cooke 1853. 25cm. [BM]
[Commentary on the pictures, pp. 1-54. Sketch, pp. 57-207.]
§2148. do. 1855. [same] Introd. by Rev. Theophilus Stork. Phil: Lindsay & Bl. viii;360p. 23cm. [LCO.BM]
[Pictorial commentary is thrown into consec. narrative.]
§2149. do. 1858. Introd. (Pp. 1-32) and a view of the reformation in England by Rev. G: Croly. L: Ward & Lock. [BM]
[Gelzer's sketch is not included. Comment on König's pictures is abr. from 1853 ed.]

GEMMINGEN-HORNBERG, O: Frhr. v. 1755-1836.
2150. (Der deutsche Hausvater.) Love's frailties. Tr. T: Holcroft. 1799. (B24).

GENÉE, Fz. F: R: 1823-95.
[NOTE. Genée was both composer and librettist, and worked much in collaboration with others: see H: Bohrmann-Riegen for "The queen's lace handkerchief," "M. West" for "A trip to Africa," C. Haffner for "The bat," and F. Zell for "Apajune, the water sprite," "The beggar student," "Boccaccio," "Countess Dubarry," "The merry war," "Nanon," "The naval cadets," "A night in Venice", "The vice-admiral."]

GENÉE and RIEGEN, Jl.
2151. Amorita: operetta by Alphons Czibulka. Copyright by Goldmark & Conreid 1897. Libr. Tw. [LCM]
[No relation to following, in either text or action.]
*2152. (Pfingsten in Florenz.) Amorita: comic opera in 3 acts by A. Czibulka. Tr. S. Rosenfeld and C. Goldmark. Libr. NY: 1885. 17p. 8. [LCM]
§2153. do. 1886. Whitsuntide in Florence. Tr. and ad. L: C: Elson. Score. Bost: White, Smith. 190p. 4. [LCM]

GENSICHEN, O: Fz. 1847- . Sel. in C169.

GENTZ, F: v. 1764-1832. Sel. in C12;191.
*2154. (Fragmente aus der neuesten Geschichte des politischen Gleichgewichts in Europa.) Fragments upon the balance of power in Europe. Tr. anon. L: For M. Peltier 1806. 335p. 22cm. [BM.LC]
2155. The orig. and princ. of the Amer. revol. compared with...the French revol. Tr. J: Q. Adams. Phil: Dickins 1800. 73p. 21cm. [LC]
2156. Reflections on the liberty of the press in Gt. Brit. Tr. anon. L: Bohte 1819. 111p. 19cm. [BM]
2157. do. 1820. [same] In "The Pamphleteer," vol. 15, pp. 455-496. [BM.LC]
*2158. (Von dem politischen Zustand...vor und nach der französischen Revolution.) On the state of Europe before and after the French revolution: being an answer to... (Citizen Hauterive). Tr. J: C: Herries. L: Hatchard 1802. cxxiv;391p. 21cm. [BM]

GENTZ, F: v.
*2159. do. 1803. [same] 2d ed. cxxiv;397p. 21cm. [BM]
*2160. do. 1803. [same] 3d ed. 397p. [LC]
*2161. do. 1804. [same] 5th ed. 397p. [BM]
*2162. do. 1804. [same] 6th ed. 397p. [BM]

GEORGE, St. 1868- . Sel. in C39*;95;423.

GERBER, Vicar at Interlaken.
2163. Interlaken. Tr. anon. 46p. il. In C294.

GERBER, N.
2164. The days of Abd-el-Kader: a tale of Algeria. Tr. Ma. E. Ireland. Elgin, Ill; Chic: Cook 1900. 94p. il. sq.8. [LC]

GERHARD, J: 1582-1637.
2165. The conquest of temptations; or, man's victory of Satan especially the great assaults at the agonie of death. Tr. Rev. R: Bruch. 2d ed. Prt. by I. H. for R: Jackson. L: 1622. 6 leaves, 186p. 13cm. [BM]
2166. (Loci communes theologici.) The summe of Christ. doctrine (aphorisms). Tr. R. Winterton. Cambridge: Roger Daniel 1640. 15 leaves, 303p. 13 x 6cm. [BM]
2167. (Meditationes sacrae.) The soules watch; or, a day-booke for the devout soule. Tr. R: Bruch. 3d ed. L: R:Jackson 1621. 11 leaves, 512p. 13cm. [BM]

GERHARDT, Pl. 1607-76. Sel. in C45-6;51;129;166;219;221-3;229;230-4;235;240;244;269*;271;273;276*;287*;372;423;443;469;486;489*; 538;570; #8904.
**2168. (Geistliche Lieder.) Spiritual songs. Tr. w. biog. sketch by J: Kelly. L: Strahan 1867. xlvi;351p. 15cm. [BM]
[77 hymns, faithful in every respect.]
2169. do. ca. 1870. [same?] NY; L: Routledge. [AC]
§2170. do. 1908. Lyra Gerhardti; or, a set of Pl. G--'s spiritual songs. Tr. by Rev. Bh. Pick. Burlington, Ia: Ger. lit. bd. 95p. 12. [NY]
See Wildenhahn, K: A:, Paul G--. #10209-12.

GERNING, J: I: v.
2171. A picturesque tour along the Rhine, from Mentz to Cologne. With (24 col.) il. (by M. Schuetz) of the scenes of remarkable events and of pop. traditions. Tr. J: Black. L: Ackermann 1820. xvi;178p. 34 x 28cm. [BM.LC]

GEROK, K: 1815-90. Sel. in C51;69;138;146;166;372;375;448;489;497.
**2172. (Palmblätter.) Palm leaves. Tr. J. E. A. Brown. L: Strahan 1869. 493p. 16cm. [Few fem. rhymes, but good flowing verse and correct sense. Seems to be complete.] [BM]

GEROK, P. Sel. in C51.

GERSCHOW, F:
*2173. Diary of the journey of Ph. Jl. duke of Stettin-Pomerania, through England in the year 1602. Ed. G. v. Bülow (and) Wilfred Powell. (Ger. and Engl.) In Royal hist. soc. transactions, new ser., vol. 6:4-67. L: Longmans 1892. 8. [BM.LC]

GERSDORF, Abh. v. 1704-84. Sel. in C269.

GERSTAECKER, F: 1816-72.
*2174. [Coll.] Tales of the desert and the bush. Tr. anon. Ed: Constable; L: Hamilton 1854. 332p. 18cm. [BM]
[§Bell-the-wolf ("Die Wolfsglocke"); *Black and white, an incident in the settler-life of Missouri ("Schwarz und Weiss");

GERSTAECKER, F: - Works
*The voyage of the Cassowary, a New Zealand sketch ("Die Schoonerfahrt"); *The German and his child, an incident in Amer. life ("Der Deutsche und sein Kind"); *The forest and the clearing, sketches from Amer. life ("Civilisation und Wildnis"); *The daughter of the Riccarees ("Die Tochter des Riccarees"); Letters from Ger. emigrants.]
*2175. do. 1859. [same] L: Philip. 332p. 17cm. [BM]
*2176. do. 1862. [same] New ed. L: Philip. [EC]
2177. Advent. in the tropics. Tr. F. L. Oswald. NY: Allison 1898. 210p. il. 12. [LC]
2178. Among the Penahuenches: a Chilian novel. NY: Appleton. ca. 1868-70. [Publisher's advt.]
2178a. Amongst the Americans. Tr. anon. "Engl. Women's Domestic Mag." 1(1860):21, etc. (B15a).
§2179. (Aus dem Matrosenleben.) A sailor's adventures. Tr. anon. L: Routledge 1859. 184p. 16cm. [BM]
2180. do. 1878. [same?] New ed. L: Routledge. 21. [EC]
*2181. (Civilisation und Wildnis.) The forest and the clearing. Tr. anon. In Nimmo's pop. tales. Ed: Nimmo 1866. vol. 6, pp. 82-123. 16cm. [Same tr. as in #2174.] [BM]
*2182. (Das alte Haus.) The haunted house. Tr. anon. L: Routledge 1857. 175p. 16cm. [BM]
2183. do. 1878. [same?] L: Routledge. 12. [EC]
*2184. (Der Deutsche und sein Kind.) Hm. Schwabe's daughter. Tr. anon. In Nimmo's pop. tales. Ed: Nimmo 1866. vol. 2. 16cm. [BM] [Same tr. as in #2174.]
*2185. (Der deutschen Auswanderer Fahrten und Schicksale.) Wanderings and fortunes of some Ger. emigrants. Tr. D: Black. L: Bogue 1848. viii;310p. 19cm. [BM.LC]
*2186. do. 1848. [same] NY; Phil: Appleton. 270p. 18cm. [LC]
*2187. (Der kleine Goldgräber in Californien.) The young gold-digger; or, a boy's advent. in the gold regions. L: Routledge 1860. viii;339p. il. 17cm. [BM]
*2188. do. 1877. [same without subtitle or il.] Routledge. [BM]
*2189. (Der kleine Walfischfänger.) The little whaler; or, the advent. of C: Hollberg. Tr. anon. L; NY: Routledge 1857. viii; 343p. il. 16cm. [BM]
[Tr. is a little stodgy. AC has: The young whaler.]
*2190. do. 1876. [same] The young whaler. Il. Harrison Weir. Routledge. [BM]
*2191. do. 1880. [same] Routledge. [EC]
*2192. (Die beiden Sträflinge.) The two convicts. Tr. anon. New ed. L: Routledge 1857. 393p. 16cm. [BM]
*2193. do. 1873. [same] Routledge. 12. [EC]
*2194. do. 1887. [same] Routledge. [EC]
§2195. (Die Flusspiraten des Mississippi.) The pirates of the M--. Tr. anon. L: Routledge 1856. vi;277p. 16cm. [BM.LC]
[Alterations in style and substance.--LC has: 12th thousand.]
2196. do. 1856. [same?] NY: DeWitt. [AC]
§2197. do. 1878. [same] New ed. Routledge. [EC]
§2198. (Die Regulatoren in Arkansas.) The feathered arrow; or, the forest rangers. Tr. anon. L: Routledge 1851. ix;420p. 17cm. [BM]
2199. do. 1857. [same?] L: Routledge. 12. [EC]
2200. do. 1857. The regulators of A--, a thrilling tale of border advent. Tr. anon. NY: Dick and Fitzgerald. 99p. 23cm. [LC]
[Chaps. 1-13.]
2201. do. 1857. Bill Johnson; or, the outlaws of A--. Tr. anon. NY: Dick & Fitzgerald. 97p. 24cm. [LC]
[Chaps. 13-25.]

GERSTAECKER, F:
2202. do. 1867. The death trail; or, the feathered arrow. Tr. anon. NY: De Witt. 100p. 16cm. [#2198 boiled down and rewritten.] [BM]
2203. do. 1872. [same as #2199] New ed. Routledge. [EC]
*2204. (Die Schoonerfahrt.) The hidden treasure. Tr. anon. In Nimmo's pop. tales. Ed: Nimmo 1866. vol. 5. 8. [BM]
[Same tr. as "The voyage of the Cassowary" in #2174.]
2205. (Die Tochter des Riccarees.) The daughter of the R--: a pict. of life in Louisiana. Tr. Mrs. F. M. Baker. Akron, O: Baker 1851. 108p. 14cm. [LC]
§2206. (Die Wolfsglocke.) Bell-the-wolf. Tr. anon. In Nimmo's pop. tales. Ed: Nimmo 1866. vol. 3. 8. [BM]
[Same tr. as in #2174.]
2207. (Fritz Waldaus Abenteuer.) Frank Wildman's advent. on land and water. Tr. and rev. by L. Wraxall. L: Routledge 1855. 8. [BM]
2208. do. 1858? [same] Bost: Crosby, Nichols. 16. [AC]
2209. do. 1863. [same] [AC]
2210. do. 1872-6. [same] NY: Routledge. il. 16. [AC]
2211. do. 1872-6. [same] Bost: Nichols & Hall. 16. [AC]
2212. do. 1872-6. [same] Phil: Lippincott. il. 12. [AC]
2213. (Germelshausen.) The strange village; and, the burgomaster's daughter. Kelly, Piet & Co. 1878. 18. [AC]
2213a. do. 1876. Germelshausen. Tr. anon. "Harper's Mag." 53(1876): 529. (B15a)
2214. do. 1888. Literally tr. anon. Cambridge, Mass: Sever. 31p. 19cm. [LC]
2215. do. 1906. Tr. Ca. M. Lathrop. NY: Crowell. 45p. 19cm. [LC]
2216. do. 1916. Lit. tr. Vivian E. Lyon. NY: Translation pub. 49p. 15cm. [AC]
§2217. do. 1919. Tr. C. W. Bell. L: Harrap. 56p. 16cm. [BM]
[Bilingual text. Not wholly satisfactory.]
*2218. (Gold! Ein californisches Lebensbild aus dem Jahre 1849.) Each for himself; or, the two adventurers. Tr. anon. L; NY: Routledge 1859. 427p. 16cm. [BM.LC]
*2219. do. 1873. [same] New ed. Routledge. 12. [EC]
*2220. do. 1893. [same] Routledge. [EC]
2221. How a bride was won; or, a chase across the pampas. Tr. Fis Jordan. NY: Appleton 1869. 274p. 24cm. [LC]
2222. do. 1872-6. [same] Appleton. il. 8. [AC]
2223. do. 1889. [same] [LC]
2224. (Mississippi-Bilder.) Western lands and western waters. Tr. anon. L: Beeton 1864. xii;388p. il. 20cm. [BM.LC]
[Up the Mississippi ("7 Tage auf einem amer. Dampfboot"); The wreck of the pirate ("Das Wrack des Piraten"); Stevens and his dog Poppy ("Jäger Stevans und s. Hund P--"); The silver mine in the Ozark mountains ("Die Silbermine in den O-- gebirgen"); A bear hunt in the western mts. ("Höhlenjagd in den westlichen Gebirgen)"; The wild man of the woods; Who did it? ("Dr. Middleton"); Lost and found ("Civilisation und Wildnis"); The planter ("Der Pflanzer"); In the backwoods ("Die Backwoodsmen Nordamerikas"); The fat widow ("Die dicke Witwe").]
2225. do. 1871. [same?] Tr. anon. L: Burns & Oates. 8. [EC]
*2226. (Pätz und Putz, oder die Lebensgeschichte zweier Bären.) Patz and Putz; or, the lives of two bears. Tr. anon. L: S. P. C. K. 1868. 96p. il. 15cm. [Tr. could be better.] [BM]
*2227. do. 1880. [same] L: S. P. C. K. [BM]
2228. (Reisen.) Narr. of a journey around the world, 1847-52. Tr. anon. L: Hurst & Blackett 1853. 3v. 360;343;351p. 19cm. [BM.LC]
[South America, California, South Sea Islands, Australia, Java. Many omissions; almost rewritten.]

GERSTAECKER, F: - Reisen
2229. do. 1853. [same] NY: Harper. [AC]
*2230. do. 1854. G--'s travels (Rio de Janeiro, Buenos Ayres, etc. to California and the gold fields). L; Ed: Nelson. 290p. il. 21cm. [Some omissions.] [BM.LC]
*2231. (Streif- und Jagdzüge durch die V. S. Nord-Amerikas.) Wild sports in the far west. Tr. anon. Il. Harrison Weir. L; NY: Routledge 1854. xi;396p. 18cm. [BM.LC]
[Not entirely complete, but well done.]
*2232. do. 1856. [same] New ed. L: Routledge. vi;314p. 16cm. [BM]
[Il. omitted. The same text.]
2233. do. 1858-60. [same?] Tr. anon. NY: Routledge. [AC]
2234. do. 1872-6. [same?] Tr. anon. NY: Routledge. 16. [AC]
2235. do. 1872-6. [same?] Tr. anon. Bost: Nichols & Hall. 16. [AC]
2236. do. 1872-6. [same?] Tr. anon. Phil: Lippincott. 12. [AC]
2237. do. 1878. [same?] New ed. Tr. anon. L: Routledge. 12. [EC]
§2238. (Unter dem Aequator.) A wife to order. Tr. Ed. Routledge. L: Routledge 1860. 12. [Cf. #2241.] [EC]
§2239. do. 1863. [same] New ed. [EC]
§2240. do. 1873. [same] New ed. [EC]
§2241. do. 1890. [same] Routledge. vii;394p. 16cm. [BM]
[Very cavalierly treated. Chapter headings added.]

GERSTENBERG, H: W: v. 1737-1823.
2242. (Ariadne auf Naxos.) Ariadne on Naxos. Sel. Tr. W: Taylor. 1830. In C533.

GERTRUD v. Hellfde, Saint, 1256-1311. Sel. in C222.
2243. (Insinuationes divinae pietatis.) The life and revelations of Saint G--. By a religious of the order of poor Clares. L: Burns & Oates 1865. xiv;565p. 18cm. [BM]
2243a. do. 1871. [same] 2d ed. [EC]

GERVINUS, G: Gf. 1805-71.
2244. (Einleitung in die Geschichte des 19. Jahrhunderts.) Introd. to the hist. of the 19th cent. W. a brief notice of the author by the tr. Tr. anon. L: Bohn 1853. xx;137p. 18cm. [BM]
See note to the following.
2245. do. 1853. The course and tendency of hist. since the overthrow of the empire of Napoleon I. Tr. by M. Sernau and J. M. Stephens, to vindicate Prof. G-- from his Engl. translator in Bohn's shilling series. L: E.Marlborough. iv;35p. 21cm. [BM]
[Tr. of pp. 149 ff. of the "Einleitung," with passages of the foregoing appended in notes, to show that that tr. is "nothing short of an adulteration," "a complete caricature."]
See Lehmann, J:, G. G. G--. #5632.

GESENIUS, W: 1786-1842. Sel. in C271;276.

GESNER, Kd. v. 1516-65.
2246. (Thierbuch das ist ein kurtze beschreybung aller vier füssigen Thieren...) The historie of foure-footed beastes. Describing the true and liuely figure of euery Beast, with a discourse...Coll. out of the volumes of C-- G-- and all other writers to the present day by E: Topsell. Tr. anon. L: W:Iaggard 1607. ff. Yyy. 33cm. [BM]
[Purporting to be natural science, this work may well be classed with imaginative lit. Topsell takes G--'s pictures, but seemingly little else.]
2247. do. 1658. [same] Rev. corr. and inlarged...L: E.Cotes for G. Sawbridge, etc. 1130p. 33cm. [BM]

GESSNER, J: G: 1765-1843.
2248. Memoirs of Lavater; also, Brief memoir of Mrs. Lavater. Tr. (abr.) by P. J. Heisch. See Lavater, J:, Memoirs etc. #5620.

GESSNER, Sl. 1730-88. Sel. in C198;373;461;469;533.
§2249. (Werke.) The works of S. G--. Tr. anon. Il. T: Stothard. L: Cadell & Davies 1802. 3v. 19cm. [BM.LC]
[Unwarranted liberties taken.--Vol. 1, xxvii;199p. front. (port.) 5 pl. The death of Abel ("Der Tod Abels"); Letter on landscape painting. --Vol. 2, viii;280p. 5 pl. Idyls ("Idyllen"); Miscellanies; The first navigator. --Vol. 3. vi;232p. 3 pl. Daphnis (do.); Evander and Alcimna; Erastus; The deluge; The wish.]
*2250. do. 1805. The works, w. crit. and explan. notes, and a copious memoir of the life of the author (by F: Shoberl). L: J. Cundee. 2v. 16cm. [BM]
[Clever revamping of the foregoing, even the rhymes being retained. But the tr. is much improved. Probably Shoberl was the reviser. --Vol. 1. lv;247p. front. (port.) by Makenzie, t.p. and 3 pl. by Uwins; *Death of Abel ("Der Tod Abels"), tr. by Shoberl, cf. note to #2295; *The first navigator ("Der erste Schiffer"), very good; *Daphnis (do.); *Idyls ("Idyllen"). --Vol. 2, 263p. 3 pl. by Uwins. Miscellanies; Evander and Alcimna, a pastoral drama; Erastus, a drama.]
†2251. do. 1797. ("Gessner's works" stamped on binding.) Tr. anon. L: T.Heptinstall. xi;275p. front. (port.) pl. by Stothard. 25cm. [BM]
[The death of Abel (by Mrs. Collyer with author's and tr.'s pref.) New idyls; The wooden leg, an Helvetic tale; Letter to M. Fuslin on landscape painting. All these by W. Hooper, as in #2319.]
2252. Sel. from the tales and idyls...tr. into verse. Kerby 1817. See "Monthly R." 84(1817): 212. (B26)
2253.[Sel.]1886. S. G--, the Swiss Theocritus. With 6 il. and... port...from drawings by T: Stothard. L: Field & Tuer; NY: Scribner & W. 27p. 20cm. [6 brief extracts from his works.] [BM]
2254. Conversation of a father with his children. (Tr. from Diderot.) Tr. H: Mackenzie. 1792. In C386.
*2255. (Daphnis.) D--. Tr. interlinearly by C: Eichhorn. L: Boosey 1811. 219p. 19cm. [BM]
[Textbook. A good and fluent tr. at the bottom of ea. page.]
§2256. (Der erste Schiffer.) The first navigator. In Chateaubriand, "Atala"...Tr. anon. L: Walker & E. etc. 1817. pp. 209-32. 12cm.
[Taken from the "Works," 1802, #2249.] [BM]
§2257. do. 1825. [same] In Chateaubriand, "Atala..." L: Baynes etc. pp. 333-59. 13cm. [BM]
†2258. (Der Tod Abels.) The death of Abel. In five books. Attempted from the German [by Mrs. Ma. Collyer]. L: Dodsley etc. 1761. xxiv; 259p. 17cm. [BM]
[Imitation rather than tr. Anon. until 1786;see #2273.]
†2259. do. 1761. [same tr.] Review with lengthy excerpts. In "Annual Reg." 4(1761): 2:286. (B26)
†2260. do. 1762. [same] 2d ed. L: Dodsley, etc. [BM]
2261. do. 1762. [same?] Phil: W. Bradford. (B6a.B48)
2262. do. 1762. [same?] Bost: Fowle & Draper. 12. (B6a.B48)
2263. do. 1762. [ad.] The thanksgiving song of Adam, on his recovery from sickness. Tr. S: Boyce. Pub. by Williams. [See "Brit. Mag." 3(1762): 382.] (B26)
†2264. do. 1763. Collyer's tr. 5th ed. L: Dodsley, etc. [BM]
*2265. do. 1763. Attempted in the style of Milton. By Rev. T: Newcombe. Davis & Reymers. 8. See "Crit. R." 16(1763): 50. (B26)
[Rev. cites lengthy passages, which are very good.]
†2266. do. 1765. Collyer's tr. 7th ed. L: Dodsley, etc. [BM]

GESSNER, Sl. - Der Tod Abels
†2267. do. 1765. [same] NY: Gaine. (B48)
[Perhaps identical with following.]
†2268. do. 1766. [same] 7th ed. NY: Hugh Gaine. (B6a).
†2269. do. 1767. [same] NY. 12. (B48)
†2270. do. 1770. [same] Phil: J. Cruikshank, J. Collins. 106p. 12.
[B48 reports: Phil: Dunlap 1770. 106p. 12.] [LC]
†2271. do. 1776. [same] 11th ed. L: Dodsley. [BM]
[Engr. front. by J. Collyer and engr. t.p.]
2272. do. 1780? New tr. L: T.Thompson. xvi;237p. 17cm. [BM]
[Engr. front. This tr. merely "edits" Collyer; he probably knew no German.]
†2273. do. 1786. "By Mrs. Collyer." L: Harrison. vii;61p. 21cm. [BM]
[The first Brit. ed. to name the tr. Prtd. in double cols. Front. by E. F. Burney.]
†2274. do. 1787. Collyer's tr. Newport (R. I.). Prtd. by P: Edes. (B6a) [Cf. 1791 ed. below.]
†2275. do. 1790. [same] Phil: Prtd. and sold by Jos. Crukshank. (B6a)
†2276. do. 1791. [same] To which is added, The death of Cain. Phil: Prtd. by W: Spotswood. viii;172; iv;68p. 24. (B6a)
[Available: AAS. JCB. Second title: The death of Cain...after the manner of the death of Abel. In five books. By a lady. Phil: Spotswood, etc. 1791. iv;68p.]
2277. do. 1791? Tr. anon. Newport (R. I.): Edes. 154p. 16. (B48).
2278. do. 1793. [same] Concord (N. H.): Prtd. by Elijah Russell. 132p. 12. (B6a)
†2279. do. 1794. "By Ma. Collyer." NY: Prtd. and sold by S: Campbell. front. 16. (B6a).
2280. do. 1795? Tr. anon. NY: Duykinck. (B48)
†2281. do. 1795. Collyer's tr. To which is added, The death of Cain. Newburyport (Mass.): Prtd. by Blunt & March. (B6a)
†2282. do. 1796. [same] L: W:Lane. xvi;203p. front. 10cm. [BM]
[Anon. Dedication and tr.'s pref. omitted.]
†2283. do. 1797. "By Ma. Collyer." Wilmington (Del.): Prtd. by P: Brynberg. 108p. 12. (B6a).
†2284. do. 1797. Collyer's tr. 30th ed. NY: Prtd. by J: Tiebout. iv;140p. 24. (B6a) [Available: AAS. NYPL]
†2285. do. 1799. [same] 20th ed. L: J.Collyer. xxiv;259p. 19cm.
[Embellished with an elegant engr. (by J. Collyer) to each book; all except t.p. different from #2271.] [BM]
†2286. do. 1800. [same] In "The sacred miscellany." Manchester: Sowler & Russell. pp. 1-112. 20cm. [BM]
2287. do. 1800? [sel. and ad.] Morning hymn, from The death of Abel. s. sh. 28 x 22cm. [BM]
[About 100 lines, rhymed couplets, roughly following Collyer.]
2288. do. 1802. With the New idyls. Tr. anon. Phil: Plowman. 275p. 8. (B48)
†2289. do. 1803. Collyer's tr. New ed. Ostell. 12. [EC]
2290. do. 180-? Tr. anon. Newburyport (Mass.) 18. (B48)
2291. do. 1806. Tr. anon. Phil: (B48)
2292. do. 1806. Tr. anon. NY: Ronalds. (B48)
*2293. do. 1806. Shoberl's tr. New ed. L: Cundee. 8. [EC]
*2294. do. 1806. [same] with memoir by Shoberl. L: Cundee. 2v. 8. [EC]
*2295. do. 1807. A new tr. by F: Shoberl, with a copious memoir of the author. 2d ed. L: Cundee. lii;131p. Front. (port.) by Makenzie, and t.p. and 3 pl. by Uwins. 16cm. [BM]
[1st ed. is doubtless #2294. Probably the same as #2293.]
†2296. do. 1807. "By Mrs. Collyer." L: Suttaby & Crosby. xxviii; 126p. Front. after R. Cook. T.p. by J. Thurston. 13cm. [BM]
[Life of G--, pp. iii-xxii, and prefs.]

GESSNER, Sl. - Der Tod Abels
†2297. do. 1807. [same] (With the New idyls. Cf. #2319.) 1st Balto. ed: Warner & Hanna. 255p. 3 pl. 16cm. [LC]
†2298. do. 1808. "By Mary Collyer." Burslem: J. Tregortha. x;120p. 21cm. [Has life of G-- and prefs. No il.] [BM]
2299. do. 1808. Tr. anon. Phil: Kite. 204p. 12. (B48)
†2300. do. 1809. Collyer's tr. Stereotype ed. w. (4) pl. (by H. Richter). L: Vernor, Hood & Sharpe etc. 148p. 17cm. [BM]
[Anon. Prefs.]
†2301. do. 1810. [same] New and impr. ed. Portsea: G. A. Stephens. 244p. front. 17cm. [Anon. No pref.] [BM]
§2302. do. 1811. Tr. w. occas. notes by W. C. Oulton. L: Hogg. viii;277p. front, and 3 pl. by R. W. Satchwell. 21cm. [BM]
[Blank verse, based chiefly on Shoberl's tr. Good verse.]
*2303. do. 1813. Shoberl's tr. Also, Death, a vision, by J: Macgowan. L: Cundee. pp. 1-150. front. (port.) t.p., 3 pl. 21cm. [Tr.'s pref. and memoir of G-- abr. from #2295.] [BM]
*2304. do. 1814. [same] w. a life of the author (as in #2296.)... The death of Cain (by Shoberl?) with pref. and introd. (Also) Death, a vision...by J: Macgowan. Oxford: Bartlett & Newman. xxvi;595p. engr. front. and t.p. 16cm. [BM]
["Death of Abel" to p. 244.]
†2305. do. 1814. Collyer's tr. Limerick: Stephen B. Goggin. 143p. 14cm. [Anon. No pref. No il.] [BM]
†2306. do. 1815. [same] L: Dean & Munday. viii;144p. front. 15cm. [Anon. No pref. by tr.] [BM]
†2307. do. 1818. [same] L: Walker etc. xxii;119p. front. and t.p. by Uwins.13cm. [Anon. Very brief sketch of G--.] [BM]
†2308. do. 1825. [same] w. life, ded., and prefs. In #2258, pp. 79-219. [HCL]
†2309. do. 1825. [same] Hartford, Conn. Andrus. [AC]
2310. do. Before 1852. Tr. anon. Pease & Co. n.d.
*2311. do. 1840. Done into blank verse from (#2258) by M. B. C. L: Hatchard. xv;193p. 17cm. [BM]
[Some passages tr. in lyric form. All very good, and better than #2302.]
2312. do. 1841. [ad.] The death of Abel: an oratorio by G: Perry. The words chiefly from the Holy Scriptures and G--'s Poem. Tr. anon. Libr. L: Howlett. 12p. 21cm. [BM]
2313. do. 1844. [same] Libr. L: J.Hart. 11p. 23cm. [BM]
†2314. do. 1853. Tr. De Benham-Yacoby. L: Prt. and pub. for the tr. iii;126p. 14cm. [Stilted and unnatural diction.] [BM]
2315. (Gedichte.) Poems...orig. and tr. or imitated from the works of G--. By Rb. Fellowes. L: Mawman 1806. See "Crit. R." (III) 8 (1806):330. (B26).
2316. (Idyllen.) Pastorals. Tr. anon. L: Newberry. See "Monthly R." 27(1762):393. (B26)
§2317. do. 1762. Rural poems. Tr. anon. L: For Becket & De Hondt. 106p. 18cm. [LC]
2318. do. 1762. Select poems from Mr. G--'s pastorals. Tr. Anne Penny. L: For the author. v;24p. 28cm. [BM]
[Three idyls in rhymed couplets.]
§2319. do. 1776. New idylles. Tr. W. Hooper, M. D. With a letter... on landscape painting and...a moral tale by M. Diderot. L: . S.Hooper & G.Robinson. 129p. 9pl. and vignets by Gessner. port. on t.p. 27cm. [Pretty bad.] [BM.LC]
§2320. do. 1798. Idyls, or pastoral poems. (Also, The wooden leg and Letter on landscape painting.) Tr. anon. Ed: Mudie & Constable. xviii;140p. Engr. front by G. Sanders and 1 pl. by R. Scott. 17cm. [BM]
[Slightly edited from #2251.]

GESSNER, Sl. - Idyllen
§2321. do. 1809. Select idyls; or, pastoral poems. Tr. G. Baker. L: Longmans. 226p. 12. [Verse tr. is very good.] [LC]
*2322. do. 1817. In #2256. L: Walker & Edwards etc. pp. 113-208. 12cm. [BM]
*2323. do. 1825. [same] In #2257, pp. 223-329.
*2324. (S. G--'s Briefwechsel mit seinem Sohne.) The letters of G-- and his family. Tr. anon. L: Vernor & Hood 1804. 248p. 20cm. [BM] [EC has: 1805.]

GEYER, A. E.
*2325. (Elly und Oswald.) Elly and Oswald; or, the emigration from Sturvis: a tale of the Grisons. From...the "Alpenrosen" [i.e., Alpenblumen: Sammlung schweizerischer Novellen.] In "Scots Mag." (II) 12(1823):47, 153. [BM]

GIEHRL, Frau Emmy (Aschenbrenner), 1837-1915.
2326. Children of Mary. Tr. anon. 1902. In C481.
2327. (Kreuzesblüten.) Blossoms of the cross, from 3d Ger. ed. Tr. and pub. by sisters of St. Joseph. Indianapolis. Carlton & Hollenbeck, printers. 1894. 296p. 18cm. [LC]
2328. Master Fridolin: a Christmas story. Tr. anon. NY; Cincin: Benziger 1897. 96p. 15cm. [LC]
2329. (Neue Märchen für grosse und kleine Kinder.) New fairy tales for children young and old, told by Aunt Emmy. Tr. Emy Gordon. Donauwörth: Auer 1889. 247p. il. 20cm. [LC]
2330. The three little kings. Tr. anon. NY; Cincin: Benziger 1897. 88p. 15cm. [LC]

GIESEKE, K: L: (Die Zauberflöte.) The magic flute. See Schikaneder, J: Ern.

GIESELER, J: K: L: 1793-1854. Sel. in C497.

"GILBERT, Jean" (i.e., Max Winterfeld, 1879- .) Operettas in collaboration: The cinema star. [See G: Okonkowski.] "Hello central." [See Fz. Arnold.] The joy-ride lady. [See J. Kren.] Katja, the dancer. [See Lp. Jacobson.] The lady of the rose. [See R. Schanzer.] The Vandemere estate. [See C. Kraatz.]

GILM zu ROSENEGG, Hm. v. 1812-64. Sel. in C73;317.

GINDELY, An. 1829-92.
*2331. (Illustrierte Geschichte des 30jährigen Krieges.) Hist. of the 30 years' war. Tr. A. Ten Brook. NY: Putnam 1884. L: Bentley 1885. 2v. xxi;456;456p. 28 il. 21cm. [LC.BM] [Introd. and concluding chap. by tr.]

GINZKEY, Fz. K: 1871- . Sel. in C28.

GIRNDT, O: 1835-1911. See G. Moser, joint author.

GISEKE, Rb. 1827-90.
2332. (Pfarr-Röschen.) The rose of the parsonage: an idyl of our own times. Tr. anon. Phil: Parry & M'Millan 1854. viii;219p. 19cm. [LC]

GITTERMANN, J: Cn. Hm. 1768-1834. Sel. in C543.

GLASENAPP, K: F: 1847-1915.
*2333. (Das Leben R: Wagners.) The life of R: W--. Tr. W: A. Ellis. L: Paul, T. & T. 1900. 6v. 23cm. [LC]

GLASSBRENNER, Ad. 1810-76. Sel. in C301;317.

GLAUBER, J: Rd. 1603?-68.
2334. Works...containing...choice secrets in medicine and alchemy. Tr. C. Packe, Philo-chymico-Medicus. L: for the author 1689.

GLAUBER, J: Rd.
3 pts. 440;220;92p. il. 38cm. [BM]
2335. A description of new philosophical furnaces, or a new art of distilling...of the tincture of gold, or the true aurum potabile. Also, The first part of the mineral work. Tr. anon. L: R:Coats for T:Williams 1651. 5 leaves; 452p; 6 leaves. 19cm. [BM]
[The five parts have sep. t.p's. ea. dated 1652. This tr. is copied verbatim in the foregoing.]
2336. The golden ass well managed, and Midas restored to reason... wherein...is Demonstrated that...Gold may be found as well in Cold as Hot regions...and be profitably extracted...And is a Work of Women and play of Children. Written at Amsterdam, 1669, by J. R. G--, The bright Sun of our Age, and Lover of Mankind, like a true Elias riding on this Golden Ass, in a Fiery Chariot. Tr. out of Latin...in briefer notes, 1670, by W(illiam) C(ooper). L: for W: Cooper 1673. 5 leaves, pp. 36-55. 17cm. [BM]

"GLAUBRECHT, O:" (i.e., Rd. L: Oeser, 1807-59).
2337. (Anna.) Anna, the leech vendor. Tr. anon. L: Wertheim 1844. 18. [EC]
2338. do. 1858-61. Anna, the leech-vender. Tr. Mrs. Clarke. Phil: Presb. bd. 18. [AC]

GLEICHEN-RUSSWURM, C: Ax. v. 1865- .
*2339. (Die Lust der Welt; schöner Frauen Liebe, Macht und Schicksal.) The world's lure: fair women, their loves, power, fates. Tr. Hannah Waller. NY: Knopf 1927. 268p. 24cm. [BM]

GLEIM, J: W: L: 1719-1803. Sel. in C17;22;25-6;43-4;67;88;106;133; 173;190;219;309;372-3;387-8;391;393;412;417;461;486;533;564.
[See Klopstock and his friends: Letters chiefly between K-- and Gleim. #5075.]

GLUCK, Cph. Wb. Ritter v. 1714-87. Sel. in C46;429.

GLUECK, Bba. Eli. 1815-94. See "Paoli, Betty."

GLUEMER, Ce. v. 1825-1906.
2340. (Frau domina.) Frau domina. Tr. anon. Hartford, Conn: Lockwood, B. & Co. 1877. 16. [AC]
2341. (Dönninghausen.) A noble name; or, Dönninghausen. Tr. Mrs. A. L. Wister. Phil: Lippincott 1883. 360p. 19cm. [LC]
2342. do. 1906. [same] [LC]

GODIN, Amélie (i.e., Amélie Linz, 1824-1904).
2343. The magician and his pupil. Tr. anon. 1897. In C126.

GOEBEL, K. v.
2343a. (W: Hofmeister: Arbeit und Leben e. Botanikers d. 19. Jahrhunderts.) W: Hofmeister: work and life of a 19th cent. botanist. Tr. by H. M. Bower. L: Dulau 1926. 213p. [EC]

GOEDE, Cn. A: Gb. 1774-1812.
§2344. (England...Reise...1802-3.) The stranger in England; or, travels in Gt. Brit. Tr. anon. L: for Mathews & Leigh 1807. 3v. viii;247;270;128p. 16cm. [Quite freely handled.] [BM]
*2345. do. 1821. A foreigner's opinion of E--. Tr. T: Horne. L: Prtd. for C. Taylor etc. 3v. 414;248;246p. 19cm. [BM]
*2346. do. 1822. [same] Bost: Wells & Lilly. 444p. 22cm. [LC]

GOEHRE, Pl. 1864- .
*2347. (Die evangelisch-soziale Bewegung.) The evang.-social movement in Germany. Abr. tr. by Janet E. K. Shuttleworth. L: Ideal publ. union 1898. 236p. 18cm. [BM]
*2348. (Drei Monate Fabrikarbeiter und Handwerksbursche.) Three months in a workshop: a practical study. Tr. A. B. Carr. Pref.

GOEHRE, Pl.-Drei Monate
note by R: T. Ely. L: Sonnenschein; NY: Scribner 1895(1894). x;219p. 19cm. [BM.LC]

GOEHREN, C:e v.
2349. (Die Waise; oder, eine gute Tat findet oft auf Erden schon ihren Lohn.) The orphan. Tr. anon. Phil: Claxton 1872. 18. [AC]

GOERING, Hg. 1827-57. Sel. in C450.

GOERLACH, W: d. 1875.
*2350. (Fürst Bismarck. Eine Lebensbeschreibung.) Prince B--: a biog. sketch. Tr. Miss M. E. v. Glehn. Lpz: Tauchnitz; L: Low 1867. 233p. 16cm. [BM]
*2351. do. 1875. [same] NY: Holt. 233p. 16cm. [LC]
*2352. do. 1882. [same] Introd. sketch by T. H. Joyce. NY: Munro. Seaside lib. 37p. il. 32cm. [LC]

GOERLING, Ad., Br. Meyer, and Af. Woltmann.
*2353. (Deutschlands Kunstschätze.) Art. treas. of Germany. Tr. anon. Bost: Walker 1873. 2v. 276;198p. front. pl. 33cm. [LC] [BM has only pt. 2 without a t.p., gives L: as place of publication. Each picture has a story related to it.]

GOERLING, Ad. 1821-77.
§2354. (Belvedere, oder die Galerien von Wien.) The galleries of V--. Text tr. W. C. Wrankmore. L: Hagger; NY: Fitzpatrick 1861-4. 336p. 28cm. [Many pictures with brief commentary.] [BM]

GOERLITZ, K: 1830-90.
2355. (Eine unvollkommene Frau.) Her only fault: comedietta in one act (and in prose). Tr. S. Rosenfeld. NY: De Witt 1882. 13p. 19cm. [LC]

GOERRES, Guido, 1805-52.
2356. The blessed N: Von der Flüe, and the deputies at the diet of Stantz. A pict. from the 15th cent. Tr. E: Cox. Pref. J: Goerres. L: Jones 1838. xvii;89p. 14cm. [BM] [Orig. pub. in "Edinb. Cath. Mag." 1837. Tr. of "God in history," part of a larger work.]
§2357. (Das Weihnachtskripplein.) The manger of the holy night; also, The tale of the Prince Schreimund and the Princess Schweigstilla (Prinz S-- und Prinzessin S--). Tr. C. E. H(awker?). L: Jos. Masters, Jas. Burns 1847. viii;150p. il. 14cm. [BM]

GOERRES, J: Js. v. 1776-1848.
2358. (Die Mystik.) The stigmata...a hist. of various cases. Tr. anon. ed. H. Austin. L: Richardson 1883. xi;225p. 16cm. [BM]
*2359. (Teutschland und die Revolution.) Germany and the revolution. Tr. J: Black. L: Longmans 1820. xix;336p. 21cm. [BM.LC]
*2360. do. 1820. [not same] Tr. liberally (from the...pamphlet... suppressed...) exclusively for the "Pamphleteer." L: Valpy. Vol. 15, pp. 497-576. [BM]
*2361. do. 1820. [Reprint of foregoing.] 80p. 22cm. [LC]

GOESCHEL, K: F: 1781-1861.
2362. The immortality of the soul. Tr. T. R. Vickroy and Susan E. Blow. 1882. In C300(11;17-20).

GOESLI v. Ebenheim, 13th cent. Sel. in C532.

GOETHE, J: Wfg. v. 1749-1832.

ARRANGEMENT

Works, Collections	Single works
Poetry	Letters, conversations
Selections	Biography

WORKS, COLLECTIONS[1]

GOETHE, J: Wfg. v.

§2363. 1845. Essays on art. Tr. S: G: Ward. Bost: Munroe. vi;263p. 17cm. [LC.BM]
[Introd. to the Propylaeum; Upon the Laocoön; The collector and his friends; Upon truth and probability in works of art; Rosalia's sanctuary; Simple imitation of nature, manner, style; Pictures of Philostratus; Ancient and modern; Landscape painting; Aphorisms, etc. Hints to young artists; Upon dilettantism.]

2364. 1848-50. Autobiography and works. Tr. anon. L: Bohn. 3v. 8. [Probably includes: Autobiog. by Oxenford, 1848, #2489; Travels in Italy by Morrison, 1849, #2927; Conversations with Soret and Eckermann by Oxenford, 1850, #3041.] [EC]

§*2365. 1848-90. Works. Tr. anon. L: Bohn. 14v. [LC]
[These tr. by different hands, mostly good or excellent--see individual titles for judgments--serve as the basis for all subsequent editions in English.--Vol. 1. Autobiog. I-XIII. Tr. by Oxenford, rev. by Minna Smith. Vol. 2, do. XIV-XX tr. by Morrison, rev. by Minna Smith. Also, Annals tr. by C: Nisbet. Vol. 3. Faust (I,II) by Swanwick. Vol. 4. Novels and tales, chiefly by Boylan, cf. #2367. Vol. 5. W: Meister (L) by Boylan. Vol. 6. Conversations tr. by Oxenford. Vol. 7. Poems by Bowring. Vol. 8. Dramas. Götz by Scott, revised; Tasso, Egmont, Iphigenia, by Swanwick; Clavigo, Wayward lover, Fellow culprits, by Bowring. Vol. 9. W: Meister (W) by E: Bell. Vol. 10. Travels in Italy by Morrison. Vol. 11. Misc. travels by Dora Schmitz. Vol. 12. Early letters by Bell. Vol. 13. Corr. with Zelter by A. D. Coleridge. Vol. 14. Reynard, West-eastern divan, Achilleid by A. Rogers.]

*2366. 1850. Dramatic works. L: Bohn. xvi;504p. front. of Goetz by Behle. 17cm. [BM]
[Faust (I), Iphigenia, Tasso, Egmont, all by Anna Swanwick, w. introd. by her; Götz by Scott, w. his introd., the tr. "carefully revised]"

*2367. 1854. Novels and tales. L: Bohn. vi;504p. 17cm. [BM]
[Elective affinities (tr. anon., see pref.). Remainder by Boylan: The sorrows of young Werther; The recreations of the German emigrants; A fairy tale (omitted from t.p.); The good women; A nouvelette (Table of contents has: A tale).]

2368. 1855. Works. W. life by Lewes. L: Nutt 1855. 2v. [EC]

2369. Before 1876. Works. Bost; NY: Bohn. 7v. 12. (B8)

2370. Before 1876. Works. NY: Appleton. 6v. 12. (B8)

2371. Before 1876. Works. Phil: Lippincott. 7v. 12. (B8)

*2372. 1879. Dram. works. L: Bohn. 543p. front. as in #2366. 18cm.
[The wayward lover, The fellow-culprits, by Bowring. Götz by Scott. Clavigo (tr. anon., by Bell?). Egmont, Tasso, Iphigenia, by Swanwick, all revised for this ed.] [BM]

*2373. 1882. Works. People's ed. Ed. F: H: Hedge and L. Noa. Bost: Cassino. 9v. (or, 9v. in 5). 8. [LC]
[Has Carlyle's tr. of "W: Meister"; poems eclectic, see B42. Other tr. as in Bohn.]

2374. 1882. Works. Identical with the foregoing. Bost: Estes & Lauriat. 9v. in 5. 12. (B42)

2375. [same] 1882. NY: Crowell. 9v. in 5. 12. (B42).

2376. [same] 1885. Bost. and NY: Crowell. (B42).

2377. [same] 1885. University ed. Bost: Cassino. 5v. 12. (B42).

2378. [same] 1895. Cambridge ed. 10v. (B42).

2379. 1882. Works. Göttingen ed. Phil. and Chic: Moore. 10v. 8 (B42) [Poetry vol. eclectic as in 2373; Hayward's prose tr. of Faust added. Otherwise same tr. as Bohn.]

*2380. 1885. Works. Il. by the best German artists. Ed. H. H. Boyesen. Phil; NY: Barrie. 5v. 30cm. [LC.BM]

[1]For fuller information on the various editions of Goethe's work, see Simmons (B42).

GOETHE--WORKS, COLLECTIONS
[Vol. 1. Life by Boyesen. Poems eclectic, with some additions. Divan. Hermann and Dorothea. Vol. 2. Faust (I, II). Egmont. The natural daughter [tr. anon.] The sorrows of young Werther. Vol. 3. Goetz. Iphigenia. Tasso. Clavigo. Stella [tr. anon.]. The brother and sister [tr. anon.]. A tale. The good women. Reineke, tr. Arnold. Vol. 4. The recreations of the German emigrants. W: Meister (L). Vol. 5. W: Meister (W). Elective affinities. Bohn translations, except as indicated.]

2381. 1885. Works. Bost: Houghton & Mifflin. 6v. 4. (B42)
[Life of G-- by Lewes. Faust by Taylor. G--'s corr. with a child. W: Meister by Carlyle. No poems.]

*2382. 1890. Reineke Fox, West-eastern divan, and Achilleïd. Tr. in the orig. metres by Ax. Rogers. L: Bohn. xiv;376p. 18cm. [BM]
[Divan is good; others excellent.]

2383. 1891. Works. Tr. J. O. Oxenford. (i.e., the autobiography?). L: 8v. (B13)

2384. 1901. Works. Göttingen ed. Same as #2379. (B42)

2385. 1901. Works. New library ed. Bost: Estes. 5v. (B13)
[Probably same as People's ed. 1882. #2373.]

2386. 1902. Works. [same as #2384] Ed. de luxe. L; Phil; Chic: Amaranth soc. 10v. (B42)

2387. 1902. Works. Weimar ed. Ed. N. H. Dole. Bost: Niccolls. 14v. 8. [Poems eclectic. W: Meister by Carlyle. Faust (I) by Martin. Reinecke by Cobb. The rest as in Bohn.] [LC]

2388. 1902. G--'s poetical works. Ed. N. H. Dole. Bost: Niccolls. 2v. 23cm. [LC]
[Faust (I, II) by Martin. Egmont by Swanwick. Clavigo and Wayward lover by Bowring. No poems.]

2389. 1905. Works. Ed. by K. Heinemann. L: Unwin. 15v. 8. [EC]

2390. 1910. Works. New imperial lib. ed. Bost: Estes. 7v. il. 8 [AC]

2391. 1915. Works. Weimar ed. [same as #2387] Bost: Niccolls. 14v. [AC]

*2392. 1921. G--'s lit. essays: a sel...arr. by J. E. Spingarn. Foreword by Viscount Haldane. L: Milford; NY: Harcourt. viii; 302p. 19cm. [BM.LC]
[The theory of art. The theory of lit. On Shakespeare. On other writers. Extracts from the conv. w. Eckermann. Appendix.]

POETRY[1]

2393. ANON. Goethe's poetical works. NY: Crowell 1882. 439p. 8. (B42)
[Tr. by various hands. This vol. used in all sets of G-- exc. Bohn.]

§2394. AYTOUN, W. E., and SIR Td. MARTIN. Poems and ballads of G--. With notes. Ed;L: Blackwood;NY: Delisser & Proctor 1859. xv;240p. 8. [BM]

§2395. do. 1860. 2d ed. Blackwood. xv;244p. [BM]
[Songs re-arranged, same contents. For slashing criticism, see J. MacCarthy in C382.]

§2396. do. 1863. NY: Gowans. [AC]

§2397. do. 1871. NY: Holt & W. (B24)

§2398. do. 1877. (42) Favorite poems. Bost: Osgood. 92p. il. 12cm. [BM]

§2399. do. 1907. 3d rev. ed. Ed;L: Blackwood. xxi;250p. 8. [BM]
[Adds 4 items.]

§2400. BOWRING, E. A. Poems of G--. L: Parker 1853. 433p. 4. [BM.LC]
[Facile and fluent, and sometimes happy; but too often he lets his fluency run away with him.]

[1] For fuller discussion of all volumes containing poems by G-- in Engl. translation, see "Hinz" (B19) and "Simmons" (B42).

GOETHE
§2401. do. 1874. Rev. and enl. ed. L: Bohn. xvi;440p. 17cm. [BM.LC]
[Adds H. & D. and Divan. Steadily reprinted in Bohn ed. of G--.]
§2402. do. 1884. Pub. anon. NY: Lovell. 12. (B8)
§2403. do. 1914. NY: Macmillan. 440p. [AC]
§2404. CHAWNER, E: G--'s minor poems. L: Pitman 1866. vii;142p. 17cm. [53 poems and some proverbs. Fair to good tr.] [BM]
†2405. DYRSEN, B. Poems tr. in orig. metres. NY: Christern 1878. 374p. 8. [Wholly negligible.] [NY.BM]
§2406. GIBSON, W. Poems...ballads and songs, and misc. sel. L: Simpkin & Marshall 1883. viii;344p. 8. [NY.BM]
[In keeping G--'s meters, Gibson does violence to the sense. Few acceptable versions.]
2407. GUTHRIE, W: NORMAN. Odes and didactic verse of G--. 1906.(B42)
§2408. LEAKE, R. Old verse--new versions. Manchester: Palmer & Howe 1901. Priv. circ. Ger. and Engl. xi;112; xxxiip. 19cm. [BM]
[Some of his versions are very good. In an appendix he prints attempts of Anster, Arnold, Aytoun, Cartwright, Hayward, Lewes, Martin, Oxenford, Swanwick, Taylor, Webb.]
2408a. MORGAN, B. Q. A book of Goethe's verse. 199p. 26cm. Tw. [115 poems. Notes include information on musical settings.] [SU]
†2409. THOMAS, W: G. Minor poetry of G--. Phil: Butler 1859. 335p. 8. [Unequal to the task; stilted and unnatural verse.] [LC.BM]

SELECTIONS[1]

2410. ANON. 1820. Lays of a wanderer. L: (B42)
2411. ANON. 1826. Two prefaces. Tr. anon. In "Feldjäger." A152-3.
2412. ANON. 1833. Literary rambler. A coll. of...stories. Ed. (B8. B42) [Contains 3 poems, and 36 of the Sprüche.]
2413. ANON. 1836. Library of romance. A coll. of traditions...L: (B42) [Two by Goethe.]
2414. ANON. 1844. The gift. Phil. (B42)
2415. ANON. 1855. Gleanings from the poets. New ed. Bost: Crosby & N. (B42)
2416. ANON. 1908. Poems and prose from W. G--. Il. H. Printz and H. Comploi. NY: Stokes. unp. Q. [AC]
2417. ANON. 1923? Revealing comments on humanity and life (literature and art). Girard, Kan: Haldeman-Julius n.d. 32p. 12cm. [BQM]
2418. ANON. 1923? Life and character. Girard, Kan: Haldeman-Julius n.d. 62p. 12cm. [Aphorisms, in 7 chapters.] [BQM]
§2419. ATTWELL, H: Gleams from G--...sel. and tr. from the prose... and...conv. L: Allen 1898. xxx;191p. 8. [BM]
[690 brief extracts, covered by a topical index, and with some expl. footnotes.--Tr. seems to be good.]
2420. do. 1900. 1901. [same?] NY: Stokes. 32. (B9, vol. 21)
2421. do. n.d. [same?] Chic: Browne's bookstore. S. [AC]
[AYTOUN, W: E. See his Poems. C13]
2422. BANCROFT, G: Life and genius of G--. Bost: Everett 1824? 24p. 8. [8 poems.] (B42)
§2423. BANNAN, MARTHA R. The fisher maiden, a vaudeville; and, The lover's caprice, a pastoral play...Tr. for the first time (cf. #2513) and in the orig. metres(?). Phil: Yorston 1899. 116p. il. 12. [LC]

[1] Volumes included in List C which have considerable amounts of G-- are listed here, but without serial numbers. Since nearly all the misc. collections include Goethe, and their contents are listed, I put in the main list only those items which contain Goethe material catalogued under other names. See #87;4082;8030.

GOETHE--SELECTIONS

2423a. BARRETT, TIMOTHY and C: J. Verses viridescent. [See "The Critic" 27(1895):267, where the trs. are censured for attempting Goethe and Homer. I find no record of the book.] [Corr.]

[BIELSCHOWSKY, Ab. Life of Goethe. #432.] [Contains many tr.]

§2424. BLACKIE, J: S. The wisdom of Goethe. Ed: Blackwood 1883. NY: Scribner 1884. lxxxiii;246p. 8. [BM.LC]

2425. BOYESEN, H. H. Essays on German lit. NY: Scribner; L: Unwin 1892. 359p. 18cm. [3 poems by G--.] [LC.BM]

2426. do. 1898. [same] 4th ed. [LC.BM].

2427. BRAUN, F: A: Marg. Fuller and Goethe. NY: Holt 1910. 271p. 19cm. [Critical discussion of her trs., also two unpub. versions.] [BM]

2428. BROWN, HORATIO R. F. J: A. Symonds. NY: Scribner; L: Nimmo 1895. 2v. [One poem in vol. 2.] [BM]

§2429. BROWN, P. Hume. The life of G--. L: Murray; NY: Holt 1913. 2v. 8. [Many fair tr.]

§2430. do. 1920. [same] L: Murray;NY: Holt. [LC]

§2431. do. The youth of G--. L: Murray 1913. xvi;304p. 22cm.[BM.LC] [8 poems.]

†BURT, Ma. A. Specimens of the...German poets. 1854. (C50.) [26 poems by G--.]

§2432. CALVERT, G:H: G--: life and works. Bost: Lee & S. 1872. 276p. 16. [A few tolerable verse tr.] [LC]

**2433. CARLYLE, T: Essay on G--. In his works; also elsewhere.[BM] [Numerous prose extracts from G--.]

§2434. CARUS, Pl. G--, with spec. consid. of his philos. Chic: Open Court 1915. 375p. 24cm. [Many verse tr., some good.] [LC.BM]

§CHAWNER, E: Gleanings from the Ger. and Fr. poets. 1879. (C67) [87 by G--.]

§2435. CLAPP, AMANDA R. G-- year book: sel. for every day...NY: Dutton 1894. 167p. 17cm. [LC.BM] [Bits of prose and verse; the latter from Bowring.]

2436. COOKE, CARRIE A. Many col. threads from...G--. Introd. by A. McKenzie. Bost: Lothrop 1885. 244p. 8. [LC.BM] [Mostly prose extracts; bits from "H. & D." and "Faust"; etc.]

2437. Coppée, ed. The classic and beautiful in literature. Phil: Simpson 1893. 6v. (B19) [3 poems by G--.]

2438. CRAWFORD, Ma. Caro. G-- and his woman friends. Bost: Little, Brown 1911. L: Unwin 1912. 452p. il. 22cm. [10 poems.] [LC.BM]

*2439. DOWDEN, E: Essays, mod. and Elizabethan. L: Dent; NY: Dutton 1910. 380p. 21cm. [BM.LC] [Many from the "West-Eastern Divan."]

2440. DUDLEY, MARION V., ed. Poetry and philos. of G--, comprising the lectures...before the Milwaukee lit. school...1886. Chic: Griggs 1887. 300p. 19cm. [Eclectic.] [HCL.BM]

2441. DUNBAR, NEWELL. J. W. v. G--, his wit, wisdom, and poetry. Bost: Cupples 1892. li;181p. 8. [Very brief bits of prose, with verse interspersed. Eclectic, no ascriptions.] [BM]

**DWIGHT, J: S. Select minor poems tr. from...G-- and Schiller, with notes. G: Ripley's Specimens of foreign standard lit., vol. 3. 1839. (C109.) [197 p. of Goethe's verse, largely by Dwight.]

2442. FULLARTON, R. M. Lallan songs and Ger. lyrics. Ed: Blackwood 1894. xii;111p. 8. [18 poems by Goethe.] [BM]

§GALLETLY, H. C. Ger. lyr. and other poems: isometrical tr. 1897. C149. [26 poems by G-- in rather mediocre tr.]

2443. GIBBERD, J. E. G--'s aphorisms, compiled. L: Siegle, H. 1912. (Langham booklets.) 96p. 32. [BM] [Pregnant quotations, probably eclectic, from a number of the great works in very good verse.]

GOETHE
§GRAY, M. Lyri·s and epigrams after G-- and other Ger. authors. 1890. C178. [28 poems, 71 "Xenien," epigrams, etc.]
†HALLER, MRS. ADELE. Metrical tr. 1862. C184. [25 poems by G--.]
2444. HARTSHORNE, GRACE. For thee alone. Poems of love sel. Bost: Estes 1899. 294p. il. D. [One from G--.] [AC]
2445. HAYWARD, A. G--. Ed: Blackwood 1878. 222p. 17cm. [BM] [Many small bits, nearly all in prose. Some citations from Scott, Swanwick, and probably others.]
**HEDGE, F: H: Prose writers of Germany. 1849. 1870. C194. [94 pages from G--.]
*2446. HUTTON, R: HOLT. Lit. essays. L: Strahan 1871. [Vol. 2 [BM] has essay on Goethe and his influence, with a few tr. pp. 3-100.]
*2447. do. 1877. [same] 2d rev. enl. ed. L: Daldy, Isbister. vol. 2, pp. 1-79.
*2448. do. [same] 1888. 3d rev. enl. ed. L; NY: Macmillan. 490p. pp. 1-89. [Other eds. 1892. 1896.]
KNORTZ, K: Representative Ger. poems...by various tr. 1885. C309. [27 from G--.]
*2449. LEE-HAMILTON, EUGENE. Poems and transcripts. Ed; L: Blackwood 1878. 171p. 8. [5 from G--, mostly quite good.] [BM]
*2450. LEONARD, W: E. The vaunt of man. NY: Huebsch 1912. 1923. 192p. 8. [one by G--.] [LC.BM]
2451. LEWES, G: H: Goethe gallery. Female characters of G-- from the orig. drawings of W. Kaulbach w...text by L--. L; Munich; NY: Bruckmann 1867. unp. 47cm. [NY]
[BM has only 2d ed. 1874. Interspersed verse, some by Lewes; citations from Aytoun, Carlyle, Martin, Scott, Swanwick.]
§2452. do. Life and works of G--. L: Nutt 1855. 2v. 786p. 12. [Some rather mediocre verse tr.] [BM.LC]
§2453. do. 1864. [same] 2d ed. L: Smith. (B42)
§2454. do. 1890. [same] 4th ed. (B42)
§2455. do. 1908. [same] Everyman's lib. (B42)
2456. LEWIS, M. G., Life and corr. of. L: Colburn 1839. 2v. 8. [BM] [One from G--.]
2457. MACDOWELL, E: Six idylls after G-- (w. music). NY: Schmidt 1901. Rev. and augmented. 19p. 4. [LCM]
2458. do. 1908. [same] In his "Verses." Bost; NY: Schmidt. 59p. 8. [LC.BM]
MARVIN, F: R. Flowers of song from many lands. 1902. C399. Also, Poems and tr. 1914. (C400.) [19 poems from G--.]
†2459. READE, J: ELMUND. The drama of life...poems...from G--. L: Saunders & Otley 1840. 162p. 21cm. [BM]
[4 passages from "Faust," one poem from "W: Meister."]
2460. REEKS, MARG. The mother of G--. L; NY: Lane 1911. 312p. 8. [9 poems and much prose, the latter very good.] [BM]
*2461. RONNFELDT, W. B. Criticisms, reflections, and maxims of G--. Tr. w. an introd. L: Scott 1897. xxxiv;261p. 8. [BM]
[G-- on Shakespeare (5 papers, in part from "W: Meister" and the "Sprüche"; G-- on Byron (4); poetry and the fine arts (9); reflections and maxims, pp. 137-261, including some of the "Sprüche in Prosa."]
2462. S., M. Thoughts from G--, compiled. L: Mayle 1905. Priory press booklets. 36p. 8. [BM]
[Chiefly "Sayings which show him in his speculative mood." A few done or rev. by compiler from conv. with Eckermann; others from Blackie's "Wisdom of G--," Carlyle's "W: Meister," and Huxley's tr. of the "Essay on nature."]
2463. SANBORN, F. B. Life and genius of G--. Bost: Ticknor 1886. 454p. 19cm. [Thirteen lectures by as many persons. Much verse and some prose, diversely rendered.] [BM]

GOETHE--SELECTIONS

2464. STRONG, A: HOPKINS. The great poets and their theology. Phil: Amer. baptist pub. soc. 1899. 531p. 21cm. [6 poems from G--.][BM]

2465. THOMAS, CALVIN. G-- and the conduct of life. U. of Mich. 1886. Pmph. 28p. (B19) [2 poems from G--.]

*2466. TOMLINSON, C: A crit. exam. of G--'s sonnets. L: Nutt 1890. 17p. 21cm. BM--Also in "Pub. of Engl. Goethe Soc." no. 7, 1893. pp. 225-45. [17 sonnets, also "Das Sonnett," and "Natur und Kunst"...No feminine rhyme, otherwise excellent.]

*WARNER, C: D. Lib. of the world's best lit. 1896. 1902. 1917. (C366.) [70p. from G-- in good or excellent tr.]

§WEBB, PHIL. G. L. Tr. from Heine and G--. 1912. (C556.)

§2467. WORSLEY, T: The Roman martyr. By Mrs. Cath. R. Worsley. W. tr. from G-- (probably by T: Worsley, who ed. the volume). L: Williams & Norgate 1859. 111p. 8. [8 poems, two scenes from "Faust," and two from "Tasso," the latter well done.] [BM]

SINGLE WORKS

*2468. (Abendmahl v. L. da Vinci zu Mailand.) Observations on L. da Vinci's pict. of the Last Supper. Tr...w. introd. and...notes by G. H. Noehden. L: J.Booth 1821. vii;37; 45p. 29cm. [BM] [Not distinguished, but mostly correct.]

**2469. (Achilleis.) Achilleid. Tr. Ax. Rogers. 1890. In #2382.

§2470. (Annalen.) Annals; or, day and year papers. Tr. w. pref. C: Nisbet. L: Bohn 1884? In #2365(2).

§2471. do. 1901. [same] Rev. ed. NY: Colonial press. 261p. 24cm. [The world's great classics, vol. 42.] [LC]

2472. (Claudina v. Villa Bella.) Fred and Alice. Tr. and ad. Wl. Scott (from the "Romance"). In C357, etc.

*2473. (Clavigo.) Clavidgo [sic]: a trag. in 5 acts (and in prose). Tr. C: L(eftley). L: Johnson 1798. 95p. 8. [NY] [Some bad blunders; style and spirit excellent.]

2474. do. 1834. In "Monthly Mag." (II) 18(1834):317;437. (B26)

2475. do. 1847. Tr. anon. In "The literary world," 2(1847):506;534. (B27)

*2476. do. 1879. Tr. anon. (perhaps by E: Bell?) In #2372. Also in #2380. Reprinted in #2387 and ascribed to E. A. Browning.

*2477. do. 1897. Tr. by members of the Manchester G-- soc. Introd. by T: Af. S(towell). L: Nutt. 136p. 8. [BM]

2478. (Das Märchen, zur Fortsetzung der Unterhaltungen deutscher Ausgewanderten.) The tale. Tr. anon. 1823. In C456.

**2479. do. 1832. Tr. T: Carlyle. In "Fraser's Mag." 6, no. 33. (B26) [Reprinted in C56.]

*2480. do. 1877. Carlyle's tr. Pref. (Pp. 3-20) by O(liver) Y(orke), pseud. (editor of "Fraser's Mag.") Bost: Osgood. 86p. 12cm. [BM] [This was evidently bound with "Favorite poems" by Aytoun and Martin, #2398, for BPL has a copy put out by Osgood, and B13 lists one for Houghton.]

§2481. do. 1854. Tr. R. D. Boylan. In #2367. [Not accurate.]

(Denkmal Ulrichs v. Hutten.) Tribute, etc. Falsely ascribed to G--. Really by Herder; see #4219.

2482. (Der neue Paris, aus "D. und W.") The new Paris, a child's tale. Tr. J: Oxenford. 1844. In C442.

*2483. do. 1889. The new Paris. Tr. W. F. Kirby. In "Pub. Eng. G-- soc." 5:28-42.

DICHTUNG UND WAHRHEIT

2484. [Sel.] 1910. Tr. anon. In C574.

2484a. 1824. Memoirs of G--: written by himself. Tr. anon. L: Colburn. 2v. viii;457;350p. port. 21cm. [BM]

GOETHE
[Tr. from the French of Aubert de Vitry, though not so stated. Biogr. notices, by the tr., of the chief persons mentioned. 3 pts. tr., i.e., 15 books, all that had been so far pub. in Germany.]
†2485. 1824. [same reprinted.] NY: Collins & Hannay. 360p. 8. (B48) [Abridged.]
*2486. 1844. Memoirs of G--. Ten books. (Tr. Parke Godwin.) NY. (B48)
*2487. 1846. Autobiog. of G--. Tr. Godwin and J. H. Hopkins. NY: Wiley & Putnam. [This ed. is cited by LC card, which says that pt. 3 was tr. by C. A. Dana, pt. 4 by J. S. Dwight.]
*2488. 1846. Autobiog.: truth and poetry of my own life. Tr. J: Oxenford. L. 3v. 8. (B8)
**2489. 1848. [same] The auto-biography of G--. Thirteen books. L: Bohn. vii;520p. 17cm. [O. admits having made use of Godwin's tr. In fact, whole sections are taken almost verbatim.] [BM.LC]
**2490. 1849. The concluding books, 14-20. Also letters from Switzerland, 2 pts., and letters from Italy. Tr. A. J. W. Morrison. L: Bohn. 544p. (B42) [Vol. 2. of #2365.]
*2491. 1850. Godwin's tr. as above. 2d ed. [LC card]
*2492. 1852-5. [same] Phil: Henderson n.d. 2v. 12. [AC]
*2493. 1872. Oxenford's tr. Bohn. [LC]
*2494. 1884. Oxenford's tr. revised. L: Bell. 2v. 19cm. [LC]
*2495. 1888. Oxenford's tr. Goethe's boyhood, 1749-64. Being the first 5 books, etc. Ed. w. pref. by E: Bell. L: Bell. 188p. 18cm. [BM]
2496. 1890. G--'s boyhood and youth. Books 1-11. Tr. anon. NY: Putnam. 2v. (B9, vol. 12)--same? Putnam 1891. 2v. 18. [EC]
*2497. 1891. [same as #2494] Bell. [LC]
*2498. 1893. [same as #2496?] G--, the boyhood and youth. Being books I to II (i.e., XI?) etc. Tr. Oxenford. L: 2v. 18. (B8)
*2499. 1901. Books 14-20, as in #2490. Also, Annals; or, day and year papers, tr. C: Nisbet. L: Bell. 518p. 18cm. [BM]
[This "stereotype ed." was first put out about 1884.]
*2500. 1904. Oxenford's tr. The early life...Books 1-9. L: Hutchinson. 378p. 17cm. [BM.LC]
**2501. 1908. Poetry and truth from my own life. 20 books. Tr. (of Oxenford and Morrison) rev. by Minna S. Smith. Introd. and bibliog. by K: Breul. L: Bell. 2v. xxxviii;401;326p. 16cm. [BM.LC]
[Very careful and thorough revision, especially effective in the prose passages; lyrics seem to me poorer.]
**2502. 1908. [same] NY: Macmillan. 2v. 16. [AC]
**2503. 1913. [same] Macmillan. 2v. 16. [AC]
**2504. 1925. [same] NY: Harcourt. 2v. 19cm. [LC]
§2505. (<u>Die Braut v. Korinth.</u>) The bride of Corinth. Tr. anon. Kingston. 1847? 13p. O. [UW]
[An unpub. tract, prt. in an unfin. state.]
2506. do. 1890. Tr. C: Tomlinson. For the author. viii p. 8. (B9, vol. 13)
†2507. do. 1911. Tr. W. A. Cox. Cambridge: Priv. prt. 9p. 22cm. [BM]
2508. (<u>Die Geschwister.</u>) The sister: a drama. Tr. W: Taylor of Norwich. L: 1792. (B8)--Also Ed: 1792. (B3)
*2509. do. 1792. The sister. Tr. H: Mackenzie. In C386.
§2510. do. 1885. Brother and sister. Tr. anon. In #2380.
[None too good, seemingly not wholly accurate.]
2511. (<u>Die guten Weiber.</u>) The good women. Tr. R. D. Boylan. 1854. In #2367 and #2380.
§2512. do. 1929? Sketches of naughty ladies. Tr. anon. Girard, Kan: Haldeman-Julius n.d. 32p. 12cm. [Tr. is not very good; old-fashioned style, and not even entirely correct.] [BQM]

GOETHE--SINGLE WORKS

**2513. (Die Laune des Verliebten.) The wayward lover. Tr. E. A. Bowring. 1879. In #2372 and #2363, also in #2387, ascribed to E. A. Browning. [Excellent, even to the handling of the difficult 12 syl. verse.]

§2514. do. 1899. The lover's caprice. Tr. Martha R. Bannan. In #2423.

DIE LEIDEN DES JUNGEN WERTHERS[1]

2515. [Sel.] Tr. anon. 1910. In C574.

†2515a. 1779. The sorrows of W--. (Tr. R: Graves.) L: Dodsley. 2v. 168;172p. 16cm. [BM]
[Tr. from French of "C. Aubry," (i.e., Count F: W: K: v. Schmettau), which is not bad, but incomplete; English still more so.]

†2516. 1780. [same] 2d ed. [Identical.] [BM]

†2517. 1780. [same] Dublin: C. Jackson. vii;105;122p. 8. (B19a)

†2518. 1782. [same] 3d ed. [15cm; otherwise identical.] [BM]

†2519. 1783. [same] 4th ed. [Identical.] (B19a)

†2520. 1784. [same] New ed. Dodsley. viii;168;166p. 16cm. [BM]
[The letterpress of vol. 2. is shortened by one line up to p. 96, then follows the foregoing page for page.]

2521. 1784. [same?] The sorrows and sympathetic attachments of Werter; a Ger. story by Mr. Goethe, doctor of the civil law. Phil: Bell. 2v. in 1. 20cm. [LC]

†2522. 1785. Graves' tr. New ed. L: Dodsley. 2v. viii; 168;168p. 15cm. [Adds a poem, "Werter to Charlotte (a little before his death)." This adds 2 pages to previous editions.] [BM]

2523. 1785. [same?]...a German story..Dublin: Chamberlaine. 2v. 8. (B3)

†2524. 1786. [same] New ed. Dodsley. 2v. 168;168p. 8. (B8)

†2525. 1786. [same] New ed. Dodsley. 1v;223p. 8. (B8)

†2526. 1786. W-- and Charlotte: a Ger. story. A new tr. from the last Leipsic ed. L: Parsons. 172p. Il. w. notes. 12. [BM]
[This is really derived from Graves' tr. by a person who probably knew no German.]

2527. 1786. The sorrows of W--: a Ger. story. Phil: Prtd. and sold by Enoch Story. 2v. (B6a)

†2528. 1788. Graves' tr. New ed. L: Osborne & Griffin. 2v. 180; 190p. 16. (B8)

†2529. 1789. [same] New ed. Dodsley. viii;223p. 8. (B19a)[Identical with #2520.]

§2530. 1789. Tr. from the genuine French ed. of "M. Aubry" (see #2515) by J: Gifford. L: Harrison. 2v. 47; 74p. (in double columns) 21cm. [BM]
[Pref. by tr., and a "Letter from a German of lit. eminence to M. Aubry." Front. by R. Smirke. Some notes by Gifford. Creditable despite disadvantages.]

†2531. 1789. Graves' tr. Litchfield, Ct: T: Collier. 94; 92p. 12. (B6a. B48) [B8 erroneously ascribes this to W: Render; cf. #2541.]

†2532. 1790. Graves' tr. Dublin. 2v. 8. Vol. 1 prt. J: Rice. 105p. Vol. 2. prt. Hannah Chamberlaine. 122p. (B8)

†2533. 1794. Graves' tr. New ed. L: Osborne & Griffin. 2v. x;180; 190p. 14cm. [BM]
[Evidently identical w. #2528. Contains poem; cf. #2522. B8 lists this for 1795.]

2534. 1794. The sorrows of W--: a Ger. story. Tr. anon. Phil: Prtd. for Rb. Campbell. (B6a)

†2535. 1795. Graves' tr. (B19a)

[1] Many judgments taken from Long, B25. Editions are listed chronologically.

GOETHE - WERTHER
2536. 1795...an affecting story. Tr. anon. NY: Prtd. for L. Wayland. 142p. 18. (B6a. B48)
2537. 1796. The sorrows of W--: an affecting story. Tr. erom [sic] the orig. Ger. anon. NY: Prtd. by Mott & Lyon. 144p. front. 24. [Available: AAS.] (B6a)
2538. 1796. same title. Tr. anon. NY: Prtd. for Nath. Bell. 16. (B6a) [Available: NYPL]
†2539. 1798. Graves' tr. W-- and Charlotte. The sorrows of W--. A Ger. story. To which is annexed, the letters of Charlotte to a female friend...(By W. James.) Bost: Thomas & Andrews. 147 (cxlix); 284p. 12. (B6a)
[Authorship revealed by a letter of W. James to the publisher Cadell, now in Speck collection at Yale.]
2540. 1799. The letters of W--. Tr. anon. Ludlow. 18. (B25) [Incomplete.]
†2541. 1801 (1800?) Tr. from...Baron Göethe, from the last Ger. ed., by W: Render. Appendix containing an account of a conversation, which the tr. had with W--, a few days preceding his death. L: Phillips. 375p. 18cm. [BM.LC]
["Another principal inducement was...the tr.'s personal acquaintance w. W--, w. Charlotte, and with their respective families." This is probably the ed. listed by B8 for 1800. T.p. by Burney.]
2542. 1802. Tr. anon. Ludlow: Nicholson. 116p. 8. (B8)
[Seems to be the same as #2540, 2544.]
†2543. 1802. Tr. F: Gotzberg (assisted by an Engl. lit. gentleman). L: Cundee for Hurst. iv; 194p. 8. [BM]
[Front. and 5 pl. by Hopwood. Tr. seems to follow Render (#2541) and apparently knows little German or ignores orig.]
2544. 1802-4. The letters of W--. Tr. anon. Pub. July 1, 1802 by G. Nicholson, Poughnill, near Ludlow. Follows a second title: The literary miscellany...1804. 119p. 12. (B19a)
[Vignette by Hawkins after Corbould.]
†2545. 1804. 1805. Graves' tr. ...a Ger. story. A new ed. Cupar-Fife: R. Tullis. iv;198p. 14cm. [BM]
[Poem as in #2522. Prefixed is engr. t.p. by J. W. Alston. Ed: Denham & Dick 1805.]
2546. 1804. Edinb. (B3)
†2547. 1807. Render's tr. Bost: Andrews & Cummings. 180p. 16. (B48)
[Identity of year and paging with the following suggests identity of tr.]
†2548. 1807. Graves' tr. Ed: Oliver. 180p. il. t.p. by C. Campbell. 16. (B8, B19a)
2549. 1807. A new tr. rev. and comp. with all the former eds. NY: Scott. 100p. 16. [NY]
[Prob. a reprint of 1st ed. of Pratt's tr. Cf. B3.--This copy could not be found in 1932.]
2550. 1807? Tr. Pratt. L: Tegg n.d. 191p. 8. (B8)
2551. 1808. The sorrows of W--. A new ed. Tr. anon. L: J.Cundee. vi;186p. sm. 8. (B19a) [Il. by 6 engr. by Hopwood.]
2552. 1809. Tr. anon. L: Jones.
[Reported by Manchester Goethe Soc.; now missing.]
†2553. 1809. Ed: Prt. by McCliesch & Campbell for Cairns, Wilson & Son, York. 180p. 24. [NY]
[Catalog says: Tr. from French, not before 1807. Suspect this is either Graves or Gifford; cf. #2548.--This copy was missing in 1932.]
†2554. 1809. A new tr. rev. and compared with all the former eds. By S: J. Pratt. 2d ed. L: Tegg & Hughes. iv;164p. front. 11cm.
[Long (B25) says he does not stick to the text.] [BM]

GOETHE--WERTHER

†2555. 1810. Graves' tr. Ed: Oliver & Boyd. 100p. il. 32. (B8)

†2556. 1810. The sorrows of W--...Baron Goethe. A new tr. rev. and comp. w. all the former eds. L: for A. K. Newman. iv;126p. 12. (B19a) [Engr. t.p. has: 1809. T.p. by J. Wallis after J. Davis. Probably Pratt's tr. and identical with #2554.]

†2557. 1813. Pratt's tr. 2d ed. L: Tegg; Dublin: Cumming; Ed: Dick. iv;191p. 16cm. [BM]
[Front. as in #2554, but dated 1813. T.p. by Thurston. Pref. by Pratt. Tr. is that of Graves through letter xv; then Pratt's tr.[1]]

†2558. 1813. Pratt's tr. 3d ed. L: Tegg; Ed: Dick; Dublin: Cumming. iv;162p. 12. (B19a)
[Engr. t.p. by Freeman after Thurston, 2d ed.]

†2559. 1815. Graves' tr. L: Lackington, Allen. v;162p. 8. [BM]
[No poem. Engr. front; t.p. by H. Corbould.]

2560. 1815. Tr. anon. L: Dean & Munday. (B8)

2561. 1816. ...a pathetic story. Tr. anon. L: Dean & Munday. 140p. 12. (B8)

2562. 1818. The sorrows of W--: a pathetic story. Tr. anon. L: Dean & Munday. 140p. 8. (B19a) [Front. by Page after Cruikshank. Engr. t.p. Probably identical with the foregoing.]

2563. 1820. Tr. anon. L: Dean & Munday. (B8)

†2564. 1823. Graves-Pratt tr. as in #2557. Chiswick: Prt. for Jennings & Tegg, L. iv;124p. 13 x 7cm. [BM]
[Engr. t.p. as in #2557, but dated Oct. 1, 1822. No poem.]

†2565. 1826. Graves' tr. L: Jones. 12. (B8)

†2566. 1826. Graves' tr. L: Dove. With letters from Yorick to Eliza, and Sterne's Sentimental journey. 216p. 24. [NY]

2567. 1829. Tr. anon. L: Blake. (B8)

2568. 1830? ...(and other miscellaneous works)...for the female sex. Tr. anon. L: C:Daly. 281p. 16. (B8)

†2569. 1838. Graves' tr. New ed. L: Osborne & Griffin. 2v. 180; 192p. 8. (B8) [Apparently a re-issue of #2528.]

†2570. 1842. Graves' tr. L: Allman. 16. (B8)
[Same combination as #2566.]

†2571. 1844. Graves' tr. New ed. Belfast: Jos. Smyth. pp. 1-135. front. 13cm. [BM]

2572. before 1852. Ithaca, NY: Andrus, Gantlett n.d. 18. [AC]

†2573. 1851. Graves' tr. L: Chapman. (The il. lit. of all nations.) 24p. 12 il. 28cm. [Separate t.p. No poem.] [BM]

†2574. 1852. Graves' tr. In Classic tales:...the most esteemed works of imagination. L: Bohn. 36p. 18cm. [Separately paged.][BM]

2575. 1855-8. Tr. anon. NY: Derby & Jackson n.d. 18. [AC]

*2576. 1854. Tr. R. D. Boylan. In #2372, and in later eds. of Bohn's lib.

2577. 1879. Tr. anon. In "The Western." St.L. (B8)

*2578. 1885. Boylan's tr. In #2385. [Slightly rev. for this ed.]

†2579. 1886. Gotzberg's tr. Introd. by H: Morley. L; NY: Cassell. 192p. 8. [Cf. #2543.] [BM]

2580. 1886. ...and other tales. Ed. and rev. by L. Noa. Bost: Bradlee Whidden. New ed. (B9, vol. 9)

2581. 1893. Tr. anon. G--'s sorrows of W--. Il. by Gambart and Marold. Bost. (B8)

2582. 1902. Tr. anon. Educ. pub. co. (B13)

2583. 1905. Caldwell. (B13)

†2584. 1905. [same as #2579] [BM]

2585. 1907-8. Tr. anon. Brooklyn: Wessels. World's best classics. (B8)

[1] Carré (B3) states that Pratt's tr. had the following reprintings: Chiswick: 1822; L: 1823, 1825, 1826, 1833, 1842, 1851, 1852. I suspect that this is due to confusion; cf. my #2564-6, 2570, 2573, 2574.

GOETHE - WERTHER
*2586. 1917. Boylan's tr. In C186.
[Erroneously ascribed to Bayard Taylor.]
2587. 1923? The love sorrows of young W--. Girard, Kan: Haldeman-Julius n.d. (Big blue books.) 128p. [Cited from catalog.]
2588. [ad.][1] 1786. The letters of Charlotte, during her connexion with Werter. Dublin: for Chamberlaine (and 15 others) 1786. 2v. 264p. 12. (Lib. of R. Priebsch)
2589. do. 1788. The sorrows of W--: a poem by Amelia Pickering. L: Cadell. xxii;69p. 27cm. [13 "letters" in 4-line stanzas.] [BM]
2590. do. 1793. Essay on novels (in verse) by Ax. Thomson, with six sonnets from Werter. Ed: Hull & Watson. pp. 17-24. 28cm. [BM]
2591. do. 1796. Werter: a trag. in three acts. Ad. by F. Reynolds. L: Woodfall. 48p. 8. [NY]
2592. do. 1797. The letters of Charlotte...NY: Davis for Duykinck et al. 2v. 240p. front. Scoles. 15cm. [BM]
2593. do. 1800? Werter and Charlotte: a Ger. story, containing many wonderful and pathetic incidents. L: Sabine. 28p. front. 18cm.[BM]
2594. do. 1813. The letters of Charlotte...L: G:Hughes. 211p. il. 17cm. [Front. by Armstrong. Engr. t.p.] [BM]

2595. (Die Metamorphose der Pflanzen.) Essay on the metamorphosis of plants. Tr. E. M. Cox. L: 1863. (B24)
2596. (Die Mitschuldigen.) The fellow culprits. Tr. E. A. Bowring. 1879. In #2372, #2365.
**2597. (Die natürliche Tochter.) The natural daughter. Tr. anon. 1885. In #2380. [Excellent both in style and substance.]
*2598. (Die Wahlverwandtschaften.) Elective affinities. [Sel.] Tr. G: Bradford. 1849. In C194.
*2599. do. 1854. Tr. anon. In #2367; also in #2380.
§2600. do. 1872. Tr. anon. Introd. by Victoria C. Woodhull. Bost: Niles. 325p. 12. [Rather poor style and not without errors.] [LC]
2601. do. 1872. [same?] Tr. anon. NY: Holt. 16. (B8)
*2602. do. 1913-15. Tr. of #2367, ed. Jas. A. Froude. In C154(2).

EGMONT

2603. [Sel.] Tr. anon. 1813. In C91.
§2604. ANON. 1848. Egmont by Goëthe. L: Saunders & Otley. iv;170p. 17cm. [BM]
[Pref. dated Frankfort-a-Main, June 1848. Fluent, but too wordy.]
*2605. BOOTT, F. Bost: Munroe & F. 1841. 150p. 17cm. [BPL.BM]
[Pref. claims this to be first Eng. ed., but cf. #2615. This is one of the best, spirited and idiomatic.]
*2606. do. 1871. [same] Bost: Sever, Francis. 150p. [LC]
*2607. COLERIDGE, A. D. With entr'actes and songs by Beethoven... and Schubert's Freudvoll und leidvoll. L: Chapman & Hall. 1868. 114p. 19cm. [Good but wordy.] [BM]
2607a. DICKENS, C: Jr. L: Williams & Norgate 1855. 12. [EC]
[In my first ed. I took this to be a school ed., but the "Amer. Bibliopolist" 1(1869):231 specifically notes such a translation.]
2608. PEARSON, E: S. Dresden: Pierson 1890. 110p. 8. (B8)
[German classical plays, no. 7.]
*2609. SWANWICK, ANNA. 1850. In #2366.
*2610. do. 1879. [same revised] In #2372.
*2611. do. 1894. [same] L: Bell. 90p. 8. (B9, vol. 23)
*2612. do. 1901. [same] Phil: McKay. 95p. S. (B9, vol. 23)
[Pocket literal tr.]
*2613. do. 1909. [same] With her "Faust" in #2791.
*2614. do. 1915. [same] In Harv. classics, vol. 19.

[1]For additional adaptations ("Wertheriaden"), see B8, p. 198 seq., and B3, p. 11 seq.

GOETHE--EGMONT
2615. TAYLOR, W: 1837. Phil: 16. (B8)
[Parts of his tr. pub. 1828 in C533.]

2616. (Erlkönig.) The erl-king. Tr. Mrs. Janna A. Morgan. Racine, Wis: 1860. (B24)
2617. The evil conscience. Tr. anon. (from the Unterhaltungen deutscher Ausgewanderten) 1895. In C559.
*2618. (Farbenlehre.) Goethe's theory of colors. Tr. Sir C: L. Eastlake. L: Murray 1840. 423p. 22cm. [BM.LC]

FAUST[1]--SELECTIONS

2619. ANON. 1813. In C91.
2620. ANON. 1820. An analysis of G--'s Faust, in illustration of Retsch's [sic]...outlines, engr...H: Moses. L: Boosey. 60p. 34cm. [BM.Yale]
2621. ANON. 1820. "Blackwoods Mag." June 1820.
[Tr. is "a young Irishman." Possibly J. C. Mangan?]
†2622. ANON. 1821. Faustus. With Retzsch's (27) outlines. L: Boosey. viii;86p. 26cm. [BM]
["Most striking passages and scenes of the original have been tr. into blank verse, and connected by a detailed description in prose."]
†2623. ANON. 1832. [same] New ed. w...append. May-day night scene, tr. P. B. Shelley. L: Lumley. vii;79p. 4. [BM]
2624. ANON. 1842. New Hampshire book. Specimens of lit., etc. Ed. C: J. Fox and S: Osgood. Nashua; N. H: Marshall; Bost: Munroe. 391p. 19cm. [One passage from "Faust."] [BM]
2625. ANON. 1875. Outlines to G--'s Faust, 26 etchings by M. Retzsch. L: Low. unp. 24 x 31cm. [BM]
[Text (in verse) follows each plate.]
2626. ANON. 1884. Songs (2 by T. Martin) and scenes from G--'s Faust. Il. A. Liezen Mayer and Ad. Lalauze. Bost: Estes & Lauriat. 44p. 21cm. [Chiefly commentary on the 20 il.] [LC.BM]
2627. ANON. 1910. In C574.
2628. ARNOLD T: J. (Selections from Faust.) Il. A. Liezen Mayer. NY: Stroefer n.d. (1872-6.) fol. [AC]
2629. BARTHOLOMEW, W. Walpurgis night. Music by Mendelssohn. Bost: Ditson n.d. (1872-6.) 8. [AC]
2630. BORROW, G: 1923. In C34.
§2631. CARLYLE, T: Essay on G--'s Helena. 1828. Reprinted in his Works, his Essays on G--, and elsewhere. [Extended passages from "Faust, II"; somewhat awkward in expression, but of course correct in sense.]
2632. CAWEIN, M. J. 1895. In C65.
2633. CLAUDY, FRANK. Sel. from...Faust. Washington, D. C: 1833.(B8)
§2634. DUCKETT, G: FLOYD. "Faust" (i.e., the "Preface" and "Prologue in Heaven"). L: 1845? 3p. 4. [BM]
["Composed at sea, on board the 'Union' transport, 1841." Duckett's prose turned into verse by Prof. Burrows. Rather poor.]
2635. do. 1885? [same] s. sh. fol. [Pub. w. Ger. parallel.] [BM]
*2636. ELBING, RAY. A study, etc. Columbus, O: Haak 1896. 118p. 19cm. [Consid. passages of pt. I in very good and acc. tr.] [LC]
2637. FUNCK, F: 1853. In C142.
†2638. GRANT, J: W. Hist. pict. from the Campagna of Rome. L: Heinemann 1867. 52p. 8. [Has some of the lyrics. Cf. #2721.] [BM]

[1]For translations of the Volksbuch and Puppenspiel, see List A.

GOETHE
2639. HAYWARD, A. Extracts from his tr. in "For. Quart. R." 12(1833):81-109. (B17) [Cf. #2723.]
2640. HEDGE, F: H: 1845. In C121. Also C193.
2641. HEPNER, ADOLPH. Dedication of Faust. Centenary...June 24, 1897. St.L: 1897. 16p. (B19) [Interlinear tr. w. notes.]
†2642. HODGES, C: 1836. In C202. [Night, Wood and cave, Dungeon. No attempt to keep meter or rhyme]
2643. MARTIN, Td. Poems orig. and tr. 1863. [C396] [3 acts from Faust II. Cf. #2765.]
§2644. NAYLOR, S: Ceracchi, a drama, and other poems. Maidenhead: Priv. prtd. 1839. 8. [Passages tr. from F--, sel. from six of the important scenes. Rather mediocre poetry.] [BM]
2645. PROWETT, C: GIPPS. Tr. and orig. pieces. Ed. C. H. Monro. Camb: Deighton; L: Bell 1862. 338p. 17cm. [Has: The archangels' song from "Faust."] [BM]
*2646. SHELLEY, P. B. (3) Passages from F--. In his Posthumous poems. L: Hunt 1824. pp. 393-415. [Also w. Hayward's tr. in #2744. See also "The Liberal" 1(1822): 121-37. Also in C166. Shelley is not wholly accurate, but his poetry is superb.] [BM]
*2647. SHIELL, A. G: (8) Songs from G--'s _Faust_. 1914. 31p. 21cm. [Some excellent, especially the grotesque.] [BM]
§2648. SOANE, G: Extracts from G--'s trag. of Faustus, explan. of the pl. by Retsch [sic]. L: Bohte 1820. 4. [A quotation, in prose, for each picture, with brief text.] [BM]
†2649. do. 1904. Soane's Faust tr. (576 lines), now first pub. (by L. L. Mackall) from the unique advance sheets sent to G-- in 1822. Braunschweig: Westermann. 20p. 22cm. [This is a separate reprint from "Herrig's Archiv" 112, p. 277-97. --Soane takes great liberties.] [LC.BM]
2650. SWANWICK, A. 1903. In C18.
2651. TAYLOR, BAYARD. Sel. from F--. Il. by P. Konewka. Bost: Roberts 1871. 17p. 30cm. [LC]
*2652. TURNER, E. J. and MORSHEAD, E. D. A. _Faust_ (I). The text, w. Engl. notes...and verse tr. L: Rivingtons 1882. vii;330p. 19cm. [Zueignung; ll. 129-160, 384-454, 906-17, 1094-1152, 1254-73, 2866-99, 2994-3014, 3236-68, 3519-59.--Blank verse very good; rhymed portions less successful.] [BM]

FAUST TRANSLATIONS[1]

2653. ANON. 1834. Faustus (I). L: Simpkin M. [By Warburton Davies; see below.] [BM]
2654. ANON. 1836. Faust (II). L: Il. by Retzsch. obl. 4. (B17) [Probably only selections; no tr. of part II is recorded before 1838.]
†2655. ANON. 1838. Faust (I,II) rend. into Engl. verse. L: prtd. by Arthur Taylor. 2v. xxiv;267; 379p. 12. [B19a says tr. was by the publisher; 50 cop. prtd. Mostly blank verse; quite feeble.] [LC]
2656. ANON. 1850. Faust and Wallenstein. Kepam. 8. [Probably Fillmore's tr.; cf. B8] [EC]
2657. ANON. 1887. Faust. Authorized ed. L: Ward, Lock. [Taylor's tr.; cf. #2818.] [BM]
2658. ANON. 1906. Faust. Il. G. James. L: Routledge. 148p. 8. [Probably Anster's tr.; cf. #2663.] [EC]
†2659. ANSTER, J: Faustus (I): a dramatic mystery. L: Longmans 1835. xliv;491p. 8. [BM]

[1] Lina Baumann (B1) has passed competent judgments on most of the Faust translations. Many of my comments derive from her study.

GOETHE--FAUST--ANSTER

[With "The bride of Corinth" and "The first Walpurgis night." Re-creation rather than tr. He expands by about one-seventh, and wholly distorts the original. The vogue of this tr. is discouraging.]

†2659a. do. 1841. [same] Frankfort o. M: Jugel. 332p. 18. [EC(Heinsius)]

†2660. do. 1864. Faust (II). L: Longmans. lxxxvii;485p. 19cm. [BM]

†2661. do. 1867. Faust (I). Lpz: Tauchnitz; L: Low. xiv;295p. 16cm. [BM]

†2662. do. 1883. Faust (I) w. Marlowe's "Faustus." L; NY: Routledge. 315p. 18cm. [BM.LC]

†2663. do. 1886. Faust (I). Introd. by H. R. Haweis. L: Routledge. 160p. 16. [BM]

†2664. do. 1886. Faust (II). The second part...w. introd. by H: Morley. L: Routledge. 287p. 18cm. [Morley's universal lib.] [BM]

†2665. do. 1886-7. Faust (I,II). NY: Harper. 2v. 18cm. [LC]

†2666. do. 1887. Faust (I). Introd. by H: Morley and H. R. Haweis. NY: Harper 290p. 8. (B8)

†2667. do. 1887. Faust (I) w. Marlowe's "Faustus." 8th ed. L: Routledge. 8. [Cf. #2662.] [LC]

†2668. do. 1887. Faust (I). Introd. H: Morley. Il. J. P. Laurens. L; NY: Routledge. 255p. 4. (B8)

†2669. do. 1888. Faust (I). NY: Munro. 329p. 8. (B8)

†2670. do. 1889. Faust (I). Introd. Burdett Mason. Il. F. M. Gregory. L: Redway. iv;71p. fol. [B8 has: NY. 1888?] [BM]

†2671. do. 1889. Faust (I?), w. Schiller's poems and ballads. Introd. H: Morley. L: Routledge. 8. [EC]

†2672. do. 1890. Faust (I?). Il. by F: J. Boston. NY: Stokes. 360p. 19cm. [LC]

†2673. do. 1893. Faust (I,II). Introd. H: Morley. L; NY: Routledge. 2 pts. 8. [Lubbock's 100 books.] [BM]

†2674. do. 1894. Faust (I). Introd. B. Mason. L: Truslove & Hanson; NY: Dodd, Mead. 250p. il. by F. M. Gregory. 22cm. [BM.LC]

†2675. do. 1895. Faust (II). 287p. D. [AC]

†2676. do. 1897. Marlowe's "Faustus" and G--'s "Faust (I)." Introd. by H: Morley. L: 604p. 8. (B8)

†2677. do. 1902. Faust (I). Unit lib. 250p. 12. [Cf. #2674.] [BM]

†2678. do. 1903. Faust. NY: Scribner. 16. [AC]

†2679. do. 1903. Faust (I). L: Newnes. 250p. 8. [Cf. #2674.] [BM]

†2680. do. 1907. Faust (I). Tr. J. Aster [sic]. L: Hutchinson. 258p. 12. [EC]

†2681. do. 1907. Marlowe's "Faustus" and G--'s Faust. Introd. A. W. Ward. L: Frowde 1907. 235p. 8. [BM]

†2682. do. 1909. Faust (I,II). People's ed. L; NY: Cassell. 419p. 18cm. [BM]

†2683. do. 1915. Faust (I) with Marlowe's "Faustus." Introd. A. W. Ward. L: Oxford press. 291p. 8. [BM]

†2684. do. 1925. Faust (I). Il. Harry Clarke. Autographed ed. Dingwall-Rock. pa. Q.[AC]--L: Harrap. 254p. [EC]

†2685. ARNOLD, T: J. Faust (I). Tr. in the orig. meters. L; Stuttgart; Munich: 1877. 157p. il. 48cm. [BM]
[50 il. after...A. Liezen Mayer...and vignettes...by R. Seitz.--Tr. is wrecked on the meters.]

†2686. VON BERESFORD. Faust (I). Cassel; Göttingen: G: H. Wigand 1862. 227p. 17cm. [BM]
[Has poetic feeling, but does not command English.]

§2687. BERNAYS, Lp. Faust (II) tr...partly in the meters of the orig., and partly in prose. With other poems...tr. L: Low; Carlsruhe: Bielefeld 1839. xx;268p. 22cm. [BM]

GOETHE--FAUST--BERNAYS
[Correct; much unrhymed verse; careless about rhythms. Poems by Goethe, Hebel, Immermann, Schiller, Uhland, Wyss.]
§2688. do. 1840. New ed. L; Carlsruhe. (B8)
†2689. "BETA." Faust (I) w. a literal tr. and notes for students. L: Nutt 1895. viii;384p. 19cm. [BM.LC]
[Little more than a copy of Hayward's tr. #2723.]
†2690. BIRCH, JONATHAN. Faust (I) w. engr. on steel after M. Retzsch. L: Black & A. 1839. 276p. 8. [BM]
["Dublin Review," 1840: "As a tr. it is bad, as a poetic tr. it is worse, but as a tr. of Faust it is worst of all."]
†2691. do. 1839-43. 2v. 276;342p. same il. 8. [BM]
†2692. do. ca. 1850. St. Helen's, Lancs. T: Beecham n.d. 128p. 24. (B19a)
†2693. do. 1886. [Issued by T: Beecham as advertisement. At the bottom of each page is printed in bold type: "Beecham's pills." (B1)
†2694. do. 1879. Faust (I,II). Re-issue of #2691. [BM]
†2695. do. 1893. [same] Re-issue. [BM]
§2696. BIRDS, JAS. A. Faust (I) chiefly in blank verse w. introd. (pp. 1-81) and notes. (pp. 321-460). L: Longmans 1880. viii;460p. 20cm. (B8) [Faithful, rarely inacc., but prosy and without insight into the spirit of Faust.] [BM]
†2697. do. 1889. Faust...The second part. L: Longmans Green. 450p. 20cm. [This forms a 2-vol. set with the foregoing. Many faulty translations of important passages.] [BM]
†2698. do. 1889. Faust (I,II). Introd. and notes. NY. 2v. 460p; 450p. [Evidently combines the two foregoing numbers.] [BM]
†2699. BLACKIE, J: S. Faust (I) w. prelim. remarks. Ed; L: Blackwood 1834. lii;288p. 8. [BM]
[Mostly weak, petty, and banal; bad rhymes and verse.]
†2700. do. 1880. [same.] 2d ed., largely rewritten. L: Macmillan. lxxvii;296p. 8. [BM]
†2701. BOWEN, C: H. Faust (I). L: Longmans 1878. 247p. 8. [BM]
[A boyish attempt sent to press after 40 years without the least revision.]
§2702. BROOKS, C: T. Faust (I). Bost: Ticknor & F. 1856. 234p. 19cm. [Succeeds best in humorous passages; struggle to retain rhyme and metre forces him to pad.] [LC]
§2703. do. 1857. 2d ed. 234p. [LC.BM]
§2704. do. 1880. 15th ed. [LC]
§2705. BUCHANAN, SIR G: Faust (I), tr. into Engl. verse, w. introd. explan. of the whole. L: Alston Rivers 1908. 200p. 8. [BM]
[Blank verse, correct but unsatisfying.]
2706. CARTWRIGHT, J: Faust (I). L: 1862. (B1)
†2707. CLARKE, W: B., an architect. Faust (I,II). Freiburg i. Br: Schmidt 1865. xxvi;460p. 18cm. [BM]
[One of the very worst; incredibly faulty and prosy.]
†2708. CLAUDY, FRANK. Faust (I). Washington, D. C. 1886. (B1)
[Lang. is Ger.-Engl; forced from beginning to end. There was a 2d ed. in 1899, unchanged.]
†2709. COLQUHOUN, W. H. Faust (I) in Engl. verse. L: Moxon 1878. 327p. 18cm. [BM]
[Literal tr., bad rhymes and verse; complete failure. He announces: "Part II of the drama is ready for publication." Evidently the public did not demand it.]
§2710. COOKSON, G. M. Faust (I). Introd. J: G. Robertson. L: Routledge; NY: Dutton 1927. lvii;216p. 8. [BM]
[Very good verse, but G-- suffers in the transmutation.]

GOETHE--FAUST--DAVIES

†2711. DAVIES, WARBURTON. Faustus (I). (cf. #2653.) L: Simpkin & M. 1834. viii;231p. 12. [BM]
[Tr.'s name is written on t.p. of copy belonging to R. Priebsch. Omits prolog, prelude, and intermezzo. Monotonous blank verse.]
†2712. FILMORE, LEWIS. Faust (I). L: Smith 1841. vi;64p. 23cm. [BM]
[Prt. in double columns. Very bald and spiritless.]
†2713. do. 1843. L. 223p. (B8)
†2714. do. 1847. [Re-issue of #2712.] New ed. L. (B8)
†2715. do. 1853. [same] L: Ingram, Cooke. Universal lib. pp. 231-96 (or 1-64). 23cm. [BM]
†2716. do. 1861. [same] New ed. L. 8. (B8)
†2717. do. 1866. [same] Masterpieces of for. lit. L: Griffin. 64p. 8. [BM]
†2718. GALVAN, J: Faust (I) tr. into Engl. verse. Dublin: Robertson 1860. ix;252p. il. 16cm. [BM.LC]
[A travesty of G--'s Faust.]
†2719. GOWER, LORD FIS. L. Faust (I). And Schiller's Song of the bell. L: Murray 1823. iv;304p. 8. [BM]
[Bowdlerized; full of errors, contradictions, and banalities.]
†2720. do. 1825. 2d rev. ed. W. tr. from the German. L: Murray. 2v. 201;205p. 8. [Lessing: "Faust." Schiller: Song of the bell and 8 poems; Körner (2); Goethe, Bürger, Salis, one each.] [UW]
†2721. GRANT, J: W. Faust (I). L: Hamilton 1867. 162p. 8. [BM]
--L: Hamilton 1868. 8. (B8)
[Only a few signed copies prt. Beneath contempt.]
†2722. GURNEY, ARCHER. Faust (II). L: Senior et al. 1842. viii; 336p. 8. --L: Nutt 1843. (B8) [BM]
[Does not follow Goethe's meters; many errors and liberties.]
§2723. HAYWARD, A. Faust (I). Tr. into Engl. prose w. remarks on former tr. L: no pub. 1833. lxxxvii;279p. 21cm. [BM]
[Surprisingly free from errors, yet wholly fails to convey the variety of the moods in the original.]
§2724. do. 1833. L: Moxon. lxxxvii;291p. 21cm. [BM]
§2725. do. 1834. 2d ed. Moxon. cviii;350p. 8. [BM]
§2726. do. 1838. 3d ed. L;NY. (B8)
§2727. do. 1840. New t.p.: First Amer. ed. (B8)
§2728. do. 1842. Reprinted from 3d Engl. ed., corr. and rev. Erfurt; Lpz: Prt. for L: Hilsenberg. 172p. 12. (B8. B19a)
§2729. do. 1847. 4th ed. L. 8. (B8)
§2730. do. 1851. Bost. [LC]
§2731. do. 1851. 5th ed. L. 12. (B8)
§2732. do. 1854. Bost. 16. (B8)
§2733. do. 1855. 6th ed. L: Moxon. xxxvi;245p. 8. [BM]
§2734. do. 1860. 7th ed. 8. (B8)
§2735. do. 1864. 8th ed. xxxvi;245p. 8. (B8)
§2736. do. 1869. New ed. (B8)
§2737. do. 1873. New ed. (B8)
§2738. do. 1874. 9th ed. w. increased notes. 12. (B8)
§2739. do. 1880. 10th ed. (B8)
§2740. do. 1882. In #2379.
§2741. do. 1889. L: Bell & S. [EC]
§2742. do. 1890. 11th ed. 282p. (B8)
§2743. do. 1892. Rev. w. introd. by C. A. Buchheim. L: Bell & S. xxvi;479p. 17cm. [BM]
§2744. do. 1908. Pref. by Roger Ingpen. Il. W. Pogány. (2) Scenes tr. P. B. Shelley. L: Hutchinson. xx;210p. 28cm. [BM]
[Prologue in heaven and May-day night by Shelley. pp. 151-67.]
§2745. do. 1927. [same?] L: Hutchinson. 8. [EC]

GOETHE--FAUST

§2746. HILLS, J: Faust (I) tr. into Eng. verse. L: Whittaker 1840. xxi;369p. 16cm. [B8 has: 1839. Hampered by meter and rhyme; often succeeds in striking the right note.] [BM]

†2747. HUTH, A. H. The trag. of Faustus (I). L: Low 1889. vii; 245p. 8. [Travesty results from attempt to combine Jacobean and mod. Engl. Meter and rhyme very faulty.] [BM]

†2748. do. 1912. 2d ed. L: Low. 191p. 8. [EC has: 1911.] [BM]

†2749. KNOX, CAPT. Faust (I). L: Ollivier 1847. viii;338p. 8. [BM] [Knows no German.]

†2750. LATHAM, A. G. Faust (I). L: Dent 1896. Temple classics. (B1) [Uneven; incredible lapses even in the midst of good passages.]

†2751. do. 1902. Dent. 281p. 15cm. [BM.LC] --Also Macmillan 1902. [AC]

†2752. do. 1905. Faust (II). L: Dent. Temple classics. 411p. 15cm. [BM.LC]

†2753. do. 1907. Faust (I,II). L: Dent; NY: Dutton. Everyman's lib. lxi,244; 410p. 17cm. [LC has: 654p.] [BM.LC]

†2754. LEFEVRE, SIR G: Faust (I) tr. into Engl. verse. L: Nutt 1841. ix;202p. 12. [BM] [Neither poetic, nor acc., nor complete.]

†2755. do. 1843. 2d ed. Frankfort o. M: Jügel. viii;207p. 14cm. [LC.BM]

§2756. MACDONALD, W: B. Faust (II) tr. into Engl. verse. Anon. Dumfries: Prtd. for the tr. by D. Halliday 1838. 83p. Lex-8. (B19a)

§2757. do. 1842. 2d ed. (somewhat revised). L: Pickering. viii; 351p. 18cm. [BM.LC] [Tr. says only a few copies of 1st ed. prtd. LC gives tr. as above; B19a likewise, with a query; BM makes no ascription; B17 says tr. was J: Macdonald Bell. --Meters frequently altered, fem. rhyme mostly lacking. Sense and spirit both good to fair. Not very musical.]

§2758. McLINTOCK, R. Faust (I), together w. "Two imps and Amor," the variants of the Göchhausen transcript, and the complete paralipomena of the Weimar ed. of 1887. L: Nutt 1897. xxxvii;375p. 23cm. [LC.BM] [No other tr. has so reproduced the varying rhythm of G--'s verse; but this formal success has crushed out the poetic content.]

†2759. MARTIN, SIR TD. Faust (I) tr. into Engl. verse. Ed; L: Blackwood 1865. 239p. 8. [BM] [Inexact: paraphrases, imitates, or expands at will.]

†2760. do. 1866. [same] 2d ed. 239p. [BM]

†2761. do. 1870. 3d ed. Blackwood. 227p. 17cm. [BM]

†2762. do. 1877. (EC: 1876.) L; Munich: Bruckmann. Il. A. v. Kreling. 140p. fol. [BM]

†2763. do. 1879. 12. (B8)

†2764. do. 1886. 8th ed. Blackwood. 227p. 12. [EC]

†2765. do. 1886. Faust (II). Ed; L: Blackwood. xiv;307p. 17cm. [BM]

†2766. do. 1887. Faust (I). 9th ed. [UW]

†2767. do. 1902. Faust (I). In #2387.

†2768. PAUL, C. K. Faust (I) tr. in rime. L: King 1873. vii;229. 19cm. [Errors and misconceptions frequent; no lyric talent; no eye for the essential.] [LC.BM]

†2769. SCOONES, W: D. Faust (I) tr. into Engl. verse. L: Trübner 1879. vi;230p. 17cm. [BM.LC] [Some good lyrics; shows dependence on Martin.]

*2770. SWANWICK, ANNA. Faust (I) and selections from Schiller. L: Manwaring 1849. (B8) [Often truly poetic; the best tr. before 1850. Somewhat over-inclined to be conventional.]

*2771. do. 1850. L: Bohn. 154p. 8. (B8)

GOETHE--FAUST--SWANWICK
*2772. do. 1850. In #2366.
*2773. do. 1879(1878). Faust (I, sel. portions of II). Il. after Retzsch. L: Bell. xvi;366p. 24cm. [BM]
[Pt. II, pp. 203-366. "Care has been taken that the progressive development of the drama (i.e., Pt. II) should not be interfered with."]
*2774. do. 1879. Faust (I,II). L: Bell. xliv;437p. 18cm. [BM]
[Second pt. newly tr. First pt. thoroughly rev., including the introd. of feminine rhymes, and resulting in considerable improvement.]
*2775. do. 1883. [same] Pt. I. ed. and annotated by F: H: Hedge. Il. by A. v. Kreling. NY: Crowell. 455p. 20cm. [LC]
*2776. do. 1883? [same] Il. after A. Liezen Mayer. NY: Crowell. 455p. 18cm. [Copyright 1882 by Cassino.] [BM]
*2777. do. 1883. Faust (I). NY: White, Stokes & Allen. 16. (B8)
*2778. do. 1884. Faust (I,II). NY: Lovell. 405p. 16. [LCO]
*2779. do. 1885. Faust (I). [same as #2777] 261p. 8. (B19a)
*2780. do. 1886. [same] L: Bell. 437p. 18cm. [LC]
*2781. do. 1888. Faust (I). Bohn's shilling lib. xliv;167p. 8. [BM]
*2782. do. 1890. [same as #2777] (B8)
*2783. do. 1893. Faust (I). New il. ed. NY: Stokes. 261p. 16cm. [LC]
*2784. do. 1893. Faust (I). [same as #2781] w. Retzsch's il. [BM]
*2785. do. 1895. Faust (I). [same as #2781] Rev. ed. Il. by Retzsch. L: Bell. 167p. 8. (B8)
*2786. do. 1898. Faust (I). Introd. by E: Brooks, Jr. Phil: McKay. 213p. 16cm. [LC]
*2787. do. 1905. Faust (I,II). Introd. by K: Breul. Macmillan. York lib. 437p. 18cm. [BM]
*2788. do. 1905. Faust (I,II). L: Bell. 508p. 12. [EC]
*2789. do. 1906. Faust (I). Il. Gilbert James. 142p. [BM]
*2790. do. 1909. [same] 437p. 18cm. [LC]
*2791. do. 1909. Faust (I). NY: Collier. (Harvard classics.) 431p. 22cm. [LC]
*2792. do. 191-. Faust (I,II). Translation pub. n.d. 15cm. [AC]
*2793. do. 191-. Faust (I). NY: Hinds & Co. Handy literal tr. [HCL]
*2794. do. 191-. Faust (I,II). Girard, Kan: Haldeman-Julius n.d. 2v. 128; 128p. 5 x 8 in. (Big blue books.) (Publisher's catalog.)
*2795. do. 1913-15. Faust (I). In C154.
*2796. do. 1914. Faust (I,II). Ed. K: Breul. L: Bell; NY: Macmillan. 437p. 12. [Cf. #2787.] [AC.EC]
*2797. do. 1925. Faust (I,II). Rev. ed. w. introd. and bibliog. by K: Breul. NY: Harcourt. [AC]
†2798. SYME, D: Faust (I). Ed: Black; Lpz: Fleischer 1834. 241p. 20cm. [LC.BM]
[Errors, abbreviations, and expansions distort the orig.]
†2799. TALBOT, R. Faust (I) attempted in Engl. rhyme. L: Smith, Elder [B1 says Wacey] 1835. xiv;263p. 8. [BM]
[Fairly acc. and painstaking, but levels everything, is chilly and conventional.]
†2800. do. 1839. 2d corr. ed. w. German text. L: Wacey. xxiv;569p. 8. [BM]
*2800a. TAYLOR, ARTHUR. See #2655.
*2801. TAYLOR, BAYARD. Faust (I,II). Bost: Houghton, Mifflin 1870. (B8)
*2802. do. 1871. [same] L: Strahan. 2v. xxiv;368; xx;507p. 8. [BM]
[Still the best Engl. version, though not uniformly ideal. Admirable both in form and spirit. Close fidelity to rhyme, meter, and sense.]
*2803. do. 1871. Faust (I). Bost: Osgood. xvi;405p. 23cm. [BM]
*2804. do. 1872. [same] Lpz. Brockhaus. 308p. (B8)

GOETHE--FAUST--TAYLOR.

*2805. do. 1873. Faust (II). Bost: Osgood. xvi;536p. 24cm. [BM]
*2806. do. 1875. Faust (I,II). Bost: Osgood. 378; 478p. [UW]
*2807. do. 1876. Faust (I). Bost. (B8)
*2808. do. 1876. Faust (II). Lpz: Brockhaus. 404p. (B8)
*2809. do. 1876. Faust. Il. E. Seibertz, A. L. Mayer, and L. Hofmann. NY. fol. (B8)
*2810. do. 1879. Faust (II). Bost. (B8)
*2811. do. 1879. Faust (I,II). Bost. 2v. (B8)
*2812. do. 1881. Faust (I). 2d ed. Lpz: Brockhaus. 308p. 8. (B8)
*2813. do. 1882. Faust (I,II). Bost: Houghton, Mifflin. 2v. in 1. 336; 463p. (B8)
*2814. do. 1883. With Konewka's il. Bost: Roberts. (B8)
*2815. do. 1884. 8th ed. Stark. 8. [EC]
*2816. do. 1886. Faust (I). L: Ward, Lock. vi;152p. 8. [BM]
*2817. do. 1886. Faust (I,II). L: Warne. Chandos classics. xxiv; 424p. 8. [BM]
*2818. do. 1887. Faust (I,II). w. biog. introd. and il. after Retzsch. L: Ward, Lock. People's standard lib. xx;636p. [B8 lists this as 1886.] [BM]
*2819. do. 1887. Faust (I). Bost. 16. [EC]
*2820. do. 1889. New ed. L: Ward, Lock. 8. [B8 has: 2d ed. of #2818.] [EC]
*2821. do. 1889. Faust (I). W. some of the minor poems, ed. w. introd. and notes Eliz. Craigmyle. L; NY: Scott. Canterbury poets. xliv;278p. 14cm. [13 poems, pp. 207-78, in fair tr., probably by Craigmyle.] [BM.LC]
*2822. do. 1890. Faust (I,II). L: Ward, Lock. Minerva lib. xxviii; 636p. 8. [3d ed. of #2818.] [BM]
*2823. do. 1898. [same] Bost; NY: Houghton, Mifflin. 2v. 20cm. [LC]
*2824. do. 1906. [same] Large paper ed. Bost: Houghton, Mifflin. 4v. 28cm. [LC]
*2825. do. 1911. [same] 4th ed? L: Ward, Lock. 664p. (B8)
*2826. do. 1911. Faust (I). Bost; NY: Houghton, Mifflin. 368p. 18cm. [LC]
§2827. TODHUNTER, J: Faust (I). Introd. J: G. Robertson. Oxford: Blackwell 1924. xvi;188p. 8. [Not equal either to Taylor or Swanwick. Lack of variety, bizarre and jarring notes, etc.] [BM]
*2828. VAN DER SMISSEN, W. H. Faust (I,II) in the orig. metres w. commentary and notes. Introd. Sir Rb. Falconer. NY: Dutton 1927. xxiv;594p. 21cm. [On the whole, very good; scholarly and faithful; slightly lacking on the poetic side.] [LC]
†2829. WEBB, T: E. Faust (I). Dublin univ. press: 1880. xxxvi; 373p. [Webb is wholly unpoetic, often lacking in taste; almost complete failure.] [BM]
†2830. do. 1881. L: Longmans. 8. [EC]
†2831. do. 1898. New ed. with the death of Faust from pt. II. L; NY: Longmans. 295p. 20cm. [BM.LC]

FAUST ADAPTATIONS

2832. BANGS, J: K. Mephistopheles: a profanation. NY: Gilliss & Turnure 1889. 97p. 17cm. [BM]
2833. BARBIER, P. J. and M. CARRÉ. Faust: opera by C: Gounod. Words founded on G--'s Faust. Libr. Engl. Melbourne: Bell 1865? 23p. 18cm. [As given by Lyster's grand opera co.] [BM]
2834. do. 1891? Book of words...by Ravenswood. Turner's Engl. opera co. 35p. 18cm. [BM]
2835. do. 1900? L: Grand opera syndicate. Libr. Fr;Engl. 30p. 24cm. [BM]
2836. do. 1900? Libr. Fr;Engl. 4. [Catalogued, but missing.] [BM]

GOETHE--FAUST--BERLIOZ

2837. BERLIOZ, HECTOR. Faust: a dramatic legend. Engl. tr. Marie Hallé. Manchester: n.d. 1880? 8p. 4. (B28)

2838. do. 1885? Libr. L: Novello. 24p. 26cm.[Not very good tr.][BM]

2839. do. 1903? Libr. Tr. W: Wallace. Lpz;L;NY: Breitkopf & H. 42p. 17cm. [Carefully done to make text singable.] [BM]

2840. BERNARD, BAYLE. Faust; or, the fate of Margaret. A romantic play, in four acts (and in verse). Ad...w. an introd. L: T:H.Lacy n.d. 67p. 19cm. [BM]
["To carry out this scheme it was of course necessary to modify some of the language of the hero...and lastly...to make some additions to the text." First performed 1866. First act, Faust's study. Second act, Easter walk, Auerbach's cellar, Faust and Marg., Martha's garden. Third act, City fountain, Brocken, Walpurgis glen. Fourth act, City gate, outskirts of city, prison. Based on some blank verse tr. of mediocre quality.]

2841. CHARLES, M. The story of Faust...told simply as a prose romance. L: Theosoph. pub. soc. 1907. x;342p. 22cm. [BM]
[An attempt at an interpretation for those who might need such help. A few quotations in tr. of Swanwick and Taylor.]

2842. "CROWQUILL, A." Faust, a serio-comic poem. L: King 1834. 32p. 8. [Travesty.] [BM]

2843. ELBING, RAY. Faust and Helena: the only Engl. drama founded on the 2d pt. of Faust; orig. mod. conception, four acts. Columbus, O: Haak 1898. 36p. 19cm. [LC]

2843a. GILBERT, W: SCHWENCK. Gretchen. A play in 4 acts. L: 1879. [BM]

2844. HALFORD, J. Faust and Marguerite: a grand operatic extravaganza. L: T: H. Lacy 1866? 46p. 18cm. [BM]
[A "Free and easy" ad. of Faust. First performed 1854.]

2845. HASELL, E. J. G--'s Faust for Engl. readers. L: St. Paul's mag., vols. 11,12. (B28) [Review with extr. from pub. tr.]

2846. PHILLIPS, AF. R. Faust: a weird story, based on G--'s play. NY: Munro 1886. 96p. 8. [BM]

2847. PHILLIPS, STEPHEN and J. W. C. CARR. Faust. L: Macmillan 1908. xv;142p. 8. [BM]
[Wholly false to G--'s spirit and intent.]

2848. do. 1908. [same] NY: Macmillan. 208p. 18cm. [LC]

2849. WILLS, W. G. Faust (I), in a prologue and 5 acts, ad. and arr. for the Lyceum theatre. n.i. 1886. 54p. (prtd. on one side.) 21cm. [BM]
[Mostly blank verse and rewritten. Prologue, Faust's study. Nuremberg, Lorenz Platz. Act I, Margaret's chamber; the city wall; Martha's house; Martha's garden. Act 2, Trees and mts; Margaret's garden. Act 3. Nuremberg, street by church. Act 4, Summit of the Brocken. Act 5, Nuremberg, dungeon. For the list of Brit. criticisms of H: Irving's production of Faust in this arr., see Engl. Goethe soc. pub. no. 2, 112-14.]

GÖTZ VON BERLICHINGEN

†2850. ANON. Goetz von B-- with the iron hand. Phil: Carey, Lea & Blanchard 1837. xxxvi;185p. 12. [LC]
["The following version...has been undertaken after a sep. tr. of each of the three pieces, and an attentive compar. of their different scenes." Ref. is to 2d vol. of G--'s nachgelassene Werke, Cotta, 1832, giving two variant forms of Götz. Actually, the tr. puts in and takes out freely, without seeming to follow G-- at all.]

*2851. LAWRENCE, ROSE (D'AGUILAR). Gortz of Berlingen [sic]...An historical drama of the 15th cent. Liverpool. 128p. 1799. 8. [BM]

GOETHE

[This is probably the tr. listed by B8 as by Rose D'Aguilar in 1795. Quite good for so early a tr.]

2852. PEARSON, E: S. Dresden. 1892. (German classical plays, no. 8.) 136p. (B8)

†2853. SCOTT, WL. L: Bell 1799. xvi;202p. 8. [BM.LC]
[Scott knew very little German.]

†2854. do. 1814. NY: Inskeep. 206p. 24. (B48)

†2855. do. 1826. [same] Paris: Galignani. 187p. 8. (B8. B19a)

†2856. do. 1829. [same] Zwickau. 254p. (B8)

*2857. do. 1850. [same, but "very carefully revised."] In #2366. --This is probably the ed. listed by B8. --Also L: 1851? (B8)

*2858. do. 1854. [same] Bohn lib. #2365.

*2859. do. 1857. [same] Phil. (B8)

*2860. do. 1879. [same] In #2372.

*2861. do. 1880. [same] In Scott's "Works," vol. 12. Edinb. [LC.BM]

*2862. do. 1898. [same] L: Bell. 12. [EC]

*2863. do. 1916. [same] In C408.

Heliodora; or, the Grecian minstrel. Falsely ascribed to Goethe, actually by W: A. Lindau. See #5842.

HERMANN UND DOROTHEA

2864. ANON. n.d. Hermann and Dorothea. Tr. written in a neat hand on 184pp. of a notebook bound in half leather. About 8 x 4 in. (R. Priebsch)

§2865. ANON. 1805. A tale (in prose). L: Longmans et al. xii;142p. 16cm. [Chapters for "Gesänge." Tr. is fairly accurate, occasional errors. B4 thinks tr. was T: Holcroft.] [BM]

2866. ANON. 1840. ...in old Engl. measure. L: Nutt. 12. [EC]
[Probably by Winter; cf. #2906.]

2867. ANON. 1848. In "The Democratic rev." NY. (B8)
[W: Whewell's tr.]

2868. ANON. 1849. ...in Engl. hexameters w. introd. essay. L: Smith & Son. 12. [W: Whewell's tr?] [EC]

2869. ANON. 1854. L: Ward, Lock.(B8)--NY: Riker, Thorn. [AC]
[Probably Porter's tr. #2896.]

2870. ANON. 1874. Ger. text w. corresponding hexameters. L: Wms. & N. 8. [Tr. by Watkins. #2900.] [EC]

2871. ANON. 1910. NY: Putnam. 32. [AC]

§2872. BOWRING, E. A. Tr. in 2d ed. of Goethe's poems, 1874. #2401.
[Takes his task too lightly.]

§2873. do. 1884. NY: Elzevir lib. (B24)

§2874. do. 1889(1888). W. etchings by Hm. Faber. Phil: Lippincott. 60p. incl. pl. 27cm. [LC]

§2875. do. 1898. L: Bell. 84p. 12. [EC]

§2876. do. 1898. Phil: McKay. 114p. 16cm. [LC]

§2877. do. 191-. NY: Hinds & Noble n.d. 83p. S. [UW]

§2878. BRANDON, VIVIAN. L: T. W. Laurie 1913. 95p. (8) Il. after Arthur W. Ramberg. 18cm. [BM]
[Tr. in 12-syl. verse, very ungainly in English.]

§2879. BROWNELL, S. E. With Alexis and Dora. NY: Prtd. for the editor 1849. 48p. 8. [LC]
[Poor verse. Lieder (B24) thinks this is Whewell's tr.]

§2880. CARTWRIGHT, J: L:Nutt 1862. 131p. 8. [BM]
[Blank verse; good, but lacks the proper melody and swing.]

§2881. COCHRANE, JAS. Oxford: M'Pherson 1853. xi;145p. 19cm. [LC]
[Poor verse; correct.]

§2882. do. 1850. Groombridge. [EC]

§2883. DALE, H: Dresden: 1859. viii;87p. 8. [BPL.BM]
[Accurate; poor poetry.]

§2884. do. 1860. L: Bohn. 8. (B8)

§2885. do. 1874. Munich; Berl; L: Bruckmann. 86p. Il. W: Kaulbach and L. Hoffmann. 4. (B8)
§2886. do. 1882. In #2393.
§2887. FROTHINGHAM, ELLEN. Bost: Roberts 1870. 165p. il. 19cm. [Verse is halting and unsatisfying.] [NY.BM]
§2888. do. 1887. [same] Bost. [NY]
§2889. do. 1909. Pub. w. Swanwick's "Faust" in Harvard Classics. #2791.
§2890. do. 1913-15. In C154(1).
2891. GOSTWICK, JOS. 1845. In C173.
†2892. HARRIS, J. B. (Prose tr.) Wilson jc.,Ia: Review press 1899. 111p. 16. [Prose indeed!] [LC]
†2893. HOLCROFT, T: L: Longmans 1801. xxii;211p. 16cm. [BM.LC] [Front. by I. Neagle, 9 pl. by F. Catel. Notes, pp. 175-211. Blank verse, with serious arbitrary omissions.]
†2894. do. 1805. Richmond, Va: Enquirer press. 133p. 16cm. [LC]
2895. MELLISH, J. C. Tr. before 1801. See t.p. to #2939.
2896. PORTER, T: C. NY: Riker, Thorne 1854. 168p. 18cm. [LC.BM] [Prose tr.]
§2897. TEESDALE, M. J. In Engl. hexameter verse. L: Wms. & Norgate 1874. 78p. 8. [Bumpy verse. Accurate enough.] [BM]
§2898. do. 1875. same. 2d ed. [BM]
**2899. TOMLINSON, C: L: Nutt 1887. 109p. 8. [NY] [B24 says this is 2d rev. ed. First ed. pub. 1849. Sense and spirit both admirably caught.]
†2900. WATKINS, F: B. Tr. in hexameters. Ger. and Engl. L: Wms. & Norgate 1875. 133p. 8. [Odd attempt to render almost word for word; the Engl. is consequently rather sad.] [BM]
†2901. WHEWELL, W: Priv. prt. n.i., n.d. L: 1840? 139p. 14 x 23cm. [Impossible hexameters.]
†2902. do. 1847. In C199.
†2903. do. 1848. In "U. S. Mag. and Democratic Review." (B24)
†2904. do. 1849. NY: Brownell. (B24)
*2905. WHITTY, J: IRWINE. Canto I and prologue. In #7844.
§2906. WINTER, M. Tr. in the old Engl. measure of Chapman's Homer. Dublin: Kelly 1850. ix;82p. 12. [BM] [Rhymed couplets. Not much good.]

IPHIGENIE AUF TAURIS

2907. ANON. Sel. 1910. In C574.
2908. ANON. NY: "Democratic rev." 24(1849). Acts 1-3, lines 1-120.
2908a. ANON. 1851. See #2911.
§2909. ADLER, G: J. NY: Appleton 1850. 155p. 12. [LC.BM] [Dull verse.]
2910. BEHR. L: Nutt 1850. 12. [Probably a school edition.] [EC]
§2911. BENNETT, ANNA R. W. other poems. Liverpool: Priv. prt. 1851. 200p. 12. [BM] [Tr. listed as anon. in BM. Copy belonging to R. Priebsch has MS dedication signed by tr. --Correct but undistinguished. --No other poems from German.]
§2912. BUTLER, F: Reading, Pa: 1898. 12. [Correct; ordinary.] [LC]
*2913. DOWDEN, ELIZ. Introd. by E: Dowden. L: Dent 1906. xv;88p. 13cm. [BPL.BM]--NY: Macmillan 1906. Temple classics. 32. [AC]
§2914. ELLIS, PHILLIS M. L: Priv. prt. 1883. 114p. sm. 8. [BPL.BM] [Close and accurate; verse rather monotonous.]
2915. HAMDON, MRS. L: 1906. (B8)
§2916. HARTWIG, G. L. Berlin: Besser; L: Black & A. 1841. 84p. 8. [Good verse; too free.] [BPL.BM]
*2917. SWANWICK, ANNA. 1843. In C515. Also 1850 in #2366.
**2918. do. 1879. "Very carefully revised." #2372.

GOETHE--HERMANN UND DOROTHEA--SWANWICK
**2919. do. 1894. L: Bell. 79p. 8. (B8)
*2920. do. 1900. Weimar text with tr. Given in Sanders' theatre, Cambridge, Mass., Mar. 22, 1900. Introd. Kuno Francke. Cambridge: Wheeler. (B24)
*2921. do. 1903. In C18.
*2922. do. 1913-15. In C154.
*2923. TAYLOR, W: of NORWICH. ...a tragedy (!) L: Johnson 1793. 126p. 8. [BM]
*2924. do. 1794. Berlin: Unger. 113p. 8. [BM]
*2925. do. 1830. In C533, vol. 3, pp. 249-304.
*2926. TUCKER, JUDGE B. In "Southern lit. messenger," Vol. 10, 1844. [LC]

§2927. (Italienische Reise.) Travels in Italy. Tr. A. J. W. Morrison. Bohn lib. 1846. 8. [No idea of retaining G--'s style.]
§2928. do. 1849. [same] With Autobiog. L: Bohn. #2490, pp. 237-450.
§2929. do. 1883. [same] With his second res. in Rome, and Fragments on Italy. L: Bell. 589p. 19cm. [LC]
[Second part tr. by C: Nisbet.]
§2930. do. 1885. [same] [LC]
§2931. do. 1892. [same] L: Bell. [BM]
*2932. (Kampagne in Frankreich.) The campaign in France in the year 1792. Tr. R. Farie. L: Chapman & Hall 1849. iv;361p. 18cm.[LC.BM]
*2933. do. 1882. Ed. L. D. Schmitz. In #2365. Cf. #2954.
§2934. (Novelle.) A tale. Tr. R. D. Boylan. 1854. In #2367. Also in vol. 4 of #2380.
*2935. do. 1832. Goethe's novel. Tr. T: Carlyle. In "Fraser's mag." No. 34. [BM]
*2936. do. 1837. [same] L: Moxon. 63p. 20cm. [BM.NY]
*2937. do. 1840. [same] In C56.
*2938. do. 1849. [same] In C194.
*2939. (Palaeophron und Neoterpe.) P-- and N--: a masque for the... 24th of October 1800. Tr. J. C. Mellish. Weimar: Gädicke 1801. 18p. col. front. 25cm. [Tr. is close and faithful, but his handling of the 12-syllable meter is clumsy.] [BM]

REINEKE FUCHS

§2940. AINSLIE, A. D. Reynard the fox, after the Ger. version of G--. L: Macmillan 1886. xx;338p. 19cm. [BM]
[Follows fairly closely, in different meter.]
2940a. ANON. History of Renard, the fox. Ad. from...Goethe. Il. w. numerous engr. designed by J. J. Grandville. Thomas 1840.
[See "Court Journal" 1840, p. 239.] (B15a)
§2941. ARNOLD, T: J. Il. by Js. Wolf. L. xvi;320p. 22cm. [BM]
[Pub. anon. Engr. t.p. has: W: Pickering 1853. Prtd. t.p. has: Nattali & Bond 1855. Heroic couplets; rather free.]
§2942. do. 1858. [same] Il. by J. Wolf. L: (B8)
§2943. do. 1860. Il. by W: v. Kaulbach. NY: Appleton; L: Trübner. vi;226p. 24cm. [LC.BM]
§2944. do. 1885. In vol. 3 of #2380.
§2945. do. 1886. Bost: Roberts. (B8)
§2946. do. 1887 (1886). L: Nimmo. 60 il. by Kaulbach. xxvii;342p. 26cm. [BM]
§2947. do. 1888. Phil. (B8)
*2948. COBB, J: S. Reynard the fox: an early apologue of renown clad in an Engl. dress, etc. With Canton's il. Bost: Damrell & Upham 1899. 386p. 12. [LC]
*2949. do. 1902. In #2387.

GOETHE--REINEKE FUCHS

?2950. JOHNSON, CLIFTON. Adapted. Springfield, Mass: Milton Bradley 1924. 155p. il. 19cm. [Really a free prose tr.] [LC]

2951. NAYLOR, S. Reynard the fox, reproduced in rhyme. L: Longmans 1845. 251p. 8. (B28) [This is an error. See A464.]

*2952. ROGERS, Ax. Reineke fox. Tr. in hexameters with an introd. L: Bell 1888. Bohn's shilling series. xiv;193p. 18cm. [BM]

*2953. do. 1890. [same] In #2382, cf. #2365.

2954. (Reisebilder.) Misc. travels, etc. Tr. R. Farie. Ed. L. Dora Schmitz. L: Bell 1882. 12. [Cf. #2365.] [EC]

2955. do. 1884. L: Bell. 424p. 18cm. [LC]

2956. do. Letters from Switzerland; letters from Italy. Tr. A. J. W. Morrison. In #2365, 2927-11.

§2957. (Römische Elegien.) Roman elegies tr. in the orig. metres by L. Noa. Bost: Schoenhof & Moeller 1876? 39p. 12. [NY.BM] [Creditable, not distinguished.]

2958. do. 1893. Tr. Td. Martin. In "Pub. Engl. G-- soc.," pp. 71-84.

*2959. (Satyros und Prometheus.) S-- and P--. Tr. J: Gray. Glasgow: Prtd. for the G-- soc. by F: Bauermeister 1898. 66p. 19cm. [LC]

2960. (Sprüche in Prosa.) Tr. anon. In the "Literary rambler": being a coll. of the most popular and entertaining stories in the Engl. lang. Ed: 1833. (B8) [Contains 36 of the "Sprüche."]

2961. do. 1853. Tr. anon. Maxims and reflections of G--. "NY Quarterly," vol. 1, pp. 109; 200. (B8)

2962. do. 1888. Tr. Mathilde Blind. Maxims and reflections..."Pub. Engl. G-- soc.," no. 4(1888), pp. 66-84. [One bit of verse from Carlyle's "Wilhelm Meister."]

§2963. do. 1893. Tr. T: B. Saunders. Maxims and reflections. L;NY: Macmillan. 223p. 19cm. [LC.BM]

§2964. do. 1906. [same] [LC]

§2965. do. 1894. Tr. T: B. Saunders. Nature aphorisms. By G. C. Tobler. In Engl. by B. Saunders. L: Macmillan. 32. [EC] [This is evidently taken from the foregoing, in which Saunders included Tobler's little essay under the heading: Nature: aphorisms.]

§2966. (Stella.) S--. Tr. anon. L: Hookham & Carpenter 1798. 113p. 8. [Tr. from the orig. form.] [BM]

§2967. do. 1890. [same] In Morley, H: Carisbrooke lib. L: Routledge. 8. [BM]

§2968. do. 1890. [same] Prtd. as appendix to "Burlesques and parodies" by Canning, Ellis, and Frere. L; NY: Routledge 1890. pp. 411-46. 21cm. [This tr. suggested the burlesque play (The rovers; or the double arrangement) by the above-named in the "Anti-Jacobin."]

2969. do. 1885. Tr. anon. In vol. 3 of #2380.

§2970. do. 1801. Tr. B: Thompson. In C535 (sep. paged.) 50p. 21cm. [Engr. front. by J. Corbett.] [LC.BM]

§2971. do. 1913. [same] In C18.

TORQUATO TASSO

2972. Sel. Tr. R. P. Gillies in "Memories of a lit. veteran." L: Bentley 1851. [BM]

2973. Sel. 1845. Tr. Jos. Gostwick. In C173.

2974. Sel. 1834. Tr. Mrs. Hemans. Scenes and passages from the Tasso of G--. In "New Monthly mag.," vol. 40: 1-8. [BM]

2975. Sel. 1870. Tr. Js. Kaines. In C303.

2976. Sel. 1831. Tr. J. F. Pries, prof. of the univ. and principal of the town-school in Rostock. Act I. Rostock. Prtd. by Adlers Erben. 31p. 4. (B19a)

GOETHE

2977. Sel. 1842. Tr. Reeve and Taylor. In C464.
2978. Sel. 1859. Tr. T: Worsley? In #2472.
*2979. CARTWRIGHT, J: L: Nutt 1861. vii;151p. 8. [Very good.] [BM]
*2980. DES VOEUX, C: With other poetry. 1827. 307p. C92--Also 1833, 1836, 1856.
["Tasso" seems to me very well done, despite the sharp censure of B22.]
§2981. FULLER, MARG. A rhythmical tr. In Ossoli, Sarah. Works, vol. 2. [Text and meter not always followed, and verse is somewhat uneven.] [BM.LC]
§2982. H., M. A. W. other poems, tr. and orig. 1855. C182. [Rather poor; wrong and stilted diction.]
2983. SWANWICK, ANNA. 1843. Sel. (Acts I,II) in C515.
2984. do. 1850. Complete in #2366.
*2985. do. 1879. "Very carefully revised." In #2372.

[A tribute to U: v. Hutten. Really by Herder. See #4216.]
2986. (Unterhaltungen deutscher Ausgewanderten.) Recreations of Ger. emigrants. Tr. R. D. Boylan. 1854. In #2367.
*2987. (West-Östlicher Diwan.) West-Eastern divan. Tr. E. A. Bowring. 1874. In #2401. Also largely in #2393.
*2988. do. 1914. The west-eastern divan in 12 books. Tr. E: Dowden. Foreword by Eliz. D. Dowden. L;Toronto: Dent. xvi;195p. 19cm. [Rather frequent is a needless obscurity of phrase.] [BM.LC]
§2989. do. Tr. Ax. Rogers. 1890. In #2382. Also in vol. 14 of #2365.
*2990. do. Tr. J: Weiss. G--'s west-easterly divan. W. introd. and notes. Roberts 1877. xxxi;264p. 15cm. [NY.BM]
[At his best Weiss is better than Dowden.]

WILHELM MEISTER

2991. Sel. Tr. T: Carlyle. 1826. In C502.
2992. Sel. 1903. Sel. from G--'s W. M. L: Simpkin, Marshall. 36p. 19 x 11cm. [Extr. from Carlyle's essay on G--. One sel. from each part of "W. M." in Carlyle's tr. Pref. signed A. M. P.] [BM]
2993. Sel. 1904. The pedagogic province; or, an outline of the scheme of education. Being extracts from Carlyle's tr. L: Chapman & H. 36p. 18cm. [BM]
2994. Sel. 1904. Goethe on Shakespeare. Carlyle's tr. L: Moring. 18. [EC]
2995. Sel. 1910. In C574.
*2996. (Lehrjahre.) W: M--'s apprenticeship. Tr. T: Carlyle. Ed: Oliver & Boyd; L: Whittaker 1824. 3v. 8. [BM]
*2997. (Wanderjahre.) W: M--'s travels; or, the renunciants. Tr. T: Carlyle. 1827. [In vol. 4 of C58.]
*2998. (L) 1828. Carlyle's tr. Bost: Wells & Lilly. (B8)
*2999. do. 1839? [same] 2d ed. (B8)
*3000. (L.W.) 1840. W: M--'s apprenticeship and travels. New ed., rev. and ed. by T: Carlyle. Phil: Lea & Blanchard. 3v. 20cm. [LC]
*3001. do. 1842. [same] L: Chapman & Hall. 3v. 12. [BM]
*3002. do. 1851. [same] Bost: Ticknor. 2v. 12. [AC]
*3003. (L) 1855. Tr. R. D. Boylan. L: Bohn. 570p. 8. [BM]
*3004. do. 1857. [same] Bost. 8. (B8)
*3005. (L.W.) 1858. Carlyle's tr. L: Chapman & Hall. 8. (B8)
*3006. do. 1865. [same] New rev. ed. Bost: Ticknor & F. 2v. 8. [BM]
*3007. do. 1871. [same] NY: Am. book exch. 16. (B8)
*3008. (L) 1872. Boylan's tr. L: Bell & Daldy. 570p. 18cm. [LC]
[Same as #3003.]
*3009. do. 1873. Tr. E. Grove. Lpz: Tauchnitz; L: Low. 2v. 322; 390p. 16cm. [BM.BPL]

GOETHE--WILHELM MEISTER

*3010. (W) 1882. Tr. A. H. Gunlogsen from enl. (i.e., 2d) ed. and ed. by E: Bell. L: Bohn. viii;438p. 8. [BM]
[B8 dates this 1881. Final decision was Bell's. New matter is shown in table of contents. Tr. not impeccable, but avoids some errors by Carlyle.]
*3011. do. 1885. [same] L: Bell. 438p. 19cm. [LC]
*3012. (L.W.) 1885. Carlyle's tr. In #2380.
*3013. (L) 1886. Boylan's tr. L: Bell & D. 570p. 19cm. [LC]
*3014. (L also W?) 1887. NY: Lovell. 3 pts. 201;440;596p. (B8)
*3015. do. 1888. Grove's tr. NY: Stokes. 2v. 322;390p. (B9, vol.11).
*3016. (L.W.) 1888. Carlyle's tr. L: Chapman & H. 3v. 12. [EC]
*3017. do. 1890. [same] Crit. introd. E: Dowden. Ed. w. notes C. K. Shorter. L: Stott. 2v. xxiii;420; 469p. 8. [BM]
[Appendices give Bell's tr. of the contin. of the Man of fifty, and Odoardo's address. B8 lists this as 1891. --Also Chic: McClurg 1890. 2v. 16. (B8)]
*3018. do. 1894. [same] L: Chapman & H. 3v. in 2. 8. [EC]
*3019. do. 1899. [same] L: Chapman & H. 2v. 472; 418p. (B8)
*3020. do. 1901. [same] Bost: Estes. 2v. (B13)
*3021. do. 1901. [same] Caldwell: 2v. (B13)
*3022. do. 1901. [same] In centenary ed. of Carlyle's works. NY: Scribner. 2v. 8. [LC]
*3023. (W) 1901. Carlyle's tr? Bost: New Atheneum ed. 2v. (B8)
*3024. (L.W.) 1902. Carlyle's tr. Ed. N. H. Dole. In #2387.
*3025. do. 1903. [same] L: Chapman & H. 3v. in 1. 750p. sm. 8. (B8)
--New Edinb. ed. NY: Scribner 1903. 3v. in 1. 16. [AC]
*3026. do. 1912. [same] L: Dent; NY: Dutton. Everyman's lib. 2v. 17cm. [BM.LC]
*3027. (W: M--s theatralische Sendung.) W: M--'s theatrical mission. Tr. G. A. Page. Introd. Harry Maync. L: Heinemann 1913. xxxiv; 341p. 19cm. [LC.BM]

3028. (Xenien.) Tr. by Pl. Carus. 1896. 1915. In C64.

CONVERSATIONS, LETTERS

(Briefe.) Bettina V. Arnim. G--'s corr. with a child. See #87-94.
*3029. do. Carlyle. Corr. w. T: C-- ed. by C: E. Norton. L: Macmillan 1887. xix;362p. 8. [G--'s letters in tr.] [BM.BPL]
§3030. do. Humboldt. Corr. w. W: v. H-- and his wife. Tr. L. H. Gray. 1913-15. In C154(2).
*3031. do. Miscellaneous. Early and misc. letters, (also) to his mother. Tr. anon. L: Bell 1884. xci;318p. 19cm. (B28)
[Tr. by E: Bell, w. notes and...biog., using Slater's Leipzig letters, and assisted by Mrs. E. Fielding and A. H. Gunlogsen. Many interspersed poems.]
3032. do. 1885. [same?] G--'s letters. NY: Scribner. (B8)
*3033. do. 1889. [same] L: Bell. 318p. [BM.LC]
*3034. do. Schiller. Corr. between S-- and G--, 1794-1805. Tr. G: H. Calvert. NY; L: Wiley & Putnam 1845. Vol. 1. 392p. 12 [BM]
3035. do. 1877-9. Schiller. Tr. from 3d ed. w. notes by L. Dora Schmitz. L: 2v. 460; 527p. 8. (B8)
3036. do. 1913-15. Sel. from the foregoing. In C154(3).
*3037. do. Zelter. Letters to Z--. Tr. A. D. Coleridge. L: Bell 1887. x;504p. 19cm. [BM.LC]
[Some verse tr. by Ma. Coleridge.]
§3038. do. 1913-15. Zelter. Sel. Tr. Fes. H. King. In C154(2).
§3039. (Gespräche.) Conversations of J: P. Eckermann w. G-- in the last years of his life. Tr. S. M. Fuller. Bost: Hilliard, Gray 1839. 414p. 8. [Two orig. vols. compressed into one, omitting G--'s experiments and theory of colors. Not slavishly done.] [LC.BM]

GOETHE--GESPRAECHE
3040. do. 1840. [same?] Wiley. 12. [EC]
*3041. do. 1850. Conv. w. E-- and Soret. Tr. J: Oxenford. L. 2v. 8.
[Excellent tr. on the whole. O. based his tr. on Fuller's.] [BM]
§3042. do. 1852. [Re-issue of #3039.] New ed. Bost. (B8)
*3043. do. 1853. G--'s opinions on the word, mankind, literature, science, and art. Tr. O: v. Wenckstern. L: Parker. viii;174p. 17cm. [BM.LC]
[Tr. appears to be well done. --Excerpts from his pub. corr...and from his...conversations. Headings on pages: Politics, Ethics, Philosophy, The Germans, etc., etc.]
*3044. do. 1874. New ed. of #3041. L: Bell. 583p. 19cm. [BM.LC]
*3045. do. 1883. [same] Rev. ed. L; NY: Bell. (B8) [Chronologically arr. Includes for the first time vol. 3 of the "Gespräche."]
*3046. do. 1892. [same] L; NY: Bell. [LC]
*3047. do. 1901. [same] Introd. by Wallace Wood. Wash;L: Dunne. 397p. 24cm. [This makes some omissions from the L. eds.] [LC]
3048. do. 1910. Sel. In C574.
3049. do. 1913-15. Sel. In C154(2)
3050. do. 1919. Goethe on the theater: sel. from the conv. w. Eckermann. Tr. J: Oxenford. Introd. W: W. Lawrence. NY: Columbia U. press. 109p. 23cm. [LC]
3051. do. 1925. Convers. w. E--. Sel. and ed. Jl. Goebel. Girard, Kan: Haldeman-Julius. 64p. 12cm. [BQM]
[Introd.; autobiog.; lit. and art; hist.; Napoleon; philos.; ethics; immortality; relig.; God; Christ; Goethe's end.]

BIOGRAPHY, Etc.

3052. Characteristics of G--, from the Ger. of Falk, v. Müller, etc. Tr. Sa. Austin. L: Wilson 1833. 3v. 331; 336; 352p. 12. [BM]
[Falk, J: Dn. G-- aus näherem persön. Umgange dargestellt.]
See Baumgart, Hm., Commentary on G--'s Märchen, #280.
See Bielschowsky, A., Life of G--, #437.
See Börne, L., G-- as a patriot, #609.
See Düntzer, H., Life of G--, #1272.
See Fischer, K., G--'s Faust, #1630.
See Grimm, Hm., Life and times of G--, #3131.
See Mendelssohn-Bartholdy, K:, G-- and Fx. v. M--, #6205.
See Muehlbach, L., G-- and Schiller, #6419.
See Reichlin-Meldegg, Ax., Exposition of Faust, #7376.
See Rosenkranz, J., Several essays, #7572 seq.
See Steffens, H., Story of my career, #9021.

GOETHE, Kta. Eli. 1731-1808.
*3053. Goethe's mother. Corr. ...w. G--, Lavater, Wieland, and others. Tr. Af. S. Gibbs w. add. biog. sketches and notes. Introd. Clar. Cook. NY: Dodd, Mead 1880. port. il. 265p. 20cm.
[Tr. seems to be very well done.] [BM]
See Arnim, B., G--'s corr. with a child, #87-94.

GOETZ, C: G. d. 1746. Sel. in C244.

GOETZ, Hm. Operas: Francesca. The taming of the shrew. See "Widmann, Js: V."

GOETZ, J: N: 1721-81. Sel. in C417.

GOETZE, A: 1840-1908.
3054. Heights: a play. Tr. Sasha Best. In "Poet Lore," vol. 25 (1914.)

GOLDBECK, J: Cn., M. D.
3055. (Metaphysik des Menschen.) The metaphysic of man; or, the pure part of the physiol. of man. Tr. S. F. Waddington., M. D.

GOLDBECK, J: Cn.- Metaphysik des Menschen
L: S. Highly et al. 1806. viii;181p. 21cm. [BM]

GOLDBECK, Rb. 1839-1908.
3056. The surprise: opera. Words & music by R-- G--. Tr. Desmond Ryan. Vocal score. Engl. L: Wessel ca. 1856. fol. [LCM]

GOLDMARK, K: 1830-1915. Operas: The cricket on the hearth. See Willner, A. M. The Queen of Sheba. See Mosenthal, S. H.
3056a. (Erinnerungen aus meinem Leben.) Notes from the life of a Viennese composer. Tr. by Mrs. Alice (Goldmark) Brandeis. NY: Boni 1927. 280p. il. D. [AC]

GOLL, Iwan. Sel. in C95.

GOLM, Rd.
§3057. (Der alte Adam und die neue Eva.) The old Adam and the new Eve. Tr. Edith Fowler. NY: Richmond; L: Heinemann 1898. xix;250p. 19cm. [Tr. mod. good.] [BM.LC]

GOLTHER, Wfg. 1863- .
*3058. (R: Wagner als Dichter.) R: Wagner as poet. Tr. Jessie Haynes. L: Heinemann 1905. 92p. il. 16cm. [BM.LC]
[Tr. not quite up to the mark.]

GOLTZ, Clr. frhr. v. d. 1843-1916. Sel. in C161.
3059. (Angeline.) Angeline: a story of the Franco-Prussian war. Tr. "J. M. Percival." Chic: Morrill, Higgins 1892. 161p. 20cm. [LC]

GOLZ, Bl. 1801-70. Sel. in C422.

GOMPERZ, Td. 1832-1912.
*§3060. (Griechische Denker.) Greek thinkers: a hist. of ancient philos. L: Murray 1901-12. 4v. 23cm. Vol. I. tr. Laurie Magnus. Vol. 2-4 tr. G: G. Berry. [LC.BM]
[Magnus is exc. tr. Berry is unwilling to follow his author's style.]

GORITZ, O:
3061. (Der süsse Papa.) Dear papa: operetta in 3 acts. Text & music by O-- G--. Tr. Alice Mattullath. Libr. Eng. 1913. 44;43;25pp. Tw. [Seemingly very little relation to orig. text.] [LCM]
§3062. do. Dear old dad. Tr. Anon. Vocal score. Ger;Engl. NY: Fischer 1917. 159p. fol. [Good singing version.] [LCM]

GOTTER, L: An. 1661-1735. Sel. in C133;229;269;272;276.

GOTTFRIED VON NEIFEN, fl. 1234-55. Sel. in C27;310;416;427;532.

GOTTFRIED VON STRASSBURG, fl. 1212. Sel. in C310,366 (under Walther).
3063. (Tristan und Isolde.) Sel. in C68;310;530. The story of Tristan and Iseult. Rendered...Jessie L. Weston. L: Nutt 1899. 2v. il. 14cm.--NY: New Amsterdam book co. 1899. 2v. 14cm. [LC.BM]
[Prose, considerably condensed; well done. Concluding portion from Hein. von Freiberg; one episode from Ulrich von Türheim.]

"GOTTHELF, Jr."(i.e., Ab. Bitzius, 1797-1854).
§3064. (Die Leiden und Freuden eines Schulmeisters.) The joys and sorrows of a schoolmaster. Tr. anon. L: Allan 1864. 390p. 12. [BM]
[Inadequate.]
*3065. (Geld und Geist, oder die Versöhnung.) Wealth and welfare. Tr. anon. L; NY: Strahan 1866. 2v. 19cm. [LC.BM]
[Not bad. Chapter headings added by tr., who has an expansive tendency.]
3066. do. 1868. [same] L; NY: Strahan 1866. [LC]
3067. do. 1872. The soul and money. Tr. Guarterick Vere. L: Tinsley 1872. 8. [EC]

"GOTTHELF, Jr."
§3068. (Käthi, die Grossmutter.) Story of an Alpine valley; or, Katie the grandmother. Tr. L. G. Smith. L: Gibbings 1896. 320p. 8. [Not adequate to the task.] [BMS]
§3069. (Uli, der Knecht.) Ulric, the farm servant. Tr. Julia Firth. Rev. and ed., with notes, by J: Ruskin. L: Orpington, Allen 1886. x;428p. 22cm. [BM]
[Not my idea of a successful tr.-"The little quot. at the heads of the chapters have been chosen by Mrs. Firth from my own books, and appear to me by no means the least valuable part of the volume!"]
3070. do. 1888. [same] Ulric the farm servant by J: Ruskin. Pts. 7, 8, 9 (conclusion). Allen. [EC]
3071. do. 1907. [same] Tr. J. Firth. L: Dent; NY: Dutton. Everyman. xii;274p. 17cm. [LC.BM]
3071a. do. 1913-15. Uli, the farmhand. abr. Tr. B. Q. Morgan. In C154(8:173-274).

"GOTTHOLD" (i.e., Cn. Scriver, 1629-93). Sel. in C271.
3072. (Zufälliger Andachten vier hundert.) Gotthold's emblems; or, invisible things understood by things that are made. Tr. R. Menzies. Ed: Clark; L: Hamilton, Adams 1857. 301p. 19cm. [BM]
[Pious meditations. 2d series, 183-376.]
3073. do. 1860. Gotthold's emblems. Tr. Hoddam. Bost: 1860. 8. [EC]
3074. do. 1862. Tr. fr. 28th German ed. by R. Menzies. Same pub. as in #3072. 472p. 18cm. [Prefs. to p. 33. Nos. 1-366.] [BM]
3075. do. 1878. [same] 4th ed. L: Hamilton 1878. 8. [BM]

GOTTSCHALD, Ern. 1826- . See "Ernst v. Elterlein."

GOTTSCHALK, Kp. F: 1772- .Sel. from the popular traditions coll. & narr. by him in C80;C477.
3076. The ring of matrimonial fidelity. Tr. G: G. Cunningham. 1829. In C80.

GOTTSCHALK, ---. Sel.in C195;417.

GOTTSCHALL, Rd. v. 1823- .Sel. in C67;317;366;395;448;469;501;551.
*3077. (Welke Blätter.) Withered leaves: a novel. Tr. Bertha Ness. L: Remington 1879. 3v. 366; 340; 320p. 18cm. [BM]

GOTTSCHED, J: Cph. 1700-66, and W. Rust.
3078. (Trauerode.) Ode of mourning. Tr. G: L. Osgood. Music by J: S. Bach. (1900). [Not seen.] [LCM]

GOTTWALT, Pl.?
3079. Christmas: a tale. Tr. Anon. 1820. In C117, pp. 83-106.

GRABBE, Cn. Dt. 1801-36. Sel. in C373.

GRAENER, Paul. The faithful sentry: opera. See Körner, K: Td.#5125.

GRAETER, F: D: 1768-1830. Sel. in C489.

GRAEVEN, O. C. v., See "Lothar."

GRAFFENRIED, Cph. v. Baron, 1661-1742.
3080. C-- von G--'s account of the founding of New Bern; ed. with an historical introd. and an Engl. tr. by Vincent H. Todd, in cooperation with Jl. Goebel. Raleigh, N. C: N. Car. Histor. Comm. 1920. 434p. 24cm. [LC]

GRAMBERG, Grd. An. Hm. 1772-1816. Sel. in C387-8.

GRAMLICH, J: An. 1689-1728. Sel. in C276 or 287.

GRANICHSTAEDTEN, Br. Rose maid: operetta. See Dörmann, F.

GRANICHSTAEDTEN, Br.
3081. (Der Orlow.) Hearts and diamonds: operetta in 3 acts. Text by Ernst Marischka and B-- G--. Ad. by P. G. Wodehouse & Laurie Wylie. Music by B-- G-- and Max Darewski. Libr. L: Keith Prowse 1926. 77p. 11cm. [No apparent relation to orig.] [BM.LCM]

GRASSER, J: Jk. Sel. in C483.

GRAUTOFF, Fd. H: 1871- .
3082. Banzai! By "Parabellum." Lpz: Weicher; NY: Baker & Taylor 1909. 320p. il. 19cm. [LC]
*3083. ("1906" - Der Zusammenbruch der alten Welt.) Armageddon 190-. By "Seestern." Tr. G. Herring. Introd. by Sir E. R. Freemantle. L: Paul, T. & T. 1907. xxiii;402p. 19cm. [BM]

GREDING, J: Ern. 1676-1748. Sel. in C273;287;#8904.

GREGOR, Cn. 1723-1801. Sel. in C244;269;273;287;489.

GREGOROVIUS, Fd. 1821-81.
3084. (Corsica.) Corsica in its picturesque, social, and historic aspects: the record of a tour...1852. Tr. R. Martineau. L: Longmans 1855. 493p. 18cm. [LC]
*3085. do. 1855. Wanderings in Corsica. Tr. A. Muir. Ed: Constable; L: Hamilton 2v. 326; 291p. 18cm. [BM]
*3086. do. 1855. Tr. E. J. Morris. Phil: Parry & McMillan vii;522p. 20cm. [Less good than Muir.] [LC.BM]
3087. (Der Kaiser Hadrian. Ein Gemälde...seiner Zeit.) The emperor Hadrian: a pict. of the Graeco-Roman world in his time. Tr. Ma. E. Robinson. L;NY: Macmillan 1898. xviii;414p. 22cm. [LC.BM]
3088. (Die Insel Capri.) The island of Capri. Tr. Lilian Clarke. Bost: Lee & Shepard 1879. 95p. 15cm. [LC]
§3089. do. 1896. The island of C--: a Mediterranean idyll. Freely tr. M. D. Fairbairn. L: Unwin. 156p. 19cm. [BM]
[Tr. understands Ger. and follows with consid. fidelity.]
*3090. (Geschichte der Stadt Rom im Mittelalter.) Hist. of the city of Rome in the middle ages. Tr. from 4th Ger. ed. by Annie Hamilton. L: Bell 1894-? 6v. 19cm. [BM.LC]
[Vol. 1 has xvi;505p. EC says: 3v. 1895. Vol. 4. 1896. 2pts.752p.]
3090a. do. 1900-9. [same] 2d rev. ed. L: Bell. 6v. 19cm. [BM]
[Vol. 1 has xxx;525p.]
*3091. (Lateinische Sommer.) Latian summers (and an excursion in Umbria). Tr. Dorothea Roberts. L: Junior army and navy stores 1902. xi;364p. 8. [BM]
[Not closely faithful, but very well done. --Six essays, five from L-- S--.]
*3092. (Römische Tagebücher.) The Roman journals, 1852-74. Ed. by F: Althaus. Tr. from 2d Ger. ed. by Mrs. G. W. Hamilton. L: Bell 1907. xxiii;473p. 21cm. [BM.LC]
3092a. do. 1911. [same] Bell. 18cm. [BM]
*3093. (Siziliana.) Siciliana: sketches of Naples and Sicily. Tr. Mrs. G. W. Hamilton. Bell 1914. vii;346p. 19cm. [BM.LC]

GRELLING, R: 1853- .
3094. (Belgische Aktenstücke.) Belgian documents: a companion volume to "The Crime." Tr. Ax. Gray. L;NY: Hodder & S. 1919. vi;308p. 22cm. [BM.LC]
*3095. (Das Verbrechen.) The crime. Tr. Ax. Gray. NY: Doran 1917-19. 4v. 22cm. [LC]
L: Hodder & S. 1917-1918. 3v. vol. 1, 1917; 2, 1918; 3, 1918. 22cm. [BM]
*3096. (J'accuse.) I accuse! By a German. Tr. Ax. Gray. NY: Doran 1915. 445p. 20cm. [LC] L: Hodder & S. viii;448p. 22cm. [BM]
[London ed. has title: "J'accuse."]

GRELLING, R:
3097. do. 1917. [same] NY: Grosset & Dunlap. [LC]

"GREIF, Mn." (i.e., F: Hm. Frey, 1839-1911). Sel. in C450;501;531.

GRILLPARZER, Fz. 1791-1872. Sel. in C93;196;311;317;366;455*;460.
3098. (Der arme Spielmann.) The poor musician. Tr. A. Remy. 1913-15. In C154(6)
*3099. (Die Jüdin von Toledo.) The Jewess of T--. Tr. G: H: and Annina P. Danton. 1913-15. In C154(6).
3100. (König Ottokars Glück und Ende.) Ottokar. [Sel.] Tr. T: Carlyle. 1840. In C56.
*3101. König Ottokar. In Gustav Pollak: "Franz Grillparzer and the Austrian drama." (2218 out of 2990 lines.) NY: Dodd, Mead 1907. xxi;440p. 21cm. [LC]
[Good, not excellent. Also selections from: Sappho; The golden fleece; The waves of the sea and love; Woe to him who lies; Esther, Libussa; The Jewess of Toledo; A brothers' feud in the House of Hapsburg.]
**3102. (Medea.) Medea: a trag. (in 5 acts and in verse). Tr. F. W. Thurstan and S. A. Wittmann. L: Nisbet 1879. vii;122p. 8. [BM]
[Very fine.]
3103. do. n.d. Medea, a trag. in 4 acts...as performed by Mlle. Fanny Janauschek and her company...NY. n.d. O. [NL]
§3104. do. 1913-15. Tr. Theodore A. Miller. In C154(6)
[English needlessly diffuse.]
*3105. (Mirjams Siegesgesang.) The song of Miriam. Cantata by Fz. Schubert. Tr. and partly rewritten by W: Duthie. Vocal score. L: Novello, Ewer 1869. 46p. 35cm. [Quite good.] [BM]
3106. do. 1872-76. Miriam's song of triumph. Tr. anon. Vocal score. Bost: Ditson n.d. 4. [AC]
§3107. do. 1877. The song of Miriam. Ad. by Rev. W. H. Milman. Vocal score. Engl. L: Novello. 50p. 25cm. [BMM]
§3108. do. 1881. Miriam's song of triumph. Tr. Lewis Novra. Vocal score. Engl. L: Augener 1881. 32p. 27cm. [BMM]
3109. My journey to Weimar. Tr. A. Remy. 1913-15. In C91(6).
†3110. (Sappho.) Sappho: a trag. (in 5 acts and in verse). Tr. J: Bramsen. L: Black & Y. 1820. 86p. 8. [NY]
[Unwarranted liberties.]
3111. do. 1821. [same] [BM]
3112. do. 1844. Sel. by T: Roscoe in "Ainsworth's Mag." 6(1844): 61. (B27)
§3113. do. 1846. Tr. E. B. Lee. In Öhlenschläger, A: G., "Correggio." Phillips & Sampson pp. 175-303. 18cm. [BM]
[Not very close, and not very poetical.]
3114. do. 1855. Tr. Lucy C. Cumming. Edinb. 8. [BM]
[EC has: L: Hamilton.]
†3115. do. 1858. Tr. Edda Middleton. NY: Appleton. 160p. 28cm. [LC]
*3116. do. 1876. Tr. Ellen Frothingham. Bost: Roberts. 136p. 15cm. [LC.BM]

GRIMM, A. Sel. in C466.

GRIMM, Ab. F: W: 1864- .
3117. (Ehrwürden Nudel.) Father Noodle. Ad. fr. romance of "Alfred Ira" by J: T. Mueller. Antigo, Wis: 1918. 236p. il. 19cm. [LC]
3118. The shadow of a crime. Based on "Seile der Liebe," by Ma. E. Ireland. St. Louis, Mo.: Concordia 1916. 127p. 19cm. [LC]

GRIMM, Ab. L: 1786-1872.
3119. Fairy tales. Il. Cruikshank. L: Tilt 1827. vi;172p. 18cm. [BM]
[The black guitar; The two foundlings of the spring; The avenging cudgel; The story of the three brothers, or, The avenging spring.]

GRIMM, Ab. L:
3120. King Roughbeard; or, the scornful Princess. A play for young people (in prose and verse). Arr. from Grimm by "Vera." L: Hatchards 1886. 31p. 16cm. [BM]
3121. Philemon and Baucis; Duller; The wicked nobody, or the golden egg. Tr. S. T. 1843. In C520.
3122. Tales: The Christmas roses; The water fairy's gifts; Lina; The hedgehog; Tony, the miller's son; The gleaner. Tr. S. T. 1845. In C519.
3123. Tales: Tony, the miller's son; The gleaner. Tr. S. T. 1846. In C521.

GRIMM, A. Th. v.
3124. Alexandra Feodorowna, empress of Russia. Tr. Lady Wallace. Ed: Edmonston & Douglas 1870. 2v. xv;325;424p. 19cm. [BM]

GRIMM, Hm. F: 1828-1901. Sel. in C469.
3125. (Albrecht Dürer.) Albert D--. Tr. anon. From the "Quarterly Ger. mag." 1872. 42p. O. [UW]
*3126. (Briefe.) Corr. between R. W. Emerson and H. Grimm. Bost; NY: Houghton 1903. 90p. 17cm. [LC]
[Ed. and prob. tr. by F: W: Holls.]
*3127. (Das Leben Michelangelos.) Life of Michelangelo. Tr. F. E. Bunnett. L: Smith Elder 1865. 2v. viii;499;471p. 19cm. [BM]
3127a. do. 1865. [same] 2d ed. [BM]
3128. do. 1896. [same] New ed. with additions. L: Dent; Bost: Little, Brown. xvi;558;536p. il. 20cm. [BM]
§3129. (Das Leben Raphaels.) Life of Raphael. Tr. Sa. H. Adams. L: Gardner 1889. vi;327p. 8. [BM]
3130. The destruction of Rome: a letter from H-- G-- Tr. Sa. H. Adams. Bost: Cupples, Upham 1886. 44p. 15cm. [BM]
*3131. (Goethe.) The life and times of Goethe. Tr. Sa. H. Adams. Bost: Little, Brown 1880. viii;559p. 21cm. [LC.BM]
[Somewhat disappointing.]
§3132. Literature: essays. Tr. Sa. H. Adams. Bost: Cupples, Upham 1886. xii;297p. 19cm. [LC.BM]
[Emerson; France and Voltaire; Voltaire and F: the Great; F: the Great and Macaulay; Dürer; Grimm brothers; Bettina v. Arnim; Dante.]

GRIMMS KINDER- UND HAUSMÄRCHEN

Note. The following entries, arr. chronologically as far as possible, represent volumes containing only the Grimm bros.' fairy tales in versions that at least pretend to reproduce the original. "Selections" and "Adaptations" are listed separately below. Following are the principal translators of the fairy tales, alphabetically arranged, with the key expressions used in designating them hereafter.

[§A-1]	1853. #3139.	[*H]	M. Hunt. #3190.
[§A-2]	1857. #3143.	[*L]	Mrs. Lucas. #3234.
[§Bn]	E. Beeson. #3345.	[§M]	B. Marshall. #3235.
[†By]	E. Boldey. #3200.	[†P]	Mrs. Paull. #3150.
[*C]	L. Crane. #3182.	[§T-1]	E. Taylor. #3133.
[§D-1]	N. Davidson. #3273.	[†T-2]	J: Taylor. #3135.
[§D-2]	M. Davis. #3142.	[†W]	L. Weedon. #3228.
[*E]	M. Edwardes. #3240.		

§3133. 1824(1823)-26. TAYLOR, EDGAR [T-1]. Ger. pop. stories. Il. by G: Cruikshank. L: Baldwyn. 2v. xii;237; 257p. 12. [BM]
[BM says vol. 1 was issued in 1823, but the "Gentleman's Mag." 92(1822):2:620 carries a notice of it. Vol. 1 has 31 stories, vol. 2 has 24. Hotten (see #3151) says vol. 1 was done by "Taylor and

GRIMM'S MÄRCHEN
a circle of relatives," whereas the second series was prepared by Taylor alone. The tr. is rather free, but in good style and spirit.]
§3134. 1839. [T-1]. Gammer Grethel; or, Ger. fairy tales, and pop. stor. from the coll. of MM. Grimm, and other sources; w...notes. New ed. L: Green. xii;325p. text. pp. 327-50, notes. [BM]
[Text is not a little revised from the foregoing. 42 stories, grouped into 12 evenings; 5 are not from Grimm: "Die Elfen" (abr.) by Tieck; "Der Ziegenhirt," by "Otmar"; "Das Märchen von der Padde," and "Kibitz," by Büsching. It has not always been possible for me to distinguish between this ed. and the foregoing.]
†3135. 1846. TAYLOR, J: E. [T-2]. The fairy ring. A coll. of tales and trad. Il. R. Doyle. L: Murray. vi;376p. 8. [BM]
[43 stories. Unwarranted liberties.]
3136. 1846. 1848. [T-1]. Gammer Grethel. L: Cundall. [EC]
[Reissue of #3134.]
3137. 1849. [T-1]. Gammer Grethel. L: Bohn. x;306p. 18cm. [BM]
3138. 1851. [T-1]. Ger. f. t. and pop. st. as told by Gammer Grethel. Il. Cruikshank. L: 12. [LCO]
§3139. 1853. ANON. [A-1]. Household st. Newly tr. 240 il. E. H. Wehnert. L: Addey. 2v. (436) 864p. 18cm. [88; 108 stories.][BM.NY]
3140. 1853. ANON. same? Ger. pop. t. and household st. NY: Francis. 2v. 12. [AC]
3141. 1854. ANON. same? Household st., 1st series. Addey. 288p. 12. [LCO]
§3142. 1855. DAVIS, MATILDA L. [D-2]. Home st. Newly tr. Il. G: Thompson. L: Routledge. viii;376p. 17cm. [BM]
[91 stories. Tr. is not closely faithful.]
§3143. 1857. ANON. [A-2]. Household st. Newly tr. 240 il. E. H. Wehnert. L: Bogue. 552p. 20cm. [BM]
[194 stories in a tr. taken from #3139 w. some revision. Fails in simple directness.]
3144. 1862. [A-1?] Household st. New ed. L: Routledge. 552p. il. sm. 4. [LCO]
3145. 1862. [A-1]. Ger. pop. t. and household st. Newly tr. Bost: Crosby & Nichols. 2v. 456; 430p. il. 12. [NY]
[90; 106 stories.]
3146. 1862. [T-1]. Gammer Grethel; or, Ger. f.t. L: Bohn. 8. [EC]
3147. 1863. ANON. Ger. f.t. and st. L: Bohn. 12. [EC]
3148. 1866. ANON. Grimm's goblins: a coll. of f.t. L: Vickers. 2v. in 1. il. 8. [This is perhaps a reissue of #3426.] [EC]
*3149. 1867. ANON. Grimm's goblins. Il. in col. after Cruikshank. Bost: Ticknor & Fields. 111p. 19cm. [13 stories.] [LC]
†3150. 1868. PAULL, MRS. H. H. B. [P]. F. t. New tr. Spec. ad. and arr. for young people. 16 il. W. J. Weigand. L: Warne; NY: Scribner. viii;575p. 17cm. [BM]
[Unwarrantable liberties. 130 stories.]
§3151. 1868. (1869?) [T-1]. Ger. pop. st. Introd. J: Ruskin. L: Hotten. xxvi;335p. 17cm. [BM]
[55 stories, w. the orig. notes, as in #3134.]
3152. 1869. ANON. Pop. t. and household st. Il. E. H. Wehnert. Phil: Porter & Coates. 2v. in 1. 12. [Probably A-1 or A-2.] [NY]
3153. 1870. ANON. Household st. New ed. NY: Miller. 12. [AC]
3154. 1872-6. ANON. Brave little tailor and other st. NY: Miller. 16. [AC]
3155. 1872-6. ANON. Grimm's f.t. NY: Miller. 16. [AC]
3156. 1872-6. ANON. Grimm's f.t. NY: Scribner & W. il. 12. [AC]
3157. 1872-6. ANON. Gammer Grethel. Phil: Lippincott. [AC]
[Probably by T-1, same as #3134.]

GRIMM'S MÄRCHEN--1872-6

3158. 1872-6. ANON. The golden bird, and other tales. NY: Miller. 16. [AC]

3159. 1872-6. ANON. The goblins. Bost: Osgood. il. sm. 4. [AC]

3160. 1872-6. [T-1]. Ger. pop. st. Introd. J: Ruskin. Little, Brown. [AC]

3161. 1872-6. ANON. Home f.t. NY: Miller. 16. [AC]

3162. 1872-6. ANON. Household st. NY: Routledge. il. 8. [AC]

3163. 1872-6. ANON. Three brothers and other st. NY: Miller. 16[AC]

3164. 1872-6. ANON. Tales and st. New tr. NY: Scribner, W. & A. il. 8. [AC]

3165. 1872-6. ANON. Stray leaves from fairy land. Phil: Bliss. il. 12. [AC]

3166. 1872-6. ANON. Pop. t. and household st. NY: Appleton. il. 12. [AC]

3167. 1872-6. ANON. The king of the swans, and other st. NY: Miller. 16. [Cf. C521. Probably A. Grimm is meant.] [AC]

3168. 1872. [P]. Grimm's f.t. Il. Weigand. 575p. [BM] [Reissue of #3150.]

3169. 1873. ANON. Household st. New ed. 12. [EC]

3170. 1874. ANON. Reissue of #3140. [BM]

3171. 1874. 1875. [D-2]. Home st. L: Routledge. 12. [EC] [Probably reissue of #3140.]

3172. 1876. [A-2]. Home st. L: Routledge. 564p. 8. [BM] [Same coll. as #3143.]

3173. 1876. [A-2]. Household st. Newly tr. Col. il. by Kronheim. Routledge. 564p. 8. [Same coll. as #3143.] [BM]

3174. 1876. [T-1]. Grimm's goblins. Grimm's household st. 24 il. after Cruikshank. L: Meek. xxiv;296p. 21cm. [BM.LC] [55 stories with notes as in #3134.]

3175. 1877. ANON. Household t. [AC]

3176. 1877. ANON. Pop. t. and household st. Reissue of #3152. [NY]

3177. 1878. [D-2]. Grimm's t. Sel. and tr...for use in schools. L: Bell's reading books. 120p. 17cm. [BM] [30 stories, slightly ed. from #3142.]

3178. 1878. [T-1]. Reissue of #3137. 306p. [BPL]

3179. 1878. [P]. Grimm's f.t. Phil: Lippincott. [AC]

3180. 1879 (1878).[D-2]. Fairy library. L: Routledge. 10v. 17cm[BM] [Same coll. as #3140, but in diff. order. Each vol. has about 20 stories, and ea. takes its title from the first story in it.]

3181. 1880. [A-2]. Household st. Newly tr. L: Routledge. 564p. 18cm. [Same coll. as #3143. No il.] [BM]

*3182. 1882. CRANE, LUCY [C]. Household st. L: Macmillan. x;269p. Il. Wl. Crane. 18cm. [LC.BM]

3183. 1882. [A-1]. Grimm's f.t. Il. E. H. Wehnert. L;NY: Routledge. 381p. 19cm. [LC]

3184. 1882. [D-2]. Grimm's f.t. L: Routledge. 64p. 28cm. [BM] [93 stories. Prtd. in triple columns. Bound with Andersen's fairy tales and the "Arabian nights."]

3185. 1883. [A-2]. Grimm's f.t. Il. E. H. Wehnert. L;NY: Routledge. 511p. 18cm. [BM]

3186. 1883. ANON. Household st. Louisville, Ky: Amer. prt. house for the blind. 150p. fol. [LC]

*3187. 1883. [C]. Household st. Il. Wl. Crane. NY: Lovell. 269p. 16. [Same as #3182.] [LC]

3188. 1883. [P]. Grimm's f.t. L: Warne. 8. [EC]

3189. 1883. [T-1?] Grimm's f.t. Il. Wl. Crane and E. H. Wehnert. Also, Grimm's goblins, il. Cruikshank. New issue. NY: Worthington. 8. [AC]

GRIMM'S MÄRCHEN--1884

*3190. 1884. HUNT, MARG. [H]. Grimm's household t. Introd. A. Lang. L: Bell. 2v. lxxv;454; 599p. [LC.BM]
[86; 124 stories. Mrs. Hunt seems to me to have followed D-2 rather closely, but correcting and improving. Tr. both with absolute fidelity and skill; the use of "thee" and "thou" is unfortunate.]

3191. 1885. ANON. Home f.t. New issue. Knox. [AC]

3192. 1885. ANON. Grimm's f.t. Routledge. 12. [AC]

3193. 1886. [A-1]. Pop. t. and household st. Phil: Porter & Coates. [AC]
[Seems to be a reissue of #3152.]

*3194. 1886. [C]. Grimm's f.t. Lothrop. [AC]

3195. 1887. [P]. do. "espec. for children." L: Warne. xii;522p. 8. [130 stories; cf. #3150.] [BM.NY]

3196. 1888. [T-1]. Ger. pop. st. and f.t. as told by Gammer Grethel. Rev. tr. by Edgar Taylor. Il. from G. Cruikshank and L: Grimm. L: Bell. xii;306p. 18cm. [BM]
[Reissue of #3134, without notes.]

3197. 1889. [T-1]. Household t. Ed. Alfonzo Gardiner. Il. by "Bertall" et al. Manchester: Heywood. xvi;255p. 17cm. [BM]
[32 stories, ed. from T-1. School text.]

3198. 1889. [T-1]. F. t. Ed. by Alfonzo Gardiner. Il. by "Bertall" et al. L: Heywood. xvi; 336p. 18cm. [38 stories, ed from T-1.][BM]

3199. 1889. ANON. Grimm's f.t. L: Ward, Lock. 12. [AC]

†3200. 1890. BOLDEY, ELLA [By]. Household f.t. newly tr. Il. R. André. NY: McLoughlin. 276p. 26 x 21cm. [97 stories.] [LC]

3201. 1890. [By]. Brave little tailor and other st. Il. André. NY: McLoughlin. 4. [LCO]

3202. 1890. [By]. The enchanted fawn and other st. Il. André. NY: McLoughlin. 4. [LCO]

3203. 1890. [By]. The golden bird and other st. Il. André. NY: McLoughlin. 4. [LCO]

3204. 1890. [By]. The magic mirror and other st. Il. André. NY: McLoughlin. 4. [LCO]

3205. 1890. [By]. The three golden hairs and other st. Il. André. NY: McLoughlin. 4. [LCO]

3206. 1890. [By]. The twelve brothers and other st. Il. André. NY: McLoughlin. 4. [LCO]
[This and the five preceding issues are evidently parts of #3200, published simultaneously with it.]

†3207. 1893. [P]. Grimm's wonder t. Tr. [P] and L. A. Wheatley. L: Warne. 12. [Probably identical with #3212.] [EC]

3208. 1893. [T-1]. Reissue of #3198. [BM]

3209. 1893. [P]. Household st. L: Warne. 12. [EC]

3210. 1893. [By]. Household f.t. L: Griffith. 4. [EC]

3211. 1893. [P]. Grimm's goblins. L: Warne. 12. [EC]

3212. 1893. [P]. Grimm's f.t. Tr.[P] and L. A. Wheatley. L: Warne. 12. [EC]

3213. 1893. [D-2]. Grimm's f.t. L: Routledge. 180p. 22cm. [BM]
[93 stories, prtd. in double columns. Same coll. as #3184.]

3214. 1893. 1894. ANON. Household st. Routledge. 8. [EC]

3215. 1894. ANON. Grimm's f.t. New rev. ed. Il. Harry S. Watson. NY: Cassell. 406p. 25cm. [LC]

3216. 1894. ANON. Grimm's f.t. L: Routledge. 8. [EC]

3217. 1894. 1895. [A-2]. F.t. from Grimm. Introd. S. Baring-Gould. Il. Gordon Browne. L: Wells Gardner. xxviii;339p. 21cm. [BM]
[44 stories.]

3218. 1895. ANON. F. t. L: King. il. 8. [EC]

†3219. 1896. ANON. Ger. f.t. NY: Maynard, Merrill. 96p. 16. [LCO]
[8 stories.]

3220. 1896. [A-2]. F. t. Il. E. H. Wehnert. New ed. L: Routledge. 384p. 8. [EC]

GRIMM'S MÄRCHEN--1896

*3221. 1896. [C]. F. t. Il. Wl. Crane. NY: Crowell. 342p. 19cm. [LC]
[No il. in this copy. 51 stories.]

3222. 1897. [P] and Wheatley. Grimm's wonder t. Reissue of #3207. [EC]

3223. 1897. [P]. Grimm's goblins. Reissue of #3211. [EC]

3224. 1897. [P]. Household st. Reissue of #3209. [EC]

3225. 1897. [P] and Wheatley. Grimm's f. t. Reissue of #3212. [EC]

3226. 1897. [T-1]. Gammer Grethel. Reissue of #3137. [LC]

§3227. 1898. ANON. F. t. Phil: Altemus. 255p. il. sq. 16. [LCO]
[33 stories. Probably same as #3197.]

†3228. 1898. WEEDON, LUCY L. [W]. F. t. Il. Ada Dennis (in col.), E. Stuart Hardy et al. L: Nister; NY: Dutton. 208p. 23cm. [BM]
[32 stories, very freely tr.]

3229. 1898. [W]. Hop o' my thumb's wanderings and other f. t. L: Nister; NY: Dutton. 104p. 23cm. [15 stories.] [BM]

3230. 1898. [W]. Little snow-white, and other f. t. L: Nister; NY: Dutton. 104p. 23cm. [BM]
[16 stories. This and the foregoing evidently derive from #3228.]

*3231. 1899. ANON. F. t. NY: McKibbin. 192p. il. 16. [26 stories.] [LC]

*3232. 1899. [C]. Household st. Reissue of #3182.

3233. 1900. ANON. F. st. supplementary to the first reader. M. Winifred Haliburton and P. P. Claxton. Richmond, Va: Johnson pub. 144p. il. 12. [LC]

*3234. 1900. LUCAS, MRS. EDGAR [L]. F. t. New tr. Il. Art. Rackham. L: Freemantle. xvii;464p. 20 x 16cm. [BM]
[62 stories. Tr. is largely taken from #3190.]

*3235. 1900. MARSHALL, BEATRICE [M]. F. t. Complete ed. L: Ward & Lock. 638p. il. 21cm. [BM]
[Very good, not excellent. Some tr. taken from C209.]

*3236. 1900. [M]. [same] Ward & Lock. 348p. [EC]

3237. 1900. [T-1]. F. t. Ed. Edric Vredenburg. Il. E. J. Andrews and S. Jacobs. L: Tuck n.d. 128p. 24cm. [BM]
[16 stories, ed. from T-1.]

3238. 190-. [P] and Wheatley. Grimm's goblins and wonder t. L: Warne. 372p. il. 8. [NY]
[69 stories. Tr. of #3150 rev. and altered, but not accurate. Not the same collection.]

3239. 1901. [A-2]. Household st. 200 il. by E. H. Wehnert. L: Routledge. viii;552p. 8. [Cf. #3143.] [BM]

*3240. 1901. EDWARDES, MARIAN [E]. Household st. Ed. and partly tr. anew by M. E--. Il. R. A. Bell. L: Dent. xvi;400p. 8. [BM]

3241. 1901. [T-1]. Reissue of #3237. [BM]

3242. 1902. [L]. Reissue of #3234. Phil: Lippincott; L: Freemantle. [LC]

3243. 1902. [T-1]. F. t. 12 il. J. Hassall. L: Sands. vi;305p. 21cm. [55 stories.] [BM]

3244. 1902. [T-1]. Gammer Grethel. Introd. Laurence Housman. Il. Cruikshank et al. L: Moring. xii;359p. 20cm. [BM.LC]
[Same as #3134, omitting one story.]

3245. 1903. ANON. F. t. Conkey. il. S. [AC]

3246. 1903. ANON. F. t. Il. Cruikshank. L: Methuen. 8. [EC]

3247. 1903. ANON. [Probably D-2.] F.t. L: Scott. 566p. 8. [EC]
[Cf. #3181, 564p.]

3248. 1903. ANON. [Probably T-1.] F. t. L: Blackie. 222p. 8. [EC]

3249. 1903. [T-1]. St. from G--. Sel. and ed. for little folk. Il. Helen Stratton. L: Blackie. unp. 25cm. [16 stories.] [BM]

3250. 1903. [same] L: Blackie. unp. 34cm. [BM]
[The same 16 stories, but in different order.]

3251. 1904. ANON. F. t. L: Collins. 448p. il. 8. [EC]

GRIMM'S MÄRCHEN--1904

3252. 1904. ANON. Reissue of #3219. [ABP]
3253. 1904. ANON. Little stor. from G--. L: Griffith & F. 4. [EC]
§3254. 1904. DAVIDSON, N. J. [D-1]. F. t. New tr. Il. L. Speed. Pearson. 416p. 8. [Cf. #3273.] [EC]
3255. 1904. [L]. F. t. Reissue of #3234. L: Constable. [EC]
3256. 1904. [T-1]. F. t. Il. Helen Stratton. L: Blackie. 336p. 8. [NY] [Reprint of #3133 w. new il.]
3257. 1904. [T-1]. Reprint of #3133. Il. by Cruikshank. L: Frowde. 2v. 8. [BM]
3258. 1904. [A-2]. F. t. L: Shaw. 256p. 24cm. [BM] [96 stories, in double columns. 79 il.]
3259. 1904. ANON. F. t. carefully chosen from the coll. etc. L: Partridge. 302p. 18cm. 12 il. A. Rackham. [BM] [76 stories, tr. by T-1 or A-2.]
3260. 1904. 1905. [A-2]. F. t. Il. E. H. Wehnert. New ed. L: Routledge. 512p. 8. [EC]
3261. 1905. ANON. F. t. Il. H. L. Shindler. L: Routledge. 480p. 8. [EC]
3262. 1905. [D-2]. F. t. L: Routledge; NY: Dutton. 392p. 12. [BM] [94 stories; no il.]
3263. 1905. [T-1]. Gammer Grethel. NY: Dodge. il. sq. 12. [AC]
3264. 1905. [T-1]. Ger. pop. st. Reissue of #3133 in one vol. xvii; 403p. 8. [BM]
3265. 1905. [T-1]. F. t. W. many il. by Helen Stratton. L: Blackie. 336p. 20cm. [54 stories, cf. #3256.] [BM]
3266. 1905. [T-1]. Grimm's t. L: Blackie. 214p. il. 19cm. [BM] [55 stories, from #3133.]
3267. 1905. [T-1]. Gammer Grethel. Reissue of #3244. [BM]
3268. 1906. ANON. Little snow-white. NY: Burt. [ABP]
3269. 1906. ANON. F. t. Collins. 232p. 8. [EC]
3270. 1906. [C]. Household st. NY: McLoughlin. 96p. il. 19cm. [LC] [9 stories.]
3271. 1906. ANON. A sel. from Grimm's f. t. Il. Gilbert James. L: Siegle. Langham ser. 63p. 16 & obl. 16. [EC] [In BM catalog, but missing.]
3272. 1906. [A-2]. Household st. Il. Dor. Furniss. L: S. P. C. K. 64p. 8. [12 stories from #3143.] [BM]
§3273. 1906. DAVIDSON, N. J. [D-1]. F. t. New tr. Il. Ambrose Dudley. L: Nisbet. vii;408p. 19cm. [121 stories. Tr. seems to be merely a revision of [A-2] (#3143). Cf. #3254.
3274. 1906. [T-1]. F. t. Il. R. A. Bell. L: Dent; NY: Dutton. Everyman's lib. xii;343p. 17cm. [BM] [66 stories, mostly from #3134.]
*3275. 1907. [L]. F. t. Reissue of #3234. [EC]
3276. 1907. [T-1 and A-2]. F. t. Reissue of #3258. [EC]
§3277. 1908. ANON. Little Snow-white and other f. t. Ed. W. T. Stead. Il. B. Le Fanu. Phil: Penn pub. co. 60p. 18cm. [LC] [7 stories.]
3278. 1908. ANON. F. t. Il. H. M. Brock and L. Speed. L: Seeley. 8. [EC]
3279. 1908. ANON. F. t. Ed. A. T. Martin. L: Macmillan. 12. [EC]
3280. 1908. [D-1]. F. t. New tr. NY: Bowman. il. D. [AC]
3281. 1908. [D-2]. F. t. L;NY: Cassell. 409p. 18cm. [BM] [94 stories.]
3282. 1908. [T-1]. F. t. Ed. and il. J. R. Monsell. L;NY: Cassell. viii;336p. 8. [Same as #3256.] [BM]
3283. 1908. ANON. Cherryblossom and other st. L: Blackie. 84p. il. 25cm. [8 stories.] [NY]
3284. 1908. [T-1]. Gammer Grethel. L: Bell. [Cf. #3244.] [EC]

GRIMM'S MÄRCHEN--1908

3285. 1908. [T-1]. Household t. Reissue of #3274. [LC]
3286. 1909. ANON. F. t. Milner. 8. [EC]
3287. 1909. ANON. F. t. L: Nimmo. il. 16. [EC]
3288. 1909. ANON. F. t. Ed. H. W. Mabie. Il. Ethel F. Betts. Phil: Stern. 117p. 28cm. [LC]
3289. 1909. ANON. F. t. L: Dent. 12. [EC]
*3290. 1909. [C]. Animal st. Il. J: Rae. NY: Duffield. 111p. 23cm. [LC]
3291. 1909. [H.] Household t. In Harvard classics, vol. 7 (pp. 51-232). NY: Collier. [41 stories.] [LC]
*3292. 1909. [L]. F. t. Il. by Rackham. L: Constable. xv;325p. 25cm. [LC.BM]
3293. 1909. [T-1]. F. t. Dodge. 336p. il. 8. [AC]
3294. 1909. [T-1]. Folk-st. Introd. J: Ruskin. L: Black. iv;96p. 17cm. [9 stories.] [BM]
3295. 1910. ANON. F. t. Ed. W. A. Jerrold. NY: Dutton. 12. [AC]
3296. 1910. ANON. F. t. Collins. 572p. 12. [EC]
3297. 1910. ANON. F. t. Il. G. James. L: Siegle, H. 64p. 8. [EC] [Cf. #3271.]
3298. 1910. ANON. The golden bird, and other t. Ed. W. H. Webster. Leeds: Arnold. 32p. il. 16. [EC]
3299. 1910. ANON. Hänsel and Gretel. Il. Maria L. Kirk. L: Gardner, Darton. 80p. 8. [EC]
§3300. 1910. ANON. The house in the wood, and other old f. st. Il. L. L. Brooke. L;NY: Warne. 89p. 24cm.[10 stories] [LC]
3301. 1910. ANON. St. from G--. Bost;NY: Caldwell. [ABP]
3302. 1910. ANON. The water of life. Ed. W. H. Webster. Leeds: Arnold. 32p. il. 16. [EC]
3303. 1910. [A-1]. Grimm's f. t. Il. in col. Alice Ross. Ed: Nimmo. 126p. 16cm. [11 stories.] [BM]
3304. 1910. [D-2]. Grimm's f. t. 4 il. Mabel L. Attwell. L: Cassell. 409p. 19cm. [94 stories.]
3305. 1910. [H]. Household t. L: Bell. 2v. 18cm. [LC] [Reissue of #3190.]
*3306. 1910. [L]. F. t. Il. Rackham. NY: Doubleday, Page. O. [AC]
3307. 1910. [M?] F. t. L: Newnes. 348p. 8. [Cf. #3236.] [EC]
3308. 1910. [T-1]. Hansel and Grettel and other st. from G--. Il. Helen Stratton. L: Blackie. unp. (84 p.) 4. [8 stories.] [NY]
3309. 1910. [T-1]. St. from G--. Il. Helen Stratton. L: Blackie. 128p. 17cm. [BM]
[8 stories, supposedly ed. for children, but little touched.]
3310. 1910. [T-1]. St. from G--. L: H:Frowde, also Hodder & S. Introd. Herb. Strang. x;256p. 17cm. [46 stories.] [BM]
3311. 1910. [T-1]. The waits of Bremen and other t. L: Blackie. 126p. 17cm. [16 stories; cf. #3249.] [BM]
3312. 1910. [W]. Grimm's f. t. Il. C. Robinson. L: Nister; NY: Dutton. 356p. 19cm. [56 stories.] [BM]
3313. 191- . ANON. Famous f. t. Girard, Kan: Haldeman-Julius n.d. 128p. (Big blue books.) 5 x 8 in. [Publisher's catalog.]
3314. 1911. ANON. F. t. NY: Platt & Peck. 176p. il. O. [ABP]
3315. 1911. ANON. Little snow-white. Bost: Palmer. [ABP]
3316. 1911. [C]. Animal stories. NY: Duffield. 95p. [NY]
3317. 1911. [D-1]. F. t. and st. Il. Lancelot Speed. L: Seeley. vi;192p. 19cm.[50 st.; page for page identical with #3273.] [BM]
*3318. 1911. [L]. F. t. L: Constable 1911. 482p. [Cf. #3234.] [EC]
3319. 1911. [T-1]. F. t. Il. C: Folkard. Introd. by Ruskin. Reissue of #3151. [LC.BM] Also NY: Macmillan. [ABP]
3320. 1912. ANON. F. t. Hurst. [ABP]
3321. 1912. ANON. F. t. McLoughlin. [ABP]

GRIMM'S MÄRCHEN--1912

3322. 1912. ANON. Ger. household t. Houghton. 2 pts. [ABP]
3323. 1912. ANON. St. from G--. NY: Cassell. [AC]
3324. 1912. [M?] F. t. NY: Harper. 637p. il. O. [Cf. #3235.] [AC]
3325. 1912. [T-1]. F. t. Il. Noel Pocock. L: Frowde; NY: Doran. 356p. 8. [AC.EC]
3326. 1913. [A-2]. F. t. Il. Hope Dunlap. Chic;NY: Rand, McNally. 275p. 23cm. [LC]
3327. 1913. ANON. F. t. Ed. A. T. Martin. L: Macmillan. 12. [EC]
*3328. 1913. [L]. F. t. Constable. Reissue of #3234. [BM]
3329. 1913. [T-1]. F. t. Il. J. R. Monsell. L: Cassell; NY: Funk & W. vii;336p. 4. [BM.AC]
3330. 1913. [T-1?] F. t. L: Gardner. 314p. 8. [EC]
[Cf. #3243, listed with 314p. in EC]
3331. 1913. [T-1]. F. t. Il. in col. Noel Pocock. L: Frowde, also Hodder and S. viii;346p. 23cm.]
[55 stories. EC and AC both list this as 1912; cf. #3325.]
3332. 1913. [T-1]. Grimm's f. t. L: Everett. 256p. 16cm. [BM]
[49 st. EC lists this as 1912.]
3333. 1913. [T-1]. Gammer Grethel. Reissue of #3244. L: Simpkin. 16. [EC]
3334. 1913. [T-1]. F. t. Reissue of #3319. [AC]
3335. 1914. ANON. F. t. Sully & Kleinteich. il. S. [AC]
3336. 1914. ANON. F. t. Ed. H. W. Mabie. Barse & Hopkins. il. Q. [AC]
3337. 1914. [A-2]. F. t. Il. G. Ridout. L: Kelly. 507p. 18cm. [BM]
3338. 1914. [A-2]. F. t. Il. Hope Dunlap. L: Duckworth. Rand McNally press. 275p. 23cm. [36 stories.] [BM]
3339. 1914. [A-2]. Golden tales from G--. Ed. Edith Robarts. L: Gardner, Darton. vii;119p. 16cm. [11 stories.] [BM]
3340. 1914. [A-2]. The ogre with the three golden hairs and other tales. Il. S. B. Pearse. NY: Stokes; L: Jack 1915 (1914). 62p. 23cm. [4 stories. AC has 1914, BM 1915.] [BM.AC]
*3341. 1914. [H]. F. t. Complete ed. Il. J: B. Gruelle. NY: Cupples & L. 419p. 25cm. [LC]
3342. 1914. [T-1]. F. t. Il. J: Hassall. NY: Stokes. 305p. O. [AC]
[Cf. #3243.]
3343. 1914. [T-1]. F. t. Il. Monroe S. Orr. L: Harrap. 333p. 23cm. [BM]
[43 stories.]
3344. 1915. [A-2]. Golden tales from Grimm. Stokes. 119p. il. S. [AC]
[Same as #3339.]
§3345. 1915. BEESON, ERNEST [Bn]. F. t. New tr. Il. G: Soper. Headley: Crowell. viii;278p. 4. [EC.AC]
[36 stories. Correct, but no real savor to the tr.]
3346. 1915. [T-1]. F. t. NY: Stokes. Same as #3343. [AC]
*3347. 1916. [L., C., E.] Household and f. t. NY: Jacobs. 377p. 20cm.
[53 stories. Eclectic vol., made up from sel. suggested by librarians and story-tellers. No individ. ascriptions.] [LC]
3348. 1916. [Bn]. F. t. Same as #3345. [BM]
3349. 1916. [T-1]. F. t. Reissue of #3319. [AC]
3350. 1917. [A-2]. F. t. Il. Ethel Betts. L: Harrap. 128p. 28cm. [BM]
[18 stories.]
*3351. 1917. [C]. Tales. New ed. NY: Crowell. [AC]
[Probably same as #3221.]
3352. 1917. [L]. Little brother and little sister, and other t. Il. Rackham. L: Constable. xi;251p. 29cm. [BM]
[40 stories ed. from Hunt's tr. Cf. #3292.]
3353. 1917. [T-1]. F. st. Reissue of #3319. [AC]
3354. 1917. [T-1]. F. t. Il. Louis Rhead. NY: Harper. 443p. O. [AC]
[Cf. #3324; 3386.]
3355. 1917. [T-1?] F. t. Il. Monroe S. Orr. Phil: McKay. 327p. D. [AC]
[Cf. #3343.]

3356. 1918. [L]. Little brother and sister, and other t. Il. Rackham. NY: Dodd. 251p. Q. [Cf. #3352.] [AC]
3357. 1919. ANON. F. t. NY: Whitman. il. O. [AC]
3358. 1919. ANON. F. t. for children and the household. Il. G: Cruikshank. L: Hutchinson. 326p. cr. 8. [EC]
3359. 1919. [T-1]. F. t. Reissue of #3319. [AC]
3360. 1919. [T-1]. Grimm's t. Cheap ed. L: Blackie. 214p. 8. [BM] [Reprint of #3124 without notes.]
3361. 1920. ANON. F. t. NY: Nelson. Golden river ser. 160p. il. T. [AC]
3362. 1920. ANON. F. t. L: Collins. 126p. Cr. 8. [Cf. #3396.] [EC]
3363. 1920. ANON. F. t. Il. Ella D. Lee. NY: Donohue. 229p. O. [AC]
3364. 1920. [C]. Animal st. [See #3290.] Il. in col. J: Rae. NY: Duffield. [AC]
*3365. 1920. [L]. Hansel and Grethel, and other t. Il. A. Rackham. L: Constable; NY: Dutton. x;160p. 25cm. [LC.BM] [Sep. issue from #3292. 30 stories.]
*3366. 1920. [L]. Snowdrop and other t. L: Constable; NY: Dutton. xii;165p. 25cm. [Sep. issue from #3292. 30 stories.] [BM]
3367. 1920. [M]. F. t. L: Ward, Lock. 320p. Cr. 8. [EC]
3368. 1920. [M]. F. t. 48 col. pl. Harry G. Theaker. L: Ward, Lock. x;344p. 20cm. [22 stories; tr. somewhat edited.] [BM]
3369. 1920. [T-1]. F. t. Il. H. Stratton. New ed. L: Blackie. 4. [Cf. #3256.] [EC]
3370. 1920. [T-1]. F. t. Il. J: Hassall. L: Gardner. 305p. 8. [EC] [Cf. #3243.]
3371. 1921. ANON. F. t. NY: Jacobs. Wash. sq. classics. il. [AC]
3372. 1921. ANON. Grimm's f. t. Ad. Edwin G. Rich. NY: Small. 240p. il. 24cm. [Fairly close to some good tr.] [LC]
3373. 1921. [A-2]. F. t. Sel. and il. Elenore Abbott [from A-2]. L: Hodder & S; NY: Scribner. vii;308p. 23cm. [38 stories.] [LC.BM]
3374. 1921. [T-1]. St. from G--. Il. H. Stratton. L: Blackie. unp. 25cm. [Same as #3249.] [BM]
3375. 1922. [A-2]. F. t. 60 il. w. col. pl. Edwin J: Prittie. Phil: Winston. 310p. 22cm. [LC]
3376. 1922. [A-2]. Grimm's f. t. Il. Anne Anderson. L: Collins. 256p. 28cm. [49 stories, edited from #3143.] [BM]
*3377. 1922. [C]. F. t. Il. Hope Dunlap. Chic: Rand McNally. New Junior lib. 321p. D. [AC]
*3378. 1922. [C]. Snow white, and other st. Il. in col. Wuanita Smith and in black and white E: Shenton. NY: Jacobs. 115p. D. [LC] [11 stories.]
3379. 1922. [E]. Household t. Reissue of #3240. [BM]
3380. 1922. [H]. F. t. Ed. by Fes. J. Olcott [from H.] Il. Rie Cramer. NY: Penn. 367p. 25cm. [LC] [51 stories. Long sentences divided and wording modernized.]
*3381. 1922. [L]. Golden bird and other st. Il. in col. by Wuanita Smith and in black and white by E: Shenton. NY: Jacobs. 116p. D. [11 stories.] [LC]
3382. 1922. [T-1]. Grimm's f. st. Col. il. J: B. Gruelle, pen-and-ink sketches R. Emmett Owen. NY: Cupples & Leon. 178p. 24cm. [LC] [25 stories.]
3383. 1922. [T-1]. F. t. Reissue of #3370. [BM]
3384. 1923. [B-1]. F. t. Il. G: Soper. L: Allen & Unwin. viii;278p. 22cm. [36 stories.] [BM]
*3385. 1923. [C]. Household st. Il. Wl. Crane. NY: Macmillan. x; 269p. 19cm. [Cf. #3182.] [LC]
3386. 1923. [T-1]. Grimm's f. t. Il. (and ed.) Louis Rhead. NY;L: Harper. 443p. 23cm. [BM] [67 st. mainly from T-1 with some verbal editing; copyright 1917, see #3354.]

GRIMM'S MÄRCHEN--1924

3387. 1924. [A-2]. F. t. 100 il. by Fes. Brundage. Akron, O: Saalfield. 310p. 23cm. [36 stories.] [LC]
3388. 1924. [A-2]. F. t. 60 il. w. col. pl. Edwin J: Prittie. Ed. Orton Lowe. Phil: Winston. x;310p. 21cm. [36 stories, same selection as foregoing.] [LC.BM]
3389. 1924. [Bn]. F. t. Il. G: Soper. NY: Doran. 278p. 22cm. [Same as #3345.] [LC]
3390. 1924. [D-1]. Grimm's f. t. Il. J. R. Monsell. L;Glasgow: Collins. 571p. 15cm. [99 stories.] [BM]
3391. 1924. [D-2]. F. t. L: Holerth press. 70p. 15cm. [11 stories.] [BM]
3392. 1924. [T-1]. F. t. Reissue of #3319. [AC]
3393. 1924. ANON. F. t. L: Collins. 8. [Cf. #3362; #3390.] [EC]
3394. 1924. ANON. Old mother frost, and other st. from G--. NY: Macmillan. 61p. il. S. [AC]
3395. 1924. ANON. F. t. NY: Sears. [AC]
3396. 1924. [A-2]. F. t. L: Low. 126p. 18cm. [11 stories. Cf. #3362.] [BM]
*3397. 1924. [L]. Grimm's f. t. Il. Rackham. L: Heinemann. xv;325p. 25cm. [60 stories.] [BM]
3398. 1924. [T-1]. Hansel and Grethel, and other st. Il. Kay Nielsen. L: Hodder & S. 275p. 30cm. [22 stories.] [BM]
3399. 1925. [T-1]. F. st. Il. Mabel L. Attwell. Ed. Capt. Edric Vredenburg. L: Tuck. 108p. 8. [Cf. #3237.] [EC]
3400. 1926. ANON. F. t. NY: Sears. 244p. 25cm. [LC]
3401. 1926. ANON. Old, old f. t. NY: Nelson. 160p. il. Q. [Cf. #3361.] [AC]
3402. 1927. ANON. F. st. Il. Attwell. L: Tuck. 280p. 8. [EC]
3403. 1927. ANON. F. t. Il. G. Ridout. Epworth press. 284p. 8. [EC]
3404. 1927. ANON. F. t. L: Gardner. [EC]
3405. 1927. ANON. Hansel and Grethel. Il. Berta and Elmer Hader. NY: Macmillan. S. [AC]
3405a. 1926. [C]. Household stories. Il. Walter Crane. NY;L: Macmillan. x;269p. D. [AC]
*3406. 1927. [E]. Household t. Il. R. A. Bell. L: Dent. 416p. 8. [Same as #3240.] [EC]
3407. 1927. [T-1]. Hansel and Grethel. Il. Kay Nielsen. NY: Doran. Q. [Cf. #3398.] [AC]

SELECTIONS[1]

See C12;68;80;82;124;128;134;154(5);163;181;190;209;366;469;477; 537;#305.

3408. 1855. PALMER, FIS. P. Old tales for the young. Il. "A. Crowquill." L: Routledge. 407p. 12. [5 from Grimm.] [BM]
3409. 1865. ANON. Ger. pop. t. Bost: Tilton 1865. 4v. 16. [Grimm and Andersen] [AC]
3410. 1871. ANON. The fairy pict. book of old st. Ed: Gall & Inglis. Col. il. n.p. 25cm. [3 by Grimm, edited. Prt. on one side.] [BM]
3411. 1883. ANON. Little tales for little readers: a coll. of interesting and amus. st. Glasgow: Marr 1883. 127p. 14cm. [Numerous woodcuts. Cinderella; Little red riding-hood.] [BM]
3412. 1883. ANON. Clever Hans. Il. J. Lawson. L: De La Rue. 23p. 22cm. [Same tr. as #3143 (A-2).] [BM]
3413. 189-. ANON. Old time st. from G-- and Andersen. Il. E. J. Andrews and S. Jacobs. L: Tuck. 72p. 4. [10 stories in a severely abridged version for children.] [NY]

[1]The following contain Grimm fairy tales as part of volumes which do not belong in List C.

GRIMM'S MÄRCHEN--SELECTIONS--1896

§3414. 1896. ANON. The gooseherd (Die Gänsemagd); King throstle-beak. L;Ed: T. Nelson. 21cm. [BM]
[Sep., 14p. ea. General title: Favorite f. t. with col. pict.]

3415. 1900. ANON. F. t. and fables. Halifax: Mackinlay. Classics for Canadian children. 48p. 17cm. [BM]

3416. 1905. ANON. F. t. old and new: A sel. of st. from...Grimm, etc. Cassell. 384p. il. 16. [EC]

3417. 1906. ANON. [T-1]. Grimm's and H. Andersen's f. t. Sel. and ed. for little folk. Il. by H. Stratton. L: Blackie. unp. 33cm.
[16 from Grimm, as in #3243.] [BM]

3418. 1909. ANON. Folk-lore and fable: Aesop, Grimm, Andersen. Collier. [Probably one vol. of the Harvard classics.] [ABP]

3419. 1913? ANON. Grimm f. t., and f. t. and legends by C: Perrault. NY book co. n.d. [AC]

3420. 1925. [T-1]. Tales from H. C. Andersen and the Brothers G--. Il. Honor C. Appleton et al. L;Ed: Nelson. 240p. 16cm. 18. [BM]
[15 stories. Tr. of E. Taylor.]

ADAPTATIONS[1]

Carsten, H: See #1053-5. Francke, A. H., #1832-44.

3421. 1810. ANON. F. t. (Chapbook.) Ed: J. Morren. 24p. 17cm. [BM]
[Cinderilla (sic), or the little glass slipper; Little red riding hood; Princess fair-star and Prince Cherry,... Retold.]

3422. 1817. ANON. F. t. Chapbook. Ed: Sanderson. 23p. 16cm. [BM]
[3 from Grimm as in the foregoing. Retold.]

3423. 1845. ANON. Household t. and trad. of England, Germany, France, etc. L: J.Burns. 188p. 16cm. [BM]
[Many from Grimm, retold. 52 in all.]

3424. 1845. LEINSTEIN, MADAME. Unlucky J: and his lump of silver. (Hans im Glück.) Tr. (i.e.,ad.) into verse, 15 col. engr. L: Dean & Munday. 31p. 14cm. [A juvenile comic tale.] [BM]

3425. 1861. ANON. Favourite f. t. Ed: Gall & Inglis. 174p. 16cm. [BM]
[Col. il. 4 from Grimm, retold.]

†3426. 1861. ANON. Fairy books for boys and girls. L: Vickers. Pts. i-vi. 240p. Col. il. from "Phiz." 24cm. [BM]
[Double columns; 84 stories, many not from Grimm. Add. and alterations.]

3427. 1865. ANON. (Aschenbrödel.) Cinderella. NY: Hurd & H. Il. 12.
[Adaptation?] [AC]

3428. 1865. ANON. do. Dramatized from the orig. f. t. NY: Gray & Green. 8. [AC]

3429. 1872. ANON. F. t. told again. L;NY: Cassell. Il. Gst. Doré. 96p. 28cm. [10 by Grimm. Retold.] [BM]

3430. 1872-6. BURNAND, F. C. Snowdrop: extravaganza. (Dornröschen.) NY: French n.d. 16. [AC]

3431. 1872-6. BURNAND, F. C. Rumpelstilskin: extravaganza. (Rumpelstilzchen.) NY: French n.d. 16. [AC]

3432. 1880. FREILIGRATH-KROEKER, KATE. Snowdrop; The bear prince. (Plays.) In Alice and other fairy plays for children. L: Sonnenschein. il. 18cm. [Pp. 65-216. 2d ed. 1880.] [BM]

3433. 1881. ANON. F. t. with fairy pict. L: S. P. C. K. Col. il. unp. 27cm. [The seven Swabians; Snow white and rosy red; The bewitched princes. Each separate. Retold.] [BM]

[1]Here are listed in chronological order publications in which the wording of the Grimms' tales is seriously modified, or perhaps only the subject matter borrowed.

GRIMM'S MÄRCHEN--ADAPTATIONS--1882

3434. 1882. ANON. Rumpelstiltskin...a new tr. Il. G. R. Halkett. L: De La Rue. 26p. 23cm. [Much adaptation.] [BM]

3435. 1883. POLLARD, JOSEPHINE. Tales of the fairy world. Rhymed by J-- P--. NY: McLoughlin. 11; 12; 12p. il. 28 x 22cm. [LC] [Bonny Belle; Brave little tailor; Snow white. Cf. #3436;#3440; #3441.]

3436. 1883. POLLARD. Brave little tailor and other stories. Rhymed by J-- P--. NY: McLoughlin. 12p. 4. [Cf. #3435.] [LCO]

3437. 1883. POLLARD. The enchanted princess. Rhymed by J-- P--. NY: McLoughlin. 4.[Cf. #3438.] [LCO]

3438. 1883. POLLARD. Hours in fairy land. Rhymed by J-- P--. NY: McLoughlin. 14; 14; 12p. il. 27 x 21cm. [LC] [Enchanted princess; White rose and red rose; Six swans. Cf. #3437;#3439;#3442.]

3439. 1883. POLLARD. The six swans. Rhymed by J-- P--. NY: McLoughlin. 12p. il. 4. [Cf. #3438.] [LCO]

3440. 1883. POLLARD. Snow white. (Sneewittchen.) Rhymed by J-- P--. NY: McLoughlin. 12p. il. 4. [Cf. #3436.] [LCO]

3441. 1883. POLLARD. The story of Bonnybelle. Rhymed by J-- P--. NY: McLoughlin. 11p. il. 4. [Cf. #3435] [LCO]

3442. 1883. POLLARD. The story of red rose and rose white. (Schneeweisschen und Rosenrot.) Rhymed by J-- P--. NY: McLoughlin. 14p. il. 4. [Cf. #3438.] [LCO]

3443. 1885. ANON. Three fairy princesses. Il. by Caro. Paterson. L;NY: Ward. unp. 17cm. [BM] [Snow white; The sleeping beauty; Cinderella. Edited.]

3444. 1889. W., E. F. R. Rumpelstilzken: a German fairy story, dramatized for children. L: Griffith, Farran & Co. 32p. front. t.p. 18cm. [Founded on Grimm's fairy tale.] [BM]

3445. 1892. PRATT-CHADWICK, MRS. MARA L. F. t. Il. Edith F. Foster; Bost;NY: Educ. pub. 19cm. [11 stories, much edited.] [LC]

3446. 1893. SPRAGUE, Ma. A., tr. The man without a heart. Il. Rose M. Sprague. Bost: Prang. 22p. 4. [Not Grimm or much altered.][LC]

3447. 1893. do. The plight of a princess. Il. Rose M. Sprague. Bost: Prang. 11p. 4. [Cf. the foregoing.] [LC]

3448. 1894-6. WILTSE, SARA E., ed. F. t. Il. Caro. S. King. Bost: Ginn. 2v. 18cm. [LC] [29 stories, edited to make proper moral effect on children.]

3449. 1895. PITT-KEITHLEY, A. F.t. from Andersen and G--. In words of one syl. L: Routledge. 96p. 16. [EC]

3450. 1895. SCOTT-GATTY, Af. The goose girl. (Die Gänsemagd.) A musical play (after Grimm) by A. S.-G. Libr. L: Boosey. 29p. 20cm. [BM]

3451. 1896. ANON. F. t. In words of one syll. By "Aunt Virginia." NY: Hurst. 162p. il. 20cm. [35 stories.] [LC]

3452. 1897. ANON. Household tales, told again in English. Bost; NY: Houghton. 2v. 17cm. [LC] [39 stories, based on #3190, much altered.]

3453. 1901. ANON. F. t. Retold in words of one syllable. Burt. 8. [AC]

3454. 1903. ANON. Best stories. Ed. and ad. for...3d reader grade. NY;Bost: Univ. pub. co. 128p. il. 18cm. [LC]

3455. 1903. TURPIN, EDNA H. L. F.t. Sel. and ed. for primary reader grades. NY: Maynard, Merrill. 207p. il. 19cm. [LC] [25 stories, severely edited.]

3456. 1904. FASSETT, JAS. H. F.t. Sel. and ed. for children in their third school year. NY;L: Macmillan. xiii;188p. 14cm. [LC] [20 stories, edited.]

3458. 1904. ANON. Old f. t. for children. L: Nister; NY: Dutton. 136p. il. 17cm. [4 from Grimm. Retold.]

3459. 1904. TURPIN. F. t. NY: Maynard, Merrill. il. 12. [Same as #3455.] [AC]
3460. 1905. ANON. F. t. old and new. Col. il. and others. L;NY: Cassell. Bks. 1 and 2 "for little folks," 96; 96p. 12 stories simplified; Bk. 3 (11) stories from Grimm. 96p. 17cm. [BM] [Consid. ed. even in Book 3.]
3461. 1905. BALDWIN, J. Fairy reader. From Grimm and Andersen by J. Baldwin. Am. bk. [ABP]
3462. 1905. ANON. F. t. Chic: Reilly & Britton. 127p. il. 10cm. [LC] [5 stories retold.]
3463. 1906. ANON. Favourite f. t. L: Gall & Inglis. 224p. il. 18cm. [8 of 18 from Grimm, retold. Same tr. as #3425.] [BM]
3464. 1906. DAVIS, LOUIS. The goose girl at the well. L: Mathews. 67p. 18cm. [BM]
3465. 1906. NORRIS, E., ed. Household st. Bost;NY: Educ. pub. co. 134p. 17cm. [13 stories, much edited.] [LC]
3465a. 1906. STEEDMAN, AMY. Same as #3471. [BM]
3466. 1906. YATES, M. T. Grimm's f. st. Aldine pub. (Little Wideawake ser.). 127p. 54 il. 18cm. [11 stories; rewritten.] [BM]
3467. 1907. FASSETT, JAS. H. Fairy tales. Sel. and ed. for children in their third school year. NY;L: Macmillan. 188p. 14cm. [LC.BM] [Same as #3456.]
3468. 1907. PERKINS, LUCY. Twenty best f. t. by Andersen, Grimm, and Miss Mulock. Comp. by L. P. NY: Stokes. [See next entry.] [ABP]
3469. 1907. [Same]. Sel. and il. (and ad.) Lucy F. Perkins. L: Harrap. 164p. 24cm. [BM]
[Cinderella; Bremen town musicians; The fair one with golden locks; Rumpelstiltzchen; The frog-prince; The wolf and the seven young goslings; Snow white and rose red; Little red ridinghood; The sleeping beauty.]
3470. 1908. ANON. Favourite t. from --- Grimm. Il. T. H. Robinson. L;Glasgow: Collins. 126p. 16cm. [26 stories; retold.] [BM]
3471. 1908. STEEDMAN, AMY. St. from G--, told to the children by A. S--. Il. Harry Rowntree. L: Jack; NY: Dutton. 116p. 15cm. [LC] [10 stories, recast quite freely.]
3472. 1909. SOWERBY, GITHA. F. t. Sel. and retold by G. S--. Il. (in col.) Millicent Sowerby. L: Richards. xv;255p. 23cm. [BM] [64 stories well told.]
3473. 1909. ANON. Grimm's tales: a sel. of favourite st. L: Frowde & Hodder & S. 54p. il. 24cm. [6 stories retold.] [BM]
3474. 1910. ANON. Little snowdrop, and other t. L: Nelson. 96p. il. 19cm. [5 stories.] [BM]
3475. 1910. SOWERBY. Same as #3472. NY: Stokes. [LC]
3476. 1912. FITZGERALD, KATHLEEN. F. t. Told by K. F--. NY: Jacobs. [AC]
3477. 1913. ABBOTT, ETHELYN. Folk tales from G--: a dramatic reader for 3d and 4th grades. Il. Dorothy Dulin. Flanagan. 126p. D. [AC]
3478. 1913. WHITE, JESSIE BRAHAM. Snow white and the seven dwarfs: a f. t. play. Mus. by Edmond Rickett. Il. C: B. Falls. NY: Dodd. 236p. O. [AC]
3479. 1914. ANON. St. from G--. L: Nelson. 160p. 16cm. [BM] [10 stories, retold.]
3480. 1915. ANON. Golden f. t. (Grimm & Andersen). L: Nelson. 316p. 18cm. [10 from Grimm, as in the foregoing.] [BM]
3481. 1915. CROSSFIELD, ELSIE J. The three feathers; Hans and Meg; The little ass. Prepared by E. J. C--. L: Arnold. 32p. 8. [EC]
3482. 1916. ANON. Fairy gold series. L: Dent. 8pt., ea. 32p. 18cm. [2 by Grimm; ed.] [BM]
3483. 1918. ANON. St. from G-- & Andersen. Melbourne: Whitcombe & Tombs. 96p. 18cm. [7 stories.] [BM]

GRIMM'S MÄRCHEN --ADAPTATIONS--1920
3484. 1920. FITZGERALD, KATHLEEN. Grimm's f. t. Retold. L: Hill. 91p. 32. [Missing. Cf. #3476.] [BM]
3485. 1920. NIGHTINGALE, Ag. Visual f. t. Containing 16 outline pict. for colouring. L: Black. 47p. 23cm. [16 stories.] [BM]
3486. 1920. TURNER, E. J. Cat who married a mouse. Retold. 3d ed. Sisson & P. Cr. 8. [EC]
3487. 1920. ANON. F. t. from G--. Il. by Louise Jacobs. L;NY: Geographia. 89p. 25cm. [14 stories.] [BM]
3488. 1921. ANON. The fairy ring. L: E: Arnold. 10pts., ea. 64p. il. 18cm. [4 from Grimm, ed.] [BM]
3489. 1922. BEISLEY, NINA C. Favourite f. t. L: Ward, Lock. Unp. il. 24cm. [3 st. retold.] [BM]
3490. 1922. ANON. Golden f. t. (G-- and Andersen.) L: Nelson. 316p. 8. [Same as #3480.] [BM]
3491. 1922. ANON. Robber bridegroom; a f. t. Il. H. J. Owen. NY: Macmillan. 39p. Q. [AC]
3492. 1922. SIDGWICK, ETHEL. The three golden hairs; The robber bridegroom. Two plays for schools (after Grimm). L: Sidgwick & J. 99p. 18cm. [BM]
3493. 1923. WILTSE, SARA E. F. t. Il. Blanche Fisher Laite. Classics for children. NY: Ginn. 2v. 254;230p. 18cm. [LC] [Prob. reissue of #3443.]
3494. 1924. WILTSE, SARA E. The queen bee and other f. t. from G--. Il. Blanche F. Laite. L: Ginn. 60p. 17cm. [BM] [Cf. #3443. Copyright 1894 and 1923. 5 stories ed. from #3143.]
3495. 1924. WILTSE, SARA E. The iron stone and other f. t. Il. B. F. Laite. L: Ginn. 96p. 17cm. [4 stories.] [BM]
3496. 1924? WILTSE, SARA E. The three crows and other f. t. Il. B. F. Laite. L: Ginn. 95p. 17cm. [7 stories.] [BM]
3497. 1925. REMY, JEAN S. F. t. retold in words of one syl. New ed. NY: Burt. [AC]
3498. 1925. WHITE, JESSIE. Snow white and the seven dwarfs: a f. t. play. Music by Edmond Rickett. Dodd: 119p., with music. No il. 18cm. [Rewritten and rev. from #3478.] [BM]
3500. 1927. ANON. Golden tales by the brothers G--. L: Brodie. 62p. 18cm. [7 stories ed. from #3143.] [BM]
3501. 1927. ANON. Bremen band. Il. Frank Dobias. NY: Macmillan. S. [Happy hour books.] [AC]

GRIMM, Jk. L: K: 1785-1863. (Deutsche Sagen.) Sel. in C477;537.
*3502. (Deutsche Mythologie.) Teutonic mythology. Tr. 4th ed. Jas. S. Stallybrass. L: Bell. 1880-8. 4v. 22cm. [BM.LC] [LC says: 1882-8.]

GRIMM, Jk. and W: See Grimm, Hm. Literature. #3132.

GRIMMELSHAUSEN, Hs. Jk. Cfl. v. 1625?-76. Sel. in C190;422;538.
**3503. (Der abenteuerliche Simplizissimus...) The adventurous Simplicissimus: being the description of the life of a strange vagabond, Melchior Sternfels von Fuchshaim. Tr. A. T. S. Goodrick. L: Heinemann 1912. xvi;431p. 19cm. [See below.] [BM]
3504. do. 1913. [same] NY: Dutton. [AC]
**3505. do. 1924. [same] Simplicissimus the vagabond, that is, the life of a strange advent. named Melchior Sternfels von Fuchshaim: namely where and in what manner he came into this world, what he saw, learned, experienced, and endured therein; also why he again left it of his own free will. Exceedingly droll and very advantageous to read. Given forth by the Ger. Schleifheim von Sulsfort (pseud.) in the year MDCLXIX, tr. by A. T: S. Goodrick...with an introd. by W: Rose. L: Routledge; NY: Dutton (1924). xxxii;377p. il. 23cm. [BM.LC]

GRIMMELSHAUSEN --Simplizissimus
[Tr. contains books I-V, being the complete first ed. Excellent tr., with faithful attention to the crabbed style.]

GRISAR, Hartmann, 1845- .
*3506. (Luther.) Luther. Auth. tr. E. M. Lamond. Ed. Luigi Cappadelta. L: Paul T. & T. 1913-17. 6v. 404; 400; 449; 327; 606; 551p. Also St.L: Herder. 21cm. [BM.LC]

GRISEBACH, E: 1845-1906. Sel. in C501.

GROB, Jean.
*3507. (Huldreich Zwingli.) The life of U: Zwingli. Tr. by Revs. I. K. Loos and G: F. Behringer. (The latter ed. the whole.) NY: Funk & W. 1883. vi;200p. 19cm. [LC.BM]
[Omits "portions...of a doctrinal and controversial nature." Not wholly exact.]

GROEBER, K:
3507a. Picturesque Palestine, Arabia, and Syria: the country, people and landscape. With 304 photogravure plates. NY: Brentano's 1925; L: Jarrolds 1926. xvi;304p. 12 x 9. [EC]

GRONAU, G:
3508. Leonardo da Vinci. Tr. (from MS) by F: Pledge. L: Duckworth; NY: Dutton. xv;190p. 15cm. [BM]
3509. do. 1914. Reissue. Duckworth. 22cm. [BM]
*3510. (Tizian.) Titian. Tr. Alice M. Todd. L: Duckworth; NY: Scribner 1904. xv;322p. il. 19cm. [BM]

GRONER, Frau A:e, 1850- .
3511. The man with the black cord. Tr. Grace I. Colbron. NY: Duffield 1911. 278p. il. 19cm. [LC] L: Chatto & Windus. 287p. [BM]
3512. (?Das Kreuz der Welser.) Joe Muller, detective. Tr. Grace I. Colbron. NY: Duffield 1917. 334p. [AC]
3513. (?Der geheimnisvolle Mönch.) The man with the black cord. Tr. Grace I. Colbron. NY: Duffield 1918. 287p. [AC]
3514. Lady in blue. By A-- G-- and G. I. Colbron. NY: Duffield 1922. 304p. 19cm. [LC]
3515. (Mene tekel.) Mene tekel: a tale of strange happenings. Tr. G. I. Colbron. NY: Duffield 1912. 243p. 19cm. [LC]

GROS, K: H:
3516. Funeral oration...in honor of the late Margrave of Brandenburg, Anspach, and Bareith. Comp. and recited at the Univ. of Erlangen...1806. Tr. from the Latin. Southampton: Baker & Fletcher et al 1807. ii;41p. front. (port.) 38 x 28cm. [BM]
[Tr. by his wife Elizabeth? She signs the pref. and writes the notes.]

GROSS, ---. Sel. in C287.

GROSS, Tb.
3517. The humming top. Tr. Blanche W. Howard. New holiday ed. Stokes 1903. S. [AC]

GROSSE, Ern. 1862- .
*3518. (Die Anfänge der Kunst.) The beginnings of art. Tr. anon. NY: Appleton 1897. xiv;327p. il. 24cm. [BM]

GROSSE, Jl. 1828-1902. Sel. in C112.

GROSSE, K: ("Graf v. Vargas"). 1761-(Death date unknown.)
3519. (Der Dolch.) The dagger. Tr. anon. L: Vernor & Hood 1796. (B26). [B43 has 1794. B47 has 1795. 12.]
3520. (Der Genius--aus den Papieren des Marquis C. v. G.) The genius: or, the mysterious advent. of Don Carlos de Grandez. Tr. Js. Trapp. L: Allen & West 1796. 2v. 12. (B26; B43; B47.)

GROSSE, K:
3521. do. 1796. Horrid mysteries. Tr. P: Will. L: Lane 1796. 4v.(B26)
§3522. do. 1927. [same]...a story from the German. L: Holden 1927. 2v. xxvi;268; 231p. 18cm. [BM]
[Reissue with pref. by Montague Summers.]

GROT, Jm. Cn. 1733-1800. Sel. in C244.

GROTH, Ks. 1819-99. Sel. in C75;311;421*;463.

GRUBE, A: W: 1816-84.
3523. (Charakterbilder aus der Geschichte und Sage, Pt. 2). Heroes of hist. and legend. Tr. J. L. Shadwell. L: Griffith & Farran 1880. xi;348p. 19cm. [BM]
[Tr. comp. with orig. and rev. by T. R. Armitage. Book intended for use of the blind.]
3523a. do. 1882. [same]. New ed. [BM]

GRUBE, Max 1854- .
3524. Wreckage: a drama in one act (and in prose). Ad. from the German by Gst. Hein. L: Capper & Newton 1893. pp. 49-69. 17cm. [BM]
[Index has: Washed ashore (Wreckage).]

GRUBER, J: Gf. 1774-1851.
3525. (Die Hölle auf Erden, oder Geschichte der Familie Fredini.) Hell upon earth. Tr. anon. L: Hughes 1804. 2v. 17cm. [BM]

GRUEBEL, J: Kd. 1736-1809. Sel. in C106.

"GRUEN, Anst." (i.e., An. Ax. Graf v. Auersperg, 1806-76). Sel. in C5; 6; 17; 32; 40-2; 50; 66; 89; 97; 111-2; 123; 141-2; 144; 149; 166; 169; 171; 173*; 196; 213; 219; 296; 309; 317; 366; 372*; 373; 380; 414; 448; 461; 469; 497; 501; #6209a; 8001.
*3526. (Der letzte Ritter.) The last knight. Tr. J: O. Sargent. NY: Hurd & Houghton 1871. 200p. 21cm. [LC.BM]
3526a. do. 1873. [same] L: Low. See "Athenaeum" 62(1873):146.

GRUENBAUM, Fr. Operettas. See Bodanzky, R.; Wilhelm, Jul.; Willner, A. M.

GRUENBAUM, Fr. and Hz. REICHERT.
§3527. (Miss Dudelsack.) Miss Dudelsack: operetta in 3 acts by R. Nelson. Tr. Grant Stewart. Vocal score. Engl. NY: Stern 1911. 164p. 27cm. [Fair translation.] [LCM.BMM]

GRUENFELD, Mx. 1879-
3528. The feast of Esther: a fairy play. Tr. Oscar Leonard. Cincin: 1911. [LC]

GRUENWALD, Af. Operettas. See Brammer, Jul.

GRUMBACH, S.
3529. (Das annexionistische Deutschland.) Germany's annexationist aims. Tr. abbrev. and introd. J. Ellis Barker. NY: Dutton; L: Murray 1917. x;148p. 19cm. [BM.LC]
[Largely by Barker, with passages quoted from G--.]

GRUPPE, O: F: 1804-76. Sel. in C41;375.

GRYPHIUS, And. 1616-64. Sel. in C233;244;423;461;533;570.

GSELL-FELS, Td. 1819-98.
3530. Switzerland, its scenery and people. Il. by eminent Swiss and Ger. artists. Text based on...Dr. G. L: Blackie 1881. xvi;472p. 34cm. [BM.LC]
[Tr. and ad. G: Goudie Chisholm. Tr. is faithful in spirit and partly in text. "Orig. has been consid. modified...for Engl. readers."]
3531. (Venedig.) Venice. Tr. by J. Gostwick. L: Bruckmann 1877. 97p. 37cm. [Il. with photographs and designs.] [BM]

GUELL, F: W: 1812-79. Sel. in C105;169;309;450.

GUENDERODE, K:e (F: L:e Mxe.) v. 1780-1806. Sel. in C90.
*3532. Günderode. Corr. with Bettina v. Arnim. Bost: Peabody 1842. xii;106p. 19cm. [First no. of Marg. Fuller's tr. Same as #95.] [LC]
**3533. do. 1861. Corr. of Fräulein G. and Bettina v. Arnim. Bost: Burnham. xii;344p. 19cm. [LC]
[Marg. Fuller's tr. compl. by Mrs. Minna Wesselhoeft, includ. those of Caro. Günderode's poems. Same as #96.]

GUENTHER, Cks. 1649-1704. Sel. in C232;244;271.

GUENTHER, Hans F: K. 1891- .
*3534. (Rassenkunde Europas.) The racial elements of European history. Tr. from 2d. German ed. by G. C. Wheeler. L: Methuen 1927. vii;279p. 22cm. [368 il. maps.] [BM]

GUERICKE, H: Ern. Fd. 1803-78.
3535. (A: Hm. Francke. Eine Denkschrift.) The life of A: Hm. Francké. Tr. S: Jackson. Intro. pref. Rev. E. Bickersteth. L: Seeley 1837. viii;296p. 16cm. [Much omitted.] [BM]
3536. do. 1847. [same] L: Bohn. 296p. [LC]

GUETZLAFF, K: F. A: 1803-51. Sel. in C469.

GUHL, Ern. K: 1819-62 and W: Koner.
*3537. (Das Leben der Griechen und Römer nach antiken Bildwerken dargestellt.) The life of the Greeks and Romans, described from antique monuments. Tr. from 3d Ger. ed. by Fis. Hueffer. NY: Appleton; L: Chapman & Hall 1875. ix;620p. 543 il. 21cm. [BM.LC]
[Some details omitted, and a concise translation consciously striven for.]
3538. do. 1878. [same] L: Chatto & Windus. 8. [EC]
3539. do. 1889. [same] New ed. Chatto. 620p. [LC]

GUMPERT, Ta. v., later v. Schober, 1810-97.
§3540. (Der Bettelknabe.) The beggar boy. Tr. anon. L: Seeley 1852. 101p. 14cm. [Tr. does not understand German.] [BM]
3541. Life's sunbeams; or, songs, birds, and flowers. Tr. anon. 1855. In C524.
3542. The nest-egg: a tale for children. Tr. anon. Berlin: Wohlgemuth 1860. 36p. 16cm. [BM]
3543. The orphans' pilgrimage. In Meade, Eliz. T., "Mou-Setsé." L: Isbister 1880. pp. 59-110. 16cm. [BM]

GUNDERT, Rev. H.
3544. Biog. of Rev. C: Isenberg. Tr. C. and M. Isenberg. L: Church Miss. Soc. 1885. vi;86p. 18cm. [BM]

"GUNDOLF" (i.e., Gundelfinger), F: 1880-1931. Sel. in C39.

GUTER, Der, 13th-14th cent. Sel. in C27;427.

GUTZKOW, K: Fd. 1811-78.
3545. Through night to light. Tr. Mrs. Faber. Lpz: Tauchnitz; L: Low 1870. 312p. 16cm. [BM]
[Wrong ascription? Cf. Spielhagen, F: #8834.]
3545a. The prince of Madagascar. Tr. anon. "Littell's liv. Age" 38 (1853): 31, 97. (B15a)
§3546. (Uriel Acosta.) U-- A--. Tr. M. M. NY: Ellinger 1860. 104p. 19cm. [LC]
§3547. do. 1867. Tr. W. J. Tuska. NY: Van der Potendyk and Cahn, printers. 86p. 17cm. [Semi-prose.] [LC]
†3548. do. 1885. Trag. in 3 acts (in verse and prose). Tr. H: Spicer. L: Paul. viii;87p. 8. [BM]
[Rewritten "for the Engl. stage, though circumstances intervened to prevent its production."]

GUTZKOW, K: Fd.
*3549. do. 1895. Tr. R: Hovey and Francois S. Jones. In "Poet-lore", vol. 7.
*3550. (Zopf und Schwert.) Sword and Queue. Tr. Grace I. Colbron. 1913-15. In C154(7).

HACKER, Fz. 1836- .
3551. (Josef Haydn. Ein Lebensbild.) Js. H--: the story of his life. Tr: from "Fz. v. Seeburg" by J. M. Toohey. Notre Dame, Ind: Lyons 1884. 349p. 20cm. [LC]

HACKLAENDER, F: W: ritter v. 1816-77. Sel. in C422;469.
*3552. (Bilder aus dem Soldatenleben im Frieden.) Military life in Prussia. First series: the soldier in time of peace. Tr. F. E. R. and H. E. R. L: Low 1873. iv;298p. 19cm. [BM]
[Good, not excellent.]
3553. do. 1874. [same] Bombardier H. and Corporal Dose; or, mil. life...L: Low. 298p. [BM]
§3554. (Bilder aus dem Soldatenleben im Kriege. Feldzug in Italien.) The Austrian campaign in Piedmont 1849. In "Scenes from the life of a soldier." Tr. anon. L: Murray 1850. pp. 1-224. 19cm. [BM]
[Tr. is not close or faithful. The remainder of the vol. to p. 245 is from anon. articles in the "Allgemeine Ztg."]
3555. (Der geheime Agent.) The secret agent: a comedy (partly from... H--) in 2 acts by J. Stirling Coyne. L: Lacy 1855. 40p. 18cm. [BM]
[Not much apparent relation.]
3556. (Der Leibschneider der Zwerge.) The dwarf's tailor and other fairy tales. Collected by Zoe D. Underhill. NY: Harper 1896. 260p. il. 12. [LCO]
3557. Enchanting and enchanted. Tr. Mrs. A. L. Wister. Phil: Lippincott 1871. 226p. il. 12. [AC says: 1870.] [LC]
3558. do. 1898. [same] Phil: Lippincott. [LC]
§3559. (Eugen Stillfried.) Katherine; and, the moment of fortune. (Der Augenblick des Glückes.) Tr. Lady Wallace. L: Bentley 1857. 3v. 19cm. [Omits rather freely.] [BM]
*3560. (Europaisches Sklavenleben.) Clara; or, slave life in Europe. Tr. anon. Pref. by Sir Archibald Alison. L: Bentley 1856. 3v. 19cm. [BM]
[Tr. has tried "to soften down or exclude whatever...might diminish the pleasure which the most fastidious must derive from its perusal." Very close and good.]
3561. do. 1856. [same] 2d ed. L: Bentley. [LC]
*3562. do. 1879(1880). European slave life. Tr. E. Woltmann. L: Tinsley. 3v. 19cm. [BM]
[Excellent tr. T.p. has 1880; BM accession stamp is 1879.]
3563. do. 1883. [same] NY: Munro. Seaside lib. 2pts. 32cm. [LC]
3564. do. 1883. [same as #3560] NY: Harper. 533p. 19cm. [LC]
*3565. (Handel und Wandel.) Behind the counter. Tr. Ma. Howitt. Lpz: Tauchnitz; L: Low 1868. 367p. 15cm. [BM]
3566. (Hinter blauen Brillen.) Behind blue glasses. Tr. Ma. A. Robinson. NY: Harper 1878. 138p. 13cm. [LC]
§3567. (Namenlose Geschichten.) Countess of St. Alban; or, lost and found. Tr. Fz. Demmler. L: Hodgson 1854. 348p. 16cm. [BM]
[Not wholly correct; omits entire opening section.]
§3568. do. 1875. The old monastery. Tr. Lady Wallace. L: Bentley. 2v. 19cm. [Same method as in #3559.] [BM]
3569. do. 1882. [same as #3567] L: Weldon 1882. 348p. 17cm. [BM]
3570. do. 1884. [same] L: Hodgson. [BM]
3571. (Verbotene Früchte.) Forbidden fruit. Tr. Rosalie Kauffmann. Bost: Estes & Lauriat 1877. 262p. 18cm. [LC]
3572. do. 1885. [same] NY: Lovell. 262p. [LC]
3573. The volunteer. Tr. Zimmern. 1880. In C575-7.

HACKMANN, H: F: 1864- .
3574. Buddhism as a religion: its histor. devel. and its present conditions...Tr. anon. Rev. and enl. by author. L; Probsthain 1910 (1909). xiii;315p. 19cm. [BM]
3575. (Die Welt des Ostens.) A Ger. scholar in the east: travel scenes and reflections. With a chapter on the position of England in India. Tr. Daisie Rommel. L: Paul, T. & T; NY: Pott 1914. 223p. il. 23cm. [LC.BM]
["With the consent of the author I have shortened the orig. considerably."]

HADELN, Detlev, Baron v.
3575a. Titian's drawings (Die Zeichnungen des Tizian). Macmillan 1927. 13 x 10. [EC]

HADLAUB, J: fl. 1302. Sel. in C27; 310; 366; 427; 532-3.

HAECKEL, Ern. 1834- . Sel. in C366*;469;574*.
3576. The answer of Ernst H-- to the falsehoods...from the Ger. pamphlet "Sandalion" and "My church departure"...Tr. Js. McCabe and T. B. Wakeman. NY: Truth seeker 1911. 46p. il. 20cm. [LC]
§3577. (Anthropogenie.) The evolution of man--pop. expos. Tr. anon. L; K.Paul. 1879. 2v. xxxviii;467; 503p. 19cm.[Not very good.][BM]
*3578. do. 1905...a popular scientific study. Tr. from 5th enl. ed. Js. McCabe. L: Watts & C. 2v. xxiv; (409) 905p. il. 19cm. [BM]
3579. do. 1906. [same] [BM]
3580. do. 1910. [same] L: Watts. xiii; (177) 364p. 22cm. [BM]
[Prtd. in double columns; same text and il. as #3578.]
3581. do. 1910.[Sel.] Tr. anon. In C574.
3582. Controversy on the creation of man. (Lectures on evolution.) Tr. anon. Girard, Kan: Haldeman-Julius. n.d. Little blue books. 64p. 12cm. [BQM]
*3583. (Der Kampf um den Entwicklungsgedanken.) Last words on evolution. Tr. from 2d. Ger. ed. by Js. McCabe. L: Owen 1906. 127p. il. 25cm. [Three lectures.] [LC.BM]
3584. do. 1910. [same] L: Watts. 127p. 22cm. [BM]
*3585. (Der Monismus als Band zwischen Religion und Wissenschaft.) Monism as connecting relig. and science: the confession of faith of a man of science. Tr. J. Gilchrist. L: Black 1894. viii;117p. [LC has: 1895.] [BM.LC]
3586. do. 1903. [same] Title: The confession of faith of a man of science. L: Black. [LC]
*3587. (Die Lebenswunder.) The wonders of life: a pop. study of biolog. philos. Supplementary vol. to "Riddle of the universe." Tr. Js. McCabe. L: Watts & Co. 1904. xiv;501p. 19cm. [BM]
3588. do. 1905. [same] NY; L: Harper. x;484p. 19cm. [LC]
3589. do. 1905. [same] L: Watts. 160p. 21cm. [BM]
[Prtd. in double columns. Somewhat abridged for the...cheap ed.]
*3590. (Die Weltraetsel.) The riddle of the universe at the close of the 19th cent. Tr. Js. McCabe. L: Watts 1900. xvi;398p. 19cm. [BM]
3591. do. 1900. [same] NY; L: Harper. 390p. 19cm. [LC]
3592. do. 1901. [same] Harper. [LC]
3593. do. 1903. [same] L: Watts. xvi;142p. 22cm. [BM]
[Prtd. in double columns.]
3594. do. 1906. [same] L: Watts. xvi;135p. 22cm. [BM]
[Omits tr's. preface.]
3595. do. 1908. [same] L: Watts. xiii;391p. [BM]
["Exact reprod. of 1st ed. 1900."]
3596. do. 1913. [same] L: Watts. xxviii;324p. 16cm. [BM]
3597. do. 1926. Substance of the riddle of the universe; summarized by Vance Randolph. NY: Vanguard Press. 116p. 18cm. [LC]

HAECKEL, Ern.
**3598. (Entwicklungsgeschichte einer Jugend.) The story of the devel. of a youth: letters to his parents, 1852-1856. Introd. sketch Hans Schmidt. Tr. G. Barry Gifford. NY;L: Harper 1923. xii;420p. 21cm. [Admirably done.] [LC.BM]
3599. Eternity: world war thoughts on death, religion, and the theory of evolution. Tr. T: Seltzer. NY: Truth seeker 1916. 173p. il. 20cm. [LC]
*3600. (Freie Wissenschaft und freie Lehre.) Freedom in science and teaching. Tr. anon. Introd. note by T: H: Huxley. NY: Appleton; L:Ed: Paul, T. & T. 1879. xxxi;121p. 19cm. [BM.LC]
3601. do. 1889. [same] NY: Humboldt pub. 1889. O. [AC]
*3602. (Gesammelte...Vorträge aus...der Entwicklungslehre.) The pedigree of man and other essays. Tr. by E: B. Aveling. L: Freethought pub. 1883. xv;352p. il. 17cm. [9 essays.] [BM]
*3603. (Indische Reisebriefe.) A visit to Ceylon. Tr. Ca. Bell. L: Kegan Paul 1883. 337p. 20cm. [First ed.] [BM]
3604. do. 1883. [same] Letters of Indian travel. Rev. by J. S. Kingsley. Bost: Cassino 1883. 12. [AC]
3605. do. 1883. India and Ceylon. Tr. Mrs. S. E. Boggs. NY: Lovell. 174p. 18cm. [LC]
3606. do. 1884. Bell's tr. L: Macmillan. [EC]
3607. do. 1881? (i.e., 1885?) Bell's tr. 3d. Amer. ed. NY: Eckler. 337p. 18cm. [LC]
3608. (Natürliche Schöpfungsgeschichte.) The hist. of creation; or, the devel. of the earth and its inhab. by the action of natural causes. A pop. expos. of the doctrine of evol. in general, and of that of Darwin, Goethe, and Lamarck in particular. Tr. rev. by E. R. Lankester. L: King 1876. 2v. xix;374; 408p. il. 20cm. [Partially rewritten.] [BM.LC]
3609. do. 1892. [same] 4th ed. L: Paul, T. & T. 2v. xxiv;422; 544p. [BM]
3610. do. 1906. 4th ed. L: Paul, T. & T. 2v. xxiv;422; 544p. xxpl. 21cm. ["Translation of new matter...by Miss (L. Dora) Schmitz from 8th Ger. ed. pub. 1889."] [BM.LC]
See Bölsche, W., Life of Haeckel. #604.

HAEHL, R:
3610a. (S: H--. Sein Leben und Schaffen auf Grund neu aufgefund. Akten, Urkunden, Briefe, Krankenberichte und unter Benützung d. gesamten in- und ausländ. homöopath. Lit.) S: Hahnemann, his life and work, based on recently discovered state papers, documents, letters, etc. Ed. J. H. Clarke and F. J. Wheeler. Homoeop. pub. 1927. 2v. 465; 530p. 10 x 7. [EC]

HAENLE, S. and K. v. Spruner.
3610b. Guide to the bathing places of Franconia: Kissingen, Bocklet, Brückenau, and their environs. Tr. S. Louis, Ph. D., M. A. Würzburg: Stahel 1845. 115p. 12. [EC(Heinsius)]

HAERING, G: W: H: 1797-1871. See "Alexis, Wilibald."

HAEUSSER, L: 1818-67.
**3611. (Geschichte des Zeitalters der Reformation.) The period of the reformation, 1517-1648. Tr. Mrs. G: Sturge. L: Strahan 1873. 2v. 20cm. [BM.LC]
[Tr. excellent, on the whole, barring some slight inaccuracy.]
3612. do. 1884. [same] Ed: Gemmell. xxiii;702p. 19cm. [BM]

HAFFNAASS, F. v. See "Hoffnass, F. V."

HAFFNER, C: and R. Genée.
3614. (Die Fledermaus.) The bat: operetta by J: Strauss. Text based on "Le Réveillon" by H. Meilhac and L. Halévy. Tr. anon. n.i.

HAFFNER, C: and R. Genée--Fledermaus
L: Prtd. by J. Miles 1895. 8p. 20cm. [Synopsis of libr.] [BM]
3615. do. 1910. Tr. by Af. Kalisch. Libr. Engl. L: T: Beecham Opera Co. 67p. 21cm. [BM]

HAGEDORN, F: v. 1708-54. Sel. in C17;88;190;373;461;533.

HAGEN, Ern. A: 1787-1880.
*3616. (Norica...Nürnberg. Novellen.) Norica; or, (16) tales of Nürnberg from the olden time. Tr. anon. L: Chapman 1851. xiv;374p. 17cm. [BM]

HAGEN, Ok. F. Lh. 1888- .
3617. Art epochs and their leaders: a survey of the genesis of modern art. NY: Scribner 1927. xxi;322p. il. 23cm. [LC]
[Tr. from MS.]

HAGENBACH, K: Rd. 1801-74. Sel. in C489.
3618. German rationalism, in its rise, progress, and decline in relation to theologians, scholars, poets, philosophers and the people. Ed. and tr. by W: L. Gage and J. H. W. Stuckenberg. L: Hamilton, Adams 1865. xix;405p. 23cm. [BM]
[Abridged "under the sanction of the author."]

HAGENBECK, K: 1844- .
3619. (Von Tieren und Menschen.) Beasts and men. Abridged tr. Hugh S. R. Elliot and A. G. Thacker. L;NY: Longmans 1909. xiii;299p. il. 24cm. [BM.LC]
[Abr. and reworked. Really a new work. No visible relation.]
3620. do. 1912. [same] [LC]

HAGER, Js.
3621. (Gemälde von Palermo.) Pict. of Palermo. Tr. Mrs. M. Robinson. L: Phillips 1800. 159p. 12. [BM]

HAHN-HAHN, Ida (Me. Lu. So. F:e Gsta.) gräfin v. 1805-80. Sel. in C12;90;191;469.
3622. (Aus Jerusalem.) From Jerusalem. Tr. E. Atcherley. L: Newby 1852. xii;202p. 19cm. [BM]
3623. (Die Erbin von Cronenstein.) Heiress of Cronenstein. (A novel.) Ad. Ma. H. Allies. NY;Cincin: Benziger 1900. 223p. 12. [LC]
3624. do. 1913. [same] Benziger. [AC]
§3625. (Ein Reiseversuch im Norden.) Travels in Sweden. Tr. J. B. S. L: Clarke 1845. 179p. 13cm. [BM]
§3626. (Eudoxia, die Kaiserin.) Eudoxia: a pict. of the fifth cent. Freely tr. anon. L: Burns, Oates 1868. 204p. 18cm. [BM]
3627. do. 1869. [same] Balto: Kelly, Piet. 287p. 19cm. [LC]
3628. The fathers of the desert, lives of. Tr. E(mily) F. B(owden). L: Richardson 1867. xxxii;520p. 19cm. [BM.LC]
3629. do. 1907. [same] L: Burns & Oates. lxxiv;520p. [BM]
3630. A few words about the Good Shepherd. Tr. by a German lady. L: Jones 1858. 172p. 16cm. [BM]
*3631. (Gräfin Faustine.) Countess F--. Tr. H. N. S. L: Clarke 1844. 301p. 13cm. [BM]
§3632. do. 1845. Tr. A. E. I. L: Ollivier. 2v. xi;335;346p. 20cm. [Quite good, but not equal to foregoing.] [BM]
3633. do. 1872. [Same as #3620.] Faustina. NY: Carleton; L: Low 298p. 19cm. [LC.BM]
3634. do. 1894. Countess Obernau. Tr. "Julien Gordon." Il. by Jas. Fagan. NY: Bonner. 281p. 19cm. [Much altered.] [LC]
§3635. (Ilda Schönholm.) Society; or, high life in Germany. Tr. anon. L: Piper, Stephenson 1854. 109p. 20cm. [BM]
[Considerable freedom. Double columns. Taken from "Aus der Gesellschaft."]

HAHN-HAHN, Ida
*3636. (Orientalische Briefe.) Letters from the orient; or, travels in Turkey, the Holy Land, and Egypt. Tr. S: Phillips. L: Moore 1845. 265p. 26cm. ["The Novel Times." 1st ed.] [BM]
*3637. do. 1845. [same] 2d. ed. L: Moore. 265p. 26cm. [BM.LC]
*3638. do. 1845. Letters of a German Countess; or, travels in Turkey, Egypt... 1843-4. Tr. anon. L: Colburn. 3v. 20cm. [Not same tr. as #3636.] [BM]
3639. do. 1845. [same] 2d. ed. Letters from Turkey, Egypt... 1843-4. L: Colburn. 3v. 8. [EC]
3640. Poems on the litany of Loretto. Tr. F. C. Husenbeth. In Orsini, "The life of the blessed virgin Mary,"... pp. 741-824. 25cm. [BM]
3641. (Ulrich.) Ullrich: a tale. Tr. anon. L: Clarke 1845. 24. [EC]
3642. (Vergib uns unsere Schuld.) Dorothea Waldegrave. Tr. Ma. Eliz., Lady Herbert. L: Bentley 1875. 2v. 286; 271p. 18cm. [EC says: 3v.] [BM]
3643. (Von Babylon nach Jerusalem.) From Babylon to Jerusalem. Tr. Eliz. Atcherley. L: Newby 1851. xiii;252p. 20cm. [EC]
See Abeken, Hm. Babylon and Jerusalem: a letter to Ida Countess of Hahn-Hahn. #6.

HAHNEMANN, S: Cn. F: 1755-1843. Sel. in C469. See Fischer, C., A biog. monument...#1618.
See Haehl, R: "S: Hahnemann, his life and work..." #3610a.

"HAIDHEIM, L." (i.e., Frau Lu. (Jäger) Ahlborn 1834-).
3644. Wife and woman. Tr. Ma. J. Safford. NY: Bonner 1891. 373p. 19cm. [LC]

HAIMBACH, Ph. 1827-1904.
§3645. Ostrolenka: grand opera in 4 acts by J: H: Bonawitz. Tr. anon. Libr. Ger;Engl. Phil: Lee & Walker 1874. 13p. 27cm. [LCM]
[Correct; no rhyme, scrubby verse.]
*3646. do. 1876. Vocal score. Ger;Engl. Bost: Ditson. 186p. 34cm. [BMM]

HALBE, Max, 1865-
*3647. (Die Rosenhagen.) The Rosenhagens. Tr. P. H. Grummann in "Poet Lore," vol. 21 (1910). [Correct; flats on the dialog.]
3648. do. 1910. [same] Bost: Badger. 87p. D. [AC]
§3649. (Mutter Erde.) Mother earth. Tr. P. H. Grummann. 1913-15. In C154 (20).
[Verbose: too anxious to get in all the particles. Germanisms.]
3650. (Jugend.) When love is young: a passion drama in three acts. Tr. and ad. C: Swickard. Chic: 1904. Tw. [LC]
3651. do. 1910. Youth and love. Tr. Harry M. Goldberg. NY. Tw. [LC]
3652. do. 1911. Ad. H. Bernstein. NY. (B19)
3653. do. 1916. Youth. Tr. Sara T. Barrows. Introd. L. Lewisohn. Garden City, NY: Doubleday Page. 131p. 18cm. [LC]

"HALDEN, Eli." (i.e., Ag. Breitzmann, 1841-).
3654. (Das Nest.) The doctor's family; or, the story of the Erlans. Tr. Ma. E. Ireland. NY: Am. tract soc. 1896. 194p. il. 19cm. [LC]

HALEM, Grd. An. v. 1752-1819. Sel. in C106.

HALIRSCH, F: L: ("K. E. Waller") 1802-32. Sel. in C173.

HALLBERG, Eme. Ea. v. 1826-62. Sel. in C318.

HALLBERG-BROICH, C: Td. Ma. Hbt. v., Baron.
†3655. Sentimental sketches...during a...journey through the north of Germany... Tr. anon. In "New voyages and travels," vol. 5. L: R.Phillips 1821. 74p. 21cm. [Rewritten.] [BM]

HALLER, Hm. and "Rideamus"
3656. (Der Vetter aus Dingsda.) The cousin from nowhere: a mus. comedy in 3 acts by E: Kunneke (i.e. Kuenneke). Ad. Fred Thompson from comedy by Max Kempner-Hochstädt. Lyrics by Adrian Ross et al. Vocal score. L: B.Feldman 1923. 135p. 30cm. [BMM.LCM]

HALLER, V: Abr. v. 1708-77. Sel. in C8;88;309;373;461;533.
*3657. (Alfred, König der Angel-Sachsen.) The moderate monarchy; or, principles of the British constitution, described in a narr. of the life and maxims of Af. the Gt. and his counsellors. Tr. anon. L: Longmans 1849. xxviii;344p. 20cm. [BM]
[Introd. and conclusion from J: v. Müller. Also notes and commentaries by Fis. Steinitz.]
†3658. (Briefe über die wichtigsten Wahrheiten der Offenbarung.) (14) Letters to his daughter, on the truths of the Christ. relig. Tr. anon. L: Murray; Ed: Creech 1780. xxxii;279p. 18cm. [BM]
3659. do. 1803. [same] New ed. L: Vernor & Hood. xxiii;257p. 19cm. [BM]
3660. do. 1807. [same] L: Vernor & Hood. xxii;206p. 16cm. [BM]
[Port. of Haller engr. by G. Cooke after Saider. Text considerably boiled down.]
3661. (Die Alpen.) The Alps: a moral and descriptive poem. Tr. H: Barrett. L: Parsons 1796. (B26. B43)
3662. Doris. Tr. W: Taylor. 1828. In C533.
†3663. (Gedichte.) The poems of Baron H--. Tr. Mrs. J. Howorth. L: J.Bell 1794. ix;155p. 18cm. [BM]
[4 in verse; all else, from p. 17 on, in prose. "The Alps" rewritten and interpreted. The poems are new poems suggested by his.]
*3664. (Usong.) U--: an eastern narr. Tr. anon. L: Newberry & Walther 1772. 2v. viii;256; 307p. 16cm. [BM]
3665. do. 1773. Usong: an oriental hist. in four books. Tr. anon. L: Wilkie. [See "Crit. R." 35(1773): 195. (B26)]

"HALM, F:" (i.e., Egs. Fz. Js. Frhr. v. Münch-Bellinghausen, 1806-71). Sel. in C108;111;116;149;196;309;378;395;407;417;448;450; 461;551;571.
3665a. (Camoens.) Camoëns: a dramatic sketch in one act. Tr. anon. "Blackwood's Mag." 48(1840):220.
†3666. (Der Fechter von Ravenna.) The gladiator of Ravenna. Tr. de Vericour (in prose). L: Blackwood 1859. x;145p. 19cm. [BM]
3667. do. 1868. Tr. W. H. Charlton. In C66, pp. 303-455.
§3668. do. 1885. Tr. Sir T. Martin. Ed: Priv. circ. 1885. 77p. 22cm. [LC] Also in Martin's "Madonna pia...", pp. 215-315. Ed;L: Blackwood 1894. 20cm. [Careless.] [BM]
†3669. (Der Sohn der Wildnis.) Ingomar, the barbarian: a play in five acts. Tr. and ad. Maria Lovell. NY: Taylor 1846. 65p. 16. [Unwarranted liberties.] [LCO]
3670. do. 1847. Son of the wilderness. Tr. anon. (Possibly by Charlton.) Dolman 1847. [EC]
[First ed. (acc. to #3672) was pub. in 1847.]
*3671. do. 1848. Tr. C: E: Anthon. NY: Ludwig. 166p. 19cm. [LC]
3672. do. 1852? Tr. W: H: Charlton? Lacy's acting ed. of plays, vol. 7. L: Lacy. 59p. 17cm. [Stamped 1852.] [BM]
3673. do. 1855. Ingomar by Lovell. From the acting copy, with remarks...by D-- G. L: Davidson. 61p. 14cm. [BM]
3674. do. 1855. [same] NY: S:French (no. 89). iv;65p. [BM]
*3675. do. 1867. Child of the wold: dramatic poem in 5 acts. (Prose). Tr. M. A. Faber. L: Williams & Norgate. 8. [BM]
3676. do. 1867. Ingomar, the barbarian. By Maria Lovell. With a scenic il. and remarks by D-- G. L: Lacy. 62p. 18cm. [BM]
[Cf. #3672; #3673.]

"HAIM, F:"
*3677. do. 1868. Son of the wilderness. Tr. W. H. Charlton. In C66 pp. 119-302.
3678. do. 1878. [same as #3669] NY: Wheat & Cornett. Vol. 3 of NY. Drama. [LCO]
**3679. (Griseldis.) Griselda: a drama in 5 acts (verse). Tr. Sir R. A. Anstruther. L: Black & Armstrong 1840. 141p. 8. [BM.LC] [Excellent translation.]
*3680. do. 1844. Griseldis...a dramatic poem. Tr. Q. E. D. L: Smith, Elder. 139p. 15cm. [Very close and good.] [BM]
3681. do. 1853. [Sel.] Griselda. Tr. F: Funck. In C142.
*3682. do. 1871. Griseldis. Tr. W. M. Sieg. L: Trübner. 136p. 16. [BM]
*3683. do. 1876. Griseldis. Tr. Mrs. G. L. Prentiss. NY: Y.W.C.A. 152p. 19cm. [LC]

HAMANN, J: G: 1730-88. Sel. in C194.

HAMERLING, Rb. 1830-89. Sel. in C3;196;311;448.
*3684. (Aspasia.) Aspasia: a romance of art and love in ancient Hellas. Tr. Ma. J. Safford. NY: Gottsberger 1882. 2v. 350; 335p. 16cm. [LC.BM]
3685. do. 1893. [same] NY: G:Gottsberger Peck. 2v. in 1. 350;335p. 19cm. [LC.BM]

HAMMER, F: Jl. 1810-62. Sel. in C112;448;460.

HAMMANN, O: 1852- .
3686. (Deutsche Weltpolitik.) The world policy of Germany, 1890-1912. Tr. M. A. Huttmann. L: Allen & U. 1927. 269p. il. 9 x 5in. [EC]

HAMPE, K: 1869- . Sel. in C563.

HAND, Fd. Ghf. 1786-1851.
*3687. (Aesthetik der Tonkunst.) Aesthetics of mus. art; or, the theory of the beautiful in music. Vol. 1. Tr. Wl. E: Lawson. L: Reeves 1880. xviii;187p. 22cm. [BM]
3688. do. 1880. [same] 2d ed. L: Reeves. [EC]
3688a. do. 1911. [same] 3d ed. L: Reeves. 187p. 20cm. [LC]

HANSJAKOB, H: 1837-1916.
3689. (Aus dem Leben eines Unglücklicken.) From the story of an unhappy life. Tr. Anon. 1902. In C481.

HANSLICK, E: 1825-1904.
3690. (Opern-Zyklus.) Operas of the great masters. Tr. anon. Il. M. v. Schwind. Rothe 1880. fol. [EC]
*3691. (Vom Musikalisch-Schönen.) The beautiful in music. 7th ed. enl. and rev. Tr. Gst. Cohen. L;NY: Novello 1891. 174p. il. 19cm. [LC]

HANSSON, La. (Mohr), 1854- .
3692. (Das Buch der Frauen.) Modern women. Tr. w. pref. Hermione C. Ramsden. L: Lane; Bost: Roberts 1896. xvi;211p. 18cm. [BM.LC]
3693. do. 1896. [same] Six modern women: Psychol. sketches. Bost: Roberts. xv; 213p. [Arrangement differs.] [BM]
§3694. (Wir Frauen und unsere Dichter.) We women and our authors. Tr. H. Ramsden. L;NY: Lane 1899. 215p. 19cm. [BM.LC] [Needless alterations.]
3695. (Zur Psychologie der Frau.) Studies in the psychol. of woman. Tr. Georgia A. Etchison. Chic;NY: Stone 1899. 348p. 20cm. [LC]
3696. do. 1899. [same] The psychol. of women. L: Richards. 295p. 19cm. [BM]

HANSTEIN, Od. v. 1869- .
3697. (Die Welt der Inca.) The world of the Incas: a socialistic state of the past. (A novel.) Tr. Anna Barwell. L: Allen & U.; NY: Dutton 1924. 189p. front. 21cm. [LC.BM]

HARDEGGER, Der, fl. 1227-75. Sel. in C427.

HARDEN, Mx. 1861- .
*3698. (Deutschland, Frankreich, England.) Germany, France & England. Tr. and ed. W: Cranston Lawton. Brentano's 1924. vi; 326p. 22cm. [LC]
*3699. (Köpfe.) Word portraits: character sketches of famous men and women. Tr. Jl. Gabe. Ed;L: Blackwood 1911. vii;425p. 22cm. [LC.BM]
[Lyrics translated moderately well by Herbert Jacobs.--Old Wilhelm; Empress F; Bismarck; J: A. Bismarck; Richter; F. V. Holstein; Af. Graf v. Waldersee; Ad. Stoecker; Gallifet; Ibsen; Böcklin; Cte. Wolter; Menzel; F: Mitterwurzer; Zola; Lenbach; Adalbert Matkowsky.]
*3700. do. 1912. [same] NY: Brentano's. [AC]
3701. (Köpfe, 2. Teil.) Monarchs and men. Tr. anon. L: Nash 1912. vii;316p. il. 8. [BM]
[King E:; Leo XIII; W: II and Bismarck; The Tsar of Russia; Fis. Js.; Ab. of Saxony; Briand; K: Lueger; Tolstoi and Rockefeller.]
*3702. (Köpfe, 4. Teil.) I meet my contemporaries. Tr. W. Cranston Lawton. Introd. by Jas. W. Gerard. NY: Holt 1925. L: Cape 1926. 287p. 22cm. [BM.LC]
[M. Harden; W. Wilson; Lloyd George; Clemenceau; The Hindenburg myth; Stinnes; King Peter of Serbia; Lenin; Sarah Bernhardt; Bonaparte in adversity. Seven of the ten chapters tr. from his "Köpfe," part 4. BM has: "My contemporaries."]

HARDENBERG, F: Lp. Frhr v. 1772-1801. See "Novalis."

HARDER, L:
3703. A family feud. Tr. Mrs. A. L. Wister. Phil: Lippincott 1877. [LC card]
3704. do. 1905. [same] 238p. 19cm. [LC]

HARDMEYER, J: Jk. 1826-1917.
3705. Milan. 64p. il.; The lake of Lucerne. 62p. il.; The Black Forest railway. 104p. il.; Locarno and its valleys. 112p. il. Tr. anon. 1884. In C294.

HARDT, Ern. 1876- . Sel. in C28;39.
3706. (Tantris, der Narr.) Tantris, the fool: drama in five acts. Tr. W. Noble and J. James. St.L: 1909. (B38)
§3707. do. 1913. Tristram, the jester. Tr. J: Heard, Jr. Bost: Badger. 185p. 19cm. [Needlessly verbose at times.] [AC]
3708. do. 1913-15. [same] In C154(20).

HARDT-WARDEN, Br. See Bodanzky, R., joint author.

HARFIN, J:
3709. Zürich and its environs. Tr. anon. 1884. 40p. il. In C294.

HARINGER, Ml.
3710. Life of the venerable servant of God Clt. Ma. Hofbauer. Tr. Ma. Eliz. Herbert. NY;Cincin: Pustet 1883. 376p. 12. [LCO]

HARMS, Claus, 1778-1855. Sel. in C244;489; #7859.

HARMS, F: 1819-80.
3711. A. Schopenhauer's philos. Tr. Mrs. Ella S. Morgan. 1879. In C300(9).

HARMS, Td.
3712. Life work of pastor Louis Harms. Tr. Ma. E. Ireland. Phil: Lutheran pub. soc. 1900. 118p. 16. [LC]

HARNACK, Ad. 1851- .
3713. (Das Christentum und die Geschichte.) Christianity and history. Tr. T: B. Saunders. L: Black 1896. 68p. 19cm. [BM]
3714. do. 1900. 2d. rev. ed. L: Black 68p. 19cm. [BM.LC]
*3715. (Das Mönchtum.) Monasticism: its ideals and history, and, the oonfessions of St. Augustine (Augustins Konfessionen.) Two lectures. Tr. E. E. Kellett...and F. H. Marseille. L: Williams & Norgate 1901. 171p. 19cm. [BM]
*3716. (Das Wesen des Christentums.) What is Christianity? 16 lectures. Tr. T: B. Saunders. L: Wms. & Norgate; NY: Putnam's 1901. 301p. 22cm. [BM]
3716a. do. 1901. 2d. rev. ed. L: Zondervan. viii;322p. O. [AC]
3717. do. 1904. [same] 3d. rev. ed. x;306p. 18cm. [BM]
3717a. do. 1933-34. 4th ed. Williams & Norgate. [AC]
*3718. (Die Mission und Ausbreitung des Christentums in den ersten drei Jahrhunderten.) The expansion of Christianity in the first three centuries. Tr. and ed. by James Moffatt. L: Wms. & Norgate; NY: Putnam's 1904,5. 2v. xv;494; 488p. 22cm. [BM]
3719. do. 1908. [same] 2d. enl. rev. ed. L: Wms. & Norgate; NY: Putnam's. 2v. xv;513; 358p. 22cm. [BM]
3720. Martin Luther, the prophet of the reformation. NY: Macmillan 1896. 16. [LCO]
3721. (Zur gegenwärtigen Lage des Protestantismus.) Thoughts on the present position of protestantism. Tr. T: B. Saunders. L: Black 1899. 64p. 19cm. [BM]

HARRING, Hr. Pl. 1798-1870. Sel. in C121.

HARTIG, Fz. de Paula, Graf v. 1789-1865.
3722. Genesis; or, details of the late Austrian revolution. Tr. W. K. Kelly, in his "History of the house of Austria." L: 1853. 18cm. (p.1-331.) [LC]

HARTLEBEN, O: Er. 1864-1905. Sel. in C28.
§3723. (Hanna Jagert.) Hanna Jagert. Tr. Sa. E. Holmes. In "Poet-Lore," vol. 24 (1913).[Errors.]
§3724. (Rosenmontag.) Love's carnival. Tr. Rud. Bleichmann. L: Heinemann 1904. 160p. 8. [BM.UW]--1914 Dramatic p. 160p. port. s. [AC]
[Played Mar. 17, 1904, St. James's theatre. Rather free version.]

HARTMANN v. AUE, fl. 1190-1210. Sel. in C27;190;427;570.
3725. (Der arme Heinrich.) Henry the leper, paraphrased by D. G. Rossetti. Bost: Bibliophile soc. 1905. 2v. il. 26cm. [LC.BM]
[Tr. made ca. 1846, pub. in vol. II of his "Poems." Follows the story of Hartmann's epic, not his verse.]
3725a. (Erec.) [Sel.] Tr. Bayard Taylor. In C530.

HARTMANN, C. F: 1743-1815. Sel. in C489.

HARTMANN, K: Rb. E: v. 1842-1906.
3726. On the dialectic method. Tr. Louis Soldan. 1876. In C300(6).
*3727. (Philosophie des Unbewussten.) The philos. of the unconscious. Tr. W: C. Coupland. L: Trübner 1884. 3v. [Engl. and For. Philos. Lib. Vol. 25-27.] 21cm. [BM]
3728. do. 1893. [same] 2d. ed. L: Paul, T. & T. 3v. 21cm. [LC]
3729. The relig. of the future. Tr. Ernest Dare. L: Stewart 1886. 119p. 18cm. [BM]
3730. The sexes compared, and (6) other essays. Sel. and tr. A. Kenner. L: Sonnenschein; NY: Macmillan 1895. xi;164p. 19cm. [LC.BM]
3731. The true and the false in Darwinism. Tr. H: I. D'Arcy. 1881-3. [C300(11, 12, 13).]

HARTMANN, Mz. 1821-72. Sel. in C17;106;112;149;296;309;311;450;497; 551;571.
*3732. (Die letzten Tage eines Königs.) The last days of a king: an histor. romance. Tr. M. E. Niles. Phil: Lippincott 1867. 198p. 19cm. [Not quite excellent.] [LC.BM]

"HARTNER, Eva" (i.e., Ea. Eva Hte. v. Twardowska, 1845-89).
3733. Pythia's pupils. Tr. Mrs. J. W. Davis. L: Routledge 1888. il. D. [AC]
3734. (Severa. Eine Familiengeschichte.) Severa. Tr. Mrs. A. L. Wister. Phil: Lippincott 1882. 354p. 19cm. [LC]

HARTWIG VON RAUTE, fl. 1190-1200. Sel. in C27;427.

HARTWIG, G: (L:) 1813-80. Sel. in C397.
*3735. (Das Leben des Luftmeeres.) The aerial world: a popular account. Tr. anon. L: Longmans 1874. xviii;566p. il. 22cm. [BM]
3736. do. 1875. [same] NY: Appleton. xviii;556p. [LC]
3737. do. 1888. Marvels over our heads. Nine chapters from "The Aerial World." Tr. anon. L: Longmans. 142p. 18cm. [BM]
3738. (Der hohe Norden.) The polar world: a popular description. Tr. anon. NY: Harper 1869. xvii;486p. il. 25cm. [LC]
3739. do. 1869. [same] L: Longmans. xviii;548p. 22cm. [BM] [Partially rewritten, not a mere reproduction of the printed German text.]
3740. do. 1874. [same] [Apparently unchanged.] [BM]
3741. do. 1882. [same] The Arctic regions: 21 sel. chapters. L: Longmans. 64p. il. 31cm. [BM] [Double columns. Text taken from the foregoing.]
3742. do. 1887. [same] Dwellers in the arctic regions. Ten chapters from "The polar world." L: Longmans. 158p. 18cm. [BM]
3743. do. 1888. [same] Heroes (i.e., explorers) of the Arctic Regions, from "The polar world." L: Longmans. 128p. il. 18cm. [BM] [Apparently some additions for this ed.]
3744. (Der hohe Norden. Die Tropenwelt.) The polar and tropical worlds. Tr. anon. Springfield, Mass.: Bill, Nichols & Co. 1871. xx;761p. il. 25cm. [LC]
3745. do. 1874. [same] Springfield: Nichols & Co.; Chic: Heron. xx;811p. il. 25cm. [LC]
3746. (Die Tropenwelt.) The tropical world: a pop. scientific account. Tr. anon. L: Longmans 1863. xx;566p. il. 22cm. [BM.LC] [Tr. is close and good where it follows orig., but deviates widely in parts; also chapters are rearranged and their order altered.]
3747. do. 1873. [same] New ed. xix;556p. il. 21cm. [BM] [Really new, based on his 1873 ed. Diff. il. in part.]
3748. do. 1887. [same] Winged life in the tropics; from Hartwig's "The tropical world." L: Longmans. vii;150p. 18cm. [BM] [Six chapters chiefly from #3747.]
3749. do. 1887. [same] Wild animals of the tropics; from "The tropical world." L: Longmans. 256p. 18cm. [BM] [16 chapters from #3747.]
3750. do. 1888. [same] Wonders of the tropical forests; from "The tropical world." L: Longmans. 128p. 18cm. [BM] [7 chapters from #3747.]
*3751. (Die Unterwelt.) The subterranean world. Tr. anon. L: Longmans 1871. 22cm. [BM] [Opening sections largely rewritten, and elsewhere alterations indicate a critical redaction of the text.]
3752. do. 1871. [same] L: Longmans. xix;522p. il. 22cm. [LC]
3753. do. 1871. [same] NY: Scribner. [LC]
3754. do. 1872. [same] L: Longmans. [LC]

HARTWIG, G: L:
3755. do. 1887. [same] Volcanoes and earthquakes: a popular description from "The subterranean world." L: Longmans. 158p. 18cm. [11 chapters.] [BM]
3756. do. 1888. [same] Marvels under our feet; from "The subterranean world." L: Longmans. 144p. il. 8. [BM]
3757. do. 1888. [same] Workers under the ground; or, mines and mining. From "The subterranean world." L: Longmans. 126p. 18cm. [19 chapters.] [BM]
3758. (Gott in der Natur.) Harmonies of nature. Tr. anon. L: Longmans 1866. xix;406p. il. 22cm. [LC]
3759. The sea and its living wonders. Tr. from 4th Ger. ed. and partly rewritten by author. Il. H: N. Humphreys. L: Longmans 1860. xviii;427p. 22cm. [26 chaps.] [BM]
3760. do. 1861. [same] 2d ed. [BM]
3761. do. 1866. [same] 3d ed. xx;518p. [BM]
[Enlarged considerably and improved. 2 new chapters; 2 rewritten; 4 enlarged; changed il.]
3762. do. 1871. The whispers of a shell: or, stories from the sea. Based on H--'s "The Sea" by Fis. F. Broderip. Il. G: Hay. L: Griffith & Farran. viii;244p. 17cm. [BM]
3763. do. 1873. [same as #3761.] 4th ed. enlarged. L. xx;518p. [BM]
3764. do. 1887. Sea-monsters and sea-birds. L: Longmans 1887. viii; 159p. 18cm. [4 chapters from #3761.] [BM]
3765. do. 1887. Denizens of the deep: an account of fishes, molluscs, crustacea. From "The sea." L: Longmans 1887. 160p. il. 18cm. [11 chapters.] [BM]

HASE, G: von. 1878- .
*3766. (Die zwei weissen Völker.) Kiel and Jutland. Tr. Art. Chambers and F. A. Holt. NY: Dutton; L: Skeffington 1922. 233p. il. 22cm. [BM has: 1921. Skeffington.] [BM.LC]
3767. do. 1927. [same] Cheap ed. L: Skeffington. 128p. il. 22cm. [BM.LC]

HASE, H: 1789-1842.
*3768. (Die griechische Altertumskunde.) The public and private life of the ancient Greeks. Tr. anon. L: Murray 1836. xi;358p. 17cm. [BM.LC]

HASE, K: A: v. 1800-90.
*3769. (Das geistliche Schauspiel.) Miracle plays and sacred dramas, an historical survey. Tr. A. W. Jackson. L: Trübner 1880. x;273p. 22cm. [BM.LC]
[Ed. by Rev. W. W. Jackson. Quotations from Lessing taken from Miss Frothingham.]

HASSLER, Fd. Rd. See Zschokke, El., Memoirs of...#10678.

HATTINGBERG, H. v.
3770. Marriage as an analytical situation. 1926. In C308.

HATZFELD, Ad. v. 1892- . Sel. in C95.

HAUFE, Ewd. 1854- .
3771. (Aus dem Leben eines freien Poedagogen.) [sic]. Passages from the life of an educational freelance. Tr. W: H: Herford. L: Isbister 1902. 204p. 19cm. [BM.LC]

HAUFF, W: 1802-27. Sel. in C67;149;152;215;309;366;422-3;448;469.
*3772. [Coll.] Select popular tales. L: Burns 1845. 4pts. il. 16cm. [The *caravan (6 stories); §The cold heart. These are paged: viii (then spec. t.p. The caravan and other tales), 120; The sheik of Alexandria and his slaves (4 stories), pp. 1-82; The legend of

HAUFF, W:
the Hirschgulden, 14p.; The portrait of the emperor (spec. t.p. 1845), 77p. The first table of contents has also: The Grünwiesel dancer, but this is not in the book.] [BM]
*3773. [Coll.] 1873? Three tales: The beggar girl of the Pont des Arts ("Die Bettlerin vom Pont des Arts"); The emperor's picture ("Das Bild des Kaisers"); The cold heart ("Das kalte Herz"). Tr. M. A. Faber. Lpz: Tauchnitz; L: Low. 326p. 16cm. [BM.LC]
3774. [Coll.] 1881. The cold heart ("Das kalte Herz"); The emperor's picture ("Das Bild des Kaisers"). NY: Munro 1881. 25p. 32cm. [LCO] [Probably from Tauchnitz ed. Cf. the foregoing.]
*3775. [Coll.] 1888. [same] Three tales. Tr. M. A. Faber. Stokes 1888. S. [The beggar girl of the Pont des Arts. The emperor's picture. The cold heart.] [AC]
§3776. (Das Wirtshaus im Spessart.) The advent. of Said. (Saids Schicksale). Tr. anon. 1897. In C126. [Free but good.]
*3777. do. 1844. The cold heart (Das kalte Herz). Tr. C. A. Feiling. 1844. In C441-2.
§3778. do. 1844. [same] Tr. anon. In C457.
3779. do. 1861. Tales of wonder; or, the inn in the Black Forest. [See #3813 below.]
3780. do. 1886. The inn in the Spessart, literally tr. by S. Mendel. L: Bell. 175p. 8. [BM]
§3781. do. 1890. The cold heart (Das kalte Herz). Tr. Ag. Henry. L: Digby & Long. 76p. 15cm. [Follows Mendel.] [BM]
3782. do. 1894. [Same as #3780] [BM]
§3783. do. 1896. The little glassman (Das kalte Herz). Tr. A. Strettell in #1017. pp. 271-328.
§3784. do. 1913. The cold heart. Tr. anon. 74p. In C493. [Same tr. as C457.]
3785. do. 1926. Coal-Munk- Peter (Das kalte Herz). Tr. anon. L: Benn. 12. S. [EC]
*3786. (Der Affe als Mensch.) The young foreigner. Tr. Chris. Morley in his Two Fables. NY: Doubleday Page 1925. xii;95p. il. 20cm. [Mostly close and good.] [LC]
3787. (Der Scheik von Alessandrien und seine Sklaven.) Nose, the dwarf. Tr. C. A. Feiling. 1844. In C441-2.
§3788. (Die Bettlerin vom Pont des Arts.) Josephine; or, the beggar-girl of the Pont-des-Arts. Tr. anon. L: Clarke 1844. 83p. 17cm. [BM]
†3789. do. 1847. The beggar-girl of the Pont des Arts. Tr. anon. In C458.
3790. do. 1880. The beggar-girl of the bridge of arts. NY: Munro. 28p. 32cm. [LCO]
§3791. do. 1893. A constant lover. Tr. J: Nisbet. L: Unwin. 193p. 19cm. [BM]
3792. (Die Karawane.) The severed hand. ("Die Geschichte von der abgehauenen Hand"). Tr. C. A. Feiling. 1844. In C442.
*3793. do. 1845. Story of a manikin, related by Muley. ("Die Geschichte von dem kleinen Muck"). Tr. S. T. In C519.
§3794. do. 1846. The false prince ("Das Märchen vom falschen Prinzen"). Tr. S. T. In C521.
§3795. do. 1862. The caravan (7 stories). Tr. anon. In C209. [Quite freely handled.]
§3796. do. 1875. The storks ("Die Geschichte von Kalif Storch"); The false prince ("Das Märchen vom falschen Prinzen"). Freely tr. by Eliz. S. Harrington. L: Sotheran. 78p. 14cm. [BM] [Follows story, but not text.]
3797. do. 1895. The severed hand ("Die Geschichte von der abgehauenen Hand"). Tr. anon. In C559.

HAUFF

*3798. do. 1898. The severed hand. Tr. anon. In C509.

3799. do. 1905. The caliph stork ("Die Geschichte von Kalif Storch"). Ad. by Rev. E. J. Cunningham. Tr. T. C. Gath. L: Sonnenschein. 9 leaves. 18 x 24cm. [In verse, good.] [BM]

3800. do. 1922. Fatma ("Die Errettung Fatmes"). Tr. anon. In C127.

3801. Fortunes of fairylore. Tr. T: Tracy. 1841. In C542.

3802. (Jud Süss.) The Jew Suss: a tale of Stutgard, in 1737. Tr. B. T. Phil: Moore 1845. 132p. 16. [NY]

*3803. (Lichtenstein.) The banished: a Swabian historical tale. Tr. anon. Ed. by Jas. Morier. L: Colburn 1839. 3v. 19cm. [BM]

*3804. do. 1846. L--; or, the Swabian league. An historical romance. Tr. Frank Woodley and W: Lander. L: Bruce & Wyld. 362p. 19cm. [BM.LC]

†3805. do. 1859? The outlaw of Würtemberg. A tale of the 16th cent. Tr. Elinor M. Swann. L: Blackwood. vi;273p. 19cm. [BM]

*3806. do. 1897. Marie of Lichtenstein: a tale of love and war. Tr. R. J. Craig. L: Digby & Long. xiv;335p. 19cm. [BM]

3807. do. 19--. Tr. anon. Translation pub. 15cm. [AC]

†3808. do. 1901. A romance...ad. for Eng. readers by Lucy L. Weedon. Il. T. H. Robinson. NY: Dutton; L: Nister. 304p. 12. [BM.UW]

3809. do. 1901. [same] Heath. (B13)

3810. (Märchen.) Mahrchen [sic] i.e., preface to his "Märchen." Also, The dwarf nose (Der Zwerg Nase).The false prince. Tr. S. T. 1843. In C520.

§3811. do. 1853. Arabian days' entertainments. Tr. H. P. Curtis. Bost: Phillips, Sampson & Co. 434p. il. 19cm. [LC]
[Includes: "Die Karawane"; "Der Scheik von Alessandrien"; "Das Wirtshaus im Spessart."]

3812. do. 1861. [same] Bost: Ticknor & F. [LC]

§3813. do. 1861. Tales of wonder; or, the inn in the Black Forest. Tr. anon. L: Cheap repos. series. 187p. il. 16cm. [BM]
[7 stories retold; some from "Die Karawane."]

§3814. do. 1872-6. [same as #3811] Bost: Osgood n.d. [AC]

3815. do. 1881. 10th ed. Bost: Houghton. 12. [AC]

§3816. do. 1881. Little Mook, and other fairy tales. Tr. P. E. Pinkerton. NY: Putnam. 303p. il. 16. [BPL]
[Longnose, the dwarf; The hist. of little Mook; The caliph turned stork; Advent. of Said; The stone-cold heart; The story of the silver florin.]

§3817. do. 1881. [same] Longnose the dwarf, and other fairy tales. Tr. P. E. Pinkerton. L: Sonnenschein. 303p. il. 8. [BM]
[Tr. is very easy-going.]

*3818. do. 1882. Tales of the caravan, inn, and palace. Tr. E: L. Stowell. Chic: Jansen, McClurg. 397p. il. 12. [LCO]
[The caravan; The inn in the Spessart; The sheik's palace; The dwarf Nosey; Little Muck; The marble heart; The caliph stork; The story of Almansor; The rescue of Fatima; The false prince; The Hirschgulden; Said's adventures; The cave of Steenfoll; Abner the Jew; The young Englishman; The amputated hand.]

*3819. do. 1886. Tales. The caravan; The sheik of Alexandria and his slaves; The inn in the Spessart. Tr. S. Mendel. L: Bell. 342p. 8. [BM]

3819a. do. 1887. [same as #3811] 11th ed. Bost;NY: Houghton. 434p. [LC]

3820. do. 1889. [same] Caravan and Sheik of Alexandria. Literally tr. by Mendel. Bell & S. 12. [EC]

§3821. do. 1891. The caravan. Said's fate. The sheik of Alexandria. In Horwitz, Carrie N., "Fairy-lure." Coll. and ad. from the German. Il. L. J. Bridgman. Bost: Lothrop. 345p. 16. [LCO]

HAUFF, W:--Märchen
*3822. do. 1893. The little glass man and other stories. Tr. S. Mendel (from #3819). L: Unwin. 176p. il. 16cm. [BM]
[Title; The story of the caliph Stork; The story of little Muck; Nose, the dwarf.]
3823. do. 1893. [same as #3817] New ed. [EC]
?3824. do. Tales. 190-? Tr. anon. Translation pub. n.d. 15cm. [AC]
§3825. do. 1903. Fairy tales. Tr. and ad. Cicely McDonnell. Il. partly in col. by Fritz Bergen. L: Dean. 224p. 18cm. [BM]
[How the caliph became a stork; The rescue of Fatima; The history of little Muck; The story of the false prince; The dwarf's nose; Almansor; The advent. of Said; The stag-florin; A heart of stone.--Fairly close tr.]
3826. do. 1905. Tales. Tr. Sybil Thesiger. L: Nimmo. 438p. il. 8. [EC]
†3827. do. 1910. Fairy tales. Tr. Lucy L. Weedon. Il. Arthur A. Dixon. L: Nister; NY: Dutton. 344p. 21cm. [NY]
[11 stories: 4 from Caravan; 3 from Sheik; 4 from Spessart. --Good style, but abandons her author and shows ignorance of German.]
§3828. do. 1912. Caravan tales and some others, freely ad. and retold by J. G. Hornstein. Il. in col. Norman Ault. L: Gardner; NY: Stokes. 337p. 21cm. [BM.LC]
[Caliph Stork; The death ship; Little Mook; The false prince; The golden whistle, or the fortunes of Said; The wonder-child; The rusty key.--Really retold, well.]
3829. do. 1914. Tales. L: Bell. 348p. 12. [EC]
[Probably a reissue of #3819.]
3830. do. 1916. Little dwarf nose ("Der Zwerg Nase"); The magic whistle ("Saids Schicksale"). Tr. E. Gordon Browne. Il. Flor. Anderson. NY: Dodd, Mead. 108p. 24cm. [BPL]
*3831. (Mitteilungen aus den Memoiren des Satan.) Memoirs of Beelzebub, extracts from. NY: Taylor 1846. 96p. 16. [BPL]
[Chapters I-IV, then scattering extracts.]
3832. do. 1921. [Sel.] From the memoirs of Satan. Tr. M. J. Rudwin. In C482.
†3833. (Phantasien im Bremer Ratskeller.) The wine-ghosts of Bremen. Tr. E. Sadler and C: R. L. Fletcher. Oxford: Blackwell; L: Simpkin & M. 1889. xxiv;64p. il. 17cm. [BM]
3834. do. 1889. [same] NY: White & A. [LC]

HAUG, J: Cph. F: 1761-1829. Sel. in C560.

HAUPT, A.
3835. Nicholas Cusanus. Tr. anon. 1902. In C481.

HAUPTMANN, C: 1858-1921.
3836. (Aus dem grossen Kriege.) The dead are singing: a play in six scenes. Tr. Ma. L. Stephenson. In "Texas Review." (Austin, Tex.) Vol. I, (1916). (B38)
§3837. (Ephraims Breite.) Tr. Ma. Harned. In "Poet Lore," Vol. 12 (1900).
3838. (Krieg, ein Tedeum.) War. Tr. A. von Ende. In "The Drama," vol. 6 (1916).
3838a. do. n.d. Tr. Lionel van Prangh. NY. Tw. [LC]

HAUPTMANN, Grt. J: Rb. 1862- . Sel. in C366*;469.
*3839. The dramatic works. Ed. Ludwig Lewisohn. NY: Huebsch (Viking Press) 1912-17. 1924. 1929. 9v. 19cm. [LC.BM]
[See individual titles for judgments. For the most part, the best Engl. versions are here collected; several tr. made for this ed. Vol. IX issued in 1929. 1. (Vor Sonnenaufgang.) Before dawn. Tr.

HAUPTMANN
Tr. Lewisohn; (Die Weber.) The weavers. Tr. Ma. Morison; (Der Biberpelz.) The beaver coat. Tr. L. L.; (Der rote Hahn.) The conflagration. Tr. L. L.; 2. (Fuhrmann Henschel.) Drayman Henschel. Tr. L. L.; (Rose Bernd.) Rose Bernd. Tr. L. L.; (Die Ratten.) The rats. Tr. L. L.; 3. (Das Friedensfest.) The reconciliation. Tr. House; (Einsame Menschen.) Lonely lives. Tr. Morison; (Kollege Crampton.) Colleague Crampton. Tr. House; (Michael Kramer.) Michael Kramer. Tr. L. L.; 4. (Hanneles Himmelfahrt.) The assumption of Hannele. Tr. Meltzer; (Die versunkene Glocke.) The sunken bell. Tr. Meltzer; (Der arme Heinrich.) H: of Aue. Tr. L. L. 5. (Schluck und Jau.) Schluck and Jau. Tr. L. L.; (Und Pippa tanzt.) And Pippa dances. Tr. Sa. T. Barrows; (Kaiser Karls Geisel.) Charlemagne's hostage. Tr. L. L. 6. (Die Jungfern vom Bischofsberg.) The maidens of the mount. Tr. L. L.; (Griselda.) Griselda. Tr. L. L.; (Gabriel Schillings Flucht.) Gabriel Schilling's Flight. Tr. L. L.; 7. (Festspiel in deutschen Reimen.) Commemoration masque. Tr. B. Q. Morgan; (Der Bogen des Odysseus.) The bow of Od. Tr. L. L.; (Elga.) Elga. Tr. L. L.; Fragments: (Helios.) Helios; (Das Hirtenlied.) Pastoral. Tr. L. L. 8. (Indipohdi.) Indipohdi. Tr. W. and E. Muir; (Der weisse Heiland.) The white Saviour; (Winterballade.) A winter ballad. 9. Florian Geyer. Tr. B. Q. Morgan. Veland. Tr. Edwin Muir.]

†3840. (Atlantis.) Atlantis. Tr. Adele and T: Seltzer. NY: Huebsch 1912. 415p. 19cm. [Outrageous liberties.] [LC]

3841. do. 1913. [same] L: Laurie. 349p. 8. [BM]

†3842. (Das Friedensfest.) The coming of peace: a family catastrophe. Tr. Janet Achurch and C. E. Wheeler. Chic: Sergel 1900. 119p. 20cm. [LC.BM]
[Translators' knowledge of German is inadequate.]

§3843. do. 1910. The reconciliation. Tr. R. T. House. In "Poet-Lore", vol. 21 (1910). [Tr. flats, and has bad errors.]

3844. do. 1914? [same] rev. by L. Lewisohn. In #3839.

3845. (Das Hirtenlied.) Pastoral (fragment). Tr. by L. Lewisohn in #3839.

*3846. (Der arme Heinrich.) Henry of Auë. Tr. L. Lewisohn. In #3839.

*3847. (Der Biberpelz.) The beaver coat. Tr. L. Lewisohn. In #3839.

†3848. do. 1905. Thieves' comedy. Tr. C: J: Horne. L: Tw. [LC]
[Examined by Scholz (B39).]

3849. (Der Bogen des Odysseus.) The bow of Odysseus. Tr. L. Lewisohn. In #3839.

3850. (Der Ketzer v. Soana.) The heretic of Soana. Tr. B. Q. Morgan. NY: Huebsch; L: Secker 1923. 192p. 19cm. [LC.BM]

†3851. (Der Narr in Christo, Emanuel Quint.) The fool in Christ, Emanuel Quint. Tr. T: Seltzer. NY: Huebsch 1911. 474p. 19cm. [Takes liberties.] [LC.BM]

3852. do. 1926. [same] [LC.BM]

3853. (Der rote Hahn.) The conflagration. Tr. L. Lewisohn. In #3839.

3854. (Der weisse Heiland.) The white Saviour. Tr. W. and E. Muir. 1924. In #3839.

§3855. (Die Insel der grossen Mutter.) The island of the great mother. Tr. Willa and Edwin Muir. NY: Huebsch 1925. 328p. 19cm. [Not very good tr. and not always accurate.] [LC]

3856. do. 1925. [same] L: Secker. 256p. 7 x 5 in. [BM]

3857. (Die Jungfern vom Bischofsberg.) The maidens of the mount. Tr. L. Lewisohn. In #3839.

3858. (Die Ratten.) The rats. Tr. L. Lewisohn. In #3839.

§3859. (Die versunkene Glocke.) The sunken bell. Tr. Ma. Harned. In "Poet-Lore," vol. 10 (1898). [Very good prose version.]

§3860. do. 1899. 1900. A fairy play, freely rendered into Engl. verse by C: H: Meltzer. NY: Doubleday, McClure. 125p. il. 20cm. [LC.BM]

HAUPTMANN, Grd. - Die versunkene Glocke
3861. do. 1900. [same] L: Heinemann. [BM]
3862. do. 19--. [same] Trans. pub. n.d. 15cm. [AC]
3863. do. 1914. [same] Doubleday, Page. 143p. 18cm. [LC]
3864. do. 1913-15. [same] In C154(18).
3865. do. 1915? [same] #3839.
3866. do. Abr. [same?] NY: Werner. (B38)
3866a. do. 1924. [same] In C420a.
§3867. (Die Weber.) The weavers: a drama of the forties. Tr. Ma. Morison. L: Heinemann 1899. 148p. 18cm. [BM]
[Flats on the style; is not scrupulously faithful.]
3868. do. 1911. [same] NY: Huebsch. 148p. 18cm. [LC]
*3869. do. 1912. [same] In #3839.
[Much revised and improved; still some errors and omissions.]
3870. do. 1913-15. [same] In C154(18).
3871. do. 1915. [same] Abr. In C453.
3872. do. 1915. [same] In C100.
*3873. (Einsame Menschen.) Lonely lives. Tr. Ma. Morison. NY: De Witt; L: Heinemann 1898. 179p. 18cm. [BM.LC]
3874. do. 1914? [same] In #3839.
§3875. (Elga.) Elga. Tr. Ma. Harned. In "Poet-Lore," vol. 17 (1906). [Errors.]
3876. do. 1909. [same] Issued in one vol. with #3902. Bost: Badger. [LC]
§3877. do. 1912. Tr. Edith Terry. NY. Tw. [LC]
[Examined by Scholz (B39).]
3878. do. 1917? Tr. L. Lewisohn. In #3839.
3879. (Festspiel in deutschen Reimen.) Commemoration masque. Tr. B. Q. Morgan. 1917? In #3839.
3879a. (Florian Geyer.) F-- G--. Tr. B. Q. Morgan. 1929. In #3839.
†3880. (Fuhrmann Henschel.) Drayman Henschel. Tr. Marion A. Redlich. Chic: Dram. pub. 1910. 149p. 21cm. [LC]
[Examined by Scholz (B39).]
3881. do. 1913? Tr. L. Lewisohn. In #3839.
3882. (Gabriel Schillings Flucht.) Gabriel Schilling's Flight. Tr. L. Lewisohn 1916? In #3839.
†3883. (Griselda.) Griselda. Tr. Alice Kauser. Binghamton book mfg. co. 1909. (B39.) [Examined by Scholz. (B39)]
3884. do. 1916? Tr. L. Lewisohn. In #3839.
*3885. (Hanneles Himmelfahrt.) Hannele: a dream poem. Tr. W: A. Archer. L: Heinemann 1894. xxi;95p. 18cm. [LC.BM]
3886. do. 1903. [same] In C18.
§3887. do. 1908. Hannele: a dream poem. Rendered into Engl. verse and prose by C: H: Meltzer. NY: Doubleday, Page. 103p. 20cm[LC.BM]
§3888. do. 1909. The assumption of Hannele: a dream poem. Tr. G: S. Bryan. Bost: Badger. ("Poet-Lore," vol. 20.) 28p. 25cm. [LC]
[Genuine colloquial style; some bad errors.]
§3889. do. 1915? [Same as #3887] In #3839.
3890. do. 1926. [same] L: Secker. 94p. 19cm. [BM]
3891. do. n.d. Abr. NY: Werner. (B39)
3892. (Helios.) Helios (fragment). Tr. L. Lewisohn. 1917? In #3839.
*3893. (Indipohdi.) Indipohdi. Tr. W. and E. Muir. 1924. In #3839.
[Awkward verse; correct.]
3894. (Kaiser Karls Geisel.) Charlemagne's hostage. Tr. L. Lewisohn. In #3839.
3895. (Kollege Krampton.) Colleague Crampton. Tr. R. T. House. Rev. by L. L. In #3839.
3896. (Michael Kramer.) Michael Kramer. Tr. L. Lewisohn. In C154 (18); also in #3839.
3897. (Parsifal.) Parsival. Tr. O. Williams. NY: Macmillan 1915. 117p. 18cm. [LC]

HAUPTMANN, Grd.
3898. (Phantom.) Phantom. Tr. B. Q. Morgan. NY: Huebsch; L: Secker 1922. 224p. 19cm. [LC.BM]
3898a. Picturesque Germany: pref. note to #4321a.
3899. (Rose Bernd.) Rose Bernd. Tr. L. Lewisohn. #3839.
*3900. (Schluck und Jau.) Schluck and Jau. Tr. L. Lewisohn. In #3839.
§3901. (Und Pippa tanzt.) And Pippa dances: a mystical tale of the glassworks. Tr. Ma. Harned. In "Poet-Lore," vol. 18 (1907). [Errors.]
3902. do. 1909. [same] Issued in one volume with #3876. Bost: Badger. [LC]
*3903. do. Tr. Sa. T. Barrows. In #3839. [Commended by Scholz (B39)]
3903a. (Veland.) V--. Tr. Edwin Muir. In #3839.
*3904. (Vor Sonnenaufgang.) Before dawn: a social drama. Tr. L. Bloomfield. In "Poet-Lore," vol. 20 (1909).
*3905. do. 1912. Tr. L. Lewisohn. In #3839.
3906. (Winterballade.) A winter ballad. Tr. W. and E. Muir. 1924. In #3839.

HAUPTMANN, Mz. 1792-1868.
3907. The letters of a Leipzig cantor. Ed. by...Af. Schöne and Fd. Hiller. Tr. and arr. A. D. Coleridge. L;NY: Novello & Ewer 1892. 2v. 243; 310p. 23cm. [BM.LC]

HAUSER, F. 1794-1870. See #3907.

HAUSER[1], Kp. 1812?-33. See Feuerbach, Ans. Caspar Hauser. #1571.

HAUSHOFER, Max, 1840-1907. Sel. in C450;501.

HAUSRATH, Ad. "G: Taylor." 1837-1909.
3908. (Antinous.) Antinous: a romance of ancient Rome. By "G: Taylor." Tr. Ma. J. Safford. NY: Gottsberger 1882. 343p. 16cm. [LC]
3909. do. 1884. Tr. J. D. Morrell. L: Longmans. 440p. 18cm. [BM]
3910. (Elfriede.) Elfriede: a romance of the Rhineland. Tr. Ellis Wright. L: Sonnenschein 1888. 2v. (232) 432p. 19cm. [BM]
3910a. (Jetta.) Jetta; or, Heidelberg under the Romans. Tr. Sutton F. Corkran. L: Trübner 1886. See "Acad." 30(1886):149 (B15a)
*3911. (Klytia.) Klytia: a story of Heidelberg castle. Tr. S. F. Corkran. Lpz: Tauchnitz 1867. 2v. 8. [See next entry.] [BM]
*3912. do. 1884. [same] NY: Munro. Seaside lib. 52p. 32cm. [LC]
[On the whole, very good. One omission and one or two slight errors noted.]
3913. do. 1884. Clytia: a romance of the 16th cent. Tr. Ma. J. Safford. NY: Gottsberger. 364p. 16cm. [LC]
3914. do. 1885. [same as #3912] NY: Munro. D. [AC]
*3915. (Pater Maternus.) Father Maternus: a romance of the 16th cent. Tr. anon. L: Dent; NY: Dutton 1911. vii;320p. 19cm. [BM]
3916. Treitschke, his doctrine of Ger. destiny and of internat. relations. Tr. anon. NY;L: Putnam 1914. 332p. 19cm. [LC]
3917. Treitschke, his life and works. Tr. anon. L: Jarrold 1914. 329p. 22cm. [LC]
[The life goes to p. 138. The remainder consists of essays by T.]
3918. do. 1914. [same] Allen & Unwin. [BM]

HAXTHAUSEN-ABBENBURG, A: Fz. L: Ma. Frhr. v. 1792-1866.
*3919. (Studien über Russland.) The Russian empire, its people, institutions, and resources. Tr. Rb. Farie. L: Chapman & Hall 1856. 2v. il. 21cm. [BM.LC]
§3920. (Transkaukasia.) Transcaucasia: sketches of the nations and races between the Black Sea and the Caspian. Il. Graeb. Tr. J: E:

[1] See also Wassermann, Caspar Hanser, in Supplementary List.

HAXTHAUSEN-ABBENBURG
Taylor. L: Chapman & Hall 1854. xxiii;448p. Col. il. 22cm. [BM.LC]
[Not wholly faithful.]
3921. The tribes of the Caucasus. Tr. J: E: Taylor. L: Chapman & Hall 1855. viii;130p. 19cm. [BM]
[Supplement to his Transcaucasia. Tr. from MS.]

HAYDN, Fz. Js. 1732-1809.
3921a. Letters. Tr. Lady Wallace. 1867. In C429.
See Hacker, Fz., Js. Haydn, the story of his life. #3551.
See Höcker, Gst., Js. Haydn, a study of his life and time for youth. #4365.
See Nohl, L:, Life of Haydn. #6906.

HAYN, Lu. Hte. v. 1744-82. Sel. in C269;287;489.

HEBBEL, Cn. F: 1813-63. Sel. in C32;38;111-2;149;151;207;309;375;378;417;448;571.
*3922. [Coll] Three plays: Gyges and his ring ("Gyges und sein Ring") and Herod and Mariamne ("Herodes und Mariamne") tr. L. H. Allen; Maria Magdalena (do.) tr. Barber Fairley. L: Dent; NY: Dutton 1914. Everyman. xxiii;237p. 17cm. [BM.LC]
*3923. (Agnes Bernauer.) Agnes Bernauer. Tr. Loueen Pattee. In "Poet-Lore," vol. 20 (1909).
*3924. (Anna.) Anna. Tr. Fes. H. King. 1913-15. In C154(5).
§3925. (Die Nibelungen.) The Niebelungs. Tr. H. Goldberger. Il. G. H. McCall. L: Siegle 1903? 256p. 4. [U. Cal.]
[Translation is correct but the verse is quite inadequate.]
*3926. do. 1913-15. (Siegfrieds Tod.) Siegfried's death. Tr. Kath. Royce. In C154(9).
3926a. do. 1928. Tr. B. Q. Morgan. 323 leaves. 25cm. tw. [SU]
3927. (Genoveva.) Partly used by R. Reinick in his opera libretto. See R--, #7388.
*3928. (Herodes und Mariamne.) Herod and Mariamne: a tragedy in five acts. Tr. Edith R. Isaacs and Kurt Rahlson. In "The Drama," no. 6 (1912).
3929. do. 1912. [same?] Tr. into blank verse by Edith J. R. Isaacs, with introd. sketch. NY: Sergel. D. [AC]
*3930. (Judith.) Judith: a tragedy. Tr. Carl van Doren. In "Poet-Lore," vol. 25 (1914).
†3931. (Maria Magdalena.) Maria Magdalena: a middle-class tragedy. Tr. Paula Green. In "Poet-Lore," vol. 25 (1914).
[Unwarranted dilution.]
3932. do. 1914. 1919. [same] Bost: Badger. [LC]
3933. do. 1913-15. Tr. P. B. Thomas. In C154(9).
3933a. (Michelangelo.) Michael Angelo: a dramatic anecdote. Ad. R: Garnett. "Macmillan's Mag." 6(1862):381. (B15a)

HEBEL, J: P: 1760-1826. Sel. in C52;169;309;366;373;529;531;#2687.

HEBEL v. Bothe. Sel. in C443.

HEBICH, S:
*3934. (S: H--) The life of S: H--. By two of his fellow-labourers. Tr. Col. J. G. Halliday. Pref. G: T. Fox. L: Seeley 1876. xiv;364p. 18cm. [BM]

HECKER, Jt. F: K: 1795-1850.
*3935. (Die grossen Volkskrankheiten des Mittelalters: Der schwarze Tod im 14. Jh.) The black death in the 14th cent. Tr. B. G. Babington. With appendices. L: Schloss 1833. xii;203p. 18cm. [BM]
3936. do. (Die Tanzwut.) 1835. The epidemics of the Middle Ages. No. II. The dancing mania. Tr. B. G. Babington. L: Sherwood, Gilbert &

HECKER
Piper. xxxiv;206p. 18cm. [BM]
3937. do. 1837. Epidemics of the Middle Ages. Phil. [AC]
[Probably combines the two foregoing.]
3938. do. 1844. [same as #3935-6] The epidemics of the Middle Ages. L: Sydenham soc. xxviii;418p. 21cm. [BM]
[Adds The sweating sickness ("Der englische Schweiss").
3939. do. 1846. [same] This ed. is identical in text to p. 380, omitting appendices.
3940. do. 1859. [same] Third ed; completed by the author's treatise on Child-Pilgrimages. (Kinder-Fahrten.) Tr. (excellently) R. H. Cooke. pp. 346-53. L: Trübner. xxiv;360p. 21cm. [BM]
3941. do. 1888. [same] The black death and the dancing mania. Tr. B. G. Babington. L: Cassell's Nat. Lib. 192p. 8. [BM]
[Combines #3935 and 3936, without B's prefaces.]

HEDEMANN, Axe. v.
*3942. (Ein Blatt der Liebe.) My friendship with Prince Hohenlohe. Ed. Denise Petit. Tr. Ethel C. Mayne. L: Nash 1912. 164p. 23cm. [Contains many of his letters. Apparently the text was dictated to the editor.] [BM.LC]

HEEREN, Arn. Hm. L: 1760-1842.
§2943. [Coll.] (3) Hist. treatises: The polit. consequences of the Reformation; The rise, progress, and practical influence in polit. theories; *Rise and growth of the continental interests of Great Britain. Tr. anon. Oxford: Talboys 1836. iv;441p. 22cm. [BM.LC]
[3 essays in 1st vol. of his "Werke." Tr. not sufficiently faithful, but no. 3 is good.]
3944. [Coll.] Hist. works. New ed. L: Bohn 1846-50. 6v. 8. [EC]
[Prob. includes: Historical researches (Asia, 3v.; Africa, 2v.; and Sketch of ancient Greece, #3954.]
*3945. (Handbuch der Geschichte des Altertums.) A manual of ancient hist. Tr. D. A. Talboys. Oxford: Talboys 1829. xix;476p. 22cm. [BM]
3946. do. 1833. [same] 2d ed. Oxford: Talboys. xxi;480p. 8. [BM]
[Corr. and improved.]
*3947. do. 1841. [same] 3d ed. improved. Oxford: Talboys. xxiii; 480p. 22cm. [BM]
3948. do. 1854. [same] 6th ed. L: Bohn. 413p. 22cm. [LC]
3949. (Handbuch der Geschichte des europäischen Staatensystems.) Hist. of the polit. system of Europe, and its colonies from the discovery of America to the independence of the Amer. continent. Tr. G: Bancroft. Northampton, Mass: Butler 1829. 2v. 22cm. [LC]
*3950. do. 1834. A manual of the hist. of the polit. system of Europe and its colonies, from its formation at the close of the fifteenth cent. to its re-establishment upon the fall of Napoleon. Tr. D. A. Talboys. Oxford: Talboys. 2v. xxix;372;xvi;464p. 21cm. [BM.LC]
3951. do. 1857. [same] L: Bohn. 540p. 23cm. [LC]
3952. (Ideen über die Politik, den Verkehr und den Handel...der alten Welt.) A sketch of the polit. hist. of ancient Greece. Tr. G: Bancroft. Phil: 1823.[Cited by BM catalog.]
3953. do. 1824. [same] Reflections on the politics of ancient Greece. Tr. G: Bancroft. Bost: Cummings, Hilliard. 350p. 23cm.[LC]
3954. do. 1829. [same] A sketch of the polit. hist. of ancient Greece. Oxford: Talboys. xii;296p. 21cm. [BM]
[Repr. from a tr. pub. 1823 at Phila. Now carefully rev. and compared with 4th ed. (1826).]
3955. do. 1834. [same] 2d ed. corr. and enl. Oxford: Talboys. x;308p. 8. [BM]
3956. do. 1842. [same] Ancient Greece. 2d Amer. ed. Bost: Little, Brown. 344p. 23cm. [LC]

HEEREN, Arn. Hm. L: - Ideen...
3957. do. 1847. [same] and hist. treatises. L: Bohn. 8. [EC]
3958. On the origin and progress of the notion concerning rewards and punishments after death, amongst the Greeks. Tr. anon. ca. 1800. In C157.

HEEREN, H. J. Sel. in C244;469.

HEERINGEN, Gst. v. 1800-51. "Tales." In Auerbach, "German evenings," #146.

HEERMANN, J: 1585-1647. Sel. in C222-3;231-3;244;269;271;273;276; 287;469;486;570;#8904.

HEGEL, G: (W: F:) 1770-1831. Sel. in C194;366*;469;574*.
3959. [Coll.] The wisdom and relig. of a Ger. philos. Coll. and ed. Eliz. S. Haldane. L: Paul, T. & T. 1897. x;138p. 20cm. [BM.LC] [Eclectic.]
3960. (Die Logik.) [Sel.] Logic. In Stirling, J. H. "The secret of Hegel." L: 1865. 2v. 8. [BM]
3961. do. 1873. [Exposition.] Outlines of Hegel's logic. Tr. W: T: Harris. In C300(3).
*3962. do. 1874. Logic. Tr. from the encyclopedia of philos. sciences by W: Wallace. Oxford: Clarendon. clxxxiv;332p. 8. [BM] [First part too free.]
3963. do. 1892. [same] Oxford: Clarendon. 439p. 20cm. [BM.LC]
*3964. (Die objektive Logik.) Doctrine of reflection. Tr. W: T. Harris. NY: Appleton 1881. 214p. 25cm. [LC]
*3965. (Die philosophie des Geistes.) Philos. of mind. Tr. from encyclopedia of philos. sciences by W: Wallace. Oxford: Clarendon 1894. 202p. 20cm. [LC]
*3966. (Die Philosophie des Rechts.) The ethics of Hegel: tr. of sel. Jas. M. Sterrett. Bost: Ginn 1893. xii;216p. 19cm. [LC.BM]
3967. (Die subjektive Logik.) The subjective logic. Tr. H. Sloman and J. Wallon. L: Chapman 1855. 96p. 19cm. [BM] [With remarks (in French) by H. Sloman. Not so much a tr. as an abstract of Hegel's views.]
*3968. do. 1869. First principle: an exposition of comprehension and idea. Tr. W: T. Harris. St.L: Knapp. 32p. 23cm. [LC] [Also in C300(3).]
*3969. do. 1912. (1. Teil.) Doctrine of formal logic. Tr. H: S. Macran. Oxford: Clarendon. 315p. 20cm. [BM.LC] [Pref. and introd. to p. 110.]
3970. (Einleitung in die Aesthetik.) The philos. of art: an introd. to the scientific study of aesthetics, by Hegel and C. L. Michelet. Tr. W: Hastie. Ed: Oliver & Boyd 1886. xv;118p. 18cm. [BM]
3971. do. 1886. Introd. to Hegel's philos. of fine art. Tr. B. Bosanquet. L: Paul, Trench. xxxiii;175p. 19cm. [BM.LC]
3972. do. 1913-15. Introd. to the philos. of art. Tr. J. Loewenberg. In C154(7).
3973. (Einleitung in die Religionsphilosophie.) Introd. to the philos. of relig. Tr. F. L. Soldan. 1888-91. In C300(18-21).
3974. (Grundlinien der Philosophie des Rechts.) [Summary.] Hegel's philos. of right. By T. C. Sandars. In "Oxford Essays." L. 1855. 8. [BM]
3975. do. 1875. Science of rights, morals, and religion. Tr. W: T. Harris. 1874. In C300(4).
*3976. do. 1896. Philos. of right. Tr. S: W. Dyde. L: Bell. xxx; 365p. 21cm. [Somewhat free, but sound.] [BM.LC]
*3977. do? 1913-15. The philos. of law. Tr. J. Loewenberg. In C154(7).
3978. (Phänomenologie des Geistes.) Phenomenology of spirit. Tr. H. C. Brockmeyer and W: T. Harris. 1872. In C300(2).

HEGEL

3979. do. 1873. "Exposition." Outlines of Hegel's phenomenology. Tr. W: T. Harris. In C300(3).

*3980. do. 1910. Phenomenology of mind. Tr. Jas. B. Baillie. L: Sonnenschein; NY: Macmillan. 2v. 23cm. [BM.LC]

3981. (Vorlesungen über die Aesthetik.)[Sel.]Aesthetics of chivalry. Tr. Sue A. Longwell. 1875-77. In C300(5,6,7).

3982. do. 1879. Philos. of art: being the second part of Hegel's "Aesthetik." Tr. W: M. Bryant. NY: Appleton. 194p. 23cm. [LC]

3984. do. 1882. On symbolic art. Tr. W: M. Bryant. In C300(12). [From the 2d French (!) ed. of C: Binard's tr. of the 2d pt. of the "Aesthetics."]

3985. do. 1882. On classic art. Tr. W: M. Bryant. In C300(12).

3986. do. 1883. On romantic art. Tr. W: M. Bryant. In C300(13).

3987. do. 1885. Aesthetics. Ed. J. S. Gedney. Chic: Griggs. 16.[LCO]

*3988. do. 1920. Philos. of fine art. Tr. F. P. B. Osmaston. L: Bell. 4v. 427; 414; 445; 376p. 19cm. [LC.BM] [First complete Engl. tr. of the 3 vols. in the coll. ed. Berlin 1835. One small error noted.]

*3989. do. 1921. [same] NY: Harcourt. [LC]

3990. (Vorlesungen über die Geschichte der Philosophie.) Philos. of Plato. Tr. W: T. Harris. 1874. In C300(4).

3991. do. 1875. On the philos. of Aristotle. Tr. W: T. Harris. In C300(5).

3992. do. 1883. On Jakob Boehme. Tr. E. D. Mead. In C300(13).

3993. do. 1890. Giordano Bruno. Tr. E. D. Mead. In C300(20).

*3994. do. 1892-6. Hist. of philos., lectures on. Tr. Eliz. Haldane and Fes. H. Simson. L: Paul, T. & T. 3v. 8. [BM]

*3995. (Vorlesungen über die Philosophie der Geschichte.) Lect. on the philos. of hist. Tr. from 3d. Ger. ed. by J. Sibree. L: Bohn 1857. xxxix;477p. 17cm. [BM]

3996. do. 1861. [same] 477p. 18cm. [LC]

3997. do. 1887. [Exposition.] Philos. of the state and of hist. By G. S. Morris. Chic: Griggs. 16. [LC]

3998. do. 1886. Philos. of the state. Tr. E. D. Mead. In C300(16).

§3999. do. 1899. [same as #3995.] Rev. ed. NY: Colonial press. 457p. 24cm. [LC]

4000. do. 1902. [same] Bell. [LC]

4001. do. 1913-15. [same] Introd. to the philos. of hist. Tr. J. Sibree. In C154(7).

4002. (Vorlesungen über die Philosophie der Religion.) On the absolute religion. Tr. Louis Soldan. 1885-6. In C300(15,16).

4003. do. 1892. On the relig. of the Old Testament. Tr. J. M. Sterrett. In C300(22).

*4004. do. 1895. Philos. of religion, lect. on. Tr. from 2d Ger. ed. E. B. Speirs and Miss J. B. Sanderson. L: Paul, T. & T. 3v. 21cm. [BM.LC]
[Also, A work on the proofs of the existence of God, tr. R. B. Haldane.]
See Rosenkranz, J: (Various articles.) #7579 seq.
See Trendelenburg, F:, Hegel's system. #9466.

HEILBRON, Ad. 1873- .

4005. The opposite sexes: a study of woman's nat. and cult. hist. Tr. J. E. Pryde-Hughes. Methuen. 1927. 160p. 18 il. 7 x 5 in.[EC]

HEILER, F: 1892- .

4006. (Sadhu sunder Singh. Ein Apostel des Ostens und des Westens.) The gospel of Sâdhu Sundar Singh. Abr. tr. O. Wyon. L: Allen & U. 1927. 277p. 9 x 6. [EC]

"HEIMBURG, W:e" (i.e., Bta. Behrens, 1850-1912.)
4007. (Aus dem Leben meiner alten Freundin.) The story of a clergyman's daughter; or, reminis. from the life of my old friend. Tr. J. W. Wylie. NY: Munro 1889. 212p. 20cm. [LC]
4008. do. 1890. The pastor's daughter. Tr. Mrs. J. W. Davis. NY: Worthington. 320p. il. 19cm. [LC]
4009. do. 1891. Martha the parson's daughter; and, Under the muses' ban. Tr. anon. NY: Street & Smith. 282p. 20cm. [LC]
4010. do. 1894. The chaplain's daughter. Also, Misunderstood, and Jascha. Tr. K. Dykers. Chic: Weeks. 217p. 20cm. [LC]
4011. Christmas stories. Tr. Mrs. J. W. Davis. NY: Worthington 1890. il. D. [AC]
4012. (Das Eulenhaus.) The owl-house. See "Marlitt, E.," The owl-house. (Finished by Heimburg.) #6022.
4013. (Die Andere.) Two daughters of one race. Tr. Mrs. D. M. Lowrey. NY: Worthington 1889. 329p. 19cm. [LC]
4014. (Ein armes Mädchen.) A penniless girl. Tr. Mrs. A. L. Wister. Phil: Lippincott 1885. 280p. 19cm. [LC]
4015. do. 1887. A penniless orphan. Tr. Edwyna Benedict. NY: Munro. 201p. 19cm. [LC]
4016. do. 1892. A poor girl. Tr. E. L. Lathrop. NY: Worthington. 257p. il. 19cm. [LC]
4016a. do. 1896. [same] Hurst. [LC]
4017. (Eine unbedeutende Frau.) An insignificant woman: a story of artist life. Tr. Mrs. M. S. Smith. Il. W. B. Davis. NY: Bonner 1891. 389p. 19cm. [LC]
4018. do. 1891. Misjudged. Tr. Ma. E. Almy. Chic;NY: Rand, McNally. 296p. 19cm. [LC]
4019. do. 1891. Misjudged. Tr. Mrs. J. W. Davis. NY: Worthington. 362p. il. 19cm. [LC]
4020. Elsie. Tr. Hettie E. Miller. Chic;NY: Rand, McNally 1891. 236p. 19cm. [LC]
4021. A fatal misunderstanding, and other stories. Tr. Elise L. Lathrop. NY: Worthington 1893. 313p. il. 19cm. [LC]
4022. (Haus Beetzen.) Beetzen manor. Tr. Elise L. Lathrop. NY;L: Internat. news 1895. 333p. 19cm. [LC]
4023. (Ihr einziger Bruder.) Her only brother. Tr. Jean W. Wylie. NY: Crowell 1888. 406p. 20cm. [LC]
4024. do. 1889. [same] New cheap ed. [AC]
4025. do. 1890. [same?] NY: Munro. Pocket ed. D. [AC]
4026. do. 1890. Sister's love. Tr. M. D. Waterman. NY: Worthington. il. D. [AC]
4027. do. 1892. Her only brother. Tr. anon. Nat. Pub. S. [AC]
4028. In the depths; The godmother; Ursula; Our Mannie. Tr. Kate Dykers. Chic: Weeks 1894. 228p. 20cm. [LC]
4029. (Kloster Wendhusen.) Cloister W--. Tr. Ma. E. Almy. Chic;NY: Rand, McNally 1890. 253p. 19cm. [LC]
4030. (Lore von Tollen.) "Lora," the major's daughter. Tr. Mrs. J. W. Davis. NY: Worthington 1889. il. D. [AC]
4031. do. 1890. Lenore von Tollen. NY: Munro. D. [AC]
§4032. do. 1891. Was she his wife? Tr. Helen Wolff. L: Eden. 271p. 18cm. [Too free.] [BM]
4033. Lucie's mistake. Tr. Mrs. J. W. Davis. NY: Worthington 1890. il. D. [AC]
*4034. (Lumpenmüllers Lieschen.) Lizzie of the mill. Tr. Christina Tyrrell. L: Bentley 1880. 2v. 312; 294p. 18cm. [BM] [Chap. I. omitted.]
4035. do. 1882. Lottie of the mill. Tr. Kath. S. Dickey. Phil. Lippincott. 289p. 18cm. [LC]
4036. do. 1889. A tale of an old castle. Tr. Mrs. M. S. Smith. NY: Munro. 185p. 19cm. [LC]

HEIMBURG

4037. Magdalen's fortunes. Tr. Mrs. J. W. Davis. NY: Worthington 1889. il. D. [AC]

4038. Maiden's choice. Tr. E. L. Lathrop. NY: Worthington 1891. il. D. [AC]

4039. (Mamsell Unnütz.) Miss Good-for-nothing. Tr. H. E. Miller. Chic: Weeks 1893. 269p. 19cm. [LC]

4040. do. 1893. Miss Mischief. Tr. Mrs. M. S. Smith. Il. W. B. Davis. NY: Bonner. 325p. 19cm. [LC]

4040a. Rube. Tr. Hasket Derby. "Littell's Liv. Age" 6(1900):816, etc. (B15a)

4041. (Trotzige Herzen.) Defiant hearts. Tr. Annie W. Ayer and Helen T. Slate. NY: Fenno 1897. 350p. 19cm. [LC]

4042. do. 1898. [same] il. D. [AC]

4043. (Trudchens Heirat.) Gertrude's marriage. Tr. Mrs. J. W. Davis. NY: Worthington 1889. 307p. il. 20cm. [LC]

4044. do. 1890. [same] Tr. Marian Ford. NY: Munro. 160p. 20cm. [LC]

4045. (Um fremde Schuld.) For another's fault. Tr. H. E. Miller. Chic: Weeks 1895. 275p. 20cm. [LC]

4046. do. 1895. For another's wrong. Tr. Annie W. Ayer and Helen T. Slate. NY: Bonner. 358p. il. 20cm. [LC]

4047. (Zwei Freundinnen.) My heart's darling. Tr. E. V. Conder. NY: Munro 1889. 200p. 19cm. [LC]

4048. do. 1889. Friendship's test. Tr. Amelia Burdette. NY: Ogilvie. 198p. 20cm. [LC]

4049. do. 1891. Hortense. Tr. Ma. E. Almy. Chic;NY: Rand, McNally. 336p. 19cm. [LC]

HEINE, H: 1797-1856.

ARRANGEMENT

Works
Poems--Selections
Poems--Collections
Prose--Selections
Single titles
Memoirs and letters

*4050. Works. 1891-1905. Tr. C: G. Leland ("Hans Breitman"), and others. L: Heinemann. 12v. 19cm. [LC.BM]
[I. Florentine nights. II. III. Pictures of travel. IV. Salon. V. VI. Germany. VII. VIII. French affairs. IX. Book of songs. Tr. T: Brooksbank. X. New poems. Tr. Marg. Armour. XI. XII. Germany. Romancero. Last poems. Tr. Marg. Armour.]

4051. do. 190-. Tr. C: G. Leland. NY: print. for subscr. only by Croscup & Sterling. 16v. il. 22cm. [LC]
[1. Florentine nights. 2. Shakespeare's maidens and women. 3-6. Pictures of travel. 7,8. The salon. Letters on the French stage. 9-12. Germany. 13-16. French affairs.]

4052. do. 1905. [same?] Ed. E. Elster. L: Unwin. 8v. [EC]

4053. 1917. Poetical works. Cheap ed. Vol. 1. Book of songs. Tr. T. Brooksbank. 289p. Vol. 2. New poems. Tr. Marg. Armour. 317p. Vol. 3. Germany, Romancero, bks. 1 and 2. Tr. Marg. Armour. 269p. Vol. 4. Romancero, bk. 3. Last poems. Tr. Marg. Armour. 278p. Heinemann. Cr. 8. [BM]
[Vols. IX-XII of #4050, cheaper reissue.]

POEMS--SELECTIONS

Sel. in C1;3;6;12;17;32;36-7;42;45;50;53;65-6;67*;69*;73;75;76*;77; 86;89;90;93;97;106*;108;111-2;115;118;123;129*;131;132*;137a;142; 144;146;149*;151;152*;163;166*;169;172-3;178;180;184;187;190;192; 193;194;195-6;205-6;208;210;216;218-9;296;301;309;311*;313;316-8; 320;366*;371;372*;373-5;378;380*;383;385;388;394-5;399;400;405a; 414-5;417;422-3;446;448;459;460-1;467;469;470*;488-9;497;501*; 504*;505;531;536*;539;551*;556*;566;574*.

HEINE--POEMS--SELECTIONS

†4054. ABBOTT, W. H. Vision: a book of lyrics. L: Mathews 1914. 69p. 18cm. [6 tr. from Heine, pp. 61-69.] [BM]

*4055. BROWNING, ELIZ. B. Complete poet. works. Bost: Houghton 1920. [Six tr. from Heine; good but not brilliant.] [LC.BM]

CRAIGMYLE, ELIZ. Poems and tr. 1886. C76. [Sixteen from Heine.]

§DIEHL, L: The sardonic smile. #1222. [Has about 35 poems besides numerous short bits of verse; some tr. not bad.]

4056. ELIOT, G: The wit of H: Heine. Girard, Kan: Haldeman-Julius n.d. 57p. 12cm. [Contains copious extracts in translation.] [BQM]

*GEIKIE, J. Songs and lyrics. 1887. C152. [Tr. from Heine, pp. 1-112. Good to excellent.]

GRAY, AX. Songs and ballads...in Scottish dialect. 1920. C177a. ["Junge Leiden"; "Lyrisches Intermezzo" (24); "Heimkehr" (23); 14 others. Very interesting.]

§GRIBBLE, J. Borrowed plumes. 1888. C180. [44 from Heine.]

4057. LAZARUS, E. Poems and translations, written between the ages of fourteen and sixteen. NY: priv. circ. 1866. 207p. 12. [LCO]

4058. do. 1867. [same] NY: Hurd & Houghton. 297p. 12. [Cf. #4079.] [LCO]

§4059. MERRICK, J: MUDGE. Nugae inutiles. Bost: Shepard 1874. 133p. 12. [LCO]

4060. MONAHAN, M. H: H--. Romance and trag. of the poet's life. NY: Brown 1923. 199p. 19cm. [LC]
[Prose passages from Leland's tr. Poetry partly from Leland, partly from Gilbert Cannan's versions.]

*ROBINSON, E. Poems of 1848 and earlier days. 1904. C470. [15 from Heine, some excellent.]

4061. SHARP, W: Life of H: H--. L: Scott; NY: Whittaker 1888. 218p. 21cm. [Tr. F. Stour, K. Freiligrath-Kroeker, W. Stigand (!), El. Craigmyle, J. Ackerlos, Emily Pfeiffer.] [LC]

[STIGAND, W: Anthea. Poems and tr. 1907. C504. Heine, pp. 261-341.]

†4062. do. Life, work, and opinions of H: H--. L: Longmans 1875. 2v. 22cm. [Many translations, cf. his other pubs. for judgment.] [BM.BPL]

*4063. THOMSON, JAS. Poetical works. Oxford: Frowde 1908. 516p. 19cm. [31 from Heine; 2 from Goethe.] [BM.LC]

§TYRRELL, G. Versions and perversions. 1909. C551. [17 from Heine, not very good.]

§WEBB, Phil. G. Tr. from H-- and Goethe. Sel. from "Heimkehr," "Lyrisches Intermezzo," "Romanzero," etc. 1912. 65p. C556. [Rather poor.]

POEMS--COLLECTIONS

§4064. ANON. n.d. Love songs. Il. Heinrich Comploi. NY: Stokes. Prtd. in Vienna. 25 leaves. unp. 4. [NY]
[24 poems, mostly pretty good versions.]

4065. ANON. 1865. Pearls from H--. Phil: Leypoldt. 16p. 4. [NY]
[Done by various hands; uneven in quality.]

4066. ANON. 1903. Book of songs. With foreword by T. Gautier. East Troy, NY: Roycrofters. 116p. 8. [Book now missing.] [NY]

4067. ANON. 191-? Poems. Translation pub. n.d. 15cm. [AC]

†4068. "ACKERLOS, J:" (i.e., J: S. Smith). Sel. from the poetry of H: H--. L: Chapman 1854. viii;66p. 16cm. [BM]
[Pretty poor, in both sel. and tr.]

*4069. ARMOUR, MARG. New poems, also, "Germany," etc. L: Heinemann 1910. 310p. 19cm. [Vols. X, XI, and XII of #4050.]

§4070. BOWRING, E. A. Poems of H-- complete. L: Longmans 1858. xxiii;553p. 8. [BM]
[Bowring seldom rises to excellence: good mediocre translation.]

HEINE--POEMS--COLLECTIONS

4071. do. 1861. L: Bohn. 8. [BM]
4072. do. 1866. New ed. Bell & D. 12. [EC]
4073. do. 1884. 2d ed. L: Bell. 560p. 12. [NY]
§4074. BRIGGS, H. B. Love songs. L: Trübner 1888. 112p. 18cm. [BM]
[Fair to poor. Taken from "Lyrisches Intermezzo" and "Heimkehr."]
4075. do. 1889. Trübner. fcp. [EC]
4076. do. 1907. [same?] Stokes. il: Q. [AC]
*4077. BROOKSBANK, T: Book of songs. L: Heinemann 1904. 278p. 19cm. [LC]
[Vol. IX of #4050.]
*4078. EGAN, T: S. Atta Troll and other poems. L: Chapman & Hall 1876. 327p. 12. [Lyrics not so good; rhymes bother him.] [BM.BPL]
*4079. FANE, JULIAN. Poems of H: H--. (not published). Vienna: Imperial court and govt. printing-office 1854. 95p. 8. [LC.BM]
4080. do. 1871.[same] In Lytton, E: Bulwer-, "Julian Fane, a memoir." L: Murray. 8. [EC]
4081. do. 1872. [same] 2d ed. 12. [LCO]
*4082. HELLMAN, Fes. Lyrics and ballads of H--, and other Ger. poets. NY: Putnam 1892. xvii;250p. 16cm. [BM]
[Chamisso, Freiligrath (5), Goethe (11), Moericke (sic), Rückert (3), Uhland (3).]
*4083. do. 1895. 2d ed. rev. and enl. NY: Putnam. xvii;256p. 16cm. [LC.BM]
§4084. HORINE, CLARA. Heine's poems; Roses and cypress. Bost: Stratford 1923. 58p. 19cm. [LC]
[53 songs, mostly "Lieder" and "Intermezzo." Translations are fair to good. Rhyme bothers her and she loses simplicity.]
†4085. JOHNSON, FRANKLIN. A romance in song: Heine's lyrical interlude. Bost: Lothrop 1884. 91p. il. 8. [LCO.BM]
[Fails in simplicity.]
§4086. JONES, H. M. Heine's poem, the North Sea. Chic: Open court 1916. 129p. 19cm. [LC.BM]
*4087. KROEKER, KATE F. Poems. L;NY: Scott 1887. 280p. 14cm. [BM.LC]
[Eclectic volume; mostly very good translations.]
4088. do. 18-? NY;L: White & Allen. 280p. 14cm. [LC]
*4089. LAZARUS, EMMA. Poems and ballads. NY: Worthington 1881. xxiv;224p. 19cm. [LC.BM]
[Contains "North Sea," "Homeward bound," and scattering poems.]
**4090. LELAND, C: G. Book of songs. Phil: Leypoldt 1864. 239p. 16.
[Not the same tr. as in #4050. Contains: "Buch der Lieder," "Romanzen," "Sonette, "Lyrisches Intermezzo," "Heimkehr," "Harzreise," "Nordsee." Mostly excellent versions.] [LC]
4091. do. 1868. [same] NY. 3d ed. 8. [BM]
4092. do. 1874. [same] [U Cal.]
4093. do. 1881. [same] [U Cal.]
4094. do. 1916. Complete poetical works. Tr. and ed. by C: G. L--. NY: Brentano's. 4v. D. [Same as Heinemann 1917 ed.] [AC]
**4095. LEVY, RB. Poems and ballads. Macmillan 1914. xxxii;246p. 12. [BM.NY]
[Knows his German thoroughly and writes good verse; almost all his translations are good, many are excellent. Especially valuable for Heine is the printing of the initial German line as subheading.]
§4096. MARTIN, SIR T. Poems and ballads, done into English. L: Blackwood 1878. xv;263p. 17cm. [BM.LC]
[Contains most of the "Traumbilder," "Lieder," "Romanzen," "Intermezzo," "Heimkehr," "Harzreise"; also some scattering poems. Fails in simplicity; some grotesque rhymes.]
4097. do. 1894. [same] 3d ed. with additions. Ed;L: Blackwood. 263p. 17cm. [BM.LC]

HEINE--POEMS--COLLECTIONS

4098. MARTIN, T., BOWRING, E. A. Book of songs. Compiled, etc. NY: White 1884. 244p. 16cm. [BM]
[About equal numbers; no individual ascriptions. No editor mentioned. No index. Memoir, pp. v-xx.]

†4099. ODDIE, J. W. Choice poems of H: H--. L;NY: Macmillan 1896. xvii;174p. 8. [Rather bad.] [BM]

§4100. PAYNE, J: Poetical works...complete. L; Villon soc. 1911. 3v. 22cm. [BM]
[Priv. subscr. and circ. Includes "Almansor" and "Ratcliff." Translations of high quality at their best; but rhymes trouble him, he breaks his lines frequently, and he is not simple enough.]

†4101. RADFORD, ERNEST. Tr. from Heine, etc. Cambridge: Johnson; L: Reeves 1882. viii;93p. 17cm. [BM]
[17 poems. pp. 1-22 Heine. Pretty bad.]

§4102. "STRATHEIR" (i.e., H. S. Jarrett). Book of songs. L: Allen 1882. viii;328p. 18cm. [BM]
["Traumbilder"; "Lieder"; "Romanzen"; "Sonette"; "Lyrisches Intermezzo"; "Heimkehr"; "Harzreise";"Nordsee"; "Letzte Gedichte"; "Anhang." Good. Not distinguished.]

4103. do. 1894. [same?] New ed. Allen. 8. [EC]

4104. do. 1913. Tr. Col. H. S. Jarrett (Stratheir). L: Constable. xiii;238p. 8. [Same as #4102. Reissue.] [BM]

†4105. STRETTELL, ALMA (afterwards Harrison). Measured steps: Sel. from the poetical works. L: Macmillan 1878. viii;115p. 18cm. [BM]
[Orig. verse and 17 poems from Heine's "Buch der Lieder," "Nordsee," "Neue Gedichte," "Letzte Gedichte." Poor translation.]

*4106. TODHUNTER, J: Book of songs. Oxford: Clarendon 1907. xvi; 279p. 18cm. [BM.LC]

§4107. TURNBULL, MONICA PEVERIL. Tr. from H--. L: Humphreys 1923. 52p. 16. [BM]
[Orig. pub. 1902 in small vol. "A short-day's worth." Poor to fair.]

**4108. UNTERMEYER, LOUIS. Poems. NY: Holt 1917. 288p. 21cm.[LC.BM]

4109. do. 1923. (325) Poems. Rev. ed. NY: Harcourt, Brace; L: Routledge. xl;288p. 21cm. [LC.BM]

*4110. WALLIS, J. E. Book of songs. L: Chapman & Hall 1856. 351p. 19cm. [BM]
[Very good as far as sampled. Youthful sorrows; "Lyrisches Intermezzo;" The return; The tour in the Hartz; The North Sea.]

§4111. WATERS, W. G. Dream pictures ("Traumbilder"). L: Glaisher 1927. 30p. 19cm. [11 poems. Rather poor tr.] [BM]

§4112. WEBB, PHIL. G: L. More tr. from Heine, L: Allen & Unwin 1920. 124p. 16cm. [BM]
[Selections from "Harzreise," "Heimkehr," "Lyrisches Intermezzo," "Twilight of the gods," "Ratcliff," "Donna Clara," "Almansor," "Romanzen" Sonnets, "Neuer Frühling," "Bimini." On the whole pretty good.]

4113. do. 1927. Poems from Heine. L: Nisbet. viii;186p. 19cm. [BM]
["I am repub. with alter. and amendments the contents of 2 previous vols. (i.e., #4112;C556) and am adding a large no. of new tr."]

PROSE--SELECTIONS

4114. ANON. Wit and wisdom. Girard, Kan: Haldeman-Julius n.d. Little Blue Books. 64p. 13cm. (BQM)

4115. ANON. 1914. Thoughts and ideas of H--. Siegle, H. 16. [EC]

4116. DUNBAR, NEWELL. Heine, his wit, wisdom, and poetry. Bost: Cupples 1892. 123p. [Eclectic volume; very brief prose extracts, poems interspersed. No ascriptions.] [LC]

HEINE

†4117. ELLIS, HAVELOCK. Prose writings. L: Scott 1887. xx;327p. 18cm. [BM.LC]
["Buch le Grand," part; English fragments: London, Wellington, the liberation; religion and philosophy in Germany; Florentine nights; Romantic school, part; confessions; gods in exile; Don Quixote.--Editor's own translations are bad; his "revisions" naturally of little account.]

†4118. FLEISHMAN, S. L. Prose miscellanies. Phil: Lippincott 1876. 302p. 8. [LC.BM]
[The salon, 1831; Memoirs of Herr v. Schnabelewopski; on the hist. of relig. and philos. in Germany; The romantic school; The Suabian school; The gods in exile; Confessions.--Cuts and is too free.]

*4119. McLINTOCK, R. Heine as novelist and dramatist, being a sel. from his longer works. L: Roper & Drowley 1890. xiii;268p. 19cm.
[The rabbi of Bacharach; Almansor; W. Ratcliff; Vitzliputzli; The slave ship; Sir Olaf; The villain of Bergen; The poet's last vision; Bimini.] [BM]

4120. do. 1896. [same] Liverpool: Jaggard. [EC]

†4121. SHARP, ELIZ. A. Heine in art and letters. L: Scott 1895. xv; 250p. 8. [LC.BM]
[Letters from the Pyrenees; Letters from Normandy; June days, 1832; The old regime, 1831; Letters from Berlin, 1822; The salon, 1831, 1833; Berlioz, Liszt, Chopin.]

§4122. SNODGRASS, J. Wit, wisdom, and pathos from the prose of H. Heine, with a few pieces from the book of songs. L: Trübner 1879. xx;338p. 18cm. [Lyrics mostly bad.] [BM.BPL]

4123. do. 1888. [same] 2d ed. L: Gardner. [BM.BPL]

§4124. STERN, S. A. Scintillations from the prose works. NY: Holt & Williams 1873. 185p. 17cm. [LC]
[Florentine nights almost entire, and miscellaneous extracts.]

SINGLE TITLES

*4125. (<u>Atta Troll.</u>) A-- T--. Tr. Herman Scheffauer. Il. W. Pogány. L: Sidgwick & J. 1913. 185p. 16cm. [BM]
[Introd. and notes by Oscar Levy; pref. by Heine.]

4126. do. 1914. [same] NY: Huebsch. 185p. [AC]

4127. (<u>Der Salon.</u>) Salon. Tr. C: G. Leland. L: Heinemann 1893. 8. [EC]
[Cf. #4050.]

4128. (<u>Deutschland.</u>) Germany. Tr. anon. L: Heinemann 1892. 2v. 8. [EC]
[Cf. #4050.]

§4129. (<u>Die Harzreise.</u>) A trip to the Brocken. Tr. R. McLintock. Macmillan 1881. vi;109p. 8. [BM]

*4130. do. 1913-15. The journey to the Harz. Tr. C: G. Leland. In C154(6).

*4131. (<u>Die romantische Schule.</u>) The romantic school. Tr. S. L. Fleishman. NY: Holt 1882. ix;273p. 18cm. [BM.HCL]

4132. do. 1913-15. Tr. C: G. Leland. In C154(6).

*4133. (<u>Englische Fragmente.</u>) English fragments. Tr. Sa. Norris. Ed: Grant; L: Simpkin 1880. vi;107p. 8. [BM]
[13 essays.--very good tr.]

4134. do. 1913-15. Tr. C: G. Leland. In C154(6).

4135. (<u>Florentinische Nächte.</u>) Florentine nights. Tr. C: G. Leland. L: Methuen 1927. vii;78p. il. 21cm. [BM]
[12 il. in col. Fx. de Gray.]

4136. (<u>Französische Zustände.</u>) French affairs (Lutèce). Letters from Paris. Tr. anon. L: Heinemann 1893. 2v. 8. [Cf. #4050.] [EC]

*4137. (<u>H: Heine über L: Börne.</u>) Ludwig Börne: recoll. of a revolutionist. Abr. and tr. T. S. Egan. L: Newman 1881. 189p. 18cm. [BM]

HEINE

*4138. (Ideen. Das Buch Le Grand.) Ideas. "Buch le grand" of the Reisebilder. Tr. I. B. L: Macmillan 1884. 120p. 8. [BM] [Excellent.]

§4139. (Italien...) Italian travel sketches... Tr. Eliz. A. Sharp. L: Scott 1892. xviii;250p. 18cm. [BM.LC] [The journey from Munich to Genoa; The town of Lucca; Conclusion; The French stage; George Sand: a supplement; The depart; Later news.]

§4140. do. 1927. [same] L: Foulis. xviii;250p. il. 19cm. [BM] [Arrangement differs from 1892 ed.: (5) Italian travel sketches; The French stage; Appendix; George Sand. She misses many a fine point.]

*4141. (Reisebilder.) Pictures of travel. Tr. C: G. Leland. Copyright 1855. [See #4143.] [LC]

4142. do. 1863. [same] 4th rev. ed. Phil: Leypoldt. 471p. [AC]

*4143. do. 1866. [same] 5th rev. ed. NY: Leypoldt and H; L: Trübner. 471p. 19cm. [BM] [The homeward journey; The Hartz journey; The North Sea (2 pts.); Ideas, a new spring; Italy (1828); English fragments.]

4144. do. 1882. [same] 9th ed. Phil. [AC]

§4145. do. 1887. Travel pictures. Tr. Fis. Storr. L: Bell. vii; 367p. 19cm. [BM] [A tour in the Harz; Book of ideas; Norderney; Romantic school.--Unequal to Heine's jokes; lacks pungent style.]

4146. do. 1891. Leland's tr. NY: Lovell. [AC]

4147. do. 1891. [same] L: Heinemann. 2v. 8. [EC]

4148. do. 1901. [same as #4145] [BM.LC]

*4149. do. 1907. Pictures of travel. New tr. R. D. Gillman. L: Low; NY: Scribners. x;408p. 8. [BM] ["Harzreise"; North Sea; Norderney; Ideas; The return home; The twilight of the gods; Ratcliffe; Donna Clara; Almansor; Pilgrim to Kevlaar; Don Quixote.]

4151. do. 191- . Travel pictures including tour in the Harz. Tr. anon. Translation pub. n.p. 15cm. [AC]

4152. do. 1925. Pict. of travel. Sel. and tr. B. Q. Morgan, with introd. note by G: S. Viereck. Girard, Kan: Haldeman-Julius Co. 63p. 13cm. [BQM]

§4153. (Shakespeares Mädchen und Frauen.) Notes on Shakespeare's heroines. Tr. Ida Benecke. Westminster: Constable 1895. 189p. 20cm. [Too free.] [BM.LC]

*4154. (Zur Geschichte der neueren schönen Literatur in Deutschland.) Letters auxil. to the hist. of mod. polite lit. in Germany. Tr. G: W. Haven. Bost: Munroe 1836. 172p. 17cm. [LC.BM]

§4155. (Zur Geschichte der Religion und Philosophie in Deutschland.) Relig. and philos. in Germany: a fragment. Tr. J. Snodgrass. L: Trübner 1882. x;177p. 8. [BM]

MEMOIRS AND LETTERS

(Briefe.)(2) Letters. Tr. anon. 1912. In C320.

§4156. EVANS, T. W. Memoirs (Mémoiren) and some newly discovered fragments. L: Bell 1884. vii;274p. 19cm. [Introd. essay to p. 133.] [BM.LC]

*4157. KARPELES, G., ed. H: Heine's life told in his own words. Tr. A. Dexter. NY: Holt 1893. vi;375p. 20cm. [BM.LC] [Lyrics fair to poor.]

*4158. do. 1910. Memoirs, from works, letters, and conversations. Tr. Gilbert Cannan. L;NY: Lane. 2v. 23cm. [BM.LC]

4159. LELAND, C: G. Family life: 122 letters. Ed. by Baron L: v. Embden. L: Heinemann 1893. xviii;276p. 8. [BM]

HEINE
4160. do. 1896. [same] 2d ed. L: Heinemann. [EC]
See Diehl, L: The sardonic smile (the romantic life of H: Heine). #1222.

HEINRICH DER ERLAUCHTE, Markgraf v. Meissen. 1221-88. Sel. in C27.

HEINRICH VI, Kaiser 1156-97. Sel. in C88;532.

HEINRICH IV, Herzog von Breslau, fl. 1253-90. Sel. in C27;416;427; 532.

HEINRICH I, Herzog von Anhalt, fl. 1199-d. 1252. Sel. in C27;532.

HEINRICH VON FRAUENBERG. Sel. in C27.

HEINRICH, Burggraf v. Lüenz, fl. 1231-58. Sel. in C27;427.

HEINRICH HETZBOLD VON WEISSENSEE, fl. 1312-45. Sel. in C27.

HEINRICH VON LAUFENBERG, fl. 1429-d. 1460. Sel. in C41;372;570.

HEINRICH VON MEISSEN (properly zur Meise), called Frauenlob, fl. 1250?-1318. Sel. in C27;310;416;427;530;570.
*4161. (Unser Frowen leich.) The lay of our lady. Tr. with introd. and notes A. E. Kroeger. St.L, Mo: Gray & Baker 1877. 22p. 22cm. [BM]

HEINRICH VON MORUNGEN, fl. 1213-21. Sel. in C27;366;427;530-2.

HEINRICH VON MUEGELN, fl. 1340-70. Sel. in C27;427.

HEINRICH VON PREUSSEN, Prinz, 1726-1802. See Frederick II, Elogy, #1983.

HEINRICH VON RUGGE, fl. 1175-91. Sel. in C27;416;427.

HEINRICH VON VELDEKE, fl. 1140?-1200? Sel. in C27;416;427.

HEINSE, J: Jk. W: 1749-1803.
4162. (Ardinghello oder die glückseligen Inseln.) Ardinghello; or, an artist's rambles in Sicily. Tr. J. D. Haas. 1839. In C183,pp. 331-44.

HEINTZ, Ab. 1822-
4163. (Die Meistersinger von Nürnberg.) The master-singers of Nuremberg...Musical explanation. Tr. from 2d Ger. ed. J: H: Cornell. NY: Schirmer 1890. 128p. 20cm. [LCM]
4164. do. 1892. Tr. C. Bache. L: Novello & Ewer. 91p. 16cm. [BM]
4165. (Parsifal.) P-- by R: W--. Its origin in the old legends and its musical motives explained with 67 mus. ex. Tr. Constance Bache. L: Novello 1892. 51p. 16cm. [BM]
4166. (Tristan und Isolde.) R: Wagner's T-- and I-- explained according to the mus. devel. of its motives. 66 mus. ex. Tr. C. Bache. L: Novello & Ewer 1892. 59p. 16cm. [BM]

HEINZELMANN. Sel. in C12.

HEINZEN, K: P: 1809-1880. Sel. in C317.
4167. Mankind the criminal: a lecture delivered in Washington, D.C. Tr. C.P. Roxbury, Mass: 1864? 19cm. [BM]

HELD, H: d. 1643. Sel. in C271;273.

HELENE Lu. Eli. duchess of Orleans, 1814-58. See Schubert, G. H., Reminiscences, etc. #8631.

HELFFERICH, K: 1872- .
4168. (Deutschlands Volkswohlstand 1888-1913.) Germany's economic

HELFFERICH, K: - Deutschlands Volkswohlstand 1888-1913
progress and national wealth... Tr. anon. NY: Germanistic soc. of America 1914. 124p. 23cm. [LC]
4169. (Die Entstehung des Weltkriegs im Lichte der Veröffentlichungen der Dreiverbandmächte.) The dual alliance vs. the triple entente: Germany's case in the supreme court of civilization. Tr. anon. NY: Fatherland corp. 1915. 46p. 23cm. [LC]
4170. do. 1915. [same] The genesis of the great war. Berlin: G: Stilke. 52p. 23cm. [LC]
4171. Money. Tr. L. Infield. Ed. with introd. by T. E. Gregory. L: Benn 1927. 2v. 356;325p. 10 x 6 in. [EC]

"HELL, Td." (i.e., K: Gf. Td. Winkler, 1775-1856.) Sel. in C512.

HELLENBACH, Lr. Frhr. v. 1827-87.
*4172. (Geburt und Tod als Wechsel der Anschauungsform.) Birth and death as a change of form of perception; or, the dual nature of man. Tr. by "V." L: Psych. press 1886. xii;223p. 21cm. [BM]

HELM, Kle. (afterwards Beyrich), 1825-96.
4173. (Backfischchens Leben und Freuden.) Gretchen's joys and sorrows. 1st Amer. from 8th Ger. ed. by H. M. D. Stack, i.e., Helen M. D. Slade. Plymouth, Mass: Avery; Bost: Williams 1877. 8. [AC]
§4174. do. 1877. A miss in her teens: a tale for girls. Tr. Rhoda E. Colborne. L: Kolckmann. 199p. 18cm. [Pretty good.] [BM]
4175. do. 1882. [same] Kolckmann. 16. [EC]
[Ascribed to C:e Helm.]
4176. Child and woman. Tr. J. Zitella Cocke. Phil: Moore 1878. 428p. 19cm. [LC]
4177. do. 1884. [same] New issue. Lilly's girlhood; or, child and woman. Ward & D. D. [AC]
4178. (Elf Goldihair.) Cecily. Tr. Eliz. P. Stork. Il. Gertrude A. Kay. Phil;L: Lippincott 1924. 298p. 24cm. [LC.BM]
4179. Princess Eve. Tr. Rosa Sachs. Bost: Lee & S. 1878. 303p. il. 16. [LCO]

HELM, Erne.
4180. The young artists. Tr. Ma. E. Ireland. Cincin: Curtis & Jennings; NY: Eaton & Mains 1896. 291p. il. 19cm. [LC]

HELMBOLD, L: 1532-98. Sel. in C240;244 (calls him "Helmbort"); 271; 570.

HELMHOLTZ, Hm. (L: Fd.) v. 1821-94. Sel. in C469. See "Koenigsberg, Leo.," #5114.
4181. Autobiog. sketch. Tr. E. Atkinson. 1891. In Pop. Lect. 2d. ser. [See #4185.] [LC]
4182. Popular lect. on scientific subjects. Tr. Ed. Atkinson. L: Longmans; NY: Appleton 1873. xvi;397p. il. 20cm. [LC]
[Other translators: H. W. Eve, A. J. Ellis, Tyndall, Pye-Smith, W. Flight.]
4183. do. 1891. [same] NY: Appleton. [LC]
4184. do. 1900. [same] NY: Appleton. [LC]
4185. Popular lect. 2d. series. Tr. E. Atkinson. NY: Appleton 1881. 291p. il. 19cm. [LC card]
4186. do. 1901. [same] NY: Appleton. [LC]

HELMKEN, Fz. Td.
§4187. (Der Dom zu Koeln.) The cathedral of Cologne, its legends, hist., etc. Tr. J. W. Watkins. Cologne: Boisserée 1881. 88p. il. 17cm. [Rearranged and not very faithfully treated.] [BM]
4188. do. 1884. [same] 2d. enl. ed. Cologne. 95p. 8. [BM]

HELMS, An. z:
*4189. (Tagebuch einer Reise durch Peru.) Travels from Buenos Ayres, by Potosi, to Lima. Containing particulars...of the various countries...in South America. Tr. anon. L: Phillips 1806. xii;287p. 17cm. [BM.LC]
[Appendix, pp. 145-287. The tr. has turned a mineralogical day-book into a picturesque travel journal. The paging leaps from 104-41.]
4190. do. 1807. [same] 2d. ed. L: Phillips. 292p. 15cm. [BM]
[Reprinted with changes in notes. Append. pp. 117-292.]
4191. do. 1807. [same] In Coll. of modern voyages and travels. L: Phillips. 21cm. [BM]
[Identical with 1st ed. pp. viii, 1-39, 40-92 (appendix).]

HELMUTH, Jt. Henry Cn. 1745-1825.
4191a. A short account of the yellow fever in Philadelphia, for the reflecting Christian. Tr. C: Erdmann. Phil: Prtd. by Jones, Hoff & Derrick 1794. 55p. 19cm. [LC]

HENCKELL, K: 1864- . Sel. in C28.

HENGSTENBERG, Ern. W: 1802-68. Sel. in C244.

HENKEL, F:e
§4192. (Die Herrin von Ibichstein.) The mistress of Ibichstein. Tr. Mrs. S. E. Boggs. NY: Holt 1884. 333p. 17cm. [LC]
[Mediocre translation.]
4193. do. 1887. Tr. Ma. J. Safford. NY: Munro. 188p. 19cm. [LC]

HENNES, Goswin Als. 1827-89.
4194. Therese Hennes and her mus. educ. A biog. sketch...by her father...Tr. H. Mannheimer. L: Tinsley 1877. 162p. 19cm. [BM.LC]
[Tr. from MS. Partly autobiog. of the father.]

HENNING, F:
4195. The maid of Orleans. Tr. G: P. Upton. Chic: McClurg 1904. 135p. il. 17cm. [LC]

"HENRION, Poly" (i.e., Kohl v. Kohlenegg, Lp. C: Dittmer)
§4196. (Die schöne Galathee.) The lovely Galatea. Opera by Fz. Suppé. Tr. W. G. Day. Vocal score. Bost: Ditson 1884. 91p. 4.
[Good, but no rhymes and a bit prosy.--LCO ascribes this text to Zell and Genée.] [LCM]
4197. do. 1884. [same] Libr. 11p. 8. [Copyright by Day.] [LCM]

HENSCHKE, Af. 1891- . See "Klabund."

HENSEL, Lu. Ma. 1798-1876. Sel. in C273;287;423;497.

HENSEL, Sb. 1830-98.
*4198. (Die Familie Mendelssohn.) The M-- family. Tr. from 2d rev. ed. by Carl Klingemann and an Amer. collaborator. L; Low 1881. 2v. 8. [8 ports. after W: Hensel.] [BM]
4199. do. 1882. [same] 2d rev. ed. NY: Harper. 2v. il. 22cm. [LC]
4200. do. 1882. [same] 3d ed. L: Low. 2v. [EC]

HENSELT, Ad. 1814-89. See Lenz, W: The great piano virtuosos of our time, #5663a.

HENTZNER, Pl. fl. 1598. Sel. in C483.

HERBERGER, Vlr. 1562-1627. Sel. in C244;271.

"HERBERT, M." (i.e., Frau Te. (Kellner) Keiter, 1859-1925.)
4201. (Flitter.) Tinsel. Tr. anon. 1902. In C481. [See also #4896.]

HERBERT, P. Sel. in C269.

HERBORD, d. 1168.
4202. (Dialogus de vita Ottonis episcopi Babenbergensis.) [Sel.] Tr. C: H. Robinson. In Ebo, "The life of Otto, etc," #1387.

HERBST, J.
4203. Claudius; or, the messenger of Wandsbeck, and his message. (Letters, essays, and fragments from his works.) Biogr. details largely from his life by J. H--. Ed. H. J. C. L: Ward 1859. 157p. 18cm. [BM]
4204. Life of Lavater. See Lavater, J. K., #5620.

HERCHENBACH, W: 1818-89.
4205. After many days. Tr. and ad. Ag. Sadlier. NY: Sadlier 1886. 119p. 16. [LCO]
4206. Angel Hilda. Tr. and ad. Ag. Sadlier. NY: Sadlier 1886. 138p. 16. [LCO]
4207. Armourer of Solingen; and, Wrongfully accused. Tr. anon. L: Simpkin 1889. il. 8. [EC]
4208. do. 1890. [same?] Tr. H. J. Gill. Dublin: Gill & son. 2v. 149; 150p. il. 18cm. [BM]
4209. As good as gold. Tr. Josephine Black. L: Simpkin 1889. 18. [EC]
4210. do. 1890. [same] and, Wilhelm, or Christian forgiveness, tr. from the French by Mrs. J. Sadlier. Dublin: Gill & son. 246p. 16cm. [BM]
4211. Bruno and Lucy; or, the ways of the Lord are wonderful. Rev. by the tr., Rev. W. H. Eyre. NY: Benziger; L: Burns & O. 1898. 301p. 17cm. [BM]
4212. The coiner's cave. Tr. Josephine Black. Dublin: Gill 1887. 226p. 8. [BM] Also L: Simpkin 1887. 12. [EC]
4213. Lucy Harding. Tr. and ad. Ag. Sadlier. NY: Sadlier 1886. 139p. 16. [LCO]
4214. Miralda: a story of Cuba. Ad. Kath. Ma. Johnston. NY; Cincin: Benziger 1915. 155p. 17cm. [LC]
4215. The voyage of the Veronica. Tr. and ad. Ag. Sadlier. NY: Sadlier 1886. 118p. 16. [LCO]

HERDER, J: Gf. v. 1744-1803. Sel. in C5*;12;15;17;31;44;63;67;69; 75;77;118;123;125;129;133;141;172;178;193;194*;296;306;309;316; 366*;372-3;375;380;387-8;391;393;395;399;400;419;438;443;461*; 469;489;497;533;537;543;#2440.
*4216. (Abhandlung über den Ursprung der Sprache.) Treatise upon the origin of language. Tr. anon. L: Longmans et al. 1827. 119p. 23cm. [BM]
*4217. (Blätter der Vorzeit.) Leaves of antiquity. Tr. Mrs. Caro. Sawyer. 3d ed. Bost: Universalist pub. 1893. 177p. 18cm. [LC]
4218. The book of Job considered as a work of art. Tr. A. E. Kroeger. 1874. In C300(4).
*4219. (Denkmal Ulrichs von Hutten.) U: v. H--, a tribute to the memory of. Tr. A. Aufrere, with remarks by the tr. (also) an appendix. L: Dodsley 1789. xvi;135p. 19cm. [BM] [Falsely ascribed to Goethe.]
*4220. (Der Cid.) The Cid. Tr. anon. L: Graves 1828. 127p. 19cm [BM]
4220a. (Fabeln.) Fables. [Sel.] Tr. anon. 1845. In C125.
*4221. (Ideen zur Geschichte der Philosophie der Menschheit.) Outlines of a philos. of the hist. of man. Tr. T. O. Churchill. L: for J. Johnson by Hansard 1800. xvi;632p. 28cm. [BM.LC]
4222. do. 1803. [same] 2d ed. 2v. xxii;518; 619p. Index. 21cm. [BM.LC]
§4223. (Vom Geist der ebräischen Poesie.) Oriental dialogues... conversations...on the...sacred poetry of the Hebrews. Tr. anon.

HERDER, J: Gf. v.
L: Cadell & Davies 1801. 384p. 8. [BM.LCO]
[Tr. of part 1 only.]
*4224. do. 1833. The spirit of Hebrew poetry. Tr. Jas. Marsh. Burlington, Vt: Smith. 2v. in one. 18cm. [LC.BM]

HERDER, J. G., A: Jk. Liebeskind, and F: Ad. Krummacher.
4225. Oriental fairy tales. New issue. NY: Knox 1886. il. D. [AC]

HERKLOTS, K: Ax. 1759-1830. Sel. in C106.

HERLOSSOHN (i.e., Herloss), K: Borromäus Sb. 1804-49. Sel. in C67; 106;309.
§4226. (Wenn die Schwalben heimwärts ziehn.) When the swallows homeward fly. Anon. tr. of the poem, with il. by Js. Lauber. NY; L: White & Allen 1888. (18)p. [Poor translation.] [LC]

"HERMANN, G:" (i.e., G: Hm. Borchardt, 1871- .)
4227. (Jettchen Gebert.) Hetty Geybert. Tr. Anna Barwell. NY: Doran 1924. 383p. 19cm. [LC]

HERMANN, J: Gf. 1707-91. Sel. in C244;271;276;486;570.

HERMANN, N: 1480?-1561. Sel. in C95;231;276;#8904.

HERMANN, N: 1611-91.
4227a. Practice of the presence of God; conversations, letters and spir. maxims of Bro. Lawrence of the Resurrection, barefooted Carmelite. Tr. Donald Attwater. Benziger 1926.xii;64p. D. [AC]

HERMANN-NEISSE, Max. Sel. in C95.

HERPORT, Rev. ---, of Berne.
4228. (Versuch über wichtige Wahrheiten, zur Glückseligkeit der Menschen.) An essay on truths of importance to the happiness of mankind. L: Baker 1768? See Crit. R. 25(1768):433. (B26)

HERRAND v. WILDONJE, fl. 1248-78. Sel. in C27;416;427.

HERRIG, Hs. 1845-1892.
4229. (Martin Luther. Festspiel.) Luther: an il. poem. Tr. Jean W. Wylie. For the author. Phil: Lutheran pub. 1890. 119p. 19cm. [LC]

HERRMANN, W: 1846-1922.
4229a. Communion of the Christian with God, descr. on the basis of Luther's statements. Tr. by J. S. Stanyon. L: Williams & Norgate 1895. 8. [EC]
4229b. do. 1906. [same] Rev. enl. and alt. in acc. with 4th ed. of 1903 by R. W. Stewart. NY;L: Putnam. xvii;356p. D. [AC]
4229c. Faith and morals. Tr. by D. Matheson and R. W. Stewart. Putnam 1904. [AC]

HERRNSCHMIDT, J: Dn. 1675-1723. Sel. in C240;269.
4230. (Beschreibung des Lebens Dr. Martin Luthers.) Life of M-- L--. Tr. anon. 1778. In "Arminian Mag." 1(1778): 68, etc. (B26)

HERTEL, Br. Sel. in C112.

HERTZ, W: 1835-1902. Sel. in C67;112;497.
*4231. (Lanzelot und Ginevra.) The story of queen Guinevere and Sir Lancelot of the lake. (pp. 1-166.) With other poems. Tr. C: Bruce. L: Longmans 1865. 19cm. [BM]
[No feminine rhyme; otherwise very good.]

HERTZBERG, Gst. F: 1826-1907.
4232. Ancient Greece. Tr. C: F. Smith. 1902. In C200(3).
§4233. Imperial Rome. Tr. J: King Lord. 1902. In C200(5).
[Anything but a strict translation.]
4234. Republican Rome. Tr. J: K. Lord. 1902. In C200(4).

HERTZKA, Td. 1845- .
*4235. (Freiland. Ein soziales Zukunftsbild.) Freeland: a social anticipation. Tr. Art. Ransome. L: Chatto & Windus; NY: Appleton 1891. xxiv;443p. 19cm. [From the orig. unabr. ed., with emendations from later eds. Excellent tr.] [BM.LC]

HERWEGH, G: 1817-75. Sel. in C3;17;41;43;89;111-2;149;196;213;301*; 309;317*;366;372-3;393;450;469;501.

HERZBERG, W:
4236. Jewish family papers; or, letters of a missionary. Tr. F: de Sola Mendes. NY: Amer. Jewish pub. 1875. 260p. 12. [LCO]

HERZOG, J: F: 1647-99. Sel. in C233.

HERZOG, Rd. 1869- .
4237. (Das Lebenslied.) The story of Helga. Tr. Mrs. Adèle Lewisohn. NY: Dutton 1913. 310p. 19cm. [LC]
4238. (Der Abenteurer.) The adventurer. Tr. J: W: van Eyndhoven. NY: Fitzgerald 1912. 378p. il. 19cm. [LC]
4239. (Der Lorbeerkranz.) The laurel wreath. Tr. E. S. Hole. L: Holerth press 1922. 36p. 18. [Ger. and Engl?] [EC]
4240. (Die Wiskottens.) Sons of the Rhine. Tr. Louise T. Lazell. NY: Fitzgerald 1914. 372p. 19cm. [LC]

HESEKIEL, J: G: L: 1819-74.
**4241. (Bismarck.) The life of B--, private and polit., with descr. notice of his ancestry. Tr. K. R. H. Mackenzie. L: Jas. Hogg 1870. xxvii;500p. il. 23cm. [BM]
[Introd., explan. notes, and append. by tr. Nearly 100 il. A poem is appended, well tr.]
4242. do. 1877. [same] Bismarck: his authentic biog. Tr. K. R. H. Mackenzie. Il. by disting. Ger. artists. NY: Ford. 596p. 23cm. [LC]
4243. do. 1877. [same] NY: Amer. book co. xxviii;641p. 23cm. [BM]
[Many...letters and...memoranda. Gen. introd. by Bayard Taylor. 120 il.]
§4244. (Zwei Königinnen und ein Simolin.) Two queens, Caro. Mde. of Denmark and Me. Antoinette of France: a hist. novel from the memoirs of Baron Simolin, with a pref. by F. Max Mueller. Tr. anon. L: Sonnenschein; NY: Macmillan 1896. 160p. 17 x 8cm. [BM]
[Needless liberties taken.]

HESS, D: 1770-1843.
4245. (Die Rose von Jericho.) The rose of J--. (Tr. from French imitation of Ger. by J. P. I. de Bottens, Baroness de Montolieu; ed. by Hon. Mrs. Norton.) L: Tinsley 1870. viii;162p. 18cm. [BM]

HESS, J. L. v.
§4246. (Ueber den Wert...der Freiheit der Hanse-Städte.) Value...of the freedom of the Hanse towns. Tr. (or rather rewritten) by B. Crusen. L: Longmans 1814. 159p. 21cm. [BM]

HESSE, Hm. 1877- . Sel. in C154(18); 423.
4247. (Blick ins Chaos.) In sight of chaos. Tr. St. Hudson. Zürich: Seldwyla; L: Zwemmer 1923. 64p. 18cm. [BM]
[The brothers Karamazoff; Thoughts on Dostoevsky's "Idiot."]
*4248. (Demian.) Demian. Tr. N. H. Priday. NY: Boni & L. 1923. 215p. 19cm. [Very good tr. One error noted.] [LC]
§4249. (Gertrud.) Gertrude and I. Tr. Adèle Lewisohn. NY: Internat. monthly 1915. 207p. 19cm. [Fair tr.; takes her task lightly.] [LC]
4250. (In der alten Sonne.) In the old "Sun." Tr. A. I. Coleman. 1913-15. In C154(19).

HESSE-WARTEGG, Ern. v. 1851-1918.
*4251. (Tunis. Land und Leute.) Tunis: the land and the people. Tr. anon. L: Chatto & Windus; NY: Dodd, Mead 1882. x;292p. il. 22cm. [BM]

HETTNER, Hm. Jl. Td. 1821-82.
*4252. (Griechische Reiseskizzen.) Athens and the Peloponnese, with sketches of northern Greece. Tr. anon. Ed: Constable; L: Hamilton, Adams 1854. 229p. 18cm. [BM]

HEUN, K: Gb. S: 1771-1854. See "Clauren, H:"

HEUSLER, Frau Dora, ed. See Niebuhr, B. G., "Life and Letters." #6732.

HEUSSER-SCHWEIZER, Meta, 1797-1876. Sel. in C229;273;375 (says "she is considered the most gifted poetess in the German language"); 486;489.
§4253. Alpine lyrics: a sel. from the poems. Tr. H. L. L. (i.e., Jane Borthwick, tr. of Hymns from the Land of Luther.) L;NY: Nelson 1875. xiv;101p. 15cm. [BM]
[AC has: NY. Randolph 1875. sq. 18. -- 33 poems of religious character.]

HEY, W: 1789-1854. Sel. in C169;229;287;423.
§4254. (Hundert Fabeln für Kinder.) The child's picture and verse book; commonly called Otto Speckter's fable book. Tr. Ma. Howitt. L: Longmans 1844. 201p. il. 18cm. [LC]
[Tr. is fair to good. Pictures by O: Speckter; see the following.]
*4255. do. 1858. Picture fables, drawn by O: Speckter, engr. by the bros. Dalziel. Rhymes tr...H: W: Dulcken. L: Routledge. 101p. 19cm. [BM]
4256. do. 1863. [same] New ed. L;NY: Routledge. viii;101p. il. 20cm. [LC]
*4257. do. 1867. Fifty fables for children, with il. by O: Speckter. Tr. So. Klingemann. Gotha: Perthes. unp. 24cm. [BM]
[Not as good as Dulcken. Has "a serious appendix": Moral verses for memorization by Rud. Löwenstein et al., with advice to parents; 40p.]
4258. do. 1868. [same as #4255] One hundred picture fables. L: Routledge. unp. 18cm. [BM]
[Il. same as above, not so good looking. Different arrangement.]
4259. do. 1869. Other fifty fables for children. Tr. So. Klingemann. Gotha: Perthes. unp. 24cm. [BM]
[No il. in this copy. Appendix of 45p.]

HEYDEN, F: A: v. 1789-1851. Sel. in C391;393.

HEYDENREICH, K: H: 1764-1801.
4260. Anecdotes of literary persons. Tr. anon. 1800? In C157(2).

HEYKING, Eli. (A:e Lu; Hle. Mlse. Mxe.(Fleming) Gans) Baronin v. 1861-1925.
§4261. (Briefe, die ihn nicht erreichten.) The letters which never reached him. Tr. anon. NY: Dutton; L: Nash 1904. 302p. 20cm. [LC.BM]
[Suspect the tr. is by the author: the Ger. and Engl. do not exactly tally, and there is a significant addition at the end of the tr.]
4262. (Ille mihi.) Lovers in exile. L: Nash 1914. 19cm. [BM.LC]
[Ad. by author and tr. by E. Andrews.]

HEYM, G: 1887-1912. Sel. in C95.

HEYMEL, Af. Wl. v. 1878-1914. Sel. in C423.

HEYNE, Cn. Glb. 1729-1812. Sel. in C33.

HEYNE, Cn. Lbt. 1751-1821. Sel. in C56;158.

HEYNICKE, Kurt, 1891- . Sel. in C95.

HEYSE, Pl. (J: L:) 1830-1914. Sel. in C116;138;180;311;366*;450; 469;501;506.

COLLECTIONS

§4263. 1857. Four phases of love. Tr. by E. H. Kingsley. L;NY: Routledge. 189p. 16cm. [BM]
[Fair; errors and ineptitudes. -- Eye-blindness and soul-blindness ("Die Blinden"); Marion (do.); La Rabbiata ("L'Arrabbiata"); "By the banks of the Tiber" ("Am Tiberufer").
§4264. 1862. [same.] Love tales. L;NY: Routledge. [BM]
[T.p. has: G. H. Kingsley.]
4265. 1867. L'Arrabbiata and other tales. Tr. Ma. Wilson. Lpz: Tauchnitz; L: Low. 274p. 16cm. [BM.LC]
[L'Arrabiata (sic); Count Ernest's home ("Im Grafenschloss"); §Blind ("Die Blinden"); §Walter's little mother ("Die kleine Mama"). -- Cf. also the following.]
§4266. 1870. The dead lake, and other stories. Tr. Ma. Wilson. Lpz: Tauchnitz; L: Low. 312p. 16cm. [BM.LC]
[She doesn't understand, or "edits." --A fortnight at the dead lake ("Am toten See"); Doomed ("Unheilbar"); Beatrice (do.); §Beginning and end ("Anfang und Ende").
*4267. 1874. Barbarossa and other tales. Tr. L(evi) C. S(heip?). Lpz: Tauchnitz; L: Low. 302p. 16cm. [BM.LC]
[From "In der Geisterstunde." The embroideress of Treviso ("Die Stickerin v. T--"); Lottka (do.); The lost son ("Der verlorene Sohn"); The fair Kate ("Das schöne Kätchen"); Geoffroy and Garcinde (do.).]
4268. 1879. Tales. Tr. anon. NY: Appleton. 281p. 18cm. [LC]
[Count Ernest's home; The dead lake; The fury ("L'Arrabbiata"); Judith Stern (do.). The first two probably by Ma. Wilson, cf. #4265-6.
4269. 1881. Fortnight at the dead lake; also, Beatrice. Tr. anon. NY: Munro. Seaside lib. 32cm. [Cf. #4266.] [AC]
4270. 1882. [same as #4267] NY: Munro. Seaside lib. 32cm. [AC]
4271. 1882. [same as #4265] NY: Munro. Seaside lib. 23p. 32cm. [LC]
4272. 1886. Selected stories. Tr. anon. Chic: Schick. 64p. 19cm [LC]
[*L'Arrabbiata (do.); Beppe, the star-gazer ("Beppo, der Sternseher"); Maria Francisca (do.).]
4273. 1887. La Marchesa, a story of the Riviera, and other tales. Tr. J: Philips. L: Stock 1887. 200p. 19cm. [BM]
[Title ("Die Frau Marchesa"); Her excellency's daughter ("Die Tochter der Excellenz"); *A divided heart ("Geteiltes Herz").]
†4274. 1888. Words never to be forgotten (Unvergessbare Worte) and, The donkey (Die Eselin). Tr. Abbie E. Fordyce. Union Springs, NY: Hoff. 139p. 17cm. [LC]
§4275. 1894. A divided heart ("Geteiltes Herz") and (2) other stories. Tr. Constance S. Copeland. NY: Brentano. 240p. 16cm. [LC]
[Rothenburg on the Tauber ("Das Glück von Rothenburg"); Minka (do.).]
4276. 1903. Tales from...P. Heyse. Tr. anon. Ormeril. (B13)
4277. 1906. Tales from...P. Heyse. Tr. anon. NY: Burt. 12. [AC]

§4278. (Andrea Delfin.) A-- D--. Tr. anon. Bost. Burnham 1864. 100p. 17cm. [Tr. by a German who is unequal to the struggle.] [BM]
†4279. (Anfang und Ende.) Beginning and end. In "The four MacNicols" by W: Black. NY: Munro 1882. Seaside lib. 21p. 32cm. [Incredibly bad.] [LC]
4280. (Beppo, der Sternseher.) Beppe, the star-gazer. Tr. anon. 1890. In C404.
§4281. (Das Haus zum ungläubigen Thomas.) The house of the unbelieving T: Tr. Fes. A. van Santford. Il. Alice C. Morse. NY: Dodd,

HEYSE, Pl.
Mead 1894. 96p. 14cm. [LC]
[General title: At the ghost hour ("In der Geisterstunde").]
4281a. (Das Glück von Rothenburg.) Rothenburg felicity. Tr. Mrs. A. L. Wister. "Lippincott's Mag." 39(1886):307. (B15a)
4282. do. 1913-15. The spell of R--. Tr. E. L. Townsend. In C154 (13).
4283. (Das Mädchen von Treppi.) The maiden of T--; or, love's victory. Tr. A. W. Hinton. NY: Hinton 1874. 16. [BPL]
†4284. do. 1907. The young girl of T--. Tr. anon. In C447.
4285. do. 1915. [same? same title] In C179.
*4286. (Das schöne Kätchen.) Fair Kate. NY: Munro 1882. Seaside lib. 20p. 32cm. [Very good -- With Björnson's "Railroad and churchyard."]
§4287. (Das Waldlachen.) The forest laugh. Tr. Fes. A. van Santford. Il. Alice C. Morse. NY: Dodd, Mead 1894. 60p. 14cm. [LC]
[Gen. title: At the ghost hour ("In der Geisterstunde").]
*4288. (Der Roman der Stiftsdame.) The romance of the canoness: a life-history. Tr. "J. M. Percival." NY: Appleton 1887. 265p. 18cm. [LC]
4289. do. 1888. [same] [BM]
§4290. (Die Blinden.) Blind. Tr. Ma. Wilson. 1913-15. In C154(13). [Wooden dialog.]
*4291. (Die Einsamen.) The solitaries. Tr. anon. Phil: Claxton, R. & H. 1870. 54p. 19cm. [LC]
*4292. do. 1870. [same?] The lonely ones (The solitaries). In Marlitt, E., "Magdalena." #6073.
*4293. (Die Hexe vom Corso.) The witch of the C--. Tr. G: W. Ingraham. NY: Munro 1882. Seaside lib. 18p. 32cm. [LC]
[Seems to be very good tr.]
4294. (Die Reise nach dem Glück.) The road to fortune. Tr. anon. Laird. (B13)
§4295. (Die schöne Abigail.) The fair A--. Tr. Fes. A. van Santford. Il. Alice C. Morse. NY: Dodd, Mead 1894. 72p. 14cm. [At the ghost hour ("In der Geisterstunde").] [LC]
4297. (Hans Lange.) H-- L--: a drama. Ed. A. A. Macdonell. Symons 1885. 12. [Possibly only a school ed?] [EC]
4298. The huntsman. Tr. Zimmern. 1880. In C575-7.
*4299. (Im Grafenschloss.) Count Ernest's home. Tr. anon. 1868. In C130.
4300. do. 1879. [same] In C168.
*4301. (Im Paradiese.) In paradise. Tr. anon. NY: Appleton 1878. 2v. 18cm. [LC]
*4302. (Kinder der Welt.) Children of the world. Tr. anon. L: Chapman & H. 1882. 3v. 19cm. [Tr. author. by Heyse.] [BM.LC]
*4303. do. 1883. Tr. anon. NY: Munro. Seaside lib. 2 pts. 32cm. [LC]
[On the whole, excellent.]
4304. do. 1890. Tr. anon. NY: Worthington. [AC]
4305. do. 1894. Tr. anon. New rev. ed. NY: Holt. 573p. 19cm. [LC]
4306. do. 19--. [same?] NY: Holt. [AC]
4307. (L'Arrabbiata.) La Rabbiata, Tr. anon. "Chambers's Journal" 24(1855):295. Also in "Littell's Liv. Age" 44:13. (B15a)
[No mention of Heyse. Cf. #4263.]
*4308. do. 1890. L'A--. Tr. anon. In C404. [Same tr. as #4272.]
†4308a. do. 1898. The fury. Tr. anon. In C509. [Repr. from #4268.]
4309. do. 1902. L'A--. Tr. W. W. Florer. Ann Arbor, Mich: Wahr. S. [AC]
4309a. do. 1908. L'A--. Tr. anon. Introd. by Hamilton W. Mabie. Repr. from Little Masterpieces of fiction. NY: Doubleday, Page. See "Outlook" 78:457.
*4310. do. 1913-15. L'A--. Tr. Ma. Wilson. In C154(13).
[Doubtless revised by the editors; cf. my judgment on #4265.]

HEYSE, Pl. - L'Arrabbiata
*4311. do. 1916. L'A--. Tr. Vivian E. Lyon. NY: Trans. pub. 39p. 15cm. [LC]
4312. do. 1926. The fury. Tr. anon. In C68.
4313. (Maria Franziska.) Maria Francisca. Tr. anon. 1890. In C404.
4314. (Maria von Magdala.) Mary of Magdala: a drama in five acts. Tr. A. I. Coleman. NY: Lederer 1900. 22p. 8. [LC]
4315. do. 1902. an histor. and romant. drama in five acts. Ad. Lionel Vale. NY: Fiske. 69p. 21cm. [LC]
4316. do. 1903. Tr. F. Hess. Tw. [LC]
4317. do. 1903. The tr. freely ad. and written in Engl. verse by W: Winter. NY;L: Macmillan. 135p. 20cm. [LC]
§4318. (Mittagszäuber.) Mid-day magic. Also, Little Lisbeth ('s Lisabethle). Tr. Fes. A. van Santford. Il. Alice C. Morse. NY: Dodd, Mead 1894. 84p. 14cm. [At the ghost hour.] [LC]
4318a. My Italian adventure. Tr. anon. "Appleton's Journal" 6(1871): 506, etc. (B?5a)
*4318b. (Nino und Maso.) N-- and M--. Tr. A. Remy. 1913-15. In C154(13).
4319. (Unheilbar.) Doomed. Tr. anon. NY: Munro 1881. Seaside lib. 32cm. [Good but undistinguished; little inaccuracies.] [LC]
§4320. do. 1890. Incurable. Tr. Mrs. H. W. Eve. L: Nutt 1890. 224p. 8. [Not bad, but certainly not very good.] [BM]
*4321. (Zwei Gefangene.) Two prisoners. Tr. anon. L: Simpkin, M. 1893. 128p. 19cm. [BM]

HIELSCHER, Kurt, 1881- .
4321a. Picturesque Germany, architecture and landscape. Pref. note by G. Hauptmann. Brentano's; Unwin 1924. xiip. il. Q. [AC]

HIEMER, Fz. K: 1768-1822. Sel. in C99.

HILDBOLD VON SCHWANGAU, 12th-13th cent. Sel. in C27;416;427.

HILDEBRAND, Ad. v. 1847-1921.
*4322. (Das Problem der Form in der bildenden Kunst.) The problem of form in painting and sculpture. Tr. Max F. Meyer and Rb. M. Ogden. NY: Stechert 1907. 141p. il. 20cm. [LC.BM] [Rather rewritten than tr.; additions, il., and comment. BM has title: Form in painting.]

HILDEBRAND, C.
4323. Winter in Spitzbergen. A book for youth. Tr. E. G. Smith. NY: Dodd 1852. 300p. il. 17cm. [LCO.BM]
4324. do. 1866. [same] L: Houlston. 12. [EC]
4325. do. 1871. [same] NY: Dodd, Mead. [LCO]

HILLE, P: 1854-1904. Sel. in C28.

HILLEBRAND, K: 1829-84.
4326. Six lect. on the hist. of Ger. thought, from the 7 yrs' war to Goethe's death. L: Longmans 1880. viii;290p. 19cm. [BM] NY: Holt 1880. [BM says: Hist of Ger. thought.] [AC]

HILLER, Fd. 1811-85.
*4327. (F. Mendelssohn-Bartholdy. Briefe und Erinnerungen.) M--. Letters and recoll. Tr. Miss M. E. v. Glehn. L: Macmillan 1874. 223p. 21cm. [BM.LC]
4329. On the hundredth anniversary of (Beethoven's) birth. In Elliot Graeme's "Beethoven." L: Griffin 1877. 184p. 18cm. [BM.LC]

HILLER, Ph. F: 1699-1769. Sel. in C234;244;276;570;#8904.

HILLERN, Hne. v. See Diemer, Hne.

HILLERN, Frau W:e (Birch) v. 1836-1916.
§4330. (Am Kreuz.) On the cross: romance of the passion play at Oberammergau. Tr. Ma. J. Safford. NY: Peck 1893. 442p. 19cm. [LC] [Careless errors.]
4331. do. 1902. [same] By W. v. Hillern and Ma. J. Safford (!) Phil: Biddle. il. [LC]
*4332. (Aus eigner Kraft.) By his own might. Tr. M. S. Phil: Lippincott 1872. 397p. 18cm. [LC]
§4333. (Die Geier-Wally.) Geier-Wally: a tale of the Tyrol. Tr. anon. NY: Appleton 1876. 237p. 16cm. [LC]
4334. do. 1876. [same] 78p. 23cm. [LC]
§4335. do. 1876. The vulture maiden. Tr. Ca. Bell and Eleanor F. Poynter. Lpz: Tauchnitz. 279p. 16cm. [BM.LC]
*4336. do. 1876. A Ger. peasant romance. Elsa and her vulture: a tale of the Tyrolean Alps. Tr. Lady Wallace. L: Longmans. viii; 272p. 19cm. [BM]
4337. do. 1879. [same as #4333] 237p. [LC]
4338. do. 1882. [Ad.] Eagle Elsa: a romantic drama in four acts. Tr. and ad. Fred Lyster and L. E. Stowell. (B38)
4339. (Doppelleben.) A twofold life. Tr. M. S. Phil: Lippincott 1873. 343p. 18cm. [LC]
4340. (Ein Arzt der Seele.) Only a girl; or, a physician for the soul. Tr. Mrs. A. L. Wister. Phil;L: Lippincott 1867. 12. [EC]
*4341. do. 1872. [same] Lippincott. 544p. 19cm. [LC]
4342. do. 1879. Ernestine. Tr. anon. L: De la Rue. 2v. 19cm. [BM] [Probably tr. by S. Baring-Gould; see the following.]
§4343. do. 1881. Ernestine. Tr. S. Baring-Gould. NY: Gottsberger. 2v. 16cm. [Vol. 1 missing in BM] [LC.BM]
4344. do. 1898. [same as #4341.]
4345. (Friedhofsblume.) A graveyard flower. Tr. Ca. Bell. Rev. and corr. NY: Gottsberger 1884. 160p. 16cm. [LC]
§4346. (Höher als die Kirche.) Higher than the church: an art legend of ancient times. Tr. Ma. J. Safford. NY: Gottsberger 1881. 74p. 16cm. [LC]
§4347. do. 1884. a tale of the olden time. Ad. M. F. P. F-G. L: Trübner. 63p. 16cm. [Errors.] [BM]
4348. do. 1916. Tr. V. E. Lyon. NY: Translation pub. 57p. 15cm. [LC]
*4349. (Und sie kommt doch!) The hour will come: a tale of an Alpine cloister. Tr. Ca. Bell. Lpz: Tauchnitz 1879. 2v. 16cm. [BM]
4350. do. 1880. [same] NY: Gottsberger. 273p. 16cm. [LC]
4351. do. 1880. [same] NY: Munro. Seaside lib. 32cm. [AC]
4352. do. 1887. [same] Lpz: Tauchnitz. 2v. [LC]

HILTY, K: 1833-1909.
4353. (Glück.) Happiness: (7) essays on the meaning of life. Tr. Fis. G. Peabody. NY;L: Macmillan 1903. x;154p. 19cm. [LC.BM] ["I have found it necessary to use much freedom...with his... style...to reproduce the tone and temper of the author."]
4354. do. 1907. The steps of life: further essays on happiness. Tr. M. Brandow. NY;L: Macmillan. ix;264p. 19cm. [LC.BM]

HINDENBURG, Pl. v. Beneckendorff u. v. 1847- .
*4355 (Aus meinem Leben.) Out of my life. Tr. F: A. Holt. NY;L: Cassell 1920. xii;458p. 24cm. [LC]
See Harden, Mx. I meet my contemporaries. #3702.

HINKEL, E. fl. 1815. Sel. in C106;215.

HINTZE, O: 1861- . Sel. in C563.

HINZE, A. P. F. Sel. in C157.

HIPPEL, Td. Gb. v. 1741-96. Sel. in C461.

HIRSCH, Fz.
4356. (Aennchen von Tharau.) Annie of T--: a song of olden times. Tr. C. Ad. Rehder. L: Siegle 1890. viii;151p. 18cm. [BM]
[In the meter of "Hiawatha."]

HIRSCHER, J: Bp. v. 1788-1865.
4357. Sympathies of the continent; or, proposals for a new reformation. Tr. and ed. w. notes and introd. (to p. 71) by Rev. A. C. Coxe. Oxford: J: H. Parker 1852. 230p. 17cm. [BM]

HIRSCHFELD, G: 1873- .
4358. (Die Mütter.) The mothers. (A drama.) Tr. L. Lewisohn. Garden City, NY: Doubleday 1916. 122p. 18cm. [LC]

HIRZEL, Hs. Kp. 1725-1803.
4359. The rural Socrates: being memoirs of a country philosopher. In Young, Arthur, "Rural oeconomy." L: 1770. 520p. 8. [BM]
[Sep. t.p. The rural S--, etc. 2d ed. 1764, with addenda. pp. 377-520. Tr. from the French.]
4360. do. 1776. The rural S--; or, a description of the oeconomical and moral conduct of a country philos. 2d ed. Tr. from the French. In Young's "Rural oeconomy." Phil: Re-prtd. and sold by J. Humphreys, junr. 8. pp. 155-345. [NY]
4361. do. 1792. [same] 3d ed. Burlington, NJ: Prtd. by I: Neale. 299p. 8. (B6a) [Available; AAS. BA. Ascribed to Jean Gaspard Hirzel.]
4362. do. 1800. The rural S--; or, an account of a celebrated philos. farmer, known by the name of Kliyogg, lately living in Switzerland. Hallowell (district of Maine), prtd. by P: Edes. 203p. 21cm. [LC.BM]
[About 82pp. derive from "Die Wirtschaft eines philosophischen Bauers." The rest is from other writings of H--, plus one orig. article. Part of the tr. is taken from Young's version of the French. This tr. follows Young so closely as to suggest that it served as a source.]

HOECKER, G:
4363. (Der Lebende hat recht.) The tell-tale watch. Tr. Meta De Vere. Il. by Jas. Fagan. NY: Bonner 1893. 284p. 19cm. [LC]

HOECKER, Gst. 1832-1911.
4364. Arnold of Winkelried, the hero of Sempach. Tr. G: P. Upton. Chic: McClurg 1908. 139p. 17cm. [LC]
4365. Js. Haydn: a study of his life and time for youth. Tr. G: P. Upton. Chic: McClurg 1907. 158p. 17cm. [LC]

HOECKER, Pl. Ok. 1865- .
4366. (Die Wappenhänse.) Dr. Armyon's wife: a play in four acts (and in prose). Ad. C: A. Mitchell. L: Internat. copyright bureau 1905. 135p. 15cm. [BM.LC]
["This is an attempt to convey the spirit...rather than...an exact verbal tr...I have thought it best, with the consent of the author, to transfer the scene to England...The name...obtained by fusion of...arms and John.]
4367. do. 1906. The doctor's wife: a play in four acts. Tr. and ad. anon. NY: Selwyn. Tw. [LC]

HOEFEL (HOFEL), J: 1600-83. Sel. in C229;486.

HOEFER, Ed. 1819-82. Sel. in C67;112.
4368. (?Das alte Fräulein.) The old countess: a novel. By the tr. of "Over yonder," "Magdalena" etc. Phil: Lippincott 1870. 205p. 12. [LCO]

HOELDERLIN, (J: Cn.) F: 1770-1843. Sel. in C5;17;38;88;151;309;366;452;461;501.
4369. (Hyperion.) Hyperion: a novel. Sel. Tr. C. F. Schreiber. 1927. In C452.
†4370. Short poems by F: H--. Tr. Pierre Loving. Girard, Kan: Haldeman-Julius 1925. 64p. 13cm. [LC]
[Re-creations in modern and very free verse, but loosely connected with the orig.]

HOELTY, L: H: Cph. 1748-76. Sel. in C17;22;25-6;44-6;50;55;88;92-3;97;106;129;133;137a;219;309;366;373;380;387;389;391;393;410-1;461;469;538.

HOENSBROECH, Pl. Kajus, Graf v. 1852- .
*4371. (14 Jahre Jesuit.) Fourteen years a Jesuit: a record of personal experience and a criticism. Tr. Alice Zimmern. L;NY: Cassell 1911. 2v. xvii;427; 495p. 23cm. [BM.LC]
[Some omissions recorded in pref.]

HOEPPL, Cn. 1826-62. Sel. in C571.

HOERMANN, Alto S.
4372. (Aners Rückkehr.) Anêr's return; or, the migrations of a soul. An allegorical tale. Tr. I. A. Bergrath. NY: O'Shea 1867. x;294p. 19cm. [LC.BM]
4373. do. 1876. [same] [AC]

HOERNLE, E. Sel. in C425.

HOFBAUER, Kl. Ma. 1751-1820. See Haringer, M., Life of the venerable, etc. #3710. See Hofer, J:s., St. Clement M. H--, #4374.

HOFER, And. 1767-1810. See Hormayr, Js., Memoirs of ---. #4579. See Mühlbach, L., A-- H-- , #6386.

HOFER, J:s 1879- .
4374. (Der heilige Kl. M. Hofbauer in seiner Spätzeit...) St. Clement Ma. H--: a biography. Tr. from 3d Ger. ed. by J: B. Haas. NY;Cincin: Pustet 1926. xxviii;551p. 21cm. [LC]

HOFF, Hinrich Ewd.
4375. The duchy of Schleswig, its place in hist. and politics. Tr. Art. Koelbing. Kiel: Lipsius & Tischer 1919. 29p. 19cm. [BM]

HOFFMANN (VON FALLERSLEBEN), A: H: 1798-1874. Sel. in C1;17;52;89;105-6;111;122;178;213;301;303;309;317;372-3;378;380;395;423;448;460;467;469.

HOFFMANN, Ern. Td. Amds. (really W:) 1776-1822. Sel. in C193;194*;366*;469;513.

COLLECTIONS

†4376. 1855. H--'s strange stories. Tr. anon. Bost: Burnham. 444p. 19cm. [LC]
[The walled-up door; Antonia's song; Berthold, the madman; Coppelius, the sandman ("Der Sandmann"); The cooper of Nuremberg ("Meister Martin der Küfner und seine Gesellen"); Cardillac, the jeweler ("Das Fräulein von Scuderi"); The pharo bank ("Spielerglück); Fascination; The agate heart ("Das steinerne Herz"); The mystery of the deserted house ("Das öde Haus"); The lost reflection; Salvator Rosa.]
4377. 1857. Fairy tales. Tr. anon. Bost: Burnham. 274p. [LCO]
[Tr. from the French version by Lafayette Burnham, who says: "The French possesses in a greater degree the ease necessary for amusing narratives, and corrects the terseness of the harsher Teutonic."]

HOFFMANN, E. T. A.--Collections
4378. 1884. Weird tales. L: Nimmo. 2v. 8. [EC]
[Tr. by Bealby? Cf. #4381.]
4379. 1884. [same?] Fantastic tales. Il. by Lalauze. NY: Worthington. 2v. 8. [AC]
4380. 1884. [same?] Fantastic tales. NY: Scribner & W. 2v. [AC]
[Possibly publisher's advance announcement of the following.]
§4381. 1885. Weird tales. New tr. by J. T. Bealby. L: Nimmo; NY: Scribner. 2v. lxxii;332; 399p. 19cm. [BM.LC]
[The Cremona violin ("Rat Krespel"); The fermata ("Die Fermate"); Signor Formica (do.); The sand-man ("Der Sandmann"); The entail ("Das Majorat"); Arthur's hall ("Der Artushof"); The Doge and Dogess ("Doge und Dogaressa"); Master Martin the cooper; Mlle. de Scuderi; Gambler's luck ("Spielerglück"); Master Johannes Wacht ("Meister J-- W--").]
4382. 1896. [same] NY. Scribner. 2v. 359; 401p. front. (port.) 19cm. [UW]
[Same contents as foregoing. Biogr. notes, vol. 2, pp. 345-401.]
4383. 1908. Stories by H--. Tr. anon. L;Ed: Jack. xx;151p. 17cm.[BM]
[The Cremona violin; Mlle. de Scudéry (ed. from Gillies' tr. C164).]
4384. 1923. Reissue of #4381 or 4382. NY: Scribner. 2v. in one. 344p. [LC]

4385. (Das Gelübde.) The vow. Tr. F: E. Pierce. 1927. In C452.
4386. (Das Majorat.) Rolandsitten; or, the deed of entail. Tr. R. P. Gillies. 1826. In C164.
4387. do. 1829. The entail. Tr. P: Will. In "The Engl. fireside upon the banks of the Rhine." An almanack for the year 1829. Heidelberg: Engelmann. 324p. il. 14cm. [LC]
§4388. (Das Fräulein von Scuderi.) Mme [sic] de Scuderi. Tr. R: Holcraft. 1826. In C203.
§4389. do. 1826. Mlle. de S--. Tr. R. P. Gillies. In C164.
§4390. do. 1908...Scudéry. Tr. Ma. Dickins. L: Gowans & G. 91p. 15cm. [Not very good.] [BM]
4391. do. 1912. The goldsmith of the rue Nicaise. Tr. C. J. T. In C518.
*4392. (Das fremde Kind.) The strange child: a fairy tale. Tr. anon. L: Rivington 1852. 77p. 14cm. [BM]
4393. (Der Elementargeist.) The elementary spirit. Tr. J: Oxenford. 1844. In C442.
4394. do. 1895. [same?] In C559.
4395. (Der goldene Topf.) The golden pot. Tr. T: Carlyle. 1827. In C58, cf. C59-60.
4396. do. 1846. [same] In C114.
4396a. The Datura Fastuosa: a botanical tale. Tr. anon. In "Dublin univ. mag." 13(1839):707. (B27)
4397. do. 1849. Tr. F: H: Hedge. In C194.
4398. do. 1913-15. Tr. Hedge. In C154(5).
4399. (Der Sandmann.) The sandman. Tr. J: Oxenford. 1844. In C441-2.
†4400. (Die Elixiere des Teufels.) The devil's elixir. Tr. anon. Ed: Blackwood 1824. 2v. 18cm. [BM.LC]
4401. do. 1826. The devil's elixer [sic]. Tr. R. P. Gillies. In C502.
4402. do. n.d. [ad.] The devil's elixir; or, the shadowless man. A mus. romance in two acts by E: Fitzball. L: Cumberland. 36p. 15cm. [Founded on H--'s story.] [LCM]
4403. (Die Jesuiterkirche in G--.) The Jesuits' church in G--. Tr. J: Oxenford. 1844. In C442.
*4404. (Die Serapionsbrüder.) Serapion brethren. Tr. Maj. Ax. Ewing. L: Bell 1886-92. 2v. 19cm. [BM.LC]

HOFFMANN, E. T. A.

4405. do. 1902. [same] Macmillan. [LC]

4406. do. 1908. [same] L: Bell. Bohn's lib. [BM]

4407. do. 1926. The story of Serapion. Tr. Ax. Ewing. In C68. [Probably from #4404, which so designates the introd. to the "Serapionsbrüder."]

*4408. (Meister Floh.) Master flea. Tr. G: Soane. 1826. In C498.

§4409. (Meister Martin der Küfner und seine Gesellen.) Master Martin and his workmen. Tr. anon. 1847. In C20.

4410. do. 1856. Master Martin...workman [sic]. Tr. anon. In C454.

4411. do. 1868. [same as #4409] In C21.

*4412. (Nussknacker und Mäusekönig.) Nut-cracker and mouse-king. Tr. Mrs. St. Simon. NY: Appleton 1853. 138p. il. 16cm. [LC.BM] [BM ascribes it to H: Hoffmann.]

*4413. do. 1892. Nutcracker and mouse king, and, The educated cat (Lebensansichten des Katers Murr). Tr. A. R. Hope. L: Unwin. 198p. 16 x 9cm. [Not as good as the foregoing.] [BM]

4414. do. 1907. [same?] New ed. L: Unwin. 12. [EC]

4415. do. ad. 1875. The hist. of a nut-cracker. Il. "Bertall." L: Routledge. 18cm. [BM] [Pp. 159-313 of a larger work. Tr. of version by Ax. Dumas, which is free retelling of the story. 234 il.]

4416. do. [same?] 1872-6. [same title] Bost: Lockwood, Brooks n.d. 8. [AC]

4417. do. [same?] 1872-6. [same title, without author's name.] NY: Appleton n.d. Grandmother's lib. il. 16. [AC]

4418. do. [same] 1920. Princess Pirlipatine and the nutcracker, by A. Dumas. Tr. and continued by O. E. Keat. Il. by Violet Dale. NY: Brentano's. 146p. il. 22cm. [LC]

4419. do. 1924. The delectable story of Princess P-- and the n--. Il. by V. Dale. L: Allan. 146p. [BM] [A tr., signed PB. MA., of A. Dumas' version.]

4420. (Rat Krespel.) The Cremona violin. Tr. anon. 1898. In C509. [Bealby's tr.]

*4421. (Signor Formica.) Signor formica. Tr. anon. NY: Taylor 1845. 90p. 8.[With Körner's "Schwertlied" in good tr. by M. S.] [BPL]

4422. Tales of H--. Retold from Offenbach's opera by Cyril Falls. Il. by A. B. Simpson. L: Chatto & Windus 1913. 22cm. [BM]

4423. do. 1919. [same] L: Jarrolds. 206p. 17cm. [BM]

HOFFMANN, Fz. 1814-82.

4424. [Coll.] Tales for my godson. Tr. and ad. F. M. Wilbraham. L: Js. Masters 1851. 254p. il. 15cm. [BM] [The golder locket; The loyal heart; The blind boy, or trust in providence; The young Robinson Crusoe; Thou shalt not steal, a tale of St. Domingo.]

4425. [Coll.] 1868. Stories from the German. 8. [BM]

4426. [Coll.] 1878. Two musicians: tales for my young people. Tr. and arr. M. M. Campbell. L: S. P. C. K. 176p. 16cm. [BM] [The youth of Mozart. L: van Beethoven.]

4427. Augustin and Wenonda: a tale. Tr. anon. L: Judd & Glass 1857. Young England's ill. lib. 98p. il. 17cm. [BM]

4428. (Aus eiserner Zeit.) The iron age of Germany. Tr. Rebecca Schively. Phil: Luth. bd. 1870. 236p. il. 17cm. [LC]

§4429. (Captal.) Captal; or, the little French count. Tr. J. Barrett. L: S. S. Inst. 1876. 128p. 16cm. [BM]

4430. Climbing the glacier. Tr. Kath. K. Walker. NY: Randolph 1865. 131p. 16cm. [LC]

4431. The count and the showman. Tr. "Janet." L: S. S. U. 1881. 116p. il. 16cm. [BM]

HOFFMANN, Fz.
4432. (Das Pfarrhaus.) The parsonage of Libenau. Tr. C: A. Smith. Phil: Luth. pub. 1880. 222p. 17cm. [LC]
4433. (Den Gerechten wird Gutes vergolten.) Dominic. Tr. Rebecca Schively. Phil: Luth. bd. 1870. 246p. il. 17cm. [LC]
4434. do. 1871. Dominic; or, a good action always has its reward. Tr. anon. L: S. P. C. K. 167p. 15cm. [BM]
4435. do. 1881. The widow's son; or, bread upon the waters. Tr. anon. L: Ward, Lock. 246p. il. 16cm. [BM]
[Evidently a reprint of #4433.]
4436. (Der alte Gott lebt noch!) The story of Father Miller. Tr. L. H. Steiner. Phil: Ref. church pub. 1869. 176p. il. 17cm. [LC]
4437. (Der Eisenkopf.) The iron head; or, an old soldier's story of Chas. XII, King of Sweden. Tr. Mrs. M. A. Manderson. Phil: Luth. bd. 1871. 239p. 17cm. [Cf. #4494.] [LC]
4438. (Der Goldsucher.) The gold-seeker. Tr. Levi C. Sheip. Phil: Luth. pub. 1883. 186p. 17cm. [LC]
4439. do. 1868. Gold-seekers and bread-winners. Tr. A. Harwood. In C189.
4440. do. 1871. [same? same title] L: S. P. C. K. 18. [EC]
4441. (Der Schatz des Inka.) The treasure of the Inca. Tr. J: F: Smith. Phil: Luth. bd. 1870. 169p. il. 17cm. [LC]
4442. do. 1879. The Inca's treasure. Ad. Jessie Young. L: Marlborough. 144p. il. 16cm. [BM]
4443. (Der Tugenden Vergeltung.) Anton the fisherman. Tr. Mrs. M. A. Manderson. Phil: Luth. bd. 1870. 172p. il. 17cm. [LC]
4444. do. 1882. [same?] Virtue triumphant; or, Anton the fisherman. Tr. anon. L: Ward, Lock, 172p. il. 16cm. [BM]
[Apparently a reprint of the foregoing.]
4445. (Des Herrn Wege sind wunderbar.) God's ways are "wonderful." By Fz. H-- and Ma. E. Ireland. Rock I., Ill: Augustana book concern 1922. 128p. il. 17cm. [LC]
4446. (Die Auswanderer.) The emigrants: a tale of the last cent. Tr. and rev. for the Am. S. S. U. by Mrs. H. C. Conrad. NY: 1883. 156p. il. 16cm. [LC]
4447. (Die Banknoten.) The three bank-notes. Tr. Rebecca Schively. Phil: Luth. bd. 1875. 170p. 17cm. [LC]
4448. (Die mit Tränen säen, werden mit Freuden ernten.) They that sow in tears shall reap in joy. Tr. anon. Jackson & W. 1863. New ed. 18. [EC]
4449. do. 1869. The story of the old schoolmaster. Tr. L. H. Steiner. Phil: Ref. church pub. 231p. il. 17cm. [LC]
4450. do. 1870. Sowing in tears and reaping in joy. Tr. Mrs. Faber. L: Nisbet. 209p. il. 14cm. [BM]
4451. (Eigensinn und Busse.) Self-will and repentance. Tr. C: A. Smith. Phil: Luth. bd. 1872. 189p. il. 17cm. [LC]
4452. (Ein Bibelblatt.) Little Hans and his Bible-leaf. Tr. and ad. Mrs. Louise Houghton. Phil: Presb. bd. 1883. 252p. il. 18cm. [LC]
4453. (Ein gutes Herz.) Leo Bertram; or, the brave heart. Tr. Ella T. Disosway. NY: Am. tract soc. 1880. 173p. il. 17cm. [LC]
4454. The forest cave: or, revenge. Tr. by a lady. L: Faithful 1863. 8. [BM]
4455. Fritz; or, filial obedience. Tr. Mrs. M. A. Manderson. Phil: Luth. bd. 1870. 125p. il. 17cm. [LC]
4456. do. 1872. Fritz; or, experience teacheth wisdom. Tr. anon. L: Warne; NY: Scribner, W. & A. 182p. il. 15cm. [BM]
4457. do. 1882. Fritz; or, the young Schiller. Ad. A. L. G. L: S. P. C. K.; NY: Young. 80p. il. 14cm. [BM]
[EC has: Fritz, or the young soldier. 1882. 16. Probably the same]
4458. (Fürst Wolfgang.) Prince Wolfgang (i.e., Prinz von Anhalt, 1492-1566): a histor. narr. Tr. J: F: Smith. Phil: Luth. bd. 1871. 316p. il. 17cm. [LC]

HOFFMANN, Fz.
4459. do. 1882. [same?] The Christian prince. Tr. anon. L: Ward, Lock. 316p. il. 8. [Apparently a reprint of the foregoing.] [BM]
4460. Geyer Wälty; or, fidelity rewarded. Tr. Mrs. M. A. Manderson. Phil: Luth. bd. 1870. 196p. 17cm. [LC]
4461. do. 1882. [same] Fidelity rewarded. L: Ward, Lock. 196p. 8 [BM]
4462. Gipsy Fred. Tr. anon. Phil: Martien n.d. (1872-6.) il. 16. [AC]
4463. (Gott lenkt.) Hilda; or, God leadeth. Tr. M. P. Butcher. Phil: Luth. pub. 1882. 201p. 17cm. [LC]
4464. (Hochmut kommt vor dem Fall.) The czar's favorite; or, pride goes before a fall. Tr. E. M. G. Phil: Moore 1878. 232p. il. 16cm. [LC]
4465. do. 1883. Pride; or, a haughty spirit before a fall. Tr. Emma L. Parry. Phil: Luth. pub. 196p. 17cm. [LC]
4466. (Im Schnee begraben.) Buried in the snow. Tr. Mrs. M. A. Manderson. Phil: Luth. bd. 1870. 161p. il. 17cm. [LC]
4467. do. 1879. [same?] L: Ward, Lock. 161p. il. 15cm. [BM] [Apparently a reprint of the foregoing.]
4468. Industry and laziness. Tr. J. King. L: Washbourne 1878. 206p. 17cm. [EC has: 1877.] [BM]
4469. do. 1884. [same] [EC]
4470. (Jeder in seiner Weise.) Adalbert and Bastel; or, every man in his place. L: S. P. C. K. 1871. 126p. 3 il. 15cm. [BM]
4471. do. 1883. Basil and Adelbert; or, each in his own way. Tr. M. P. Butcher. Phil: Luth. pub. 144p. 17cm. [LC]
4472. (Kindesliebe.) The Greek slave. Tr. J. C. Brodführer. Phil: Luth. bd. 1870. 239p. il. 17cm. [LC]
4473. do. 1881. [same?] The Greek slave; or, filial love. L: Ward, Lock. 239p. il. 16cm. [Apparently a reprint of the foregoing.] [BM]
4474. Leo's whaling voyage. By Fz. H-- and Ma. E. Ireland. Rock I., Il. Augustana book concern 1923. 127p. il. 18cm. [LC]
4475. The little dauphin. Tr. G: P. Upton. Chic: McClurg 1905. 150p. 17cm. [LC]
4476. (Ludwig van Beethoven.) Ludvig van B--. Tr. G: P. Upton. Chic: McClurg 1904. 117p. 17cm. [LC]
4477. Max Wild the merchant's son. Tr. anon. 1874. In C567.
4478. Money, and its influence. Tr. by a lady. L: Wertheim & Macintosh 1852. viii;126p. 17cm. [BM]
4479. (Mozarts Jugend.) Mozart's early days. Tr. Mrs. C. A. Smith. 1873. [AC]
4480. do. 1874. [same] New ed. Bost: Hoyt. 16. [AC]
4481. do. 1887. A boy musician; or, the early days of Mozart. (With: Violetta, a romance of the later life of M-- by E. Polko.) L: Blackie 1887. 126p. il. 17cm. [BM]
4482. do. 1904. M--'s youth. Tr. G: P. Upton. Chic: McClurg. 119p. 17cm. [LC]
4483. (Mutterliebe.) Maternal love. Tr. H. J. K. Lemcke. Phil: Luth. bd. 1870. 200p. il. 17cm. [LC]
4484. do? 1879. [same?] The lost child. Tr. anon. L: Ward, Lock, 200p. il. 15cm. [This seems to be a reissue of the foregoing.] [BM]
4485. The orphans: a tale for youth. L: Wertheim, Macintosh & H. 1861. 124p. 17cm. [BM]
4486. Paul Arnold: a tale of life in Peru. Tr. J: Henderson. L;Ed: Chambers 1870. 139p. 14cm. [BM]
4487. René. Tr. J: F: Smith. Phil: Luth. bd. 1870. 176p. il. 17cm. [LC]
4488. do. 1881. [same] Trust in God: the story of René the little Savoyard. Tr. anon. L: Ward, Lock. 176p. il. 15cm. [BM]
4489. Rich and poor. Ward 1862. 16. [Ascribed to D. Hoffman.] [EC]
4490. do. 1863. [same] New ed. Jackson & W. 18. [EC]

HOFFMANN, Fz.

4491. (Ritter und Bauer.) Knight and peasant. Tr. D. P. Rosemüller. Phil: Luth. bd. 1872. 194p. il. 17cm. [LC]

4492. (Selig sind die Barmherzigen, denn sie werden Barmherzigkeit erlangen.) Alli; or, blessed are the merciful, for they shall obtain mercy. Tr. Ph. C. Croll. Phil: Luth. pub. 1886. 176p. 17cm. [LC]

4493. Seppi. Ad. M. M. Campbell. L: S. P. C. K.; NY: Pott, Young 1877. 160p. il. 16cm. [BM]

4494. The stiff-necked king: stories from the life of Chas. XII of Sweden. Tr. J: Henderson. L;Ed: Chambers 1870. 161p. 14cm. [BM] [Probably from Der Eisenkopf; cf. #4437.]

4495. (Unter der Erde.) Under the earth. Tr. Rebecca Schively. Phil: Luth. bd. 1870. 134p. il. 17cm. [LC]

4496. (Weihnachten.) Christmas: a story for my friends. Tr. H: Harbaugh. Phil: Luth. bd. 1875. 114p. il. 17cm. [LC]

4497. (Wen Gott lieb hat, den züchtiget er.) Advent. of Leo Rembrandt. Tr. L. H. Steiner. Phil: Ref. church pub. 1869. 241p. il. 17cm. [LC]

4498. (Wie die Saat, so die Ernte.) The Hartz boys; or, as a man sows, so must he reap. L: S. P. C. K. 1871. 128p. il. 18cm. [BM]

4499. do. 1872-6. [same?] Bost: Lothrop n.d. il. 16. [AC]

4500. do? 1883. Martin Bernhard; or, seed-time and harvest. Enl. by Mrs. S. K. Porter. Easton, Pa: Riegel. 256p. 18cm. [LC]

HOFFMANN, Fz. and Hoffmann, Jl.

4501. Little things, the germs of greatness. 38p. Floating on the ice. 20p. Tr. anon. Phil: Hoffmann & Morwitz 1872. il. 16cm. [LC]

HOFFMANN, Fz. 1804-81.

4502. Philosophy of Baader. Tr. A. Strothotte. 1875. In C300(5).

4503. Theism and pantheism. Tr. D. J. Snider. 1871. In C300(1).

HOFFMANN, F: Sel. in C450.

HOFFMANN, Gf. 1658-1712. Sel. in C229.

HOFFMANN (or Hoffmann-Donner), H: 1809-94.

§4504. (Konig Nussknacker und der arme Reinhold.) King nut-cracker; or, the dream of poor R--. With Hoffmann's il. Tr. J. R. Planché. Lpz: Volckmar; L: Tegg and Joseph, Myers & Co. 1853. 28p. 28cm. [Verse is free, but good.] [BM]

*4505. do. 1854. King nutcracker and the poor boy, R--: a Christmas story. Tr. A. H. L: W: S. Orr. 40p. 18cm. [BM]

4506. do. 1927. King nutcracker freely rendered by J. R. Planché. With the Engl. "Struwwelpeter." In Rhys, E. "Book of nonsense." il. pp. 73-108. [BM]

4507. Prince Greenwood and Pearl-of-Price, with their good donkey, kind and wise! Tr. Mrs. Matilda Despard. Il. Eleanor Greatorex. Washington, D. C: Peters 1874. 17p. 30cm. [LC]

*4508. (Struwwelpeter.)[1] The Engl. Struwwelpeter; or, pretty stories and funny pictures for little children. Tr. anon. 4th ed. Lpz: Volckmar 1848. 24p. 24cm. [Mostly quite good.] [BM]

*4509. do. 1860? Pauline and the matches. Tr. anon. NY: McLoughlin. unp. il. 16cm. [Il. not the same as in the foregoing.] [BM]

4510. do. 1880. Tr. anon. 27th ed. on linen. Griffith. 4. [EC]

4511. do. 1885. Tr. anon. Slovenly Peter; or, pleasing stories and funny pictures. New issue. NY: Knox. il. sq. O. [AC]

§4512. do. 189-? Slovenly Peter. Tr. anon. Phil: Winston. 90p. il. 4. [Not a close tr.] [NY]

4513. do. 1893. Struwwelpeter minor. Tr. J. Trojan. Engl. ed. L: Jarrold. 8. [EC]

4514. do. 1896. [same] [EC]

[1] Imitations of Struwwelpeter have not been included.

HOFFMANN, H: - Struwwelpeter
4515. do. 1897. [same] [EC]
4516. do. 1898. [same?] Struwwelpeter junior. Tr. J. Trojan. New ed. Jarrold. 24p. long 4. [EC]
4517. do. 1898. Struwel Peter; a picture book for boys and girls. Tr. anon. NY: McLoughlin. 34p. il. fol. [Without ascription.] [LC]
4518. do. 1902. [same as #4512] [NY]
4519. do. 1903. The Engl. Struwwelpeter; on linen. Tr. anon. L: Blackie. 4. [EC]
4520. do. 1904. [same title] New ed. Griffith & F. 4. [EC]
4521. do. 1904. Struwel Peter: a picture book for boys and girls. Tr. anon. NY: McLoughlin. 48p. il. 28 x 22cm. [Cf. #4517.] [LC]
4522. do. 1905. The Engl. Struwwelpeter. Tr. anon. L: Dean's rag book co. 16p. il. 30cm. [BPL]
4523. do. 1909. S--. New ed. L: Routledge. 24p. 26cm. [BM] [Same as #4508? Same paging and size.]
4524. do. 1909. S--. On linen. L: Routledge. 8. [EC]
4525. do. 1911. S--. Frowde. [EC]
4526. do. 1916. Slovenly Peter. L: Warne. Q. [Cf. #4511-2.] [AC]
4527. do. 1918. Slovenly Peter. Tr. Annis Lee Furness. Pict. and verses as remembered by the children of R. W. Emerson. Il. E: Waldo Emerson. Bost: Houghton. D. [AC]
4528. do. 1927. [same as #4508.] In Rhys, E. "Book of nonsense," pp. 142-69. [Cf. #4506.]
4529. do. [ad.] 1901. Shock-headed Peter: a children's farce with song in two acts. Ad. by Ph. Carr and Nigel Playfair. Music by Wl. Rubens. L: Enoch; NY: Boosey 1901. 58p. 4. [LC]
4530. do. [ad.] 1905. Peter Teeter stories, ad. from the famous Ger. S--, with orig. add. by Prof. H. L. Schwetzky. Il. R. H. Garman. Chic: Thompson & Thomas. 63p. il. 23 x 30cm. [LC]

HOFFMANN, Jl.
4531. Floating on the ice. Tr. anon. 1872. In #4501.
4532. do. 1872. With, Grandfather's darling. Phil: Claxton. 18. [AC]
4533. Grandfather's darling: a tale. Tr. St. W. White. Phil: Hoffman & Morwitz 1872. 64p. il. 16. [LCO]
4534. "Oh, I see you!" A tale. Tr. anon. Phil: Hoffman & Morwitz 1873. 87p. il. 18. [LCO]
4535. Thou shalt not steal; The faithful watcher. Two tales. Tr. anon. Phil: Hoffman & Morwitz 1873. 63; 22p. il. 18. [LCO]

HOFFMANN, Max, 1869- .
4536. (Der Krieg der versäumten Gelegenheiten.) War of lost opportunities. Tr. A. E. Chamot. NY: Internat. pub. 1925. 246p. 22cm. [LC]

HOFFMEISTER, Wr. F: L: Ab. 1819-45.
*4537. (Briefe aus Indien.) Travels in Ceylon and continental India, etc. Tr. anon. Ed: Kennedy 1848. xii; 527p. 20cm. [BM.LC] [Memoir of author, and appendices.]

HOFFNASS, F. V.
*4538. (Christoforus. Legende.) Christophorus: a legend, in 2 pts. (composed) by Js. Rheinberger. Tr. Seymour Egerton. Vocal score. Ger; Engl. Lpz: Kistner 1881. 93p. 27cm. [BMM]
4538a. do. 1915. [same] Bost: Birchard. [AC]

HOFMANN, F: 1813-88.
§4539. (Der Rattenfänger von Hameln.) The piper of Hamelin: opera in 5 acts by V: Nessler. Text by H-- after J. Wolff. Engl. ad. by H: Hersee. Vocal score. Ger; Engl. L: Hutchings & Romer 1882. 215p. 26cm. [Quite freely ad., with considerable omissions.] [BMM]

HOFMANN VON HOFMANNSWALDAU, Cn. 1617-79. Sel. in C461.

HOFMANNSTHAL, Hg. Hofmann, Edler v. 1874-1929. Sel. in C28;39; 154(17);366(2d ed.);423.

§4540. (Ariadne auf Naxos.) A-- on N--: opera by R: Strauss. Tr. Af. Kalisch. Libr: Engl. Berlin;Paris: Fürstner 1913. [LC]

*4541. do. 1922. Ariadne. Tr. Af. Kalisch. Vocal score. Engl. Berlin: Fürstner. 250p. fol. [LCM] [New version, improvement over the foregoing.]

4542. do. 1924. [same] Libr. Ger;Engl. Fürstner. 51p. 25cm. [LCM] [With H--'s "Prelude."]

*4543. (Cristinas Heimreise.) Cristina's journey home. Tr. Roy T. House. In "Poet-Lore" 28(1917). [Very good tr.]

4544. do. 1916. [same] Bost: Badger. 25cm. [LC]

§4545. (Das gerettete Venedig.) Venice preserved, a tragedy. Tr. Elis. Walter. In "Poet-Lore" 26(1915).

4546. (Der Abenteurer und die Sängerin.) The adventurer and the singer. Sel. Tr. B. Q. Morgan. 1917-18. In C366 (3d ed.)

†4547. (Der Rosenkavalier.) The rose-bearer. Opera by R: Strauss. Tr. A. Kalisch. Libr. Berlin: Fürstner 1912. 130p. 12. [NY] [Incomplete; true neither to sense nor to meter.]

*4548. do. 1912 (1911). Tr. Af. Kalisch. Score. Ger;Engl. Berlin; Paris: Fürstner. 451p. fol. [LCM.BMM] [Excellent singing version. Copyright 1911.]

*4549. do. 1926. The knight of the rose. Tr. C: H: Meltzer. Libr. n.i. 30cm. Tw. [Close and good.] [LCM]

§4550. (Der Tor und der Tod.) Death and the fool. Tr. Max Batt. In "Poet-Lore" 24(1913). [No rhymes; forced verse.]

§4551. do. 1913-15. Tr. J: Heard, Jr. In C154(17).

§4552. do. 1914. Tr. Elis. Walter. Bost: Badger. 45p. 19cm. [LC] [Poor tr.; errors.]

4552a. do. 1923. In C420b.

§4553. (Der Tod des Tizian.) The death of Titian. Tr. J: Heard, Jr. 1913-15. In C154(17).

4554. do. 1920. [same] Bost: Four seas co. 27p. 18cm. [LC]

4555. (Die Hochzeit der Sobeide.) The marriage of S--. Tr. B. Q. Morgan. 1913-15. In C154(20).

§4556. (Elektra.) Electra. Tr. Art. Symons. NY: Brentano's 1908. 83p. 20cm. [Style excellent; errors.] [LC.BM]

†4557. do. 1909. Tr. C: T. Mason. Libr. Fr;Engl. Berlin: Fürstner. 43p. 8. [LC]

*4558. do. 1910. Tr. Af. Kalisch. Libr. Engl. Berlin: Fürstner. 58p. 18cm. [BM.LC]

4559. do. 1910 (1909). [same] Vocal score. Ger;Engl. Berlin: Fürstner. 226p. fol. [LCM]

*4560. (Gedichte.) Lyrical poems...Tr. C: W. Stork. New Haven, Ct: Yale U. pr. 1918. x;83p. 19cm. [LC]--L: Milford 1918. [EC] [On the whole, very good.--Reprinted in part from period. and includes tr. by M. Münsterberg, Daisy Broicher, Elis. Walter.]

4561. Introd. to Holdt, "Picturesque Greece," tr. by L: Hamilton. #4560.

§4562. (Jedermann.) The play of everyman, based on the old Engl. morality play; new version by H-- set to blank verse by G: Sterling in collab. with R: Ordynski. San Franc: Robertson 1917. 95p. 17cm. [LC.BM] [Tr.'s verse is not even close in sense, and he adds not a little matter of his own.]

4563. (Madonna Dianora.) M-- D--: a play in verse. Tr. Mrs. Harriet Boas. Bost: Badger 1916. 44p. 19cm. [LC]

4564. do. 1919. [same] Bost: Four seas co. [BM]

†4565. (Prolog zu Anatol.) The prologue to Anatol. Tr. Trevor Blakemore. See Schnitzler, "Liebelei," #8514.

HOFMANNSTHAL, Hg. v.
See Strauss, R: Corr. between R: S-- and Hg. v. H--. #9230.

HOGSENIUS, ---. Sel. in C240.

"HOHENAU, Pl. v." See Cohn, Pl.

HOHENHAUSEN, Ele. Phe. Ame. 1789-1857. Sel. in C90.

HOHENLOHE-SCHILLINGSFUERST, Cg. K: V: Fürst zu, 1819-1901.
*4566. (Denkwürdigkeiten...) Memoirs. Ed. F: Curtius. Engl. ed. supervised by G: W. Chrystal. NY: Macmillan 1906. 2v. vii;406; 501p. 24cm.[Could be better, but is faithful and honest.] [LC.BM]
See Hedemann, Axe. v., "My friendship, etc.," #3942.

HOHLFELDT, ---. Sel. in C543.

HOJER, Kd. 16th cent. Sel. in C271;287.

HOLBEIN, Hs. 1497-1543. See Knackfuss, H., Hs. H--., #5085. See Woltmann, A., H--. #10341 seq.

HOLD, Ern.
4567. The young Savoyard. See Krummacher, F., "Alfred, etc.," #5453.

HOLDT, Hanns.
4568. (Griechenland: Baukunst, Landschaft, Volksleben.) Picturesque Greece: architecture, landscape, life of the people. Introd. Hg. v. Hofmannsthal; tr. L: Hamilton. NY: Architectural bk; L: Unwin 1923. xivp. 176p. of il. 24cm. [LC]
[Photographs by Holdt, Hamann, and M. Zachos.]

HOLLAENDER, Fx. 1868- .
4569. (Der Eid des Stefan Huller.) The sins of the fathers. Tr. Sara J. I. Lawson. Payson & Clarke 1927. 350p. D. [AC]

HOLM, Ad. 1830-1900.
*4570. (Griechische Geschichte.) Hist. of Greece from the commencement to the close of the indep. Greek nation. Tr. F: Clarke. L; NY: Macmillan 1894-98. 4v. 21cm. [BM.LC]
[Vol. 1, 1894; vol. 2, 1895; vol. 3, 1896; vol. 4, 1898. LC has: 1878-1900.--Clarke tr. vol. 4, revised the others.]

HOLSTEIN, Fz. v. 1826-78. Sel. in C501.

HOLSTEIN, F. V. 1839-1909. See Harden, Mx. Word portraits, #3699.

HOLTEI, K: v. 1798-1880. Sel. in C106;295.

HOLTHAUS, P. Dd.
4571. Wanderings of a journeyman tailor through Europe and the East, 1824-40. Tr. from 3d Ger. ed. W: Howitt. L: Longmans 1844. xv;286p. 18cm. [BM.LC]
4572. do. 1849. [same] L: Bohn. 12. [EC]

HOLTZ, ---. Sel. in C501.

HOLTZ, E. v.
4573. The unsigned will. See Werner, E., "The stolen vail," #10073.

HOLTZENDORF, Fz. v. 1829- . Sel. in C301.

HOLUB, El. 1847-1902.
4574. (Sieben Jahre in Süd-Afrika.) Seven years in South Africa: travels, researches, and hunting advent. 1872-9. Tr. Ellen E. Frewer. Bost: Houghton 1881. 2v. 200 il. 22cm. [LC]
§4575. do. 1881. [same] 2d ed. L: Low. 2v, 426;479p. [BM.LC]
[Tr. quite freely, with omissions and rewording.]

HOLZ, Arno, 1863-1929. Sel. in C28;95;423.

HOMBURG, Ern. Cph. 1605-81. Sel. in C269;271.

HOMMEL, Fr. 1854- .
4576. The civilization of the east. Tr. Jas. H. Loewe. L: Dent;NY: Macmillan 1900. Temple primers. xii;141p. il. 15cm. [BM.LC]

HOPFEN, Hs. 1835-1904. Sel. in C448.
4577. The fortunes and fate of little Spangle; Trudel's ball ("Trudels Ball"). Tr. anon. 1890. In C404.

HOPFEN, Hs. and Ern. Eckstein.
4578. Novels and humorous sketches. Chic: Schick 1885. 3 pts. in 1 v. 19cm. [LC]
[Contains the foregoing and Eckstein's "Against the stream." See #1399.]

HOPFENSACK, J: Cn. W; A: 1801-74. Sel. in C244.

HORMAYR ZU HORTENBURG, Js. Freiherr v. d. 1782-1848.
4579. Memoirs of the life of Andrew Hofer. Tr. C: H: Hall. L: Murray 1820. lxiii;198p. 22cm. [BM.LC]

HORN, G: 1831-97.
4580. Count Silvius: a romance. Tr. Ma. J. Safford. NY: Harlan 1882. 463p. [LCO]
§4581. (Voltaire und die Markgräfin von Baireuth.) The margravine of B-- and V--. (Correspondence.) Tr. Princess Cn. of Schleswig-Holstein. L: Stott 1888. 184p. 22cm. [BM.LCO]
["I have endeavoured to tr...literally, but...have...omitted some passages." Not my idea of fidelity.]

HORN, H: Mz. 1814-74.
4582. (Der Rose Pilgerfahrt.) The rose's pilgrimage: a legend. Ad. to the music of Rb. Schumann by H: Cobb. Libr. St.L: Studley 1862. 10p. 8. [LCO]

"HORN, W. O. v." (i.e., Ph. F: W: Oertel, 1798-1876).
4583. [Coll.] The schoolmaster of Abbach, and other stories. From.. van Horn. Phil: Claxton, R. & H. 1870. 354p. 18cm. [LC]
4584. The beaver trappers (Pp. 1-112) and other stories (not by Horn). Tr. from...Horan [sic] by J: Henderson. L: Tegg 1870. 207p. 16cm. [BM]
4585. (Der Leibhusar.) The snow-king's trumpeter, by H. I. M. G. Il. F. Dadd. L: S. P. C. K. 1884. 79p. 17cm. [BM]
["The plot of this tale was suggested by Horn's 'Leibhusar.'"]
*4586. (Drei Tage aus Gellerts Leben.) Three days from the life of G--. Tr. K. K. L: Whittaker 1859. 40p. 16cm. [BM]
[Some errors, but honest attempt to be faithful.--A true story, chiefly based on Gellert's corr.]
4587. do. 1858-61. Trust in God; or, three days...Tr. anon. NY: Carter & bros. 16. [AC]
*4588. do. 1861. Three days in G--'s life. Founded on facts. Tr. anon. L: Jarrold. 48p. 16cm. [Very good.] [BM]
§4589. do. 1862. The advent. of a hymn; or, three days, etc. Tr. anon. L: Dalton. 32p. 18cm. [Poor style.] [BM]
4590. do. 1864. Cn. G--; or, trust in God. Tr. anon. L: Knight. 63p. 14cm. [BM]
[Somewhat abr. and simplified; seemingly derived from foregoing.]
4591. do. 1874. Lending unto the Lord; or, three days, etc. By Baron Conway and Mrs. J. Russell Endean. Il. by Hon. Cte. Ellis. L: Kerby & Endean. xxii;124p. 15cm. [Retold] [BM]
4592. do. 1881. [same?] Lending unto the Lord. L: Kerby. 16. [EC]

"HORN, W. O. v."
*4593. (Friedel. Eine Geschichte aus dem Volksleben.) Friedel: an autobiog. Tr. Mrs. C. M. Sawyer. Phil: G. Collins 1856. 3d ed. 349p. il. 15cm. [BM]
4594. How the French took Algiers; or, the Janissary's slave. Tr. J. Latchmore. Ed: Oliphant, A. & F. 1881. 190p. il. 17cm. [BM]
4595. Leonhard, the runaway. Tr. from van Horn [sic]. Phil: Luth. bd. 1871. 74p. 16. [LCO]
4596. Maria Theresa. Tr. G: P. Upton. Chic: McClurg 1905. 141p. 17cm. [LC]
4597. The military chest: an incident of the war between Prussia and France (Pp. 1-117) and other stories (not by Horn). Tr. from Horan [sic] by J: Henderson. L: Tegg 1870. 16cm. [BM]
§4598. (Olaf Thorlacksen.) Olaf Thorlaksen: an Icelandic narr. Tr. Rev. M. Sheeleigh. Phil: Luth. bd. 1870. 211p. 17cm. [BM] [Inadequate tr. Pref. pp. 11-19.]
4599. do. 1882. [same] The boy pilot; or, Olaf T--. Tr. M. Sheeleigh. L: Ward, Lock. 211p. il. 16cm. [BM]

HORNFECK, F: 1822-82.
†4600. The human heart (a poem). Tr. G: A. Muller. 1891. In Schiller, Lay of the bell. #7934.

HORST, Jl. 1864- . See Engel, Ax., joint author., #1456.

HOSEMANN, Td. 1813-75.
4601. A laughter book for little folk. Tr. Mme. de Chatelain. L: Cundall & Addey 1851. 19p. col. il. 24cm. [BM]

HOTTINGER, J: Jk. 1783-1860.
*4602. (Huldreich Zwingli und seine Zeit.) The life and times of U: Z--. Tr. Rev. T. C. Porter. Harrisburg, Pa: Scheffer 1856. 421p. 12. [LC.BM]

HOUWALD, Cph. Ern. Frhr. v. 1778-1845.
4603. (Der Christ und der Muhamedaner.) The Christian and the Mahometan. Tr. S. T. 1845. In C519.
4604. The goldsmith; The new year's wish. Tr. anon. 1841. In C426.

HRABANUS MAURUS, 776?-856. Sel. in C235.

HROTSUITHA [the spelling varies], 932?-1000? Sel. in C190;469.
4605. [Coll.] The plays...Tr. by Cph. St. John (i.e., Christabel Marshall), with introd. by Cardinal Gasquet and crit. pref. by the tr. L: Chatto & Windus 1923. xxxv;160p. 17cm. [BM.LC] [Prefaces of Roswitha; Gallicanus; Dulcitius; Callimachus; Abraham; Paphnutius; Sapientia.]
4606. [Coll.] 1923. The plays of Roswitha. Tr. H. J. W. Tillyard. L: Faith pr. xix;123p. 21cm. [Six plays, as in foregoing.] [BM]
4607. (Abraham.) A--: a play by R--, the nun of Gandersheim. Tr... into Engl. prose by R: S. Lambert and il. by Agnes Lambert. L: Stanton pr. 1922. 37p. 23cm. [BM]
4608. (Callimachus.) C--: a play by R--, the nun of Gandersheim. Tr. by R: S. Lambert and il. by Agnes Lambert. L: Stanton pr. 1923. 35p. 23cm. [BM]
4609. (Dulcitius.) D--. Tr. Art. F. McCann. Elmira, NY: Priv. prt. 1916. 16p. 23cm. [Tr. made for the use of students at Cornell Univ.] [LC]
4610. The lost child (extr.). Tr. anon. 1906. In C190.

HRUSSOCZY, Me. Edle v. 1821-98. See "Tenger, Mariam."

HUBER, Fz. X:
4611. (Das unterbrochene Opferfest.) The oracle; or, the interrupted sacrifice. Opera in two acts by P: V. Winter. Tr. Hampden Napier. Arr. by W: Hawes. Pianoforte score. L: 1825? fol. [BMM]

HUBER, Fz. X: - Das unterbrochene Opferfest
4611a. do. 1870. [same] Vocal score. L: Royal harmonic instit. 288p. 34cm. [BMM]
4611b. do. n.d. [same] L: Welsh & Hawes. 288p. fol. [LCM]

HUBER, Te. 1764-1829.
4612. Female experience. Tr. Miss Eliza C--. 1800? In C430.
4613. Francis & Josepha: a tale. Tr. W: Fardely. Leeds: 1807. See "Crit. R." (III)11(1807):213. (B26)

HUBER, V: Aimé, 1800-69.
4614. (Die englischen Universitäten.) The Engl. universities. Unabr tr. ed. by Fis. W. Newman. L: W: Pickering 1843. 2v. lxi;450; 740p. il. 22cm. [BM]
[Tr. done by J. Palgrave Simpson, then recast and ed. by Newman. "...immense abridgment of the earlier chapters, and consid. condensation in all but the last..." No important fact omitted, no opinion suppressed or altered.]
*4615. (Skizzen aus Spanien.) Stories of Span. life. Ed. (and tr.) with histor. introd. (pp. 1-66) by Jas. Robertson Craufurd. L: H: Colburn 1837. 2v. 264;338p. 19cm. [BM]
[Contains Huber's "Vorwort und Einleitung" and the novel "Dolores."]

HUCH, R:a. 1864- . Sel. in C28;154(18);423.
4616. (Erinnerungen von Ludolf Ursleu dem Jüngeren.) Recoll. of L-- U-- the younger. Tr. (abr.) by Muriel Almon. 1913-15. In C154(18).
4617. Romantic marriage. 1926. In C308.

HUEBNER, ---. Sel. in C105.

HUEBNER, J: 1668-1731.
4618. (Biblische Historien.) Easy introd. to the study of the holy script. Tr. D. Bellamy. See "Crit. R." 1(1756):240. (B26)

HUEBNER, Js. Ax. Graf v. 1811-92.
*4619. (Ein Spaziergang um die Welt. Promenade autour du monde.) A ramble around the world. Tr. Lady Herbert. L;NY: Macmillan 1874. 2v. 463;491p. 21cm. [BM.LC]
[H-- published in French and German. LC gives the French title as original.]
4620. do. 1878. [same] Macmillan. 657p. 19cm. [BM.LC]

HUEGEL, Carl Ax. Ans. Frhr. v. 1796-1870.
§4621. (Kaschmir und das Reich der Seik.) Travels in Kashmir and the Panjab. Tr. anon. Notes by Maj. T. B. Jervis. L: Petheram 1845. xvi;423p. il. 25cm. [Rather freely tr.] [BM.LC]

HUELSEN, Cn. C: F: 1858- .
*4622. (Das Forum Romanum, seine Geschichte und seine Denkmäler.) The Roman forum: its history and its monuments. Tr. from 2d Ger. Ed. Jesse B. Carter. Rome: Loescher; NY: Stechert 1906. xi;259p. il. 17cm. [LC.BM]
4623. do. 1909. [same] xv;271p. [BM]

HUFELAND, Cph. W: 1762-1836.
4624. (Von der Kunst das menschliche Leben zu verlängern.) The art of prolonging life. Tr. anon. 1797. (Orig. of the following.)
4625. do. 1874. [same] Ed. by J. M. L: Ward, Lock & Tyler. 240p. 18cm. [Reprint of foregoing. Tr. is completely rev. and adapted.] [BM]

"HUFFUMBOURGHAUSEN, baron"
'4626. The congress of the beasts...for negotiating a peace between the...quadrupedes at war: a farce of two acts. Written orig. in High Dutch. Tr. J. J. Heidegger. To which is prefixt a curious print of the last scene...by an eminent hand. L: W.Webb 1748. 50p. 20cm. [A satire on the congress at Aix-la-Chapelle.] [BM]

"HUFFUMBOURGHAUSEN, baron"
4627. do. 1748. [same] 2d ed. Corr. and amended in the print (19 x 22cm.) By a different hand. L: Webb. 61p. 20cm. [BM]
4628. do. 1748. [same] another ed. L: Webb. 30p. 17cm. [BM]
[Has vignette on t.p.]
4629. do. 1748. [same] 4th ed. L: Webb. 68p. [LCO]
4630. do. 1748. [same] 2d ed. Corr. and amend. in the print. Phil: Gedruckt bey Godhard Armbruster. (B6a)
[The name is spelled "Huffumboarghausen"; also in the following.]
4631. do. 1748. [same] NY: Sold by Catharine Zenger in Stone-Street. (B6a)

HUGO VON MONTFORT, 1357-1423. Sel. in C27.

HUGO VON TRIMBERG, fl. 1260-1313. Sel. in C190;422.

HUGO VON WERBENWAG, fl. 1258-79. Sel. in C27;416;532.

HUHN, Art. Ern. v. 1851-
4632. The kidnapping of Prince Ax. v. Battenberg...Tr. anon. Stanford 1887. 8. [EC]

HUMBOLDT, Ax. and W: Sel. in C12;366;461*;469;574. Lives of, by Klencke and Schlesier. See Klencke, P. #5030.

HUMBOLDT, (F: W: H:) Ax. Frhr. v. 1769-1859. Sel. in C366.
4633. Works. NY: Appleton n.d. (ABP 1876) 9v. 12. [AC]
[Cosmos, 5v. Narr. of trav. in America, 3v. Views of nature.]
*4634. (Ansichten der Natur.) Aspects of nature, in diff. lands and diff. climates. Tr. Mrs. Eliz. Sabine. L: Longmans 1849. 2v. xix; 301;347p. 17cm. [BM.LC]
[EC dates this 1848. Also pub. by J: Murray.]
4635. do. 1849. [same] Phil: Lea & Blanchard. 475p. 20cm. [LC]
4636. do. 1850. [same] L: Longmans. 2v. in one. [LC]
4637. do. 1850. [same as #4635] [LC]
*4638. do. 1850. Views of nature; or, contemplations on the sublime phenomena of creation. Tr. Elise C. Otté and H: G: Bohn, with collab. of R. H. Whitelocke and E. A. Bowring (who transl. one poem). L: Bohn. 452p. 18cm. [BM.LC]
*4639. (Briefe an Varnhagen von Ense.) Letters, 1827-58, to Varnhagen v. Ense, and other matter. Tr. anon. L: Trübner 1860. xv;334p. 22cm. [BM.LC]
[Extr. from Varnhagen's diaries, and letters from V-- and others to H--. Taken from vol. ed. by Ludmilla Assing. Author. tr. with explan. notes.]
4640. do. 1860. Tr. from 2d ed. by Fried. Kapp. NY: Rudd & C. 407p. 19cm. [LC]
4641. Copernicus and the ancient astronomers. (From the "Cosmos.") Bost: Old South leaflets. 1888. 12p. 12. [LCO]
4642. (Essai politique sur l'île de Cuba.) Polit. essay on the island of Cuba. Tr. Helen M. Williams. L: Longmans 1822. 8. [LCO]
[Vol. 7 of #4659.]
*4643. do. 1856. The island of Cuba. Tr. from the Spanish (tr. of the French orig. by D. J. B. de V. Y. M.) by J: S. Thrasher, with prelim. essay (to p. 95). NY: Derby & Jackson. 397p. 18cm.
[Tr. seems to be very good, but omitted H--'s views on slavery, of which he publicly complained. Vol. ends with "A trip to Trinidad." --EC has: L: Low 1856.] [LC]
*4644. (Essai politique sur le royaume de la nouvelle Espagne.) Polit. essay on the kingdom of New Spain (i.e., Mexico). Tr. J: Black. L: Longmans et al. 1811. 2v. xvii;cxlv;289;531p. 21cm. [BM]
[Part of his "Voyage aux régions équinoctiales." Geograph. introd.]
4645. do. 1811-22. [same] 4v. [LC]
[Vols. 1-3 have: 3d ed. 1822. Plates of vol. 2 have spec. t.p. dated 1811.]

HUMBOLDT, Ax. v. - Essai politique...
4646. do. 1811 [same] NY: Riley. 2v. [LC]
[No more of this ed. published.]
4647. do. 1813. An abridgement of H--'s...essay...by a citizen of Maryland. Balto: Wane & O'Reilly. 41p. 21cm. [LC]
4648. do. 1824. Sel. from the works...relating to...Mexico. With notes and introd. by J: Taylor. L: Longmans xxxiii;310p. 21cm. [Chiefly from his "Essai"; also from a scientific work on rocks.] [BM.LC]
*4649. (Kosmos. Entwurf einer physischen Weltbeschreibung.) Cosmos: a general survey of the physical phenomena of the universe. Tr. A. Prichard. L: H:Baillière 1845. 2v. xix;482; 534p. 20cm. [BM]
[Criticized by Otté, I think too severely.]
4650. do. 1845. Tr. anon. NY: Harper & bros. 64p. 24cm. [LC]
[Prtd. in double columns. Probably Prichard's tr. Unbound part (I) of an issue in parts.]
*4651. do. 1846-58. Tr. Mrs. Eliz. Sabine. L: Longmans. 4v. 17cm. [LC has: 1850-58. -- Otté calls this tr. "singularly accurate and elegant," but says the tr. makes consid. omissions. In my judgment Prichard is better.] [BM.LC]
4652. do. 1848. [same as #4649] [BM]
*4653. do. 1849-50. Cosmos: a sketch of a physical description of the universe. Tr. E. C. Otté, B. H. Paul, and W. S. Dallas. L: Bohn. 5v. 18cm. [Complete tr. Otté tr. vols. 1-3; Otté and Paul vol. 4, 1852; Otté and Dallas vol. 5.] [BM.LC]
4654. do. 1852? [same] NY: Harper. 2v. 20cm. [LC]
[Vols. 1 and 2 of the foregoing.]
4656. do. 1859. Ottè's tr. NY: Harper. [AC]
4657. do. 1872-6. [same] NY: Harper n.d. 5v. 12. [AC]
4658. Preface to Moellhausen's diary. See #6255.
*4659. (Voyage aux régions équinoctiales.) Personal narr. of travels to the...new continent...1799-1804. Tr. Helen M. Williams. L: Longmans et al. 1814-29. 7v. il. 21cm. [BM.LC]
[LC has: 7v. in 9.]
4660. do. 1814. [same] L: Longmans, etc. 2v. 289; 299p. 8. [LCO]
[Vols. 1 and 2 of the foregoing.]
4661. do. 1815. [same] Phil: Carey. 7v. 21cm. [BM]
[Text is ident. with #4659, but paging differs.]
4662. do. 1815. [same] Phil: Carey. 432p. 22cm. [LC]
[Reprint of books 1-2 of #4659. Perhaps the same as #4660.]
4663. do. 1822-29. [same] 2d ed. L: Longmans, etc. [LC]
4664. do. 1822. [same] 3d ed. L: Longmans, etc. [LC]
4665. do. 1832. The travels and researches...being a condensed narr. of his journeys in...America (1801) and in Asiatic Russia. By W. MacGillivray. Ed: Oliver & Boyd; L: Simpkin & Marshall 1832. 424p. il. 16cm. [BM]
4666. do. 1833. [same] 2d ed. 424p. [BM.LC]
4667. do. 1840. H--'s travels and discoveries in South America. L: Parker. 278p. il. 14cm. [BM]
[Condensed from the "Voyage"...with extracts in tr.]
4668. do. 1840? [same as #4665?] Travels in America and Asiatic Russia. Crosby & N. n.d. 18. [AC]
4669. do. 1842. [same as #4665] NY: Harper. 367p. il. 15cm. [LC.BM]
*4670. do. 1847. Personal narrative, etc. Tr. and ed. Thomasina Ross. L: Bohn. 3v. 17cm. [BM]
4671. do. 1853. [same] L: Bohn. 3v. [EC]
4672. do. 1857. [same as #4665] Nelson. [EC]
4673. do. 1859. Life, travels, and researches. L: Nelson. 420p. il. 17cm. [Same as #4665.] [BM]
4674. do. 1860. [same?] L: Nelson. [Same tr. as #4665.] [EC]
4675. do. 1872-6. [same as #4665] NY: Harper n.d. il. 18. [AC]
4676. do. 1872-6. [same tr. as #4670] 3v. Bohn. [AC]

HUMBOLDT, Ax. v.
4677. do. 1872-6. [same tr. as #4670] Bost: Little, Brown. [AC]
4678. do. 1872-6. [same tr. as #4670] Phil: Lippincott. [AC]
4679. do. 1872-6. [same tr. as #4670] NY: Scribner & W. [AC]
4680. do. 1881. [same as #4670] L: Bell. 3v. 19cm. [LC]
4681. do. 1895. Travels to equinoctial America, 1799-1804. L: Routledge. 3v. 8. [Probably same as #4670.] [EC]
4682. (Vues des Cordillères.) Researches concerning...the ancient inhabitants of America. Tr. Helen M. Williams. L: Longmans, etc. 1814. 2v. in one. il. 22cm. [LC]
4683. The life, travels, and books of Ax. v. H--, by R. H. S. With introd. by Bayard Taylor. NY: Rudd & Carleton 1859. xx;482p. 18cm. [BM]
[Biog. largely from Klencke (cf. #5030); remainder is mainly from his accounts of his travels, in the tr. of Ross, Sabine, Williams, and Black; also material from Taylor's "Encyclopedia of modern travel."]
4684. do. 1859. [same?] Life, travels, and books of H--, by B. Taylor. L: Low 1859. 8. [Probably British ed. of foregoing.] [EC]
4685. do? 1860. [same?] Life and travels. Blackwood. 12. [EC]
4686. do. 1865. [same as #4683] [AC]
4687. do. 1892. [same as #4685] L: Nelson. New ed. 8. [EC]
See "Bruhns, K:," "Life of A. v. H--," #810. See Loewenberg, J., "A. v. H--. Youth and early manhood," #5858. See Schwarzenberg, F., "Ax. v. H--," #8692.

HUMBOLDT, (F:) W: (Cn. K: Fd.) Frhr. v. 1767-1835.
*4688. (Briefe an eine Freundin.) Letters to a female friend (Cte. Diede). Complete tr. from 2d. Ger. ed. by Cath. M. A. Couper. L: Chapman 1849. 2v. xx;348; 244p. 19cm. [BM.LC]
[Couper did not do most of vol. 1. The other tr. was perhaps Dr. Stebbing. See the following.]
4689. do. 1849. Tr. Dr. Stebbing. L: Hall. 8. [EC]
[Probably same as the foregoing.]
*4690. do. 1849. Thoughts and opinions of a statesman. Tr. anon. L: Pickering 1849. 166p. 17cm. [BM]
[Sel. from the "Briefe," freshly tr. Really relig. thoughts, see #4692.]
4691. do. 1850. [same] 2d ed. [LC]
4692. do. 1851. [same] Relig. thoughts and opinions. Bost: Crosby & N. 171p. 17cm. [LC.BM]
4693. do. 1852. [same as #4688] L: Chapman. 2v. 8. [EC]
4694. do. 1864. Letters to a lady. Tr. anon. Introd. C: G. Leland. Phil: Leypoldt; NY: Christern. 257p. 17cm. [LC]
[Probably from Couper's tr.]
4695. do. 1873. [same as foregoing] New ed. NY: Holt. [AC]
4696. The early romantic school. Tr. Jas. T. Hatfield. 1913-15. In C154(4).
*4697. (Ideen zu einem Versuch, die Grenzen der Wirksamkeit des Staates zu bestimmen.) The sphere and duties of government. Tr. J. Coulthard, Jr. L: Chapman 1844. xv;203p. 19cm. [BM]
4698. do. 1854. [same] [LC]
4699. Schiller and the progress of his intellectual development. Tr. Fes. H. King. 1913-15. In C154(4).
See Goethe, Corr. with W: v. H-- and his wife, #3030.

HUMPERDINCK, En. 1854-1921. Operas. Hänsel and Gretel, see Wette, Ade. Königskinder, see Rosmer, Ern.

HUONDER, An. 1858-1926.
4700. (Vater Renés letzte Fahrt.) Father René's last journey. Tr. Helena Long. 1897. In C370a.

HUTTEN, U: v. 1488-1523. Sel. in C88;190;469;570.
See Herder, J. G. "A tribute to U: v. H--," #4219. See Strauss, D:, "Life and times," #9223.

IFFLAND, A: W: 1759-1814.
4701. (Das Gewissen.) Conscience. Tr. B: Thompson. 1801. In C535.
4702. do. 1903. [same] In C18.
4703. do. n.d. Education: a comedy in five acts by T: Morton. L: Cumberland. [Borrowed in part from #4701.] [LC]
§4704. (Das Mündel.) The nephews: a play. Freely tr. H. E. Lloyd. L: Spilsbury 1799. 104p. 21cm. [Very free indeed.] [BM.LCO]
*4705. (Die Advokaten.) The lawyers: a drama in five acts (and in prose). Tr. C: Ludger. L: Myers for West 1799. 106p. 21cm. [BM]
§4706. (Die Hagestolzen.) The bachelors: a comedy in five acts (and in prose). Tr. anon. L: Myers for Pitkeathley 1799. 109p. 21cm. [German misunderstood.] [BM]
§4707. (Die Jäger.) The foresters: a picture of rural manners. A play in five acts (and in prose). Tr. Bell Plumptre. L: Vernor & Hood 1799. 119p. 21cm. [E.g.: "It is not evening all day."] [BM]
4708. (Die Nachbarschaft.) The good neighbor: an interlude in one act. Altered...by W: Dunlap. NY: Longworth 1814. 12p. 12. [LCO]
*4709. (Verbrechen aus Ehrsucht.) Crime from ambition: a play in five acts (and in prose). Tr. Ma. Geisweiler. L: Geisweiler 1800. 131p. 20cm. [BM]

IHERING, Rd. v. 1818-92.
*4710. (Der Kampf ums Recht.) The struggle for law. Tr. from 5th Ger. ed. by J. J. Lalor. Chic: Callaghan 1879. 130p. 12. [LC] [Very good tr.]
*4711. do. 1883. The battle for right. Tr. P. A. Ashworth. L: Stevens. xii;84p. 21cm. [Lalor's tr. is better.] [BM]
4712. do. 1915. Lalor's tr. 2d ed. 138p. [LC]
*4713. (Der Zweck im Recht.) Law as a means to an end. Tr. I: Husik, with edit. pref. by Js. H. Drake, and with introd. by H: Lamm and W. M. Geldart. Bost. bk. co. 1913. lix;483p. 21cm. [LC] [Tr. includes first vol. of orig. work. Also, in Appendix I, Rd. v. Ihering by Ad. Merkel, tr. by Ab. Kocourek.]
4714. do. 1921. [same (reissue)] Macmillan. [LC]
*4715. (Vorgeschichte der Indo-Europäer.) The evolution of the Aryan. Tr. A. Drucker. L: Sonnenschein 1897. xviii;412p. 23cm. [BM.LC]

IHNE, W: 1821-1902.
4716. Early Rome, to its destruction by the Gauls. Tr. anon. L: Longmans, Green 1876. xix;207p. 15cm. [BM.LC] [A popular condensation of his larger work.]
4717. do. 1882. [same] 3d ed. Longmans. [LC]
4718. do. 1886. [same] NY: Scribner. xx;217p. 16cm. [LC]
4719. do. 1891. [same] 7th ed. Longmans. [LC]
4720. do. 1904. [same] L: Longmans. [ABP]
4721. do. 1907. [same] NY: Scribner. [ABP]
*4722. The history of Rome. L: Longmans 1871-82. 5v. 8. [BM.LC] [Tr. or rather rewritten from the orig. by the author.]

IMHOFF, afterwards Helwig, Ame. Freiin v. 1776-1831. See Auerbach, "Deutsche Abende," #146.

IMMANUEL, ---. Sel. in C296.

IMMERMANN, K: Lbt. 1796-1840. Sel. in C17;366;372;391;393;469;489;499; #2687.
4723. The wonders in the Spessart. Tr. J: Oxenford. 1844. In C441-2.
§4724. The Oberhof. Tr. P. B. Thomas. 1913-15. In C154(7).

INGERSLEBEN, Frau Eme. (v. Loga) v. 1822-71. See "Rothenfels, E. v."

INGOLSTETTER, An. J: 1633-1711. Sel. in C229.

"IRA, Af." See Grimm, A. F. W.

ISELIN, I: 1728-82. Sel. in C12.

ISENBERG, C. See Gundert, H., Biog. of C. I--. #3544.

ITALIENER, H:
†4725. (Der Rattenfänger von Hameln.) The rat-charmer of Hamelin: comic opera in four acts. Ad. by Neuendorff. Vocal score. Engl; Ger. NY: Schuberth 1881. 198p. 4. [A very free version.] [LCM]

JACOBI, F: H: 1743-1819. Sel. in C12;194;469.

JACOBI, J: G: 1740-1814. Sel. in C17;22;25-6;31;43;137a;178;269; 306;309;373;380;489;533;560.

JACOBS, F: Cn. W: 1764-1847. Sel. in C12;158.
**4726. (Hellas. Vorträge...) Hellas; or, the home, history, lit., and art of the Greeks. Tr. J: Oxenford. L: Parker 1855. xii;335p. 17cm. [Posthumous, ed. by E. F. Wüstemann. Lect. deliv. 1808-9 before Prince L: of Bavaria. Tr. seems to be excellent.] [BM]

JACOBSON, Lp. Operettas. See Bernauer, Rd., and Doermann, F.

JACOBSON, Lp. and Rd. Oesterreicher.
4727. (Katja, die Tänzerin.) Katja, the dancer: musical play in 3 acts by "Jean Gilbert." Tr. anon. Libr. Engl. 1923. 107p. Tw[LCM]
4728. do. 1925. Ad. by F: Lonsdale and Harry Graham. Vocal score. Engl. L: Ascherberg, Hopwood & Crew. 97p. 31cm. [LCM]
4729. do. 1926. [same] Libr. n.i. 39;30; 30p. 28cm. Tw. [LCM]

JAEGER, A: 1864- . Sel. in C42.

JAEGER, ---. Sel. in C173.

JAGOW, Gb. v. 1863- .
*4730. Reply (to Lichnowsky memorandum). Tr. Munroe Smith. 1918. In C160. [German and English.]

JAHN, K.
4731. Augusta, grand duchess of Mecklenburg-Schwerin. A biog. sketch. Tr. J. Rafter. Schwerin: A. Hildebrand 1864. 90p. 15cm. [BM]

JAHN, O: 1813-69.
*4732. (Mozart.) The life of M--. Tr. Pauline D. Townsend. With pref. by G: Grove. L: Novello 1882. 3v. 28cm. [BM.LC]

JAKOB VON DER WARTE. Sel. in C88.

JANITSCHEK, D. Sel. in C102.

JANSSEN, J:s, 1829-91.
*4733. (Geschichte des deutschen Volkes seit dem Ausgang des Mittelalters.) Hist. of the Ger. people at (i.e., after) the close of the middle ages. L: Paul, T. & T. 1896-1925. 17v. 23cm. [Vols. 1-2 tr. M. A. Mitchell and A. M. Christie; remainder tr. by Christie. Vol. 17 is index, pub. sep. by Herder, 1925.][BM.LC]

JARNO, G: 1868-1920. The girl and the Kaiser. Operetta. See Buchbinder, B., #818.

JAROSY, Rd.
4734. (Im Schneegestöber.) A warm reception: a comedietta, in one act. Tr. ad. for Amer. stage by Mabel Morse. NY: De Witt 1890. 11p. 19cm. [LC]

JEGERLECHNER, J:s.
4734a. Alp legends (ed. by J--). Tr. I. M. Witworth; il. R. Munzer; col. il. M. Todhunter. Sherrat & Hughes 1926. 229p. 8. [EC]

JEILER, Igs.
4735. (Leben der ehrwürdigen Klosterfrau M. C. Höss.) Life of the venerable Mary Crescentia Höss. Tr. C. Deymann. NY: Benziger 1886. 357p. 12. [LCO]

JENBACH, Bela. Operettas. See Gatti, E. v., #2124. See Stein, Leo., #9035.

JENBACH, Bela and Rb. Pohl.
§4736. (Madame Troubadour.) Madame Troubadour: operetta in 3 acts by Albini. Tr. Js. W. Herbert. Vocal score. NY: Stern 1910. 148p. fol. [Quite free.] [LCM]

JENSEN, W: 1837-1911. Sel. in C67;112;423;501.
4737. (Die Insel.) Fair isle: a tale in verse. Tr. by a Shetlander. Kirkwall: W. Peace; Ed: Menzies 1881. 65p. front. vignettes. 18cm. [BM]
*4738. (Gradiva. Ein pompejanisches Fantasiestück.) Gradiva: a Pompeian fancy. Tr. Helen M. Downey. In Freud, "Delusion and dream." 1917. #1892. [Not ideal, but very good.]
4739. do. 1918. [same] Gradiva, etc. NY: Moffat, Yard. 118p. 19cm. [Sep. publication.] [LC]
*4740. (Karin von Schweden.) Karin. Tr. Lillie A. Mercur. Towanda, Pa: Mercur 1882. 50p. 22cm. [On the whole, excellent.] [LC]
§4741. do. 1894. Karin of Sweden. Tr. Mrs. Ellen Waugh. NY: Collier. 208p. 18cm. [Fairly good.] [LC]
†4742. do. 1896. Karine: a story of Swedish love. Tr. Emma A. Endlich. Chic: McClurg. 211p. 17cm. [LC]
[Bad tr.; she tries to be poetic.]
4743. (Runensteine.) Runic rocks: a North-Sea idyl. Tr. Marianne E. Suckling. With pref. by G. Fiedler. L: Stock 1895. xv;269p. 8. [BM]
4744. do. 1898. [same] Cheap ed. [BM]

JERITZA, Ma. (Baronin v. Popper), 1891- .
4745. Sunlight and song: a singer's life. Tr. F: H. Martens. NY;L: Appleton 1924. 262p. il. 21cm. [LC.BM]

JERRMANN, E: 1795-1859.
*4746. (Unpolitische Bilder aus St. Petersburg.) Pictures from St. P--. Tr. F: Hardman. L: Longmans 1852. 2 pts. 276p. 17cm. [BM]
4747. do. 1855. [same] St. P--: its people, their character and institutions. NY: Barnes. 234p. 19cm. [LC]

JERUSALEM, J: F: W: 1709-89.
4748. Life of prince Ab. H: of Brunswick Luneburg [sic]. Tr. anon. L: Curtis, etc. 1763. 46p. 19cm. [BM]
[Name also spelled Hierusalem.]

JERUSALEM, W: 1854-1923.
4748a. Introd. to philos. Auth. tr. from 4th ed. by C: F. Sanders. Macmillan 1910. x;319p. D. [AC]

JIRICZEK, O: Luitpold, 1867- .
§4749. (Nordische Heldensagen.) Northern hero legends. Tr. M. Bentinck Smith. L: Dent 1902. 146p. 15cm. [BM.LC]
[Tr. seems to alter arbitrarily.]

JOACHIM, Js. 1831-1907.
*4750. Letters from and to...sel. and tr. Mrs. Nora Bickley. With pref. by J. A. Fuller-Maitland. L: Macmillan 1914. xiii;470p. il. 23cm. [BM.LC]

JOACHIM, Js.- Letters
[A relatively small sel., includ. 25 letters exch. w. Brahms, and giving something like a chronol. survey of his career.]

JOANNES DE HILDESHEIM, fl. 1358, d. 1375.
4751. (Historia trium regum.) The three kings of Cologne. An early Engl. (abr.) tr. ca. 1400. Tr. anon. In Early Engl. text soc. 1886. xxi;312p. 21cm. [Engl., Lat., and readings.] [BM]

JOHANN Ern. I., Herzog v. Sachsen-Weimar, 1594-1626. Sel. in C483. See Neumayr v. Ramssla, J:, #6701.

JOHANN F:? prince of Württemberg, 1582-1628. Sel. in C483.

JOHANN VON BRABANT, Herzog (Jan I), fl. 1269-94. Sel. in C27;416; 427.

JOHANNE Jne., Gräfin v. Reden. See Reuss, E., "A pietist of the Napol. wars," #7405.

JOHN, Ege. 1825-87. See "Marlitt, E."

JOLSDORF, Gf. See "Ottfried."

JONAS, Jt. 1493-1555. Sel. in C570.
4752. True hystorye of the Christen departynge of...D. Martyne Luther, collected by J. J--, Ml. Celius, and Joannes Aurifaber. Tr. Johan Bale. Marburg? Hans Luft? 1546. 32fol. 8. [BM]

JORDAN, W: 1819-94. Sel. in C450.

JORGENS, J. L., d. 1827. Sel. in C244.

JOSEPH II, Kaiser, 1741-90.
*4754. (Recueil de lettres originales de l'empereur Js. II au général D'Alton...) Letters...to Gen. D'Alton, commander of the troops in the Austrian Netherlands. Tr. anon. L: Robinson 1790. ff. a-c, 198p. 17cm. [BM]
[Tr. includes the lengthy and censorious pref. to the "Recueil," Paris, 1790.]
*4753. (Briefe J's II.) Letters...to disting. princes and statesmen (now first tr. from the Ger.) Tr. anon. L: Pamphleteer. Vol. 19, 1821. pp. 1-96. Vol. 20, 1822. pp. 273-96. 21cm. [BM.LC]
[A special group of 54 letters "recently published in Germany."]
See Mühlbach, L., "Jos. II and his court," #6428.

JOSEPHSON, L: 1809- . Sel. in C287.

JUENGER, J: F: 1759-97.
4755. (Wilhelmine, oder alles ist nicht Gold, was glänzt.) Wilhelmine: a novel. L: Lowndes 1807. 2v. Ryl. 18. [EC]

JUENGST, Ane. 1845-1918.
4756. A brother's sacrifice. Ad. Aloysius J. Eifel. Techny, Il. Soc. of the divine word 1909. 222p. 19cm. [LC]
4757. Quo vadis: musical drama by Fx. Nowowiejski. Text based on novel by Henryk Sienkiewicz. Tr. J: Bernhoff. Libr. Engl. text w. notes,... Fulda: Maier 1912. 36p. [Copyright 1909.] [LCM]
4758. Sister Angela. Tr. anon. 1902. In C481.

"JUNCKER, E." (i.e., Frau Else (Kobert) Schmieden, 1841-96).
4759. (Lebensrätsel.) Margarethe; or, life-problems. Tr. Mrs. A. L. Wister. Phil: Lippincott 1878. 12. [AC]
4760. do. 1883. [same] Margaret's ordeal; or, life-problems. L: Ward, Lock. 224p. 17cm. [BM]
4761. do. 1906. [same] Phil: Lippincott. 336p. 19cm. [LC]

"JUNCKER, E."
4762. Lucy; or, married from pique. A story of real life. Tr. Js. A. Sigmund. Bost: Loring 1868. 52p. 23cm. [LC.BM]

JUNG, C: Gst. 1875-
4763. Marriage as a psychol. relationship. Tr. 1926. In C308.

JUNGHANS, So. 1845-1907.
4764. (Die Erbin wider Willen.) The heiress against her will. Tr. Lilian Field. L: Lit. soc. 1885. 245p. 19cm. [BM]
[Author's name spelled: Yunghaus.]

JUNG-STILLING, J: H: 1740-1817.
*4765. [Coll.] Interesting tales. Tr. S: Jackson. L: Hamilton, Adams 1837. 12. [BM]
[Ten stories pub. by his daughter Caroline. Includ. incidents connected with his life which do not appear in his biog.-- Conrad the good ("Kd. der Gute"); The emigrant ("Der Emigrant"); The noble youths ("Die edlen Jünglinge"); Blind Leonard and his guide ("Leonhard und Bernhardine"); The watchman and his daughter ("Der Nachtwächter und seine Tochter"); The way to the throne ("Der Weg zum Thron"); Gotthard and his sons ("G-- und seine Söhne"); A holy family ("Auch eine heilige Familie"); The poor weaver ("Der arme Leinweber"); An extraordinary effect of the imagination ("Eine ausserordentliche Wirkung der Einbildungskraft").]
4766. (H: Stillings Jugend, Jünglingsjahre und Wanderschaft.) Life. Tr. E. L. Hazelius. Gettysburg, Pa: Neinstedt 1831. 416p. 8.[LCO]
*4767. do. 1835-6. H: S--. Part 1. Childhood. L: Hamilton, Adams 1835. 371p. Part 2. His domestic life and years of tuition. 1835. 445p. Part 3. Sequel to H: S--, containing S--'s old age (H: S--'s Alter); his last hours, a supplement, by his son-in-law (i.e., grandson, W. H. E. Schwarz); and letters to S-- from Lavater, Oberlin, Moser, Baroness v. Krudener, Prince C: of Hesse-Cassel. 1836. 342p. Tr. S: Jackson. 12. [BM.LCO]
4768. do. 1842. [same] L: Hamilton. 8. [EC]
4769. do. 1843. [same] 2d ed. L: J: Wright; also Hamilton, Adams. 173p. 24cm. [BM]
[Contains all of #4767 except the letters of part 3. Prt. in double columns.]
4770. do. 1844. [same?] Autobiog. Tr. S: Jackson. NY: Harper. 188p. [LCO]
4771. do. 1845. [same?] Autobiog. Tr. S: Jackson. NY: Harper. [LCO]
4772. do. 1847. Life, by Jackson, abr. by Wright. L: Houlston. 32. [EC]
4773. Introd. to Stahlschmidt's Pilgrimage. Tr. S: Jackson. 1837. In #9013.
4773a. Sel. Tr. S. Jackson. 1833. 32. [EC]
4774. (Szenen aus dem Geisterreiche.) Scenes in the world of spirits. Tr. from 3d orig. ed. by Gb. Shober. New-Market: Prt. by A. Henkel 1815. 282p. 18cm. [LC]
§4775. (Theobald oder die Schwärmer.) Theobald; or, the fanatic. A true history. Tr. S: Schaeffer. Phil: Hooker; NY: Saxton & Miles 1846. 286p. 20cm. [Tr. expands and "interprets."] [LC.BM]

JUNKER, W: J: 1840-92.
*4776. (Reisen in Afrika.) Travels in Africa, 1875-86. Tr. A: H: Keane. L: Chapman & Hall 1890-2. 3v. il. 23cm. [BM.LC]
["In this tr. the spirit of the Ger. text has been adhered to, with condensation of non-essential details throughout."]

JUST, Ad.
4777. (Kehrt zurück zur Natur!) Return to nature. Author. tr. by H. A. Nesbitt. L: Routledge; NY: Dutton 1912. viii,460p. il. 22cm.[BM]

JUST, Coelestin, A:
4778. Sketch of the life of Novalis. Tr. W: Hastie. 1888. In #6960.
4779. do. 1891. Tr. J. Hope. In #6961.

JUST, Gst.
4780. Life of Luther. Tr. Mn. Sommer and F: W: Herzberger. St.L: Concordia 1903. 103p. il. 19cm. [LC]

KADELBURG, Gst. 1851-1925. See Blumenthal, Ok., and Schönthan, Fz., joint authors.

KADEN, Wol. 1838- . See Stieler, K., joint author.

"KAHLENBERG, H. v." (i.e., Frau He.--v. Mombart--Kessler, 1870-). Sel. in C422.

KAHLERT, K. F. See "Flammenberg, Lz."

KAISENBERG, Mz. Lp. Ld. v. 1837-1910.
4781. Memoirs of the Baroness Cecile de Courtot, cómpiled from the (17) letters (in French)...to Frau v. Alvensleben...and the diary (also in French) of the latter by her great-grandson...Tr. from the Ger. by Jessie Haynes. NY: Holt 1900. xiv;298p. 22cm. [LC.BM]

KAISER, G: 1878- .
**4782. (Gas.) Gas: a play in five acts (and in prose). Tr. H. G. Scheffauer. Bost: Small, Maynard; L: Chapman & Dodd 1924. 96p. 19cm.[The translator's art can go no further.--Gas I only.][LC.BM]
*4783. (Von Morgens bis Mitternachts.) From morn to midnight: a play in seven scenes (and in prose). Tr. Ashley Dukes. L: Hendersons 1920. 58p. 7 x 5 in. [BM]
4784. do. 1920. [same] In "Poet-Lore" 31:317-363.
4785. do. 1922. [same] NY: Brentano's. 154p. il. 19cm. [LC]

KALB, J: 1721-81. See Kapp, F:, Life of Major J: Kalb, etc., #4859.

KALBERER, John.
4786. Margaret: dramatic scenes from the life of St. Marg. Ma. Alacoque. Author. tr. and ad. by a friar minor. Cincin: Franciscan fathers, 42 Calhoun St. 1923. 85p. S. [AC]

KÁLMÁN, Emmerich. Operettas. See Bakony, K: v.; Bodansky, R; Brammer, Jl.; Wilhelm, Jl. See also the gipsy princess, A211.

KALM, ---. Sel. in C67.

KANT, Im. 1724-1804. Sel. in C12;194*;366*;461;469;574*.

COLLECTIONS

*4787. 1798. Elements of the crit. philos: essays and treatises on moral, polit., and various philos. subjects. Tr. by the tr. of the "Principles of crit. philos." (cf. #306), i.e., A. F. M. Willich. L: W:Richardson 1798, 99. 2v. xv;432; xix;444p. 21cm. [Tr. seems excellent. This vol. includes "Synopsis of the critique of pure reason" by Johannes Schultz, probably translated (see Wellek, "Kant in England," 1931, p. 268) by J: Colquhoun. --Correspondent.] [BM]
†4788. 1819. The metaphysical works. Tr. J: Richardson. L: Simpkin & Marshall. 2 pts. 21cm. [BM]
[Later trs. are united in the opinion that R. knew neither German nor philos.--Part 1. Logic. Introd. (to p. 124), 244p. Part 2. Prolegomena. xviii;216p.]
4789. 1836. [same] L: Simpkin & M. 3 pts. 21cm. [BM]
[Parts 1 and 2 same as foregoing. Part 3. An enquiry...into the... proof for the existence of God. (Der einzige mögliche Beweisgrund zu einer Demonstration des Daseins Gottes.) Prt. in 1819, but now first published. xx;262p. (introd. to p. 50.)

KANT, Im.--Collections

*4790. 1873. Theory of ethics, or practical philos. Tr. T: K. Abbott. L: Longmans. viii;262p. 18cm. [BM]
[Fundamental principles of the metaphysic of morals ("Grundlegung zur Metaphysik der Sitten"); Dialectic and methodology of practical reason ("Kritik der praktischen Vernunft," extract); On the radical evil in human nature (Part 1 of "Die Religion innerhalb der...blossen Vernunft").]

4791. 1879. [same] Critique of practical reason and other works on the theory of ethics. L: Longmans. 8. [EC]
[Enl. ed. of the foregoing; cf. next entry.]

*4792. 1883. [same] Theory of ethics, etc. 3d rev. and enl. ed. with memoir and port. L: Longmans. lxiv;368p. 22cm. [BM]
[Completes tr. of "Kritik der praktischen Vernunft"; adds Introd. to the metaphysic of morals (from two sources); Also a new appendix on "The right to lie."]

4793. 1889. [same] 4th ed. lxiv;368p. [BM]

§4794. 1891. Principles of politics, includ. his essay on perpetual peace. Ed. and tr. W: Hastie. Ed: Clark; L: Hamilton; NY: Scribner. xliv;148p. 19cm. [BM.LC]
[Idea of universal hist.; Principles of polit. right; The principle of progress; Perpetual peace.]

4795. 1895. Fundamental principles of the metaphysics of ethics. Extr. from K--'s Critique of pract. reason and other works on the theory of ethics. Tr. T: K. Abbott. 3d ed. L;NY: Longmans. 102p. 19cm. [BM]

4796. 1898. Critique of practical reason, etc. 5th rev. ed. (cf. #4791-2). L;NY: Longmans. 368p. [LC]

*4797. 1900. K--'s cosmogony, as in his essay on the retardation of the rotation of the earth and his nat. hist. and theory of the heavens. With introd., append., and a port. of T: Wright of Durham. Ed. and tr. W: Hastie. Glasgow: Maclehose. cix;205p. 20cm. [BM.LC]

4798. 1907. [same as #4795] 3d ed. Longmans. 102p. [BM.LC]

4799. 1909. [same as #4796] 6th ed. [LC]

4800. 1914. Eternal peace, and other internat. essays. Tr. W: Hastie. Introd. by Edwin D. Mead. Bost: World peace foundation. xxiv;179p. 20cm. [LC]

4801. [Sel.] The principles of crit. philos., sel. from the work... and expounded by Jas. S. Beck...Univ. of Halle. Tr. by an auditor of the latter, i.e., A. F. M. Willich (cf. #4787). L: J.Johnson, W: Richardson 1797. lxxx;454p. 22cm. [BM]
[Apparently no direct citation of Kant; rather a digest and exposition by Beck.]

*4802. [Sel.] 1888. The philos. of K-- as contained in extracts from his own writings. Sel. and tr. J: Watson. Glasgow: Maclehose. x;356p. 20cm. [BM]

4803. [Sel.] 1901. [same] New ed. Glasgow: Maclehose; NY;L: Macmillan. [LC]

4804. [Sel.] 1911. Attempt to introd. conception of neg. quant. into philos. Concerning the first ground of the difference of environs in space; A new theory of motion and rest, and the consequent results for the rudiments of nat. science. In D: Irvine, "Metaphysical rudiments of liberalism," L: Watts. pp. 117-83. [BM]

4805. [Sel.] 1919. [same as #4802] Macmillan. 356p. [LC]

4806. (Anthropologie in pragmatischer Hinsicht.) Anthropology. Tr. A. E. Kroeger. In C300(9-11, 13-16).

†4807. (De mundi sensibilis atque intelligibilis forma et principiis.) Inaugural dissertation of 1770. Tr. W: J. Eckoff.

KANT, Im.
NY: Columbia coll. 1894. 101p. 24cm. [LC]
[Tr. adds and elaborates, and is not faithful to K--'s language.]
§4808. (Die Religion innerhalb der Grenzen der blossen Vernunft.) Relig. within the boundary of pure reason. Tr. J. W. Semple. Ed: Clark 1838. x;275p. 8. [BM.LCO]
4809. do. 1848. [same] 2d ed. (B6)
†4810. (Grundlegung zur Metaphysik der Sitten.) The metaphysic of morals, divided into metaphys. elements of law and of ethics. Tr. J: Richardson. L: W: Richardson 1799. 2v. xli;132; lix;84p. 18cm. [BM]
[Cf. #4788.]
†4811. do. 1836. Tr. with introd. and append. by J. W. Semple. Ed: Clark. 378p. 21cm. [BM.LC]
[Part of "Kritik der prakt. Vernunft." Also, "Metaphysische Anfangsgründe der Tugendlehre."]
4812. do. 1869. [same] New ed. with introd. by H. Calderwood. Ed: Clark. xvi;307p. 19cm. [BM.LC]
4813. do. 1871 [same] 3d ed. xx;315p. 19cm. [BM.LC]
4814. do. 1886. [same] 4th ed. (B6)
§4815. do. 1887. Philos. of law. Tr. W: Hastie. Ed: Clark. xxxvi; 265p. 19cm. [Verbose.] [BM.LC]
4816. do. 1910. Fundamental principles of the metaphysic of morals. Tr. T: K. Abbott. In C119. Also in C370. [Cf. #4790.]
4817. (Ideen zu einer allgemeinen Geschichte in weltbürgerlicher Absicht.) Idea of a universal hist. Tr. anon. 1800? In C157.
4818. do. 1927. Idea of a universal hist. on a cosmo-political plan. Tr. T: De Quincey. Hanover, N. H: Sociological press. 14p. O. [AC]
†4819. (Kritik der reinen Vernunft.) Critick of pure reason. Tr. Fis. Haywood. L: Pickering 1838. xxxvi;655p. 22cm. [BM.LC]
[Severely criticized by Meiklejohn, #4822.]
4820. do. 1844. An analysis...(by Fis. Haywood). L: W:Pickering. 215p. 22cm. [An epitome of K--'s work.] [BM]
4821. do. 1848. [same] 2d ed., with notes and explan. of terms. L: Pickering. xlvi;625p. 22cm. [BM]
*4822. do. 1855. Critique of pure reason. Tr. J: M. D. Meiklejohn. L: Bohn. xliii;517p. 18cm. [Includes K--'s two prefs.] [BM]
4823. do. 1872. [same] L: Bell & D. 517p. [LC]
*4824. do. 1881. Im. Kant's critique of pure reason. Tr. F: Max Müller, with an hist. introd. by L. Noiré. Centenary ed. L: Macmillan. 2v. 22cm. [BM.LC]
*4825. do. 1881. Textbook to Kant. The critique of pure reason: aesthetic categories and schematism. Tr., reproduction, commentary, index, with biog. sketch, by J. H. Stirling. Ed: Oliver & Boyd. xxviii;548p. 23cm. [BM]
4826. do. 1884. Critic of pure reason criticised and explained by himself. Tr. A. E. Kroeger. In C300(14).
4827. do. 1889. K--'s crit. philos. for Engl. readers. By J. D. Mahaffy and J: H: Bernard. New and completed ed. Vol. 1. L: Macmillan. xix;389p. 19cm. [BM]
[The Kritik of the pure reason expl. and defended. Commentary and tr. mingled.]
4828. do. 1896. [same as #4824] 808p. 21cm. [LC]
4829. do. 1899. [same as #4822] Rev. ed. NY: Colonial press. 480p. il. 24cm. [LC]
4830. do. 1907. [same as #4824] 2d rev. ed. NY: Macmillan. lxxxii; 808p. [LC.BM]
4831. do. 1918. Norman K. Smith. A commentary... L: Macmillan. lxi; 615p. 22cm. [Has much from the "Kritik" in his own tr.] [BM]
4832. do. 1923. [same] 2d rev. and enl. ed. lxi;651p. [BM]

KANT, Im.

*4833. (Kritik der Urteilskraft.) Critique of judgment. Tr. w. introd. and notes by J: H: Bernard. L;NY: Macmillan 1892. xlviii; 429p. 23cm. [BM.LC]

§4834. do. 1911. Critique of aesthetic judgment. Tr. Jas. C. Meredith. With 7 introd. essays, notes, and anal. index by tr. Oxford: Clarendon. clxx;333p. 19cm. [BM.LC]

4835. do. 1914. Bernard's tr. 2d rev. ed. Macmillan. xlviii; 429p. [BM]

*4836. (Logik.) Introd. to logic, and, Essay on the mistaken subtilty of the four figures. Tr. T: K. Abbott, with a few notes by Coleridge. L: Longmans 1885. 100p. 22cm. [BM]

4837. On the infinite divisibility of space. Tr. J: Watson. 1890. In C300(20).

†4838. (Prolegomena zu einer jeden künftigen Metaphysik.) Prolegomena to every future metaphysic. Tr. J: Richardson. L: Simpkin & Marshall 1819. xviii;206p. 22cm. [BM]
[Bax severely criticizes this, and Mahaffy says it is full of errors. Cf. #4788.]

*4839. do. 1872. K--'s crit. philos. for Engl. readers, by J. P. Mahaffy. Prolegomena, etc. L: Longmans. xiii;281p. 21cm. [BM]
[Append., pp. 191-281.]

*4840. do. 1883. Proleg. and metaphys. foundations of nat. science. Tr. E. B. Bax. L: Bell & sons. cix;254p. 18cm. [BM]

4841. do. 1889. Tr. with notes and append. by J. P. Mahaffy and J: H: Bernard. Rev. ed. Macmillan. 239p. 19cm. [BM]

4842. do. 1891. Bax's tr. 2d rev. ed. L: Bell. 254p. 18cm. [LC]

*4843. do. 1902. Proleg. to any future metaphysics. Tr. Pl. Carus. Chic: Open court; L: Paul, T. &. T. v;301p. 19cm. [LC.BM]

4844. do. 1915. [same as #4841] 3d ed. Macmillan. [BM]

*4845. (Träume eines Geistersehers.) Dreams of a spirit-seer. Tr. E. P. Goerwitz. L: Sonnenschein; NY: Macmillan 1900. xiv;161p. 19cm. [BM.LC]

4846. (Ueber ein vermeintes Recht, aus Menschenliebe zu lügen.) Concerning a pretended right to lie from motives of humanity. Tr. A. E. Kroeger. 1877. In C300(7).

*4847. (Ueber Pädagogik.) K-- on education. Tr. Annette Churton. Introd. by Mrs. Rhys Davids. L: Paul, T. & T. 1899. xix;121p. 19cm. [BM.LC]

*4848. do. 1904. Educational theory. Tr. E: F. Buchner. Phil;L: Lippincott. xvi;309p. [Has bibliog. of translations.] [LC.BM]

4849. do. 1906. [same as #4847] Bost: Heath. [LC]

4850. do. 1908. [same as #4848] [LC]

4850a. ("Von der Macht des Gemüts, durch den blossen Vorsatz, seiner krankhaften Gefühle Meister zu sein. Streit der Fakultäten," part 3.) Tr. by J: Colquhoun in "The code of health and longevity," ed. Sir J: Sinclair. L: 1806, III:245.[Correspondent.]

§4851. (Zum ewigen Frieden.) Project for a perpetual peace: a philos. essay. Tr. anon. L: Vernor & Hood 1797. See "Monthly Mirror" 3(1797): 166. (B26)
[Tr. is smooth but not very close and not always accurate.]

4852. do. 1849. Plan of an everlasting peace. Tr. Cabot. In C194.

*4853. do. 1884. A philos. treatise on perpetual peace. By J. D. Morell. L: Hodder & Stoughton. ix;88p. 16cm. [BM]

*4854. do. 1897. Perpetual peace. Tr. B: F. Trueblood. Bost: Amer. peace soc. 53p. 19cm. [One bad error on first page.] [LC.BM]

**4855. do. 1903. Perpetual peace: philos. essay, 1795. Tr. w. introd. and notes by M. Campbell Smith. Pref. by Prof. Latta. L: Sonnenschein. x;203p. 17cm. [BM]
[This seems to me the best tr.-- Introd. to p. 105.]

4856. do. 1915. [same] Macmillan. xi;196p. D. [AC]

KANT, Im.
4857. do. 1915. [same] Cheaper ed. L: Allen & Unwin. [EC]
*4858. do. 1927. Perpetual peace. Tr. Helen O'Brien. L: Sweet & Maxwell. 59p. 21cm. [Excellent tr.] [LC]
See Chamberlain, H., I. Kant...a comparison with Goethe etc., #1080.
See Fischer, K., A critique of Kant, #1627, etc.
See Paulsen, F., Kant, his life and doctrine, #7045.
See Stählin, L., A crit. exam. of Kant, etc., #9011.

KANZLER, Der, 13th cent. Sel. in C416;532.

KAPP, F: 1824-84.
*4859. (Leben des...J: Kalb.) Life of J: Kalb, major general in the revolutionary army. Tr. anon. NY: Holt 1884. ix;337p. 20cm. [Possibly tr. by Bancroft; cf. next entry.] [LC.BM]
*4860. (Leben...F: W: v. Steuben.) Life of F: W: v. Steuben, major general in the revolutionary army. Tr. anon. Introd. by G: Bancroft. NY: Mason 1859. xvi;735p. 20cm. [LC]
[The tr. omits and adds like a historian rather than a mere translator; possibly Bancroft did the tr. himself.]
4861. do. 1859. [same] 2d ed. [BM]

KARG, Cassian.
4861a. In the school of Jesus: introd. to the interior life. Tr. Ed. Krautkraemer. Detroit: Capuchin fathers 1927. 5v. vol. 1. 65p. [AC]
4861b. Little secret: key to the interior life. Tr. by a Capuchin father of St. Joseph's province. 4th ed. Detroit: Capuchin fathers 1926. 44p. S. [AC]

KARL DER GROSSE, 742-814. See Eginhardus, Life of emperor Karl the Great, #1424.
See Hauptmann, G., Kaiser Karls Geisel, #3883. See Prutz, Hs., The age of Charlemagne, #7248.
See Schmidt, Fd., Charlemagne, #8439.

KARL F: v. Sachsen-Weimar, 1783-1853.
4862. Travels through North America in 1825-6. Tr. anon. Phil: Carey, Lea & Carey 1828. 2v. 8. [AC]

"KARLSTEIN, H: Ok. v." (i.e., F. C. Valentine). [Gotham and the Gothamites, listed in my first edition, is not a translation.]

"KARLWEIS, Marta" (i.e., Marta Wassermann, 1889-).
4863. Marriage and the changing woman. Tr. 1926. In C308.

KARPELES, G. 1848-
4864. Jewish lit. and other essays (i.e., addresses). Tr. anon. Phil: Jewish pub. soc. of America. 1895. 404p. 8.[14 essays.] [BM]
4865. Jews and Judaism in the 19th cent. (Lectures.) Tr. anon. from unpub. MS. Phil: Jewish pub. soc. 1905. 83p. 17cm. [BM]

KARSCHIN, Anna Lu. 1729-91. Sel. in C90.

KASTNER, Leo and Af. Möller.
4866. "Yvonne." Musical play in three acts by Jean Gilbert. Engl. by Percy Greenbank. Libr. L: G:Edwardes. 1926. 30cm. Tw. [LCM]
[Partly paged.]
4867. do. 1926. Music by Jean Gilbert and Vernon Duke. Vocal score. L: Ascherberg, Hopwood & Crew. 105p. 31cm. [LCM]

KATSCH, Gst. Ad. 1813- .
4868. (Unter dem Storchnest.) Under the storks' nest: a romance. Tr. Emily R. Steinestel. Phil: Lippincott 1875. 233p. 19cm. [LC]

KAUFFMANN, K: F: 1863- .
4869. (Deutsche Mythologie.) Northern mythology. Tr. M. Steele Smith. L: Dent. Temple primers. 1903. xii;106p. 15cm. [BM.LC] [Cover-title has: D. F. Kauffmann.]

KAUFMANN, Ax. 1821-93. Sel. in C67.

KAUN, Hg. 1863- . The ring of fate: opera. See Drobegg, W:, #1269.

KAUTSKY, K: 1854- .
4870. The capitalist class. Tr. and ad. to America by D. De Leon. NY: Socialist labor party 1911? 32p. 18cm. [LC]
4871. The class struggle. Tr. W: E: Bohn. Chic: Kerr 1910. 217p. 17cm. [LC]
4872. do. 1911. Tr. and ad. to America by D. De Leon. NY: Nat. ex. com. of soc. labor party. 32p. 17cm. [LC]
4873. Communism in central Europe at the time of the reformation. Tr. J. L. and E. G. Mulliken. L: Unwin 1897. 293p. 22cm. [BM]
4874. (Der Ursprung des Christentums.) The origin of Christianity. Tr. anon. NY: Boni & Liveright 1917. [BM]
*4875. do. 1925. Foundations of Christianity. Author. tr. from 13th Ger. ed. L: Allen & U;NY: Internat. pubs. 480p. 24cm. [BM.LC]
4876. (Der Weg zur Macht.) The road to power. Author. tr. by A. M. Simons. Chic: Bloch 1909. 127p. 20cm. [LC]
4877. (Die Diktatur des Proletariats.) The dictatorship of the proletariat. Tr. H. J. Stenning. Manchester: Nat. labour press 1918. vii;149p. 18cm. [BM]
4878. do. 1920. [same] [BM.LC]
4879. (Die proletarische Revolution und ihr Programm.) The social revolution. Tr. A. M. and May W. Simons. Chic: Kerr 1903. 189p. 17cm. [LC]
4880. do. 1925. The labour revolution. Tr. H. J. Stenning. L: Allen & U. 287p. 18cm. [Pp. 1-63 of orig. omitted.] [BM]
§4881. (Ethik und materialistische Geschichtsauffassung.) Ethics and the materialist conception of history. Tr. J: B. Askew. Chic: Kerr 1907. 206p. 17cm. [Poor English style.] [LC]
4882. Frederick Engels: his life, his work, and his writings. Tr. May W. Simons. Chic: Kerr 1890. 32p. 19cm. [LC]
§4883. (Georgien, eine sozialdemokratische Bauernrepublik.) Georgia, a social-democratic peasant republic. Tr. H. J. Stenning and rev. by the author. L: Internat. bookshops 1921. 111p. 18cm. [LC] [Rather poor tr., due to inadequate mastery of German.]
4884. The high cost of living. Tr. Austin Lewis. Chic: Kerr 1914. 114p. 17cm. [LC says: published 1913.] [LC]
4885. (K: Marx' ökonomische Lehren.) The economic doctrines of K: M--. Tr. H. J. Stenning. L: Black 1925. 248p. 20cm. [BM.LC]
*4886. (Rasse und Judentum.) Are the Jews a race? Tr. anon. from 2d Ger. ed. L: Cape 1926. 255p. 20cm. [BM]
4887. The social revolution; and, On the morrow of the social revolution. (Two addresses.) Tr. J: B. Askew. Author. and rev. by author. L: Twentieth cent. press 1903. 50; 43p. 21cm. [LC]
4888. do. 1909. [same?] Rev. by author. 1909. 2 pts. 8. [BM]
4889. The socialist republic, tr. and ad. to America by D. De Leon. NY: Labor news 1911. 48p. 18cm. [LC]
*4890. (Terrorismus und Kommunismus.) Terrorism and communism: contribution to the nat. hist. of revolution. Tr. W. H. Kerridge. L: Allen & U. 1920. 234p. 19cm. [LC]
4891. do. 1920. [same] Manchester; L: Nat. labour press. 234p. 18cm. [Diff. t.p.; otherwise identical.] [BM]
4892. (T: More und sein Utopia.) T: More and his Utopia. Tr. H. J. Stenning. L: Black 1927. 250p. 19cm. [BM]
*4893. (Wie der Weltkrieg entstand.) The guilt of W: Hohenzollern. Tr. anon. L: Skeffington 1920. 272p. 22cm. [BM.LC]

KAUTSKY, K:
4894. The working class...Tr. and ad. to America by D. De Leon. NY: Labor news 1911. 32p. 18cm. [LC]

KAYSER-LANGERHANNSS, Ag. 1818-1902. Sel. in C497.

KEIL, G:
4895. (Neue Märchen für meine Enkel.) New fairy stories for my grandchildren. Tr. S. W. Lander. NY: Appleton 1861. 84p. il. sq. 16. [LÇO]

KEITER, Te. Kellner ("M. Herbert"), 1859-1925.
4896. Poems of Therese. Tr. Ellen Frothingham. NY;L: Putnam 1899. 97p. 16cm.[See also #4201.] [LC]

KELLER, A:n, 1805-81. Sel. in C438.

KELLER, Gf. 1819-90. Sel. in C3;311;317;366*;422-3;469.
4897. [Coll.] The funeral; Clothes make men (abr.). Tr. Zimmern. 1880. In C575-7.
*4898. [Coll.] 1891. A selection of his tales. Tr. Kate F. Kroeker. L: Unwin. 291p. 8. [BM]
[Clothes maketh man ("Kleider machen Leute"); The abused love letters ("Die missbrauchten Liebesbriefe"); Dietegen (do.).]
4899. [Coll.] 1894. [same] Clothes maketh man and other Swiss stories. [BM]
†4900. [Coll.] 1919. Seldwyla folks: three singular tales. Tr. Wolf v. Schierbrand. NY: Brentano's. x;327p. 19cm. [LC]
[Three decent combmakers ("Die drei gerechten Kammacher"); Dietegen (do.); Romeo and Juliet of the village ("Romeo und Julia auf dem Dorfe"). --Tr. of third story is awkward and bungling. First paragraph omitted.]
4901. [Coll.] 1925. The fat of the cat, and other stories. Freely ad. by Louis Untermeyer. Il. Ab. Sallak. NY: Harcourt, Brace. 283p. 21cm. [LC]
[Not a tr., but delightfully done. --The fat of the cat ("Spiegel, das Kätzchen"); Clothes make the man ("Kleider machen Leute"); Hungry Hans (not in coll. works); The virgin and the knight, The nun and the statue (from his "Sieben Legenden").
4902. (Das Fähnlein der sieben Aufrechten.) The company of the upright seven. Tr. B. Q. Morgan. 1913-15. In C154(14).
4903. do. 1917. The banner of the upright seven. Tr. Muriel Almon. In C186.
†4904. (Das Meretlein.) Little Meret. Tr. Lilaise R. Smith. In "Poet-Lore" 17(1906). [Taken from "Der grüne Heinrich," chap. v. Arbitrary.]
4905. (Das Tanzlegendchen.) A legend of the dance. Tr. M. Wyness. 1926. In C68. [Taken from #4916.]
4906. (Der Landvogt von Greifensee.) The governor of G--. Tr. P. B. Thomas and B. Q. Morgan. 1913-15. In C154(14).
4907. (Die Jungfrau und die Nonne.) The virgin and the nun. Tr. M. Wyness. 1927. In C367. [Taken from #4916.]
*4908. (Dietegen.) Dietegen: a novel. Literally tr. anon. NY? n.i. 1894. 48p. 23cm. [BM]
4909. do. 1894. [same?] Tr. Oscar Block. NY. (B13)
4910. (Kleider machen Leute.) Clothes make the man. Tr. A. S. Newcastle-upon-Tyne. 1876. (B13)
§4911. (Romeo und Julia auf dem Dorfe.) A village Romeo and Juliet. Tr. and condensed by H. T. P(orter) and C. P(orter). In "Poet-Lore" 9(1897). [Good style, but needless changes and some errors.]
4912. do. 1913-15. Tr. P. B. Thomas and B. Q. Morgan. In C154(14).
*4913. do. 1914. Tr. A. C. Bahlmann. Introd. by Edith Wharton. NY:

KELLER, Gf. - Romeo und Julia auf dem Dorfe
Scribner. xxv;155p. 19cm. [Not quite excellent.] [LC]
4914. do. 1915. [same] L: Constable. [BM]
4915. do. [ad.] Romeo and Juliet: a music drama in 6 scenes by F: Delius. Text founded on the novel of G. Keller. Libr. n.i. 1910. 27p. 24cm. [Follows the story quite closely.] [BM]
*4916. (Sieben Legenden.) Seven legends. Tr. from 56th Ger. ed. by Mn. Wyness. Introd. R: M. Meyer. L;Glasgow: Gowans & Gray 1911. xii;105p. 19cm. [BM]
§4917. do. 1911. Legends of long ago. Tr. C: H. Handschin. Chic: Abbey. 96p. 16cm. [Not strictly faithful.] [LC]
4918. do. 1912. Wyness' tr. NY: Stokes. xii;112p. [AC]
4920. (Ursula.) Ursula. Tr. B. Q. Morgan. 1913-15. In C154(14).

KELLER, Js. An.
4921. Angeli Dei; or, stories of angels. Tr. O. S. B. L: Washbourne 1887. x;174p. 16cm. [BM]
[Sel. and ad. from "Zweihundertzehn Engelsgeschichten."]
4922. do. 1888. [same] NY;Cincin: Benziger. [AC]
4923. do. 1893. [same] 2d enl. ed. 182p. [BM]
4924. Maria Sanctissima. Tr. O. S. B. L: Washbourne 1899. xiii; 411p. 18cm. [BM]
4925. The sacred heart: incidents...Also, lives of B. Marg. Mary and P. de la Colombière. Sel...by O. S. B. L: Washbourne 1898. 255p. 18cm. [BM]
4926. St. Joseph's help; or, stories of...intercession. Tr. O. S. B. L: Washbourne 1888. x;278p. 16cm. [BM]
4927. Stories for first communicants. Cincin;NY: Benziger 1888. [AC]

KELLER, S., See "Schrill, Ern."

KELLERMANN, Bh. 1879- .
*4928. (Das Meer.) Sea. Tr. Sasha Best. NY: McBride 1924. 281p. 20cm. [Has the idea, but not quite the execution; misses the concise and pregnant style.] [LC]
4929. do. 1925. [same] L: Cape. 288p. [BM]
§4930. (Der neunte November.) The ninth of November. Tr. Caro. V. Kerr. NY: McBride 1925. 443p. 19cm. [LC.BM]
[Fair tr., not scrupulously exact nor accurate.]
4931. do. 1925. [same] L: Cape. 414p. [BM]
§4932. (Der Tunnel.) The tunnel. Tr. anon. NY: Macaulay 1915. 322p. 19cm. [Too ready to abandon his author.] [LC]
4933. do. 1915. [same] L: Hodder & Stoughton. 319p. [BM]
4934. God's beloved. Tr. Kath. Royce. 1913-15. In C154(20).

KEMNITZ, Mde. v.
4935. Marriage as a fulfilment. Tr. 1926. In C308.

KEMPER, J.
4936. Maximilian in Mexico. Tr. G: P. Upton. Chic: McClurg 1911. 133p. 17cm. [LC]

KEMPFF, J: d. 1625. Sel. in C271.

KEMPNER-HOCHSTAEDT, Max.
4937. (Der Vetter aus Dingsda.) The cousin from nowhere. Ad. from a comedy of K-H by Hm. Haller and "Rideamus." Mus. by Ed. Künnecke. Ad. by F: Thompson. Vocal score. L: Feldman 1923. 135p. fol. [LCM]

KENNER, J. Sel. in C137a.

KEPPLER, Pl. W: v. 1852-1926.
4938. (Mehr Freude.) More joy...Ad. J. McSorley. St.L: Herder 1914. 257p. 20cm. [LC.BM]

KEPPLER, Pl. W: v.
4939. do. 1914. [same] 2d ed. Herder. viii;257p. [AC]
4940. do. 1919. [same] 4th ed. Herder. xiv;257p. [AC]
4941. do. 1926. A little more joy: some hints for parents and teachers...by Js. McSorley. Paulist press. 31p. D. [AC]

KERN, Cn. Gb. 1792-1835. Sel. in C287;489.

"KERNER, H." (i.e., Hm. Cardanus, 1847-1925).
4942. The good dean Ensfried. Tr. anon. 1902. In C481.

KERNER, Jts. (And. Cn.) 1786-1862. Sel. in C17;40-2;44;67;77;89;90; 106;123;129;149;152;166;195;215;219;295-6;317;366;372;375;378; 380;388;391;393*;394-5;412;417;438;448;450;497;500-1;539;571.
§4943. (Die Seherin von Prevorst.) The seeress of P--: being revelations concerning the inner life of man. Trs. Mrs. Cath. Crowe. L: Moore 1845. xii;338p. 17cm. [BM.LC]
["A literal tr...out of the question...I have therefore thought it advisable to make a free tr." Where she follows closely, the tr. is very good.]
4944. do. 1845. [same] NY: Harper. 120p. front. 24cm. [BM]
4945. do. 1849. [same] NY: C: Partridge. 120p. 23cm. [BM]
[No front. in this ed.]
4945a. (Goldner.) Goldner. Tr. G: G. Cunningham. 1829. In C80.
[Falsely ascribed to Koerner.]

KERNER, Tb. 1817-1907.
4945b. (Natur und Frieden.) Nature and peace. Tr. anon. Heidelberg: Bangel & Schmidt 1861. 247p. 8. [EC]

KERST, F: 1870-
Beethoven, the man and the artist, etc. See "Beethoven," #337.
Mozart, the man and the artist, etc. See "Mozart," #6366.

KEYSERLING, E: (H: N:) Graf v. 1855-1918.
*4946. (Abendliche Häuser.) Twilight. Tr. Jas. Ashton and E. D. Arundel. NY: Macaulay 1927. 311p. 19cm. [LC.BM]
[Twilight; Harmony; Kersta.]
*4947. do. 1927. Twilight. Tr. Amy Wesselhoeft v. Erdberg and A. W. Erdberg. L: Holden. 311p. 7 x 5 in. [BM]
4948. (Bunte Herzen.) Gay hearts. Tr. B. Q. Morgan. 1913-15. In C154(19).

KEYSERLING, Hm. (Ax.) Graf v. 1880-
4949. The correct statement of the marriage problem; Marriage as an eternal problem; The proper choice of partners. Tr. 1926. In C308.
**4950. (Das Reisetagebuch eines Philosophen.) The travel diary of a philosopher. Tr. J: H. Reece. L: Cape 1925. 2v. 338; 400p. 23cm. [BM.LC]
[Tr. carefully revised by author, and as nearly correct as possible. Cf. p. 4]
4951. do. 1927. [same] Complete ed. in one vol. L: Cape. 745p. 9 x 6 in. [EC]
4952. (Die neuentstehende Welt.) The world in the making. Tr. Maurice Samuel. NY: Harcourt, Brace 1927. 293p. 21cm. [LC]
4953. do. 1927. [same] L: Cape. 283p. 8 x 5 in. [BM]

KEYSSLER, J: G: 1693-1743.
*4954. (...neueste Reise durch Deutschland...) Travels through Germany, Bohemia, Hungary, Switzerland, Italy, and Lorrain. Containing an accurate description of the present state and curiosities of those countries. Tr. from 2d Ger. ed. Anon. L: A. Linde & T. Field 1756-7. 4v. il. w. copper-pl. 26cm. [BM]
[Vols. 2-4 dated 1757. --Excellent tr.]

KEYSSLER, J: G: - ... neueste Reise durch Deutschland...
4955. do. 1758. 2d ed. Travels, etc. Also, the life of the auther [sic] by M. Godfrey Schutze (pp. iii-xv). L: J:Scott. 4v. 17cm. [Not the same tr. as the foregoing. Rather freely treated, but essentially faithful.] [BM]
4956. do. 1760. Travels, etc. Giving a true and just description of the present state of those countries. 3d ed. L: Prt. for G. Keith 1760. 4v. il. 21cm. [LC]
4957. do. 1778. Mr. Keysler's travels through Swisserland, Germany, and Hungary. In The world displayed...voyages and travels, selected...3d ed. corr. Vol. 19, pp. 171-216. L: Carman & Newbery. 14cm. [Merest epitome of the orig.] [BM.LC]
4958. do. 1785? Travels, etc. In Moore, J. H. New and complete coll. of voyages, etc. Vol. 2. pp. 1013ff. 35cm. [BM] [Much cut down from first ed. K--'s travels run on into something else without a break.]

KIECHEL, S: 1563-1619. Sel. in C483.

KIEFER, F. J.
†4959. (Die Sagen des Rheinlandes.) The legends of the Rhine from Basil [sic] to Rotterdam. Tr. L. W. Garnham. Mayence: D: Kapp 1868. 313p. front. 2 pl. 17cm. [BM]
[Errors and poor English. Adds some verse.]
4960. do. 1869. [same] 2d ed. [BM.LC]
4961. do. 1881. Legends of the Rhine for children by "Luigi." (Based on Kiefer.) L: Simpkin. 200p. 17cm. [BM]

KIEL, Ts. 1584-1627. Sel. in C287.

KIELMANSEGG, F: Graf v. 1728-1800.
4962. Diary of a journey to England, 1761-2. Tr. (from MS) by Countess Kielmansegg. L;NY; Bombay: Longmans 1902. 287p. il. 20cm. [BM.LC]

KIENZL, W: 1857- . Song of the cowherd. (Der Kuhreigen.) Opera. See Bartsch, R. H.
§4963. (Der Evangelimann.) Der Evangelimann: opera in 2 acts, words and music by W: K--. Engl. version by P. Pinkerton. Libr. Ger; Engl. L: Aschenberg 1897. 65p. 21cm. [BM]
[Tr. gives the sense but abandons the form, mostly.]

KIESEL, O: Er.
4964. Visitor's guide to Hamburg. Ed. by O. E. K. Tr. W. J. Eggers. Hamb: Broschek 1922. 109p. il. 19cm. [BM]

KIESEWETTER, Rl. G: 1773-1850.
*4965. (Geschichte der europäisch-abendländischen oder unserer heutigen Musik.) Hist. of the mod. mus. of west. Europe, from the first cent. to the present day. Tr. Rb. Müller. L: Newby 1848. xii;300p. 39p. music. 22cm. [BM]

KIESSLING, J: Ts. See "Schubert, G.," Life of ---, #8635.

KILLIAS, E:
4966. Coire and its environs. 58p. il. Tr. anon. 1884. In C294.

KIND, J: F: 1768-1843. Sel. in C44;165;295.
§4967. (Das Nachtlager von Granada.) A night in Granada: opera by K. Kreutzer. Text ad. from Kind's drama by J: K. Braun. Tr. anon. Libr. Ger;Engl. NY: Acad. of mus. 1864? 17p. 8.[Prose,good.] [LCM]
*4968. (Der Freischütz.)[1] Music...in the celebrated melodrame, called, Der Freischütz, or, The seventh bullet. A romantic opera

[1] See Genest, 9:283-5, for versions of Der Freischütz acted but probably not published.

KIND, J: F:
in three acts by K: Ma. v. Weber. Tr. W. McG. Logan. L: Royal harmonic institution 1824. Vocal score. 182p. 33cm. [BMM]
4969. do. 1824. Freischütz; or, the seventh bullet. Etch. by Cruikshank. Baldwyn. 12. [EC]
4970. do. 1825. Altered by Soane. L: [LC]
[Not a translation: dialog virtually new, songs "rewritten."]
4971. do. 1832? Der Freischutz; or, the seventh bullet. L: Cumberland. (C--'s British theatre, vol. 9.) Libr. 41p. 15cm. [LC]
[Tr. and ad. by Logan. Reissued in Davidson's shilling vol. of Cumberland's plays, Vol. 10.]
§4972. do. 1832. Der Freischutz. Tr. anon. Libr. Ger;Engl. L: G. Schulze. 101p. 15cm. [BM]
[Verse is very good, prose is poor and inaccurate.]
'4973. do. 1835? Logan's tr. Weber's celebrated opera Der Freischütz, or, The seventh bullet. Vocal score. L: Cramer, Addison & Beale. 230p. 35cm. [BMM]
§4974. do. 1841? Der F--. 4th ed. rev. and retranslated. Anon. Libr. Ger;Engl. L: Schloss. 49p. 18cm. [BM]
[Verse tr., unrhymed, fairly close line for line. Some errors, or misprints?]
4975. do. 1842. [same] Manager's ed. The 5th, rev. and retranslated. L: Schloss. 49p. 17cm. [BM]
†4976. do. 1845. Tr. C: B. Burkhardt. Libr. NY: Ward. 17p. 8. [LCO]
*4977. do. 1849. The free-shooter: a lyric folk-drama. Ed. W. S. Rockstro. Tr. J. Wrey Mould. Vocal score. L: Boosey. xxviii;258p. 25cm. [BMM]
4978. do. 1856. [same as #4976] Libr. [Contains some music.][NY.LC]
§4979. do. 1859. Der F--; and the music of the principal airs. Libr. Ger;Engl. L: Davidson. 26p. 24cm. [BMM]
[Tr. (or ed?) by Macfarren. Much of tr. exactly like Logan's version. --Prtd. in double columns.]
*4980. do. 1860. Freyschutz [sic]. Tr. anon. Libr. Ital;Engl., also music. Bost: Ditson? [Same tr. as #4987.] [LCM]
4981. do. 1861. (extracts.) Tr. W. E. Gladstone. In C165.
4982. do. 1861. Der Freischutz. Tr. anon. Melbourne: Abbott. Libr. Engl. 24p. 17cm. [BM]
[Prose very poor; verse very good, largely from Logan's tr. Text is consid. edited.]
4983. do. 1866. Der Freischutz. Tr. J: Oxenford. Libr. Engl. L: Lacey. 39p. front. of Samiel. 22cm. [BM]
[Prose rewritten. Verse largely borrowed from Logan's tr.]
§4984. do. 1871. Der Freischutz. Tr. anon. Libr. NY: Bryant. 35p. 8. [Some lyrics taken from Logan's tr., otherwise independent.][LCO]
4985. do. 1872. The freeshooter. Ed. and in part tr. by Natalia Macfarren. Vocal score. Engl;Ger. L: Novello. 142p. 26cm. [Cf. #4978.] [BMM.LCM]
*4986. do. 1872. [same] Vocal score. Ital;Engl;Ger. Ed. A. Sullivan and J. Pittman. L;NY: Boosey. 213p. 25cm. [BMM.LCM]
4987. do. 1888. [same as #4980] Libr. Ital;Engl. Bost: Ditson. 25p. 8. [Ital. cuts slightly. Some music.] [LCO]
*4988. do. 1904. Ed. and tr. N. Macfarren and Th. Baker. Vocal score. Ger;Engl. NY: Schirmer. 171p. fol. [LCM]
[Baker has improved the tr.]
4989. do. 1923. same. New version, with few orig. recitatives by Artur Bodanzky. Ed. and tr. N. Macfarren and Th. Baker. Vocal score. Ger;Engl. NY: Schirmer. 191p. 28cm. [LCM.BMM]
[Speaking parts condensed and set to music. Otherwise unchanged.]
4990. do. n.d. Soane's tr. Vocal score. L: Goulding, D'Almaine. 164p. fol. [LCM]
4991. do. [ad.] 1924. The wild huntsman by Washington Irving. Introd. by G: S. Hellman. Bost: Bibliophile soc. 1924. 113p. 24cm. [LC.BM]

KIND, J: F:--Der Freischütz
[From a hitherto unpub. MS of 1823-4. Irving alters the names, uses only prose, and changes the action.]
4992. do. [ad.] 1925. Der Freishchütz [sic]. Retold by J. McSpadden. 1925. In C390.
4993. Körner's oak, a fantasy. Tr. G. F. Richardson. 1827. In #5120.

KINDERMANN, Henny.
4994. Lola; or, the thought and speech of animals. Tr. Ag. Blake. With a chap. on thinking animals by Dr. W: Mackenzie. L: Methuen 1922. ix;188p. 19cm. [BM]

KINKEL, Gf. 1815-82. Sel. in C17;42;106;380;399;400;448.
*4995. (Der Hauskrieg.) A family feud. Tr. F: Hardman. In "Tales from Blackwood," new series, vol. XI, 1880. pp. 148-96. [BM.LCO]
[Pub. in "Blackwood's Mag." 68(1850):174.]
*4996. (Tanagra. Idylle aus Griechenland.) Tanagra: an idyl of Greece. Tr. Mrs. Fes. Hellman. Il. by Edwin H. Blashfield. NY: Putnam 1893. xix;79p. 20cm. [LC.BM]

KINKEL, J:a, 1810-58.
4997. Twelve stories of earth, air, and water. In "Mamma's stories, etc." L: Ward, Lock 1872. pp. 133-76. 17cm. [BM]

KIRCHBACH, Wfg.
*4998. (Lili-Tsé.) Lili-Tsé: operetta by Fz. Curti. Tr. Ruth Mayhew and H. Zschalig. Libr. Lpz: Breitkopf & Haertel 1896. 38p. 8.
[On the whole, very good.] [BM.LCM]

KIRCHHOFF, Af. 1838-1907.
4999. Graphic pict. of native life in distant lands, ill. the typical races of mankind. Depicted by H. Leutemann with text by K--. Tr. G: Philip, Jr. L: Philip 1888. 54p. 12 pl. in col. 28cm.
[Probably from his "Länderkunde von Europa."] [BM]

KIRCHMEYER, T: called Naogeorgus, 1511-63.
5000. (Regnum papisticum.) The popish kingdom or reigne of Antichrist. Tr. B. Googe. L: H:Denham 1570. 60p. 4.
[The only perfect copy is in the Cambridge Univ. lib.]
5001. do. 1880. reprint. Ed. w. brief memoir...by Rb. C: Hope. L: Satchell. xviii;74p. 22cm. [BM]
5002. Spiritual husbandrie. Tr. B. Googe, ca. 1570. Two books: 918; 978 lines. [Bound with #5000.]

KIRCHNER, Hm.
5003. An oration in praise of trauell in generall.--Another, in praise of the trauell of Germanie in particular. In "Coryat's crudities." L: W. S. 1611. ff. B-Di, Dd-Ee3. 20cm. [BM]
[Orations pronounced in the University of Marpurg.]

KIRSCHNER, Lula (i.e., Aloisia), 1854-. See "Schubin, Ossip."

KLAATSCH, Hm. (A: L:) 1863-1916.
*5004. (Der Werdegang der Menschheit.) Evolution and progress of mankind. Ed. and enl. by Ad. Heilborn and tr. Js. McCabe. L: Unwin; NY: Stokes 1923. 316p. il. 26cm. [BM.LC]

"KLABUND" (i.e., Af. Henschke, 1891-1928). Sel. in C95.
*5005. (Bracke, ein Eulenspiegel-Roman.) Brackie, the fool. Tr. H. G. Scheffauer. Il. Arn. Hall. NY;L: Putnam 1927. 261p. 19cm [LC.BM]
*5006. (Pjotr, Roman eines Zaren.) Peter the czar. Tr. H. G. Scheffauer. NY: Putnam 1925. 156p. 19cm. [LC.BM]
5007. do. 1926. 3d printing. Putnam. [LC]

KLAMER-SCHMIDT, Eb. K: 1746-1824. See Schmidt, Klamer.

KLAPROTH, H. Jl. v. 1783-1835.
*5008. (Reise in den Kaukasus und nach Georgien.) Travels in the Caucasus and Georgia...1807-8. Tr. F. Shoberl. L: Colburn 1814. xv;421p. 28cm. [EC dates it 1813.] [BM]

KLARWILL, V: ed.
*5009. (Fugger-Zeitungen.) The Fugger news letters, 1568-1605. Author. tr. by Pauline de Chary. With 30 contemp. il. Foreword by H. Gordon Selfridge. L: Lane 1924. xlv;284p. 22cm. [BM]
5010. do. 1926. [same] 2d series, being a further selection, spec. ref. to Queen Eliz. and...England. Tr. L. S. R. Byrne. L: Lane. li;353p.22cm. [Orig. not yet pub.] [BM]

KLEE, Ghd. L: 1850-1916.
5011. (Grundzüge der deutschen Literaturgeschichte.) A brief hist. of Ger. lit. By G: M. Priest. NY: Scribner 1909. xii;366p. 20cm. [Freely altered to suit American conditions, these changes being indicated in the pref.] [LC.BM]
5012. Heldensagen (Hagen und Hilde, Gudrun) literally tr. by S. Mendel. L: Cornish 1894. 12. [EC]
*5013. do. 1896. [same] 63p. 18cm. [BM]

KLEIN, Hm. I. and O: W: Thomé.
*5014. (Die Erde und ihr organisches Leben.) Land, sea, and sky; or, the wonders of life and nature. Tr. J. Minshull. L;NY: Ward, Lock 1881-2. viii;832p. il. 24cm. [BM]
5015. do. 1884? [same in 2 pts.] God's glorious creation (to p. 376); The creator's wonders in living nature (to p. 822). Index is prefixed. [Date is that of the BM stamp.] [BM]

KLEIN, K: 1838-98.
*5016. (Fröschweiler Chronik. Kriegs- und Friedensbilder aus dem Jahre 1870.) The pastor's narrative; or, before and after the battle of Wörth, 1870. Tr. Mrs. F. E. Marshall. L: Longmans 1879. 264p. 19cm. [Some errors.] [BM]

KLEIST, Ewd. Cn. v. 1715-59. Sel. in C17;22;25-6;44;88;133;157(1); 317;372-3;489;533.
5017. (Der Frühling.) Kleist's vernal season. Tr. G. H. Egestorff. L: 1814? See "Gentleman's Mag." 84(1814):1:248. (B26)
5018. do. 1818. [same] 2d ed. L: Souter. 32p. 21cm. [BM] [Sketch of the author's life. Imitation, not tr.: hexameters into blank verse.]

KLEIST, H: v. 1777-1811. Sel. in C366*.
§5019. (Briefe.) Letters. Tr. 1875. In #5025.
*5020. (Die Familie Schroffenstein.) The feud of the Schroffensteins. Tr. Ma. J. and L. M. Price. In "Poet Lore" 27(1916):457-576. Also issued sep. by Badger. 1916. [LC]
5021. (Die heilige Cäcilie oder die Gewalt der Musik.) St. Cecilia; or, the power of music. Tr. J: Oxenford. 1844. In C442.
§5022. (Käthchen von Heilbronn.)[Sel.] Kate of Heilbronn. Tr. E. B. Impey. 1841. In C295, pp. 443-520.[Poor tr.]
5023. do. 1927. Kaethchen of Heilbronn. Tr. F: E. Pierce. In C452.
5024. (Michael Kohlhaas.) M-- K--. Tr. J: Oxenford. 1844. In C441-2.
5024a. do. 1853. Tr. anon. In "Dublin univ. mag." 41(1853):556.(B27) [Kleist not mentioned, nor is it called a translation.]
*5025. do. 1875. In "Prussia's representative man" (i.e., Kleist). By Fis. Lloyd and W: Newton. L: Trübner. 12. [BM]
5026. do. 1896. (Extract) in C366(23pp.).
5027. do. 1913-15. Tr. Fes. H. King. In C154(4).
†5028. (Prinz F: von Homburg.) Prince Friedrich von H--. Tr. 1875. In #5025. [Unwarranted liberties.]

KLEIST, H: v.--Prinz F: von Homburg.
*5029. do. 1913-15. Tr. Herman Hagedorn. In C154(4).

KLEMM, W: Sel. in C95.

KLENKE, K:e Lu. (Karsch) v. 1754-1802. Sel. in C90.

KLENCKE, Ph. F: Hm. 1813-81. See "Maltitz, Hm. v."

KLENCKE, Ph. F: Hm. and G. Schlesier.
*5030. Lives of the brothers Humboldt. Tr. and arr. Juliette Bauer. L: Ingram, Cooke 1852. 431p. 19cm. [BM.LC]
[Ax. v. H-- (pp. 1-245) by K--. Sep. t.p., continuous paging.]
5031. do. 1853. [same] NY: Harper. [AC]
5032. do. 1872-6. [same] NY: Harper. 12. [AC]

KLESHEIM, An. Freiherr v. 1812-84. Sel. in C36.

KLETKE, Gst. Hm. 1813-86. Sel. in C450;501.
5033. (Der Kinderkreuzzug.) Robert of Marseilles; or, the crusade of the children. Tr. Rebecca Schively. Phil: Luth. pub. 1883. 16. [AC]
§5034. (Die Savoyardenkinder.) The Savoyard boy and his sister. Ad. J. D. Haas. Il. (in col.) J: Absolon. L: Orr 1844. 38p. 17cm.[BM]
[None too good.]

KLINGEMANN, Ern. A: F: 1777-1831. Sel. in C33.
5035. (Faust.) Sel. Tr. T: Carlyle. 1840. In C56.

KLINGEMANN, K:
5036. (Heimkehr aus der Fremde.) Son and stranger: operetta by Fx. Mendelssohn-Bartholdy. Freely ad. by H: F. Chorley. Vocal score. Lpz: Breitkopf; L: Ewer 1851. 115p. 36cm. [BMM]
5037. do. 1860? [same] Orchestral score. Ger;Engl. Lpz: Breitkopf & Haertel; L: Ewer. 174p. 26 x 33cm. [BMM]
5038. do. 1902? [same tr.] Vocal score. Engl. L: Novello. 119p. 4. [LCM]

KLINGER, F: Mx. v. 1752-1831.
5039. (Der Faust der Morgenländer.) Partly tr. in Lewis, M. G., Amorassam. (B31)
5040. (Die neue Arria.) The modern Arria: a tragedy in five acts (and in prose). Tr. anon. L: Boosey & Escher 1795. 92p. 20cm.[BM]
§5041. (Fausts Leben, Taten und Höllenfahrt.) Faustus: his life, death, and descent into hell. Tr. G: Borrow. L: 1825. 8. [BM]
5042. do. 1864. [same] L: Kent. 302p. 19cm. [LC]
[Good spirit, but needless liberties taken.]
5043. (Reisen vor der Sündflut.) Travels before the flood: an interesting oriental record...interpreted in...conversations... between the Caliph of Bagdad and his court. Tr. from the Arabic. L: Johnson 1796. 238; 217p. 16cm. [Of course a hoax.] [BM]

KLOEDEN, C: F: v. 1786-1856.
*5044. (Jugenderinnerungen.) The self-made man: autobiog. Ed. with sketch of his after life by M. Jahn. Tr. A. M. Christie. L: Strahan 1876. 2v. 358;383p. 22cm. [BM.LCO]

KLOPSTOCK, F: Gb. 1724-1803. Sel. in C8;17*;22;25-6;31;44;50;67;88; 91;129;133;171-2;184;190;193;229;273;295;303;366;372-3;375;391; 393;410;423;428;461*;469;486;489;501;530;533;543;570;574.
†5045. (Der Messias.) The Messiah. Attempted...by Js. Collyer (i.e., begun by Ma. Collyer and completed by Js.). L: Dodsley, etc. 1763. 2v. xlviii;232; 299p. 16cm. [Prose, inaccurate. --Cantos 1-10, to which is prefixed his introd. on divine poetry.] [BM]
5046. do. 1769. [same] L: Dodsley. xlviii;240; 287p. 16cm. [BM]
[Engr. front. and t.p. by Collyer. Front of vol. 2 not signed.]

KLOPSTOCK--Messias

5047. do. 1788. [same] In 15 books. Elizabeth-Town (N.J.): Prtd. and sold by Shepard Kollock. xvi;383p. 16. (B6a, B48.) [Available: AAS. Reprint of #5045 plus cantos 11-15.]

5048. do. 1795. [same] NY: Prtd. by G: Forman for Duykinck. 403p. 12. [LC]

5049. do. 1808. New ed. in one vol. Bungay. C. Brightly. 464p. 21cm. [Pref. omitted. 4 pl., two by Craig. No indication who tr. cantos 11-15. Perhaps not Collyer? They seem more accurate than the earlier books.] [BM]

5050. do. 1810. The M--: a poem. Attempted in Engl. blank verse. By Sl. Halling. Georgetown, S. C. Baxter. 37p. 8. [LCO] [A versification of Canto I apparently made from Collyer.]

§5051. do. 1810. Elegant extracts from K--'s Messiah. To which is added, never before translated, an Ode on God. Tr. G. H. C. Egestorff. L: Cradock & Joy. 157p. 17cm. [BM] [Messiah in prose. To Fanny, and The bands of roses also included, tr. in verse. --Tr. is not very good.]

5052. do. 1811. Collyer's tr. Bost: West. 2v. 299; 272p. 16. (B48)

5053. do. 1811. [same]...a sacred poem. L: J.Walker. 2v. 12cm. [BM] [Cantos 1-16 by Mrs. Collyer, the remainder by Mrs. Meeke. Vol. 1 (xii;244p.) includes introd. on divine poetry. Vol. 2 (328pp.) has explan. notes, pp. 317-28, on books 16-19. Vol. 1 has front. by W. Hilton and full engr. t.p; vol. 2 has front. by H: Corbould and full engr. t.p.]

5054. do. 1811. [same]...Memoirs of the life of the author. New ed. L: R.Edwards and R.Evans. xv;559p. 8. (B46)

5055. do. 1814. A new tr. The last five books prepared for the press by T. Raffles. L: Underwood. 3v. 16. [BM.LCO] [Raffles is much closer than Collyer; knows more German.]

5056. do. 1817. The M-- by K--. Collyer's tr. L: S. A. Oddy. 463p. 21cm. [BM] [15 cantos. Memoirs of K--, pp. iii-xiv, as in Shoberl's ed., slightly reworded. Engr. t.p. by J. Wallis shows "Eloa and Grabriel [sic] at the altar of Messiah."]

5057. do. 1817? The M--. descriptive of the principal events attending the passion and crucifixion...Tr. F: Shoberl. Memoir of the life. L: Cundee et al. Albion press ed. 475p. 22cm. [BM] [18 cantos. "Collyer's tr...has been taken for the groundwork of the present volume, but...revised throughout..." Overfaithfulness to Collyer prevents even such success as might be attained in prose.]

5058. do. 1819. Collyer's tr. L: T.Kelly. xiv;463p. 21cm. [BM] [Text and paging identical with #5156. Front; t.p. same as #5156. 4 pl., 3 by R. Taylor.]

†5059. do. 1820? Poems of F: W: Cronhelm; with an hexametrical tr. (or rather imitation) of part of the 2d book of K--'s M--. L: Longmans. 200p. 17cm. [BM] [Very strange hexameters. Sense conveyed with moderate accuracy. pp. 155-200.]

5060. do. 1821. [same as #5053] L: Rivington. xxviii;618p. 13cm. [BM] [19 cantos, notes as in #5053. Introd. on divine poetry. Later books more accurate but more prosy. Front. and t.p. by T. Uwins.]

§5061. do. 1821-2. K--'s M--: a poem in 20 cantos. Tr. into Engl. verse by G. H. C. Egestorff. Hamburgh: Pub. by and for the author. viii;690p. 21cm. [4 vols. paged continuously. Vols. 2-4, 1822, each w. sep. t.p., 5 cantos per volume. Tr. into tolerable blank verse, which follows the sense quite well. He says: "I never could prevail on myself to submit it to the rev. of any other person." Of the earlier

KLOPSTOCK--Messias
versions he writes: "It may justly be said, that, in their tr., K--'s M-- has been crucified a second time."]
5062. do. 1823. Gethsemane, a poem; founded on (or rather an abridgment of) the M--. By Mrs. Montolieu. L: Bensley. 2v. vi;142; 160p. 17cm. [BM]
[Rhymed couplets. Good verse, but remoter from sense than Egestorff or Miss Head. 6 cantos.]
5063. do. 1826. [same as #5061, with new t.ps.] No pref. [BM]
§5064. do. 1826. The seven first cantos of the M--, a poem. By F. T. [sic] K--. Tr. into Engl. verse ("by Miss [i.e., Catharine] Head," written on t.p.). L: Longmans. 2v. 313; 318p. 21cm.[BM.LC]
[LC says: Books I-XV. "The tr...has not scrupled to make...such abridgments as...indispensably requisite." These omissions are listed at the end. Blank verse, almost as correct as Egestorff, better as poetry.]
5065. do. 1839. [same as #6060?] L: Rivington. 24. [EC]
5066. do. 1866. Book I, tr. into Engl. heroic metre. Cambridge: Prtd. for the author by T: Dixon. 40p. 16cm. [BM]
[Blank verse, good; sense not so good or close.]
§5067. (Der Tod Adams.) The death of Adam: a tragedy in 3 acts [verse]. Tr. Rb. Lloyd. L: D.Leach for Becket & De Hondt 1763. ix;60p. 16cm. [BM]
[Blank verse from orig. prose, rather flowery and high-flown. None too close in sense.]
5068. do. 1810. [same]...intended as a companion to the "Death of Cain." Portsea: Stephens. 88p. 17cm. [BM]
[No pref.; adds learned commentaries. Otherwise quite the same.]
§5069. (Briefe.) Memoirs (i.e., mainly letters) of F: and Marg. Klopstock. Tr. Miss Eliz. Smith. Bath: R: Cruttwell; L: Cadell & Davies 1808. xii;236p. 18cm. [BM]
[Taken from Klamer Schmidt's "Klopstock und seine Freunde." Letters from and to K--, pp. 53-217. Also, (7) odes, with pref., pp. 219-32. Tr. of these is quite good, mostly in blank verse and accurate.]
5070. do. 1809. [same] In "Fragments in prose and verse." By Eliz. Smith. Bath, etc. 2v. [BM]
[Memoirs are vol. 2. xiv;242p. 20cm. Entirely reprinted from the foregoing.]
5071. do. 1809. [same as #5069] 3d ed. Bath: Cruttwell; L: Hatchard. (B26)
5071a. do. 1810. [same as #5070] Bath: Cruttwell; L: Cadell & D. 2v. 21cm. [Memoirs are vol. 2. xiv;242p.] [BM]
5071b. do. 1810. [same] Bost: Munroe & Francis, and S: Parker. 240p. [BM]
[Front. (port.) by J. Barker. This ed. has nothing by K--.]
5071c. do. 1810. [same] Memoirs, etc. Phil: Earle; Bost: Farrand, Mallory. 252p. 17cm. [LCO says: Phil: Nicklin.] [LC]
5072. do. 1811-2. [same] Fragments, etc. New ed. Bath: Cruttwell; L: Cadell & D. 2v. in one. [BM]
[Memoirs are vol. 2, dated 1812. xiv;242p. 21cm.]
5073. do. 1812. [same] Memoirs, etc. Bath etc. 242p. [BM]
[Memoirs, i.e., vol. 2 of foregoing, issued sep. with port. instead of t.p.]
5074. do. 1814. [same] Fragments. New ed. L: Cadell & D. 8. [EC]
†5075. do. 1814. K-- and his friends: a series of familiar letters ...1750-1803. Tr. w. biogr. introd. by Miss Benger. L: Colburn. xxxiii;309p. 8. [BM.LC]
[Taken from Klamer Schmidt. Tr. is inaccurate.]
5076. do. 1818. [same as #5072] Fragments, etc. New ed. L: Cadell & D. 2v. 21cm. [BM]

KLOPSTOCK--Briefe
[Vol. 2, xiv;242p. Inserted fly-leaf reads: Fragments, etc. Vol. II. Vol. I (Fragments 274p.) has: End of vol. I, on last page. Otherwise there is no mention of vol. number.]
5077. do. 1826. [same] Memoirs, etc. L: Cadell. xiv;242p. 21cm. [BM]
[Cover t.p. says: Fragments, etc. Vol. 2. No port.]
5078. do. 1842. [same] Fragments, etc. New ed. with essays, etc. Memoirs, etc. L: J:Murray. 20cm. (227) 437p. 20cm. [BM]
[Essays to p. 502.]
§5079. (Oden.) Odes, 1747-80. Tr. W: Nind. L: Pickering 1848. 310p. 16. [True to sense but not to form.] [BM.LCO]
*5080. (Salomon.) Solomon: a sacred drama in 5 acts [verse]. Tr. Rb. Huish. L: Hatchard, Sherwood 1809. xii;261p. 8. [BM]
[Quite good blank verse; a trifle expanded.]

KLUCKHOHN, A: 1832-93.
*5081. (Luise, Königin von Preussen.) Louise, queen of Prussia: a memorial. Tr. Eliz. H. Denio. Cambridge, Mass: Riverside press 1881. 83p. front. (port.) 20cm. [Tr. is fair to good.] [LC.BM]

KLUGE, F: 1856- . See Lublin, Isabel T., Primer of Ger. lit., C379.

KLUNZINGER, K: B: 1834-1914.
*5082. (Bilder aus Oberägypten.) Upper Egypt; its people and its products: a descriptive account. Pref. notice by G: Schweinfurth. Tr. anon. L: Blackie; NY: Scribner & A. 1878. 408p. il. 23cm. ["Tr...prepared by arr. w. the author, and w. his active co-op. and assistance." "Il. by addit. engr. after his own sketches," not in Ger. ed.] [BM.LC]

KLUSEN, ---
5083. My grandmother: a tale. Tr. G: G. Cunningham. 1829. In C80.

KNACKFUSS, Hm. 1848-1915.
*5084. (Dürer.) Dürer. Tr. C. Dodgson. Lpz: Velhagen & Klasing; L: Grevel 1900. vii;152p. il. 26cm. [BM.LC]
*5085. (Holbein der Jüngere.) Holbein. Tr. C. Dodgson. Lpz: Velhagen & Klasing; L: Grevel 1899. 160p. il. 26cm. [BM.LC]
*5086. (Raffael.) R--. Tr. C. Dodgson. Lpz: Velhagen & Klasing; L: Grevel 1899. 132p. il. 26cm. [BM]
*5087. (Rembrandt.) R--. Tr. C. Dodgson. Lpz: Velhagen & Klasing; L: Grevel 1899. xiii;160p. il. 26cm. [BM]
*5088. (Rubens.) R--. Tr. Louise M. Richter. Lpz: Velhagen & Klasing; L: Grevel 1904. 168p. il. 26cm. [BM]
*5089. (Van Dyck.) Van Dyck. Tr. C. Dodgson. Lpz: Velhagen & Klasing; L: Grevel 1899. vi;83p. il. 26cm. [BM]

KNAPP, Ab. ("Pl. Speratus.) 1798-1864. Sel. in C234-5;273;287;489; #8904.

KNAUST, H: Sel. in C373.

KNEBEL, K: L: v. 1744-1834. Sel. in C12;373.

KNIGGE, Ad. Fz. F: L: Freiherr v. 1752-96.
5090. (Briefe auf einer Reise aus Lothringen nach Niedersachsen geschrieben.) Brieven; or, letters written on a journey from Lorraine to Lower Saxony. Tr. 179-. (B43)
5091. (Geschichte des Amtsrats Gutmann.) The hist. of the Amtsrath G--. Written by himself. Tr. anon. L: Vernor & Hood 1799. (B26, B43) [B47 has: L: 1800. 12.]
§5092. (Geschichte Peter Clausens.) The Ger. Gil Blas; or, the advent. of P: Claus. Tr. from...Baron Kuiegge [sic]. Tr. anon. L: Kearsley 1793. 3v. 18cm. [BM]
[The French tr. was entitled: "Le Gil Blas allemand." --Tr. is free and easy.]

KNIGGE
*5093. (Ueber den Umgang mit Menschen.) Pract. philos. of social life; or, the art of conversing with men. Tr. P: Will. L: Cadell & Davies 1799. 2v. xli;270; 322p. 18cm. [BM]
[Tr. seems to be quite good.]
5094. do. 1805. [same] 1st Amer. ed. Lansingburgh, NY: Pennimann & Bliss. 368p. 21cm. [Reprint of the foregoing.] [LC]

KNOBELSDORFF-BRENKENHOFF, Ny. A:e Ame. Hne. (v. Eschstruth) v. 1860- . See Eschstruth, Ny. v.

KNOPKE (KNOEPKE), An. d. ca. 1530. Sel. in C271.

KNORR VON ROSENROTH, Cn. 1636-89. Sel. in C229;269;271;276;#8904.

KNORRING, So. (Tieck) Bernhardi v. 1775-1833.
5094a. The peasant and his landlord. Tr. Ma. Howitt. L: Bentley 1848. 2v. See "Athenaeum" 1848, p. 238. (B15a)

KNORTZ, K: 1841- . Sel. in C216;309;450.

KNOTTNERUS-MEYER, Td.
5095. Birds and beasts of the Roman zoo: observations of a lover of animals. Tr. B. Miall. L: Allen & U. 1927. 378p. 22cm. [BM.LC]

KOBELL, Fz. v. 1803-82. Sel. in C372.

KOBELL, Lu. v. 1828-1901. See Döllinger, J., Conversations, etc., #1258.

KOCH, Ad.
*5096. Prince Ax. of Battenberg: reminisc. of his reign in Bulgaria, from authentic sources. Tr. J. F. Davis, Miss H. F. Powell, Miss P. C. Evans. L: Whittaker 1887. viii;280p. il. 8. [BM.LC]

KOCH, Ern. 1808-58.
5097. (Prinz Rosa-Stramin.) Prince Rosa-Stramin by "E: Helmer." Tr. from latest Ger. ed. by A. v. Beresford. Göttingen: G: H. Wigand 1860. viii;156p. 16cm. [BM]

KOCH, Jl. 1866- .
5098. Roman history. Tr. L. D: Barnett. L: Dent. Temple primers. 1900. viii;160p. 15cm. [BM]
5099. do. 1901. [same] 2d ed. [LC card]
5100. do. 1905. [same] 3d ed. [LC]

KOCH, K: H: El. 1809-79.
5101. The Crimea; with a visit to Odessa. Tr. anon. L: Routledge 1855. 8th thous. 183p. il. 17cm. [BM]
5102. do. 1855. [same] [Another copy with a different t.p.] [BM]
5103. do. 1855. Tr. Joanna B. Horner. L: Murray. 323p. 19cm. [LC]

KOCH, Rle.
5104. The faithful dog; The generous enemy. Tr. "Trauermantel." 1857. In C544.
5105. Country cousins; The little ragman; The picture. Tr. "Trauermantel." 1859. In C548.
5106. Holly and mistletoe: tales. Tr. "Trauermantel." Bost: Crosby, Nichols 1860. 249p. il. 16. [LCO]

KOEHLER, B: F: 1730-96. Sel. in C273;543.

KOEHLER, J: Gb. F: 1788-1855. Sel. in C233.

KOEHLER, Wfg. 1887- .
5107. (Intelligenzprüfungen an Menschenaffen.) The mentality of apes. Tr. from 2d rev. ed. by Ella Winter. L: K.Paul 1925. 342p. 22cm. [BM]
5108. do. 1927. [same] 2d rev. ed. L: Paul. 336p. 9 pl. 22cm. [BM]

KOELLNER, W: H: E: 1806- .
5108a. The return to faith: exemplified in the life of W-- K--. Written by himself. Tr. S: Jackson. L: Jackson & Walford 1836. 304p. front. (Port.) 16cm. [BM]
[Has a letter from his son C: relating his death. Appendix of letters to him by a friend and patron.]

KOENIG KONRAD DER JUNGE, 1252-68. See Konradin.

KOENIG, E: 1846- .
5109. (Bibel und Babel.) The Bible and Babylon: a brief study in the hist. of ancient civilization. With ref. to Delitzsch, "Babel und Bibel." Tr. from 9th rev. and enl. ed. by C: E. Hay. Burlington, Ia: Ger. lit. bd. 1903. 64p. 20cm. [LC]
*5110. do. 1905. Tr. Rev. W: T. Pilter. Pref. by H: Wace. L: Relig. tract soc. xvi;137p. 18cm. [BM]

KOENIG, Ewd. A: 1833-88.
5111. Wooing a widow. Tr. Ma. A. Robinson. Il. Jas. Fagan. NY: Bonner 1894. 380p. 19cm. [LC]

KOENIG, Pl.
§5112. (Die Fahrt der Deutschland.) The voyage of the "Deutschland." Tr. anon. NY: Hearst's internat. lib. 1916. 247p. il. 19cm. [BM]
[Fair tr.]
§5113. do. 1917. Tr. Vivien Ellis. L: Pearson. 126p. 8. [BM]
[Many errors.]

KOENIGSBERG, Leo, 1837- .
*5114. Hm. v. Helmholtz. Tr. Fes. A. Welby. Pref. by Lord Kelvin. Oxford: Clarendon 1906. xvii;440p. 24cm. [BM.LC]
[Somewhat abridged.]

KOENIGSMARCK, Hs. Ad. Erwein Max, Graf v. 1865- .
*5115. (Die Engländer in Indien.) A Ger. staff officer in India. Tr. P. H. O. Williams. L: Paul, T. & T. 1910. xiv;339p. il. 25cm.
[Il. w. photos and drawings by the author and others.] [BM.LC]
5116. The Markhor: sport in Cashmere. Tr. Norah Bashford. L: Paul, T. & T. 1910. xv;151p. il. 16. [BM]

KOENIGSMARCK, Me. Au. Gräfin v. 1670-1728.
5117. Memoirs of the love and intrigues of the court of H(anover) from the marriage of the Princess of Z(elle) to the tragical death of Count K...k (Königsmarck). Written orig. in High German by the celebrated countess of K...k (Königsmarck). Tr. anon. L: Prtd. for J. H. 1743. 119p. 21cm. [BM]
5118. do. 1744? [same] A home truth: being memoirs of the love and state-intrigues of the court of H(anover). 2d ed. L: J.Robinson. 119p. 20cm. [Copious MS notes.] [BM]

KOERBER, Ph.
5119. The herdsman of Dambach; or, "vengeance is mine, I will repay, saith the Lord." Tr. Sa. A. Flory. Phil: Luth. bd. 1875. 156p. 16. [LCO]

KOERNER, Cn. Gf. 1756-1831. Sel. in #5132.
§5120. Life of Carl T. Körner...with sel. from his poems, tales, and dramas (and letters). Tr. G. F. Richardson. L: 1827. 2v. 8. [BM]
[Knows German, but is no poet; lyrics undistinguished, blank verse good, prose excellent. --Poems, pp. 73-147; prose tales, pp. 151-208. Vol. 2 has "Zriny," "Joseph Heyderich."]
5121. do. 1833. [same] Phil. Greenbank. Vol. 1. 8. [LCO]
[Probably a reprint of the foregoing.]
5122. do. 1845. [same] 2d ed. L: Nutt. 2v. 367;387p. 12. [BM.LCO]
See Corr. of Schiller with K--., #8241.

KOERNER, K: Td. 1791-1813. Sel. in C8;9;17;29;31;37;42-3;44*;45-6; 48;67*;69;88-9;101;106;111;123;129;131-3;142-4;149;153;166;172; 177;182;184;192;195;215;219;295-6;306;309;366*;372-3;375;380-1; 391;393;417;423;428;439;443;448;467;469;471;486;489;497;499;500-1; 511;539;#2720;4421;8023.

*5123. [Coll.] A selection from the poems and dramatic works. Tr. Mme. Lucien Daviésiès de Pontès L: Williams & N. 1850. xxiii; 399p. 20cm. [BM]
[On the whole, excellent. Has the life of K--. The expiation ("Die Sühne"); Antonia ("Toni"); Hedwig (do.); Rosamond ("Rosamunde"); The fisherman's daughter ("Das Fischermädchen"); On hate and love; The spirits of the mountain ("Die Bergknappen"); The fight with the dragon ("Der Kampf mit dem Drachen"); Alfred the great ("Af. der Grosse"); The doves ("Die Tauben"); The harp ("Die Harfe"); The roses ("Die Rosen"); 38 poems.]

*5124. (Briefe.) Letters, to friends and family. Tr. G. F. Richardson. 1827. In #5122, vol. 1, pp. 135-270.

*5125. (Der vierjährige Posten.) The faithful sentry: opera in one act by Pl. Graener. Tr. S: Gordon. Vocal score. Ger;Engl. L: St. Cecilia 1899. 83p. 4. [Very good.] [LCM]

5126. (Die Harfe.) The harp. Tr. G. F. Richardson. 1827. In #5122.

5127. (Die Reise nach Schandau.) The journey to S--. Tr. G. F. Richardson. 1827. In #5122.

(Goldner.) Goldner. [This ascription is erroneous. See Kerner, J.]

5129. (Hans Heilings Felsen.) Hans Heiling's rocks. Tr. G. F. Richardson. 1827. In #5122.

*5130. (Hedwig.) Hedwig; or, love and gratitude. A drama in 3 acts. [verse]. Tr. Mrs. Burton Daveney. Norwich: Miller 1878. 70p. 16cm. [Also L: Simpkin, M.] [BM]

5131. (Josef Heyderich.) Js. H--. Tr. G. F. Richardson. 1827. In #5122.

**5132. (Leier und Schwert.) The lyre and the sword...with a life of the author and extracts from his letters. Tr. W. B. Chorley. L: Hamilton, Adams; Liverpool: Marples 1834. x;248p. front. (port.) 16. [BM]
[36 poems, besides some on K-- by Tiedge, Wolfart, Theremin, Caro. Pichler, Cn. Gf. Körner.--Pref. to p. 82. --Excellent tr.]

5133. do. 1839. [same] L: Hamilton. 32. [EC]

§5134. do. 1841. Lyre and sword. Tr. anon. with notes. Ed: Smith; L: Whittaker. xii;94p. 22cm. [36 poems, rather poorly done.] [BM]

*5135. (Rosamunde.) Rosamond. Tr. G. F. Richardson. 1827. In #5122.

5136. do. 1830. Tr. anon. L: W:Kidd, and Simpkin & M. iv;63p. 21cm. [BM]

†5137. do. 1878. Rosamunda: a trag. in 4 acts. Tr. J: Chapman. Folkestone: Prtd. by Goulden. 26p. 17cm. [LC]
[Hardly recognizable; a mere skeleton of the orig.]

*5138. To the people of Saxony. Tr. G. F. Richardson. 1827. In #5122.

5139. Woldemar (do.); The harp (Die Harfe). Tr. R: Holcraft. 1826. In C203.

*5140. do. 1827. Tr. G. F. Richardson. In #5122.

*5141. (Zriny.) Zriny. Tr. G. F. Richardson. 1827. In #5122.

5142. do. 1830. [Sel.] Tr. W: Taylor. In C533.

KOESTLIN, Jl. 1826-1902.

*5143. (Luthers Leben.) The life of L--. Tr. anon. L: Longmans; NY: Scribner 1883. xvi;587p. 58 il. 20cm. [BM.LC]

*5144. do. 1883. Life of Mn. L--. Ed. J: G. Morris. Tr. by different hands. Phil: Luth. pub. 496p. il. 25cm. [LC.BM]
[Not as good as #5143.]

5145. do. 1895. [same as #5143] 2d ed. L: Longmans. xvi;496p. [BM]

KOESTLIN, Jl.--Luthers Leben
5146. do. 1898. [same] [EC]
5147. do. 1903. [same as #5143] NY: Scribner. [LC]
5148. do. 1912. [same] [AC]
5149. (Martin Luther, der deutsche Reformator.) Mn. L--, the reformer. Tr. Eliz. P. Weir. 3d ed. L: Cassell 1883. x;145p. port. 16cm. [Much abr., epitomized.] [BM]

KOETTSCHAU, C.
*5150. (Der nächste deutsch-französische Krieg.) The coming Franco-German war: a military-political study. Tr. J: Hill. L: Ward & Downey 1887. 295p. 20cm. [Rather disappointing.] [BM]

KOHL, Horst
*5151. (Wegweiser durch Bismarcks Gedanken und Erinnerungen.) A guide through B--'s "Reflections and reminiscences." Tr. C. Bell. L: Dent 1899. xii;278p. front.(port.) after Lenbach. 19cm. [BM]

KOHL, J: G: 1808-78.
§5152. [Coll.] (Reisen in Irland. Reisen in Schottland. Reisen in England und Wales.) Ireland, Scotland, and England. Tr. anon. L: Chapman & Hall 1843-4. 3 pts. 248; 100; 202p. [BM.LC]
[Pt. 1, Ireland, 1843. Pt. 2, Scotland, 1844. Pt. 3, England and Wales, no t.p.--Considerably condensed, but this is not stated.]
5153. [Coll.] 1850? Travels in Russia, Austria, Scotland, England, and Wales. NY: Carey & Hart n.d. (before 1852). [AC]
*5154. (Geschichte der Entdeckung Amerikas von Columbus bis Franklin.) A popular hist. of the discovery of America, from Columbus to Franklin. Tr. R. R. Noel. L: Chapman & Hall 1862. 2v. 275; 284p. 20cm. [BM]
*5155. (Hundert Tage auf Reisen in den österreichischen Staaten.) Austria...Hungary, Bohemia. Also, The conclud. vol. of his work on Russia, containing his remarks on the Bukovina, Galicia, and Moravia. L: Chapman & Hall 1843. 532p. 21cm. [BM.LC]
[Condensed tr., good as far as it goes.]
5156. do. 1844. Austria. Phil: Carey & Hart. 104p. 28cm. [LC]
[Contains only Bohemia, and Upper and Lower Austria.]
*5157. (Kitschi-Gami, oder Erzählungen vom Obern See.) Kitchi-gami: wanderings round Lake Superior. Tr. Sir F. C. L. Wraxall. L: Chapman & Hall 1860. xii;428p. il. 8. [BM.LC]
[Omits certain portions, e.g., Indian legends, which had been pub. in his other works.]
5158. (Petersburg in Bildern.) Russia and the Russians in 1842. Tr. anon. L: Colburn 1842. 2v. 340; 341p. il. 19cm. [BM.LC]
5159. do. 1842. [same] L: Chapman & Hall. 530p. 21cm. [BM]
["Abstract of nine...vols. descriptive of...a large portion of the Russian empire."]
5160. do. 1850. [same] New ed. L: Bohn. 8. [EC]
5161. do. 1852. Panorama of St. Petersburg. L: Simms & McIntyre. 224p. 18cm. [BM.LC]
[Name spelled Köhl. Phrases omitted right and left, otherwise the tr. is clever. This is taken from #5159, pp. 1-210.]
§5162. (Reisen in Canada, New-York und Pennsylvania.) Travels in Canada, and through the states of NY and Penn. Tr. Mrs. Percy Sinnett, rev. by the author. L: Manwaring 1861. 2v. 345; 357p. 19cm. [Differs somewhat from the orig. as printed.] [BM.LC]
§5163. (Reisen in England und Wales.) Travels in E--. Tr. T: Roscoe. L: Sherwood, etc. 1845. 4 pts. 420p. 17cm. [BM]
[T.p. as above. Pt. 4 has extra t.p.: Travels in England and Wales. Heading on p. 1 reads: England and Wales. --Tr. puts in his own ideas.]

KOHL, J: G:
5164. (Reisen in Irland.) Ireland. Tr. anon. NY: Harper 1844. 115p. 24cm. [Cf. #5152.] [LC]
*5165. (Reisen in Schottland.) Travels in S--. Tr. J: Kesson, with notes by the tr. L: Bruce & Wyld 1844. xiv;253p. 19cm. [BM]

KOHLER, Js. 1849-1919.
*5166. (Lehrbuch der Rechtsphilosophie.) Philos. of law. Tr. Adalbert Albrecht, with ed. pref. by A. Kocourek and introds. by Orrin M. Carter and W: Caldwell. Bost: Bost. bk. 1914. xliv;390p. 21cm. [LC]
5167. do. 1921. [same] NY: Macmillan. xliv;390p. [LC]

KOHLRAUSCH, H: F: Td. 1780-1865.
5168. The character of Charlemagne. Tr. J. D. Haas. 1839. In C183.
5169. A hist. of Germany; from the earliest period to the present time. Tr. Jas. D. Haas. L: Chapman & Hall 1844. 700p. 22cm. [Either from an orig. unknown to me, or much reworked.] [BM.LC]
5170. do. 1847. [same] NY;Phil: Appleton. 480p. 23cm. [LC]
5171. do. 1848. [same?] L: Bohn. 8. [EC]

KOHN, Sl. 1825- .
*5172. (Gawriel, histor. Erzählung aus dem 30jähr. Kriege.) Gabriel: a story of the Jews in Prague. Tr. Arthur Milman. Lpz: Tauchnitz; L: Low 1875. 267p. 16cm. [BM]
5173. do. 1882. [same] NY: Munro. Seaside lib. 30p. 32cm. [LCO]

KOHNEN, L.
5173a. (Editorial contributions to Schreiber's Guide to the Rhine.) 1834. In #8620.

KOITSCH, Cn. Jk. 1671-1735. Sel. in C229;269.

KOLB, P: 1675-1726.
5174. The present state of the Cape of Good Hope. Written...by P: Kolben. Done into Engl...by Mr. (Guido) Medley. Il. w. copper pl. L: Innys & Manby 1738, 31. 2v. xviii;365; 363p. 19cm. [BM.LC]
5175. do. 1773. The voyage of P: K-- to the Cape of Good Hope. In "The world displayed," vol. X, 3d corr. ed., pp. 44-123. L: Carman & Newberry. 14cm. [BM]
5176. do. 1787. A coll. of voyages and travels, containing...The voyage of P: Kolben, A. M., to the Cape of Good Hope. Phil: Prtd. by W: Spotswood. (B6a)

KOLDEWEY, K: 1837- .
5177. (Die zweite deutsche Nordpolarfahrt...) The Ger. arctic exped. of 1869-70. Tr. and abr. by L. P. Mercier. Ed. H. W. Bates. L: Low 1874. 590p. 24cm. [BM.LC] [Woodcuts, maps, ports., and 4 col. ils.--Cut down from 2 vols. to 1; tr. is faithful as far as it goes.]

KOLDEWEY, Rb. 1855- .
§5178. (Das wieder erstehende Babylon.) Excavations at B--. Tr. Ag. Johns. L;NY: Macmillan 1914. xix;335p. 255 il. 24cm. [BM.LC] [Tr. is good but not impeccable.]

KOLLO, Wl. The girl on the film. Musical farce. See Bernauer, K.

KOLLONITZ, Pla. Gräfin v. 1830- .
*5179. (Eine Reise nach Mexico...1864.) The court of Mexico. Tr. J. E. Ollivant. L: Saunders & O. 1867. 8. [EC] [EC spells name Kollowitz.]
5180. do. 1868. [same] 3d ed. xix;303p. 22cm. [BM.LC]

KOLMAS, Der v., 12th. cent. Sel. in C27;427.

KOMPERT, Lp. 1822-86. Sel. in C179.
§5181. [Coll.] Scenes from the Ghetto: studies of Jewish life. Tr. anon. L: Remington 1882. 340p. 18cm. [BM]
[Schlemiel (do.); Old Babele ("Alt B--"); The randar's children ("Die Kinder des Randars"); Without authorization ("Ohne Bewilligung").--Tr. is incorrect.]
5182. [Coll.] 1883. [same?] Stories of Jewish life; or, scenes from the Ghetto. Tr. anon. NY: Munro. Seaside lib. 36p.32cm. [LCO]
§5183. [Coll.] 1895. Christian and Leah (Lea), and other Ghetto stories. Tr. Ax. S. Arnold. Il: F. H. Jackson. L: Dent. 246p. 16cm. [BM]
[Also: A ghetto violet; Debby and her door.--Very free and not always correct.]
5184. A ghetto violet. Tr. A. S. Arnold. 1898. In C509.
[Probably from the foregoing.]
5185. The silent woman. Tr. C: F. McClumpha. In "Modern ghosts." NY: Harper 1890. 225p. 18cm. [LC]

KONEBERG, Hm.
5186. Blessed ones of 1888: Clement Ma. Hofbauer...Tr. Eliza A. Donnelly. NY: Benziger 1888. 188p. 18. [LCO]

KONEWKA, Pl. 1840-71. Black Peter. See Trojan, J. Konewka is silhouette artist.

KONRAD VON KIRCHBERG, 13th cent. Sel. in C171;190;532.

KONRAD VON QUEINFURT. Sel. in C570.

KONRAD VON WUERZBURG, d. 1287. Sel. in C27;171;366;416;530-2.

KONRADIN, König, 1252-68. Sel. in C27;88;427.

KOPISCH, A: 1799-1853. Sel. in C17;41;106;169;215;372;394;450;499.

KORNGOLD, Er. Wfg. 1897- . Violanta. Opera. See Müller, Hs.,#6502.

KORTUM, K: Arn. 1745-1824.
*5187. (Die Jobsiade.) The Jobsiad: a grotesco-comico-heroic poem. Tr. C: T. Brooks. Phil: Leypoldt 1863. xviii;181p. il. 18cm.
[Il. W: Busch.] [LC.BM]
5188. do. 1867. [same] NY. xviii;181p. [BM]

KOSEGARTEN, L: Gtd. 1758-1818. Sel. in C44;182;219;309;373;375;469; 489.

"KOSEWITZ, W. F. v." (i.e., C: Rb. Forrester, 1803-50.)
[The "Eccentric tales," 1827, are not translated.]

KOSSAK, Ern. 1814-80. Sel. in C422.

KOSZTOLANYI, Desider (Deszö), 1885- .
5188. Bloody poet: a novel about Nero. Pref. letter by T: Mann. Macy-Masius 1927. 344p. D. [AC]
5189. do. 1928. Tr. C. P. Fadiman. Gollancz. 288p. 7 x 5 in. [EC]

KOTTENKAMP, Fz.
5190. (Der Rittersaal. Eine Geschichte des Rittertums...) Hist. of chivalry and ancient armour. Tr. Rev. A. Löwy. L: Willis & Sotheran 1857. 110p. 62 col. engr. 22 x 28cm. [BM.LCO]
[Considerable condensation, otherwise good.]

KOTTER, Cph.
5191. (Göttliche Offenbahrungen so...C. K. (1616-1624) widerfahren.) The lives, prophecies, visions and revelations of C. Kotterus and C. Poniatonia. In "Prophetical extracts." L: G. Terry 1804? pp. 1-24. 21cm. [BM]

KOTZEBUE, A: (F: Fd.) v. 1761-1819. Sel. in C26;44;67;106;132-3; 152;214;295;373;391;393;422.
5192. [Coll.] The dramatic works. Tr. C: Smith. NY: Prtd. for Smith & Stephens. 1800. 3v. 8. (B48)
[Only three tr. by Smith; all pub. sep. by him. See individ. titles.]
†5193. [Coll.] 1800. The beauties of K--: containing the most interesting scenes, sentiments, speeches, etc., in all his admired dramas. Freely tr., connected and digested under approp. heads, alphabet. arr. w. biogr. anecdotes of the author, a summary of his dramatic fables, and cursory remarks, by W. C. Oulton. L: Crosby & Letterman. xxxix;402p. 17cm. [BM]
5194. [Coll.] 1802. The dramatic works. Tr. B: Thompson. L: 3v. See "Monthly Mirror" 14(1802):259. (B26)
[Perhaps the same as #5192. Cf., e.g., #5207.]
5195. [Coll.] 1806. The pastor's daughter (and other stories). Tr. anon. L: Colburn. 4v. 12. [BM]
[The pastor's daughter ("Des Pfarrers Tochter"); The masquerade; The protecting spirit ("Der Schutzgeist"); The subterranean passage ("Der unterirdische Gang"); The revenge ("Die Rache"); The romantic wife.]
§5196. [Coll.] 1807. Novelettes. Tr. anon. L: Phillips. 3v. 16cm. [BM]
[Tr. is not very good.--The grave on the hill; Shun even the appearance of vice ("Meide den Schein"); The guardian angel ("Der Schutzgeist"); The revenge ("Die Rache"); The pigeon ("Die Taube"); The enthusiast ("Die geheilte Schwärmerei"); The vicar's daughter ("Des Pfarrers Tochter"); The little lie ("Die kleinste Lüge ist gefährlich"); Schad, a Benedictine monk; Insolent arrogance; The unhappy husbands' complaint ("Die klagenden Ehemänner"); The maid of Orleans as wife and mother ("Die Jungfrau von Orleans als Frau und Mutter"); The mysterious cavern.]
5197. [Coll.] 1807. Histor., lit., and polit. anecdotes and miscellanies. Tr. anon. L: Colburn. 3v. 16. [LCO]
§5198. [Coll.] 1834? The beauties of K-- sel. from his works by Af. Howard. L: Davison for T: Tegg. 187p. front. (port.) engr. by W. T. Fry. 14cm. [BM]
[26 sel., includ. 2 complete tales, 2 acts and some scenes from plays, anecdotes, scenes of travel, etc. Appar. the tr. is newly done.]
5199. [Coll.] 1872-6. Plays. Tr. anon. NY: French n.d. 4v. 16. [AC]
§5200. (<u>Adelheid von Wulfingen.</u>) Adelaide of W--: a tragedy (in 4 acts and in prose). Tr. B: Thompson. L: Vernor & Hood 1798. 108p. 21cm. [BM]
["Exemplifying...barbarity...13th cent."--I incline to the view that T. knew little German. Cf. my comment on C535.]
5201. do. 1800. [same] NY: Prtd. for Smith & Stephens. 67p. 8.(B48)
§5202. do. 1801. [same] L: Vernor & Hood. 82p. 21cm. [BM]
[This is part of C535, but has sep. t.p. and paging. Verbal revision for this ed.]
*5203. (<u>Armut und Edelsinn.</u>) Poverty and nobleness of mind: a play in 3 acts [prose]. Tr. Ma. Geisweiler. L: C.Geisweiler 1799. 126p. 21cm. [BM]
5204. do. 1799. [same] 2d ed. [BM]
§5205. do. 1799. Sighs; or, the daughter: a comedy in 5 acts [prose] With alterations by Prince Hoare. As performed at the theater-royal. L: Prtd. for Machell Stace. vii;87p. 20cm. [BM]
[Adds a postscript of 4 p. The adaptation is considerable; probably Ma. Geisweiler's tr. was the source.]
5206. do. 1800. [same] Prtd. in Charlestown for Larkin in Boston. 71p. 12. (B48)
5207. do. 1800. [same as #5203?] Indigence, and nobleness of mind. NY: Prtd. for Smith & Stephens. 64p. 8. (B48)

KOTZEBUE, A: v.--Armut und Edelsinn
5208. do. 1802. Hoare's tr. Sighs, etc. Dublin: N. Kelly. Advt. 88p. epilogue. 17cm. [BM]
5209. (Blind geladen.) How to die for love: a farce in 2 acts [prose]. Ad. by abridgment, alteration of scene numbering, etc., from a sketch in one act. Tr. anon. L: Chapple 1812. 45p.20cm. [BM]
5210. do. 1812. [same] 3d ed. 22cm. [BM]
[This ed. adds: First performed...21st of May, 1812.]
5211. do. 1816. [same] [BM]
[This ed. adds: with additional songs, which appear on p. 46. Otherwise identical.]
5212. do. 1833. [same] Phil: Turner & Son. 30p. 15cm. [LC]
5213. do. n.d. [same] Prtd. from the acting copy, with remarks by D.-G. (pp. 5-7). Front. by R. Cruikshank. L: J:Cumberland. 34p. 14cm. [BM]
[Vol. 40 of "Cumberland's British Theatre," pub. from 1829 on.]
§5214. (Das Kind der Liebe.) Lover's vows; or, the child of love. A play in 5 acts [prose]. Tr. St. Porter. with a brief biogr. L: Prtd. for Parsons, sold by Hatchard 1798. vii;111p. 20cm. [BM.LC]
[None too faithful, for all his protestations.]
5215. do. 1798. Lovers' vows. Tr. Mrs. Inchbald. L: Robinson. iv; 90p. plus epilogue. 21cm. [BM]
["Performing at the Theatre Royal."--Mrs. I. knew no Ger. and worked from "a literal tr...by a German...in broken Engl." Her pref. gives a succinct account of her alterations.]
5216. do. 1798. [same] 7th ed. [BM]
5217. do. 1798. [same] 9th ed. [BM]
*5218. do. 1798. The natural son: a play in 5 acts, being the original of Lovers' vows (i.e., Mrs. Inchbald's adaptation). Tr. Anne Plumptre. L: R.Phillips. vii;83p. 20cm. [BM]
[Tries to be quite faithful, does not wholly succeed.]
5219. do. 1798. [same] 2d ed. [BM]
5220. do. 1798. [same] Dublin: Fitzpatrick. xi;108p. 17cm. [BM]
[Sketch of author's life appended.]
5221. do. 1798. [same] 4th rev. ed. L: [BM]
[One name is corrected, and the biog. sketch is partly rewritten.]
5221a. do. 1799. Mrs. Inchbald's tr. Bost: West. 56p. 12.
[Available: AAS.] (B6a)
5221b. do. 1799. [same] NY: Repr. for Judah. 86p. 8. (B6a) [AAS]
*5222. do. 1800. Lovers' vows; or, the natural son. Tr. B: Thompson. L: Vernor & Hood. 99p. In C535. Front. by H. Smith.
[Tr. not exactly accurate, but good. He seems to have used Plumptre's version.]
5223. do. 1802. [same] Balto: Prtd. for Thomas, A. & B. 66p. 8. (B48)
5224. do. 1806. Mrs. Inchbald's tr. Dublin. T: Burnside. 63p. 17cm.
[Has no pref.] [BM]
5225. do. 1808. [same] In "Inchbald's Brit. theatre." L: Longmans. 74p. 15cm. [Prtd...from the prompt book. Orig. pref. and added remarks. Front. after painting by Howard.] [BM]
5226. do. 1809. Lovers' vows. Altered from the tr. of Mrs. Inchbald and B: Thompson by J. H. Payne. Balto: Dobbin & Murphy. 90p. 16.
[In reality, he combines the two versions.] [LCO]
5227. do. 1814. Lovers [sic] vows: a play in 5 acts. From the Ger. of Rotzebue [sic]. By W: Dunlap, as performed at the New-York theatre. NY: D: Longworth. 74p. 15cm. [LCO.BM]
[Dunlap chiefly abridged Plumptre's version.]
5228. do. 1826? Inchbald's tr. In "The Lond. stage." L: G:Balne.16p. 22cm. [Date 1826 is printed on front of vol. Il. I. R. Dodd.] [BM.LC]
5229. do. 1829. [same]. In "Cumberland's Brit. theatre," vol. 17. From the acting copy, with remarks by D.-G. L: J:Cumberland. 58p. 14cm.[Her pref.omitted. Front. by G.W. Bonner after R.Cruikshank.] [BM]

KOTZEBUE, A: v.--Das Kind der Liebe
5230. do. 1830? [same] In "The penny nat. lib." L: F:Lawrance. 25cm. [Pp. 308-20. Last 3 pages missing.] [BM]
5231. do. 1834. [same] In "The acting drama." L: Mayhew, Isaac & Mayhew. 24cm. [Pp. 308-23.] [BM]
5232. do. 1872. [same] In "The British drama," vol. 10. L: J:Dicks. 18cm. [Pp. 130-48. One il.] [BM]
5233. do. 1883. [same] In "Dicks' standard plays," no. 184, pp. 129-48. [Same text and il. as the foregoing.] [BM]
*5234. (Das Schreibepult.) The writing-desk; or, youth in danger. A play in 4 acts [prose]. Tr. anon. L: Robinson 1799. 114p. 20cm. ["Literally tr."] [BM]
5235. do. 1799. The wise man of the east: a play in 5 acts. Now performing at the theatre royal. Tr. Mrs. Inchbald. L: Robinson. 80p. 20cm. [Much altered from the foregoing. Cf. note to #5215.] [BM]
5236. do. 1799. [same] 2d ed. [BM]
[This prints epilogue at end; otherwise identical.]
5237. do. 1801. [reprint of #5234?] NY: Prtd. for Smith. 72p. 8. [LCO]
*5238. (Der Graf von Burgund.) The count of Burgundy: a play in 4 acts [prose]. Tr. Anne Plumptre. L: Phillips 1798. 77p. 20cm. [BM] [Not flawless.]
5239. do. 1798. [same]. 2d ed. [BM]
5240. do. 1798. [same] 3d ed. [BM]
5241. do. 1799. [same] Dublin: N.Kelly. 103p. 17cm. [BM]
5242. do. 1800. Tr. C: Smith. NY: Smith & Stephens. 69p. 8. [LCO] [Cf. #5192.]
5243. (Der Mann von 40 Jahren.) The man of 40: a comedietta in one act [prose], as performed June 29, 1880. Ad...by W: Poel. L;NY: French 1883. 20p. 17cm. [BM]
*5244. (Der Opfertod.) Self-immolation; or, the sacrifice of love. A play in 3 acts [prose]. Tr. H: Neuman. L: R.Phillips 1799. viii; 49p. 19cm. [BM]
5245. do. 1799.[same]. Family distress; or, self-immolation, etc. As...now performing verbatim from this tr. L: Phillips. viii;49p. 21cm. [2d ed. of the foregoing.] [BM]
5245a. do. 1799. [same] Dublin: Folingsby. vi;60p. 17cm. [BM]
5246. do. 1799. [same] Bost: Prtd. for Blake. 57p. 12. (B48)
5247. do. 1800. [same] NY: Prtd. for Smith & Stephens. 54p. 8. (B48)
§5248. (Der Schutzgeist.) The guardian angel: a story for youth. L: Vernor & Hood 1802. 117p. front. 14cm. [BM]
[Singular and plural die confused.]
§5249. (Der Taubstumme). Deaf and dumb; or, the orphan. An histor. drama in 5 acts [prose], from the French of Bouilly. Tr. B: Thompson. L: Vernor & Hood 1801 (C535). 60p. front. by Thurston. 21cm. [Here T. seems to be quite astray; Cf. #5200 and C535.] [BM]
5250. do. 1801. [same] 60p. 16cm. [BM]
[Sep. ed. without front; margins trimmed, otherwise ident.]
5251. do. 1801. Deaf and dumb; or, the orphan protected. Tr. anon. Performed...Feb. 24, 1801. Dublin: J. Stockdale. iv;73p. 17cm. [BM]
5252. do. 1801. [reprint] Abbé de l'Epée; or, the orphan. NY: Prtd. for Smith. 42p. 8. [Probably Thompson's tr.] [LCO]
§5253. (Der Wildfang.) The wild goose chace: a play in 4 acts [prose]. Tr. W: Dunlap. 1798. (B41)
§5254. do. 1800. [same] NY. Prtd. by Hopkins for W. Dunlap. x;106p. 21cm. [Life by K-- prefixed. Notes give the variations from the orig., which are consid. Front. (port.) by Gilbert Fox. Also port. by W. Dunlap of Hodgkinson as Wellinghorst.] [BM]
5255. do. 1800. The wild youth: a comedy for digestion. Tr. C: Smith. NY: Smith & Stephens. 72p. 8. [Cf. #5192.] [LCO]
5256. do. 1806. Of age to-morrow. Ad. by T: Dibdin. L: (Cited by B48). [Probably Dibdin used Dunlap's version. See B41.]

KOTZEBUE, A: v.--Der Wildfang
5257. do. 1808. [same] NY: Longworth. (B48)
*5258. (Der weibliche Jakobiner-Clubb.) The female Jacobin-club: a polit. comedy in one act [prose]. Tr. J. C. Siber. Liverpool: Coddington; L: Vernor & Hood 1801. 41p. 17cm. [BM]
[EC has: Vernor 1802.]
*5259. (Der Wirrwarr.) The confusion; or, the wag. A play in 5 acts [prose]. Tr. E. F. F. Cambridge: J. Hall; L: Whittaker 1842. iii; 89p. 19cm. [Quite good, not impeccable.] [BM]
§5260. (Die Beichte.) The confession: a comedy in one act [verse]. Tr. anon. Phil: Hall & Atkinson 1820. 23p. 18cm. [BM]
[Orig. is in 12-syl. verse. Tr. struggles vainly with it.]
§5261. (Die beiden Klingsberg.) Father and son; or, family frailties. A comedy in 5 acts [prose]. Tr. anon. In "The new British theatre." Vol. 3, 1814, pp. 484-510. 21cm. [BM]
[Good, with liberties taken. K. has only 4 acts.]
*5262. (Die Corsen.) The Corsicans: a drama in 4 acts [prose]. Tr. anon. 2d ed. L: J.Bell 1799. 91p. 20cm. [BM]
*5263. do. 1800. Tr. by "Eleanor." In "Lady's Mag." 31(1800):37, etc. (B26) [Note that "Eleanor H---" tr. Lessing's Miss Sara Sampson. One or two of the names are changed.]
5264. do. 1814. [reprint of #5262.] NY: Longworth. 79p. 16. (B48)
*5265. (Die edle Lüge.) The noble lie: a drama in one act [prose]. A continuation of..."The stranger," now acting, etc. Tr. Ma. Geisweiler. L: C.Geisweiler 1799. Advt., pref. 43p. 22cm. [BM]
[See Menschenhass und Reue below. #5393 seq.]
5266. do. 1799. [same] 2d ed. [BM]
5267. do. 1799. The noble lie: a comedy, being the conclusion of The stranger. Tr. anon. L: Pitkeathley. 39p. 8. [LCO]
5268. (Die Flucht.) The escape: a narr. Tr. B: Thompson. L: Vernor & Hood 1799. (B26) [From "Jüngste Kinder meiner Laune."]
5269. do. 1814. The hist. of Js. Pignata. Tr. anon. In "Theatrical Inquisitor" 5(1814): 151, etc. (B26)
5270. do. 1821. The hist. and surprising advent. of Js. Pignata. Tr. G. Beech. L: Dean & Munday. 26p. 17cm. [LC]
5271. (Die Hussiten vor Naumburg.) The patriot father: a historical play. Ad. by F: Shoberl. Truro. 1818. See "Gentleman's Mag." 80 (1819):1:440. (B26)
§5272. do. 1830. [same] A histor. play in 5 acts [verse]. L: Kirby. x;60p. 17cm. [BM]
[Blank verse is excellent, rhymed verse not very successful.]
5273. do. 1850. [same] L: Priv. prtd. 66p. 21cm. [LC]
§5274. (Die Indianer in England.) The Indians in E--: a comedy in 3 acts [prose] by President K--. Tr. Ax. Thomson. 1796. In C534, pp. 1-132. 17cm. [He does not understand the German.] [BM]
5275. do. 1799. [same] The East Indian: a comedy. Tr. anon. L: Longman & Rees. 94p. 22cm. [BM]
5276. do. 1800. [same] The East Indian. Dublin: G. Burnett, etc. 106p. 17cm. [BM]
5277. do. 1800. [reprint?] NY: Prtd. for Smith & Stephens. 88p. 8. (B48)
§5278. do. 1800. The Indian exiles. Tr. B: Thompson. L: Vernor & Hood. (C535) 84p. 21cm. [Front. Thurston.] [BM]
5279. (Die Kreuzfahrer.) Alfred and Emma: a play in 5 acts [prose], founded on the Red cross knights. Tr. anon. L: for the author by J. Whiting 1806. 72p. 21cm. [BM]
[Fairly close in text, but names are substituted.]
*5280. (Die Leiden der Ortenbergischen Familie.) The sufferings of the family of Ortenberg: a novel. Tr. P: Will. L: Geisweiler 1799. 3v. 17cm. [Initial verse is poor; prose is good.] [BM]
5281. do. 1799. [same] Dublin: Prtd. for Moore. 2v. 17cm. [LC]

KOTZEBUE, A: v.--Die Leiden der Ortenbergischen Familie
5282. do. 1800. [reprint] Phil: Prtd. for Rice. 2v. in one. 154;160p. 18cm. [LC]
*5283. (Die Negersklaven.) The negro slaves: a dramatic-historical piece in 3 acts [prose]. Tr. anon. from...the President de K--. L: Cadell & Davies 1796. x;142p. 21cm. [BM]
5284. do. 1800. [same] New. t.p. and front. [BM]
*5285. (Die Organe des Gehirns.) The organs of the brain: a comedy in 3 acts [prose]. Tr. Lieut.-Col. Capadose. L: E:Bull 1838. 68p. 22cm. [BM]
5286. (Die Ruinen von Athen.) The ruins of Athens: cantata by Beethoven. Engl. words written and ad. by Pl. England. Books of words, with analytical notes by F. G. Edwards. L: Novello 1898. 8p. 25cm. [10 choruses, quite freely treated, but singable.] [BM]
5287. (Die schöne Unbekannte.) The beautiful unknown: a dramatic hist. Tr. C: Smith. NY: Burnton & Darling 1803. 50p. 18cm. [LC] [Bound with "Zaida."]
*5288. (Die silberne Hochzeit.) The happy family: a drama in 5 acts [Prose]. Tr. B: Thompson. L: Vernor & Hood 1799. 102p. 22cm. [BM]
5289. do. 1800. [reprint]. NY: Prtd. for Smith & Stephens. 84p. 8. (B48)
5290. do. 1801. [same] L: Vernor & Hood. (C535). 95p. 21cm. [BM] [Front. Thurston.]
5290a. do. 1847. The silver wedding: a drama in five acts. Tr. J: Hofstetter. Lpz;Vienna: Hunger. 141p. 12. [EC (Heinsius)] [Listed as: Select dramatic works of the Ger. theatre.]
*5291. (Die Sonnenjungfrau.) The virgin of the sun: a play in 5 acts [prose]. Tr. Anne Plumptre. L: R.Phillips 1799. vi;96p. 19cm. [BM] [Pretty good.]
5292. do. 1799. [same] 2d ed. [BM]
*5293. do. 1799. Rolla; or, the virgin of the sun. Tr. B: Thompson. L: Vernor & Hood. 130p. 21cm. [BM]
5294. do. 1799. Tr. W: Dunlap. L: Fauleder. See "Crit. R." (II)26 (1799):476. (B26)
*5295. do. 1800. Tr. J. Lawrence, with notes. NY: Prtd. by Hopkins for W. Dunlap. 80p. 21cm. [BM]
5296. do. 1801. [same as #5293]. L: Vernor & Hood. (C535). 93p. 21cm. [Front. T. Thurston.] [BM]
5297. do. 1812. Ad. Reynolds. See "Quarterly R." 1812, p. 227. (B41)
5298. (Die Spanier in Peru, oder Rollas Tod.) Rolla; or, the Peruvian hero. Tr. M. G. Lewis. 1797. [This publ. is cited by Max Rentsch, "M. G. Lewis." 1902. I have no other record.]
**5299. do. 1799. [same]: a tragedy in 5 acts [prose]. L: J.Bell. 108p. 22cm. [Admirable dialog.] [BM]
†5300. do. 1799. Pizarro in Peru; or, the death of Rolla. Being the orig. of the new trag. now performing, etc. Tr. from last Ger. ed. ...with notes by T: Dutton. L: West. 120p. 22cm. [BM] [General remarks at end. Insufferable expansion.]
5301. do. 1799. [same] 2d ed. [BM] [Notes point out the differences between Mr. Sheridan's play and the orig., with strictures on the performers, etc. The text is ident. with first ed., also the notes, only the t.p. differs.]
5302. do. 1799. Pizarro: a trag. in 5 acts, differing widely from all other Pizarros...By a North Briton. Hurst 1799. See "New London R." 2(1799):292. (B26)
[Sellier (B41) has: Pizarro, or the Peruvian mother. Tr. by Dr. Ainslie (in blank verse "with some additions and alterations"). See also Genest, S. A. 7:419ff.]
5303. do. 1799. Pizarro in Peru. Tr. R: Heron. Macpherson. See "New Lond. R." 2(1799):299. (B26)

KOTZEBUE, A: v.--Die Spanier in Peru, oder Rollas Tod
*5304. do. 1799. The Spaniards in Peru; or, the death of Rolla. Being the orig. of the play now performing etc. 6th ed. rev. Tr. Anne Plumptre. L: R.Phillips. vi;93p. 22cm. [BM]
[Fairly correct, not as good as Lewis.]
5305. do. 1799. Pizarro: a trag., as performed at the Theatre-Royal. Ad. to the Engl. stage by R: B. Sheridan. L: Jas. Ridgway. Advt. Dedication. Prologue. 76p. Epilogue. 21cm. [BM]
[Sheridan seems to have based his very free ad. on Lewis's tr.]
5306. do. 1799. [same] Dublin. J. Moore. 76p. 17cm. [BM]
[Prol. and epil. both precede the drama; otherwise ident. with L: ed.]
5307. do. 1799. [same] reprint. Phil: Prtd. for Rice. 59p. 19cm. [LC]
5308. do. 1799. [same] NY: Judah. 74p. 16. (B48)
5309. do. 1799. [same] 5th ed. [BM]
5310. do. 1799. [same] 7th ed. [BM]
5311. do. 1799. [same] 9th ed. [BM]
5312. do. 1799. [same] 11th ed. [BM]
5313. do. 1799. [same] 13th ed. [This adds publisher's advt.] [BM]
5314. do. 1799. [same] 15th ed. [Has a different advt.] [BM]
5315. do. 1799. [same] 20th ed. [BM]
[T.p. offers "an elegant front...designed by Buck and engr. by Milton...Mr. Kemble as Rolla...Price 1s."]
5315a. do. 1799. [same] 1st Charleston ed. from 20th L: ed. Charleston. Cox. (B6a)
5315b. do. 1799. [same] Charleston: Blake. 60p. 12. [NYPL]
5315c. do. 1799. [same] NY: Judah. 74p. 16. [LCO]
5315d. do. 1799. [same] Phil: Rice. 59p. pl. 12. (B6a)
5316. do. 1800. [same] 26th ed. [T.p. advt. reduced.] [BM]
5317. do. 1800. [same] 26th ed. With a tr. back into German by C. Geisweiler. L: Geisweiler. 76; 77p. 21cm. [BM]
[Sep. t.p. in German. The pages of the 26th ed. are interleaved with Geisweiler's tr. Only prol. and epil. are not tr.]
5318. do. 1800. Pizarro; or, the Spaniards in Peru. A trag. in 5 acts. Tr. anon. NY: Prtd. for Smith & Stephens. 62p. 18. (B48)
[Taken from #5305, but act V is expanded to follow the German.]
5319. do. 1800. Pizarro in Peru; or, the death of Rolla. Tr. W: Dunlap. NY: Hopkins. 92p. 8. [LCO]
[Bound with "The wild goose chace."]
*5320. do. 1800. Pizarro; or, the death of Rolla. Tr. B: Thompson. In C535. 92p. 21cm. [Front. Thurston. Thompson certainly knew and used #5304. Pretty good version.]
5321. do. 18-. [Identical with #5308?] Pizarro. Ad. by Sheridan. NY? 74p. 18. [LCO]
5322. do. 1805. [same as #5305]. Dublin: Macwilliam. 64p. 17cm. [LC]
5323. do. 1809. [reprint of #5305]. Bost. (B48)
5324. do. 1818. [same] Bost: West & Richardson. 69p. 17cm. [LC]
5325. do. 1819. [same] NY: Longworth. 68p. 18. [LCO]
5326. do. 1823. [same] Phil: Turner. 58p. 24. [LCO]
5327. do. 1824. [same] Pizarro: a trag. by R. B. Sheridan. With pref. remarks. The only ed. which is faithfully marked with the stage business...by W. Oxberry. L: Simpkin & Marshall. (xiii)61 (ii)p. 21cm. [BM.LC]
[Front. B: Holl after Wageman: Mr. Kemble as Rolla.]
5328. do. 1824. [same] In "The Lond. stage," vol. 1, 16p. 22cm. L: Balne. [Il. Mason. Prologue at end.] [BM.LC]
5329. do. 1824. [same] In "Dolby's British Theatre." L: Dolby. 60p. 15cm. [BM]
[Prtd. from the prompt book with notes, etc. Drawing by White after R. Cruikshank.]

KOTZEBUE, A: v.--Die Spanier in Peru
5330. do. 1826. [same] In "British drama," vol. 2. L: Jones & Co. 21cm. [Pp. 982-1000. Prologue at end.] [BM]
5331. do. 1826-7. [same] In "Acting Amer. theatre." Phil: Poole. Vol. 13, no. 4. 12. [The plays carefully corrected from the prompt books of the Phil. theater.] [LCO]
5332. do. 1830? [same] In "Penny nat. lib.," vol. 5, pp. 95-111. 25cm. [No prol. or epil.] [BM]
5333. do. 1834. [same] In "The acting drama." L: Mayhew, etc. 24cm. [Identical with foregoing, pp. 95-111.] [BM]
5334. do. 1846. [same] NY: Taylor. 60p. 16. [LCO] [Cf. paging of #5329.]
5335. do. 1850. [same] In "The British drama," vol. 2. Phil. [LC]
5336. do. 1856. [same] Pizarro: a play in 5 acts. Pref. J: H: Anderson and T: H. Lacy. L: Lacy. x;50p. 18cm. [BM] [No prol. or epil. Some revision of the text.]
5337. do. 1856. [same] Sheridan's tragic play of Pizarro. Arr. for rep...with historic notes, by C: Kean. Performed Sept. 1, 1856. L: J:Chapman. ix;67p. 21cm. [Text consid. revised and pruned.][BM]
5338. do. 1864. [same as #5305.] In "British drama," vol. 1. L: Dicks. 18cm. [Pp. 65-81. One il.] [BM]
5339. do. 1877. [same] In "New York drama," vol. 3. NY: Wheat & Cornett. 8. [LCO]
5340. do. 1883. [same as #5338] In Dicks' standard plays, no. 15, pp. 65-81. 18cm. [BM]
*5341. (Die Taube.) The pigeon: a tale. Tr. by a Philadelphian. Phil: H: Sweitzer 1802. 77p. 15cm. [BM] [From "Die jüngsten Kinder meiner Laune."]
§5342. (Die Verleumder.) The force of calumny: a play in 5 acts [prose]. Tr. Anne Plumptre. L: Phillips 1799. 108p. 19cm. [BM] [Neither close nor accurate.]
5343. do. 1800. [reprint.] NY: Prtd. for Smith & Stephens. 124p. 8. (B48)
*5344. (Die Versöhnung.) The reconciliation; or, the birth-day. A comedy in 5 acts [prose]. Tr. C. Ludger. L: Jas. Ridgway 1799. 120p. 20cm. [Paging jumps from 58-65.] [BM]
5345. do. 1799. [same] 3d ed. [BM]
5346. do. 1799. [same] 4th ed. 114p. [This ed. corrects paging.][BM]
5347. do. 1800. The birth-day. As performed at the Theatre-Royal. Ad. to the Engl. stage by T: Dibdin (from #5344). L: Longman & Rees. viii;80p. 19cm. [LC has: 22cm.] [BM.LC]
5348. do. 1801. Fraternal discord. Tr. anon. NY: Prtd. for Smith. 74p. 8. (B48) [Cf. the following.]
5349. do. 1809. Fraternal discord. Altered...W. Dunlap. Performed... in the New-York theatre. NY: Longworth. 69p. 15cm. [LC.BM] [Ad. from #5344.]
5350. do. 1815. [same as #5348.] In Inchbald, "Coll. of farces," vol. 2. L: Longmans. 46p. 16cm. [Prtd. from the prompt book.][BM.LCO]
*5351. (Die Verwandtschaften.) Kindred: a comedy in 5 acts [prose]. Tr. Lieut.-Col. Capadose. L: E:Bull 1837. 83p. 21cm. [BM]
*5352. (Die Witwe und das Reitpferd.) The widow and the riding-horse: a dram. trifle in one act (and in prose). Tr. Anne Plumptre. L: R.Phillips 1799. 20p. 21cm. [BM]
5353. do. 1799. [same] Dublin: S: Kathrens. 24p. 12. [BM]
5354. do. 1799. The horse and the widow: a farce. As performed... Theatre-Royal. Altered...ad. T. Dibdin (from #5352). L: J.Barker. 31p. 21cm. [BM.LC]
5355. do. 1800. [reprint of #5352?] NY: Prtd. for Smith & Stephens. 26p. 8. (B48)
5356. (Eduard in Schottland.) The wanderer; or, the rights of hospitality. A drama in 3 acts [prose]. Altered by C: Kemble. L: Prtd. for Appleyards 1808. 64p. 21cm. [Much altered.] [BM]

KOTZEBUE, A: v.--Eduard in Schottland

5357. do. 1808. [same?] L: Scales 1808? 28p. 19cm. [LC]
[LC says: K--'s play is a free tr. of Duval's "Edouard en Ecosse."]
5358. do. 1808. [reprint?] NY: Longworth. (B48)
5359. (Einige Züge aus dem Leben des guten Musäus.) Life of M--. Tr. Anne Plumptre. 1800. In #6649.
*5360. (Erinnerungen aus Paris...) Travels from Berlin, through Switzerland, to Paris...1804. Tr. anon. L: R.Phillips 1804. 3v. 16cm. [BM]
5361. do. 1805. [same (summary)] In R. Phillips, A coll. of mod. and contemp. voyages and travels, vol. 1. L: 64p. 22cm. [BM.LC]
5362. do. 1806. [same] 4th ed. 3v. in one. [LC]
§5363. (Erinnerungen von einer Reise aus Liefland nach Rom und Neapel.) Travels through Italy...1804...1805. Tr. anon. New rev. ed. L: Phillips 1807. 4v. 16cm. [Expanded and "interpreted."] [BM]
5364. do. 1807. [same] 4v. in 2. 17cm. [LC]
5365. do. 1807? [same (summary)] In R. Phillips, Coll. of modern voyages, etc., vol. 4. 44p. [Pp. 1-8 missing in BM copy.] [BM.LC]
*5366. (Falsche Scham.) False shame: a comedy in 4 acts [prose]. Tr. anon. L: Vernor & Hood 1799. 74p. 20cm. [BM]
§5367. do. 1800. False delicacy: a drama in 5 acts (K. has 4). Tr. B: Thompson. L: Vernor & Hood. (C535) 68p. 21cm. [BM.LC]
[Front. Thurston. Tr. is too free.]
5368. do. 1800. False shame; or, the American orphan in Germany. Tr. anon. Charleston, S.C: Young. 76p. 12. (B48)
[Possibly a reprint of #5366.]
5369. do. 1801. [reprint of #5366] Newark, N. J: Prtd. for Smith in NY. 63p. 23cm. [LC]
5370. (Gefährliche Nachbarschaft.) The party wall; or, in and out. Altered by W: T: Moncrieff. NY: Clayton; Phil: Neal 1842. 24p. 15cm. [LC]
*5371. (Geprüfte Liebe.) The constant lover; or, William and Jeannette. A tale. Prefixed an account of the literary life of the author. Tr. anon. L: Bell 1799. 2v. xxvii;288; 302p. 17cm. [BM]
5372. do. 1799. [same title] Bost: Prtd. for Bumstead. 2v. in one. 12. (B48) [Probably a reprint of the foregoing.]
5373. do. 1799. [same?] NY: Prtd. for Judah. 2v. 12. (B48)
5374. do. 1801. [same?] NY: Jansen. 2v. 12. (B48)
*5375. (Graf Benjowski.) Count Benyowsky; or, the conspiracy of Kamtschatka. A tragi-comedy in 5 acts (and in prose). Tr. W: Render. 2d ed. with an elegant front. (by J. Thurston). L: Richardson, etc. 1798. 205p. 22cm. [BM]
5375a. Count Bergowsky; or, the conspiracy of Kamtschatka. Tr. by Rev. W. Reader [sic] teacher...in the Univ. of Cambridge. NY: Judah 1799. (B6a)
§5376. do. 1800. A drama in 5 acts. Tr. B: Thompson. L: Vernor & Hood. (C535) 120p. 21cm. [BM.LC]
[Front. Stothard. Tr. is better than most of his, style very good.]
5377. do. 1800. [reprint] 1st Amer. from 2d L: ed. Bost: Manning & Loring. 98p. 16. [LCO]
5378. do. 1803. [reprint] Balto: Prtd. for Thomas, A. & B. 76p. 8. [LCO]
5379. (Herr Gottlieb Merks, der Egoist und Kritikus.) Egotist and pseudo-critic. Tr. W. H. H. Chambers. 1903. In C18.
*5380. (Ildegerte, Königin von Norwegen.) I--, queen of Norway. Tr. B: Thompson, Jr. L: Lane 1798. 2v. 12. [BM]
5381. do. 1800. [same] Phil: Prtd. for Campbell. 2v. in one. 103; 91p. 17cm. [Reprint of the foregoing.] [LC]
5382. (Johanna v. Montfaucon.) J-- of M--. Tr. anon. L: Geisweiler 1800. See "Monthly R." 32(1800):326. (B26)

KOTZEBUE, A: v.--Johanna v. Montfaucon
[Probably tr. by Ma. Geisweiler, and very likely used by Cumberland, see B41.]
5383. do. 1800. Joanna of M--: a dram. romance of the 14th cent. Formed upon the plan...and ad. to the Engl. stage by R: Cumberland. L: Lackington, Allen. xiv;88p. 19cm. [BM]
[Cumberland states that he knew no German and based his play on an Engl. tr., probably the foregoing. The general outline is the same, and there are many verbal resemblances. The pref. discusses his alterations. Sellier (B41) seems to be somewhat confused here.]
5384. do. 1800. [same] 2d ed. [BM.LC]
5385. do. 1800. [same] 3d ed. [BM]
§5386. (La Peyrouse.) La-Peyrouse: a drama in 2 acts (and in prose). Tr. Anne Plumptre. L: R.Phillips 1799. 34p. 21cm. [BM]
§5387. do. 1799. La Perouse. Tr. B: Thompson. L: Vernor & Hood. 40p. 21cm. [BM]
5388. do. 1800. La Peyrouse. Tr. C: Smith. NY: Prtd. for Smith & Stephens. 40p. 8. (B48) [Cf. paging with the foregoing.]
5389. do. 1801. [ad.] Pérouse; or, the desolate island. Pantomim. drama by J. Fawcett. 8. (B41)
5390. (Leontine.) Leontina. Tr. anon. 3v. See "Crit. R." 14(1809): 272 (B26)
5391. (Meide den Schein.?) Appearances deceive. Tr. B: Thompson. 1797. (B43)
5392. do. 1798. Appearances deceive: an old proverb confirmed by a new example. Tr. in "Monthly Mirror" 6(1798):151. (B26)
§5393. (Menschenhass und Reue.) The stranger: a comedy in 5 acts [prose]. Freely tr. A. Schink. L: C.Dilly 1798. 67p. 20cm. [BM]
[Tr. is accurate but omits largely.]
5394. do. 1798. [same] 2d ed. [BM]
5395. do. 1798. [same] 6th ed. [BM]
*5396. do. 1798. The stranger; or, misanthropy and repentance. A drama. Tr. G: Papendick, "sub-librarian to H.R.H. the Prince of Wales." L: Wingrave. 8. [BM]
5397. do. 1799. [reprint] NY. (B48)
5397a. do. 1799. Papendick's tr. Bost: Russell. 76p. 12. [AAS]
5397b. do. 1799. [same] Salem: Macanulty. 84p. 12. [AAS]
5397c. do. 1799. Schink's tr. NY: Judah. vi;56p. 12. [NYPL]
5398. do. 1799. Misanthropy and repentance: a novel. Tr. Mr. (J:?) Hemet. L: Bellamy. See "Monthly Mirror" 8(1799):97. (B26)
§5399. do. 1800. The stranger: a drama in 5 acts, as performed at the Theatre-Royal. Tr. B: Thompson. L: Vernor & Hood. (C535) 71p. 21cm. [Front. Thurston. Thompson's claim not to have seen #5393 is borne out by his text. Sellier (B41) thinks this one of T's best tr. I disagree: it is rewritten and curtailed.] [BM]
5400. do. n.d. [reprint of #5396.] Bost: Russell. 12. (B48)
5401. do. 1801. [reprint of #5399?] Phil. (B48)
5402. do. 1802. [same as #5399] L: Longman & Rees. 78p. 21cm. [BM]
5403. do. 1806. [same] [BM]
5404. do. 1808? [same] NY: Longworth. (B48)
5405. do. 1816? [same] In Inchbald, "British theatre," vol. 24. From the prompt book, with remarks by Mrs. I. L: Longmans, etc. 72p. 15cm. [Front. engr. by C. Heath from painting by Howard, pub. by Longman & Co. March 1816.] [BM]
5406. do. 1826. [same] In "Lond. stage," vol. 3. L: Balne. 16p. one il. 22cm. [BM.LC]
5407. do. 183-? [same] In "Cumberland's British theatre," vol. 14. From acting copy, with remarks (pp. 5-9)...by D-G. As now performing, etc. L: Cumberland. 60p. 14cm. [BM]
[Engr. front. G. W. Bonner after R. Cruikshank.]

KOTZEBUE, A: v.--Menschenhass und Reue
5408. do. 1830. [same] In "The penny nat. lib.," vol. 5, pp. 291-307. 25cm. [No pref., prol., or epil.] [BM]
5409. do. 1834. [same] In "The acting drama." L: Mayhew, etc. [BM] [Identical with foregoing.]
5410. do. 1846. Tr. anon. NY: Taylor. 59p. 16. [LCO]
5411. do. 1849. Thompson's tr. In B. Webster, The "acting nat. drama," vol. 15, 54p. 18cm. [BM]
[As performed Jan. 23, 1849. Front. Brewer.]
5412. do. 1849. [same] In B. Webster, "The series of dram. entertainments...at Windsor Castle," 1849. pp. 191-251. 24cm. [BM.LC]
5413. do. 1855? [same] In "Lacy's acting ed. of plays," vol. 22, no. 326. L: T:H.Lacy. 58p. 18cm. [BM]
5414. do. 1864. [same] In "The British drama," vol. 1. pp. 257-74. one il. 18cm. [BM]
5415. do. 1873-6. [same?] In "NY drama." Wheat & Cornett. Vol. 1, no. 3. [LCO]
5416. do. 1883. [same as #5414.] In "Dicks' standard plays." L: Dicks. [Identical.] [BM]
*5417. (Ueble Laune.) The peevish man: a drama in 4 acts [prose]. Being his last production. Tr. C. Ludger. L: Jordan Hookham 1799. 106p. 21cm. [BM]
*5418. (Zaida, oder die Entthronung Muhamed des Vierten.) Zaida; or, the dethronement of Muhamed IV. A novel, founded on hist. facts. Tr. C: Smith. NY: Burnton & Darling 1803. 213p. 18cm. [LC]
5419. do. 1811. Bound with "The beautiful unknown," #5287.

BIOGRAPHY

§5420. (Das merkwürdigste Jahr meines Lebens.) The most remarkable year in the life of A: v. K--. Written by himself. Tr. B. Beresford. L: Phillips 1802. 3v. 12. [BM]
5421. do. 1802. [reprint] NY: Prtd. for Caritat. 309p. 16. [LCO]
5422. (Die Geschichte meines Vaters, oder wie es zuging, dass ich geboren wurde.) The hist. of my father; or, how it happened that I was born. A romance. Tr. anon. L: W. Treppass 1798. See "Brit. Crit." 11(1798):681. (B26)
§5423. (Mein literärischer Lebenslauf, etc.) Sketch of the life and lit. career...with the journal of his tour to Paris, 1790. Written by himself. Tr. Anne Plumptre. L: Symonds 1800. 384p. 8. [BM]
[Rather more freely tr. than necessary.--Sketch of my lit. career. My flight to Paris ("Meine Flucht nach P--"). Postscript and dedication.--Front. (port.) by Holl.]
5424. do. 1801. [reprint] NY: Ward. 276p. 16cm. [BM]
5425. do. 1801? [reprint] Life, written by himself. Phil. (B48)
5426. do. 1820. The life of A: v. K--, from the German. Tr. anon. L: Boosey. 293p. 18cm. [BM]
[Rewritten from his autobiogr. works: "Lebenslauf," "Flucht," "Reisen," etc.]
5427. do. 1826. Sketch of the life and lit. career of K--, with the journal of his exile to Siberia. Tr. anon. In "Autobiographies," vol. 9, 10. L: Hunt & Clark. 2v. 285; 274p. 14cm. [BM.LCO]
[Introd. Sketch of my lit. career (as in #5423). My flight to Paris (as in #5423). The most remarkable year of my life. Appendix. Sequel to the life of K--. "A full and complete repub. of the most comprehensive tr...in the Engl. language."]

KOTZEBUE, Mz. v. 1789-1861.
*5428. (Der russische Kriegsgefangene unter den Franzosen.) The Russian prisoner. Ed. with pref. and postscript by A: v. K--. Tr. anon. L: Gale & Fenner 1816. 320p. 21cm. [BM]

KOTZEBUE, Mz. v.
§5429. Narr. of a journey into Persia, in the suite of the imperial Russian embassy, in the year 1817. Ed. by A: v. K--. Tr. anon. L: Longmans 1819. 328p. il. 21cm. [Fair tr., not very careful.][BM.LC]
5430. do. 1820. [same] Phil: Carey. 8. [AC]

KRAATZ, Curt, 1857-1925. See Laufs, K:, joint author.

KRAATZ, Curt, G. Okonkowski, and Af. Schönfeld.
5431. (Die polnische Wirtschaft.) The Vandemere estate: a (musical) farce in 3 acts by Jean Gilbert. Ad. by Milton Goldsmith. Libr. 1917. Partly paged. Tw. [LCM]

KRABBE, C. F.
*5432. (Leben Bernard Overbergs.) The life of B-- O--. Tr. by Rev. G: Spencer. Derby: Prtd. by T: Richardson for the Catholic bk. soc. 1843. 184p. 12cm. [BM]

KRABBE, Hg. 1857- .
**5433. (Die moderne Staats-Idee.) The mod. idea of the state. Author. tr. with introd. by G: H. Sabine and Wl. J. Shepard. The Hague: Nijhoff; NY: Appleton 1922. lxxxi;281p. 24cm. [LC.BM]
[Very clever tr.]

KRAFT VON TOGGENBURG, fl. 1260. Sel. in C27;366;416;532.

KRAMER, see K: G. Cramer and Cne. Naubert.

KRAPF, J: L:
5434. (Reisen in Ost-Afrika...1837-55.) Travels, researches, and missionary labors during an 18 years' residence in eastern Africa. L: Trübner 1860. li;566p. il. 22cm. [BM]
[Tr. or rewritten, chiefly by the author, from the Ger. work or its substrata, "with numerous important additions."]

KRATTER, Fz. 1758-1830.
5435. (Das Mädchen von Marienburg.) The maid of M--: a drama in 5 acts. Tr. anon. L: Allen 1798. See "Brit. Crit." 12(1798):668. (B26, B43)
†5436. (Die Verschwörung wider P: den Grossen, oder Menzikoff und Natalia.) Natalia and Menzikoff; or, the conspiracy against P: the Great. A trag. in five acts (and in prose). Tr. anon. L: M. Allen for W. Treppass, etc. 1798. 204p. 20cm. [BM]
[Misunderstandings, no style.]

KRAUS, El.
5437. The advent. of Count G: Ab. of Erbach: a true story. Tr. H.R.H. Beatrice, princess H: of Battenberg. L: Murray 1890. 322p. ports. and il. 20cm. [BM.LC]

KRAUSE, Jth. 1701-62. Sel. in C276;287.

KRAUSE, K: Cn. F: 1781-1832.
5438. The ideal of humanity and universal federation. (3 essays) Ed. in Engl. by W: Hastie. Ed: Clark 1900. xix;191p. 19cm. [BM.LC]

KRAUSE, K: L:
5439. What is the Ger. nation dying for? Tr. Adèle S. Seltzer. NY: Boni & Liveright 1918. 303p. 19cm. [LC.BM]

KREBS, En. Gst. Hs. 1881- .
5439a. Little book on Christian charity. Tr. Isabel Garahan. Herder 1927. 156p. D. [AC]

KREISSLE VON HELLBORN, H: d. 1869.
*5440. (Fz. Schubert.) The life of Fz. S--. Tr. A. D. Coleridge. Appendix by G: Grove (pp. 297-336). L: Longmans 1869. 2v. 318;

KREISSLE VON HELLBORN
336p. front. (port.) 19cm. [BM.LC]
5441. do. 1866. Fz. S--, a musical biogr. Tr. E: Wilberforce. L: Allen. xii;287p. 20cm. [BM.LC]
["The pres. vol. is consid. condensed" with the author's permission. "I have not adhered either to his words or his arrangement, and...sometimes put in opinions...not...in the orig."]

KREMER, Frau Ida.
5442. The struggle for a royal child, Anna Monica Pia. My experiences as governess in the household of the Countess Montignoso. L: J:Long 1907. 284p. 19cm. [BM]

KREN, Jean.
5443. (Autoliebchen.) The joy-ride lady: musical farce in 3 acts by "Jean Gilbert." Engl. verse and lyrics by Art. Anderson and Hartley Carrick. Vocal score. L: Ascherberg, Hopwood & Crew 1914. 129p. 27cm. [BMM]

KRETSCHMER, E. 1888- .
5444. Physical and spiritual harmony in marriage. Tr. 1926. In C308.

KREUTZER, Conradin, 1780-1849. A night in Granada. Opera. See Braun, J: K:

KREUZ, Rd. Jr.
5445. Captain Zillner: a human document. Tr. W. J. Ax. Worster. L: Hodder & Stoughton 1919. 326p. 19cm. [Orig. pub. in Scandinavia under the title: "Den store frase" (The great phrase).]
5446. do. 1919. [same] 2d ed. NY: Doran. 326p. [AC]

KREYENBERG, Ghd. Sel. in C112.

KRUEGER, Fr. Kd. 1887- .
5447. Government and politics of the Ger. empire. Tr. anon. NY: World bk. 1915. xi;340p. il. 18cm. [LC]

KRUEDENER, Jne. (v. Vietinghoff), Freifrau v. 1764-1824.
5448. Letters. In H: Jung-Stilling's autobiog. #4767.

KRUESI, Hm. 1817-1903.
†5449. Pestalozzi: his life, work and influence. Tr. anon. Cincin; NY: Wilson, Hinkle 1875. x;248p. front. (port.) 22cm. [LC.BM]
[Conscienceless tr. of sel. from P--.]
5450. do. 1903. [same] NY: Amer. bk. x;248p. il. 22cm. [LC]
5451. Sketch of the life and character of Pestalozzi. In Amer. inst. of instruction. Lectures, 1853. Bost: Ticknor, R. & F. 1854. 12. [Pp. 27-52. Derived from the orig. of #5449.] [LCO.BM]

KRUG, W: Traugott, 1770-1842.
5452. (Fundamentalphilosophie, oder urwissenschaftliche Grundlehre.) Fundamental philos.; or, elements of primitive philos. Tr. H. N. Day. Sawyer, Ingersoll 1852. 18. [AC]

KRUGER, J: Sel. in C489.

KRUMMACHER, F: Ad. 1767-1845. Sel. in C31;43-6;125*;158;229;233;273; 287;319;372;461;469.
5453. Alfred and the little dove. Tr. by a lady. Ed: Johnstone, Hunter; L: Hamilton, Adams 1862. 96p. 13cm. [BM]
[Contains also "The young Savoyard," by E. Hold.]
5454. Cornelius the centurion. Tr. Rev. J: W. Ferguson, with notes and biogr. In "The biblical cabinet," vol. 22. Ed: Clark; L: Rivington 1838. ix;210p. 15cm. [BM]
5455. (Fabeln.) (17) Fables. Tr. 1845. In C125.

KRUMMACHER, F: Ad.--Fabeln
5456. do. 1852. Tr. anon. In C319.
5457. Oriental fairy tales. Tr. anon. 1886. In #4226.
*5458. (Parabeln.) Parables. Tr. F: Shoberl. L: Ackermann 1824. viii; 316p. 14cm. [114 parables.] [BM]
*5459. do. 1839. Tr. Miss F. Johnstone. L: Nisbet. 218p. 16cm. [BM]
5460. do. 1844. Tr. anon. L: Parker. 83p. 16cm., [BM]
[29 parables. Rewritten from Shoberl?]
5461. do. 1847. [same] L: Gilpin. 30p. 14cm. [Slightly edited.] [BM]
5462. do. 1849, [same as #5459] Nisbet. 12. [EC]
5463. do. 1852. Tr. L. Lermont. 1852. In C319.
5464. do. 1852. [same] Phil: Prtd. for the tr. 95p. 16. [LCO]
5465. do. 1853. L: Cooke. il. 4. [EC]
[Probably ident. with the following.]
5466. do. 1854. Shoberl's tr., from the 7th Ger. ed., edited. 40 il. J. R. Clayton; engr. Dalziel bros. L: N.Cooke. xii;280p. 17cm. [BM.LC]
5467. do. 1854. Tr. anon. Phil. Lindsay & Blakiston. 8. [AC]
5468. do. 1857. The robins and other parables for children. Tr. anon. Phil.: Lindsay & Blakiston. [AC]
5469. do. 1858. [same as #5466] same il. L: Bohn. 362p. 17cm.[BM.LC]
5470. do. 1861. Simple similitudes; or, fables, etc. Tr. anon. L: S.P.C.K. Books for the young, packet no. 9. 32p. front. 14cm. [BM]
[Seems to be ed. from Shoberl's tr.]
5471. do. 1872-6. [same as #5469] NY: Scribner n.d. 12. [AC]
5472. do. 1872-6. [same as #5469] Phil: Lippincott. n.d. 12. [AC]
5473. do. 1872-6. [same as #5469] Bost: Little, Brown n.d. 12. [AC]
5474. do. 1872-6. [same as #5469?] McCauley n.d. 12. [AC]
5475. do. 1892. Strength and beauty; for boys and girls. Ad. from Prof. J: H. Agnew's tr. of K--'s parables. Plainfield, N. J: Dalziel. 63p. 22cm. [LC]

KRUMMACHER, F: W: 1796-1868.
*5476. (Eine Selbstbiographie.) Autobiogr. Ed. by his daughter. Tr. Rev. M. G. Easton. Pref. Rev. J: Cairns. Ed: Clark; L: Hamilton 1869. 351p. front. (port.) 20cm. [BM]
[Tr. is none too sure of the German.]
5477. do. 1869. [same] NY: Carter. 350p. 8. [LCO]
5478. do. 1871. [same] With new biogr. supplement by the editor. Ed: Clark. 383p. 20cm. [BM]
5479. Gems of --- by P. C. Hirschfeld. L: Wertheim 1847. 18. [EC]

KRUMMACHER, Gf. Dl. 1774-1868. Sel. in C45.

KRUMMACHER, M.
5480. (Unsere Mutter. Ein Lebensbild von M. K.) Our mother: a life picture by M. K. From the Ger. by X. Y. Z. Ed: J. Gemmel 1882. 271p. 17cm. [Life of Ctte. (Pilgeram) K--.] [BM]
5481. do. 1883, 1884. [same] L: Simpkin. 12. [EC]

KRUPP, Af. 1812-87. See Niemeyer, V:, Af. K--: a sketch of his life and work, #6744.

KRUSE, H: 1815-1902.
5482. The crystal dagger; Oath and conscience. Tr. Rb. Gillies. 1826. In C164.

KRUSENSTERN, Am. J: v. 1770-1846.
5483. Memoirs and corr. Tr. his daughter, Mme. Cte. Bernhardi. Ed. Sir J: Ross. L: Longmans 1856. 75p. 23cm. [LC]
*5484. (Reise um die Welt...) Voyage round the world, 1803-6. Tr. R: B. Hoppner. L: Prtd. for Murray 1813. 2v. xxxii;314; 404p. col. front. 28 x 22cm. [LC has 2v. in one] [BM]

KUEBLER, Td.
5485. General ("Chinese") Gordon, the Christian hero. Tr. G: P. Upton. Chic: McClurg 1912. 111p. front. 17cm. [LC]

KUECHLER, C: Gb. F: 1869- .
5486. Elizabeth (Consort of Fis. Js. I), empress of Austria and queen of Hungary. Tr. G: P. Upton. Chic: McClurg 1909. 139p. 17cm. [LC]

KUEGELGEN, W: (G: Ax.) v. 1802-67.
*5487. (Jugenderinnerungen eines alten Mannes.) Bygone days; or, an old man's reminiscences of his youth. Ed. by Ph. v. Nathusius, with pref. Tr. anon. L: Chapman & Hall 1871. 3v. 19cm. [BM.LC]

KUEHN, Fz. 1814-76.
5488. Barbarossa. Tr. G: P. Upton. Chic: McClurg 1906. 167p.17cm [LC]

KUEHNE, A: 1829-83. See "Dewall, J:s van"

KUEHNE, J:s. See Ramseyer, F:, joint author.

KUEHNEMANN, Eg. 1868- .
§5489. Schiller. Tr. 3d Ger. ed. Mrs. Kath. H. Royce. Bost; L: Ginn 1912. 2v. 21cm. [LC.BM]

KUEHNEN, ---. Sel. in C470.

KUELPE, Os. 1862- .
§5490. (Die Philosophie der Gegenwart in Deutschland.) The philos. of the present in Germany. Tr. from 5th Ger. ed. by Maud L. Patrick and T: W. Patrick. L: Allen 1913. 256p. 19cm. [BM.LC]
[Only fair to good; not sufficiently painstaking.]
*5491. (Einleitung in die Philosophie.) Introd. to philos: a hand-book for students. Tr. W. B. Pillsbury and E. B. Titchener. L: Sonnenschein 1897. x;256p. 19cm. [BM]
5492. do. 1901. [same] NY: Macmillan. 256p. [LC]
5493. do. 1907. [same] Sonnenschein. [EC]
5494. do. 1916. [same] L: Allen & U. 256p. [EC]
5495. do. 1927. [same] Allen & U. 256p. [EC]

KUEMMEL, Kd. 1848- .
5496. In the Turkish camp, and other stories. Tr. Ma. R. Gray. St. L: Herder 1899. 136p. 16. [LC]

KUENNEKE, E: 1885- . The cousin from nowhere. Musical comedy. See Haller, Hm., and "Rideamus."

KUERENBERG, Der v., early 12th cent. Sel. in C27*;421;423;427.

KUETTNER, K: Glb. 1755-1805.
5497. (Reise durch...Dänemark, Schweden...1798-9.) Travels through Denmark, Sweden, Austria, etc. Tr. anon. In "Coll. of mod. voyages," vol. 1. L: R:Phillips 1805. 200p. 21cm. [BM.LC]
[Very much abridged.]

KUGLER, Fz. Td. 1808-58. Sel. in C105.
*5498. (Handbuch der Geschichte der Malerei in Italien.) Hand-book of the hist. of painting. Part I. Italian schools. Tr. Mrs. Marg. Hutton. Ed. C. L. Eastlake. L: J:Murray 1842. xxxii;444p. 19cm. [Additions by K-- for this ed., which takes his text as basis rather than copyist's model.] [BM]
*5499. do. 1846. Handbook of the hist. of painting. Part II. The German, Flemish, and Dutch schools. Tr. Mrs. Marg. Hutton. Ed. Sir Ed. Head, with notes. L: Murray. lii;377p. 17cm. [BM.LC]
5500. do. 1851. Schools of painting in Italy. 2d rev. and enl. ed. (of #5498). L: Murray. 2v. xxviii;(270); 539p. 20cm. [BM.LC]

KUGLER, Fz. Td.- Handbuch der Geschichte der Malerei....
5501. do. 1854. Part II. Also, Spanish and French schools. Ed. with notes by Sir E. Head. L: Murray. 2v. xlviii;377; xiv;373p. il. 20cm. [BM.LC]
[Note that later eds. of part II, from 1860 on, are so remote from Kugler as hardly to count as translations, and are therefore omitted from my list.]
5502. do. 1855. Italian schools. 3d ed. L: Murray. 2 pts. 100 il.[BM]
[Pt. 1 missing; pt. 2, 583p.]
5503. do. 1867. [same?] New ed. Murray. 2v. 8. [EC]
5504. do. 1874. [same] 4th ed. Rev. by Lady Eastlake. L: Murray. 2 pts. xxv;(288); 620p. 19cm. [BM]
5505. do. 1887. [same] 5th ed. Rev. by A. H. Layard. L: Murray. 2 pts. 8. [BM]
5506. do. 1902. [same] 6th ed. rev. and in part rewritten by A. H. Layard. L: Murray. 2v. il. 8. [BM.LC]
§5507. (Geschichte F:s des Grossen.) Hist. of F: the Great. Tr. E: A. Moriarty. 500 orig. designs by A. Menzel. L: Virtue 1844. 616p. 25cm. [Expands in flowery style; correct.] [BM]
5508. do. 1845. [same?] Pictor. hist. of Germany during the reign of F: the Gt. Tr. anon. Il. by Ad. Menzel. L: Bohn. 616p. 25cm. [LC]
[Paging is identical.]
5509. do. 1877. [same title as the foregoing.] L: Routledge. 8. [EC]
5510. do. 1902. [same?] Life of F: the Gt. NY: Perkins. 453p. il. 19cm. [LC]

KUH, El. 1828-76. Sel. in C501.

KUHN, A: 1784-1829. Sel. in C391;393.

KUHNEL, Ernst and Goetz, Hm.
5510a. India book painting from Fahangir's album, State Lib., Berlin. With 74 pl., 26 in col. Paul 1926. 83pp. 14 x 10. [EC]

KULMANN, Eli. 1808-25. Sel. in C17;399;400;461.

KUNTH, J: Sg. 1700-79. Sel. in C166;222-3.

KUPFFER, Elisario v. 1872- . Sel. in C63.

KURTSCHEID, Bertrand, 1877- .
5510b. Hist. of the seal of confession. Auth. tr. F. A. Marks, ed. Art. Preuss. Herder 1927. xxxi;342p. D. [AC]

KURZ, Hm. 1813-73.
5511. (Falstaff und seine Gesellen.) F-- and his companions. Tr. C. C. Shackford. Plates by Pl. Konewka. Bost: Roberts 1872. 18p. 12. [LC]

KURZ, Iso. (i.e., Ka. Mge.) 1853- . Sel. in C154(18); 423.
*5512. (Florentinische Novellen.) Tales of Florence. Tr. Lilian Dundas. L: Melrose 1919. 309p. 18cm. [BM]
[The marriage of the dead ("Die Vermählung der Toten"); Saint Sebastian ("Der heilige Sebastian").]

"KYRBURG, Fritz v. d." See Bilse, Os. Fr., 1878-.

LACHMANN, He., afterwards Landauer, 1868-1918. Sel. in C28.
*5513. (Salome.) Salome: opera in one act by R: Strauss. Tr. anon. Libr. Ger;Engl. NY: Theatre ticket off. 1906. 53p. [LC]
*5514. do. 1911. Tr. Af. Kalisch. Libr. Ger;Engl. Berlin; Paris: Fürstner. 31p. 8. [LC]
5515. do. 1923. R: Strauss' "Salome." By Td. M. R. v. Keler. Girard, Kan: Haldeman-Julius. 56p. 12cm. [BQM]
[Synopsis, extracts from libr., musical il.]

LACHMANN, P. d. 1715. Sel. in C244.

LAFONTAINE, A: (H: Jl.) 1758-1831. ("Gst. Freier.") Sel. in C513.
5516. [Coll.] Love and gratitude; or, traits of the human heart. Six novels. Prepared for the press by Mrs. Parsons. Brentford: Norbury; L: Longmans 1804. 3v. 12. [BM]
[Love and gratitude; Love and greatness of soul; Love and esteem; Love put to the test; Love and probity; Love and vanity.]
5517. Age and youth; or, the families of Abendstedt. A novel. Tr. anon. L: A. K. Newman 1813. 4v. 19cm. [BM]
5518. Baron de Fleming, the son; or, the rage of systems. A novel. Tr. anon. L: Lane, Newman 1804. 3v. 18cm. [BM]
[Said to be a continuation of "Baron de Fleming," by Gst. Freier (which is, however, a name assumed by Lafontaine): See "Ed. R." 4(1804):498. No Ger. orig. for this novel has been found; see B26.]
5519. (Clara Duplessis und Clairaut.) Ca. D-- and C--: the hist. of a family of French emigrants. Tr. anon. L: Longmans 1797. 3v. See "Crit. R." (II)21(1797):355. (B26)
§5520. (Das Haus Bärburg, oder der Familienzwist.) Family quarrels: a novel. Tr. anon. L: Dean 1811. 3v. 19cm. [Poor stuff.] [BM]
5521. (Das Nadelöhr, oder die Schwärmerei.) The village of Friedewalde; or, the enthusiast. A novel. Tr. J. Powell. L: Hughes 1806. 3v. 17cm. [BM]
5522. (Der Naturmensch.) The man of nature; or, nature and love. Tr. W: Wennington. ca. 1800. Cited in C157(2). Ascribed to "Miltenberg."
5523. do. 1807. [same] New enl. ed. L: Prtd. for the tr. 447p. 22cm. [LC]
5524. (Der Sonderling.) Odd enough, to be sure! or, Emilius in the world. Tr. J: Hemet. L: Lane & Newman 1802. 2v. 12. [BM]
5525. (Die Familie von Halden.) The family of H--: a novel. Tr. anon. L: J.Bell 1799. 4v. 17cm. [BM]
5526. Edward and Annette: a moral tale. Tr. anon. L: J.F.Weise 1807. 239p. front. engr. G: Cooke. 17cm. [BM]
§5527. (Fedor und Marie, oder Treue bis zum Tode.) Dolgoroncki and Menzikoff: a Russian tale. Tr. anon. L: Lane, Newman 1805. 2v. 17cm. [BM]
5528. do. 180-. Ma. Menzikoff and Fedor Dolgoroncki: a Russian tale founded on fact. Tr. anon. L: Bailey. 280p. 17cm. [LC]
5529. The haunted castle. Tr. R: Holcraft. 1826. In C203.
§5530. (Henrietta Bellmann. Ein Gemälde schöner Herzen.) Henriette Bellman; or, the new family picture. Tr. anon. L: Vernor & Hood 1804. 2v. 16cm. [Inadequate tr.] [BM]
5531. Hermann and Emilia. Tr. anon. 1805? 4v. See "Ed. R." 7(1805): 256. (B26)
5532. Hulkem. Tr. anon. ca. 1800. In C157(1).
5533. Idda of Tokenburg; or, the force of jealousy. Tr. anon. In "Lady's Mag." 32(1801):28, etc. (B26)
5534. do. 1802. Tr. anon. In "Hibernian Mag." 32(1802):80, etc. (B26)
5535. (Leben eines armen Landpredigers.) The village pastor and his children: a novel. Tr. anon. L: Lane, Newman 1803. 4v. See "Crit. R." (II)39(1803):236. (B26)
5536. do. 1810. [same] NY: Longworth. 4v. in 2. 246; 238p. (B48)
[Reprint of the foregoing.]
§5537. do. 1849. Family pictures; or, the life of a poor village pastor and his children. Tr. anon. L: Simms & M'Intyre. Parlour lib. 304p. 16cm. [Very free indeed.] [BM]
5538. do. 1857. Family portraiture; or, the hist. of a Ger. country pastor and his family. Tr. (into French) by Mme. I. de Montolieu ...freely rend. from the French by Mrs. J. D. W. Digby. L: Hall. 259p. 16cm. [BM]

LAFONTAINE, A: H:
5539. (Leben und Taten des Freiherrn Quinctius Heymeran v. Flaming. Von Gustav Freier.) Baron de Fleming. From the Ger. of A: Lafontaine. L? 3v. See "Ed. R." 4(1804):498. (B26)
5540. Maria. Tr. Miss Eliza C--. ca. 1800. In C430.
5541. (Neue moralische Erzählungen.) New moral tales. Tr. by Ni--ce Bickerstaff. 1803. See "Brit. Crit." 21(1803):314. (B26)
5542. The rake and the misanthrope. Tr. anon. L? 2v. See "Universal Mag." (II)1(1804):52. (B26)
5543. Raphael; or, peaceful life. Tr. Mrs. Green. L: Taylor 1812. 2v. 200; 222p. 18cm. [BM]
5544. The reprobate: a novel. Tr. Ma. Charlton. L: Lane, Newman 1802. 2v. 334; 300p. 17cm. [BM]
5545. do. 1804. [ad.] Guilty or not guilty: a comedy in 5 acts. By T: Dibdin. NY: Longworth. 79p. 14cm. [Based on the foregoing tr.][LC]
5546. The rigid father; or, paternal authority too strictly enforced. A novel in a series of letters. Tr. anon. In "Lady's Mag." 33(1802): 42, etc. (B26)
5547. (Romulus.) Romulus: a tale of ancient times. Tr. P: Will. L: Phillips 1799. 2v. See "New Lond. R." 2(1799):389. (B26)
5548. do. 1814. [same?] A tale of ancient times, entitled Romulus. Balto: Mauro. 314p. 17cm. [Probably a reprint of the foregoing.][LC]
5549. (Rudolph v. Werdenberg. Eine Rittergeschichte.) Rodolphus of W--: a novel. By La Fontane [sic]. L: Hughes 1805. 2v. 154; 160p. 17cm. [BM]
5550. do? 1807. The monk of Dissentis: founded on the revolution of Switzerland in the 13th and 14th cent. Tr. J. Powell. 3v. See "Universal Mag." (II)7(1807):88. (B26)
[Subtitle of R. v. Werdenberg is: "Rittergeschichte aus der Revolutionszeit Helvetiens."]
5551. (Saint Julien.) Saint J--; or, memoirs of a father. Tr. anon. L: Bell 1798. 279p. 17cm. [BM]
5552. do. 1799. Saint J--. By Augustin [sic] La Fontaine. Tr. anon. With additional notes. L: Lane. 2v. 342; 311p. 17cm. [BM]
[Derived by slight editing from the foregoing.]

LAGERSTROEM, Anga. v. See "Moeller, A. v."

LA MOTTE-FOUQUÉ, F: H: K: Freiherr de, 1777-1843. See Fouqué.

LAMERDIN, E: Sel. in C497.

LAMEY, A: 1816-96. Sel. in C391;393.

LAMPADIUS, W: Ad. 1812-92.
*5553. (Fx. Mendelssohn-Bartholdy. Ein Denkmal...) Life of Fx. M.-B. Tr. W: L. Gage. NY;Phil: Leypoldt 1865. xi;271p. front. (port.) 17cm. [LC.BM]
[Gage is competent, but has also reworked his material to some extent.]
*5554. do. 1876. [same] With suppl. sketches and notes by C. L. Grüneisen. L: Reeves. xiv;243p. 20cm. [BM]
*5555. (Fx. Mendelssohn-Bartholdy. Ein Gesamtbild...) The life of Fx. M.-B. Tr. W: L. Gage. New and enl. ed. Bost: Ditson 1887. 333p. 20cm. ["I have...exercised a certain liberty of condensation ...most sparingly."] [LC.BM]

LAMPE, F: Ad. 1683-1729. Sel. in C223-4.

LAMPING, Cl.
5556. The soldier of the foreign legion. (Reminiscences.) Tr. Lady Duff-Gordon. In "The French in Algiers," pp. 1-89. L: Murray 1845. 17cm. [BM]

LAMPRECHT, Pfaffe, early 12th cent. Sel. from "Alexander," in C88; 171;190.

LAMPRECHT, K: (Gtd.) 1856-1915.
*5557. (Moderne Geschichtswissenschaft.) What is history? Five lect. on the mod. science of hist. Tr. E. A. Andrews. NY;L: Macmillan 1905. ix;277p. 20cm. [BM.LC]

LAMSZUS, W:
5558. (Das Menschenschlachthaus. Bilder vom kommenden Krieg.) The human slaughter-house: scenes from the war that is sure to come. Tr. Oakley Williams. L: Hutchinson 1913. 127p. 18cm. [BM.LC]
5559. do. 1913. [same] NY: Stokes. 116p. 18cm. [LC]

LANDESMANN, H: 1821-1902. See "Lorm, Hieronimus."

LANG, G: 1836- .
5560. Pixy's holiday journey. Tr. Ma. E. Ireland. Chic;Akron: Saalfield 1908. 252p. il. 19cm. [LC]

LANGBECKER, Em. Cn. Gb. 1792-1843. Sel. in C229;486;489.

LANGBEIN, A: F: Ern. 1757-1835. Sel. in C41-2;44;106;184;295;387-8; 499;513.
§5561. [Coll.] The bridegroom's probation ("Die Bräutigamsprobe"); The broken leg ("Der Beinbruch"). Tr. R: Holcraft. 1826. In C203.
§5562. [Coll.] 1826. Marianne Richards ("M-- Richard"); Seven marriages, and never a husband ("Sieben Hochzeiten und keine Brautnacht"); The irreconcilable man ("Der Unversöhnliche"); Albert Limbach, or a martyr to the fair ("A-- L--, oder der Märtyrer des schönen Geschlechts"); An hour's instruction in political economy; The lady's palfrey. Tr. T: Roscoe. In C477.
5563. The lady's palfrey. Tr. anon. 189-. In C56.
[Probably from the foregoing.]

LANGE, Ern. 1650-1727. Sel. in C229;231-2;273;486.

LANGE, Ern. Ph. K: 1813-99. See "Galen, Ph."

LANGE, F: Ab. 1828-75.
*5564. (Geschichte des Materialismus und Kritik seiner Bedeutung in der Gegenwart.) Hist. of materialism and criticism of its present importance. Author. tr. E. C. Thomas. L: Trübner 1877-81. 3v. 20cm. [Vol. 1, 1877, xx;330p. Vol. 2, 1880, 397p. Vol. 3, 1881, 376p.] [BM]
*5565. do. 1890. [same] 3d ed. Introd. by Bertrand Russell. L: Paul, T. & T. 3v. 22cm. [LC]
*5566. do. 1925. [same] 3d ed. L: K.Paul; NY: Harcourt. 3 pts. xlii; 330; 397; 376p. 22cm. [BM]

LANGE, Jm. 1670-1744. Sel. in C269.

LANGE, J: Cn. Sel. in C240;269.

LANGE, J: P: 1802-84. Sel. in C240;273;489.

LANGE, Lz.
5567. Journey from Petersburg to Peking. In "The present state of Russia, etc.," vol. 2. Tr. anon. L: W.Taylor, etc. 1722. 92p. 19cm. [BM]
5568. do? 1746. Travels in China, 1717. In "A new coll. of voyages and travels," vol. 3. pp. 575-84. 26cm. [BM]
5569. do? 1763. Journal of the residence of Mr. De Lange...at... Pekin...1721-22. Tr. from the French. In Bell, J., of Autermony, "Travels, etc." Vol. 2, pp. 169-321. Glasgow: Prtd. for the author. 24cm. [BM]

LANGHANS, W: 1832-92.
5570. Hist. of music in twelve lectures. Tr. from 2d enl. ed. by J: H: Cornell. NY: Schirmer 1886. 184p. 25cm. [LC]

LANGSDORFF, G: H: Freiherr v. 1774-1852.
*5571. (Bemerkungen auf einer Reise um die Welt...1803-7.) Voyages and travels...Tr. anon. Il. from orig. drawings. L: Colburn 1813-14. 2v. xxi;362; 386p. 28cm. [BM.LC]
*5572. do. 1817. [same] Carlisle, Pa. Prtd. by G: Philips, for sale in Phil. by Carey. xvi;617p. 2 pts. 22cm. [LC.BM]
5572a. do. 1927. Narr. of the Rezanov voyage to Nueva California in 1806, being that division of...Bemerkungen auf einer Reise um die Welt, when as a personal physician he accompanied R-- to Nueva California from Sitka, Alaska, and back; an English tr. rev. with the Teutonisms of the original Hispaniolized, Russianized, or Anglicized, by T: C. Russell. Il. w. port. and a map. Priv. prtd. xiv;158p. autog. ed. Q. [Contains facsimiles of title pages of orig. Ger. (Frankfurt 1812) and orig. English (L: 1814) editions.]

LAPPE, C: 1773-1843. Sel. in C137a.

LA ROCHE, (Me.) So. (Gutermann), 1731-1807.
5573. (Geschichte des Fräuleins v. Sternheim.) The hist. of lady Sophia S--, attempted from the Ger. of Mr. Wieland [sic] by J. Collyer. L: Collyer 1776. 8. [Merely pub. by Wieland.] [BM]
5574. do. 1776. The advent. of Miss Sophia S--. Tr. E: Harwood. L: Becket. 2v. See "Lond. R." 4(1776):306. (B26)
[Ascribed to Wieland. Another title: Memoirs of Miss Sophy S--.]
5575. do. 1786. [same as #5573.] L: Prtd. for J. Collyer & T. Jones. 2v. viii;252; 212p. 18cm. [BM]

L'ARRONGE, Ad. 1838-1908.
5576. (Die Sorglosen.) Dollars and sense: a comedy...in 3 acts by A. Daly. NY: Prtd. for the author 1885. 71p. 22cm. [Adapted from L'A--.] [LC]
5577. (Doktor Klaus.) Dr. Klaus: a comedy in 5 acts [prose]. Tr. and ad. A. Neuendorff. 1878. (B38)
5578. (Hasemanns Töchter.) Our daughters: a society comedy in 4 acts [prose]. By F: L. Greenwood. Clyde, O: Ames 1883. 44p. 19cm. [LC]
5579. (Mein Leopold.) My boy: a comedy in 3 acts [prose] and 6 tableaux, tr. and ad...by A. Neuendorff. (B38)
5580. do. 1915. My son: a comedy drama in one act [prose] by Ruth C. Mitchell (Mrs. Young). NY: Tw. [LC]

LASAULX, Ame. v. 1815-72.
*5581. (Erinnerungen an Ame. von L--.) Sister Augustine. Superior... at Bonn. Tr. anon. L: K.Paul 1880. xiv;338p. 20cm. [BM]
*5582. do. 1881. [same] NY: Holt. 338p. [LCO]

LASKER-SCHUELER, Else, 1876- . Sel. in C28;95.

LASSALLE, Fd. (J: Gb.) 1825-64. Sel. in C154(10).
§5583. (Franz v. Sickingen.) Fz. v. S--: a tragedy in 5 acts [verse]. Tr. D. De Leon. NY: NY labor news 1910. 149p. 19cm. [LC]
[Stumbling verse.]
*5584. What is capital? Freely tr. from chap. IV of "Herr Bastiat Schulze v. Delitsch (i.e., Delitzsch)" by F. Keddell. Reprint from "Justice." L: Justice print. 1889. 13p. 20cm. [BM]
[Tr. is fairly close and good.]
See Bernstein, E., F. L-- as a social reformer, #405.

LATZKO, (Ad.) And. 1876- .
*5585. (Friedensgericht.) Judgment of peace. Tr. Ludwig Lewisohn. NY: Boni & Liveright 1919. 280p. 19cm. [LC]
[On the whole, excellent; but careless slips are not rare.]

LATZKO, (Ad.) And.
†5586. (Menschen im Krieg.) Men in battle. Tr. Adèle S. Seltzer. NY; L: Cassell 1918. 237p. 8.[Errors; unable to handle the style.][LC]
†5587. do. 1918. [same] NY: Boni & Liveright. 264p. 19cm. [LC]

LAUFENBERG, H: v. See Heinrich v. L--.

LAUFER, Bh.
5588. The white Indian: a wild west drama in 4 acts. Tr. W: Sinnhold. Buffalo, NY: 1889. 64p. 24. [LCO]

LAUFS, K: 1858-1900.
5589. (Ein toller Einfall.) Crazy idea: a comedy in 4 acts. Tr. Maurice Hagemann. Chic: Chic. dram. soc. 1897. (B38)

LAUFS, K: and Kurt Kraatz.
5590. (Die Logenbrüder.) Are you a mason? Ad. by Leo Ditrichstein. NY: Lederer & Herrmann 1901. 83p. 8. [AC]
5591. do. n.d. Are you an Odd Fellow? Farce comedy. Ad. by W. Brandon. Paola, Kan. (B38)

LAUKENAU, H. v. and L. v. d. Oelsnitz.
5592. Russia, past and present. Ad. Mrs. Hta. M. Chester. L: S. P. C. K; NY: Young 1881. 434p. il. 20cm. [LC]

"LAUN, F:" (i.e., F: A: Schulze, 1770-1849).*
5593. The blind passenger. Tr. anon. 1826. In C498.
5593a. The two New Year's nights. Tr. anon. In "Court Mag." 1(1839): 120. (B27)

LAURENTII, Las. 1660-1722. Sel. in C223;229;269;273;287;489.

LAURILLARD, ---. Sel. in C501.

LAUTENSCHLAEGER, Othmar, 1809-78.
5594. The young crusaders. From the Ger. NY: Strong n.d. (1872-76) 18. [AC]

LAVATER, Anna. See Ziethe, W., Anna L--, a picture of Swiss pastoral life, #10618. Cf. also #5620.

LAVATER[2], J: Kp. 1741-1801. Sel. in C6;118;194;231-2;269;271;273; 489;497;574*;#5963.
§5595. (Ein Wort eines freien Schweizers an die französische Nation.) Remonstrance...to the...directory of the French republic, against the invasion of Switzerland. From the French, anon. L: Debrett & Longman 1798. 31p. 21cm. [Expanded.] [BM]
*5596. do. 1798. Energetic address to the French directory...Engl., Fr., and Ger. By Obadiah Prim, one of the people called Quakers. L: Sold by W. Richardson. 31p. 21cm. [BM]
[Prtd. in triple columns. Contains the Ger. orig., with a pref. by Prim.]
5597. do. 1798. Remonstrance, etc. Dublin: Milliken. 16p. 8. [LCO]
5598. do. 1798. Remonstrance. Graisberry & Campbell. 14p. 8. [LCO]
§5599. do. 1799. Letter to the French directory. Tr. anon. L: Hatchard. 33p. 8. [Tr. condenses, and also sharpens the tone.][BM]
5599a. do. 1799. Remonstrance. First NY ed. Repr. by J: Tiebout. 22p. 8. [NYHS]
*5600. (Geheimes Tagebuch von einem Beobachter seiner selbst.) Secret journal of a self-observer; or, confessions and familiar letters of...Tr. P: Will. L: Cadell & Davies 1770. 2v. viii;280; 372p. 18cm. [BM.LCO]
*5601. do. 1795. [same] [BM]

[1] I cannot trace a collection of "Tales of F. Laun pub. lately [before 1823] by Ackermann."

[2] The essays on physiognomy are not included.

LAVATER, J: Kp.
5602. (Hundert Sentenzen vom seligen Lavater.) The pastor's legacy; or, devotional fragments from...L--. By Hta. J. Fry (in verse). L: Hamilton, Adams 1842. xii;152p. 11cm. [BM]
5603. Of design, colouring, and writing. In Lumley, E. "The art of judging...character...from...handwriting." L: J: R. Smith 1875. 14cm. [Pp. 160-76.] [BM]
5604. On the nature, excellency, and necessity of faith. Tr. P: Will. L: Prtd. for the author 1805. 39p. 18cm. [BM]
5605. Orig. maxims for the young. Tr. Eliz. A. MacCaul, afterwards Finn. L: Wertheim 1838. 71p. 8cm. [BM]
5606. (Privatbriefe von Saulus und Paulus.) Letters of St. Paul the apostle, written before and after his conversion. Tr. anon. L: 1804. See "Christian observer" 4(1805):369. (B26)
5607. (Vermischte unphysiognomische Regeln zur Selbst- und Menschenkenntnis.) Aphorisms on man. Tr. J. H. Fuseli. L: Johnson 1788. vi;224p. 8. [BM]
[643 aphorisms. Front. engr. by Blake. L. to Fuseli: "I give you liberty not only to make improvements, but to omit what you think false or unimportant." Tr. is also spelled Fuesseli, Fuessli.]
5608. do. 1788. [same] Tr. from the orig. MS of the Rev. J: Cp. L--, citizen of Zuric. By J: H: Fuessli. Embellished w. an elegant front. Phil: Prtd. for T: Dobson. (B6a)
5609. do. 1790. [same] Phil: Spotswood. 100p. 16. (B6a; B48) [Available: AAS. JCB]
5610. do. 1790. [same] 3d ed. L: prtd., NY: reprtd. by T. & J. Swords. 114p. front. 16. (B6a) [Available: AAS.]
5611. do. 1790. [same] 3d (Amer.) ed. NY: Berry & Rogers. 114p. 16. (B48) [Ident. with the foregoing?]
5612. do. 1790. [same] 3d ed. Dublin: Sleater & Byrne. vi;222p. 12. [This begins like #5607, then becomes wholly different.] [BM]
5613. do. 1790. [same] 4th (Amer.) ed. Bost: Prtd. by I. Thomas & E. T. Andrews. 112p. plate. 16. [Available: AAS] [LCO]
5614. do. 1793. [same] 5th (Amer.) ed. Newburyport, Mass: G: J. Osborne. 109p. 17cm. [633 aphorisms; uses Roman numerals.] [LC.BM]
5615. do. 1794. [same] 3d ed. L: Prtd. for W. Johnson. 224p. 16.[LCO]
5616. do. 1794. [same] In "The gentleman's pocket lib." Bost: Prtd. and sold by W. Spotswood. 256p. 12. (B6a) [Available: AAS]
5617. do. 1795. [same] 5th ed. Catskill, NY: Reprtd. by Mackay, Croswell. 76p. 16cm. [LC]
5618. do. 1830. [same] 1st Amer. ed. Lancaster, Pa: Albright. 140p. 13cm. ["First" probably means: "original edition."] [LC]
†5619. (Worte des Herzens.) Words of consolation for friends of love and of faith. Tr. G. G. Moore. L: Nisbet 1881. 62p. 15cm. [BM]
[Tr. turns his rhythmical prose into very bald stuff, not always correct.]
5620. Memoirs of J. C. L--, compiled by Ph. J. Heisch chiefly from the biog. of G. Gessner and J. Herbst. With memoir of his widow (from Gessner). Also, L--'s corr. with the Oberlins. Tr. anon. L: Bagster 1842. 317p. il. 14cm. [BM.LC]
5621. (Briefe.) Letters. Tr. S: Jackson. 1836. In #4767.

LAVATER, L:
5622. (De spectris...lemuribus, magnis...fragoribus...) Of ghostes and spirites walking by nyght, and of strange noyses, crackes, and sundry forewarnynges, which commonly happen before the death of menne, great slaughters and alterations of kyngdomes. Tr. into Englyshe by R. H. L: Prtd. by H: Benneyman for R: Watkins 1572. 8 leaves, 220p. 18cm. [BM]
5623. do. 1596. [same] L: T:Creede. 10 leaves, 220p. 17cm. [BM]

"LEANDER, R:" (i.e., R: v. Volkmann, 1830-89). Sel. in C422;450;501.
5624. [Coll.] The meadow sprite, and other tales of mod. Germany. By Gert. R. Schottenfels. Bost; NY: Educ. pub. 1909. 166p. il. 19cm. [Stories from Rd. Baumbach and R: v. V--.] [LC]
*5625. (Träumereien an französischen Kaminen.) Fantastic stories. Tr. Paulina B. Granville. L: King 1873. xi;157p. il. by M. Fraser-Tytler. 19cm. [14 stories.] [BM]
5626. do. 1878. The organ builder (Die künstliche Orgel); The invisible kingdom (Vom unsichtbaren Königreiche.) Tr. anon. In C159.
*5627. do. 1886. Dreams by a French fireside. Tr. Ma. O'Callaghan. Il. by Fred Roe. L: Chapman & Hall. xi;271p 19cm. [BM] [22 stories; tr. not as good as Raleigh's.]
5627a. do. 1887. Ger. fantasies by French firesides. Tr. Pauline C. Lane. NY: Putnams. 203p. 17cm. [LC]
*5628. do. 1890. Dreams by French firesides. Tr. J. Raleigh. Il. by Louis Wain. Ed: A. & C.Black. xii;203p. 20cm. [22 stories.] [BM]
5629. do. 1897. The story of the invisible kingdom (Vom unsichtbaren Königreiche.) Tr. anon. In C126.

LEDDERHOSE, K: F: 1806-90.
5630. The life of A: Gb. Spangenberg. Tr. anon. L: W.Mallalieu 1855. 118p. 19cm. [BM]
5631. Life of Ph. Melanchthon. Tr. Glb. F: Krotel. Phil: Lindsay & Blakiston 1855. 364p. 18cm. [LC]

LEHÁR, Fz. 1870- . Operettas. Alone at last. Count of Luxembourg. Eva. Gipsy love. See Willner, A. M. Merry widow. See Leon, Victor.

LEHMANN, (J: F: W:) El.
*5632. (G: Gf. Gervinus.) G. G. G--. Tr. Edith Dixon. L: Chapman & Hall 1872. 69p. 21cm. [BM]

LEHMANN, J. F.
5633. (Deutschlands Zukunft bei einem guten und einem schlechten Frieden.) Germany's future with a good peace and a bad peace. Tr. anon. Introd. by Edwyn Bevan. L: Darling 1918. 56p. 8. [BM]

LEHMANN, Lilli, 1848- .
§5634. (Mein Weg.) My path through life. Tr. Alice B. Seligmann. NY; L: Putnam 1914. xiii;510p. il. 23cm. [LC.BM] [Tr. is weak in knowledge of German.]

LEHMANN, Marcus, 1831-90.
5635. Akiba. Tr. Aaron Schaffer. NY: Jewish forum pub. 1925. 367p. 19cm. [LC]

LEHMUS, J: Am. 1707-88. Sel. in C244.

LEIBNIZ, Gf. W: Freiherr v. 1646-1716.
*5636. [Coll.] A coll. of papers...between...L-- and Dr. S: Clarke... 1715 and 1716, relating to...nat. philos. and relig. In Clarke, S:, "A collection," etc. L: Jas. Knapton 1717. 416p. 19cm. [BM] [French and Engl.]
**5637. [Coll.] 1890. The philos. works. Tr. fr. Latin and French by G: M. Duncan. New Haven, Conn. Tuttle, Morehouse & Taylor. 392p. 23cm. [Carefully done. Better than Montgomery's tr.] [LC.BM]
*5638. [Coll.] 1898. Monadology and other philos. writings. Tr. w. introd. and notes by Rb. Latta. Oxford: Clarendon 1898. x;437p. 20cm. [BM]
*5639. [Coll.] 1902. Discourse on metaphysics; corr. with Arnauld; and monadology. Tr. G: R. Montgomery. Chic: Open court; L: Paul, T. & T. xxi;272p. 19cm. [LC.BM]
*5640. [Coll.] 1925. [same as #5638] 2d. impr. L: Milford.437p.[BM.LC]

LEIBNIZ, Gf. W: Freiherr v.
5641. (Consilium aegyptiacum.) A summary account of Leibnitz's [sic] memoir...to Louis the fourteenth, recommending...the conquest of Egypt. Tr. anon. L: Hatchard 1803. xiii;89p. 21cm. [BM]
5642. (Essai de Théodicée sur la bonté de Dieu...) Abridgment of his theodicy. Tr. A. E. Kroeger. 1877. In C300(7).
*5643. (La monadologie.) Monadology. Tr. F: H: Hedge. 1871. In C300(1).
5644. A letter...to the author of the reflections on the origin of Mahometanism. In Reeland, Adrian, "Of the Mahometan religion," pt. 3, pp. 245-54. 1712. 19cm. [BM]
5645. A letter...to Mr. Burnet of Kenney, 24th Aug. 1697. French and Engl. In Thueming, L. P., "A defence of the late Dr. S: Clarke, etc.," pp. 110-57. L: Knapton 1744. 20cm. [BM]
5646. (3) Letters. In G. Burnet, "A memorial...to the princess Sophia." L: Mawman 1815. 24cm. [BM]
5647. New system of nature. Tr. A. E. Kroeger. 1875. In C300(5).
5648. (Nouveaux essais sur l'entendement humain.) Critique of Locke. Tr. Af. G. Langley. 1879-82. In C300 (19, 21, 22). [Cf. the following entry.]
*5649. do. 1896. New essays concerning human understanding. Tr. Af. G. Langley. NY;L: Macmillan. xix;861p. 20cm. [LC.BM] [Also has several pieces on Locke, and some appended matter.]
*5650. do. 1916. [same] 2d ed. Chic: Open court. xix;861p. [LC.BM]
5651. On the doctrine of a universal spirit. Tr. A. E. Kroeger. 1875. In C300(5).
5652. On the nature of the soul. Tr. T. Davidson. 1872. In C300(2).
5653. On Platonic enthusiasm. Tr. T. Davidson. 1873. In C300(3).
5654. A refutation recently discovered of Spinoza by Leibnitz [sic]. Tr. O. F. Owen. Pref. and introd. A. Foucher de Careil. Ed: Constable; L: Hamilton, Adams 1855. xix;155p. 18cm. [BM.LC]
5655. (Systema theologicum.) A system of theology. Tr. w. introd. and notes C: W: Russell. L: Burns & Lambert 1850. cliv;232p. 22cm. [BM]
5656. do. 1855. [same] New ed. Burns. 8. [EC]
5657. Life of L--. Tr. J. M. Mackie. Wiley 1847. 12. [EC]

LEINER, L.
5658. Constance and its environs. 40p. il. Tr. anon. 1884. In C294.

LEINHAAS, G. A.
*5659. (Erinnerungen an...Kaiserin...) Reminiscences of Victoria Empress Frederick. Mainz: Victor & Zabern 1902. 53p. 20cm. [BM]

LEININGEN, Graf v. fl. 1214-39. Sel. in C427.

LEIPOLDT, W:
*5660. (H. E. Rauschenbusch in seinem Leben und Wirken dargestellt.) A memoir of H. E. R--, late pastor...at Elberfeld. Tr. R. F. Walker. L: Seeley 1843. vii;400p. 17cm. [BM]

LEISEWITZ, J: An. 1752-1806.
§5661. (Julius v. Tarent.) Julius of Tarentum: a tragedy. Tr. P: Will. ca. 1800. In C157(2). [Tr. is fair to good.]

LEITENBERGER, O. Sel. in C169.

LEITNER, K: Gf. Ritter v. 1800-90. Sel. in C41;137a;174;372(3).

LEMCKE, K: v. 1831-1913. Sel. in C102.

"LENAU, N:" (i.e., N: Niembsch v. Strehlenau, 1802-50). Sel. in C5*; 17;36;38;41;67;89;90;97;112;123;137;151-2;173;195-6;219;296;309; 311;317;372;378;380;395;417;423;448;460;497;501;571*;#6209a.

LENBACH, Fz. v. 1836-1904. See Harden, M., #3688.

LENGERKA, Cs. v. 1803-55. Sel. in C112.

LENZ, Max, 1850- .
*5662. (Napoleon.) N--: a biogr. study. Tr. Frederic Whyte. L: Hutchinson 1907. viii;391p. front. 50 il. 22cm. [BM]
*5663. do. 1918. [same] L: Hutchinson. 336p. front. (port.) no other il. 16cm. [BM]

LENZ, W: v. 1808-83.
*5663a. (Die grossen Pianoforte-Virtuosen unserer Zeit...) The great piano virtuosos of our time, from personal acquaintance. Tr. Madeleine R. Baker. NY: Schirmer 1899. 169p. 12. [LC].
[Liszt, Chopin, Tausig, Henselt.]

LENZEN, Ma. (di Sebregondi; later ten Brink), 1814-82.
5664. Not in their set; or, in different circles of society. Tr. M. S. Bost;NY: Lee & Shepard 1874. 375p. 18cm. [LC]

LEO, F:A: 1820-98. Sel. in C112.

"LEON, V:" (i.e., V: Hirschfeld, 1860-). See Feld, L., joint author.
5665. (Die geschiedene Frau.) The girl in the train: musical play in 2 acts by Leo Fall. Ad. by Adrian Ross. Libr. L: Enoch 1908? 22p. 21cm. [BM]
5666. do. 1910. [same] Vocal score. Engl. L: Enoch. 119p. 28cm. [BMM]
*5667. do. 1910. Tr. Harry B. Smith. Vocal score. NY: Witmark. 233p. 4. [Fairly free, but clever and good.] [LCM]

LEON, V: and Leo Stein.
5668. (Die lustige Witwe.) The merry widow: operetta in 3 acts by Lehár. Ad. by Basil Hood. Vocal score. Engl. L: Chappell 1907. 207p. 4. [LCM]
5669. do. 1907. [same] Vocal score. Engl. NY: Chappell. 192p. 4. [LCM]
5670. do. 1907. [same] Libr. L: 43; 29; 16p. Dialog. Tw. [LCM]
5671. do. [Ad.] The merry widow: a novel founded on the opera. anon. L: Unwin 1909. 331p. il. 18cm. [BM]

LEONHARDT, Rd. 1889- . Sel. in C95.

LEONHARDT-PIERSON, ---. Sel. in C448.

LEPSIUS, J:s. 1858-1926.
§5672. (Armenien und Europa. Eine Anklageschrift.) Armenia and Europe: an indictment. Ed. by J. Rendel Harris. L: Hodder & Stoughton 1897. xx;331p. 19cm. [BM.LC]
[Tr. supv. by Harris and Miss A. W. Richardson. Certainly not correct or faithful.]

LEPSIUS, (K:) R: 1810-84.
*5673. (Briefe aus Aegypten, Aethiopien und der Halbinsel des Sinai.) Letters from Egypt, Ethiopia, and the peninsula of Sinai. Tr. Leonora and Joanna B. Horner. L: Bohn 1847. 578p. 17cm. [BM]
[Some revision by author, and some add. matter.]
*5674. do. 1852. [same] L: Bentley. 455p. il. 22cm. [LC]
*5675. do. 1872-6. [same] Bost: Little, Brown. n.d. 12. [AC]
*5676. do. 1872-6. [same] NY: Scribner. n.d. 12. [AC]
5677. do. 1872-6. Phil: Lippincott. n.d. 12. [AC]
*5678. (Reise...von Theben nach der Halbinsel des Sinai.) A tour from Thebes to the peninsula of Sinai. ...1845. Tr. C: H. Cottrell. L: Petheram 1846. 92p. 17cm. [BM]
*5679. do. 1847. [same] Petheram. 8. [EC]
See Ebers, G:, R: Lepsius, a biogr., #1358.

LESIMPLE, A:
*5680. R: Wagner: Personal recoll. Tr. C. Armbruster. L: Lucas, Weber 1884. 40p. 12. [BM]
[Not as good as his tr. of Wilsing (cf. #10274); lapses from strict accuracy.]

LESSING, Ghd. Ep. 1729-81. Sel. in C5;12;17;67;118;123;125*;140;163; 172;190;193-4;309;319;366*;373;375;387-8;398-9;400;405a*;419;461; 469;530;533*;574*;#2720;3769.

COLLECTIONS

§5681. 1838. Three comedies. Tr. by Rev. J. J. Holroyd. Colchester: Totham. xx;281p. 17cm. [BM]
[His knowledge of German is not adequate. --The freethinker ("Der Freigeist"); The treasure ("Der Schatz"); Minna v. Barnhelm, or the soldier's fortune ("Minna v. B--").]
†5682. 1862. Cambridge free thoughts and letters on bibliolatry. Tr. H. H. Bernard. L: Trübner. xl;144p. 8. [BM.LCO]
[Contains "Eine Parabel" and the "Anti-Goetziana."]
5683. 1878. Dramatic works. Ed. Ern. Bell. L: Bell. 2v. xxxi;382; 413p. 18cm. [BM.LCO]
[Probably much of the tr. by E: Bell. --Vol. 1. Tragedies. Memoir. *Miss Sara Sampson; Philotas; *Emilia Galotti, tr. R. D. Boylan; *Nathan the wise, tr. Boylan. Vol. 2. Comedies. Damon, or true friendship ("Damon, oder die wahre Freundschaft"); The young scholar ("Der junge Gelehrte"); The old maid ("Die alte Jungfer"); The woman-hater ("Der Misogyn"); The Jews ("Die Juden"); The free-thinker ("Der Freigeist"); The treasure ("Der Schatz"); Minna v. Barnhelm. The tr. of the last three based on #5681.]
*5684. 1879. Select prose works. Tr. E. C. Beasley and Helen Zimmern. L: Bell. xxiv;493p. front. 18cm. [BM]
[Laocoön ("Laokoon"); How the ancients represented death ("Wie die Alten den Tod dargestellt haben"); Dramatic notes ("Hamburgische Dramaturgie"). See #5687 below.]
5685. 1888. [same as #5683.] [LC]
5686. 1888. Nathan the wise and Minna v. Barnhelm. Ed. E. Bell. Tr. R. D. Boylan. L: Bohn. 239p. 18cm. [BM]
[Nathan by Boylan. Minna revised by Bell from Holroyd as in #5683.]
5687. 1890. [same as #5684] New rev. ed. L: Bell. 493p. [LC]
[Tr. of Laocoön is by Beasley, revised; the remainder by Zimmern.]
5688. 1891. [same as #5683] [LC]
5689. 1895. A brief account, etc. Bost;NY: Silver, Burdett. [LC]
[Contains 7 prose fables, and Nathan in tr. of W: Taylor.]
*5690. 1895. Laocoön and other prose. Tr. and ed. w. introd. W. B. Rönnfeldt. L: Scott. xx;289p. 17cm. [BM.BPL]
[Dramatic notes ("Hamburgische Dramaturgie"); 7 sel. from The education of the human race ("Die Erziehung des Menschengeschlechts").]
5691. 1895. [same as #5683] [LC]
5692. 1900. [same as #5687] [LC]
5693. 1914. Laocoön, and, How the ancients represented death. L: Bell 1914. 246p. 12. [AC has: NY. Macmillan 1914. xx;226p.] [EC]

5694. (Damon, oder die wahre Freundschaft.) Damon; or, true friendship. Tr. anon. 1878. In #5683.
5695. (Der Freigeist.) The free-thinker. Tr. J. J. Holroyd. 1838. In #5681.
5696. do. 1878. [same, revised] In #5683.
5697. (Der junge Gelehrte.) The young scholar. Tr. anon. 1878. In #5683.
5698. (Der Misogyn.) The woman-hater. Tr. anon. 1878. In #5683.

LESSING, Ghd. Ep.
5699. (Der Schatz.) The treasure. Tr. J. J. Holroyd. 1838. In #5681.
5700. do. 1878. [same, revised] In #5683.
5701. (Die alte Jungfer.) The old maid. Tr. anon. 1878. In #5683.
5702. (Die Erziehung des Menschengeschlechts.) The educ. of the human race. Tr. signed by H. C. R. (H: Crabb Robinson?) In"Monthly Repos. of theol." 1(1806):412, 467. (B26)
*5703. do. 1858. Tr. F: W: Robertson. L: Smith, Elder. 79p. 17cm. [BM.LC]
[Not a really strong translation.]
*5704. do. 1872. [same] 3d ed. L: King. 16. [BM]
*5705. do. 1881. [same] 3d ed. L: Paul. 79p. 16cm. [LC]
*5706. do. 1896. [same] 4th ed. rev. by C: B. Robertson. L: Paul. xvi;79p. 16cm. [BM]
*5707. do. 1909. [same] NY: Collier. Harvard classics, vol. 32.
*5708. do. 1910. [same] In C370.
*5709. do. 1910. [same] In C119.
*5710. do. 1927. [same] L;NY: Anthroposoph. pub. 24p. 25cm. [BM]
*5711. do. 1927. [same] L;NY. 24p. 16cm. [BM]
[Reprint from "Anthroposophy."]
5712. (Emilia Galotti.) E-- G--. Tr. by Berrington. L: 1794. (B8)
†5713. do. 1800. A trag. in 5 acts [prose]. Tr. B: Thompson. In C535. [Front. Corbould. 75p. 21cm.]
†5714. do. 1805. Tr. Fanny Holcroft. In C204, pp. 365-409.
†5715. do. 1810. [reprint] In "The mirror of taste and dram. recorder," vol. 2, no. 3. Phil: Bradford & Inskeep. 18p. 22cm. [LC]
†5716. do. 1810. [same] Bost: McIlhenry. (B48)
†5717. do. 1810. [same] Balto: Coale. (B48)
†5718. do. 1810. [same] Charleston, S. C: Morfodd, Wellington. (B48)
5719. do. 1842. Tr. anon. In "King's college mag." 2(1842):265, etc. (B27)
5719a. do. 1847. Tr. J: Hofstetter. Lpz;Vienna: Hunger. 101p. 12.
[Listed as: Select dram. works of the Ger. theatre.][EC(Heinsius)]
5720. do. 1867. Tr. G: Marlow. As performed by Mlle. Fanny Janauschek. NY. O. [NL]
*5721. do. 1868. Tr. C: L. Lewes. Lpz: Tauchnitz ed., vol. 9, pp. 177-298. [BM.LC]
*5722. do. 1878. Tr. R. D. Boylan. In #5683.
5723. do. 1912-17. Tr. anon. NY: Translation pub. 15cm. [AC]
*5724. (Ernst und Falk. Gespräche für Freimaurer.) L--'s masonic dialogues. Tr. w. introd. and notes Rev. A. Cohen. L: Baskerville 1927. iv;126p. 17cm. [BM]
§5725. (Fabeln.) Fables and parables. Tr. J. Richardson. York: Etherington 1773. xiii;168p. 16cm. [BM]
[90 prose fables. Flowery expansion.]
†5726. do. 1825. Fables and epigrams, w. essays on fable and epigram. Tr. anon. L: Hunt. viii;208p. 18cm. [BM.LC]
[89 fables; epigrams, pp. 147-64.]
†5727. do. 1829. Fables. In three books. Ger. and Engl. L: J:Taylor. 88p. 18cm. [BM]
[Textbook. Literal tr. without style. 90 fables. Engl. paged sep.]
5728. do. 1845. Sel. from L--'s fables. Tr. anon. In C125.
5729. do. 1849. Sel. Tr. anon. (F. H. Hedge?) In C194.
5730. do. 1860. L--'s Ger. fables in prose and verse. With a close Engl. tr. Ger. and Engl. L: Nutt. 117p. 18cm. [BM]
[Close, but neither good nor accurate. The verse tr. is particularly choice. 90 fables in prose, 11 in verse.]
5731. (Faust.) L--'s "Faust" fragments. Tr. Gower. 1825. In #2720.
*5732. (Hamburgische Dramaturgie.) Dram. notes (not complete). Tr. Helen Zimmern. 1879. In #5684.
5733. (Laokoon.) Laocoön. Tr. anon. 1767. 8. (B8)

LESSING, Ghd. Ep.--Laokoon
*5734. do. 1836. L--; or, the limits of poetry and painting. Tr. W: Ross. L: Ridgway. xxv;373p. 22cm. [Has engr. t.p.] [BM]
5735. do. 1847. Tr. J: Hofstetter. Vienna;Lpz. 12. (B8) [Not recorded in Heinsius.]
5736. do. 1853. Tr. E. C. Beasley. Introd. Rev. T. Burbidge. L: Longmans. xviii;255p. 17cm. [Cf. #5741.] [BM.BPL]
*5739. do. 1874. Tr. Ellen Frothingham. Bost: Roberts. 245p. 18cm. [LC.BM]
†5738. do. 1874. Tr. Sir Rb. Js. Phillimore. L: Macmillan. 336p. 15cm. [BM]
5739. do. 1877. A condensation of L--'s L--. Cambridge, Mass: Sever. 24p. 25cm. [LC]
[A brief statement of L--'s general contentions, cleverly done.]
*5740. do. 1877. [same as #5737] [UCal]
*5741. do. 1878. Tr. E. C. Beasley. In #5684. [Revised tr.]
5742. do. 1888. Tr. Beasley. rev. ed. L: Bohn. xxiv;169p. 8. [BM]
*5743. do. 1894. [same as #5737] [UCal]
*5744. do. 1904. [same as #5737] Bost: Little, Brown. 250p. 17cm. [LC]
†5745. do. 1905. [same as #5738] L: Routledge; NY: Dutton. 336p. 15cm. [BM has: Macmillan 1905. 336p.] [LC]
†5746. do. 1910. [same] L: Macmillan. 336p. [BM.LC]
*5747. do. 1910. [same as #5737] [UCal]
†5748. do. 1910. [same as #5738] L: Routledge. [EC]
5749. do. 1912-17. Tr. anon. Translation pub. n.d. 15cm. [AC]
†5750. (Minna v. Barnhelm.) The disbanded officer; or, the baroness of Bruchsal. A comedy in 5 acts [prose]. Altered by Jas. Johnstone. As performed at the Theatre-Royal. L: T.Cadell 1786. xvi;71p. 20cm. [Fairly close and in good style, but not Lessing.] [BM]
§5751. do. 1799. The school for honor; or, the chance of war. Tr. anon. L: Vernor & Hood. 106p. 8. [NY]
[Probably tr. by Rb. Harvey, see "Notes & Queries" 4(1875):260.--Good in spirit, but not a close version. Just is Trim, Minna is Louisa, Host is Shark, Servant is Tryell, Widow is Mrs. Shadley, etc.]
†5752. do. 1806. Minna v. B--. Tr. Fanny Holcroft. In C204, pp. 217-58.
§5753. do. 1858. Minna v. B--; or, a soldier's fortune. Tr. W. C. Wrankmore. Lpz: Prtd. for A. Gumprecht. iv;79p. 21cm. [BM]
[Rather poor tr.]
§5754. do. 1864. [same] NY: Holt. [AC]
§5755. do. 1876. [same] New ed. [AC]
§5756. do. 1878. A soldier's fortune. In #5683. Rev. by E: Bell from #5681.
5757. do. 189- . Tr. anon. NY: Hinds. Handy literal tr. 83p. 16. [NY]
§5758. do. 1899. M. v. B.; or, a soldier's luck. Tr. w. introd. and notes by P. Maxwell. L: Univ. press. xi;287p. 21cm. [BM]
§5759. do. 1899. [same as #5683] Phil: McKay. Pocket literal tr. 113p. 16. [LC]
§5760. do. 1901. Bell's tr. In C409.
§5761. do. 1903. Tr. Ern. Bell (probably same as #5683). In C18.
§5762. do. 1909? Bell's tr. In The Harvard classics, vol. 26. NY: Collier.
§5763. do. 1910. Bell's tr. In C72.
§5764. do. 1916. Bell's tr. In C408.
*5765. do. 1917. Minna; or, soldier's fortune. Tr. O: Heller. NY: Holt. lxxii;152p. 19cm. [LC]
[Correct; but uses bookish language for Just.]
5766. (Miss Sara Sampson.) Lucy Sampson; or, the unhappy heiress. A trag. in 5 acts [prose]. Tr. by a citizen of Phil. (D: Rittenhouse). Phil: Prtd. and sold by C: Cist 1789. 88p. 8. [HCL]

LESSING, Ghd. Ep.--Miss Sara Sampson
5767. do. 1799. The fatal elopement. Tr. anon. In "Lady's Mag." 30(1799):30, etc. (B26)
[Tr. is named by Todt (B44) as Eleonore H--. Cf. #5263.]
*5768. do. 1878. Tr. anon. (probably by Bell). In #5683.
5769. do. 1912-17. Miss Sara Simpson [sic]. Tr. anon. Translation pub. n.d. 15cm. [AC]
†5770. (Nathan der Weise.) N-- the wise: a philos. drama in 5 acts [prose]. Tr. R. E. Raspe. L: J.Fielding 1781. 103p. 21cm. [BM]
[Not even close; clumsy prose.]
§5771. do. 1791. Tr. W: Taylor of Norwich. Norwich: Stevenson & Matchett. 293p. 8. [NY]
§5772. do. 1805. [same]...a dramatic poem. L: Philips. 293p. 24cm.
[Ident. with the foregoing, but with new t.p., offering for pub. sale the remaining copies of the 1st ed.] [BM]
§5773. do. 1828. [same] In C533.
§5774. do. 1860. Tr. Dr. Adolphus Reich. L: Bennett. xxxv;219p. 20cm. [Biogr. of L--, etc.] [BM.LC]
*5775. do. 1867. Tr. Ellen Frothingham. With Kuno Fischer's essay. NY: Holt. 259p. 17cm. [LC]
*5776. do. 1868. [same] rev. ed. NY: Leypoldt & Holt. xxiii;259p. 17cm. [Brief account of L-- and K. Fischer's essay.] [LC.BM]
§5777. do. 1868. [same as #5771] Tauchnitz ed., vol. 9. [BM]
§5778. do. 1868. Tr. by Rb. Willis? L: Trübner. xxxviii;214p. 18cm.
[Not equal to the task. Introd. on Lessing and the "Nathan," signed R. W., M. D.] [BM]
†5779. do. 1869. Tr. into Engl. prose by Dr. Isidore Kalisch. NY: Waldemar & Zenn. 212p. 16. [LCO]
†5780. do. 1874. Abr. and tr. by E. S. H. L: Sotheran. 128p. 22cm.
[Prose, redone.] [BM]
§5781. do. 1877. Tr. Andrew Wood. L;Ed: Nimmo. xxiv;212p. 19cm. [BM]
[Awkward verse.]
5782. do. 1877. A dramatic poem. Tr. anon. L: Williams & N. 8. [EC]
[Probably Taylor's tr.]
*5783. do. 1878. Tr. R. D. Boylan. In #5683.
*5784. do. 1883. Tr. with introd. and notes E. K. Corbett. L: K.Paul. lvi;185p. 19cm. [BM.HCL]
§5785. do. 1886. Taylor's tr. Introd. by H: M(orley?) L;NY: Cassell. 192p. 13cm. [BM]
§5786. do. 1888. [same] Cassell. 192p. [BM]
§5789. do. 1894. Tr. anon. New Orleans: Hopkins. 181p. 8. [LCO]
[Correct; poor verse.]
§5790. do. 1894. Tr. W: Jacks. Introd. F: W. Farrar. Etchings by W: Strang. Glasgow: Maclehose. xxxiv;252p. 18cm. [Wretched verse][BM]
§5791. do. 1895. Taylor's tr. In Hoyles, Euretta A., "Lessing." NY; Bost;Chic: Silver, Burdett. 212p. 12. [LC]
§5792. do. 1895. Tr. Patrick Maxwell. L: Scott. xxii;264p. 8. [BM]
§5793. do. 1895. [same] NY: Bloch. 388p. 12. [LC]
5794. do. 1903. Sel. Tr. Ern. Bell. In C18.
5795. do. 191-. Tr. anon. Girard, Kan: Haldeman-Julius n.d. Big blue books. 128p. 5 x 8 in. (Publisher's catalog.)
5796. do. 1912-17. Tr. anon. Translation pub. n.d. 15cm. [AC]
§5797. do. 1917. [same as #5793] Ed. with introd...G: Kohut. NY: Bloch. 388p. il. [LC]
5798. (Philotas.) P--. Tr. anon. Translation pub. n.d. 15cm. [AC]
5799. (Vom Alter der Oelmalerei.) Tr. R. E. Raspe. L: 1781. 4. (B8)
5800. (Wie die Alten den Tod dargestellt haben.) How the ancients represented death. Tr. Helen Zimmern. 1879. In #5684.
See Stahr, Ad., Life and works. #9014.
See "The philosopher." A421. [Falsely ascribed to Lessing.]

LESSING, Jl. 1843- .
5801. (Altorientalische Teppichmuster.) Ancient oriental carpet patterns. After pict. and orig. of the 15th and 16th cent. Tr. anon. 30 col.pl. L: Sotheran 1879. 25p. 49 x 34cm. [BM]
[Text is very freely treated.]

LEUTHOLD, H: 1827-79. Sel. in C423;450;501.

LEUTOLT VON SEVEN, fl. 1220-30. Sel. in C532.

LEVY, Ok.
*5802. (Das 19. Jahrhundert.) The revival of aristocracy. Tr. L. A. Magnus. L: Probsthain 1906. xvi;119p. 8. [BM]
[Some differences from the published ed. requested by the author, who wrote a new Engl. introd. for this issue.]
5803. Nietzsche in England. Tr. Pl. V. Cohn. In #6816(18).

LEWALD-STAHR, Fanny, 1811-89.
5804. [Coll.] Stories and tales. Tr. anon. Chic: Schick 1885. 2 pts. 19cm. [The aristocratic world; The maid of Oyas.] [LC]
5805. do. 1890. [same] In C404.
5806. The aristocratic world. Tr. anon. 1895. In C405.
5806a. The captain's self-devotion. Tr. anon. "Harper's Mag." 3(1851): 689. (B15a)
**5807. (Der Seehof.) Lake-house. Tr. Nathaniel Greene. Bost: Ticknor & Fields 1861. 304p. 19cm. [Excellent tr.] [LC]
5808. (Die Erlöserin.) Hulda; or, the deliverer. A romance. Tr. Mrs. A. L. Wister. Phil: Lippincott 1874. 394p. 18cm. [LC]
*5809. (Italienisches Bilderbuch.) The Italians at home. Tr. Countess d'Avigdor. L: T: C. Newby 1848. 2v. 322; 362p. 19cm. [Mostly excellent; some doubtful liberties.] [BM.LC]
5810. do. 1852. The Italian sketch-book. Tr. anon. In "The book-case," vol. 3. L: Simms & M'Intyre. 224p. 18cm. [BM]
[Consid. condensation, but in excellent style.]
5811. The mask of beauty: a novel. Tr. Ma. M. Pleasants. Il. F. A. Carter. NY: Bonner 1894. 340p. 19cm. [LC]
*5812. (Stella.) Stella. Tr. Beatrice Marshall. Lpz: Tauchnitz 1884. 2v. 296;280p. 15cm. [BM]
*5813. do. 1885. [same] NY: Munro. Seaside lib. 199p. 18cm. [LC]

LHOTZKY, H: 1859-1931.
5814. (Die Seele deines Kindes.) The soul of your child. Tr. Anna Barwell. L: Allen & Unwin 1924. 175p. 7 x 5 in. [EC]

LICHNOWSKY (von und zu Arco-Zinneberg), Fürstin v. 1879- .
5815. Marriage as a work of art. 1926. In C308.

LICHNOWSKY, K: Max, 1860-1928.
*5816. The L-- memorandum. Tr. Munroe Smith. 1918. In C160.
[Ger. and Engl. given.]

LICHTENAU, W:e (Encken) Rietz, Gräfin v. 1752-1820.
5817. (Geheime Papiere der Gräfin v. Lichtenau, vulgo Minchen Encken.) Confessions of the celebrated Countess of L--. Drawn from orig. papers. Tr. R: B-t-n. L: Myers 1799. ix;68p. front. 21cm. [Engr. port. after an orig. painting.--Pt. 2 (pp. 36-68) is a good tr. of the Geheime Papiere, probably a forgery by H: Husen, who signs the pref. of the Ger. ed.] [BM.LC]

LICHTENBERG, G: Cph. 1742-99.
*5818. (Gedanken und Maximen.) The reflections of L--. Sel. and tr. Norman Alliston. L: Sonnenschein 1908. 168p. 19cm. [BM.LC]
[Tr. from 1844 ed., 8 general subheads given. Very good tr. Pref. to p. 19.]

LICHTENSTEIN, Af. Sel. in C95.

LICHTENSTEIN, Mt. H: K: 1780-1857.
*5819. (Reisen im südlichen Afrika.) Travels in southern Africa, 1803-6. Tr. Anne Plumptre. L: Colburn 1812-15. 2v. xii;383;368p. 28cm. [Appendices.] [BM]

LICHTERFELD, ---. Sel. in C37.

LICHTWER, Mg. Gf. 1719-82. Sel. in C17;443;461.

LIEBER, Fz. 1800-72. Sel. in C43.

LIEBESKIND, A: Jk. See Herder, J. G., Oriental fairy tales.
5819a. Oriental fairy tales. Tr. anon. 1886. In #4225.

LIEBICH, Ehf. 1713-80. Sel. in C229;231;244;489;#8904.

LIEBIG, Jt. 1803-73. Sel. in C574.

LIEBKNECHT, K: (Pl. A: F:) 1871-1919.
5820. The future belongs to the people. (Speeches made since the beginning of the war.) Ed. and tr. Savel Zimand. Introd. Wl. Weyl. L;NY: Macmillan 1918. 144p. 19cm. [LC.BM]
§5821. Militarism. Tr. anon. NY: Huebsch 1917. xviii;178p. 19cm. [LC] [Sel. from a book revised from a lecture delivered in 1906.--On the whole, good; some errors noted.]
5822. do. 1918. Militarism and anti-militarism, with spec. regard to the internat. young socialist movement. Tr. anon. Socialist labour press. xv;176p. 7 x 5 in. [Tr. A. Sirmis; cf. next entry.] [EC]
5823. do. 1919. [same] 2d ed. Glasgow: Socialist labour press. xv; 176p. 18cm. pa. [BM]

LIEBKNECHT, W: Ph. Cn. Mn. L: 1826-1900.
5824. (K: Marx zum Gedächtnis.) K: M--: Biogr. memoirs. Tr. Ern. Untermann. Chic: Kerr 1901. 181p. 17cm. [LC]

LILIENCRON, Dv. Freiherr v. 1844-1909. Sel. in C28;95;366;423.

LIMAN VON SANDERS, O: 1855-1929.
*5825. (Fünf Jahre Türkei.) Five years in Turkey. Tr. Carl Reichmann. U. S. naval inst. 1927. x;326p. il. O. [BM]

LINDAU, C: The love-cure. Operetta. See Stein, Leo., joint author.

LINDAU, Pl. 1839-1919. Sel. in C422.
5826. Diana; or, father and son. A play in 5 acts. Tr. L. J. Frank. NY: 1873. (B38)
§5827. (Hängendes Moos.) Hanging moss. Tr. W. Ayer and Helen Folger. NY: Appleton 1892. 300p. 18cm. [LC] [Fair tr. They insist on improving the orig.]
5828. Helen Young. Tr. P. J. McFadden. Chic;NY: Rand, McNally 1892. 183p. 19cm. [LC]
§5829. (Herr und Frau Bewer.) Klaus Bewer's wife. Tr. Ca. S. Fleishman. NY: Holt 1886. 253p. 17cm. [Fair tr.] [LC]
5830. (Maria und Magdalena.) M-- and M--: a play in 4 acts. Ad. L. J. Hollenius. NY: De Witt 1874. 44p. 12. [LCO]
5831. do. 1874. [same] Chic. dram. soc. (B38)
5832. (Spitzen.) Lace: a Berlin romance. Tr. anon. NY: Appleton 1889. 324p. 19cm. [LC]
5833. Unter den Linden. Tr. anon. In "The great streets of the world," pp. 173-210. NY: Scribner 1892. xiii;253p. il. L: Osgood; NY: Scribner 1892. xiii;253p. il. 25cm. [LC.BM]

LINDAU, Rd. 1829-1910.
5834. [Coll.][*Gordon Baldwin (do.) and, The philosopher's pendulum (Das Glückspendel). Tr. anon. NY: Appleton 1878. 163p. 16cm [LC.BM]

LINDAU, Rd.
*5835. [Coll.] 1878. Liquidated (Liquidiert) and The seer (Der Seher). Tr. anon. NY: Appleton 1878. 179p. 16cm. [LC.BM]
5836. [Coll.] 1883. The philosopher's pendulum, and other stories. Ed;L: Blackwood. 322p. 19cm. [BM]
[The philosopher's pendulum ("Das Glückspendel"), a tale from Germany; Gordon Baldwin (do.); Weariness, a tale from France; The seer ("Der Seher"); Fred ("Fred"), a tale from Japan.--Nos. 1, 2, and 4 as in two preceding entries.]
5837. [Coll.] 1885. Stories and novels. Tr. anon. Chic: Schick. 3 pts. 94;42;10p. 19cm. [LC]
[Hans the dreamer; All in vain ("Verlorenes Mühen"); First love ("Erste Liebe").]
5838. [Coll.] 1890. [same] In C404.
5839. (Das Glückspendel.) The philosopher's pendulum. In "Tales from Blackwood," 2nd ser., vol. 10, 1879, pp. 160-204. [BM.LCO]
[Same tr. as in #5834. Pub. in "Blackwood's Mag." 120(1876):211.]
5840. do. 1898. [same?] Tr. anon. In C509.
5840a. A deadly feud: a tale from France. Tr. anon. "Blackwood's Mag." 126(1879):408. (B15a)
5840b. Second sight. Tr. E. W. Latimer. "Littell's Liv. Age." 137 (1878):337, etc. (B15a)
5841. (Die kleine Welt.) Our little world. Tr. Cornelia D. Wilder. St. Paul, Minn: Price, McGill 1889. 149p. 17cm. [LC]

LINDAU, W: Ad. 1774-1849.
5842. (Heliodora oder die Lautenspielerin aus Griechenland.) H--; or, the Grecian minstrel. Tr. (anon.) from the Ger. of Baron Goethe [sic]. L: Dutton 1894. 3v. 12. [BM]

LINDEMANN, J: fl. 1580-1630. Sel. in C287;486.

LINDEN, A:e
5843. Children's trials; or, the little rope-dancers and other tales. Tr. "Trauermantel." Bost: Crosby & Nichols; NY: Evans and Dickerson 1855. 238p. 17cm. [BM]
[Flodvard and Ermenax, or the little rope-dancers; Gabrielle; The gray woman of Scharfenstein; Mother Ingeborg and her children; The true son.]
5844. do. 1868. [same] NY: O'Shea. [AC]
5845. do. 1876. [same] [AC]
5846. Titania: tales and legends. Tr. "Trauermantel." Bost: Crosby & Nichols; Cincin: G. S. Blanchard 1857. 236p. 17cm. [BM]
[The page; The mountain-elf's gift; The dear reckoning; Filial love]
5847. do. 1868. [same] NY: O'Shea. [AC]
5848. do. 1876. [same] [AC]

LINGG, Hm. 1820-1905. Sel. in C112;149;151-2;196;309;311;397;448; 450;501;566;571.

LINK, H: F: 1767-1851.
*5849. (Bemerkungen auf einer Reise durch Frankreich, Spanien und vorzüglich Portugal.) Travels in Portugal and through France and Spain. Tr. J: Hinckley. L: Longman 1801. vii;504p. 21cm. [BM.LC]
5850. do. 1806-8. In Pelham, Cavendish, compiler. "The world, etc.," vol. 11, pp. 345-400. L: [LC]

LINSINGEN (afterwards Meineke), C:e v. 1768-1815.
*5851. C. v. L-- and W: IV. Unpub. love-letters. Tr. T. G. Arundel. L: Sonnenschein & Allen 1880. iv;183p. 19cm. [BM.LC]
*5852. do. 1881. [same] 2d ed. [EC]

LIPPMANN, F. 1839-1903.
*5852a. (Der Kupferstich.) Engraving and etching: a handbook for the use of students and print collectors. Tr...from 3d ed. (rev. Max Lehrs) by Mn. Hardie. L: Grevel 1906. xvii;312p. il. 23cm. [BM.LC]
5852b. The gipsy in music. Tr. Edwin Evans. Reeves 1926. 2v. 228; 165p. 7 ports. 8. [EC]

LISCOVIUS (Lischkow), Slm. 1640-89. Sel. in C233;244;269.

LISZT, Fz. 1811-86.
*5853. (Briefe.) Letters. Coll. and ed. by "La Mara." Tr. (from the French) Constance Bache. L: Grevel 1894. 2v. 20cm. [BM.LC]
See Lenz, W: v., The great piano virtuosos of our time, #5663.
See Nohl, L., Life of L-- , #6907.
See Ramann, Lina, F. L--, artist and man, #7315.
See Wagner, R:, Corr..., #9892.

LITZMANN, Bd. 1857-1926.
*5854. (Ka. Schumann.) Ca. S--: an artist's life based on...diaries and letters. Tr. and abr. from 4th ed. by Grace E. Hadow. Lpz: Breitkopf & Haertel; L: Macmillan 1913. 2v. 24cm. [BM.LC]

LOEBELL, J: W: 1786-1863. See Niebuhr, B. G., Life and letters, #6732.

LOEHER, Fr. v. 1818-92.
5855. (Cypern...Reiseberichte...) Cyprus, histor. and descriptive. Ad. with much add. matter by Mrs. A. B. Joyner. L: Allen 1878. xvi;308p. 19cm. [Thoroughly rewritten.] [BM]
5856. do. 1878. [same] NY: Worthington. 324p. il. 21cm. [LC]

LOËN, J: Ml. Freiherr v. 1694-1775.
5857. (Der Adel.) The analysis of nobility, in its origin, etc. Tr. from...v. Lowhen [sic]. L: Prtd. and sold by Robinson 1754. 317p. 17cm. [LC]

LOEWE, Fdr. 1816-90. Sel. in C231;309;375;417;450;571.

LOEWENBERG, Jl.
*5858. (Ax. v. Humboldt. Sein Reiseleben in Amerika und Asien.) Ax. v. H--. Youth and early manhood. Travels in America and Asia. In Bruhns, C., Ax. v. Humboldt, etc., vol. 1, pp. 253-390. See #810.

LOEWENSTERN, Mts. Ap. v. 1594-1648. Sel. in C269;273;287;486.

LOEWY, Em. 1857- .
*5859. (Die Naturwiedergabe in der älteren griechischen Kunst.) The rendering of nature in early Greek art. Tr. J: Fothergill. L: Duckworth 1907. xii;109p. 20cm. [BM.LC]

LOGAU, F: v. 1604-55. Sel. in C371;530;570.

LOHMANN, Eme. F:e So. 1783-1830.
*5860. (Die Entscheidung bei Hochkirch.) Self-devotion; or, the Prussians at H--. A free tr. anon. Lichfield. Lomax;L: Masters 1849. 82p. 15cm. [Pretty good tr.] [BM]

LOHMANN, F:e, 1749-1811.
5861. [Coll.] The pilgrim; The mill of the vale; The night on the mountain. Tr. G: G. Cunningham. 1829. In C80.

LOHMEYER, Jl. 1835-1903.
5862. Prince Fridolin's courtship. Verses by J-- L-- and Frieda Schanz. Tr. Sydney Clifton. 1888. See Schanz, #7688.

LOHR, Fr.
5863. A day in ancient Rome: being a revision of "Aus dem alten Rom"

LOHR, Fr.--A day in ancient Rome
by E. S. Shumway. NY: Chautauqua press 1885. 96p. il. 20cm. [LC]
5864. do. 1887. [same] 40th thous. Bost: Heath 1887. [LC]

LORENTZ, F:
§5865. (Alcuins Leben.) Life of A--. Tr. J. M. Slee. L: Hurst 1837. 284p. 8. [Seems to me interpreted rather than translated, and I feel subtle shifts of emphasis in the change of form.] [BM]

"LORM, Hieronimus" (i.e., H: Landesmann, 1821-1902). Sel. in C309; 450*;501.

LORTZING, Gst. Ab. 1801-51.
*5866. (Czar und Zimmermann.) Peter the great in Saardam: comic opera in 3 acts. Words and music by L-- (from the French). Tr. Hans Balatka. Libr. Chic: Chic. mus. union 1864. 16p. 8. [LCM]
*5867. do. 1866. The czar and the carpenter; or, P: the great in Saardam. Libr. Phil: Ledger job print. off. 28p. 8. [LCO] [This is Balatka's tr.; cf. following entry.]
*5868. do. 1868. [same] Phil: Ledger job prt. off. 28p. 8. [LCM] [Balatka's tr.]
*5869. do. 1871. P: the shipwright. Tr. anon. Vocal score, Engl. L; NY: Boosey. 257p. 27cm. [Good, rhymed.] [BMM.LCM]
§5870. do. 1879. The two Peters. Tr. anon. Libr., with music. NY: Rullman. 24p., 4p. music. sm. 4. [Fair to good; rhymed.] [LCM]
5871. do. 1880. [same?] The two peters. Libr. NY: Theatre ticket off. 24p. [LCO]

LOSKIEL, G: H: 1740-1814.
5872. Extempore on a wagon: a metrical narr. of a journey from Bethlehem, Pa. to...Goshen, O...1803. Tr. Js. Mx. Hark. Lancaster, Pa: Zahm 1887. 45p. front. 24cm. [LC]
*5873. (Geschichte der Mission der evangelischen Brüder...in Nordamerika.) Hist. of the mission of the United Brethren among the Indians in North America. Tr. C. I. La Trobe. L: Prtd. for the Brethren's soc. 1794. 3 pts. 21cm. [BM]
5874. do. 1838. Hist. of the Moravian mission among the Indians, etc. Tr. anon. L: Allman. vi;316p. 17cm. [LC]--L: Seeley. 316p. [BM] [Based on Loskiel's work. "by a member of the Brethren's church."]

LOSSIUS, Kp. F: 1753-1817.
5875. (Gumal und Lina.) Gumal and Lina; or, the African children. Tr. from French (of J. L. A. Dumas) S. B. Moens. L: Prtd. for the tr. 1817. 2v. 262; 256p. plates. 18cm. [BM] ["The French tr...has been followed in pref. to the orig...The... tr. has not scrupled to make a few further deviations."]
5876. do. 1839. [same] 4th ed. L: Duncan & Malcolm. xii;418p.15cm. [BM]

"LOTHAR" (i.e., O: C: v. Graeven)
5877. [Coll.] The arch rogue ("Der Erzgauner"); Castle Christburg ("Die Christburg.") Tr. T: Roscoe. 1826. In C477.

LOTHAR (really Spitzer), Rd. 1865- .
5878. (König Harlekin.) The harlequin king: a play in 4 acts. Tr. J. Severance. 1906. Tw. [Founded on L--'s play.] [LC]
*5879. (Tiefland.) Tiefland: music drama in a prelude and 2 acts by E. d'Albert. Text after "Terra baixa" by A. Guimera. Tr. Rosie H. Elkin. Libr. Engl. L: A. H. Crew 1908. 74p. 21cm. [BM] [Orig. is in irreg. unrhymed verse.]
*5880. do. 1908. [same] Libr. Ger;Engl. NY: Boosey. 74;74p. 22cm. [LCM]

LOTZE, (Rd.) Hm. 1817-81.
5881. (Grundzüge der Aesthetik.) Outlines of aesthetics. Dictated

LOTZE, (Rd.) Hm.
portions of the lectures. Tr. and ed. G: T. Ladd. Bost: Ginn 1886. viii;113p. 19cm. [LC.BM]
*5882. (Grundzüge der Logik und Enzyklopädie der Philosophie.) Outlines of logic and of encyclopedia of philos. Dictated portions, etc. Tr. and ed. G: T. Ladd. Bost: Ginn 1887. 184p. 19cm. [LC.BM]
*5883. (Grundzüge der Metaphysik.) Outlines of metaphysic. Dictated portions, etc. Tr. and ed. G: T. Ladd. Bost: Ginn, Heath 1884. xii;166p. 19cm. [LC.BM]
*5884. (Grundzüge der Philosophie.) Outlines of philos. Dictated portions, etc. Tr. and ed. G: T. Ladd. Bost: Ginn, Heath 1884-7. 4v. [This is a collective title for the foregoing entries, and the next following.] [LCO]
*5885. (Grundzüge der praktischen Philosophie.) Outlines of practical philosophy. Dictated portions, etc. 1885. ix;156p. 19cm.[LC.BM]
*5886. (Grundzüge der Religionsphilosophie.) Outlines of the philos. of relig. Dictated portions, etc. Tr. and ed. G: T. Ladd. Bost: Ginn, Heath 1885. 162p. 19cm. [LC.BM]
*5887. do. 1887. [same] L: Dickinson. viii;158p. 8. [BM]
*5888. do. 1892. Outlines of a philos. of relig. Ed. F. C. Conybeare Tr. begun by Emily Ma. Müller, compl. and ed. by her husband, F. C. Conybeare. L: Sonnenschein. xx;176p. 19cm. [BM]
*5889. (Mikrokosmus. Ideen zur Naturgeschichte und Geschichte der Menschheit.) Microcosmus: an essay concerning man and his relation to the world. Tr. Eliz. Hamilton and E. E. Constance Jones. Ed: Clark 1885. 2v. xxvi;714;740p. 22cm. [BM.LC]
[Hamilton tr. vol. 1 to p. 659; Jones ed. Hamilton and tr. the rest. She is better as independent tr.]
*5890. do. 1894. [same] 4th ed. L: Simpkin. 2v. 8. [EC]
5891. do. 1895. An outline of the microcosmus. By H: C. King. Oberlin, O: Pearce & Randolph. 105p. 24cm.[Derived from Engl. tr.][LC]
5892. On the ideal and real. Tr. Max Eberhardt. 1876. In C300(6).
*5893. (System der Philosophie. Logik. Metaphysik.) System of philos. Pt. 1. Logic. Pt. 2. Metaphysics. Tr. ed. B. Bosanquet. Oxford: Clarendon 1884. 2 pts. xx;xxiii; 538; xvi;539p. 22cm. [BM.LC]
[LC lists this as two sep. vols.]
*5894. do. 1887-8. [same] 2d ed. Oxford: Clarendon. 4v. [BM]

LUCKA, El. 1877- .
§5895. (Die drei Stufen der Erotik.) Eros: the devel. of the sex relation through the ages. Tr. w. introd. Ellie Schleussner. L;NY: Putnam 1915. xx;379p. 20cm. [LC]
[Not wholly faithful, and some errors.]
5896. do. 1923. [same] The evolution of love. L: Allen & Unwin. 303p. 9 x 5 in. [EC]

LUCKNER, Fx. Graf v. 1881- .
5897. Count L--, the sea devil. By Lowell J. Thomas. NY: Doubleday 1927. x;308p. il. O. [Really a tr. of Luckner's own account.] [AC]

LUDAEMILIA Eli., Prinzessin v. Schwarzburg-Rudolstadt, 1640-72. Sel. in C233.

LUDENDORFF, Er. v. 1865- .
*5898. (Meine Kriegserinnerungen.) My war memories. Tr. anon. L: Hutchinson 1920. 2v. (401), 792p. front. maps. 22cm. [BM]
[Tr. appears to be excellent; not very hard to do, as the style is simple.]
*5899. do. 1920. [same] L--'s own story, Aug. 1914-November 1918. NY: Harper. 2v. 477; 473p. 21cm. [LC]

LUDOLF, Hiob W. 1624-1704.
5900. Curious observations concerning the products of Russia. In

LUDOLF, Hiob W.
Brand, "Am., Journal, etc." #741.

LUDWIG I. (K: A:) König v. Bayern, 1786-1868. Sel. in C50;63;303; 317;388;#6209a.
§5901. (Gedichte.) A sel. from the poems...imitated...by G: Everill. L: Smith, Elder 1837. xiv;150p. 16cm. [BM]
[Correct; not very poetical.]
§5902. do. 1844. [same] 2d ed. Munich: Franz. 108p. 12. [LCO]
[55 poems.]
*5903. (Walhallas Genossen.) A translation of Walhalla's inmates, described by L: I. With a description of Walhalla, etc. By G: Everill. Munich: G: Franz 1845. 217p. 20cm. [BM]

LUDWIG F:, prince of Wirtemberg, 16th cent. Sel. in C483.

LUDWIG, prince of Anhalt-Cöthen, 1579-1649. Sel. in C483.

LUDWIG Sr. (Ma. Js. J: Bp. Dc. Renier Fd. C: Zb. Ant.) Erzherzog v. Oesterreich, 1847-1915.
§5904. (Die Karawanen-Strasse v. Aegypten nach Syrien.) The caravan route between Egypt and Syria. Tr. Ern. Hesse-Wartegg. 23 il. by the author. L: Chatto & Windus 1881. x;68p. 22cm. [BM.LC]
[Very free and easy.]
§5905. (Levkosia, die Hauptstadt von Cypern.) L--, the capital of Cyprus. Tr. anon. L: K.Paul 1881. 12 il. 70pp. 24cm. [BM]
[Same comment as on foregoing. Same translator?]

LUDWIG (really Cohn), El. 1881- .
5910. (Bismarck, Geschichte eines Kämpfers.) Bismarck: the story of a fighter. Tr. E. and C. Paul. L: Allen & Unwin; Bost: Little, Brown 1927. 646p. 9 x 6 in. [EC.AC]
[See also #5914; possibly the same.]
5910a. do. 1927. Bismarck: the trilogy of a fighter. Putnam. 418p. il. 8. [EC]
*5911. (Genie und Charakter. 20 männliche Bildnisse.) Genius and character. Tr. K. Burke. L: Cape 1927. 330p. ports. 20cm. [BM]
[Germans included are: F: the Gt, Stein, Bismarck, Rathenau, Goethe and Schiller, Dehmel; also, Portrait of an officer.]
*5912. do. 1927. [same] NY: Harcourt. 246p. ports. 20cm. [BM]
[Instead of essay on Machiavelli, this ed. has: Lord Byron and Lassalle.]
*5913. (Napoleon.) N--. Tr. E. and C. Paul. L: Allen & Unwin 1927. xii;707p. ports. 21cm. [BM]
*5914. (Volk und Krone. 1870. Die Entlassung.) Bismarck, the trilogy of a fighter. (Three plays.) King and people. Union. Dismissal. Tr. anon. L: Putnam 1927. xiii;464p. 22cm. [BM]
*5915. (Wilhelm II.) Kaiser W: II. Tr. Ethel C. Mayne. L;NY: Putnam 1926. xvi;459p. il. 22cm. [LC.BM]
*5916. do. 1927. [same] Putnam. xviii;528p. il. 24cm. [LC]

LUDWIG, J. M.
*5917. Pontresina and its neighborhood. Tr. F. S. Reilly. L: Longmans; Lpz: Engelmann 1876. 108p. 15cm. [BM]
*5918. do. 1879. [same] 4th (2d Engl.) ed. L: E.Stanford. 148p. 14cm. [BM]

LUDWIG, O: 1813-65.
5919. (Der Erbförster.) The hereditary forester. Tr. Af. Remy. 1913-15. In C154(9).
§5920. do. The forest warden. Tr. Paula Green. "Poet-Lore," vol. 24(1913). [Fails in the colloquial style.]
§5921. do. 1912. [same] Bost: Badger. [Separate issue of foregoing.] [AC]
5922. (Zwischen Himmel und Erde.) Between heaven and earth. Tr. anon. L;Glasgow: Gowans & Gray 1911. viii;294p. 18cm. [BM]
[Possibly by A. Gowans; see translator list.]

LUDWIG, O:
5923. do. 1913-15. Tr. Muriel Almon. In C154(9).
5923a. do. 1928. Tr. B. Q. Morgan. 206 leaves. 25cm. Tw. [SU]

"LUDWIG, O:" (i.e., El. Frhr. v. Puttkamer, 1802-75)
5923b. (Der Tote von St. Annas Kapelle.) The dead man of St. Anne's chapel, a criminal story in four parts. Tr. anon. "Blackwood's Mag." 47(1840):575, etc. (B15a)

LUEBKE, W: 1826-93.
5924. (Geschichte der Kirchenbaukunst.) Ecclesiastical art in Germany during the middle ages. Tr. from 5th Ger. ed. by L. A. Wheatley. Ed: Jack; L: Simpkin, Marshall 1870. 299p. il. 24cm. [BM] [LC has: Cassell 1870, same paging.]
5925. do. 1873. [same] 2d ed. Ed: Jack. [LC]
5926. do. 1877. [same] 4th ed. [LC]
*5927. (Geschichte der Plastik.) Hist. of sculpture. Tr. Fanny E. Bunnètt. L: Smith, Elder 1872. 2v. xii;409; 500p. il. 26cm. [BM.LC]
*5928. do. 1878. [same] New ed. [EC]
*5929. (Grundriss der Kunstgeschichte.) Hist. of art. Tr. from 4th Ger. ed. by Fanny E. Bunnètt. L: Smith, Elder 1868. 2v. xvi;466; 473p. il. 24cm. [LC has 1869.] [BM.LC]
*5930. do. 1875. [same] 3d ed. [EC]
*5931. do. 1878. [same] 2d ed. [LC]
*5932. do. 1878. Outlines of the hist. of art. New tr. from the 7th Ger. ed. Ed. by C. Cook. NY: Dodd, Mead. 2v. xvii;571; 695p. il. 24cm. [LC.BM]
[Cook censures Miss Bunnett's tr. and claims this is entirely new under the supervision of E: L. Burlingame. In fact, entire sections of her tr. (which I consider very good) are taken over verbatim with little or no alteration.]
*5933. do. 1880. [same] 2v. [AC]
*5934. do. 1881. [same] Student's ed. 2v. [AC]
*5935. do. 1904. [same] Minutely rev. and largely rewritten by R. Sturgis. NY: Dodd, Mead. 2v. x;626; 557p. il. 25cm. [LC.BM]
["The basis...is (#5932)...and the text of that tr. has been retained where no change has seemed desirable."]
*5936. do. 1922. [same] reissue. NY: Dodd, Mead. [BM]
5937. (Vorschule zur Geschichte der Kirchenbaukunst des Mittelalters) Introd. to a hist. of church architecture. Tr. W: Bell and condensed. In Bell, W:, "Altertümliches Wortregister der Baukunst, etc." L: Parker 1855. pp. vii-xx. 21cm. [BM]

LUECKE, F: 1791-1855.
5938. Reminiscences of Schleiermacher. In #8293, pp. 3-86.

LUEGER, K: 1844-1910. See Harden, Mx., Monarchs and Men, #3701.

LUETZOW, K: F: Arn. v. 1832-97.
5939. The Belvedere gallery (in Vienna): 40 etchings after old masters by W: Unger. Descriptive text by L--. Tr. anon. 1893. 48p. text. 68 x 52cm. [BM]
5940. (Die Kunstschätze Italiens.) Art treasures of Italy. Tr. Susan T. Hooper. Bost: Fine art pub. 1888. 2v. in 12 pts. il. 45 x 32cm. [LC]
5941. Restoration of the Venus of Melos by A. Wittig. Tr. Lewis J. Block. 1875. In C300 (5).

LUISE Anete. Ma., consort of F: A:, crown prince of Saxony.
*5942. (Mein Lebensweg.) My own story. Tr. anon. L: Nash 1911. 285p. il. 22cm. [Assisted by Mrs. Maude Ma. Chester ffoulkes in the prep. of the book.] [BM]

LUISE A:e W:e Ame. 1776-1810, Königin v. Preussen. Sel. in C12.
See Kluckhohn, A:, A memorial, #5081.
See Merz, H:, Louise, queen of Prussia, #6215a.
See Mühlbach, Lu., Napoleon and the queen of Prussia, #6460.

LUISE Hte., Kurfürstin v. Brandenburg, 1627-67. Sel. in C232;244;269;271;273;486;489;570;#8904.

LUTHER, Hs. 1879- . Sel. in C563.

LUTHER[1], Mn. 1483-1546.

ARRANGEMENT

Collections
Selections
Hymns
Letters
Table Talk
Biography

COLLECTIONS

*5943. 1883. The first principles of the reformation. The 95 theses and the three primary works. Tr. w. introds. H: Wace and C. A. Buchheim. L: Murray. lxxxviii;245p. front. (port.) 22cm. [BM] [Address to the nobility of the Ger. nation; Concerning Christian liberty; On the Babylonian captivity of the church.]
*5944. 1896. [same] Luther's primary works. L: Hodder & Stoughton. xvi;492p. 20cm. [Adds the short and greater catechism. Essays by Wace and Buchheim are appended.] [BM]
5945. 1904. Precious and sacred writings of Mn. L--. Ed. by J. N. Lenker. Minneapolis, Minn: Lutherans in all lands co. 21cm. (In progress.) [LC]
**5946. 1915. Works. Phil: Holman. 21cm. (In progress.) [LC] [Done in collaboration and with great care; should become definitive Engl. ed.]

SELECTIONS

Sel. in C12;43;45-6;56;86;106;129;131;166;190;193;194*;195;208;230-5;244*;269;271*;273;276;366*;373;388*;399;400;423;469;486;489*;530;538;570;574.
5947. CHARLES, MRS. ELIZ. Watchwords for the warfare of life. NY: Dodd 1868. [Probably identical with the following.] [AC]
5948. do. 1869. [same title] L;NY: Nelson. xix;354p. 19cm. [BM] [Sel. and tr. chiefly from his letters and table talk.]
5949. do. 1884. [same] Nelson. [AC]
5950. GRIGNON, R. S. The 95 theses, and, Concerning Christian liberty. Also, Address...respecting the reformation of the Christian estate, tr. C. A. Buchheim. In The Harvard Classics, vol. 36, pp. 265-397. NY: Collier 1910. [LC]
5951. HIRSCHFELD, Ph. C: Gems of L--. L;Dublin: Tims 1838. 111p. 15cm. [BM]
[329 brief prose extracts. "I have gathered these pebbles out of the brook of L--, endeavouring in the tr. to retain their orig. pointedness."]
5952. do. 1841. [same?] Manna of the heart. Groombridge. 18. [EC]
5953. MACAULAY, DR. Luther anecdotes...gathered from his books, letters, and history. L: Relig. tract soc. 1883. 160p. 17cm. [BM] [AC has: NY: Scribner & W. 1883.]
5954. MORRIS, J: GOTTLIEB. Quaint sayings and doings concerning L--. Phil: Lindsay & Blakiston 1859. 284p. 12. [LC] [Many selections from German writers, unascribed.]
5955. MUELLER, J: TD. Five minutes daily with L--: daily lessons. NY: Macmillan 1926. vii;375p. 21cm. [LC]

[1]Sermons and strictly theological matter not included.

LUTHER, Mn.
5956. O'CONNER, H: L--'s own statements concerning his teaching and its results, from the earliest and best ed. of his Ger. and Lat. works. NY: Benziger 1884. 12. [AC]
5957. STEINHÄUSER, AB. T. W. Luther primer: a little book of goodly excerpts. Columbia, S. C: Survey pub. 1917. viii;178p. 18cm. [LC]
5958. Bondage of the will. Tr. H: Cole. Eedes 1823. 8. [EC]
5959. do. 1823. Tr. Vaughan. L: Hamilton. 8. [EC]
5960. The favour of princes. Tr. anon. L: Macmillan 1899. 270p.8[EC]
5961. The interpretation of M. Luther...of a moonkish calfe, etc. In Melanchthon, Ph., "Of two wonderful popish monsters, etc.," #6182.
5962. Treatise touching the liberty of a Christian man. Tr. Jas. Bell. L: Longmans 1817. 12. [EC]

HYMNS

§5963. 1845. Hymns of the reformation by Dr. Mn. L-- and others from the German...his life...P. Melanchthon. Tr. H. J. Fry. L: Gilpin. viii;231p. 12cm. [BM]
[Other hymn-writers are: Gellert, Lavater, D. P. Nicolai, J. Ringwald, J. Rist (2), Spitta, J. Walther.]
5964. 1847. Hymns. Tr. by Rev. J. Anderson. Collins. 12. [EC]
§5965. 1853. [same as #5963] L: Partridge, Oakey. [BM]
§5966. 1853. The spiritual songs of Mn. L--. Tr. J: Hunt. L: Hamilton, Adams. 190p. 18cm. [BM]
[Front. (port.) by E: Schuler after Dietrich. Mostly very free adaptations.]
§5967. 1854. Mn. L--'s spiritual songs. Tr. R. Massie. L: Hatchard. xviii;92p. 18cm. [BM.LCO]
5968. 1875. Luther as a hymnist. (Compilation of L--'s hymns) by B. Pick. Luth. bk. store. 12. [Translations? Cf. #6965.] [AC]
§5969. 1883. (36) Hymns set to their orig. melodies. Ed. L. W. Bacon. NY: Scribner. 70p. 24 x 18cm. [BM.LCO]
[Other translators are: F. E. Cox, R. Massie, A. T. Russel, C. Winkworth. Bacon's own tr. seem to me the best.]
*5970. 1897. Luther's song-book. Tr. G: Macdonald. In his "Rampolli." C385. [Quite good.]
*5971. 1917. L--'s hymns. Tr. Jas. F. Lambert. Introd. J: A. W. Haas. United Lutheran pub. xviii;160p. il. 22cm. [LCM]

LETTERS

*5972. 1865. (Dr. Mn. L--'s Briefe an Frauen.) L--'s letters to women. Tr. Mrs. Malcolm. L: Chapman & Hall. vii;168p. 19cm. [BM]
[64 letters coll. by K. Zimmermann.]
§5973. 1908. The letters of ---. Sel. and tr. Marg. A. Currie. L: Macmillan. xxxv;482p. 23cm. [Style is inadequate.] [BM.LC]
*5974. 1913-18. L--'s corr. and other contemp. letters. Tr. and ed. Preserved Smith. Phil: Luth. pub. soc. 2v. 22cm. [LC]
[Vol. 2 tr. in part by C: Ml. Jacobs.]

TABLE TALK

*5975. 1652. Dris. Martini Lutheris colloquia mensalia; or...divine discourses at his table. Coll. first...by Dr. Antonius Lauterbach and afterwards disposed...by J: Aurifaber, w. pref. by him. Tr. Capt. Henrie Bell. L: W:Du-Gard. ff. A-C, 541p. 33cm. [BM]
[Really excellent tr. Front. (full length port.) engr. W.Trevethen.]
*5976. 1791. [same] 2d ed. Colloquia mensalia; or, the familiar discourses...at his table. Prefixed, the life and character...by J: Gb. Burckhardt. Also Pref. J: Ryland. L: Heptinstal. xxiv;502p. 37cm. [BM]

LUTHER, Mn.--Table Talk
[Same text as before; spelling modernized. Front. (port. appar. taken from 1st ed.) engr. C. Warren.]
*5977. 1818. [same] The familiar discourses, etc. New rev. ed. by Js. Kerby. Lewes: Baxter; L: Baldwin, Craddock & Joy, etc. xliv; 476p. 21cm. [BM.LCO]
[Some passages omitted from 1st ed. Front. (port.) after painting by Ab. Durenin.]
†5978. 1832. Table talk; or, some choice fragments from the familiar discourse, etc. L: Longmans. xxvi;323p. 12. [BM]
[P. Smith (in #5988) says this book transforms L. into an unctuous Engl. clergyman, grave and formal.]
*5979. 1848. Table talk. Ed. and tr. W: Hazlitt. L: Bogue. xxvi;390p. 18cm. [Really only a revision of Bell's tr., perhaps without even consulting the German. Contains about one-fourth of Aurifaber; see #5988. No port.] [BM.LCO]
*5980. 1857. [same] New ed. with life of L-- by Ax. Chalmers. Also with add. after Michelet and Audin. L: Bohn. cii;390p. 17cm.
[Port. Hinchliff after Cranach.] [BM.LC]
*5981. 1875. [same] New ed. L: Bell. [LC]
*5982. 1883. Table talk. 4th centenary ed. Sel. and ed. (and tr?) Prof. J: Gibb. L: Unwin. 141p. 14cm. [BM]
[Very small sel. competently tr.]
*5983. 1883. Table talk. Extracts sel. by Dr. Macaulay. L: Relig. tract soc. 127p. 15cm. [These sel. made from #5976.] [BM]
5984. 1883. L-- at table: a few elegant extracts from his talk. By W. H. Anderdon. L: Burns & Oates. 32p. 18cm. [BM]
[The term "elegant" is ironic. The Roman Catholic author set out to make L. as odious as possible. Commentary added.]
*5985. 1886. Selections from the table talk. Tr. Capt. H: Bell. L: Cassell. 192p. 13cm. [Modernized; otherwise unedited.] [BM]
*5986. 1893. NY: Stokes. 141p. 18. [Probably same as #5982.] [LCO]
*5987. 1902. [same as #5980] L: Bell. 390p. 18cm. [LC]
*5988. 1915. Conversations. Sel. tr. and ed. Preserved Smith and H. P. Gallinger. Bost;NY: Pilgrim press. 260p. il. 19cm. [LC]

BIOGRAPHY

5989. The autobiogr. of Mn. L--. Tr. J: P. Lawson. L: Smith & Elder 1836. 8. [BM]
["The present vol. may therefore be regarded both as a new work, and as a tr. of M. Michelet." (Cf. following entry.) It was, however, quite independently planned and executed.]
*5990. 1846. (Mémoires de L-- écrits par lui-même.) Life of L. written by himself. Coll. and arr. by M. Michelet. Tr. W: Hazlitt. L: Bogue. xv;471p. 18cm. [Front. (port.) after Cranach.] [BM]
§5991. 1846. do. Life of L. gathered from his own writings by M. Michelet. Tr. G. H. Smith. L: Whittaker. 108p. 23cm. [BM]
[Prtd. in double columns. Not so good: makes free with the orig.]
5992. 1846. do. NY: Appleton. 314p. [Probably Hazlitt's tr.] [LCO]
§5993. 1853. [same as #5991] Universal lib. Biogr. vol. 1. 108p. 23cm. [Front. (port.) and t.p. engr. by Dalziel.] [BM]
Liber vagatorum. Ed. by Luther. 1528. See A307.
See Burckhardt, J: Life and character, etc., #938; 5976.
See Döllinger, J. Luther, a succinct view, #1250.
See Fick, Hm., Life and deeds, #1617.
See Freytag, Gst., Doktor L--, #1941.
See Gelzer, H:, Life of M. L--. #2147.
See Grisar, H., L--, #3498.
See Harnack, A., M. L--, the prophet of the reformation, #3709.
See Just, G., Life of L--, #4780.
See Köstlin, J., Life of L--, #5143 seq.

LUTHER, Mn.--Biography
See Melanchthon, Ph., #6180 seq.
See Meurer, M., Life of M. L--, #6220.
See Nebe, A., L-- as spiritual adviser, #6695.
See Pfeilschmidt, Ern., L-- at Coburg, #7139.
See Pfizer, G., Life of L--, #7146.
See Rein, W:, The life of M. L--, #7380.
See Scheibel, J. G., Life of M. L--, #7720.
See Schücking, L., L-- in Rome, #8663.
See Stein, A., Count Erbach, #9031; Kath. v. Bora, #9028; L-- and the cardinal, #9027. Prince Abr. of Brandenburg, #9033.
See Tischer, J., Life of L--, #9409.
See Uhlhorn, G., L-- and the Swiss, #9497.
See Wildenhahn, C:, The blind girl of Wittenberg, #10203; The diet of Augsburg, #10206.

LUTROW, ---, Sel. in C36.

MACKAY, John Henry, 1864- .
*5994. (Die Anarchisten.) The anarchists: a pict. of civil. at the close of the 19th cent. Tr. G: Schumm and Sa. E. Holmes. Bost: Tucker 1891. x;305p. 19cm. [LC.BM]

"MADELEINE, Me." (i.e., Me. Madeleine (Günther), Freifrau v. Puttkamer, 1881- .) Sel. in C28.
5995. Hydromel and rue. Tr. Fd. E. Kappy. L: Griffiths 1907. 91p. 19cm. [BM]

MAEDER, Alphonse
5996. Marriage and self-development. Tr. 1926. In C308.

MAEURER, W: Sel. in C50*.

MAGDEBURG, Jm. d. 1565. Sel. in C244;271.

MAHLER, Gst. 1860- . See Stefan-Grünfeldt, Pl., G. M--, #9018.

MAHLMANN, Sf. A: 1771-1826. Sel. in C44;51;67;106;152;371;387-9;391; 393;543.

"MALTITZ, Hm. v." (i.e., Hm. Klencke, 1813-81). Sel. in #6209a.

MANDELSLO, J: Abr. v. 1616-44.
5997. (Morgenländische Reisebeschreibung.) The voyages and travels (of M--) into the East Indies, 1638-40. In 3 books. Il. with maps and figs. Tr. J: Davies of Kidwelly. L: Prtd. for Dring & Starkey 1662. 287p. 29cm. [BM]
[Bound with Olearius' "Voyages and travels." This account was written by Olearius from M--'s notes.]
5998. do. 1669. [same] 2d ed. corr. L: Starkey & Basset. 11, leaves, 232p. 32cm. [Bound with Olearius' "Voyages, etc."] [BM.LC]
5999. do. 1705. Voyages and travels, etc. In Harris, J:, "Navigantium atque itinerantium biblioteca," or, a complete coll. of voyages and travels. Tr. by J: Harris? Vol. 2, pp. 115-176. 38cm. [BM]
6000. do. 1744. The remarks and observations made by M-- in his passage...through several countries of the Indies. In Harris, J:, "Navigantium, etc.," vol. 1. pp. 749-810. L: T.Woodward, etc. 41cm. [Somewhat less in quantity than #5997.] [BM]

MANN, F. O.
6001. The devil in a nunnery. Tr. M. J. Rudwin. 1921. In C482.

MANN, H: 1871- .
§6002. (Der Untertan.) The patrioteer. Author. tr. Ern. Boyd. NY: Harcourt 1921. 388p. 19cm. [LC]

MANN, H: - Der Untertan
[Apparently not completely master of the German.]

MANN, Klaus, 1906- .
6003. (Kindernovelle.) The fifth child. Tr. L. A. Shears. NY: Liveright 1927. 141p. D. [AC]

MANN, T: 1875- .
*6004. [Coll.] Death in Venice. Tr. K. Burke. NY: Knopf 1925. 284p. 19cm. [Death in Venice ("Der Tod in Venedig"); Tristan (do.); *Tonio Kröger (do.).--Judging by the last, very good.] [LC]
*6005. (Buddenbrooks.) Buddenbrooks. Tr. H. T. Lowe-Porter. L: Secker; NY: Knopf 1924. 2v. 389; 359p. 19cm. [BM.LC]
[The Engl. is smooth and the general sense is well caught; but there is much in the orig. not preserved in the tr.]
6006. (Das Eisenbahnunglück.) A railway accident. Tr. W. Katzin. 1927. In C367.
*6007. (Der Zauberberg.) The magic mountain. Tr. H. T. Lowe-Porter. L: Secker; NY: Knopf 1927. 2v. 446; 471p. 19cm. [BM.LC]
[Cf. comment on #6005. On the whole, excellent.]
*6008. (Herr und Hund.) Bashan and I. Tr. H. G. Scheffauer. NY: Holt; L: Collins 1923. 247p. 19cm. [LC.BM]
[Excellent despite one error in the first part, and the breaking up of Mann's sentences.]
*6009. do. 1927. [same] Cheap ed. L: Collins. 247p. [EC]
*6010. (Königliche Hoheit.) Royal highness. Tr. A. C. Curtis. L: Sidgwick & Jackson 1916. ix;362p. 19cm. [BM]
*6011. do. 1926. [same] NY: Knopf. ix;339p. 19cm. [LC]
6012. Marriage in transition. Tr. 1926. In C308.
6013. (Tonio Kröger.) T-- K--. Tr. B. Q. Morgan. 1913-15. In C154(19).

MANTEUFFEL, Ula. Zöge v., Frau v. Trebra-Lindenau, 1850- .
6014. Violetta: a romance. Tr. Mrs. A. L. Wister. Phil: Lippincott 1886. 368p. 18cm. [LC]

MARCKS, Er. 1861- . Sel. in C563.

MARENHOLTZ-BUELOW, Bta. Ma. Baronin v. 1810-93.
6015. (Erinnerungen an F: Froebel.) Reminisc. of F: Froebel. Tr. Mrs. Horace Mann. Bost: Lee & Shepard; NY: Dillingham 1877. 359p. 17cm. [LC.BM]
6016. do. 1887. [same] NY: Scribner & W. [AC]
6017. do. 1892. [same] Scribner. 19cm. [LC]
6018. do. 1905. [same] Scribner. 20cm. [LC]

MARGGRAFF, Hm. 1809-64. Sel. in C50.

"MARHOLM, La." See Hansson, La. (Mohr), 1854- .

MARIA THERESIA, 1717-80. Sel. in C288.
See Horn, W. O. v. Ma. T--. #4596.

MARIA, queen of Hungary, 1505-58. Sel. in C276.

MARISCHKA, Ern. See Granichstaedten, Bruno.

MARKGRAF VON BRANDENBURG. See Albrecht.

MARKGRAF VON BRANDENBURG-ANSPACH. See Gros, K: H:, #3508.

MARKGRAF VON HOHENBURG (Diepold v. Vohburg). fl. 1212-25. Sel. in C27;310;427.

MARKGRAF O: VON BRANDENBURG MIT DEM PFEIL, fl. 1266-1309. Sel. in C27;366;532.

"MARLITT, E." (i.e., Ege. John, 1825-87).

"MARLITT, E."
*6019. (Amtmanns Magd.) The bailiff's maid: a romance. Tr. Mrs. A. L. Wister. Phil: Lippincott 1881. 272p. 19cm. [Very good tr.] [LC]
*6020. do. 1881. [same] NY: Munro. Seaside lib. 32cm. [LC]
*6021. do. 1888. [same] NY: Munro. Pocket ed. 204p. 19cm. [LC]
6022. (Das Eulenhaus.) The owl-house: a posthumous novel (finished by by W. Heimburg). Tr. Ma. S. and G. H. Smith. NY: Munro 1888. 275p. 19cm. [LC]
6023. do. 1888. The owl's nest. Tr. Mrs. A. L. Wister. Phil: Lippincott. 362p. 18cm. [LC]
6024. do. 1893. The owl's nest. Tr. Hettie E. Miller. Chic: Weeks. 269p. 20cm. [LC]
6025. do. 1900. Wister's tr. Lippincott. [LC]
6026. do. 1912. [same] [LC]
*6027. (Das Geheimnis der alten Mamsell.) The old mam'selle's secret. Tr. Mrs. A. L. Wister. Phil: Lippincott 1868. 297p. 19cm. [LCO.BM]
*6028. do. 1869. [same] Lippincott. 312p. 19cm. [LC]
*6029. do. 1871. The old maid's secret. Tr. H. J. G. L: Strahan. 350p. 19cm. [BM]
*6030. do. 1876. [same as #6028] [LC]
§6031. do. 1882. Old ma'm'selle's secret. Tr. Mrs. M. S. Smith. NY: Munro. Seaside lib. 47p. 32cm. [Not very good.] [LC]
6032. do. 1882. The old maid's secret. New ed. L: Ward, Lock. 12[EC] [Probably same as #6029.]
6033. do. 1886. The old mam'selle's secret. NY: Lovell. D. [AC] [Probably Wister's tr.]
*6034. do. 1886. [same as #6028] [LC]
§6035. do. 1886. Smith's tr. (#6031). NY: Munro. 259p. 18cm. [LC]
*6036. do. 1896. [same as #6028] [LC]
*6037. do. 1911. [same] [LC]
§6038. (Das Heideprinzesschen.) The princess of the moor. Tr. anon. Lpz: Tauchnitz 1872. 2v. 331; 307p. 16cm. [BM]
*6039. do. 1876. The little moorland princess. Tr. Mrs. A. L. Wister. Phil: Lippincott. 408p. 19cm. [LC]
*6040. do. 1881. [same] L: Ward, Lock. 387p. 18cm. [BM]
§6041. do. 1883. The little princess. Tr. Blanche E. Slade. L: Remington. 2v. 324; 296p. 18cm. [Tr. is weak on her German.] [BM]
§6042. do. 1888. The princess of the moor. NY: Munro. 301p. 19cm [LC] [Probably same tr. as #6038.]
*6043. do. 1900. [same as #6039] [LC]
6044. (Die Frau mit den Karfunkelsteinen.) The lady with the rubies. Tr. Mrs. A. L. Wister. Phil: Lippincott 1885. 334p. 19cm. [LC]
6045. do. 1885. Tr. Ma. S. Smith. NY: Munro. Seaside lib. 72p. 32cm. [LC]
6046. do. 1885. [same] NY: Munro. Pocket ed. 273p. 16. [LC]
6047. do. 1886. The lady with the garnets. Tr. Baroness Langenau. L: Stock. 318p. 19cm. [BM]
6048. do. 1895. The lady with the rubies. Tr. Hettie E. Miller. Chic: Weeks. 370p. il. 20cm. [LC]
6049. (Die zweite Frau.) The second wife: a romance. Tr. Mrs. A. L. Wister. Phil: Lippincott 1874. 302p. 18cm. [LC]
§6050. do. 1875. Tr. Annie Wood. L: Bentley. 3v. 18cm. [BM] [Begins with chapter 3 and rewrites freely.]
§6051. do. 1880. Wood's tr. NY: Munro. Seaside lib. 52p. 32cm. [LC]
§6052. do. 1881. The second wife: a romance of Castle Schönwerth. Tr. anon. L: Ward, Lock. 318p. 17cm. [Too free.] [BM]
§6053. do. 1887. Wood's tr. NY: Munro. Pocket ed. 263p. 18cm. [LC]
6053a. do. 1891. Brave woman. Tr. M. P. Waterman. NY;L: 12. [EC]
6054. do. 1902. Wister's tr. [same as #6049.] [LC]
6055. Fighting with fate. A novel. Tr. anon. L: Remington 1881. 323p. 18cm. [BM]

"MARLITT, E."
§6056. (Goldelse.) Gold Else. Tr. W. C. Wrankmore. Lpz: W. Baensch 1868. 2v. 164; 160p. 15cm. [BM]
*6057. do. 1868. Gold Elsie. Tr. Mrs. A. L. Wister. Phil: Lippincott. 344p. 18cm. [LC,BM]
*6058. do. 1873. [same] L: Strahan. 344p. 18cm. [BM]
6059. do. 1881. Gold Elsie. Tr. Ma. S. Smith and son. NY: Munro. Pocket ed. 284p. 18cm. [LC]
*6060. do. 1883. [same as #6057] [LC]
6061. do. 1887. Gold Elsie. Tr. anon. NY: Lovell. 235p. 19cm. [LC]
*6062. do. 1896. [same as #6057] [LC]
6063. (Im Hause des Kommerzienrates.) At the councilor's; or, a nameless history. Tr. Mrs. A. L. Wister. Phil: Lippincott 1876. 356p. 18cm. [LC]
§6064. do. 1876. In the counselor's house. Tr. anon. L: Bentley. 3v. 8. [Poor, loose and incorrect. "Academy" (10(1876):379) says tr. is Annie Wood.] [BM]
6065. do. 1880. Tr. anon. NY: Munro. [AC]
[Probably by Annie Wood; see next entry.]
§6066. do. 1888. In the counselor's house. Tr. Annie Wood. NY: Munro. Pocket ed. 294p. 19cm. [LC]
6067. do. 1904. [same as #6063] [LC]
6068. (Im Schillingshof.) In the Schillingscourt. Tr. Mrs. A. L. Wister. Phil: Lippincott 1879. 386p. 19cm. [LC]
§6069. do. 1879. Tr. Emily R. Steinestel. NY: Munro. Seaside lib. 47p. 32cm. [Fair to good tr.] [LC]
§6070. do. 1888. [same] NY: Munro. Pocket ed. 248p. 19cm. [LC]
6071. do. 1896. Tr. Hettie E. Miller. Chic: Weeks. 488p. il.20cm. [LC]
6072. do. 1901. [same as #6068] [LC]
6073. Magdalena. Tr. Mrs. A. L. Wister. Phil: From "Lippincott's mag." 1870. 49p. 22cm. [BM]
[Magdalena, pp. 1-34. Also, The lonely ones, by Pl. Heyse.]
6074. do. 1872-6. Tr. Mrs. Elgard. Phil: Lippincott n.d. il. 8. [AC]
6075. do. 1877. [same as #6073?] Tr. Mrs. Wister. Phil: Lippincott. 49p. (B12)
6076. Over yonder: novelette. Tr. anon. Phil: Lippincott 1869. 43p. 8. [Reprinted from "Lippincott's mag." Cf. the following.] [LC]
6077. do. 1872-6. Tr. Mrs. Elgard. Phil. Lippincott n.d. [AC]
*6078. (Reichsgräfin Gisela.) The countess Gisela. Tr. anon. L: Macmillan 1870. 358p. 19cm. [BM]
[Mostly excellent, but with some errors.]
6079. do. 1872-6. Tr. A. Nahmer. NY: Harper n.d. 8. [AC]
6080. do. 1879. Tr. Mrs. A. L. Wister. Phil: Lippincott. 424p. 18cm. [LC]
6081. do. 1879. Tr. anon. NY: Munro. Seaside lib. 60p. 32cm. [LC]
6082. do. 1888. [same] NY: Munro. Pocket ed. 317p. 19cm. [LC]
6083. do. 1897. [same as #6080.] [LC]
*6084. (Zwölf Apostel.) The twelve apostles. Tr. Helen Zimmern. 1880. In C575-7.

MARNER, Der, fl. 1230-70. Sel. in C310;366 (under Walther); 427;530; 532.

MARPERGER, Bh. Wl. 1681-1746. Sel. in C276;486.

MARSCHNER, H: 1795-1861. The templar and the Jewess. Opera. See Wohlbrück, W. A.

MARTELL, K: ca. 688-741. Sel. in C123.

MARTIN, Ern. 1841-1910.
6085. The minnesingers in Thuringia and the contest of the singers in the Wartburg. Tr. G. A. Greene. 1907. In C555.

MARTIN, Rd.
6086. (Die Zukunft Russlands und Japans.) The future of Russia. Tr. Hulda Friederichs. L: Smith, Elder 1906. xx;305p. 20cm. [BM]
[The tr. is good where it follows closely; done in sections.]

MARTIUS, K: F: Ph. v. 1794-1868, and J: B. Spix.
*6087. (Reise in Brasilien.) Travels in B--...1817-20. Tr. H. E. Lloyd. L: Longmans 1824. 2v. xix;327; 298p. 9 pl. 21cm. [BM.LC]
[Only vol. 1 of orig. is tr.]

MARX, Ad. Bh. 1795-1866.
6088. Beethoven's F minor sonata. Tr. A. E. Kroeger. 1874. In C300(4).

MARX, K: F: H: 1796-1877.
*6089. (Akesios. Blicke in die ethischen Beziehungen der Medizin.) The moral aspect of medical life. Tr. Jas. Mackness. L: Churchill 1846. xiv;348p. 20cm. [BM.LC]
6090. (Ueber die Abnahme der Krankheiten durch die Zunahme der Zivilisation.) On the decrease of disease effected by the progress of civilization. Tr. R. Willis. L: Longmans 1844. vii;102p. 17cm.
["I have rather paraphrased than tr. my friend."] [BM]

MARX, K: H: 1818-83. Sel. in C366*;574*.
6091. [Coll.] The Paris commune; includ. The first manifesto of the International on the Franco-Prussian war, The second manifesto of the International on the Franco-Prussian war, The civil war in France. With introd. F: Engels. Notes to the Amer. ed. by Lucien Sanial. NY: NY labor news 1902. xxxv;117p. 19cm. [LC]
6092. [Coll.] 1919. [same] NY: NY labor news. 117p. [LC]
*6093. [Coll.] 1926. Selected essays. Tr. H. J. Stenning. NY: Internat. pub. 207p. 19cm. [LC.BM]
[A criticism of the Hegelian philos. of right ("Zur Kritik der Hegelschen Rechtsphilosophie"); On the Jewish question ("Zur Judenfrage"); On the king of Prussia and social reform ("Kritische Randglossen zu dem Artikel: Der König von Preussen und die Sozialreform"); Moralizing criticism and critical morality ("Die moralisierende Kritik und die kritische Moral"); A polemic against K: Heinzen; Proudhon (do.); French materialism; The English revolution.]
*6094. (Das Elend der Philosophie.) The poverty of philos. A tr. of "Misère de la philosophie" (A reply to "La philosophie de la misère" of M. Proudhon). Pref. F: Engels. Tr. H. Quelch. L: 20th cent. press 1906. xix;195p. 19cm. [BM]
*6095. (Das Kapital.) Capital: a crit. analysis. Tr. from 3d ed. by S: Moore and E: B. Aveling, and ed. F: Engels. L: Sonnenschein 1887. 2v. 816p. 22cm. [Only book 1 of the orig. is tr.] [BM.LC]
*6096. do. 1890? [same] NY: Humboldt pub. xviii;506p. 23cm. [LC]
*6097. do. 1893. The theory of value, complete...the first 9 chapters of..."Capital." Tr. anon. L: W:Reeves. Bellamy lib. 189p. 21cm. [BM]
*6098. do. 1895. [same] L: Reeves. 189p. [BM]
*6099. do. 1896. [same as #6095] 5th ed. L: Sonnenschein. xxxi; 816p. [BM]
*6100. do. 1897. The first nine chapters of Capital. Tr. from 3d Ger. ed. by Moore and Aveling. Ed. Engels. Reprtd. from stereotyped plates of complete work. L: Sonnenschein. xxxi;213p. 21cm.
[Taken from #6095.] [BM]
*6101. do. 1906-9. Capital: a critique of polit. econ. Chic: Kerr. 3v. 23cm. [LC]
[Vol. 1 is same as #6095 with rev. and amplif. from 4th Ger. ed. by Ern. Untermann. Vol. 2. tr. from 2d Ger. ed. by Untermann. Vol. 3. tr. from 1st Ger. ed. by Untermann. Untermann's work not quite as good as that of Aveling and Moore.--BM has: vol. 2., 618p.

MARX, K: H:--Das Kapital
Chic: Kerr; L: Sonnenschein 1907. Vol. 3, 1048p. Chic: Kerr 1909.]
*6102. do. 1908. [same as #6097] 4th ed. L: Reeves. 189p. [BM]
*6103. do. 1919. [same as vol. 1 of #6101] Chic: Kerr. [LC]
6104. do. 1920...A critical analysis of capitalistic production. New ed. L: Glaisher. 8. [Probably same as #6095.] [EC]
6105. do. 1921. The people's Marx. Abr. pop. ed. of Capital. Ed. by Julian Borchardt. Tr. Stephen L. Trask. L;Potsdam: Internat. bookshops. vii;284p. 8. [BM]
6106. do. 1925. Capital. In "Marxian econ. handbook and glossary," by W. H. Emmett. NY: Internat. pub; L: Allen & Unwin. 350p. 22cm. [LC]
*6107. (Die Klassenkämpfe in Frankreich.) Class struggles in France, 1848-50. Introd. F: Engels. Tr. H: Kuhn. NY: NY labor news 1924. x;207p. port. 19cm. [LC.BM]
6107a. The Eighteenth Brumaire of Louis Bonaparte. Tr. Eden and Cedar Paul. Allen 1926. 192p. 8. [EC]
6108. Free trade. A speech...Brussels...1848. Tr. Flor. K. Wischnewetsky. Bost: Lee & Shepard; NY: Dillingham 1888. 48p. 22cm. [Cover title reads: A discourse on free trade.] [LC.BM]
6109. The Gotha program, by K: Marx, and, Did Marx err? by D. De Leon. NY: Socialist labor party 1922. 64p. 19cm. [LC]
6110. (Lohnarbeit und Kapital.) Wage-labour and capital. Tr. J. L. Joynes. New and cheaper ed. L: Modern press 1886. 15p. 23cm. [BM]
6111. do. 1897. [same] New ed. L: 20th cent. press. 24p. 18cm. [LC]
*6112. do. 1902. Wage-labor and capital. Tr. Harriet E. Lothrop. NY: NY labor news. 60; 43p. [Appended: Free trade; tr. Flor.Kelley.][LC]
6113. do. 1908. Joynes' tr. Glasgow: Socialist labour party. 32p. 18cm. [BM]
6114. do. 1918. [same] With introd. F: Engels. Chic: Kerr. 54p.D[AC]
*6115. do. 1925. Tr. Flor. Baldwin. Introd. F: Engels. L: Communist party. 32p. 21cm. [BM]
6116. (Manifest der kommunistischen Partei.) Tr. Miss Helen McFarlane. 1850. In Harvey's "Red Republican."
*6117. do. 1883. Manifesto of the communists, by K: Marx assisted by F: Engels. Tr. S: Moore. 2d ed. L: Internat. working men's assoc; NY: Schaerr & Frantz. 28p. 20cm. [BM]
*6118. do. 1886. [same] L: Internat. pub. 29p. 17cm. [BM.LC]
*6119. do. 1887? [same] 29p. [This copy has no t.p.] [BM]
*6120. do. 1888. Author. Engl. tr. ed. and annotated by F: Engels. 5th ed. L: Reeves. 31p. 17cm. [BM.LC] [Moore's tr., rev. by Moore and Engels.]
*6121. do. 1898. [same] author. Engl. tr. ed. and annotated F: Engels. 2d ed. NY: Socialist labor party. 60p. 18cm. [LC]
6122. do. 1902. [same?] Chic: Kerr. 64p. 15cm. [LC]
6123. do. 1912. [same?] NY: Socialist lit. co. 62p. S. [AC]
6124. Secret diplomatic hist. of the 18th cent. Ed. by E. M. Aveling. L: Sonnenschein 1899. 96p. 18cm. [BM]
6125. Value, price, and profit. Addressed to working men. Ed. Eleanor M. Aveling. L: Sonnenschein 1898. vi;94p. 18cm. [BM]
6126. do. 1908. [same] Glasgow: Socialist labour party. 54p. plus 2p. of "definitions." 18cm. [BM]
6127. do. 1925. [same] L: Allen & Unwin. 94p. 7 x 5 in. [BM]
*6128. (Zur Kritik der politischen Oekonomie.) A contrib. to the critique of polit. econ. Tr. from the 2d Ger. ed. by N. I. Stone. With an appendix containing Marx's introd. to the critique recently published among his posthumous papers. NY: Internat. lib. pub. co. 1904. 314p. 20cm. [LC]
*6129. do. 1904. [same] 2d rev. ed. L: Paul, T. & T. 314p. [BM]
*6130. (Zur Kritik des sozialdemokratischen Programms von Gotha.) The socialist programme. Tr. E. and C. Paul. Glasgow. Socialist

MARX, K: H:
series, no. 1. 1919. 16p. 24cm. [BM]
See Beer, Max, Life and teaching of K: M--, #328.
See Kautsky, K:, Econ. doctrines of K: M--, #4885.
See Liebknecht, W:, K: M-- zum Gedächtnis, #5824.

MASCOV, J: Jk. 1689-1761.
*6131. (Geschichte der Teutschen bis zum Anfang der Franckischen Monarchie.) Hist. of the ancient Germans. Tr. T: Lediard. L: Prtd. Jas. Mechell for the tr. 1737-8. 2v. 25 x 20cm. [BM.LC]

MATHESIUS, J:s, 1504-65. Sel. in C244;269;570.

MATHILDE VON HELLFDE, MATHILDE VON MAGDEBURG. See Mechtild.

MATHILDE, consort of prince Louis of Saxe-Coburg-Gotha, 1877-1906.
6132. (Traum und Leben.) Life-dreams: the poems of a blighted life. Attrib. to Princess M-- of Bavaria. Tr. J: Heard, Jr. Bost: Badger 1913. 78p. 19cm. [LC]

MATKOWSKY, Adalbert, 1858-1909. See Harden, Mx., word portraits #3699.

MATTHISSON, F: v. 1761-1831. Sel. in C10;17;22;25-6;54;88;129;133; 137a;149;171;182;187;219;309;371-3;380;387*;388*;391;399;400;410-1;470-1;531;533;539.
6133. Letters...1785-94: containing...anecdotes relative to the present state of lit. in Germany. Tr. Anne Plumptre. L: Longman & Rees 1799. xvi;544p. 21cm. [BM.LC]
[Letters to von Köpken, Salis, and (chiefly) to C: v. Bonstetten.]

MATZERATH, Cn. Js. 1815-76. Sel. in C174;372.

MAU, A: 1840-1909.
*6134. (Pompeii in Leben und Kunst.) Pompeii, its life and art. Tr. F. W. Kelsey. NY;L: Macmillan 1899. xxii;509p. il. 22cm. [LC.BM]
*6135. do. 1902. [same] New rev. and cor. ed. Macmillan. xxv; 557p. [LC.BM]

MAUTHNER, Fritz, 1849-1923.
**6136. (Aristoteles. Ein unhistorischer Essay.) Aristotle. Tr. C: D. Gordon. Introd. by G: Brandes. L: W.Heinemann 1907. 111p. il. 16cm. [Excellent.] [BM]
§6137. (Xantippe.) Mrs. Socrates. Tr. Jacob W. Hartmann. NY: Internat. pub; L: Nash & Grayson 1927. 254p. 19cm. [LC.BM]
[Tr. omits orig. pref., and thinks he is smarter than the author.]

MAUTNER, E: 1824-89.
6138. Battaglia near Padua. Tr. anon. 1884. 41p. il. In C294.

MAXIMILIAN, emperor of Mexico, 1832-67.
§6139. (Aus meinem Leben.) Recoll. of my life. Tr. anon. L: Bentley 1868. 3v. 20cm. [BM.LC]
[Not very good; tr. does not understand German. This issue omits poems and aphorisms of the orig. ed.]
6140. (Mein erster Ausflug.) On the wing. Tr. A. M. Lushington. L: Saunders & Otley 1868. 343p. 21cm. [LC]
See Kemper, J., M-- in Mexico, #4936.
See Kollonitz, Pla., The court of Mexico, #5179.
See Salm-Salm, Fx., My diary in Mexico, #7653.

MAY, Dr.
6141. The baths of Kreuth in the Bavarian Alps. Tr. anon. 1884. 40p. il. In C294.

MAYER, K: 1786-1870. Sel. in C138;309;450.

MAYER, Pl. Sel. in C95.

MAYREDER, Frau Rosa (Obermayer), 1858- .
6142. Survey of the woman problem. Tr. H. G. Scheffauer. L: Heinemann; NY: Doran 1913. xi;215p. 21cm. [BM.LC]

MAYRHOFER, J: N. 1787-1836. Sel. in C137a,222.

MECHTILD VON HELLFDE (Mde. v. Hackeborn-Wippra), 1242-99. Sel. in C222.
6143. Love of the Sacred Heart. Foreword by Lord Bishop of Salford. L: Oates; NY: Benziger 1922. 169p. [AC]

MECHTILD VON MAGDEBURG, 1210?-85.
§6144. (Offenbarungen der Schwester M-- v. M--.) Matelda and the cloister of Hellfde. Extracts...Mrs. Fes. Bevan. L: Nisbet 1896. viii;159p. 8. [Tr. admits inability to cope with orig. verse.][BM]

MECKLENBURG. See Ad. F: Herzog von.

MEDING, Ok. 1829-1903. See "Samarow, Gregor"

MEGERLE, U: 1644-1709. Sel. in C469.

MEGISER, Hrns., ca. 1553-1618.
*6145. (...Beschreibung der...Insul Madagascar...) An ancient accont of M--, A.D. 1608. Introd. by Jas. Sibree, Jr. Antananarivo. Friends for. miss. assoc. 1877. 28p. 21cm. [BM]
[Tr. made by an English lady.]

MEHLIS, G: 1878- .
*6146. (Einführung in ein System der Religionsphilosophie.) The quest for God: an introd. to the philos. of relig. Tr. Gert. Baker. Foreword W. Tudor Jones. L: Williams & Norgate 1927. viii;167p. 7 x 5 in. [BM]

MEIER, G: F: 1718-77.
6147. (Gedancken von Schertzen.) The merry philosopher; or, thoughts on jesting. Containing rules...and the criterion for distinguishing true and genuine wit, etc. L: Newberry 1764. 2v. 213p. 16cm. [BM has only one vol.--Much abridged, almost an epitome, but not bad.] [BM.LC]
6148. do. 1789. [same] Phil: Prtd. by H: Taylor. (B6a)

MEIER-GRAEFE, Jl. 1867- .
6149. Cezanne. Tr. J: H. Reece. L: Benn; NY: Scribner's 1927. 66p. il. 29cm. [BM]
*6150. (Degas.) Degas. Tr. J: H. Reece. L: Benn 1923. 87p. il. 29cm. [Mrs. Reece's collab. in the tr. seems to me not to have improved it.] [BM]
*6151. (Entwicklungsgeschichte der modernen Kunst.) Mod. art: being a contrib. to a new system of aesthetics. Tr. Flor. Simmonds and G: W. Chrystal. L: Heinemann; NY: Putnam 1908. 2v. 325; 337p. il. 29cm. [LC]
6152. (Spanische Reise.) The Spanish journey. Tr. J: H. Reece. Drawings by J. Sima, and 9 paintings by El Greco. L: Cape 1926. 464p. 24cm. [AC has: NY: Harcourt 1927.] [LC]
*6153. (Vincent.) V. van Gogh: a biogr. study. Tr. J: H. Reece. L: Medici soc. 1922. 2v. il. 4. [BM]
6153a. do. 1926. [same] W. 102 il. after the works of the artist. Medici soc. 2v. 156;118p. 11 x 9. [EC]

MEINECKE, F: 1862- . Sel. in C563.
*6154. (Die deutsche Erhebung von 1914.) The warfare of a nation. Lectures and essays. Tr. J: A. Spaulding. Worcester, Mass: Davis press 1915. 60p. 24cm. [LC.BM]
[Two of the orig. essays omitted as too restricted in appeal.]

to

MEINERS, Cph. 1747-1810.
*6155. (Geschichte des weiblichen Geschlechts.) Hist. of the female sex. Tr. F: Shoberl. L: Colburn 1808. 4v. 16cm. [BM.LC]
6156. (Grundriss der Geschichte aller Religionen.) Plan of a hist. of all religions (100 pp.). Tr. anon. In "Maty's New Rev." 9(1786): 1, etc. (B26)

MEINHOLD, J: W: 1797-1851. Sel. in C235;244;287;366*.
*6157. (Maria Schweidler, die Bernstein-Hexe.) The amber witch. Tr. E. A. Friedländer. L: Clarke 1844. xii;262p. 13cm. [BM]
*6157a. do. 1844. Tr. Lady Duff Gordon. L: Murray. Colonial and home lib. [Info. from special bibliog.]
6157b. do. 1844. Tr. anon. NY: Winchester. [Info. from special bibliog.]
*6158. do. 1845. Ma. Schweidler, the amber witch. Tr. Lady Duff Gordon. NY: Wiley & Putnam. 180p. 18cm.[Reprinted from #6157a.][LC]
6159. do. 1846. Tr. Lady Duff Gordon. L: Murray. Traveller's lib. [This ed. cited in BM catalog. Cf. #6162. See also "Athenaeum." 17 (1844):731.
6160. do. 1852. [same as #6157] L: 12. [BM] [Issued with Beckford's "Vathek."]
6161. do. 1861. [same] New ed. Murray. [EC]
*6162. do. 1888. Tr. Lady Duff Gordon. L;NY: Cassell. 192p. 14cm. [BM.LC]
*6163. do. 1894. [same] Cassell. [EC]
*6164. do. 1895. [same] Introd. by Js. Jacobs. Il. by P. Burne-Jones. L: Nutt; NY: Scribner. xxxviii;221p. 19cm. [BM]
*6165. do. 1903. [same] Decorated by C. S. Ricketts. L: Hacon & Ricketts. L;NY: Lane. clvi p. 29cm. [BM.LC]
6165a. A royal whim. Tr. anon. "Colburn's Mag." 97(1853):300. Also in "Littell's Liv. Age." 37:226. (B15a)
*6166. (Sidonia v. Bork.) Sidonia, the sorceress. Tr. Mrs. W. R. Wilde. L: Simms & M'Intyre 1849. Parlour lib. 2v. xi;286; 292p. 16cm. [BM]
6167. do. 1849. [same?] Hodgson. 12. [EC]
6168. do. 1849. [same?] NY: Harper & bros. 8. [AC]
*6169. do. 1852. [same] L: Simms & M'Intyre. 2v. in one. [EC]
6170. do. 1860. [same?] NY: Harper. 230p. (B12) [NY]
*6171. do. 1893. [same] L: Morris, Kelmscott press. xiv;455p. 29cm. [BM]
*6172. do. 1894. Sidonia the sorceress, the supposed destroyer of the whole reigning ducal house of Pomerania. Tr. Lady Wilde. And, Mary Schweidler, etc. Tr. Lady Duff Gordon. L: Reeves & Turner. 2v. 20cm. [BM.LC]
*6173. do. 1926. Tr. Lady Wilde. Il. T: Lowinsky. L: Benn. xviii; 481p. 29cm. [225 cop. prtd. white vellum.] [BM.LC]

MEINLOH VON SEVELINGEN, 12th cent. Sel. in C27*;427.

MEISEL-HESS, Grete, 1879- .
§6174. (Die sexuelle Krise.) The sexual crisis: a critique of our sex life. Author. tr. E. and C. Paul. Introd. W: J. Robinson. NY: Critic & guide co. 1917. 345p. 21cm. [Not sufficiently accurate.] [LC]
§6175. do. 1922. [same] Cosmopolis press. [AC]

MEISSNER, Af. 1822-85. Sel. in C17;97;125;149;195;216;309;310;395; 450.

MEISSNER, A: Gb. 1753-1807. Sel. in C157.
6176. [Coll.] The nutshell, a tale; A genuine dialogue; Bianca Capello (do.), a dram. narr; The hist. of Lamberg; The Ger. theatre at Venice, a true anecdote; In what language should an

MEISSNER, A: Gb.
author write? Tr. Ax. Thomson. 1796. In C534.

MEISSNER, Me. 1851- .
6177. (?Aus meiner Welt.) From the land of stories: a book...for children...mostly from...Meissner. Tr. ad. and arr. P. P. Claxton. Richmond, Va: Johnson 1902. 92p. il. 18cm. [LC]
6178. do. 1911. [same] Atlanta;Richmond: Johnson. 102p. il.18cm.[LC]

MEISSNER, O. Af. [?]
6179. Ode to harmony. Tr. for Bost. acad. of mus. by S. A. Eliot. Bost: Perkins & Marion 1837. 4p. 8. [LCO]

MEISTER, K: Sel. in C318.

MEISTER, Cph: L: G: 1783-1811. Sel. in C106.

MELANCHTHON (i.e., Schwarzerd), Ph. 1497-1560. Sel. in C469;486.
6180. The hist. of the lyfe and actes of M. Luther. In "A famous and godly history, etc.," by H: Bennet. L: J:Awdely 1561. 14cm. [BM] [Consid. expanded from the orig. Latin.]
*6181. do. 1845. A hist. of the life...of...M. Luther. Tr. H. J. Fry. In "Hymns of the reformation," #5963; #5965, pp. 159-231.
§6182. (Deuttung der zwo grewlichen Figuren Bapstesels zu Rom und Munchkalbs zu Freyberg in Meyssen funden.) Of two Woonderful Popish Monsters, to wyt, Of a Popish Asse which was found at Rome in the riuer of Tyber, and of a Moonkish Calfe, calued at Friberge in Misne, etc. Tr. from French by J: Brooke of Assh, next Sandwich. These bookes are to be sould in Powles Churchyard (L.) at the signe of the Parat. Imprinted by T: East 1579. 19p. 18cm. [BM] [Very freely done.]
*6183. Memoirs of Mn. Luther. In Luther, "Thirty-four sermons, etc." L: Gale & Fenner 1816. pp. i-xlviii. 8. [BM]
6184. An oracyon or precesse rehearsed off Ph. M-- at the buryall of ...M. Luther. Tr. (from Latin) by Johan Bale. In "The true hystorie, etc." by J. Jonas. n.i. 1546. 15cm. [BM] [Not at all close.]
6185. A very godly defense...defending the mariage of preistes, gathered by Ph. M-- and sent unto the Kyng of Englond, Henry the aight. Tr...lewes beuchame...1541. Prynted at Lipse by Ubryght Hoff. ff. A-D. 14cm. [BM]
6186. do? 1547. The epistle of...Ph. M-- made unto...Kynge Henry the Eight. Tr. out of Laten into Englishe by J. C. Prtd. at Weesell. ff. A-B. 13cm. [BM]
See Ledderhose, C., Life of M--, #5631.

"MELENA, Elpis" (i.e., Me. Esperance (Brandt) v. Schwartz, 1818-99).
6187. (Blätter aus dem afrikanischen Reise-Tagebuch einer Dame.) Leaves from a lady's diary of her travels in Barbary. Tr. anon. L: Colburn 1850. 2v. ix;285; ix;281p. 19cm. [BM]
*6188. (Blicke auf Calabrien und die Liparischen Inseln.) Calabria and the Liparian Is. in the year 1860. Tr. anon. L: Saunders 1862. vi;29p. 22cm. [BM]

MELLIN, ---, Graf v. Sel. in C44.
[Perhaps this is Gst. Henrik M--, 1803-76, Swedish pastor and poet.]

"MELS, A." (i.e., Mn. Cohn, 1829-94).
6189. Baron Leo v. Oberg, M. D. A story of love unspoken. Tr. Js. A. Sigmund. Bost: Loring 1868. 92p. 23cm. [LC.BM] [Prtd. in double columns.]
6190. (Clelia. Erzählung.) Clelia. From family papers. Tr. for "Littell's Living Age," anon. Bost: Littell & Gay 1870. 8. [LCO]
6191. do. 1870. [same?] Tr. T. H. Fairfax. Bound in one vol. with Detlef's Clemence D'Orville, #1195.

MELTZER, Ad. H.
6192. (Laura, oder der Kuss in seiner Wirkung.) Laura; or, the influence of a kiss. Tr. 1796. [Ascribed by Stokoe (B43) to Sl. Gessner.]

MENCKEN, Lüder, 1658-1726. Sel. in C269.

MENDELSSOHN, Moses, 1729-86. Sel. in C157;190;193;194*;469.
*6193. (Phaedon, oder über die Unsterblichkeit der Seele.) Phaedon; or, the death of Socrates. Tr. C: Cullen. L. Prtd. for the author by J. Cooper 1789. viii;lx;212p. 21cm. [Imitation of Plato.] [BM]
See Auerbach, B., Poet and merchant, #147.

MENDELSSOHN-BARTHOLDY, (Jk. L:) Fx. 1809-47. Sel. in C366*;429. Son and stranger. Operetta. See Klingemann, C.
*6194. (Briefe.) Letters, 1833-47. Tr. Lady Wallace. L: Longmans 1863. 468p. 19cm. [BM.LC]
*6195. do. 1864. [same] New ed. 437p. [BM]
*6196. do. 1866. [same] NY: Leypoldt & Holt; Bost: Ditson. vi;421p. il. 17cm. [LC]
*6197. do. 1868. [same] [LC]
§6198. (Briefe an...Moscheles.) Letters...to Ignaz and Cte. M--. Tr. anon. Bost: Ticknor; L: Trübner 1888. xx;306p. il. 22cm. [LC.BM]
*6199. (Reisebriefe.) Letters from Italy and Switzerland, 1830-33. Tr. Lady Wallace. L: Longmans 1862. vii;357p. 19cm. [BM.LC]
*6200. do. 1862. [same] 2d ed. [BM.LC]
*6201. do. 1864. [same] 3d ed. [BM.LC]
*6202. do. 186-? [same] NY;Bost: Ditson. xv;360p. il. 16cm. [LC]
§6203. Selected letters. Tr. and ed. W: F. Alexander. Introd. Sir G: Grove. L: Sonnenschein; NY: Macmillan 1894. viii;133p. port. 17cm. [BM.LC]
*6204. Sel. letters. In "Letters of dist. musicians." Tr. Lady Wallace. 1867. C429.
See Devrient, E., My recoll. of Fx. M--, #1224.
See Hensel, S., The M-- family, #4198.
See Hiller, Fd., M--, letters and recoll., #4327.
See Lampadius, W:, Life of Fx. M--, #5553.
See Polko, E., Reminisc. of Fx. M--, #7231.

MENDELSSOHN-BARTHOLDY, K: 1838-97.
*6205. (Goethe und Mendelssohn.) G-- and M--, 1821-31. Tr. Miss M. E. v. Glehn. L: Macmillan 1872. xx;159p. port. 19cm. [BM.LC] [Excellent in the main. "Autocrat" for Autodidakt is a bad blunder.]

MENGE, Rd. 1845-1912.
*6206. (Einführung in die antike Kunst.) An introd. to ancient art. Tr. Lilian B. Worthington. 2d enl. ed. L: Mansell 1887. xi;206p. 21cm. [BM]

MENGER, Rd. 1824-96.
6207. (Gräfin Loreley.) Countess Loreley: a novel. Tr. Miss Dandridge. NY: Appleton 1889. 237p. 18cm. [LC]

MENSEL, Wfg. 1497-1563. Sel. in C269.

MENTZEL, O: F:
6208. A geogr. and topogr. description of the Cape of Good Hope. Tr. H. J. Mandelbrote. Cape Town: Van Riebeeck soc. 1921, 5. 2 pts. 21cm. [BM]

MENTZER (or Mentzner), J: 1658-1734. Sel. in C244;271;276;287.

MENZEL, Ad. v. 1815-1905. See Harden, Mx., Word portraits, #3699.

MENZEL, Wfg. 1798-1873. Sel. in C142.

MENZEL, Wfg.
*6209. (Die deutsche Literatur.) Ger. lit. Tr. C. C. Felton. Bost: Hilliard, Gray; L: Wiley 1840. 3v. 19cm. [LC.BM]
[Verse tr. is not very good.]
§6209a. do. 1840. Tr. T: Gordon. Oxford;L: Talboys. 4v. 19cm. [LC]
[Solid translations, some very good.]
*6210. (Europa im Jahre 1840.) Europe in 1840. Tr. anon. Ed: Black; L: Longmans 1841. viii;240p. 20cm. [BM.LC]
*6211. (Geschichte der Deutschen bis auf die neueste Zeit.) The hist. of Germany from the earliest period to 1842. Tr. Mrs. G: Horrocks. L: Bohn 1848-9. 3v. 18cm. [BM.LC]
[Fronts. of Charlemagne, C: V, Metternich.]
*6212. do. 1892-9. [same] L;NY: Bell. 3v. 19cm. [LC]

MERKEL, Ad.
6213. Rd. v. Ihering. Tr. Ab. Kocourek. 1913. #4713.

MERKEL, Garlieb Helwig, 1769-1850. Sel. in C12.

MERLAU, J:a Elre. v.
6213a. The nature and necessity of the new creature in Christ. Tr. Fis. Okely. L: Lewis 1772. See "Monthly R." 46(1772):548. (B26)
6214. do. 1772. [same] 2d ed. L: Lewis. 34p. 17cm. [BM]

MERZ, H:
6215. Eminent women of the Ger. reformation. Tr. S: Jackson. L: Seeley, Jackson 1856. vi;159p. 17cm. [BM]
[Cath. Luther; Cath. Melanchthon; Argula v. Grumbach; Eliz. duchess of Brunswick-Luneburg; Cath. Zell; Anna Zwingle; Wilibrandis Rosenblatt; Valeria Anselm; Marg. Blaarer.]
6215a. Louise, queen of Prussia. Tr. G: P. Upton. Chic: McClurg 1909. 128p. il. 17cm. [LC]

MESSMER, J: J.
6216. (Im Strom der Zeit.) Red Carl. Tr. Ma. E. Ireland. NY: Crowell 1888. 295p. il. 17cm. [LC.BM]

METHFESSEL, Ab. 1785-1869. Sel. in C106;309.

METTERNICH (-WINNEBURG), Clt. Lt. Wz. Fürst v. 1773-1859.
*6217. Memoirs (written in French), 1773-1829. Tr. Robina Napier. L: Bentley 1880-2. 4v. 22cm. [BM.LC]
*6218. do. 1881. [same] NY: Munro. 4 pts. in one vol. 33cm. [LC]
*6219. do. 1881. Memoirs, 1773-1835. NY: Harper. 5v. 30cm. [LC]
[Pt. 5, 1830-35, tr. excellently by Gerard W. Smith.]

METZGER, Amb. Sel. in C106.

MEURER, Mz.
*6220. (Luthers Leben aus den Quellen erzählt.) The life of Mn. L--. Tr. by a pastor, etc. NY: Ludwig 1848. 695p. 16 engr. 22cm.[LCO.BM]

MEYER, Arn. Ok. 1877- .
*6221. (England und die katholische Kirche unter Elisabeth und den Stuarts.) England and the Catholic church under Queen Eliz. Author tr. by Rev. J: R. McKee. L: Paul, T. & T; St.L: Herder 1916. xxi; 556p. 22cm. [Tr. seems to be excellent.] [BM.LC]

MEYER, Br. 1840- . See Goerling, Ad., joint author, #2353.

MEYER, Cd. Fd. 1825-98. Sel. in C38;154(14);366*;423.
6222. (Der Heilige.) Thomas a Becket the saint: a novel. Tr. M. V. Wendheim. Lpz: Haessel 1885. 243p. 8. [Heinsius cat.]
6223. do. 1887. The chancellor's secret: a tale of the 12th cent. Tr. M. J. Taber. New Bedford, Mass: Lawton. S. [AC]
†6224. (Die Hochzeit des Mönchs.) The monk's wedding: a novel. Tr. Sa. H. Adams. Bost: Cupples & Hurd 1887. 169p. 19cm. [LC]

MEYER, Cd. Fd.
[Omits arbitrarily.]
*6225. do. 1913-15. The monk's marriage. Tr. W: G. Howard. In C154 (14).
§6226. (Die Versuchung des Pescara.) The tempting of P--. Tr. Ca. Bell. Rev. and corr. NY: Gottsberger 1890. 184p. 17cm. [LC.BM]
[She cannot manage the difficulty of the style.]
*6227. (Plautus im Nonnenkloster.) Plautus in the convent. Tr. W: G. Howard. 1913-15. In C154(14).

MEYER, E. L. E. v.
6228. Love and friendship's rosary. NY: Kelly 1865. 16. [AC]
[Translation?]

MEYER, E: 1855- .
§6229. (England, seine staatliche und politische Entwicklung und der Krieg gegen Deutschland 1915.) England: its polit. organization and devel. and the war against Germany. Tr. Helene S. White. NY: Ritter 1916. xix;328p. 19cm. [LC]
[She can't handle the involved style, and makes mistakes.]

MEYER, Hs. (H: Js.) 1858- .
6230. (In den Hoch-Anden von Ecuador.) In the high Andes of Equador. Chimborazo-Cotopaxi. Tr. anon. L: Williams & Norgate 1908. 24p. 38 x 30cm. [BM has only the album.] [BM]
*6231. (Zum Schneedom des Kilimandscharo.) Across East African glaciers: an account of the first ascent of Kilimanjaro. Tr. E. H. S. Calder. L: Philip 1891. xx;404p. il. 28 x 22cm. [BM.LC]

MEYER-FOERSTER, W: 1862- .
§6232. (Alt-Heidelberg.) Old Heidelberg. (Novel.) Tr. Max Chapelle. NY: Dodge & Metcalf 1903. 173p. 19cm. [Careless and loose.] [LC]
§6234. do. 1904. [same] Il. N. W. Brinckerhoff. NY: Wessels. 173p. 19cm. [LC]
*6235. do. 1906. Karl Heinrich: a tale. Orig. form of the play "Old H--." Tr. Grace B. v. Wentzel. 12 il. Ad. Wald. L;Glasgow: Gowans & Gray. 227p. 19cm. [BM]
6236. (Alt-Heidelberg. Schauspiel.) Old H--: a sentimental comedy in 5 acts [prose]. Tr. R. Bleichmann. L: 1903. (B38)
6237. do. 1905. Tr. anon. L: Siegle. 119p. 19cm. [BM]
[Probably same as the following.]
*6238. do. 1924? Tr. Cath. Pochin. L;NY: French. 119p. 18cm. [LC]
[On the whole, very good. Some errors.]

MEYER, F. Sel. in C105.

MEYERN-HOHENBERG, Gst. Freiherr v. 1826-78.
6239. (Teuerdanks Brautfahrt.) A perilous advent.; or, the days of Ma. of Burgundy. Tr. M. Hall. L: Warne 1884. 312p. 18cm. [BM]
6240. do. 1896. [same] Il. Gordon Browne. 312p. [BM]

MEYER VON SCHANENSEE, Lu.
6241. A storm on the lake of Lucerne. Tr. anon. Frome. J: Hodges; L: Simpkin, Marshall 1869. 55p. 14cm. [BM]

MEYFAHRT, J: Mts. 1590-1642. Sel. in C222-3;232;271;287;489.

"MEYRINK, Gst." i.e., Meyer-Meyrink, Gst. 1868- . See Roda Roda, joint author.

MICHAELIS, J: B: 1746-72. Sel. in C443;461.

MICHAELIS, J: D: 1717-91.
6242. (Ueber den Einfluss der Sprachen...) A dissertation on the infl. of opinions on language, and of lang. on opin....together with an enquiry into the advis. and practicability of an universal learned lang. Tr. anon. L: W. Owen & W.Bingley 1769. viii;92p. 26cm. [BM]

MICHAELIS, J: D: - Ueber den Einfluss der Sprachen...
6243. do. 1771. [same] 2d ed. L: W.Owen, J.Johnson & W.Bingley. 92p. 24cm. [BM]
Obituary notice by Schlichtegroll in C157(3). Tr. ca. 1801. By C. Geisweiler.

MICHEL, F: 1862-1922.
6244. (Schneider und Geiger.) Tailor and fiddler. Tr. "Trauermantel". 1859. In C549.

MICHELET, K: L: 1801-93.
6245. The dialectic and the principle of contradiction. Tr. Louis Soldan. 1875. In C300(5).
6246. M--'s philos. of art as the science of aesthetics. In Hegel, G., The philos. of art, etc. 1886. pp. 47-118. 18cm. [BM] [Cf. #3970.]

MIEGEL, Ag. 1879- . Sel. in C28*;154(18);423.

MIETHE, A.
6246a. Photography from airplane. Tr. E. and C. Paul. 1925. In Mittelholzer, Wl., "By airplane towards the north pole," #6252.

MILLER, J. B. d. 1824. Sel. in C244.

MILLER, J: Mn. 1750-1814. Sel. in C44;97;133;244;269;391.
§6247. (Siegwart. Eine Klostergeschichte.) Sigevart: a tale. Tr. by H.L. Chelsea, Eng: Prtd. for Polidori 1799. 2v. 270; 225p. 13cm. [BM.LC]
*6248. do. 1806. Siegwart: a monastic tale. Tr. with pref. by Laetitia M. Hawkins. L: Carpenter. 3v. 18cm. [BM]

MILLER, J:s, 1756-90. Sel. in C269.

MILLOECKER, K: 1842-99. Operettas: Apajune; The beggar student; Countess Dubarry; Gasparone; The vice-admiral. See Zell, F. The black hussar. See "Wittmann, H."

"MILOW, St." (i.e., St. v. Millenkovich, 1836-1915). Sel. in C501.

"MILTENBERG" (i.e., A: H: v. Lafontaine), see #5522.

MILTITZ, K: Borromäus, 1791-1841.
*6249. Explanations of M. Retzsch's outlines to Bürger's ballads. Tr. F: Shoberl. 1840. In #847.

"MIRZA SCHAFFY" See F: v. Bodenstedt.

MISKY, P. Sel. in C240.

MITTELBERGER, Gb.
6250. (G. M--s Reise nach Pennsylvanien im Jahre 1750...1754.) G. M--'s journey to P--...1750 and return to Germany...1754. Tr. C. T. Eben. Phil. Prtd. for Jeanes 1898. 129p. 8. [LC.BM]
6251. do. 1898. [same] Phil. McVey. [LC]

MITTELHOLZER, Wl., and others.
*6252. (Im Flugzeuge dem Nordpol entgegen.) By airplane towards the north pole. An account of an expedition to Spitzbergen in the summer of 1923. Tr. E. and C. Paul. L: Allen & Unwin; NY: Houghton 1925. 175p. il. 21cm. [BM.LC]
[Introd. by Kurt Wegener; A. Miethe, Photography from airplane; H. Boykow, Geogr. value of the photographs; Wl. Mittelholzer, The first arctic aviation.]

MITTERWURZER, F: 1844-97. See Harden, Mx., Word portraits, #3699.

MOELLER, Af. Yvonne. Operetta. See Kastner, Leo.

"MOELLER, A. V." (i.e., Anga. v. Lagerström)
6253. Little Paul and his moss-wreaths; or, the king and the little boy who kept his word. L: Hogg 1861. 67pp. 16. [BM]
6254. do. 1861. [same] L: G:Bell. 121p. col. il. 16cm. [BM]

MOELLHAUSEN, Bld. 1825-1905.
*6255. (Tagebuch einer Reise vom Mississippi nach den Küsten der Südsee.) Diary of a journey from the M-- to the coast of the Pacific. Tr. Mrs. P. Sinnett. Pref. by Ax. v. Humboldt. L: Longmans 1858. 2v. xxx;352; 397p. 22cm. [BM.LC]
[Il. in chromo-lithography.]

MOELLING, K: Erdwin.
*6256. (Fausts Tod.) Faust's death: a tragedy in 5 acts [verse] Phil: Lippincott 1865. 136p. 18cm. [LCO.BM]
[Tr. by the author? Very good.]

MOERIKE, E: 1804-75. Sel. in C17;38;41;73;97;195;309;311;366;372; 391;422-3;448;460;501;#4082.
†6257. (Mozart auf der Reise nach Prag.) Mozart's journey from Vienna to Prague. Tr. Flor. Leonard. 1913-15. In C154(7).
[Outrageous liberties.]

MOESER, Jt. 1720-94. Sel. in C12;194;461;469.
*6258. (Harlekin, oder Verteidigung des Grotesk-Komischen.) Harlequin; or, a defence of grotesque comic performances. Tr. Jn. An. F: Warnecke. L: W.Niccoll 1766.xv;104p. 16cm. [BM]
6259. (Schreiben an den Herrn Vicar in Savoyen.) Letter to the Rev. Vicar of Savoy. Tr. Jn. An. F: Warnecke. L: Dodsley. See "Monthly R." 33(1765):305. (B26)

MOEWES, H: 1793-1834. Sel. in C229;273.
*6260. (Der Pfarrer von Andouse.) The minister of A--. Tr. S: Jackson. Ed: Clark; L: Hamilton 1839. 272p. 16cm. [BM]
Memoir...principally translated. See Appuhn, W., #74.

MOHNIKE, Gb. Cn. 1781-1841. Sel. in C446.

MOHR, Js. 1792-1848. Sel. in C42;269.

MOHR, N: C: E: 1828-76.
6261. (Nach den Viktoria-Fällen des Zambesi.) To the Victoria Falls of the Z--. Tr. Nancy D'Anvers. L: Low 1876. 462p. il. 22cm. [LC]

MOLESCHOTT, Jk. 1822-93. Sel. in C461.

MOLLER, G: 1784-1852.
*6262. An essay on the orig. and progress of Gothic architecture. Tr. anon. L: Priestley & Weale 1824. xvi;141p. 19cm. [BM.LC]
[From the "Einleitung" to his "Denkmäler der deutschen Baukunst."]
6263. do. 1835. M--'s memorials of Ger. gothic architecture. Tr. W. H. Leeds. L: Weale. 2v. fol. Text. 8. [EC]
[See following entry. The folio vols. evidently contain Moller's plates.]
6264. do. 1836. [same] L: Weale. xvi;176p. 23cm. [BM.LC]
[This reprints #6262, but adds consid. matter, partly by M--, also by von der Hagen and Stieglitz. Front. of Church of St. Eliz. at Marburg; rose window of Strassburg cath. in col. on t.p.]

MOLLER (or Moeller), Mn. 1547-1606. Sel. in C271.

MOLTKE, Hlm. (K: Bh.) Graf v. 1800-91. Sel. in C154(10), tr. by E. v. Mach, Grace Bigelow, Ca. Bell, H: W. Fischer, Ma. Herms.
[See entries below.]
*6265. [Coll.] Moltke: his life and character, sketched in journals, letters, memoirs, a novel, and autobiog. notes. Tr. Ma. Herms. NY:

MOLTKE, Hlm. (K: Bh.) Graf v. - Moltke: his life and character... Harper 1892. 332p. il. 23cm. [LC.BM]
[Tr. of vol. 1 of M--'s "Gesammelte Schriften," Berlin 1892, which is followed in both matter and arrangement. On the whole, very good.]
*6266. [Coll.] 1893. Essays, speeches, and memoirs. Tr. (respectively) C: F. McClumpha, C: St. L. Barter, and Ma. Herms. L: Osgood, McIlvaine; NY: Harper. 2v. 23cm. [BM.LC]
[Memoirs are less well tr. than the other two sections.]
*6267. (Briefe.) Letters...to his mother and his brothers. Tr. Ca. Bell and H: W. Fischer. L: Osgood 1891. 2v. 256; 244p. il. 22cm[BM]
*6268. do. 1892. [same] NY: Harper. 317p. il. 22cm. [LC]
6269. do. 1893. Field-marshal count v. M-- as corr. Tr. Ma. Herms. L: Osgood; NY: Harper. 309p. il. 23cm. [LC]
*6270. do. 1896. Letters to his wife and other relatives. Tr. J. R. McIlraith. Introd. by Sidney Whitman. L: Paul, T. & T. 2v. xv;303; 362p. 2 ports. 8. [BM.LC]
*6271. (Briefe aus Russland.) Letters from Russia. Tr. Robina Napier. L: K.Paul 1878. xxxi;163p. 19cm. [BM.LC]
§6272. do. 1878. Tr. Grace Bigelow. NY: Harper. 181p. 12cm. [LC]
[Fair; errors.]
*6273. do. 1881. [same as #6271] New ed. L: K.Paul. 12. [EC]
6274. (Briefe, 1870-71.) Extracts from...corr. pertaining to the war of 1870-71. Tr. Harry Bell. Ft. Leavenworth, Kan: Army press 1911. 229p. 20cm. [LC.BM]
*6275. The Franco-German war of 1870-71. Tr. Ca. Bell and H: W. Fischer. L: Osgood, McIlvaine 1891. 2v. 274;304p. 21cm. [BM]
[From vol. 3 of his "Gesammelte Schriften."]
*6276. do. 1893. [same] Rev. by Archibald Forbes. Map, notes, etc. L: Osgood, McIlvaine. xi;447p. 22cm. [BM]
[Revision not always an improvement.]
*6277. (Wanderbuch...Aufzeichnungen aus dem Reisetagebuch.) Notes of travel: extracts from the journals. Tr. anon. L: K.Paul 1880. 196p. 19cm. [BM]
[Wanderings near Rome; Spanish journal; Letters from Paris.]
*6278. do. 1881. [same] New ed. 12. [EC]
See Dressler, F:, M-- in his home, #1273.
See Müller, W:, Moltke, 1800-78, #6529.

MOLTKE, Mx. 1819-94. Sel. in C67;395.
6278a. (Der 4. Juli. 1776. 1826. 1851.) The fourth of July. A poem. The Engl. tr. by H. A. Franklin. Berlin: 1863. 32p. 8. [EC]

MOMBERT, Af. 1872- . Sel. in C28*;95.

MOMMSEN, Td. 1817-1903. Sel. in C321;366*;469;574*.
*6279. (Römische Geschichte.) The earliest inhab. of Italy. Tr. G: Robertson. Pref. by L. Schmitz. L: Parker 1858. 63p. 21cm. [BM]
*6280. do. 1862-6. The hist. of Rome. Tr. W: P. Dickson. L: Bentley. 4v. 18cm. [BM]
[Vols. 1,2, 1862; vol. 3, 1863; vol. 4, 1866. Index pub. 1875; hence BM lists this ed. as 1862-75.]
*6281. do. 1868. [same] New ed. Pref. by L. Schmitz. L: Bentley. 4v. 22cm. [BM lists this as 1868-86; see below, #6293.] [BM]
*6282. do. 1870. [same] New ed. NY: Scribner. 4v. 20cm. [LC]
*6283. do. 1887. [same] Scribner. 21cm. [LC]
*6284. do. 1888. The hist. of the Roman republic, abr. from the hist. by Prof. M--. Tr. C. Bryans and F. J. R. Hendy. L: Bentley. xviii;542p. 19cm. [Largely taken from Dickson's tr.] [BM]
*6285. do. 1894. [same as #6281] New ed. rev. with add. from the 8th Ger. ed. L: Bentley. [BM]
*6286. do. 1903. [same as #6283] New rev. ed. NY: Scribner. 5v. 21cm. [Vol. 5 is probably index; cf. #6280.] [LC]

MOMMSEN, Td.
*6287. do. 1906. Dickson's tr. L: Dent;NY: Dutton. Everyman lib. 4v. 17cm. [Introd. (xxxvi p.)E: A: Freeman.] [BM.LC]
*6288. do. 1908. Dickson's tr. Rev. with recent add. L: Macmillan. 5v. 8. [BM]
*6289. do. 1908. [same as #6284] NY: Scribner. xviii;542p. 19cm. [LC.BM]
6290. (Römische Geschichte. Bis 44 vor Christo.) Rome from earliest times to 44 B.C. Ed. Arthur C. Howland. Phil: Morris 1906. 418p. 24cm. [De luxe ed.] [LC]
6291. do. 1913. [same] NY: Collier. 21cm. [LC]
6292. do. 1916. [same] NY: Collier. il. 23cm. [LC]
*6293. (Römische Geschichte. Band 5.) The provinces of the Roman empire from Caesar to Diocletian. Tr. W: P. Dickson. L: Bentley 1886. 2v. xvi;367;366p. 22cm. [BM]
[This has cover t.p. "The hist. of Rome." Hence the date 1886 on #6281 in BM catalog. Really a separate work.]
*6294. do. 1887. [same] NY: Scribner. 2v. 21cm. [LC]
*6295. do. 1909. [same] The tr. rev. and corr. (much needed) by F. Haverfield. L: Macmillan. 2v. xvi;367;374p. 23cm. [BM.LC]
6296. To the people of Italy...Two letters. Tr. from Italian by I. C. 1871. In C321, pp. 1-40.

MORAHT, Ad. 1805-84. Sel. in C229.

MORGENSTERN, Cn. 1871-1914. Sel. in C28;95.

MORITZ, A:
6297. [Coll.] The hymn-book; Kasem the miser; W: the little chimney-sweeper. Tr. "Trauermantel." 1858. In C546.
6298. [Coll.] 1859. The benefactor's portrait; The gardener's daughter; Patience removes mountains; The ways of providence. Tr. "Trauermantel." 1859. In C549.
6299. Kasem the miser. Tr. E. Perry. 1840. In C449.

MORITZ, Gst.
6300. Duty and affection: a tale. Ed: Chambers 1850. 162p. front. 14cm. [BM]

MORITZ, K: Ph. 1757-93.
*6301. (Anton Reiser. Ein psychologischer Roman.) Anton Reiser: a psych. novel. Tr. P. E. Matheson. L;NY: Oxford 1926. xv;456p. 15cm. [BM.LC]
6302. Mythological fictions of the Greeks and Romans. Oxford. Talboys 1830. 12. [Probably the original of the following.] [EC]
6303. do. 1830. Tr. from 5th ed. by C. F. W. Jaeger. NY: Carvill. 276p. il. 16. [LCO]
§6304. (Reisen eines Deutschen in England im Jahre 1782.) Travels, chiefly on foot, through several parts of England, in 1782, described in letters to a friend. Tr. by a lady. L: Robinsons 1795. See "Engl. R." 26(1795):186. (B26)
§6305. do. 1798. [same] In Mavor, W: F. "The British tourists." L: Newbery. pp. 1-138. 14cm. [Tr. is not very close.] [BM]
§6306. do. 1800. [same] 2d ed. [BM.LC]
§6307. do. 1808-14. [same] In Pinkerton, J:, "A general coll. of... voyages and travels," vol. 2, pp. 489-573. L: 27cm. [BM.LC]
[The text is completed, and this ed. is the source of #6309.]
§6308. do. 1809. [same as #6305] 3d impr. enl. ed. L: R:Phillips. 14cm. [Same tr. as in #6305. Pp. 1-121.] [BM]
§6309. do. 1886. [same as #6307] Pref. by H: Morley. L: Cassell. 192p. 13cm. [The passages omitted by the orig. tr. are competently done, but her errors are left untouched.] [BM]
§6310. do. 1924. [same as #6304] reprint. Introd. by P. E. Matheson. L: Milford. xx;239p. il. 17cm. [LC]

MORNING, R. Sel. in C89.

MOSCHELES, Cte. (Embden), d. 1889.
*6311. (Aus Moscheles' Leben.) Life of M--, with sel. from his diaries and corr., by his wife. Ad. by A. D. Coleridge. L: Hurst & Blackett 1873. 2v. xvi;333; 318p. 19cm. [BM.LC]
[Two verse tr. by C: S. Calverley. Don't quite like the tr.]
*6312. do. 1875. [same] New ed. NY: Holt. 12. [AC]

MOSCHELES, Ig. 1794-1870.
6313. Life of Beethoven. See Schindler, An., #8250.
See Mendelssohn-Bartholdy, Fx., Letters to...Moscheles, #6198.

MOSEN, Jl. 1803-67. Sel. in C17;67;69;149;309;311;371-3;391;448;469; 489;571.
*6314. (Bilder im Moose). Ishmael ("Ismael"). *The Italian novel ("Die italienische Novelle"). Helena Vallisneriana (do.). The picture of the mermaid ("Das Ondinenbild"). Tr. G. F. Crossthwaite. 1842. In C79. [The tr. is quite good.]

MOSENTHAL, Sl. Hm. Ritter v. 1821-77. Sel. in C36.
§6315. (Deborah.) Deborah: a drama in 4 acts [prose]. Tr. anon. Libr. Ger;Engl. NY: Acad. of mus. 1867. 37p. 4. [LCM]
[Prose passages good. Verse tr. in prose and abridged.]
*6316. (Die Königin von Saba.) The queen of Saba: opera in 4 acts by K: Goldmark. Tr. J: H: Cornell. Vocal score. Engl. Hamburg: Pohle; NY: Schirmer 1881. 276p. 4. [Close unrhymed tr.] [LCM]
*6317. do. 1881. [same] Libr. Engl. Hamburg: Pohle; NY: Schirmer. 52p. 15cm. [LCM.BM]
*6318. do. 1885. The queen of Sheba. Tr. anon. Libr. with mus. NY: n.i. [Somewhat better than Cornell's tr.] [LCM]
§6319. (Die lustigen Weiber von Windsor.) The merry wives of Windsor: opera in 3 acts by O: Nicolai. Text based on Shakespeare. Tr. anon. Libr. Ger;Engl. NY: Herbert 1863. 34p. 8. [LCM]
[Tr. is fair to good.]
§6320. do. 1885. Tr. anon. Libr. Engl. L? n.i. 37p. 22cm. [BM]
[None too good.]
*6321. (Erzählungen aus dem jüdischen Familienleben.) Stories of Jewish home life. Tr. anon. Phil: Jewish pub. soc. 1907. 387p. 19cm. [LC.BM]
[Aunt Guttraud ("Tante G--"); Schlemihlchen ("Schlemilchen"); Rav's mine ("Raaf's Mine"); Jephthah's daughter ("Jephthahs Tochter"); Raschelchen (do.).]
6322. The golden cross: opera in 2 acts by Ignaz Brüll. Tr. J: P. Jackson. Libr. L: Carl Rosa opera co. 1878. 40p. 21cm. [BM]
[Text after M--, who ad. it from "La croix d'or" of Brazier and Melleville.]
6323. Gyda: a play. Ad. J. Schönberg. 1875. (B38)
6324. (Isabella Orsini.) I-- O--: a romantic drama in 4 acts. Tr. and ad. H: L. Williams. NY: De Witt. (B38)
6325. Leah, the forsaken: a play in 5 acts. Tr. A. Daly. NY: Author's private ed. 1886. 50p. 22cm. [First acted 1862.] [LC]
6326. do. 1890. [same]. [LC]
6327. do. n.d. Tr. W. Benneux and ad. A. Daly. L: French. (In NY lib.) (B38)
6328. (Madeleine Morel.) M-- M--: a play in 4 acts. By A. Daly. NY: Prtd. as MS for the author 1884. 67p. 22cm. [First acted 1873.][LC]

MOSER, And. 1859-1925.
*6329. (Js. Joachim.) Js. J--: a biog., 1831-99. Tr. Lilla Durham. Introd. J. A. Fuller Maitland. L: Wellby 1901. xvi;336p. port. il. 23cm. [BM.LC]

MOSER, E. See Schönthan, Fz., joint author.

MOSER, F: K: Freiherr v. 1723-98.
6330. (Briefe.) Letters by him. Tr. S: Jackson in Jung-Stilling's autobiogr. #4767.

MOSER, Gst. v. 1825-1903.
6331. Alfred: comedy in 4 acts [prose]. Tr. Sidney Wittmann. L: 1886. 29; 31; 24; 24p. 26cm. Tw. [BM]
6332. An artist taylor: A dram. composition in 4 acts [prose]. Ad. Hilmar Stephany. Chic: 1881. (B38)
6333. Confidential clerk. Ad. Sydney Wittmann and Shedden Wilson. (B38) [Perhaps from "Der Bibliothekar"?]
6334. (Der Bibliothekar.) The secretary. Ad. W: Gillette. NY: 1882. (B38)
6335. do. 1884. The private secretary. Ad. by C: Hawtrey. L: French (B38) [Cf. #6338 below.]
6336. do. 1885. The librarian. Ad. H. G. Dresen and E. S. Rheem. Washington, D. C. (B38)
6337. do. 1907. [same as #6335] (B38)
6338. do. 1921. [same as #6335] L;NY: French. 90p. 18cm. [BM] [Clever ad., fairly close. Orig. prod. Nov. 14, 1883. Copyright 1907.]
*6339. (Der Salontyroler.) The swell Tyrolean: a comedy in 4 acts [prose]. 1884. 39;38;45;33p. Tw. 33cm. [BM] [Mostly correct, but speech is often wooden.]
6340. (Der Schimmel.) The white horse: comedy in one act [prose]. Tr. anon. Cambridge, Mass: Wheeler 1887. 18p. 20cm. [LC] [Perhaps identical with the following.]
6341. do. 1888. White horse. Cambridge, Mass: Sever. 12. [AC]
§6342. (Die Leibrente.) The annuity: comedy in 5 acts [prose]. Tr. S. Wittmann. L: Miles 1885. 75p. 20cm. [Well enough.] [BM]
6343. (Die Versucherin.) The marble arch: comedietta in one act. Ad. by E: Rose and A. J. Garraway. L: Lacy 1887. 15p. 17cm. [BM]
6344. do. 1891. [same] [BM]
6345. A foolish investment: comedietta in one act. Ad. by Miss M. Morse. NY: De Witt 1888. 15p. 12. [LCO]
6346. (Harun al Raschid.) An Arabian night; or, Haroun al Raschid and his mother-in-law. A comedy in 4 acts [prose]. Tr. A. Daly. NY: Prtd. as MS for the author. 1884. 84p. 22cm. [LC]
6347. do. 1893. The Arabian nights: farce in 3 acts [prose]... founded on the Ger...by S. Grundy. L;NY: French. 49p. 17cm. [BM] [Produced Nov. 5, 1887.]
6348. (Ich werde mir den Major einladen.) "I shall invite the major." A petite comedy in one act [prose]. Liberally tr. by Sydney Rosenthal. NY: De Witt 1875. 16p. 19cm. [LC]
6349. Lot 49: farce...W. J. Fisher. L;NY: French 1893. 20p. 17cm. [First produced Jan. 17, 1888.] [BM]
6350. Medium: a comedy in 4 acts [prose]. Ad. R. Rudelius. San Francisco: 1880. (B38)
6351. On 'change: farce in 3 acts [prose]. arr...Miss Eweretta Lawrence. L;NY: French 1895. 53p. 17cm. [BM] [First produced Aug. 22, 1885.]
6352. Our regiment: farcical comedy. Ad...H. Hamilton. L;NY: French 1893. 55p. 17cm. [First produced Feb. 13, 1883.] [BM]
6353. (Reif-Reiflingen.) Our English friend: a comedy in 4 acts [prose]. Ad. A. Daly. NY: Prtd. as MS for the author 1884. 78p. 22cm. [First acted 1882.] [LC]
6354. (Ultimo.) Ultimo; or, bulls and bears. A comedy in 4 acts [prose]. Ad. Bartley Campbell. San Francisco: 1875. (B38)
6355. do. 1875. The big bonanza. Ad. A. Daly. [LC] [Probably refers to the following.]

MOSER, Gst. v. - (Ultimo)
6356. do. 1884. [same] Prtd. as MS for the author. 77p. 22cm. [LC]
[First acted 1875.]
6357. The violet eater: a drama in 3 acts [prose]. MS prompt book[NY]

MOSER, Gst. v. and O: Girudt (i.e., Girndt).
6358. The shooting star: comedy in 4 acts [prose] L: 1886. 29;28;26;
29p. Tw. 25cm. [BM]

MOSER, Gst. v. and Fz. v. Schönthan.
6359. (Krieg im Frieden.) The passing regiment: a play in 5 acts
[prose]. Ad. A. Daly. NY: Prtd. as MS for the author 1884. 79p.
23cm. [First acted 1880.] [LC]
6360. do. 1886. [same] (B38)

MOSES, Ad.
6361. Luser the watchmaker: an episode of the Polish revolution. Tr.
Mrs. A. de V. Chaudron. Cincin: Bloch 1883? 125p. 24cm. [BM]
[Prtd. in double columns.]

MOSZKOWSKI, Ax. 1851- .
6362. (Die Inseln der Weisheit.) Isles of wisdom. Tr. H. J. Stenning.
L: Routledge 1924. 322p. 19cm. [LC]
6363. (Einstein, Einblicke in seine Gedankenwelt.) Einstein, the
searcher: his work explained from dialogues with E--. Tr. H: L.
Brose. L: Methuen 1921. NY: Dutton 1922. xi;246p. O. [EC.AC]

MOSZKOWSKI, Mz. 1854- . Boabdil. Opera. See Wittkowsky.

MOZART, J:s Cms. Wfg. Gb., called Wfg. Amds. 1756-91.
§6364. (Briefe.) Letters. In Holmes, E:, "Life...includ. his corr."
L: Chapman & Hall 1845. 12. [LCO]
*6365. do. 1865. The letters of W. A. M--, 1769-91. Tr. Lady
Wallace. L: Longmans. 2v. 19cm. [BM.LC]
*6366. Mozart, the man and the artist, as revealed in his own words.
Comp. by F: Kerst. Tr. H: E: Krehbiel. NY: Huebsch 1905. 143p.
20cm. [LC]
*6367. do. 1906. [same] L: Gay & Berd. [BM]
*6368. do. 1926. [same] reissue. L: G.Bles. 8. [BM]
Operas: Hoodwinking the impressario. See Louis Schneider. The
magic flute. See J: Schikaneder.
See Hoffmann, Fz., Mozart's early days, #4479. Two musicians,
#4426.
See Jahn, O:, Life of M--, #4732.
See Mörike, E:, M--'s journey from Vienna to Prague, #6257.
See Nohl, L:, Life of M--, #6910.
See Rau, H., The tone king etc., #7340-1.
See Schlichtegroll, Ad., The life of M--, #8297.]

MUECHLER, K: 1763- . Sel. in C26;93;133;152.
6369. Personal anecdotes of F: the Gt. Tr. J. D. Haas. 1839. In
C183, pp. 392-99.

MUECKE, Hlm. v. 1881- .
*6370. (Ayesha.) The Ayesha: being the advent. of the landing squad
of the Emden. Tr. Helene S. White. Bost: Ritter 1916. vi;223p. il.
19cm. [LC.BM]
*6371. do. 1921. [same] NY: Four seas co. 222p. il. D. [AC]
*6372. (Emden.) The Emden. Tr. Helene S. White. Bost: Ritter 1917.
viii;219p. il. 19cm. [LC]
[On the whole, excellent, with some needless padding.]

MUEFFLING, F: K: Fd. Freiherr v. 1775-1851.
*6373. (Aus meinem Leben.) Passages from my life. Tr. anon. L:
Bentley 1853. viii;520p. 22cm. [BM]

MUEFFLING, F: K: Fd. Freiherr v. 1775-1851.
*6374. do. 1853. [same] 2d rev. ed. Bentley. viii;528p. [BM.LC]
[Includes as pt. 3 "campaigns of the Silesian army...1813-14."]
*6375. do. 1855. [extracts] Narr. of my missions to Constantinople and St. Petersburg, 1829 and 1830. Tr. D: Jardine. L: Longmans. xv;166p. 17cm. [BM.LC]

MUEGGE, Td. 1806-61.
*6376. (Afraja.) Afraja, a Norwegian and Lapland tale; or, life and love in Norway. Tr. E: J. Morris. Phil: Lindsay & Blakiston; L: Low 1854. 571p. 20cm. [LC.BM]
*6377. do. 1858. [same?] Life and love in Norway. 6th ed. [LC]
*6377a. do. 1865. [same] 7th ed. Phil: Lindsay & Blakiston. See "Nation" 1(1865):504.
6378. do. 1876. [same?] Afraja. Phil: Porter. [AC]
6379. (Arvor Spang.) A peasant prince. Tr. (i.e., summarized) by G. Gordon. 1861. In C170.
6379a. The breaking of the dykes: a thrilling sketch. Tr. E: J. Morris. "Graham's Mag." 48(1856):305. (B15a)
6380. Chas. I and Cromwell: an hist. novel. NY: Appleton. ca. 1868-70. [Publisher's announcement.]
6381. (Die Schweiz und ihre Zustände.) Switzerland in 1847, and its condition, political, social, moral, and physical, before the war. Ed. Mrs. P. Sinnett. L: Bentley 1848. 2v. xi;304; 335p. 19cm. ["The present tr. is greatly abridged...by the gen. condensation of the whole work."] [BM.LC]
6382. Toussaint l'Ouverture. Novel? NY: Appleton. ca. 1868-70. [Publisher's announcement.]

"MUEHLBACH,[1] Lu." (i.e., Frau Ka. (Müller) Mundt, 1814-73). Sel. in C469.
6383. [Coll.] Hist. romances of Louisa M--. NY;L: Appleton 1898. 20v. 22cm. [Also pub. separately; see titles below.] [LC]
6384. [Coll.] 1912. [same] Univ. soc. [AC]
§6385. (Der alte Fritz und seine Zeit.) Old Fritz and the new era. Tr. P: Langley. Il. Gaston Fay. NY: Appleton 1868. 271p. 24cm. [Tr. is rather free, not otherwise bad. -- This is pt. 1 of "Deutschland in Sturm und Drang." BM has title: Germany in storm and stress. Old Fritz, etc. The early eds. were mostly prtd. in double columns, hence the discrepancy in paging.] [LC.BM]
§6385a. do. 1898. [same] 407p. 22cm. [LC]
§6385b. do. 1915. [same] Marion co. [AC]
6386. Andreas Hofer: an historical novel. Tr. F. Jordan. Il. G. Fay. NY: Appleton 1868. 261p. 23cm. [LC.BM]

[1]The following novels were announced for publication by Appletons' about 1868 (probably most of them never appeared): Chas. II and his court (Karl II und sein Hof). Count Benjowski; or, F: the Gt. in Bohemia (Der Graf v. Benjowsky). Court histories (Hofgeschichten?). Emperor Leopold and his time (Kaiser Leopold II und seine Zeit). Empress Claudia; or, the princess of Tyrol. (Kaiserin Claudia, Prinzessin v. Tirol). Eva (Eva). Franz Rakoczy, a Hungarian tale (Fz. R--). The gay world (Eine Welt des Glanzes). Gisela (do.). The great elector and his children (Der grosse Kurfürstuund seine Zeit). Hist. sketch-book (Historisches Bilderbuch). Last days of the Empress Catherine (Die letzten Lebenstage Katharinas II). Maria Theresa and Trenck (Maria Theresia und der Pandurenoberst T--). Memoirs of a man of the world (Memoiren eines Weltkindes). Napoleon and the Vienna congress (Napoleon in Deutschland). Prince Louis Ferdinand. The princes and the poets. Rich by the wind. The serf. Urban. The world and the stage (Welt und Bühne).

MUEHLBACH, Lu.--Andreas Hofer
6387. do. 1893. [same] 499p. 19cm. [LC]
6388. do. 1898. [same] 499p. 22cm. [LC]
6389. do. 1915. [same] Marion co. [AC]
6390. (Berlin und Sanssouci.) The romance of a court; or, B-- and S--. A novel. Tr. A. G. Vaughan. L: Bentley 1866. 3v. 20cm. [BM]
6391. do. 1867. B-- and S--; or, F: the Gt. and his friends. Tr. Mrs. C. Coleman and her daughters. NY: Appleton. 391p. 20cm.[LC.BM]
6392. do. 1889. [same] New cheap ed. Appleton. [AC]
6393. do. 1898. [same] Appleton. 497p. 22cm. [LC]
6394. do. 1915. [same] Marion co. [AC]
6395. Bernthal; or, the son's revenge. NY: Harper 1867. 96p. 24cm. [Prtd. in double columns.] [LC.BM]
6396. (Bonners, oder Geschichte eines Millionärs.) The story of a millionaire. Tr. Nathaniel Greene. NY: Appleton 1872. 356p. 18cm. [LC]
6397. A conspiracy of the Carbonari. Tr. Ma. J. Safford. NY: Neely 1896. 236p. 16cm. [LC]
6398. (Der grosse Kurfürst und seine Zeit.) The reign of the great elector. Tr. M. S. Smith. NY;L: Appleton 1898. 426p. 22cm. [LC]
6399. do. 1915. [same] Marion co. [AC]
6400. (Der junge Kurfürst.) The youth of the great elector: an historical romance. Tr. M. S. Smith. NY: Appleton 1896. 470p. 19cm. [LC]
6401. do. 1898. [same] Appleton. 22cm. [LC]
6402. do. 1915. [same] Marion co. [AC]
6403. (Die Tochter einer Kaiserin.) The daughter of an empress: an historical novel. Tr. Nath. Greene. NY: Appleton 1869. 255p. il. 24cm. [Pub. in 1867; see "Catholic world" 6(1868):713.] [LC.BM]
6404. do. 1887. [same?] NY: Lovell. D. [AC]
6405. do. 1893. [same] Appleton. 453p. 19cm. [LC]
6406. do. 1898. [same] 22cm. [LC]
6407. do. 1915. [same] Marion co. [AC]
6408. F: the Gt. and his merchant. Tr. Lady Wallace. L: Bentley. 1858. 2v. 8. [Cf. #6423. This may be from the same original.] [BM]
6409. (Friedrich der Grosse und seine Geschwister.) F: the Gt. and his family: an hist. novel. Tr. Mrs. C. Coleman and her daughters. NY: Appleton 1867. 300p. il. 24cm. [Prtd. in double columns.][LC.BM]
6410. do. 1893. [same] 572p. 19cm. [LC]
6411. do. 1898. [same] 22cm. [LC]
6412. do. 1915. [same] Marion co. [AC]
6413. (Friedrich der Grosse und sein Hof.) F: the Gt. and his court: an hist. romance. Tr. Mrs. C. Coleman and her daughters. NY: Appleton 1866. 434p. 20cm. [LC]
6414. do. 1887. [same] Appleton. [AC]
6415. do. 1887. [same?] NY: Merrill & Baker. 299p. il. 21cm. [LC]
6416. do. 1887. [same?] NY: Lovell. D. [AC]
6417. do. 1898. [same as #6413] Appleton. 433p. 22cm. [LC]
6418. do. 1915. [same] Marion co. [AC]
6419. (Goethe und Schiller.) G-- and S--: an hist. romance. Tr. C. Coleman. Il. by G. Fay. NY: Appleton 1868. 283p. 23cm. [LC.BM]
6420. do. 1887. [same?] NY: Lovell. D. [AC]
6421. do. 1898. [same as #6419] Appleton. 494p. 22cm. [LC]
6422. do. 1915. [same] Marion co. [AC]
6423. (Johann Gotzkowsky.) The merchant of Berlin: an hist. novel. Tr. Amory Coffin. NY: Appleton 1867. 394p. 19cm. [LC.BM] [Cf. also #6408.]
6424. do. 1868. [same] Also, Ma. Theresa and her fireman (Ma. Theresia und ihr Heizer). Appleton. 291p. il. 24cm. [LC]
6425. do. 1889. [same as #6423] New ed. Appleton. [AC]
6426. do. 1898. [same] Appleton. 420p. 22cm. [LC]

MUEHLBACH, Lu.--Johann Gotzkowsky.
6427. do. 1915. [same] Marion co. [AC]
6428. (Kaiser Js. II und sein Hof.) Js. II and his court: an hist. novel. Tr. A. de V. Chaudron. Mobile, Ala: Goetzel 1864. 4v. in one. 19cm. [Wall-paper covers.] [LC]
6429. do. 1868. [same] NY: Appleton. 343p. 23cm. [BM]
[Prtd. in double columns.]
6430. do. 1884. [same] il. 23cm. [LC]
6431. do. 1898. [same] Appleton. 672p. 22cm. [LC]
6432. do. 1915. [same] Marion co. [AC]
*6433. (Kaiserin Josephine.) The empress J--: an hist. sketch of the days of Napoleon. Tr. by Rev. W. Binet. Il. G. Fay. NY: Appleton 1867. 280p. 23cm. [Prtd. in double columns.] [LC.BM]
*6434. do. 1898. [same] 524p. 22cm. [LC]
*6435. do. 1911. [same] 19cm. [LC]
*6436. do. 1915. [same] Marion co. [AC]
6437. (König H: VIII und sein Hof.) Katharine Parr; or, the court of H: VIII. An hist. romance. Tr. J: R. Atkins. L: Newby 1862. 3v. 19cm. [BM]
6438. do. 1865. H: VIII and his court; or, Catharine Parr. Tr. anon. Mobile, Ala: Goetzel. 2v. 142; 143p. 19cm. [Wall-paper covers.][BM]
6439. do. 1867. H: VIII and his court, etc. Tr. H: N. Pierce. NY: Appleton. 418p. 20cm. [LC]
6440. do. 1868. [same] Appleton. 2v. in one. 418p. 20cm. [BM]
6441. do. 1887. [same] New ed. Appleton. [AC]
6442. do. 1898. [same] Appleton. 418p. 22cm. [LC]
6443. do. 1915. [same] H: VIII and Catherine Parr. Marion co. [AC]
6444. (Königin Hortense.) Queen Hortense: a life pict. of the Napoleonic era. An hist. novel. Tr. C. Coleman. NY: Appleton 1870. 187p. 24cm. [LC]
6445. do. 1888. [same?] Queen H--: a pict. of life in the time of Napoleon. NY: Lovell. 210p. 18cm. [LC]
6446. do. 1898. [same as #6444] Appleton. 383p. 22cm. [LC]
6447. do. 1915. [same] Marion co. [AC]
6448. (Ma. Theresia und ihr Heizer.) Maria Theresa and her fireman. Tr. anon. NY: Appleton 1868. 24cm.
[Bound with "The merchant of Berlin," see #6424; but also issued sep., and listed by AC as in print in 1876.]
6449. (Marie Antoinette und ihr Sohn.) Marie A-- and her son: an hist. novel. Tr. W: L. Gage. NY: Appleton 1867. 301p. il. 23cm[LC]
6450. do. 1869. [same] [BM]
6451. do. 1898. [same] 566p. 22cm. [LC]
6452. do. 1915. [same] Marion co. 1915. [AC]
6453. (Mehemed Ali und sein Haus.) Mohammed Ali and his house: an hist. romance. Tr. C. Coleman. Il. A. Fredericks. NY: Appleton 1872. 229p. 23cm. [LC]
6454. do. 1898. [same] Appleton. 463p. 22cm. [LC]
6455. do. 1915. [same] Mohammed Ali. Marion co. [AC]
§6456. (Napoleon und Blücher.) N-- and B--: an hist. novel. Tr. F. Jordan. NY: Appleton 1867. 301p. il. 24cm. [LC.BM]
[Prtd. in double columns.]
§6457. do. 1893. [same] 507p. 19cm. [LC]
§6458. do. 1898. [same] 22cm. [LC]
§6459. do. 1915. [same] Marion co. [AC]
§6460. (Napoleon und Königin Luise.) N-- and the queen of Prussia: an hist. novel. Tr. F. Jordan. NY: Appleton 1867. 245p. il. 24cm.
[Prtd. in double columns.] [LC.BM]
§6461. do. 1868. [same] [LC]
§6462. do. 1893. [same] Appleton. 509p. 19cm. [LC]
§6463. do. 1898. [same] Appleton. 22cm. [LC]
§6464. do. 1915. [same] Marion co. [AC]

MUEHLBACH, Lu.
§6465. (Prinz Eugen und seine Zeit.) Prince Eugene and his times: an hist. novel. Tr. A. de V. Chaudron. Il. G. Fay. NY: Appleton 1869. 316p. 23cm.[Prtd. in double columns. Quite freely handled.][LC.BM]
§6466. do. 1898. [same] 549p. 22cm. [LC]
§6467. do. 1915. [same] Marion co. [AC]
6468. (Rastatt und Jena.) Louisa of Prussia and her times: an hist. novel. Tr. F. Jordan. NY: Appleton 1867. 277p. il. 24cm. [LC]
6469. do. 1877. [same] New ed. Appleton. [AC]
6470. do. 1898. [same] Appleton. 516p. 22cm. [LC]
6471. do. 1915. [same] Marion co. [AC]
6472. A royal marriage. Tr. (i.e., condensed and retold) G. Gordon. 1861. In C170.
6473. (Zwei Lebenswege.) Two life-paths: a romance. Tr. Nathaniel Greene. NY: Appleton 1869. 157p. 23cm. [LC]

MUEHLER, H: v. 1812-74. Sel. in C106.

MUEHLMANN, J: 1543-1614. Sel. in C271;275.

MUEHLON, W:
*6475. (Die Verheerung Europas. Aufzeichnungen aus den ersten Kriegsmonaten.) Dr. M--'s diary: notes written early in the war. Tr. anon. L;NY: Cassell 1918. xii;247p. 21cm. [BM.LC] [Seems to be excellent.]
*6476. do. 1918. The vandal of Europe: an exposé of the inner workings of Germany's policy of world domination, and its brutalizing consequences. Tr. with introd. by W: L. McPherson. NY;L: Putnam. xvi;335p. 19cm. [Excellent tr.] [LC]
*6477. Memoranda and letters of Dr. M--. Tr. Munroe Smith. NY: Amer. assoc. for internat. concil. 1918. 51p. 19cm. [LC.BM]
*6478. do. 1918. [same] In C160.
§6479. Revelations of an ex-director of Krupp's: dr. M-- memorandum and his letter to Herr v. Bethmann-Hollweg. Tr. anon. NY: Doran 1918. 8p. 18cm. [Not very skillful or good.] [LC]
§6480. do. 1918. [same] L;NY: Hodder & Stoughton. 11p. 21cm. [BM.LC]

MUELLER, Adalbert v. 1802-79.
6481. (Donaustauf und Walhalla.) D-- and W-- described by Ethelbert [sic] M--. Tr. from 6th ed. and enl. with the (abr.) biogr. of Walhalla's inmates. Anon. Ratisbon: G:J.Manz 1846. 80p. engr. 23cm. [Done evidently by a German in very naive literal style. The biogr. is not in orig. EC says: Regensburg 1847.] [BM]

MUELLER, Ad. 1839-1901. The king's fool. Opera. See Wittmann, Hg., #10316.

MUELLER, Art. 1826-73. Sel. in C554.

MUELLER, D:
6483. (Geschichte des deutschen Volkes.) See Charlton T. Lewis, "A hist. of Germany," founded on...NY: Harper 1874. 799p. 20cm. [BM] [Some parts are closely tr., but Lewis rewrote much of it, drawing on other sources.]

MUELLER, (F:) Max, 1823-1900.
*6484. (Ansprache am Friedensfest...am 1. Mai 1871.) Speech at the Ger. peace festival in London...(Ger;Engl.) L: Williams & Norgate 1871. 16p. 22cm. [BM]
6485. (Das Pferdeburla.) The Silesian horse-herd. Tr. O. A. Fechter. Pref. J. E. Carpenter. L: Longmans 1903. 230p. 8. [EC]
*6486. (Deutsche Liebe.) German love. From the papers of an alien. Tr. Susannah Winkworth. L: Chapman & Hall 1858. 153p. 12. [BM.LC]
*6487. do. 1875. Memories: a story of Ger. love. Tr. G: P. Upton. Chic: Jansen, McClurg. 173p. 18cm. [LC.BM]

MUELLER, (F:) Max--Deutsche Liebe
*6488. do. 1877. Tr. from 4th ed. by Georgina A. Mueller. L: Mullan. 152p. 12. [This supposedly new version is not orig., but borrows quite shamelessly from #6486.] [BM.LC]
*6489. do. 1879. [same as #6487] [LC]
*6490. do. 1884. [same as #6488] L: Sonnenschein. 152p. [BM]
*6491. do. 1887. [same] 2d ed. [BM]
6491a. do. 1887. Tr. "Gowan Lea" in C417.
*6492. do. 1898. [same as #6488] New ed. L: Longmans. 152p. [BM]
*6493. do. 1902. [same as #6487] New ed. Il. Blanche Ostertag. Chic: McClurg. 134p. 22cm. [LC]
*6494. do. 1906. [same] New il. ed. Il. Marg. and Helen M. Armstrong. Chic: McClurg. 135p. 23cm. [LC]
*6495. do. 1909. [same as #6488] Pocket ed. L: Longmans. xiv;161p. port. 16cm. [BM]
*6496. do. 1914. [same as #6487] 60th thousand. Chic: McClurg. [LC]
6497. Vedanta philos. NY: Longmans 1920. [AC]
6498. Letters. In his Life and letters, ed. by his wife. L: Longmans 1902. 2v. il. 8. [BM]
[Contains many of his letters in Engl. tr. Mrs. R. Corbet, Mabel Peach, and Mrs. M--.]

MUELLER, Grd. F: 1705-83.
6499. Voyages from Asia to America, for completing the discoveries of the northwest coast of America. Tr. from...S. Muller [sic]. By T: Jefferys. L: Jefferys 1761. 76p. 26 x 21cm. [BM.LC]
6500. do. 1764. [same] 2d ed. viii;120p. 27 x 21cm. [BM.LC]

MUELLER, Hs. 1882- .
6501. (Die blaue Küste.) The love coast: comedy in 3 acts. Ad. Mrs. C: A. Doremus. Libr. NY: Carczak pub. 1915. Tw. [LC]
§6502. (Violanta.) V--: opera in one act by Er. Korngold. Tr. K. H. B. de Jaffa. Libr. Ger;Engl. NY: Ricordi 1927. 61p. 23cm. [LCM.BM]
[In part quite good, but not wholly correct. Rhythmical prose.]

MUELLER, H: of Rostock, 17th cent.
§6503. (Geistliche Erquickungsstunden.) Hours of spir. refreshment. Tr. Rev. M. Geneste. L: Relig. tract soc. 1840. xxiv;280. 12cm. [Not very good. Brief memoir added.] [BM]
6504. do. 1886. Hours of refreshing. Pref. A. Melville. Glasgow: D. Bryce. 134p. 8. [BM]
6505. do. 1887. House (i.e., hours) of refreshing. NY: Armstrong. S. [AC]

MUELLER, H: Ern. 1866- .
6506. (Der Weltkrieg und das Völkerrecht.) "Who are the Huns?" The law of nations and its breakers. Tr. R. L. Orchelle. Berlin: Reimer; NY: Stechert 1915. 405p. 24cm. [LC]
§6507. (Die Braut v. Messina.) The bride of M--: opera in 3 acts by J: H: Bonawitz. Text ad. from Schiller. Tr. H. M. Wetherill. Libr. Phil: Lee & Walker 1874. 12p. 29cm. [Poor verse, correct.] [LCM]
*6508. do. 1874. Tr. anon. Vocal score. Ger;Engl. Phil: Lee & Walker. 183p. 34cm. [Blank verse, very good.] [LCM.BMM]

MUELLER, Hg. 1831-81.
§6509. (Adelaide.) Beethoven: a dramatized episode from his life. In one act. Introducing his two songs "Adelaide" and "Joyful and mournful." Tr. Gst. Hein. Aberdeen: Milne 1879. 31p. 16cm. [BM]
[Verse tr. is rather poor.]
6510. do. 1897. Adelaide: a play in one act. Ad. D: Bispham. NY: Tw. [LC]

MUELLER, J: Am.
*6511. The authentic narr. of J. A. Miller, the German prophet. Tr.

MUELLER, J: Am.
by an Episc. Ger. clergyman, I. I. G. Fisher. Greenwich: Eliz. Delahoy 1817. xiii;28p. 8. [BM]
[Tr. from "Der neue Prophet; oder der Bauer J. A. Müller von Mekesheim in Baden," Frankfurt 1816. The condensation may have been done by the editor of the German work. The Engl. is much reduced from Müller's "Erzählung." Tr. seems correct.]

MUELLER, J:s.
6512. (Hemmungen des Lebens.) Hindrances of life. Tr. F. F. Strecker. NY: Kennedy 1909. 32p. 19cm. [LC]
6512a. (Unser Tageslauf.) Hidden springs. Auth. tr. Hilda Bell. Bagster 1926. 42p. 18. [EC]

MUELLER, J:s v. 1752-1809. Sel. in C12;158.
*6513. (Vierundzwanzig Bücher allgemeiner Geschichte.) Universal hist. Tr. Jas. C. Prichard. L: Prtd. for Longmans 1811. 3v. 21cm. [Tr. is not strictly close, but very good.] [BM.LC]
*6514. do. 1834. [same] Bost: Cottons & Barnard. 4v. 20cm. [BM]
*6515. do. 1837. [same?] Bost. 4v. 12. [AC]
6516. do. 1840. The hist. of the world...to...1783. Compared with the orig., rev.corr....Ax. H. Everett. Bost: Marsh, Capen, Lyon & Webb. 4v. 19cm. [BM]
[Has biogr. of author. LC has vols. 1-2 of this ed.]
6517. do. 1872-6. [same] Rev. by A. Everett. NY: Harper n.d. 4v. [AC]
6518. Topogr. and mil. description of Germany. Egerton 1813. 8. [EC]
See Virchow, Rd., J: Mueller, an eloge, #9547.

MUELLER, K: Otfried, 1797-1840. Sel. in C12.
6519. Attica and Athens. Tr. J: G. Lockhart. L: Groombridge 1842. 194p. 21cm. [LC]
*6520. (Die Dorier.) Hist. and antiq. of the Doric race. Tr. H: Tufnell and G: C. Lewis. L: Murray 1830. 2v. xxxv;547;551p. 22cm. [BM.LC]
6521. (Die Etrusker.) Manners and customs, relig. and arts of the Etruscans. Freely tr. by Mrs. E. C. Gray, in her "Hist. of Etruria," pt. 3, pp. 71-314. L: Hatchards 1843, etc. 19cm. [BM.LC]
*6522. (Handbuch der Archäologie der Kunst.) Ancient art and its remains; or, a manual of the archaeology of art. Tr. from 2d ed. by J: Leitch. L: Fullarton 1847. xv;526p. 22cm. [BM.LC]
*6523. do. 1850. [same] New enl. ed. with numerous add. by F. G. Welcker. L: Fullarton. xv;634p. 22cm. [BM]
*6524. (Prolegomena zu einer wissenschaftlichen Mythologie.) Introd. to a scientific system of mythology. Tr. J: Leitch. L: Longmans 1844. x;353p. 22cm. [BM.LCO]

MUELLER, K. W. Sel. in C41;372.

MUELLER, L: Ern. Sg. 1766-1804. Sel. in C287.

MUELLER, Ml. 1673-1704. Sel. in C231;269;469.

MUELLER, M.
6525. Hist. of the principal monarchies and states, prior to the Christian era. From the German. L: Bingley 1768. See "Crit. R." 26(1768):233. (B26)
[The author is "head master of the grammar school at Hall, in Saxony."]

MUELLER, N: 1770-1851. Sel. in C47;309.

MUELLER, O: 1816-94.
*6526. (Cte. Ackermann.) Cte. A--: a theatrical romance, founded upon...the life of a young artist of the last cent. Tr. Mrs. C.

MUELLER, O:
Coleman and her daughters. Phil: Porter & Coates 1871. 357p. 18cm. [LC.BM]
§6527. (Der Stadtschultheiss von Frankfurt.) Dr. Goethe's courtship: a tale of domestic life. Tr. by V. S. L;NY: Routledge 1866. xv; 271p. 17cm. [Quite freely handled.] [BM.LC]
6528. (Der Tannenschütz.) The forester of Altenhain. Tr. F: Shoberl. L: Saunders & Otley 1852. 201p. 20cm. [BM]

MUELLER, W: 1794-1827. Sel. in C3;17;25-6;37;41;45-6;67;86;106;111; 123;129;137a*;149;152;195;309;311*;366*;371-4;378;380;391;395-7; 405a;421;423;448;467;469;470;538;571;#8001.
[Mueller's 44 songs, "Die schöne Müllerin" and "Winterreise," were composed by Franz Schubert and are found in translation in bilingual editions of Schubert's songs.]

MUELLER, W: 1820-92.
*6529. (Generalfeldmarschall Graf Moltke.) Field marshal count M--, 1800-78. Tr. P. C. Pinkerton. Ed. Capt. H. M. Hozier. L: Sonnenschein 1879. viii;203p. front. (port.) 20cm. [Not flawless.] [BM]
*6530. do. 1880. [same] 2d. L: Sonnenschein & Allen. [BM]
6531. Polit. hist. of recent times, 1816-75, with spec. ref. to Germany. Tr. J: P. Peters. NY: Harper 1882. 692p. 20cm. [LC]

MUELLER, W: 1845-1914.
6532. Hagar: opera in one act by Ad. Neuendorff. Tr. anon. Libr. Engl. n.i. 1894. 32p. Tw. [LCM]

MUELLER, Wfg. 1816-73. Sel. in C17;67;152;309;372.

MUELLER-LYER, Fz. C: 1857- .
*6533. (Phasen der Kultur.) Hist. of social devel. Tr. Mrs. Eliz. C. Lake and Hilda A. Lake. Introds. L. T. Hobhouse and E. J. Urwick. L: Allen & Unwin 1920. 362p. 22cm. [BM]
[My judgment derived from the preface; the orig. before me did not correspond fully with the tr., which may have been based on another ed.]
*6534. do. 1921. [same] NY: Knopf. [LC]

MUELLNER, Amand Gf. Ad. 1774-1829. Sel. in C461;543.
*6535. (Der 29. Februar.) The 29th of Feb.: a dram. sketch in blank verse. Tr. R. P. Gillies. 1820. In "Blackwood's Mag." 6:397. [Good verse and correct as to sense, but one misses the rhymes of the orig.]
†6536. (Die Schuld.) Guilt; or, the gipseys prophecy. A tragedy in 5 acts [verse]. Followed by Schiller's "Ideal" and "The cranes of Ibycus." Tr. W: E: Frye. L: Prtd. for the author 1819. 88p. 21cm. ["A free tr...I have...taken some liberties with the original." Blank verse from M--'s rhymed trochaics.] [BM]
*6537. do. 1819. Guilt; or, the anniversary. A tragedy in 4 acts [verse]. Tr. R. P. Gillies. Ed: Priv. prtd. 103p. 21cm. [BM]
[50 cop. prtd."...a rapid sketch in blank verse..." On the whole, quite good: correct in sense and clever verse.]
*6538. do. 1888. Guilt. Tr. J. Cockle. L: Williams & Norgate. 108p. 19cm. [A better tr. than that of Gillies.] [BM]
*6539. (König Ingurd.) King I--: A trag. in 5 acts [verse]. Tr. (by R. P. Gillies) in large part, with summaries of omitted portions, in the series "Horae germanicae," "Blackwood's Mag." 7(1840):407, 545. (B26)

MUENCH-BELLINGHAUSEN, Egs. Fz. Jz. Freiherr v. 1806-71. See "F. Halm."

MUENCHHAUSEN, Börries v., 1874- . Sel. in C154(18);423.

MUENCHHAUSEN, K: F: Hrns. Baron v. 1720-97. Sel. in C469.

MUENCHHAUSEN,[1] K: F: Hrns. Baron v. and Gf. A: Bürger.
6540. Baron Munchausen's narr. of his marvellous travels and campaigns in Russia, etc. Tr. anon. Oxford: 1786. 49p. 12. [BM]
[Unique copy, ending with "God bless great George our King," supposedly issuing from the thawing horn of the postilion. Tr. by Rd. Er. Raspe; see footnote.]
6541. do. 1786. 2d Engl. ed. Pref. dated April 20, 1786.
[Unique copy in lib. of Göttingen university. This was the source of Bürger's first ed. Tr. Raspe; see footnote.]
6542. do. 1787. Gulliver revived; containing singular travels, campaigns, voyages and advent. By Baron Munchausen. 5th enl. ed. L: Kearsley. xxiv;208p. 12. [BM]
[20 chapters. Pref. to the 4th ed., here reprinted, says, "The first ed. contained no more than was written by Baron M-- and includes chapters (2-6) only. All the other chapters are the production of another pen." Chap. 6 ends with the frozen horn. Thereafter comes new matter, partly taken from Lucian's "True history."]
6543. do. 1787. Gulliver revived. Also, an account of a voyage into the moon, with...particulars relative to the cooking animal in that planet...the human species. Bost: Prtd. and sold by B: Edes & son. (B6a)
6544. do. 1787. [same] 4th ed. enl. L: Prtd. Newport (R. I.): Reprtd. by P: Edes. 2; 4; 40p. 16. (B6a) [Available: CLS]
6545. do. 1787. [same] 4th ed. consid. enl. NY: Prtd. for S: Campbell. (B6a)
6546. do. 1792. [same] NY: Prtd. for S: Campbell. (B6a)
6547. do. 1792. Sequel. L: Symonds & Owen. 243p. [BM]
[14 chaps. No relation to German.]
6548. do. 1793. [same as #6542] 7th ed. consid. enl. and ornamented with...orig. designs. L: Kearsley. 12. [BM]
[Some alterations in text, pruning, etc.]
6549. do. 1795. [same as #6543] Haverhill (Mass.): Prtd. by P: Edes. (B6a)
6550. do. 1796. Sequel. [same as #6547] 239p. [BM]
6551. do. 1797. [same as #6543] NY. 18. (B6a)
6552. do. 1799. Gulliver revived; or, the vice of lying properly exposed. 8th ed. L: Kearsley. 199p. il. 16. [LCO]
6553. do. 1801. Sequel to the advent. of Baron M--. L: Simonds. xvii;184p. il. 16. [With "Gulliver revived."] [LC]
6554. do. 1808. Supplement, etc. L: Mawman. 84p. [BM]
[Three songs at back. No relation to the German.]

[1]The actual claim of the Baron to the authorship of the stories which commonly go by the name "Munchausen," while the complete facts cannot be ascertained, appears to be rather slight. In the Vademecum für lustige Leute, Berlin 1781, there appeared 18 stories, most if not all of which derived from M--'s big tales to his friends. These were very terse, hardly more than anecdotes. It has been suggested that they were put to paper by Rd. Er. Raspe, but from the "Nachwort" by Dr. Er. Ebstein in the ed. issued by the Gesellschaft der Bibliophilen in Weimar (1925), I am strongly inclined to believe that the writer of them was Bürger, who did in fact publish two editions of the work, with additions that can be ascribed only to him. Seventeen stories from the Vademecum were tr. into Engl. by Raspe, who elaborated on them considerably. This coll. went into a 2d ed. in 1786. On it Bürger based his first ed. of the stories, retaining Raspe's elaborations and adding some of his own, and also adding 8 further stories to Raspe's 17. In 1788 Bürger published a 2d ed., which contained 7 further stories; these 7 are not found in the English ed. of 1787.

MUENCHHAUSEN, Baron v.
6555. do. 1809. Surprising advent. of Baron M--. Il. by T. Rowlandson. L: Tegg. viii;144p. 12. [BM]
[25 chaps. 1-5 are "Ur-Münchhausen"; 6-12 as in #6542; 13-25 as in #6547. Consid. omissions; also addition of voyage to moon and dog-star.]
6556. do. 1809. Sequel. [same as #6547] L: Lane, Newman. 184p. [BM]
[14 chapters]
6557. do. 1810. Surprising advent. Chapbook. 8p. 8. [BM]
[Very brief; sel. and condensation.]
6558. do. 1810? Surprising advent. of the renowned Baron M--. Chapbook. L: Dean & Munday. 32p. 12. [BM]
6559. do. 1811. Voyages, etc. of the renowned Baron M--. (No other data.) [EC]
6560. do. 1811. M-- at Walcheren. Engr. Cruikshank. Johnston. 12 [EC]
6561. do. 1814. Surprising advent. Gainsborough: Mozley. 72p. [BM]
["Abridged." 25 chaps.; same text as #6555.]
6562. do. 1821. Surprising advent. Derby: Mozley. 74p. [BM]
[Same as foregoing. Rare ed.]
6563. do. 1822. Surprising travels and advent. etc. New ed. L: Jones. xvi;288p. il. 12. [BM.LCO]
[BM has 228p. LC copy was not to be found. Contains the Sequel, through chap. 20; chaps. 21-24 contain the Supplement. This ed. omits allusion to intercourse with moon and dog-star.]
6564. do. 1823. [same] New and complete ed. L: Hughes & Bysh. [BM]
[24 chaps., as in foregoing. 70p. plus sequel of 61p.]
6565. do. 1827. Life and exploits of Baron M--. Glasgow: Griffin. 104p. 12. [BM]
[Has chapter headings and summaries. Text based on #6548, edited.]
6566. do. 1830. [same as #6548, abr.] L: Allman. 28p. [BM]
[No division into chapters.]
6567. do. 1840? [same as #6548, abr.] Surprising advent....of... Baron M--. Derby: Richardson. 24p. 12. [BM]
[Selection, without chaps. but under subtitles.]
6568. do. 1842. Surprising travels and advent. Francfort o/M. 2 pts. (70) 137p. 16. [Same as #6548 plus Sequel.] [BM]
6569. do. 1845. Curious and entertaining advent. and travels...NY: Farmer & Daggers. iv;56p. 22cm. [LC]
[Somewhat pruned, and chap. 11 and most of 20 omitted; after that greater liberties are taken.]
6570. do. 1858. Surprising travels and advent. Ed: Black. 159p. 8.
[26 chaps. 1-21 same as #6548. Sequel much condensed.] [BM]
6571. do. 1859. Travels and surprising advent. Il. "A. Crowquill." L: Trübner. 194p. 8. [34 chaps.] [BM]
6572. do. 1861? Travels of Baron M--. L: Vickers. 2 pts. 32p. col. il. 4. [35 chaps. 1-6 are "Ur-Münchhausen."] [BM]
6573. do. 1863. Advent. New ed. L: Bohn. 8. [EC]
6574. do. 1865. Advent. of Baron M--. New and rev. ed. Introd. T. T. Shore. Il. Gustave Doré. L: Cassell, Petter & Galpin. xv;216p. 32cm. [LC]
[This ed. shifts stories around and prunes them. 17 chaps. 1-5 are "Ur-M--."]
6574a. do. 1866. [same] [BM]
6575. do. 1867. Travels and surprising advent. Il. G. Cruikshank. L: Tegg. 268p. 8. [34 chaps. plus Supplement. 1-6 are "Ur-M--."] [BM]
6576. do. 1869. [same as #6574] Cassell. 4. [EC]
6577. do. 1869. Advent. L: Tegg. 8. [EC]
6578. do. 1870. [Sel.] In Ma. Howitt's "Treasury of old favourite tales, etc.", pp. 212-20. Ed: Gall & Inglis. 347p. 17cm. [BM]
6579. do. 1876. NY: Radde. 12. pa. [AC]
6580. do. 1876. Baron M--'s narr. of his marvellous travels and campaigns in Russia, etc. Oxford. 12. [BM]

MUENCHHAUSEN, Baron v.

6581. do. 1877. Baron M--: his life travels, and extraord. advent. New ed. L: Ward, Lock. 163p. 8. [34 chaps. plus Supplement.] [BM]

6582. do. 1878. Advent. of Baron M-- from the best Engl. and Ger. eds. Col. ils. by A. Bichard. L: Warne. 104p. 4. [BM] [27 chaps., wholly new arrangement; incorporates Bürger's additions to the 2d Ger. edition.]

6583. do. 1879. [same; reissue] xvi;201p. 8. [BM]

6584. do. 1879. Travels and surprising advent. Il. "Af. Crowquill." NY: Munro. Seaside lib. 31p. 32cm. [LC]

6585. do. 1879. Travels and surprising advent. NY: Amer. bk. exch. xxiii;283p. 18cm. [LC]

6586. do. 1879. Travels, with "Gulliver's travels" and "The vicar of Wakefield." Ed;L: Blackwood. 8. [EC]

6587. do. 1881. Advent. New ed. Il. G. Doré. L: Cassell. 8. [EC] [Cf. #6574.]

6588. do. 1882. Travels and surprising advent. NY: Lovell. 125p. 18cm. [Cf. paging of #6590.] [LC]

6589. do. 1884. Travels and surprising advent. Il. Cruikshank. L: Warne. Chandos classics. xii;268p. 8. [BM] [34 chaps. plus Supplement.]

6590. do. 1885. Travels and surprising advent. L: Maxwell. 125p. il. 8. [34 chaps. plus Supplement. Cf. paging of #6588.] [BM]

6591. do. 1889. Orig. travels and surprising advent. New ed. Il. "Af. Crowquill." L: Trübner. 253p. 8. [BM] [34 chaps. plus Supplement.]

6592. do. 1894. Advent. Il. A. Bichard. New ed. L: Warne. fol. [EC] [Cf. #6582.]

6593. do. 1895. Surprising advent. Il. W: Strang and J. B. Clark. Introd. T: Seccombe. L: Lawrence & Bullen. li;299p. 22cm. [LC.BM] [34 chaps. plus Supplement. EC dates this 1894.]

6594. do. 1896. Travels and surprising advent. L: Biggs. 125p. il. 8. [Reprint of #6590.] [BM]

6594a. do. 1898. Surprising travels and advent. Il. A. Nobody. L: Wells, Gardner & Darton. xx;268p. 8. [BM] [34 chaps. plus Supplement. EC lists this with 290p. Cf. paging of #6589.]

6594b. do. 1899. Gulliver revived; or, the vice of lying properly exposed. 8th ed. L: Kearsley. iv;199p. il. 16. [LC] [7th ed. was pub. in 1793. Cf. #6548.]

6594c. do. 1900. Tales from the travels of Baron M--. Ed....E: E. Hale. Il. after G. Doré. Bost: Heath. ix;78p. 19cm. [LC]

6594d. do. 1902. Advent. NY: Crowell. xxii;250p. il. 17cm. [LC]

6594e. do. 1902. Surprising travels and advent. Il. in col. W. Heath Robinson. L: Richards. 256p. 7 x 4 in. [Same text as #6591.] [BM]

6595. do. 1903. Advent. of Baron M-- by Rd. Er. Raspe. Introd. J. H. Willard. Phil: Altemus. xii;194p. il. 19cm. [LC]

6596. do. 1903. Wonderful advent. Ad. for children by Doris Hayman. L: Dean. 192p. [23 chaps., edited.] [BM]

6596a. do. 1907. Tales. NY: Hurst. 283p. 12. [AC]

6597. do. 1907. Travels and surprising advent. Greening. 270p. il. 7 x 4 in. [EC]

6598. do. 1908. Tales from the travels. Certified as strictly true by Gulliver, Sindbad, and Aladdin. Ed. W: T. Stead. Phil: Penn pub. 62p. il. 18cm. [LC]

6599. do. 1914. Advent. of Baron M-- by Rd. Er. Raspe. NY: Brentano's. Lotus lib. [AC]

6600. do. 1915. Travels and advent. Retold for children by G: S. Duncan. Il. in col. W. H. Margetson. L: Nelson. 160p.[17 chaps.] [BM]

6600a. do. 1921. Children's M--, retold by J: Martin. Il. Gordon Ross. Houghton 1921. xv;185p. il. O. [AC]

MUENCHHAUSEN, Baron v.
6601. do. 1922. Surprising advent. Girard, Kan: Haldeman-Julius. 63p. 12cm. [LC]
6602. do. 1922. [same as #6599] [AC]
6603. do. 1922. The children's M--. Retold by J: Martin. Il. G. Ross. L: Batsford. 185p. Ryl. 8. [EC]
6604. do. 1923. Travels of Baron M--. Gulliver revived, etc. Ed. W: Rose. Il. "Af. Crowquill." L: Routledge; NY: Dutton. 253p. 19cm. [Rose's introd. discusses the hist. of the stories.] [LC]
6605. do. 1926. Travels and surprising advent. Il. 37 curious engr. from the baron's own designs and 5 il. G: Cruikshank. L: Warne. 294p. 7 x 5 in. [Called a reissue. Cf. #6589 and #6591.] [EC]

MUENSTER, Sb. 1489-1552.
6606. (Cosmographia universalis.) A treatyse of the newe India... after the...uniuersall cosmographie. Tr. Rycharde Eden. L: E:Sutton 1553. 4 leaves, ff. A-M. 15cm. [BM.LC] [From book 5 of the orig.: "Nova India," etc.]
6607. do. 1572. A Briefe Collection and compendious extract of straunge and memorable thinges, gathered oute of the Cosmographye of S. Munster. L: T:Marshe. ff. 100. 14cm. [BM]
6608. do. 1574. [same] ff. 102. [BM]
6609. do. 1885. [reprint of #6606] In E: Arber, "The first three Engl. books on America," pp. 1-42. Birmingham. 29cm. [BM.LC]

MUENSTER-LEDENBURG, G: Hb. Fürst Münster v. Derneburg, Graf zu, 1820-1902.
§6610. (Politische Skizzen über die Lage Europas.) Polit. sketches of the state of Europe, 1814-67. Tr. Gräfin Harriet Münster-Ledenburg. Ed: Edmonston & Douglas 1868. 287p. 23cm. [BM.LC] [Not very close or accurate.]

MUENSTERBERG, Hg. 1863-1916. (See also "Hg. Terberg.")
§6611. (Die Amerikaner.) The Americans. Tr. E. B. Holt. NY: McClure, Phillips 1904. 619p. 24cm. [LC.BM]
§6612. do. 1905. [same] [LC]

MUENTER, Blr. d. 1793. Sel. in C244.
6613. (Bekehrungsgeschichte...) A faithful narr. of the conversion and death of Count Struensee, formerly prime minister of Denmark. L: Linde 1773. 308p. 8. [This is the 1st ed. of the tr. by G. F. A. Wendeborn. Not in BM or LC]
6614. do. 1773. [same] Together with letters...To which is added, The hist. of Count Enevold Brandt etc. Tr. by Mr. Wendeborn. Embellished with heads and coats of arms. Phil: Rb. Bell. (B6a) [Evidently a reprint of the foregoing.]
*6615. do. 1774. [same] 2d ed. L: Linde. xii;308p. 21cm. [BM.LC]
*6616. do. 1824. [same] A narr. etc. Introd. with notes by T: Rennell. L: Rivington. xxiv;238p. 22cm. [BM.LC] [Same text as the foregoing.]
*6617. do. 1825. [same] 2d ed. L: Rivington. 238p. [LC]
*6618. do. 1826. [same] 3d ed. L: Rivington. [BM]
6619. do. 1853. Count Struenzée, the sceptic and the Christian. Tr. from the French tr. of the German by Mrs. J. H. Wilson. Bost: J: P. Jewett; L: Low. xi;243p. 18cm. [LC.BM] [Anything but a tr. Really a dramatized narr. from the French version.]

MUHEIN, ---. Sel. in C438.

MULDENER, ---. Sel. in C128.

MULNHUSEN. See "Wachsmut von Mühlhausen."

MUMBEL, E. R. Sel. in C425.

MUNCKER, Fz. 1855-1926.
§6620. (R: Wagner. Eine Skizze seines Lebens und Wirkens.) R: W--: his life and works. Tr. by D. Landmann. Il. H: Nisle. L: Williams & Norgate 1891. 106p. 19cm. [BM]
[Front. of W-- by H. Herkomer. Tr. correct, but marred by Germanisms.]

MUND, E. D. See "Pochhammer, Max v."

MUND, Rld. Sel. in C571.

MUNDLICH, ---. Sel. in C169.

MUNDT, Frau Ka. (Müller), 1814-73. See "Lu. Mühlbach."

MUNDT,[1] Td. 1808-61.
§6621. (Graf Mirabeau.) Count M--. an hist. novel. Tr. Thérèse J. Radford. NY: Appleton 1868. 273p. il. 24cm. [LC.BM]
[This tr. cannot handle anything at all difficult.]
*6622. (Krim-Girai, ein Bundesgenosse F:s des Grossen.) Krim-Girai, Khan of the Crimea. Tr. W: G. C. Eliot. L: Murray 1856. xvi;192p. 20cm. [BM]

MUSAEUS, J: K: A: 1735-87. Sel. in C194;372;469.
*6623. (Volksmärchen der Deutschen.) Pop. tales of the Germans. Tr. W: Beckford. L: Murray 1791. 2v. xi;264; 284p. 18cm. [BM]
[Beckford can translate admirably when he chooses, but makes free when he doesn't.--Richilde, or the progress from vanity to vice ("Richilde"); The chronicles of the three sisters ("Die Bücher der Chronika der drei Schwestern"); Stealing of the veil, or the tale à la Mongolfier ("Der geraubte Schleier"); Elfin-freaks, or the seven (i.e., five) legends of Number-Nip ("Legenden von Rübezahl"); The nymph of the fountain ("Die Nymphe des Brunnens.")]
*6224. do. 1801. [same] L: Murray. (B26)
6225. do. 1800? [same?] Pop. tales of the Germans. Lpz: Joachim. 2v. 8. [Notice in Lpz. catalog of the Easter fair, 1800, reprtd. in C157(2). Probably Beckford's tr.]
6626. do. 1823. *The treasure-seeker ("Der Schatzgräber"), wrongly ascribed to Tieck; The spectre barber; Legends concerning Number-Nip ("Legenden v. Rübezahl"); Richilda, or the progress from vanity to vice ("Richilde"); The stealing of the veil, or the tale a la Mongolfier ("Der geraubte Schleier").Tr. anon. in C456. [Tr. of the first story is quite good. The last two probably by Beckford.]
6627. do. 1827. Dumb love ("Stumme Liebe"); Libussa (do.); Melechsala (do.). Tr. T: Carlyle. In C58. Cf. also C59-62.
6628. do. 1845. Popular tales. Hughes. 12. [EC]
[Probably from Beckford's tr.]
*6629. do. 1845. The enchanted knights; or, the chronicle of the three sisters ("Die Bücher der Chronika der drei Schwestern"). Also, The demon of the ring. Tr. A. Sagorski. L: Cunningham. 2 pts. 68; 31p. 16cm. [Somewhat lacking in English style.] [BM]
§6630. do. 1845. Legends of Rubezahl [sic] and other tales. L: Cundall. Hazlitt's holiday lib. xviii;254p. 17cm. [BM]
[Front. and 3 il. J. Erxleben. --§The books of the chronicles of the three sisters ("Die Bücher der Chronika der drei Schwestern"),

[1] The following tr. were announced by Appleton about 1868 (it is doubtful if they were published): Carmola, or the enbaptized; Mendoza, or the father of a rogue; The matador; No divorce; Robespierre, an hist. novel.

MUSAEUS, J: K: A:
tr. Mme. de Chatelain; §(5) Legends of R--; §The hen with the golden eggs ("Ulrich mit dem Bühel"). The last two tr. W: Hazlitt, who is too independent. Pref. Hazlitt and prelim. notice Wieland.]
6631. do. 1845. Select pop. tales. Tr. anon. L: Burns. 168p. 12. [LC says: Lumley 1845. same paging.--*Mute love ("Stumme Liebe"); The nymph of the fountain ("Die Nymphe des Brunnens"); Peter Bock, or the treasure-seeker of the Harz ("Der Schatzgräber"); The three sisters ("Die Bücher etc."); Richilda ("R--"); Roland's squires ("R--s Knappen"); Legends of Rubezahl ("Legenden etc."); The princess's flight; The rescued lover; The countryman and his family. --Tr. is mostly quite good. Perhaps done by Jas. Burns?] [BM.LC]
6632. do. 1850? [same] L: Lumley. 168p. 16. [LCO]
*6633. do. 1865? Pop. works. Tr. J. T. Hanstein. L: Neal. 136p. 15cm. [The squires ("Rolands Knappen"); (3) Legends of Rübezahl; Richilda; The treasure-seeker.] [BM]
6634. do. 1866. Libussa, Duchess of Bohemia ("Libussa"). Also, The man without a name ("Die Entführung"). Tr. J. T. Hanstein. L: Macdonald & Neal. xi;112p. 16cm. [BM]
6635. do. 1866. The chronicles of the three sisters ("Die Bücher, etc."); Mute love ("Stumme Liebe"). Tr. J. T. Hanstein. L: Macdonald & Neal. 134p. 16cm. [BM]
6636. (Die Bücher der Chronika der drei Schwestern.) The arm! The sword! and the hour! or, the legend of the enchanted knights. Freely versified and amplified M. G. Kennedy. L: Longmans 1850. viii;173p. 19cm. [BM]
6637. do. 1857. [same] Longmans. 8. [EC]
6638. do. 1861. The three sons-in-law: a free version (in verse)... by A. F. Frere. L;NY: Nelson. 72p. 24cm. [Very amusing.] [BM]
§6639. do. 1868. Chronicles of the three sisters. Tr. Mark Lemon. In his "Fairy tales." L: [BM]
[Quite freely done. Probably taken from Beckford's tr. (#6623); cf. #6646.]
6640. do. 1871. [same as #6637] [EC]
*6641. do. 1877. Reinald, the wonder-child; or, the chronicles of the three sisters. Tr. Pabke and Pitman. In C444.
6642. (Die Entführung.) The elopement. Tr. anon. 1800? In C157.
6643. do. 1826. Tr. the Misses Corbett. In C436.
6644. (Die Nymphe des Brunnens.) The nymph of the fountain. Tr. anon. In "Ladies Pocket Mag." 4(1825):27, etc. (B26)
6645. (Legenden von Rübezahl.) A legend of Number Nip [Tr. the Misses Corbett? In "Tales and legends," by the authors of the "Odd volume" (C436), vol. 2, 1828.] [BM]
6646. do. 1864. (5) Legends of Number Nip. (Comp. from a tr. of M--'s works pub. in L. shortly after his death; i.e., #6623.) By Mark Lemon. L: Macmillan. xi;140p. 17cm. [BM]
[Lemon claims in his pref. to have corrected Beckford; but only the slightest verbal revision was actually made.]
6647. do. 1870. [same] Macmillan. [EC]
6648. (Libussa.) Libussa. Tr. J: Oxenford. 1844. In C441-2.
6649. (Physiognomische Reisen.) Physiognomical travels, preceded by a physiognomical journal. With his life by Kotzebue. Tr. Anne Plumptre. L: Longman & Rees 1800. 3v. 17cm. [BM]
6650. (Rolands Knappen.) Roland's squires: a legend of the time of Charlemagne. Tr. Harriet P. Huse. NY: Jenkins 1891. 39p. (B12)[NY]
6651. (Stumme Liebe.) The dumb lover. Tr. T: Roscoe. 1826. In C477.
*6652. do. 1849. Dumb love. Tr. T: Carlyle. Pref. the Amer. editor. Phil: Joy. 84p. 21cm. [Also in C156; C194.] [BM]

MUSCULUS (properly Müslin or Meuslin), Wfg. 1497-1563.
6653. (Loci communes sacrae theologiae.) Common places of Christian

MUSCULUS, Wfg.--Loci communes sacrae theologiae
Religion, gathered by...two other treatises...one of Othes, and an other of Vsurye. Tr. J: Man. L: Reginald Wolfe 1563. 5 leaves, ff. 587, 31 leaves. 28cm. [Engr. t.p. and initial.] [BM]
6654. do. 1578. [same] 2d ed. L: H:Bynneman. 5 leaves; 1340; 42p.; 47 leaves. 21cm. [BM]
6655. A ryght godly treatise of matrimony...Tr. (from Lat.) Rychard Ryce. In "The right institucion, etc." L: A.Scoloker 1548? 7 leaves. 13cm. [BM]
6656. do. 1550. [same] A ryght godlye treatyse of matrymonye...In "The right instytucion of baptisme, etc." Tr. Rychard Ryce. L: A.Scoloker & Wylyam Seres. 8 leaves. 12cm. [BM]
6657. The temporysour, that is to saye: the obseruer of tyme, or he that chaungeth with the tyme. Compyled in Latyn...tr. into Frenche by M. Vallerain Pullain. And out of Frenche into Inglishe by R. P. no pub. 1555. ff. A-G. 13cm. [4 dialogs.] [BM]

MUTHER, R: 1860-1909.
§6658. (Geschichte der Malerei im 19. Jahrhundert.) The hist. of mod. painting. Tr. E. C. Dowson, G: A. Greene, and A. C. Hillier. L: Henry 1895-6. 3v. il. 27cm. [BM.LC]
[The tr. is not scrupulously close, but seems correct.]
§6659. do. 1907. [same] Rev. ed. continued by the author to the end of the 19th cent. L: Dent; NY: Dutton. 4v. il. 26cm. [BM.LC]
[The tr. is often inept or even slightly faulty.]
*6660. Hist. of painting, from the 4th to the early 19th cent. Tr. G: Kriehn. NY;L: Putnam 1907. 2v. il. 22cm. [LC.BM]
[Not without errors.]
6661. Leonardo da Vinci. Tr. F. F. Cox. L: Siegle, Hill 1907. xii; 69p. il. 16cm. [BM]
6662. Rembrandt. Tr. Fis. F. Cox. L: Siegle, Hill 1910. 74p. il. 16cm. [BM]

MYCONIUS (really Geisshüsler), Os. 1488-1552.
6663. Life of Zwingli. Tr. H: Bennet. L: 1561. In #10796.

NACHTENHOEFER, ---. Sel. in C271.

NACHTIGAL, J: Kd. Cph. 1753-1819. See "Othmar."

NAOGEORGUS. See Kirchmeyer, T:

NATALIA, queen of Servia.
6664. Sketches from her diary. See H: Buettner, #907.

NATHUSIUS, Frau Ma. K:e Eli. Lu. (Scheele) v. 1817-57. Sel. in C41.
*6665. [Coll.] Two stories: Joachim von Kamern ("Jm. v. K--"); The diary of a poor young lady ("Tagebuch eines armen Fräuleins.") Tr. Miss Thompson. Lpz: Tauchnitz; L: Low 1869. 333p. 16cm. [BM]
6666. Christfrid's first journey. Tr. anon. 1874. In C567.
§6667. (Die Kammerjungfer.) Above her station: the story of a young woman's life. Tr. Mrs. Herman Philip. Ed: Strahan; L: Hamilton, Adams 1859. 222p. 17cm. [Too literal.] [BM]
§6668. do. 1862. [same] NY: Follett, F. & co. 12. [AC]
§6669. do. 1865. [same] NY: Bradburn. 12. [AC]
§6670. (Elisabeth. Eine Geschichte, die nicht mit der Heirat schliesst.) Elizabeth: a story which does not end in marriage. Tr. S. A. Smith. Ed: Grant; L: Simpkin & Marshall 1860. 2v. 345; 444p. 17cm. [Rather feeble tr. --EC has: L: Simpkin 1859.] [BM]
§6671. do. 1871. [same] [EC]
6672. do. n.d. Tr. Mrs. M. A. Shryock. vii;493p. 18cm. [LC]
[T.p. missing.]

NATHUSIUS, Frau Ma. K:e Eli. Lu. v.
6673. (Langenstein und Boblingen.) Katie von Walden; or, Langenstein and Bobbingen. Tr. Ma. A. Robinson. Phil;NY: Amer. S. S. U. 1892. 381p. 19cm. [LC]
6674. (Tagebuch eines armen Fräuleins.) Louisa v. Plettenhaus: the diary of a poor young lady. Tr. anon. Bost;NY: Francis 1857. 233p. 17cm. [LC]
§6675. do. 1860. Step by step; or, the good fight. (Heading of story reads: the poor governess; or, pride and humility.) Tr. anon. L: Bentley. 236p. 17cm. [Pretty good.] [BM]
§6676. do. 1860. [same] Step by step; or, the poor governess. New ed. Bentley. [EC]
†6677. do. 1869. Diary of a poor young lady. Tr. Emily Ritzerow. Ed. with pref. Rev. J. H. Bryant. L: W.Macintosh. viii;148p. 16cm. [BM] [Free and false.]

NAUBERT, Cne. Bne. Ege. 1756-1819. See "Cramer, K: Glb."
§6678. (Alfons von Duelmen, oder Geschichte Kaiser Philipps und seiner Tochter.) Alf von Deulmen; or, the hist. of the Emperor Ph. and his daughters. Tr. Miss A. E. Booth. L: Bell 1790. 2v. xx;300; 305p. 21cm. [Much abridged.] [BM]
6679. (Barbara Blomberg.) Lindorf and Caroline. By "Kramer." Tr. Ma. J. Young. Crosby 1803. 3v. 12. [EC]
6680. (Der kurze Mantel.) The mantle. Tr. G: Soane. 1826. In C498.
§6681. (Hermann von Unna. Eine Geschichte aus der Zeiten der Vehmgerichte.) Hm. of Unna: a series of advent. of the 15th cent. With pref. by "Prof. Kramer" (i.e., Cramer, pseud.). Tr. anon. L: Robinson 1796. 3v. 12. [Some omissions and more errors.] [BM]
6682. (Walther v. Montbarry.) Wl. de Monbary: a romance by "Kramer." Tr. anon. 2d ed. L: Newman 1816. 4v. 12. [EC]

NAUMANN, El. 1827-88.
*6683. (Illustrierte Musikgeschichte.) The hist. of music. Ed. by Sir F. A. G. Ouseley, Bart. Tr. F. C. W. Praeger. L;NY: Cassell 1882-86. 2v. (758) 1332p. il. 22cm. [BM]
[Not without error.--LC dates this: 1886.]
*6684. do. 1888-91. [same; reissue] [BM]
*6685. do. 1894-97. [reissue] [BM]
*6686. do. 1898-1900. [reissue] [BM]

NAUMANN, F: 1860-1919.
*6687. (Mitteleuropa.) Central Europe. Tr. Christabel M. Meredith. Introd. W. J. Ashley. L: King 1916. xix;354p. 22cm. [BM.LC]
*6688. do. 1917. [same] NY: Knopf. 351p. 21cm. [LC]

NEANDER, Jm. 1640-80. Sel. in C166;229;231;235;240;244;269;271;287; 423;469;486;489;570.

NEANDER, J: A: W: 1789-1850.
6689. The emperor Julian and his generation: an histor. pict. Tr. G: V. Cox. L: Parker 1850. 180p. 27cm. [LC]
[Probably from his "Allgemeine Geschichte der christlichen Religion und Kirche."]
6690. do. 1850. [same] NY: Riker. 191p. 19cm. [LC]
*6691. (Das Leben Jesu Christi...) The life of Jesus Christ in its hist. connection and hist. devel. Tr. from 4th Ger. ed. by J: M'Clintock and C: E. Blumenthal. L: Bohn 1851. xxxii;499p. 18cm. [BM]
*6692. (Denkwürdigkeiten aus der Geschichte des christlichen Lebens.) Light in dark places. Tr. Mrs. Eliz. Charles. L: Low 1850. viii; 365p. 17cm. [BM]
*6693. do. 1851. Light in the dark places: memorials of Christian life in the middle ages. NY: Lane & Scott. 344p. 17cm. [LC.BM]

NEANDER, J: A: W: - Denkwürdigkeiten...des christlichen Lebens
6694. do. 1852. Memorials of Christian life in the early and middle ages. Tr. J. E. Ryland. L: Bohn 538p. 12. [BM.LCO]

NEBE, A:
6695. (Luther als Seelsorger.) L-- as spiritual adviser. Tr. C: A. Hay and C: E. Hay. Phil: Luth. pub. 1894. 242p. 12. [LCO]

NEFF, Fx. 1798-1829.
6696. Conversations on sin and salvation...with a sketch of his life. Tr. from the Ger. L: Relig. tract soc. 1838. 160p. 10cm.[BM]
See Schubert, Gotthilf, Memoirs, etc., #8643.

NEIDHART VON REUENTHAL, fl. 1216-45. Sel. in C27*;310;416*;427.

NEITSCHMANN (properly Nietschmann), 1840- . See "A. Stein."

NELSON, Rd. Miss Dudelsack. Operetta. See Fritz Grünbaum.

NEMBACH, Andrew. Harvest home. Opera. See Roescher, L., #7250.

NESSLER, V: E. 1841-90. The trumpeter of Sackingen [sic] Opera. See Rd. Bunge, #922.

NEUBECK, Vlr. W: 1768-1850. Sel. in C26;373;411;469.

NEUENDORFF, Ad. 1843-97. Operas: Hagar. See Mueller, W:, #6532. Rat-charmer of Hamelin. See H. Italiener, #4725.

NEUFFER, Cn. L: 1769-1839. Sel. in C173.

NEUMANN, Angelo, 1838-1910.
§6698. (Erinnerungen an R: Wagner.) Personal recoll. of W--. Tr. from 4th ed. by Edith Livermore. NY: Holt 1908. 329p. il. 23cm. [Takes liberties with text.] [LC]
§6699. do. 1909. [same] L: Constable. 329p. [BM]

NEUMANN, Arno.
6700. Jesus. Tr. Maurice C. Anney, M. A. Pref. P. W. Schmieden. L: Black 1906. xxxii;180p. 18cm. [BM]

NEUMANN, Gf. fl. 1700-36. Sel. in C231.

NEUMANN, Hm. Kb. 1808-75. Sel. in C111-2;149;378;551.

NEUMANN, J: N. See Berger, J:, Life of the right rev. J. N. N-- , #365.

NEUMANN, Kp. 1648-1715. Sel. in C276.

NEUMANN, L. Freiburg (Baden) and its environs. Tr. anon. 1884. 40p. il. In C294.

NEUMARK, G: 1621-81. Sel. in C106;230;269;271;276;486;489.

NEUMAYR VON RAMSSLA, J: W:
6701. Visit to King James I at Theobalds in 1613...by J: Ern. duke of Saxe-Weimar. Tr. W. B. Rye. 1865. In C483.
[From his "Reise in Frankreich, England und die Niederlande des Fürsten J: Ern. des Jüngeren Hertzogen zu Sachsen."]

NEUMEISTER, Erdmann, 1671-1756. Sel. in C222-3;229;233;244;269;271.

NEUNHERZ, J: 1653-1737. Sel. in C276;287.

NEUSS, H: G: 1664-1716. Sel. in C231-2.

NICOLAI, Cph. F: 1733-1811. Sel. in C193.
**6702. (Das Leben und die Meinungen des Herrn Magister Sebaldus Nothanker.) The life and opinions of Sebaldus N--. Tr. T: Dutton. L: C.Lowndes 1798. 3v. 17cm. [BM.LC]

NICOLAI, Cph. F:
[Excellent tr. Vol. 1 seems to have been pub. 1796. See "Analyt. R." 26(1797):75. (B26)]
6703. An account of the apparition of several phantasms. Tr. anon. ca. 1800. In C157.

NICOLAI, O: 1810-49. The merry wives of Windsor. Opera. See Mosenthal, S., #6319.

NICOLAI, Ph. 1556-1608. Sel. in C41;223;230;232;234;269;271;273;287; 486;489;543;570;#5963.
6704. A (p)rophesie of Doomesday...shortly coll. and augm. by Niels Michelsone. Tr. out of Germane and Deuce tongue...by D: Forbes. Ed: J: Wreittoun 1631. ff. Av-Dii. 13cm. [BM]

NICOLAY, L: Sel. in C372.

NIEBUHR, Barthold G: 1776-1831. Sel. in C12;366;469;486.
*6705. (Carsten Niebuhrs Leben.) Life of C-- N--. Tr. Prof. Robinson. Append. by J. D. Michaelis. Ed: Clark 1836. 77p. 16cm. [BM]
6706. A dissertation on the geogr. of Herodotus. Tr. anon. Oxf: Talboys 1830. 86p. 8. [LCO]
*6707. (Griechische Heroen-Geschichten.) Stories of the gods and heroes of Greece. Tr. Lady Duff-Gordon. Ed. S. Austin. L: Parker 1843. vii;52p. 18 x 10cm. [BM.LCO]
6708. do. 1843. Stories from Greek hist. L: Nutt 47p. 21cm. [BM]
*6709. do. 1844. Heroic tales of ancient Greece, related by B-- N-- to his little son Marcus. Ed. with notes by "Fx. Summerly" (i.e., H. Cole). L: Cundall. viii;116p. 17 x 12cm. [BM]
*6710. do. 1844. [same] 4 col. ils. by H. J. Townsend. L: Chapman & Hall n.d. viii;146p. 17 x 12cm. [BM.LC]
[The t.p. is pasted in. The date 1843 given by LCO is incorrect.]
*6711. do. 1849. [same] Bohn. 16. [EC]
*6712. do. 1879. Greek hero-stories. Tr. B: Hoppin. Il. A: Hoppin. NY: Dodd, Mead. 120p. 19 x 14cm. [LC.BM]
[The voyage of the Argonauts; Stories of Hercules; The Herakleidae and Orestes.]
*6713. do. 1880. [same] L: Shaw. 120p. [BM.LC]
*6714. do. 1903. The Greek heroes: stories tr. from N-- with additions. 4 col. pl. and other ils. A. Rackham. L;NY: Cassell. 96p. 17cm. [Adds The story of Perseus and The story of Theseus.] [BM]
*6715. do. 1910. [same] Cassell. 18 x 12cm. [BM.LC]
6716. Lect. on the hist. of Rome, from the first Punic War to the death of Constantine. Ed. (i.e., tr. and ed.) Leonhard Schmitz. L: Taylor & Walton 1844. 2v. xxxvii;434; 406p. front. (port.) 22cm. [Second t.p. has: The hist. of Rome, etc., and calls this vol. 4 of the entire work. This ed. from Schmitz's own notes of unpub. lectures, 1828-9, compared with notes of other students.] [BM.LC]
6717. Lect. on ancient ethnography and geogr. Tr. from ed. of Dr. Isler by L. Schmitz, with add. and corr. from his own notes. L: Walton & Maberly 1853. 2v. x;314; 375p. 22cm. [BM.LC]
6718. Lect. on the hist. of Rome from the earliest time to the commencement of the first Punic War. Ed. by M. Isler. Tr. with many add. from MSS by L. Schmitz. L: Taylor & Walton 1848. xxii; 552p. front. (port.) 22cm. [BM]
6719. Lect. on Roman hist. Tr. from the ed. of Dr. M. Isler by H. Le M. Chepmell and F. C. F. Demmler. L: Fullarton 1849-50. 3v. xvi;581; 408; 480p. 17cm. [Vol. 3 is dated 1850.] [BM]
6720. Lect. on the hist. of Rome from earliest times to the fall of western empire. Tr. L. Schmitz. 2d ed. L: Taylor, Walton & Maberly 1849-50. 3v. 22cm. [This is the 2d ed. of #6716 and #6718.][BM.LC]
6721. Lect. on Roman hist. L: Bohn 1850. 3v. 12. [EC]
[Either the same as #6719, or a reissue.]

NIEBUHR, B. G.
6722. Lect. on the hist. of Rome, etc. 3d ed. L: Walton 1870. xxvi; 811p. 19cm. [3d ed. refers to #6720. Prtd. in double columns.] [BM]
6723. do. 1873. [same] 4th ed. Lockwood. 8. [EC]
6724. do. 1898. [same] 5th ed. Taylor. 840p. 8. [EC]
6725. Lect. on ancient hist. from the earliest period to the taking of Alexandria by Octavianus. Tr. L. Schmitz. L: Taylor, Walton & Maberly; Phil: Blanchard & Lea 1852. 3v. 22cm. [BM.LC] [Taken from students' notes of unpub. lect., and compared with Schmitz's own notes.]
*6726. (Römische Geschichte.) The Roman hist. Tr. F. A. Walter. L: Rivington 1827. 2v. xviii;480; 564p. 21cm. [BM]
**6727. do. 1828-42. Hist. of Rome. Tr. from 2d ed. Jl. C. Hare and Connop Thirlwall. Cambridge: Prtd. for J: Taylor in L. 3v. 21cm. [Excellent tr. Vol. 1, 1828, xvi;556p. Vol. 2, 1832, x;641p. Vol. 3, 1842, xvi;717p. Vol. 3 tr. W: Smith and L. Schmitz and pub. Taylor & Walton in L.] [BM.LC]
*6728. do. 1831. [same] 2d ed. rev. with additions in the 3d Ger. ed. Cambridge: Prtd. for J: Taylor. vol. 1 only. xxii;615p. 21cm. [BM]
6729. do. 1836-7. An epitome of N--'s hist. of Rome...by Travers Twiss (from the tr. of Hare and Thirlwall, whose language is retained wherever possible). Oxford: Talboys. 2 pts. xliii;359; 269p. 21cm. [BM]
6730. do. 1847-51. 4th ed. of #6727. L: Taylor, Walton & Maberly. 3v. 22cm. [Vol. 1, 4th ed., xxxiv;626p. Vol. 2, new ed., 1851, xii;644p. Vol. 3, new ed., 1851, xvi;717p.] [BM]
6731. do. 1859. [same] New ed. L: Walton. 3v. 8. [EC]
6732. (Lebensnachrichten über B. G. N--.) The life and letters of B. G. N--, with essays on his character and influence by C. K. J. Bunsen, Cn.A: Brandis, and J: W: Lorbell (i.e., Loebell). Tr. Susannah Winkworth. L: Chapman & Hall 1852. 2v. xix;424; 453p. 22cm. [Contains about half the letters pub. in the Ger. work.] [BM.LC]
6733. do. 1852. [same] NY: Harper. 563p. 20cm. [LC]
6734. do. 1852. [same] The life and letters, and sel. from his minor writings, ed. and tr. S. Winkworth. L: Chapman & Hall. 2d ed. 3v, 22cm. [Vol. 3, 297p. contains: Letters from Holland, 1808-9, Polit. fragments, Misc. selections.] [BM.LC]

NIEBUHR, Carsten, 1733-1815.
6735. (N-s Reisebeschreibung nach Arabien und anderen umliegenden Ländern.) Travels through Arabia, and other countries in the East ...Tr. Rb. Heron. Ed: Morison 1792. 2v. xx;454; 439p. il. 21cm. ["...the whole...of his travels...is not comprized in these volumes...As to the translation, I cannot indeed say much for it."] [BM.LC]
6736. do. abr. In Pinkerton, J., "A general coll. of voyages, etc." L: 1808, etc. Vol. 10, pp. 1-221. 4. [BM.LC]

NIEDIECK, Pl.
6737. (Kreuzfahrten im Beringmeer.) Cruises in the Bering sea. Tr. R: A. Ploetz. L: Ward; NY: Scribner 1909. xv;252p. 73 pl., 56 il. 23cm. [BM.LC]
6738. (Mit der Büchse in fünf Weltteilen.) With rifle in five continents. Tr. H. B. Stanwell. L: Ward 1908. xiv;426p. 206 il. 23cm. [BM]
6739. do. 1909. [same] NY: Scribner. 426p. [LC]

NIEMANN, (W: O:) A: 1839-1919.
6740. (Bakchen und Thyrsosträger.) Ephraim; or, the many and the few. A novel. Tr. Christina Tyrrell. L: Bentley 1883. 3v. 18cm [BM]

NIEMANN, A:
6741. The baroness Blank: a novel of the new German empire. Tr. anon. NY: Bonner 1890. 320p. il. 19cm. [LC]
**6742. (Der Weltkrieg; deutsche Träume.) The coming conquest of England. Tr. J: H: Freese. NY: Putnam; L: Routledge 1904. vii; 384p. 19cm. [Excellent tr.] [BM.LC]
6743. (Pieter Moritz, der Burensohn vom Transvaal.) The Boer boy of the T--. Tr. Kate M. Rabb. Phil: Penn pub. 1900. 348p. il. 12. [LC]

NIEMEYER, V: 1812-87.
6744. (Af. Krupp. Ein Bild seines Lebens und Wirkens.) Af. K--: a sketch of his life and work. Tr. Kate W. and O. E. Michaelis. NY: Prosser 1888. 72p. il. 24cm. [LC]

"NIENDORF, Emma" i.e., Emma (v. Pappenheim) v. Suckow, 1807-76. Sel. in C90.

NIENDORF, M. An. 1826-78. Sel. in C501 (spells him Niondorf).

NIERITZ, (K:) Gst. 1795-1876.
6745. [Coll.] Swan maiden and other tales. Tr. anon. Phil: Lippincott, Grambo n.d. (1852-5) 18. [AC]
6746. [Coll.] 1854. Tales of old times. Tr. anon. C: Scott. 16. [AC]
6747. [Coll.] 1855. The foundling, or the school of life; The siege of Magdeburg, a tale of 1631. Tr. anon. In C524. [The foundling in same tr. as #6786.]
*6748. [Coll.] 1880. The exiles of Salzburg ("Die protestantischen Salzburger und deren Vertreibung"), and other stories. Tr. Mrs. L. H. Kerr. L: Relig. tract soc. li; 256p. il. 18cm. [BM]
[The king of Prussia's tall soldier; The belfry of Dresden. -- Some omissions from the first story.]
6749. (Ax. Menzikoff, oder die Gefahren des Reichtums.) Ax. M--; or, the perils of greatness. Tr. Mrs. H. C. Conant. NY: Scribner 1853. 226p. 16. [LCO]
6750. do. 1854. [same] Scribner. 18. [AC]
6751. do. 1855. Ax. Menschikoff, the founder of a family. Tr. anon. Ed: Constable; L: Hamilton. 125p. 13cm. [BM]
6752. do. 1865. The perils of greatness: the story of A. Menschikoff. Ed: Nimmo. 124p. col. front. 16cm. [BM]
6753. do. 1894. Menzikoff; or, the danger of wealth. Tr. Mrs. Ax. Kerr. L: Relig. tract soc. 159p. il. 19cm. [BM]
6754. do. 1902. In the days of P: the Gt. Tr. from 17th Ger. ed. by Ma. E. Ireland. Dayton, O: United brethren. 135p. 17cm. [LC]
6755. (Betty und Tomas, oder Dr. Jenner und seine Entdeckung.) Betty's decision. Tr. Ma. E. Ireland, Phil: Luth. pub. house 1886. 145p. 18. [LCO]
6756. Busy hands and patient hearts; or, the blind boy of Dresden and his friends. Tr. Annie Harwood. L: Jackson, Walford & Hodder 1863. viii;112p. il. 18cm. [BM]
6757. do. 1864. [same] Phil: Ashmead & Evans. 168p. 16cm. [BM]
6758. do. 1868. [same] 2d thous. L: Hodder & Stoughton. viii;94p. 18cm. [BM]
6759. do. 1869. [same] Phil: Lippincott. sq. 12. [AC]
6760. do. 1873. [same] 3d thous. L: Hodder & Stoughton. viii;181p. il. 16cm. [BM]
6761. do. 1877. [same] New ed. Hodder. 12. [EC]
6762. do. 1885. [same] New ed. Hodder. 12. [EC]
6763. do. 1889. [same] New ed. Hodder. 12. [EC]
6764. Christian Beck's grandson. Tr. Ma. E. Ireland. Richmond, Va: Presb. com. of pub. 1894. 232p. 19cm. [LC]

NIERITZ, Gst.
6765. The cobbler, the clerk, and the lawyer of Liebstein. Tr. Annie Harwood. 1868. In C189.
6766. (Der Hirtenknabe und sein Hund.) The shepherd boy and his dog. Tr. Rebecca Schively. Phil: Ref. church pub. 1889. il. 16. [LCO]
6767. do. 1894. The shepherd's family. Tr. Ma. E. Ireland. Richmond, Va: Presb. com. of pub. 111p. 19cm. [LC]
6768. (Die Bären von Augustusburg.) The bears of Augustusberg: an episode in Saxon hist. Tr. anon. Bost: Crosby & Nichols 1856. 18. [AC]
6769. do. 1868. [same] NY: O'Shea. 16. [AC]
6770. do. 1872-6. [same] NY: O'Shea n.d. 16. [AC]
6771. The crown prince and his scapegoat; or, truth and falsehood. Tr. E. M. G. Phil: Moore 1877. 242p. 18. [LCO]
*6772. (Der Kerkermeister von Norwich, oder das 7. Gebot.) The jailer of N--; or, the eighth commandment. Tr. anon. NY: Gen. prot. episc. S.S.U. 1863. 186p. il. 15cm. [LCO.BM]
6773. (Die arme Gertrud.) Her first and only school friend. Tr. Ma. E. Ireland. Dayton, O: United brethren 189-? 165p. 17cm. [LC]
6774. (Die Ausgestossene.) Driven out. Tr. Ma. E. Ireland. Richmond, Va: Presb. com. of pub. 1893. 156p. 19cm. [LC]
§6775. (Die Belagerung von Freiberg in Sachsen.) The young carpenters of Freiberg: a tale of the 30 years' war. Tr. J. Latchmore, Jr. Ed: Oliphant 1880 (1879). 192p. il. 17cm. [BM]
[Quite free, omissions. --Catalogued in BM under Freiberg.]
6776. (Die Haideschule.) The school on Lüneburg heath. Tr. Ma. E. Ireland. Richmond, Va: Presb. com. of pub. 1895. 148p. 19cm. [LC]
§6777. (Die Hussiten vor Naumburg.) The weaver of N--; or, a city saved by children. Tr. anon. L: Relig. tract soc. 1874. 157p. 16cm. [Pretty good tr.--Catalogued by BM under Naumburg.] [BM]
§6778. do. 1879. [same] 17cm. [BM]
6778a. (Die protestantischen Salzburger und deren Vertreibung.) The Salzburger exodus. Tr. anon. Phil: Lutheran pub. n.d.[Fatherland series; see list A.] il. 17cm. [AC]
6779. (Drei Mütter zu einem Kind.) The plum-woman; or, the child with three mothers. Tr. Mrs. H. C. Conant. NY: Scribner 1855. 201p. 16. [LCO]
6780. The dumb boy of Fribourg; or, the pilgrim and the dragon. A tale of the discovery of gunpowder. Tr. J. B. J. Champagnac. Rev. Anna T. Sadlier. NY: Sadlier 1873. 166p. 18. [LCO]
6781. The emigrants. Tr. Eliz. F. Bell. In "People's and Howitt's Mag." 9(1850): 82, etc. (B27)
6782. Erna, the forest princess; or, the pilgrimage of the three wise men to Bethlehem. Tr. Mrs. H. C. Conant. Rochester, NY: Darrow 1855. 12. [AC]
6784. Faithful unto death. Tr. M. A. Manderson. Phil: Luth. bd. 1871. 287p. il. 16. [LCO]
6785. do. 1881. [same] The noble wife; or, faithful unto death. L: Ward. Lock. 287p. il. 16cm. [BM]
6786. The foundling; or, the school of life. Tr. anon. Ed: Paton & Ritchie 1850. 139p. il. 14cm. [BM]
6787. do. 1869. [same] L: Houlston. 18. [EC]
[Probably identical with the following.]
6788. do. 1870. [same] Ed: Gall & Inglis. 136p. il. 14cm. [BM]
[The ils. differ from #6786.]
6789. Gottlieb Frey; or, honesty is the best policy. Tr. from... Meritz [sic]. Anon. Phil: Luth. bd. 1870. 16. [AC]
6790. do. 1871. [same] 226p. il. 16. [LCO]
*6791. (Gustav Vasa, oder König und Bauer.) Gustavus Vasa; or, king and peasant. Tr. J. F: Smith. Phil: Luth bd. 1872. 258p. 16. [LCO]

NIERITZ, Gst.--Gustav Vasa, oder König und Bauer
*6792. do. 1881. [same] The faithful servant; or, the king and the peasant. L: Ward, Lock. 258p. il. 16cm. [With notes.] [BM]
6793. Gutenberg and the lost child. Tr. anon. L: Blackwood 1860? 167p. 14cm. [Catalogued by BM under Gutenberg.] [BM]
6794. do. 1873. The noble printer and his adopted daughter: a tale of the first printed Bible. Tr. with additions by Campbell Overend Ed: Oliphant. 319p. 17cm. [BM]
[Not the same tr. as the foregoing. Listed by BM as anonymous.]
*6795. (Hans Egede, der Grönlandsfahrer.) The faithful missionary; or, life in Greenland. Tr. Rev. W: H. Gotwald. L: Ward, Lock 1882. viii;233p. il. 16cm. [The heading is: Hans Egede.] [BM]
6795a. do. 1872-6. Tr. anon. Phil: Lutheran pub. n.d. il. 17cm. [AC]
[One of the Fatherland series; see list A.]
6796. In fair Silesia. Tr. Ma. E. Ireland. Presb. com. 1894. 156p. 19cm. [LC]
6797. Lenchen's brother and the Platzbäcker of Plauen. Tr. Ma. E. Ireland. Phil: Presb. bd. 1887. 313p. il. 18cm. [LC]
6798. The little drummer; or, filial affection. A story of the Russian campaign. Tr. H: W: Dulcken. L: Addey 1852. viii;132p. 17cm. [4 ils. by Dalziels after Gilbert.] [BM]
6799. do. 1853. Tr. Mrs. H. C. Conant. NY: Scribner. 200p. il. 16. [LCO]
6800. do. 1856. [same as #6798] L: Routledge. 12. [EC]
6801. (Nach Sibirien verbannt.) The Siberian exile. Tr. Ma. E. Ireland. Richmond, Va: Presb. com. of pub. 1894. 122p. 19cm. [LC]
6802. One offence punished: a Swiss tale. Tr. E. M. M. Dublin: Hodges, Smith 1859. 48p. 14cm. [BM]
6803. Otto, the miner's child; or, honesty is the best policy. Tr. anon. Manchester: J: Heywood; L: Simpkin 1861. 145p. il. 16cm. [Page heading is: The little miner.] [BM]
6804. do. 1878. The little miner; or, honesty rewarded. Tr. Ellen M. Gifford. Phil: Moore. 18. [AC]
6805. The rat catcher; or, the magic fife. A story of the olden time. Tr. Mrs. H. C. Conant. NY: Scribner 1855. 166p. 16. [LCO]
6806. The rich man and the poor man. Tr. Rev. W: H. Gotwald. Phil: Luth. bd. 1875. 120p. 17cm. [LC]
6807. do. 1881. [same] Help in need; or, rich and poor. L: Ward, Lock. 120p. il. 15cm. [BM]
[Heading reads: The rich man and the poor man. No tr. named.]
6808. Seppel; or, the burning of the synagogue at Munich. Tr. anon. L: Hodder & Stoughton 1879. 179p. front. 16cm. [BM]
["Athenaeum" (74:276) says tr. is by Mrs. Kerr.]
6809. do. 1883. [same] Hodder. 18. [EC]
6810. The smuggler's revenge; or, the lost child. Tr. Lady Lentaigne New ed. L: Simpkin 1884. 12. [EC]
6811. do? Stolen for ransom. Tr. Ma. E. Ireland. Dayton, O: United Brethren 1901. 138p. 15cm. [LC]
6812. The three kings. Tr. Rebecca Schively. Phil: Luth. bd. 1871. 223p. 17cm. [LC]
6813. do. 1881. [same] The pilgrim kings; or, the star of Bethlehem. Tr. anon. L: Ward, Lock. 223p. il. 16cm. [BM]
6813a. A village tale. Tr. anon. In "Athenaeum" 26(1854):60, etc. (B27)

NIESE, Cte. 1854-1936. ("Lucian Bürger")
6814. The story of the little mamsell. Tr. Miss E. C. Emerson. 1915. In C179.

NIETSCHMANN, Hm. O: See "Armin Stein."

NIETZSCHE, F: (W:) 1844-1900. Sel. in C154(15);366* (2d ed.).

WORKS

6815. Works. Ed. and tr. Ax. Tille, T: Common, and others. L: Henry; NY: Macmillan 1896- . Also L: Unwin 1899. 21cm. [BM.LC] [Apparently this ed. was in part fused with the following; this has created a bibliog. tangle which I could not wholly straighten out. --LC has: Vol. VIII. Thus spake Zarathustra. Tr. Ax. Tille. 1896. Vol. X. Genealogy of morals. Tr. W: A. Haussmann. Poems. Tr. J: Gray. 1897. Vol. XI. Case of Wagner. Twilight of the idols. Nietzsche contra Wagner. Tr. T: Common. 1896. LC also has: The case of Wagner. Nietzsche contra Wagner. The twilight of the idols. Antichrist. Tr. T: Common. L: Henry 1896. BM has: Vol. 1. (Also numbered X.) A genealogy of morals. Tr. W: A. Haussmann. Poems. Tr. J: Gray. Vol. 2 (or XI). The case of Wagner. The twilight of the idols. Antichrist. Tr. T: Common.]

6816. Complete works of F: N--. Ed. by Dr. Oc. Levy. Ed;L: Foulis 1909-13 (or 1910-14). 18v. 20cm. [BM.LC] [See individual titles for judgments on the translations. --1. On the birth of tragedy. Tr. W: A. Haussmann. 2. Early Greek philos. and other essays. Tr. Mx. A. Mügge. 3. On the future of our educ. institutions. Homer and class. philol. Tr. J. M. Kennedy. 4.5. Thoughts out of season. Tr. A. M. Ludovici and Adrian Collins. 6.7. Human, all-too human. Tr. Helen Zimmern and Pl. V. Cohn. 8. The case of Wagner. Tr. Ludovici. We philologists. Tr. J. M. Kennedy. 9. The dawn of day. Tr. J. M. Kennedy. 10. The joyful wisdom. Tr. T: Common. Poems. Tr. Cohn and Maude D. Petre. 11. Thus spake Zarathustra. Tr. T: Common. 12. Beyond good and evil, a prelude to the philos. of the future. Tr. H. Zimmern. 13.14. The will to power. Tr. Ludovici. 15. The genealogy of morals. Tr. H. B. Samuel. Peoples and countries. Tr. J. M. Kennedy. 16. The twilight of the idols. The Antichrist. Tr. Ludovici. 17. Ecce homo. Poetry mostly by Cohn, some by Hm. Scheffauer, Fis. Bickley, G. T. Wrench. 18. Index by Rb. Guffy. Quotations tr. by Cohn. Essay on N-- in England by Levy.]

6817. Complete works. The first complete and auth. Engl. tr. Ed. by Oc. Levy. NY: Macmillan 1925. 18v. [AC] [Complete contents listed by AC show the following differences from the foregoing ed. Vol. 8 appears to have no aphorisms; vol. 10 appears to have no poems; vol. 13 equals vol. 15; vol. 14-15 equals vol. 13-14; vol. 16 also has Notes to Zarathustra and Eternal recurrence, tr. by Ludovici; vol. 17 seems to have no poems.]

POEMS

§6818. BICKLEY, FIS. In #6816(17) (epigrams).
*6819. COHN, PL. V. In #6816(10 and 17).
*6820. GRAY, J: In #6815. [Not excellent, but good.]
§6821. PETRE, MAUDE D. In #6816(10).
*6822. SCHEFFAUER, HM. G: In #6816(17).
§6823. WRENCH, G. T. In #6816(17), two poems.

SELECTIONS

6824. ANON. 1909. The quintessence of N--. L: Laurie. xiv;364. front. (port.) 19cm. [BM] [An expos. largely based on quot. from N--'s writings, many newly tr. for this ed.]

6825. ANON. 1914. [same] A pop. rev. ed. (with new pref.) 192p. 18cm. [BM]

6826. ANON. 191-. Epigrams of power. Girard, Kan: Haldeman-Julius n.d. Little blue books. 12cm. [Publisher's catalog.]

NIETZSCHE, F:--Selections
6827. ANON. 1927. Guilt and bad conscience. Girard, Kan: Haldeman-Julius n.d. Little blue books. 62p. 12cm. [BQM]
6828. ANON. 1927. What is good and evil? Girard, Kan: Haldeman-Julius n.d. Little blue books. 62p. 12cm. [BQM]
[Includes: Peoples and countries.]
6829. COMMON, T: N-- as critic, philos., poet, and prophet. Choice sel. from his works compiled by T: C--. L: Richards; NY: Dutton 1901. lxv;261p. 20cm. [BM.LC]
6830. KENNEDY, J.M. N--: his maxims of life. Sel. and arr. by J. M. K--. Maxims of life series 1913. 115p. front. (port. by Max Klein.) 13 x 6cm. [Topics under six headings.] [BM]
6831. MENCKEN, H. L. The gist of N--, arr. by H. L. M--. Bost: Luce 1910. 60p. 19cm. [LC]
6832. ORAGE, A.R. N-- in outline and aphorism. Ed;L: Foulis 1907. 188p. 17cm. [BM]
[Eleven groups of utterances, with introd. for each group.]
6833. WEISBERG, C: Epigrams of N--. Sel. C: W--. Girard, Kan: Haldeman-Julius 1925. Little blue books. 32p. 12cm. [BQM]
6834. (Also sprach Zarathustra.) Thus spake Z--. Tr. Ax. Tille. 1896. In #6815. [EC says: Henry 1896. 512p.]
6835. do. 1901. [same] L: Reeves. 8. [EC]
*6836. do. 1906-9. Tr. T: Common. 2d rev. ed. In "The good European lib." 4 pts. 62;61;71;80p. 8. [BM]
6837. do. 1908. Tille's tr. L: Unwin. New ed. 8. [EC]
*6838. do. 1909-13. Tr. T: Common. xxvi;458p. 20cm. In #6816(11).
6839. do. 1913-15. Sel. in C154(15).
6840. do. 1917. Common's tr. NY: Boni & Liveright. 325p. 17cm. [LC]
6841. do. 1924. [same] NY: Macmillan. [AC]
[Same paging as #6838; evidently part of #6817.]
6842. (Der Antichrist.) Antichrist. Tr. T: Common. 1896. In #6815.
6843. do. 1909-13. Tr. A. M. Ludovici. In #6816(16).
6844. do. 1920. Tr. with introd. H: L. Mencken. NY: Knopf. 182p. 19cm. [LC]
6845. do. 1922. [same] [AC]
6846. (Der Fall Wagner. Nietzsche contra Wagner.) The case of W--; N-- contra W--. Tr. T: Common. 1896. In #6815.
6847. do. 1909-13. Tr. A. M. Ludovici. In #6816(8).
6848. (Der Wille zur Macht.) The will to power. Tr. A. M. Ludovici. In #6816(13-14).
6849. do. 1924. [same] Macmillan. 2v. 20cm. [Part of #6817.] [LC]
**6850. (Die Geburt der Tragödie.) The birth of tragedy. Tr. W: A. Haussmann. 1909? In #6816(1). [Nearly perfect.]
**6851. do. 1927. Tr. C. P. Fadiman. In #6858 below.
*6852. (Die fröhliche Wissenschaft.) The joyful wisdom. Tr. T: Common. 1909-13. In #6816(10).
*6853. do. 1918? [same] With poetry by Cohn and Petre. 2d ed. L: Foulis. viii;370p. 20cm. [LC]
6854. Early Greek philos. and other essays. Tr. Mx. A. Mügge. 1909-13. In #6816(2).
6855. (Ecce homo.) Ecce homo. Tr. anon. 1909-13. In #6816(17).
[Probably by Ludovici; see below.]
§6856. do. 1911. Tr. anon. Portland, Me: Smith & Sale. 60p. 19cm. [LC]
6857. do. 1912. Ecce homo (N--'s autobiog.). Tr. A. M. Ludovici. Also poetry by Cohn and others. NY: Macmillan. xiv;214p. D. [AC]
[This appears to be the same as #6816, vol. 17.]
**6858. do. 1927. Ecce homo and The birth of tragedy. Tr. C. P. Fadiman. NY: Mod. lib. x;340p. 17cm. [Excellent tr.] [LC]
6859. do. 1927. Tr. Ludovici. Ed. Levy. Pocket ed. L: Allen & Unwin. 157p. 7 x 4 in. [EC]

NIETZSCHE, F:--Selections
6860. Eternal recurrence. Tr. A. M. Ludovici. 1925. In #6817(16). Cf. #6864.
6861. (Götzendämmerung.) The twilight of the idols. Tr. T: Common. 1896. In #6815.
6862. do. 1909-13. Tr. Ludovici. In #6816(16).
6863. do. 1912. [same] NY: Macmillan. xviii;281p. D. [AC] [Probably the same as vol. 16 of #6816.]
6864. do. 1927. [same] With The Antichrist, Notes to Zarathustra, and Eternal recurrence. L: Allen & Unwin. 299p. 8 x 5 in. [EC] [Same as vol. 16 of #6817.]
§6865. (Homer und die klassische Philologie.) Homer and class. philol. Tr. J. M. Kennedy. 1909-13. In #6816(3). [Seems to have inadequate knowledge of German.]
*6866. (Jenseits von Gut und Böse.) Beyond good and evil. Tr. Helen Zimmern. L;NY: Macmillan 1907. xv;268p. 20cm. [BM.LC]
6867. do. 1909-13. In #6816(12).
*6868. do. 1914. [same as #6866] Ed;L: Foulis. 268p. 20cm. [BM.LC]
*6869. do. 1917. [same] Introd. by Willard Huntington. NY: Boni & Liveright. xv;237p. 17cm. [LC]
*6870. do. 1924. [same] 268p. [LC]
§6871. (Menschliches, Allzumenschliches.) Human, all-too human. Tr. Ax. Harvey. Chic: Kerr 1908. 182p. 17cm. [LC] [Considerable error on first page.]
*6872. do. 1909-13. Pt. 1. Tr. Helen Zimmern. In #6816(6). [Some minor errors.]
*6873. do. 1909-13. Pt. 2. Tr. Pl. Cohn. In #6816(7).
*6874. do. 1912. [same] NY: Macmillan. x;366p. [AC]
*6875. (Morgenröte.) The dawn of day. Tr. J:a Volz. L: Unwin 1903. 387p. 24cm. [LC]
6876. do. 1909-13. Tr. J. M. Kennedy. In #6816(9).
6877. Peoples and countries. Tr. J. M. Kennedy. 1909-13. In #6816 (16).
†6878. (Ueber die Zukunft unserer Bildungsanstalten.) On the future of our educational institutions. Tr. J. M. Kennedy. 1909-13. In #6816(3). [Poor and in some cases inaccurate.]
§6879. (Unzeitgemässe Betrachtungen.) Thoughts out of season. Tr. A. M. Ludovici. 1909-13. In #6816(4). [Loose and arbitrary.]
§6880. do. Pt. 2. Tr. Adrian Collins. 1909-13. In #6816(5). [Too free.]
6881. (Wir Philologen.) We philologists. Tr. J. M. Kennedy. 1909-13. In #6816(8).
6882. (Zur Genealogie der Moral.) The genealogy of morals. Tr. W: A. Haussmann. 1896. In #6815.
6883. do. 1909-13. Tr. H. B. Samuel. In #6816(15).
6884. do. 1912. [same] NY: Macmillan. xii;192p. D. [AC]
6885. do. 1918. [same] NY: Boni & Liveright. xii;193p. 17cm. [LC]
6886. do. 1920. [same] [AC]
6887. do. 1924. [same] With Peoples and countries tr. by Kennedy. NY: Macmillan. 229p. 20cm. [LC]
6888. (Briefe.) Selected letters. Ed. by Oc. Levy. Tr. A. M. Ludovici. Garden City, NY;Toronto: Doubleday, Page. L: Heinemann 1921. xiii;364p. port. 21cm. [BM.LC]
6889. (Briefe.) Nietzsche-Wagner corr., ed. by Elis. Förster-Nietzsche. Tr. Caro. V. Kerr. Introd. H. L. Mencken. NY: Boni & Liveright; L: Duckworth 1922. xvii;312p. 21cm. [LC.BM]
See Förster-Nietzsche, Eli., The life of N-- , The lonely Nietzsche, #1647-9.

NIKOLAUS VON BASEL (i.e., N: v. Flüe, 1417-87?). Sel. in C224.

NIONDORF. See Niendorf.

NIPPOLD, Otfried, 1864- .
*6890. (Das Erwachen des deutschen Volkes.) The awakening of the Ger. people. Tr. Ax. Gray. L: Allen & Unwin 1918. 60p. 21cm. [BM]
*6891. do. 1918. [same] NY: Doran. 49p. 20cm. [LC]
*6892. do. 1918. [same] NY: Amer. Assoc. for internat. concil. 31p. 19cm. ["A tr. of part 1..."] [LC]
*6893. (Die Gestaltung des Völkerrechts nach dem Weltkriege.) The devel. of internat. law after the world war. Tr. Amos S. Hershey. L: Milford; NY: Oxford press 1923. xvi;242p. 25cm. [BM.LC] [Not completely satisfactory, but very good; a little heavier than need be.]
6894. (Gefährlicher Optimismus.) Dangerous optimism. Tr. anon. L: Allen & Unwin 1918. 20p. 21cm. [BM.LC]

NITSCHE, G: 1633-1729.
6895. Golden thoughts on a holy life. Tr. M. A. C. Glasgow: Bryce 1883. 128p. 32. [BM]

NITSCHMANN, Anna, 1715-60. Sel. in C269.

NOE, H: A: 1835-96.
6896. The southern railway of Austria: The line through Carynthia and the Pustertal. 111p. From Germany to Italy: The Brenner railway. 112p. From the Danube to the Adriatic. 111p. Tr. anon. 1884. il. In C294.

NOELDECHEN, W:
6897. Baron and squire: a story of the 30 years' war. Tr. Sa. M. S. Clarke. L: Nisbet 1892. 392p. 16 il. 19cm. [BM]

NOESSELT, F: A: 1781-1850
6898. (Lehrbuch der Mythologie.) Mythol., Greek and Roman. Tr. Mrs. Angus W. Hall. L: Kerby & Endean 1885. xiv;578p. 19cm. [BM]
6899. do. 1890. [same] [EC]

NOHL, J:s, 1882- .
**6900. (Der schwarze Tod. Eine Chronik der Pest.) The black death: a chronicle of the plague (1348-1720). Compiled from contemp. sources. Tr. C: H. Clarke. L: Allen & Unwin 1926. 284p. il. 22cm. [Excellent.] [BM.LC]

NOHL, (K: F:)L: 1831-85.
§6901.(Beethoven nach den Schilderungen seiner Zeitgenossen.) B-- depicted by his contemporaries. Tr. Emily Hill. L: Reeves 1880. 374p. 19cm. [BM.LC]
§6902. (Beethovens Leben.) Life of B--. Tr. J: Js. Lalor. Chic: Jansen, McClurg 1881. 201p. 19cm. [Rather feeble reflection.] [LC]
§6903. do. 1884. [same] 2d ed. L: Reeves. xii;168p. 19cm. [BM.LC]
§6904. do. 1893. [same] [EC]
§6905. (Eine stille Liebe zu Beethoven. Nach dem Tagebuche einer jungen Dame.) An unrequited love: an episode in the life of B--. From the diary of a young lady (Fanny Giannatasio del Rio). Ed. L. N--. Tr. Annie Wood. L: Bentley 1876. 250p. 22cm. [BM.LC] [Tr. does not fully understand the German.]
6906. Life of Haydn. Tr. G: P. Upton. Chic: Jansen, McClurg 1883. 195p. 19cm. [LC]
6907. Life of Liszt. Tr. G: P. Upton. Chic: Jansen, McClurg 1884. 198p. 19cm. [LC]
6908. do. 1897. [same] 18cm. [LC]
6910. Life of Mozart. Tr. J: Js. Lalor. Chic: Jansen, McClurg 1880. 236p. 19cm. [LC]
6911. Life of Wagner. Tr. G: P. Upton. Chic: Jansen, McClurg 1884. 204p. 19cm. [LC]
*6912. (Mozarts Leben.) Life of M--. Tr. Lady Wallace. L: Longmans 1877. 2v. xxx;260; 320p. 20cm. [BM.LC]

NOHL, L:
6913. Facts about Beethoven's ninth symphony. See Elterlein, #1448. See Letters of distinguished musicians, 1867, C429.

NOIRÉ, L: 1829-89.
*6914. (Die Entwicklung der abendländischen Philosophie...) The critique of pure reason as il. by a sketch of the devel. of occidental philos. In Kant, "Critique of pure reason." Tr. Max Müller. L: Macmillan 1881. pp. 1-359. #4824.
*6915. do. 1900. [same] A sketch of the devel. of philos. thought from Thales to Kant. L: Macmillan. 359p. 8. [BM]
6916. Max Müller and the philos. of language. (5 essays.) Tr. anon. L: Longmans 1879. 102p. 22cm. [BM]
6917. do. 1917. The origin and philos. of language. 2d rev. enl. ed. (8 essays.) Tr. anon. Chic;L: Open court. 159p. 20cm. [BM] [One addition tr. by T. J. McCormack; others probably by Paul Carus.]
6918. Problem of anthropology. Tr. M. B. Bonner. 1888. In C300(18).

NOLTE, Vincent (O.), 1770-1856.
*6919. (Fünfzig Jahre in beiden Hemisphären.) Fifty years in both hemispheres; or, reminiscences of a merchant's life. Tr. anon. NY: Redfield 1854. xix;476p. 19cm. [LC.BM]

NORDAU, Max Sm. 1849-1923. Sel. in C469.
6920. (Biologie der Ethik.) Morals and the evolution of man. Tr. Me. A. Lewenz. NY: Funk & Wagnalls; L: Cassell 1922. 278p. 22cm. [LC]
6921. (Das Recht zu lieben.) The right to love: a drama in 4 acts. Tr. El. Blum. Allegheny, Pa: 1892. (B38)
*6922. do. 1895. Tr. Ma. J. Safford. NY;Chic: Neeley. L: Chatto & Windus. xi;169p. 19cm. [LC.BM]
6923. do? 1907. A question of honor: a tragedy of the present day. In 4 acts. Tr. Ma. J. Safford. Bost;L: Luce. 169p. 20cm. [LC] [Possibly a reissue of the foregoing? Note the paging.]
6924. Deliverance. Tr. anon. 1907. In C447.
6925. do. 1915. [same?] Tr. Euphemia Johnson. In C179.
§6926. (Der Sinn der Geschichte.) The interpretation of history. Tr. M. A. Hamilton. L: Rebmann 1910. 376p. 22cm. [BM.LC]
§6927. do. 1911. [same] NY: Moffat, Yard. 414p. 21cm. [LC]
*6928. (Die konventionellen Lügen der Kulturmenschheit.) The conventional lies of our civilization. Tr. anon. From the 7th Ger. ed. Chic: Schick 1884. 364p. 8. [BM]
*6929. do. 1895. [same] Chic: Laird & Lee; L: Heinemann. 346p. 22cm. [LC.BM]
*6930. do. 1906. [same] Popular ed. 346p. 21cm. [BM]
6931. do. 1925. Conventional lies... Ed. by Leo Markun. Girard, Kan: Haldeman-Julius. Little blue books. 63p. 12cm. [LC] [Much abridged. Introd.; Mene, tekel, upsharin [sic]; The lie of religion; The political lie; The economic lie; The matrimonial lie.]
†6932. (Die Krankheit des Jahrhunderts.) The malady of the century. Tr. anon. L: Heinemann 1896. 308p. 19cm. [BM] [Tr. knows little German, and makes no attempt to be faithful.]
6933. do. 1898. [same?] L;NY: Neely. 433p. 12. [LC]
6934. (Doktor Kohn.) Doctor Kohn. A trag. of the present day. Tr. M. A. Safford. Washington, D. C. 1899. (B38)
*6935. (Drohnenschlacht.) The drones must die. Tr. anon. NY: Dillingham 1897. 526p. 20cm. [LC]
*6936. do. 1899. [same?] L: Heinemann. 416p. 8. [BM]
*6937. (Entartung.) Degeneration. Tr. anon. From the 2d Ger. ed. L: Heinemann 1895. xiii;560p. 22cm. [BM]
*6938. do. 1895. [same] 2d-7th ed. [EC]

NORDAU, Max
*6939. do. 1895. [same] 4th ed. NY: Appleton. 566p. 23cm. [LC]
*6940. do. 1898. [same] Popular ed. L: Heinemann. 514p. 8. [EC]
*6941. do. 1913. [same] Popular ed. Heinemann. xiii;560p. 22cm. [BM]
*6942. do. 1913. [same] Popular ed. Heinemann. 514p. 8. [EC]
*6943. (Gefühlskomödie.) The comedy of sentiment: a novel. Tr. anon. NY;Chic: Neely 1895. 278p. 19cm. [LC]
*6944. do. 1895. Tr. Jessie Haynes. L: Heinemann. 231p. 19cm. [BM] [Some errors.]
*6945. (Märchen, seiner Maxa...erzählt.) The dwarf's spectacles, and (19) other fairy tales told by M. N. to his Maxa. Tr. Ma. J. Safford. L;NY: Macmillan 1905. 390p. il. 19cm. [LC.BM] [Il. H. A. Hart, F. P. Safford, R. McGowan.]
*6946. (Morganatisch.) Morganatic: a novel. Tr. Eliz. Lee. L: Chatto & Windus 1904. 396p. 19cm. [BM]
6947. (Paradoxa.) Paradoxes. Chic: Laird & Lee 1895. 377p. 18cm. [LC]
§6948. do. 1896. Tr. from the 5th Ger. ed. by J. R. McIlraith. L: Heinemann. x;343p. 22cm. [BM] [Seems to me too wordy and not wholly correct.]
§6949. do. 1906. [same] Popular ed. Heinemann. 8. [BM]
6950. Paris sketches. Tr. anon. Chic: Schick 1890. 162;30p. 19cm. [LC]
6951. do. 1895. [same?] Chic: Laird & Lee. 162p. il. 12. [LCO]
*6952. (Seelenanalysen.) How women love, and other tales (soul analysis). Tr. anon. NY;Chic: Neely 1896. 282p. 19cm. [LC] [Simple style; tr. had easy task.]
6953. The shackles of fate: a play in 5 acts. Tr. anon. NY;L: Neely 1897. 189p. 16cm. [LC]
6954. Soap bubbles, etc. Tr. Ma. J. Safford. L;NY: Neely 1896. 203p. 16. [LC]
*6955. (Von Kunst und Künstlern.) On art and artists. Tr. W. F. Harvey. L: Unwin; Phil: Jacobs 1907. 351p. front. (port.) 21cm. [BM.LC]

NOSSIG, Af.
*6956. Manru: opera in 3 acts by I. Paderewski. Tr. and ad. by H: E: Krehbiel. Vocal score. Ger;Engl. NY: Schirmer 1901. 412p. 29cm. [LCM.BMM]
*6957. do. 1901. [same] Libr. Engl;NY: Schirmer. 29p. 8. [BM]
*6958. do. 1902. [same] Libr. Ger;Engl. NY: Rullman. 77p. 8. [LCM]

NOSTITZ, Gräfin Ple. (i.e., Mde. Ple. (de Granges) Helfer, Gräfin Nostitz-Rokitnitz)
*6959. (J: W: Helfers Reisen in Vorderasien und Indien.) Travels... in Syria, Mesopotamia, Burmah. Tr. Jane Sturge. L: Bentley 1878. 2v. x;297;346p. 21cm. [Some small omissions.] [BM]

NOSTIZ VON JAENCKENDORFF, Glb. Ad. Ern. v., 1765-1836. Sel. in C26.

NOTHANKER, Sbl. See Nicolai, C., Life and opinions..., #6702.

NOTKER Balbulus, 840?-912. Sel. in C269;276.
Life of Charlemagne. See Eginhardus, #1427.

"NOVALIS" (i.e., F: Lp. Freiherr v. Hardenberg, 1772-1801). Sel. in C12;17;44;56;88;129;133;142;154(4);184;190;193-4;229;244;273;276;287;366;383*;384;385*;388;395;419;423;452;461;464;469;486;489;543.
**6960. [Coll.] Hymns and thoughts on religion. Tr. W: Hastie. L: Hamilton 1888. lxii;135p. 19cm. [BM] [Excellent tr. Biog. sketch by Just; Hymns to night, pp. 1-30; Spiritual songs, pp. 31-72; Thoughts on relig., under five subheads, pp. 73-135.]
*6961. [Coll.] 1891. His life, thoughts, and works. Ed. and tr. M. J. Hope. L: Stott. 246p. 12. [BM]

"NOVALIS" (i.e., F: Lp. Freiherr v. Hardenberg)
[Not as good as the foregoing.--Tr.'s pref., 22p; Life by Just; H: v. Osterdingen [sic] with Tieck's conclusion; Fugitive thoughts; Thoughts on philos. and physics; (5) Hymns to the night.]
*6962. [Coll.] 1903. The disciples at Sais and other fragments. Tr. F. V. M. T. and U(na) C. B(irch?). Introd by Una Birch. L: Methuen. 176p. 17cm. [BM]
[Fem. rhymes abandoned; otherwise very good. --Sketch of N-- the man and the author; Sel. from the spiritual songs; Thoughts on philos., love, and religion; The disciples at Sais; Flower pollen; bibliog. and index.]
*6963. (Die Christenheit oder Europa.) Christianity or Europe. Tr. by Rev. J: Dalton. L: Chapman 1844. 34p. 19cm. [BM]
*6964. (Gedichte.) Spiritual songs. Tr. G: Macdonald. 1876. In C383, pp. 3-37.
6965. do. 1910. The devotional songs of N--. Coll. and ed. Bernhard Pick. Chic: Open Court. 114p. 16cm. [LC]
*6966. (Heinrich v. Ofterdingen.) H: of O--. Tr. anon. Cambridge, Mass: Owen 1842. xviii;236p. 20cm. [LC.BM]
["The life...chiefly drawn from the one written by (Tieck)." Also includes Tieck's completion of part II.]
*6967. do. 1853. [same] NY: H. H. Moore. xvii;236p. [LC.BM]
[EC has: L: Wiley 1853.]
§6968. (Hymnen an die Nacht.) (8) Hymns... Tr. Helen Lowe. 1841. In her Prophecy of Balaam...and other poems. Exeter. Hannaford; L: Murray. pp. 216-229. [Rather good, somewhat too free.] [BM]
6969. do. 1845. 6 hymns. Tr. H: Morley. In C419.
6970. do. 1889. [same] In C492.
6971. The story of Hyacinth and Roseblossom. Tr. Lillie Winter. 1913-15. In C154(4).

NOWOWIEJSKI, Fx. 1877- . Quo vadis? Opera, see A. Jüngst.

NUECHTER, F:
6972. Abr. Dürer: his life and a sel. of his works, with explan. comments by Lucy D. Williams. Introd. Sir Mn. Conway. L: Macmillan 1911. 96p. il. fol. [BM.LC]

OBERLIN, J: F: 1740-1826.
6973. Letters. In #4767. Cf. also #5620.
See Schubert, G., Memoirs, etc., #8643.

ODELEBEN, Ern. O: Iz. Freiherr v. 1777-1833.
*6974. (Napoleons Feldzug in Sachsen.) A circumstantial narr. of the campaign in Saxony...1813. Tr. Af. J: Kempe. L: Murray 1820. 2v. 343;459p. 21cm. [BM]
*6975. do. 1822. [same] [LC]

OECHSLI, W: 1851-1919.
6975a. Hist. of Switzerland, 1499-1914. Tr. Eden and Cedar Paul. Cambridge: Univ. press 1922. xiii;480p. 22cm. [BM]
[AC has: NY: Macmillan. il.]

OELSCHLAEGER, Hm.
*6976. (Wunderliche Leute.) Strange folk: a novel. Tr. Lt.-Col. F. Grant. L: Longmans 1872. 2v. 310;311p. 20cm. [BM]
[Noted one bad error.]

OELSCHLAEGER, J: See Olearius.

OELSNITZ, L. v. d. See Laukenau, H. v, joint author, #5592.

OER, Max v. Sel. in C173;451.

OER, Dom Sb. v.
6977. A day in the cloister. Ad...Dom Bede Camm. L: Sands 1900. xv; 291p. 8. [BM]

OER, Dom Sb. v.
[Orig. tr. by a nun, ed. by Camm. "It is now not a tr. but an ad... passages...omitted...altered, and a few...inserted."]
6978. Our failings. Tr. from 10th ed. by Countess Af. v. Bothmer. St.L: Herder 1914. 10; 271p. O. [AC]

OERTEL, Ph. F: W: 1798-1867. See "Horn, W. O. v."

OERTZEN, G: v. 1829-1910. Sel. in C195.

OESER, Rd. L: 1807-59. See "O. GLAUBRECHT."

OESTERREICH, Tt. Kst. 1880- .
§6979. (Der Okkultismus im modernen Weltbild.) Occultism and mod. science. Tr. anon. From 2d Ger. ed. L: Methuen; NY: McBride 1923. 181p. 14cm. [BM.LC]
[Poor tr.: in an effort to condense and make smooth English, the tr. commits blunders and sometimes perverts the sense.]

OESTERREICHER, Rd. 1881- . See Jacobsohn, Lp., joint author. See Schönthan, Fz. v., joint author.

OHRWALDER, Js. 1856-1913.
6980. Ten years' captivity in the Mahdi's camp, from orig. MSS. By Maj. F. R. Wingate. Il. W. C. Horsley and from photos. L: Low 1892. xiii;460p. 22cm. [BM]
[Rewritten by W. from a rough Engl. tr. of the orig.]
6981. do. 1892. [same] 8th ed. unchanged. [LC]
6982. do. 1893. [same] 10th ed., rev. and abr. xvi;471p. il. 19cm. [BM]
6983. do. 1893. [same] 13th ed. 18cm. [BM.LC]
6984. do. 1903. [same] 14th ed. [BM]

OKEN (properly Okenfuss), Lz. 1779-1851. See Ecker, Ax., Lz. O--, a biog. sketch, #1395.

OKONKOWSKI, G: Operettas, see Arnold, Fz. See Kraatz, Kurt.
6985. (Die keusche Susanna.) The girl in the taxi: mus. play in 3 acts by "Jean Gilbert." Tr. F: Fenn and Art. Wimperis. Vocal score. L: Ascherberg 1912. 164p. 28cm. [BMM]

OKONKOWSKI, G: and Jl. Freund.
6986. (Kinokönigin.) The cinema star: operetta in 3 acts by "Jean Gilbert." Ad. Jack Hulbert and Harry Graham (lyrics by him). Vocal score. L: Chappell 1914. 214p. 27cm. [BMM.LCM]
[Hardly any relation to the original.]

OLEARIUS, Am. 1599?-1671.
*6987. (Oft begehrte Beschreibung der neuen orientalischen Reise...) The voyages and travels of the ambassadors sent by Frederick, duke of Holstein, to the great duke of Muscovy, and the king of Persia ...1633-39. Whereto are added the travels of J: Ab. de Mandelslo ...into the East-Indies. Tr. J: Davies, of Kidwelly. L: T: Dring & J: Starkey 1662. 2v. 11 leaves; 424; 287p.; 5 leaves. il. 29cm. [Sep. t.ps. Seems to be very good tr.] [BM.LC]
*6988. do. 1669. (Vermehrte neue Beschreibung der muscovitischen und persischen Reise.) [same title, same tr.] 2d corr. ed. L: Prtd. for Starkey & Basset. 2v. in one. 10 leaves, 316; 232p.; 5 leaves. 32cm. [BM copy is misbound.] [BM.LC]
6989. do. 1774-75. abr. In "The world displayed," vol. 3(1774), pp. 104-91, vol. 14(1775), pp. 1-124.

OLEARIUS, J. 1611-84. Sel. in C231;271.

OLIVEN, Fritz. See "Rideamus."

OMPTEDA, Cn. F: W: Freiherr v. 1765-1815.
*6990. (Ein hannoversch-englischer Offizier vor hundert Jahren.)

QMPTEDA, Cn. F: W: Freiherr v.
A Hannoverian-Engl. officer a hundred years ago. Memoirs of Baron O--. Tr. J: Hill. L: Grevel 1892. viii;320p. front. (port.) 22cm. [Ed. Freiherr L: v. O--, grandnephew of Freiherr Cn. v. O--.] [BM]
*6991. do. 1894. [same] Title: In the king's Ger. legion. Memoirs, etc. L: Grevel. 320p. [LC]

ONCKEN, Hm. 1869- . Sel. in C563.
6992. Mn. Luther in the Wartburg; The Burschenschaft and the Wartburg festival. Tr. G. A. Greene. 1907. In C555.

OPITZ, Mn. 1597-1639. Sel. in C309;366;371;446;461;530-1;570.

OPPERMANN, And. 1827-96.
§6993. (Ern. Rietschel.) Ern. R-- the sculptor, and the lessons of his life. Tr. Mrs. G. Sturge. L: Hodder & Stoughton 1875. xiv;213p. 19cm. [BM]
[Quite free in omissions, which rather shift the emphasis and alter the color.]

ORLICH, Lp. v. 1804-60.
*6994. (Reise in Ostindien in Briefen an Ax. v. Humboldt und C: Ritter.) Travels in India...1842-43. Tr. H. E. Lloyd. L: Longmans 1845. 2v. xv;278; 314p. il. 22cm. [Not without faults.] [BM]
*6995. do. 1846. [same] L: Bohn. [EC]

ORTLEPP, Ern. 1800-64. Sel. in C213;388.

ORTMANN, Rld.
6996. Görbersdorf. Tr. anon. 1884. 56p. il. In C294.

OSIANDER, Cn. Nl. 1781-1855. Sel. in C106.

OSTEN, Mary.
6997. Grandmother's curiosity cabinet. Tr. Anna B. Cooke. Bost: Dutton 1869. 255p. 16. [LCO]

OSTERWALD, W: 1820-87. Sel. in C69;112;450.

OSWALD VON WOLKENSTEIN, 1377-1445. Sel. in C27.

"OSWALD, E." (i.e., Frau Bhe. Schulze-Smidt, 1846-1920.)
6998. A madonna of the Alps. Tr. N. H. Dole. Bost: Little, Brown 1895. 207p. 18cm. [LC]
6999. Vain forebodings. Tr. Mrs. A. L. Wister. Phil: Lippincott 1885. 305p. 19cm. [LC]

OSWALD, H: Sg. 1751-1834. Sel. in C231-2;235;269.

OTFRID VON WEISSENBURG, fl. 868. Sel. in C96;530;533;570.
7000. Krist.[Sel.] Tr. E. H. Dewar. 1845. In C96.

"OTHMAR" (i.e., J. K. C. Nachtigal)
7001. (Volkssagen nacherzählt von O--, Bremen 1800.)[Sel.] Tr. T: Roscoe. 1826. In C477.
7002. do. 1834.[Sel.] Tr. W. J. Thoms. In C537.

OTTE, Fr. Sel. in C438.

"OTTFRIED" (i.e., Gf. Jolsdorf).
7003. (Schubert-Novellen.) Schubert fantasies. Ad. by A. Foxton Ferguson. Bost: Four seas co. 1914. 127p. 19cm. [LC]
[The erl-king; Withered flowers; The organ grinder; The angler; The linden tree; The phantom double.]

OTTO VON BOTENLAUBEN, 1175?-d. 1245. Sel. in C27;416;470;532.

OTTO ZUM TURME. Sel. in C416.

OTTO IV mit dem Pfeile, Markgraf v. Brandenburg, 1266-1309. See Markgraf Otto.

OTTO I, Bischof von Bamberg, 1060-1139. See Ebo, The life of O:, #1387.

OTTO, son of Moritz, Landgraf v. Hessen.
7004. Visit to England...1611. Tr. W. B. Rye. 1865. In C483.

OTTO, (K: L:) Rd. 1869- .
§7005. (Das Heilige.) The idea of the holy: an inquiry into the non-rational factor in the idea of the divine and its relation to the rational. Tr. J: W. Harvey. L: Milford; NY: Oxford 1924. xvi;228p. 22cm. [Tr. gets into trouble by abandoning his author.] [BM.LC]
§7006. do. 1925. [same] rev. ed. xx;237p. [BM]
*7007. (Leben und Wirken Jesu.) Life and ministry of Jesus according to the histor. and crit. method. (Three lectures.) Tr. from 3d unalt. ed. by H: J. Whitby. L: K.Paul; Chic: Open court 1908. 85p. 20cm. [BM.LC]
7008. (Naturalistische und religiöse Weltansicht.) Naturalism and religion. Tr. J: A. Thompson and Marg. R. Thompson. Ed. with introd. by Rev. W. D. Morrison. L: Williams; NY: Putnam 1907. xi; 374p. 19cm. [BM.LC]

OVERBECK, Cn. Ad. Sel. in C26;31;133;387-8;443.

OVERBERG, Bh. 1754-1826.
See Krabbe, C., Life of..., #6432.
See Schubert, G., Memoir of..., #8629.

PAALZOW, Frau Hte. (Wach) v. 1788-1847.
*7009. (Godwil-Castle. Aus den Papieren der Herzogin von Nottingham.) Godway castle; or, the fortunes of a king's daughter. Tr. Fes. K. Barnard. L: Bruce & Wyld 1846. 504p. 19cm. [BM.LC]
§7010. (Sainte Roche.) St. Roche. Tr. H. S. and A. B. I. P. Ed. by J. Morier. L: Bentley 1847. 3v. 19cm. [Dialog occasionally curtailed. Trs. seem to have an inferiority complex, see pref.] [BM]
*7011. (Thomas Thyrnau.) The citizen of Prague. Tr. Ma. Howitt. L: Colburn 1846. 3v. in one. 20cm. [Somewhat too literal.] [BM]

PADEREWSKI, Ignacy (Jan), 1859- . Manru. Opera. See A. Nossig,#6956.

PALLESKE, El. 1823-80.
*7012. (Schillers Leben.) S--'s life and works. Tr. Lady Wallace. L: Longmans 1860 (1859). 2v. xi;436; 452p. 20cm. [BM.LC]
[EC has: Bohn 1859, 1860. 2v. --Poetry tr. by H: Inglis. Blank verse good, also a humorous poem. Rhymed verse less successful. Brief sel. from poems.]

PANOFKA, Td. 1800-58.
§7013. (Griechinnen und Griechen nach Antiken skizziert.) Manners and customs of the Greeks. Il. G: Scharf. Ed. Sir C. T. Newton. L: Newby 1849. v;40p. 28cm. [BM.LC]
[Tr. has made consid. changes in arrangement; also the rendering is not literal, many omissions.]

"PAOLI, Betty" (i.e., Bba. Eli. Glück, 1815-94.) Sel. in C309;450.

PAPPUS, J: 1549-1610. Sel. in C271;287.

"PARABELLUM" See Grautoff, Fd. H:

"PARACELSUS" (i.e., Ph. Aurs. Tps. Bts. v. Hohenheim, 1493-1541.)
7014. [Coll.] Paracelsus of the supreme mysteries of nature, of the spirits of the planets, occult philos., the magical, sympathetical, and antipathetical cure of wounds and diseases. The mysteries of

the 12 signs of the Zodiac. Tr. R. Turner. L: Prtd. by J. C. for N. Brook and J. Harrison. 1656. 158p. 16cm. [BM]
[On t.p. the last fig. of date is stricken through, and 1655 is written in beside it. Cf. following for Turner as tr.]

§7015. [Coll.] 1657. Paracelsus of the chymical transmutation, genealogy and generation of metals and minerals. Also, of the Urim and Thummim of the Jews. Tr. Rb. Turner. L: Prtd. for Rich. Moon at the seven stars and Hen. Fletcher at the three gilt cups in Paul's church-yard. 1657. pp. 1-78. 17cm. [BM.LC]

7016. [Coll.] 1894. The hermetic and alchemical writings of P--. Ed. with pref...notes...vocab...by Art. E: Waite. L: Elliot. 2v. 30 x 24cm. [Vol. 1, Hermetic chemistry, xvi;394p. Vol. 2, Hermetic medicine and hermetic philos., 396p.] [BM.LC]

7017. [Coll.] 1910. [same] Chic: De Laurence, Scott. 2v. 29cm. [LC]

7018. Sel. The first part (the second part) of the key of philosophie...by...Theophrastus Paraselius [sic], now pub. in English... by J: Hester. L: V.Simmes 1596. 2 pts. 111p. (continuous paging) 14cm. [BM]

7019. Sel. 1633. The secrets of physick and philos...Tr. J: Hester. L: Prtd. for W: Lugger. 196p. 12. [A reprint of his Key to philos.]

7020. Sel. 1887. The life of...P--...and the substance of his teachings. Extr. and tr. from his...works and...MSS by Fz. Hartmann. L: Redway. xiii;220p. 22cm. [BM.LC]

7021. Sel. 1891. See Hartmann, Fz., Life and doctrines of...P-- etc. NY: Lovell. xvi;367p. 19cm. [LC]

7022. Sel. 1896. [same as #7020] [BM]

7023. (<u>Archidoxorum liber x.</u>) P-- his archidoxes...in ten books. Disclosing the genuine way of making quintessences, arcanums, magisteries, elixirs, etc. Tr. J(ames) H(owell?), Oxon;L: Prtd. for W. S. and...sold by S: Thomson 1661. 2pts. 160p. 15cm. [BM]

7024. (<u>Auroram philosophorum thesaurum.</u>) P--, his aurora, and treasure of the philosophers, as also, the water-stone of the wise men, describing the matter of, and manner how to attain the universal tincture. Englished and pub. by J(ames) H(owell?), Oxon: Prtd. for Giles Calvert 1659. 3 leaves; 229p. 14cm. [BM]

7025. (<u>Centum quindecim curationes.</u>) A hundred and foureteene Experiments and Cures...Tr. J: Hester. L: Prtd. by Valentine Sime dwelling on Adling hill at the signe of the White Swanne. 1596. 7 leaves; 82p. 18cm. [BM]

7026. do. 1652. [same] L? Prtd. by G. Dawson. In Fioravante, L., 3 exact pieces, etc. 5 leaves; 14p. 18cm. [BM]
[Date on t.p. is treated like that of #7014.]

7027. (<u>Des hocherfahrnen...Herrn P. T. v. H-- philosophiae an Athenienses drei Bücher.</u>) Three books of philos. written to the Athenians. Done into Engl...by a young seeker of truth and holines. In Pinnell, H., "Philos. reformed." L: Prtd. by M. S. for L: (sic for Lodowick) Lloyd 1657. 70p. 17cm. [BM]
[Engr. port. of P-- as front. of vol.]

7028. (<u>Dictionarium T-- P--, continens obscuriorum vocabulorum.</u>) A chymicall dictionary, explaining hard places and words...in the writings of P-- and other obscure authors. By M. Sendivogius. L: R: Cotes for T: Williams. 1650. ff. Aaa-Fff. 19cm. [BM]

7029. (<u>Medicina diastatica.</u>) <u>Medicina diastatica</u>, or sympatheticall mumie, containing many mysterious and hidden secrets in philos. and physick. By the construction, extraction, transplantation and application of microcosmical and spiritual mumie. Teaching the magneticall cure of diseases at distance... Abstracted from the works...by...Andrea Teutzelius. Tr. F. Parkhurst. L: Prtd. by T. Newcomb for T. Heath 1653. 12 leaves; 128p. 14cm. [BM]

"PARACELSUS"
7030. Of the nature of things, nine books, with a new light of alchymie, etc. Tr. by J. F., M.D. L: R:Cotes for T: Williams 1650. 3 leaves; 145p. 19cm. [BM]

PARROT, J: Jk. F: W: v. 1791-1841.
*7031. (Reise zu Ararat.) Journey to A--. Tr. W: D. Cooley. L: Longmans 1845. xii;375p. il. 22cm. [BM.LC]
[In "The world surveyed in the 19th cent; or, recent narratives..." Tr. and (where necessary) abr. W: D. Cooley.]
*7032. do. 1846. [same] NY: Harpers. 389p. il. 18cm. [LC]

PAUL, B.
7033. The flower monster. Tr. Pabke and Pitman. 1877. In C444.

PAULI, Gst. 1866- .
*7034. (Venedig.) Venice. Tr. P. G. Konody. L: Grevel; NY: Scribner 1904. 173p. il. 24cm. [First paragraph omitted.] [BM.LC]

PAULI, Rld. 1823-82.
*7035. Pictures of old England. Tr. Elise C. Otté under supv. of author. L: Macmillan 1861. xii;457p. 18cm. [BM]
*7036. do. 1877. [same] Macmillan. 12. [AC]
*7037. do. 1906. [same] L: Routledge; NY: Dutton. New univ. lib. xii;387p. [First two chaps. entirely different from #7035.] [BM]

PAULSEN, Eli. 1879- . Sel. in C28.

PAULSEN, F: 1846-1908.
*7038. (Das deutsche Bildungswesen.) Ger. educ. past and present. Tr. T. Lorenz. L: Unwin 1908. xx;310p. 19cm. [BM.LC]
§7039. (Die Universitäten und das Universitätsstudium.) The Ger. universities and university study. Tr. F. Thilly and W: W. Elwang. NY: Scribner 1906. xii;xvi;451p. 23cm.
[Irritating alterations.] [LC.BM]
7040. (Einleitung in die Philosophie.) Introd. to philos. Tr. F. Thilly. 1st Amer. from 3d Ger. ed. NY: Holt 1895. 437p. 22cm. [LC]
7041. do. 1898. [same] 2d Amer. ed. [LC]
7042. do. 1901. [extract] The problem of cosmology, abr. and ed. E. B. Andrews. Lincoln, Neb: Ivy press. 83p. 12. [LC]
7043. do. 1907. [same as #7040] NY: Holt;L: K.Paul. [LC]
[EC has: K. Paul 1906.]
7044. do. 1911. [same] 2d Amer. from 3d Ger. ed. NY: Holt. xxii;437p. [BM]
*7045. (Kant.) Im. Kant, his life and doctrine. Tr. from rev. Ger. ed. by J. E. Creighton and Ab. Lefevre. L: Nimmo; NY: Scribner 1902. xix;419p. front. (port.) 21cm. [BM.LC]
*7046. (System der Ethik.) System of ethics. Ed. and tr. from 4th rev. and enl. ed. F. Thilly. L: K.Paul; NY: Scribner 1899. 723p. 8. [LC]
*7047. do. 1906. [same] [LC]
*7048. (Wesen und Entwicklung der deutschen Universitäten.) The Ger. universities: their character and devel. Tr. E: D. Perry. NY;L: Macmillan 1895. xxxi;254p. 20cm. [BM.LC]

PAULUS, Beatè (Hahn), 1778-1842. Life of, see Paulus, Ph., #7050.

PAULUS, E: 1837-1907. See Stieler, K:, joint author.

PAULUS, N: 1853- .
*7049. (Der Ablass im Mittelalter als Kulturfaktor.) Indulgences as a social factor in the middle ages. Tr. J. Elliot Ross. Foreword Eugene C. Barker. NY: Devin-Adair 1922. 121p. 19cm. [BM]

PAULUS, Ph. 1809-78.
7050. The miracles of faith: a sketch of the life of Beatè Paulus. By Mary Weitbrecht. NY: Dodd 1872. viii;103p. 15cm. [LC]
7051. do. 1874. [same] Introd. C: S. Robinson. NY: Dodd, Mead. 103p. 17cm. [BM]

PAULUS, Ph. - The miracles of faith
7052. do. 1875. [same] Faith's miracles; or, the power of prayer exemplified in the life of Beatè P--. Introd. Rev. Adolph Saphir. New ed. L: Shaw. xiii;108p. 14cm. [BM]

PAYER, Jl. Ritter v. 1842-1915.
*7053. (Die österreichisch-ungarische Nordpolexpedition.) New lands within the arctic circle: narr. of the discoveries of the Austrian ship "Tegetthof," 1872-4. Tr. anon. L: Macmillan 1876. 2v. xxxi; 335; 303p. il. 23cm. [BM.LC]
*7054. do. 1876. [same] Macmillan. cvi;696p. [BM]
*7055. do. 1877. [same] NY: Appleton. xxiv;399p. il. 22cm. [LC]

PECHOFF, H. Sel. in C67.

PERL, Frau Hte. 1845- ("Henry Perl")
*7056. (Venezia. Beschrieben von Henry Perl.) Venezia. Ad. by Mrs. Art. Bell. L: Low, Marston 1894. vii;248p. 32cm. [BM.LC]
[Orig. drawings by Bartoluzzi, Berti, Brugnoli, Grubhofer, Lancerotto, Tito.]

PERLS, R: Sel. in C39.

PERNER, --- Dr.
7057. Kindness and cruelty; or, the advent. of Edward and Stephen. A tale. Tr. anon. L: Addey 1852. 32p. il. 19cm. [BM]

PERNISCH, J.
7058. The Upper-Engadine. Tr. anon. 40p. il. In C294.

PERTHES, C:e.
7059. C. Perthes, the perfect Christian wife. Condensed from life of F: C. P-- by Mrs. L. C. Tuthill. NY: Carter & Bros. n.d. (1858-60) 12. [AC]

PERTHES, Cl. Td. 1809-67.
§7060. (F: Perthes' Leben, nach dessen schriftlichen und mündlichen Mitteilungen aufgezeichnet.) Life and times of F: P--. Ed: Constable; L: Hamilton 1856. viii;464p. front. (port.) 19cm. [BM]
[Abr. by S. S. L(aurie). Really an adaptation, but very good.]
*7061. do. 1856. Memoirs of F: P--; or, literary, relig., and polit. life in Germany, 1789-1843. Tr. anon. Ed: Constable; L: Hamilton. 2v. xii;448; viii;491p. 21cm. [BM]
[Probably by Laurie; see foregoing. "Not...a lit. tr. of Ger. work."] [LC]
*7062. do. 1857. [same] 3d ed. [LC]
*7063. do. 1858. [same] New ed. [BM]
*7064. do. 1878. [same] L;Ed: Nimmo. [BM]
*7065. do. 1872. [ad.] Christ in a Ger. home, as seen in the married life of F: and C:e P--. NY: Amer. tract soc. 228p. 17cm. [LC]
[Arr. by Alice H. Goodwin from Engl. tr.]

PERTHES, F: (Cph.) 1772-1843. See Perthes, Cl. Td., #7060ff.

PERTHES, F: Mts.
*7066. (Des Bischofs J: Chrysostomus Leben, nach den Forschungen Neanders, Böhringers und anderer dargestellt.) Life of J: C--. Tr. Alvah Hovey and D:B.Ford. Bost: Jewett 1854. vi;239p. 18cm. [BM]

PERUTZ, Leo, 1884- .
§7067. (Der Marquis de Bolibar.) The marquis de B--. Tr. Graham Rawson. L: Lane 1926. 306p. 19cm. [Lacking in accuracy.] [BM.LC]
§7068. do. 1927. [same] NY: Viking press. 303p. [AC]
§7069. (Zwischen neun und neun.) From nine to nine. Tr. Lily Lore. NY: Viking press 1926. 224p. 19cm. [Loose and free.] [LC]
§7070. do. 1927. [same] L: Lane. 224p. 7 x 5 in. [BM]

PESTALOZZI, J: H: 1746-1827. Sel. in C12;469.
7071. [Sel.] A biog. sketch of the struggles of P-- to estab. his system; compiled and tr. chiefly from his own works, by an Irish

PESTALOZZI, J: H:
traveler (-- Synge). Dublin: W: Folds 1815. 115p. 21cm. [BM]
[Mostly the story is told in the 3d person; direct tr. only in spots.]
†7072. Sel. 1875. In Kruesi, Hm. "Pestalozzi," #5449.
[Consid. extracts from his writings, rather badly tr.]
†7073. (Lienhard und Gertrud.) Leonard and Gertrude: a pop. story... tr. into French, and now attempted in Engl.; with the hope of its being useful to the lower orders of society. Tr. anon. Bath: S. Hazard; L: Cadell & Davies 1800. 367p. 18cm. [100 chaps. 7 children reduced to five, and consid. other liberties taken.]
7074. do. 1801. [same] Phil. Prtd. for Js. Groff. 276p. 17cm. [LC]
[Reprint of the foregoing.]
*7075. do. 1824. "A book for the poor." Tr. from the Ger. by Eliza Shepherd. Geneva: Prtd. by W. Fick. x;322p. 20cm. [BM]
[On the whole, very good. 100 chaps.]
§7076. do. 1825. ...or, a book for the people. Tr. anon. L: Mawman. 2v. xvi;223; 241p. 17cm. [BM]
[73 chaps., but the same conclusion; frequent small inaccuracies.]
§7077. do. 1885. P--'s Leonard and Gertrude. Tr. and abr. by Eva Channing. Introd. G. Stanley Hall. Bost;NY: Heath. x;181p. 19cm.
[Really retold, apparently with judgment and skill.] [LC.BM]
§7078. do. 1926. [reissue of the foregoing] Bost: Heath. 181p. [BM]
*7079. (Wie Gertrud ihre Kinder lehrt.) How G-- teaches her children. Tr. Lucy E. Holland and Fes. C. Turner. Introd. and notes Ebenezer Cooke. L: Sonnenschein 1894. li;254p. 18cm. [BM]
*7080. do. 1900. [same] [BM]
*7081. do. 1904. [same] [BM]
*7082. do. 1915. [same] ...an attempt to help mothers to teach their own children. 5th ed. Syracuse, NY: Bardeen. li;256p. 18cm. [LC]
7083. (Briefe.) Letters on early education. Addressed to J. P. Greaves, Esq., by P--. Tr. from...MSS with a memoir. anon. L: Sherwood, Gilbert & Piper 1827. xlv;157p. 22cm. [BM.LC]
7084. do. 1830. Letters of P-- on the educ. of infancy. Addressed to mothers. Bost: Carter & Hendee. viii;51p. 18cm. [LC]
7085. do. 1850. Letters to Greaves. L: Gilpin. xxxviii;179p. front. 18cm. [BM]
7086. do. 1851. [same] [BM]
7087. do. 1898. [reprint of #7083] Syracuse, NY: Bardeen. 180p. 17cm. [LC]
See Kruesi, Hm., P--, #5449.
See Raumer, K., Life and system...,#7350.

PETERS, K: 1856-1918.
§7088. (Das goldene Ophir Salomos.) King Solomon's golden ophir: a research into the most ancient gold production in history. Tr. K. Karuth. L: Leadenhall press 1899 (1898). 117p. front. (port.) 18cm. [BM]
*7089. (Die deutsche Emin Pascha Expedition.) New lights on dark Africa; being the narr. of the Ger. Emin Pasha expedition. Tr. H: W: Dulcken. L;NY;Melbourne: Ward, Lock 1891. xviii;597p. il. 25cm. [BM.LC]
*7090. (England und die Engländer.) England and the English. Tr. anon. L: Hurst & Blackett 1904. vi;400p. 19cm. [BM]
*7091. (Im Goldland des Altertums.) The Eldorado of the ancients. Tr. anon. Il. by Tennyson Cole. L: Pearson 1902. x;447p. front. (port.) 22cm. [BM.LC]

PETERSEN, J: W: 1649-1727. Sel. in C240;269.

PETERSEN, Me. 1816-59.
§7092. (Die Irrlichter.) The will o' the wisps; or, St. John's eve in the forest. Tr. anon. Ed: W: Kennedy 1865. 163p. 17cm. [BM]
§7093. do. 1870. The wandering lights (ascribed to Ploennies). Also, Princess Ilse (Prinzessin Ilse). Tr. Lizzie S. Eden. In C113.

PETERSEN, Me.--Die Irrlichter
†7094. do. 1874. The will-o'-the-wisp. Tr. M. M. B. L: Simpkin, Marshall. 164p. 13cm. [BM]
*7095. do. 1883. Tr. Cte. I. Hart. L: Chapman & Hall. x;264p. il. 19cm. [BM]
§7096. do. 1892. Tr. Mrs. Brathwaite Skeete. L: Sonnenschein. 114p. 16cm. [Fails to get the finer shades of meaning.] [BM]
*7097. (Prinzessin Ilse.) Princess Ilse: a story of the Harz Mts. Tr. Helen Burrows. Devizes: Priv. prt. 1856. 24p. 20cm. [BM] [Reprinted from a newspaper.]
*7098. do. 1856. A legend. Tr. Lady Maxwell Wallace. L: Bell & D. viii;63p. il. 18cm. [BM]
*7099. do. 1859. [same] [EC]
7099a. do. 1859. The Princess Ilse. Tr. anon. "Russell's Mag." 4 (1859):50.
*7100. do. 1867. The princess Ilsée: a fairy tale. Tr. anon. Il. E. Froment. L: Saunders & Otley. xiv;59p. 24cm. [BM]
7101. do. 1867. A story of the Harz Mts. (ascribed to L. v. Ploennies.) Tr. from 24th Ger. ed. Introd. J. L. Lincoln. Bost: Gould & Lincoln. 81p. il. 23cm. [LC]
7102. do. 1867? [same?] Bost: Tilton.[Cf. the following entry.] [AC]
§7103. do. 1868. A story of the Harz Mts., and, The will-o'-the-wisps. Bost: Tilton. 259p. il. 17cm. [LC.BM]
7103a. do. 1868. Princess Ilse. Tr. Harriet C. Sterling. "Northern Monthly." 2(1868): 321.
*7104. do. 1876. Tr. C. A. Girdlestone. L: Char. cross pub. 47p. 18cm. [BM]
7104a. do. 1876. Tr. Eliz. McClellan. "Scribner's Mag." 12(1876):609
*7105. do. 1880. or, the hist. of a river, and other stories (not from the German). Tr. anon. L: Lond. bk. soc. 128p. 36 ils. 16cm. [BM]
7106. do. 1891. Tr. Flor. M. Cronise. Il. J. E. Bundy. Chic: Albert, Scott. 82p. 20cm. [LC]
§7107. do. 1898. A legend of the Harz Mts. Tr. A. M. Deane. L: Leadenhall press; NY: Scribner. ix;106p. [BM]

PETISCUS, A. H.
7108. (Der Olymp oder Mythologie der Griechen und Römer.) The gods of Olympus. Tr. and ed. from the 20th Ger. ed. by K. A. Raleigh. Pref. Jane E. Harrison. L: Unwin 1892. xv;271p. front. (port.) 21cm. [Large alterations and additions, practically rewritten.] [BM]

PETZEL, Rosa. See "Claudius, Mn."

PETZOLD, Alfons
7108a. Raw life. Tr. by E. Bennett. Allen 1926. 320p. 8. [EC]

PFAFF, K.
7109. Heidelberg. Tr. anon. 1884. 80p. il. In C294.

PFARRIUS, Gst. 1800-84. Sel. in C17;75;112;184;309;450.

PFAU, L: 1821-94. Sel. in C301.

PFEFFEL, Gf. Kd. 1736-99. Sel. in C44-6;111;125;219;309;373;443;504-5.

PFEFFERKORN, G. M. 1646-1732. Sel. in C44;244.

PFEIFFER, Ida (Reyer), 1797-1858.
7110. [Coll.] The story of I. P-- and her travels in many lands. L; Ed;NY: Nelson 1879. 207p. il. 16cm. [BM] [Four chaps., one of biog., the others each summarizing one of her travel books: Journey round the world, Northward, Last travels.]
*7111. (Eine Frauenfahrt um die Welt.) A lady's voyage round the world. A selected tr. With an introd. by Mrs. P. Sinnett. L: Longmans 1851. Traveller's lib. 2 pts. vii;272p. (continuous paging) 17cm. [BM]

PFEIFFER, Ida--Eine Frauenfahrt um die Welt
*7112. do. 1852. A woman's journey round the world. An unabr. tr. anon. L: Ingram, Cooke. (Nat. il. lib.) xii;338p. front. il. (tinted engravings) 18cm. [BM]
7113. do. 1852. [same] 2d ed. xvi;338p. [BM]
*7114. do. 1852. A lady's travels round the world. Tr. W: Hazlitt. L: Routledge. viii;409p. 16cm. [BM]
*7115. do. 1854. [same as #7112] 4th ed. [LC]
7116. do. 1855-8. A lady's voyage, etc. NY: Harper n.d. 12. [AC]
[Cf. title of #7111.]
7117. do. 1868. [ad.] Round the world: a story of travel compiled from the narr...by D. Murray Smith. L: Nelson. vii;208p. front. il. 16cm. [Condensed version told in 3d person, with additions to suit the needs of the times.] [BM]
7118. do. 1893. Journey round the world. L: Nelson. 12. [EC]
[Cf. title of #7112.]
7119. Margaret; or, the motherless. L: Hurst & Blackett 1861. 8. [EC]
7120. (Meine zweite Weltreise.) A lady's second journey round the world. L: Longmans 1851. 16. [EC]
[Probably the first ed. of #7122 below.]
7121. do. 1854. Second journey round the world. L: Routledge. 12 [EC]
7122. do. 1855. A lady's second journey, etc. Tr. Jane Sinnett. L: Longman, Brown. 2v. xii;451; 423p. 20cm. [BM]
[Cf. #7120, which would appear to be the 1st ed.]
7123. do. 1855. [same?] L: Bohn. [EC]
7124. do. 1856. A lady's second journey, etc. NY: Harper 1856. 500p. 20cm. [Probably Sinnett's tr.] [LC]
7125. do. 1856. Second journey, etc. L: Ward, Lock. il. 8. [EC]
*7126. (Reise einer Wienerin in das heilige Land.) Visit to the Holy Land, Egypt, and Italy. Tr. H: W: Dulcken. L: Ingram, Cooke 1852. 336p. il. 20cm. [BM.LC]
*7127. do. 1853. [same] 2d ed. 19cm. [LC]
*7128. do. 1862. [same] New ed. L: Ward, Lock. 8. [EC]
*7129. (Reise nach dem skandinavischen Norden.) Journey to Iceland.. Sweden, and Norway. Tr. Cte. F. Cooper. L: Bentley 1852. ix;363p. 20cm. [BM.LC]
*7130. do. 1852. [same] NY: Putnam. 273p. 18cm. [LC]
7131. do. 1852. Visit to Iceland and the Scandinavian north. Tr. anon. L: Ingram, Cooke. Nat. il. lib. 354p. il. 19cm. [BM]
7132. do. 1854. Tr. anon. NY: Riker. 12. [AC]
7133. do. 1856. Tr. anon. Visit to Iceland and north Scandinavia. L: Ward, Lock. 8. [Title suggests reissue of #7131.] [EC]
*7134. (Reise nach Madagascar.) The last travels...visit to M--. With biog. memoir. Tr. H: W: Dulcken. L: Routledge 1861. xliv; 338p. 19cm. [BM.LC]
*7135. do. 1863. [same] New ed. [EC]
7136. Valisneria; or, a midsummer day's dream. A tale. Tr. anon. L: Longmans 1857. 12. [EC]

PFEIL, J: Glb. 1732-1800.
*7137. (Geschichte des Grafen P.) The memoirs of the count of P--. Tr. F. W. Streit. L: W.Franklin 1767. 2v. vii;262; 317p. 17cm. [BM]

PFEILSCHIFTER, G: 1870- .
*7138. (Deutsche Kultur, Katholizismus und Weltkrieg.) Ger. culture, catholicism, and the world war. Tr. Js. Matt. Author. Amer. ed. St. Paul, Minn: Wanderer 1916. 448p. 23cm. [LC.BM]

PFEILSCHMIDT, Ern. H: 1809-94.
7139. (Luther in Coburg.) L-- at C--. Tr. J: G. Morris. Phil: Luth. pub. 1882. 142p. 17cm. [LC]

PFISTER, Ab. v.
7140. The voyage of the 1st Hessian army from Portsmouth to NY, 1776. Also, extr. from the diary of J. G. Seume. Tr. C: F. Heartman. NY: Heartman 1915. 31p. 18cm. [110 cop. prtd.] [LC.BM]

PFISTER, Ok. Rb. 1873- .
*7141. (Der psychologische und biologische Untergrund des Expressionismus.) Expressionism in art: its psychol. and biol. basis. Author tr. Barbara Low and Mx. A. Mügge. L: K.Paul; NY: Dutton 1923. vii; 272p. il. 19cm. [BM.LC]
[On the whole, good to excellent; needless liberties here and there.]
7142. (Die Liebe des Kindes und ihre Fehlentwicklungen.) Love in children and its aberrations: a book for parents and teachers. Tr. E. and C. Paul. L: Allen & Unwin; NY: Dodd, Mead 1924. 576p. 22cm. [BM.LC]
**7143. (Die psychoanalytische Methode.) The psychoanalytic method. Author. tr. by C: R. Payne. NY: Moffat, Yard 1917. xviii;588p. il. 23cm. [Seems to be unimpeachable.] [LC]
*7144. (Was bietet die Psychoanalyse dem Erzieher?) Psycho-analysis in the service of education, being an introd... Author. tr. L: Kimpton 1922. xii;176p. 19cm. [BM.LC]
[Tr. begun by C: R. Payne, contin. by F. Gschwind, and rev. by Bba. Low.]
*7145. (Zum Kampf um die Psychoanalyse.) Some applications of psycho-analysis. Author. Engl. version, anon. L: Allen & Unwin; NY: Dodd, Mead 1923. 352p. 22cm. [BM.LC]

PFIZER, Gst. 1807-90. Sel. in C137;173;309;366;373.
*7146. (Martin Luthers Leben.) Life of L--. Tr. T. S. Williams. L: Soc. for promotion of pop. instruc. 1840. xxxi;197p. 25cm. [BM]
[Prtd. in double columns. Slight variations, some omissions.]

PFIZER, Pl. Acs. 1801-67. Sel. in C317.

PFLEIDERER, O: 1839-1908.
7147. [Coll.] Evolution and theol., and other essays. Ed. Orello Cone. L: Black 1900. 306p. 19cm. [BM.LC]
7148. (Das Christusbild des urchristlichen Glaubens in ihrer geschichtlichen Beleuchtung.) The early Christian conception of Christ... Tr. anon. L: Williams & Norgate; NY: Putnam 1905. 170p. 19cm. [BM.LC]
**7149. (Das Urchristentum.) Primitive Christianity: its writings and teachings in their historical connections. Tr. anon. NY;L: Putnam 1912. 4v. 22cm. [On the whole, an excellent tr.] [LC.BM]
*7150. (Die Entstehung des Christentums.) Christian origins. Tr. Dl. A. Huebsch. Author. ed. NY: Huebsch 1906. 295p. 19cm. [LC.BM]
7151. (Die Entwicklung des Christentums.) The devel. of Christianity. Author. ed. Tr. Dl. A. Huebsch. NY: Huebsch 1910. 319p. 19cm. [LC]
*7152. (Religion und Religionen.) Religion and historic faiths. Author. ed. Tr. Dl. A. Huebsch. NY: Huebsch; L: Unwin 1907. 291p. 18cm. [LC.BM]
*7153. (Religionsphilosophie auf geschichtlicher Grundlage.) The philos. of relig. on the basis of its hist. Tr. from 2d ed. by Ax. Stewart and Allan Menzies. L: Williams & Norgate 1886-88. 4v. 22cm. [Theol. transl. fund. Menzies did vols. 2-4. AC has: NY: Scribner & W. 1885-88.] [BM]
7154. (Religionsphilosophie...) Philos. and the devel. of religion. The Gifford lectures 1894. Tr. anon. Ed;L: Blackwood 1894. 2v. 331; 356p. 20cm. [BM]

PFLUGK-HARTTUNG, Jl. v. 1848-1919.
7155. The early middle ages. Tr. anon. 1902, 1905. In C201(7).
?7156. The great migrations. Tr. anon. 1902, 1905. In C201(6).
[No apparent relation to the orig. before me.]

PFORDTEN, Hm. L: Freiherr v. d. 1857- .
7157. A plain handbook to Wagner's "Ring of the Nibelung"...Tr. F. Speed. Berlin: Trowitsch 1892-7. 4 pts. 177p. 17cm. [LCM]
7158. A plain handbook to the plot and text of Wagner's "Tristan"... Tr. anon. Berlin: Trowitsch 1892? 50p. 18cm. [BM]

PFRANGER, J: G: Sel. in C450.
7159. The monk of Libanon. Tr. W: Taylor. 1829. In C533.

PFROEPFER, ---. Sel. in C84.

PFUHL, Ern. 1876- .
7160. (Meisterwerke griechischer Zeichnung und Malerei.) Masterpieces of Greek drawing and painting. Tr. J: D. Beazley. L: Chatto & Windus; NY: Macmillan 1926. viii;150p. 126 pl. 28cm. [BM.LC]

PFUNGST, Art. (Js.) 1864-1912.
*7161. (Ein deutscher Buddhist -- Oberpräsidialrat Td. Schultze. Biographische Skizze.) A Ger. Buddhist: a biog. sketch. Tr. L. F. De Wilde. L: Luzac 1902. 79p. 20cm. [BM]
*7162. do. 1902. [same] 2d ed. [BM]
7163. (Gedichte.) Poems. Tr. E. F. L. Gauss. Pref. W. Rhys Davids. L: K.Paul 1906. xii;145p. 8. [BM]

PFUNGST, Ok.
7164. (Der kluge Hans.) Clever Hans. Tr. Carl L. Rahn. NY: Holt; L: Bell 1911. vi;274p. il. 19cm. [LC]

PHILIPP Jl., Herzog v. Stettin-Pommern. See Gerschow, F:, Diary of the journey, etc., #2173.

PHILIPPI, Ad. 1843- .
*7165. (Florenz.) Florence. Tr. P. G. Konody. L: Grevel; NY: Scribner 1905. 187p. 170 ils. 24cm. [BM.LC]

PHILIPPI, Fx. 1851-1921.
7166. (Das grosse Licht.) The great light. Tr. and ad. C. Swickard. NY: 1903. Tw. (B38)
7167. (Wer war's?) Anonymous: a drama in three acts. Ad. Emily Howard. St.L: 1899. (B38)

PHILIPPSON, L: 1811-89.
7168. The Marannos: a novel. Tr. I. Koplowitz. Phil: Levy type co. 1898. 146p. 12. [LC]

PHILIPPSON, Mn. 1846-1916.
7169. The age of F: the Gt. Tr. anon. 1902, 1905. In C201(15).
7170. The age of the Reformation. Tr. Louis Pollens. 1902, 1905. In C201(11).
7171. The age of the European balance of power. Tr. anon. 1902, 1905. In C201(14).
7172. The relig. wars. Tr. anon. 1902. 1905. In C201(12).

PICHLER, Frau C:e (Greiner) 1769-1843. Sel. in C155; #5132.
7173. [Coll.] Quentin Matsys (do.), pp. 1-58; Johannes Schoreel, pp. 59-124. Tr. anon. 1877. In C21. Cf. also C20.
7174. The count of Barcelona. Tr. G: G. Cunningham. 1829. In C80.
§7175. (Die Belagerung Wiens.) The siege of Vienna. Tr. anon. L: Smith, Elder. Ritchie's lib. of romance. 1834. 337p. 16cm. [BM] [Somewhat abr., giving the effect of a renarration.]
7176. do. 1835. [same?] Phil. Waldie's select circulating lib., vol. 5. 4. [LCO]
*7177. do. 1877. ...A tale of 1683. Tr. anon. L: Tinsley. 3v. 19cm. [BM]
*7178. (Die Schweden in Prag.) Waldstein; or, the Swedes in Prague. Tr. J. D. Rosenthal, afterwards Haas. L: T.Rodwell 1828. 2v. viii;280; 293p. 18cm. [BM]

PICHLER, Frau C:e--Die Schweden in Prag
*7179. do. 1839. [same] The Swedes in Prague; or, the signal-rocket. In C183, pp. 49-290.
*7180. do. 1845. [same, same title] A romance of the 30 yrs' war. L: Burns. 192p. 16cm. [Somewhat revised for this ed. On Cover page: Wallenstein and the Swedes in Prague.] [BM]
*7181. do. 1845. [same] With her "Quentin Matsys." L: Lumley. 192; 58p. il. 16cm. [LC]
7182. do. 1875. The signal rocket. L: Warne. 12. [EC] [See following entry.]
*7183. do. 1878. [same] The signal rocket: a tale of the 30 yrs' war. Tr. anon. L: Warne. viii;182p. 17cm. [BM] [Shortened and somewhat modernized.]
§7184. G: Selding. Tr. R. P. Gillies. 1826. In C164.
7185. J:s Schoreel. Tr. anon. 1847. In C20. [Cf. also C21.]
7186. (Quentin Matsys.) Q-- M--; or, the blacksmith. Tr. anon. L: Burns. Fireside lib. 1845. iv;58p. front. 12. [BM] [Cf. also #7181 above.]
7187. do. 1877. Tr. anon. In C21. [Probably same as foregoing.]

PICHLER, Lu. (i.e., Frau Lu. Zeller, 1823-89).
7188. A daughter of Rome: a romance of the Fatherland. Tr. J. M. Colles. L: Digby 1893. 344p. 19cm. [BM]
7189. The red mantle. Tr. K. E. Heyser. Phil: Luth. pub. soc. 1884. 124p. 17cm. [LC]

"PICK, Is." (i.e., Jesaja Berlin, 1725?-99.)
*7190. ("Israel hat eine Idee zu tragen." Ein Wort an mein Volk.) Life from the dead: a word to my people. Tr. anon. Ed: Johnstone & Hunter 1854. x;31p. 18cm. [BM]

PICTORIUS, G.
7191. The nature of spirits. Tr. Rb. Turner. 1655. In Agrippa, H., "Fourth book...," #36.

PIETSCH, L: 1824-1911.
*7192. (Die deutsche Malerei der Gegenwart.) Contemp. Ger. art at the centenary festival of the Royal acad. of arts, Berlin. Tr. N. D'Anvers Bell. L: Bell; NY: Scribner 1888. 2v. 91;110p. pl. 31cm. [BM.LC]

PILLERSDORF, Fz. X: Frhr. v. 1786-1862.
*7193. (Rückblicke auf die politische Bewegung in Oesterreich...) Austria in 1848 and 1849. Tr. G: Gaskell. L: Bentley 1850. 143p. 19cm. [BM.LC]

PINSKY, D: 1872- .
7194. [Coll.] Temptations: a book of short stories. Tr. from Yiddish Dr. I: Goldberg. NY: Brentano 1919. xiii;325p. 18cm. [BM] [Beruriah; The temptations of Rabbi Akiba; Johann the high priest; Zerubbabel; Drabkin, a novelette of proletarian life; The black cat; A tale of a hungry man; In the storm.]
7195. do. 1921. [same] [BM]
7196. The treasure: a drama in 4 acts. Tr. L. Lewisohn. NY: Huebsch 1915. 194p. 19cm. [LC]

PLATEN-HALLERMUENDE, (K:) A: (G: Max) Graf v. 1796-1835. Sel. in C38;41-2;50;63;75;77;90;123;129;149;151;166;171;173*;178;184;195; 295;309;311;313;317;366;371-3;423;448;460;497;501;531;571.
§7197. Sonette. Sonnets from Venice. Tr. R. B. Cooke. Madison, Wis: Priv. prt. 1914. 26p. 17cm. [See #7202.] [LC]
7198. do. 1919. To Cardenio. Tr. R. B. Cooke. Ithaca, NY: Priv. prt. 13 leaves. 17cm. [See #7202.] [LC]

PLATEN-HALLERMUENDE, A: Graf v.--Sonette
7199. do. 1920. To K: Td. German. Tr. R. B. Cooke. Ithaca, NY: Priv. prt. 56p. 17 x 14cm. [100 cop. prtd. See #7202.] [LC]
7200. do. 1921. Misc. sonnets. Tr. R. B. Cooke. Ithaca, NY: Andrus & Church. 30p. 18cm. [75 cop. prtd. See #7202.] [LC]
7201. do. 1922. Sonnets to lit. personages. Tr. R. B. Cooke. Ithaca, NY: Andrus & Church. 17 leaves. 18cm. [LC]
[40 cop. prtd. See #7202.]
*7202. do. 1923. Sonnets...Tr. R. B. Cóoke. Bost: Badger. 142p. 20 x 15cm. [LC]
[Combines most or all of the earlier issues. On the whole, very good. Cooke is painstaking and careful, understands the German, writes good Engl. verse. Later tr. show improvement over earlier ones.]

PLATTER, T: 1499-1582.
*7203. (T: Platers [sic] Leben.) The autobiog. of T: P--, a school-master of the 16th cent. Tr. Eliz. A. McCaul, afterwards Finn. L: Wertheim 1839. iv;106p. il. front. (port.) 15cm. [BM]
[Opening paragraphs omitted; slightly condensed. Cf. Barth, C. G., who edited the Ger. orig., #231]
*7204. do. 1846. [same] New ed. [EC]

PLEHN, M. C.
7205. Emin Pasha (i.e., E: Schneider). Tr. G: P. Upton. Chic: Mc-Clurg 1912. ix;125p. il. 17cm. [LC]

PLIENINGER, Gst.
7206. D: Livingstone. Tr. G: P. Upton. Chic: McClurg 1912. 143p. il. 17cm. [LC]

PLOENNIES, Lu. v. 1803-72. Sel. in C41;90;448;450;501.
Princess Ilse. The wandering lights. False ascription, see Petersen, Me.

PLOENNIES, W: v. 1828-71. See J. W. Wolf, joint author.

PLOETZ, K: 1819-81.
7207. (Auszug aus der alten, mittleren und neueren Geschichte.) Epitome of ancient, medieval, and mod. hist. Tr. and enl. W: H. Tillinghast. Bost;NY: Houghton; L: Blackie 1884. xii;618p. 19cm. [BM.LC]
7208. do. 1884. [same] 2d ed. Houghton. [BM]
7209. do. 1884. [same] another ed. L: 618p. [BM]
7210. do. 1897. [same] Houghton. [LC]
7211. do. 1898. [same] Houghton. [LC]
7212. do. 1905. [same] New rev. ed. Houghton. 660p. 20cm. [LC.BM]
7213. do. 1911. [same] [LC.BM]
7214. do. 1914. [same] A handbook of universal hist., from the dawn of civil. to the outbreak of the great war of 1914. Bost;NY: Houghton. 624p. 20cm. [LC.BM]
[Also bears title: A manual of universal hist.]
7215. do. 1915. [same] Houghton. [LC]
7216. do. 1915. [same] In Tappan, Eva M., "The world's story," vol. 14. Houghton 1914-18. [LC]
7217. do. 1916. [same] Houghton. xii;642; 63p. 20cm. [LC]
[Has supplement to May 31, 1916.]
7218. do. 1918. [same] Houghton. xii;658; 63p. [LC]
[Has supplement to Nov. 11, 1918.]
7219. do. 1919. [same] Rev. ed. Houghton. [AC]
7220. do. 1925. [same] Rev. by Harry Elmer Barnes et al. 2d rev. ed. NY: Houghton. xvii;766;lxxxixp. 21cm. [LC]
[Title: Manual of universal hist.]
7220a. do. 1926.[same.] Harrap. 873p. 8. [EC]

PLUESCHOW, Gr.
*7221. (Die Abenteuer des Fliegers von Tsingtau.) My escape from Donington Hall. Also, The siege of Kiao-Chow in 1915. Tr. Pauline de Chary. L: Lane 1922. vii;244p. ports. 19cm. [BM]

POCCI, Fz. Graf v. 1807-70.
§7222. (Ein Büchlein für Kinder.) Rhymes and pictures for children. Tr. anon. Littlemore: Masson 1850. 29ff. 13cm. [BM]

"POCHHAMMER, Max v." (i.e., E. D. (v. P--) Mund.)
7223. Six stories narr. by...written with an apprec. by Evelyn Everett-Green. 12 page il. by Ambrose Dudley. L: Leadenhall press 1900. xxvii;292p. 18cm. [BM]
[The minister's marriage; The soldier's stratagem; A perplexing patient; The professor's peril; A sailor's sacrifice; "No!"]

POELLNITZ, K: L: 1692-1775.
*7224. (La Saxe galante.) La Saxe galante; or, the amorous advent. of F: A: II. Tr. from French by a gentleman of Oxford. L: Prtd. and sold by the booksellers 1750? 307p. 16cm. [BM]
*7225. (Mémoires...) The memoirs of Charles-Lewis, Baron de Pöllnitz. Tr. Stephen Whatley. Dublin: 1738. 5v. [Correspondent]
[Tr. made from the French orig.]
*7226. do. 1739. [same] 2d ed. L: Browne. 2v. 19cm. [BM]
*7227. do. 1745. [same] The mémoires...3d ed. with additions. L: Browne. 5v. 16cm. [BM]

POESCHMANN, Fr. Sel. in C44.

POETZL, E: 1851-1914. Sel. in C405a;422.

POLAND, Fz. 1857- , E. Reisinger, and R. Wagner
*7228. (Die antike Kultur in ihren Hauptzügen.) The culture of ancient Greece and Rome. Author. tr. from 2d Ger. ed. by J: H: Freese. Bost: Little, Brown; L: Harrap 1926. 335p. il. 24cm. [WAGNER: Literature; Philos. and science; Relig. REISINGER: art. POLAND: Private life; Army; Constitution.] [LC.BM]

POLENZ, W: v. 1861-1903.
§7229. (Das Land der Zukunft.) The land of the future. Tr. Lily Wolffsohn. Berlin: Fontane; NY: Brentano's 1904. 301p. 21cm. [LC]
[Questionable liberties.]
*7230. (Der Büttnerbauer.) Farmer Büttner. Tr. (and abr.) E. v. Mach. 1913-15. In C154(17).

"POLIANDER" (i.e., J: Graumann, 1487-1541.) Sel. in C244.

POLKO, Frau Ele. (Vogel) 1822-99.
*7231. (Erinnerungen an Fx. Mendelssohn-Bartholdy.) Reminisc. of F. M.-B: a social and artistic biog. Tr. Lady Wallace. L: Longmans 1869. x;251p. front. (port.) 20cm. [BM.LC]
7232. Flower picture. Tr. Sa. W. Lander. NY: Appleton n.d. (1858-60) 16. [AC]
7233. Lulu's novel. Tr. anon. NY: Munro 1880. Seaside lib. 32cm. [AC]
*7234. (Musikalische Märchen. Phantasien und Skizzen.) Musical sketches. Tr. from 6th ed. by Fanny Fuller. Phil: Leypoldt; NY: Christern 1864. 297p. 17cm. [LC.BM]
[22 sketches. Tr. is good, not perfect.]
§7235. do. 1875. Musical tales, phantasms, and sketches. 1st series. Tr. Ma. P. Maudslay. L: Tinsley. [Cf. the following.] [EC]
§7236. do. 1876-7. [same] 2d series. L: Tinsley. 2v. 342; 357p. 19cm. [Not very good.] [BM.LC]
*7237. do. 1892. [same as #7234] Bost;NY: Ditson. 20cm. [LC]
7238. do. 1909. Tr. from 15th Ger. ed. anon. NY: Sturgis & Walton. 345p. 19cm. [LC]

POLKO, E.--Musik. Märchen
7239. do. 1915. [same] Phil: Presser. 345;ixp. il. D. [AC]
7239a. She writes. (A story.) Tr. anon. "Old and New" 1(1870):294, etc.
§7240. do.[Ad.] Violetta: a romance of the later life of Mozart. Tr. anon. 1887. In Hoffmann, Fz., "A boy musician," pp. 113-26, #4481. [Extr. from the "Mus. Märchen," but quite freely treated, without much attempt to tr. faithfully.]

POPP, Frau Ade. 1869- .
7241. The autobiog. of a working woman. Tr. from 3d Ger. ed. Edith C. Harvey. With introd. A: Bebel and J. Ramsay Macdonald. L;Lpz: Unwin 1912. 135p. 2 ports. 19cm. [BM.LC]
7242. do. 1913. [same] Chic: Browne. [LC]

POSCHINGER, H: Ritter, 1845-1911. See Bismarck, Table Talk, #467-9.

POSCHINGER, Mge. (Landau) Edle v. 1862- .
*7243. ("Kaiser Friedrich.") Life of the emperor F: Ed. by Sidney Whitman. NY;L: Harper 1901. xiv;459p. front. (port.) 22cm. [LC.BM] [Somewhat condensed, but well done.]
See Friedrich III for her ed. of his diary, #2020.

PRANGER, see Pfranger.

PRECHT, V. Sel. in C105.

PREISS, L: and ROHRBACH, Pl.
7243a. Palestine and Transjordania. 214 photogr. and pl. 21 col. ils. Sheldon 1926. 12 x 9.[EC]--Macmillan 1926. xvi;230p. Q. [AC]

PREISWERK, S: 1799-1871. Sel. in C287.

PRINZ H: v. Preussen, 1726-1802. See F: II, Elogy, etc., #1983.

PROHL, He. 1823-86.
§7244. (Das Glückskind.) Christel: a tale of true luck. Tr. Philippa M. Pearson and Gertraud Wegner. Il. F. Dadd. L: S. P. C. K. 1885. front. 222p. 18cm.[They do not get the finer shades of meaning.] [BM]
§7245. do. 1887. [same] NY: Young. il. 16. [AC]
7246. (Im trauten Daheim.) Tannenwiese; or, a happy home. A sequel to "Where is heaven?" Tr. M. P. Butcher. Phil: Luth. pub. 1886. 204p. 17cm. [LC]
7247. (Wo ist der Himmel?) Where is heaven? Tr. M. P. Butcher. Phil: Luth. pub. 1884. S. [AC]

PRUTZ, Hs. 1843- .
?7248. The age of Charlemagne. Tr. Hm. W. Hayley. 1902, 1905. In C201(8). [No apparent relation to the orig. before me.]
7249. The age of feudalism and theocracy. Tr. Frank E. Zinkeisen. 1902, 1905. In C201(9).
7250. The age of the Renaissance. Tr. F. E. Zinkeisen. 1902, 1905. In C201(10).

PRUTZ, Rb. E: 1816-72. Sel. in C50;112;317;378;395;448;539;571.

PRUEWER, Jl. See O: Roese, joint author, #7521.

PUCHTA, Cn. Rd. H: 1808-58. Sel. in C287.

PUECKLER-MUSKAU, Hm. L: H: Fürst v. 1785-1871. Sel. in C142.
*7251. (Aus Mehemed Alis Reich.) Egypt and Mehemet Ali. Tr. anon. L: Newby 1845. 3v. 19cm. [BM.LC]
[Tr. improves if anything on the fine writing of the orig.]
*7252. do. 1845. Egypt under Mehemet Ali. Tr. H. E. Lloyd. L: Colburn. 2v. in one. xxiv;323;vii;374p. 19cm. [BM]
*7253. (Briefe eines Verstorbenen. Ein fragmentarisches Tagebuch...) Tour in England, Ireland, and France...1828-29...in a series of

PUECKLER-MUSKAU, Hm. L: H: Fürst v.--Briefe eines Verstorbenen... letters. By a Ger. prince. L: E.Wilson 1832. 2v. in one. xxi;358; 304p. 18cm. [BM]
[Tr. is doubtless by Mrs. Austin, cf. following entries. Publishers' announcement is for 1831. See B26.]
*7254. do. 1832. Tour in Germany, Holland, and England, 1826-28. In a series of letters, etc. Tr. Mrs. Sa. Austin. L: E.Wilson. Vols. 3,4. front. (port.) 19cm. [BM.LC]
[A continuation of the foregoing. Vol. 3, xvi;384p. Vol. 4, x; 389p. Vol. 3 says: in 4 vols.]
*7255. do. 1833. [same title as #7253]...1826-29. Tr. Mrs. Sa. Austin. Phil: Carey, Lea & B. 499p. 22cm. [LC]
7256. (Semilasso in Afrika.) S-- in A--. Tr. anon. L: Bentley 1837. 3v. 19cm. [BM]
7257. do. 1837. [same] 2d ed. [LC]
7258. do. 1839. [same] Title: Travels and advent. in Algiers, etc[LC]
7259. (Tutti Frutti. Aus den Papieren des Verstorbenen.) Tutti frutti. Tr. Capt. Edm. Spencer. NY: Harper 1833. 226p. 20cm. [LC]
[Probably based on P--'s "Tutti Frutti," pub. 1835 in 5 vols.
7260. do. 1833? [same] L: Bach & co. 2v. See "Monthly R." (IV)11 (1834):413. (B26)
7261. do. 1836. [same] T-- f--; or, the sketch-book of the author of "The tour of a Ger. prince." L: Simpkin & M. 2 pts. in 1v. 19cm.
[Cf. following entry.] [LC]
*7262. do. 1839. The Ger. sketch-book: scenes and sketches of a tour in the Riesengebirge. Tr. Edm. Spencer. L: Simpkin & M. 2v. xxviii;260;240p. 19cm. [BM]

PUENJER, G: Cn. Bh. 1850-85.
*7263. (Geschichte der christlichen Religionsphilosophie.) Hist. of the Christian philos. of relig., from the Reformation to Kant. Tr. W: Hastie. Pref. Rb. F. Flint. Ed: Clark 1887. xix;660p. 22cm. [BM.LC]

PUETTER, J: St. 1725-1807.
*7264. (Historische Entwicklung der heutigen Staatsverfassung des teutschen Reiches.) An histor. devel. of the pres. polit. constitution of the Germanic empire. Tr. Josiah Dornford. L: Payne 1790. 3v. 32cm. [Large paper ed.] [BM.LC]
*7265. do. 1790. [same] 21cm. [BM]

PUETZ, E. v. (i.e., Frau Everilda Eleanora Felicité (v. Klenze) Pütz zu Pütz, 1843-1926.)
7266. Sacrifice. Tr. anon. 1902. In C481.

PUETZ, W: 1806-77.
7267. (Grundriss der Geographie und Geschichte der alten, mittleren und neuen Zeit. Teil 1.) Manual of ancient geog. and hist. Tr. anon. NY: Appleton 1849. 12. [AC]
7268. do. 1853. Handbook of ancient geog. and hist. Ed. by T: K. Arnold. L: Rivington. xv;396p. 18cm. [BM]
7269. (Grundriss...Teil 2.) Handbook of medieval geog. and hist. Tr. R. B. Paul. L: Rivington 1849. xii;208p. 17cm. [BM.LC]
7270. do. 1850. [same] NY: Appleton. 211p. 19cm. [LC]
7271. do. 1854. Survey of the geog. and hist. of the middle ages, 476-1492. Tr. Prof. Stigell. L: Varty & Owen. vii;334p. 18cm.[BM.LC]
7272. do. 1855. [same] Gover. 12. [EC]
7273. (Grundriss...Teil 3.) Manual of mod. geog. and hist. Tr. Rb. B. Paul. 1st Amer. ed. rev. and cor. from L. ed. NY: Appleton 1851. 336p. 19cm. [LC.BM]
7274. do. 1859. Mod. geog. and hist. by Paul and Arnold. Rivington. 12. [EC]

PUFENDORF, S: Frhr. v. 1632-94.
7275. (De jure naturae et gentium.) Of the law of nature and of nations. Tr. Basil Kennett. Oxf: Prtd. for Churchill 1703. 4;27; 400;262p. 33cm. [Book V tr. by W: Percivale.] [BM.LC]
7276. do. 1710. [same] 2d ed. carefully corr. and compared with Mr. Barbeyrac's French tr. Oxf: Prtd. by Lichfield for Churchill. 724p. 33cm. [BM]
7277. do. 1716. [same] ...Abr. from the orig...Compared with the respective last eds. of Mr. Barbeyrac's...tr...By J. Spavan. L: Prtd. for Vanan & Osborne. 2v. 371;339p. front. (port.) 20cm. [BM.LC]
7278. do. 1729. [same] 4th ed. carefully corr. L: Walthoe, Wilkin. 14;84;878p. 36 x 24cm. [BM.LC]
7279. do. 1749. [same] 5th ed. carefully corr. To which is prefix'd, M. Barbeyrac's prefatory discourse done into Engl. by Mr. Carew. L: Bonwicke. 4;75;883p. 38cm. [BM.LC]
7280. (De officio hominis et civis juxta legem.) The whole duty of man according to the law of nature. Now made Engl. Anon. L: Prtd. for Harper 1698. 336p. 18cm. [LC]
7281. do. 1698. [same] 2d ed. L: B:Motte for C:Harper & J:Jones. 336p. port. [BM]
7282. do. 1716. [same] 4th ed. with additions by A. Tooke. L: B.Tooke. 387p. 20cm. [BM]
*7283. (Einleitung zu der Historie der vornehmsten Reiche und Staaten, etc.) An introd. to the hist. of the principal states of Europe. Tr. J. Crull. 3d ed. with additions. L: Prtd. for M. Gilliflower & T. Newborough 1699. Pref., 515p., index. 19cm. [BM]
*7284. do. 1702. [same] 5th ed. with additions. L: Prtd. for T: Newborough. 515p. 19cm. [BM]
*7285. do. 1706. [same] 6th ed. L: Prtd. for T: Newborough at the golden ball. 670p. 19cm. [BM]
["From the orig. High-Dutch, with appendix never prtd. before containing introd. to the hist. of the principal sovereign states of Italy."]
*7286. do. 1719. [same] 8th ed. L: Prtd. for Tooke. 646p. 19cm. [BM]
*7287. do. 1748. ...Begun by Baron P--, and contin. down to...1743 by M. Martiniere. Improved from the French by Js. Sayer. L: Prtd. for Knapton. 2v. xiv;412;382p. 20cm. [BM.LC]
*7288. do. 1764. [same] L: Knapton. 2v. xiii;412;382p. [BM.LC]
7289. (Vom Verhältnis der Religion gegen den Staat.) Relig. in ref. to civil society (Of the nature and qualification of relig.);which may serve as an appendix to the author's "Duty of man." Tr. anon. L: Prtd. by D. E. for A. Roper 1698. 182p. 18cm. [BM]
[From his "Der geistlichen Rechtsgelahrtheit I und II Teil."]
7290. do. 1719. Of the relation between church and state; or, how far Christian and civil life affect each other. Tr. anon. L: Prtd. for J: Wyat. 173p. 16cm. [BM]

PUTTKAMER, El. Frhr. v. 1802-75. See "Otto Ludwig."

PUTTKAMER, Me. M. v. 1881- . See "Me. Madeleine."

PUTLITZ, Gst. H: Gans, edler Herr von und zu, 1821-90.
7291. Orig. of the Christmas tree. Tr. E. E. H. NY: Dutton 1869. 18. [AC]
*7292. (Was sich der Wald erzählt.) What was said in the woods. Tr. anon. L: Longmans 1851. 163p. 13cm. [BM]
§7293. do. 1855. What the woods talk about. Tr. H: W. Carstens. In his "A trifolium." pp. 11-81. Bost: Munroe. 18cm. [LC.BM]
[Awkward English.]
7294. do. 1866. Forest voices. Ed. C. A. Smith. Albany, NY: Munsell. 102p. 18cm. [LC]

PUTLITZ, Gst. H: Gans--Was sich der Wald erzählt
7295. do. 1870. What the wood whispers to itself. Tr. E. E. H. NY: Appleton. 72p. il. 16. [AC lists this for 1869.] [LCO]
7296. The young lady's house. In Speed, "Stories of patriotism, etc." [LCO]

PUTTMANN, ---. Sel. in C301.

PYRKER, J: Ladislaw, v. Felsö-Cör, 1772-1847. Sel. in C112.

QUIDDE, L: 1858- .
**7297. The Kaiser's double: being a tr. by Claud H. A. Field of the...pamphlet...entitled "Caligula." n.p. n.d. 16p. 18cm. [LC] [Excellent tr.]

QUINIUS, A:a.
7298. My dear friend Malta. Tr. J: G: Quinius. n.p. 190-? 35p. (B12) [NY]

RAABE, W: 1831-1910. Sel. in C405a;422.
*7299. (Abu Telfan, oder die Heimkehr vom Mondgebirge.) Abu Telfan; or, the return from the Mountains of the Moon. Tr. Sofie Delffs. L: Chapman & Hall 1881. 3v. 19cm. [BM.LC]
*7300. (Der Hungerpastor.) The hunger-pastor. Tr. "Arnold." L: Chapman & Hall 1885. 2v. 308;320p. 18cm. [BM]
§7301. do. 1913-15. Tr. Muriel Almon. In C154(11). [Unable to cope with his style.]

RABENER, Gb. W: 1714-71.
7302. A dream upon the occupations of departed souls. Tr. anon. ca. 1800. In C157(1).
§7303. (Satyren.) Satirical letters. Tr. anon. L: Linde 1757. 2v. 317; 325p. 16. [Not wholly faithful nor wholly correct.] [LCO]

RACOVITZA, He. (v. Dönniges), afterwards Friedmann, afterwards v. Schewitsch, 1845-1911.
7304. The evil that women do: a novel. Tr. A. Howard. NY: Dillingham 1890. 332p. 18cm. [LC.BM]
§7305. (Von Anderen und mir.) Princess Helene v. R--: an autobiog. Tr. Cecil Mar. NY: Macmillan; L: Constable 1910. xiii;420p. 24cm. [Tr. conventionalizes her style, normalizes her punctuation, omits freely.] [LC.BM]

RADKERSBERG-RADNICKY, Mary v.
7306. Ardent natures, and, In hard days, by "Redeatis." Tr. Rev. L. A. Rendter. NY: Soc. of the divine word 1913. 184p. D. [AC]

RAIMUND, Fd. 1790-1836.
7306a. (Der Alpenkönig.) The king of the Alps. A romantic drama in 3 acts. Tr. ed. J: Baldwin Buckstone. In Lacy's acting ed. of plays, no. 6. 1850? [R. F. Arnold.]

"RAIMUND, Golo" (i.e., Bta. (Heyn) Frederich, 1825-82.)
7307. (Ein neues Geschlecht.) A new race. Tr. Mrs. A. L. Wister. Phil: Lippincott 1880. 221p. 19cm. [LC]
7308. do. 1900. [same] [LC]
7309. do. 1908. [same] [LC]
7310. (Gesucht und gefunden.) Sought and found. Tr. Adelaide S. Buckley. NY: Funk & Wagnalls 1888. 171p. 20cm. [LC.BM]
7311. A hard heart. By S. H. Phil: Lippincott 1884. 243p. 19cm. [LC]
7312. (Von Hand zu Hand.) From hand to hand. Tr. Mrs. A. L. Wister. Phil: Lippincott 1882. 372p. 19cm. [LC]
7313. do. 1902. [same] [LC]

RAINER FAMILY. See C460a.

RAINER, Js. 1845- .
7314. A noble priest: Js. Salzmann. Tr. Js. W: Berg. Milwaukee, Wis: Olinger & S. 1903. 254p. il. 20cm. [LC]

RAISNER, i.e., Reisner? 17th cent. Sel. in C276.

RAMANN, Lina, 1833-1912.
*7315. (Fz. Liszt als Künstler und Mensch.) Fz. L--, artist and man, 1811-40. Tr. Miss E. Cowdery. L: Allen 1882. 2v. xxvi;413;400p. 19cm. [BM.LC]

RAMBACH, J: Jk. 1693-1735. Sel. in C232;244;269;287;486.
7316. Considerations on the sufferings of Christ. Tr. anon. L: Linde 1759? 3v. See "Crit. R." 7(1759):467. (B26)
7317. Memoirs of the life and death of the late Rev. Mr. Anthony W: Boehm. Tr. J: Cn. Jacobi. L: R:Ford 1735. 72p. 19cm. [BM]

RAMLER, K: W: 1725-98. Sel. in C88;219;244;373;389.

RAMSEYER, F: A:
7318. Dark and stormy days at Kumassi, 1900. Compiled Rev. Pl. Steiner. Tr. Miss Meyer. Pref. T: Nicol. L: Partridge 1901. 240p. 18cm. [BM]

RAMSEYER, F: A: and J:s Kuehne.
7319. (Vier Jahre gefangen in Asante. Nach den Tagebüchern...) Four years in Ashantee. Ed. Mrs. Weitbrecht (from their diaries). Introd. Dr. Gundert, pref. Prof. Td. Christleib. L: Nisbet; NY: Carter 1875. xv;320p. il. 20cm. [BM.LC]
7320. do. 1877. [same] 2d ed. Nisbet. [BM]
*7321. do. 1901. Four years' captivity in Ashanti. Related (from their diaries)...by Rev. Pl. Steiner. L: Partridge. 119p. il. 18cm. [BM]

RANKE, Lp. v. 1795-1886. Sel. in C366*;469;574*.
7322. (Deutsche Geschichte im Zeitalter der Reformation.) Hist. of the Reformation in Germany. Tr. Sa. Austin. Phil: Lea & Blanchard 1844. 453p. 24cm. [LC]
*7323. do. 1845-7. [same] 2d ed. L: Longmans. 3v. 8. [BM.LC] [LC has 1st ed. of vol. 3.]
7324. do. 1905. [same] Ed. R. A. Johnson. L: Routledge; NY: Dutton. xxiv;792p. 23cm. [BM.LC]
7325. Ferd. I and Mx. II of Austria: an essay on the polit. and relig. state of Germany immediately after the Reformation. Tr. Lady Duff Gordon. L: Longmans 1853. Travelers Lib. 135p. 8. [BM]
*7326. (Geschichte der romanischen und germanischen Völker.) Hist. of the Latin and Teutonic nations, 1494-1514. Tr. Ph. A. Ashworth. L: Bell 1887. 388p. 18cm. [LC]
7327. do. 1909. [same] Tr. rev. by G. R. Dennis. Introd. by E: Armstrong. L: Bell. xxxvi;448p. 19cm. [BM.LC]
7328. do. 1915. [same] Macmillan. xxxvi;448p. [BM]
*7329. (Neun Bücher preussischer Geschichte.) Hist. of the Prussian monarchy from its rise to the present time. Tr. F. Demmler. L: Newby 1847-8. 2v. 22cm. [BM]
*7330. do. 1849. Memoirs of the house of Brandenburg...17th and 18th cent. Tr. Sir Ax. and Lady Lucie Duff-Gordon. L: Murray. 3v. 22cm. [BM.LC]
*7331. (Weltgeschichte.) Universal hist. Tr. D. C. Tovey and G: W. Prothero. L: K.Paul 1884. xvi;501p. 8. [BM]
*7332. do. 1885. [same] NY: Harper. 494p. 22cm. [LC]

RAPP, G: 1798-1868. Sel. in C372.

RATICH (Ratichius, Ratke), Wfg. 1571-1635. See Raumer, K: v., R--, Comenius, and Basedow, #7354.

RATHENAU, Wl. 1867-1922.
*7333. (Die neue Gesellschaft.) The new society. Tr. anon. L: Williams & N. 1920. 147p. 19cm. [BM]
[On the whole, very good. Tr. abandons the pungent and crisp style by needless expansion.]
*7334. do. 1921. [same] NY: Harcourt, Brace & Howe. 147p. [LC]
*7335. (Von kommenden Dingen.) In days to come. Tr. E. and C. Paul. L: Allen & U;NY: Knopf 1921. 286p. 22cm. [BM.LC]

RATZEL, F: 1844-1904.
*7336. (Völkerkunde.) Hist. of mankind. Tr. from 2d Ger. ed. by A. J. Butler. Introd. E. B. Tylor. L: Macmillan 1896-98. 3v. il. 25cm. [BM.LC]

RAU, Heribert, 1813-76.
7337. (Beethoven.) B--: a biogr. romance. Tr. S. E. Randolph. Bost; NY: Ditson 1880. 332p. 17cm. [LC]
7338. do. 1908. [same] 20cm. [LC]
§7339. (Der Raub Strassburgs.) A royal robber. Tr. Ag. A. E. Blake. Chic: Morrill, Higgins 1893. 556p. 21cm. [Not faithful.] [LC]
7340. (Mozart, ein Künstlerleben.) M--: a biogr. romance. Tr. E: R. Sill. NY: Leypoldt & Holt 1868. 323p. 19cm. [LC]
§7341. do. 1899. The tone king: a romance of the life of M--. Tr. J. E. St. Q. Rae. L: Jarrold. 480p. 19cm. [Errors.] [BM]
§7342. do. 1900. [same] NY: Dodd, Mead. 387p. 19cm. [LC]

RAUMER, F: L: G: v. 1781-1873. Sel. in C158.
7343. (Beiträge zur neueren Geschichte, etc.) Contributions to mod. hist. Vol. 2, F: II and his times. Tr. anon. L: Knight 1837. xvi; 467p. 19cm. [This book was missing from BM.] [BM.LC]
*7344. (Briefe aus Paris zur Erläuterung der Geschichte des 16. und 17. Jahrhunderts.) Hist. of the 16th and 17th centuries. Tr. anon. L: Murray 1835. 2v. xvii;480; 455p. 19cm. [BM.LC]
*7345. (Die Vereinigten Staaten von Nordamerika.) America and the Amer. people. Tr. W: W. Turner. NY: Langley 1846. 512p. 22cm [LC.BM]
*7346. (England im Jahre 1835.) E-- in 1835: being a series of letters. Tr. Sa. Austin and H. E. Lloyd. With memoir of v. R--. L: Lee 1836. 3v. 19cm. [BM]
[Vols. 1,2 tr. by Austin; vol. 3 tr. by Lloyd.]
*7347. do. 1836. [same] Phil: Carey, Lea & B. 512p. 23cm. [LC]
[With "England in 1841."]
*7348. (England im Jahre 1841.) E-- in 1841: being a series of letters. Tr. H. E. Lloyd. L: Lee 1842. 2v. 292; 323p. 18cm. [BM.LC]
[A continuation of #7346.]
*7349. (Italien.) Italy and the Italians. Tr. anon. L: Colburn 1840. 2v. x;351; 371p. 20cm. [BM]

RAUMER, K: G: v. 1783-1865.
*7350. (Geschichte der Pädagogik. Teil 2.) Life and system of Pestalozzi. Tr. J. Tilleard. L: Longmans 1855. 80p. 22cm. [BM.LC]
[Extr. from the Ger. work.]
7351. (Geschichte...Bd. 4.) German universities. Tr. F. B. Perkins. NY: Brownell 1859. 256p. 8. [Reprint from "Amer. journ. of educ."] [LC]
7352. do. 1859. [same] Tr. from last Ger. ed. by F. P. Perkins. NY: Brownell. 198p. 23cm. [Reprint from "Amer. journ. of educ."] [BM]
7353. do. n.d. [same?] Hartford, Conn: Barnard. 8. [AC]
7354. Ratich, Comenius, and Basedow. Tr. anon. Hartford, Conn: Barnard n.d. (1872-6.) 8. [AC]

RAUPACH, Ern. B: Bn. Sl. 1784-1852. Sel. in C412.
§7355. (Der Niebelungen Hort.) The Nibelungen treasure: a tragedy. Tr. Mme. L. Davésiès de Pontès. L: Williams & N. 1847. xxiii;126p. 17cm. [BM.LCO]

RAUPACH, Ern. B: Bn. Sl.
[Good verse; one omission noted, and tr. is somewhat lacking in faithful accuracy.]
7355a. (Die Schule des Lebens.) Won: not Wooed. A drama in 5 acts [verse]. Ad. from the German. 1877. 2d rev. ed. See A515.
§7356. (Die Tochter der Luft.) The daughter of the air: a mythic trag. in 5 acts [verse] after the idea of P. Calderon. Tr. anon. L: Marsh 1831. xii;102p. 12. [BM.LC]
[Fairly close in sense, but verse is irreg. and uncouth.]
7357. (Isidor und Olga.) The serf: a trag. in 5 acts [verse]. Altered...and ad. to Engl. stage by R. Talbot. L: Cumberland 1828. 54p. 15cm. [LC]
7358. do. 1828. [same] 2d ed. L: Cumberland. 18cm. [BM]
7359. do. 1837? [same] In "Cumberland's Brit. theatre," vol. 19. 54p. [BM.LCO]

RAUSCHENBUSCH, Hilmar Ern. See Leipoldt, W:, Memoir of H. E. R--, #5660.

RAUWOLFF, Lh. ("Flaminius, L.")
*7360. (Reyss ins gelobte Land.) Itinerary into the eastern countries, as Syria, Palestine, etc. Tr. N: Staphorst. In Ray, J:, "A coll. of curious travels and voyages," tome 1, 1693. L: Prtd. for S. Smith & B. Walford. 2 pts. 396p. 19cm. [BM]
*7361. do. 1738. [same] 2d ed. corr. and improved. L: Prtd. for Walthoe, 338p. 19cm. [Travels through the low countries, V.2.][BM]

RAVEN, Frau Mde. (Beckmann) 1817- .
7362. (Eine Familie aus der ersten Gesellschaft.) The two brothers; or, the family that lived in the first society. Tr. anon. L: Bentley 1850. 2v. 299; 289p. 19cm. [BM.LC]
7363. do. 1853. [same] Bentley. Railway lib. 221p. 17cm. [BM]

REBER, Fz. v. 1834-1919.
*7364. (Kunstgeschichte des Altertums.) Hist. of ancient art. Tr. and augm. Js. T. Clarke. NY: Harper 1882. xx;482p. il. 23cm[BM.LC]
[Orig. pub. 1871.]
*7365. (Kunstgeschichte des Mittelalters.) Hist. of medieval art. Tr. Js. T: Clarke. NY: Harper 1887. xxxi;743p. il. 23cm. [LC.BM]

RECK, Ph. G: F: v.
7366. An extract of the journals of Mr. Commissary v. Reck, who conducted the first transport of Saltzburgers to Georgia; and of the Rev. Mr. Boltzius, one of their ministers. Tr. anon. L: S. P. C. K. 1734. 72p. 16cm. [BM.LC]
7367. do. 1836? reprint. In Force, P., Tracts, vol. 4. Washington, D. C: 1836-46. 23cm. [LC]
7368. do. 1846. [same] Washington, D. C: Force. 38p. 8. [LC.BM]

RECKE-VOLMERSTEIN, Ma. Gräfin v. d.
*7369. (Erinnerungen aus dem Leben...) Recoll. of the life of Mda. (v. Pfeil und Klein-Ellguth) v.d. R.-V. Tr. Marg. Fox. Introd. Lord Bishop of Bath and Wells. L: Seeley 1874. xiii;326p. front. (port.) 18cm. [BM]

"REDEATIS" See Radkersberg-Radnicky, Mary.

REDEN, J:e Jne. F:e, Gräfin v. See Reuss, E., A pietist of the Napoleonic wars, #7405.

REDENBACHER, W: 1800-76.
7370. The emerald. Tr. A. H. Lochman. Phil: Luth. bd. 1872. 199p. il. 18cm. [LC]
7371. The little cloister ruin: a narr. Tr. by Rev. J. Oswald. Phil: Luth. bd. 1871. 130p. 18. [LCO]

REDWITZ, Ok., Baron v. 1823-91. Sel. in C17;112;309;395;450.
7371a. (Amaranth.) Amaranth. Tr. anon. "Engl. Rev." 16(1852):445. (B15a)

RÉE, Pl. J:s, 1858- .
*7372. (Nürnberg.) Nuremberg and its art to the end of the 18th cent. Tr. G. H. Palmer. L: Grevel; NY: Scribner 1905. 181p. il. 24cm. [BM.LC]

REGENBOGE, Barthel, fl. 1300-18. Sel. in C310;427.

REGNET, C. Sel. in C102.

REICHENAU, Rd. 1817-79. Sel. in C174.
§7373. (Aus unseren vier Wänden. Bilder aus dem Kinderleben.) Child-life. Ad. by C. Campbell. Il. by Oc. Pletsch. L: Routledge 1871. 148p. 18cm. [BM]

"REICHENBACH, Mz. v." (i.e., Valeska--v. Reiswitz--Gräfin v. Bethusy-Huc, 1848-)
7374. (Die Eichhofs.) The E--. Tr. Mrs. A. L. Wister. Phil: Lippincott 1881. 322p. 18cm. [LC]
7375. do. 1909. [same] 322p. (B12)

REICHERT, Heinz. Operettas. See Grünbaum, Fritz: Willner, A. M.

REICHLIN-MELDEGG, Ax. Freiherr v. 1801-77.
7376. (Die deutschen Volksbücher v. J: Faust.) An expos. of Goethe's Faust. Tr. R: H. Chittenden. NY: Miller 1864. 2v. in one. 18cm. [LC]

REICHMANN, Rd. Sel. in C169.

REIL, (J: AM.) F: v. Sel. in C137a.

REIMARUS, H. S., i.e., J: Ab. H: 1729-1814.
7377. (Die Wahrheiten der natürlichen Religion.) Principal truths of nat. relig. defended and illustrated. Tr. Wynne. L: Law 1766? See "Monthly R." 34(1766):370. (B26)

REIN, J. Jt. 1835-1918.
*7378. (Japan, nach Reisen und Studien.) Japan: travels and researches. Tr. anon. L: Hodder & Stoughton; NY: Armstrong 1884. 543p. il. 25cm. [EC lists this for 1883.] [BM.LC]
*7379. do. 1889. [same] 2d ed. Hodder & S. [EC]

REIN, W: 1847- .
7380. (Das Leben D. Mn. Luthers dem deutschen Volk erzählt.) The life of M. L--. Tr. and ed. by Rev. G: F. Behringer. NY: Funk & W. 1883. 219p. 19cm. [LC]

REINECKE, Abh. d. 1760. Sel. in C221;489.

REINECKE, ---. Sel. in C123.

REINECKE, K: H: Carsten, 1824-1910.
*7381. (Die Beethovenschen Klaviersonaten.) The B-- pianoforte sonatas: letters to a lady. Tr. E. M. T. Dawson. L: Augener 1898. 142p. 19cm. [BM.LC]

REINHARD, Fz. Volkmar, 1753-1812.
*7382. (Geständnisse.) Memoirs and confessions. Tr. O. A. Taylor. Bost: Peirce & Parker 1832. 164p. front. (port.) 18cm. [LCO.BM]

REINHARD, K: v.
*7383. ("Ich dien." Der Armee gewidmet.) "Ich dien." The soldier's life: its dignity and honour. Tr. J: T. Ferrier. L: Clowes 1856. 77p. 15cm. [BM]

REINHARDT, H: 1865- . The spring maid. Operetta. See Wilhelm, Jl.

"REINHOLD, C." (i.e., Cn. Rld. Köstlin, 1813-56.) Sel. in C318;423.

REINHOLD, C:e
*7384. (Die Abendglocke.) The evening bell; or, the hour of relating entertaining anecdotes for dear young people. Tr. Rev. C.S. Mangan. Dublin: McGlashan; L: Orr 1858. 243p. col. front. and 2 pl. 19cm. [BM] [Ger. and Eng. interpaged. Faithful tr.: terrible in both languages.]
*7385. do. 1858. [same] ...or, tales and entertaining anecdotes for young people. Dublin: McGlashan & Gill; L: Simpkin & Marshall. [BM] [Dupl. of preceding, with a new t.p. and a longer list of errata.]

REINICK, Rb. 1805-52. Sel. in C97;106;112;116;152;169;192;195;296; 309;372;395;448;497;501;571.
*7386. (Die Wurzelprinzessin.) The king of root valley and his curious daughter: a fairy tale. Tr. anon. Il. (in col.) by T. v. Oer and R. Reinick. L: Chapman & Hall 1856. 34p. 24cm. [BM]
*7387. do. 1865. The root princess: a Christmas story. Tr. Fanny Fuller. Phil: Leypoldt. 32p. il. in col. 22cm. [LCO.BM] [A better tr. than the foregoing.]
*7388. (Genoveva.) G--: opera in 4 acts by Rb. Schumann. Text based on L: Tieck and F: Hebbel, esp. the latter, and rev. by the composer. Ad. (i.e., tr.) by Louisa Vance. Vocal score. Engl;Ger. L;NY: Novello n.d. 1890? 202p. 26cm. [BMM.LCM]
7389. The road to fortune, with other tales. Tr. anon. Bost: Crosby, Nichols 1852. 12. [AC]

REINMAR VON BRENNENBURG (Der Brennenberger), fl. 1238-75. Sel. in C427.

REINMAR VON HAGENAU, fl. 1150-1210. Sel. in C27*;421;427*;570.

REINMAR VON ZWETER, fl. 1219-52. Sel. in C27*;171;427*.

REISCHACH, Hg. Baron v. 1854- .
*7390. (Unter drei Kaisern.) Under three emperors. Tr. Prince Blücher. L: Constable 1927. vii;264p. front. (port.) 22cm. [BM.LC]

REISINGER, Ern. 1884- .
7391. The art of ancient Greece and Rome. In Poland, Fz., "The culture...," #7228.

REISSMANN, A: 1825-1903.
*7392. (Rb. Schumann, sein Leben und seine Werke.) Life and works of Rb. S--. Tr. from 3d ed. Abby L. Alger. L: Bell 1886. Bohn lib. vi;276p. 19cm. [BM.LC]

REISNER, Am. 1471-1563. Sel. in C244 (spelled Reissner).

REISNER, Fd. 1721-89. Sel. in C276 (spelled Raisner).

REITHARDT, J: Jk. 1805-57. Sel. in C438*.

REITZENSTEIN, K: Freiherr v., fl. 1792.
7393. Count Koenigsmark. Tr. B: Thompson. 1801. in C535.

RELLSTAB, L: 1799-1860. Sel. in C137a;470.
*7394. (1812, ein historischer Roman.) Eighteen hundred and twelve: histor. novel. Tr. Ma. Norman. L: Bentley 1849. 3v. 19cm. [BM] [Tr. acknowledges that some few liberties have been taken with the text.]
7395. do. 1849. [same?] Eighteen hundred and twelve; or, Napoleon's invasion of Russia. NY: Stringer & T. 8. [AC]
*7396. do. 1853. The Polish lancer; or, 1812: a tale of Napoleon's invasion of Russia. Tr. anon. L: Routledge. 376p. 16cm. [BM] [This reads better than the foregoing: tr. condenses in part by omitting adjectives. 74 chaps., fine type and close print.]
*7397. do. 1878. [same] New ed. L: Routledge. [EC]

REMY, Nahida (i.e., Mrs. Nahida Anna Ma. Ruth--Remy--Lazarus.)
*7398. (Das jüdische Weib.) The Jewish woman. Author. tr. Mrs.

REMY, Nahida--Das jüdische Weib
Louise Mannheimer. Cincin: Krehbiel 1895. 264p. front. (port.) 20cm. [LC.BM]
*7399. do. 1916. [same] 3d enl. ed. NY: Bloch. 294p. O. [AC]

REU, J: Ml. 1869- .
7400. Life of Mn. Luther. Tr. El. H. Rausch. Chic: Wartburg 1917. 297p. 92 ils. 19cm. [LC]

REUMONT, Af. v. 1808-87. Sel. in C466*.
*7401. (Die Carafa von Maddaloni. Neapel unter spanischer Herrschaft.) The carafas of Maddaloni. Naples under Span. dominion. Tr. anon. L: Bohn 1854. xiv;465p. front. (port.) 8. [BM]
*7402. (Lorenzo de Medici, il Magnifico.) L-- de' M--. Tr. Rb. Harrison. L: Smith, Elder 1876. 2v. xiv;489; 500p. 22cm. [BM]
7403. (Rheinlands Sagen.) Ruins of the Rhine, their times and traditions. Ed. C. White. Aix-la-Chapelle: Kohnen 1838. 356p. il. 8. [LC]
7404. Sir F: Adam: a sketch of mod. times. Tr. anon. Priv. prtd. 1855. 56p. 18cm. [BM]

REUSS, --- (i.e., Erdmuthe Dora v. Zinzendorf?) Sel. in C497.

REUSS, Elre. F:e, Gräfin v. Reden, 1835-1903.
7405. (Ein Lebensbild nach Briefen und Tagebüchern.) A pietist of the Napoleonic wars and after: the life of J:e Jne. Gräfin v. Reden. Tr. Mrs. C: E: Barrett-Lennard and Miss M. W. Hoper. Introd. note R. S. Tait. L: Dutton; NY: Murray 1905. xi;375p. il. 22cm. [Ad. and abr., almost retold.] [BM.LC]

REUTER, (H: L: Cn. F:) Fritz, 1810-74. Sel. in C366*;422;463;469.
7405a. (Dörchläuchting.) His little serene highness. Tr. anon. "Littell's Living Age" 116(1873):20, etc. (B15a)
§7406. (Ut de Franzosentid.) In the year '13: a tale of Mecklenburg life. Tr. C: L. Lewes. Lpz: Tauchnitz 1867. 299p. 16cm. [LC.BM]
§7407. do. 1868. [same] NY: Leypoldt & Holt. sq. 16. [BM]
§7408. do. 1878. [same] NY: Munro. Seaside lib. 29p. 32cm. [LC]
§7409. (Ut mine Stromtid.) Seed-time and harvest; or, during my apprenticeship. Tr. anon. Phil: Lippincott 1871. 292p. 23cm. [LC.BM]
7409a. do. 1871. [same?]"Littell's Living Age" 108(1871): 19, etc.
§7410. do. 1878. [same] New ed. [AC]
§7411. do. 1878. An old story of my farming days. Tr. M. W. Macdowall. Lpz: Tauchnitz. 3v. 16cm. [LC.BM]
§7412. do. 1886. [same] NY: Munro. Pocket ed. 2v. in one. [LC]
7413. do. 1913-15. [extract] The Bräsig episodes...Tr. M. W. Macdowall and E. v. Mach. In C154(8).
7413a. (Woans ick tau 'ne Fru kam.) How I won a wife. Tr. by M. S. "Littell's Living Age" 128(1876):17. (B15a)
*7414. do. 1883. How I came by a wife: a humorous story. Tr. P. C. Glave. Denver: Echo pub. 32p. 15cm. [LC]
[Misses many chances, but is correct enough.]

REUTER, Gle. 1859- .
7415. (Nippsachen und Schicksale.) Bric-a-brac and destinies. Tr. Grace I. Colbron. 1915. In C179.

REVENTLOW, Ern. Cn. Einar L: Dv. Graf zu, 1869- .
§7416. (Der Vampir des Festlandes.) The vampire of the continent. Tr. G: Chatterton-Hill. NY: Jackson press 1916. xiii;225p. 19cm.
[Not fully in command of German.] [LC.BM]

RHEGIUS, Urbanus, 1449-1541.
7417. (Novae doctrinae ad veterem collatio.) A cõparison betweene the Olde learnynge and the Newe. Tr. out of Latin in Englysh by Wyliam Turner (Dean of Wells). Prynted in Southwarke by me James Nicolsõ anno. 1537. ff. A-G. 14cm. [BM]
[Also has: "To the reader" under + .

RHEGIUS, Urbanus--Novae doctrinae ad veterem collatio
7418. do. 1538. [same] ...latyn... Nicolson. ff. A-Hiv. 13cm. [BM]
[Printer's name on colophon; t.p. has only the date.]
7419. do. 1548. [same] The olde learnyng and the new, compared together wherby it may easely be knowē which of them is better and more agreyng with the euerlasting word of God. Newly corr. and augm. by Wyllyam Turner. Imprinted at L. by Rb. Stoughton, dwelling within Ludgate, at the sygne of the Bysshops Myter. ff. A-H. 13cm. [BM]

RHEINBERGER, Js.
7420. The daughter of Jairus: cantata. Tr. and ad. W. A. Barrett. Vocal score. Engl. L: Augener; NY: Schirmer 1879. 22p. 27cm. [BMM]

RHEINWALD, G: F: H:
*7421. (Die evangelischen Zillerthaler in Schlesien.) The protestant exiles of Zillerthal, their persecutions, and ex-patriation from the Tyrol. Tr. J: B. Saunders. L: Hatchard 1840. xv;125p. 17cm [BM]
*7422. do. 1840. [same] 2d ed. xix;128p. 17cm. [BM]
*7423. do. 1842. [same] 1st Amer. from 2d L. ed. NY: Moore. xiii; 107p. 18. [LCO]
*7424. do. 1848. [same] L: Hatchard. [EC]

"RHODEN, Emma v." (i.e., Frau Emmy F:e Cte.--Kühne--Friedrich, 1832-85.)
7425. (Der Trotzkopf.) An obstinate maid. Tr. from 21st Ger. ed. Ma. E. Ireland. Il. I. Waugh. Phil: Jacobs 1898. 323p. 12. [LC]
7426. do. 1898. Taming a tomboy. Tr. from 25th ed. and ad. by Fx. L. Oswald. NY: Allison. 236p. il. 19cm. [LC]
7427. do. 1916. [same as #7425] Jacobs. il. D. [AC]
7428. The young violinist. Tr. from 12th Ger. ed. Ma. E. Ireland. Il. C. B. Williams. NY;Akron: Saalfield 1906. 140p. 19cm. [LC]

RICHTER, Cn. F: 1676-1711. Sel. in C222-3;232;240;269;271;276;489; #8902;#8904.

RICHTER, Eg.
*7429. (Sozialdemokratische Zukunftsbilder.) Pictures of the socialistic future, freely ad. from Bebel. Author. tr. H: Wright. L: Sonnenschein 1893. 134p. 8. [BM]
[Tr. is competent, but improves on the orig.]
*7430. do. 1907. [same] Cheap ed. Introd. T. Mackay. L: Sonnenschein. x;134p. [BM]

RICHTER, Gg. d. 1650. Sel. in C271.

RICHTER, J: Pl. F: ("Jean Paul") 1763-1825. Sel. in C12;31;44;56;91; 98;122;158;163;172;190;193;194*;366;372;391;419;422;461*;464;469; 471;500;543;560;574*.
*7431. [Coll.] The death of an angel, and other pieces. Tr. A. Kenney. L: Black 1839. xxx;289p. 8. [68 prose selections.] [BM.NY]
*7432. [Coll.] 1864. The Campanerthal, and other writings. Bost: Ticknor & Fields. 383p. 18cm. [LC.BM]
[Title ("Das Kampaner Tal"), tr. Juliette Bauer, cf. #7445; Life of Quintus Fixlein ("Leben des Q-- F--"), tr. T: Carlyle, cf. C58; Schmelzle ("Des Feldpredigers Schmelzle Reise nach Flätz"), tr. Carlyle, cf. C58; Analects from R--, tr. T: De Quincey, cf. #7435; Misc. pieces.]
7433. [Sel.] Anon. 1859. Sketches of and from J. P. R--. L: Bennett. 84p. 19cm. [BM.LCO]
["The writer has interwoven a short biog. sketch with...sel. from his works."]
7434. [Sel.] Chatterton, Georgiana Lady. Extr. from the works. Sel. and tr. by...L: Parker 1859. 240p. 17cm. [BM]

RICHTER, Jean Paul
7435. [Sel.] De Quincey, T: Uncoll. writings. L: Sonnenschein 1890. 2v. 19cm. [Last will and testament; The house of weeping.] [BM.LC]
7436. [Sel.] Sharman, K. B. A prose poet of childhood, J. P. R--. Sel. by... L: Mayle 1901. 79p. 19cm. [BM] [Extr. from Levana, passages from autobiog.]
*7437. (Blumen-, Frucht- und Dornenstücke.) Flower, fruit, and thorn pieces; or, the married life, death, and wedding of the advocate of the poor, Firmian Siebenkäs. Tr. E: H: Noel. L: Smith 1845. 2v. 16cm. [BM.LC]
*7438. do. 1845-52. [same] Bost: Munroe. n.d. 2v. [AC]
*7439. do. 1863. [same] Bost: Ticknor & F. 2v. 19cm. [LC]
*7440. do. 1870? [same] Lpz: Tauchnitz. 2v. 16cm. [BM]
*7441. do. 1877. ...or, the wedded life, death, and marriage... Tr. Ax. Ewing. L: Bohn. 565p. 17cm. [BM]
*7442. do. 1888. [same] Bost: Little, Brown. [AC]
*7443. do. 1888. [same] NY: Scribner. [AC]
*7444. do. n.d. [same] NY: Macmillan. (B12)
*7445. (Das Kampaner Tal, oder über die Unsterblichkeit der Seele.) The Campaner Thal; or, discourses on the immortality of the soul. Tr. Juliette Gowa (i.e., Bauer? Cf. #7432). L: Gilpin 1848. xii; 104p. 18cm. [BM]
*7446. do. 1857. [same] 2d rev. and cor. ed. Gilpin. [BM]
§7447. (Der Mond.) The moon: a tale of the imagination. Tr. R: Holcraft. 1826. In C203.
*7448. do. 1844. Tr. J: Oxenford. In C442.
§7449. (Der Tod eines Engels.) The death of an angel. Tr. R: Holcraft. 1826. In C203.
*7450. do. 1845. Tr. H: Morley. In C419.
§7451. do. 1847. Tr. anon. In C20; cf. C21.
*7452. (Des Feldpredigers Schmelzle Reise nach Flätz...) Army chaplain S--'s journey to Flätz. Tr. T: Carlyle. 1827. In C58, cf. C59-62; #7432.
7453. The diadem. Tr. Miss L. Osgood. Phil: Carey & Hart 1846. (Cited in C120.)
*7454. (Die unsichtbare Loge.) The invisible lodge. Tr. C: T. Brooks. NY: Holt 1883. 406p. 17cm. [LC]
*7455. (Erinnerungen aus den schönsten Stunden für die letzten.) Recoll. from the most beautiful hours, for the last hours of life. Tr. A. Kenney. 1839. In #7431.
§7456. do. 1841. Reminisc. of the best hours of life for the hour of death. Tr. anon. Bost: Dowe. 52p. 18. [LCO]
§7457. do. 1841-52. [same] Bost: Munroe. n.d. 24. [AC]
§7458. (Flegeljahre.) Walt and Vult; or, the twins. Tr. Mrs. Eliza B. Lee. Bost: Munroe; NY: Wiley & P. 1846. 2v. 17cm. [LC.BM]
*7459. (Hesperus oder 45 Hundsposttage.) Hesperus; or, forty-five dog-post-days. Tr. C: T. Brooks. Bost: Ticknor & F. 1865. 2v. 18cm. [LC.BM]
*7460. (Leben des Quintus Fixlein aus fünfzehn Kästen gezogen.) Life of Q-- F--. Tr. T: Carlyle. 1827. In C58; Cf. C59-62; #7432.
*7461. do. 1913-15. [extract] Q-- F--'s wedding. Tr. Carlyle. In C154(4).
7462. (Leben des vergnügten Schulmeisterleins Maria Wuz in Auenthal.) Maria Wuz. Tr. F. and R. Storr. 1881. In C510, pp. 5-45.
*7463. (Levana oder Erziehungslehre.) Levana; or, the doctrine of education. Tr. A. H. L: Longmans 1848. xx;487p. 21cm. [BM.LC] [The following entry examined and rated.]
*7464. do. 1863. [same] Bost: Ticknor & F. xxi;400p. 18cm. [LC]
*7465. do. 1866. [same] 3d ed. xxi;400p. 18cm. [BM]
*7466. do. 1876. [same] Preceded by a short biog. of the author and his autobiog., a fragment. L: Bohn. xliv;413p. 17cm. [BM]

RICHTER, Jean Paul--Levana oder Erziehungslehre
*7467. do. 1886. [same] Bost: Little, Brown. [AC]
*7468. do. 1886. [same] NY: Scribner & W. [AC]
*7469. do. 1886. [same as #7466.] Bost: Heath. 413p. [LC]
7470. do. 1887. Ed. for Engl. readers by Susan Wood. L: Sonnenschein. xx;110p. 8. [BM]
*7471. do. 1897. [same as #7466] L: Bell. 16. [UW]
7472. The new year's night of an unhappy man. Tr. Hm. Bokum. 1836. In C31. [From Die Neujahrsnacht eines Unglücklichen.]
*7473. do. 1927. Tr. A. Kenney. In C367.
*7474. The opening of the will. Tr. Fes. H. King. 1913-15. In C154(4). From his "Flegeljahre".]
*7475. Rome. Tr. C: T. Brooks. 1913-15. In C154(4).
*7476. (Titan.) Titan. A romance. Tr. C: T. Brooks. Bost: Ticknor;L: Trübner 1862. 2v. 18cm. [LC]
*7477. do. 1863. [same] 2d ed. 19cm. [LC]
*7478. do. 1868. [same] xv;522; 521p. front. (port.) 18cm. [BM]
§7479. (Wahrheit aus Jean Pauls Leben.) Autobiog. Tr. Mrs. Eliza B. Lee, in her Life of J. P. F. R--. L: Chapman 1845. 478p. 19cm. [BM.LCO]
§7480. do. 1849. [same] 2d ed. [BM]
§7481. do. 1851. [same] [EC]
7482. do. 1876. In #7466; cf. also the following entries.
7483. (Weisheitssprüche.) Wit, wisdom, and philos. Ed. Giles P. Hawley. NY;L: Funk & W. 1884. 228p. 19cm. [LC.BM]
[Brief sel. under headings; at least partly eclectic.]
See Harden, M., Word portraits, #3699.

RICHTER, Lina.
7484. Family life in Germany under the blockade. Tr. anon. Pref. by Bernard Shaw. L: Nat. labour press 1919. 60p. 19cm. [BM]

RICHTHOFEN, Md. Abr. Frhr. v. 1892-1918.
7485. (Der rote Kampfflieger.) The red battle flyer. Tr. J. Ellis Barker. Pref. and notes C. G. Grey. NY: McBride 1918. vii;222p. il. 19cm. [LC]
*7486. do. 1918. The red air fighter. 2d ed. L: 'Aeroplane' etc. 140p. il. 18cm. [BM.LC]
7487. do. 1927. [sel.] In Floyd Gibbons, "The red knight of Germany." L: Heinemann. 383p. il. 20cm. [BM]

"RIDEAMUS" i.e., Fritz Oliven. The cousin from nowhere. Operetta. See Haller, Hm.

RIEDEL, Gst.
7488. Blind William. Phil: Claxton 1872. il. 16. [Tr?] [AC]

RIEDESEL, F:e Cte. Lu. (v. Massow), Freifrau v. 1746-1808.
*7489. (Die Berufsreise nach Amerika.) Letters and memoirs relating to the war of Amer. independence, and the capture of Ger. troops at Saratoga. Tr. anon. NY: Carvill 1827. 323p. 19cm. [LC.BM]
[Tr. has omitted passages out of deference to the sensitive feelings of his readers.]
*7490. do. 1867. Letters and journals... Tr. W: L. Stone. Albany, NY: Munsell. 235p. il. 22cm. [LC.BM]

RIEDESEL, F: Ad. v. See Eelking, Max v., Memoirs...., #1421.

RIEDESEL, J: Hm. v.
§7491. (Reise durch Sicilien und Grossgriechenland.) Travels through Sicily and that part of Italy formerly called Magna Graecia. Tr. J. R. Forster. L: Dilly 1773. vii;383p. 21cm.
[Correct but rather free.]

RIEHL, Alois, 1844-1924.
**7492. (Der philosophische Kritizismus.) The principles of the crit. philos.: introd. to the theory of science and metaphysics. Tr. Art. Fairbanks. L: Paul, T. & T. 1894. xvi;346p. 21cm. [BM.LC]
[Excellent; much of the tr. was read by author--see Pref.]

RIEHL, W: H: 1823-97. Sel. in C154(8);422.
§7493. (Burg Neideck.) Castle N--. Tr. A. M. Reiner. 1907. In C447. Also 1915 in C179.

RIEMANN, (C: W: Jl.) Hg. 1849-1919.
7494. Catechism of musical aesthetics. Tr. by Rev. H. Bewerunge. L: Augener 1895. iv;67p. 19cm. [BM.LC]

RIESBECK, J: Kp. 1754-86.
7495. (Briefe eines reisenden Franzosen über Deutschland an seinen Bruder zu Paris.) Travels through Germany, in a series of letters. Tr. by Rev. P. H. Maty. L: Cadell 1787. 3v. 21cm. [LC]
7496. do. 1809. [same] In J: Pinkerton, "A...coll...of...travels." L: 1808-14. 27 x 21cm. Vol. 6(1809), pp. 1-292. [LC]

RIETSCHEL, Ern. 1804-61.
7497. (Selbstbiographie.) Autobiog. of early years. Tr. Mrs. G. Sturge. 1875. In A. Oppermann, "E. R-- the sculptor," pp. 1-88. L: Hodder & Stoughton. [BM]

RIETZ, W:e (Encken), 1752-1820. See Lichtenau, W:e., #5817.

RILKE, Rainer Ma. 1875-1926. Sel. in C28*;95*;154(18);423*.
7498. (Auguste Rodin.) A: R--. Tr. Jessie Lemont and Hans Trausil. NY: Sunwise turn 1919. 80p. 22cm. [LC]
*7499. (Das Marien-Leben.) The life of the Virgin Mary. Tr. R. G. L. Barrett. Würzburg. n.d. (1922) 27p. D. [UW]
[Enormously difficult, quite well done.]
§7500. Gedichte. Poems. Tr. Jessie Lemont. NY: Wright 1918. xxxvi; 65p. 21cm. [Tr. only fair. She has no feeling for rhythm and ruins his melody and meter.] [LC]

RINCKART, Mn. 1586-1649. Sel. in C230;232;235;244;269;271;287;423; 570.

RING, Max, 1817-1901.
7501. (Fürst und Musiker.) Prince and musician. Tr. Hettie E. Miller. Chic: Donohue, Henneberry 1892. 319p. il. 20cm. [LC]
*7502. (J: Milton und seine Zeit.) J: M-- and his times: an histor. novel. Tr. F. Jordan. Il. Gaston Fay. NY: Appleton 1868. 308p. 23cm. [LC.BM]
*7503. do. 1889. Tr. J. Jefferson. Manchester: Heywood. 472p. 18cm. [BM]

RINGHOFFER, K: 1854-1906.
7504. (Im Kampfe für Preussens Ehre.) The Bernstorff papers: the life of Count A. v. B--. Tr. Mrs. Barrett-Lennard and Miss M. W. Hoper. Introd. Blennerhassett. L;NY: Longmans 1908. 2v. 23cm. [BM.LC]

RINGWALDT, Bms. 1530-99. Sel. in C230;235;269;486;489;570; #5963.

RIO, Fanny (Giannatasio) del. See Nohl, L:, An unrequited love... #6905.

RIST, J: 1607-67. Sel. in C15;232-3;269;271;273;276;287;461;538;570; #5963.
§7505. An account of the Ger. morality play entitled Depositio Cornuti Typographici. Also, a reprint of the...orig. version... partly in Plaat-Deutsch [sic] by Pl. De Vise...1621. With a

RIST, J:
rhythmical tr. of the Ger. version (by J: R--) of 1648. By W: Blades. L: Trübner 1885. xii;113p. 23cm. [BM]
[Not bad, but not very good either.]

RITSCHL, Abr. 1822-89. See Staehlin, L., Crit. exam. of Kant, Lotze, and R--, #9011.

RITTER, (A:) H: 1791-1869.
*7506. (Geschichte der Philosophie.) The hist. of ancient philos. Tr. A. J. W. Morrison. Oxf: Talboys 1838-46. 4v. 22cm. [BM.LC]

RITTER, Jk. 1627-69. Sel. in C231.

RITTERMANN, K: V: Sel. in C554.

RITTERSHAUS, El. 1834-97. Sel. in C67;112;195;309;311;450.
§7507. (Fest-Gedicht für die Humboldt-Feier in Amerika.) For the H-- festival in America. Tr. Mrs. Kate Freiligrath-Kroeker. NY: Schmidt 1869. 7p. 23cm. [LC]
[Tr. fair to good, but orig. is miserable.]

ROBERTHIN, Rb. 1600-48. Sel. in C570.

ROCHAU, A: L: v. 1810-73.
*7508. (Italienisches Wanderbuch.) Wanderings through...Italy in 1850 and 1851. Tr. Jane Sinnett. L: Bentley 1853. 2v. xii;321; 335p. 19cm. [BM.LC]

ROCHLITZ, F: 1769-1842. Sel. in C106;137a;215.

RODA RODA, Ax. F: Ladislaus, 1872- and "Gst. Meyrink."
7509. The slave girl from Rhodus. Comic opera in 3 acts by E. d'Albert. Text after the Eunuchus of Pub. Terentius Afer. Tr. Jas. L. A. Burrell. Libr. Engl. n.i. 1923. 132p. Tw. [LCM]

RODENBERG (i.e., Levy), Jl. 1831-1914. Sel. in C116;167;309;448;501.
§7510. (Der Turm zu Babel.) The tower of B--: sacred opera in one act by A. Rubinstein. Tr. Mrs. M. L. Michels. Vocal score. Cincin. festival assoc. Cleveland, O: Brainard 1879. 131p. 4. [LCM]
[Fairly close, prosy; little rhyme.]
7511. do. 1880. Tr. Josiah Pittman. Libr. Engl. L: Chappell. 19p. 21cm. [BM]
*7512. do. 1883. Tr. F. W. Rosier. Vocal score. NY: Schirmer. 159p. 4. [On the whole, very good.] [LCM]
*7513. (Die Grandidiers.) The G--: a tale of Berlin life. Tr. W: Saville. L: Low 1881. 3v. 18cm. [BM]
*7514. (Die Insel der Heiligen.) The island of the saints: a pilgrimage through Ireland. Tr. Sir F: C: L. Wraxall. L: Chapman & Hall 1861. 323p. 19cm. [LC]
*7515. do. 1861. [same] L: Bentley. [BM]
§7516. (Gedichte.) Poems. Tr. W: Vocke. Chic: Western news 1860. 129 leaves. (Ger;Engl.) 16. [For a native German, very creditable tr.] [UW]
§7517. do. 1869. [same] 19cm. [BM]
*7518. (Studienreisen in England.) England, literary, and social, from a Ger. point of view. Tr. anon. L: Bentley 1875. ix;442p. 23cm. [BM.LC]
§7519. (Von Gottes Gnaden.) King "by the grace of God": an histor. romance. Tr. anon. L: Bentley 1871. 3v. 18cm. [BM]
[Retold rather than tr.]

RODIGAST, S: 1649-1708. Sel. in C244;271;287;489.

ROECKEL, A: See Wagner, R:, Letters..., #9896.

ROESCHER, L.
§7520. (Sichelhängen.) Harvest home: opera in 3 acts by Andrew Nembach. Tr. anon. Libr. Ger;Engl. w. music. Cincin: Hawley 1884.

ROESCHER, L.- Sichelhängen
32p. 8. [Good tr. except for lack of rhyme.] [LCM]

ROESE, O: 1853- . and Jl. Prüwer.
§7521. R: Strauss: Elektra: a guide to the music. Tr. A. Kalisch. Berlin: Fürstner; NY: Schirmer 1910. 43p. il. 18cm. [LCM]
[Good but faulty.]

ROESEMEIER, Hm.
*7522. (Deutsches Volk, wach' auf!) A German to Germans: an open letter. Tr. Julian Grande. L: Hodder & S. 1917. 42p. 18cm. [BM.LC]

ROESSLER, C: 1864- .
§7523. (Die fünf Frankfurter.) The five Frankfurters: a comedy in 3 acts. Tr. Jas. Fuchs. NY: Fly 1913. 127p. il. 20cm. [LC]
[Tr. flats.]

ROFFHACK, Ab. 1837-1906. Sel. in C28.

ROGGE, Bh. 1831- .
§7524. (Die evangelischen Geistlichen im Feldzug von 1866.) The chaplain in the field of war: being the experiences of the clerical staff during the Prussian campaign of 1866. Condensed (and tr.) from the official report...G. Gladstone. L: Bell & Daldy 1870. vi;216p. 19cm. [BM]
[Pref. says the tr. is substantially the same, but it is really much altered; otherwise good.]

ROH, Jan ("Johann Horn"), d. 1547. Sel. in C244;269;570.

ROHDE, Erw. 1845-98.
7525. (Psyche; Seelenkult.) Psyche: cult of souls...among the Greeks. Tr. from 8th ed. by W. B. Hillis. L: Paul; NY: Harcourt 1925. xvi; 626p. 22cm. [BM.LC]

ROHE, Charles Henry, 1846- .
7526. Thamar and the destruction of Jerusalem. Tr. Ma. E. Ireland. Columbus, O: Luth. bk. concern 1919. 127p. il. 19cm. [LC]

ROHLFS, Grd. 1831-96.
*7527. (Reise durch Marokko.) Advent. in Morocco and journeys through the oases of Praa and Tofilet. Tr. anon. Introd. Winwood Reade. L: Low 1874. viii;371p. 22cm. [BM.LC]

ROHRBACH, Pl. 1869- .
7528. (Der deutsche Gedanke in der Welt.) Ger. world policies. Tr. E. v. Mach. NY: Macmillan 1915. 243p. 19cm. [LC]
7529. (Der Krieg und die deutsche Politik.) Germany's isolation: an exposition of the economic causes of the war. Tr. P. H. Phillipson. Chic: McClurg 1915. 186p. 19cm. [LC]

ROLLE, R., d. 1349. Sel. in C222.

ROLLETT, Hm. 1819-1904. Sel. in C309; 501.
§7530.(Gedichte.)Poems. Tr. H. Phillips, Jr. Phil: Priv. prt. 1887. 30p. 16cm. [BM]
[200 cop. for priv. distrib. Tr. is not bad, but not very good.]

RONGE, J:s, 1813-87.
*7531. (Rechtfertigung.) Vindication of J. R--, the Luther of the 19th cent. Tr. R. Taylor. L: Painter 1845. 58p. 21cm. [BM]
7532. do. 1845. Justification. Tr. anon. In J: Ronge, "The holy coat of Treves and the new German-Catholic church." Ed;L: Nelson. 120p. front. 19cm. [BM]
7533. do. 1846. Autobiog. and justification of J. R--. Tr. from 5th ed. by J. Lord. L: Chapman bros. 70p. 17cm. [BM]

RONGE, J:s
7534. The reformation of the 19th cent. Part first: Histor. devel. from 1844 to 1852. Tr. anon. L: Deutsch 1852. x;93p. 19cm. [BM]
7535. do. 1852. Part second. Tr. anon. Manchester: Oswald & Covacs. vii;93p. 18cm. [BM]

ROQUETTE, O: 1824-96. Sel. in C112;152;195;448;497;501;571.
7536. Conrad Hagen's mistake. Tr. Mrs. Crozer. Phil: Lippincott 1881. 216p. 19cm. [LC]
7537. The curate of Orsières. Ad. by Ma. A. Robinson. NY: Harper 1878. 81p. 12cm. [LC]

ROSEGGER, P: (Petri Kettenfeier), 1843-1918. Sel. in C422;574*.
*7538. (Das ewige Licht.) The light eternal. Tr. anon. L: Unwin 1907. 352p. 19cm. [BM]
*7539. (Der Gottsucher.) The God-seeker. Tr. Fes. E. Skinner. NY;L: Putnam 1901. 475p. 20cm. [LC.BM]
§7540. (Die Schriften des Waldschulmeisters.) The forest schoolmaster. Tr. Fes. E. Skinner. NY;L: Putnam 1901. 333p. 19cm. [LC.BM] [Unwarranted liberties.]
7541. do. 1913-51. [same (abr.)] In C154(16).
§7542. (Erdsegen.) The earth and the fulness thereof: a romance of modern Styria. Tr. Fes. E. Skinner. NY;L: Putnam 1902. 397p. 20cm. [Tr. flats.] [LC]
*7543. (I.N.R.I. Frohe Botschaft eines armen Sünders.) I.N.R.I.: a prisoner's story of the cross. Tr. Eliz. Lee. Il. C. K. Linson. NY: McClure, Phillips; L: Hodder & S. 1905. 340p. 20cm. [LC]
*7544. do. 1905. [same] L: Hodder & S. 324p. 18cm. [BM]
*7545. do. 1907. [same] Hodder. 8. [EC]
*7546. do. 1911. [same] Pop. ed. 328p. [EC]
*7547. (Mein Himmelreich.) My kingdom of heaven. Tr. anon. L: Hodder & S. 1907. vii;330p. 19cm. [BM]
*7548. (Peter Mayr, der Wirt an der Mahr.) A fight for freedom; or, P: M--, landlord of the Mahr. Tr. Ma. Dougherty. Dublin: Gill 1913. vi;392p. 19cm. [Some bad errors.] [BM.NY]
*7549. (Waldheimat.) The forest farm: tales of the Austrian Tyrol. Tr. Maude E. King and A. T. de Mattos. L: Fifield 1912. 226p. front. and port. 20cm. [BM.NY]
*7550. do. 1913-15. Forest home (abr.). Tr. L. Fossler. In C154(16).
7551. When the bright nights were. In "Famous stories from for. countries." Tr. Edna W. Underwood. Bost: Four seas 1921. 150p. 19cm. [LC]

ROSEMANN, ---. Sel. in C44.

"ROSEN, Erw." (i.e., Erw. Carlé, 1876-1923.)
*7552. (In der Fremdenlegion.) In the for. legion. Tr. anon. L: Duckworth 1910. xiv;285p. 22cm. [BM.LC]
*7553. do. 1912. [same] Cheaper reissue. 8. [EC]
"ROSEN, Jl. v." (i.e., N: Duffek, 1833-92).
7554. (Defizit.) Deficit: a comedy in 4 acts. Tr. anon. n.i. 1884. 60p. 20cm. [BM]
7555. Grisette: a tale of Paris and NY. L: Drane 1889. Lovell lib. 8. [EC]
7556. (Halbe Dichter.) Half-poets: comedy-farce in 3 acts based upon an idea of B. Busch. Tr. anon. Berlin? 1884. 19; 16; 16p. 32cm. Tw. [BM]
7557. do. 1884. Nancy and co: a comedy in 4 acts. Tr. A. Daly. NY [LC]
7558. do. 1886. [same] ...an eccentric piece in 4 acts. Tr. A. Daly. NY: Prtd. as MS for the author. 63p. 8. [LCO]
7559. A model husband: a comedy in 4 acts. Ad. by A. Stein. Phil: 1880. (B38)

"ROSEN, Jl. v."
7560. (O diese Männer!) Oh, these naughty men: comedy in 4 acts. Tr. and ad. by A. Neuendorff. 1877. (B38)
7561. do. 1878. [same] L: (lithographed.) 21; 19; 17; 19p. 25cm. [BM]
7562. (Starke Mittel.) Needles and pins: a comedy in 4 acts. Tr. A. Daly. NY: 1880. [LC]
7563. Quits; or, a game of tit-for-tat. A comedy in 4 acts. Tr. A. Daly. NY: 1881. (B38)
7564. A triple courtship: a comedy ad. and augm. W: D. Eaton. Chic: 1878. 49; 43; 33 leaves. sm. 4. Tw. [LCO]

ROSENBERG, A. Sel. in C102.

ROSENCREUTZ, Cn. See Andreä, J:, The hermetick romance, #60.

ROSENGARTEN, ---, Sel. in C486.

ROSENGARTEN, Paul.
7564a. Handbook of architect. styles. Tr. by W. Collet-Sanders. Chatto 1926. New ed. 531p. 639 ils. 9 x 6. [EC]

ROSENKRANZ, J: K: F: 1805-79.
*7565. (Die Pädagogik als System.) Pedagogics as a system. Tr. Anna C. Brackett. St.L: Studley 1872. 148p. 23cm. [BM]
[Said to be reprtd. from the "Journal of spec. philos." (C300), but cf. #7567 below.]
*7566. do. 1872. [same] Philos. of education; or, pedagogics as a system. Tr. A. C. Brackett. St.L: Gray, Baker. 8. [AC]
7567. do. 1876. In C300(6, etc.).
*7568. do. 1886. [same] 2d rev. ed. NY: Appleton. xxviii;286p. 18cm. [LC]
*7569. do. 1902. [same] 2d rev. ed. NY: Appleton. xxviii;292p. 18cm. [BM]
*7570. do. 1903. [same] 292p. [LC]
7571. do. [Ad.] Science of education. St.L: Jones 1878. 48p. 24cm. [LC]
[Paraphrase of #7565 by Anna C. Brackett.]
7572. (Goethe und seine Werke.) Second part of..."Faust." Tr. D. J. Snider. 1871. In C300(1).
[I assume that this and the following were taken from the work cited.]
7573. do. 1872. Goethe's social romances. Tr. T: Davidson. In C300 (2).
7574. do. 1874. Goethe's "W: Meister." Tr. T: Davidson. In C300(4).
7575. do. 1874. Composition of Goethe's social romance. Tr. D. J. Snider. In C300(4).
7576. do. 1875. Goethe's story of the snake (i.e., "Das Märchen"). Tr. Anna C. Brackett. In C300(5).
7577. do. 1879. On Goethe's "Faust." Tr. Anna C. Brackett. In C300(9).
7578. do. 1881. Second part of "Faust." Tr. Anna C. Brackett. In C300(11).
7579. (Hegel als deutscher Nationalphilosoph.) Hegel as the national philosopher of Germany. Tr. G. S. Hall. St.L: Gray, Baker 1874. 8. [AC]
7580. do? 1872. Difference of Baader from Hegel. Tr. T: Davidson. In C300(2).
[This and the following probably derive from the work on Hegel.]
7581. do? 1875. Introd. to Hegel's encyclopaedia. Tr. W: R. Walker. In C300(5).
7582. do? 1876. On Hegel's phenomenology; On Hegel's logic; On Hegel's philos. of right; On Hegel's philos. of hist. Tr. G. S. Hall. In C300(6).
7583. do? 1877. Hegel's aesthetics; Hegel's philos. of relig. Tr. G. S. Hall. In C300(7).

ROSENKRANZ, J: K: F:--Hegel als deutscher Nationalphilosoph
7584. do? 1881. Hegel and his contemporaries. Tr. G. S. Hall. In C300(11).

ROSENKREUZ, Cn. See Andreä, J:, The hermetick romance, #60.

ROSENROTH, C. Knorr v. See Knorr v. R--.

ROSKOWSKA, Ma. v. 1828-89.
7585. (In Mitten der Nordsee.) Die Halligen; or, in the midst of the North Sea. Tr. J. F: Smith. Phil: Luth. bd. 1870. 159p. il. 16. [LCO]

"ROSMER, Ern." (i.e., Else Porges Bernstein, 1866- .)
§7586. (Dämmerung.) Twilight. Tr. P. H. Grummann. In "Poet Lore," vol. 23 (1912). [Fails in the dialect.]
7587. (Johannes Herkner.) J: H--. Tr. Ma. Harned. In "Poet Lore," vol. 22 (1911).
§7588. (Königskinder.) Kingly children: opera by Humperdinck. Tr. C: H: Meltzer. Libr. Engl;Ger. NY: Rullman 1910. 69p. 4. [LC]
§7589. do. 1911. [same] Engl. singing words by C. H. M--. Berlin: Fischer; Lpz: Brockhaus. 95p. 20cm. [BM]
[Either he misunderstands or ignores.]
7590. do.[Ad.] 1911. The royal children: a fairy tale founded on the opera. Told for children by Anna Alice Chapin. NY;L: Harpers. xii; 276p. il. 19cm. [LC]
7591. do. do. 1925. The king's children. Retold by J. McSpadden. In C390.

ROSNER, K: 1873- .
7592. (Der König.) The king. Tr. Ag. Blake. Introd. by Viscount Haldane. L: Methuen 1922. viii;245p. 19cm. [BM]

ROSTHIO (?) Sel. in C106.

ROSWITHA, See Hrotsuitha.

ROTH, Abh.
7593. The Doldenhorn and Weisse Frau. Ascended for the first time by A. R. and Edm. v. Fellenberg. Tr. anon. Coblenz;Lpz: Baedeker 1863. 82p. il. map. 25cm. [BM.LC]

ROTH, J. 1818-92. See Schubert, G. H., joint author.

ROTH, R: 1835-1915.
7594. (Der Burggraf und sein Schildknappe.) Prince F: and the dawn of the Reformation. Tr. from 5th ed. by Ma. E. Ireland. Burlington, Ia: Ger. lit. bd. 1913. 167p. 17cm. [LC]
7595. (Kaiser, König und Papst.) Kaiser, king, and pope. Tr. Ma. E. Ireland. Minneapolis: Augsburg pub. 1917. 198p. 20cm. [LC]
7596. King Otto's crown. Tr. Ma. E. Ireland. St.L: Concordia pub. 1917. 139p. 19cm. [LC]
7597. Stanley's journey through the dark continent. Tr. G: P. Upton. Chic: McClurg 1912. 139p. il. 17cm. [LC]

ROTHE, J: And. 1688-1758. Sel. in C222-3;244;271;273;486.

ROTHE, R: 1799-1867.
7598. (Stille Stunden. Aphorismen.) Still hours. Tr. Jane T. Stoddart. Introd. essay by Rev. J: Macpherson. L: Hodder & S. 1886. 425p. 20cm. [BM]

ROTHENBURG, Frau Ade. Kta. Mde. (v. Zastrow) v. 1837-91.
7599. (Die Nähterin von Stettin.) The seamstress of S--. Ad. by "Cornelia McFadden." Cincin: Cranston & Stowe; NY: Hunt & Eaton 1889. 327p. 19cm. [LC]

"ROTHENFELS, Emmy v." (i.e., Frau Eme.--v. Loga--v. Ingersleben, 1822-71.)
7600. Eleonore. Tr. Fes. E. Bunnett. Phil: Lippincott 1872. 303p. 19cm. [LC]
7601. (Haideblume.) Little heather blossom. Tr. Ma. J. Safford. Il. W. B. Davis. NY: Bonner 1891. 470p. 19cm. [LC]

ROTHER, ---. Sel. in C269.

ROTTECK, K: Wzs. Rodecker v. 1775-1840.
*7602. (Allgemeine Weltgeschichte.) Gen. hist. of the world...to 1831. Tr. and cont. to 1840 by F: Jones. 1st Amer. ed. Phil: Stollmeyer 1840-41. 4v. il. 23cm. [LC.BM]
*7603. do. 1842. [same] L: Longmans. 4v. 8. [BM]
*7604. do. 1851. [same] Phil: Leary. 4v. in 2. 23cm. [LC]
*7605. do. 1872-6. [same...continued]...C: J. Peterson. Phil: Leary & Getz. 4v. in 2. [AC]
*7606. do. n.d. [same.] 4v. in one. [AC]
*7607. do. 1885. [same] New rev. ed. NY: Worthington. 4v. [AC]

ROTTENBURGER, G. Sel. in C425.

RUBIN, 13th cent. Sel. in C27;427.

RUDOLF Fis. C: Js. Erzherzog und Kronprinz v. Oesterreich, 1858-89.
*7608. (Eine Orientreise im Jahre 1881.) Travels in the east, includ. a visit to Egypt and the Holy Land. Tr. anon. Il. Pausinger, etc. L: Bentley 1884. 380p. 26cm. [BM]
*7609. (Jagden und Beobachtungen.) Notes on sport and ornithology. Tr. C. G. Danford. L: Gurney & Jackson 1889. viii;648p. front. (port.) 22cm. [BM.LC]

RUDOLF VON FENIS, fl. 1158-92. Sel. in C416;427.

RUDOLF VON ROTENBURG, 13th cent. Sel. in C27;532.

RUDOLPHI, K:e, 1750-1811. Sel. in C443.
7610. The king of the swans; The children's spring. Tr. S. T. 1843. In C520, cf. C521.
7611. The tales of the stork, fox, and magpie; The labyrinth. Tr. S. T. 1845. In C519.

RUECKERT, F: 1789-1866. Sel. in C3;5*;15;17;31;40-2;43*;44;50;63;67;69;73;75;106;111-2;129;137a;141*;149;151-2;166-7;169;171-3;178;184;192*;195;208;273;295-6;301;309;311;313;317;366*;372-5;378;380;391;393-7;399;400;407;414-5;423;446;448;460;464;467;469;470;486;489;497;500-1;504-5;529;531;538-9;543;551;570-1;#4082;#6209a.
§7612. (Des fremden Kindes heiliger Christ.) The alien child's holy Christ. Tr. E. Hodges. Newcastle: Richardson 1846. 17p. 19cm. [BM] [Incorrect. Ger;Engl.]
*7613. (Die Weisheit des Brahmanen.) The wisdom of the Brahmin: a didactic poem. Tr. C: T. Brooks. Bost: Roberts 1882. xii;252p. 18cm. [Books I-VI.] [LCO.BM]
*7614. do. 1898. The vision of God as represented in R--'s fragments. Tr. in Engl. rhyme by W: Hastie. Glasgow: Maclehose. 33p. 22cm. [Extracts under subject headings.] [BM]
§7615. do. 1910. The Brahman's wisdom. Tr. Eva M. Martin. L: Rider. 44p. 8. [Good verse, but sense sometimes astray.] [BM]

RUEDIGER, Mrs. Minna, 1841- .
7616. [Coll.] It is better to give than to receive: a Christmas story; and other stories. Tr. anon. NY: Kaufmann 1912. 96p. il. S. [AC]
7617. (Um des Glaubens willen.) For the sake of the faith: four stories of the times of the Reformation. Tr. anon. Burlington, Ia: Ger. lit. bd. 1905. 128p. 18cm. [LC]

RUEDIGER, Mrs. Minna
*7618. (Waldtraut.) W--: a story of the forest. Tr. Sophy G. Colvin. Ed;L: Oliphant 1896. 223p. front. 19cm. [BM]
7619. do. 1898. W--, according to the chronicle of the pastor of Hinrichshagen. Tr. Corinth Crook. Il. Dorothy Cole. Chic: Elliott. 284p. 17cm. [LC]

RUEMMER, Fz.
7620. Great secret of the saints. Tr. Isabel Garahan. St.L: Herder 1926. xi;119p. 19cm. [LC.BM]
7621. True life: a little book on grace. Tr. Isabel Garahan. St.L: Herder 1926. v;106p. 19cm. [LC.BM]

RUESTOW, F: W: 1821-78.
*7622. (Der Krieg um die Rheingrenze 1870 politisch und militärisch dargestellt.) The war for the Rhine frontier, 1870: its polit. and mil. hist. Tr. J: L. Needham. Ed;L: Blackwood 1871-72. 3v. 21cm. [BM.LC]

RUETE, Frau Eme. 1844- .
*7623. (Memoiren.) Memoirs of an Arabian princess. Tr. Lionel Strachey. NY: Appleton 1888. viii;307p. front. (port.) 8. [BM]
*7624. do. 1907. [same] NY: Doubleday, Page. xvi;227p. il. 23cm [LC.BM]

RUHKOPF, Jle.
7625. Stories. Tr. "Trauermantel." 1858. In C546.

RUMI, ---. Sel. in C223.

RUMOHR, K: F: Fx. v. 1785-1843. Sel. in C12.

RUMPF, A.
7626. Thusis. Tr. anon. 1884. 40p. il. In C294.

RUNDT, C: Gf. 1713-64.
7627. Sel. from diary. Tr. 1916. In C19.

RUNGE, Ph. O: 1777-1810. Sel. in C391;393.

RUPERTI, F: Sel. in C395;450.

RUPPIN, Art.
7627a. The agricultural colonisation of the Zionist organ. In Palestine. Tr. by R. J. Friwel. Hopkinson 1926. 217p. 8. [EC]
*7628. (Die Juden der Gegenwart.) The Jews of today. Tr. Margery Bentwich. Introd. by Js. Jacobs. L: Bell; NY: Holt 1913. xxii; 310p. 8. [BM]

RUPPIUS, O: 1819-64.
7629. (Das Vermächtnis des Pedlars.) The peddler: a romance of Amer. life. Tr. Emily R. Steinestel. Cincin: Bloch 1877. 83p. il. (B12) [NY]
7630. (Der Prairie-Teufel.) José. Ed. by Lillie E. Myers. NY: Street & Smith 1890. 301p. 20cm. [LC]
7631. (Zwei Welten.) Two hemispheres: a romance. Tr. C. L. W. Phil: Claxton, R. & H. 1870. 245p. 18cm. [LC]

RUSS, K:
7631a. The Budgerigar. Tr. by M. Burgers. 7th ed. rev. by K. Neunzig. "Cage Birds" 1927. 142p. il. 8 x 6. [EC]

RUST, W: See Gottsched, J. C., joint author.

RUTILIUS, Mn. 1550-1618. Sel. in C287.

SAALFELD, Am. F: W:
7632. A philos. discourse on the nature of dreams. Tr. anon. L: Becket & de Hondt 1764. 136p. 15cm. [BM]

SAAR, Fd. v. 1833-1906. Sel. in C154(18);423.
§7633. (Die Steinklopfer.) The stonebreakers. Tr. A. M. Reiner. 1907. In C447.

SACER, Gf. W: 1635-99. Sel. in C231-2;273;276.

SACHER-MASOCH, Lp. v. 1836-95.
7634. The bookbinder of Hort. Tr. anon. 1898. In C509.
*7635. (Der neue Hiob.) The new Job. Tr. Harriet L. Cohen. NY: Cassell 1891. vii;270p. 19cm. [LC.BM]
*7636. (Eine Schlittenfahrt.) The sledge-ride. Tr. Zimmern. 1880. In C575-7.
7637. (Judengeschichten.) Jewish tales. Tr. from the French by Harriet L. Cohen. Chic: McClurg 1894. 317p. 18cm. [LC]
*7638. (Russische Hofgeschichten.) Venus and Adonis, and other tales of the court of Cath. II. Tr. anon. L: Mathieson 1896? 187p. 17cm. [BM]
[Title; The art of making oneself loved ("Die Kunst geliebt zu werden"); Disgrace at any price ("Ungnade um jeden Preis"); Eating cherries; A woman on outpost duty ("Eine Frau auf Vorposten"); Cupid with the corporal's cane ("Amor mit dem Korporalstock").
7639. Seraph: a tale of Hungary.. Tr. Emma M. Phelps. NY: Allen 1893. 159p. 19cm. [BM]
7640. Thou shalt not kill. Tr. Harriet L. Cohen. 1907. In C447. Also in C179.

SACHS, Hs. 1494-1576. Sel. in C88;190;208;234;244;287;366*;422;469; 530-1;570.
§7641. [Coll.] 1910. Merry tales and three Shrovetide plays. Now first done into Engl. verse by W: Leighton. L: Nutt. xv;270p. 20cm. [BM.LC]
[The plays are: The horse thief ("Der Rosdieb zu Fünsing"); The hot iron ("Das heiss Eisen"); The traveling scholar ("Der farendt Schüler im Paradeis").
*7642. [Coll.] 1926. The farmer in Purgatory ("Der Bauer im Fegfeuer") and The student in Purgatory. Tr. H: G. Atkins. L: Macdonald 1926. 32p. 18cm. [BM]
7642a. [Coll.] Three Shrovetide comedies. Tr. into Engl. verse by B. Q. Morgan. 35p. 26cm. Tw. 1912. [SU]
[The scholar bound for Paradise ("Der farendt Schüler im Paradeis"), same as #7642b; The merchant's basket ("Der Krämerskorb"); The hot iron ("Das heiss Eisen").]
7642b. ("Der farendt Schüler im Paradeis.") The scholar bound for Paradise. A Shrove-tide comedy. Tr. B. Q. Morgan. In "The Playbook," I(1913):16-27. [UW]
§7643. do. 1922. The wandering scholar from Paradise. Ed. by S: A. Eliot. Bost: Little, Brown 1922. (Little theater classics. vol. 4.) vii;281p. il. 19cm. [Pretty good.] [LC]
†7644. (Der farend Schüler mit dem Teufelbannen.) Raising the devil. Tr. W. H. H. Chambers. 1903. In C18.
[Very bald prose, not wholly accurate.]
7645. Goodly dysputacion between a Christen showmaker and a Papysshe Person...done within the famous citie of Norembourgh...Tr. Anthony Scoloker. L: 1648.
[Cited by B16, who says the tr. is crude and faulty.]
7646. (St. Peter und die Geis.) St. Peter and the goat. Tr. anon. 1906. In C190.
See Wildenhahn, A., Hs. Sachs: a family tradition, #10201.

SACHSE, Cn. F: H: 1785-1860. Sel. in C229.

SACHSENDORF, der (U:?) v., 13th cent. Sel. in C27.

SACHSEN-WEIMAR, Herzog v. See Karl F:

SALIS, J: Gaudenz v. 1762-1834. Sel. in C10;17;22;25-6;42;44;50;54-5;
86;88;111-2;133;142;166;177;219;306;309;366;371;373;380;383;385;
387-8;391;393-4;410;412;461;469;471;499;501; #2720.

SALIS-MARSCHLINS, K: Uls. v. 1762-1818.
*7647. (Reisen in verschiedenen Provinzen des Königreichs Neapel.)
Travels through various provinces of Naples, in 1789. Tr. A.
Aufrere. L: Cadell & D. 1795. viii;527p. il. 21cm. [BM.LC]
[Il. w. engr., map, and col. plates.]

SALLET, F: v. 1812-43. Sel. in C17;123;149;152;216;309;417;469;501;
571.
*7648. (Der starke Hakon.) H-- the strong: cantata von Gustave
Lazarus. Tr. Isidora Martinez. Vocal score. Ger;Engl. Bost: Ditson
1914. 31p. 27cm. [AC has: 1913.] [BMM]

SALM-SALM, Ag. (Leclerq) Prinzessin zu, 1840-1912.
*7649. (Zehn Jahre aus meinem Leben.) Ten years of my life. Tr.
anon. L: Bentley 1875. 2v. xvi;328;x;280p. front. (port.) 20cm[BM]
*7650. do. 1876. [same] Bentley. 2v. [LC]
7651. do. 1877. [same?] Detroit. Belford. 385p. 18cm. [LC]
7652. Leaves from the diary. In #7653.

SALM-SALM, Fx. Cst. Ax. J: Nk. Prinz zu, 1828-70.
7653. (Queretaro. Blätter aus meinem Tagebuch in Mexico.) My diary
in Mexico in 1867, includ. the last days of the emperor Mx. With
leaves from the diary of the Princess S.-S. Tr. anon. L: Bentley
1868. 2v. xiv;320; 328p. fronts. (ports.) il. 20cm. [BM.LC]
[Rewritten]

SALTEN (i.e., Salzmann), Fx. 1869- .
7654. The love of life. Ad. by Js. H. Neebe. Chic: 1910. Tw. [LC]

SALUS, Hg. 1866- .
7655. Children: a Märchen. Tr. Aletheia C. Caton. L: Priv. prt.
1910. 24p. 15cm. [BM]
7656. do. 1912. [same] rev. ed. L: A.C.Caton. 26p. [BM]

SALZMANN, Çn. Glf. 1744-1811.
§7657. (Moralisches Elementarbuch.) Elements of morality, for the
use of children. Tr. Ma. Wollstonecraft (while learning the
language). L: Johnson 1790. 2v. in one. xxxiii;196; 175p. 17cm.
[Tr. is rather free. 45 chaps.] [BM]
§7658. do. 1792. [same] 3d. ed. il. with 50 copper pl. L: J.Johnson.
3v. xxxii;168; 190; 200p. 17cm. [BM]
[Front. is dated 1790; all plates but one in vols. 2 and 3 are
dated 1791. 46 chaps.]
§7659. do. 1793. [same] L: Johnson. [BM]
[Identical with #7657, except for new t.p.]
§7660. do. 1795. [same] With an introd. address to parents. 1st
Amer. ed. Providence, (R. I.): Prtd. by Carter and Wilkinson.
306p. plate. 12. (B6a; B48) [Available: AAS. BPL. JCB. RIHS.]
§7661. do. 1796. [same] 3d Amer. ed. Wilmington, Del: Prtd. by J.
Johnson. 232p. 17cm. [LC]
§7662. do. 1796. [same] Phil: Hoff & Kammerer (B48: Kaemmerer). Il.
w. 20 copper pl. by Weston. 2v. 240;259p. 12. (B6a) [AAC]
§7663. do. 1803? [same] NY. 12. (B48)
7664. do. 181-. [same?] Il. W: Blake. L: Prtd. for J. Sharpe. 2v.
18cm. [LC]
§7665. do. 1811. [same] 1st Balto. ed. rev. and corr. Balto:
Robinson. xvi;267p. 17cm. [BM]

SALZMANN, Cn. Glf.--Moral. Elementarbuch
*7666. do. 1821. [same] A new and improved ed. il. w. engr. Ed: Prtd. for Oliver & Boyd. L: Whittaker and Hailes. xxiv;268p. [BM]
[Tr. is improved also.]
7667. do. 1852-5. [same?] Stories for children, or, elements of morality. NY: Francis n.d. 18. [AC]
7668. do? 1858-60. Charles and Mary; or, stories to help in the training of children. NY: Miller n.d. 12. [AC]
[I suspect this to be from the "Moral. Elementarbuch."]
7669. What God does is well done. Tr. E. T. Disosway. Cincin: Hitchcock & Walden 1875. 304p. 16. [LCO]

"SAMAROW, Gg." (i.e., Ok. Meding, 1827- .)
*7670. (Um Szepter und Krone.) For sceptre and crown. Tr. anon. L: King 1875. 2v. 312; 424p. 19cm. [BM]

SANDER, Cn. Lävinus F: Sel. in C26; 533.

SAPHIR, Mz. Gb. 1795-1858. Sel. in C422.

SAPHIR, Ph.
7671. Letters and diaries of Ph. S--, ed. by his brother. Pref. note by C. J. Brown. Ed: Johnstone & Hunter 1852. iv;130p. 17cm. [BM]

SARRE, F. Pl. Td. 1865- .
7671a. Old oriental carpets; text by F: S-- and Hm. Trenkwald. Tr. A. F. Kendrick. Vienna: Schroll 1926-9. 2v. pl. F. [AC]
Vol. 1. Quaritch 1926. 25 ils. 35 col. ils. 23 x 18. [EC]

SARTORIUS, C: Cn. W: 1796-1872.
7672. Mexico: landscapes and pop. sketches. Ed. Dr. Gaspey. Engr. from sketches by M. Rugendas. Darmstadt: Lange; NY: Lang & Kronfeld 1858. 202p. il. 28 x 22cm. [Copyright 1855.] [LC.BM]
7673. do. 1859. [same] L: Trübner. [BM.LC]

SASSEN, S. E. W:e. Sel. in C8;9.

SASTROW, Bms. 1520-1603.
*7674. (Deutsches Bürgertum und der Adel im 16. Jahrhundert.) Social Germany in Luther's time: being the memoirs of B. S--. Tr. Ab. D. Vandam. Introd. Herb. A. L. Fisher. Westminster: Archibald; Ed: Constable 1902. xxv;349p. front. 20cm. [BM.LC]
*7675. do. 1903. [same] NY: Dutton. [AC]
*7676. do. 1905. [same] Title: Memoirs of a Ger. burgomaster. Constable. [EC]

SAUERWEIN, W: Sel. in C317.

SAUPE, Ern. Jl. 1809-71.
7677. (Schiller und sein väterliches Haus.) Tr. with slight abridgments, transposals, and additions by T: Carlyle in his "Life of Schiller." NY: Scribner 1901. pp. 239-337. 21cm. [LC.BM]
[See also appendix.]

SAVIGNY, F: K: v. 1779-1861. Sel. in C12.

SCALIGER, Js. 1540-1609.
7677a. Autobiography. Tr. J. W. Robinson. Oxford 1927. 8. [EC]

"SCHACHING, O: v." (i.e., V: Mt. O: Denk, 1853-1921.)
7678. Afra. Tr. anon. 1902. In C481.
7679. (Der verrückte Junker.) The mad knight: a merry tale. Ad. K. Denvir. NY;Cincin: Benziger 1915. 175p. 17cm. [LC]
[Ad. from "Don Quixote."]
7680. (Der Geigenmacher von Mittenwald.) The violin maker. Tr. (i.e., ad.) Sa. T. Smith. NY;Cincin: Benziger 1905. 175p. 17cm. [LC]
[AC has title: The violin maker of Mittenwald.]

"SCHACHING, O: v."
7681. (Der Glockenhof.) The bell foundry. Tr. anon. NY;Cincin: Benziger 1907. 171p. 17cm. [LC]
7682. do. 1915. [same] [AC]

SCHACHT, Hjalmar, 1877- .
*7683. (Die Stabilisierung der Mark.) The stabilization of the mark. Tr. Ralph Butler. L: Allen & Unwin 1927. 247p. front. (port.) 22cm. [BM.LC]

SCHACK, Ad. F: Graf v. 1815-94. Sel. in C450.

SCHADE, J: Kp. 1666-98. Sel. in C233;240;269;287.

SCHAFFNER, Jk. 1875- .
7684. The iron idol. Tr. Mrs. Amelia v. Ende. 1913-15. In C154(19).
7685. (Die Weisheit der Liebe.) The wisdom of love. Tr. Anne Banvell. (B37)

"SCHAFFY, Mirza." See F: Bodenstedt.

SCHAFHAEUTL, K. El. v.
7686. Theobald Böhm. Tr. El. Reich. In "Hist. of the Boehm flute," pp. 151-269. L: Rudall 1892. 21cm. [BM]
7687. do. 1896. [same] [BM]

SCHALL, K: 1780-1833. Sel. in C215.

SCHALLING, Mt. 1532-1608. Sel. in C244;271;273;287.

SCHANENSEE, L. M. v. See Meyer v. Schanensee.

"SCHANZ, Frieda" (i.e., Frieda--Schanz--Soyaux, 1859-)
7688. Prince Fridolin's courtship. Verses by Jl. Lohmeyer and F. S--. Il. Jl. Kleinmichel. Tr. Sydney Clifton. NY: Sackett & Williams 1888. 40p. col. il. 24 x 27cm. [LC]
7689. The strawberry thief. Tr. anon. 1897. In C126.

SCHANZER, Rd. and Ern. Welisch.
7690. (Die Frau im Hermelin.) The lady of the rose: opera by Jean Gilbert. Ad. F: Lonsdale. Vocal score. Engl. L: Ascherberg, Hopwood & Crew 1921. 145p. 30cm. [BMM.LCM]

SCHARRELMANN, W: 1875- . See Wiegand, J., joint author.

SCHAUFUSS, L: W:
†7691. (Correggio's träumende Magdalena.) C--'s dreaming Magdalene. Tr. anon. Dresden: Weiske 1873. 30p. (Ger;Engl.) 28cm. [BM]
[Ludicrously bad; see p. 4 for citation.]

SCHAUMBERGER, H: 1843-74. Sel. in C422.

SCHAUKAL, R: 1874- . Sel. in C28*.

SCHEDE, Mn.
7691a. The acropolis of Athens. Tr. by H. T. Price. Batsford 1927. 8. [EC]

SCHEER, Rh. K: F: H: 1863-1928.
*7692. (Die Hochseeflotte im Weltkrieg.) Germany's high seas fleet in the world war. Tr. anon. L;NY: Cassell 1920. xiv;376p. front. (port.) 24cm. [BM.LC]

SCHEERER, L: Sel. in C450.

SCHEFER, (Gb.) Lp. (Im.) 1784-1862. Sel. in C17;151;171;412;461;469; 489;501.
*7693. (Der Weltpriester.) The world-priest. Poems. Tr. C: T. Brooks. Bost: Roberts 1873. ix;373p. 17cm. [LC.BM]

SCHEFER, Lp.
*7694. (Ein Weihnachtsfest in Rom.) The bishop's wife: a tale of the Papacy. Tr. Mrs. J: R. Stodart. L: Chapman 1851. 200p. 17cm. [BM]
*7695. (Künstlerehe.) The artist's married life: being that of Abr. Dürer. Tr. Mrs. J: R. Stodart. L: Chapman 1848. xx;226p. il. 16cm. [BM]
7696. do. 1849. [same?] Bost: Munroe. 257p. NY. (B12)
*7697. do. 1853. [same] L: Chapman. 98p. 19cm. [BM]
*7698. do. 1861. [same] Rev. ed. Bost;Cambridge: Munroe. 204p. 18cm. [Cf. the following entry.] [LC]
*7699. do. 1862. [same] Rev. ed. with memoir. NY: Jas. Miller. xxvii;204p. 18cm. [BM]
*7699a. do. 1867. [same] NY: Miller. See "Nation" 4:313.
*7700. do. 1872-6. [same] NY: Miller n.d. [AC]
*7701. (Laienbrevier.) The layman's breviary; or, meditations for every day in the year. (Poems.) Tr. C: T. Brooks. Bost: Roberts 1867. iv;452p. front. 17cm. [Tr. in blank verse, excellent.] [LC]
*7702. do. 1896. [same] 3d ed. [LC]
*7703. do. 1904. [same. sel.] Thoughts from "The layman's breviary." Tr. C: T. Brooks. L: Priory Press. 35p. 19cm. [BM]

SCHEFFEL, Js. V: v. 1826-86. Sel. in C3;190;196;309;311;366*;372; 422-3;448;469.
§7704. (Bergpsalmen.) Mountain psalms. Tr. Mrs. Fis. Brünnow. L: Trübner 1882. 62p. il. 16cm. [BM]
§7705. (Der Trompeter von Säkkingen.) The trumpeter of S--. Tr. Mrs. Fis. Brünnow. L: Chapman & Hall; NY: Scribner 1877. 302p. 12. [Poor verse.] [BM.NY]
*7706. do. 1893. The trumpeter: a romance of the Rhine. Tr. from 20th ed. by Jessie Beck and Louise Lorimer. Introd. Sir Td. Martin. Ed: Blackwood. xiv;215p. 19cm. [BM.LC]
*7707. do.[Ad.] 1887. Opera by V. Nessler. Text ad. from S-- by Rd. Bunge. Sel. from S--'s poem tr. in pref. by J: P. Jackson. Libr. NY: Metrop. opera house. xiv;25p. 8. [LC]
[Cf. also #923 for another translation of the libretto.]
§7708. (Die Schweden in Rippoldsau.) The Swedes at R--, A. D. 1643. Tr. anon. L: Ballantyne 1879. (Priv. prt.) pp. 1-21. 22cm. [BM]
[With Eckstein, Eternal laws of morality, pp. 22-39. Ger;Engl.]
§7709. (Ekkehard.) E--: a tale of the 10th cent. Tr. Sofie Delffs. Lpz: Tauchnitz 1872. 2v. 16cm. [Cf. #7714.] [LC.BM]
§7710. do. 1881. [same] NY: Munro. Seaside lib. 71p. 32cm. [LC]
§7711. do. 1890. [same] NY: Gottsberger. 2v. 16cm. [LC]
§7712. do. 1895. [same] NY;Bost: Crowell. 2v. il. 17cm. [LC]
*7713. do. 1911. Tr. Helena Easson. L: Dent;NY: Dutton. Everyman's lib. xx;391p. 17cm. [BM.LC]
§7714. do. 1913-15. abr. Tr. S. Delffs and Rd. Tombo, Jr. In C154 (13). [Severely abridged; archaic style wholly lost.]
7715. do. 1916? NY: Transl. pub. n.d. Literal translations.15cm.[AC]
7716. do.[Ad.] 1879. The monk of St. Gall: A dram. adaptation in 5 acts [verse] ...by R. S. Ross. L: Bell 1879. 8. [BM]
*7717. (Gaudeamus!) Gaudeamus! Humorous poems tr. from S-- and others by C: G. Leland. Bost: Osgood; L: Trübner 1872. 154p. 13 x 9cm. [LC.BM]
[Contains anonymous songs and one each by Caspary and Schlippenbach.]
7718. In the Rhaetian Alps. Tr. A. I. Coleman. 1913-15. In C154(13).

SCHEFFER (Schefferus), J:s, 1621-79.
7719. (...Lapponia...regionis Lapponum...nova...description..) The hist. of Lapland, wherein are shewed the orig. manners, habits, marriages, conjurations, etc. of that people. Tr. anon. Oxf: At the theater 1674. 147p. il. 29cm. [BM.LC]

SCHEFFLER, J: Angelus, 1624-77. See "Angelus Silesius."

SCHEIBEL, J: Gf.
7720. Life of Dr. M. Luther. Tr. by Rev. J. P. Menge with alt. and add. L: Pigott 1862. 20p. 21cm. [BM]

SCHEIN, J: Hm. 1586-1630. Sel. in C271.

SCHELLING, F: W: Js. v. 1775-1854. Sel. in C12;194*;469.
7721. Academical lectures. Tr. Mrs. Ella Morgan. 1883. In C300(13).
*7722. (Das Verhältnis der bildenden Künste zu der Natur.) The philos. of art: an oration on the relation between the plastic arts and nature. Tr. anon. L: Chapman 1845. 34p. 19cm. [BM]
[Bost. pub. lib. says this was tr. by A. Johnson.]
*7723. do. 1913-15. On the relation of the plastic arts to nature. Tr. J. E. Cabot. In C154(5).
7724. The histor. construction of Christianity. Tr. Mrs. Ella Morgan. 1882. In C300(12).
7725. (Ideen zu einer Philosophie der Natur.) Introd. to the philos. of nature. (Extract.) Tr. T: Davidson. 1871. In C300(1).
7726. On medicine and the theory of organic nature; On the sciences of the fine arts. Tr. Mrs. Ella Morgan. 1885. In C300(15).
7727. On natural science in general. Tr. Mrs. Ella Morgan. 1884. In C300(14).
7728. (System des transzendentalen Idealismus.) Introd. to idealism. Tr. T: Davidson. 1871. In C300(1).
7729. (Ueber die Methode des akademischen Studiums.) Method of university study. Tr. Mrs. Ella Morgan. 1881. In C300(11).
7730. (Zur Geschichte der neueren Philosophie.) Practical effects of mod. philos. (Extract.) Tr. C: L. Bernays. 1873. In C300(3).
See Steffens, H: Reminisc. of Schelling. In "Story of my career," #9022.

SCHENK VON LIMBURG, 13th cent. Sel. in C416.

SCHENK, H: Tb. 1656-1727. Sel. in C231-2;235;271;276.

SCHENKENDORF, Fd. Gf. Mx. v. 1784-1812. Sel. in C17;29;67;106;137; 154(5);388;391;393;423;428;#6209a.

SCHERENBERG, Ern. 1839-1905. Sel. in C123;195 (ascribed to El. S--), 207;395.

SCHERER, Vl. 1878- .
7731. (Dürer...mit einer biographischen Einleitung.) The work of D--...introd. abr. from Vl. S--. Tr. anon. NY: Brentano's 1907. 16; 382p. il. 27cm. [LC]

SCHERER, W: 1841-86. Sel. in C417;469.
*7732. (Geschichte der deutschen Literatur.) Hist. of Ger. lit. Tr. from 3d ed. by Mrs. F. C. Conybeare. Oxf: Clarendon 1886. 2v. xv; 401;425p. 23cm. [BM.LC]
*7733. do. 1891. [same] Oxf: Clarendon. vii;335p. 19cm. [BM]
*7734. do. 1893. [same] NY: Scribner. 2v. 20cm. [LC]
*7735. do. 1906. [same] Ed. F. Max Müller. L: Frowde. 2v. 401;357p. 19cm. [BM]

SCHERR, J:s, 1817-86. Sel. in C301;422.
*7736. (Schiller und seine Zeit.) S-- and his times. Tr. Elis. McClellan. Phil: Kohler 1880. 454p. il. 12. [LCO]
[On the whole, excellent.]

SCHERZER, K: Ritter v. 1821-1903.
*7737. (Reise der österreichischen Fregatte Novara um die Erde.) Narr. of the circumnavigation of the globe by the Austrian frigate "Novara," in 1857-59. L: Saunders & O. 1861-63. 3v. il. maps.

SCHERZER, K: Ritter v.
25cm. [Apparently tr. by the author.] [BM.LC]
*7738. (Wanderungen durch die mittel-amerikanischen Freistaaten.) Travels in the free states of Central America. Tr. anon. (by the author?) L: Longmans 1857. 2v. 320;253p. 20cm. [BM.LC]
[Has an added first chapter.]

SCHEU, A. Sel. in C301.

SCHEURLIN, G: 1802-72. Sel. in C108;116;309;450.

SCHICK, Louis.
7738a. (Führer durch Bad Homburg und seine Umgebungen.) Guide to Homburg and its environs. Tr. Fr. Steinhäusser. Homburg: Schick 1855. xi;127p. 8. [EC (Heinsius)]

SCHICKELE, René, 1883- . Sel. in C95.

SCHIEBELER, Dn. 1741-71. Sel. in C231;244.

SCHIEMANN, Td. 1847-1921.
*7739. (Ein Verleumder.) A slanderer. Tr. anon. NY: Issues & events 1916. 46p. 19cm. [A reply to "J'accuse." Cf. #3096. seq.] [LC.BM]

SCHIKANEDER, J: Em. 1751-1812. Sel. in C133.
†7740. (Die Zauberflöte.)[1] Die Zauber Flöte [sic]; or Il flauto magico. An heroi-comic opera in two acts (by W. A. Mozart). As repr. at the King's theatre in the Haymarket for the benefit of Signor Naldi, June 6, 1811. Tr. from the German by Signor Gamerra, poet to the emperor of Germany. Libr. Ital;Engl. L: Brettell 1811. 85p. 18cm. [BM.LCM]
[Ital. is quite free; Engl. (in prose) follows Italian. Engl. tr. is by W. Js. Walter, cf. the following.]
†7742. do. 1819. The magic flute; or, the mysteries of Isis. Grand romantic opera in two acts as repr. etc. Tr. W. Js. Walter. Libr. Ital;Engl. L: W.Glindon. v;113p. 18cm. [BM]
[Engl. and Ital. both same as in #7740. This is also Prtd. by W. Winchester 1819. same paging. 17cm. BM]
?7743. do. 1838. Magic flute. Ad. T. Cooke. Libr. Engl. L: Theatre royal. 28p. 8. [Much altered.] [LC]
§7744. do. 1841. The magic flute. Tr. anon. Libr. Ger;Engl. L: Schloss. 72p. 17cm. [BM]
[Tr. follows line for line, giving only the sense of the orig.]
§7745. do. 1841. Ad. W. H. Latham. Libr. Engl. Phil: Meignen. 39p. 16. [Very free.] [LCM]
*7746. do. 1852. The magic flute: a lyric drama. Tr. J. Wrey Mould. Mus. ed. W. S. Rockstro. Vocal score. L: Boosey. 286p. 25cm. [BMM]
§7747. do. 1860. The magic flute. Tr. anon. Libr. Ital;Engl. Bost: Ditson. 31p. 8. [Bald prose tr. of German, fairly close in sense.] [LCM]
*7748. do. 1871. Il flauto magico. Vocal score. Ed. Art. Sullivan and J. Pittman. L;NY: Boosey. 208p. 25cm. [same tr. as #7746][BMM]
§7749. do. 1874. The magic flute. Tr. Natalia Macfarren. Vocal score L: Novello. n.d. 174p. 26cm. [BMM.LCM]
[Not so close to orig., but good to sing.]
†7750. do. 1880. Tr. anon. Libr. Ital;Engl. NY: French. 28p. 4. [LC]
[My 1st ed. said: Tr. from Italian, which slaughters the German. Very likely this is a reprint of Signor Gamerra's masterpiece.]
§7751. do. 1888. [same as #7747] Libr. Bost: Ditson. 31p. 8. [LC]
§7752. do. n.d. [same as #7747] Libr. Ital;Engl. NY:...Acad. of mus[LC]

[1] For conclusive evidence that K: L: Giesecke was not even the co-author of this libretto (as, e.g., stated by Kosch and BM), see Otto Rommel's introduction to vol. 1 of "Barocktradition" in Reclams "Deutsche Literatur," 1935.

SCHIKANEDER, J: Em.--Die Zauberflöte
?7753. do. 1911. Tr. E: J. Dent for the performance at Cambridge. Libr. Cambridge: Heffer. 57p. 12. [BM.LC]
[Text differs from both the Ger. versions before me.]
?7754. do. 1913. [same] Mozart's opera, The magic flute. Freely tr. E: J. Dent. 2d ed. L: Heffer. 58p. 18cm. [BM]

SCHILLER, Fx. 1805-53.
*7755. (München, dessen Kunstschätze...) Munich, its treas. of art and science, manners and customs. Tr. an Engl. tourist (J: Palm). Munich: J. Lendner 1852. iv;274p. steel engrs. front. map. 14cm. [BM]

SCHILLER, (J: Cph.)F: v. 1759-1805.

ARRANGEMENT

Collections[1]
Selections
Poems
Single works
Letters
Biography

COLLECTIONS

7756. 1802. Select plays...performed at the principal theatres. Vol. 2. Balto: Warner & Hanna. 24. [BPL]
[Robbers, 108p; Fiesco, 120p; Cabal and love, 103p.]
*7757. 1824. Mary Stuart and The maid of Orleans. Tr. Rev. H: Salvin. With life of author. L: Longman et al. xii;381p. 22cm. [BM]
[Style is excellent, but there are some errors.]
7758. 1828. Historical works. Tr. G: Moir. Ed: Constable; L: Hurst. (Constable's miscellany.) 2v. xxxv;300; 360p. 14cm. [BM.LC]
[Vol. 1 has on t.p. port. of S-- engr. by W. Archibald after Graff; vol. 2 has port. of Wallenstein engr. by T. Dick after Vandyke.--Thirty years' war; Trial of Egmont and Horn; Siege of Antwerp.]
7759. 1830. Poetic and prose works. L: Black. 8. [EC]
[Inclined to think this was an edition of the works in German; few trs. this early.]
7760. 1844. Philos. and aesthet. letters. Tr. J: Weiss. Pref. J. Chapman. L: Chapman. Catholic series. xii;318p. 12. [BM]
7761. 1845. [same] L: Chapman. [BM]
[Ident. with the foregoing, exc. for the t.p.]
7762. 1845. [same] L: Bohn. [EC]
§7763. 1845. Essays. The aesthetic letters, essays, and the philos. letters. Tr. J: Weiss. Bost: Little, Brown. 380p. 16. [LCO.BM]
[Free; not incorrect.]
7764. 1846-49. Works, histor. and dram. L: Bohn. 4v. 8. [BM]
[Vol. 1. Thirty years' war, Revolt of the Netherlands. Vol. 2. Revolt of the Netherlands, Wallenstein, W: Tell. Vol. 3. Don Carlos, Mary Stuart, Maid of Orleans, Bride of Messina. Vol. 4. Robbers, Fiesco, Love and intrigue, Demetrius, Ghost-seer.]
7765. 1847. Hist. of the revolt of the Netherlands. Trial and execution of Counts Egmont and Horn. The siege of Antwerp. Tr. A. J. W. Morrison. NY: Harper. 333p. 16. (B29)
7766. 1853. [same as #7764] Bohn. 4v. [UW]
7766. 1853. [same as #7764] Bohn. 4v. [UW]
7767. 1855. [same as #7765] NY: Harper. (B29)
7768. 1861. Complete works. Ed. C: J. Hempel. Phil: Kohler. 2v.
[Cited by LC and by B49, who says it is the first complete Engl. ed. For contents, see the following entry.]
*7769. 1870. Complete works. Ed. with careful revisions and new tr. C: J. Hempel. Phil: Kohler. 2v. 27cm. [LC.BM]

[1] For critical judgments see individual titles.

SCHILLER, F: v.--Collections
[Vol. 1. Poetic works tr. Bulwer-Lytton ("Semele" by Hempel); The robbers tr. H. G. Bohn; Fiesco, do; Love and intrigue, do; The misanthrope; Homage of the arts tr. Hempel; Don Carlos tr. R. D. Boylan; Mary Stuart tr. J. C. Mellish; Maid of Orleans tr. A. Swanwick; On the use of chorus in trag., The bride of Messina, both tr. A. Lodge; Camp of Wallenstein tr. J. Churchill; Piccolomini and Wallenstein's death tr. S. T. Coleridge (with previous omissions chiefly tr. G. F. Richardson); W: Tell tr. Td. Martin; Demetrius; Warbeck; The Maltese; The children of the house. Vol. 2. Hist. of the revolt of the united Netherlands, rev. tr.; Trial and execution of Counts Egmont and Horn, Siege of Antwerp, Hist. of the thirty years' war, all tr. A. J. W. Morrison; Philos. writings tr. Hempel; Criminal from lost honor; Sport of destiny tr. H. G. Bohn; Ghost-seer tr. H. G. Bohn; Miscellaneous writings, Aesthetical writings, both tr. Hempel.]

7770. 1872. Dramatic works. L: Bell. [LC]
[Same as vol. 3 of #7764. Don Carlos tr. Boylan; Mary Stuart tr. Mellish(from prompter's copy), revised; Maid of Orleans by Swanwick; Bride of Messina and Essay on the use of chorus in tragedy by Lodge.]

*7771. 1875. Essays aesthetical and philosophical. Tr. by various hands. L: Bell. 435p. 18cm. [No tr. named. Introd. to p. 23.] [BM.LC]

7772. 1883. Works, il. by the greatest Ger. artists. Ed. J. G. Fischer. Phil: Barrie. 4v. il. 30cm. [LC.BM]
[Vol. 1. Poems tr. by Bowring; Robbers, Fiesco, Love and intrigue, as in #7764. Vol. 2. Don Carlos, Wallenstein, complete, Mary Stuart, Maid of Orleans, as in #7764; Misanthrope, anon. Vol. 3. Bride of Messina, Tell, Demetrius, Ghost-seer, Revolt of Netherlands, as in #7764. Criminal from lost honor, Warbeck, The Maltese, The children of the house. Vol. 4. Revolt of Netherlands, continued; Thirty years' war, as in #7764. Fragments of Schiller's translations (in German). Life of S-- by H. H. Boyesen.]

7773. 1884. Works. Household ed. NY: J: D. Williams n.d. Bost: Cassino 1884. 4v. il. 16. [UW]
[Vol. 1. Thirty years' war; Revolt of Netherlands. Vol. 2. Ghost-seer; Sport of destiny; Robbers; Fiesco; Love and intrigue, Wallenstein, complete. Vol. 3. Tell, Don Carlos, Demetrius, Mary Stuart, Maid of Orleans, Bride of Messina; these tr. as in #7764. Vol. 4. Poems and essays; the poems are by Bowring and Lytton, almost alternately chosen and in slightly changed order--thus, the poems by Bowring are: 2, 4-7, 11-13, 15, 18, 20, 21, 23, etc.

7774. 1884? Works. Household ed. NY: Lovell 188- . 4v. 19cm. [LC]
[Same contents as the foregoing.]

7775. 1888. S--'s dramas. L: Bell. Bohn's shilling series. 436p. 18cm. [Mary Stuart by Mellish; The maid of Orleans by Swanwick] [BM]

7776. 1889. Dramatic works. L: Bohn. 419p. 19cm. [BM]
[Wallenstein by Churchill and Coleridge, Tell by Martin. EC has: Wallenstein and Wilhelm Tell. L: Bell 1889.]

7777. 1889. Poems and plays. L;NY: Routledge. xxxvi;889p. 20cm. [BM]
[Poems by Lytton; Robbers by C. W. Mann; Fiesco by Noehden and Stoddart; Cabal and love by Lewis (1797); Don Carlos by Lord J: Russell (see note); Wallenstein's camp by Gower; Piccolomini and Death of Wallenstein by Coleridge; Mary Stuart by Mellish; Maid of Orleans by Drinkwater; Bride of Messina by Lodge; Tell by S. Robinson. --The tr. of Don Carlos bears no apparent relation to Schiller's drama.]

7778. 1890. do. [same] L: Routledge. xxxvi;889p. [BM]
[Ident. with the foregoing except for the t.p.]

7779. 1897-1903. Works. L: Bell. 7v. 19cm. [LC]
[Vol. 1. Revolt of Netherlands (orig. tr. Eastwick, carefully rev.

SCHILLER, F: v.--Collections
and to some extent rewritten by Morrison); Egmont and Horn by Morrison; Siege of Antwerp, by Morrison? Relig. disturb. in France, tr. L. Dora Schmitz. Vol. 2 (marked Vol. I on the inside). Thirty years' war by Morrison. Vol. 3. Don Carlos by Boylan; Mary Stuart by Mellish, with revisions by Bohn; Maid of Orleans by Swanwick, as completed in 1847; Bride of Messina and Essay on the use of chorus in tragedy by Lodge. Vol. 4. Robbers by Bohn (Pref. dated 1849); Fiesco, tr. rev. from that of Noehden and Stoddart (by Bohn?), almost a new version; Love and intrigue, by Bohn? Ghost-seer, tr. anon; Demetrius by Martin; Sport of destiny, tr. anon. Vol. 5. Poems tr. by Bowring, none by Lytton as in #7773; this is the same as the rev. ed. #7820. Vol. 6. Essays aesthet. and philos., tr. anon., same as #7771. Vol. 6. Wallenstein's camp by Churchill, Piccolomini and Wallenstein's death by Coleridge, with additions by G. F. Richardson, the translator of Körner's poems (#5120);Tell by Martin, as revised in 1894.]

7780. 1902. Works. Ed. de luxe. Ed. N. H. Dole. Bost: Niccolls. 8v. il. 23cm. [LC]
[Includes Düntzer's life of Schiller, tr. by Percy Pinkerton, cf. #1274. Revolt of Netherlands in rev. tr. of #7769. Otherwise the tr. are those of #7764, except for the poems. Arnold-Forster signs the tr.'s pref., but I examined 38 poems, all tr. either by Bowring or Lytton. Probably this volume is taken over from #7773. Vols. are not numbered. (1.2.) Aesthet. and philos. letters and essays. (3.) Poetical works. (4.) Revolt of Netherlands. (5.) Thirty years' war. (6.) Maid of Orleans, Bride of Messina, Tell, Demetrius. (7.) Wallenstein. (8.) Robbers, Fiesco, Love and intrigue.]

7781. 190- ? [same] Works. NY: Williams n.d. 8v. [NY]
[Cheap reissue of the foregoing.]

7782. 1903. Dramatic works, [same as #7776] L: Bell. 420p. 19cm. [LC]

7783. 1905. Works. Ed. by L. Hermann. L: Unwin. 8v. 8. [EC]
[Probably the same as #7781.]

7784. 1910. Dramatic works [same as #7776] L: Bell. [UW]

7785. 1914. Wallenstein and Tell. L: Bell. [LC]
[Same as vol. 7 of #7779, prtd. from stereotyped plates.]

7786. 1915. Works. Bost: Niccolls. 10v. [Cf. #7780.] [AC]

SELECTIONS

Sel. in C3;7;8;9;12;17*;22;25-6;31;35;37;40;42-3;44*;48;50*;54*;56; 63-4;67;69;71;75*;76-7;86;89;90;92-3;97-9;101;103-4;106;108;109*; 111-2;118;120-1;123;129;132;133*;137a;141-4;146;149*;150;153;158; 163;165-6;172-3;176-8;180;182;184;190;193-6;199*;208;215;218-9; 293;295-6;299;306*;309*;313;316;366*;372*;373*;374-5;378;380-1; 383;385*;387-8;391*;393*;395;396*;397*;399;400;405a;410-1;412*; 423;428*;438-9;443;445;448*;459;460;461*;467;469;471;486;488-9; 499;500-1;507;516;530-1;533;538-9;543;554;560;562*;566;574*;#2687; 2720;5120;6536;7859;7931;7948;8001;8023;8030;8141.

7787. ANON. 1823. Illustrations of Shakespeare, Goethe, and Schiller. By M. Retzsch. Tilt 1823. obl. 4. [This undoubtedly contains some text; I believe it is in BM, but was unable to find it.] [EC]

7788. ANON. 1836. The laurel: a gift for all seasons. Poems by (48) Amer. authors. Bost: Broaders. 252p. 24. (B29)
[Contains: The exile ("Der Flüchtling"), a free tr. by C. Sherry.]

7789. ANON. 1848. Gems of poetry from 48 Amer. poets. With ports. Hartford, Ct: S. Andrus. 252p. 16. (B29) [Reissue of foregoing.]

7790. ANON. 1856. Hill-side flowers. Introd. Rev. Bishop Simpson. NY: Prtd. for the author by Carlton & Phillips. 240p. 12. (B29)
[Contains 2 from Schiller, also other tr. from Ger., Ital, French, etc.]

SCHILLER, F: v.--Selections

7791. ANON. 1895. S--'s poems in relation to his character, etc. An address by E. T. G. L: W.Hall & Lovitt. 33p. 20cm. [BM] [Contains citations in Lytton's tr.]

7792. BELL, ROSALIE. Lilies and violets; or, thoughts in prose and verse on the true graces of maidenhood. NY;Cincin: Derby 1855. Also Bost: Phillips, Sampson. 442p. 12. (B29) [Contains: The empire of woman ("Die Macht des Weibes"), tr. anon.]

7793. BULFINCH, ST. Poems. Charleston, S.C: Burges 1834. 108p. 24. (B29) [Contains: The ideals ("Die Ideale"); The immensity of creation ("Die Grösse der Welt").

*7794. CARLYLE, T: Life of S--, comprehending an exam. of his works. L: Taylor & Hessey 1825. vi;352p. 8. [BM] [Variously repub. in C--'s works and elsewhere. Has fairly extensive sel. from "Don Carlos," "Jungfrau," "Wallenstein," "W: Tell."]

7795. CARLYLE, T: Schiller (essay). Bost: Osgood 1877. 80p. 12cm.[BM]

7796. CARUS, Pl. F: Schiller, a sketch of his life and an appreciation of his poetry. Chic: Open ct. 1904. 102p. il. 24cm. [LC.BM] [Carus cites and edits tr. by Baskerville, Bowring, Bulwer. Editing is not extensive, but to the point.]

7797. COLMAN, MISS. Wild flowers: a coll. of gems from the best authors. Bost: Colman 1846. 126p. 12cm. (B42) [Two brief sel. from S--.]

7798. do. 1848. [same] Ladies' vase of wild flowers. (B42)

7799. do. 1850. [same] Auburn: Alden. 126p. 12cm. [LC]

7800. DAWES, RUFUS. Geraldine, Athenia of Damascus, and misc. poems. NY: Colman 1839. 343p. 16. (B29) [Contains: The division of the earth ("Die Teilung der Erde").]

§7801. ELLET, MRS. ELIZ. F. The characters of S--. Bost: Otis etc. 1839. 296p. 19cm. [A consid. sel. from the dramas, all by the author exc. Wallenstein (Coleridge's tr.). Fair to good tr.] [LC]

7802. do. Poems, tr. and orig. Phil: Key & Biddle 1835. 229p. 17cm. [Contains one from Schiller.] [BM]

7803. HALE, MRS. SA. J. The white veil: a bridal gift. Phil: Butler 1854. 324p. il. 12. (B29) [Contains: The dignity of woman ("Würde der Frauen").]

7804. HALL, MRS. JAS. Phantasia and other poems. NY;L: Putnam 1849. 144p. 12.[Contains: Sir Toggenburg. A ballad ("Ritter T--").] [BM]

7805. HODGES, C: Orig. poems, etc. 1836. C202. [Contains: Demetrius, part of The bride of Messina.]

7806. HOPPIN, JAS. M. Notes of a theol. student. NY;L: Appleton 1854. 256p. 16. [Contains most of "An die Freude."] [BM]

7807. HYNEMAN, MRS. REBEKAH. The leper, and other poems. Phil: A. Hart 1853. 216p. 16. [Contains: The dignity of woman ("Würde der Frauen"), same tr. as in #7803.] [BM]

7808. NACK, JAS. Earl Rupert, and other tales and poems. NY: Adlard 1839. xx;220p. 19cm. [BM] [Contains: "The bell song." Partly from the <u>Lied von der Glocke</u>. He omitted the technical passages as of no general interest.]

*7809. NEVINSON, H: W. Life of F: S--. L;NY: 1889. 203p. 20cm. [LC] [Small bits, mostly by author, some from Coleridge. Excellent.]

*7810. ROYCE, KATH. In Eg. Kühnemann's "Schiller," #5489.[Sel. partly from Lytton, mostly done very well by the tr. of the biog.]

*7811. SIME, JAS. Schiller. Phil: Lippincott 1882. 214p. 17cm. [LC] [Poems by Lytton. Wallenstein by Coleridge (extr.); sel. from "Maria Stuart," "Jungfrau," "Braut von Messina," "W: Tell" by author; these excellent.]

*7812. THOMAS, CALVIN. Life and works of S--. NY: Holt 1901. 481p. il. 22cm. [Not much verse quoted. Some citations from Lytton, some verse excellently done by author.] [LC]

7813. WERNER, F: The characteristics of S--'s dramas, etc. L:

SCHILLER, F: v.--Selections
Longman et al. 1859. 55p. 19cm. [BM]
[Many brief sel, tr. by the author in rhythmical prose.]

POEMS

7814. ANON. 1821. Poems and tr. from S--. L: Rodwell. 8. [EC]
[This is very likely by G. T. Gallop; see below, #7825.]
7815. ANON. 1896. Ballads: a literal tr. NY: Hinds & N. 92p. 15cm.
[Prose; correct.] [LC]
7816. ANON. 1912-17. Poems. Literal trs. Transl. pub. n.d. 15cm. [AC]
*7817. ARNOLD-FORSTER, E. P. Sel. from S--'s poems. L: Hamilton, Adams 1888. 124p. 12. [20 poems, includ. Song of the bell, The diver, The walk. Tr. seems to be excellent.] [BM]
*7818. do. 1902. L: Heinemann. xi;360p. 8. [BM]
[367 poems. AC has: NY: Holt 1902.]
§7819. BOWRING, E. A. Poems of S--, complete, including all his early suppressed poems. L: Parker 1851. xix;377p. 17cm. [BM]
[Extracts from the dramas, pp. 361-77. See my remarks on Bowring's tr. of Goethe's poems, #2400.]
§7820. do. 1874. [same] 2d rev. ed. L: Bell. 377p. 18cm. [LC]
§7821. do. 1884. [same] NY: Lovell. 344p. 16. [LCO]
†7822. CLARK, GILBERT. Ballads and shorter poems. L: Williams & N. 1901. xv;408p. 16cm. [Cf. #7873.] [BM]
7823. FEBECK, BARON. German muse, Worth of woman, The song of the bell. L: Treuttel, Würz 1831. See "Lit. Gazette" 15(1831):633. (B26)
7824. FRYE, W. E. Ideals and The cranes of Ibycus. Porter 1819. See "Monthly R." 92(1820):331. (B26)
†7825. GALLOP, G. T. Poems. L: Prtd. for Rodwell & Martin 1823. 62p. 12. [(Copy in lib. of Rb. Priebsch.) Contains: The bell; The diver; The glove; Worth of women; Farewell to the reader.]
§7826. HICKSON, S: Specimens of tr. from the poems. L: Priv. circ. 1849. 28p. 12. [BM.LC]
§7827. JOHNSTON, J. PYM. Lyrics and song of the bell. L: Senior 1839. 55p. 8. [Mediocre tr. Cf. #7910.] [NY]
†7828. LYTTON, E: Lord. (Bulwer-Lytton.) Poems and ballads. NY: Harper 1844. 424p. 19cm. [LC]
[A fluent versifier and good poet but a conscienceless translator.]
†7829. do. 1844. [same] Lpz: Tauchnitz. 104; 284p. S. [UW]
†7830. do. 1844. [same] Ed;L: Blackwoods. 2v. 8. [BM]
†7831. do. 1852. [same] 2d ed. Ed;L: Blackwoods. xx;382p. 18cm. [BM]
["Many...tr. have been wholly rewritten, most of them carefully retouched."]
†7832. do. 1875. With "Odes of Horace." Introd. H: Morley. L: Routledge. 18cm. [Sep. paged. Schiller section is xiv;276p.] [BM]
†7833. do. 1877. Favorite poems. Bost: Osgood. 96p. il. 12cm. [BM]
[23 poems, includ. Diver, Glove, Toggenburg, Cranes, Ceres, Eleus. festival, and others.]
†7834. do. 1887. [same as #7832] L: Routledge. 492p. 18cm. [BM]
†7835. do. 1887. Part I of #7832. Introd. H. Morley. xiv;276p. 18cm. [BM]
†7836. do. 1887. [same as the foregoing] L: Warne. Chandos classics. xv;384p. 8. [Introd. (Life of S--) to p. 98.] [BM]
†7837. do. 1898. Louisville, Ky: Amer. print. house for the blind. 72p. fol. [LC]
*7838. MERIVALE, J: H. Minor poems of S-- of the 2d and 3d periods, with a few of those of earlier date. L: Pickering 1844. 8. [BM]
[Cf. C412, and my note.]
§7839. MILLS, ART. The song of the bell, The gods of Greece, and (2) other ballads. Paraphrased. L: Bickers 1876. 40p. 17cm. ["An attempt to render (in verse)...the general meaning of the orig."] [BM]
7840. PRYM, J. Lyrics from the Ger. of S--. L: 1839. 55p. 12. (B8)

SCHILLER, F: v.--Poems

†7841. R(OBINSON), S(AMUEL). Specimens of...minor poems. L: Williams & N. 1867. 122p. 8. [35 poems, including the Bell, very bad.] [BM]

7842. SOTHEBY, W. W. Poems, complete. L: 1851. (B50) [Cannot verify this reference;possibly an error.]

†7843. TRELAWNY, ANNE, afterwards GIBBONS. Lyrical ballads from... S--. By the tr. of "Ma. Stuart." Devonport: Prtd. by W. Byers 1838. 68p. 18cm. [Bell, Fridolin, Hapsburg, 5 others. Not much.] [BM]

†7844. WHITTY, J: I. The Gods of Greece / from the German of / Schiller / with the celebrated suppressed stanzas restored / also/ Prologue and First Canto / of / Goethe's / Hermann and Dorothea / accurately translated / No word whatsoever of the slightest importance in the original of / either Masterpiece being uninterpreted. / And other poems / by / John Irwine Whitty. L: Grocock & Condliff 1892. 41p. 20cm. [Also contains: The invincible Armada by S--. H. and D. is very good, but S. is impossible.] [BM]

7845. WIREMAN, H: D. Poems...complete. (Ger;Eng.) Phil: Kohler 1871. 871p. 18cm. [A few tr. by the editor, but most of them taken from Bowring, Dwight, Lytton, Mangan.] [LC]

SINGLE WORKS

7846. (<u>An die Freude</u>.) Tr. J. Beresford. Berlin: 1810. (B8)

7847. do. Tr. Julian Fane. Wien: 1855. (B8)

DAS LIED VON DER GLOCKE

7848. ANON. 1821. The song of the bell. In #7814. Cf. #7825.

7849. do. 1827. L: [This tr. is by F: Page; see below, #7935.] [BM]

7850. do. 1828. Bath. [Also by F: Page, #7937.] [BM]

7851. do. 1833. Retzsch's il. to the song...L: Black. obl. 4. [EC] [Probably by Page; see below, #7938-40.]

7852. do. 1837. Il. Retzsch. L: Black & Armstrong. obl. 8. [NY] [Probably by Page; see below, #7938-40.]

7853. do. 1839. Ger. and Engl. NY: Radde. 24p. 16. (B29)

7854. do. 1845. [Tr. is by Eliot; see B29, and #7883 below.] [NY]

7855. do. 1850. Il. of human life. 16...il. to S--'s Song of the bell, designed by M. Retzsch, and engr. Phil: Hazard & Mitchell. 16. (B29)

†7856. do. 1857. Dublin: McGlashan & Gill. 24p. 15cm. [BM] [Rea (B32) says: mere doggerel.]

7857. do. 1857. Il. M. Retzsch. Stuttgart: Cotta; NY: Appleton, also Radde. 12; 12p. fol. [Cf. #7853.] [NY]

7858. do. 1859. L: [Tr. of Lord Lytton; see below, #7915.] [BM]

§7859. do. 1863. The lay of the bell. With other tr. and orig. pieces. Norwich: Prtd. by J. Fletcher. 32p. 15cm. [BM] [One additional poem each by Harms, Schiller, Spitta. --Not as bad as Rea (B32) paints it, but bad enough.]

†7860. do. 1873. The lay of the bell. L: Priv. prt. 17p. 24cm. [Done by C. K. F. Quite worthless. See #7888.] [BM.LC]

7861. do. 1880. The song of the bell. Grand mus. entertainment by the Harmonic Soc. Dayton, O., May 5, 1880. 16p. 4. [NY] [Same tr. as #7857.]

7862. do. 1883. The lay of the bell, and, The diver. L: Partridge. 8. [Probably by J. W. Grant; see below, #7901.] [EC]

7863. do. 1912-17. Song of the bell. Transl. pub. n.d. 15cm. [AC]

§7864. ARNOLD, T: J. The lay of the bell. L: Nutt, xii;37p. 16cm. [Rea says: Neither elegant nor poetical.] [BM]

7865. ARNOLD-FORSTER, E. P. Bradford. 1886-7. (B8)

§7866. do. 1888. In #7817. [Rea says: Follows form pretty closely, uses too much iambic meter; a good deal of merit.]

§7867. ASHER, A. Berlin: 1834. 31p. 32. [BPL]

§7868. BASKERVILLE, Af. 1863. In C17. [He grows flowery and loses S--'s force.]

SCHILLER, F: v.--Das Lied von der Glocke
§7869. do. 1904. In #7796. [Ed. and improved by Pl. Carus.]
§7870. BOWRING, E. A. The lay of the bell. 1851. In #7819.
†7871. BROMWELL, H. P. The song of the bell. 1919. In C40.
†7872. CAMPBELL, J. J. 1836. In C54.
†7873. CLARK, G. 1901. In #7822.
[Rea (B32): One of the most slovenly, inelegant, and careless translations of a great work that we have ever seen.]
§7874. COLOMB, CAPT. (later Col.) G. H. The song of the bell. Gibraltar: Garrison lib. 1862. 20p. 21cm. [BM]
§7875. do. 1878. With Bürger's Lenore. In #871.
7876. CUTLER, A. W. Bost: 1887. (B50)
§7877. DWIGHT, J. S. The song of the bell. 1839. In C109. [Not very good.]
§7878. do. 1844. Ger;Engl. Phil: Schreiber & Schwacke. 8p. 8. (B29)
§7879. do. 1845-8. Phil: Schwacke. 27p. 16. (B29)
†7880. EGESTORFF, G: H: Cph. The song of the bell. L: Nutt 1844. 32p. 21cm. [Terrible! --One of a projected series of textbooks: A sel. of Ger. poetry with elucidations, translations, and notes for self-tuition.] [BM]
§7881. ELIOT, S: A. The song of the bell. Tr. for Bost. acad. of music. Bost: Perkins & Marvin 1837. 16p. 8. [LCO.BM]
§7882. do. 1838. [same] [LCO]
§7883. do. 1845. (Sung at a concert given by the Handel Soc. of the W. R. College, Aug. 14, 1845.) 4 leaves. 8. [NY]
§7884. do. 1845. In C373.
§7885. do. 1851. Tr. and ad. to the music of Romberg. 2d ed. Bost: Ditson; NY: Gordon. obl. 4. (B29)
§7886. do. 1852. 2d ed. of #7881. Bost: Johnson. 16p. 12. (B29)
§7887. ELLIS (i.e., ELIOT?), S. A. 1905. In C163.
†7888. F., C. K. The lay of the bell. L: Priv. prt. 1873. 17p. 24cm. [Quite worthless.] [BM.LC]
†7889. do. 1873. [same] In C123.
7890. FEBECK, BARON. 1831. In #7823.
†7891. FOSTER-BARHAM, A. G. The lay of the bell. Il. W. A. Phillips. L: Unwin 1896. 52p. 21 x 28cm. [BM]
*7892. FURNESS, W: H: The song of the bell. 1850. In C143. Cf. C144-6. [Adheres strictly to S--'s meters; though impure rhymes are frequent, the tr. is on the whole very good.]
*7893. do. 1859. Phil: Schäfer & Konradi. 8p. 8. [NY]
*7894. do. 1874. Il. C. Jaeger and A. Mueller. L: F:Bruckmann. 22p. 33cm. [BM]
*7895. do. 1879. Vignettes by R. Seitz. Munich: Stroefer; NY: Kirchner. 55p. 32cm. [LC]
*7896. do. 1880. [same] 32 il. after A. L. Mayer and vignettes, etc. by Rd. Seitz. Munich: Stroefer; L: Hachette. 55p. fol. [BM]
*7897. do. 1883. Il. A. Liezen-Mayer and E. H. Garrett. Bost: Estes & Lauriat. 46p. 21cm. [LC]
*7898. do. 1889. In C309.
†7899. GOSTWICK, JS. 1845. In C173.
†7900. GOWER, LORD FIS. 1823. In #2720.
†7901. GRANT, J. W. The lay of the bell, and, The diver. L: Hamilton 1867. 8. [EC]
[Rea (B32): "not very brilliant." But cf. his "Faust" translation, #2721.]
7902. do? 1883. L: Partridge. 8. [Probably a reissue of #7901.] [EC]
†7903. GRIBBLE, J. D. B. 1888. In C180.
§7904. HEDLEY, F. H. 1876. In C196. [Correct but too flowery in spots.]
§7905. HICKSON, S. 1849. In #7826.
§7906. HOLMES, G. B. S--'s lay of the bell. An attempt to accommodate an Engl. version...to the music of Romberg. L: Kent 1877. 16p. 17cm. [Rea (B32): Faithful, but tame.] [BM]

SCHILLER, F: v.--Das Lied von der Glocke
†7907. IMPEY, E. B. The lay of the bell. 1841. In C295.
†7908. do. 1842. Il. by M. Retzsch. 2d ed. L: Simpkin, Marshall. 122p. obl. 4. [LCO]
[Possibly the first ed. was the foregoing.]
†7909. do. 1850. [same] 2d ed. L: Simpkin. obl. 4. [EC]
†7910. JOHNSTON, J. P. 1839. In #7827.
7911. L., C. R. The lay of the bell. In "Tait's Ed. Mag." 11(1844): 82. (B27)
§7912. LAMBERT, C: R. 1850. In C313.
§7913. LIVESEY, T. J. and FZ. HAGELÜKEN. L: Allman 1876. iv;42p. 18cm. [Allman's pop. elementary series (i.e., textbook). Interlinear tr. and a fluent prose tr., the latter very good.] [BM]
§7914. LYTTON, E: LORD. The lay of the bell. 1844. In #7828. [Worden (B50) calls this one of the worst tr. Rea (B32) says: "Although far from perfect, this version shows a mastery of the art of translation..." I cannot agree with either judgment. Lytton is a poet and turns S--'s verse into excellent English, but he forsakes at times both meter and sense.]
§7915. do. 1859. ...with a biogr. sketch. Centenary festival, Nov. 10, 1859. L: Petsch. 14p. Ger;Engl. 24cm. [BM]
§7916. do. 1865. 42 il. T: Scott and J. D. Cooper after M. Retzsch. L: Low. 30p. 22 x 27cm. [BM]
§7917. do. 1874. In "Catalogue of...bells," prtd. for Meneely & Co., West Troy, NY, by Wied, Parsons, Albany, NY. 8. [LCO]
§7918. do. 1875. [same as #7916] New ed. L: Low. il. 4. [EC]
§7919. do. 1877. The lay of the bell, and, Fridolin. Bost: Osgood. 79p. il. 12cm. [BM]
§7920. do. 1895. Il. J. A. Symington. L: Nister; NY: Dutton. 48p. 14cm. [BM]
§7921. do. 1905. Lay of the bell, also, The walk. L: Routledge; NY: Dutton. Broadway booklets. 62p. 14cm. [BM]
[Cover il. J. E. Millais.]
§7921. do. 1905. Lay of the bell; The walk. L: Routledge; NY: Dutton. Broadway booklets. 62p. 14cm. [Cover il. J. E. Millais.] [BM]
*7922. MANGAN, JAS. C. The lay of the bell. 1845. In C391. [Has very good spots.]
†7923. MARTIN, RENIRA H. A. Exeter. J. H. Wallis 1849. 24p. 16cm. [BM]
[Rea (B32): Tolerably faithful, but very prosaic.]
§7924. MARTIN, SIR TD. 1889. In C397. [He alters the metrical form; cf. comment on his "Faust" tr., #2759.]
†7925. MAURER, G. P. 1840. In C410. [Rea (B32): can hardly show one good line.]
§7926. MEESON, H: A. Song...with...literal tr. and vocab. L: Longmans 1846. 18p. 16cm. [BM]
[Tr. is on opposite pages, done line for line; seems to be correct]
*7927. MERIVALE, J. H. Song of the bell. 1844. In C412. Cf. #7838. [Rea (B32): On the whole, very faithful; one of the best we have.]
*7928. do. 1856. Ed;L: Williams & Norgate. 31p. 16cm. [BM]
*7929. do. 1869. [same] Ger;Engl. 39p. 18cm. [BM]
7930. MILLS, ART. Song...(paraphrase). 1876. In #7839. [Not bad as a paraphrase.]
†7931. M(ONTAGU), M. Song of the bell and (7) other poems. L: Hatchard 1839. xxvi;111p. 22cm. [Notes given.] [BM]
†7932. do. 1854. [same] [BM]
§7933. MUENSTERBERG, MARG. 1916. In C423.
†7934. MULLER, DR. G: A. Also, The human heart (a poem), by F. Hornfeck. Paris;Nice: Galignani 1891. 30p. 17cm. [Quite poor.] [BM]
†7935. PAGE, F: The song of the bell. L: Treuttel & Würtz, and Hatchard 1827. vii;45p. Ger;Engl. 19cm. [BM]
[Cf. #7849. Entirely devoid of merit, says Rea (B32).]

SCHILLER, F: v.--Das Lied von der Glocke
†7936. do. 1828. In C445.
†7937. do. 1828. Engl. only. Prtd. by B. Higman in Bath for J: Upham, Walks. vi;21p. 19cm. [Same as #7850.] [BM]
7938. do? 1833. Retzsch's outline to the song...L: Black. obl. 4.[EC] [I assume that this is Page's tr.; see the two following.]
7939. do? 1837. Il. Retzsch. L: Black & Armstrong. obl. 8. [NY] [Cf. the following, which seems to justify ascribing this and the foregoing to Page.]
†7940. do. 1840. The song of the bell. Tr. anon. With explan. of the outlines of M. Retzsch. L: Black & Armstrong. 16p. 22 x 30cm. [BM] [This is Page's tr.]
*7941. PAGE, GREG. A. The song of the bell. L: Jordan 1903. 19p. 21cm. [Strictly faithful in meter, which results in considerable harshness. Perhaps it can't be better done.] [BM]
§7942. PEARSON, E. S. 1879. In C448.
†7943. ROBINSON, R. 1828. In C471.
†7944. ROBINSON, S: 1867. In #7841.
†7945. SKRINE, H: D. Bath. Priv. prt. 1870. 21p. 17cm. [BM] [Absolutely worthless.]
†7946. TRELAWNY, ANNE. 1838. In #7843.
†7947. WHEWELL, W: 1847. In C562.
§7948. WOOD, AND. Lay of the bell and (6) other ballads. Ed: Nimmo 1879. 147p. Ger;Engl. 19cm. [BM] [Introd. to p. 36. --Rea (B32): style is tame.]
*7949. WORDEN, J. P. ...acc. to the metre and rime of the orig. (With histor. introd., Ger. text, review of several other tr., and a bibliography of all known versions in English.) Halle: Niemeyer 1900. xiv;149p. il. 15cm. [LC.BM] [Perhaps the most accurate version, not the most poetical.]
†7950. WYTTENBACH. L: Hatchard 1839. 8. [EC] [Worden (B50) has seen this and says it is no good.]
†7951. ZIMMERMANN, T: C. Reading, Pa: Priv. prt. 1889. 26p. Ger; Engl. 22cm. [Pp. 9-26 are made up of newspaper clippings, commendations, etc. I find little ground for Worden's praise.] [BM]
†7952. do. 1896....and other poems. 2d ed. Reading, Pa: Priv. prt. (B50)

7953. (Demetrius.) D--. Tr. C: Hodges. 1836. In C202.
*7954. do. 1849? Tr. Sir Td. Martin. In #7764. Also in subsequent editions.
*7955. (Der Gang nach dem Eisenhammer.) Fridolin; or, the road to the iron foundry. Tr. J. P. Collier. 8 engr. Moses after Retsch [sic]. L: Prowett 1824. 43p. Ger;Engl. 25cm. [BM.LC] [LC has it bound with The fight with the dragon (#7972), 27 x 21cm.]
7956. do. 1857. Anon. (Tr. Lytton.) Fridolin; or, an errand to the iron foundry. Stuttgart: Cotta; NY: Appleton. 7p. 8 il. obl. 4. [NY]
*7957. do. 1875. Collier's tr. L: Low. 8p. of text bound with alternate plates. 24 x 31cm. [BM]

DER GEISTERSEHER

7958. ANON. 1832. The ghost-seer. Paris. 1832. 2v. (B8) [This is probably Render's tr. See below, #7969.]
*7959. ANON. 1843. No t.p. n.d. 48p. 8. [NY] [Parry (B29) says this was pub. NY: Sun office 1843.]
*7960. ANON. 1845. The visionary; from the papers of the Count de O--. NY;Phil: Ferrett. 96p. 25cm. [LC]
7960a. ANON. 1850. The ghost seer, or, apparitionist, from the papers of Count O-- . Tr. anon. The "Press" (L.) 1(1850):79, etc.
7961. ANON. 1857. Ghost seer: a tale. Blackwoods. 12. [EC]
†7962. ANON. 1895. The ghost-seer. In C559.

SCHILLER, F: v.--Der Geisterseher

*7963. BOHN, H: G. The ghost-seer. 1849. In #7764 and subsequent editions.

§7964. BOILEAU, D. The ghost-seer, or apparitionist. L: Vernor 1795. 242p. 16cm. [Abr. and without the letters.] [BM]

7965. do? 1796. The ghost-seer; or, the apparitionist. Charleston, S. C: Prtd. by W. P. Young. (B6a) [Probably a reprint of foregoing.]

7966. do. 1796. The ghost-seer; or, apparitionist. NY: Prtd. for T. & J. Swords. 120p. 12. (B6a;B48)

†7967. RENDER, W: The Armenian; or, the ghost seer. A hist. founded on fact. L: Symonds 1800. 4v. in 2. 18 x 10cm. [BM.LC] [This ed. includes the "continuation" by Follenius, see #1650.]

7968. do. 1801. Reprint. Phil. n.d. 2v. 12. (B48) [Parry (B29) dates this 1801.]

7969. do. 1831. The ghostseer! L: Colburn & Bentley. 2v. 18cm. [Cf. #7958, probably the same.] [BM.LC]

*7970. ROSCOE, T: The apparitionist: a fragment. 1826. In C477.

7971. (Der Kampf mit dem Drachen.) The fight with the dragon. Tr. anon. With Retzsch's outlines. L: Boosey 1825. 4. [EC] [Cf. #7955, also the following. Probably Collier's tr.]

*7972. do. 1825. Tr. J. P. Collier. Il. with 16 engr. H. Moses after Retsch [sic]. 31p. text, Ger;Engl. 32cm. [BM.LCO]

7973. do. 1857. Anon. (Tr. Lytton.) Il. Retzsch. Stuttgart: Cotta; NY: Appleton. obl. 4. [NY]

*7974. do. 1873. Collier's tr. L: Low. 16p. of text bound with alternate plates. No Ger. 24 x 31cm. [BM:LCO]

7975. (Der Malteser.) The Maltese: a fragment. Tr. anon. 1883. In #7772.

*7976. (Der Menschenfeind.) The misanthrope. Tr. anon. 1883. In #7772. [Excellent tr.]

Der Neffe als Onkel. Der Parasit. Tr. by S-- from the French of L. B. Picard. Not included.

*7977. (Der Spaziergang.) The walk. Tr. E. P. Arnold-Forster. 1888. In #7817.

*7978. do. Tr. E. A. Bowring. 1851. In #7819.

*7979. do. Tr. Sir J. W. Herschel. L? 1843? Priv. circ. 23p. 14 x 18cm. [On p. 23 is printed: Collingwood. December 13, 1842. Possibly this was sent out to friends as a Christmas gift. Probably pub. not later than 1843.] [BM.LC]

*7980. do. 1847. In C199.

§7981. do. Tr. Lord Lytton. 1844. In #7828.

§7982. do. Tr. J. H. Merivale. 1844. In C412. [Fairly correct, lacks the freshness and strength of the German, says Rea (B32).]

§7983. do. Tr. R: Roscoe. A walk among the linden-trees. 1826. In C477. [Rather poor.]

§7984. (Der Taucher.) The diver. Tr. anon. In Ida Pfeiffer's "Visit to Iceland," pp. 342-46. See #7131.

§7985. do. 1878. Ballads of S--. No. 1. The diver. With notes Rev. F: K. Harford. L: Bickers. viii;71p. 28cm. [BM] [Pref., transl., copious notes. Fair tr.]

DER VERBRECHER AUS VERLORENER EHRE

*7986. ANON. The criminal. 1800? In C157. Tr. by F. [Not excellent.]

7987. ANON. 1818. The criminal from lost honour. In "Brit. ladies mag." 2(1818): 57, etc. (B26)

§7988. ANON. 1837. Christian Wolf: a true story. L: Berger. pp. 97-112. il. 21cm. [Fair tr.] [BPL]

*7989. ANON. 1841. The criminal, in consequence of lost reputation. L: Clements. (Tr. for "The Romancist.") 13p. 22cm. [BM.LC] [Pretty good.]

SCHILLER, F: v--Der Verbrecher
§7990. HOLCRAFT, R: The dishonoured irreclaimable. 1826. In C203.
*7991. OXENFORD, J: The criminal from lost honour. 1844. In C441-2. [Spelling changed to "honor" in #7772.]
*7992. ROSCOE, T: The criminal; or, martyr to lost honour. A true story. 1826. In C477. [Not as good as the foregoing.]
7993. T., C. J. The host of "The sun." 1912. In C518.
†7994. WAPLER, L. The criminal become so from lost [sic] of honour. Augsburgh: Prtd. by J. Rösl. 34p. 17cm. [BM]
[Probably by a German; incorrect. Entire introd. omitted.]

DIE BRAUT VON MESSINA

7995. Sel. Tr. F: Funck. 1853. In C142.
7996. Sel. (75 p.) Tr. C: Hodges. 1836. In C202.
7996a. ANON. Bride of M--. (Ger. and Engl.) München: Franz 1839. 280p. gr. 8. [Heinsius]
7997. ANON. Bride of M--. (Literal tr.) Transl. pub. n.d. 1912-17. 15cm. [AC]
§7998. ALLFREY, EMILY. L: Trübner 1876. vi;110p. 18cm. [BM]
[Blank verse very good, choruses rather poor. Sense is well given.]
§7999. IRVINE, G. L: J:Macrone 1837. vi;172p. 22cm. [BM.LCO]
[Choruses poor, blank verse better; expansive tendency.]
†8000. LODGE, AM. L: Bohn 1841. xvi;136p. 22cm. [BM]
[Rea (B32) says: paraphrase rather than a tr. This version is used in #7764 and subsequent editions of the works.]
†8001. do. 1863. 3d ed. ...with other poems. L: Day. xxxi;168p. 21cm. [BM]
[Includes (pp. 1-14) S--'s essay "On the use of the chorus in tragedy." Also poems: K: Ebert, Grün, W. Müller, Schulze, Uhland, one each, and 3 by S-- in fair tr.]
†8002. PERCIVAL, E: LOCKWOOD. München: G:Franz 1839. 275p. (Ger; Engl.) 21cm. [Incredibly bald and prosy.] [BM]
8003. TOWLER, J. A trag. with choruses. Carlsruhe; Bielefeld 1850. 119p. 8. [Heinsius]
See Mueller, Hm., The bride of Messina, #6507.

8004. (Die Kinder des Hauses.) The children of the house. Tr. anon. 1883. In #7772.
*8005. (Die Huldigung der Künste.) The homage of the arts. Tr. C: T. Brooks. 1847. In C43.
†8006. do. 1861. Tr. C: J. Hempel. In #7768.
*8007. do. 1913-15. Tr. A. I. Coleman. In C154(3).

DIE JUNGFRAU VON ORLEANS

8008. Sel. Tr. anon. 1813. In C91.
8009. Sel. Tr. T: Carlyle. 1825. In #7794. Also 1840. In C56.
8010. Sel. Tr. W. Herbert. 1804. In C198.
8011. Sel. Tr. E. B. Impey. 1841. In C295 (pp. 421-42).
8012. CALVERT, G: H: The maid of O--. Cambridge, Mass: Priv. prtd. Riverside press 1873. 134p. sq. 16. [Calvert bibliog.]
8013. do. 1874. NY: Putnam. 234p. sq. 12. [AC]
[Somewhat revised, according to Calvert bibliog.]
*8014. DRINKWATER-BETHUNE, J. E. L: Priv. prt. 1835. 210p. 21cm.[BM]
[Blank verse very good, but without fem. endings; lyrics poor. Correct. Rea (B32): "It is evident at a first glance that the tr. is a man of genius."]
*8015. do. 1848. In "Specimens of Swedish and Ger. poetry." L: Murray. 8. [LCO]
§8016. EGESTORFF, G: H: C. L: Black & Young 1836. 109p. 22cm. [BM]
[As a native German, he has inadequate command of English.]
§8017. FILMORE, L. L: Griffin 1882. iv;124p. front. (port.) H. Adlard after C. Jaeger. 18cm. [BM]

SCHILLER, F: v.--Die Jungfrau von Orleans
†8018. LUCAS, N. I. Bremen: C:Schünemann; L: Black & Armstrong 1841. xv;168p. 20cm. ["That I have endeavoured to do justice to my author I...aver; but that I have taken great liberties is equally true." Certainly pretty bad.] [BM]
†8019. do. 1845. L: Black. 8. [EC]
§8020. MAXWELL, P. L: Nutt 1889. 96p. 19cm. [BM]
[Contains only the Prolog and Acts I-II.]
§8021. do. 1892. L: Scott. 12. [Complete tr., writes a correspondent.] [EC]
†8022. PEARSON, E. S. Dresden;Lpz: E. Pierson 1887. 158p. 15cm. [UW]
†8023. PETER, W: ...and other poems. Cambridge, Mass: Owen 1843. 229p. 16cm. [Poems by Körner and Schiller.] [LC.BM]
*8024. SALVIN, H. Tr. 1824. In #7757.
[Blank verse is very good, Johanna's song rather poor.]
*8025. SWANWICK, ANNA. Tr. 1843. In C515. [Incomplete: has chiefly "those scenes in which she (Johanna) is introduced."]
*8026. do. 1848? Complete. In #7764.
*8027. do. 1888. In Schiller's dramas. Bohn's shilling series. #7775.
*8028. do. 1899. Phil: McKay. Pocket literal tr. 158p. 16. [LC]
†8029. THOMPSON, H: L: Burns 1845. xxii;146p. 17cm. [The tr. "has thought it advisable to shorten and alter some passages."] [BM.LC]
*8030. TURNER, E. S. and F. J. [ladies]. The maid of O-- and other poems tr. from the German. L: Smith, Elder 1842. 247p. 17cm. [BM]
[More literal than #8814, less poetic. --Has also: Goethe (3), Schiller (6), Stolberg, Uhland (2).]
8031. [Ad.] Anon. Joan of Arc: a trag. in 5 acts. After...S--. n.i. 18--. 15 leaves fol. MS. [NY]
[With mus. score. Prompter's copy of an abr. acting version, enclosing a program of the performance at Phil. in 1865.]
8032. [Ad.] Viereck, G: S. The maid of O--. Girard, Kan: Haldeman-Julius n.d. Big blue books, 5 x 8 in., 128p. [Publisher's catalog.]

DIE RÄUBER

8033. Sel. Tr. T: Carlyle. 1840. In C56.
†8034. ANON. The robbers. Perth. 1800. [Cited in #7766 by H: Bohn, who says it is a piracy of Tytler's tr., and a worse version.]
*8035. BOHN, H: G. Tr. 1849. In #7764, reprinted in subsequent editions. [Probably the best tr. we have. Willoughby (B49) states, however, that some of the "exceptionable passages" were omitted.]
†8038. CRAVEN, KEPPEL. Tr. and altered from the Ger. With a pref., prologue, and epilogue...by...the margravine of Anspach (i.e., Lady Craven). As performed at Brandenburgh-house theater 1798. L: Prtd. for Wigstead & Hooper 1799. 104p. 21cm. [Made by Lady Craven's son from Tytler's tr. Severely pruned, omitting all the "jacobinical speeches that abound in the original." See B49.] [BM]
8039. DICKS, J. L: J:Dicks. 1885. 19p. 12. [BM]
8040. LEWIS, M. G. 1794. [This entry derives from Max Rentsch, "M.G. Lewis," Lpz: 1902, p. 12: "Er übersetzte 'Die Räuber' von Schiller unter dem Titel 'The robbers'..." On the other hand, the statement is challenged by Railo (B31), p. 342.]
†8041. MANN, C. W. "College mag.," 1842. (B49) [Willoughby (B49) says his knowledge of German was inadequate, the style wooden.]
†8042. do. 1889. In #7777
§8043. RENDER, W: L: Symonds 1799. 195p. 22cm. [BM]
[Front. Neagle after Thurston. Based on stage edition. Rather good, but in a pinch he reveals his ignorance of the original. He makes free use of Tytler's tr. Willoughby (B49) says he is pedantic, literal, sometimes inaccurate, and prone to bowdlerize.]
§8044. THOMPSON, B: Tr. 1800. 99p. Front. Raimbach after Thurston. 21cm. In C535. [Willoughby (B49) says T. was the most successful and accurate of early successors to Tytler, whose version he

SCHILLER, F: v.
probably used. Some lines from "Schauspiel" were included. For my doubts about Thompson, see note to C535.]
§8045. do. 1802. In "Select plays," vol. 2. Balto. 16. [BPL]
[Reprint of the foregoing.]
§8046. TYTLER, Ax. F., Lord Woodhouselee. L: Robinsons 1792. xviii;220p. 21cm.[Based on stage ed. Tr. is fairly good, but shows errors.][BM]
§8047. do. 1792. Dublin. (B49)
§8048. do. 1793. Anon. NY: Prtd. by S: Campbell. 120p. 8. [LC]
[Reprint of #8046.]
§8049. do. 1795. 2d ed. Corr. and impr. L: Robinsons. xvi;144p. 20cm.[BM]
[Willoughby (B49) finds this tr. has at least 75 bad errors, but says it is on the whole an adequate and literary rendering of the stage version. Subsequent trs. borrowed largely from it.]
§8050. do. 1795. 2d ed. Dublin. (B49)
§8051. do. 1795. 2d Amer. ed., as ad. for representation by Mr. Marriott, and performed...NY. The passages marked with inverted commas were omitted, and those included with crotchets added, in the performance. NY: Prtd. and sold by S: Campbell. 102p. 12. (B6a) [Available: AAS. 2d ed. doubtless refers to #8048.]
§8052. do. 1797. 3d ed. L: Robinsons. (B49)
§8053. do. 1797. 3d ed. Dublin. (B49)
§8054. do. 1800. 4th ed. corr. and impr. L: Robinsons. xxii;176p. front. R. Scott after I. Foulis. 21cm. [BM.NY]
[Contains a challenge to Render "to point out those scenes and characters which he asserts to be omitted."]
§8055. do. 1808. Anon. NY: Longworth. 108p. 24.[This is not Thompson's tr., but based on Tytler, says Willoughby (B49)] [NY]
§8056. do. 1821. Anon. Balto. J. Robinson. 103p. 12. (B29)
[Willoughby (B49) says this also is based on Tytler.]
§8057. do. 1854. NY: French n.d. 57p. 12. [Abr. as acted at the Bowery theatre in 1853. Text is based on Tytler, says Willoughby (B49).] [NY]
§8058. do. 1854. [same] NY;Balto: Taylor. 57p. 16. [LCO]
§8059. do. 185- . [same] In "Dick's standard plays," no. 332. 19p. 18cm. [Prtd. in double cols. One il. as heading.] [BM]
8060. [Ad.] ANON. 1836. The brigands: a serious opera in three acts by Mercadante, as represented...June 1836. Libr. Ital. and Engl. L: Brettell. 93p. 16cm. [BM]
8061. [Ad.] GANDY, E. LORENZO. The outcast son: a tragic drama, founded on...L: Simpkin & M. 1823. 103p. 21cm. [BM]
8062. [Ad.] HOLMAN, J. G. The red-cross knights: a play in 5 acts. Founded on...L: Cawthorn 1799. 68p. 8. [Willoughby (B49) says that whole scenes were lifted bodily from Tytler's tr.] [BM]

DIE VERSCHWOERUNG DES FIESKO ZU GENUA

†8063. ANON. Fiesco; or, the conspiracy of Genoa. A tragedy. L: Saunders & O; Ed: Bell & Bradfute 1841. 140p. 22cm. [BM]
[H: Bohn in #7766 condemns it; Rea praises it. Bohn is right, and Rea's judgment proves either ignorance or carelessness. This tr. knows no German.]
*8064. BOHN, H: G. Tr. 1849. In #7764, reprinted in subsequent eds. [Founded on Noehden and Stoddart, but thoroughly revised.]
†8065. D'AGUILAR, SIR G. C. Fiesko... Dublin: Milliken; L: Longmans 1832. 8. [Rea (B32) says: Prose and blank verse mingled; full of errors and interpolations.] [BM]
†8066. NOEHDEN, G. H. and J. STODDART. L: Johnson 1796. 228p. 8. [Very faulty.] [BM.NY]
§8067. do. 1802. In "Select plays," vol. 2. Balto: 12. [BPL]
†8068. REINBECK, DR. Tr. ca. 1824. (B32, p. 31)
8069. Ad. ANON. Fiesko; or, the revolt of Genoa. An histor. play in

SCHILLER, F: v.--Die Verschwoerung
5 acts. Altered from S--. L: Wright 1850. 8. [BM]
[EC ascribes this to Planché.]

DON CARLOS

8070. Sel. Tr. T: Carlyle. 1825. In #7794.
8071. Sel. Tr. F: Funck. 1853. In C142.
8072. ANON. 1795. (B32, p. 40.)
[Lieder (B23) says this tr. is of "doubtful authenticity."]
?8073. ANON. 1822. Tr. and rendered into verse. L: Reynolds. xxiii; 148p. 22cm. ["I have found it necessary to retrench one half...to leave out the underplot, make many changes, some additions, and to compose an entirely new catastrophe. In short, I have adapted it to the Engl. stage." The paging is ident. with that of the Paris ed. by Simon Sabba, see below.] [BM]
8074. ANON. 1912-17. Literal tr. Translation pub. n.d. 15cm. [AC]
*8075. BOYLAN, R. D. Tr. 1848, reprinted in subsequent eds.
[Both Rea (B32) and Lieder (B23) call this the best Engl. version.]
*8076. BRUCE, J: W. Mannheim: Schwan & Goetz; L: Black & Armstrong 1837. 311p.12. [BM.NY]
*8076a. do. 1843. [same] 2d ed. Mannheim. 12. [EC (Appendix)]
8077. CALVERT, G: H: Balto: W: & Js. Neal 1834. 223p. 16.
[Cited in bibliog. of the works of Calvert. Newport, R. I. 1900.]
§8078. COTTRELL, C. H. L: Longmans 1843. 265p. 8. [BM.LCO]
[Correct; poor verse. EC has: L: Smith, Elder 1843.]
§8079. do. 1844. [same] 2d ed. [BM.LCO]
8080. DUNLAP, W: (Adapted.) NY: 1799. (B23)
§8081. EGAN, T. S. L: Williams & N. 1867. 288p. 17cm. [Introd. to p. 8. Rea (B32) says it is faithful, wanting in inspiration.] [BM]
§8082. NOEHDEN, G. H. and J. STODDART. L: Miller 1798. 327p. 8. [BM]
[Fairly good prose tr.]
?8083. SABBA, SIMON. Tr. and altered...and ad. for the Engl. stage. Paris. 1821. 148p. 8. (B8)
[Taken from the prose stage version of 1808. Cf. #8073.]
†8084. SYMONDS (?; see B23). 3d ed. L: Prtd. for Richardson 1798. 320p. 23cm. [Prose tr. of 1st Ger. ed. Abridges, slurs over difficulties, and mistranslates.] [BM.LC]
8085. TAYLOR, BAYARD. Unpub. MS. (B23)
†8086. THOMPSON, B: Don Carlos, infant of Spain. Tr. 1801. 172p. [Front. by J. Neagle after T. Thurston. 21cm. In C535. Prose, neither close nor accurate.]
§8087. TOWLER, I. Carlsruhe: Nöldeke 1843. iv;267p. 17cm. [BM]
[Rea (B32) says this is tolerably faithful, but the style is careless and unpoetical.]
§8088. do. 1844. L: Williams & N. 12. [EC]
§8089. WOOD, AND. Tr. into Engl. blank verse. Ed: Nimmo 1873. xxx; 291p. 19cm. [Fairly good.] [BM]
8090. [Ad.] WILLIAMS, ESPY. Don Carlos: an histor. play in 4 acts. Founded on... NY: 190-. 56 leaves 4. Tw. [NY]
§8091. (Eine grossmütige Handlung aus der neuesten Geschichte.) Fraternal magnanimity. Tr. T: Roscoe. 1826. In C477.
8092. do. 189- . [same?] In C156.
8093. (Geschichte des Abfalls Der vereinigten Niederlande.) The revolt of the Netherlands, books I-V. The Ger. text with a literal word for word tr. by Heinrich Apel. L: Cornish 1860. 222p. 14cm. [Ger. and Engl. words form one continuous text, very odd looking and very confusing.] [BM]
8094. do. 1880. [same] Cornish. [EC]
*8095. do. Eastwick, E. B. Hist. of the defection of the United Netherlands from the Span. empire. Frankfort on the Main: B: Krebs

SCHILLER, F: v.--Geschichte des Abfalls...
1844. 532p. 17cm. [BM]
*8096. do. do. 1846. Revolt of the United Netherlands. Tr. (i.e., revised from Eastwick) by A. J. W. Morrison. 1846. In #7764.
*8097. do. do. 1897. Revised by L. Dora Schmitz. In #7779.
§8098. do. Horne, T: Hist. of the rise and progress of the Belgian republic, until the revolution under Philip II. L: Coxhead 1807. 238p. 18cm. [Not quite all of S--'s first book is here given. Tr. is expansive. This tr. was probably announced for pub. in 1805; see "Brit. Crit." 30(1807):457. (B26)] [BM]
*8099. do. Moir, G: Tr. 1828. In #7758.
8100. (Geschichte des dreissigjährigen Krieges.) Hist. of the thirty years' war. Tr. anon. NY: Harper n.d. (before 1852) [AC] [Probably from #7764.]
8101. do. Anon. 1905. NY: Burt. 12. [Probably from the Bohn ed.] [AC]
8102. do. Anon. 1912-17. Literal tr. Transl. pub. n.d. 15cm. [AC]
§8103. do. Blaquiere, Capt. Pref. by Wieland. L: Miller 1799. 2v. xxviii;305; 351p. 22cm. [BM.LC] [Front. (port.) of S-- by A. Smith after Graff; 16 other ports. in vol. 1. 9 pl., mostly ports., in vol. 2.]
§8104. do. do. 1842. Frankfort o. M. 18. (B8)
§8105. do. Duncan, J. M. L: Simpkin 1828. 2v. 224; 260p. 22cm. [BM]
8106. do. Martin, Jas. Key to German. Hist...book I. Construed and literally tr. L: Cornish 1873. 104; 104p. Ger;Engl. 14cm. [Printed in irreg. lines, so that orig. and tr. follow line for line. The tr. is probably as good as a lit. tr. can be made.] [BM]
*8107. do. Morrison, A. J. W. Tr. 1846. In #7764, reprinted in subsequent eds.]
*8108. do. do. 1846. NY: Harper. iv;370p. 16. (B29)
*8109. do. do. 1913-15. Last campaigns of Gustavus Adolphus. In C154(3).

KABALE UND LIEBE

*8110. BOHN, H: G. Love and intrigue. Tr. 1849. In #7764, reprinted in subsequent eds. [Contains not a few errors.]
†8111. LEWIS, M. G. The minister: a tragedy in 5 acts. L: J.Bell 1797. 220p. 21cm. [Paraphrase; omission on every page, also much amplification and distortion.] [UW]
†8112. do. 1798. [same] 2d ed. [BM]
†8113. do. 1813. The harper's daughter; or, love and ambition. Tr. by M. G. Lewis...and now pub. with consid. alterations, as performed (in 1803) at the Phil. and Balto. theatres. Phil: Carey. 76p. 15cm. [LCO.BM]
8114. PAYNE, J: H. Love and intrigue. Tr. ca. 1817-20. 161p. 4. MS. [He knew little German.] [LCO]
†8115. TIMÄUS, J. J. B. Cabal and love. L: Boosey 1795. 119p. 20cm. [BM ascribes this to P. Colombine; Goedeke (B8) and recently Willoughby (B49) assign it as here. --The tr. seems to me impossible, despite Willoughby's defence.] [BM.LC]
8116. do? 1795. Cabal and love. Phil: (B6a)
†8117. do. 1796. L;Lpz: Boosey & Reinicke. 110p. 18cm. [BM]
†8118. do. 1797. 2d ed. L: Boosey. [Identical with #8115.] [BM]
†8119. do. 1802. reprint. In "Select plays," vol. 2. Balto. 12.[BPL]
*8120. WILKINSON, T: C. L: Sonnenschein 1884. 155p. 16cm. [BM] [I find some faults in it, but the general style is excellent.]
8121. [Ad.] 1851. Power and principle: a drama in 3 acts. Founded on ... by Morris Barnett. L: Lacy. 31p. 17cm. [Prompter's copy. A play of this title was performed in L. in 1850. Main lines as in Schiller, but the dénouement is altered. See B32.] [BM.NY]
8122. [Ad.] Clarke, J: B. Ravenna; or, Italian love. A tragedy in 5 acts. [Produced at Covent Garden in 1824. The plot is not much altered. Blank verse.] [BM]

SCHILLER, F: v.--Kabale und Liebe

8123.[Ad.] Cammarano, Salvadore. Luisa Miller: tragic opera in 3 acts by G. Verdi. Text after S--. Tr. anon. Libr. Engl. Music of the principal airs. L: Davidson 1858. 30p. 24cm. [BMM]

8124. [same] 1860? Written and ad. by C: Jefferys. Libr. Engl. L: Theatre royal. 34p. 17cm. [BM]
[Quite free except for rhymed choruses and arias; these fairly done.]

8125. [same as the foregoing] 1871? Melbourne: Shaw, Harnett. 34p. 17cm. [BM]

8126. [same] 1874. Tr. anon. Libr. Ital;Engl. L: Prtd. by G. Stuart. iv;65p. 18cm.[The Engl. follows the Italian fairly closely, but without rhyme or meter.] [BM]

8127. [same] 1874. Jefferys' tr. Vocal score. L: C.Jefferys. 241p. 28cm. [BMM]

MARIA STUART

8128. Sel. ANON. ca. 1801. In C157(2).

8129. Sel. ANON. 1813. In C91.

8130. ANON. 1833. Mary Stuart. L: Longmans. 8. [EC]

8130a. ANON. 1843. Mary Stuart: a tragedy. See "Monthly Rev." 162 (1843):182. (B27)

8131. ANON. 1912-17. (Literal tr.) Transl. pub. n.d. 15cm. [AC]
[Probably Mellish's tr.; cf. #8136-7.]

*8132. MELLISH, JS. C: L: Prtd. by G. Auld for Cotta in Tubingen [sic] 1801. xvi;224p. 21cm. [Tr. from first MS copy, hence does not wholly agree with printed eds.] [BM.NY]

*8133. do. 1848? In #7764, reprinted in subsequent eds. Revised for this ed.

8134. do. 1870.[Abr.] As performed by Mme. Marie Seebach. NY. 52p. 8. [LCO]

*8135. do. 1888. Bohn's shilling series. In #7775.

*8136. do. 1898. Phil: Mckay. Pocket literal tr. 165p. 16. [NY]

*8137. do. 1902? NY: Hinds & N. Handy literal tr. 122p. 16. [NY]

†8138. PEARSON, E. S. Dresden;Lpz: E. Pierson 1885? 15cm. [UW]

†8139. PERCIVAL, E. L. Munich. no.pub. 1839. 209p. Ger;Engl. 22cm. [Here I agree with Rea (B32), who says the tr. has not the slightest notion of verse. --The tr. ends with III, 1.] [BM]

†8140. PETER, W: Phil: Perkins 1840. New ed. 255p. 16. [NY]

†8141. do. 1841. [same] With (notes and) other versions of some of his best poems, i.e.,"chiefly attempted paraphrases or imitations." Heidelberg: Winter; L: Ridgway. 262p. 17cm.[5 poems after S--.][BM]

*8142. SALVIN, H: 1824. In #7757.

†8143. TRELAWNY, ANNE, afterwards GIBBONS. Devonport: Prtd. by W. Byers 1838. 162p. 17cm. [Rea (B32) says she is mostly faithful and poetical; I call the tr. neither faithful nor poetical.] [BM]

†8144. do. 1838. [same] L: Schloss. [Identical,with new t.p.] [BM]

§8145. WHITE, L. L: K.Paul 1882. 431p. Ger;Engl. 19cm. [Here I find Rea too severe: he says it is dull and prosaic. Really, the tr. is faithful, and the verse not bad.] [BM]

8146. [Ad.] Tr. (or rather ad.) by Mrs. Fanny K. Butler in her "Plays." L: Longmans, etc. 1863. pp. 1-423. 20cm. [Abridged acting version. Names and action changed, e.g., Eliz. is omitted!][BM.NY]

8147. [Ad.] MAFFEI, ANDRÉ, expressly for Mme. Ristori. Tr. T: Williams. L: Francis 1856. 139p. Ital;Engl. 18cm. [Prose tr. of Italian verse, much condensed from S--.] [BM]

8148. [same] 1866. NY: Sanford, Harroun. 41p. 8. [LCO]

8149. [Ad.] WINGFIELD, LEWIS...as performed by Mme. Helene Modjeska. Indianap: Hasselman-Journal co. 1883. 57p. 12. [This abridges #8133. Last act remodelled to conform more to history.] [NY]

8150. [same] 1904. Ed. from the prompt book of Mme. Mojeska [sic] by M.A. Bost: Baker. 72p. 19cm. [LC]
[The present version is substantially the "Wingfield version."]

SCHILLER, F: v.

8151. (Pegasus im Joche.) P-- in the yoke. Tr. anon. Lytton's tr. Il. M. Retzsch. Stuttgart: Cotta; NY: Appleton, also Radde 1857. 2p. 2 leaves fol. [NY]

§8152. (Ritter Toggenburg.) The knight of T--. Tr. anon. (By W: Whewell.) Prtd. for sale at the Shelford bazaar. Shelford: 1842. 9 unnumb. leaves prtd. on one side. 24cm. [BM.LC]

8153. do. 1916. The knight of Toggenberg. Tr. anon. Music by W. W. Gilchrist. Bost: Ditson. [AC]

*8154. (Spiel des Schicksals.) The sport of destiny. Tr. T: Roscoe. 1826. In C477.

8155. do. 1884. Tr. anon. In #7773.

8156. do. ca. 1900. [same?] In #7779.

Turandot. Tr. by S-- from Gozzi. Not included

8157. (Ueber den Gebrauch des Chors in der Tragödie.) On the use of chorus in tragedy. Tr. Am. Lodge. 1863. In #8001. Also in #7779. Also in C154(3).

8158. (Ueber die ästhetische Erziehung des Menschen.) Letter upon the aesthet. educ. of man. Tr. anon. 1910. In C119; C370. [Taken from #7771.]

*8159. (Ueber naive und sentimentalische Dichtung.) Upon naive and sentimental poetry. Tr. anon. 1849. In C194.

*8160. do. 1900. Tr. anon. In C118. [Probably from C194.]

WALLENSTEIN[1]

8161. Sel. ANON. 1839. In C55.

8162. Sel. ANSTER, J: 1864. In C7.

*8163. Sel. CARLYLE, T: 1825. In #7794.

8164. Sel. COLERIDGE, S. T. 1903. In C18.

8165. Sel. FUNCK, F: 1853. In C142.

8166. Sel. W(ILL?), P(ETER). 1800. In C157(1).

8167. ANON. (P) The Piccolominis: a drama in 5 acts. L: Chapple 1805. See "Brit. Crit." 25(1804):684. (B26) [Probably Coleridge's tr.]

†8168. ANON. (L) "Dublin univ. mag." 8(1836). [Rea (B32) says very faulty.]

8169. ANON. (L,P,T) W--'s camp, P--, and death of W--. (Literal tr.) Transl. pub. n.d. 1912-17. 15cm. [LC]

†8170. CHURCHILL, JAS. (L) W--'s camp. "Fraser's mag." 1846. [Rea (B32) says: very mediocre, dull, prosy. Frequently issued with Coleridge's tr.]

†8171. do. 1847? [same] In #7764 and subsequent eds.

†8172. do. 1895. [same] W--'s camp and Piccolomini (probably by Coleridge). L: Bell. 8. [EC]

†8173. do. 1903. [same] In C18.

*8174. COLERIDGE, S: T. (P) L: Longman & Rees 1800. 214p. 8. [BM] [Some omissions and errors. Cf. #8178.]

*8175. do. 1800. (T) L: Longman & Rees. 157p. 8. [BM] [Likewise has some omissions and errors.]

*8176. do. 1805. (P) NY: Longworth. 173p. 16. (B48)

*8177. do. 1842. (P,T) Tragedies: The Piccolomini, etc. L: W.Smith. 8. [EC]

*8178. do. 1847? (P,T) In #7764 and subsequent eds. [Carefully revised, this is the best Engl. version.]

*8179. do. 1852. (P,T) In C--'s sel. poet. works. L: Bohn. pp. 111-280, 281-392. 14cm. [BM] [Probably does not contain the revisions of the foregoing.]

*8180. do. 1853. (P,T) In "Universal lib." vol. 1. L: Ingram, Cooke. pp. 297-387 or viii;1-83. front. 23cm. [BM]

[1] In the following entries, L, P, and T, stand, respectively, for Lager, Piccolomini, and Tod.

SCHILLER, F: v.--Wallenstein.
*8181. do. 1860. (P,T) [same as #8177] New ed. L: Griffin. [EC]
*8182. do. 1866. (P,T) In "Masterpieces of for. lit." (C403) L: C:Griffin. pp. 1-97. [Same paging and get-up as #8180.] [BM]
*8183. do. 1889. (P,T) In #7776.
*8184. do. 1895. (P) In #8172.
*8185. do. 1913-15. (T) In C154(3).
§8186. GOWER, LORD FIS. (L) The camp of W-- (and orig. poems). L: Murray 1830. 167p. 17cm. [Pretty good in spirit, not always correct; grotesque humor well conveyed. One add. poem by S--.][BM]
*8187. HUNTER, J. A. W. (LP,T) L: K.Paul 1885. lxvii;421p. 19cm. [BM] [Very superior tr.; "Larger" admirably done.]
§8188. LOCKHART, C: G. N. (P,T) L: Blackwood 1887. xviii;407p. 17cm. [Correct, lacks interest.] [BM]
§8189. MARTIN, SIR TD. (L) In his "Madonna pia," and three other dramas. Ed: Blackwood 1894. pp. 161-214. 20cm. [BM] [I do not like it much.]
*8190. MOIR, G: (P,T) Ed;L: Simpkin 1827. 2v. xxviii;217; 307p. 18cm. [Rea's severity seems to me unjustified; the tr. is in fact very good, though not equal to Hunter's.] [BM]
8191. do. 1830? (L) no pub. n.d. 56p. Pmph. [Lib. of Rb. Priebsch.] [Prob. pub. about 1830, as extracts were printed in "For. Quart. R." some months before Gower's tr. appeared.]
§8192. do. 1837. (L) Bost: Munroe. 142p. 12. [LCO]
8193. do. 1845. (P,T) L: Simpkin. 2v. 8. [EC] [Very likely includes the "Lager" also.]
8194. PEARSON, E. S. (L,P,T) Dresden: 1886. (B32)
†8195. THORNTON, E: (L) Frankfort on the Main. Prtd. by Reinhold Baist. 1854. 67p. 15cm. [No rhyme; prosaic stuff.] [BM]
§8196. WALKINGTON, W. R. (P) L: Smith & Elder 1862. 120p. 8. [BM]
†8197. WIRGMANN, T. (L) L: Nutt 1871. viii;103p. Ger;Engl. 18cm.[BM] [S--'s terse speech is expanded into a prosy chatter.]
8198. (Warbeck.) W--: fragment. Tr. anon. 1861. In #7768.
8199. (Was kann eine gute stehende Schaubühne eigentlich wirken?) What are the particular effects of the stage? An essay. Tr. anon. In "Monthly Mirror" 8(1799):357 and 9(1800):42. (B26)

WILHELM TELL

8200. Sel. ANON. 1813. In C91.
8201. Sel. ANON. 1836. In "Carlton Chronicle," 1836, p. 137. (B27)
*8202. Sel. CARLYLE, T: 1825. In #7794.
8203. Sel. FUNCK, F: 1853. In C142.
†8204. Sel. SCHAFER, JS. The Swiss patriots: a scene (Melchthal scene from Act I) from S--. Valley City, N. D: 1898. 15p. S. [UW]
§8205. ANON. 1829. L: Bull 1829. viii;212p. 21cm. [BM]
8206. ANON. 184- . [Same] L: Lumley n.d. (B46)
§8207. BANFIELD, T: C. W-- T--: a dramatic poem. L: Black, Y. & Y. 1831. v;166p. 18cm. [Fair tr.] [BM]
8208. BRAUNFELS, LUDWIG. Bonn. 1841. (B8) [See following entries.]
8209. do. 1847. Ger;Engl. L: Williams & Norgate. 8. [EC]
8210. do. and ARTHUR C. WHITE. Ger. text with an interlinear tr., etc. 2d ed. rev. and impr. L: Williams & N. 1859. 19cm. [BM] [Purely interlinear tr. without aesthetic value.]
*8211. BROOKS, C: T. Providence, R.I: Cranston 1838. 120p. 12. [LC]
*8212. do. 1842. [same] Bost: Munroe. [AC]
§8213. CAMPBELL, D. C. Tr. with an introd. essay. L: Williams & N. 1878. lxi;173p. 19cm. [Seems to me pretty poor.] [BM]
†8214. CARTWRIGHT, J: L:Nutt 1869. vii;180p. 19cm. [BM] [Has little poetic talent or knowledge of German.]
8215. DES VOEUX, C: ? In "Kaleidoscope" 7(1827):225, etc. (B26)
*8216. LATHAM, A. G. L: Dent 1904. 303p. front. (port.) 15cm. [BM]

SCHILLER, F: v.--Wilhelm Tell
[Mostly quite good, some bad lapses. --AC has: NY: Macmillan. Temple classics.]
8217. MCMURRY, C: A. Tr. and ad. to school use. NY;Bost: Silver, Burdett 1902. 120p. il. 18cm. [LC]
*8218. MARTIN, SIR TD. 1847. In #7764.
[Excellent tr., the only really good version available in Engl.]
*8219. do. 1889. In #7776.
*8220. do. 1901. In C409.
*8221. do. 1910. In C72.
*8222. do. 1913-15. In C154(3).
*8223. do. 1916. In C408.
†8224. MASSIE, E: Oxf: Clarendon; NY: Macmillan 1878. 343p. Ger; Engl. 17cm. [BM]
§8225. MAXWELL, P. L: Scott 1893. xxvi;214p. 17cm. [Fair tr.] [BM]
†8226. PEARSON, E. S. Dresden; Lpz: E. Pierson 1885. 15cm. [UW]
†8227. PETER, W: Heidelberg. Winter 1839. viii;200p. 18cm. [BM.NY]
†8228. do. 1840. W: T-- and other poems. New ed. Phil: Perkins. 234p. 24. (B29)
†8229. do. 1851. Phil. (B8)
†8230. do. 1856. [same as #8227] Lucerne: Kaiser. [NY]
†8231. do. 1867. [same] An hist. play...with notes and il. 2d ed. Lucerne. Prtd. for Gebhardt. viii;200p. 18cm. [BM]
†8232. do. 1874. [same as #8230?] Lucerne. (B8)
§8233. do. 1915. 5th ed. rev. and cor. by T: Johnson. Lucerne: O: Wicke. vii;185p. 17cm. [Still not better than fair.] [BM]
8234. ROBINSON, S: L: Hurst 1825. 8. [EC]
§8235. do. 1834. L: 12. [See note to #8236.] [NY]
§8236. do. 1892. L: Routledge. 180p. 19cm. [BM]
[Rea (B32) overrates this tr., which is only fair in quality.]
§8237. TALBOT, R. L: Prtd. by Plummer & Brewis 1829. xii;180p. 21cm. [BM]
[Blank verse fair to good, lyrics poor. "A few copies only will be printed."]
†8238. TARKARI. L: Hamilton; Ed: Menzies 1879. 207p. 16cm. [BM]
[Tr. knows neither Ger. nor Engl.]
§8239. THOMPSON, H: L: Burns 1845. 135p. 17cm. [LC]
[Blank verse so-so; lyrics poor.]

*8240. (Xenien.) Xenions. Tr. Pl. Carus. See Goethe, #3028.

LETTERS

Correspondence with Goethe, #3034.
§8241. Corr. with Körner, comprising sketches and anecdotes of Goethe, the Schlegels, Wieland, and other contemp. With biogr. sketches and notes. Tr. Leonard Simpson. L: Bentley 1849. 3v. 19cm. [Ports. of S--, Goethe, and W: v. Humboldt.] [BM]
8242. Letters...prior to his marriage. (1782-90) Tr. J. L. Weisse. Bost: Dickinson 1841. 134p. 12. [NY]

BIOGRAPHY

See Düntzer, H., Life of S--, #1274.
See Humboldt, W: v., S-- and the progress of his intellectual devel., #4699.
See Kühnemann, E., S--, #5489.
See Mühlbach, Lu., Goethe and S--, #6419.
See Palleske, El., S--'s life and works, #7012.
See Scherr, J:s, S-- and his times, #7736.
See Steffens, H:, Reminisc. of S--, in his Story of my career, #9022.

SCHILLINGS, K: G: 1865- .
*8243. (In Afrikas Wildkammern als Forscher und Jäger.) In wildest

SCHILLINGS, K: G: In Afrikas Wildkammern--
Afrika. Tr. F: Whyte. L: Hutchinson 1907. 2v. xiv; (318); 716p. il. 24cm. [BM]
*8244. do. 1907. [same] NY;L: Harpers. xvi;716p. il. 24cm. [LC]
*8245. (Mit Blitzlicht und Büchse.) With flashlight and rifle. Tr. F: Whyte. Introd. Sir H. H. Johnston. L: Hutchinson 1906 (1905). 2v. xxvii;(376); 782p. il. 24cm. [BM]
8246. do. 1905. Tr. and abr. by H: Zick. NY: Harper. xii;420p. il. 23cm. [LC]
*8247. do. 1906. [same as #8245] 2d and pop. ed. Hutchinson. 814p. il. 8. [EC]

SCHILLINGS, Max, 1868- . Mona Lisa. Opera. See Dovsky, B.

SCHILTBERGER, Hs. 1380- . (death date unknown).
*8248. (Reisen des J:s S-- aus München in Europa, Asia und Afrika... 1394-1427.) The bondage and travels of J. S., a native of Bavaria, ...Tr. Commander J. B. Telfer. L: Prtd. for Hakluyt Soc. 1879. xxxii;263p. 21cm. [BM.LC]

SCHIMMER, K: A: 1800-63.
8249. (Wiens Belagerung durch die Türken.) The sieges of Vienna by the Turks. From...S-- and other sources. Borrowed and tr. the Earl of Ellesmere. L: Murray 1847. iv;172p. 17cm. [BM.LC]

"SCHINDERHANNES" (i.e., J: Bueckler or Bickler, fl. 1783-1803).
8249a. S--, the robber of the Rhine. Tr. anon. (1852-6.) Phil: Perry n.d. [Perhaps a tr. of "Der berühmte Räuberhauptmann Schinderhannes" (novel) by Ig. Fd. Arnold, ca, 1800.] [AC]

SCHINDLER, An. Fx. 1796-1864.
*8250. Life of Beethoven, includ. his corr. with his friends, and H. Döring's Life and characteristics. Ed. I. Moscheles. Tr. anon. L: Colburn 1841. 2v. in one. xxvi;298, 387p. 19cm. [BM.LC] [Some music.]
*8251. do. 1870. [same] Bost: Ditson n.d. 390p. 12. [AC]

SCHIRMACHER, Kaethe, 1865- .
*8252. (Die moderne Frauenbewegung.) The mod. woman's rights movement: a histor. survey. Tr. from 2d Ger. ed. C. C. Eckhardt. L;NY: Macmillan 1912. xvi;280p. 19cm. [BM.LC]

SCHLECHTA VON WSCHEHRD, Fz. Baron, 1796-1875. Sel. in C137a.

SCHLEGEL, A: and F: Sel. in C12;17;40;91;101;133;140;142;166;193; 194*;295;366*;461;469.
See Schiller, Corr. with Koerner, etc., #8241.

SCHLEGEL, A: W: v., 1767-1845.
*8253. (Ueber dramatische Kunst und Literatur.) A course of lect. on dram. art and lit. Tr. J: Black. L: Prtd. for Baldwin, Cradock & Joy 1815. 2v. 21cm. [BM.LC]
*8254. do. 1840. [same] 2d ed. Introd. by R. H. Horne. L: J.Templeman. 2v. xxxi;400;404p. 12. [BM]
*8255. do. 1845. [same] Rev. accord. to the last Ger. ed. by J. W. Morrison. L: Bohn. 535p. 18cm. [BM.LC]
8256. do. 184- . [same?] Phil: Hogan & Thompson n.d. [AC]
*8257. do. 1886. 2d ed. Rev. by Morrison. L: Bell. 535p. 19cm. [LC]
*8258. do. 1902. [same] [LC]

SCHLEGEL, J: Ad. 1721-93. Sel. in C244.

SCHLEGEL, J: Els. 1719-49. Sel. in C391;393.

SCHLEGEL, (K: W:) F: v. 1772-1829.
8259. [Coll.] The aesthet. and misc. works of F: v. S--. Tr. Ellen J. Millington. L: Bohn 1849. xxiii;533p. 18cm. [BM.LC]

SCHLEGEL, (K: W:) F: v.
[Style is inadequate. --Letters on Christian art; An essay on the romance-poetry of the middle ages and on Shakspere; On the limits of the beautiful; On the lang. and wisdom of the Indians.]
§8260. [Coll.] 1889. [same] L: Bell. [LC]
*8261. (Geschichte der alten und neuen Literatur.) Lect. on the hist. of lit. ancient and mod. Tr. J: G. Lockhart. Ed: Blackwood 1818. 2v. 346; 310p. 21cm. [BM.LC]
[LCO has: Phil: Dobson 1818. 2v. 346; 130p. 8.]
*8262. do. 1841. [same] New ed. viii;430p. 18cm. [BM]
8263. do. 184- ? [same?] Moss n.d. [AC]
8264. do. 1846. New ed. Ed;L: Blackwood. viii;423p. 17cm. [BM]
*8265. do. 1846. [same as #8262] L: Bohn. 430p. 18cm. [BM]
8266. do. 1853. With questions by J: Frost. Moss. 12. [AC]
*8267. do. 1859. L: Bohn. xii;420p. 18cm. [BM]
8268. do. 1861. New ed. L: Bohn. 8. [EC]
*8269. do. 1865. [same as #8267] L: Bell & D. 420p. 18cm. [LC]
*8270. do. 1871. [same] L: Bell & D. [LC]
*8271. do. 1876. [same] L: Bell. [LC]
*8272. do. 1896. [same] L: Bell. 420p. [LC]
§8273. (Lucinde.) Lucinda. Tr. P. B. Thomas. 1913-15. In C154(4). [Errors.]
*8274. (Philosophie der Geschichte.) The philos. of hist. Tr. Jas. B. Robertson. L: Saunders & O. 1835. 2v. lxxxvi;359; 336p. 22cm. [Vol. 1 has memoir.] [BM.LC]
*8275. do. 1841. [same] NY: Appleton. 2v. 19cm. [LC]
*8276. do. 1846. [same] L: Bohn. xii;498p. front. (port.) 18cm. [BM]
*8277. do. 1888. [same] 7th rev. ed. L: Bell. 498p. 19cm. [LC]
§8278. (Philosophie des Lebens.) The philos. of life and philos. of lang... lect... Tr. A. J. W. Morrison. L: Bohn 1847. 567p. 18cm. [LC]
8279. do. 1852-55. [same] NY: Harper. n.d. [AC]
*8280. (Ueber die neuere Geschichte.) A course of lect. on mod. hist...hist. essays on the beginning of our history. Tr. L. Purcell and R. H. Whitelock. L: Bohn 1849. 423p. 18cm. [BM.LC]
[LCO has: L: 1847.]

SCHLEIDEN, Mt. Jk. 1804-81.
*8281. (Die Bedeutung der Juden für Erhaltung und Wiederbelebung der Wissenschaften.) The importance of the Jews for the preservation and revival of learning during the middle ages. Tr. from 4th rev. and augm. ed. by Maurice Kleimenhagen. Introd. Rev. Prof. Hm. Gollancz. L: Siegle, Hill 1911. 63p. 20cm. [BM]

SCHLEIERMACHER, F: (Ern. Dn.) 1768-1834. Sel. in C194.
*8282. (Die Weihnachtsfeier.) Christmas eve: a dialog on the celebration of Christmas. Tr. W: Hastie. Ed: Clark 1890. xv;80p. 19cm. [Awkward in spots.] [BM]
8283. Introds. to the dialogues of Plato. Tr. W. Dobson. Cambridge: Deighton; L: Parker 1836. 432p. 23cm. [BM.LCO]
[Taken from his tr. of Plato.]
8284. do. 1840. In The apology of Socrates, Crito, etc., with... S--'s introds. L: Taylor & Walton. xix;211p. 19cm. [LC]
*8285. (Monologen.) Soliloquies. Tr. H. L. Friess. Chic: Open court 1926. 176p. 20cm. [Excellent tr.] [LC]
8286. On the social element in religion. Tr. G: Ripley. 1913-15. In C154(5).
8287. On the worth of Socrates as a philosopher. Tr. Connop Thirlwall. In Wiggers, "Life of Socrates." 1840. [BM.LC]
8288. do. 1858. and, Introd. to the Apology of Socrates. Tr. anon. 3d ed. L: Walton & Maberly. 45p. 19cm. [BM]
8289. do. 1863. [same] 4th ed. [BM]

SCHLEIERMACHER, F:--On the worth of Socrates as a philosopher
8290. do. 1880. [same as #8287] In Xenophon's "Memorabilia, etc." NY: Harper. xxxiii;458p. 19cm. [Pref. is dated 1848.] [LC]
*8291. (Ueber die Religion. Reden an die Gebildeten unter ihren Verächtern.) On religion: speeches to its cultured despisers. Tr. J: Oman. L: Paul, T. & T. 1892. lviii;287p. 21cm. [BM.LC] [BM dates this 1893.]
*8292. Life of S--, as unfolded in his autobiog. and letters. Tr. Frederica Rowan. L: Smith, Elder 1860. 2v. xx;386; 339p. 20cm. [Carefully done.] [BM.LC]
8293. Brief outline, etc. With reminisc. of S-- by F: Lücke. Tr. W: Farrer. Ed: Clark; L: Hamilton, Adams 1850. xvi;220p. 20cm. [BM]

SCHLESIER, Gst. See Klencke, P., joint author.

SCHLESINGER, J:
8294. The orphan of Lowood: a play in two parts and 4 acts. Dram. from Cte. Brontë's novel "Jane Eyre." Written and ad. from the Ger. MS. NY: 1863. 2v. 60; 34 leaves (Ends at Act III, sc. 8.) [LCO]

SCHLESINGER, Max, 1822-81.
*8295. (Wanderungen durch London.) Saunterings in and about L--. Tr. O: v. Wenckstern. L: Cooke 1853. 290p. il. 19cm. [BM.LC] [EC has: L: Ward, Lock 1853.]
8296. War in Hungary. Tr. J: E: Taylor. L: Bentley 1850. 2v. lxxxvii;262; 334p. 8. [BM]

SCHLICHT, Ern. L: 1714-69. Sel. in C269.

"SCHLICHT, Freiherr v." See Baudissin, Wf. Graf v. 1867- .

SCHLICHTEGROLL, Ad. H: F: 1765-1822.
8297. The life of Mozart. Tr. anon. In Beyle, Marie H., "The lives of Haydn and M--." L: Murray 1817. pp. 335-493. 21cm. [BM]
8298. do. 1818. [same] L: pp. 334-418. 22cm. [BM.LC]
8298a. Obituary notice of J: D: Michaelis. Tr. C(onstantin) G(eisweiler). ca. 1801. In C157(3).

SCHLIEMANN, H: 1822-90. Sel. in C469;574.
*8299. (Ilios. Stadt und Land.) Ilios, the city and country of the Trojans. Tr. anon. Pref. Prof. Virchow. L: Murray 1880. xvi;800p. 24cm. [Includes an autobiogr. ("Selbstbiographie.")] [BM.LC]
*8300. (Trojanische Altertümer.) Troy and its remains. Tr. L. Dora Schmitz, rev. by ed., Philip Smith. L: Murray 1875. lv;392p. il. Lii pl. 23cm. [BM.LC]

SCHLIPPENBACH, Ab. Graf v. 1859- . Sel. in C318;422;#7717.

SCHLOSSER, F: Cph. 1776-1861.
*8301. (Geschichte des 18. Jahrhunderts und des 19. bis zum Sturz des französischen Kaiserreichs.) Hist. of the 18th cent. and of the 19th cent. till the overthrow of the French empire. Tr. D. Davison. L: Chapman & Hall 1843-52. 8v. 21cm. [BM.LC] [Tr. compared in part by author and is correct. The tr. craves (and needs) indulgence for the style (his first essay in tr.).]

SCHLUETER, Js.
*8302. (Allgemeine Geschichte der Musik.) A gen. hist. of music. Tr. F. Cecilia Tubbs. L: Bentley 1865. v;359p. 20cm. [BM.LC]

SCHMID, Cn. F. See below, after Cph. Schmid.

SCHMID, Cph. v. 1768-1854. Sel. in C125;153;438.

COLLECTIONS

8303. 1839. The basket of flowers ("Das Blumenkörbchen") and other tales. Tr. anon. L: Simpkin. 12. [EC]

SCHMID, Cph. v.--Collections
8304. 1843. The castle of Falkenburg, and other tales from the German (i.e., of Schmid). Tr. anon. L: J.Burns. 142p. 14cm. [BM]
[The castle of F--, or the dove ("Das Täubchen"); The valley of Schwarzenfels, or the canary bird ("Der Kanarienvogel"); Heinrich and Blanca; Count Sternfeld, or the nightingale ("Die Nachtigall"); The overseer of Mahlbourg, or the cherries ("Die Kirschen").]
8305. 1843. The bird's nest and other tales from the German. Tr. anon. L: Burns. 58p. 14cm. [BM]
[§The bird's nest ("Das Vogelnestchen"); The daisies; The cherries ("Die Kirschen"); The sluggard; The lobsters; The festival of roses. Nos. 1 and 3 are by Schmid, possibly the others as well.]
*8306. 1843. The red and white roses, and other stories. Tr. anon. L: J.Burns. 176p. 14cm. [BM]
[The red and white roses ("Die roten und die weissen Rosen"); Gottfried, or the island hermitage ("Gottfried, der junge Einsiedler"); Isaac Pinchpenny, or the unmasked hypocrite; Henry of Eichenfels ("Wie H: v. Eichenfels zur Kenntnis Gottes kam").]
§8307. 1843. The redbreast and other tales. Tr. anon. L: J.Burns. 57p. front. and tail-piece. 14cm. [BM]
[Title ("Das Rotkehlchen"); The forget-me-not ("Das Vergissmeinnicht"); Ingratitude; Vanity; Appearances are deceitful; Veronica.]
§8308. 1846. Tales designed chiefly for the young. New and independent tr. Anon. Dublin. Duffy. 3v. il. 19cm. [BM]
[Trs. are fair to very good. --Vol. 1. The wooden cross ("Das hölzerne Kreuz"); Angelica, The fire, The melon; The rose-bush ("Der Rosenstock"); The crayfish; Titus and his family; The best inheritance; The inundation of the Rhine ("Die Wasserflut am Rheine"); The nightingale ("Die Nachtigall"); Clara, or the red and white roses ("Die roten und die weissen Rosen"). Vol. 2. §Christmas eve ("Der Weihnachtsabend"); *The easter eggs ("Die Ostereier"); The bird's nest ("Das Vogelnestchen"); The water pitcher; The carrier pigeon ("Das Täubchen"); How H: of Eichenfels came to the knowledge of God ("Wie H: v. E-- zur Kenntnis Gottes kam"); The forest chapel ("Die Waldkapelle"); The jewels; Lewis, the little emigrant ("L: der kleine Auswanderer"); The dumb girl. Vol. 3. The lamb ("Das Lämmchen"); The madonna ("Das Marienbild"); The forget-me-not ("Das Vergissmeinnicht"); Godfrey, the little hermit ("Gottfried, der junge Einsiedler"); The cherries ("Die Kirschen"); The cakes ("Die Kuchen"); The chapel of Wolfsbuhl ("Die Kapelle bei Wolfsbühl"); Anselmo; The firefly; The redbreast ("Das Rotkehlchen"); The canary bird ("Der Kanarienvogel"); The copper coins and the gold coins; The hop blossoms ("Die Hopfenblüten"); The daisy; The old castle; The diamond ring. --See #8335 and my note.]
8309. 1848. Histor. tales, sel. from S--. Tr. anon. L: Burns. 18. [EC]
8310. 1849. The shepherd boy ("Das Vogelnestchen") and other tales. L: Burns. 32p. 10cm. [BM]
[Also, The festival of roses; The daisies. Cf. #8305.]
§8311. 1849. The cake ("Der Kuchen") and other tales. Tr. anon. L: Richardson. 15;12;8;14;12p. 15cm. [BM]
[Also, Titus and his family; The forget-me-not ("Das Vergissmeinnicht"); The overseer of Mahlbourg ("Die Kirschen"); Bear-hunt in the Pyrenees.]
8312. 1853. Christmas eve ("Der Weihnachtsabend") and other tales. Tr. anon. New ed. rev. and cor. by J: Tillotson. L: T:Allman. vi; 152p. front. engr. t.p. 12cm. [BM]
[Title; The water-pitcher; The dumb girl. Retold with additional moralizing.]
8313. 1853. How little H: came to the knowledge of God ("Wie H: v. Eichenfels ...") and other tales. New ed. rev. and cor. by

SCHMID, Cph. v.--Collections
J: Tillotson. L: T:Allman. v;152p. 12cm. [BM]
[Title; †The bird's nest ("Das Vogelnestchen"); The mother's gift.]
8314. 1853. The rose-bush ("Der Rosenstock"): a tale for young persons. New ed. rev. and cor. by T. M. Ready. L: T:Allman. 160p. 12cm. [BM]
[Also, The strawberries; The forget-me-not ("Das Vergissmeinnicht").]
8315. 1858. The two roads of life. (14) Tales designed to show that honesty is the best policy. Tr. anon. Dublin: Duffy. 355p. front. il. t.p. 16cm. [BM]
[Part of a new ed. of #8308, tales being classified by subjects.]
8316. 1862. [same as #8303] L: Simpkin. 8. [EC]
8317. 1867. [same?] Basket of flowers and other tales. Milner. 32[EC]
8318. 1872-6. Tales. Tr. anon. NY: Strong n.d. 6v. 18. [AC]
[Possibly a reissue of the 6 pts. of #8326.]
8319. 1875. The boy adventurers. Histor. tales. L: Warne. il. 18[EC]
[Cf. #8309.]
8320. 1876. Canary bird ("Der Kanarienvogel"), dove ("Das Täubchen"), inundation ("Die Wasserflut am Rheine"), rose-tree ("Der Rosenstock"), etc. (Separate.) L: Simpkin. 12. [EC]
§8321. 1892. Godfrey the little hermit ("Gottfried, der junge Einsiedler") and other tales. New ed. L: Art & book co; NY;Cincin: Benziger. 310p. 16cm. [BM]
[Same tr. as #8311. Errors. Includes: Hop blossoms ("Die Hopfenblüten"); §The cake ("Der Kuchen"); Titus and his family; The forget-me-not ("Das Vergissmeinnicht"); The overseer of Mahlbourg ("Die Kirschen"); Title.]
8322. 1893. The black lady and other tales. Tr. anon. L: Art & book co; NY;Cincin: Benziger. 298p. 16cm. [BM]
[Title; The easter eggs ("Die Ostereier"); The chapel of the forest ("Die Waldkapelle"); The robin redbreast ("Das Rotkehlchen"); The rose bush ("Der Rosenstock").
8323. 1900. Short stories, series 2, NY: Wildermann (The Catholic lib.) 64;64;64p. 16. [LC]
[Vol. 39. The nightingale ("Die Nachtigall"); The forest chapel ("Die Waldkapelle"). Vol. 49. The wooden cross ("Das hölzerne Kreuz"); The old castle. Vol. 59. The rose bush ("Der Rosenstock"); The cakes ("Die Kuchen").]
8324. 1905. The basket of flowers and other tales. L: Milner. 286p. 8. [Cf. #8317; 8303.] [EC]
8325. 1906. [same] [EC]
8326. DRUGULIN, W: E. Moral tales for young people. A new pictorial ed. (in 10 pts.) Stuttgart: Müller 1850-52. 6 pts. 16cm. [BM]
[Sep. t.ps. Pt. 1 missing.--Pt. 2. 1851. §Christmas eve ("Der Weihnachtsabend"); The glow-worm ("Das Johanniskäferchen"). Pt. 3, 1851. The nightingale ("Die Nachtigall"); The rose-bush ("Der Rosenstock"). 2 woodcuts. Pt. 4, 1852. *Henry v. Eichenfels ("Wie H:"etc.); Louis the little emigrant ("Ludwig," etc.) Pt. 5. 1852. Timothy and Philemon. ("Timotheus und P--"). 80p. One steel engr. Pt. 6, 1852. Eustace ("Eustachius"); The brothers ("Die zwei Brüder"). 60; 67p. --From Heinsius it appears that part 1 was The flower-basket, 147p., 1848.]
8327. G(ill), H. J. Tales, newly tr. L: Simpkin 1875. 12. [EC]
[For contents, see #8329.]
8328. do. 1888. [same?] Dublin: Gill. 384p. il. 17cm. [LC]
8329. do. 1890. Tales. Dublin: Gill; L: Simpkin. 384p. il. 18cm. [BM]
[§The canary bird; The forget-me-not; The rose tree; Trust in God ("Wie H: v. Eichenfels, etc."); The dove; Three parables; The wooden cross; The garden; The better land; The inundation; The fly and the spider; The sack of earth; The king's

SCHMID, Cph. v.--Collections
page; The water-jug; Titus and his family.--Tr. is not wholly correct.]
8330. do. 1902. New enl. ed. 17th thous. Il. T. J. Reynolds. Dublin: Gill. 368p. 8. [EC]
8331. HALL, MRS. SARAH J. The crocus: a fresh flower for the holidays. NY: Dunigan 1849. 277p. il. 18cm. [LC]
[Includes: The rosebush; The forget-me-not; The cakes; The cherries; The dumb girl.]
8332. JENKINS, REV. T: J. Canon Schmid's new tales of good fortune. Ad. Akron, O;Chic;NY: McBride 1897. 189p. il. 16. [LCO]
8333. do. 1897. [same?] 144p. [LCO]
8334. RUSSELL and KELLY, Revs. Catholic tales. L: Richardson 1847. 3v. 8. [Probably the same as #8308; cf. the following entry.] [EC]
8335. do? 1911. Catholic tales. Dublin: Cath. truth soc. Each no. 32p. 18cm. [BM]
[The trs. are the same as in #8308; probably taken from the foregoing. --No. 2. Angelica; The melon; The crayfish. No. 3. *Easter eggs ("Die Ostereier"). No. 4. The black lady. No. 6. How H: of Eichenfels came to the knowledge of God ("Wie H: v. E-- etc."). No. 9. The jewels. No. 10. Christmas eve ("Der Weihnachtsabend"), 36p. No. 12. The nightingale ("Die Nachtigall"). Others missing.]
8336. SMITH, MRS. F. H. Canary bird ("Der Kanarienvogel") and other tales. NY: Amer. tract soc. 1883. il. 16. [AC]

DAS BLUMENKÖRBCHEN

8337. ANON. 1834. The flower-basket. In "The juvenile miscellany," 3d series, vol. 4, pp. 109-73. Bost: Putnam ca. 1834. 14cm. [LC]
8338. ANON. 1858-60. The flower basket: a Catholic tale. Phil: McGrath n.d. 32. [AC]
*8339. ANON. 1869. The basket of flowers; or, piety and truth triumphant. Tr. from orig. Ger. ed. L: Warne; NY: Scribner, Welford. Lansdowne gift books. xi;191p. 19cm. [BM]
8340. ANON. 1894. ...A tale for the young. L: Blackie. 192p. 18cm. [A new tr., somewhat expanded and rewritten.] [BM]
8341. ANON. 1912. [same] L: Everett. 221p. col. front. and cover-title. 16cm. [BM]
8342. BEDELL, G. T. The basket of flowers; or, piety and truth triumphant. Tr. from the French and altered and arr. Phil: Perkins; Bost: Perkins & Marvin 1833. 144p. il. 15cm. [See note to #8344.] [LC]
8343. do. 1840? [same] Phil: McVey n.d. 143p. [NY (B12)]
[Probably a reissue of the foregoing; title and paging the same.]
8344. do. 1851. [same title] Halifax: Milner & Sowerby. ix;153p. 12cm. ["The tr. is a very free one, and in many places large omissions are made, and...consid. additions."] [BM]
8345. do. 1856. L: Hall, Virtue. vii;160p. 11cm. [BM]
8346. do. 1862. New ed. L: Routledge. 128p. front. 12cm. [BM]
8347. do. 1862. L: Ward & Lock. 123p. front. il. t.p. 12cm. [BM]
8348. do. 1865. New ed. L: Routledge. viii;149p. col. front. and cover-title. 15cm. [BM]
8349. do. 1869. L: Blackwood. ix;173p. front. and one il. 14cm. [BM]
8350. do. 1870. [ad.]The basket of flowers: a tale. Tr. from the German. Ed: Hislop. 127p. col. front. 15cm.
[Really rewritten from Bedell.] [BM]
8351. do. 1872. Bedell's tr. L: Ward, Lock. 158p. front. 15cm. [BM]
8352. do. 1873. L: Ward, Lock. Beeton's books. 158p. 16. [BM]
8353. do. 1879. Introd. G. T. B(edell). L;NY: Routledge. viii;192p. il. col. front. 17cm. [BM]
[Pref. note omits the admission of free tr.]
8354. do. 1882. Ed: Gemmell. vi;150p. 16cm. [No.il.] [BM]
8355. do. 1884. L: Sonnenschein. 127p. il. 13cm. [BM]
[Tr. given as Beddell. Same paging as #8350.]

SCHMID, Cph. v.--Das Blumenkörbchen
8356. do. 1887. L: Hodder & Stoughton. 150p. front. 17cm. [BM]
8357. do. 1889. The basket of flowers: a tale. Tr. from the Ger. L: Houlston. 128p. front. and one il. 17cm. [BM]
[Really rewritten from Bedell; about the same as #8350.]
8358. do. 1908. Il. in col. by Watson Charlton. L: Melrose. 151p. 17cm. [Edited from Bedell.] [BM]
?8359. ST. A., J. H. The basket of flowers: a tale for the young. Tr. from the French. L;Ed;NY: Nelson 1866. iv;203p. il. 16cm. [BM]
[Quite different from the orig. German.]
8360. do. 1872. [same] 161p. il. col. front. and cover-title. 16cm. [BM]
8361. do. 1904. [same] Nelson. Col. front. and cover-title. [BM]
8362. do. 1919. [same] Nelson. 128p. col. front. 18cm. [BM]

§8363. (Das hölzerne Kreuz.) The little wooden crucifix. Tr. anon. 1841. In C426.
8364. do. 1854. The orphan child; or, the story of little Sophia. Tr. anon. New ed. rev. and cor. by T. M. Ready. L: Allman. vi; 152p. front. t.p. vign. 12cm. [BM]
8365. (Das Lämmchen.) The pet lamb; or, the little strawberry girl. Tr. anon. New. ed. rev. and cor. by T. M. Ready. L: Allman 1853. viii;152p. front. engr. t.p. and vign. 12cm. [Rewritten.] [BM]
8366. do. Anon. 1870. The pet lamb. A tale. Ed: Oliphant. 130p. col. front. 15cm. [BM]
§8367. do. Graham, M. E. W. Dublin: Gill 1884. 78p. 16cm. [BM]
[EC has: L: Simpkin, and ascribes the story to H. Schmid.]
8368. do. Jackson, (S:?) The little lamb. A tale. L: Hamilton, Adams 1839. 18. [EC]
8369. (Das Marienbild.) The madonna. Tr. anon. NY: Dunigan 1848. 56p 18. [LCO]
8370. do. Howitt, Ma. The picture of the Virgin. Ad. Il. in col. by J: Absolon. L: Orr 1844. 24p. il. 18cm. [BM]
§8371. (Das Rotkehlchen.) Little Martin; or, the redbreast. Tr. anon. L: Burns 1849. 20p. 11cm. [Same tr. as in #8307.] [BM]
8372. (Das Täubchen.) The carrier pigeon. Tr. anon. NY: Dunigan 1849. 70p. il. 18. [Probably the same tr. as #8308.] [LCO]
8373. (Das Vergissmeinnicht.) Forget me not. Tr. Lizzie S. Eden. 1870. In C113.
8374. (Das Vogelnestchen.) The bird's nest; or, the keeping of a promise rewarded. Tr. anon. Introd. by J. W. Welman. L: Seeley, Jackson & Halliday 1872. 58p. il. 20cm. [BM]
[Retold with moral underscored.]
*8375. (Der Eierdieb.) The egg-thief: a comedy in one act [prose]. Tr. M. Trautwein. L: J. W. Kolckmann 1882. 39p. Ger. and Engl. 17cm. [Quite good.] [BM]
*8376. (Der Weihnachtsabend.) Christmas eve. Tr. anon. L: Burns 1843. 74p. 14cm. [BM]
§8377. do. 1849. or, the story of little Anton. Tr. anon. L: Cundall. 110p. front. 15cm. [BM]
§8378. do. 1850. Christmas-eve; The glow-worm. Tr. W: E. Drugulin. Stuttgart: J. B. Müller; L: Orr. 90p. woodcuts. 16cm. [BM]
[Same as part 2 of #8326, but with different date.]
§8379. (Die Hopfenblüten.) The hop blossoms. Tr. anon. Derby: Richardson 1845. 68p. 15cm. [BM]
8380. do. 1853. [same?] Honesty the best policy; or, the hop blossoms. New ed. rev. and cor. by T. M. Ready. L: T:Allman. vi; 152p. front. t.p. vign. 12cm. [BM]
[Also contains (not by Schmid): The old castle; A story of Renard the fox; The family of martyrs.]
8381. do. 1872. The hop blossoms. Tr. J. F: Smith. Phil: Luth. bd.

SCHMID, Cph. v.--Die Hopfenblüten
174p. 16. [LCO]
*8382. (Die Kirschen.) The cherries. Also, The sluggard. Tr. anon. L: Burns 1849. 28p. one il. 11cm. [BM]
8383. do. 1849. The cherries. Tr. anon. NY: Dunigan. 38p. 18. [LCO]
§8384. (Die Nachtigall.) The nightingale; or, a kind act is never lost. A tale of the Russian war, forty years ago. Tr. anon. NY: Dana 1856. 91p. 16cm. [LCO.BM]
§8385. do. 1861. The boy and the man. From the Ger. of Christopher von Schmidt [sic]. Tr. Ma. Howitt. In C211, pp. 129-68.
8386. do. 1866? [same] In Cassell's story books for the young. pp. 52-89. 17cm. [BM]
8387. do. 1872-76. [same title as #8384] Claremont, N.H: Claremont n.d. 18. [AC]
8388. do. 1872-76. [same title] NY: Dutton n.d. 18. [AC]
*8389. (Die Ostereier.) The easter eggs: a tale for children. Tr. anon. L: Harvey & Darton 1829. v;99p. front. 14cm. [BM]
8390. do. 1839. Tr. (S:?) Jackson. L: Hamilton, Adams. 18. [EC]
*8391. do. 1846. C. v. S--'s easter eggs. Tr. H: J: Whitling, for the use of schools and...instruction. Nuremberg: Prtd. by J. L. Schrag. 64p. of text. 16cm. [BM]
8392. do. 1846. Tr. by U. Derby: Richardson. 48p. 14cm. [BM]
[Retold quite freely.]
†8393. do. 1870. and, red and white roses ("Die roten und die weissen Rosen"). Tr. anon. Ed: W: Oliphant. 128p. 16cm. [BM]
8394. do. 1870. a story...for children. Tr. L. H. Steiner. Phil: Ref. church pub. 95p. 16. [LCO]
8395. do. 1872-6. Tr. anon. NY: Dutton n.d. 18. [AC]
8396. do. 1877? The easter eggs, intended to be an easter present for children, and tr. appropriately by E. G. for her grandchildren. Belfast: Prtd. by Ward. 88p. 13cm. [LC]
8397. do. 1908. Tr. anon. Il. M. W. Wheelhouse. L: Bell. 68p. 25cm. ["Reprint--slightly curtailed" from #8308.] [BM]
§8398. (Die roten und die weissen Rosen.) Red and white roses. Tr. anon. Ed: Hislop 1870. 34p. 14cm. [BM]
*8399. (Die Waldkapelle.) The chapel of the forest, and, The robin redbreast ("Das Rotkehlchen"). Tr. anon. Derby; L: Richardson 1845. 28; 14p. 14cm. [Varies only slightly from #8308.] [BM]
*8400. (Genoveva.) G-- of Brabant: a tale of old times. Tr. anon. L: Burns 1845? vi;76p. 17cm. [Same tr. as #8403.] [BM]
8401. do. 1845? Genevieve. Balto: Lucas n.d. 18. [AC]
8402. do. 1848. [same as #8400?] G-- of Brabant: a tale. L: Burns. 16. [EC]
*8403. do. 1855. Genevieve of Brabant: a legend of the middle ages. Tr. C. W. R. Dublin: Duffy. vii;204p. 14cm. [BM]
8404. do. 1872-6. [same?] Genevieve de Brabant: tale of antiquity. NY: Cath. pub. n.d. 18. [AC]
8405. (Gottfried der junge Einsiedler.) The little hermit; or, the Ger. Robinson Crusoe. New ed. rev. and cor. by T. M. Ready. L: T:Allman 1853. vi;151p. front. t.p. vignettes. 12cm. [BM]
§8406. (Klara, oder die Gefahren der Unschuld.) Clara; or, the dangers of innocence. Tr. "Heliodora." Augsburg: Prtd. by F. C. Kremer. 1843. 92p. 20cm. [BM]
[Done by a 15-year-old Ger. girl. Not bad.]

KURZE ERZÄHLUNGEN

§8407. ANON. Short tales for little children. Dublin: Jas. Duffy 1855. viii;234p. 14cm. [BM]
8408. ANON. 1855-8; One hundred and forty short tales and parables for children. NY: Sadlier n.d. [AC]

SCHMID, Cph. v.--Kurze Erzählungen
8409. ANON. 1872-6. Hundred short tales for children. NY: Sadlier n.d. 16. [AC]
§8410. HALES, R: C. A series of tales for children. 2d ed. L: Simpkin 1859. viii;128p. front. 16cm. [BM]
8411. do. 1861. [same] 2d ed. Simpkin. 8. [EC]
8412. JOHNSTONE, MISS F. First tales for children. Bath: Binns & Goodwin; L: Hamilton, Adams 1845. 76p. 15cm. [BM]
[This ed. has: Johnston, 2d has: Johnstone. 93 tales, retold.]
8413. do. 1846. [same] 2d ed. [BM]
8414. T., S. Sel. Tr. 1842. In C522.
§8415. WELLS, F. B. Hundred short tales for children. L: Bosworth 1853. viii;184p. front. il. t.p. 16cm. [BM]
[From the 3d group of the orig. stories.]
§8416. do. 1853. [same] 2d ed. Bosworth. 18. [LCO]
8417. do. 1853. [same?] NY: Carter & bros. 16. [AC]
8418. do. 1859. [same?] Bosworth. [EC]
§8419. do. 1869. [same] New ed. Frome Selwood. Hodges; L: Simpkin, Marshall. viii;134p. 14cm. [BM]
[Same front. as #8415; diff. il. on t.p.]
*8420. WHITLING, H: J: Fifty short stories...First reading book for the use of students of the Engl. lang. Nuremberg: Riegel & Wiessner 1846. x;102p. 17cm. [BM]
8421. (Ludwig, der kleine Auswanderer.) The little emigrant: a tale of the French revolution. Tr. anon. New ed. rev. and cor. by J. Tillotson. L: T:Allman 1853. vi;152p. front. il. t.p. vignettes. 12cm. [Retold] [BM]
8422. The rings; or, the two orphans. Tr. arr. and alt. by C: A. Wyeth. Phil: Martien 1854. 153p. 16. [LCO]
8423. (Rosa von Tannenburg.) Rosa of T--: a tale of ancient times for parents and children. Tr. anon. Stuttgart: Verlagsmagazin 1847. 189p. 8. [Heinsius]
§8423a. do. 1857. [same?] a tale of the olden time, etc. L: C: Dolman. 181p. 17cm. [BM]
*8424. do. 1860. Rosa v. T--: a tale, etc. Tr. anon. L: Booth. 150p. 17cm. [EC says: new ed.] [BM]
*8425. do. 1881. Tr. Lucie A. Archer. NY: Scott. 172p. 12. [LCO]
[Good, not excellent.]
8426. do. 1883. [same] NY: Ward & Drummond. 12. [AC]
8427. (Wie H: v. Eichenfels zur Kenntnis Gottes kam.) The stolen child; or, how H: E-- came to the knowledge of God. Tr. J. Bachman and J. Miller. 2d ed. Harrisburg, Pa: Winebrenner 1836. 103p. 13cm. [LC]
8427a. do. 1843. In what manner H: of E-- came to the knowledge of God: a story for children. Tr. anon. Dresden: Bromme. 120p. 16. [EC (Heinsius)]
§8428. do. 1848. H: of E--; or, how a child learned to know that there is a God. Ed;L: J:Johnstone. viii;132p. il. 13cm. [BM]
8429. do. 1848. H: of E--, and, Christmas eve ("Der Weihnachtsabend"). By Flower. Cleaver. 18. [EC]
*8430. do. 1852. H: of E--; Louis the little emigrant ("Ludwig, der kleine Auswanderer"). Two moral tales for young people. Stuttgart: J: B. Müller. 48; 66p. fronts. 16cm. [BM]
[Same as part 4 of #8326; tr. W: E. Drugulin.]
8431. do. 1856. H: of E--. Tr. anon. L: Groombridge. 16. [EC]
8432. do. 1898. How H: of E-- came to the knowledge of God. Tr. A. M. Grussi. Collegeville, Ind: St. Joseph's coll. press. 86p. il. 16. [LC]
8433. The wonderful doctor. An Eastern tale. Tr. anon. McGrath n.d. 1858-60. [AC]

SCHMID, Cn. F: 1794-1852.
8434. (Christliche Sittenlehre.) General principles of Christian ethics. Abr. by W. J. Mann. Phil: Luth. bookstore 1872. 153p. 12. [LCO]

SCHMID, Hm. Td. v. 1815-80. Sel. in C112.
*8435. (Der Habermeister.) The habermeister: a tale of the Bav. mts. Tr. anon. NY: Leypoldt & Holt 1869. 379p. 17cm. [LC.BM]
*8436. do. 1875. [same] New ed. Holt. [LC]
§8437. (Der Kanzler von Tirol.) The chancellor of the Tyrol. Tr. Dorothea Roberts. L: Unwin 1885. 2v. 323; 318p. 19cm. [BM]
[Condensed; good tr. per se.]

SCHMID, Hm. Td. v. and K: Stieler.
8438. (Aus den Bergen.) The Bav. highlands and the Salzkammergut. Profusely il., with an account of the peasantry. Tr. anon. L: Chapman & Hall 1874. viii;205p. 35cm. [BM.LC]

SCHMIDT, Fd. 1816-90.
8439. Charlemagne. Tr. G: P. Upton. Chic: McClurg 1910. 101p. 17cm. [LC]
8440. Gods and heroes. Tr. and ad. from S-- and C: F: Becker by G: P. Upton. Chic: McClurg 1912. 123p. 17cm. [LC]
8441. Gudrun. Tr. G: P. Upton. Chic: McClurg 1906. 134p. 17cm. [LC]
8442. Herman and Thusnelda. Tr. G: P. Upton. Chic: McClurg 1907. 128p. 17cm. [LC]
8443. The Nibelungs. Tr. G: P. Upton. Chic: McClurg 1906. 174p. 17cm. [LC]
8444. William Tell. Tr. G: P. Upton. Chic: McClurg 1904. 117p. il. 17cm. [LC]
8445. The youth of the Great Elector. Tr. G: P. Upton. Chic: McClurg 1909. 144p. 17cm. [LC]

SCHMIDT, Harry
*8446. (Das Weltbild der Relativitätstheorie.) Relativity and the universe: a pop. introd. in Einstein's theory of space and time. Author. tr. K: Wichmann. L: Methuen 1921. xiii;136p. 19cm. [BM]
*8447. do. 1922. [same] NY: McBride. [LC]

SCHMIDT (VON LUEBECK), G: Ph. 1766-1849. Sel. in C31;73;123;137a; 372;380;470;500.
8448. Conjectures respecting Caspar Hauser's place of confinement. In Anselm Feuerbach, "Caspar Hauser." 2d ed. pp. 161-77. L: Simpkin 1834. 18cm. [BM]

SCHMIDT, J: Esb. 1669-1745. Sel. in C44;244;271;511.

SCHMIDT, J: Kp. 1806-50. See "Stirner, Max."

SCHMIDT, Klamer Eb. K: 1746-1824. Sel. in C450.
[See "Klopstock and his friends," #5069 seq.]

SCHMIDT, Max
*8449. (Völkerkunde.) The primitive races of mankind. Tr. Ax. K. Dallas. L: Harrap 1926. 360p. il. 22cm. [BM.LC]

SCHMIDT, O: Ern. 1862- . See "Ernst, O:"

SCHMIDT, W. Sel. in C102.

SCHMIDT, (P: H:) W: 1855- .
8450. Ben Juda, the shepherd. Tr. Pl. W. Neoper. Luth. bk. 1926. 319p. D. [AC]
8451. (Goldene Quelle.) The golden fountain. Tr. M. E. Ireland. Columbus, O: Lutheran bk. 1916. 96p. 18cm. [LC]
8452. Star eye: a story of the Amer. revolution. Concordia n.d. 300p. il. D. [AC]

SCHMIDT-PHISELDECK, Cd. G: F: Els. v. 1770-1832. Sel. in C296.
§8453. (Europa und Amerika, oder die künftigen Verhältnisse der zivilisierten Welt.) Europe and America; or, the relative state of the civilized world at a future period. Tr. Js. Owen. Copenhagen: Schlesinger 1820. viii;257p. 16cm. [Good tr.] [LC.BM]

SCHMIEDEN, Frau Else (Kobert) 1841-96. See "Junker, E."

"SCHMITHOF, E:" (i.e., E: Schmidt, 1819-96).
8454. (Kaffeeklatsch.) Six cups of chocolate: a piece of gossip in one act. Freely Englished...Edith V. B. Matthews. NY: Harper 1897. 32p. 16. [LC]

SCHMITT, Hs. 1835-1907.
8455. (Ueber die natürlichen Gesetze...) The nat. laws of mus. expression. Tr. Fes. A. Van Santford. Chic: Summy 1894. 47p. 17cm. [LC]

SCHMITZ, Ok. A. H.
*8456. (Das Land ohne Musik.) The land without music. Tr. H. Herzl. L: Jarrolds 1926. 230p. 23cm. [BM.LC]

SCHMOEGER, K: Ehd. 1819-83.
8457. (Das Leben der gottseligen...) Life of Anna Catharina Emmerich. Tr. Helen Ram. L: Quarterly series, vol. 10. 1874. xvi;231p. 19cm. [Large portions (e.g., visions) omitted.] [BM.LC]
8458. do. 1885. 2v. 19cm. [This is probably more nearly complete.] [LC]

SCHMOLCK (or Schmolke), B: 1672-1737. Sel. in C51;229;231-5;244;269; 271;273;276;287;486;489.

SCHMOLLER, Gst. v. 1838-1917. Sel. in C563.

SCHMOLZÉ, K: H: 1823-59.
8459. An artist's poems. Written and il. by C: H: S--. Tr. C: G. Leland. Phot. from orig. lead pencil drawings. Pub...for the benefit of the great central fair...Phil: Leypoldt 1864. 9 leaves. front. 6 pl. 33 x 26cm. [Text and tr. in parallel columns.] [LC]

SCHNAUFFER, K: H: 1822-54. Sel. in C497.

SCHNECKENBURGER, Max, 1819-49. Sel. in C29;40;309;366;372;531.
§8460. (Die Wacht am Rhein.) The watch on the Rhine. Tr. anon. Il. G. W. Brenneman. Bost: Brown 1892. 32p. 23cm. [Fair tr.] [LC]

SCHNEE, (Ab. Hm.) H: 1871- .
8461. (Die koloniale Schuldlüge.) German colonisation, past and future: the truth about Ger. colonies. Introd. by W: H. Dawson. L: Allen & U;NY: Knopf 1926. 176p. 34 il. 22cm. [BM.LC]

SCHNEEGAZ (Schneegass), Cyriacus, d. 1597. Sel. in C271.

SCHNEER, Js.
*8462. (Alassio und seine Umgebung.) Alassio. "A pearl of the Riviera." Tr. anon. L: Trübner 1887. xii;80p. 18cm. [BM]

SCHNEESING, J: fl. 1522-d. 1567. Sel. in C271;273;287.

SCHNEIDER (i.e. Schnitzer), E: See "Emin Pasha."

SCHNEIDER, H. G.
8463. Hansina Hinz: a true story of Moravian missions in Greenland. Tr. freely E. F. K. L: Rel. tract soc. 1901. 95p. front. (port.) 18cm. [BM]
8464. Working and waiting for Tibet: a sketch of the Moravian mission to the western Himalayas. Tr. and rev. by Art. Ward. L: Morgan & Scott 1891. vi;95p. il. 8. [BM]

SCHNEIDER, Louis, 1805-78.
8465. (Der Schauspieldirektor.) Hoodwinking the impressario; or, the wiles of the prima donna. Music borrowed from Mozart's "Singspiel" and from Taubert. Tr. H: E: Krehbiel. Libr. 1916. 18p. Tw. [LCM]

SCHNEIDER, W: 1847-1909.
*8466. (Das andere Leben.) The other life. Tr. and ad. from the 11th ed., rev. and ed. by Rev. Herbert Thurston, S. J. NY: J. F. Wagner 1920. vi;410p. 21cm. [LC.BM]

SCHNEZLER, A: 1809-53. Sel. in C41;152;219;296;372;391;393.

SCHNITZER, E: See "Emin Pasha."

SCHNITZER, Ig.
8467. (Der Zigeunerbaron.) The gypsy baron: operetta in 3 acts by J: Strauss. Text ad. from M. Jokai. Tr. anon. Libr. NY: 1897. 46p. Tw. [LCM]

SCHNITZLER, Art. 1862-1931. Sel. in C366*.
*8468. [Coll.] Björkman, E. A. Three plays. NY: Kennerley 1915. 323p. 19cm. [LC]
[Clever, genuine dialog, few errors. --The lonely way ("Der einsame Weg"); Intermezzo (do.); Countess Mizzie ("Comtesse Mizzi").]
8469. [Coll.] Colbron, Grace I. Anatol, etc. Tr. Grace I. Colbron. Introd. Ashley Dukes. NY: Boni & Liveright 1917. xiii;226p. 17cm. [LC]
[*Prolog. to Anatol; §Anatol (do.), too much expanded; *Living hours ("Lebendige Stunden"); *The green cockatoo ("Der grüne Kakadu"); The lady with the dagger ("Die Frau mit dem Dolche"); Last masks ("Die letzten Masken"); *Literature ("Literatur").]
§8470. [Coll.] Eisemann, F. Viennese idyls. Bost: Luce 1913. 182p. 12. [NY]
[Correct but flat: style wholly lost. --Flowers ("Blumen"); Blind Geronimo and his brother ("Der blinde G-- und sein Bruder"); Andreas Thameyer's last letter ("A-- Thameiers letzter Brief"); The sage's wife ("Die Frau des Weisen"); The farewell ("Ein Abschied"); The dead are silent ("Die Toten schweigen").]
8471. [Coll.] Jacques, Agnes. Beatrice, a novel. tr. by Ag. Jacques, and other stories tr. by Elsie M. Lang. L: Laurie 1926. vii;247p. 8. [BM]
[Beatrice; Flowers ("Blumen"); A farewell ("Ein Abschied"); The wife of the wise man ("Die Frau des Weisen"); The hour of fame ("Der Ehrentag"); The dead are silent ("Die Toten schweigen").]
§8472. [Coll.] Loving, Pierre. Comedies of words, and other plays. Cincin: Stewart & Kidd 1917. 182p. 20cm. [LC]
[Tr. shows errors or improves the orig. --The hour of recognition; The big scene; The festival of Bacchus; †Literature ("Literatur"); †His helpmate ("Die Gefährtin").]
8473. [Coll.] Samuel, H. B. The green cockatoo ("Der grüne Kakadu") and other plays. L;Ed: Gay & H. 1913. ix;123p. 19cm. [BM.LC]
[Includes: The mate ("Die Gefährtin"); Paracelsus (do.).]
§8474. [Coll.] Theis, O. F. The shepherd's pipe and other stories. NY: Brown 1922. 169p. 17cm. [LC]
[Title ("Die Hirtenflöte"); The murderer ("Der Mörder"); Blind Geronimo and his brother ("Der blinde G-- und sein Bruder"). --Not wholly accurate nor respectful.]
§8475. (Anatol.) Anatol: a sequence of dialogues...paraphrased for the Engl. stage by Granville Barker. L: Sidgwick & Jackson; NY: Kennerley 1911. 125p. 20cm. [Clever but not Schnitzler.] [BM.LC]
8476. (Blumen.) Flowers. Tr. anon. 1927. In C367.
§8477. (Casanovas Heimfahrt.) C--'s homecoming. Tr. Eden and Cedar Paul. NY: Priv. prt. 1921. 201p. 25cm. [LC]
[Correct, but they alter his sentences and ruin his style.]

SCHNITZLER, Art--Casanovas Heimfahrt
§8478. do. 1922. [same] L: Brentano; NY: Seltzer. 175p. 21cm.[BM.LC]
8478a. (Comtesse Mizzi.) Countess Mizzie. 1923. In C420b. [Probably from 8468.]
8479. (Das Märchen.) Tr. C. E. Wheeler and Granville Barker. (B38)
*8480. (Das Vermächtnis.) The legacy: a drama in 3 acts. Tr. Ma. L. Stephenson. In "Poet Lore," vol. 22 (1911). [Excellent dialog.]
8481. do. 1911. [same] Bost: Badger. Poet Lore plays. 25cm. [LC]
8481a. (Der einsame Weg.) The lonely way. 1924. In C420a. [Probably from #8468.]
§8482. (Der grüne Kakadu.) The duke and the actress. Tr. Hans Weysz. In "Poet Lore," vol. 21 (1910).[He does not understand the German.]
8483. do. 1913-15. Tr. H. B. Samuel. In C154(20).
†8484. (Der tapfere Cassian.) Gallant C--: a puppet play in one act. Tr. from 3d ed. by Am. L. Gowans. L: Gowans & Gray 1914. 10; 45p. 12. [A very dull imitation.] [BM.NY]
†8485. do. 1921-4. [same] Leroy Phillips. 45p. D. [AC]
†8486. do. 1925. [same] Girard, Kan: Haldeman-Julius. Little blue books. 30p. 12cm. [BQM]
*8487. (Der Weg ins Freie.) The road to the open. Author. tr. by H. B. Samuel. L: Allen & U; NY: Knopf 1923. 412p. 21cm. [BM.LC] [Perhaps a trifle too literal, but very careful and exact.]
8488. (Die dreifache Warnung.) The triple warning. Tr. B. H. Clark. 1926. In C68.
§8489. (Die Frage an das Schicksal.) Questioning the irrevocable. Tr. W. H. H. Chambers. 1903. In C18. [Good but faulty. --From Anatol.]
8490. (Die Frau mit dem Dolche.) The woman with the dagger. Abr. Tr. Anon. International, vol. 4.(1911)(B38)
§8491. do. 1904. Tr. H. T. Porter. In "Poet Lore," vol. 15. [Not much good.]
8492. do. 1909. Tr. H. B. Samuel. In "Fortnightly Rev.," vol. 91.
8493. (Die Gefährtin.) The wife. Abr. Tr. anon. In "Current lit.," vol. 39 (1905).
§8494. (Die Toten schweigen.) The dead are silent. Tr. C. H. Young. 1907. In C447. [He improves on his author.]
§8494a.do. 1915. [same] In C179.
†8495. (Dr. Graesler, Badearzt.) Dr. G--. Tr. E. C. Slade. NY: Seltzer 1923. 180p. 21cm. [LC]
[Tr. prunes freely, and also makes errors.]
8496. do. 1924. [same?] L: Chapman & Hall. 186p. 8. [BM]
§8497. (Frau Beate und ihr Sohn.) Beatrice. Tr. Ag. Jacques. NY: Simon & Schuster 1926. iv;173p. 19cm. [Improved.] [LC]
8498. (Frau Bertha Garlan.) B-- G--. a novel. Tr. anon. Goschen 1913. 272p. 8. [Cf. #8501.] [EC]
8499. do. 1913. [same?] Vienna ed. Bost: Badger. D. [AC]
§8500. do. 1918. Tr. anon. NY: Boni & Liveright. 246p. 17cm. [LC]
[Poor style and some errors.]
*8501. do. 1914. Tr. J. H. Wisdom and Marr Murray. L: Goschen. 267p. 18cm. [BM]
8502. (Fräulein Else.) Fräulein Else. Tr. F. H. Lyon. L: Philpot 1925. 149p. 7 x 5 in. [BM]
§8503. do. 1925. Tr. Rb. A. Simon. NY: Simon & Schuster. 145p. 19cm. [Ruins the choppy style.] [LC]
8504. (Freiwild.) Free game: a drama in 3 acts. Tr. anon. Bost: Badger 1913. Vienna ed. D. [AC]
8505. The hour of recognition. Tr. Pierre Loving. In "The international," vol. 10(1916).
†8506. (Lebendige Stunden.) Living hours. Tr. H. T. Porter. In "Poet Lore," vol. 17(1906). [Gnädiger Herr tr. als "worshipful sir."]
8507. do. 1910. [abr.] Vital moments. Tr. anon. In "The international," vol. 3 (1910).

SCHNITZLER, Art.--Lebendige Stunden
8508. do. 1913. Living hours: four one-act plays. Tr. anon. Bost: Badger. Vienna ed. D. [AC]
8509. do. 1921. Tr. G. I. Colbron. In C100a.
*8510. (Leutnant Gustl.) "None but the brave." Tr. R: L. Simon. NY: Simon & Schuster 1926. 74p. 19cm. [Quite good.] [LC]
8511. (Liebelei.) The reckoning. Tr. Grace I. Colbron. NY: 1907. (B38)
8512. do. 1912. Light-o'-love. Tr. B. Q. Morgan. In "The drama," no. 7 (1912).
8513. do. 1912. [same] Sergel. [AC]
*8514. do. 1914. Playing with love. Tr. P. Morton Shand. L: Gay & H. ix;101p. 19cm. [Also contains Hofmannsthal's Prolog to Anatol, very badly tr. by Trevor Blakemore.] [BM.LC]
8515. (Literatur.) Literature. Tr. Elsie Plaut. (B38)
8516. do. 1908. The literary sense. Tr. and ad. by C: H. Genung. NY: Copyright by Wl. H. Lawrence. (B38)
*8517. do. 1913-15. Tr. A. I. Coleman. In C154(20). [Very good, not quite right.]
†8518. do. 1915. Tr. P. Loving. In "The international," vol. 9(1915). [Very poor.]
†8519. (Professor Bernhardi.) Prof. B--. Ad. in Engl. by Mrs. El. Pohli. San Fran: Elder 1913. 64p. 20cm. [Unwarranted liberties.] [LC]
8520. do. 192-? The anti-Semites. (Prof. Bernhardi: a play.) Tr. anon. Girard, Kan: Haldeman-Julius n.d. Little blue books. 63p. 12cm. [BQM]
*8521. do. 1927. Prof. B--: a comedy in 5 acts. Tr. Hetty Landstone. L: Faber & Gwyer. 160p. 19cm. [BM]
*8522. (Reigen.) Hands around: a cycle of ten dialogues. Tr. anon. NY: Priv. prt. 1920. 223p. 24cm. [Good, but could be better; fine points not brought out, and even small errors made.] [LC]
8523. (Spiel im Morgengrauen.) Daybreak. Tr. W: A. Drake. NY: Simon & Schuster 1927. 204p. D. [AC]

SCHOBER, Fz. v. 1798-1882. Sel. in C137a.

SCHOBERT, Frau He. (Harnisch) 1858- .
8524. (Das Kind der Strasse.) Picked up in the streets: a romance. Tr. Mrs. A. L. Wister. Phil: Lippincott 1888. 335p. 18cm. [LC]
8525. do. 1893. The flower girl of Paris. Tr. Laura E. Kendall. Chic;NY: Rand, McNally. 232p. 21cm. [LC]

SCHOEBERL, F. Passion play at Oberammergau. See "Oberammergau," A385 seq.

SCHOEMANN, G: F: 1793-1879.
*8526. (Griechische Altertümer.) The antiquities of Greece. Vol. 1. The state. Tr. E. G: Hardy and Jas. S. Mann. L: Rivingtons 1880. xi;583p. 21cm. [BM.LC]
8526a. Dissertation of the assemblies of the Athenians. Tr. from the Latin. anon. Cambridge: Grant 1838. 361p. 22cm. [LC]

SCHOEN, W: E: Frhr. v. 1851- .
*8527. (Erlebtes.) Memoirs of an ambassador: a contrib. to the polit. hist. of mod. times. Tr. Constance Vesey. L: Allen & Unwin 1922. 254p. 22cm. [BM]
*8527a. do. 1923. [same] NY: Brentano's. [LC]

SCHOENAICH, Cph. O: Freiherr v. 1725-1807.
§8528. (Hermann, oder das befreite Deutschland.) Arminius; or, Germania freed. Tr. from the 3d ed. by "Baron Cronzeck." With histor. and crit. pref. by...Gottsched. L: Prtd. for Becket & de Hondt 1764. 2v. liv;192; 216p. 15cm. [BM.LC]
[Verse done into rhythmical prose; sense very well rendered.]

SCHOENAICH-CAROLATH, El. zu, Prinz, 1852-1908. Sel. in C28;154(18); 423.
*8529. (Tauwasser.) Melting snows. Tr. Marg. Symonds. L: Nimmo 1895. 238p. 19cm. [BM]
[EC has: 1894. 1895.--Contains also (from "Geschichten aus Moll"): The queen of Thule ("Die Königin v. T--"), pp. 240-259; The moth ("Der Nachtfalter"), pp. 263-80.]

SCHOENBACH, ---. Sel. in C448.

SCHOENBERG, (Wf.) Er. v. 1812-83.
8530. Travels in India and Kashmir. Tr. anon. L: Hurst & B. 1853. 2v. 337;310p. front. 19cm. [BM.LC]

SCHOENBORN, Wl. 1883- . Sel. in C563.

SCHOENER, Rld. 1849- .
8531. Rome...Condensed and ed. by Mrs. Art. Bell. L: Low; NY: Scribner 1898. viii;296p. il. 33cm. [BM.LC]

SCHOENFELD, Af. Operetta. See Kraatz, Curt, joint author.

SCHOENHERR, K: 1869- .
8532. (Glaube und Heimat.) Faith and fireside. Tr. E. v. Mach. 1913-15. In C154(16). [Correct, flats on the style.]

SCHOENTHAN Edler v. Pernwald, Fz. 1849-1913. Sel. in C422.
8533. (Das letzte Wort.) The last word: a comedy in 4 acts [prose]. Tr. A. Daly. NY: 1890. [BM]
8534. (Klein Dorrit.) The Dorrits: a comedy in 3 acts [prose]. Tr. Marg. Mayo. NY: 1909. Tw. [Founded on Dickens's "Little Dorrit."] [LC]
8535. (Maria Theresia.) Marie Theresa: a play in 4 acts [prose]. Tr. J. H. Sprange. NY: 1907. Tw. [LC]
8536. A night off; or, a page from Balzac. A comedy in 4 acts [prose] Tr. A. Daly. NY: Dick & Fitzgerald 1885. (B38)
8537. do. 1897. [same] NY: Roorbach. 99p. 18cm. [LC]
8538. Nobody's fault; or, the child of the Marshalsea. A play in 3 acts [prose]. Tr. anon. NY: Selwyn & co. (copyright) 1906. Tw. [LC.BM]

SCHOENTHAN, Fz. and Pl. (1853-1905).
*8539. (Der Raub der Sabinerinnen.) The rape of the Sabine women, by F. and P. Schöuthau [sic]. Comedy farce in 4 acts [prose]. Tr. anon. Berlin: 1884. 34;39;35;22p. 33cm. Tw. [BM]
8540. do. 1884. The Sabine women. Tr. A. Daly. NY. (B38)
8541. do. 1898. The professor's play; or, the kidnapping of the Sabine women. A comedy in 4 acts. Tr. Ludmilla Krueger. Alameda, Cal. (B38)
8542. (Der Schwabenstreich.) Seven-twenty-eight; or, casting the boomerang. A comedy in 4 acts [prose]. Tr. A. Daly. NY: Dick & Fitzgerald 1883. (B38)
8543. do. 1886. The hurly-burly; or, 7-20-8. A farcical comedy in 3 acts. Alt. and ad. by H. Hendricks. L: French. 48p. 17cm. [BM]
8544. do. 1890. A kettle of fish: a farcical comedy in one act. Ad. Anon. Bost: Baker. 53p. 16. [LCO]
8545. do. 1897. [same as #8542] NY: Roorbach. 103p. 18cm. [LC]
*8546. (Die goldene Spinne.) The gold spider: comedy farce in 4 acts [prose]. Tr. anon. Berlin? 1885. 11;14;18;12p. 33cm. Tw. [BM]

SCHOENTHAN, Fz. and G. Kadelburg.
8547. (Goldfische.) The railroad of love: a comedy in 4 acts [prose] Tr. A. Daly. NY: Prtd. as MS for the author. 1887. 72p. 8.[LCO.BM]

SCHOENTHAN, Fz. and E. Moser.
8548. (Krieg im Frieden.) The lancers: a comedy in 3 acts [prose]. Tr. J. Hartley Manners. NY: 1907. Tw. [LC.BM]

SCHOENTHAN, Fz. and Rd. Oesterreicher.
8549. (Graf Pollinger.) Miss Patsy; or, "Der dumme August." Ad. by Sewell Collins. NY: (Copyright by H: Savage.) 1909. Tw. [LC]

SCHOENTHAN, Fz. and Freiherr v. Schlicht (i.e., Wf. v. Baudissin).
8550. (Im bunten Rock.) Military mad: a comedy in 3 acts [prose]. Tr. Leo Ditrichstein. 1904. [BM]

SCHOEPF, J: D:
8551. (Reise durch einige der...nordamerikanischen Staaten...) Travels in the confederation, 1783-4. Tr. and ed. Af. J. Morrison. Phil: Campbell 1911. 2v. 20cm. [LC]

SCHONER, J. G., d. 1818. Sel. in C244.

SCHOPENHAUER, Art. 1788-1860. Sel. in C118;366*;461*;469;574.

COLLECTIONS

*8552. ANON. 1891. Selected essays. With a biogr. introd. and sketch of his philos. by Ern. B. Bax. L: Bell. lii;359p. 17cm. [BM]
8553. ANON. 1914. [same]. L: Bell; NY: Macmillan. Bohn's pop. lib. liii;359p. [EC.AC]
8554. ANON. 1924. Essays in ethics. Girard, Kan: Haldeman-Julius. Little blue books. 64p. 12cm. [LC]
[Human nature; Free-will and fatalism; Character.]
8555. ANON. 1924. Essays on relig. and pantheism. Girard, Kan: Haldeman-Julius. Little blue books. 60p. 12cm. [BQM]
8556. ANON. 1925? The Christian system, and other essays. Girard, Kan: Haldeman-Julius. Little blue books. 59p. 12cm. [BQM]
[Title; Physiognomy; Psychol. observations; The metaphysics of fine art.]
8557. ANON. 1926. Essays. NY: Harcourt n.d. Bohn lib. [AC]
[Probably the same as #8553.]
8558. BERNAYS, C. L. Dialogue on immortality; Doctrine of the will. 1871. In C300(1).
8559. DANNREUTHER, E: An essay on visions, etc; On the metaphysics of music. Tr. 1880. In #9628.
*8560. DIRCKS, MRS. R. Essays of S--. L: Scott 1897. xxxiv;224p. 17cm. [BM]
*8561. DROPPERS, GARRETT and C: A: P. DACHSEL. Select essays. Milwaukee: Sentinel co. 1881. 178p. 20cm. [Some errors.] [LC.BM]
*8562. HILLEBRAND, MME. K: Two essays. Tr. from 4th Ger. ed. L: Bell 1889. xxviii;380p. 18cm. [BM.LC]
[On the fourfold root of the principle of sufficient reason ("Vierfache Wurzel des Satzes vom zureichenden Grunde"); On the will in nature ("Ueber den Willen in der Natur").]
*8563. do. 1891. [same] Rev. ed. L: Bell. 380p. [LC]
8564. JOSÉFÉ, C: Thoughts on philos. and its method; Thoughts on logic and dialectic. Tr. 1875. In C300(5).
8565. SAUNDERS, T: B. Essays, sel. and tr. NY: Burt 1893? 455p. 12. [Wisdom of life; Counsels and maxims; Relig. and other essays; Art of lit.; Studies in pessimism.] [LC]
8566. do. 1896. The art of controversy, and other posthumous papers. Sel. and tr. L: Sonnenschein; NY: Macmillan. 116p. 18cm. [BM.LC]
8567. do. and E. B. Bax. 1901. Wisdom of life, and other essays. L; Washington, D.C: Dunne. 332p. 8. [LC]

8568. [Sel.] With introd. by R. Dinsdale Stocker. Phil: McKay n.d. 77p. Fe. [AC]
8569. [Sel.] 1902. The wisdom of S--, sel. by T: B. Saunders. NY: Wieners. 127p. 16cm. [LC]
8570. [Sel.] 1911. Wisdom of S-- as revealed in some of his principal writings. Sel. and tr. Wl. Jekyll. L: Watts. xii;442p. front.

SCHOPENHAUER, Art.--Selections
(port.) 20cm. [BM]
8571. [Sel] 1912. Sel. from S--. Tr. anon. L: Siegle, H. Langham booklets. 77p. 9cm. [BM]
8572. (Aphorismen zur Lebensweisheit, I.) Wisdom of life...Tr. T: B. Saunders. L: Sonnenschein 1890. xxvi;135p. 19cm. [BM.LC]
8573. do. 1891. [same] [LC]
8574. do. 1902. [same] 3d ed. [LC]
8575. do. 191- . [same?] Girard, Kan: Haldeman-Julius n.d. Big blue books. 128p. 5 x 8 in. [Publisher's catalog.]
*8576. (Aphorismen...II.) Counsels and maxims...Tr. T: B. Saunders. L: Sonnenschein 1890. 162p. 19cm. [BM]
*8577. do. 1891. [same] 2d ed. 162p. [LCO]
*8578. do. 1895. [same] 4th ed. Sonnenschein. 162p. 19cm. [BM]
*8579. do. 1899. [same] L: Sonnenschein; NY: Macmillan. 162p. 19cm. [LC]
8580. do. 191- . [same?] Girard, Kan: Haldeman-Julius n.d. Big blue books, 128p. 5 x 8 in. [Publisher's catalog.]
*8581. (Die Grundlage der Moral.) The basis of morality. Tr. A. B. Bullock. L: Sonnenschein 1903. 285p. 19cm. [BM.LC]
*8582. do. 1915. [same] 2d ed. L: Allen & Unwin; NY: Macmillan. xxviii;288p. [BM]
8583. (Die Welt als Wille und Vorstellung.) Sel. Tr. R: B. Haldane and J: Kemp. 1913-15. In C154(15).
*8584. do. 1883-6. The world as will and idea. Tr. R: B. Haldane and J: Kemp. L: Trübner. 3v. 21cm. [BM.LC]
*8585. do. 1896. [same] L: Paul, T. & T. [LC]
8586. On the intellect. Tr. C: Joséfé. 1878. In C300(8).

PARERGA UND PARALIPOMENA

8587. 1889. Religion, a dialogue, and other essays. Sel. and tr. T: B. Saunders. L: Sonnenschein. viii;117p. 19cm. [BM]
8588. 1890. [same] 2d ed. 117p. [LC]
8589. 1891. [same] 3d enl. ed. Sonnenschein. 140p. 19cm. [BM.LC]
8590. 1891. The art of literature: a series of essays. Sel. and tr. T: B. Saunders. L: Sonnenschein. xiv;149p. 18cm. [BM]
*8591. 1891. Studies in pessimism. A series of essays. Sel. and tr. T: B. Saunders. 2d ed. L: Sonnenschein. 142p. 19cm. [BM.LC]
[He takes some questionable liberties.]
8592. 1893. Studies in pessimism. L: Temple. 12. [EC]
[Cf. the following entry.]
8593. 1896. do. Tr. W: M. Thomson. L: Temple. After-dinner series. vi;184p. 16cm. [BM]
8594. 1898. do. [reissue of #8592] [EC]
8595. 1899. [reissue of #8587] L: Sonnenschein; NY: Macmillan. [LC]
8596. 1900. [reissue of #8590] L: Sonnenschein; NY: Macmillan. 149p. 19cm. [LC]
*8597. 1903. [reissue of #8591] L: Sonnenschein; NY: Macmillan. [LC]
*8598. 1906. [same] 7th ed. Sonnenschein. 8. [EC]
*8599. 1908. [same as #8597] [LC]
8600. 1910. [same as #8590] 6th ed. Sonnenschein. [EC]
8601. 1913-15. [Sel.] Parerga and paralipomena. Tr. T: B. Saunders. In C154(15).
8602. 1917. Studies in pessimism. Tr. anon. NY: Boni & Liveright. 182p. S. [AC]
8603. 1925? do. Tr. anon. Girard, Kan: Haldeman-Julius n.d. Little blue books. 64p. 12cm. [BQM]
[On the sufferings of the world; On suicide; On women; Further psychol. observations.]

*8604. (Transzendente Spekulation über die anscheinende Absichtlich-

SCHOPENHAUER, Art.
keit im Schicksal des Einzelnen.) Transcendent speculations on apparent design in the fate of the individual. Tr. D: Irvine. L: Watts 1913. 56p. 18cm. [BM]
[A popularization of the orig. Cover-title has: "In memoriam Richard Wagner, 1813-83."]
8605. (Ueber den Willen in der Natur.) Will in nature. Tr. anon. NY: Eckler 1900. D. [AC]
*8606. (Zur Ethik. Zur Rechtslehre und Politik.) On human nature. Essays on ethics and politics. Sel. and tr. T: B. Saunders. L: Sonnenschein 1897. 132p. 19cm. [BM.LC]
[For convenience, orig. chaps. have been divided into sections and named.]
*8607. do. 1902. [same] L: Sonnenschein; NY: Macmillan. 132p. 19cm. [BM.LC]
8608. do. 1906. [same] 3d ed. L: Sonnenschein. 146p. 8. [EC]
8609. do. 1910. [same] 4th ed. Sonnenschein. [EC]
*8610. do. 1926. [reissue] L: Allen & Unwin. [LC]

SCHOPENHAUER, J:a Hte. (Trosiener) 1766-1838. Sel. in C12.
*8611. (Die arme Margarete.) Poor Margaret: a tale. Tr. Ag. Fraser. L: Pub. by Com. of patriotic art exhib. 1855. 20p. il. with 13 orig. drawings. 22cm. [BM]
*8612. (Jugendleben und Wanderbilder.) My youthful life, and pict. of travel. Tr. E.W. L: Longmans 1847. 2v. xxviii;283; 320p. 16cm. [BM.LC]

SCHOPPE, Ama. (Ea. So. Kta.) (Weise) 1791-1858.
8613. Henry and Mary; or, the little orphans. Tr. Susan Cobbett. L: Simpkin 1860. 148p. 18cm. [BM]
8614. do. 1863. [same] Simpkin. [EC]

SCHOTT, Pl.
8615. (Die tote Stadt.) The dead city: opera in 3 acts by Er. Wfg. Korngold. Text founded on G. Rodenbachs "Das Trugbild." Tr. R. H. Elkin. Libr. Ger;Engl. NY: G. Ricordi. 1921. 95p. 23cm. [BM]
[Line for line tr.; close, rather prosy.]

SCHOTTEL(IUS), Jt. G: 1612-76. Sel. in C41.

SCHRADER, Fd.
8616. (F: der Grosse und der 7jährige Krieg.) F: the Gt. and the seven years' war. Tr. G: P. Upton. Chic: McClurg 1905. 145p. 17cm. [LC]

SCHRECKENBACH, Pl. 1866-1923.
†8617. (Der König v. Rothenburg.) The king of R--: a histor. romance. Mrs. Ma. A. Bookstaver. Bost: Badger 1914. 315p. 19cm. [LC]
[Tr. is quite ruthless.]

SCHREIBER, der tugendhafte, early 13th cent. Sel. in C27;532.

SCHREIBER, Als. (W:) 1761-1841. Sel. in C6;106;125;319;372;391;393; 415;466.
8618. (Anleitung...den Rhein...zu bereisen.) The traveler's guide down the Rhine. Tr. anon. New ed. L: S:Leigh 1823. viii;399p. 14cm. [BM]
8619. do. 1830. [same]...and...describing the Moselle. New ed. L: Leigh. viii;453p. 14cm. [LC]
8620. do. 1834. [same] New ed. with corr. and add. by L. Kohnen. Brussels: Ad. Wahlen. xxxiv;384p. 14cm. [BM]
8621. do. 1835. A complete guide on a voyage on the Rhine...on the Mosella, etc. Tr. new moulded...Rev. P: Will. Heidelberg. Engelmann. xiv;374p. 17cm. [BM]

SCHREIBER, Als.
[Also, Saws and legends of the Rhine, Oden-forest, by C: V. Incledon (based on Schreiber). Heidelberg. 84p.]
8622. do. 1836. The traveler's guide to the Rhine, orig. compiled from A. S--. 4th ed., consid. augmented. L: Leigh. xxiv;428p. 14cm. [BM]
8623. (Sagen aus den Rheingegenden, dem Schwarzwalde und den Vogesen...) Traditions of the countries of the Rhine. Tr. C: V. Incledon and Rev. P: Will. Heidelberg: Engelmann 1836. 120p. il. w. engr. 17cm. [Rewritten and expanded.] [BM.LC]

"SCHRILL, Ern." (i.e., S: Keller, 1856-1924).
8624. (Am freien Glauben. Erzählung aus Südrussland.) His heir: a novel of mod. life in Southern Russia. Tr. W. Eickmann. L;NY: Neely 1899. 478p. 12. [LC]

SCHROEDER, F: U: L: 1744-1816.
8625. (Der Fähndrich.) The ensign: a comedy in 3 acts [prose]. Tr. B: Thompson. 1801. In C535.

SCHROEDER, J: H: 1666-99. Sel. in C231-2;244;273;276;466;489.

SCHUBART, Cn. F: Dn. 1739-91. Sel. in C17;26;123;133;137a;171;229;309;372;388;394;461;560;#6209a.

SCHUBERT, Fz. P: 1797-1828. The conspirators: opera. See Castelli.
Miriam's song of triumph: cantata. See Grillparzer, Fz.
See Kreissle v. Hellborn, H:, Fz. S--, #5440.

SCHUBERT, Glf. H: v. 1780-1860. Sel. in C88.
8626. The cripple of Rottenstein...a narr. of facts. Tr. Mrs. W. H. L: Nickisson 1843. 52p. 16cm. [BM]
*8627. (Der Meeresstrom.) The ocean current. Tr. anon. L: Rivingtons 1849. 64p. front. 15cm. [BM]
8628. (Die Geschichte der Natur.) Nat. hist. of the animal kingdom for the use of young people, in 3 pts. Tr. W. F. Kirby. L: S.P.C.K. 1889. 66p. il. w. plates. 33cm. [BM]
§8629. (Erinnerungen an Bernard Overberg, 1838.) A memoir of B-- O--, taken from a somewhat larger life by Krabbe. With a short account of the system of nat. educ. in Prussia. Tr. anon. L: Seeley 1838. xxvii;104p. 12. [BM]
8630. do. 1840. Memoirs of B-- O--. Tr. freely Mrs. S. Williams. In C569.
8631. (Erinnerungen aus dem Leben der Herzogin He. Lu. v. Orléans.) Reminisc. of the life, and some of the letters, of H.R.H. Helene Louise, the late duchess of Orleans. Tr. anon. Bath: Binns & Goodwin 1862. xvi;246p. 19cm. [BM.LC]
8632. do. 1862. In Harcourt, Jeanne Paule, "Memoir of the duchess of O--." 2d ed. NY: Scribner. 391p. 19cm. [LC]
[Tr. from the French for this ed.]
8633. Frederic Lambert; or, the student of Leipzig. Tr. anon. L: Rivingtons 1848. 101p. 14cm. [BM]
8634. do. 1852. [not the same] The Leipsic student; or, the old debt. A tale. Tr. anon. L: Houlston & Stoneman. 181p. front. 14cm. [BM]
8635. (J: Ts. Kiessling.) The life of J: T. Kiessling. Tr. anon. L: Relig. tract soc. 1837. 118p. 15cm. [BM]
[Much condensed from the orig.]
8636. Js. Paehler; or, "The man who would be rich." Tr. anon. L: Rivingtons 1848. 56p. 14cm. [BM]
8637. Mirror of nature. Phil: 1849. 12. [EC]
8638. Palästina. New album of the Holy Land, etc. See Fraas, O., joint author, #1837.
8639. The schoolmaster. Tr. anon. L: Rivingtons 1848. 70p. 14cm. [BM]

SCHUBERT, Glf.
8640. A treatise on the existence of a good and evil principle in man. Tr. Rev. W. Lobscheid. Hong Kong: Shortrede 1861. 18p. 18cm. [BM]
8641. The twin brothers: a tale. Tr. Mrs. Stanley Carr. L: Partridge 1846. 68p. 15cm. [BM]
8642. The whirlpool. Tr. anon. Bath: Binns & Goodwin; L: Whittaker 1852. 32p. 12cm. [BM]
*8643. (Züge aus dem Leben des J: F: Oberlin.) Memoirs of J: F: O--, late pastor in Steinthal. Tr. Mrs. S. Williams. 1840. In C569.

"SCHUBIN, Ossip" (i.e., Lula Kirschner, 1854- .)
*8644. (Asbeïn. Aus dem Leben eines Virtuosen.) Asbeïn: from the life of a virtuoso. Tr. Elise L. Lathrop. NY: Worthington 1890. 341p. 19cm. [Seems to be very good.] [LC.BM]
8645. Blanche: the maid of Lille. Tr. Sa. H. Adams. Bost: Priv. prt. 1902. 93p. 19cm. [LC]
§8646. (Die Geschichte eines Genies.) The story of a genius. Tr. E. H. Lockwood. NY: Fenno 1898. 212p. 12. [LC]
[Not very good, but not bad; some twisting of her style. --Title; The nobl' Zwilk; What happened to Holy St. Pancras of Evolo.]
*8647. (Erlachhof.) Erlach court. Tr. Mrs. A. L. Wister. Phil: Lippincott 1889. 367p. 19cm. [LC.BM]
8648. Felix Lanzberg's expiation. Tr. Elise L. Lathrop. NY: Worthington 1892. 311p. il. 19cm. [LC]
8649. (Gebrochene Flügel.) Broken wings. Tr. anon. NY: Collier 1893. 284p. 18cm. [LC]
*8650. (Gloria victis.) Gloria victis. Tr. Ma. Maxwell. NY: Gottsberger 1886. 319p. 16. [Very good tr.] [LC]
*8651. (Gräfin Erikas Lehr- und Wanderjahre.) Countess Erika's apprenticeship. Tr. Mrs. A. L. Wister. Phil: Lippincott 1891. 425p. 19cm. [LC.BM]
[Author called this "faithful and picturesque rendering."]
*8652. do. 1892. [same] L: [Another copy with a new t.p.] [BM]
8653. The hand of destiny. Tr. Ma. A. Robinson. NY: Worthington 1892. 272p. 20cm. [LC]
*8654. (O du mein Oesterreich!) "O thou, my Austria!" Tr. Mrs. A. L. Wister. Phil: Lippincott 1890. 429p. 19cm. [LC.BM]
8655. (Peterl. Eine Hundegeschichte.) Peterkins, the story of a dog. Tr. Mrs. J: Lane. Il. C. Taylor. L;NY: Lane 1906. 180p. 20 x 17cm. [BM.LC]
*8656. (Torschlusspanik.) The closing door. Tr. Marie D. Gurney. L: Dent 1896. 197p. 16cm. [Well enough; correct.] [BM]
8657. (Toter Frühling.) A leafless spring. Tr. Ma. J. Safford. Phil: Lippincott 1893. 295p. 19cm. [LC]
8658. (Unter uns.) Our own set. Tr. Ca. Bell. Rev. and corr. NY: Gottsberger 1884. 280p. 16cm. [LC]
8659. do. 1888. One of us: a novel in three parts. Tr. Harriet F. Powell. L: Stott. 8. [EC]
8660. do. 1893. One of us. Tr. Mrs. Ellen Waugh. NY: Collier. 288p. 18cm. [LC]
8661. (Woher tönt dieser Missklang durch die Welt?) Chords and discords: a story of souls astray. Tr. A. H. L. NY: Collier 1894. 2v. in one. 18cm. [LC]

SCHUECKING, (Cph. Bh.) Levin, 1814-83.
8661a. (Die barmherzige Schwester.) The sister of mercy: an advent. of the campaign of 1870. Tr. anon. "Colburn's Mag." 148(1871): 290. (B15a)
8662. (Feuer und Flamme.) Fire and flame. Tr. Mrs. Evangeline O'Connor. NY: Appleton 1876. 175p. 23cm. [LC]

SCHUECKING, (Cph. Bh.) Levin
8662a. Frau von Bernard's valet. Tr. anon. "Every Sat." 3(1867):426, 467. (B15a)
8662b. How the baron got him a wife. Tr. W. H. Furness. "Penn Monthly" 9(1878):819. (B15a)
*8663. (Luther in Rom.) L-- in Rome; or, Corradina, the last of the Hohenstaufen. A religio-histor. romance. Tr. Mrs. Eudora South. Bost: Thayer 1890. 377p. il. front. (port.) 24cm. [LC.BM] [First two chaps. omitted.]
8664. (Pulver und Gold.) Powder and gold: a story of the Franco-Prussian war. Tr. anon. NY: Hinton n.d. 1872-6. 16. [AC]

SCHUETZ, J: Jk. 1640-90. Sel. in C232;235;239;269;287.

SCHUETZE, Gf.
8665. Life of J. G. Keyssler, as pref. to #4955. Tr. 1758.

SCHULTS, Ad. 1820-58. Sel. in C301;438.

SCHULTZ, Alwin, 1838-1909. Sel. in C102.

SCHULTZ, Jm. Cph. F:
§8666. (Moritz, ein kleiner Roman.) Maurice: a Ger. tale. Tr. from the French. Anon. L: Vernor & Hood 1796. 2v. 227; 193p. 18cm. [BM]

SCHULTZE, ---. Sel. in C31;67;216;417.

SCHULZ, Ab. ("San-Marte") 1802-93.
8667. An essay on the influence of Welsh trad. on the lit. of Germany, France, and Scand. Tr. Mrs. Berrington. Llandovery: W. Rees 1841. 140p. 22cm. [BM]

SCHULZ, E: 1813-42. See "Ferrand, E:"

SCHULZE, Ern. Kd. F: 1789-1817. Sel. in C17;43;88;152;373;533;#8001.
*8668. (Die bezauberte Rose.) The enchanted rose: a poem in three cantos. Tr. W. Waddilove. Hamburg: Fabricius & Rathgen 1835. viii;89p. 21cm. [No fem. rhyme; otherwise excellent.] [BM]
§8669. do. 1844. A romaunt in three cantos. Tr. Caro. de Crespigny. L: Longmans. xiii;134p. 17cm. [BM]

SCHULZE, F: A: 1770-1849. See "Laun, F:"

SCHULZE, Fritz.
8670. The legendary in Ger. lit. Tr. W. C. Sawyer. 1904. In "Teutonic legends, etc." pp. 13-48. See "Wagner, R:" Ring of the Nibelungen, #9692.

SCHULZE-SMIDT, Frau Bhe. 1846-1920. See "Oswald, E."

SCHUMACHER, Gb.
8671. Across the Jordun, being an explor. and survey of part of Haurân and Jaulân. Tr. anon. L: Bentley 1886. xv;342p. il. 19cm. [BM]
8672. The Jaulân: surveyed for the Ger. soc. for the explor. of the Holy Land. Tr. anon. L: Bentley 1880. xi;304p. il. 20cm. [BM]
8673. do. 1888. [same] 304p. [LC]
8674. Northern 'Aljûn, "within the Decapolis." Tr. Ax. P. Watt. L: Bentley 1890. 207p. 20cm. [BM]

SCHUMACHER, H: Vollrat.
8675. The fair enchantress. Tr. anon. L: Hutchinson 1912. 307p. il. 19cm. [BM]
*8676. (Lord Nelsons letzte Liebe.) N--'s last love. Tr. anon. L: Hutchinson 1913. 355p. il. col. front. (port.) 20cm. [BM]

SCHUMACHER, Hm. 1868- . Sel. in C563.

SCHUMACHER, Tony.
8677. The tower angel. Tr. Ma. E. Ireland. Chic;Akron: Saalfield 1908. 197p. il. 19cm. [LC]

SCHUMANN, Ege.
*8678. (Erinnerungen.) The memoirs of E--S--. Tr. Marie Busch. L: Heinemann 1927. xi;218p. ports. 22cm. [BM]
[Includes: "Erinnerungsbüchelchen für unsere Kinder," by Rb. Schumann. --AC has title: Schumanns and J:s Brahms; the memoirs. Dial press 1927. il.]

SCHUMANN, Ka. 1819-96. See Litzmann, B., C. S--, an artist's life, #5854.
*8679. (Ka. Schumann und J:s Brahms. Briefe, 1853-96.) Letters of Ca. S-- and J:s B--. Ed. by B. Litzmann. Tr. anon. L: Arnold 1927. xiv;299; 310p. 22cm. [LC]
[Many letters and passages omitted, but with good judgment; many of those omitted had already been pub. in #5854.]

SCHUMANN, Rb. (Ax.) 1810-56.
§8680. [Coll.] Music and musicians: essays and criticisms. Tr. Fanny Ritter. NY: Schuberth; L: Reeves 1877. 418p. 20cm. [LC.BM]
8681. [Coll.] 1880. do. 2d series. 540p. 20cm. [LC.BM]
8682. [Coll.] 1920. do. 2d series. 4th ed. L: Reeves. 540p. [BM]
§8683. (Briefe.) The life...told in his letters. Tr. May Herbert. L: Bentley 1890. 2v. 19cm. [BM.LC]
§8684. (Briefe.) Letters. Sel. and ed. Dr. K: Storck. Tr. Ha. Bryant. L: Murray 1907. xviii;299p. 23cm. [BM.LC]
8685. (Erinnerungsbüchelchen für unsere Kinder.) A little book of memories for our children. Tr. Marie Busch. 1927. In Memoirs of Ege. Schumann, pp. 205-18. #8678.
Genoveva: opera. See Reinick, Rb., #7388.
§8686. (Jugendbriefe.) Early letters. Tr. May Herbert. L: Bell 1888. xii;307p. 20cm. [BM.LC]
§8687. (Musikalische Haus- und Lebensregeln.) Advice to young musicians. Tr. H: Hg. Pierson. Lpz;NY: Schuberth; L: Ewer 1860. 35p. Ger;Engl. 14cm. [BM]
[Tr. is complete and reasonably faithful, but not very expert.]
§8688. do. 1876. [not the same] Advice to young musicians. Tr. anon. L: Millereau. 8p. 13cm. [BM]
[Also complete; free, and about as good as the foregoing.]
*8689. do. 1878. Rules and maxims for young musicians. Tr. F. R. Ritter. L: Reeves. 11p. 18cm. [Good, not excellent.] [BM]
*8690. do. 1879. Rules of life and conduct from a musical point of view. Tr. anon. L: Rb. Cocks & Co. 14p. 17cm. [BM]
[Not ideal, but better than the others.]
See Reissmann, A:, Life and works of R. S--, #7392.
See Wasiliewski, W:, Life..., #9915.

SCHURZE, C. H. An artist's poems. (AC) Error for "Schmolze, K. H.," q.v.

SCHWAB, Gst. (B:) 1792-1850. Sel. in C17;40;97;215;296;309;372;388; 414-5;438;539.
*8691. (Die Legende von den heiligen drei Königen v. Hildesheim, bearbeitet...) The legend of the three holy kings. Freely tr. W: A. Gardner. L: Priv. prt. 1845. 44p. 20cm. [BM]
[Excellent in sense and form; no fem. rhyme.]

SCHWAB, Michel. Sel. in C301.

SCHWARTZKOPPEN, Cde. v. Sel. in C112.

SCHWARZENBERG, F. A.
8692. Ax. v. Humboldt; or, what may be accomplished in a lifetime. L: Rb. Hardwicke 1866. 207p. 19cm. [BM]
[Based on Klencke's "Denkmal." Cf. #5030. EC has: Life and labours of Ax. v. Humboldt. L: Hardwicke 1866.]

SCHWARZENBURG, Ad.
8693. True newes of a notable victorie obtayned against the Turkes. By the Right honorable Lorde, Adolph Baron of Swatzburg, 18th day of March, 1598. Tr. out of high dutch by W. S. R. L: Prtd. for R: Oliue 1598. 14p. il. (2 ports.) 18cm. [BM]

SCHWEDLER, J: Cph. 1672-1730. Sel. in C269.

SCHWEGLER, F: K: Ab. 1819-57.
*8694. (Geschichte der Philosophie im Umriss.) Hist. of philos. in epitome. Tr. J. H. Seelye. NY;L: Appleton 1856. xiv;365p. 19cm. [LC.BM]
*8695. do. 1867. Hand book of the hist. of philos. Tr. J. H. Stirling. Ed: Edmonston & Douglas. viii;417p. 17cm. [BM] [Correct, choppy, formal. No annotations.]
*8696. do. 1868. [same] 2d ed. Ed;L: xiv;486p. 17cm. [BM] [Annotations, pp. 343-476.]
*8697. do. 1871. [same] 3d ed. xviii;486p. 17cm. [BM] [With life of S--.]
8698. do. 1874. [same] 5th corr. ed. Edmonston & Douglas. 486p. 18cm. [LC]
*8699. do. 1877. [same] 6th ed. xviii;486p. 17cm. [BM]
*8700. do. 1879. [same] 7th ed. xviii;486p. 18cm. [BM]
*8701. do. 1880. Seelye's tr. rev. by B: E. Smith. Appleton. xiv; 469p. 20cm. [LC]
*8702. do. 1881. [same] [BM]
*8703. do. 1884. Stirling's tr. 9th ed. Ed: Oliver & Boyd. xviii; 486p. [BM]
*8704. do. 1888. [same] 10th ed. Ed: Oliver & Boyd; L: Simpkin. xviii;486p. [BM]
*8705. do. 1908. [same as #8700] [LC]

SCHWEIGER-LERCHENFELD, Amand v. 1846-1910.
8706. (Das Frauenleben der Erde.) Woman in all lands. Tr. A. S. Meyrick. Roper 1880. 4. [AC]

SCHWEINFURTH, G: (A:) 1836- .
*8707. (Im Herzen von Afrika.) The heart of Africa: three years' travels and advent...1868-71. Tr. Ellen E. Frewer. L: Low 1873. 2v. 559; 521p. il. 21cm. [BM.LC]
*8708. do. 1874. [same] NY: Harper. 2v. il. 24cm. [LC]
*8709. do. 1878. [same] L: Low. 2v. 308; 297p. il. 18cm. [BM]

SCHWEINICHEN, Hs. v. 1552-1616.
8710. (Des schlesischen Ritters Hans v. Schweinichen und Mertschuetz abenteuerlicher Lebenslauf.) A sketch of a Silesian knight of the 16th cent. Tr. Mrs. Percy Sinnett in "Byways of hist. from the 12th to the 16th cent." L: Bentley 1854. pp. 363-401. 19cm. [BM] [Condensed from the orig.]

SCHWEINITZ, Hs. Cph. v. 1645-1722. Sel. in C229.

SCHWEINITZ, L: D: v. 1780-1834.
8710a. Journey to Goshen (Indiana)...in 1831. Tr. Adolf Gerber. Ind. hist. soc. 1927. 205-85p. O. [AC]

SCHWEITZER, Ab. 1875- .
*8711. (Aus meiner Kindheit und Jugendzeit.) Memoirs of childhood and youth. Tr. C: T: Campion. L: Allen & Unwin; NY: Macmillan 1925. 103p. front. 19cm. [Admirable tr.] [BM.LC]
8712. (Das Abendmahl.) The mystery of the kingdom of God: the secret of Jesus' messiahship and passion. Tr. with introd. by Wl. Lowrie. NY: Dodd 1914. 275p. 19cm. [LC]
8713. do. 1925. [same] L: Black. 279p. 8 x 5 in. [BM]

SCHWEITZER, Ab.
8714. (Das Christentum und die vier Weltreligionen.) Christianity and the religions of the world. Tr. J:a Powers, with foreword by Nath. Micklem. L: Allen & Unwin 1923. 86p. 7 x 5 in. [BM]
8715. do. 1923. [same] NY: Doran. xv;193p. 19cm. [LC]
8716. (Geschichte der Leben-Jesu Forschung.) The quest of the histor. Jesus. Tr. W: Montgomery. Pref. F. C. Burkitt. L: Black 1910. x; 410p. 8. [BM]
8717. do. 1911. [same] 2d ed. [BM]
8718. do. 1922. [same] 2d ed. Black. [EC]
8719. (Geschichte der paulinischen Forschung.) Paul and his interpreters: a crit. hist. Tr. W: Montgomery. L: Black; NY: Macmillan 1913. xiii;253p. [BM.LC]
*8720. (J: Sb. Bach.) J. S. Bach. Tr. Ern. Newman. Lpz;L;NY: Breitkopf & H. 1911. 2v. xiv;428; 500p. 3 il. 23cm. [BM.LC] [First ed. in collab. with M. Hubert Gillot and written in French, 1905. This tr. into Ger. and expanded, 1908. Newman tr. from German, but with alterations and additions by S--, thus making a 3d enl. ed.]
*8721. do. 1923. [same] Pref. C. M. Widor. L: Black; NY: Macmillan. xiv;428; 500p. il. 23cm. [LC]
8722. (Kulturphilosophie.) The philos. of civilization. L: Black; NY: Macmillan 1923. 2 pts. xvi;105;xxvi;298p. [LC] [Pt. 1, Decay and the restoration of civilization, tr. by C: T: Campion. Pt. 2, Civilization and ethics, tr. by J: P. Naish. -- Also issued separately; see below.]
*8723. (Kulturphilosophie. 1. Verfall und Wiederaufbau der Kultur.) Decay and the restoration of civilization. Tr. C: T: Campion. L: Black; NY: Macmillan 1923. xvi;105p. 22cm. [BM.LC]
8724. (Kulturphilosophie. 2. Kultur und Ethik.) Civilization and ethics. Tr. J: P. Naish. L: Black; NY: Macmillan 1923. xxvi;298p. 22cm. [BM.LC]
*8725. (Zwischen Wasser und Urwald.) On the edge of the primeval forest: exper. and observations of a doctor in equatorial Africa. Tr. C: T: Campion. L: Black; NY: Macmillan 1922. 180p. il. 19cm. [BM.LC]

SCHWEITZER, G:
8726. Emin Pasha, his life and work. Compiled from his journals, letters, etc. by G: S--. Introd. R. W. Felkin. Tr. anon. Westminster: Constable 1898. 2v. xliv;330;339p. 23cm. [BM.LC] [Slightly abbreviated.]

SCHWERIN, Jse. Eli. Felicitas, Gräfin, 1836- .
8727. (Drei Jahre.) Three years. Tr. Ma. J. Safford. Chic;NY: Rand, McNally 1889. 210p. 19cm. [LC]

SCRIVER, Cn. 1629-93. See "Gotthold."

"SEALSFIELD, Charles"[1] (i.e., K: Postl, 1793-1864.) Sel. in C469.
8728. ("Das Kajütenbuch, oder nationale Charakteristiken.") Advent. in Texas. 1. A scamper in the prairie of Jacinto. "Blackwoods Mag." 54(1843):551-564. 2. A trial by jury, ibid. 777-799. 3. The struggle, ibid. 55(1844):18-33. (B7) [Probably by F: Hardman; not called a tr. Abr. from chapters I-III, X-XVI.]
8729. do. 1843. A sketch in the tropics; From a supercargo's log. "Blackwoods Mag." 54(1843):362-373. (B7) [Not called a translation. Probably by Hardman.]

[1] My data on translations from Sealsfield in "Blackwood's Magazine" have been somewhat augmented and considerably clarified by T. H. Leon, whose dissertation (Washington Univ., St. Louis) deals with "The Mexican Novels of Charles Sealsfield," and who kindly wrote me some of the results of his studies.

SEALSFIELD, Charles--Das Kajütenbuch

8729a. do. [same] In "The Anglo-American," I(1843):534-538. [Leon]

8729b. do. [same] In "Travel, adventure and sport from Blackwood's," I(1844):144-175. [Leon]

8730. do. 1844. The cabin book; or, Sketches of life in Texas. Tr. by Professor C: F: Mersch. NY: Winchester. 155p. 22cm. [LC] [Includes "Life in the new world." See #87.]

8731. do. 1845. [same] Title: Life in Texas. Phil: Colon & Adriance. 155p. 21cm. [LC]

*8732. do. 1852. The cabin book; or, National characteristics. Tr. by Sarah Powell. L: Ingram, Cooke. 296p. il. 19cm. [BM.LC] [Cf. #8739.]

8733. do. 1852. Scenes and advent. in Central America. Ed. [i.e., tr.] by Fis. [i.e., F:] Hardman. Ed: Blackwood. 298p. 18cm. [BM.LC] [Consists of articles printed in "Blackwoods Mag."]

8734. do. 1853. Frontier life; or, Scenes and advent. in the south west. By Fis. [i.e., F:] Hardman. NY: Derby & Miller. (B7) [A 'rifacimento' from the German.]

8735. do. 1856. [same] Auburn; NY: Miller, Orton & Mulligan. 376p. il. 19cm. [LC]

8736. do. 1856. [same] NY: Miller & Orton. [LC]

8737. do. 1859. [same] NY: Saxton. 376p. il. 19cm. [LC]

8738. do. 1859. Advent. in Texas. 1. A scamper in the prairie. 2. Lynch law. Abr. by F: Hardman. In "Tales from Blackwood," no. 113. 112p. 16cm. [BM]

*8739. do. 1871. [same as #8732] NY: St. John & Coffin. 273p. il. with numerous engravings. 21cm. [BM.LC]

8740. do. 1881. Frontier life; or, Tales of the southwestern border. By Fis. [i.e., F:] Hardman. Phil: Coates. 376p. 12. [AC] [Evidently same as #8734. No mention of Sealsfield.]

8741. (Der Legitime und die Republikaner.) The Americans and the aborigines. A tale of the shorter war. "Blackwoods Mag." 59(1846): 554;677. Also vol. 60 (1846). (B7) [Abr. tr. without mention of author or tr.]

8741a. do. 1846. Abr. by F. Hardman. In "Travel, advent. and sport from Blackwood's," vol. 6. (Sealsfield named as author.) [Leon]

8742. (Der Virey und die Aristokraten.) German-American romances: The viceroy and the aristocracy, or Mexico in 1812. In "Blackwoods Mag." 57(1845). [Anon. but undoubtedly by Hardman. Abr. tr. (in that order) of chaps. 16, 1, 2, 17-20, (21 and 22 summarized), 23, 24, 32, 41, 42.] [Leon]

8743. (Die deutsch-amerikanischen Wahlverwandtschaften.) Rambleton: a romance of fashionable life in NY during the great speculation of 1836. NY: Winchester 1844. 285p. 23cm. [LC]

8744. do. [same] 1846. By Seatsfield [sic]. NY: Wm. Taylor. 285p. 8. [Jacket title is: Flirtations in America; or, High life in NY and Saratoga.] [Leon]

8744a. do. [same] Flirtation in America. NY: Berford n.d. [Before 1852.] [AC]

8745. (Geo. Howards Brautfahrt. Ralph Doughbys, Esq. Brautfahrt.) 1. My first love: a sketch in NY. In "Blackwood's Mag." 56(1844):69-77. 2. The stolen child: a true tale of the backwoods, ibid. 56 (1844): 227-237. 3. A night on the banks of the Tennessee, ibid. 56(1844): 278-289. 4. My last courtship; or, Life in Louisiana, ibid. 56(1844): 507-524. 5. Up-stream; or, Steamboat reminiscences, ibid. 56(1844): 640-652. [Abr. No mention of author or tr.] [Leon]

8746. do. 1845. (Ralph Doughby...) Settled at last; or, Red River recollections. In "Blackwood's Mag." 57(1845):18-30. (B7) [No mention of author or tr.]

8747. do. 1844. (Ralph Doughby...) Upstream: on the Red River. In "Travel, advent. and sport from Blackwood's," no. 4, vol. 2(1844). [Leon]

SEALSFIELD, Charles
[No mention of author or tr.]
*8748. (Lebensbilder aus d. westlichen Hemisphäre.) Life in the new world; or, Sketches of Amer. society. Tr. G. C. Hebbe and J. A. Mackay. NY: Winchester 1842. 349p. 21cm. [LC]
*8749. do. 1844. [same] [Name printed Seatsfield.] [LC.BM]
8751. (Nathan, der Squatter-Regulator. Pflanzerleben.) Advent. in Louisiana. The blockhouse. The prairies and the swamp: an advent. in Louisiana. In "Blackwood's Mag." 54(1843):234-243, 43-51. [From chap. 3 of the former, chaps. 4 and 5 of vol. 2 of the latter. No mention of author or translator.] [Leon]
8752. do. [same] In "The Anglo-American," I(1843): 415-419, 291-295. [Leon]
8753. do. 1846? [same] In "Travel, advent. and sport from Blackwood's," vol. 6. [Leon]
*8754. (Süden und Norden.) North and South; or, Scenes and advent. in Mexico. Tr. Joel T. Headley. NY: Winchester 1844. 118p. 23cm. [BM dates it 1845. Name spelled Seatsfield.] [LC.BM]
8755. do. 1844. Two nights in southern Mexico. A frag. from the journal of an Amer. traveller. In "Blackwood's Mag." 55;18; 55:449. [Chaps. 17, 18, 25, 26. Abr. tr.] (B7)
8755a. do. (same) In "Travel, adventure and sport from Blackwood's," 3(1844):57-95. [Leon]
[Tokeah; or, The white rose. Phil: Lea & Carey 1829. 19cm.] [LC]
[This was orig. pub. in Engl., afterwards enl. and repub. under the title, "Der Legitime und die Republikaner."]

"SEEBURG, Fz. v." (i.e., Fz. Hacker, 1836-94).
8756. Honor thy father and thy mother. Ad...Art. Preuss. NY: Soc. of the divine word. 1913. 47p. D. [AC]
8757. (Js. Haydn. Ein Lebensbild.) Js. H--: the story of his life. Tr. from "Fz. v. Seeburg" by J. M. Toohey. Notre Dame, Ind: Lyons 1884. 349p. 20cm. [LC]

SEEGER, L. Sel. in C317.

SEEMANN, O: 1825-1901.
*8758. (Kleine Mythologie der Griechen und Römer.) The mythol. of Greece and Rome w. ref. to its use in art. Tr. anon. L: M.Ward 1877. 275p. il. 18cm. [BM]
8759. do. 1877. [same] NY: Harper. il. 16. [AC]
8760. do. 1877. [same] NY: Scribner. il. cr. 8. [AC]
8761. do. 1887. Tr. G: H: Bianchi. L: Chapman. New ed. 8. [EC]
*8762. do. 1923. [same] Ed. G: H: Bianchi. New rev. ed. L: Chapman & Hall. 275p. il. 19cm. [BM dates this 1924.] [BM.LC]

"SEESTERN" See Grautoff, Fd. H., 1871-

SEIDEL, H: 1842-1900. Sel. in C67.
§8763. (Leberecht Hühnchen.) A Ger. Christmas eve. Tr. Jane H. White. Chic: Abbey 1910. 22p. 16cm. [LC]
*8764. do. 1913-15. Leberecht Hühnchen. Tr. A. Werner-Spanhoofd. In C154(13).

SEIDL, J: Gl. 1814-75. Sel. in C36;41;111;137;137a;196;309;372;375;486;497;501;571.

SEILER, ---. Sel. in C241.

SEILING, Max, 1852- .
8765. (Theosophie und Christentum.) Theosophy and Christianity...w. afterword by Dr. Rd. Steiner. Author. tr. by "A. R." (i.e., Ca. F. Barnett). Chic: Rand 1913. 66p. 19cm. [LC]

SELL, K: 1845-1914.
8766. Alice, grandduchess of Hesse, Princess of Gt. Britain and Ireland: biogr. sketch and letters. L: Murray 1884. 12; 415p. il. 20cm. [BM.LC]

SELL, K:
[Memoir by Sell, tr. by Princess Christian. The letters were written in Engl.]
8767. do. 1884. [same] NY: Munro. Seaside lib. 57p. 32cm. [LCO]
8768. do. 1884. [same] NY: Munro. Pocket ed. 212p. 18cm. [LC]
8769. (Aus der Geschichte des Christentums.) The church in the mirror of hist. Tr. Eliz. Sterling. Ed: T. & T. Clark 1890. viii; 250p. 19cm. [BM]

SELNECKER(-neccer, i.e., Schellenecker), N: 1530-92. Sel. in C271; 287;486;570.

SENGENBERG, ---. Sel. in C269.

SENDIVOGIUS, M. Dictionarium, etc. See Paracelsus, #7028.

SEUME, J: Gf. 1763-1810. Sel. in C17;461;489.
8770. Advent. of the Hessian recruit. (Letter from Halifax, 1782.) Tr. anon. In "Mass. Hist. Soc. Proceedings." Bost: 1889. 2d ser., vol. 4, pp. 2-12. [LC.BM]
8771. Extract from diary. In Pfister, Ab. v. #7140.
§8772. (Mein Sommer.) A tour through Germany, Poland, Russia, Sweden, Denmark, etc...1805. L: Prtd. for Phillips 1807. 102p. 22cm. In Phillips, R:, "A coll. of voyages," 1st ser., Vol. VII. [Free, not very accurate.] [BM.LC]

SEYPPEL, K: Ma. 1847- .
§8773. (Er-sie-es.) He-she-it: Egyptian court chronicle B.C. 1302. A veracious and truthful version preserved and transcribed for general use by the peerless poet laureate of Rampsinnit III. Tr. anon. L: Stock 1884. 42p. il. 27cm. [BM.LC]
[Clever, but not faithful to the orig. form.]
8774. do. 1884. [same] NY: Bouton. [AC]
8775. do. 1885. [same] NY: White, Stokes, Allen. il. 4. [AC]
8776. My book: an old Egyptian MS quaintly and humorously il. w. descr. text tr. from Ger. of v. Bodenstein. Anon. NY: White & Allen 1887. 8. [AC]
*8777. (Schlau, schläuer, am schläusten.) Sharp, sharper, sharpest: humorous tale of old Egypt. Tr. anon. Düsseldorf. 1885. 40p. 27cm. [Prtd. (hand lettering) on brown cardboard with burlap covers, imitated seal, copious ils. --Tr. not as good as the orig.] [BM]
8778. do. 1885. [same?] NY: White, Stokes, Allen. il. 4. [AC]
8779. Smith and Schmidt in Africa: Hottentot blue-book. Engl. words by E. H. Jones. NY: White & Allen 1888. il. nar. O. [AC]

SIEBEL, K: 1836-68. Sel. in C309;450;501;571;#8904.

SIEBOLD, Ax. v.
*8780. (Der Eintritt Japans in das europäische Völkerrecht.) Japan's accession to the comity of nations. Tr. with introd. by C. Lowe. L: K.Paul 1901. xiii;119p. 8. [BM]

SIEBOLD, Ph. Fz. v. 1796-1866.
8781. Manners and customs of the Japanese. Tr. anon. L: Murray 1841. xi;423p. 19cm. [BM.LC]
[Only in part from S--. AC has: NY: Harper 1841.]
8782. do. 1841? [same] NY: Harper. 8. [AC]
8783. do. 1845. [same] NY: Harper. 298p. front. 15cm. [BM]

SIEGFRIED, ---. Sel. in C26.

SIEVEKING, Ame. W:e, 1794-1859.
*8784. Life. Ed. by Cath. Winkworth. L: Longmans 1863. xxviii;520p. il. 19cm. [BM.LC]

SIEVEKING, Ame. W:e
8785. The principles of charitable work--love, truth, and order--as set forth in the writings of A.W.S--. Compiled and tr. by S***. L: Longmans 1863. xxvii;123p. 20cm. [BM]
[Not a tr. of any existing work, but very little orig. matter. Substance taken from reports of the Female soc. for the care of the sick and poor in Hamburg. Condensed.]

SILBERSTEIN, Ad. 1845-99.
*8786. (Strategie der Liebe.) Love's strategy. Studies on the art of winning and retaining love. Tr. anon. Chic: Schick 1884. 226p. 17cm. [LC]
*8787. do. 1888. [same] L: Maxwell. 226p. [BM]
*8788. do. 1897. [same] Chic: Laird & Lee. 226p. il. 20cm. [LC]

SILBERSTEIN, A: 1827-1900. Sel. in C112;450.

SIMROCK, K: 1802-76. Sel. in C17;105-6;123;142;167;296;309;318;372-3;391;393;438;469.

SINOLD, Ph. Blr. 1657-1742. Sel. in C276.

SOEHNGEN, Ern. See Stein, Leo, joint author.

SOHN, G:, professor at Heidelberg.
8789. (Disputatio...quod Papa Romanus sit antichristus ille.) A briefe and learned treatise...of the antichrist. Tr. by N. G. Cambridge: J: Legate 1592. 38p. 14cm. [BM]

SOLF, W: 1862- . Sel. in C563.

SOMMERFELD, Ad. 1870- .
†8790. (Frankreichs Ende im Jahre 19??) "How Germany crushed France" (the story of the greatest conspiracy in history). Tr. Louis G. Redmond-Howard. L: Everett 1914. 158p. 18cm. [LC]
[Tr. takes great liberties.]

SONNENBURG, Fd.
8791. Bismarck: his life and times. Tr. Ida L. Saxton and Grace H. Webb. L;NY: Neely 1898. 200p. il. 12. [LC]
8792. The hero of Danzig; or, Konrad, the standard bearer. Tr. by "Luigi," author of "Legends of the Rhine for children." L: Partridge 1882. 253p. front. il. 18cm. [BM]

SONNLEITHNER, Js. 1766-1835, and G. F: Treitschke.

FIDELIO

†8793. n.d. Fidelio: opera in 3 acts by Beethoven. Text ad. freely from the French of Bouilly: "Léonore; ou, l'amour conjugal." Tr. anon. Libr. Ger;Engl. NY: Acad. of mus. n.d. [LC]
8794. n.d. Tr. T: Oliphant. In "The vocal score." L: [LC]
§8795. n.d. Tr. T: Oliphant. Vocal score. L: Cramer, Addison & Beale. 152p. fol. [Good verse, but too remote from the orig.] [BMM.LCM]
8796. 1810. Fidelio. Orig. called Leonora. Tr. T: Oliphant. Piano acc. rev. by C. Lucas. Vocal score. L: Cramer, Addison & Beale. 152p. 36cm. [BMM]
§8797. 1836. F--; or, constancy rewarded. As performed at the theatres royal. Written and ad. to the Engl. stage by W. McGregor Logan. Libr. Engl. L: Brettell. 21p. 17cm.[Tr. is quite free.][BM]
†8798. 1839. [same title] Tr. anon. Libr. Engl. NY: Kimber. 30p. 12. [Poor tr.] [LCM]
*8799. 1851. F--. Tr. J. Wrey Mould. Mus. rev. by W. S. Rockstro. Vocal score. Ger;Engl. L: Boosey. xii;302p. 25cm. [BMM]
†8800. 1851. Tr. anon. Libr. Ital;Engl. L: Her majesty's theatre. 72p. 18cm. [LCM]

SONNLEITHNER and Treitschke--Fidelio
†8801. 1859. Tr. anon. Libr. Engl. (and Ital.) and the music of the principal airs. L: Davidson. 26p. 24cm. [BMM]
[Prtd. in double columns. Engl. tr. the Ital., which is quite far from the German.]
†8802. 1864. Tr. anon. Libr. Ger;Engl. Bost. 24p. [LC]
*8803. 1870. Tr. anon. (Mould's tr.) Ed. by Art. Sullivan. Vocal score. Ital;Engl. L;NY: Boosey. 223p. 25cm. [BMM]
§8804. 1871. Tr. and cor. by Natalia Macfarren. Vocal score. L;NY: Novello. 263p. 26cm. [BMM.LCM]
[Not very good: the rhymes bother her.]
†8805. 1892. [same as #8802] [LC]
*8806. 1907. Tr. Td. Baker. Vocal score. NY: Schirmer. xiv;262p. 4. [LCM]
*8807. 1926. [same] New version with note and orig. recitatives by Art. Bodanzky. Essay by H: E: Krehbiel. Vocal score. NY: Schirmer. [LCM.BMM]
8808. [Ad.] 1808. The fortress of Sorrento: a petit histor. drama in 2 acts. NY: Longworth. 28p. 12. (B48)
[Ad. with very slight change from "Leonore," i.e., "Fidelio."]
8809. [Ad.] 1925. Fidelio. Retold by J. McSpadden. In C390.

SOPHIE, consort of Ern. A: elector of Hanover, 1630-1714.
*8810. (Memoiren.) Memoirs, 1630-80. Tr. H. Forester (from the French). L: Bentley 1888. xx;270p. 21cm. [BM.LC]

SOPHIE Do. Kurprinzessin v. Hannover, consort of G: I of England, 1666-1726.
8811. An authentic narr. of the life, persecutions, and sufferings of the Princess of Zell. Tr. anon. L: Lee 1820? unp. 21cm. [BM]
8812. do. ca. 1820. [same] L: Dean & Munday. 30p. front. 17cm. [LC]
8813. (Briefe.) The love of an uncrowned queen. (Corr. with Count Königsmarck.) Tr. from the French by W: H: Wilkins. L: Hutchinson 1900. 2v. xiii;(341);673p. 42 ports. and ils. 22cm. [BM]
8814. do. 1903. [same] Wilkins, W: H:, The love of...S-- D-- and her corr. with Ph. Cn. Count K--. Now first pub. from the originals (in French). New and rev. ed. L;NY: Longmans. xiv;673p. il. 20cm. [BM.LC]
8815. Memoirs of...chiefly from the secret archives of Hanover, Brunswick, Berlin, and Vienna; includ. a diary of the conversations of illustrious persons of those courts, il. of her hist., with letters and other documents. Now first pub. from the originals. Ed. Rb. F. Williams. L: H:Colburn 1845. 2v. xii;452; 452p. front. (ports.) 22cm. [BM.LC]
8816. Memoirs of the love and state intrigues of the court of Hanover (extr.), pp. 14-47. Also, An old courtier to a young prince ("Ein alter Hoffmeister an einem jonger Kron Prinsen"), pp. 48-71. Also, Princess So. Do's journal, etc., pp. 71-120. In Brown, J:, "Anecdotes and characters of the house of Brunswick." L: Allman 1821. 22cm. [BM]

SORGE, Rev. ---.
8817. Extracts of two letters...in Ger...Oct. 1758...giving an account of the horrid cruelties...committed by the Russians on the king of Prussia's dominions...Tr. anon. L: prtd. Bost: reprtd. and sold at Fowle & Draper's printing-office...in Marlborough street, 1759. 23p. 17cm. [LC]

SPALDING, J: Jm. 1714-1804. Sel. in C244.

SPANGENBERG, A: Gb. 1704-92. Sel. in C19;271;287.
8818. Diary. Tr. 1916. In C19.
8819. (Leben des Herrn...Zinzendorf.) Life of N: L. Count Z--. Tr. S: Jackson. L: Holdsworth 1838. xxxv;511p. 20cm. [BM.LCO]

SPANGENBERG, A: Gb.
[Introd. cites a tr. of vol. 1, ca. 1777, comprising first two pts. issued in Germany in 1772.]
8820. do. 1844. Abr. The banished count: a true history. By the author of "Peep o' day." (F. L. Mortimer.) L: J:Snow. 54p. 12cm. [BM]
[Taken from the foregoing.]
See Ledderhose, K: F:, Life..., #5630.

SPEE, F: 1591-1635. Sel. in C287;372;570.

SPENER, Ph. Jk. 1635-1705. Sel. in C287;372;570.
8821. (Das geistliche Priestertum.) The spiritual priesthood. Tr. A. G: Voigt. Phil: Luth. pub. 1917. 34p. 16cm. [LC]
8822. Memoirs...Compiled from the Ger. Rev. by Com. of Publ. Phil: A.S.S.U. 1830. front. (port.) 144p. 14cm. [BM]
See Wildenhahn, K: A., Ph. Jk. Spener, #10213.

SPENGLER, Os. 1880-1936.
*8823. (Der Untergang des Abendlandes.) The decline of the west. Author. tr. by C: Fis. Atkinson. L: Allen & Unwin; NY: Knopf 1926. 2v. xviii;443; 507p. 23cm. [BM.LC]

SPERATUS, Pl. 1484-1551. Sel. in C244;271;487.

SPERGER, Abbe Hagel.
8824. The adopted son. Tr. by U. Derby: T: Richardson 1846. 35p. 15cm. [BM]

SPERL, Js. 1761-1837. Sel. in C229.

SPERO, Eg. Operettas, see Brammer, Jl., Bernauer, Rd., and Willner, A. M.

SPERVOGEL (I and II), early and late 12th cent. Sel. in C27*;423;427; 489;570.

SPIEGEL, ---. Sel. in C388.

SPIEGEL VON UND ZU PECKELSHEIM, Ad. K: G: Edgar, Freiherr, 1885- .
§8825. (Kriegstagebuch. U 202.) The advent. of the U-202: an actual narr. Tr. anon. NY: Century 1917. vii;202p. 8. [LC.BM]
[Correct but wooden.]
*8826. do. 1919. U Boat 202: the war diary of a Ger. submarine. Tr. Capt. Barry Domvile. L: Melrose. viii;169p. 18cm. [BM.LC]
[One bad mistake in the first sentence.]

SPIELHAGEN, F: 1829-1911. Sel. in C366*;469.
§8827. (Clara Vere.) Lady Ca. de Vere: a story. Tr. anon. NY: Appleton 1881. 181p. 16cm. [LC]
[Rather severely pruned and altered.]
*8828. (Das Skelett im Hause.) The skeleton in the house. Tr. J. Marsden. Dessau: Kolckmann 1881. 167p. 18cm. [BM]
[Very good, not excellent.]
8829. do. 1881. Tr. Ma. J. Safford. NY: Harlan. 16. [AC]
8830. (Deutsche Pioniere.) Block house on the prairie: Ger. pioneers. Tr. anon. City of Lond. co. 1882. 8. [EC]
[Athenaeum (79:247) says tr. is by Ida Veramy.]
§8831. do. 1891. The Ger. pioneers: a tale of the Mohawk. Tr. Levi Sternberg. Chic: Donohue, Henneberry. 250p. 20cm. [LC]
[Not wholly correct.]
§8832. (Die Dorfkokette.) The village coquette. Tr. J. L. Laird. L: Chapman 1875. 157p. 19cm. [Too free.] [BM]
8833. (Die von Hohenstein.) The Hohensteins: a novel. Tr. Prof. M. S. De Vere. NY: Leypoldt & Holt 1870. 584p. 18cm. [LC]
§8834. (Durch Nacht zum Licht.) Through night to light: a novel. Tr. M. S. De Vere. NY: Leypoldt & Holt 1870. 569p. 18cm. [LC]

SPIELHAGEN, F: --Durch Nacht zum Licht
§8835. do. 1888. [same] Holt. 16cm. [LC]
8835a. (Hammer und Amboss.) Hammer and anvil. Tr. anon. "Statesman" 1(1868):135, etc. (B15a)
§8836. do. 1870. Tr. W: Hand Browne. NY: Leypoldt & Holt. 691p. 16. [Better than De Vere, but ruthless.] [UW]
*8837. do. 1880. [extr.] The storm. Tr. Zimmern. In C575-7.
8838. (In Reih' und Glied.) In rank and file. Tr. anon. NY: Leypoldt & Holt 187- . 16. [Publishers' announcement.]
§8839. (Problematische Naturen.) Problematic characters. Tr. M. S. De Vere. NY: Leypoldt & Holt 1869. 507p. 18cm. [LC] [Rather poor; errors.]
§8840. do. 1888. [same] Holt. 16cm. [LC]
*8841. (Quisisana.) Quisisana; or, rest at last. Tr. H: E: Goldschmidt. L: Nimmo & Bain 1881. 316p. 18cm. [See #8843.] [BM]
8842. do. 1882. [same] NY: Munro. Seaside lib. 32cm. [AC]
*8843. do. 1884. [same] NY: Lovell. 316p. 18cm. [LC] [Not without some questionable spots.]
8844. Rose (Röschen vom Hofe) and The village coquette (Die Dorfkokette). Tr. anon. NY: Leypoldt & Holt 187- . 16. [Publishers' announcement.]
*8845. (Sturmflut.) The breaking of the storm. Tr. S. E. A. Stephenson. L: Bentley 1877. 3v. 8. [BM] [Acc. to a reviewer, Misses E. and A. Stephenson were the translators.]
*8846. do. 1913-15. Abr. Tr. Marion D. Learned. In C154(11).
8847. (Susi.) Baroness Susan. Tr. anon. Maclaren 1904. 8. [EC]
8848. do. 1905. Tr. Hilda Skae. NY: Brentano's (B13)
8849. (Ultimo.) Ultimo. 1874? (B15)
8850. (Was die Schwalbe sang.) What the swallow sang: a novel. Tr. M. S. NY: Holt & Williams 1873. 306p. 17cm. [LC]

SPIESS, Cn. H: 1755-99.
8851. [Coll.] 1809. The fallen minister, and other tales. Tr. W. B. Hewetson. L: Newman. 2v. 213; 223p. 12. [BM] [Vol. 1. The murderer; The revenue collector; The fallen minister; Vanity, or the merchant. Vol. 2. Charles; Paulina; Jealousy, or the curate.]
*8852. (Das Petermännchen.) The dwarf of Westerbourg. Tr. anon. L: Morgan 1827. 2v. 249;248p. il. 12. [BM] [Name spelled Spietz. Beautiful col. ils.]
8853. The mountain cottager; or, wonder upon wonder. Tr. Annabelle Plumptre. L: Lane 1798. See "Analyt. R." 18(1798):518. (B26)
8854. do. 1800. [same title] A tale. Phil: Prtd. for Hyndman. 228p. 17cm. [Probably a reprint of the foregoing.] [LC]

SPIKER, (S.) H: 1786-1858.
*8855. (Reise durch England, Wales und Schottland.) Travels through E--, W--, and S--, in the year 1816. Tr. anon. L: Lackington 1820. 2v. xx;325;283p. 19cm. [BM has: 2v. in one.] [BM.LC]

SPILLMANN, Js., S. J. 1842-1905.
8856. (Der Neffe der Königin.) The queen's nephew: an histor. narration from the early Japanese mission. Tr. Helena Long. St.L: Herder 1896. 149p. 17cm. [LC]
8857. (Der Zug nach Nicaragua.) The trip to N--. a tale of the days of the Conquistadores. Tr. Ma. R. Gray. St.L;Freiburg: Herder 1907. 148p. 17cm. [LC]
8858. do. 1913. [same] 2d ed. [AC]
8859. (Die beiden Schiffsjungen.) The cabin boys: a story for the young. Tr. Ma. R. Gray. St.L;Freiburg (Baden): Herder 1907. 137p. 17cm. [LC]

SPILLMANN, Js., S. J.--Die beiden Schiffsjungen
8860. do. 1912. [same] 2d ed. [AC]
8861. (Die englischen Märtyrer unter H: VIII und Elisabeth.) Grandfather and grandson: some pages from the family hist. of the Worthingtons of Blainsco. A tale of the persecutions endured by the Engl. Catholics under Queen Eliz. Tr. M. C. E. Wells. The vista 1890. 108p. 16cm. [BM]
8862. (Die Marienkinder.) Children of Mary: a tale of the Caucasus. Tr. Helena Long. St.L: Herder 1896. 122p. 17cm. [LC]
8863. (Die Schiffsbrüchigen.) The shipwreck: a story for the young. Tr. Ma. R. Gray. St.L;Freiburg: Herder 1906. 126p. 17cm. [LC]
8864. (Die wunderbare Blume von Woxindon.) The wonderful flower of W--: an histor. romance of the time of queen Eliz. Tr. anon. St.L: Herder 1896. 494p. 19cm. [LC]
8865. (Ein Opfer des Beichtgeheimnisses.) A victim to the seal of confession: a true story. Tr. anon. St.L: Herder 1898. [AC]
[Tr. by Miss Clarke.]
8866. do. 1913. [same] 8th ed. St.L: Herder. 321p. O. [AC]
8867. do. 1926. [same] 13th ed. [AC]
8868. (Fronleichnamsfest der Chiquiten.) The Chiquitan festival of Corpus Christi day: a tale of the old missions of South America. Tr. Ma. R. Gray. St.L;Freiburg: Herder 1906. 129p. 17cm. [LC]
8869. (Kämpfe und Kronen.) Crosses and crowns. Tr. Ma. R. Gray. St.L;Freiburg: Herder 1906. 141p. 17cm. [LC]
8870. do. 1912. [same] 2d ed. [AC]
8871. (Kreuz und Chrysanthemum.) Cross and chrysanthemum: an episode from Japanese history. Tr. anon. St.L: Herder n.d. viii;398p. 8. [Publisher's catalog.]
8872. (Liebet eure Feinde.) Love your enemies: a tale of the Maori insurrections in New Zealand. Tr. Helena Long. St. Francis, Wis: St. Aemilianus' asylum 1895. 86p. il. 17cm. [LC]
8873. do. 1896. [same] St.L: Herder. 86p. il. 16cm. [BM]
8874. do. 1897. [same] 2d ed. St.L: Herder. 117p. 17cm. [LC]
8875. do. 1911. [same] 4th ed. Herder. 117p. [AC]
8876. The little martyr of Prague. Tr. M. C. E. L: Art & book co. 1892. vi;146p. front. il. 18cm. [BM]
8877. Long Philip. Tr. anon. 1902. In C481.
8878. (Lucius Flavus.) L-- F--. an histor. tale of the time immed. preced. the destruction of Jerusalem. Tr. anon. St.L: Herder 1901. 619p. 20cm. [LC]
8879. do. 1913. [same] 4th ed. Herder. 619p. [AC]
8880. do. 1925. [same] 6th ed. Herder. 619p. 20cm. [LC]
[Maron, the Christian youth of Labanon. St.L: Herder. [AC]
[This is really by Ad. v. Berlichingen, q.v.]
8881. (Selig die Barmherzigen.) Blessed are the merciful: a tale of the negro uprising in Haiti. Tr. Ma. R. Gray. St.L: Herder 1906. 135p. 17cm. [LC]
8882. (Tapfer und treu.) Valiant and true: advent. of a young officer of the Swiss guards at the time of the French Revolution. Tr. anon. L: Sands 1905. xvi;424p. il. 19cm. [BM]
8883. do. 1912. [same] St.L: Herder. 16;417p. il. O. [AC]

SPINDLER, K: 1796-1855. Sel. in C155.
*8884. (Der Bastard.) The natural son: a Ger. tale descriptive of the age of the emperor Rd. II. Tr. Lord A. Conyngham. L: Mitchell 1835. 3v. in one. 18cm. [Very good.] [BM.LC]
8885. do. 1845. The bastard; or, the brother's revenge. A romantic tale. Tr. A. Braunfels. NY: Winchester. 234p. 23cm. [LC]
8886. do. 1849. [same] Archibald Werner; or, the brother's revenge. NY: Stringer & Townsend. 234p. 23cm. [BM]
†8887. (Der Jesuit.) The Jesuit: a novel. Tr. anon. L: Saunders & O. 1832. 3v. 393p. 16cm. [BM.LC]

SPINDLER, K:--Der Jesuit
[Condensed and altered; complete distortion.]
8888. do. 1834. [same] ...characteristic of the early portion of the 18th cent. L: Smith & Elder. 393p. 16cm. [BM]
§8889. do. 1839. ...a pict. of manners and characters from the 1st quarter of the 18th cent. Tr. anon. L: Bull. 2v. 292;264p. 20cm. [Tr. has good spots, but shows misunderstanding of the orig.] [BM.LC]
8890. do. 1844. ...a histor. romance, il. the principles and practices of the celebrated society...during the early portion of the 18th cent. Tr. anon. NY: Winchester. 110p. 23cm. [LC]
8891. do. 1854. Bryce. [EC]
*8892. (Der Jude.) The Jew: a novel. Tr. anon. L: Bull 1832. 3v. in one. 379p. 19cm. [Excellent.] [BM]
8892a. do. 1844. The Jew. Tr. anon. "Orion" 4(1844):150. (B15a)
8893. do. 1872-6. [same?] NY: Harper n.d. 8. [AC]
8894. (Der Schwärmer.) The enthusiast. Tr. anon. L: Smith, Elder 1835. 288p. 16cm. [Altered from the German.] [BM]
8895. St. Sylvester's night. Tr. anon. 1844. In C457.
8896. do. 1844. [same] Cambridge;L: Rugeley. Juvenile Englishman's lib. 63p. front. 14cm. [BM]

SPINDLER, K:
*8897. (Das geheimnisvolle Schiff.) Gun running for Casement in the Easter rebellion, 1916. Tr. W. Montgomery and E. H. McGrath. L: Collins 1921. viii;242p. 18cm. [BM]

SPITTA, Jl. A: Ph. 1841-94.
*8898. (J: Sb. Bach.) J: S. Bach: his work and influence on the music of Germany. Tr. Ca. Bell and J. A. F. Maitland. L;NY: Novello 1899. 3v. 23cm. [BM has: 3v. in one, xvi;656p.] [BM.LC]

SPITTA, K: J: Ph. 1801-59. Sel. in C51;107;122;166-7;222-3;229*;235; 269;273*;287;309;375;450;486;489;571;#5963;#7859.
8899. (Psalter und Harfe.) Sel. In Durand, Lady, "Imitations from S-- and Tersteegen." C107, pp. 1-72.
§8900. do. 1860. Lyra domestica: Christian songs for domestic edification. Tr. R: Massie. L: Longmans. xv;142p. front. (port.) 16cm. [Contains most of "Psalter und Harfe."] [BM.LCO]
§8901. do. 1861. [same] 2d ed. identical. [BM]
§8902. do. 1861. [same title and tr.] Bost: Dutton. 300p. 16. [LCO] [This contains only a portion of #8900, but adds other hymns, mainly English.]
§8903. do. 1862. [same as #8900] 3d ed. identical. [BM]
§8904. do. 1864. Lyra domestica, 2d series. From...S-- and other hymn-writers. Tr. R: Massie. L: Longmans. xii;163p. 16cm. [BM.LCO] [Two pts. Pt. 1 contains conclud. portions of "Psalter und Harfe." Pt. 2 has: L. H. C. v. Brandenburg, J: Franck, Freylinghausen, Gerhardt (8), Greding, N: Hermann, F. K. Hiller, A. Knapp, Knorr v. Rosenroth, E. Liebich, C. F. Richter.]

SPITTELER, C: 1845-1924. Sel. in C28;154(14);423.
†8905. (Die Mädchenfeinde.) Two little misogynists. Tr. Vicomtesse de Roquette-Buisson. Il. A. Helene Carter. NY: Holt 1922. 132p. 26cm. [A very free adaptation.] [LC]
*8906. (Lachende Wahrheiten.) Laughing truths. Tr. Jas. F. Muirhead. Apprec. of the author by Romain Rolland. L;NY: Putnam 1927. xv; 243p. 19cm. [BM.LC]

SPIX, J: Bp. v. 1781-1826 and C. F. P. v. Martius.
*8907. (Reise in Brasilien...) Travels in Brazil...1817-20. Tr. H. E. Lloyd. L: Longmans 1824. 2v. in one. il. 8. [BM.LC] [Only the first vol. of the orig., four books, is given. Tr. is excellent.]

SPOHR, L: 1784-1859.
*8908. (Selbstbiographie.) Autobiog. Tr. anon. L: Reeves & Turner 1878. 2v. in one. 23cm. [LC]
*8909. do. 1865. [same] L: Longmans. 2v. in one. 327;342p. 22cm. [EC has: 1864.] [BM]
Operas: "Faust," see Bernard, J.; "Jessonda," see Gehe, E.
See Hauptmann, Mz., Letters..., #3907.

SPRINGER, An. H: 1825-91.
8910. Text-book to the illustrations of the hist. of art. Tr. Mrs. Marg. Volkmann. Bost: Prang 1883. 362p. 22cm. [LC.BM]

SPRINGER, Balthasar, fl. 1509.
8911. The voyage from Lisbon to India, 1505-6. Tr. from the Flemish (tr. of the orig. Lat.) by G: F: and Mrs. Janet Barwick. In Harrisse, H: "Americus Vespuccius." L: Stevens 1895. [LC]

SPYRI, Frau J:a (Heusser) 1827-1901.

COLLECTIONS

8912. 1884. Red-letter stories: Swiss tales. Tr. Lucy Wheelock. Bost: Lothrop. 94p. 17cm. [LC]
[Wisa's Christmas; Basti's song in Altorf.]
8913. 1885. Rico and Wiseli. Tr. Louise Brooks. Bost: De Wolfe, Fiske. 2v. in one. 18cm. [LC]
[Rico and Stineli; How Wiseli was provided for.]
†8914. 1887. Swiss stories. Tr. Lucy Wheelock. Bost: Lothrop. 208p. 8. [Adapted rather than tr.--In safe keeping; Rosenresli; Lisa's Christmas; Basti's song in Altorf; Toni.] [BPL]
8915. do. 1889. [same] L: Blackie. 208p. il. 18cm. [BM]
§8916. 1906. Moni, the goat boy ("Moni der Geissbub"), and other stories. Tr. Edith F. Kunz. School ed. Bost: Ginn. viii;211p. il. 17cm. [Large liberties.--Also contains: Without a friend; The little runaway.] [LC]
8917. 1907. [same] [AC]
8918. 1912. Heimatlos: two stories for children. Tr. Emma S. Hopkins. Il. F. Richardson. Bost;NY: Ginn. 231p. 17cm. [LC.BM]
[Lake Sils and Lake Garda; Wiseli finds her place.]
8919. 1914. [same as #8916] [AC]
8920. 1916. [same as #8916] [AC]
8921. 1919. Little curly head; the pet lamb. Tr. Helen B. Dole. NY: Crowell. 77p. il. 20cm. [LC]
8922. 1922. [same as #8913] NY: Crowell. 509p. col. il. 20cm. [LC]
8923. 1925. Children of the Alps. Tr. Eli. P. Stork. Il. in col. by Marg. J. Marshall. Phil;L: Lippincott. 318p. 21cm. [LC.BM]
[Francesca at Hinterwald; The fairy of Intra; Gay little Herbli.]
8924. 1926. [same as #8916] [AC]
8925. 1926. Stories of Swiss children. Tr. Helen B. Dole. NY: Crowell. vii;425p. col. il. 22cm. [LC]
[Toni, the little wood carver; Little curly-head; The rose-child ("Rosenresli"); The children's carol; Little Miss Grasshopper; Jo, the little machinist; What Sami sings to the birds ("Was Sami mit den Vöglein singt"); Moni, the goat-boy ("Moni, der Geissbub"); Trini, the little strawberry girl; Tiss, a little Alpine waif.]
8926. 1926. Eveli, the little singer. Tr. Eli. P. Stork. Il. in col. Blanche Greer. Phil;L: Lippincott. 272p. 21cm. [LC.BM]
[Peppino; Eveli; The Stauffer mill ("Die Stauffer-Mühle").]

8927. Arthur and squirrel. Tr. Helen B. Dole. NY: Crowell 1925. 248p. 20cm. [LC]
8927a. Chel: a story of the Swiss mountains. Tr. Helene H. Boll. NY: Eaton & Mains; Cincin: Jennings & Graham 1913. 126p. 18cm. [LC]

SPYRI, J:a
8928. The children's carol. Tr. Helen B. Dole. NY: Crowell 1925. 58p. 19cm. [LC]
8929. Cornelli. Tr. Eli. P. Stork. Introd. C: W. Stork. Il. in col. Ma. L. Kirk. Phil: Lippincott 1920. 275p. 20cm. [LC.BM]
8930. do. 1921. [same] de luxe ed. 24cm. [LC]
8931. do. 1926. Cornelli, her childhood. Tr. C. W. Coumbe. Il. Fes. Brundage. Akron, O;NY: Saalfield. 250p. il. 18cm. [LC]
8932. Dora. Tr. Eli. P. Stork. Il. in col. Ma. L. Kirk. Phil;L: Lippincott 1924. 215p. 21cm. [LC.BM]
8933. Dorris and her mountain home. Tr. Ma. E. Ireland. Richmond, Va: Presb. com. 1902. 166p. il. 19cm. [LC]
8934. Erick and Sally. Tr. Helene H. Boll. Bost: Beacon press 1921. xi;73p. il. 21cm. [LC]
8935. Eveli and Beni. Tr. Helen B. Dole. NY: Crowell 1926. 62p. 19cm. [LC]
8936. The fairy of Intra. Tr. Eli. P. Stork. Col. il. Marg. J. Marshall. Phil: Lippincott 1925. 98p. D. [Cf. #8923.] [AC]
8937. Francesca at Hinterwald. Tr. Eli. P. Stork. Il. in col. by Marg. J. Marshall. Phil;L: Lippincott 1925. 134p. 19cm. [BM] [Cf. #8923.]
8938. (Gritlis Kinder.) Gritli's children: a story for children. Tr. Louise Brooks. Bost: Cupples & Hurd 1887. 2v. in one. 18cm. [LC]
8939. do. 1923. [same] NY: Crowell. 2v. in one. 196;201p. il. O. [AC]
8940. do. 1924. Tr. Eli. P. Stork. Il. in col. Ma. L. Kirk. Gift ed. Phil;L: Lippincott. 264p. 24cm. [LC.BM]
8941. do. 1927. [same?] Lippincott. 8. [EC]

HEIDI

8942. ANON. 1884. Heidi's early experiences: story for children, etc. L: Low. 8. [Probably tr. by Brooks; see #8956.] [EC]
8943. ANON. 1884. Heidi's further experiences: for children, etc. L: Low. 8. [Probably tr. by Brooks; see #8956.] [EC]
8944. ANON. 1918. Phil: McKay 356p. il. 20cm. [LC]
8945. ANON. 1919. New ed. Akron. O;NY: Saalfield. D. [AC] [Cf. #8949.]
8946. ANON. 1922. Il. Jessie W. Smith. Phil: McKay. 380p. O. [AC]
8947. ANON. 1923. [same as #8944?] Il. by Gst. Tenggren. Bost;NY: Houghton. 356p. 22cm. [LC]
§8948. ANON. 1924. Ed. by Adeline B. Zachert. Il. (partly in col.) by Clara M. Burd. Phil;Chic;Toronto: Winston. 290p. 21cm. [LC.BM] [Consid. edited from the following.]
§8949. ANON. 1924. With 100 il. by Fes. Brundage. Akron, O;NY: Saalfield. 307p. il. 23cm. [Not wholly correct; stilted dialog.] [LC]
§8950. ANON. 1925. [same tr. as the foregoing] Il. L: Rhead. NY;L: Harper. 333p. il. 23cm. [LC]
§8951. ANON. 1926. [same tr. as #8949] Il. Gertrude Welling. NY: Sears. 243p. il. 25cm. [LC]
8952. ABBOTT, MABEL. 1916. Il. with 33 pict. in col. and in black and white by Alice Carsey. Chic: Whitman. [AC] [Tr. not named; I infer Abbott from the following.]
§8953. do. 1924. Heidi. Directly tr. Mabel Abbott, and with over 80 col. il. by Violet M. Higgins. Chic: Whitman. 284p. 23cm. [LC] [Much altered. Pretty well told, but conversation is rather wooden.]
*8954. ALLEN, Ph. S. 1921. Il. Maginel W. Enright. Chic: Rand. viii;368p. 23cm. [Not a strictly faithful rendering, but very good.] [LC]
*8955. do. 1925. Introd. by Kath. L. Bates. Il. Do. L. Gregory and Milo Winter. Chic;NY: Rand, McNally. 404p. il. 18cm. [LC]
8956. BROOKS, LOUISE. Heidi, her years of wandering and learning. Bost: De Wolfe, Fiske 1884. 2v. in one. 12. [AC]

SPYRI, J:a--Heidi
8957. do. 1927. L: Nelson. 256p. il. 16cm. [BM]
*8958. DOLE, MRS. HELEN B. Tr. from 13th Ger. ed. Bost: Ginn 1899. 363p. il. 18cm. [LC]
[She does not wholly understand the German, and she prunes somewhat; still it has style.]
*8959. do. 1907. [same] 20cm. [LC]
*8960. do. 1927. [same] Centennial ed. Il. Marguerite Davis. Bost: Ginn. vi;410p. 17cm. [BM]
§8961. MELCON, H. A. Heidi: a story for girls. Il. J. W. Davis. NY: Burt 1901. 367p. 19cm. [LC]
[Rather bungling and not quite correct. Both parts.]
§8962. STORK, ELI. P. Gift ed. Il. in col. Maria L. Kirk. Phil;L: Lippincott 1915. 319p. 23cm.[Disappointing;not wholly accurate.][BM]
§8963. do. 1915. Il. Kirk. Lippincott. 318p. 21cm. [LC]
§8964. do. 1919. Introd. by C: W. Stork. 14 il. in col. by Maria L. Kirk. Gift ed. Phil;L: Lippincott. 319p. 23cm. [LC.BM]
§8965. do. 1920. Il. with scenes from the photoplay. NY: Grosset. 318p. D. [AC]
§8966. do. 1921. 9th impr. Lippincott. 319p. 8. [EC]
§8967. do. 1922. NY: Grosset. [AC]
§8968. do. 1925. Introd. C: W. Stork. NY: Grosset. Children's favorites series. 318p. D. [AC]
†8969. WATKINS, SHIRLEY. Il. Edna C. Shoemaker. Phil: Macrae Smith 1925. 305p. col. il. 20cm. [LC]
[Very free tr., regardless of orig. Rewritten.]
§8970. WHITE, HELENE S. Heide. NY: Crowell 1902. 338p. il. 17cm.[LC]
[Tr. improves the orig. Both parts.]
§8971. do. 1906. L: Dent; NY: Dutton. Everyman's lib. ix;262p. il. 17cm. [Introd. signed M. E.] [BM]
8972. do. 1907. Bost: Ginn. il. O. [AC]
§8973. do. 1909. Il. in col. Lizzie Lawson. L: Dutton. ix;319p. 19cm. [Same introd. as in #8971.] [BM]
§8974. do. 1910. [same as #8971.] [LC]
§8975. do. 1913. NY: Crowell. 433p. il. 21cm. [LC]
8976. do. 1917. NY: Crowell. Children's favorite classics. [AC]
8977. do. 1917. [reprint of #8973] [BM catalog.]
8978. do. 1923. [reprint of #8973] [BM catalog.]
§8979. do. 1924. Il. Anne Anderson. L: Harrap. 329p. 20cm. [BM]
§8980. do. 1927. [reprint of #8973] [BM]

8981. In safe keeping: a tale. Tr. Lucy Wheelock. L: Blackie 1896. 48p. front. 15cm. [BM]
8982. Jo, the little machinist. Tr. Helen B. Dole. NY: Crowell 1923. 76p. 20cm. [LC]
8983. Jörli: the story of a Swiss boy. Tr. from 11th ed. by Fis. T. Clayton and Olga Wunderli. Chic;NY: Sanborn 1924. xii;111p. il. 18cm. [LC]
8984. The little Alpine musician. Tr. Helen B. Dole. NY: Crowell 1924. 4;345p. il. 20cm. [LC]
8985. Little Miss Grasshopper. Tr. Helen B. Dole. NY: Crowell 1918. 76p. il. 20cm. [LC]
8986. A little Swiss boy. Tr. C. W. Coumbe. Il. Fes. Brundage. Akron, O;NY: Saalfield 1926. 251p. il. 18cm. [LC]
8987. Maxa's children. Tr. C. W. Coumbe. Il. Fes. Brundage. Akron, O;NY: Saalfield 1926. 244p. il. 18cm. [LC]
8988. Mäzli: a story of the Swiss valleys. Tr. Eli. P. Stork. Col. il. Maria L. Kirk. Phil;L: Lippincott 1921. 320p. 20cm. [LC.BM]
8989. do. 1923. [same] Gift ed. 24cm. [LC]
*8990. (Moni der Geissbub.) Moni, the goat boy. Tr. Helen B. Dole. NY: Crowell 1914. 43p. il. 19cm. [Very good.] [LC]

SPYRI, J:a--Moni der Geissbub
§8991. do. 1916. Tr. Eli. P. Stork. Il. Maria L. Kirk. NY;L;Phil: Lippincott. 72p. 19cm. [Very free.] [LC]
§8992. do. 1926. Tr. C. W. Coumbe. Il. Fes. Brundage. Akron, O;NY: Saalfield. 90p. 20cm. [Very cavalier performance.] [LC]
8993. The new year's carol. Tr. Alice H. Goodwin. Il. Grace E. Wesson. Bost;NY: Houghton 1924. 34p. 19cm. [LC.BM]
8994. Peppino. Tr. Eli. P. Stork. Il. in col. Phil;L: Lippincott 1927. 114p. 19cm. [BM]
8995. do. 1927. [same] [EC]
*8996. (Rosenresli.) Rose child. Tr. Helen B. Dole. NY: Crowell 1916. 62p. il. 19cm. [Seems excellent.] [LC]
8997. Story of Rico. Tr. Helene H. Boll. Bost: Beacon press 1921. xi;163p. il. 21cm. [LC]
8998. Tiss, a little Alpine waif. Tr. Helen B. Dole. Il. in col. G: Carlson. NY: Crowell 1921. 78p. 20cm. [LC]
8999. Toni, the little wood-carver. Tr. Helen B. Dole. NY: Crowell 1920. 78p. 20cm. [LC]
9000. Trini, the little strawberry girl. Tr. Helen B. Dole. Il. in col. G: Carlson. NY: Crowell 1922. 92p. 20cm. [LC]
†9001. Uncle Titus: a story for children. Tr. Lucy Wheelock. Bost: Lothrop 1886. 201p. 18cm. [Hardly a translation.] [LC]
9002. do. 1886. Uncle Titus and his visit to the country. Tr. Louise Brooks. Bost: Cupples, Upham. 16. [BPL]
9003. do. 1924. [same] NY: Crowell. 268p. D. [AC]
9004. do. 1926. Uncle Titus in the country. Tr. C. W. Coumbe. Il. Fes. Brundage. Akron, O:NY: Saalfield. 245p. 18cm. [LC]
9005. Veronica and other friends. Tr. Louise Brooks. Bost: Cupples & Hurd 1886? 12. [BPL]
9006. do. 1924. [same] NY: Crowell. 248p. col. il. 20cm. [LC]
9007. Vinzi: a story of the Swiss Alps. Tr. Eli. P. Stork. Il. in col. Maria L. Kirk. Phil;L: Lippincott 1923. 297p. 21cm. [LC.BM]
9008. (Was Sami mit den Vöglein singt.) What Sami sings with the birds. Tr. Helen B. Dole. NY: Crowell 1917. 90p. il. 20cm. [LC]
See Ulrich, Anna, Recollections, etc., #9500.

STACKELBERG, Na. v. baroness.
*9009. (Aus Carmen Sylvas Leben.) The life of C-- S--. Tr. Baroness Deichmann. L: K.Paul 1890. vi;306p. il. ports. 22cm. [BM]

STADEN, Hs., 16th cent.
*9010. (Wahrhaftig Historia...und Beschreibung...) The captivity of Hanse Stade of Hesse...1547-55, among the wild tribes of eastern Brazil. Tr. A. Tootal. L: Hakluyt soc. 1874. xcvi;169p. 22cm.[BM.LC]

STADLER, Ern. 1883-1914. Sel. in C95.

STAEHLIN, Lh.
*9011. (Kant, Lotze, Abr. Ritschl. Eine kritische Studie.) Crit. exam. of Kant, Lotze, and Ritschl. Tr. D. W. Simon. Ed: T. & T. Clark. xxxii;327p. 22cm. [BM]
[Correct; a little labored at first.--EC has: Hamilton 1889. AC has: NY: Scribner & W. 1889.]

STAEHLIN VON STORCKSBURG, Jk. 1710-85.
*9012. (Das von den Russen...entdeckte nördliche Insel-Meer.) An account of the new northern archipelago...in the seas of Kamtschatka and Anadir. Tr. C. Heydinger and Matthew Maty. L: Prtd. for Heydinger 1774. 20;118p. 19cm. [LC says: 22cm.] [BM.LC]

STAHL, K:e (Dumpf), 1776-1837. Sel. in C155.

STAHL, W: The authentic memoirs and sufferings of Dr. W: S--, a Ger. physician. Written by himself. 2d ed. [BM]
[This is cited by B43, but seems to have been written in English.]

STAHLSCHMIDT, J: Cn.
9013. Pilgrimage by sea and land. Introd. by Jung-Stilling. Tr. I. (i.e., S:) Jackson. L: Hatchard 1837. xxxii;355p. 15cm. [BM]

STAHR, Ad. (W: Td.) 1805-76. Sel. in C112.
*9014. Life and works of G. E. Lessing. Tr. E. P. Evans. Bost: Spencer 1866. 2v. xvi;383;442p. 20cm. [LCO.BM]
*9015. Rafael's Bible, called the Loggie, with a pref. on the Loggie by A. S--. Tr. anon. "Prachtausgabe." L: Trübner 1861. unp. il. 33cm. [BM]

STAMMLER, Rd. 1856- .
*9016. (Die Lehre von dem richtigen Rechte.) The theory of justice. Tr. I: Husik. L;NY: Macmillan 1925. xli;591p. 21cm. [BM.LC]

STAMPFER, F:
*9017. From Versailles to peace. Tr. H. G. Scheffauer. Berlin: Vorwärts 1920. 128p. 21cm. [BM]
[The work of this tr. is always excellent.]

STARK, J: F: 1680-1756. Sel. in C231.

STARKE, E. Sel. in C106.

STARKE, Ghf. W: Cph. 1762-1830. Sel. in C106.

STEFAN-GRUENFELDT, Pl. 1879- .
*9018. (Gustav Mahler.) G-- M--: a study of his personality and work. Tr. T. E. Clark. NY: Schirmer 1913. viii;132p. 21cm. [LC.BM]

STEFFENS, Henrich, 1773-1845. Sel. in C469.
9019. The mysterious wedding: a Danish story. Tr. G: G. Cunningham. 1829. In C80.
*9020. (Was ich erlebte.) Advent. on the road to Paris...1813-14. Extr. from the autobiog. Tr. anon. L: Murray 1848. viii;167p. 17cm. [BM]
*9021. do. 1863. The story of my career, as stud. at Freiberg [sic] and Jena, and as prof. at Halle, Breslau, and Berlin. Tr. W: L. Gage. Bost: Gould & Lincoln. xiv;284p. 18cm. [LC.BM]
[He begins with the opening of vol. 4; chaps. 9 and 10, already translated, he incorporates at second hand (probably from the foregoing.) He has rejected useless matter, he says. Tr. is free but good.]
*9022. do. 1874. [same] German university life. The story of my career...with personal reminisc. of Goethe, Schiller, Schelling, and others. Phil: Lippincott. xiv;284p. 18cm. [LC.BM]

STEGEMANN, Hm. 1870- .
*9023. (Der Kampf um den Rhein.) The struggle for the Rhine. Tr. Georges Chatterton-Hill. L: Allen & Unwin 1927. 432p. 22cm. [BM]
["The tr. has been made from an abr. version of the orig. work specially prepared by the author for that purpose." Somewhat expansive tendency.--AC has: NY: Knopf.]

STEGMANN, C: Mn. Ritter v. 1832-95, and H. A. Geymüller.
9024. (Die Architektur der Renaissance in Toscana.) The architecture of the Ren. in Tuscany, il. the most important churches, palaces, villas, and monuments. Pref. Guy Lowell. Tr. anon. NY: Architectural bk. 1924. 2v. il. 41cm. [LC]

STEGMANN, Hs. 1862- .
§9025. (Die Plastik des Abendlandes.) The sculpture of the west. Tr. Marian Edwardes. L: Dent 1907. Temple primers. viii;162p. il. 15cm. [Largely rewritten, with some errors.] [BM.LC]

STEGMANN, Josua, 1588-1632. Sel. in C269;287.

STEIN, Am.
9026. Schoolboys abroad and at home; Anna's vacation; Julian's experience. Tr. "Trauermantel." 1857. In C544.

"STEIN, Armin" (i.e., Hm. O: Nietschmann, 1840- .)
9027. (Das Buch vom Dr. Luther.) Luther and the cardinal: a historic biogr. tale. Tr. Julie Sutter. L: Relig. tract soc. 1883. x;374p. 18cm. ["An adaptation...not so much a tr. as a reprod. in kind with liberty of handling."] [BM]
9028. Katharine v. Bora...a pict. from life. Tr. Emma A. Endlich. Phil: Frederick 1890. 294p. 12. [LCO]
9029. do. 1890. Kath. v. Bora, Luther's wife. Tr. M.P. Paisley; L: J. & R. Parlane. 171p. il. front. (port.) 18cm. [BM]
9030. Little Anna: a story for pleasant little children. Tr. anon. Bost: Ticknor & F. 1864. 134p. il. sq. 16. [LCO]
9031. (Martin Luther und Graf Erbach.) Count Erbach: a story of the Reformation. Tr. Jas. I. Helm. NY: Randolph 1882. 248p. 19cm. [LC]
9032. do. 1889. [same] L: Houlston. 8. [EC]
9033. Prince Abr. of Brandenburg: a story of the Reformation. Tr. Ma. E. Ireland. Burlington, Ia: Ger. lit. bd. 1907. 199p. 18cm. [Very free; almost an adaptation.] [LC]

"STEIN (i.e., Rosenstein), Leo" (Wl.), 1858- . See Leon, V:, joint author.

"STEIN, Leo" and L: Heller.
9034. The house next door. An adaptation by J. Hartley Manners. Bost: Baker 1912. (B38)

"STEIN, Leo" and Bela Jenbach.
9035. The blue paradise: a Viennese operetta in a prologue and 2 acts by Ed. Eysler and Sigmund Romberg. Tr. Edgar Smith. Vocal score. NY;L: Schirmer 1915. 106p. 30cm. [BMM]

"STEIN, Leo" and C: Lindau.
§9036. (Künstlerblut.) The love-cure: operetta in 3 acts by Ed. Eysler. Ad. Oliver Herford. Vocal score. NY: Schirmer 1909. 137p. 28cm. [Very free adaptation.] [LCM.BMM]

"STEIN, Leo" and Ern. Soehngen.
9037. The affair of the barracks. Ad. by C. M. S. McLellan. NY: (copyright by Lieber & co.) 1911. Tw. [LC]

"STEIN, Leo" and A. M. Willner.
9038. (Die Sirene.) The siren: operetta in 3 acts by Leo Fall. Tr. Harry B. Smith. Vocal score. NY: Stern 1911. 154p. 28cm. [LCM.BMM]

STEINACH, ---. Sel. in C27.

STEINACKER, Ed.
9039. Budapest. Tr. anon. 1884. 108p. il. In C294.

STEINBACH, F.
9039a. California: a tale. Tr. Y. S. N. In "Sharpe's Lond. Mag." 30 (1859):189, etc. (B27)

STEINER, Rd. 1861- .
9040. An address (on eurhythmy). Tr. anon. L: 1924. 4p. 19cm. [BM]
9041. The Bible and wisdom. Tr. anon. Ed. by H. Collison. L: Anthroposoph. pub. 1923. 36p. 18cm. [BM]
9042. Christ and the human soul. Four lect. Tr. anon. L;NY: 1927. pp. 23-71. 24cm. [BM]
9043. The Christ impulse and the devel. of the ego-consciousness. Seven lect. Tr. anon. L: Anthroposoph. pub. 1926. 88p. 24cm. [BM]
9044. Christmas. Author. tr. under the editorship of H. Collison. L: Anthroposoph. pub. 1923. 28p. 18cm. [BM]

STEINER, Rd.
9045. Cosmic and human metamorphoses. Seven lect. L: Anthr. pub. 1926. 85p. 25cm. [BM]
9046. (Das Christentum als mystische Tatsache und die Mysterien des Altertums.) Christianity as mystical fact and the mysteries of antiquity. Tr. Harry Collison. NY;L: Putnam 1910. viii;241p. 19cm. [BM]
9047. do. 1914. [same] 3d rev. and enl. ed. x;241p. 19cm. [LC]
*9048. (Das Vater Unser.) The Lord's prayer. Author. tr. by A. M. W. L: Theosoph. pub. 1913. 47p. 17cm. [BM]
*9049. do. 1927. [same] L: Anthr. soc. 48p. 17cm. [BM]
*9050. (Der dreigliedrige soziale Organismus.) The triorganic social organism...Tr. O. H. Frederick. Detroit, Mich: Goetheanum press 1920. 135p. il. 20cm. [LC.BM]
*9051. do. 1920. The threefold state, the true aspect of the social question. Author. Engl. tr. (by E. Bowen-Wedgwood.) L: Allen & Unwin. 201p. 19cm. [This tr. is not as good as Frederick's.] [LC]
*9052. (Die Geheimwissenschaft im Umriss.) An outline of occult science. Author. tr. from 4th ed. Ed. by Max Gysi. Chic;NY: Rand, McNally 1914. xvi;469p. 20cm. [LC.BM]
*9053. (Die Kernpunkte der sozialen Frage.) The threefold commonwealth. Author. tr. by E. Bowen-Wedgwood. L;NY: The threefold commonwealth pub. 1922. xi;206p. 19cm. [See note to following.] [LC]
*9054. do. 1923. [same] L: Anthrop. pub. xxxii;147p. 18cm. [LC]
["This is a tr. of the 2nd (1920) ed. of 'Die Kernpunkte der sozialen Frage,' the first ed. of which (April 1919) was tr. and pub. in England three years ago under the title 'The threefold state.' Note by the publishers." --There appears to be no essential difference between this and the 1st ed. Paragraphing is the same for 30 odd pages, and the tr. is unchanged, though newly set in type.]
*9055. (Die Mystik im Aufgang des neuzeitlichen Geisteslebens und ihr Verhältnis zu modernen Weltanschauungen.) Mystics of the Renaissance and their relation to mod. thought, including Meister Eckhard, Tauler, Paracelsus, Jacob Boehme, Giordano Bruno, and others. Author. tr. by Bertram Keightley. NY;L: Putnam 1911. 278p. 19cm. [BM.LC]
9056. (Die Pforte der Einweihung.) The way of initiation; or, how to attain knowledge of the higher worlds. Tr. Max Gysi. Biogr. notes by Edouard Schuré. Foreword Annie Besant. L: 1908. iii;237p. 18cm. [BM]
9057. do. 1910. [same] 1st Americanized ed. NY: Macoy pub. and masonic supply co. 163p. 20cm. [LC]
9058. (Die Philosophie der Freiheit.) The philos. of freedom: a mod. philos. of life. Tr. Mr. and Mrs. Rld. F. Af. Hoernlé. Ed. H. Collison. L;NY: Putnam 1916. viii;301p. 19cm. [LC.BM]
9059. do. 1922. [same] The philos. of spiritual activity. Enl. and rev. ed. of "The philos. of freedom," together with the orig. thesis on "Truth and science." Putnam. xv;382p. 19cm. [LC]
*9060. (Die Schwelle der geistigen Welt.) The threshold of the spiritual world. Author. Engl. tr. ed. by H. Collison. L;NY: Putnam 1918. xii;140p. 18cm. [Excellent tr.] [BM.LC]
9061. Earthly death and cosmic life. Seven lect. Tr. anon. L: Anthr. pub. 1927. 70p. 24cm. [BM]
9062. The east in the light of the west. Tr. S. M. K. Gandell and Miss D. Osmond. L;NY: Putnam 1922. xxi;222p. 19cm. [BM]
9063. The educ. of children from the standpoint of theosophy. Author. tr. from 2d Ger. ed. by W. B. L: Theosoph. pub. 1911. 83p. 17cm. [BM.LC]
9064. do. 1911. [same] Amer. ed. Ed. Max Gysi. Chic: Rajput press. 105p. 16cm. [LC]

STEINER, Rd.--The educ. of children from the standpoint of theosophy.
9065. do? 1922. The educ. of the child in the light of anthroposophy. Tr. G: and Ma. Kaufmann. L: Threefold commonwealth 1922. 64p. 16cm. [BM]
9065a. do. 1927. Tr. anon. Anthroposoph. press. 71p. S. [AC]
9066. The effect of occult devel. upon the bodies and self of man. A course of ten lect. at the Hague, 1913. Tr. anon. L: Anthrop. soc. 1925. unp. 25cm. [BM]
9067. The essentials of educ. Five lectures...Stuttgart, 1924. Tr. anon. L: Anthrop. pub. 1926. 98p. 18cm. [BM]
9068. Evol. in the aspect of reality. Six lect. L: Anthrop. soc. 1925. 63p. 25cm. [BM]
9069. Evol. of the world and of humanity. Thirteen lect. at Penmaenmawr, 1923. Tr. anon. L: Anthrop. pub. 1926. xi;246p. 22cm. [BM]
9070. The forming of destiny and life after death. Six lect. Tr. anon. L: Anthrop. pub. 1927. 80p. 25cm. [BM]
*9071. Four mystery plays. Tr. and ed. with author's permission by H. Collison, S. M. K. Gandell, and R. T. Gladstone. L;NY: Putnam 1920. 2v. vii;265; 295p. 19cm. [BM.LC]
[Vol. 1. The portal of initiation; The soul's probation. Vol. 2. The guardian of the threshold; The soul's awakening.]
*9072. do. 1925. [same] 2d ed. 2v. vii;267; 295p. [BM]
9072a. do. 1926. [same] Anthroposoph. pr. 2d ed. 2v. [EC]
9073. Gates of knowledge...(Also) Philosophy and theosophy. Author. tr. ed. by Max Gysi. NY;L: Putnam 1912. 187p. 19cm. [LC.BM]
*9074. (<u>Goethe als Vater einer neuen Aesthetik</u>.) Goethe as the founder of a new science of aesthetics. Tr. G. Metaxa. Ed. by H. Collison. L: Anthrop. pub. 1922. 30p. 22cm. [BM]
*9075. (<u>Goethes Geistesart in ihrer Offenbarung durch seinen Faust und durch das Märchen "Von der Schlange und der Lilie."</u>) G--'s standard of the soul as ill. in "Faust" and in the fairy story "Of the green snake and the beautiful lily." Tr. Miss D. S. Osmond. L: Anthrop. pub. 1925. 112p. 18cm. [BM]
9076. How the spiritual world interpenetrates the physical. Two lect. at Cassel, 1914. L;NY: Anthrop. pub. 1927. 71p. 25cm. [BM]
9077. (<u>Der Hüter der Schwelle</u>.) Initiation and its results: a sequel to "The way of initiation." Tr. Clifford Bax. 1st Amer. ed. NY: Macoy pub. and masonic supply co. 1909. 134p. 20cm. [LC]
9078. do. 1909. [same] L: Theosoph. pub. xi;185p. [BM.LC]
9079. Investigations in occultism, showing its practical value in daily life, based upon lect... Pref. signed H. Collison. NY;L: Putnam 1920. xii;253p. 19cm. [BM.LC]
9080. Knowledge and initiation, and Knowledge of the Christ through anthroposophy. Two lect. in L. Tr. G: Kaufmann. L: Anthrop. pub. 1922. 48p. 22cm. [BM]
9081. Knowledge of the higher worlds and its attainment. Tr. G. Metaxa. L;NY: Putnam 1923. 221p. 19cm. [BM]
9082. A lect. on eurhythmy given at Penmaenmawr 1923. Author. tr. anon. L: Anthrop. pub. 1926. 43p. 18cm. [BM]
9083. Lect. to teachers. Tr. anon. L: Anthrop. pub. 1923. 112p. 18cm. [BM]
9084. The manifestations of Karma. A course of eleven lect. Hamburg 1910. Tr. anon. L: Anthrop. soc. 1925. 141p. 24cm. [BM]
9085. Man's life on earth and in the spiritual worlds. Six lect. in England 1922. Tr. anon. L: Anthrop. pub. 1925. 69p. 25cm. [BM]
9086. Mysteries of Christianity and of the East (Four priv. lect.); Christ and the spiritual world (Six priv. lect.). Tr. anon. L: Anthrop. pub. 1925. 2 pts. 68p. 25cm. [BM]
9087. The occult significance of blood: an esoteric study. Author. tr. by Max Gysi from...lect. Bost: Occult and mod. thought book centre 1912. 47p. 16cm. [LC]

STEINER, Rd.--The occult significance of blood
9088. do. 1912. [same] L: Theosoph. pub. [BM]
*9089. (Praktische Ausbildung des Denkens.) Practical training in thought. Tr. W: R. Nedella. Introd. H: B. Monges. Chic: Anthrop. lit. concern 1922. 38p. 19cm. [LC.BM]
[BM dates this 1921. 39p. --Tr. not wholly satisfactory.]
9090. A road to self-knowledge. Described in 8 meditations. Author. tr. ed. H. Collison. L;NY: Putnam 1918. x;124p. 18cm. [LC]
9091. A road to self-knowledge and the threshold of the spiritual world. Tr. anon. L;NY: Putnam 1922. viii;210p. 19cm. [BM]
9092. The secrets of the biblical story of creation. Eleven lect. Munich 1910. Tr. anon. L: Anthrop. pub. 1925. 88p. 25cm. [BM]
9093. The spiritual beings in the heavenly bodies and in the kingdom of nature. Ten lect. Helsingfors 1912. Tr. anon. L: Anthrop. pub. 1925. 127p. drawings. 25cm. [BM]
9094. The spiritual guidance of man and of mankind. Author. Engl. tr. ed. by H. Collison. Bethlehem, Pa: Prtd. by Times pub. 1915. 100p. 19cm. [LC]
9095. Spiritual science, Christianity, and the future of mankind. Tr. and annotated by G: Kaufmann. L: Threefold commonwealth 1921. 32p. 19cm. [BM]
9096. Spiritual science and the art of educ. Address to school teachers at Bale 1919. Tr. anon. L: Threefold commonwealth 1921. 24p. 22cm. [BM]
9097. The submerged continents of Atlantis and Lemuria, their hist. and civilization. Being chaps. from the Akashic records. Author. tr. by Max Gysi. Amer. ed. Chic: Rajput press 1911. 241p. 18cm [LC]
9098. do. 1911. [same] L: Theosoph. pub. 202p. 19cm. [BM.LC]
9099. do. 1923. Atlantis and Lemuria. Tr. Ag. Blake. L: Anthrop. pub. 131p. 18cm. [BM]
*9100. Theosophy: an introd. to the supersensible knowl. of the world and the destination of man. Tr. with permission of the author from 3d Ger. ed. by Mrs. Eli. D. S(hields). Chic;NY: Rand, McNally 1910. 230p. 19cm. [LC]
*9101. do. 1910. [same] L: K.Paul. xvi;212p. 20cm. [BM.LC]
9102. do. 1922. [same?] L: K.Paul. xii;144p. 18cm. [BM]
9103. Three essays on Haeckel and Karma. Tr. Max Gysi. L: Theosoph. pub. 1914. 223p. 18cm. [BM]
9104. True and false paths in spiritual investigation. Eleven lect. Ed. by H. Collison from shorthand report, unrevised. L: Anthrop. pub. 1927. xxxi;224p. 22cm. [BM]
9105. Universe, earth and man: their nature and devel. Eleven lect. Stuttgart 1908. Tr. anon. L: Anthrop. pub. 1925. 113p. 24cm. [BM]
9105a. (Wahrheit, Schönheit, Güte.) Truth, beauty, goodness. Tr. anon. Anthrop. pr. 1927. 16p. S. [AC]
9106. (Wege zu einem neuen Baustil.) Ways to a new style in architecture. Five lect. 1914. Tr. ed. by H. Collison. L;NY: Anthrop. pub. 1927. viii;60p. il. 31cm. [BM]

STEINER, Rd. and Ita Wegmann.
9107. Fundamentals of therapy. Tr. anon. L: Anthrop. pub. 1925. ix; 169p. 22cm. [BM]

STEINMANN, F: Arn. 1801-75. Sel. in C466.

STEINMAR, Bertold, fl. 1276. Sel. in C27;366 (under Walther);427;532.

STEKEL, W: ("Willy Bojan," "Dr. Serenus") 1868- .
9107a. (Störungen des Trieb- und Affektlebens. 4. Die Impotenz des Mannes.) Impotence in the male: the psychic disorders of sexual function in the male. Auth. tr. by Oswald H. Boltz. Liveright 1927. 2v. O. [AC]

STENGEL, ---. Sel. in C497.

STERN, Ad. ("Ad. Ernst") 1835-1907.
9108. Andreas Heimberger; or, the miner of Berchtesgaden. Tr. Mrs. B. Mallon. 1873. 12. [AC]

"STERN, Dv."
9109. Without home, without faith. Tr. Nellie H. Simpson. L: Blackwood 1886. 369p. 18cm. [BM]

STERN, Maurice Rld. v. 1860- . Sel. in C28.

"STERNAU, C. O." (i.e., Pius Ax. Wolff, 1782-1828). Sel. in C97.

STERNBERG, Adt. Wcs. H: Lp. Ma. Graf v. 1868- .
*9110. (Die Barbaren von Marokko.) The barbarians of Morocco. Tr. Ethel Peck. Col. il. Douglas Fox-Pitt. L: Chatto & Windus 1908. xi;177p. 21cm. [BM.LC]
*9111. (Meine Erlebenisse und Erfahrungen im Burenkrieg.) My exper. of the Boer war. Tr. G: F: R: Henderson. L;NY;Bombay: Longmans 1901. xlii;268p. 20cm. [BM.LC]
[Good but not absolutely dependable, nor wholly complete.]

STERNBERG, Ax. Freiherr v., see "Ungern-Sternberg."

STERNHEIM, C: 1878- .
9112. (Fairfax.) Fairfax. Tr. Af. B. Kuttner. NY: Knopf 1923. 66p. 24cm. [LC]

STERNHOLD, ---. Sel. in C230.

STETTENHEIM, Jl. 1831- . Sel. in C422.

STEUBEN, F: W: v. 1730-94. See Kapp, F:, Life..., #4860.

STEUDING, Hm. 1850- .
9113. Greek and Roman mythol. and heroic legend. Tr. Lionel D. Barnett. L: Dent 1901. Temple primers. vii;134p. il. 15cm. [BM.LC]
9114. do. 1903. [same] 2d ed. [LC]

STIEFF, Hte.
9115. The Jewess, Christian, and heathen. Tr. Mrs. Trees. L: Wertheim 1862. 284p. 17cm. [BM]

STIEGLITZ, H: 1801-49. Sel. in C450.
9116. The church year: talks to children. Tr. Anthony B. Kruegler. NY: Macmillan 1923. xx;217p. 19cm. [LC]
9117. do. 1924. [same] Ed;L: Sands. [BM]

STIELER, Js.
*9118. (Deutsche Tonmeister.) The great Ger. composers: biogr. notices...ad. to young minds. Tr. C. P. S. L: Augener; NY: Schirmer 1879. 216p. il. 25cm. [BM.LC]

STIELER, K: 1842-85. See Schmid, Hm., joint author.
9119. C: v. Piloty. Tr. Ca. Bell. in Dumas, F. G. "Il. biog. of mod. artists." 1882. pp. 171-92. 49cm. [BM]
9120. Italy from the Alps to the Arno. Tr. Fes. E. Trollope. L: Chapman & Hall 1892. 186p. il. fol. [LC]

STIELER, K:, E. Paulus and W. Kaden.
9121. Italy from the Alps to Mt. Etna. Tr. Fes. E. and T: A. Trollope. L: Chapman & Hall 1877. xiii;468p. il. 34cm. [BM.LC]

STIELER, K:, Hs. Wachenhausen, and F: W: Hacklaender.
*9122. (Rheinfahrt.) The Rhine from its source to the sea. Tr. Sir G: C. Bartley. Phil: Lippincott 1878. 373p. profusely il. 34cm. [LC]
*9123. do. 1878. [same] L: Bickers. 35 x 27cm. [BM.LC]
*9124. do. 1899. New rev. and corr. ed. Phil: Coates. 2v. 20cm. [LC]

STIER, (Ewd.) Rld. 1800-62. Sel. in C229.

STIEVE, F: 1884- .
*9125. (Iswolski und der Weltkrieg.) Isvolsky and the world war. Tr. E. W. Dickes. L: Allen & Unwin 1926. 254p. 22cm. [BM]
[Mostly good; he mistakes foreword by the daughter for a pref. to the daughter.]
9125a. do. 1926. [same] based on...documents...NY: Knopf. 300p.O.[AC]

STIFTER, Adt. 1805-68.
9126. [Coll.] Rural life in Austria and Hungary. Tr. Ma. Norman. L: Bentley 1850. 3v. in one. 8. [BM]
[Vol. 1. *My great-grandfather's note-book ("Die Mappe meines Urgrossvaters"). 299p. Vol. 2. Abdias the Jew ("Abdias"), 149p. The Hochwald ("Der Hochwald"), pp. 150-307. Vol. 3. Crazy castle ("Die Narrenburg"), 159p. Maroshely, pp. 161-256. The village on the heath ("Das Haidedorf"), pp. 257-309.
*9127. [Coll.] 1852. Pict. of life. Tr. Ma. Howitt. L: Hodgson. The parlour lib. 254p. 16cm. [BM]
[Angela, 120p. The castle of fools ("Die Narrenburg"), pp. 121-221. The village on the heath ("Das Haidedorf"), pp. 225-54.]
9128. (Abdias.) Abdias, the Jew: a story. L: Bentley 1850. 8. [EC]
[Probably vol. 2 of #9126.]
9129. The balloon ascent; The heath. Tr. Zimmern. 1880. In C575-7.
9130. (Bergkristall.) Mount Gars; or, Marie's Christmas-eve. Tr. anon. Oxf;L: Parker 1857. 50p. 16cm. [BM]
[First pub. under title: "Der heilige Abend."]
*9131. do. 1913-15. Rock crystal. Tr. Lee M. Hollander. In C154(8).
*9132. (Das Haidedorf.) Heather village. Tr. C. C. Mackley. L: Marlborough 1868. 50p. 18cm. [BM]
9132a. (Der Condor.) The condor. Tr. anon. "Dem. Rev." 27(1850):231. (B15a)
9133. (Die Mappe meines Urgrossvaters.) My great grandfather's note book. Tr. anon. L: Bentley 1851. 8. [Probably vol. 1 of #9126][EC]
9134. (Die Narrenburg.) Castle crazy and Maroshely: stories. Tr. anon. L: Bentley 1851. 8. [Probably vol. 3 of #9126.] [EC]

STILGEBAUER, E: 1868- .
9135. (Das Schiff des Todes.) The ship of death: a novel of the war. Author. tr. M. T. H. Sadler. L: Constable 1918. 280p. 18cm. [BM]
9136. do. 1918. [same] NY: Brentano's. 232p. 19cm. [LC]
9137. (Inferno.) Love's inferno. Tr. Carel Thieme. L: S.Paul;NY: Brentano's 1916. x;306p. 19cm. [BM.LC]
9138. do. 1917. [same] 7th ed. Brentano's. [LC]
9139. The star of Hollywood. Tr. E. E. Wilson. L: S.Paul 1927. 256p. 19cm. [BM]

STINDE, Jl. (Ern. W:) 1841-1905. Sel. in C405a;422.
9140. (Buchholzens in Italien.) The Buch-holzes in Italy. Tr. from 37th ed. by Harriet F. Powell. L: Bell 1887. x;167p. 19cm. [BM]
§9141. (Die Familie Buchholz.) The B-- family: sketches of Berlin life. Tr. L. Dora Schmitz. NY: Scribner 1886. 2v. 19cm. [LC]
[Correct, but loses the long-winded style.]
§9142. do. 1887. [same] pt. 2. L: Bell. 228p. 19cm. [BM]
§9143. do. 1887. [same] pt. 1. Tr. from 49th ed. Hamburg. vi;251p. 19cm. [BM]
9144. do. 1890. [both?] 4th ed. L: Bell. 8. [EC]
§9145. (Frau W:e.) Frau W:e: the concluding part of the B-- family. Tr. Harriet F. Powell. NY: Scribner 1887. 267p. 19cm. [LC]
§9146. The hausfrau rampant. Tr. E: V. Lucas. NY: Doran 1916. 357p. 19cm. [LC]
[Condensed. Not tr. directly from the German, but taken from the Bell translations; in very good style and spirit.]
§9147. do. 1925. [same] Masterful W:e. Cheaper ed. L: Methuen. xi; 242p. 19cm. [BM]
9148. do. 1927. [same] Masterful W:e. Methuen. 254p. [EC]

STINDE, Jl.
*9149. (Waldnovellen.) Woodland tales. Tr. Ellis Wright. L: Unwin 1887. 199p. 18cm. [BM]
[AC has: NY: Whittaker. --Very good, some errors. --Aunt Juliana; His stupid wife; Brother Johannes; Three times ten years; Bells; Princess Goldhair.]

STINNES, Hg. 1870-1924. See Harden, Mx., I meet my contemp., #3702.

"STIRNER, Max" (i.e., J: Kp. Schmidt, 1806-50.)
*9150. (Der einzige und sein Eigentum.) The ego and his own. Tr. Steven T. Byington. NY: Tucker 1907. xx;506p. 17cm. [LC.BM]
[Admirably done, with extraordinary pains.]
*9151. do. 1918. [same] Introd. by J. L. Walker. NY: Boni & Liveright. xiv;387p. 17cm. [LC].

STOCKMAR, Cn. F: Freiherr v. 1823-63. See the following name.

STOCKMAR, Ern. Af. Cn. Freiherr v. 1823-86. Sel. in C371.
*9152. (Denkwürdigkeiten aus den Papieren des Freiherrn C. F. v. Stockmar.) Memoirs of Cn. F: Baron S-- by his son. Tr. Georgiana Müller. L: Longmans, Green 1872. 2v. cx;391;xiii;555p. 18cm.
[Accurate and faithful; some intentional omissions.] [BM.LC]

STOEBER, Ad. 1811-92. Sel. in C97;375.

STOEBER, A: 1808-84. Sel. in C438;450.

STOEBER, Dn. Ehf. 1779-1835. Sel. in C173.

STOEBER (or Stober), K:
9153. The curate's favorite pupil. Tr. Ma. Howitt. Il. in col. J: Absolon. L: Orr 1844. 22p. 18cm. [BM]

STOECKER, Ad. 1835-1909. See Harden, Mx., Word portraits, #3699.

STOECKL, Abr. 1823-95.
*9154. (Lehrbuch der Geschichte der Philosophie.) Handbook of the hist. of philos. Tr. T: A. Finlay. Vol. 1. Dublin: Gill 1887. vi; 285p. 24cm. [BM]
*9155. do. 1903. [same] Hist. of philos. Tr. T: A. Finlay. Dublin: Fallon. 2v. Vol. 1, 446p. 24cm. [BM]
*9156. do. 1911- . [same tr.] 2d ed. L;NY: Longmans. 25cm. [LC]
[In progress.]

STOLBERG, Anna, Gräfin, fl. 1600. See Wellmer, Arn., Anna countess zu W-- S--, #10003.

STOLBERG, Cn. Graf zu, 1748-1821. Sel. in C373.

STOLBERG, F: Lp. Graf zu, 1750-1819. Sel. in C7;17;22;25-6;31;44;88; 95;123;133;142;157;219;309;373-4;378;380-1;387-8;391;393;461;469; 501;533;551;#8030.
9157. (Hymne an die Erde.) Hymn to the earth. Tr. J: Whitehouse. L: Cadell. 1801. 4. [EC]
9158. A little book of the love of God. Tr. Rev. J: Dalton. L: Burns 1849. viii;208p. 13cm. [BM]
*9159. (Reise in Deutschland, der Schweiz, Italien und Sizilien.) Travels through Germany, Switzerland, Italy, and Sicily. Tr. T: Holcroft. L: Robinson 1796-7. 2v. xx;506;xi;656p. 27cm. [BM.LC]
*9160. do. 1797. [same] 2d ed. [LC]
9161. do. 1801. [same] L: Robinson. 4v. 8. [EC]
*9162. do. 1806. [same abr.] In Pelham, Cavendish, "The world," Vol. 2, pp. 401-52. L: [BM.LC]

STOLL, H: W: 1819-90.
9163. (Die Götter und Heroen...) Handbook of the relig. and mythol. of the Greeks, with a short account of the relig. system of the Romans. Tr. R. B. Paul. L: Rivington 1852. vii;189p. il. 19cm.[BM]

STOLLE, L: Fd. (properly Anders), 1806-72. Sel. in C41;571.
9163a. Courtship under difficulties. Tr. anon. In "Blackwoods Mag." 78(1855):718. (B27)

STOLTERFOTH, Ade. Freiherrin v. (i.e., W:e Jle. Ade. K:e--v. Stolterfoth--Zwierlein, 1800-75.) Sel. in C17;41;67;153;182;372;395;571.
9164. (Rheinische Lieder und Sagen.) The Rhenish minstrel: a series of ballads, traditional and legendary, of the Rhine. Tr. anon. Frankfort on the Main. Jugel 1835. 19; 65p. il. 22 x 27cm. [LC.BM] [Ballads not tr., but the principal incident in each is summarized; histor. notices which accompany them are translated. --EC has: L: Schloss 1835. Long 4.]

STOLZ, Alban, 1808-83.
9165. (Diamant oder Glas.) Diamond or glass. Tr. Js. Cauvin. L;Derby: Richardson 1871. 108p. 13cm. [BM]
*9166. (Die Hexenangst der aufgeklärten Welt.) The witch-mania; or, the learned world. Tr. anon. L: T:Richardson 1872. 32p. 16cm. [BM]
9167. The everlasting salutation. Tr. from 5th ed. by Js. Cauvin, LL.D.,Ph.D. L: T:Richardson 1872. 160p. 13cm. [BM]

STOLZ, Alban
9168. "Give us this day our daily bread." Tr. M. A. C. Pref. Rev. And. Melville. Glasgow: Bryce 1886. Worthy books. 83p. 17cm. [BM] ["The tr. seems to have hit a very happy medium between freedom and literalism."]
9169. do. 1897. [same] thoughts on the 4th petition of "the Lord's prayer." Glasgow: Bryce. Worthy books. 32p. 18cm. [BM]
9170. The sting of death: its antidote. Tr. anon. from 20th Ger. ed. L: St. Anselm soc. 1892. vi;88p. 18cm. [BM]
9171. Whither shall we go? Tr. anon. L;Derby: Richardson 1872. 74p. 13cm. [BM]

STOLZ, Rb. The great name: operetta. See A217.

STORCH, H: F: v. 1766-1835.
*9172. (Gemälde von St. Petersburg.) The pict. of Petersburg. Tr. anon. L: Longmans 1801. xviii;591p. front. 21cm. [BM.LC]

STORCH, L: 1803-81.
9173. (Der Knabe mit der Bibel.) The boy with the Bible. With an inter-lined Engl. tr. for the use of Engl. scholars by J. F. A. Schmidt. L: D:Nutt 1858. 121p. 19cm. [BM]
9174. do. 1859. [same] 2d ed. L: Williams & Norgate. [BM]

STORM, (Hs.) Td. (Woldsen), 1817-88. Sel. in C38;112;138;366*;415; 423;448;450;501.
*9175. (Aquis submersus.) Aquis submersus. Tr. Jas. Miller (or rather Millar). L;Glasgow: Gowans & Gray 1910. 94p. 15cm. [BM]
*9176. (Der Schimmelreiter.) The rider of the white horse. Tr. Muriel Almon. 1913-15. In C154(11).
9177. do. 1917. The rider on the white horse. Tr. Marg. Münsterberg. In C186.
*9178. (Eekenhof.) Eekenhof. Tr. Jas. Millar. L;Glasgow: Gowans & Gray 1908. 54p. 14cm. [BM]
*9179. (Ein Fest auf Haderslevhuus.) A festival at H--. Tr. Jas. Millar. L;Glasgow: Gowans & Gray 1909. 88p. 15cm. [BM]

IMMENSEE

9179a. 1858. I--: a dream of youth. Tr. anon. In "Colburn's new monthly mag." 112:230. (B27)[Author not named.]
§9180. 1863. Immensee; or, the old man's reverie. Tr. H. Clark. Munster: E. C. Brunn. 68p. 14cm. [BM]

STORM, Td.--Immensee
[Too loose, inaccurate; correct in spots.]
§9181. 1863. [same] Also, Grandmother and granddaughter by Louise Esche. Tr. Caro. R. Corson. Phil: Leypoldt; NY: Christern. 112p. 17cm. [LC]
§9182. 1881. Immen Lake. Tr. Mark Briton. L: Charing cross pub. 63p. 18cm. [Loses the charm of the orig.] [BM]
9183. 1896. [same?] Immensee. L;Glasgow: Gowans & Gray. 64p. [EC]
*9184. 1902. Tr. Bertha M. Schimmelfennig. NY: Crowell. 46p. 18cm. [Conversation is not so very good.] [LC]
*9185. 1902. Tr. Irma A. Heath. Portland, Me: Mosher. (On vellum.) 88p. 13cm. [LC]
*9186. 1903. [same] L: S. C. Brown. (Vellum.) ix;77p. 14cm. [BM]
*9187. 1904. Tr. P. K. Allen. NY: Hinds, Noble & E. Handy lit. tr. 46p. 15cm. [LC]
*9188. 1907. Tr. G: P. Upton. Il. by Marg. and Helen Armstrong. Chic: McClurg. 130p. 22cm. [LC]
§9189. 1916. Tr. Vivian E. Lyon. NY: Translation pub. 58p. 15cm. [LC]
*9190. 1919. Tr. C. W. Bell. L: Harrap. ff. 55. Ger;Engl. 8. [BM]
[Very good; some doubtful liberties, and some stilted language.]
9191. 1920. [same?] NY: Brentano's. B--'s bilingual series. [AC]

*9192. (Renate.) Renate. Tr. Jas. Millar. L;Glasgow: Gowans & Gray 1909. 76p. 14cm. [BM]
9193. Stormy wedding. Tr. Mrs. Bryan. Street & S. 1906. (B13)
*9194. (Zur Chronik von Grieshuus.) A chap. in the hist. of G--. Tr. Jas. Millar. L;Glasgow: Gowans & Gray 1908. 117p. 14cm. [BM]

STRACHWITZ, Mz. Graf v. 1822-47. Sel. in C17;51;138;152;195;309;448; 450.

STRALENBERG, Ph. J: Tabbert v. 1676-1747.
*9195. (Das nord- und östliche Teil von Europa und Asia.) An histori-geograph. description of the north and eastern parts of Europe and Asia. Tr. anon. L: Innys & Manby 1736. ix;463p. il. 23cm. [BM catalog spells Strahlenberg.] [BM]
*9196. do. 1738. [same] [BM.LC]

STRAMM, A: 1874-1915.
9197. (Die Haidebraut.) The bride of the moor: a play in one act. Tr. E: J. O'Brien. "Poet-Lore," vol. 25 (1914).
9198. The song of a May night: a play in one act. Tr. E: J. O'Brien. "Poet-Lore," vol. 25 (1914).

STRAPOLOLA (perhaps Straparola, Giov. Francesco?)
9199. The golden mermaid; The green man. Tr. Jas. B. Laurie. 1861. In C315.

STRASBURGER, E: 1844-1912.
*9200. (Streifzüge an der Riviera.) Rambles on the Riviera. Tr. O. and B. C. Casey. Il. Louise Reusch. L: Unwin; NY: Scribner 1906. xxiii;444p. 23cm. [BM.LC]

STRATZ, Rd. 1864- .
9201. (Der lange Preusse.) The countess Valeska: a romantic drama in 4 acts. Ad. NY: 1898. (B38)
9202. (Der weisse Tod.) Where snow is sovereign: a romance of the glaciers. Tr. Ma. J. Safford. NY: Dodd, Mead 1909. 282p. il. 19cm. [LC]
*9203. (Eine englische Frau.) His Engl. wife. Tr. A. C. Curtis. L: Arnold; NY: Longmans 1905. 335p. 19cm. [BM.LC]

STRAUS, Oc. 1870- . Operettas: The chocolate soldier. See Bernauer, R. The dancing Viennese. See Brammer, J. Waltz dream. See Doermann, F.

STRAUSS, D: F: 1808-74. Sel. in C321;366*;469.
*9204. (Der alte und der neue Glaube, ein Bekenntnis.) The old faith and the new...Author. tr. from the 6th ed. Mathilde Blind. 2d ed. L: Asher 1873. viii;439p. 20cm. [BM]
*9205. do. 1873. [same] Amer. ed. The tr. rev. and partly rewritten, and preceded by an Amer. version of the author's "prefatory postscript" (by J. Fitzgerald). NY: 2v. in one. xxxiii;223; 224p. 18cm. [BM]
*9206. do. 1874. [same] 3d Engl. ed. Tr. (with final pref.) and an orig. memoir of the author by M. Blind. L: Asher. 2v. liii;223; 263p. port. 17cm. [BM]
9207. do. 1885. [same] Amer. ed. NY: Truth seeker. 2v. in one. D.[AC]
*9208. (Leben Jesu.) The life of Jesus; or, a critical exam. of his hist. Tr. anon. Birmingham. 1842-44. 4v. in one. 17cm. [BM]
[Tr. Marian Evans, afterwards Cross ("George Eliot").]
*9209. do. 1846. [same] Tr. from 4th Ger. ed. L: 3v. 22cm. [BM]
9210. do. 1855. [same?] Life of Jesus critically exam. NY: C. Blanchard. 8. [AC]
*9211. do. 1860. [same] NY: Blanchard. 2v. 24cm. [LC]
*9212. do. 1865. New life of J--. Author. tr. L: Williams & Norgate. 2v. xxiv;440; 439p. 21cm. [BM]
*9213. do. 1865. New life of J-- written for the use of the Ger. people. Author. ed. L: 16p. 21cm. [BM]
[Taken from his revision of the orig. work.]
9214. do. 1876 (in print). NY: Scribner, W. & A. 2v. 8. [AC]
*9215. do. 1892. 2d ed. L: Sonnenschein. xxxviii;784p. 23cm. [BM]
9216. do. 1893. Life of J-- crit. exam. from 4th Ger. ed. by G: Eliot. New cheaper ed. in 1 vol. NY: Macmillan. 8. [AC]
*9217. do. 1898. [same as #9215] Life of Jesus. Tr. from 4th Ger. ed. by G: Eliot. L: Sonnenschein. xxxviii;784p. 23cm. [BM]
*9218. do. 1906. [same] 5th ed. Introd. O: Pfleiderer. 784p. [UW]
9219. Letter to Ernest Renan. Tr. anon. 1871. In C321.
9220. (Sendschreiben.) The opinions of D: F: S-- as embodied in his letter, with an address to the people of Zürich by Prof. Orelli. Tr. from 2d ed. of orig. Anon. L: Chapman 1844. 31p. 21cm. [BM]
9221. do. 1865. [same] L: Scott. pmph. 30p. 18cm. [BM]
9222. Soliloquies on the Christian religion. Tr. anon. L: Chapman 1845. 67p. 21cm. [As literal as possible.] [BM]
*9223. (U: v. Hutten.) U: v. H--: his life and times. Tr. Mrs. G. Sturge. L: Daldy, Isbister 1874. xii;386p. 19cm. [BM]
[Considerably abridged, but nothing important omitted. --AC has: L;NY: Routledge 1874.]
Reminisc. of a Lutheran clergyman. L: 1838.[EC]Really by Gerh. Strauss, see below.
See Ulrici, Hm., S-- as a philosophical thinker, #9501.
See Zeller, E:, Life...Strauss and Renan, #10596; 10611.

STRAUSS, El. 1866- .
*9224. (Mara.) Mara. Tr. W: G. Howard. 1913-15. In C154(19).

STRAUSS, F: Ad. 1817-88.
*9225. (Sinai und Golgatha: Reise in das Morgenland.) Sinai and Golgotha: a journey in the east. Tr. anon. Introd. H. Stebbing. L: Blackwood 1849. xii;390p. il. 17cm.[BM has: L: Collins 1849][LC]

STRAUSS, (Gh.) F: (Abh.) 1786-1863. Sel. in C196.
9226. (Glockentöne. Erinnerungen aus dem Leben eines jungen Geistlichen.) The chime of the bells. Tr. Hm. Bokum. Bost: Peirce 1836. 118p. 19cm. [LC]
*9227. do. 1838. Reminisc. from the early life of a Lutheran clergyman. Tr. S: Jackson. L: Smith, Elder. viii;352p. 17cm. [BM.LC]
9228. (Helons Wallfahrt nach Jerusalem.) Helon's pilgrimage to Jerusalem: a novel. Tr. J: Kenrick. L: Mawman 1824. 2v. xxiv;371; 396p. 19cm. [BM.LC]

STRAUSS, F:--Helons Wallfahrt nach Jerusalem
9229. do. 1835. [same] Rev. and abr. by Baron Stow. Bost: Ticknor. xii;298p. 18cm. [LC]
9229a. do. 1859. [same] The glory of the house of Israel; or, the Hebrew's pilgrimage to the Holy City. Comprising a pict. of Judaism in the cent. preceding the birth of our savior. Tr. J: Kenrick. Phil: Lippincott. xxiii;480p. 19cm. [LC]

STRAUSS, J: 1804-49. Operettas. The queen's lace handkerchief, see Bohrmann-Riegen, H:, #690. The gipsy baron, see Schnitzer, Ig., #8467. A night in Venice, see Zell, F., #10582.

STRAUSS, R: 1864- . Operas: Ariadne on Naxos. Elektra. The rose-bearer, see Hg. v. Hofmannsthal. Salome, see Lachmann, Hedwig. See Roese, O:, Elektra. See Tiessen, Heinz, The legend of Joseph.
*9230. (Briefwechsel mit Hg. v. Hofmannsthal.) Corr. between R: S-- and H. v. H--. Tr. Pl. England. L: Becker; NY: Knopf 1927. x;355p. 22cm. [BM.LC]

STRAUSS UND TORNEY, Lulu v. 1873- . Sel. in C154(18);423.

STRAUSS UND TORNEY, V: v. 1809-99. Sel. in C112;287;501.
§9231. Religion in earnest: tales illustrative of Christian life in Germany. Tr. Mrs. Stanley Carr. L: Hamilton 1857. ix;334p. 18cm. [She could but wouldn't. --The pastorate ("Das Pfarramt"); The peasantry ("Die Bauern"); Mammon (do.).] [BM]

STRECKFUSS, Ad. 1823-95.
9232. (Das einsame Haus.) The lonely house. Tr. Mrs. A. L. Wister. Il. by Cte. Weber-Ditzler. Phil;L: Lippincott 1907. 286p. 20cm. [BM.LC]
9233. (Verschwunden.) Quicksands. Tr. Mrs. A. L. Wister. Phil: Lippincott 1884. 356p. 19cm. [LC card]
9234. do. 1902. [same] [LC]
9235. (Von Hohenwald.) Castle Hohenwald: a romance. Tr. Mrs. A. L. Wister. Phil: Lippincott 1879. [LC card]
9236. do. 1906. [same] 355p. 19cm. [LC]
9237. (Zu reich.) Too rich: a romance. Tr. Mrs. A. L. Wister. Phil: Lippincott 1787. [LC card]
9238. do. 1906. [same] 370p. 19cm. [LC]

STRICKER, der, 13th cent. Sel. in C56.

STROEBEL, H:
*9239. (Die deutsche Revolution.) The Ger. revol. and after: its disasters and its hopes. Tr. H. J. Stenning. L: Jarrolds; NY: Seltzer 1923. 320p. 23cm. [BM.LC]
9240. (Sozialisierung.) Socialisation in theory and practice. Tr. H. J. Stenning. L: King 1922. vi;341p. 19cm. [BM.LC]

STRZYGOWSKI, Js. 1862- .
9241. (Ursprung der christlichen Kirchenkunst.) Origin of Christian church art: new facts and principles of research. Eight lect...at Upsala...(also) On Christian art in Britain. Tr. O. M. Dalton and H.J.Braunholtz. L: Milford;NY: Oxford 1923. xx;268p. il. 26cm.[BM.LC]

STUDER-GOLL, Claire. Sel. in C95.

STURM, Cph. Cn. 1740-86. Sel. in C3;67;112;180;244;366;395;448;450; 489;497;501;571.

STURM, Jl. 1816-96. Sel. in C195; #8902.

STURZ, Helfrich P. 1736-79. Sel. in C12;461.

SUABE, ---. Sel. in C133.

SUDERMANN, Hm. 1857-1928. Sel. in C366*;469.
9242. [Coll.] 1918. Iolanthe's wedding. ("Iolanthes Hochzeit.") Tr. Adèle S. Seltzer. NY: Boni & Liveright. 159p.19cm. [LC.BM]

SUDERMANN, Hm.
[Also: The woman who was his friend ("Die Freundin"); The new year's eve confession ("Des Hausfreunds Silvesterbeichte"); The gooseherd ("Der Gänsehirt").]

§9243. [Coll.] 1911. The Indian lily ("Die indische Lilie") and other stories. Tr. Ludwig Lewisohn. NY: Huebsch. 327p. 18cm. [LC.BM]
[Competent but careless. --Also: The song of death ("Das Sterbelied"); The purpose ("Der Lebensplan"); The victim ("Die leidende Dritte"); Autumn ("Herbst"); Merry folk ("Fröhliche Leut'"); Thea ("Thea").]

†9244. (Das Bilderbuch meiner Jugend.) The book of my youth. Tr. Wyndham Harding. L: Lane; NY: Harper 1923. 394p. 21cm. [BM.LC]
[The style is positively trampled upon and maltreated.]

*9245. (Das Glück im Winkel.) The vale of content. Tr. W: E. Leonard 1915. In C100.

*9246. (Das hohe Lied.) The song of songs. Tr. T: Seltzer. NY: Huebsch 1909. 640p. 19cm. [LC]

*9247. do. 1910. [same] NY: Huebsch; L: Lane. 640p. [BM]

*9248. do. 1913. Tr. Beatrice Marshall. L: Lane. xxii;487p. 19cm. [Not perfect, but very good.] [BM]

*9249. do. 1919. [same as #9246] New issue. Huebsch. [LC]

*9250. do. 1923. [same] 13th printing. [LC]

*9251. do. 1926. [same] 14th printing. [LC]

9252. do.[Ad.] 1913. On approval: an episode in two scenes from "Das Hohelied." Dramatized by Alison M. Lederer. NY. Tw. [LC]

9253. do.[Ad.] 1914. The song of songs. (Drama.) By E: Sheldon. n.i. 110p. 19cm. [LC.BM]

*9254. (Der gute Ruf.) A good reputation: a play in 4 acts [prose]. Tr. Marg. Holz and Olga Marz. NY: 1915. Tw. [LC]
[Exam. by Scholz, see B39.]

†9255. (Der Katzensteg.) Regine. Tr. Hettie E. Miller. Chic: Weeks 1894. 195p. 20cm. [Slovenly and inaccurate.] [LC.BM]

§9256. do. 1905. Regina; or, the sins of the fathers. Tr. Beatrice Marshall. L;NY: Lane. 347p. 19cm. [BM.LC]

*9257. do. 1910. [same] [LC]

*9258. (Der Wunsch.) The wish. Tr. Lily Henkel. Biogr. introd. by Eli. Lee. L: Unwin 1894. 309p. 19cm. [B13 says: Unwin 1891.] [BM]

9259. do. 1895. [same] NY: Appleton. 309p. [LC]

9259a. (Des Hausfreunds Silvesterbeichte.) A new year's eve confession. Tr. Grace I. Colbron. 1907. In C447.

9260. do. 1915. [same] In C179.

9261. do. 1926. [same] In C68.

†9262. (Die drei Reiherfedern.) The three heron's feathers. Tr. Helen T. Porter. In "Poet-Lore," vol. 12 (1900).
[Mostly in prose, which is not even faithful.]

9263. (?Die Ehre) What money cannot buy: a drama in 4 acts. Ad. Maurice Magnus. Berlin: 1906. (B39)

§9264. (Die Ehre.) Honor: a play in 4 acts [prose]. Tr. Hilmar R. Baukhage. NY: French 1915. 104p. 20cm. [LC]

9265. (Die ferne Prinzessin.) The far away princess. Tr. anon. NY: French. (B39)

9266. do. 1922. [same] The far-away princess. In Lewis, B: R., "Contemp. one-act plays." NY;Chic: Scribner. [LC]

§9267. (Die Geschichte der stillen Mühle.) The silent mill. Tr. anon. NY: Brentano's 1919. 204p. 19cm. [LC]
[Seems to be fairly good.]

9268. (Die leidende Dritte.) The victim. Tr. L. Lewisohn. 1927. In C367.

§9269. (Es lebe das Leben.) The joy of living: a play in 5 acts [Prose]. Tr. Edith Wharton. NY: Scribner 1902. vii;185p. 20cm. [LC.BM]
[Needless small liberties.]

SUDERMANN, Hm.--Es lebe das Leben
9270. do. 1914. [same] L: Duckworth. 194p. 8. [EC]
§9271. (Es war.) The undying past. Tr. Beatrice Marshall. L;NY: Lane 1906. 382p. 20cm. [Errors, expansions.] [BM.LC]
§9272. (Frau Sorge.) Dame Care. Tr. Bertha Overbeck. NY: Harper 1891. 314p. 17cm. [Errors; and why Meyerhofer for Meyhöfer?][LC.BM]
§9273. do. 1891. [same] L: Osgood & McIlvaine. 294p. 8. [BM]
§9274. do. 1902. [same as #9272] 314p. 18cm. [LC]
9275. do. 1913. [same] NY: Translation pub. n.d. 314p. 15cm. [AC]
9276. do. 1917. [same] NY: Boni & Liveright. 311p. S. [AC]
9277. (Fritzchen.) Fritzchen. Tr. anon. New Haven, Conn.: Yale dram. soc. (B39)
§9278. (Heimat.) Magda: a play in 4 acts [prose]. Tr. C: E. A. Winslow. Bost;NY: Lamson, Wolffe 1896. 161p. 17cm. [LC.BM] [He knows little German.]
9279. do. 1907. New tr. Claude Sykes. Eastbourne: Devonshire Park. (B39)
9280. do. n.d. Tr. Count Bonzenta. (B39)
9281. do. n.d. Tr. Louis N. Parker. (B39)
*9282. (Johannes.) Johannes. Tr. W. H. Harned and Ma. Harned. In "Poet-Lore," vol. 11 (1890).
*9283. do. 1902. John. Tr. Nelly M. Bauman and Gertrude P. Dingee. Chic. Tw. (B39) [Exam. by Scholz; see B39.]
§9284. do. 1909. John the baptist: a play in 5 acts [verse]. Tr. Beatrice Marshall. L;NY: Lane. vi;202p. 22cm. [BM.LC]
*9285. do. 1913-15. [same] In C154(17). [Probably revised.]
9286. do. 1915. John the baptist (abr.). Tr. anon. In C453.
§9287. (Johannisfeuer.) St. John's fire. Tr. Cte. Porter and Helen T. Porter. In "Poet-Lore," vol. 15 (1904). [Tr. flats.]
9288. do. 1904. [same] Bost: Badger. [AC]
9289. do. 1904. Fires of St. John: a drama in 4 acts [prose]. As presented for the first time on the Amer. stage in Bost. Tr. and ad. C: Swickard. Bost: Luce. 139p. 20cm. [LC]
§9290. do. 1905. St. John's fire. Tr. Grace E. Polk. Minneapolis: Wilson. 108p. 23cm. [Banalities and errors.] [LC]
9290a. do. 1924. Fires of St. John. In C420a.
9291. do. 1906. Tr. and ad. Fernanda Eliscu. NY. Tw. [LC]
*9292. (Morituri: Teja.) Morituri: Teias. Tr. Ma. Harned. In "Poet-Lore," vol. 9 (1897). [Noted one error.]
9292a. do. 1923. Teias. In C420b.
†9293. (Morituri.) Morituri: three one-act plays. Tr. A. Alexander. NY: Scribner 1910. 156p. 19cm. [LC] [Teja pretty well done, but Fritzchen and The eternal masculine badly.]
†9294. do. 1912. [same] L: Duckworth. [BM]
*9295. (Rosen.) Roses: four one-act plays. Tr. Grace Frank. NY: Scribner 1909. 183p. 19cm. [LC.BM] [Examined by Scholz, see B39. Streaks of light; The last visit; Margot; The far-away princess.]
*9296. (Schmetterlingsschlacht.) The battle of the butterflies: a play in 4 acts [prose]. Tr. A. H. Schwarz. NY: (Copyright by C: Kraus.) 1914. Tw. [Examined by Scholz; see B39.] [LC]
9297. (Sodoms Ende.) The man and his picture. Tr. anon. L: 1903. (B39)

SUENNER, Pl. 1881- .
9298. (Gehirn und Seele.) The brain and the mind. Tr. C. Harry Brooks. NY: Frank-Maurice; L: Allen & Unwin 1926. 112p. 19cm. [LC.BM]

SUESSKIND VON TRIMBERG, late 13th cent. Sel. in C416.

SULZER, G. Sel. in C317.

SULZER, J: G: 1720-79.
9299. (Allgemeine Theorie der schönen Künste.) Illustrations of the theory and principles of taste...as...applicable to the fine arts. Tr. Eli. de Brusasque. L: Mawman 1806. 417p. 18cm. [LC]

SUNECK, Der v., late 13th cent. Sel. in C27;427.

SUPPÉ, Fz. v. 1820-95. Operettas: Boccaccio. Fatinitza. The Prince of Palermo. See Zell and Genée. A trip to Africa. See "West, M." and Genée.

SUREN, Hans.
9300. (Der Mensch und die Sonne.) Man and sunlight. Tr. D. A. Jones. Forew. C. W. Saleeby. Sollux pub. 1927. 207p. il. 8. [EC]

SUSMAN, Mge. 1874- . Sel. in C28.

SUSO, H: ca. 1300-66. Sel. in C221*;224.

SUTER, Halb. 14th-15th cent. Sel. in C373.

SUTER-LERCH, H. J.
*9303. (Deutschland sein eigener Richter.) Germany her own judge: reply of a cosmopolitan Swiss to German propaganda. Tr. anon. NY: Houghton 1918. xiii;145p. 20cm. [Excellent tr.] [LC.BM]
*9304. do. 1918. [same] L: Allen & Unwin. 128p. 21cm. [BM.LC]

SUTTNER, Art. Gundaccar, Frhr. v. 1850-1902.
9305. Djambek the Georgian: a tale of mod. Turkey. Tr. H. M. Jewett. NY: Appleton 1890. 258p. 18cm. [LC]

SUTTNER, Bta. (Fce. So.) (Kinsky), Freifrau v. 1843-1914.
*9306. (Der Menschheit Hochgedanken.) When thoughts will soar: a romance of the immediate future. Tr. N. H. Dole. Bost;NY: Houghton 1914. 448p. 21cm. [BM has: L: Constable.] [LC.BM]
†9307. (Die Waffen nieder.) "Ground arms!" The hist. of a life. Tr. Alice A. Abbott. Chic: McClurg 1892. 286p. 18cm. [LC]
[Incomplete and inaccurate.]
*9308. do. 1892. Lay down your arms: the autobiog. of Martha v. Tilling. Tr. T. Holmes, rev. the author. L;NY: Longmans. 435p. 19cm. [BM]
*9308a. do. 1894. [same] [BM]
*9309. do. 1906. [same] 2d ed. Longmans. [LC]
†9310. do. 1906. [same as #9307] 7th ed. McClurg. 411p. 20cm. [LC]
†9311. do. 1908. [same] [LC]
§9312. do. 1913. Disarm! Disarm! Ad...Mrs. Andrea Proudfoot. L;NY: Hodder & Stoughton. xi;308p. 20cm. [Loose.] [BM.LC]
9313. do. 1914. [same] Pop. ed. Hodder. [EC]
9314. do. 1914. [same] War ed. Hodder. [EC]
*9315. (Memoiren.) Memoirs...the records of an eventful life. Tr. anon. Bost;L: Ginn 1910. Prtd. for Internat. school of peace. 2v. 21cm. [LC.BM]

SWOBODA, H: 1856- .
9316. (Griechische Geschichte.) Greek hist. Tr. L. D. Barnett. L: Dent 1900. Temple primers. viii;168p. 15cm. [BM.LC]

SYBEL, (K: Ld.) H: v. 1817-95.
*9317. (Die Begründung des deutschen Reiches durch W: I.) The founding of the Ger. empire by W: I. Tr. M. L. Perrin and G. Bradford, Jr. NY: Crowell 1890-8. 7v. il. 22cm. [LC.BM]
9318. The hist. and lit. of the crusades. Ed. Lady Duff Gordon. L: Chapman & Hall 1861. viii;356p. 19cm. [BM.LC]
[Pt. 1 a tr. of three lect., 1855. Pt. 2 from pref. of his "Geschichte des ersten Kreuzzuges."]
9319. do. 1905. [same] L: Routledge. xii;272p. 12. [BM]
[EC dates this 1906.]

SZCZEPANSKI, Pl. v. 1855- .
*9320. (Spartanerjünglinge.) The Prussian cadet: letters from a cadet to his mother. Also, A story of cadet life ("Das edle Blut"), by Ern. v. Wildenbruch. Tr. W. D. Lowe. L: Routledge;NY: Dutton 1910. 135p. 19cm. [BM.LC]
*9321. do. 1914. [same] [BM]

TAFINGER, W. F. 1691- . Sel. in C244.

TALER, Der, 13th cent. Sel. in C27.

TANNHAEUSER, fl. 1240-70. Sel. in C27;190;310;427;440;470;530.

TAULER, J:s, ca. 1300-61. Sel. in C221-2;224;273;489;570.
9322. [Sel.] Golden thoughts from the book of spiritual poverty. Tr. M. A. C. Glasgow: Bryce. 120p. 18cm. [BM]
9323. [Sel.] 1897. Golden thoughts on the higher life. Sel. from the "Medulla animae" and "Nachfolgung des armen Lebens Christi." Tr. M. A. C. Glasgow: Bryce. 128p. 18cm. [BM]
9324. [Sel.] 1898. The golden alphabet, sel...for every day of the month. Ed. by Fis. E. Clark. Bost;Chic: United soc. Christ. endeavor. 47p. 18cm. [LC]
9325. (Colloquium theologi et mendici.) A short dialogue, between a learned divine and a beggar. Tr. anon. Norwich. Prtd. 1787. 8p. 16 x 9cm. [LC]
9326. The hist. and life of the Rev. Dr. J: Tauler. Tr. Susanna Winkworth. Pref. C: Kingsley. L: Smith, Elder 1857. 426p. 21cm. [EC dates this 1856. Includes 25 of his sermons.] [BM.LCO]
9327. do. 1878. Sel. from the life and sermons. Abr. from the foregoing by M. W. T. Bost: Roberts. iv;155p. 13cm. [LCO.BM]
9328. do. 1905. [same as #9326] L: H. R. Allenson. 426p. 21cm. [BM]
9329. do. 1907. Life...Eaton & Mains. O. [AC]
9330. Meditations on the life and passion of our Lord Jesus Christ. Tr. by a secular priest (A. J. P. Cruikshank). L;Dublin;Derby: T:Richardson 1875. vii;446p. 19cm. [BM]
9331. do. 1904. [same] Meditations, attributed to Tauler. Tr. by Cruikshank. Pref. by Wilberforce. 3d ed. L: Art & book co. x;446p. 19cm. [BM]
9332. do. 1925. [same] L: Burns & Oates. xiii;345p. 19cm. [BM] [AC has: Benziger 1925. 345p.]
§9333. (Nachfolgung des armen Lebens Christi.) The following of Christ. Tr. J. R. Morell. L;NY: Burns & Oates 1886. xxxix;328p. 13cm. [BM]
§9334. do. 1918. [same] L: Watkins. xxxix;328p. 16cm. [BM]
9335. Plain path to Christian perfection. Tr. from French by A. Benezet. Phil: Crukshank 1772. xi;124p. 16cm. [LC]
9336. The sermons and conferences of J: Tauler...First complete Engl. tr. by Very Rev. Wl. Elliott. Brookland station, Washington, D.C.: Apostolic mission house 1910. 780p. 23cm. [LC]
See Arnold, Gf., Life of Taulerus, #103.

TAUND, Eg. (von Szyll-), 1856- . The little genius: opera. See A190.

"TAURINIUS, Zacharias"
[See a pamphlet: Of the shoe-maker, Schrödter, the printer, Taurinius, and the cabinet-maker, Damberger, three travellers who never traveled at all (and were the same person). L: Geisweiler 1801. 19p. 21cm. [BM]
This perhaps written by Geisweiler himself? Travels pub. under the names of Taurinius and Damberger were fictitious, written up from other books and his imagination. The real person who did the fabrication is suspected to have been one Junge of Wittenberg, M. A., and Taurinius-Damberger was merely his stool-pigeon.

"TAURINIUS, Zacharias"
Geisweiler issued a tr. in 1801, done by W: Tooke assisted by Hinkely. Another ed. issued 1801 by Phillips. A third by Stockdale appeared in the same year.]
9337. (Beschreibung einiger See- und Landreisen nach Asien, Afrika und Amerika.) Travels in the interior of Africa, etc. Tr. anon. L: Longman & Rees 1801. 2v. in one. il. 21cm. [LC]
9338. do. 1801. Travels through the interior of Africa, etc. Tr. anon. Bost: E. & S. Larkin. Prtd. by S. Etheridge in Charlestown. xxiv;523p. 21cm. [Tr.'s pref. is dated London 1800.] [LC]
9339. do. 1801. [reprint of #9337] NY: Durell. 2v. in one. 18cm. [LC] [Omits map and explanation.]

TAUSIG, K: 1841-71. See Lenz, W:, The great piano virtuosos..., #5663a.

"TAYLOR, G:" See Hausrath, Ad.

TEMME, Jodocus Donatus Hubertus, 1798-1881.
9340. (Anna Hammer.) Anna H--: a tale of contemp. Ger. life. Tr. A. H. Guernsey. NY: Harper 1852. 127p. 24cm. [LC]

"TENGER, Mariam" (i.e., Me. Edle v. Hrussoczy, 1821-98).
*9341. (Beethovens unsterbliche Geliebte.) Recoll. of Countess Teresa (v. Braunschweig). Tr. Gert. Russell. L: Unwin 1893. 94p. 20cm. [BM]
9342. (Der Amulettmann.) The Hungarian girl: a novel. Tr. S. E. Boggs. Il. by W. B. Davis. NY: Bonner 1892. 325p. 19cm. [LC]

TENNEMANN, W: Gb. 1761-1819.
*9343. (Grundriss der Geschichte der Philosophie.) A manual of the hist. of philos. Tr. by Rev. A. Johnson. Oxf: Talboys 1832. xi; 494p. 22cm. [LC]
9344. do. 1852. [same] Rev. enl. and continued by J. R. Morell. L: Bohn. xii;532p. 18cm. [BM.LC]
*9345. (System der platonischen Philosophie. Erster Teil.) Life of Plato. Tr. by Edwards. In Edwards and Park, Sel. from Ger. lit. Andover;NY. 1839. 22cm. pp. 311-367. [BM]

TERBERG (i.e. Münsterberg), Hg. 1863-1916. Sel. in C423. [See also "Münsterberg, Hg."]

TERSTEEGEN, Grd. 1697-1769. Sel. in C86;107;221*;222*;223;229;230-3; 235;269;273;276;287;486;489;570.
9346. [Sel.] Spiritual crumbs. Tr. S: Jackson. L: Shaw 1837. viii; 306p. 16cm. [BM]
9347. (Der Frommen Lotterie.) Spiritual lottery. Tr. E. A. Durand. L: Elliot Stock 1874. 79p. 14cm. [BM]
9347a. (Geistliches Blumengärtlein.) Sel. tr. Lady Durand. 1873. In C107.
9347b. God and thyself: a treatise on godly living. Ed. H. E. Govan. Ed: Christian lit. co. 1900. 46p. 8. [BM]
[Reprint of tr. by S: Jackson.]
9347c. Hymns of Ter Steegen, Suso and others. Tr. Fes. Bevan. 1895-7. In C221-2.
9347d. Life and writings by S: Jackson. Allan 1832. 12. [EC]
9347e. do. 1838. [same] Life and character of G. T--. With sel. from his letters and writings. Tr. S: Jackson. 2d ed. carefully rev. L: Black, Young & Young. viii;431p. 17cm. [BM]
9347f. do. 1846. [same] Life and writings by Jackson. W. Allen. 12. [EC]
9347g. do. 1902. Life of G. T. with sel. from his writings. Ed. by H. E. Govan. L: Nisbet. 256p. 18cm. [BM]
[Based on Jackson, but not greatly improved.]

TEZNER, F: 1856- . Sel. in C563.

"THARAU, Hs." (i.e., Anna v. Weling, 1837-1900).
9348. (Die Studiengenossen.) The fellow-students. Tr. J:a S. Rockwood. NY: Amer. tract soc. 1884. 262p. il. 18cm. [BM]

THAUSING, Mz. 1838-84.
*9349. (Dürer - Geschichte seines Lebens und seiner Kunst.) Ab. D--: his life and works. Tr. anon. L: Murray 1882. 2v. xiii;376;347p. il. 23cm. [BM.LC]

THEBESIUS, ---. Sel. in C271.

THEREMIN, (L: F:) Fz. 1780-1846. Sel. in #5132.
*9350. (Adalberts Bekenntnisse.) The confessions of Adalbert. Tr. S: Jackson. L: Wertheim 1838. vii;264p. 17cm. [BM.LCO]
9351. The awakening: a pious dialog. Tr. anon. Bost: T. R. Marvin 1849. 16p. 12cm. [BM]
9352. do. 1855. [same?] Tr. anon. Bost: Warin. 30p. 24. [LCO]

THIBAUT, An. F: Jt. 1772-1840.
*9353. (Ueber Reinheit der Tonkunst.) On purity in musical art. Tr. W: H: Gladstone. L: Murray 1877. viii;194p. 19cm. [LC]
§9354. do. 1882. Purity in music. Tr. J: Broadhouse. L: Reeves. vi; 103p. 18cm. [Rather clumsy and bungling.] [LC]
§9355. do. 1885. [same] [BM]

THIELMANN, Max Fz. Guido, Frhr. v. 1846- .
*9356. (Streifzüge im Kaukasus.) Journey in the Caucasus, Persia, and Turkey in Asia. Tr. C: Heneage. L: Murray 1875. 2v. xv;308; 302p. il. 19cm. [BM.LC]

THIERSCH, H: W: Josias, 1817-85.
9357. Abyssinia. Tr. Sa. M. S. Pereira. L: Nisbet 1885. 128p. 17cm. [BM]
*9358. (Das Wesen des christlichen Staates.) On Christian commonwealth. Tr. and ad. (notes omitted) under direction of the author by J. W. Watkins. Ed: T. & T. Clark 1877. ix;272p. 22cm.[BM]
[The tr. has reproduced the clear, terse, and classical style.]
*9359. (Ueber christliches Familienleben.) Christian family life. Tr. J. R. Gardiner. L: Bosworth & Harrison 1856. vii;195p. 18cm[BM]

THIESS, Frank.
*9360. (Das Tor zur Welt.) The gateway to life. Tr. H. T. Lowe-Porter. NY: Knopf 1927. 325p. 21cm. [BM]
[In the main, very good; some inept expressions.]

THILO, Vl. 1607-62. Sel. in C271.

THOLUCK, F: A: Gtg. 1799-1877. Sel. in C5;69;469.
*9361. (Die Lehre von der Sünde.) Guido and Julius: the doctrine of sin and the propitiator...exhib. in the corr. of two friends. Tr. J. E. Ryland. L: W:Ball 1836. xxxvii;263p. 16cm. [BM]
[Ryland is more restrained than Martin.]
*9362. do. 1854. [same] G-- and J--; or, sin and the propitiator, exhib. in the true consecration of the sceptic. Tr. Ryland. Bost: Gould & Lincoln. 238p. 16. [LCO]
*9363. do. 1855. The two students, G-- and J--; or, the true consecration of the doubter. Tr. from 7th Ger. ed. by Jas. Martin. L: J:Shaw. vii;173p. 19cm. [BM]
[A bit extravagant. Appendices abbreviated.]

THOMA, L: 1867- .
9364. (Der heilige Hies.) Matt the holy. Tr. B. Q. Morgan. 1913-15. In C154(19).
9365. (Moral.) Morality. Tr. Hm. Bernstein. NY: 1909. Tw. [LC]

THOMA, L:--Moral
§9366. do. 1916. "Moral": a comedy in 3 acts [prose] Tr. C: Recht. NY: Knopf. 94p. 19cm. [LC]
§9367. do. 1921. [same] In C100a.

THOMASIN VON ZERKLAERE, d. 1235. Sel. in C108;440.

THOMÉ, O: W: See Klein, Hm., joint author.

THUEMMEL, Mz. A: v. 1738-1817.
*9368. (Reise in die mittäglichen Provinzen von Frankreich.) Journal of sentimental travels in the southern provinces of France, shortly before the Revolution. Tr. anon. Abr. L: Ackermann 1821. 291p. il. 25cm. [BM.LC]

THUILLE, L: W: A: M:a, 1861-1907. Merrydance: operetta. See O: J. Bierbaum.

THUN-HOHENSTEIN, Pl. Graf v. 1884- .
9369. The marriage of convention in Europe. 1926. In C308.

TIECK, L: 1773-1853. Sel. in C12;17;44;56;88;158;190;193-4;219;295; 309;366*;373;380;388;391;393-4;412;422;461;469;507;543.

COLLECTIONS

9370. 1823. The sorcerers; The enchanted castle ("Das Zauberschloss"); Wake not the dead; *Auburn Egbert ("Der blonde Eckbert"); §Elfinland ("Die Elfen"). Tr. anon. In C456.
*9371. 1825. The pictures ("Die Gemälde"); The betrothing ("Die Verlobung"). Tr. anon. L: Whittaker. xxxix;255p. 8. [BM]
9372. 1826. §Auburn Egbert ("Der blonde Eckbert"); *The faithful Eckart and the Tannenhäuser ("Der getreue E-- und der T--"); Love magic ("Liebeszauber"). Tr. T: Roscoe. In C477.
[The first is pruned and altered; the second is excellent, even the verse is very good.]
*9373. 1827. The fair-haired Eckbert ("Der blonde E--"); *The trusty Eckart ("Der getreue E--"); The Runenberg ("Der R--"); *The elves ("Die Elfen"); The goblet ("Der Pokal"). Tr. T: Carlyle. In C58, cf. C59-62. [Excellent tr.; fem. rhyme retained.]
9374. 1831. Tales. Tr. anon. L: Moxon. See "Athenaeum" 4(1831):245. (B26) [Grimm (B12) lists for NY: The old man of the mountain. Tr. J. C. Hare. L: Moxon 1831. 335p. Three tales: The old man of the mountain ("Der alte vom Berge"); The love charm ("Liebeszauber"); Pietro of Abano ("P-- v. A--"). This is doubtless the first ed. of #9377.]
9375. 1843. The faithful Eckart ("Der getreue E--"); The mysterious cup ("Der Pokal"); The runenberg ("Der R--"). Tr. anon. In C473.
†9376. 1845. Tales from the Phantasus. L: Burns. sep. paged. 8.[BM.NY] Tr. J. C. Hare, J. A. Froude, and others.--†The white Egbert ("Der blonde Eckbert"): †The Tannenhäuser ("Der blonde Eckbert und der Tannenhäuser"); †The faithful Eckart ("Der getreue Eckart"); †The love-charm ("Liebeszauber"); †The elves ("Die Elfen"); †The mysterious cup ("Der Pokal"); §The runenberg ("Der R--"). Not in Phantasus: The reconciliation ("Die Versöhnung"); The friends ("Die Freunde"); The brothers ("Die Brüder").
9377. 1860. [same as #9374?] Tales from the German. 2d ed. L: Parker. 210p. 17cm. [BM.LCO]
*9378. 1879. Tales of fairyland. Tr. anon. Pref. by J. A. F. L: Routledge. xviii;197p. il. 16cm. [BM]
[Awkwardly faithful.--The reconciliation ("Die Versöhnung"); The friends ("Die Freunde"); The elves; The white Egbert; Faithful Eckart; The Tannenhäuser; The Runenberg; The mysterious cup ("Der Pokal"); The love charm; The brothers ("Die Brüder").]

TIECK, L:--Collections
9379. 189- . *The goblet ("Der Pokal"); *Love magic: some centuries ago ("Liebeszauber"). Tr. anon. In C156.
[The goblet by Carlyle; tr. of Love magic pads needlessly.]
9380. 1895. The bracelet; The Klausenburg ("Die K--"). Tr. C. A. F. In C559.

*9381. (Der Aufruhr in den Cevennen.) The rebellion in the Cevennes: an histor. novel. Tr. Mme. Burette. L: Nutt 1845. 2v. 12. [BM.NY]
[Very good; not without faults.]
*9382. (Der blonde Eckbert.) Fair E--. Tr. P. B. Thomas. 1913-15. In C154(4).
§9383. (Der gestiefelte Kater.) Puss in boots. Tr. Lillie Winter. 1913-15. In C154(4). [Rather severely edited and pruned.]
9384. (Der Runenberg.) The r--. Tr. T: Carlyle. 1927. In C452.
9385. (Der Tod des Dichters.) Camoens; or, the death of the poet. Tr. anon. 1847. In C20. Cf. C21.
*9386. (Dichterleben.) The life of poets: a novel. Tr. anon. Leipsic: 1830. 140p. 8. [Very good.] [BM]
*9387. (Die Elfen.) The elves. Tr. T: Carlyle. 1845. In C114.
*9388. do. 1913-15. [same] In C154(4). [Slightly revised from C58.]
9389. (Die Freunde.) The friends. Tr. anon. 1927. In C367.From #9376.
9390. (Die Gemälde.) The pictures. Tr. G: G. Cunningham. 1829. In C80.
§9391. do. 1883. The legacy. Tr. G. G. Moore. L: Remington. 153p. 18cm. [BM]
9392. (Die Klausenburg.) The K--. Tr. C. A. Feiling. 1844. In C442.
9393. (Die sieben Weiber des Blaubart.) Der Blaubart, ein Märchen, with translation by Apel. L: Simpkin n.d. 1833? 12. [EC]
[See "Blackwoods Mag." 33(1833):206 for considerable extracts.(B26)]
§9394. (Die Sommernacht.) The midsummer night; or, Shakespeare and the fairies. Tr. Ma. C. Rumsey. L: Whittingham 1854. 35p. 8.
[Fair to good. Agreeable verse, sense pretty well caught; Tieck's meters mostly abandoned.] [BM.LCO]
†9395. (Fermer, der geniale.) Fermer the genius: a novel. Tr. Fd. Marckwort. Brunswic: Lucius; L: Black & Armstrong 1837. 100p. Ger;Engl. 12. [Very bad tr.] [BM]
9396. (Leben und Tod der heiligen Genoveva.) Genoveva. See Reinick, R., Genoveva.
9397. (Leben und Tod des kleinen Rotkäppchens.) The life and death of Little Red Riding-hood: a tragedy. Ad. by Jane B. Smith. Il. J: Mulready. L: Groombridge 1851. 58p. 18cm. [BM]
9398. Leonhard and Kunigunde. Tr. C. F. Schreiber. 1927. In C452.
9398a. (Pietro v. Abano.) P-- of A--. Tr. anon. In "Blackwood's Mag." 46(1839):288. (B27)
9399. Precipitation. Tr. G. F. Crossthwaite. 1842. In C79.
9400. Remarks on the Sistine Madonna. Tr. C. L. Bernays. 1877. In C300(7).
§9401. (Vittoria accorombona.) The Roman matron; or V-- a--. A novel. Tr. anon. L;Bury St. Edmunds: Newby 1845. 3v. 362;283;226p. 12. [Too flowery.] [BM]
9402. Conclusion of Novalis' H: v. Ofterdingen. See Novalis, #6966 seq.
9403. Life of Novalis. See Novalis, #6966.

TIEDGE, Cph. A: 1752-1840. Sel. in C17;41;309;371;373;391;393;443; 501;#5132.

TIESSEN, Heinz, 1887- .
9404. (R: Strauss, op. 63. Josephslegende. Ein Führer durch das Werk.) R: S--, The legend of Joseph: A guide to the music. Tr. Af. Kalisch. Berlin; Paris: Fürstner 1914. xiii;61p. il. 18cm. [LCM]

TIETZ, F: 1803-79.
9405. (Erinnerungs-Skizzen aus Russland, der Türkei und Griechenland...) St. Petersburg, Constantinople...in 1833-4. Richter 1836. 2v. 8. [EC]
9406. do. 1836. [same?] Tr. J. D. Haas. NY: Foster. 227p. 12. [LC]

TILKE, Max
9406a. The costumes of eastern Europe. Benn; Weyhe 1925. (EC: Benn 1926.) 32p. 96 col. pl. 12 x 9. [EC]

TIRPITZ, Af. P. F: v. 1849- .
*9407. (Erinnerungen.) My memoirs: being the recoll. and letters... Tr. anon. L: Hurst & Blackett; NY: Dodd 1919. 2v. 377;428p. 23cm. [BM.LC]

TISCHENDORF, Lobegott F: Cst. 1815-74.
9408. (Reise in den Orient.) Travels in the east. Tr. W: E: Shuckard. L: Longmans 1847. xvi;287p. 18cm. [BM.LC]

TISCHER, J: F: W:
9409. (Luthers Leben und Taten.) Life, deeds, and opinions of Dr. M. L--. Tr. J: Kortz. Hudson: Clark 1818. 260p. 12. [LCO]
9410. do. 1872. abr. In Luther's commentary on St. Paul's epistle to the Galatians. Phil: Quaker city pub. 8. pp. 25-77. [LCO]

TISCHNER, Rd. E. 1879- .
9411. Telepathy and clairvoyance. Tr. W. D. Hutchinson. L: Paul 1925. ix;227p. NY: Harcourt. xi;226p. il. 22cm. [BM]

TITIUS (Tietze), Cph. 1641-1703. Sel. in C287.

TOERRING-GUTTENZELL, Js. A: Graf v. 1753-1826.
9412. (Agnes Bernauerinn. Ein vaterländisches Schauspiel.) The tournament, a tragedy in 5 acts [verse], imitated from the celebrated Ger. drama...written by a nobleman of high rank, and founded on fact, that occurred in Bavaria about the year 1435. By Mariana Starke. L: Prtd. for R. Phillips 1800. 64p. 20cm. [BM] [The orig. is in prose. "The imitator has ventured to deviate from the truth by preserving the life of Agnes."]
9413. do. 1803. [same] As performed at the NY:theatre. From the prompt book. NY: Longworth. 60p. 14cm. (In "The NY Theatre," vol. 1.) [LC]

TOLLENS, ---. Sel. in C388. [A Dutchman?]

TOLLER, Ern. 1893- .
*9414. (Das Schwalbenbuch.) The swallow-book. Tr. Ashley Dukes. L: Milford; NY: Oxford 1924. 54p. 19cm. [BM.LC]
§9415. (Die Maschinenstürmer.) The machine-wreckers: a drama of the Engl. Luddites in a prologue and 5 acts. Tr. Ashley Dukes. L: Benn; NY: Knopf 1923. viii;113p. 20cm. [BM.LC] [This tr. is "dressed up."]
9416. do. 1926. [same] 194p. 8. [BM]
9416a. do. 1926. [same] Benn. 95p. 8. [EC]
*9417. (Hinkemann.) Brokenbrow: a tragedy. Tr. Vera Mendel. Il. G: Grosz. L: Nonesuch 1926. 50p. 23cm. [BM.LC]
*9418. (Masse-Mensch.) Man and the masses: a play of the social revolution in seven scenes. Tr. L: Untermeyer. The Theatre guild version, with six il. from photographs of the...production. NY: Doubleday, Page 1924. xxix;109p. 20cm. [LC]
*9419. do. 1924. Masses and man. Tr. Vera Mendel. L: Nonesuch. x; 57p. 8 x 5 in. [BM]

TORGE, Else, 1885- .
9420. (Das Urteil des Salomo.) The judgment of Solomon: a drama in 4 acts and an interlude. Tr. Thekla M. Bernays. St.L. 1914. Tw.[LC]

TOVOTE, Heinz, 1864- .
9421. (Im Liebesrausch.) "Love's delirium." Tr. Hettie E. Miller. Chic: Morrill, Higgins 1892. 286p. il. 21cm. [LC]

TOZE (Totze), Eobald, 1715-89.
*9422. (Der gegenwärtige Zustand von Europa.) The present state of Europe. Tr. T: Nugent. L: J.Nourse 1770. 3v. 20cm. [BM]

TRAEGER, Ab. 1830-1912. Sel. in C112;152;309;448;497;501;571.

TRAKL, G: 1887-1914. Sel. in C95.

TRAUT, So. Sel. in C169.

TREBITSCH, Sf.
§9423. (Frau Gittas Sühne.) Jittas atonement: a play in 3 acts. 82p. 17cm. In Bernard Shaw's "Translations and tomfooleries." L: Constable 1926. 246p. [BM]
[Delightfully Shavianized, but de-Trebitschized.]

TREITSCHKE, H: (Gtd.) v. 1834-96. Sel. in C161.
9424.[Coll.] Tr. anon. 1914. In A. Hausrath's Treitschke. #3917. [The army; Internat. law; First attempts at Ger. colonization; Two emperors ("Zwei Kaiser"); Germany and the neutral states; Austria and the Ger. empire ("Oesterreich und das deutsche Reich"); The alliance between Austria and Prussia; *Freedom ("Die Freiheit").]
9425. [Coll.] 1915. Germany, France, Russia, and Islam. (Essays and lectures.) Tr. anon. L: Jarrold. 327p. 23cm. [BM.LC]
[*Turkey and the great nations ("Die Türkei und die Grossmächte"); Germany and the oriental question ("Deutschland und die orientalische Frage"); *What we demand from France ("Was fordern wir von Frankreich?"); The incorporation of Alsace-Lorraine in the Ger. empire; The memory of the great war; *Luther and the Ger. nation ("L-- und die deutsche Nation"); Gustavus Adolphus and Germany's freedom ("G-- A-- und Deutschlands Freiheit"); Our empire ("Unser Reich").--What we demand from France is reprinted from #9431.]
*9426. (Deutsche Geschichte im 19. Jahrhundert.) Hist. of Germany in the 19th cent. Tr. Eden and Cedar Paul. L: Jarrold; NY: McBride, Nast 1915-19. 7v. 22cm. [BM.LC]
*9427. (Die Feuerprobe.) The fire-test of the North-German Confederation. Tr. F: A. Hyndman. L: Longmans 1870. 35p. 18cm.[BM]
[Very good, yet disappoints by not being better; lacks the sure touch.]
9428. Life of F: the Gt. In "Les matinées royales, etc." See F: II, #2003.
*9429. (Politik.) Politics. Tr. Blanche Dugdale and Torben de Bille. L: Constable; NY: Macmillan 1916. 2v. xliii;406;643p. 23cm. [BM.LC]
*9430. do. 1914. Selections from...lect. on politics. Tr. Am. L. Gowans. L;Glasgow: Gowans & Gray. 128p. 18cm. [BM.LC]
[Tr. follows the orig. closely and prefers a somewhat bald literalness to more fluent English; exact sense given.]
*9431. (Was fordern wir von Frankreich?) What we demand from France. Tr. anon. L: Macmillan 1870. 109p. 18cm. [BM]
See Hausrath, Ad., T--, his life and works, #3917; T--, his doctrine of German destiny, #3916.

TRENCK, Fz. Freiherr v. d. 1711-49.
9432. "Life and actions of the illustrious Fis. Baron T--." Memoirs ...written by himself and done...into English. Tr. anon. L: Owen 1747. 108p. 20cm. [BM]
9433. The hist. of Fis. baron T--, a partisan colonel, and commander

TRENCK, Fz. Freiherr v. d.
in chief of the Pandours, in the service of her majesty the empress-queen. Written by F: Baron Trenck, as a necessary supplement to his own history. Phil: Prtd. and sold by W. Woodhouse, 1712 (i.e., 1792). pp. 271-309. [LC]
9434. do. 1792. Tr. T: Holcroft. In #9438.

TRENCK, F: Freiherr v. d. 1726-94.
9435. (Merkwürdige Lebensgeschichte...) Life...containing his advent., his cruel and excessive sufferings, during ten years' imprisonment at the fortress of Magdeburg, by command of the late king of Prussia. Also, anecdotes historical, political, and personal. Tr. T: Holcroft. L: Robinson 1788-93. 4v. 18cm. [Cf. note on #9438]
9436. do. 1789. [same] Phil: Prtd. by W: Spotswood. Vol. I (-II). 2v. in one. iv;152;159p. port. 12. (B6a) [Available: AAS.NYPL.]
9437. do. 1791. abr. Sketch of the life of F: Baron T--, with engraving. In Webster's calendar; or, the Albany almanac...1792. Albany (NY): Webster. 36p. 12. (B6a) [Available: AAS.LC.]
9438. do. 1792. [same as #9435] Bost: Belknap & Young. 417p. Front. by S. Hill 16cm. [BM]
[Tr. mainly from the Berlin ed., with additions via the French from the Vienna ed. "Greater liberties must be taken, of omitting and compressing certain passages...than...in any other work." In point of fact Holcroft seems to have followed the French, and quite closely, including matter not in the Ger. but in the French ed. Life of F: extends to p. 342, then comes hist. of Fis. Trenck to p. 382, then anecdotes of the life of Ax. Schell, and finally apologies and vindications. He tr. quite closely where he follows his source.]
9439. do. 1792. [same] Phil: Woodhouse. 345p. plate. 16cm. [LC]
[Has second title: The life...as contained in the fourth volume; being the most important.]
9440. do. 1793. Life and advent. etc. Windsor: Prtd. by Alden Spooner. (B6a) [No anecdotes mentioned.]
9441. do. 1793. Life, etc. Bost: Prtd. by P: Edes for Thomas & Andrews. 200p. front. 12. (B6a)
[Available: AAS.NL. No anecdotes mentioned.]
9442. do. 1793. Life of Baron F: T--. Vol. fourth, and most important. Bost: Prtd. for Larkin. 110 (i.e., 120)p. 12. (B6a)
[Available: NYPL. No anecdotes mentioned.]
9443. do. 1794. Life, etc. Also, anecdotes. Also, second title, as in #9439. Phil: Prtd. for Rb. Campbell. 256;68p. port. 16. (B6a)
[Available: AAS.JCB]
9444. do. 1794. The life...as contained in the fourth vol., being the most important. Phil: Campbell. 68p. 16cm. [LC]
[Evidently part of the foregoing.]
9445. do. 1794. Life, etc. Also, anecdotes. Albany (NY). Prtd. for T: Spencer. 345p. port. 12. (B6a) [Available: AAS. Also contains, with sep. title: Hist. of Fis. Baron T--, pp. 271-345.]
9446. do. 1795. [same as #9435, but in 3 vols.] L: Robinson. 3v. viii;390;356;386p. 17cm. [BM]
[Vol. 3 has the anecdotes and apologies, to. p. 65, then a new t.p.: The life of F: Baron T--. This from a supplementary 4th vol., not done by Holcroft.]
9447. do. 1796. Life, etc. (With anecdotes of the life of Ax. Schell ...written as a supplement to my own history.) Tr. Holcroft. NY: Prtd. and sold by W: Durell. 187p. plate. 24. (B6a)
[Available: AAS.]
9447a. do. 1798. The life and advent...containing his cruel and excessive sufferings etc. Phil. 12. (B6a)
9448. do. 1800. [same as #9446] 3d ed. 3v. in one. [BM]
[Pref. xiip. Otherwise identical. No front. in this copy, though the description of it is retained.]

TRENCK, F: v. d.--Lebensgeschichte
9449. do. 1802. The life and surprising advent...Carefully corr. and abr. To which is added a short supplement, etc. Chapbook. Stirling: Randall. 24p. 16cm. [BM]
9450. do. 1808. Holcroft's tr. abridged. Providence, R. I: Heaton. 108p. 16cm. [LC]
9451. do. 1810. Holcroft's tr. abridged. Phil: Johnson & Warner. 121p. 14cm. [LC]
9452. do. 1817. [same as #9448] 4th ed. L: Newman. 3v. xii;345;311; 359p. 19cm. [No front., no description of it.] [BM]
9453. do. 1820. [same as #9449] The surprising advent...How he was confined in a dungeon, with chains of 68 pounds weight, etc. Chapbook. Falkirk: Johnston. 24p. 15cm. [BM]
[The text is that of #9449, with some additions near the end.]
9454. do. 1826. The surprising advent. etc. Chapbook. Stirling: Prtd. by W. Macnie. 24p. 17cm. [BM]
[Not quite the same as the foregoing.]
9455. do. 1835. [same as #9448] L: 12. [This copy is now lost.] [BM]
9456. do. 1843. Holcroft's tr. New ed. Halifax. Milner. 472p. 13cm. [LC]
9457. do. before 1852. Life, advent. etc. Phil: Gihon n.d. 18. [AC]
9458. do. before 1852. Life, advent. etc. Phil: Anners n.d. [AC]
9459. do. 1853. Life...abridged. Albany, NY: Munsell. 100p. 23cm. [Probably the same as #9450.] [LC]
9460. do. 1858-60. Prison life; or, interesting biographies of... and Baron Trenck. NY: Barnes & Burr n.d. 16. [AC]
*9461. do. 1878. Memoirs...written by himself. Tr. anon. L;NY: Routledge. 157p. double cols. 19cm. [BM]
[Life to p. 144; supplement of one page; Abridgment of the life of Fis. Trenck; The advent. of Lieut. Schell. Not Holcroft's tr. Done either from French or the Ger. orig. Col. cover from orig. front.]
9462. do. 1886. Life...Tr. Holcroft. L: Cassell. 2v. in one. 192; 192p. 13cm. [BM]
[H: M(orley) in his pref. to vol. 2 states that H. tr. from the French. This is only true in a limited sense; see my note to #9438. This ed. is somewhat abridged; it omits the anecdotes of Schell, and ends with the hist. of Fis. Trenck.]
9463. do. 1886. Memoirs...written by himself. Tr. anon. Introd. Rev. H. R. Haweis. L;NY: Routledge. 160p. 16cm. [BM]
[This is ident. with #9461 as far as the end of the life on p. 144.]
9464. do. 1893. [same as #9461] Caxton novels. 23cm. [BM]
[Large paper ed. of #9461. Col. cover from the orig. front.]
9465. do. 1927. The strange advent. of F: Baron Trenck (an abridgment). Ed. Ph. Murray. L: Allan. viii;279p. front. il. 22cm. [BM]
[Based on Holcroft's tr. Pref. says: "The present version...has been entirely rewritten," but a cursory comparison reveals little or no change of Holcroft's wording. 14 chapters, giving only the life.]

TRENDELENBURG, F: Ad. 1802-72.
9466. Hegel's system. Tr. T. Davidson. 1875-6. In C300(5,6).

TREVIRANUS, Ld. Cn. 1779-1864.
9467. Memoir of the life of J. R. T. Vogel. Tr. by Rev. M. J. Berkeley. In Hooker's "Niger flora." L: Hippolyte 1849. xv;21p. 22cm. [BM]

TRINIUS, ---. Sel. in C2;296.

TRINIUS, A: 1851-1919.
9468. The Wartburg in legend and poetry; Modern life in the Wartburg Tr. G. A. Greene. 1907. In C555.

TRITHEIM (or Trithemius), J:s, 1462-1516.
9469. Book of secret things and Doctrine of spirits. Tr. Fis. Barrett. In his "The magus," pp. 129-40. L: Lackington, Allen 1801. 4. [BM.LCO]
9470. do. 1875. [reprint] [BM]

TROELTSCH, Ern. 1865-1923. Sel. in C563.
*9471. (Der Historismus und seine Ueberwindung.) Christian thought, its hist. and application: lect...1923. Tr. by various hands. Ed. by Baron F. v. Hügel. L: Univ. press; NY: Doran 1923. xxxi;179p. 18cm. [Tr. are: Ma. E. Clarke, Mx. A. Muegge, Miss Durban, H: G. Atkins, F. v. Hügel, Principal Barker.] [BM.LC]
*9472. (Die Bedeutung des Protestantismus...) Protestantism and progress. Tr. W. Montgomery. L;NY: Putnam 1912. xi;210p. 19cm [BM.LC]

TROJAN, J:s, 1837-1915.
9473. (Der schwarze Peter.) Black Peter: scissor pict. (by Pl. Konewka), with rhymes from the German. Tr. anon. NY: Hurd & Houghton 1872. 21p. 23cm. [LC]
9474. (Die Geschichte vom kleinen Rehbock.) The little roebuck. Pict. by F. Lossow, and rhymes by J. T--. Tr. J. S. S. Rothwell. L: Griffith & Farran 1873. 23cm. [BM]
[16 leaves, one verse and pict. to each. Rather sad stuff: neither sense nor rhyme.]
9475. Struwwelpeter junior. Tr. anon. L: Jarrold 1893. il. 30cm. [BM]
[Cf. H: Hoffmann.]

"TROMLITZ, A. v." (i.e., K: A: F: v. Witzeleben, 1773-1839.)
9476. (Romantische Wanderung durch die sächsische Schweiz.) Saxon Switzerland. Tr. Miss Henningsen. In "Romantic and picturesque Germany," section 1. L: Schloss 1838. 32p. il. with steel engr. 25cm. [No more pub. in this series.] [BM]

TROTZNOU (?). Sel. in C486.

TRUCHSESS VON SANKT GALLEN. See U: v. Singenberg.

TSCHABUSCHNIGG, Ad. Ritter v. 1809-77. Sel. in C450.

TSCHERNING, And. 1611-59. Sel. in C461.

TSCHINK, Cajetan, d. 1809.
9477. (Geschichte eines Geistersehers.?) The victim of magical delusion; or, the mystery of the revolution of P...l. Tr. P: Will. L: 1795. 3v. 8. [BM]

TSCHUDI, F: v. 1820-86.
*9478. (Das Tierleben der Alpenwelt.) Sketches of nature in the Alps. Tr. anon. L: Longman etc. 1856. Traveller's lib. 2 pts. 246p. 17cm. [Chapters on "Animal life" omitted, as well as several of the biographies; condensed.] [BM]

TSCHUDI, J: Jk. v. 1818-89.
§9479. (Peru. Reiseskizzen...) Travels in Peru...1838-42. Tr. Thomasina Ross. L: Bogue 1847. 506p. 21cm. [BM.LC]
[Tr. cuts quite freely, making comparison difficult.]
§9480. do. 1847. [same] NY: Wiley & Putnam. 2 pts. in one. 19cm. [LC]
9481. do. 1854. [same?] NY: Riker. 12. [AC]

TUERCK, Hm. 1856- .
*9482. (Der geniale Mensch.) The man of genius. Tr. from 6th Ger. ed. by G: J. Tamson. Additions of 7th ed. Tr. Mrs. Eliz. Deibel. L: Black 1914. 483p. 23cm. [BM.LC]

TUGENDHAFTE SCHREIBER, Der. See Schreiber.

TURLERUS, Hrns. d. 1602. Sel. in C483.

TURLERUS, Hrns.
9483. The traveiler of Jerome Turler, devided into two bookes. The first conteining a notable discourse of the maner, and order of traveiling oversea, or into strange and forrein countreys. The second comprehending an excellent description of the most delicious realme of Naples in Italy. (From the Latin.) Tr. anon. L: Veale 1575. 192p. 14cm. [BM]

TWARDOWSKA, Ea. Eva Hte. v. 1845-89. See "Hartner, E."

UEBERSBERGER, Hs. Ph. 1877- . Sel. in C563.

UEBERWEG, F: 1826-71.
*9484. (Grundriss der Geschichte der Philosophie von Thales...) A Hist. of philos. from Thales to the present time. Tr. from 4th ed. by G: S. Morris. NY: Scribner 1872-4. 2v. 24cm. [LC]
[Judgment from review in C300(8).]
*9485. do. 1874. [same] L: Theol. and philos. lib. 2v. xv;487;viii; 561p. 24cm. [BM]
[BM also has: Vol. 1, xi;487p. L: Hodder & Stoughton 1872. 25cm.]
*9486. do. 1876. 2d (English) ed. L: Hodder & Stoughton. 2v. same paging. 22cm. [BM]
9487. do. 1876. [same] New ed. NY: Scribner. 2v. [AC]
*9488. do. 1892. [same] Scribner. 2v. 23cm. [LC]
*9489. (System der Logik.) System of logic and hist. of logical doctrine. Tr. T: M. Lindsay. L: Longmans 1871. xx;590p. 22cm. [BM.LC]

UEXKUELL, J. v.
9489a. (Theoretische Biologie.) Theoret. biol. Paul 1926. 378p. 8. [EC]

UHLAND, (J:) L: 1787-1862. Sel. in C1-3;12;17;28;31;32*;36-7;40-3; 44*;45-7;50;65*;67*;69;73;75*;77*;86;89;92-3;97-9;106;111-2;116; 123;129;131;132*;133;137a;141-4;146*;149;151-3;166*;169;171-3; 182*;184*;192*;195-6;208;215-6;219;273;295-6;299;306-7;309*;311; 313;316-8;366*;371-2;373*;375;378;380;383;385;387-8;391;393;395; 396*;397*;410;412;417;423;428;438;448;450;452;460;464;467;469;470; 486;489;499;500-1;504-6;516-7;531;538;539*;543;554;564;571;#2687; 4082;6209a;8001;8030.

SELECTIONS

9490. ANON. Flowers from the fatherland. Tr. by various hands. 1870. See C132. [58 poems tr. from U--.]
§9491. BUTLER, W: ALLEN. Poems. Bost: Osgood 1871. vi;263p. 16. [BM]
--Also, Nothing to wear and other poems. NY: Harper 1899. 240p. 8. [10 poems tr. from U--.] [LC]
*9492. PLATT, Ax. Poems. Lpz: Volckmann 1848. 12. [BM.NY]
[Nearly complete. Many excellent renderings.]
§9493. SANDARS, W: C. Poems... L: Ridgway 1869. 180p. 19cm. [BM.LC]
[Some very good; but his taste is imperfectly educated.]
*9494. SKEAT, W. W. Songs and ballads of U--. L: Williams & Norgate 1864. 456p. 20cm. [BM.LC]
[At his best, S-- is unsurpassed; he does not always retain the meter.]

9495. The herd-boy, a fairy tale in Engl. verse. Tr. anon. L: Routledge 1856. 16. [EC]

UHLEMANN, Mx. Ad.
*9496. (Drei Tage in Memphis.) Three days in M--; or, sketches of the public and private life of the old Egyptians. Tr.'s notice signed E. Goodrich Smith. Phil: Lippincott 1858. xii;253p. il. 19cm. [Faithful transcript of the orig.] [LC.BM]

UHLHORN, Grd. 1826-1901.
9497. (Luther und die Schweizer.) L-- and the Swiss. Tr. G. F. Krotel. Luth. book-store 1876. 12. [AC]
[From one of 3 lect. on the Reformation.]

UHLIG, Td. See Wagner, R:, Letters to his Dresden friends, #9897.

UKLANSKI, K: Td. Freiherr v.
†9498. (Briefe über Polen.) Travels in Poland, Austria, Saxony, Bavaria, and the Tyrol in 1807-8. Tr. anon. L: J.Soulter 1815. 243p. 16cm. [Tr. knows no German.] [BM]
*9499. (Briefe über Polen, II. Teil.) Travels in upper Italy, Tuscany, and the Ecclesiastical State. Tr. anon. L: J.Soulter 1816. 2v. 243;198p. 16cm. [Occasional poems, pp. 183-98.] [BM]

ULRICH VON LICHTENSTEIN, fl. 1227-74. Sel. in C1;27;88*;310;366;416; 427;532.

ULRICH VON SACHSENDORF, fl. 1240. Sel. in C27.

ULRICH VON SINGENBERG, Truchsess (Sewer) v. Sankt Gallen, fl. 1209-28. Sel. in C27;427.

ULRICH VON WINTERSTETTEN, fl. 1241-69. Sel. in C27;310;427;530.

ULRICH, Anna.
9500. Recoll. of J:a Spyri's childhood. Tr. Helen B. Dole. NY: Crowell 1925. 54p. il. 19cm. [LC]

ULRICHS, K: H: d. 1894. Sel. in C63.

ULRICI, Hm. 1806-84.
*9501. (Der Philosoph Strauss.) S-- as a philosophical thinker. A review...Tr. with introd. by C. P. Krauth. Phil: Smith, English; Ed: Clark 1874. 167p. 12. [Admirable tr.--Introd., pp. 9-72.] [BM]
9502. Shakspeare's dram. art and his relation to Calderon and Goethe. Tr. anon. L: Chapman 1846. 554p. 21cm. [BM]
[From "Ueber S--'s dramatische Kunst." Goethe, pp. 512-54.]

UMLAUFT, F: 1844- .
*9503. (Die Alpen.) The Alps. Tr. Louisa Brough. L: K.Paul 1889. 523p. il. 24cm. [Effective abridgment.] [BM.LC]

UMLAUFT, Pl. 1853- .
*9504. (Evanthia.) Evanthe: price (i.e., prize) opera in one act, words and music by Pl. U--. Tr. F: Corder. Vocal score. Ger;Engl. L: Schott 1894. 155p. fol. [LCM]

UNGERN-STERNBERG, Ax. Freiherr v. 1806-68.
9505. (Die Brüder.) The Breughel brothers: an art romance. Tr. G. H: Lodge. Designs by H. Billings. Bost: Little; Brown 1854. 187p. il. 21 x 15cm. [LC.BM]
9506. do. 1873. [same] Bost: Osgood. 187p. [LC.BM]
[AC dates this 1872.]

UNGERN-STERNBERG, Léonie
9507. The marriage of the future. Tr. 1926. In C308.

UNZER, J: Cph. 1747-1809.
9508. (Diego und Leonore.) The inquisitor: a trag. in 5 acts. Altered...Jas. P. Andrews and H: J. Pye. L: Hatchard 1798. 76p. 22cm. [LC]
9509. do. 1798. Tr. T: Holcroft. L: Robinsons. See "Monthly R." 27 (1798):347. (B26)

USTERI, J: Mt. 1763-1827. Sel. in C106;438.

UZ, J: P: 1720-96. Sel. in C93.

VACANO, El. Als. Fd. 1840-92.
9510. The honor of a heart. Tr. Ma. J. Safford. Il. F. A. Carter.

VACANO, El. Als. Fd.
NY: Bonner 1893. 265p. il. 19cm. [LC]
9511. The last grave of the Nibescos. Tr. E. Wilhelmina Spencer. L: Remington 1877. iv;223p. 18cm. [BM]

VAIHINGER, Hs. 1852- .
*9512. (Die Philosophie des als ob.) The philos. of 'as if': a system of the theoret., pract., and relig. fictions of mankind. Tr. C: K. Ogden. L: Paul, T. & T; NY: Harcourt, Brace 1924. xlviii; 370p. 22cm. [BM.LC]

VALENTINER, W: Rld. 1880- .
9513. (Aus der niederländischen Kunst.) The art of the Low Countries. Studies. Tr. Mrs. S. van Rensselaer. NY: Doubleday, Page; L: Ax. Moring 1914. xx;251p. 24cm. [LC.BM]
9514. do. 1920. [same] Il. Ax. Moring. L: De la More press. [BM]

VALENTINUS, Basilius
9515. (Currus triumphalis antimonii.) The triumphal chariot of antimony: being a conscientious discovery of the many real transcendent excellencies included in that mineral. Faithfully Englished and pub. for the common good by J: H(arding). L: S.Thomson 1661. 175p. 14cm. [BM.LC]
9516. do. 1678. [same?] Basil Valentine, his triumphant chariot of antimony. L: Newman. 176p. il. 18cm. [BM.LC]
9517. do. 1893. Tr. A. E. Waite. L: Elliott. xxiii;204p. il. 20cm. [BM.LC]
9518. (Fratris B. V. geheime Bücher oder letztes Testament.) B. V-- ...his last will and testament...wherein he...declared the wayes he wrought to obtain the philosopher's stone... 4 pts. 1657. 175p. Also, his XII keyes, and, Treatise about the great stone of philosophers. 1656. 40p. Repetition, 25p. Conclusions and experiments, 21p. 5th and last part of his testament, 9p. Microcosme, 23p. no pub. 14cm. [BM]
9519. do. 1671. The last will and testament, to which is added two treatises, Manual operations, Natural and supernatural. Partly tr. and corr. by J.W. L: Brewster. 8 pts. 534p. il. 16cm. [BM]
9520. (Von den natürlichen und übernatürlichen Dingen.) Of natural and supernatural things...Tr. (and ed.) by D. Cable. L: M.Pitt 1670. 238;122p. 14cm. [BM dates this 1671.] [BM.LC]

VAN DER VELDE, K: Fz. 1779-1824.
*9521. [Coll.] Tales...Tr. Nath. Greene. Bost: J: B. Russell 1837. 2v. 354;352p. 19cm. [LC.BM]
[Vol. 1. Arwed Gyllenstierna (do.). Vol. 2. The Lichtensteins ("Die Lichtensteiner"); The sorceress ("Die Trude Hiorba"); The anabaptist ("Die Wiedertäufer ").
§9522. (Arwed Gyllenstierna.) A-- Gyllensterna: a tale of the early part of the 18th cent. Tr. anon. L: Lloyd 1827. 2v. 247;251p. 18cm. [BM]
9523. do. 1846. A. Gillenstern; or, the robber captain's bride. A tale of love - treason - and mystery. Tr. anon. L: Pratt. 448p. 12cm. [Lifted without acknowledgment from #9521.] [BM]
*9524. do. 1879. A son of Sweden: a tale of the last cent. Tr. Christina Tyrrell. L: Remington. 2v. 277;271p. 18cm. [BM]
*9525. (Die Lichtensteiner.) Oswald Dorn: an episode of the 30 years' war. Tr. J. F. Hanstein. L: Horne 1857. 128p. 16cm. [BM]
[Lifted with slight changes from #9521.]
9526. (Die Patrizier.) The patricians. Tr. G: Soane. 1826. In C498.
9527. (Erzstufen. Teil 3.) Axel; a tale of the 30 years' war. Tr. C. A. Feiling. 1844. In C441-2.

VARNHAGEN VON ENSE, K: A: L: Ph. 1785-1858. Sel. in C56;317.

VARNHAGEN VON ENSE, K: A: L: Ph.
9528. (Denkwürdigkeiten des eignen Lebens.) Sketches of Ger. life and scenes from the war of liberation. Sel. and tr. from memoirs... Sir A. Duff Gordon. L: Murray 1847. vi;340p. 17cm. [BM]
9529. do. 1861. [same] New ed. Murray. 340p. 18cm. [LC]
9530. Extr. from diaries and letters to Ax. v. Humboldt. See Humboldt, #4639.

VARNHAGEN, Rahel Ane. F:e, 1771-1833. Sel. in C12.
†9531. Rahel: her life and letters. By Mrs. Vaughan Jennings. L: King 1876. 268p. 12. [Unjustifiable garbling.] [BM]

VEHSE, K: E: 1802-70.
*9532. (Geschichte des österreichischen Hofs.) Memoirs of the court, aristocracy, and diplomacy of Austria. Tr. Fz. Demmler. L: Longmans 1856. 2v. xiv;503;viii;532p. 20cm. [BM.LC]
[Abr. from the orig.]
*9533. do. 1896. [same] L: Nichols. 2v. xv;448;xii;504p. 22cm. [BM]
[Edition limited to 500 cop.]
*9534. (Geschichte des preussischen Hofs.) Memoirs of the court of Prussia. Tr. Fz. Demmler. L: Nelson 1854. 532p. 19cm. [BM.LC]

"VELY, Ea." (i.e., Frau Ea.--Couvely--Simon, 1848-).
9535. (Die Erbin des Herzens.) True daughter of Hartenstein. Tr. Ma. J. Safford. Il. W. B. Davis. NY: Bonner 1892. 377p. il. 19cm. [LC]

"VERENA, So." (i.e., Frau So.--Mödinger--Alberti, 1826-92).
9536. Above tempest and tide. Tr. "Auber Forestier." Phil: McKinney 1873. 395p. 18cm. [LC]

VERNALEKEN, F: Td. 1812-1907.
*9537. (Oesterreichische Kinder- und Hausmärchen.) In the land of marvels: folk-tales from Austria and Bohemia. Tr. anon. Pref. E. Johnson. L: Sonnenschein 1884. 363p. 8. [BM]
[On the whole, excellent. 60 Märchen, supplementing the Grimms' collection. These were told to V--, who wrote them down on the spot.]
9538. do. 1889. [same] il. [BM]

VICTORIA, consort of Emperor Frederick. See Harden, Mx., Word Portraits, #3699.

"VIEBIG, Ca." (i.e., Frau Ca.--Viebig--Cohn, 1860-).
*9539. (Absolvo te.) Absolution. Tr. H. Raahauge. L: Lane 1908. 318p. 19cm. [BM.NY]
9540. (Brennende Liebe.) Burning love. Tr. W: G. Howard. 1913-15. In C154 (19).
*9541 (Das tägliche Brot.) Our daily bread. Tr. Marg. L. Clarke. L: Lane 1909. 356p. 19cm. [BM.NY]
*9542. (Einer Mutter Sohn.) The son of his mother. Tr. H. Raahauge. L;NY: Lane 1913. 340p. 19cm. [BM.LC]
9543. (Margrets Wallfahrt.) Margret's pilgrimage. Tr. Grace I. Colbron. 1913-15. In C447.
*9544. (Töchter der Hekuba.) Daughters of Hecuba. Tr. Anna Barwell. L: Allen & Unwin 1922. 308p. 19cm. [LC]
[Correct but flattens out the style.]

VIERORDT, H: 1855- . Sel. in C311.

VILMAR, A: F: Cn. 1800-68.
9545. Hist. of Ger. lit. by Rev. F: Metcalfe. Based on...V--. L: Longmans 1858. 531p. 18cm. [BM.LC]

VIRCHOW, Rd. 1821-1902. Sel. in C574.
§9546. (Die Freiheit der Wissenschaft im modernen Staat.) The freedom of science in the mod. state. Tr. anon. L: Murray 1878. xxiii;65p. 16cm. [Correct, but awkwardly expressed.] [BM]

VIRCHOW, Rd.
*9547. (J: Mueller, eine Gedächtnisrede.) J: M--: an eloge. Tr. and ed. A. M. Adam. Ed: Sutherland & Knox 1859. 30p. 8. [BM]

VISCHER, F: Td. 1807-87.
9548. A rabid philosopher (from "Auch Einer"). Tr. H. Müller-Casenov. 1909. In C422.

VISCHER, R. Sel. in C102.

VITZTHUM VON ECKSTAEDT, K: F: Graf v. 1819-95.
*9549. (St. Petersburg und London...) St. P-- and L-- in the years 1852-64. Reminisc. Tr. E: F. Taylor. L: Longmans 1887. 2v. xix; 383;xiv;375p. 22cm. [Very competent.] [BM.LC]

VOELCKER, K: H: W:
*9550. (Winkelried.) W--: a trag. in 5 acts [verse] Tr. by Rev. Js. McAlister. L: Smith & Elder 1837. 198p. Ger;Engl. 12. [BM] [Very good tr. Written by author for school performance, later revised. Name is spelled Voelker.]

VOGEL, H:
*9551. (Beschreibung seiner dreissigjährigen...Seereisen.) The advent. and travels, in various parts of the world. Tr. anon. In "Universal mag." (II)12(1809):1, etc. (B26) [Incomplete; three instalments prtd. Tr. is for the most part very good.]

VOGEL, Jl. R. T.
9552. Journal of the voyage to the Niger. Tr. F. Scheer. 1849. In Hooker, Sir W. J., "Niger flora," pp. 22-87. L: Hippolyte 1849. 22cm. [Has also: Memoir of the life of Vogel, 21p.] [BM]

VOGELWEIDE. See Walther v. d. V--.

VOGET, F: L.
9553. (Lebensgeschichte der Giftmörderin...) Life of Gesche Margarethe Gottfried (geb. Timm), executed at Bremen...1831, for having poisoned her parents...and...other persons. Tr. Ern. Friederici. Gettysburg, Pa: Neinstedt 1832. 79p. 12. [LCO]

VOGL, J: 1802-66. Sel. in C36*;105;132;309;372;414-5;423;460;466; 497;501;571.

VOGTS, Af. Sel. in C95.

VOGRICH, Max, 1850- .
*9554. The highland widow: dram. scene after Wl. Scott. Words and music by M. V--. Tr. Td. Baker. Vocal score. NY: Schirmer 1897. 59p. 4. [LCM]
*9555. (König Arthur.) King A--: opera in 3 acts and a prolog. Words and music by M. V--. Tr. N. H. Dole. Vocal score. Ger;Engl. NY: Schirmer 1893. xxxvi;241p. 4. [LCM]

VOIGT, Frau J:a (Ambrosius), 1854- . Sel. in C366.
§9556. Gedichte. Poems. Tr. Ma. J. Safford from 26th Ger. ed. Memoir by Hm. Grimm. Bost: Roberts 1896. 247p. il. 20cm. [LC.BM]
§9557. do. 1910. Poems of J:a A--. Tr. Ellen Kullmann. L: Sherratt & Hughes. 103p. front. (port.) 17cm. [BM] [Poor form and not always correct. Prt. on one side of the paper.]

VOLCKHAUSEN, Frau Jle. Adle. (Voigt) 1823-93.
9558. (Das Kind aus dem Ebräergang.) Why did he not die? Or, the child from the Ebräergang. Tr. Mrs. A. L. Wister. Phil: Lippincott 1871. 372p. 18cm. [LC]

VOLKMANN, R: v. 183-89. See "Leander, R:"

VOLLMAR, Ag. 1836-1910.
9559. [Coll.] 1922. The white house. Tr. anon. Rock Island, Ill: Augustana bk. 128p. il. 17cm. [LC]
[Title; David; What came of Patty's prayer.]
§9560. [Coll.] 1923. Winter roses ("Rosen im Winter"). Also, Christmas eve. Tr. anon. Rock Island, Ill: Augustana bk. 151p. il. 18cm. [Much altered.] [LC]
9561. [Coll.] 1925. Heaven sought and found. (Three stories.) Tr. anon. Rock Island, Ill: Augustana bk. 126p. il. 18cm. [LC]
9562. Bread upon the waters. Tr. anon. Rock Island, Ill: Augustana bk. 1922. 142p. il. 18cm. [AC]
9563. (Das Pfarrhaus in Indien.) The parsonage in India. Ad. by Cornelia McFadden. Cincin: Walden & Stowe 1881. 297p. 16. [LCO]
9564. (Drei Weihnachtsabende.) The Christmas eves. Ad. by Cornelia McFadden. Cincin: Walden & Stowe 1881. 313p. 16. [LCO]
9565. The parsonage in the Hartz. Tr. and ad. by Cornelia McFadden. Phil: Pres. bd. 1873. 288p. il. 16. [LCO]
9566. (Sibylle.) Sibylla. Ad. by Cornelia McFadden. Cincin: Cranston & Stowe; NY: Phillips & Hunt 1888. 396p. 19cm. [LC]

VOLLMAR, G: H: v. 1850- .
9567. Socialism and the Ger. Kaiser. Two speeches by V-- and A: Bebel. Tr. C. and Ax. M. Thompson. L: Clarion 1903. 12p. 21cm. [LC]

VOLLMOELLER, K: Gst. 1878- . Sel. in C39.

VOSS, J: H: 1751-1826. Sel. in C17;22;25-6;111;132;190;307;309;372-3; 387-8;469;499;533.
§9568. (Luise.) Louisa. (A poem.) Tr. J. Cochrane. Ed: Johnstone 1852. 201p. 24cm. [Correct, poor style.] [BM]
9569. do. 1829. Sel. Tr. W: Taylor. In C533.

VOSS, R: 1851-1918.
9570. (Alexandra.) A--: a drama. Tr. and ad. by W. L. Hubbard. Chic: 1888. (B38)
9571. (Amata.) A--. Tr. R. S. G. Boutell. Washington, D. C. Neale 1901. 116p. 12. [LC]
9572. (Daniel Danieli.) D-- D--: a drama in 4 acts. Ad. Sara M. Friedman. Winnetka, Ill: 1912. Tw. [LC]
9573. (Das Wunder.) The miracle: a legend drama in 4 acts. Tr. and ad. by Marie Walsh and Ma. J. Safford. NY: 1906. (B38)
*9574. (Der neue Gott.) The new god: a tale of the early Christians. Tr. Ma. A. Robinson. NY;L: Harper 1899. 240p. il. 17cm. [LC.BM]
9575. (Die Mutter der Catonen.) Mother of the Catos. Neely. (B13)
9576. The monk and the hangman's daughter. (Founded on V.) By A. Bierce and G. A. Danziger. Il. T. Hampe. L: Low 1892. 166p. 19cm. [BM]
9577. (Nubia.) N-- of Saracenescu. Tr. Hettie E. Miller. Akron, O: Saalfield. (B13)
9578. (Schuldig!) Guilty: a drama in 3 acts. Tr. and ad. Ruth C. Mitchell. Five Islands, Me. ca. 1892. Tw. [LC]
9579. (Sigurd Ekdals Braut.) Sigurd Ekdal's bride: a romance of the far north. Tr. Ma. J.Safford. Bost: Little, Brown 1900. 235p. il. 18cm. [LC.BM]
9580. Vera Varces: a drama. Ad. by Ethel Guernsey. NY: 1890. (B38)
9581. A walk through the Wartburg. Tr. G. A. Greene. 1907. In C555.

VOSS, So. W:e Cte. Me. (v. Pannwitz), Gräfin v. 1729-1814.
*9582. (69 Jahre am preussischen Hofe.) Sixty-nine years at the court of Prussia. Tr. Emily and Ag. Stephenson. L: Bentley 1876. 2v. 20cm. [LC]

VULPIUS, Cn. A: 1762-1827.
9583. The mystery: a comedy in 5 acts. Tr. M(aria) G(eisweiler). ca. 1800. In C94.

VULPIUS, Cn. A:
9584. (Rinaldo Rinaldini, der Räuberhauptmann.) The hist. of R-- R--. Tr. T. Hinckley. L: Longmans 1800. 3v. See "Brit. Crit." 16(1800):440. (B26)
9585. do. 1810. R-- R--; or, the great banditti. A trag. in 5 acts. NY: Prtd. for the author. 82p. 12. (B48)
[A servile adaptation from the foregoing.]
9586. do. 1831. [same as #9584?] R-- R--: a novel. L: Newman. 3v. 12. [EC]
9587. do. 1841. [same?] R-- R--, captain of banditti: a tale of the last cent. 4th ed. L: Clements. ("The Romancist," new ser., vol. 1.) 136p. 21cm. [BM.LC]
9588. do. 1872-6. [same? same title] Cincin: James n.d. 8. [AC]

WAAGEN, Gst. F: 1794-1868.
*9589. (Kunstwerke und Künstler in England und Paris.) Works of art and artists in England. Tr. H. E. Lloyd. L: Murray 1838. 3v. 19cm. [He tr. angeregt by "gratified."] [BM]
9590. do. 1854. Treasures of art in Gt. Brit. Tr. Eliz. Lady Eastlake. L: Murray. 3v.(BM: 4v.) 21cm. [BM.LC]
[The work has: 3v. Vol. 4 in BM has sep. t.p.: Galleries and cabinets of art in Gt. Brit. See next entry.]
9591. do. 1857. Galleries and cabinets of art in England...more than 40 collections...visited...and described. Supplemental...to the Treasures of art...Tr. anon. L: Murray. vii;560p. 22cm. [LC]
9592. do. 1857. [same as #9589] Murray. 3v. 8. [EC]
*9593. (Ueber den Maler Petrus Paulus Rubens.) P: Pl. R--, his life. Tr. Rb. R. Noel. Ed. by Mrs. Jameson. L: Saunders & Otley 1840. xix;132p. 19cm. [Waagen made emendations and corr. Mrs. Jameson says the tr. will be found very faithful.] [BM]

WACHENHUSEN, Hs. 1823-98.
9594. (Des Herzens Golgatha.) The Golgotha of the heart. Tr. Hettie E. Miller. Chic;NY: Rand, McNally 1889. 282p. 19cm. [LC]
9595. (Die bleiche Gräfin.) A tangled web; or, the pale countess. Tr. Ma. J. Safford. Chic;NY: Rand, McNally 1898. 284p. 12. [LC]
9596. For a woman's sake; or, the mysteries of the castle. Tr. M. S. Bost: Gill 1875. 184p. (B12) [NY]

WACHSMUTH, Ern. W: Gb. 1784-1866.
*9597. (Hellenische Altertumskunde aus dem Gesichtspunkte des Staates.) The histor. antiquities of the Greeks, with ref. to their polit. institutions. Tr. E. Woolrych. Oxf: Talboys 1837. Vol. 1-2. xxv;472;574p. 22cm. [No more pub.] [BM.LC]

WACHSMUTH VON MUEHLHAUSEN, fl. 1250. Sel. in C27;310;427.

WACKENRODER, W: H: 1773-98. Sel. in C452.

WACKERNAGEL, W: 1806-69. Sel. in C97;380.

WAECHTER, G: Ph. L: Lh. 1762-1837. See "Weber, Veit."

WAEGNER, J: W: Ern. 1800-86.
9598. (Bilder-Cyklus aus der nordisch-germanischen Göttersage.) Asgard and the gods: tales and traditions of our northern ancestors. Told for boys and girls (by M. W. Macdowall). L: Sonnenschein 1880. 326p. 21cm. [BM]
9599. do. 1882. [same] New ed. Sonnenschein. [EC]
*9600. (Nordisch-germanische Götter und Helden.) Asgard and the gods: a manual of Norse mythol. Ad. M. W. Macdowall. 3d ed. L: Sonnenschein 1884. xvi;326p. il. 22cm. [BM]
[3d ed. refers to #9598. Passage examined very close and good.]
*9601. do. 1917. [same] NY: Dutton. xvi;326p. il. 22cm. [LC]

WAEGNER, J: W: Ern.
§9602. (Unsere Vorzeit: Deutsche Heldensagen, Deutsche Volkssagen.) Epics and romances of the middle ages. Ad. M. W. Macdowall. Ed. W. S. W. Anson. L: Sonnenschein 1883. 488p. il. 21cm. [BM]
[Rather freely adapted. Publishers state the first ed. to have been pub. 1882, 2d in 1883, but EC gives 2d ed. as 1884.]
§9603. do. 1884. [same] 2d ed. [BM]
9604. do. 1886. [same] 3d ed. (Publishers.)
9605. do. 1887. [same] 4th ed. (Publishers.)
9606. do. 1889. [same] 5th ed. (Publishers.)
9607. do. 1890. [same] 6th ed. (Publishers.)
9608. do. 1892. [same] 7th ed. (Publishers.)
§9609. do. 1896. [same] 8th ed. Sonnenschein. [LC]
9610. do. 1903. [same] 9th ed. (Publishers.)
§9611. do. 1904. [same] [BM]
§9612. do. 1906. [same] Romances and epics of our northern ancestors, Norse, Celt, and Teuton. L;NY: Norroena soc. 343p. il. 23cm. [LC]
9613. (Unsere Vorzeit: Deutsche Volkssagen.) Teutonic legends in the Nieblungen Lied and the N-- Ring, by W. C. Sawyer. 1904. 8. [BM]
9614. Prose version of the Nibelungenlied. See A377.

WAGENER, Z:
9615. A short account of the voyages of Z: W--. Taken out of his own journal. In Churchill's "Coll. of voyages and travels." L: 1732. Vol. 2, pp. 496-500. 35cm. [BM]
9616. do. 1744. [same] 3d ed. [BM]
9617. do. 1752. [same] pp. 474-78. [BM]

WAGNER VON LAUFENBURG, Sel. in C438.

WAGNER, Ern. 1769-1812. Sel. in C244.

WAGNER, F:
9618. (Schamyl, als Feldherr, Sultan und Prophet des Kaukasus.) Schamyl and the Circassians. Tr. K. R. H. Mackenzie. L: Routledge 1854. 188p. 16cm. [BM.LC]
9619. do. 1854. S--, the sultan, warrior, and prophet of the Caucasus. Tr. L. Wraxall. L: Longmans. Trav. lib. vii;144p. 17cm. [Lascelles Wraxall, who sel., arr. and tr. the material, found that Wagner's work did not guarantee the solidity which could alone render it acceptable to the Engl. reader, and so was compelled to add copious extracts from Bodenstedt's "Die Völker des Kaukasus."] [BM]

WAGNER, Mz. 1813-87.
9620. (Reise nach Persien und dem Lande der Kurden.) Travels in Persia, Georgia, and Koordistan. Tr. anon. L: Hurst & B. 1856. 3v. 19cm. [BM.LC]
9621. (Reisen in der Regentschaft Algier.) The tricolor on the atlas; or, Algeria and the French conquest. Tr. Fis. A. Pulszky. Ed;L;NY: Nelson 1854. 402p. 21cm. [BM]
[From Wagner and other sources. His 1st vol. condensed, 2d translated. A gen'l account given of the rest, includ. French blue book. Tinted double page front.]

WAGNER, R:, (Naturalist)
9622. Stories from nat. hist. Tr. G. S. L: Macmillan 1904. viii;177p il. 17cm. [BM]

WAGNER, R: 1813-83. Sel. in C63;320;366*;469;574*.

WAGNER, R:

ARRANGEMENT

Prose works
Operas [1]
Letters
Biography

PROSE WORKS

*9623. [Coll.] 1875. Art life and theories. Sel. and tr. E: L. Burlingame. NY: Holt. 305p. il. 19cm. [LC.BM]
[Autobiog.; The love-veto ("Das Liebesverbot"?); A pilgrimage to Beethoven ("Eine Pilgerfahrt zu B--"); An end in Paris; "Der Freischütz" in Paris; The music of the future ("Zukunftsmusik"); Account of the production of "Tannhäuser" in Paris; The purpose of the opera. Musical criticism; Extracts from a letter...; The legend of the Nibelungen; The opera-house at Bayreuth.]

*9624. [Coll.] 1892-9. Prose works. Tr. W: A. Ellis. L: Paul, T. & T. 8v. 23cm. [BM.LC]
[LC dates the first vol. 1893. Vol. 1, Art work of the future. Vol. 2, Opera and drama. Vol. 3, Theatre. Vol. 4, Art and politics. Vol. 5, Actors and singers. Vol. 6, Religion. Art. Vol. 7, In Paris and Dresden. Vol. 8, Posthumous, etc. Each vol. also pub. separately.]

9625. [Coll.] 1913-15. Tr. W: A. Ellis. In C154(15).
[Doubtless taken over from the foregoing.--Art and revolution; Man and art in general; The art of tone; The art of sculpture; Outlines of the art work of the future; Opera and the nature of music; A communication to my friends; Beethoven. Speech at Weber's grave.]

*9626. (Beethoven.) B--. Tr. A. R. Parsons. Indianapolis, Ind: Benham 1872. 151p. 20cm. [LC]

9627. do. 1872. [same] 2d ed. [BM]

*9628. do. 1880. Tr. E: Dannreuther. L: Reeves. viii;177p. 19cm. [BM]
[With a supplement from the philos. works of Schopenhauer. See #8559.]

*9629. do. 1883. [same as #9626] 3d ed. NY: Schirmer. 125p. 19cm [LC]

*9630. do. 1893. [same as #9628] 2d ed. Reeves. [BM]

§9631. (Das Judentum in der Musik.) Judaism in music...being the orig. essay together with the later supplement. Tr. Edwin Evans. L: Reeves 1910. xv;95p. 19cm. [LC]

*9632. (Eine Pilgerfahrt zu Beethoven.) A pilgrimage to B--: a novel. Tr. O: W. Weyer. Chic: Open ct. 1897. vii;39p. 21cm. [LC.BM]

§9633. (Oper und Drama.) Opera and drama. Tr. Edwin Evans, Sr. NY: Scribner; L: Reeves 1913. 2v. 790p. 19cm. [Bad blunders.] [LC.BM]

§9634. (Ueber das Dirigieren.) On conducting: a treatise on style in the execution of classical music. Tr. E: Dannreuther. L: Reeves 1887. 122p. 19cm. [He tones down too much.] [BM]

§9635. do. 1897. [same] 2d ed. Reeves. 127p. [LC]

*9636. (Was erzählt R: W-- über die Entstehung seines Nibelungengedichtes...) What does R: W-- relate concerning...his Nibelungen poem...1853-1903? Compiled...Sb. Röckl. Tr. Constance Parrish. L: Breitkopf & H. 1907. 32p. 22cm. [BM.LC]

*9637. do. 1908. [continuation] What does R: W-- relate concerning ...The ring of the Nibelungs? Compiled Sb. Röckl. Tr. Constance Parrish. L: Breitkopf & H. 27p. 22cm. [BM.LC]

§9638. (Zukunftsmusik.) The music of the future, a letter...Tr. E: Dannreuther. L: Scott;NY: Schirmer 1873. 54p. 21cm. [BM.LC]

[1]Purely musical selections, and selections from the operas, e.g., arias, etc., not included.

WAGNER, R:

OPERAS[1]

9639. [Coll.] Sämtliche Musikdramen. Vocal score. Ger;Engl. Tr. by various hands. Lpz: Breitkopf & Haertel 1914. 4. [LCM] [All of these are listed below under individual titles. 1. Rienzi. Tr. Fanny S. Copeland. #9817. 2. Der fliegende Holländer. Probably tr. by Newman, see #9661. 3. Tannhäuser. Probably tr. by Newman, see #9853. 4. Lohengrin. Tr. H. and F. Corder. #9751. 5. Tristan und Isolde. Tr. H. and F. Corder. #9872. 6. Die Meistersinger von Nürnberg. Tr. by Newman. #9711. 7. Rheingold. Tr. by Newman. #9812. 8. Die Walküre. Tr. by Newman. #9727. 9. Siegfried. Tr. by Newman. #9833. 10. Götterdämmerung. Tr. by Newman. #9737. 11. Parsifal. Tr. by Newman. #9788. 12. Das Liebesverbot. Tr. E: Dent. (Copyright 1922.) #9646.]

9640. [Sel.] (Wagner festival...May 1877. Sel. from the Ger. texts of Der Ring des Nibelungen, Rienzi, Tannhäuser, Der fliegende Holländer, Lohengrin, etc. Tr. by Dr. Hueffer, A. Forman, J: P. Jackson...and J: Oxenford. L: Hodge & Essex 1877. 8 pts. 30;36;26;64; 27;22;35;47p. Ger. and Eng. 27cm. [BM]

9641. [Ad.] McSpadden, Js. W. Stories (11) from W--. L: Harrap 1905. xiv;231p. il. 19cm. [BM]

9642. [Ad.] McSpadden, Js. W. The stories of W--'s operas. il. Fd. Lecke and Hm. Hendrich. L: Harrap 1915. xv;282p. 19cm. [BM] [Same text as the foregoing.]

§9643. (Das Liebesmahl.) The holy supper of the apostles. Tr. anon. Vocal score. Engl. L: Novello 1876. 40p. 25 x 34cm. [BMM]

*9644. do. 1892. The feast of Pentecost (for male cho. and orch.) Tr. F: Corder. Lpz: Breitkopf & H. (Eulenburgs Partitur-Ausgabe.) 94p. 18cm. [BMM]

*9645. do. 1892. [same] Vocal score. Lpz: Breitkopf & H. 83p. 27cm. [BMM]

§9646. (Das Liebesverbot.) The ban on love. Text after Shakespeare's "Measure for Measure." Tr. E: Dent. Vocal score. Lpz: Breitkopf & H. 1922. 594p. 8. [Fair to good tr.] [LCM]

*9647. do. 1923. [same] Vocal score. Breitkopf & H. 590p. 27cm. [BMM] [Good singing version; rhymes bother the tr. As a translation, only fair to good.]

DER FLIEGENDE HOLLÄNDER

9648. ANON. n.d. The flying Dutchman. Libr. unbound. n.p., n.d. 48p. 0. [UW]

†9649. ANON. 1876. Libr. Ger;Engl. NY: Theatre ticket off. 8; 8p. 8. [Poor version; free, poor rhymes.] [LCM]

9650. ANON. 1908. Libr. L: Jack. 46p. 16. [EC]

*9651. BAKER, TD. and J. TROUTBECK. Vocal score. Ger;Engl. NY: Schirmer 1897. 248p. 4. [LC] [Consid. revision of Troutbeck's tr., and improvement of it.]

§9652. BERNHOFF, J: Vocal score. Ger;Engl. L: Schott 1912. 265p. 27cm. [BMM.LCM]

†9653. DU TERREAUX, L. H. F. L'Olandese dannato. Tr. into Ital. by Salvatore de C. Marchesi. Libr. Ital;Engl. L: Cramer 1870. 63p. 17cm. [Ital. cuts down somewhat; Engl. is good but remote from orig.] [BM]

†9654. do. 1876. [same] [BM]

†9655. ENGLAND, PL. Libr. Ger;Engl. Berlin. Fürstner 1895. 44 (i.e., 88)p. 8. ["Free" tr.] [LC.BM]

†9656. do. 1904. [same] Full score. Berlin: Fürstner. 415p. fol. [LCM]

§9657. JACKSON, J: P. Libr. Engl. L: Carl Rosa opera co. 1876. 42p. 12. [LC]

[1]Most of the English commentaries, which are very numerous, tell the stories of the operas. It has not seemed advisable to follow up all these publications, but straight adaptations (including the retelling of the stories) have been included.

WAGNER, R:--Der fliegende Holländer

§9658. do. 1876. Engl. ad. by J: P. Jackson. Ed. by J. Pittman. Vocal score. Ger;Engl. L: Boosey. 276p. 25cm. [BMM]

§9659. do. 1877. Libr. Ger;Engl. NY: Metropolitan opera house. 17; 17p. 8. [LCM]

§9660. do. 1889. [same] [LCM]

*9661. NEWMAN, ERN. Libr. Eng. L: Breitkopf & H. 1912. 38p. 4.[BM.LC] [Perhaps the best tr.; not perfect.]

*9662. do. 1912. Piano score; text Ger;Engl. Breitkopf & H. 158p. 31cm. [BMM]

*9663. do. 1912. Vocal score. Text rev. by W. Golther. Ger;Engl. Breitkopf & H. 259p. 27cm. [BMM.LCM]

9664. do? 1914. Vol. 2 of #9639.

§9665. PITTMAN, JOSIAH. Il vascello fantasma: a grand romantic opera. Libr. Ital;Engl. L: Prtd. for the Royal Ital. opera co. 1876. 63p. 18cm. [A little closer than #9653;not as good verse.[BM]

*9666. TROUTBECK, REV. J. Vocal score. L: Novello; Bost;NY;Phil: Ditson 1877. 228p. 28cm. [Very good tr.] [BMM]

*9667. do. 1886. Libr. Engl. NY: Koppel. 44p. with music. 24cm.[LCM]

*9668. do. 1894. Libr. Engl. Burnley: Nuttall. 24p. 18cm. [BM]

*9669. do. 1899. Libr. Ger;Engl. in parallel columns. L: Novello; NY: Gray. 34p. 24 x 18cm. [BM]

9670.[Ad.] The flying Dutchman: a dram. poem...freely tr. in poetic narr. form by Oliver Huckel. NY: Crowell 1914. 53p. il. 19cm. [LC] [He tr. longer speeches fairly closely, connects them with description and comment. Very well done.]

DER RING DES NIBELUNGEN[1]

9671. ANON. Ring of the Nibelungs. L: Jack 1907. 64p. 16. [EC]

*9672. ARMOUR, MARG. The ring of the Niblung. Il. Art. Rackham. L: Heinemann; NY: Doubleday, Page 1910. Vol. 1. 160p. 29cm. [BM] [Rhinegold and Valkyrie. See note on the following.]

*9673. do. 1911-12. [same] L;NY: Heinemann. 2v. 8. [LC] [She seems to lean rather heavily on Jameson's tr.]

9674. do. 1911. [same] Ed. de Luxe. Heinemann. 4. [EC] [Vol. 2 has 194p.]

*9675. do. 1923. [same] Il. Rackham. NY: Doubleday, Page. viii;341p. 25cm. [LC] [Half-title of pt. 1 of two-vol. ed. is retained here.]

*9676. CORDER, H. and F: The Nibelung's ring. Libr. Ger;Engl. Mainz;L: Schott 1882. 4pts. 17cm. [BM] [Each part has double paging: 75 (i.e.,150); 84; 98; 86p.]

*9677. do. 1882? Vocal scores. Ger;Engl. Mainz: Schott n.d. 4v. 4. [Also listed separately. Rheingold, 221p. Walküre, 309p. Siegfried, 337p. Götterdämmerung, 340p.] [LCM]

§9678. FINCK, H: T. Vocal score. Ger;Engl. Cincin: Church 1903. 4v. 4. [Also listed separately.] [LCM]

*9679. FORMAN, A. The Nibelung's ring: a festival play for three days and a fore-evening. Engl. words...in allit. verse. L: Schott, also Dulau 1877. 351p. 18cm. [BM]

*9680. JAMESON, F: The Niblung's ring. Libr. Mainz; L: Schott 1896. 349p. 8. [BM]

*9681. do. 1899. 1900. Vocal scores. Ger;Engl. Mainz: Schott. 4v. 4. [Also listed separately.] [LCM]

*9682. do. 1904. Vocal scores. Ger;Engl. NY: Schirmer. 4v. 4. [LCM] [Also listed separately.]

*9683. do. 1905-7. The ring of the Niblung. Libr. Ger;Engl. Mainz;L: Schott. 4pts. 17cm. [Each part has double paging, as in #9676. Siegfried, 1905, 98p. Rhinegold, 1906, 75p. Twilight of the gods,

[1] This caption refers only to publications which contain the cycle; see below for the individual operas.

WAGNER, R:--Der Ring des Nibelungen
1906, 86p. Valkyrie, 1907, 84p.] [BM]
*9684. NEWMAN, ERN. The ring of the Nibelung. Ger. Text revised by W. Golther. Vocal scores. Ger;Engl. L: Breitkopf & H. 1910. 4v. 4. [Also listed separately.] [LCM]
9685. [Ad] 1888. R: Wagner's poem "The ring of the Nibelung" explained and in part tr. by G: T. Dippold. NY: Holt 1888. v;240p. 19cm. [BM]
9686. [Ad] 1896. The four stories of the N-- ring. By A. L. Watson. L: Stock. 35p. 19cm. [BM]
9687. [Ad] 1897. The stories of "Der Ring des N--" and "Parsifal." By W. F. Sheppard. L: Nutt. 69p. 19cm. [BM]
9688. [Ad] 1898. Der Ring des N--. Being the story concisely told (of all four operas). By N. Kilburn. L: Reeves 1898. 50p. 16cm. [BM]
[No umlaut anywhere: e.g., Gotterdammerung, Walkure, etc.]
9689. [Ad] 1899-1901. Tr. (i.e., ad.) by J. R. L. Rankin. L;NY: Longmans. 2v. 18cm. [BM.LC]
[Similar to Huckel's versions: a poetic recasting rather than a tr]
9690. [Ad] 1903. The ring of the N--...interpret. embodying W--'s own explan. By Alice L. Cleather and Basil Crump. L: Methuen. 150p. 12. [EC]
9691. [Ad] 1904. Siegfried: a romance founded on W--'s operas...By S. Baring-Gould. Il. C: Robinson. L: Dean. 351p. 20cm. [BM]
9692. [Ad] 1904. Teutonic legends in the Nibelungenlied and the N-- ring. By W. C. Sawyer. Introd. essay by Fritz Schulze. Phil;L: Lippincott. 343p. 19cm. [BM]
9693. [Ad.] 1905-7. The ring...synopsis of the four parts, with introd. sketch and notes on text and music. By O. Kramer. L: Owen. 4 pts. 14cm. [BM]
[Rhinegold, 1905; 40p; port. after Lenbach. Valkyrie, 1907; 37p.; front. after Th. Pixis. Siegfried, 1907; 45p.; front. after Th. Pixis. Twilight of the gods, 1907; 39p.; front. after Th. Pixis.]
9694. [Ad] 1907. The story of "The Ring." A short analysis of the plot...with the principal musical "motives." By S. H. Hamer. 4 col. pl. by H. Rountree. L;NY: Cassell. 53p. 20cm. [BM]
9695. [Ad] 1913. The ring of the N--. Engl. version by Randle Fynes. L: Smith, Elder. 206p. 19cm. [BM]
["An attempt to render in simple Engl. verse W--'s poem...reproducing the spirit rather than the letter of the orig."]
9696. [Ad] 1925. The ring of the N--. Retold by Js. McSpadden. In C390.
See Pfordten, Hm., A plain handbook..., #7157.
See Wolzogen und Neuhaus, Hs., Guide..., #10353.

*9697. (Die Feen.) The fairies: a romantic opera in 3 acts. Tr. and arr. by Td. Reuss. Engl. lyrics by A. V. Sinclair. Libr. L: 1906. 28p. 19cm. [Copyright NY: 1894.] [BM]

DIE MEISTERSINGER VON NÜRNBERG

9698. ANON. The master-singers of Nuremberg. Libr. L: Jack 1907. 48p. 16. [EC]
*9699. CORDER, H. and F: Libr. Ger;Engl. Mainz: Schott 1882. 135; 135p. 18cm. [Very clever.] [BM]
*9700. do. 1882. Vocal score. Ger;Engl. Mainz; Schott. 467p. 28cm. [BMM]
*9701. do. 1885? Libr. Ger;Engl. NY: Metropolitan opera house, season 1885-6. Pref. signed C. A. B. [Tr. not named.] [NY]
*9702. do. 1889. Libr. Ger;Engl. Bost: Ditson. 81p. 8. [LC]
[Has some music.]
*9703. do. 1891? Libr. Ger;Engl. NY, n.i. 43; 43p. 23cm. [LCM]
§9704. do. 1912. Libr. Ed. W. J. Henderson. NY: Dodd, Mead. 511p. 14cm. [Revision of the foregoing; not an improvement, to my

WAGNER, R:--Die Meistersinger
thinking. Ger. and Engl. on opp. pages.] [LC]
§9705. JACKSON, J: P. Libr. Engl. L;NY;Munich: Dickens & Evans 1892. 40p. 8. [BM.LC]
*9706. JAMESON, F: The mastersingers...Vocal score. Ger;Engl. L: Schott; NY: Schirmer 1903. 569p. 29cm. [BMM.LCM]
[Excellent singing version, but sacrifices too many rhymes.]
*9707. do. 1909. Libr. Engl. Mainz: Schott. x;135p. 17cm. [BM]
*9708. NEWMAN, ERN. The mastersingers...Vocal score. Ger;Engl. L: Breitkopf & H. 1911. 567p. 27cm. [BMM.LCM]
*9709. do. 1911. Piano score with text. L: Breitkopf & H. 283p. 31cm. [BMM]
*9710. do. 1912. Libr. Ger;Engl. L: Breitkopf & H. 111p. 25cm.[BM.LC]
*9711. do. 1914. Vocal score. Vol. 6 of #9639.
9712.[Ad.] 1912. By Oliver Huckel. NY: Crowell. 127p. il. 19cm. [LC]
[Done in the same manner as #9670.]
See Dinger, Hg., The mastersingers...,#1240.
See Heintz, Ab., The master-singers..., #4163.
See Wilsing, H:, The mastersingers...,#10274.

DIE WALKÜRE

†9713. ANON. The Walkyre. Libr. Ger;Engl. NY: Theatre ticket office 1877. 43p. 8. [LC]
9714. ANON. 1885. Libr. Ger;Engl. Bost: Ditson. 46p. 24cm. [LCM]
[Has some music. Could not identify it.]
*§9715. CORDER, H. and F: Vocal score. Mainz: Schott n.d. 309p. 4.
[Earlier version than #9719.] [LCM]
*§9716. do. 1900? Libr. Ger;Engl. Mayence;L: Schott. 84; 84p. 17cm. [BM]
§9717. FINCK, H: T. Vocal score. Cincin: Church 1903. 391p. 4. [LCM]
9718. JACKSON, J: P. The Valkyr. Libr. NY: 1885. 59p. unbound.O.[UW]
*9719. JAMESON, F: The valkyrie. Vocal score. Mainz;L: Schott 1899. 305p. 29 x 21cm. [BMM.LCM]
*9720. do. 1904. [same] NY: Schirmer. [LC]
*9721. do. n.d. Libr. Engl. Mainz: Schott n.d. 84p. 17cm. [LCM]
*9722. NEWMAN, ERN. The valkyrie. Vocal score. Ger;Engl. L: Breitkopf & H. 1910. 334p. 27cm. [BMM.LCM]
*9723. do. 1912. [same] [BMM]
*9724. do. 1912. Piano score with text. Breitkopf & H. 208p. 31cm. [BMM]
*9725. do. 1913. Libr. Engl. L: Breitkopf & H. 72p. 21cm. [BM]
*9726. do. 1914. [same] [LC]
*9727. do. 1914. Vocal score. Vol. 8 of #9639.
9728.[Ad.] 1903. The valkyries: a romance founded on W--'s opera by E. F. Benson. Il. T. Noyes Lewis. L: Dean. xviii;259p. 20cm. [BM]
9729.[Ad.] 1909. By Oliver Huckel. NY: Crowell. 95p. il. 19cm. [LC]
[Done in the same manner as #9670.]

GÖTTERDÄMMERUNG

*§9730. CORDER, H. and F. Dusk of the gods. Libr. Ger;Engl. Bost: Ditson 1888. 45p. 25cm. [Omits the Norns in the Vorspiel.] [LC]
*9731. do. 1900? Libr. Ger;Engl. Mainz: Schott. 86; 86p. 17cm. [BM]
*9732. do. n.d. Vocal score. Mainz: Schott. (1900) 340p. 4. [LCM]
§9733. FINCK, H: T. Vocal score. Cincin: Church 1903. 422p. 4. [LCM]
*9734. JAMESON, F: The twilight of the gods. Vocal score. Ger;Engl. Mainz;L: Schott 1900. 340p. 29cm.[Corders' tr. is better.][BMM.LCM]
*9735. do. 1904. [same] NY: Schirmer. 29 x 21cm. [LCM]
9736. MELTZER, C: H: Dusk of the gods. Libr. n.i. 1922. 4. Tw. [LCM]
*9737. NEWMAN, ERN. Vocal score. Ger;Engl. Lpz;L: Breitkopf & H. 1914. 418p. 4. [Same as vol. 10 of #9639.] [LCM]

WAGNER, R:--Götterdämmerung
9738.[Ad.] By Oliver Huckel. NY: Crowell 1911. 100p. il. 19cm. [LC]
[Cf. #9670 and note.]
9739.[Ad.] 1923. G--. By Td. M. R. v. Keler. Girard, Kan: Haldeman-Julius. Little blue books. 60p. 12cm. [BQM]
[Synopsis, extr. from libr., music.]

LOHENGRIN

*9740. ANON. L--: a romantic opera. Libr. Engl. L: Hope 1857. 64p. 19cm. [EC has: 1858.] [BM]
*9741. ANON. 1875? Libr. Ital;Engl. NY: Wynkoop & Hallenbeck. 31p. 6p. music. 25cm. [LCM]
9742. ANON. 1880? Libr. Ital;Engl. L: Davidson. 55p. 18cm. [BM]
[Action much reduced; Engl. text is line for line with Ital.]
†9743. ANON. 1881? Libr. Ital;Engl. NY;L: French n.d. some music. [LC]
[Line for line, merely to give the sense of the Ital.]
*9744. ANON. 1883. [same as #9741] NY: Theatre ticket office, 1883-4. 31p., 6p. music. 25cm. [LCM]
*9745. ANON. 1896. [same] NY: Rullman. [LCM]
*9746. ANON. 1907? [same tr. as #9741] Libr. Ger;Engl. NY: Rullman. 45p. 25cm. [LCM]
9747. ANON. 1907. Libr. L: Jack. 48p. 16. [EC]
*9748. CORDER, H. and F: Vocal score. Ger;Engl. Lpz: Breitkopf & H. 1890. 350p. 27cm. [BMM]
*9749. do. 1894. Libr. Engl. L: Breitkopf & H. 63p. 16cm. [BM]
*9750. do. 1906. Full score. Ger;Engl;Ital. Breitkopf & H. 1906. 851p. fol. [LCM]
*9751. do. 1914. Vocal score. Vol. 4 of #9639.
*9752. JACKSON, J: P. W--'s grand romantic opera L-- musically and pictorially illustrated. Tr. and arr. J. P. J--. Libr. Engl. L: Bogue 1881. 62p. 31cm. [BM]
§9753. JAMESON, F: Vocal score. Ger;Engl. L: Schott 1913. 389p. 28cm. [BMM.LCM]
[Sense is correct; form is unsatisfying, and there are errors.]
§9754. do. 1913. Libr. Engl. L: Schott. 54p. 18cm. [BM]
§9755. MACFARREN, NATALIA. Vocal score. Ger;Engl. L: Novello 1873. 266p. 26cm. [BMM]
9756. do. 1872. Libr? L: Novello. 8. [EC]
§9757. do. 1880? Libr. Engl. NY: Tretbar. 28p. 24cm. [LCM]
§9758. do. 189- . Libr. Ger;Engl. anon. NY: Tretbar n.d. 43p. 8. [NY]
§9759. do. 1896? Libr. Ger;Engl. NY: Caulon. 40p. 23cm. [LCM]
§9760. do. 1897. Vocal score. Ger;Engl. NY: Schirmer. 341p. 4. [LCM]
*9761. MELTZER, C: H: Libr. Engl. n.i. 1922. 23; 29; 20p. 4. Tw. [LCM]
[Not fully satisfying.]
§9762. OXENFORD, J: Vocal score. Ital;Ger;Engl. L: Boosey 1872. xvi; 383p. 25cm. [BMM]
§9763. do. 1875. Tr. anon. Libr. Ital;Engl. As represented at the Royal Ital. opera. Covent Garden. L: Miles. 72p. 18cm. [BM]
§9764. do. 1876. Libr. Ital;Engl., with music. L: Davidson. 32p. 24cm. [Tr. is erroneously said to have been done from Italian] [BMM]
§9765. do. 1900? Tr. anon. Libr. Ger;Engl. L: Grand opera syndicate. 31p. 24cm. [BM]
9766.[Ad.] 1880. The legend, the poem, the musical gems. L: Bogue. 4. [EC]
9767.[Ad.] 1905. By Oliver Huckel. NY: Crowell. 76p. il. 19cm. [LC]
[Cf. #9670 and note.]
9768.[Ad.] 1913. The story of W--'s L--. Retold...F: Colin Tilney with 6 pict. in col. by the author. L: Routledge; NY: Dutton. 95p. 21cm. [BM]
9769.[Ad.] 1913. The tale of L--, the knight of the swan (in verse). By T. W. Rolleston. Presented by Willy Pogány. L: Harrap. unp. 8.

WAGNER, R:--Lohengrin
[Some col. plates. The entire book is a marvel.] [BM]
9770.[Ad.] 1916. Lohengrin, retold from the opera by Js. W. McSpadden. L: Harrap. 62p. col. front. 13 x 7cm. [BM]
9771.[Ad.] 1923. L--. By Td. M. R. v. Keler. Girard, Kan: Haldeman-Julius. Little blue books. 54p. 12cm. [BQM]
[Synopsis, extr. from libr., music.]
9772.[Ad.] 1925. L-- retold by Js. McSpadden. In C390.

PARSIFAL

*9773. AVELING, CLAUDE. Parsifal: a sacred festival drama. Vocal score. Ger;Engl. L: Novello; NY: Gray 1919. 318p. 27cm. [BMM]
[Close and good, but no rhyme.]
*9774. CORDER, H. and F: P--: a festival drama. Libr. Engl. Mayence; Lpz: Schott 1879. 62p. 16cm. [Very good tr.] [BM]
*9775. do. 1884. Vocal score. Ger;Engl. Mayence;L: Schott. 279p. 29cm. [BMM.LCM]
*9776. do. 1903. Parsifal: the story of this solemn festival play. Foreword by C: H: Meltzer. NY: Ogilvie. 127p. 19cm. [LC]
[Contains the libr. in the Corders' tr.]
*9777. do. 1903. Libr. Ger;Engl. Bost: Ditson. 44p. 24cm. [LC]
§9778. FORMAN, AF. Libr. Engl. NY;L: Macmillan 1899. xv;71p. 12. [BM.LC]
9779. do. 1899. [same?] Author 1899. 84p. 8. [EC]
*9780. GLYN, MARG. H. Libr. Engl. Mainz;L: Schott 1890. 61p. 17cm. [BM]
*9781. do. 1902. Vocal score. Ger;Engl. Mainz: Schott 1902. 277p. 30cm. [Excellent singing version; she dodges the rhymes.] [BMM.LCM]
*9782. do. 1904. Vocal score. NY: Schirmer. 4. [LCM]
*9783. do. 1909. Vocal score. Cincin;NY: Church. 355p. 28cm. [LCM]
*9783a. do. 1914. Libr. L: Schott. 35p. 8. [BM]
*9784. JACKSON, J: P. Libr. Engl. L: Dickens & Evans; NY: Schuberth 1890. 20p. il. 8. [Not as good as the Corders' tr.] [BM.LC]
§9785. KREHBIEL, H: E: Tr. and ad. for performance. Vocal score. Ger;Engl. NY: Harms & Francis, Day & Hunter 1920. 283p. 30cm. [BMM]
[Not so good; awkward; one bad error noted.]
§9786. do. 1920. Libr. Engl. NY: Harms & Francis. 48p. 8. [LCM.BM]
§9787. MELTZER, C: H: Libr. Engl. n.i. 1922. 4. Tw. [LCM]
[Seems to me inadequate.]
*9788. NEWMAN, ERN. Vocal score. Ger;Engl. Lpz: Breitkopf & H. 1914. 297p. 4. [Same as vol. 11 of #9639.] [LCM]
§9789. PHELPS, G: T. Libr. Ger;Engl. Bost: Badger 1904. 85p. 18cm.
[Correct, but bald and prosy.] [LC]
§9790. TESCHEMACHER, E: Vocal score. Ger;Engl. L: Boosey 1914. 364p. 4. [Not as good as Krehbiel.] [LCM]
§9791. WEBBER, AMHURST. The sacred festival-drama of P--. The argument, the musical drama, and the mystery. By C: T. Gatty. L: Schott 1894. 152p. 18cm. [Libr. in prose, close and good.] [BM]
§9792. do. 1914. [same] L;NY: Boosey. 152p. [BM]
9793.[Ad.] 1897. The story of P--. By W. F. Sheppard. In #9687.
9794.[Ad.] 1903. P--, a mystical drama...retold in the spirit of the Bayreuth interpretation by Oliver Huckel. NY: Crowell 1903. 70p. il. 20cm. [Cf. #9670 and note.] [LC]
9795.[Ad.] 1913. The story of P-- told in simple language, with notes, bibliog. etc. By R: Northcott. L: Lindley. 23p. 18cm. [BM]
9796.[Ad.] 1914. P-- and Tristan and Isolde: the stories of R: Wagner's dramas told in Engl. (blank verse) by R. Fynes and L: N. Parker. L: Smith, Elder. 88p. 18cm. [Excellent verse.] [BM]
9797.[Ad.] 1916. P-- retold from the opera by Js. McSpadden. L: Harrap. col. front. 63p. 13 x 7cm. [BM]
9798.[Ad.] 1925. Retold by Js. McSpadden. In C390.

WAGNER, R:--Parsifal
See Heintz, A., Parsifal...explained, #4165.
See Wolzogen und Neuhaus, Hs., Thematic guide..., #10359.

RHEINGOLD

*9799. ARMOUR, MARG. The Rhinegold and the Valkyrie. Il. Art. Rackham. L: Heinemann; NY: Doubleday, Page 1910. 159p. 26cm. [Cf. #9672, of which this is vol. 1.] [LC]
9800. do. 1910. [same] De luxe ed. Heinemann. 170p. 4. [EC]
*9801. do. 1912. [same as #9799] [LC]
*9802. CORDER, H. and F: Vocal score. Ger;Engl. Mainz: Schott n.d. (1899.) 221p. 4. [LCM]
§9803. FINCK, H: T. Vocal score. Ger;Engl. Cincin: Church 1903. 281p. 4. [LCM]
*9804. JACKSON, J: P. Libr. Ger;Engl. NY: 1888. 29 (i.e., 58) p. O. [UW]
*9805. JAMESON, F: Vocal score. Ger;Engl. Mainz: Schott 1899. 221p. 29 x 21cm. [LCM.BMM]
*9806. do. 1900? Libr. Engl. Mainz;L: Schott. 75p. 17cm. [BM]
*9807. do. 1904. [same as #9805] NY: Schirmer. 221p. [LCM]
*9808. NEWMAN, ERN. Piano score with text, Ger. and Engl. L: Breitkopf & H. n.d. 154p. 31cm. [BMM]
*9809. do. 1910. Ger. text rev. by W. Golther. Vocal score. Ger; Engl. L: Breitkopf & H. 268p. 27cm. [LCM]
*9810. do. 1912. [same] [BMM]
*9811. do. 1913. Libr. Engl. L: Breitkopf & H. 64p. 21cm. [BM]
*9812. do. 1914. Vocal score. In #9639, vol. 7.
9813. [Ad.] 1907. Oliver Huckel. NY: Crowell. 102p. il. 19cm. [Cf. #9670 and note.] [LC]
9814. [Ad.] 1925. The story of R--. Told for young people (by Anna A. Chapin). NY;L: Harper. xx;138p. pl. and mus. il. 20cm. [BM]

RIENZI

§9815. ANON. Libr. Ger;Engl. NY: Theatre ticket office 1877. 23 (i.e., 46)p. 8. [LC]
§9816. BERNHOFF, J: R--, the last of the tribunes. Vocal score. Ger;Engl. L: Schott 1911. 630p. 27cm. [BMM.LCM]
*9817. COPELAND, FANNY S. Vocal score. Lpz: Breitkopf & H. 1914. 596p. 4. [LCM]
§9818. JACKSON, J: P. Libr. With overture and princ. airs of the opera. L: Carl Rosa opera co. 1879. 59p. 21cm. [BMM]
†9819. PITTMAN, JOSIAH. Vocal score. Ger;Engl;Ital. Berlin: Fürstner 1878. 339p. 27cm. [LCM.BMM]
9820. [Ad.] Oliver Huckel. NY: Crowell 1914. 72p. il. 19cm. [Cf. #9670 and note.] [LC]

SIEGFRIED

9821. ARMOUR, MARG. Siegfried and the twilight of the gods. Il. A. Rackham. L: Heinemann; NY: Doubleday, Page 1911. 181p. 25cm. [Cf. #9672, of which this is vol. 2.] [LC]
*9822. CORDER, H. and F: Libr. Ger;Engl. NY: Rullman 188- . 48p. 4. [Close and acc. in the main; awkward at times.] [NY]
*9823. do. 1889. Libr. Ger;Engl. Bost: Ditson. 58p. 25cm. [LC]
*9824. do. 1900? Libr. Ger;Engl. Mayence;L: Schott. 98; 98p. 17cm. [BM]
*9825. do. 1900? Vocal score. Ger;Engl. Mainz: Schott. 337p. 4. [LCM]
*9826. do. 1913. Libr. Ger;Engl. Tr. anon. NY: Rullman. 64p. 26cm [LCM]
§9827. FINCK, H: T. Vocal score. Ger;Engl. Cincin: Church 1903. 426p. 4. [LCM]
*9828. JACKSON, J: P. Libr. Ger;Engl. NY: Metropolitan opera house 1887. 37; 37p. 8. [Preserves the alliteration.] [LCM]

WAGNER, R:--Siegfried
*9829. JAMESON, F: Vocal score. Mainz: Schott 1900. 337p. 30cm. [LCM.BMM]
*9830. do. 1904. [same] NY: Schirmer. 337p. 29 x 21cm. [LCM]
*9831. MELTZER, C: H: n.i. 1923. 121p. Tw. [LCM]
[Misses the alliteration; otherwise very good.]
*9832. NEWMAN, ERN. Vocal score. Ger;Engl. Lpz: Breitkopf & H. 1910. 365p. 4. [LCM]
*9833. do. 1914. [same] Vol. 9 of #9639.
9834. [Ad.] 1880. Argument...with libr. of 3d act. NY. 15p. 8. [LCO]
9835. [Ad.] 1909. The story of S--. Retold by Js. McSpadden. L: Harrap. 125p. il. 18cm. [BM]
9836. [Ad.] 1910. Oliver Huckel. NY: Crowell. 105p. il. 19cm. [LC]
[Cf. #9670 and note.]

TANNHÄUSER

9837. ANON. 1876. T-- as represented at the Lond. Ital. opera-houses. Libr. Ital;Engl. L: Davidson. 32p. 24cm. [BM]
[Engl. from Ital., which is quite free.]
9838. ANON. 1900? [same tr.] Libr. Ger;Engl. L: Grand opera syndicate. 23p. 24cm. [BM]
9839. ANON. 1907. Libr. L: Jack. 48p. 16. [EC]
†9840. ENGLAND, PL. Vocal score. L;NY: Boosey 1900. 299p. 26cm. [BMM.LCM]
*9841. JACKSON, J: P. T-- and the tournament of song on the Wartburg. Libr. Engl. L;NY: no pub. 1875. 51p. 18cm. [BM]
*9842. JAMESON, F: T-- and the minstrel's contest at Wartburg. Vocal score. Ger;Engl. L: Schott 1912. 354p. 27cm. [BMM.LCM]
§9843. MACFARREN, NATALIA. T-- and the tournament of song at Wartburg. Vocal score. L: Novello, also Simpkin & M. 1872. 272p. 26cm. [Not very good as tr.; pretty good as singing version.][BMM]
§9844. do. 1872. Libr? L: Novello. 8. [EC]
§9845. do. 1877. Tr. anon. Libr. Ger;Engl. NY: Wynkoop & Hallenbeck. 22p. 25cm. [LCM]
§9846. do. 1889? Libr. Ger;Engl. n.p. n.d. For use at the Metropolitan opera house. 28p. 23cm. [LCM]
§9847. do. 18- . Libr. Engl. NY: Tretbar n.d. 38p. 24cm. [LCM]
§9848. do. 190- . Libr. Ger;Engl. NY: Rullman n.d. 32; 8p. 4. [NY]
§9849. do. 19- ? Vocal score. Ger;Engl. NY: Schirmer. 343p. 4. [LCM]
§9850. do. 1911? Tr. anon. Libr. Ger;Engl. with music. Bost: Ditson. 28p. 24cm. [Cf. #9846.] [LCM]
§9851. do. 1911. Tr. anon. Libr. Ger;Engl. NY: Rullman. 32p. 25cm. [LCM]
*9852. MORGAN, MRS. J: P. Libr. Ger;Engl. Berlin: Fürstner 1891. 48(i.e., 96)p. 12. [LCM]
*9853. NEWMAN, ERN. T-- and the tournament of song on the Wartburg. Vocal score. L: Breitkopf & H. 1910. 390p. 27cm. [BMM.LCM]
*9854. do. 1912. Piano score with text. L: Breitkopf & H. 173p. 30cm. [BMM]
*9855. do. 1914. Vocal score. In #9639, vol. 3.
9856. [Ad.] 1906. Oliver Huckel. NY: Crowell. 68p. il. 19cm. [LC]
[Cf. #9670 and note.]
9857. [Ad.] 1911. Freely tr. in poetic narr. form by T. W. Rolleston. Il. W. Pogány. L: Harrap. ff. A-Q. 28cm. [BM]
[Cf. #9769, parallel volume.]
9858. [Ad.] 1914. Text ed. by B. R. Sharon. Bost: Birchard. Laurel octavo ed. of famous operas. 49p. 4. [No relation to Wagner's text.] [LCM]
9859. [Ad.] 1916. Retold by Js. McSpadden. L: Harrap. 60p. front. 16. [BM]

WAGNER, R:--Tannhäuser

9860. [Ad.] 1923. T--. By Td. M. R. v. Keler. Girard, Kan: Haldeman-Julius. Little blue books. 52p. 12cm. [BCM]
[Synopsis, extr. from libretto, music.]

9861. [Ad.] 1925. Tannhauser [sic]. Retold by Js. McSpadden. In C390.

9862. [Ad.] 1927. [same as #9857.] 25cm. [AC has: NY: Brentano's 1927.] [BM]

TRISTAN UND ISOLDE

9863. ANON. Libr. L: Jack 1908. 46p. 16. [EC]

*9864. CHAPMAN, H: G. Vocal score. Ger;Engl. NY: Schirmer 1906. 301p. 4. [LCM]

*9865. CORDER, H. and F: Tristan and Isolda. Libr. Ger;Engl. Lpz: Breitkopf & H. 1882. 58p. 26cm. [BM.LC]

*9866. do. 1882. Libr. Engl. Lpz: Breitkopf & H. 96p. 16cm. [BM]

*9867. do. 1882. Vocal score. Engl. L: Novello; NY: Schirmer. 260p. 27cm. [BMM]

*9868. do. 18-? Libr. Ger;Engl. NY: Rullman n.d. 36p. 26cm. [LCM]

*9869. do. 1890. [same as #9865] [BM]

*9870. do. 1894. Vocal score. Ger;Engl. L: Novello; NY: Schirmer. 276p. 28cm. [BMM]

*9870a. do. 1904-5. Full score. Ger;Engl;French. Lpz: Breitkopf & H. 1025p. 12. [LCM]

§9871. do. 1912. Ed. (and slightly revised) by W. J. Henderson. Libr. Ger. and Engl. (on opp. pages). NY: Dodd, Mead. 321p. 14cm. [LC]
[Revision seems to me not an improvement.]

§9872. do. 1914. Vocal score. In #9639, vol. 5.

*9873. FORMAN, AF. Tr. in allit. rhyming meters. Libr. Engl. L: Reeves & Turner 1891. 76p. 20cm. [BM]

9874. do. 1897. 8. [EC]

*9875. JACKSON, J: P. Tristan and Ysolde. Libr. Ger;Engl. NY? 1885. 33; 33p. 24cm. [Alliteration retained; close and good.] [LCM]

*9876. JAMESON, F: Tristan and Isolde. Libr. Engl. Priv. prt. 1886. 76p. 19cm. [BM]

*9877. do. 1906. Vocal score. L: Schott. 387p. 30cm. [BMM.LCM]

*9878. do. 1913. Libr. Engl. L: Schott. 56p. 8. [BM]

*9879. LE GALLIENNE, R: Il. G: A. Williams. Text. NY: Stokes 1909. 358p. 28cm. [LC.BM]

*9880. MELTZER, C: H: Libr. Engl. n.i. 1923. 98p. Tw. [LCM]

9881. [Ad.] 1913. Oliver Huckel. NY: Crowell. 72p. il. 19cm. [LC]
[Cf. #9670 and note.]

9882. [Ad]. 1914. T-- and I--. Told in (excellent) English (blank verse) by L: N. Parker. In #9796.

See Heintz, A., Tristan...explained, #4166.

See Pfordten, Hm. v.d., A plain handbook to the plot and text of ...Tristan, #7158.

See Wolzogen und Neuhaus, Hs., Guide to Tristan, #10355.

LETTERS

*9883. BOZMAN, M. M. Letters of R: W--. Sel. and ed. by W: Altmann. L;Toronto: Dent 1927. Internat. lib. of books on music. 2v. xiii; 358; 333p. port. 22cm. [A little too faithful.] [BM]

§9884. ELLIS, W: A. Letters...to E. Heckel. L: Richards 1899. viii; 154p. 18cm. [BM.LC]

*9885. do. 1899. Letters to Wesendonck et al. L: Richards. xi;180p. 18cm. [BM.LC]
[O: Wesendonck; Malvida v. Meysenbug, Frau Eliza Wille.]

9886. do. 1905. Letters to Mde. Wesendonck. NY: Scribner. xii;386p. il. 23cm. [LC.BM]

*9887. do. 1909. R: to Minna Wagner. Letters to his...first wife. L: Grevel. 2v. xviii;812p. front. (ports.) 22cm. [BM]

*9888. do. 1909. [same] NY: Scribner. 2v. 834p. [LC]

WAGNER, R:--Letters
§9889. do. 1910. [reissue of #9884] [LC]
9890. do. 1911. Family letters. L: Macmillan. vi;307p. 21cm. [BM.LC]
9891. do. 1911. [same as #9886] 3d ed. L: Grevel. 8. [EC]
**9892. HUEFFER, FIS. Corr. of W-- and Liszt, 1841-61. L: Grevel 1888. 2v. xvi;352; 340p. 20cm. [BM]
["This tr. of the corr. is intended to be an exact facsimile of the Ger. orig." Done with scrupulous, almost worshipful faithfulness. Vol. 1, 1841-53. Vol. 2 , 1854-61.]
**9893. do. 1897. [same] New rev. ed. Grevel. 2v. 748. 20cm. [BM.LC]
*9894. KERR, CARO. V. The story of Bayreuth as told in the Bayreuth letters of R: W--. Tr. and ed. by C. V. K. Bost: Small, Maynard 1912. 364p. il. 21cm. [LC.BM]
9895. do. 1913. [same] L: Nisbet. 8. [EC]
*9896. SELLAR, ELEANOR C. Letters to A: Roeckel. Introd. H. S. Chamberlain. Bristol: Arrowsmith 1897. 178p. 19cm. [BM.LC]
§9897. SHEDLOCK, J: S. Letters to his Dresden friends, Td. Uhlig, W: Fischer, and Fd. Heine. L: Grevel 1890. xi;512p. 21cm. [BM.LC]
[Fails at important points.]
See Nietzsche, F:, N-- W-- corr., #6889.

BIOGRAPHY

*9898. (Mein Leben.) My life. Tr. anon. L: Constable; NY: Dodd, Mead 1911. 2v. 926p. 23cm. [One error noted.] [BM.LC]
9899. do. 1915. [same] Pop. ed. NY: Dodd. 2v. 911p. O. [AC]
*9900. do. 1924. [same] NY: Dodd. vii;911p. 23cm. [LC]
*9901. W-- and his Isolde. By Gst. Kobbe. Tr. anon. NY: Dodd, Mead 1905. 255p. 18cm. [LC]
[Letters and journals anent Mde. Wesendonck, connected with comment and narr.]
See Bahr-Mildenburg, Anna, Bayreuth and the W-- theatre, #183.
See Chamberlain, H., R: W--, #1077.
See Glasenapp, C:, Life of R: W--, #2333.
See Golther, W., R: W-- as poet, #3058.
See Muncker, Fz., R: W--, #6620.
See Neumann, A., Personal recoll., #6698.
See Nietzsche, F:, The case of W--, #6848.
See Nohl, L:, Life of W--, #6911.
See Wolzogen und Neuhaus, Hs., Recoll. of R: W--, #10358.

WAGNER, R: An. 1860- . See Poland, Fz., joint author.

WAGNER, Sf. 1869-1931.
*9902. (Der Bärenhäuter.) Der Bärenhäuter. Author. tr. by W: A. Ellis. Libr. Ger;Engl. Lpz: Brockhaus 1899. 115; 115p. 16. [LCM]
[Good, undistinguished, clumsy verse.]

WAGNER VON LAUFENBURG, --. Sel. in C438.

WAHL, L: Sel. in C572.

WALDERSEE, Af. Graf v. 1832-1904.
*9903. (Denkwürdigkeiten.) A field marshal's memoirs: from the diary, corr., and reminiscences. Condensed and tr. by F: Whyte. L: Hutchinson 1924. xix;286p. 23cm. [BM]

WALDMANN, Emil, 1880- .
9903a. (Die Nürnberger Kleinmeister.) Little masters. Priv. ptd. 1927. 44p. il. T. (From chapter 4.) [AC]
See Harden, Mx., Word portraits, #3699.

WALDSTEIN, Abr. See "Wallenstein."

WALDSTEIN, Louis, 1853-1915.
9904. The subconscious self and its relation to educ. and health. Tr. O: Veraguth. L: Richards 1897. 171p. 19cm. [BM]

WALDSTEIN, Louis.--The subconscious self
9905. do. 1926. New ed. With the pref. to the Ger. ed. tr. by Mrs. Gertrud Veraguth. A biogr. sketch by Sir C: Walston, etc. NY: Scribners 1926. lxvii;171p. 19cm. [LC.BM]

"WALL, An." (i.e., Cn. Lbt. Heyne), 1751-1821.
9906. (Amathonte, ein persisches Märchen.) Amatonda. Tr. H: Crabb Robinson. L: Longmans 1811. 288p. 17cm. [LC]
9907. Two tales. Tr. anon. ca. 1800. In C157(3).

WALLENSTEIN (properly Waldstein, orig. Waldenstein), Abr. Esb. Wz. 1583-1634. Sel. in C486.
9908. The relation of the death of...the duke of...Fridland... Together with the cause thereof. Tr. anon. L: T:Harper for Butler & Bourne 1634. 36p. 16cm. [BM]
See Pichler, C: E., Waldstein, or the Swedes in Prague, #7178-83.

"WALLING, Günther" (i.e., "K: Ulrici," 1839-96). Sel. in C180.

WALLOTH, W: 1856- .
*9909. (Das Schatzhaus des Königs.) The king's treasure house: a romance of ancient Egypt. Tr. Ma. J. Safford. NY: Gottsberger 1886. 353p. 16cm. [LC.BM]
9910. (Oktavia.) Empress Octavia: a romance of the reign of Nero. Tr. Ma. J. Safford. Bost: Little, Brown 1900. 378p. 8. [LC]

WALTER, Fd. 1794-1879. Sel. in C12.

WALTHER VON DER VOGELWEIDE, fl. 1198-1230. Sel. in C27*;88;129;171; 190;309;310*;366;372;416;423;427*;470;530-2;570.
§9911. Songs and sayings. Tr. Frank Betts. Oxf: Blackwell; NY: Longmans 1917. 54p. 15cm. [Prose, correct. BM dates this 1918] [LC.BM]
*9912. Selected poems. Tr. W. A. Phillips. L: Smith, Elder 1896. xliii;126p.il. 8. [BM.LC]

WALTHER VON METZ, d. 1270? Sel. in C27;416;427.

WALTHER, J: fl. 1520-64. Sel. in C287;#5963.

WALTHER, Oc.
§9913. Lorraine: comic operetta in 3 acts by Rd. Dellinger. Ad. W. J. Henderson. Libr. Chic: 1887. [LC]
[Excellent singing version, rather far from orig.]

WASILIEWSKI, W: Js. v. 1822-96.
*9914. (Das Violoncell und seine Geschichte.) The violoncello and its hist. Tr. Isobella S. E. Stigand. L;NY: Novello 1894. x;225p. il. 22cm. [BM.LCM]
*9915. (Rb. Schumann, eine Biographie.) Life of Rb. S--. Tr. Abby L. Alger. Bost;NY: Ditson 1871. 275p. 17cm. [LC]
*9916. do. 1878. [same] with letters (1833-52). xii;299p. 19cm. [BM]

WASMANN, Er.
9917. Christian monism: meditations on Christian truths in the lang. of mod. thought. Tr. by Rev. Spencer Jones. L: Burns, Oates 1923. xxx;123p. 8. [BM]
9918. Mod. biol. and the theory of evol. Tr. from 3d Ger. ed. by A. M. Buchanan, M.A. L: K.Paul 1910. xxxii;539p. 23cm. [BM]

WASSERMANN, Jk. 1873- .
9919. [Coll.] World's ends. Tr. Lewis Galantière. NY: Boni & Liveright 1927. 278p. (B37)
[Adam's son ("Am. Urbas"); Golovin ("Golowin"); Lukardis (do.); Erasmus ("Erasmus Ungnad"); Jost (do.).]
9920. The beast. Tr. 1927. In C367.
9921. Bourgeois marriage. Tr. 1926. In C308.

WASSERMANN, Jk.
*9922. (Christian Wahnschaffe.) The world's illusion. Tr. Ludwig Lewisohn. NY: Harcourt 1920. 2v. 383; 405p. 19cm. [LC.BM]
[Vol. 1, Eva. Vol. 2, Ruth.]
*9923. do. 1921. [same] L: Hodder & Stoughton. [BM]
*9924. do. 1926. [same] 10th printing. NY: Harcourt. [LC]
*§9925. (Das Gänsemännchen.) The goose man. Author. tr. by Allen W. Porterfield. NY: Harcourt 1922. 470p. 19cm. [LC.BM]
[Chaps. I and pt. of II done by Lewisohn, excellent; the remainder by A. W. Porterfield, rather faulty.]
*9926. (Der Aufruhr um den Junker Ernst.) The triumph of youth. Tr. O: P. Schinnerer. NY: Boni & Liveright 1927. 205p. 19cm. [LC]
*9927. (Die Schwestern.) Clarissa Mirabel. Tr. Julia Franklin. 1913-15. In C154(20).
*9928. (Faber, oder die verlorenen Jahre.) Faber; or, the lost years. Tr. Harry Hansen. NY: Harcourt 1925. 347p. 19cm. [LC]
[Has some errors.]
9929. (Laudin und die Seinen.) Wedlock. Tr. Ludwig Lewisohn. NY: Boni & Liveright 1926. 344p. 19cm. [LC]
§9930. (Oberlins drei Stufen.) Oberlin's three stages. Tr. A. W. Porterfield. NY: Harcourt, Brace 1925. 350p. 19cm. [LC]
[Good, but style is violated and errors occur.]
§9931. (Ulrike Voytich.) Gold. Author. tr. by Mrs. Louise C. Willcox. NY: Harcourt 1924. vi;431p. 19cm. [LC]
[Fair to good; she is unequal to the stylistic task.]

WASSERMANN, Moses, 1811-92.
*9932. (Judah Touro.) J-- T--: a biogr. romance. Tr. Harriet W. Mayer. NY: Bloch 1923. 275p. 19cm. [Some questionable liberties.][LC]

WATTEROTH, Rev. Ig.
9933. Life of Mother Clare Fey, foundress of the Congregation of the poor child Jesus, 1815-94. A free tr...with add. from the...work of O: Pfulf...by a member of the congregation. L: Burns, Oates 1923. v;276p. 18cm. [BM]
9934. do. 1923. [same] Pref. by J: McIntyre. St. Louis: Herder. xvi; 276p. il. O. [AC]

WEBER, Abr.
9934a. India and the West in old days. Tr. Emily Hawtrey. Madras: Lawrence asylum press 1887. 27p. 23cm. [BM]
[One of four lect. entitled "Indische Skizzen." Some omissions.]

WEBER, Eugen
9934b. (Vinzenz Pallotti. Ein Apostel und Mystiker.) Ven. Vincent P--, modern apostle and mystic. Abr. and ad. Js. de Maria. Milwaukee: Pallottine fathers 1927. 60p. il. D. [AC]

WEBER, F: W: 1813-94.
*9935. (Dreizehnlinden.) Corvey Abbey: a lyrical epopee thought into Engl. verse by Mx. A. Muegge. L: Burns, Oates 1923. xiii; 177p. [On the whole, a remarkable transmutation. AC has: Introd. by Cardinal Bourne. St.L: Herder n.d. Q.] [BM]
9936. (Goliath.) Goliath: a tragic love tale (in verse) of the north. Tr. Marie C. Buehrle. Soc. of the divine word 1914. 92p. D. [AC]

WEBER, G: 1808-88.
*9937. (Lehrbuch der Weltgeschichte.) Outlines of universal hist. from the creation of the world to the present time. Tr. Dr. M. Behr. L: Whittaker 1851. xvi;483p. 22cm. [BM.LC]
*9938. do. 1853. [same] Rev. and corr. Bost: Jenks, Hockling & Swan. 559p. 23cm. [Has the hist. of the U. S. A. tr. by Fis. Bowen.][LC]
9939. do. 1853. [same?] Bost: Little, Brown. 8. [AC]
9940. do. 1872-6. [same] Bost: Ware n.d. 8. [AC]

WEBER, G:--Lehrbuch der Weltgeschichte
*9941. do. 1894. [another tr.] Hist. of the world from the creation of man to the present day. Profusely il. Phil;St.L: Ziegler. 1030p 28cm. [Seemingly a complete translation of the orig. "Lehrbuch" (1847), exc. for Amer. hist., rewritten by C: J. Little.] [LC]
*9942. do. 1896. [same] The story of the nations. [LC]

WEBER, K: Ma. (F: Em.) Frhr. v. 1786-1826. Sel. in C12. Operas: Euryanthe, see Chezy, Hna. Der Freischütz, see Kind, F: Preciosa, see Wolff, P.
9943. The life of a musician, a humourous sketch; The discordant harmonists, a dream. Tr. J. D. Haas. 1839. In C183, pp. 321-30.
9944. Letters. Tr. Lady Wallace. 1867. In C429.
9945. Letters. In "Oberon"...To which are prefixed three unpub. letters by the composer to M. Planché. L: 1842. 12. [BM]
See Weber, K. Max Ma. v., The life of an artist.

WEBER, Max Ma. Frhr. v. 1822-81. Sel. in C12;429.
9946. (K: Ma. v. Weber. Ein Lebensbild.) Carl Maria v. W--: the life of an artist. Tr. J: P. Simpson. L: Chapman & Hall 1865. 2v. ix; 404; 483p. 19cm. [Condensed and in part reconstructed.] [BM.LC]

WEBER, Norbert, 1870- .
9947. With the heralds of the cross: thoughts on the foreign mission. Tr. T: J. Kennedy. Soc. of the divine word 1924. viii; 331p. D. [AC]

WEBER, Or, 1860- . Sel. in C563.

WEBER, P.
9948. Architectural hist. of the Wartburg; Old and new works of art in the Wartburg. Tr. G. A. Greene. 1907. In C555.

"WEBER, Veit" (i.e., G: Ph. L: Lh. Wächter, 1762-1837). Sel. in C372-3.
9949. (Der Müller des Schwarztals.) The black valley: a tale. Tr. anon. L: Johnson 1796. See "Analyt. Rev." 23(1796):507. (B26) [Tr. is said to be the same as of "The sorcerer." Rb. Huish?]
9950. do. 1801. [same, reprint] Alexandria. Prtd. for Thomas. 172p. 15cm. [LC]
9951. (Die Teufelsbeschwörung.) The sorcerer: a tale. Tr. Rb. Huish? L: Johnson 1795. 210p. 19cm. [BM]
§9952. (Sagen der Vorzeit: Wolf.) Wolf; or, the tribunal of blood. Tr. J. Powell. L: Hughes 1806. 2v. in one. 193; 173p. 17cm. [BM] [Not very close or acc. Part prose, part dialog.]
§9953. do. 1841. [same] Woman's revenge; or, the tribunal of blood. L: Clements. (Romancist and novelist's lib.) 42p. 21cm. [BM.LC]

WECKHERLIN, G: Rodolf, 1584-1653.
9954. (Triumf newlich bey der F. kindtauf zu Stutgart gehalten. Beschriben durch...Stutgart 1616.) Triumphall shewes set forth lately at Stutgart. Written first in German, and now in English. Tr. by himself. Stutgart: Resslin 1616. 167p. 15cm. [BM]

WEDEKIND, Frank, 1864-1918. Sel. in C28.
9955. [Coll.] 1911. Rabbi Ezra; The victim. Two stories. Tr. Fis. J. Ziegler. Phil: Brown. 37p. 20cm. [LC]
9956. [Coll.] 1919. Princess Russalka (Die Fürstin R--). Tr. F: Eisemann. Bost: Luce. xxxiv;138p. port. 19cm. [LC] [On eroticism; Title; The grisly suitor; I am bored; The burning of Egliswyl; Les Halles; The victim; The inoculation; Rabbi Esra.]
9957. [Coll.] 1923. Tragedies of sex. Tr. with introd. S: A. Eliot, Jr. NY: Boni & Liveright; L: Henderson. xxiv;347p. 21cm. [LC] [Spring's awakening ("Frühlings Erwachen"); *Earth-spirit ("Der Erdgeist"); Pandora's box ("Die Büchse der Pandora"); Damnation

WEDEKIND, Frank
("Tod und Teufel"). --The one examined excellent, both the verse prolog and the dialog.]
§9958. (Die Büchse der Pandora.) Pandora's box: a trag. in 3 acts. Tr. S: A. Eliot, Jr. NY: Boni & Liveright 1918. 79p. 19cm. [LC]
[Arbitrary treatment of stage directions; not wholly correct, nor in just the right tone.]
*9959. (Der Erdgeist.) Earth-spirit: a trag. in 4 acts. Tr. S: A. Eliot, Jr. NY: Boni & Liveright 1914. 93p. 12. [LC]
9960. (?Der Kammersänger.) The heart of a tenor. Ad. by André Tridon. "Smart Set" 1913. (B38)
*9961. (Der Kammersänger.) The court singer. Tr. Ab. W: Boesche. 1913-15. In C154(20).
9961a. do. 1923. In C420b.
§9962. (Frühlings Erwachen.) The awakening of spring: a trag. of childhood. Tr. Fis. J. Ziegler. Phil: Brown 1909. 161p. 21cm. [Careless.] [LC.BM]
§9963. do. 1910. [same] [LC]
§9964. do. 1916. [same] 5th ed. [LC]
9965. The grisley suitor: a story. Tr. Fis. J. Ziegler. Phil: Brown 1911. 33p. 20cm. [LC]
*9966. (So ist das Leben.) Such is life: a play in 5 acts. Tr. Fis. J. Ziegler. Phil: Brown 1912. 127p. 21cm. [LC]
*9967. do. 1916. [same] [LC]
9968. The virgin and the white slaver: a play in one act. Ad. André Tridon. NY: "Internat. Mag." Vol. 7(1913).

WEDEL, Lupold v.
*9969. Journey through England and Scotland...1584 and 1585. Tr. Gf. v. Bülow. In "Royal hist. soc. transactions." L: Longmans 1895. Vol. 9, pp. 223-70. 21cm. [BM.LCO]
[Tr. from Wedel's diary, dictated by him to a secretary from his notes. The journey to England forms one small portion.]

WEERTH, G: d. 1856. Sel. in C301.

WEGELER, Fz. Grd. 1765-1848.
9970. (Biographische Notizen über L: van Beethoven.) Furioso; or, passages from the life of L: van B--. Altered from the diary of F. G. W-- by W. Mueller. Tr. ed. O. Glover. Cambridge: Deighton, Bell 1865. 214p. 19cm. [BM.LC]

WEGELIN, Josua, d. 1640. Sel. in C273;287.

WEGENER, Hm.
9971. Heroes of the mission field; or, abridged lives of famous missionaries and martyrs of our time. Tr. E. McCall. Mission Press 1916. 298p. il. D. [AC]

WEGENER, Kurt
9972. Introd. to Wl. Mittelholzer, "By airplane towards the North Pole," #6252.

WEGENER, R. C. (i.e., Rhingulph E:?) Sel. in C152;571.

WEGENER, T:
9973. (Das wunderbare innere und äussere Leben...) Sister Anne Kath. Emmerich...The marvellous interior life of this servant of God. Tr. from the French ed. by Fis. X. McGowan. NY;Cincin: Benziger 1898. 317p. 20cm. [LC]

WEGENER, W.
9974. Great reformer. Tr. by Rev. F. D. Wyneken. Concordia 1917. 127p. il. D. [AC]

WEGLEITER, Cph. 1659-1706. Sel. in C231.

WEGNER, Armin T. 1886- . Sel. in C95.

WEHL, Feodor, 1821-90. Sel. in C112.

WEICHARDT, C: F: W: 1846-1906.
9975. (Das Schloss des Tiberius und andere Römerbauten auf Capri.) Tiberius's villa and other Roman buildings on the isle of C--. Expounded and il. Tr. H. Brett. Lpz: Köhler; NY: Stechert 1900. 124p. il. 28cm. [LC]

WEIGAND, W: 1862- . Sel. in C28.

WEIGL, J. F.
9976. Othello; The word of honor. Tr. Louisa Addison. 1841. In #480.

WEIKONE, A. M. See Willner, A. M., joint author.

WEILEN (i.e., Weil Ritter v. Weilen), Js. 1828-89.
9977. (Drahomira.) Agramahra: a trag. in 5 acts. Tr. H. Bernstein. Ad. Mattilda Heron. 1871. (B38)

WEILL, Ax. (orig. Abraham) 1811-99.
*9978. (Sittengemälde aus dem elsässischen Volksleben.) Village tales from Alsatia. Tr. Sir A. C. Duff Gordon. L: Cundall 1848. 247p. 18cm. [See A3 and A4, with notes.] [BM.LC]

WEINGAERTNER, Sgs. 17th cent. Sel. in C271;570.

WEINGARTNER, (Pl.) Fx. Edler v. Münzberg, 1863- .
9979. Bayreuth, 1876-96. A crit. of the performance of Wagner's work. Tr. Lily Antrobus. L: Weekes 1898. 48p. 17cm. [BM]
†9980. (Die Symphonie nach Beethoven.) The symphony since B--. Tr. from 2d Ger. ed. by Maude B. Dutton. Bost;NY: Ditson 1904. 98p. 19cm. [LC]
§9981. do. 1906. The post-Beethoven symphonists. Tr. from 2d ed. by Art. Bles. NY: Scribner. 163p. il. 19cm. [LC]
§9982. do. 1907. [same] L: Reeves. 12 ports. 19cm. [BM]
§9983. do. 1925. [same] 2d imp. With notice of the author's own no. 5 symphony by D. C. Parker added to this issue. L: Reeves. vii; 168p. 12 ports. 19cm. [BM.LC]
9984. (Ratschläge für Aufführungen der Symphonien Beethovens.) On the performance of B--'s symphonies. Tr. Jessie Crosland. Lpz;L: Breitkopf & H. 1907. x;195p. 21cm. [BM]
*9985. (Ueber das Dirigieren.) On conducting. Tr. Ern. Newman. Lpz; L: Breitkopf & H. 1906. 56p. 22cm. [BM]

WEININGER, O: 1881-1902.
*9986. (Geschlecht und Charakter.) Sex and character. Author. tr. from 6th Ger. ed. anon. L: Heinemann 1906. xxii;356p. 22cm. [BM]

WEINMANN, K: 1873- .
*9987. (Geschichte der Kirchenmusik.) Hist. of church music. Tr. anon. Ratisbon;NY: Pustet 1910. vii;216p. 17cm. [LC.BM]

WEISER, Cd. 1696-1760.
9988. C-- W--'s tour to the Ohio, 1748. In Thwaites, Reuben G., "Early western travels." Cleveland: 1904. Vol. 1, pp. 15-44. 24cm. [LC.BM]
9989. Narr. of a journey from Tulpehocken...Penn. to Onondago...in 1737. Tr. Hiester H. Muhlenberg. Phil: Pennington 1853. 72p. 8. [LC]
9990. do. 1854. [same] In Schoolcraft, H. R., "Information respecting the Indian tribes of the U. S." Phil: Lippincott, Grambo. Vol. 4, pp. 324-41. 4. [LCO]
9991. Translation of a Ger. letter, wrote (1746) by C-- W--, Esq., interpreter, on Indian affairs, for the province of Penn. Phil: B. Franklin & D. Hall 1757. 7p. 8. (B6a)

WEISFLOG, K: 1770-1828.
9992. Measure for measure: a tale. Tr. G: G. Cunningham. 1829. In C80.

WEISMANN, A: 1834-1914.
*9993. (Aufsätze über Vererbung und verwandte biologische Fragen.) Essays upon heredity and kindred biological problems. Ed. E: B. Poulton, S. Schönland, and Art. E. Shipley. Tr. Shipley. Oxf: Clarendon 1889. x;455p. 8. [BM]
*9994. do. 1891-2. [same] Oxf: Clarendon. 2v. xv;455; 226p. [BM]
9995. The evolution theory. Tr. with author's co-op. by J. Art. Thompson and Marg. R. Thompson. L: E.Arnold 1904. 2v. xvi;416; 415p. il. 24cm. [BM]
[Lect. delivered to a mixed audience, hence not narrowly technical.]

WEISS, Bh.
9996. Life of Christ. Tr. anon. Ed: Hope 1883. For. theol. lib. xvi; 393p. 22cm. [BM]

WEISS, Cn. 1774-1853? or Cph. 1818-83? Sel. in C271.

WEISS, Ml. ca. 1480-1540. Sel. in C244;269;273;287.

WEISSE, A:
9997. (Das grüne Auto.) The mystery of the green car. Tr. Ax. T. de Mattos. L: Nelson 1913. 379p. col. front. 18cm. [BM]

WEISSE, Cn. Fx. 1726-1804. Sel. in C17;22;25-6;106;235;269;461;489.
9998. The modish young lady; The birthday; Filial piety. (Plays.) Tr. anon. 1801. In C302.
9999. Moral songs for children. Tr. anon. L: Searle 1789. xii;60p. front. 17cm. [BM]
†10000. (Rosemunde.) Rosamond: a trag. in 5 acts [verse]. Tr. Fanny Holcroft. 1806. In C206, vol. 2, pp. 359-97.
[Rhymed 12-syl. verse turned into blank verse, none too good; sense not fully given.]

WEISSEL, G: 1590-1635. Sel. in C269;273;276;486;489.

WEISSENBORN, E: W:
10001. Homeric life. Tr. and ad. to the needs of Amer. students by G. C. Scoggin and C: G. Burkitt. NY: Amer. bk. co. 1903. 144p. il. 19cm. [LC.BM]

WEISSENBORN, J. Sel. in C244.

WEISSMANN, Ad.
10002. (Die Musik in der Weltkrise.) Problems of mod. music. Tr. M. M. Bozman. L: Dent;NY: Dutton 1925. xxiv;244p. il. 19cm. [BM.LC]
[Rewritten.]

WEITBRECHT, K: 1847-1904. Sel. in C448.

WEITZ, W: 1806-90. Sel. in C466.

WELISCH, Ern. See Bernauer, Rd., joint author. See Schanzer, Rd., joint author.

WELLMER, Arn.
*10003. (Anna, Gräfin zu Stolberg-Wernigerode.) Anna, countess zu S-- W--: a story of our own times. Tr. D.M.P. L: Routledge 1873. 199p. 18cm. [BM]

WENCK, K:
10004. Earliest hist. of the Wartburg; St. Elizabeth; Hist. of the landgraves and of the Wartburg as a princely seat, 13th-15th cent. Tr. G. A. Greene. 1907. In C555.

WENDEBORN, Gebhard F: A: 1742-1811.
*10005. (Der Zustand des Staates, der Religion, der Gelehrsamkeit und der Kunst in Grosbrittanien gegen das Ende des 18. Jahrhunderts.) A view of England towards the close of the 18th cent. Tr. ...by the author. L: Robinson 1791. 2v. xiv;442; 488p. 22cm. [BM.LC]
[Author was preacher in London. Some chaps. omitted for the Engl. public; some of the rest abridged.]
*10006. do. 1791. [same] Dublin: Prtd. for Wogan. 2v. 18cm. [LC]

WENZEL VON BOEHMEN, König, fl. 1286-1305. Sel. in C27;427;532.

WERFEL, Fz. 1890- . Sel. in C95.
10007. (Bocksgesang.) Goat song: a drama in 5 acts. Tr. Ruth Laugner. NY: Doubleday 1926. xiii;161p. 19cm. [LC]
*10008. (Der Tod des Kleinbürgers.) The man who conquered death. Tr. C. P. Fadiman and W: A. Drake. NY: Simon & Schuster 1927. 134p. [LC]
[On the whole, excellent.]
*10009. do. 1927. [same] The death of a poor man. L: Benn. 186p. 18cm. [BM]
§10010. (Juarez und Maximilian, dramatische Historie.) J-- and M--: a dram. hist. in three phases and thirteen pict. Tr. Ruth Laugner. NY: Simon & Schuster 1926. 172p. 19cm. [LC]
[Rather an adaptation than a tr.]
§10011. (Verdi, Roman der Oper.) Verdi: a novel of the opera. Tr. Helen Jessiman. NY: Simon & Schuster 1925. vii;438p. 21cm. [LC.BM]
[No idea of real faithfulness: omissions, alterations, broken sentences, etc.]
10012. do. 1926. [same] L: Jarrolds. 384p. 9 x 5 in. [EC]

WERNE, Fd.
*10013. (Expedition zur Entdeckung der Quellen des weissen Nil.) Exped. to discover the sources of the White Nile...1840-1. Tr. C: W: O'Reilly. L: Bentley 1849. 2v. in one. 346; 354p. 19cm. [BM.LC]
*10014. (Feldzug von Sennaar nach Taka...) African wanderings...Tr. J. R. Johnston. L: Longmans 1852. 267p. 17cm. [BM.LC]
[Somewhat abridged to advantage.]

"WERNER, E." (i.e., Eli. Bürstenbinder, 1838-1918). Sel. in C469.
10015. [Coll.] 1879. A hero of the pen ("Ein Held der Feder") and other stories. Tr. anon. NY: Worthington. 8. [AC]
§10016. [Coll.] 1894. Lover from across the seas ("Der Egoist"); In the hands of the enemy; Fountain of youth. Tr. Ma. J. Safford. NY: Bonner. 292p. il. 19cm. [LC]
[Numerous errors. Il. by V: Perard and H. M. Eaton.]
10017. (Am Altar.) At the altar. Tr. J. S. L. Phil: Lippincott 1872. 343p. 18cm. [LC]
10018. do. 1874. [same] Bound by his vows; or, at the altar. [LC]
*10019. do. 1878. At the altar. Tr. Mrs. Parker. L: Low. 2v. 299; 265p. 19cm. [BM]
*10020. do. 1878. Sacred vows. Tr. Bertha Ness. L: Remington. 3v. 18cm. [BM]
*10021. do. 1885. [same] L: Ward & L. 307p. 17cm. [BM]
10022. do. 1895. At the altar. Tr. E. F. Hart and E. van Gerpen. NY: Munro. 214p. (B12) [NY]
10023. (Der Egoist.) Partners. Tr. H. G. Goodwin. L: Remington 1882. 283p. 18cm. [BM]
*10024. do. 1882. [same? same title] NY: Munro. Seaside lib. 19p. 32cm. [LC]
10025. (Die Alpenfee.) The fairy of the Alps. Tr. M. S. Smith and G. H. Smith. NY: Munro 1889. 285p. 19cm. [LC]
10026. do. 1889. The Alpine fay. Tr. Mrs. A. L. Wister. Phil: Lippincott. 356p. 18cm. [LC]
10027. do. 1897. [same] 19cm. [LC]

"WERNER, E."
10028. (Ein Gottesurteil.) Danira. Tr. Ma. J. Safford. Chic: McNally 1888. 194p. 19cm. [LC]
*10029. do. 1889. Judgment of God. Tr. M. S. and G. H. Smith. NY: Munro. Seaside lib. 32cm. [LC]
10030. (Ein Held der Feder.) Hero of the pen. Tr. Fes. A. Shaw. Bost: Gill 1875. 166p. (B12) [NY]
10031. do. 1878. Tr. Sa. Phillips. L: Low. 2v. 8. [EC]
10032. do. 1883. Tr. M. S. Smith. NY: Munro. Seaside lib. 48p. 32cm. [LC]
10033. do. 1895. Quill-driver. Tr. Hettie E. Miller. Chic: Weeks. 238p. 20cm. [LC]
10034. Fickle fortune. Tr. Christina Tyrrell. L: Bentley 1881. 2v. 286; 276p. 18cm. [BM]
10035. do. 1884. [same] Bentley. 3v. 8. [BM]
10036. do. 1888. [same] New ed. Bentley. 336p. 19cm. [BM]
10037. (Flammenzeichen.) His word of honor. Tr. anon. NY: Street 1890. 284p. il. 20cm. [LC]
10038. do. 1891. Beacon-fires. Tr. anon. L: Bentley. 3v. 18cm. [BM]
10039. do. 1891. Flames. Ad. anon. Chic: Donohue, Henneberry. 385p. il. 20cm. [LC]
10040. do. 1891. The northern light. Tr. Mrs. D. M. Lowrey. NY: Bonner. 373p. il. 19cm. [LC]
10041. do. 1899. Beacon lights. Tr. M. S. Smith and G. H. Smith. NY: Munro. 289p. 12. [LC]
10042. do. 1902. The sign of flame. Tr. Eva F. Hart and E. van Gerpen. NY: Burt. 425p. 18cm. [LC]
10043. (Freie Bahn.) "Clear the track!" Tr. Ma. S. Smith. NY: Internat. news 1893. 319p. 18cm. [LC.BM]
10044. (Frühlingsboten.) What the spring brought. Tr. anon. NY: Munro 1881. Seaside lib. 49p. 32cm. [AC dates this 1880.] [LC]
10045. do. 1891. The master of Ettersberg. Tr. anon. NY: Street. 321p. 19cm. [LC]
10046. do. 1894. [same as #10044] NY: Munro. Pocket ed. 188p. 19cm. [LC]
10047. (Gebannt und erlöst.) Banned and blessed. Tr. Mrs. A. L. Wister. Phil: Lippincott 1884. 390p. 19cm. [LC]
*10048. do. 1884. Raymond's atonement. Tr. Christina Tyrrell. L: Bentley. 3v. 18cm. [BM]
*10049. do. 1885. [same] NY: Munro. Seaside lib. 32cm. [LC]
§10050. do. 1885. Enthralled and released. Tr. H: Raphael. NY: Knox. 504p. 19cm. [Rather inaccurate.] [LC]
10051. do. 1892. [same] NY: Worthington. D. [AC]
§10052. do. 1896. Banned and blessed. Tr. Hettie E. Miller. Chic: Weeks. 445p. il. 20cm. [Moderately good.] [LC]
10053. (Gesprengte Fesseln.) Broken chains. Tr. Fes. A. Shaw. Bost: Osgood 1875. 133p. 23cm. [LC]
10054. do. 1877. Riven bonds. Tr. Bertha Ness. L: Remington. 2v. 286; 288p. 18cm. [BM]
10055. do. 1885. [same] L: Ward & L. 292p. 17cm. [BM]
10056. do. 1890. [same as #10053] L: Routledge. 133p. 22cm. [BM]
*10057. (Glück auf!) Good luck! Tr. Fes. A. Shaw. Bost: Osgood 1874. 153p. 12. [LC]
10058. do. 1878. [same] New issue. Bost: Estes. 8. [AC]
10059. do. 1883. [same?] NY: Munro. Seaside lib. 49p. 32cm. [LC] [AC dates this 1882.]
*10060. do. 1890. [same as #10057] L: Routledge. 153p. 22cm. [BM]
*10061. do. 1912. [same] NY: Burt. 419p. 19cm. [LC]
*10062. (Heimatklang.) Home sounds. Tr. E. W. Conduit. NY: Munro 1888. 133p. 19cm. [LC]

"WERNER, E."--Heimatklang
10063. do. 1888. The spell of home. Tr. Mrs. A. L. Wister. "Lippincott's monthly mag." Vol. 41(1888), pp. 143-214.
*10064. (Hermann.) Hermann. Tr. Helen K. Brown. L: Remington 1879. 241p. 18cm. [BM]
10065. do. 1883. Tr. M. S. Smith. NY: Munro. Seaside lib. 25p. 32cm. [LC]
10066. Her son. Tr. Christina Tyrrell. L: Bentley 1887. 3v. 18cm [BM]
10067. (Sankt Michael.) Saint M--. Tr. Mrs. A. L. Wister. Phil: Lippincott 1887. 411p. 18cm. [LC]
10068. do. 1910. [same] [LC]
10069. She fell in love with her husband. Tr. anon. NY: Street 1892. D. [AC]
10070. do. 1896. Tr. anon. Chic: Laird & Lee. D. [AC]
10071. do. 1896. Tr. anon. Chic: Rand, McNally. D. [AC]
10072. The stolen vail. Tr. Ma. J. Safford. In Hopkins, Seward W. "Two gentlemen of Hawaii." NY: Bonner 1894. 244; 63p. il. 19cm [LC]
10073. do. 1892. [same] Also, The unsigned will, by E. v. Holtz, tr. Mrs. D. M. Lowrey. NY: Bonner. 160p. 18cm. [LC]
*10074. (Um hohen Preis.) No surrender. Tr. Christina Tyrrell. L: Bentley 1879. 3v. 18cm. [This is the best tr.] [BM]
10075. do. 1879. At a high price. Tr. M. S. Smith. Bost: Estes. 12. [Cf. note to #10079.] [AC]
*10076. do. 1881. [same as #10074] New ed. Bentley. 443p. 19cm. [BM]
10077. do. 1883. [same] NY: Munro. Seaside lib. 54p. 32cm. [AC]
10078. do. 1884. [same as #10075] NY: Dodd. 12. [AC]
*10079. do. 1885. [same] NY: Lovell. 384p. 18cm. [Excellent despite some errors.] [LC]
10080. do. 1885. At a high price. Tr. Tyrrell. NY: Munro. Pocket ed. D. [AC]
10081. do? 1890. A heavy reckoning. Tr. anon. L: Bentley. 3v. 19cm. [BM]
*10082. do. 1891. The price he paid. (Tr. Tyrrell.) NY: Street & Smith. 307p. 20cm. [LC]
10083. do. 1896. [same] Chic: Rand, McNally. D. [AC]
10084. do. 1897. [same as #10075] Fenno. D. [AC]
10085. Success, and how he won it. Tr. Christina Tyrrell. L: Bentley 1876. 3v. 18cm. [EC dates this 1877.] [BM]
10086. do. 1877. [same] L;Ed: Bentley. 444p. 8. [BM]
*10087. (Vineta.) Under a charm. Tr. Christian Tyrrell. L: Bentley 1877. 3v. 18cm. [BM]
10088. do. 1877. Vineta, the phantom city. Tr. Fes. A. Shaw. Bost: Estes. 12. [AC]
*10089. do. 1878. [same as #10087] 3d ed. Bentley. [BM]
10090. do. 1882. [same] NY: Munro. Seaside lib. 32cm. [AC]
§10091. do. 1886. [same as #10088] NY: Lovell. 414p. 18cm. [Pruned.] [LC]
10092. do. 1891. [same?] Vineta. NY: Munro. Pocket ed. D. [Cf. #10090. Possibly Tyrrell's tr. with altered title.] [AC]

WERNER, (F: L:) Z: 1768-1823. Sel. in C56;93;469.
*10093. (Der 24. Februar.) The twenty-fourth of Feb: a tragedy... Tr. by Rev. E. Riley. L: Hughes 1844. 60p. 16cm. [Prolog omitted.] [BM]
10094. do. 1903. Tr. W. H. H. Chambers. In C18.
§10095. (Söhne des Tales: Die Kreuzesbrüder.) The brethren of the cross: a dram. poem...Tr. Mrs. Eliz. Lewis. L;NY: Bell 1892. xx; 283p. 21cm. [BM.LC]
*10096. (Söhne des Tales: Die Templer auf Cypern.) The Templars in Cyprus: a dram. poem. Tr. Mrs. Eliz. Lewis. L: Bell 1886. 262p. 18cm. [BM.LC]

WERNER, Z:
10097. (Söhne des Tales.) Sons of the valley. Sel. Tr. anon. (Perhaps by Bates?) 1903. In C18.

WERNER, G: 1607-71. Sel. in C287.

WERNHER, Bruder, 12th cent. Sel. in C88 (ascribed to Wernher v. Tegernsee).

WERTHEIMER, Pl. 1874-1937. Sel. in C28.

WESENDONCK, Mde. 1828-1902. See Wagner, R:, Letters..., #9886. See G. Kobbe, Wagner and his Isolde, #9901.

WESENDONCK, O: See Wagner, R:, Letters..., #9885.

WESSENBERG, Ig. H: K: 1774-1860. Sel. in #6209a.
*10098. (Das Volksleben zu Athen im Zeitalter des Perikles nach griechischen Schriften.) Life in Athens in the time of Pericles. Tr. anon. L: Painter 1844. xxxiii;307p. 17cm. [BM]

"WEST, M." (i.e., Mz. Nitzelberger) and R: Genée.
*10099. (Die Afrikareise.) A trip to A--: operetta by Fz. Suppé. Tr. El. Schwab. Libr. Bost: Hyatt 1884. 32p. 8. [LCM]
*10100. do. 1884. [same] Vocal score. Ger;Engl. Bost: White, Smith. 187p. 4. [LCM]

WETTE, Frau Ade. (Humperdinck) 1858- . Sel. in C487;489.
§10101. (Hänsel und Gretel.) Hänsel and Gretel: a fairy opera in 3 acts by E. Humperdinck. Tr. Constance Bache. Libr. Engl. Elberfeld. S: Lucas. 42p. 19cm. [BM]
§10102. do. 1895. [same tr.] Vocal score. Mayence: Schott. 179p. 4. [LCM]
§10103. do. 1901. [same as #10101] 42p. [BM]
§10104. do. 1905. [same tr.] Libr. Ger;Engl. NY: 34p. 8. [LC]
10105. do. 1909. a fairy opera ad. from the Ger. Tr. Norreys J. O'Conor. Il. Maria L. Kirk. NY: Stokes. 75p. 24cm. [LC.BM]
10106. do. 1910. [same] L: Wells, Gardner & Darton. 75p. 24cm. [BM]
10107. do.[Ad.] Retold by Js. McSpadden. 1925. In C390.

WETTE, W: Mn. Lbt. de, 1780-1849.
10108. (Christliche Sittenlehre.) Human life; or, practical ethics. Tr. S: Osgood. Bost: Munroe; L: J:Green 1842. 2v. xxii;368;xxiii; 409p. 19cm. [LCO.BM]
10109. do. 1856. [same] [LC]
10110. do. 1872-6. [same] Bost: Dennett n.d. 2v. 12. [AC]
10111. (Theodor, oder des Zweiflers Weihe.) Theodore; or, the sceptic's conversion. Hist. of the culture of a protestant clergyman. Tr. Jas. F. Clarke. Bost: Hilliard, Gray 1841. 2v. xlv; 311;xv;422p. 19cm. [LCO.BM]
10112. do. 1856. [same] 2v. 18cm. [LC]
10113. do. 1872-6. [same] Bost: Burnham n.d. 2v. in one. 12. [AC]

WETZEL, Kd. Sel. in C391;393-4;486.

WEULE, K: 1864- .
10113a. (Die Kultur der Kulturlosen. Ein Blick in die Anfänge menschlicher Geistesbetätigung.) The culture of the barbarians: a glimpse in the beginnings of the human mind. Il. after photos. and drawings by K. Reinke. Simpkin 1926. 80p. 8. [EC]
10113b. (Kulturelemente der Menschheit. Anfänge und Urformen der materiellen Kultur.) Cultural elements in mankind: commencements and primitive forms of material culture. Il. after photos. and drawings by K. Reinke. Simpkin 1926. 88p. 8. [EC]
*10114. (Negerleben in Ostafrika.) Native life in East Africa. Tr. Alice Werner. L: Pitman 1909. xxiv;431p. il. 23cm. [BM.LC]
[On the whole, satisfactory.]

WEYDEN, E. Sel. in C466.

WEYL, Hm. 1885- .
10114a. (Raum, Zeit, Materie.) Space - time - matter. Tr. H: L. Brose. Dutton; Methuen 1922. xi;330p. O. [AC]

WICHERT, Ern. 1831-1902.
10115. (Das grüne Tor.) The green gate. Tr. Mrs. A. L. Wister. Phil: Lippincott 1875. 374p. 19cm. [LC]
10116. do. 1906. [same] Lippincott. 374p. (B12) [NY]
*10117. (Der jüngste Bruder.) The youngest brother. Tr. by "Kannida." Chic: Laird & Lee 1891. 291p. 20cm. [Some errors noted.] [LC]

WICKHOFF, Fz. 1853-1909.
10118. Roman art: some of its principles and their application to early Christian painting. Tr. Mrs. S. Art. Strong. L: Heinemann; NY: Macmillan 1900. xiv;198p. il. 32 x 24cm. [BM.LC]

WIDMANN, Js. V: 1842-1911. Sel. in C366(14);423.
10119. Francesca: opera in 3 acts. Orig. Ger. book by Js. V: W--, rewritten by H. Goetz. Tr. Marmaduke Browne. Westminster: Nichols 1908. 48p. 8. [BM]
10120. (Der Widerspenstigen Zähmung.) The taming of the shrew: opera in 4 acts by H. Goetz. Free ad. of Shakespeare's comedy. Tr. J. Troutbeck. Libr. Engl. L: Augener; NY: Schirmer 1878. 63p. Some music. 18cm. [Tr. in verse.] [BM]
*10121. do. 1916. [same?] Tr. anon. Libr. Ger;Engl. NY: Rullman. 59p.[Prose tr., very good, assigned to Troutbeck by LCM.][LCM. BM]
See Dietrich, Ab., joint author, Recoll. of J:s Brahms. #1228.

WIED-NEUWIED, Mx. Ax. Ph. Prinz v. 1782-1867.
*10122. (Reise nach Brasilien.) Travels in Brazil, 1815-7. Pt. 1. Tr. anon. L: Colburn 1820. xi;335p. il. 27cm. [BM]
§10123. do. 1820. Abr. anon. ...Brazil, to which a number of travellers have recently been attracted. In "New voyages and travels," vol. 3. L: Phillips. iv;130p. il. 21cm. [BM]
10124. (Reise in das innere Nord-Amerika.) Travels in the interior of North America, 1832-4. Tr. H. E. Lloyd. L: Ackermann 1843. 520p. il. 32cm. [BM.LC]
10125. do. 1906. [same] Cleveland, O. Clark. 3pts. il. 24cm. [LC.BM] [Early western travels, ed. by R. G. Thwaites.]

WIEDEMANN, Fz.
10126. A day out of the life of a little maiden. (6 poems.) Studies from life (i.e. drawings) by M. Scherer and H. Engler. Text by F. W--. Tr. anon. Dresden: Schwager 1878. 6p. 35cm. [BM] [EC has: L: Low.]

WIEDMANN, Fz.
10127. The treasure-digger. Tr. M.H. Ed: Johnstone & Hunter 1870. 63p. front. 14cm. [BM]

WIEGAND, J:s 1874- .
10128. (Der Fall Henner. ?) The bachelor's will: a comedy in 3 acts. Ad. by Amelia v. Ende. NY: 1910. Tw. [LC]
10129. The last trick: a sea drama in one act. Tr. Amelia v. Ende. NY: 1904. [LC]
10130. (Macht.) Power: a social drama in 4 acts. Ad. by Amelia v. Ende. NY: 1910. Tw. [LC]

WIEGAND, J:s and W: Scharrelmann.
*10131. (Krieg.) The wages of war. Tr. Amelia v. Ende. "Poet-Lore," vol. 19 (1907).

WIELAND, Cph. Mn. 1733-1813. Sel. in C17;88;118;142;158;172;190;192-3;194*;216;309;366*;373;461*;469;530;533*.

WIELAND, Cph. Mn.
*10132. [Coll.] 1775. Dialogues: Araspes and Panthea; or, the effects of love. ("A-- und P--, eine moralische Geschichte in einer Reihe von Unterredungen"). Socrates and Timocles, on apparent and real beauty. Tr. anon. L: Leacroft. 270p. 8. [LCO]
10133. [Coll.] 1795. Phaon; On the liberty and licentiousness of the press; On the liberty of reasoning on matters of belief; (4) Olympic dialogues; An excursion to the realms below. Tr. W: Tooke. In C553.
10134. [Coll.] 1796. Select fairy tales. By the tr. of The sorcerer of the black valley of Weber (i.e., R. Huish?). L: Johnson. 2v. See "Brit. Crit." 9:559. (B26)
10135. [Coll.] 1810. The relig. of Psammis (from his "Danishmend"); Koxkox and Kikequetzel. Ed. (and tr?) by W: Taylor. In C520.
10136. [Coll.] 1829. Dialogues of the dead; The golden mirror ("Der goldene Spiegel"), abr.; Oberon, abr.; "Wintermärchen." Tr. W: Taylor. In C533.
10137. [Coll.] 1849. Sketches and anecdotes. In Schiller's corr. See #8241.
10138. (Der geprüfte Abraham.) The trial of A--. Tr. anon. L: Becket & De Hondt. 8. See "Crit. R." 17(1764):180. (B26)
§10139. do. 1777. [same?] The trial of A--, in four cantos. Tr. anon. Norwich: J: Trumbull. v;60p. 17cm. [BM.NY]
[Prose from verse, not even wholly correct.]
10140. (Der goldene Spiegel.) The golden mirror; or, the kings of Scheschian. Tr. anon. In "The Hibernian mag." 28(1798):1, etc. Also in "Lady's Mag." 29:34, etc. (B26)
§10141. (Die Abderiten, eine sehr wahrscheinliche Geschichte.) The republic of fools: being the hist. of the state and people of Abdera, in Thrace. Tr. H: Christmas. L: Allen 1861. 2v. 19cm.
[Consid. omissions.] [BM.LC]
10142. (Die Abenteuer des don Sylvio von Rosalva, oder der Sieg der Natur über die Schwärmerei.) Reason triumphant over fancy; exemplified in the singular advent. of Don Sylvio de Rosalva. Tr. anon. L: J.Wilkie, S.Leacroft, and C.Heydinger 1773. 3v. 247; 231; 211p. 12. [Data from W. Kurrelmeyer, "MLN" 32(1917):225.]
*10143. do. 1904. [reprint] Advent. of Don Sylvio de R--. Introd. Ern. A. Baker. L: Routledge; NY: Dutton. xxxiii;443p. 21cm.[BM.LC]
[Lacks the wit of the orig.]
§10144. (Die Grazien.) The graces: a class. allegory, interspersed with poetry, and il. by explan. notes. Together with a poet. fragment entitled Psyche among the Graces. Tr. anon. L: Whittaker 1823. 148p. 12. [Prose well done, verse badly. Pref. signed with monogram S. T. Perhaps Sa. (Taylor) Austin?] [BM.LCO]
§10145. (Diogenes v. Sinope.) Socrates out of his senses; or, dialogues of D-- of S--. Tr. Mr. Wintersted. L: Davies. 2v. 115; 134p. front. 15cm. [BM]
§10146. do. 1797. [reprint] Newburgh (NY): Prtd. by D. Denniston. 2v. in one. xvi;105; 119p. 14cm. [LC]
§10147. (Gandalin.) G--; or, love for love. A poem. Tr. F. Hope. L: Longmans 1838. 190p. 19cm. [Good poem, but it falls short of W-'s charm and grace; not enough variety in verse and rhyme.] [BM]
*10148. (Geheime Geschichte des Philosophen Peregrinus Proteus.) Private hist. of Peregrinus Proteus, the philosopher. Tr. anon. L: Johnson 1796. 2v. in 1. 17cm. [LC]
10149. do. 1804. Abr. Confessions in elysium; or, the advent. of a platonic philosopher. Tr. J: B. Elrington. L: Bell. 3v. in one. 17cm.
[Contains long extr. from "Agathon," some 275 pp. in all.] [BM.LCO]
10150. (Geron, der Adelich.) Geron the courteous. Tr. W: Taylor. 1829. In C533.

WIELAND, Cph. Mn.
§10151. (Geschichte des Agathon.) The hist. of A--. Tr. anon. L: Cadell 1773. 4v. 18cm. [BM.LC]
[Tr...with pref. by the translator, i.e., Justamond? See K: H: Jördens 5:355, and Kurrelmeyer, "MLN" 32:226.]
10152. do. 1804. [extr.] In #10149.
§10153. (Göttergespräche.) Dialogues of the gods. Tr. W: Taylor. L: Johnson 1795. 181p. 18cm. [LC]
Henrietta of Gerstenfeld. Wrongly ascribed to W--; really by Am. Beuvius, q.v.
*10154. (Krates und Hipparchia.) Crates and H--: a tale. Tr. C. R. Coke. L: Longmans 1823. xii;132p. 17cm. [BM]
[On the whole, excellent.]
*10155. (Oberon.) O--. Tr. W: Sotheby. L: Cadell & D. 1798. 2v. in one. 206; 234p. 18cm. [BM]
[Does not retain fem. rhymes, otherwise excellent.]
*10156. do. 1805. [same] 2d ed. Cadell & D. 2v. 203; 229p. 16cm. [BM]
[12 pl. after H. Fuseli, engr. by diff. hands.]
*10157. do. 1805. [same] 2d ed. Cadell & D. 2v. 203; 229p. 23cm. [BM]
[No plates. Same letter press and paging as the foregoing, large paper ed.]
*10158. do. 1810. [same] 1st Amer. from 3d Lond. ed. Newport (R.I.) Rousmaniere; Bost: Belcher. 2v. 203; 231p. 17cm. [LC]
*10159. do. 1826. [same] 3d ed. L: Murray. 2v. 203; 229p. 16cm. [BM.LCO]
*10160. do. 1844. [same] L: Clarke. viii;299p. 13cm. [BM]
10161. do. [Ad.] 1816. Oberon's oath; or, the palladin of the princess. A melo-dram. romance in two acts. Ad. B: Thompson. with biogr. memoir of the author. L: Miller. 41p. 21cm. [Memoir, pp. 1-14.] [BM]
10162. do. [Ad.] 1826. Oberon; or, the charmed horn. Ad. T: Cooke. L: Tabby. 46p. 8. [NY]
Ad. by Planché (Weber's opera) not included.
10163. Prelim. notice to Musaeus' "Volksmärchen." Tr. anon. 1845. In #6630.
10164. (Sympathieen.) The sympathy of souls. Attempted from the French and rev. after the orig. German, by F. A. Winzer. L: Bladon. ca. 1787. See "Crit. R." 64(1787):394. (B26)
10165. do. 1795. [same] L: Prtd. for the editor. xii;191p. 18cm. [BM]
[Tr. says he received copy of German ed. too late for a minute revision...in some instances...he finds it impossible to render fully the elegance of the orig.]
See Schiller, Corr. with Koerner, #8241.

WIESENMAYER, Burckard, fl. 1635-45. Sel. in C232.

WIGGERS, Gst. F:
10166. (Sokrates als Mensch, als Bürger und als Philosoph.) Life of S-- (abr.), tr. anon., and Schleiermacher, On the worth of S--, tr. by Rev. Connop Thirlwall. L: Taylor & Walton 1860. cxv. p. 18cm. [BM]

WILBRANDT, Ad. v. 1837-1911.
10167. (Arria und Messalina.) Messalina: an improved trag. in 5 acts. Tr. and ad. anon. NY: (Copyright P. Salisbury.) 1877. (B38)
*10168. (Der Lotsenkommandeur.) The pilot captain. Tr. anon. 1890. In C404.
10169. (Der Meister v. Palmyra.) The master of P--: a drama in 5 acts. Tr. C: Gordon. Brooklyn: Copyright Blanche Walsh. 1899. (B38)
†10170. do. 1901. Tr. Harriott S. Olive. In "Poet-Lore," vol. 13 (1901). [Knows no German.]
10171. do. 1904. The love of life. Ad...by E. Cayley. Hamburg: Copyright by Lillie Cayley Robinson. (B38)

WILBRANDT, Ad. v.--Der Meister v. Palmyra
10172. do. 1909. Tr. Blanco and Guido Marburg. [NY.LC]
*10173. do. 1913-15. Tr. C: W. Stork. In C154(16).
*10174. (Die Osterinsel.) A new humanity; or, the Easter Island. Tr. Dr. A. S. Rappoport. L: Maclaren 1905. viii;360p. 19cm. [BM]
10175. (Die Tochter des Herrn Fabricius.) The daughter of F--: a drama in 4 acts. Tr. Ludmilla Krueger. Alameda, Cal: Copyright Marian F. Delanoy. 1898. (B38)
§10176. (Fridolins heimliche Ehe.) F--'s mystical marriage: a study of an original, founded on the reminisc. of a friend. Tr. Ca. Bell. NY: Gottsberger 1884. 241p. 16cm. [LC]
10177. Thusnelda: a drama in one act. Tr. Deborah K. Janowitz. NY: 1911. Tw. [LC]

WILBRANDT, Cd.
*10178. (Des Herrn F: Osts Erlebnisse...) Mr. East's experiences in Mr. Bellamy's world. Tr. Ma. J. Safford. NY: Harper 1891. 255p. 21cm. [LC.BM]

WILD, F: K: d. 1869.
10179. The valley mill; or, extract from the diary of a Ger. tradesman. Tr. Joel Swartz. Phil: Luth. bd. 1871. 227p. 16. [LCO]

WILD, H: Sel. in C169.

WILDENBRUCH, (Am.) Ern. v. 1845-1900. Sel. in C422.
*10180. (Claudias Garten.) Claudia's garden. Tr. H. T. P(orter), Cte. Porter, and Helen A. Clarke. In "Poet-Lore," vol. 8(1896).
§10181. (Das edle Blut.) Noble blood: a Prussian cadet story. Tr. C: King and Anne W. Ward. (Also, A West Point parallel, by C: King.) NY: Neely 1896. 211p. 16cm. [LC]
§10182. do. 1907. Good blood. Tr. anon. In C447.
*10183. do. 1910. A story of cadet life. Tr. W. D. Lowe. In #9320, pp. 85-135. [Rather free, but very good.]
*10184. do. 1913-15. Noble blood. Tr. Muriel Almon. In C154(17).
§10185. do. 1915. [same as #10182] Tr. anon. In C179.
§10186. (Das Hexenlied.) The witchsong. Tr. C. S. Cole. NY: 1916. 16p. 19cm. [LC]
10187. (Das Märchen von den zwei Rosen.) The tale of two roses. Tr. Kath. W. Evans. NY: Pott 1895. 32p. 18cm. [LC]
§10188. (Der Letzte.) The captain's last child. Tr. Marg. C. Wirtz. Chic: Donohue 1909. 62p. 18 x 14cm. [LC]
10189. (Der Meister v. Tanagra.) The master of T--: a sculptor's story of ancient Greece. Tr. M. Baroness v. Lauer. Westermann 1886. [AC] --L: Grevel. 8. [EC]
10190. do. 1887. [same] L: Grevel. New ed. [EC]
*10191. (Die Danaide.) The Danaid: an episode from the Franco-German war. Tr. Bertha Young. L: Simpkin 1902. 61p. 18cm. [BM]
10192. (Die Haubenlerche.) The bird in the cage. Ad. by Clyde Fitch. (B38)
*10193. (Die Rabensteinerin.) Barseba of Rabenstein. Tr. R: v. Appiano and W: Nobbe. St.L: Prtd. by Frederick. ca. 1909. 49p. 19cm. [LC]
†10194. (Francesca von Rimini.) F-- da R--. Tr. "Kannida." Chic: Laird & Lee 1891. 300p. 20cm. [Slovenly.] [LC]
*10195. (Harold.) H--. Tr. O: Heller, done into Engl. verse by Hugh A. Clarke. In "Poet-Lore," vol. 3(1891). [On the whole, excellent.]
10196. do. 1891. H--: a play in 5 acts. Tr. anon. Phil;L: 16. [EC]
10197. The inner life of the second-class cab-driver. Tr. H. Müller-Casenov. 1909. In C422.
§10198. (König H:) King Henry: a drama in 4 acts with a prologue. Tr. Rb. M. Wernaer. In "The Drama," vol. 5 (1915). [He fails to get the archaic effect and makes errors.]

WILDENBRUCH, Ern. v.--König H:
10199. do. 1913-15. [same] In C154(17). [Probably revised for this ed]
*10200. (Neid.) Envy. Author. tr. Elise Traut. Bost: Four seas 1921. 144p. 19cm. [Needless deviations, but born of desire to be faithful; general spirit is excellent.] [LC]

WILDENHAHN, K: A: 1805-68.
10201. (Hans Sachs. Einer Familiensage nacherzählt.) Hs. Sachs: a family trad. retold. Tr. H. R. Krauth. Easton, Pa: Riegel 1881. 321p. 12. [AC has: Phil: Smith 1881.] [LCO]
10202. (J. Arndt. Ein Zeitbild.) J: Arndt: a historical life-picture. Tr. C. F. Welden. Ed. J. K. Shryock. Easton, Pa: Riegel 1882. 519p. 12. [AC has: Phil: Smith 1882.] [LCO]
10203. (Mn. Luther.) The blind girl of Wittenberg: a life-picture of the times of L--. Tr. J: G. Morris. Phil: Lindsay & B. 1856. 30p. 19cm. [First part of the orig.] [LC]
10204. do. 1876. [same] New ed. NY: Dodd. [AC]
10205. do. 1882. Mn. L--: a histor. life-picture. Tr. G. T. Spieker. Easton, Pa: Riegel 1882. 434p. 12. [LCO]
[Probably a tr. of the whole work.]
10206. (Mn. Luther: Der Tag zu Augsburg.) The diet of A--. a histor. life-picture. Tr. J: G. Morris. Phil: Smith 1880. 419p. 19cm. [LC]
10207. do. 1881. [same] Easton, Pa: Riegel. [LCO]
10208. Pastor and prince: a sequel to Pl. Gerhardt. New ed. L: Knight 1861. 12. [EC]
§10209. (Pl. Gerhardt.) Pl. G--: an histor. tale of the Lutherans and Reformed in Brandenburg under the Great Elector. Tr. Mrs. Stanley Carr. L: Knight 1847. 2v. in one. xviii;264; 270p. 19cm. [Too free, liberties taken.] [BM]
§10210. do. 1854. [same] [New t.ps.; otherwise identical.] [BM]
10211. do. 1861. [same] New ed. Knight. [EC]
10212. do. 1881. Pl. G--: a histor. life-picture. Tr. G. A. Wenzel. Ed. J. K. Shryock. Easton, Pa: Riegel. 553p. 12. [LCO]
[AC has: Phil: Smith.]
10213. (Ph. Jk. Spener.) Ph. Jk. Spener: a histor. life-picture. Tr. G. A. Wenzel. Easton, Pa: Riegel 1881. 468p. 12. [LC]
10214. (Vollbrechts Wallfahrt.) The pilgrimage; or, rationalism in the bud, the blade, and the ear. A tale for our times. Tr. Mrs. Stanley Carr. Ed: Oliver & Boyd 1847. 404p. 19cm. [BM]

WILDERMUTH, Ote. Rooschütz, 1817-77.
*10215. [Coll.] 1865. By daylight ("Im Tageslicht"); or, pict. from real life. Tr. and ed. by Anne Pratt. L: Routledge. viii;437p. il. 16cm. [BM]
[Excellent tr. Engl. ed. does not include all of the orig. --The cheerful spirit; The proud heart; Herr Wezler and his wife ("Herr Welzer und seine Frau"); Re-union ("Wiedersehen"); The good granny; The stranger; In front of the last house ("Vor dem letzten Haus"); Old Jenny; Eugenie (do.).]
10216. [Coll.] 1865. Stories for the little folks. Tr. anon. Bost: Dutton. 16. [AC]
10217. [Coll.] 1866. [same?] Ottilie's stories for the little folks. Tr. anon. Bost: Dutton. 16. [AC]
10218. [Coll.] 1872. Household stories. Tr. Eleanor Kinmont. Cincin: Hitchcock & Walden; NY: Nelson & Phillips. 4v. il. 18cm. [Dwarf's mirror, etc. Cherubino and Seraphina, etc. Emma's pilgrimage, etc. Little brother and sister.] [LC]
10219. [Coll.] 1872-6. [same] Cincin: Method. book concern n.d. 4v. il. 16. [AC]
§10220. (Bärbeles Weihnachten.) Barbara's Christmas. Tr. anon. L: S.P.C.K. 1873. 32p. front. 14cm. [Free and incorrect.] [BM]

WILDERMUTH, Ote. Rooschütz.
§10221. (Der Sandbub, oder wer hat's am besten?) The little sand boy; or, who is best off? Tr. anon. Ed: Oliphant 1877. 63p. col. front. 16cm. [BM]
§10222. (Die Ferien auf Schloss Bärenburg.) The holidays at Barenburg [sic] castle. Tr. Ma. Howitt. 1861. In C211, pp. 281-317. [Not wholly accurate. Spelling Bärenburg used in title of story.]
§10223. do. 1865. Midsummer holidays at Castle B--. Tr. anon. L: S.P.C.K. 64p. front. 14cm. [BM]
10224. do. 1866? [same as #10222] In Cassell's story books for the young. 1866, etc. pp. 67-103. il. 17cm. [BM]
10224a. (Eine Königin.) A queen: a story for girls. Tr. Anna B. Cooke. Genl. Prot. Episc. S. S. U. 1864. See "Nat. Quart. Rev." 10:201. (B15a)
10225. do. 1865.[same] Bost: Dutton. 123p. 16. (B15a) [LCO]
§10226. do. 1868. [same?] L: Warne. 123p. Col. front. and t.p. 14cm. [Padded, inaccurate.] [BM]
10227. do. 1871. [same] L: Warne. 18. [EC]
10228. Leon and Zephie; or, the little wanderers. Tr. Anna B. Cooke. Bost: Dutton 1865. 120p. 18. [LCO]
10229. The little dwarf's mirror. Tr. A. L. G. 1878. In C147.
10230. (Margaretens Silvesterabend.) Nurse Margaret's two St. Sylvester's eves: a tale. L: S.P.C.K. 1871. 79p. 15cm. [BM]

WILDONJE. See Herrand v. Wildonje.

WILHELM I, Deutscher Kaiser, 1797-1888.
§10231. The corr. of W: I and Bismarck, with other letters from and to Prince Bismarck. Tr. J. A. Ford. NY: Stokes 1903. 2v. il. 23cm. [Some errors.] [LC.BM]
§10232. do. 1915. [same] Pop. ed. L: Heinemann. xxx;237p. [BM]
*10233. Wit and wisdom. Tr. Julie Liebe. L: Ward & D. 1888. 96p. 18cm. [Seems excellent.] [BM]
See Harden, Mx., Word portraits, #3699.
See Sybel, H: v., The founding of the Ger. empire..., #9317.

WILHELM II, Deutscher Kaiser, 1859- . Sel. in C161.
10234.[Sel.] 1907. Words of W: II, being 39 articles sel. from his sayings by P. L. L: Burns & Oates. 19cm. [BM]
10235. [Sel.] 1914. The war lord: a character study...by means of his speeches, letters, and telegrams. Compiled by J. M. Kennedy. L: Palmer. 96p. 16cm. [BM.LC]
10236. [Sel.] 1914. The Kaiser in his own words. Tr. anon. NY: Doubleday. il. [AC]
*10237. [Sel.] 1915. The Ger. emperor as shown in his public utterances. Tr. C. F. Gauss. NY: Scribner. xvi;329p. 19cm. [LC.BM] [Each item complete.]
10238. (Erinnerungen und Gestalten...1878-1918.) The Kaiser's memoirs...1888-1918. Tr. R: R. Ybarra. NY;L: Harper 1922. 365p. 22cm. [LC]
*10239. do. 1922. My memoirs, 1878-1918. L;NY: Cassell. 348p. 24cm. [BM.LC]
10240. The Kaiser vs. Bismarck: suppressed letters...and new chaps. from the autobiog. of the iron chancellor. Tr. Bernard Miall. NY; L: Harper 1921. xxi;202p. il. 22cm. [LC.BM]
10241. do. 1921. New chaps. of Bismarck's autobiog. L: Hodder & S. 343p. 22cm. [LC]
10242. My early life (?Aus meinem Leben, 1859-88.) Tr. anon. NY: Doran 1926. 353p. il. 22cm. [LC]
10243. do. 1926. [same?] Tr. anon. L: Methuen. xiv;346p. 40 il. col. front. [BM]
10244. My ideas and ideals. Tr. anon. Bost: Luce 1914. 96p. 20cm. [Paging suggests identity with #10235.] [LC]

WILHELM II
*10245. Speeches, forming a character portrait. Tr. and ed. Wolf v. Schierbrand. NY;L: Harper 1903. 332p. 23cm. [LC]
[Virtually a tr. of Klaussmann's compilation.]
*10246. Speeches...a sel. from...speeches, edicts, letters, and telegrams. Tr. L: Elkind. L;NY;Bombay: Longmans 1904. 335p. 22cm. [BM.LC]
[Tr. of Klaussmann's compilation.]
10247. Speeches. Tr. E. v. Mach. 1913-15. In C154(15).
10248. (Vergleichende Geschichtstabellen.) Comparative hist., 1878-1914. Tr. F: A. Holt. L: Hutchinson 1922. 190p. il. 22cm. [LC]
See Fried, A. H., The Ger. emperor and the peace of the world, #1959.
See Harden, Mx., Word portraits, #3699.
See Ludwig, El., Kaiser W: II, #5915.
See Vollmar, G:, Socialism and the German Kaiser, #9567.

WILHELM, Kronprinz v. Preussen, 1882- . Sel. in C161.
*10249. (Aus meinem Jagdtagebuch.) From my hunting day-book. Tr. J. E. Hodder Williams. NY;L: Hodder & S. 1912. xv;131p. il. 20cm. [BM.LC]
[Excellent tr.]
*10250. (Erinnerungen des Kronprinzen W:) Memoirs. Tr. anon. NY: Scribner's 1922. vi;375p. il. 22cm. [LC]
*10251. do. 1922. [same] L: Butterworth. 299p. il. 22cm. [BM.LC]
*10252. (Ich suche die Wahrheit.) I seek the truth:...responsibility for the war. Tr. Ralph Butler. L: Faber & Gwyer 1926. xvi;325p. 23cm. [BM.LC]
*10253. do. 1926. [same] NY: Sears. xvi;352p. 22cm. [LC]
*10254. (Meine Erinnerungen.) My war experiences. Tr. anon. L: Hurst & B. 1922. viii;363p. il. 23cm. [BM.LC]
[On the whole, excellent. AC has: NY: McBride 1923. 364p.]

WILHELM II, Herzog v. Sachsen-Weimar, 1598-1662. Sel. in C269;271.

WILHELM, Jl.
10255. (Brüderlein fein.) Darby and Joan: operetta in one act by Leo Fall. Ad. Art. Anderson. Vocal score. L: Enoch 1912. 43p.28cm.[BMM]

WILHELM, Jl. and Fritz Grünbaum.
10256. (Der Zigeunerprimás.) Sari: operetta in two acts by E. Kálmán. Ad. by C. C. S. Cushing and E. P. Heath. Vocal score. Engl. NY: Stern 1914. 122p. 28cm. [LCM.BMM]
10257. do. 1914. [same] Libr. Toronto: Solman. 57p. 23cm. [BM]

WILHELM, Jl. and A. M. Willner.
§10258. (Die Sprudelfee.) The spring maid: operetta in two acts by H: Reinhardt. Tr. Harry B. and Rb. B. Smith. Vocal score. NY: Stern 1910. 151p. 28cm. [Fairly close.] [LCM.BMM]

WILHELM, R: 1873-1930.
10259. The Chinese conception of marriage. Tr. 1926. In C308.

"WILHELMI, Ax." (i.e., Ax. V: Zechmeister, 1817-77).
§10260. (Einer muss heiraten!) One of you must marry. Ad. anon. L: Lacy 1866. (Acting ed. of plays, vol. 71.) 20p. 18cm.
[Wooden. Name spelled Wilhelme.]
10261. do. 1879. One must marry! A comedy in one act. Tr. C. W. Ritch. NY: Happy hours co. 18p. 12. [LCO]
10262. do. 1879. Roorbach. 12. [AC]

WILHELMINE V. BAYREUTH. See "F:e So. W:e."

WILHELMINE VON GRAEVENITZ
?10263. A Ger. Pompadour: being an extraord. hist. of W:e v. G--, Landhofmeisterin of Wirtemberg. A narr. of the 18th cent. By Ag. B. M. Hay. NY: Scribner 1909. 358p. 22cm. [LC]
[Not a tr., but a pieced-out narr., partly imaginative.]

WILLAMOW, J: Jk. 1736-77. Sel. in C125.

WILLIBALD, ca. 700-81.
*10264. The life of St. Boniface. Tr. G: W. Robinson. Cambridge, Mass: Harvard univ. press; L: Oxf. univ. press 1916. 114p. 21cm. [LC.BM]

WILLNER, Af. M. d. 1929. Operettas: See Stein, Leo, joint author. See Wilhelm, Jl., joint author.
*10265. (Das Heimchen am Herd.) The cricket on the hearth: opera in 3 acts by C: Goldmark. Text ad. from C: Dickens. tr. Percy Pinkerton. Libr. Engl. L: Ascherberg 1900. 26p. 20cm. [BM]
*10266. do. 1912. Tr. C: H: Meltzer. Libr. Ger;Engl. NY: Rullman. 37p. 8. [LCM]

WILLNER, A. M. and Rb. Bodanzky.
10267. (Der Graf v. Luxemburg.) The count of Luxembourg: operetta in 2 acts by Fz. Lehár. [Ad.] by Basil Hood. Vocal score. Engl. L: Chappell 1911. 179p. 28cm. [BMM.LCM]
10268. do. 1911. [same] Lyrics by Basil Hood and Adrian Ross. Libr. Engl. L: Chappell. 31p. 21cm. [No dialog given.] [BM.LCM]
10268a. do. 1911. Ad. The novel of the play. By Harold Simpson. L: Mills & Boon. 18cm. [BM]
10268b. (Zigeunerliebe.) Gipsy love: operetta in 3 acts by Fz. Lehár. Ad. Harry B. Smith. Vocal score. L: Chappell 1911. 157p. 28cm. [LCM]
10268c. do. 1912. Tr. Basil Hood. Vocal score. Engl. L: Chappell. 210p. 28cm. [LCM]
10268d. do. 1912. [same] Libr. (Book of lyrics.) Lyrics by Adrian Ross. L: Chappell. 34p. 21cm. [No dialog given.] [BM.LCM]
§10268e. (Baron Trenck.) The Pandour: operetta in 3 acts by Fx. Albini. Tr. F: F. Schrader. Vocal score. NY: Remick 1911. 188p. fol. [LCM]
[Very free; really a rewriting. Ascribed to A. H. Willner.]

WILLNER, A. M., Rb. Bodanzky, and E. Spero.
10269. Eva: operetta in three acts by Fz. Lehár. Tr. Glen Macdonough. Vocal score. Engl. NY: Schirmer 1912. 125p. fol. [LCM]

WILLNER, A. M., Rb. Bodanzky, and A. M. Weikone.
10270. (Endlich allein.) Alone at last: operetta in 3 acts by Fz. Lehár. Tr. Mt. Woodward, Edg. Smith, and Js. Herbert. Libr. Engl. NY: Karczag 1916. 17p. 8. [No dialog given.] [LCM]

WILLNER, A. M. and F. Grünbaum.
10271. (Die Dollarprinzessin.) The dollar princess: operetta in 3 acts by Leo Fall. Ad. Basil Hood. Vocal score. Engl. L: Ascherberg, Hopwood & Crew 1909. 204p. 28cm. [BMM.LCM]
10272. do. 1909. [Ad.] The dollar princess: the novel of the play. By Harold Simpson. L: Mills & Boon. 18cm. [BM]

WILLNER, A. M. and Heinz Reichert.
10273. (Das Dreimäderlhaus.) Lilac-time: operetta, partly based on "Schwammerl" by Rd. Hs. Bartsch. Music after Fz. Schubert. Ad. by Adrian Ross. Vocal score. Engl. L: Chappell 1922. 122p. 28cm. [LCM]

WILSING, H:
*10274. (R: Wagner: Die Meistersinger von Nürnberg.) R: Wagner: The mastersingers of Nuremberg. A guide to the music and the drama. Tr. Carl Armbruster. L: Schott 1892. 68p. some music. 8. [BM]

WINCKELMANN, J: Jm. 1717-68. Sel. in C287.
10275. Description of Apollo Belvedere. Tr. Mrs. Ella Morgan. 1873. In C300(3).
10276. Essay on the Laokoön; Remarks on the torso of Hercules. Tr. T: Davidson. 1872. In C399(2).

WINCKELMANN, J: Jm.
†10277. (Gedanken über die Malerei und Bildhauerkunst der Griechen.) Reflections on the paintings and sculpture of the Greeks. Tr. H: Fusseli. L: Prtd. for the tr. Sold by A. Millar 1765. 287p. 20cm. [BM]
[Very bad translation: he omits and alters at will. --Seven letters on the above; A letter containing objections to the foregoing reflections; An account of a mummy in the Royal cabinet of antiquities at Dresden; An answer to the foregoing letter, and a further explication of the subject; Instructions for the connoisseur on grace.]
†10278. (Gedanken über die Nachahmung der griechischen Werke in der Malerei und Bildhauerkunst.) Reflections concerning the imitation of the Grecian artists in painting and sculpture, in a series of letters. Glasgow: R. Urie 1766. 158p. 17cm. [BM]
[Almost as bad as the foregoing: ruthless omissions. Seven letters; he includes instructions for the connoisseur, and an Essay on grace in works of art.]
*10279. (Geschichte der Kunst des Altertums.) The hist. of ancient art. Tr. G. H: Lodge. B: Osgood 1849-73. 4v. il. 26cm. [LC]
*10280. do. 1850. Hist. of ancient art among the Greeks. Tr. G. H: Lodge. L: Chapman. xx;254p. 22cm. [BM]
[Only one part of the orig.; this is a reprint of an earlier Amer. ed., apparently not the same as the foregoing; date unknown to me.]
10281. do. 1852. [same] [EC]
*10282. do. 1856. [same] Bost: Little, Brown. 2v. xi;459;ix;270p. 25cm. [Books I-V. Vol. 2. of LC copy has imprint: Munroe 1849] [LC.BM]
*10283. do. 1880. [same] Bost: Osgood. 4v. il. 31cm. [LC]
*10284. do. 1880. [same] Bost: Osgood. 4v. in 2. xvi;491;xx;507p. 22cm. [BM]
*10285. do. 1881. [same] L: Low. [BM]
[Ident. with foregoing except for t.ps.]

WINDELBAND, W: 1848-1915.
*10286. (Einleitung in die Philosophie.) Introd. to philos. Tr. Js. McCabe. L: Unwin 1921. 365p. 22cm. [BM]
[Some things not quite right.]
*10287. do. 1923. [same] [LC]
*10288. (Geschichte der alten Philosophie.) Hist. of ancient philos. Tr. from 2d Ger. ed. by H. E. Cushman. NY: Scribner 1899. 393p. 21cm. [LC]
*10289. do. 1900. [same] L: Low. xv;393p. [BM]
*10290. (Geschichte der Philosophie.) A hist. of philos. with spec. ref. to the formation and devel. of its problems and conceptions. Tr. Jas. H. Tufts. NY;L: Macmillan 1893. 640p. 23cm. [LC.BM]
[BM has: xiii;659p.]
*10291. do. 1901. [same] 2d rev. and enl. ed. 726p. [LC]

WINKELRIED, Arn. v., d. 1386. See Hoecker, Gst., A. of W--, the hero of Sempach, #4364. See also Winkelried, A579. See Voelcker, K. H. W., W--, a tragedy, #9550.

WINKELMANN, F: d. ca. 1807. Sel. in C287.

WINKLER, J: H:
†10292. (Anfangsgründe der Physik.) Elements of natural philos. Tr. from 2d ed. anon. L: Linde. 1758. 2v. 8. See "Monthly R." 18 (1758):28. (B26)
[The tr. "seems to have been done by a person unacquainted...with the Engl. lang....and with the terms of philos."]

WINKLER, J: Js. 1670-1722. Sel. in C222-3;276.

WINLI, 13th cent. Sel. in C310.

"WINTER, Ame." (i.e., Ame. v. Salbach, afterwards v. Gross).
10293. Michaelo and the twins: a tale. Binns & G. 1851. 16. [EC]
10294. A simple tale of love. Tr. anon. 189- . In C156.

WINTER, P: v. 1754-1825. The oracle: opera. See Fz. X. Huber.

WINTERFELD, Ad. (W: Ern.) v. 1824-88.
10295. (Ein bedeutender Mensch.) A distinguished man: a humorous romance. Tr. W. Laird-Clowes. L;Ed: Paul 1879. 3v. 281;256;260p. 19cm. [BM]
10296. The matrimonial agent of Potsdam. A humoro-social romance. Tr. "El Rapha" (H: Raphael). NY: Knox 1887. 479p. 18cm. [LC]
10297. do. 1890. [same] NY: Worthington. 478p. (B12) [NY]

WISLIZENUS, F: Ad. 1810-89.
*10298. (Ein Ausflug nach den Felsen-Gebirgen...) A journey to the Rocky Mts. in the year 1839. Tr. F: A. Wislizenus. St.L: Missouri hist. soc. 1912. 162p. port. 22cm. [Has a sketch of his life, 13p.] [LC]

WISSMANN, Hm. v. 1853-1905.
*10299. (Meine zweite Durchquerung...Afrikas.) My second journey through equatorial Africa...1886-7. Tr. Minna J. A. Bergmann. L: Chatto & W. 1891. xiv;326p. il. 22cm. [BM.LC]

WITKOWSKI, G: 1863- .
§10300. (Das deutsche Drama des 19. Jahrhunderts.) The Ger. drama of the 19th cent. Tr. L. E. Horning. NY: Holt 1909. x;230p. 19cm. [Serious errors.] [LC.BM]

WITT, K: 1815-91.
10301. (Der trojanische Krieg und die Heimkehr des Odysseus.) The Trojan war. Tr. Fes. Younghusband. Pref. W. G. Rutherford. L: Longmans 1884. v;102p. 17cm. [BM]
10302. do. 1885. [same] The wanderings of Ulysses: sequel to the Trojan war. Tr. Fes. Younghusband. L: Longmans, Green. x;242p. 18cm. [BM]
10303. do? 1891. Tales of Troy. Tr. and ad. C: De Garmo. Bloomington, Ill: Public school pub. 68p. il. 17cm. [LC]
10304. (Griechische Götter- und Heldengeschichten.) Classic mythol. Tr. Fes. Younghusband. NY: Holt 1883. 268p. 19cm. [LC]
*10305. do. 1883. [same] Myths of Hellas; or, Greek tales. Tr. Fes. Younghusband. Pref. by A. Sidgwick. L: Longmans. xiv;268p. front. 18cm. [Simplicity of style well retained.] [BM]
10306. The retreat of the 10,000. Tr. Fes. Younghusband. Pref. H. G. Dakyns. L: Longmans 1891. xiv;191p. il. 19cm. [BM]

WITTE, El.
10307. (Aus einer deutschen Botschaft.) Revelations of a Ger. attaché: ten years of German-American diplomacy. Tr. Flor. C. Taylor. NY: Doran 1916. 264p. 20cm. [LC]

WITTE, K: (H: Gf.) 1767-1845. Sel. in C438.
*10308. (K: Witte, oder Erziehungs- und Bildungsgeschichte desselben.) The educ. of K: W--; or, the training of the child. Tr. Leo Wiener. NY: Crowell; L: Harrap 1914. xl;312p. 20cm. [LC.BM] [Long introd. by the tr.]

WITTELS, Fritz.
10309. (Die Vernichtung der Not.) An end to poverty. Tr. Eden and Cedar Paul. L: Allen & Unwin 1925. 223p. 19cm. [BM.LC]
10310. (Der Juwelier von Bagdad.) The jeweller of Bagdad. Tr. F: H. Martens. L: Cape 1927. 192p. 20cm. [BM]
--NY: Doubleday 1927. 228p. il. D. [AC]

WITTELS, Fritz.
10311. Sigmund Freud: his personality, his teaching, and his school. Tr. Eden and Cedar Paul. L: Allen & Unwin; NY: Dodd & Mead 1924. 287p. port. 22cm. [BM.LC]

WITTENBAUER, Fd. 1857-1922.
10312. (Filia hospitalis.) Filia hospitalis. Tr. Prof. Farr. New Haven, Ct: Yale dram. assoc. 1909. (B38)

WITTIG, L. Sel. in C301.

WITTKOWSKY, C:
*10313. (Boabdil, der letzte Maurenkönig.) B--, the last of the Moorish kings: opera by Mz. Moszkowski. Tr. Helen D. Tretbar. Libr. with music. NY: Tretbar 1893. 36p. 25cm. [LCM]

WITTMANN, Hg. 1839?- and Jl. Bauer.
10314. Child of fortune: comic opera in 3 acts by Millöcker. Tr. H. F. Tretbar. Vocal gems. NY: Pond 1892. 40p. fol. [LCM]
10315. (Der arme Jonathan.) Poor Jonathan: operetta in 3 acts by Millöcker. Tr. Ambrose Davenport. Vocal gems. Bost: White-Smith 1891. 34p. fol. [LCM]
10316. do. 1891. Tr. J: P. Jackson and Ralph A. Weill. Vocal gems. NY: Pond. 40p. 4. [LCM]
10317. do. 1900? Ad. C. H. E. Brookfield. Lyrics by Harry Greenbank. Libr. L: Prince of Wales theatre. 48p. 21cm. [BM]
10318. (Der Hofnarr.) The king's fool: comic opera in 3 acts by Ad. Müller. Tr. anon. Libr. NY: Copyright by H: Conried, 1888. Prtd. by Pusey. n.p. 8 leaves. [LCM]

WITTMANN, Hg. and Als. Wohlmuth.
*10319. (Der Feldprediger.) The black hussar: operetta in 3 acts by Millöcker. Tr. Sydney Rosenfeld. Libr. NY: Brentano 1885. 51p. 16. [Close and good, clever.] [LCM]
10320. do. 1886. Tr. G. E. Jackson. Vocal gems. Bost: Evans. n.p. fol. [LCM]

WITZEL, ---. Sel. in C67.

WITZLEBEN, K: A: F: v. 1773-1839. See "A. v. Tromlitz"

WITZSTAEDT, Hs. 16th cent. Sel. in C244.

WOBESER, W:e K:e v.
10320a. (Elisa, oder das Weib, wie es sein sollte.) Eliza; or, the pattern of women. A moral romance. Tr. from the Ger. of Ma. Regina Roche [sic]. Lancaster, Pa: Hutter 1802. 178p. 17cm. [LC] [Book published anonymously.]

WOELFFLIN, H. 1864- .
*10321. (Die klassische Kunst in der italienischen Renaissance. Eine Einführung.) The art of the Italian renaissance: a handbook for students and travelers. Tr. anon. Pref. note by Sir W. Armstrong. L: Heinemann; NY: Putnam 1903. xv;290p. il. 23cm. [Very good.] [BM.LC]
*10322. do. n.d. New ed. xvii;436p. il. 16cm. [AC has: new rev. ed. 1913.] [LC]
10323. do. 1926. Putnam. xvii;436p. [AC]

WOERMANN, K: 1844- . ~~Sel. in C102.~~ See Woltmann, Af., joint author.

WOHLBRUECK, W: A:
§10324. (Der Templer und die Jüdin.) The templar and the Jewess: opera in 3 acts by H. Marschner. Text after W. Scott's "Ivanhoe." Now performing at the Theatre-Royal, Drury Lane. Tr. anon. Libr. Ger;Engl. L: Schloss 1842? 69p. 17cm. [Line for line, unrhymed and unmetered.] [BM]

WOHLMUTH, Als. 1849- . See Wittmann, Hg., joint author.

WOLF, J: W: 1817-55, and W: v. Ploennies.
§10325. (Deutsche Hausmärchen.) Fairy tales, coll. in the Odenwald by J. W. W. Ed. with pref. by K. R. H. Mackenzie. L;NY: Routledge 1855. x;337p. 17cm. [BM]
[This has Wolff on cover and back, not on t.p. 46 stories out of original 51, 12 written by Ploennies. He says: "In the ad...for Engl. Children, I have attempted to throw mod. Engl. lights upon these wild old stories." The rendering is fairly close, however, only it prettifies and pads.]
10326. do. 1856. (2) Fairy ballads...rendered into Engl. verse by R. O. C. L: Bell & Daldy. viii;115p. 12cm. [BM]
["An attempt to versify two stories" (from the foregoing). --The fisher-boy and the two horses; The golden kingdom.]

WOLFERSDORFF, Elise, Freiin v., 1846-1921. See "C. Berkow."

WOLFF, Cn. Freiherr v. 1769-1754.
10327. (Vernünftige Gedanken...) Logic; or, rational thoughts on the powers of the human understanding. Tr. anon. L: Hawes, Clarke, and Collins 1770. lxiv;228p. 20cm. [BM]
[Introd. contains life of the author.]
10328. The real happiness of a people under a philosophical king. L: M.Cooper 1750. 96p. 20cm. [LC]
["An abstract drawn from the abridgement of Wolfius's philos. by Mr. (Jean) Deschamps."]

WOLFF, Jk. Gl. 1684-1754. Sel. in C269.

WOLFF, Jl. 1834-1910.
10329. (Das Recht der Hagestolze.) Fifty years, three months, two days: a tale of the Neckar valley. Tr. from 15th Ger. ed. by W. H: and Eliz. R. Winslow. NY: Crowell 1890. 291p. 19cm. [LC]
†10330. (Der Raubgraf.) The robber count: a story of the Hartz country. Tr. from 23d Ger. ed. by W. H: and Eliz. R. Winslow. NY: Crowell 1890. 326p. 19cm. [Unconscionable liberties.] [LC]
*10331. (Der Sülfmeister.) The salt master of Lüneburg. Tr. from 21st Ger. ed. by W. H: and Eliz. R. Winslow. NY: Crowell 1890. 395p. 20cm. [LC]
*10332. (Der wilde Jäger.) The wild huntsman: a legend of the Hartz. Tr. Ralph Davidson. NY;L: Putnam 1905. 224p. il. 21cm. [LC]
[Some songs omitted and some condensation; style and spirit excellent.]
10333. (Tannhäuser, ein Minnesang.) Tannhäuser: minnesinger and knight templar. A metrical romance. Tr. C: G. Kendall. Bost: Badger 1903-4. 2v. il. D. [AC]

WOLFF, Ok. L: Bh. 1799-1851. Sel. in C309;443.

WOLFF, Ok. and J: M. H. Doering.
10334. The German tourist for MDCCCXXXVII. Tr. H. E. Lloyd. L: Acker 1836. 200p. il. 20cm. [LC]
10335. do. 1837. [same] The German tourist. L: Nutt. 200p. [BM.LC]
[BM copy is 25cm. LC has 20cm.]

WOLFF, Pius Ax. 1782-1828.
*10336. (Preciosa.) P--: opera by K: Ma. v. Weber. Eng. words tr. from version of "C. O. Sternau" by Rev. J. Troutbeck. Vocal score. Ger;Engl. L: Novello 1879. 65p. 26cm. [BMM]

WOLFF, Frau Ulla (Hirschfeld) 1850- . See "U: Frank."

WOLFGANG, Prinz. v. Anhalt, 1492-1566. See Hoffmann, Fz., Prince W--, a histor. narr., #4458.

WOLFRAM VON ESCHENBACH, 12th-13th cent. Sel. in C27;190;310;366;427; 532;570.

WOLFRAM VON ESCHENBACH
10337. Parzival, Titurel.[Sel.] Tr. Bayard Taylor. 1879. In C530.
*10338. (Parzival.) P--: a knightly epic. Tr. into Engl. verse by Jessie L. Weston. L: Nutt 1894. 2v. 20cm. [BM.LC]
10339. do. 1911. The story of P--, the templar. Retold...Ma. B. Sterling. NY: Dutton. 285p. il. 21cm. [LC]
*10340. do. 1912. [Reprint of #10338] NY: Stechert. 2v. 20cm. [LC]

WOLFSKEHL, K: 1869- . Sel. in C39.

WOLTER, Cte. 1834-97. See Harden, Mx., Word portraits, #3699.

WOLTERSDORF, Ern. Gb. 1725-61. Sel. in C229;244.

WOLTMANN, Af. F: Gf. Ab. 1841-80. Sel. in C102.
10341. (Holbein und seine Zeit.) Holbein and his times. Tr. F. E. Bunnètt. NY: Macmillan 1871. 4. [AC]
*10342. do. 1872. Tr. F. E. Bunnètt. L: Bentley. 468p. il. 22cm. [BM.LC]
10343. do. 1873. [same] L: Reeves & T. 4. [EC]
10344. do. 1879. Hs. H--. Tr. Js. Cundall. L: Low; NY: Scribner. 116p. 20cm.[A brief study--7 from 27 chaps. --based on W--.] [LC]
See Goerling, Ad., joint author. Art treasures of Germany, #2353.

WOLTMANN, Af. and K: Woermann.
*10345. (Geschichte der Malerei.) Hist. of painting. Ed. by Sidney Colvin. L: K.Paul 1880-7. 2v. il. 26cm. [BM.UW]
[BM has only vol. I, xxiv, 505p. BM ascribes entire tr. to Clara Bell; UW assigns vol. 1 to Colvin. Vol. 1 of orig., "Altertum," written by Woermann. Vol. 2, "Mittel und Neuzeit," by Woltmann. Tr. often sacrifices the letter of the orig. for the sake of better comprehension.]
*10346. do. 1894. [same] NY: Dodd, Mead. 2v. il. 25cm. [LC]

WOLTMANN, K:e (v. Lengefeld) v. 1763-1847. Sel. in C112.
10346a. (Agnes v. Lilien.) Agnes de Lilien: a novel. Tr. anon. L: W:Lane 1801. 3v. 263; 264; 332p. 17cm. [BM]
10346b. (Die weisse Frau.) The white lady (also Fouqué's "Undine"). Tr. anon. L: Pickering 1844. 90; 126p. il. 17cm. [BM]
[Tr. is C. L. Lyttelton. Very much abr. and freely tr. Orig. derives from "Neue Volkssagen der Böhmen by C. v. W--." Vol. is richly vignetted.]
*10346c. do. 1845. The white lady. Tr. Jas. D. Haas. L: Burns. Fireside lib. 64p. front. 16cm. [BM]
10347. do. 1859. [same as #10346b (without "Undine")] L: Bell & Daldy. 122p. il. 16cm. [Same ils.] [BM]

WOLZOGEN (U. NEUHAUS), Ern. (L:) Frhr. v. 1855- .
10348. (Das dritte Geschlecht.) The third sex. Tr. Grace I. Colbron. NY: Macaulay 1914. 285p. 19cm. [LC]
*10349. (Der Kraft-Mayr.) Florian Mayr: a humorous tale of musical life. Tr. E: Breck and C: H. Genung. NY: Huebsch 1914. 402p. 19cm. [Easy-flowing tr.] [LC.BM]
§10350. (Feuersnot.) Beltane fire: opera by R: Strauss. Tr. W: Wallace. Libr. Engl. Berlin: Fürstner 1910. 51p. 12. [LC]
§10351. do. 1910. [same] Vocal score. Engl. Berlin: Fürstner. 203p. fol. [LCM]
†10352. do. 1910. The fire of St. John's eve. Tr. C: T. Mason. Libr. French;Engl. Berlin: Fürstner. 31p. 4. [LC]

WOLZOGEN (U. NEUHAUS), Hs. (Pl.) Frhr. v. 1848- .
*10353. (Der Ring des Nibelungen, ein thematischer Leitfaden.) Guide through...Ring of the Nibelung. Tr. E. v. Wolzogen. 2d ed. L: Schulz-Curtius 1882. 79p. 18cm. [BM.LC]
[Excellent tr. Orig. introd. omitted.]
10354. do. 1895. Guide...a thematic key. Tr. N. H. Dole. NY: Schirmer. 122p. 18cm. [LC.BM]

WOLZOGEN, Hs. v.
§10355. (Ein Leitfaden...) Guide to the legend, poem, and music of ...Tristan and Isolde. With extr. from Swinburne's "Tristran of Lyonesse." Tr. B: L. Mosely. Lpz: Breitkopf & H. 1884. 52p. 19cm. [Good but with undue liberties.] [BM]
*10356. do. 1889. Guide through...Tristan and Isolde. Tr. anon. Lpz; NY: Reinboth. 47p. 19cm. [BM]
§10357. do. 1902. Guide to the legend, poem, and music...Tr. B: L. Mosely. Lpz: Breitkopf & H. 52p. 18cm. [LC]
*10358. (Erinnerungen an...Wagner.) Recoll. of R: W--. Tr. Ag. and Carnegie Simpson. Bayreuth. Giessel 1894. 103p. 16cm. [LC]
*10359. (Thematischer Leitfaden...) Key to "Parsifal." Tr. W: A. Ellis. L: Chappell 1889. 80p. 18cm. [BM]
[Engl. intended for use, faithful to orig.]
*10360. do. 1891. Thematic guide through the music of P--. Tr. from 6th ed. by J: H: Cornell. NY: Schirmer. 100p. 18cm. [LC.BM]

WORRINGER, W:
10360a. (Formprobleme der Gothik.) Form in Gothic. Tr. ed. w. introd. by H. Read. Original ils. Putnam 1927. 197p. 10 x 7. [EC]

WUCKE, L: 1807-83. Sel. in C450.

WUELFFER, Dn. 1617-85. Sel. in C43;231-2;276;486;489.

WUERDIG, L: 1818-89.
10361. Prince Eugene, the noble knight. Tr. G: P. Upton. Chic: McClurg 1910. 145p. il. 17cm. [LC]

WUERKERT, L: F: 1800-76. Sel. in C41.
*10362. Payne's il. hist. of the church of Christ. Tr. Js. Temple. L: Hagger 1861. 2v. in one. 416; 416p. il. 29cm. [BM]

WUNDT, W: (Max), 1832-1920.
*10363. (Ethik...Tatsachen und Gesetze des sittlichen Lebens.) Ethics: an invest. of the facts and laws of the moral life. Tr. from 2d Ger. ed. by E: B. Titchener, Julia H. Gulliver, and Marg. F. Washburn. L: Sonnenschein; NY: Macmillan 1897-1901. 3v. xii; 339;viii;196;xii;308p. 22cm. [BM.LC]
[Vol. 1. tr. by Gulliver and Titchener, vols. 2 and 3 by Washburn. Each vol. also issued sep.]
*10364. do. 1902. [same] 2d ed. [BM]
*10365. (Ueber den wahrhaften Krieg.) Concerning true war. Tr. Grace E. Hadow. L;NY: Oxford press 1915. (Oxford pamphlets.) 27p. 18cm. [Excellent.] [BM.LC]

WUTTKE, K: F: (Ad.) 1819-70.
*10366. (Handbuch der christlichen Sittenlehre.) Christian ethics. Tr. J: P. Lacroix. Ed: T. & T. Clark 1873. 2v. xiii;378;xvi;348p. 19cm. [Tr. aims at the truest practical reproduction.] [BM]
10367. do. 1873. [same] NY: Nelson & Phillips. 2v. 12. [LCO]
10368. do. 1873. [same] Cincin: Meth. book concern. 2v. 12. [AC]
10369. do. 1872-6. [same] Bost: Lee & S. 2v. 12. [AC]
*10370. do. 1901. [same] NY: Eaton & Mains; Cincin: Jennings & Pye. 2v. 12. [LC]

WYSS, J: D: 1743-1818, and J: Rd. 1781-1830. Sel. in C415;469;539; #2687.

DER SCHWEIZERISCHE ROBINSON

[Note: J. D. W-- was the originator of this story; J. R. W--, his son, revised the MS and had it printed. Jeanne Isabelle Polier de Bottens, Baronne de Montolieu, tr. the work into French, but added a better ending; also she tr. rather freely. Her additions have been

WYSS, J: D:--Der Schweizerische Robinson
variously accepted by German publishers, and appear in the most popular Engl. editions. It has not seemed feasible, in view of the indicated variations in the German texts, to distinguish translations and adaptations. Since many of the Engl. versions name no translator, a chronological arrangement is probably the best.]

§10371. 1814. The family Robinson Crusoe; or, journal of a father shipwrecked, with his wife and children, on an uninhabited island. Tr. from...M. Wiss. anon. L: M. J. Godwin. 2v. in one. xxii;144; 202p. front. and 3 pl. after H: Corbould. 17cm. [BM]
[16 chaps. Fairly close rendering, but moralizingly expansive.]

10372. 1818. [same] The Swiss family Robinson; or, advent. of a father and mother and four sons on a desert island, etc. Tr...from M. Wiss. L: Godwin. 2v. xxiv;343; 380p. il. 17cm. [BM]
[36 chaps. Vol. 1 ident. with the foregoing, text and plates; vol. 2 has map and one add. plate by Corbould. See note to #10378.]

10373. 1824. [same] 5th ed. L: 2v. 12. (B45)

10374. 1848. Swiss f. R. 2d series. Tr. from French by J. De Clinton Locke. NY: Harpers. 2v. 237; 237p. 16. [LCO]
[Cf. 10378 and note.]

10375. 1848? [same?] NY: Harper n.d. 4v. 18. [AC]
[Very likely this is ident. with the foregoing.]

10376. 1849. The S. f. R.; or, advent. on a desert island. Forming a second series or continuation...Tr. anon. Il. with notes and engr. L: Low. 399p. 18cm. [BM]
[35 chaps. Not very close to the Ger. text available in BM. Story begins with the anniversary of the rescue.]

10377. before 1852. S. f. R. Tr. anon. Bost: Francis n.d. [AC]

§10378. 1852. The S. f. R.; or, advent. of a father and mother and four sons in a desert island. Tr. J. De Clinton Locke. New ed. 1st and 2d series. Il. with notes and engr. L: Simpkin & Marshall, etc. viii;525p. 17cm. [BM]
[49 chaps. Text is edited from #10372 with omissions and verbal alterations.]

§10379. 1852. The S. f. R.; or, the advent. of a father and his four sons on a desert island. Tr. anon. L;Ed: Nelson. viii;384p. il. 15cm. [49 chaps. New tr., fair. EC dates this 1851.] [BM]

10380. 1853. [same] L;Ed: Nelson. viii;377p. il. 17cm. [BM]
[49 chaps.]

10381. 1855. [same as #10378] viii;525p. il. 17cm. [BM]

10382. 1855-8. Tr. anon. NY: Derby & Jackson n.d. 12. [AC]

10383. 1856. Tr. anon. L: C.H.Clarke. viii;288p. il. 16cm. [BM]
[42 chaps. Text seems to be abr. from #10379. EC calls it: Cheap ed.]

10384. 1862. New ed. with plates. L: Simpkin. 12. [Cf. #10378.] [EC]

10385. 1863. Abr. L: Laurie. 18.[Possibly the same as #10383?] [EC]

10386. 1864. Ed. and rev. by C. Hartley. NY: Hurd & H. il. 8. [AC]

10387. 1864. [same] 16. [AC]

10388. 1865. [same?] New ed. NY: Hurd & H. 16. [AC]

10389. 1865. Gall. Tr. anon. 8. [EC]

10390. 1865. Tr. anon. New ed. with woodcuts. L: Routledge. [EC]

10391. 1868. New and unabr. tr. by Mrs. H. B. Paull, with add. of Baroness Montolieu. Orig. ed. L: Warne. Chandos classics. 8. [EC]
[Cf. #10424, 10453.]

10392. 1869. In words of one syllable by Ma. Godolphin. L;NY: Routledge. 165p. col. il. 16cm. [BM]
[AC has: NY: Appleton. sq. 12.]

10393. 1869. In words of one syl. by I. F. W. Abr. and ed. from the orig. story. L;NY: Cassell, Petter & Galpin. 227p. col. il. 17cm. [BM]

WYSS--Swiss family Robinson

10394. 1869. Tr. anon. L: Nelson. 20 il. 8. [Cf. #10379-80.] (B45)
10395. 1869? [same as #10374] Phil: Porter & C. [NY]
10396. 1869. Tr. J: Lovell from Stahl's "Nouveau Robinson Suisse." L;NY: Cassell, Petter & Galpin. xiv;358p. numerous il. 23cm. [BM]
[45 chaps. The very interesting pref. notes the considerations which led Lovell to recast the entire story, though following the orig. plot; e.g., he sought the judgment of his four boys as to what they didn't like, and why!]
10397. 1870. The S. f. R.; or, advent of a shipwrecked family on a desolate island. New and unabr. tr. by W. H. Davenport Adams. Introd. from the French of C: Nodier. L;Ed;NY: Nelson. 690p. 19cm.
[13 chaps. and conclusion. Tr. has "followed the French tr. of Mme. Voïart, which is, perhaps, superior even to the orig. in style; is more lucid, spirited, and expressive."] [BM]
10398. 1870. In words of one syl. Anon. NY: Felt & Dillingham. sq. 16. [AC]
10399. 1872? [same as #10396] 4th ed. Springfield, Mass: Holland. 358p. il. 8. [LCO]
10400. 1872. [same] NY: Cassell n.d. il. 8. [AC]
10401. 1872. Tr. anon. L;Ed: Blackwood. il. 12. [EC]
10402. 1872. Tr. anon. L: Warne. il. 8. [Cf. #10391] [EC]
10403. 1872-6. Tr. anon. NY: Harper n.d. 2v. Sequel 2v. il. 18. [Cf. #10375.]
10404. 1872-6. Tr. anon. Phil: Lippincott n.d. il. 12. [AC]
10405. 1872-6. Tr. anon. Phil: Porter n.d. il. 12. [AC]
10406. 1872-6. Tr. anon. NY: Scribner n.d. il. 8. [AC]
10407. 1872-6. Tr. anon. NY: Scribner n.d. il. 12. [AC]
10408. 1872-6. Tr. anon. NY: Miller n.d. 12. [AC]
10409. 1872-6. Tr. anon. NY: Routledge n.d. il. 12. [AC]
10410. 1872-6. Tr. anon. NY: Routledge n.d. il. 16. [AC]
10411. 1872-6. Tr. anon. NY: Routledge n.d. Presentation ed. il. 16. [AC]
10412. 1872-6. Tr. anon. NY: Clark & Maynard n.d. il. 16. [AC]
10413. 1872-6. Tr. anon. NY: Appleton n.d. il. 12. [AC]
10414. 1872-6. Tr. anon. NY: Carleton n.d. il. 12. [AC]
10415. 1872-6. Tr. anon. NY: World pub. n.d. il. 12. [AC]
10416. 1872-6. Tr. anon. Bost: Estes n.d. il. 8. [AC]
10417. 1872-6. Tr. anon. NY: Nelson n.d. il. 12. [AC]
10418. 1872-6. Tr. anon. NY: Nelson n.d. (Household ed.) il. 8. [AC]
10419. 1872-6. Tr. anon. Bost: Lee & Shepard n.d. Household series. il. 16. [AC]
10420. 1872-6. Tr. anon. Bost: Lee & Shepard n.d. Crusoe series. il. 12. [AC]
10421. 1877. Tr. anon. NY: Munro. Seaside lib. 33p. 32cm. [LCO]
10422. 1877. Tr. anon. The S. f. R.; or, advent. in a desert island. New tr. L;NY: Routledge. 409p. 16cm. [BM]
[57 chaps. and conclusion. Rather free version, somewhat ed. and abr. from #10383 or #10379.]
10423. 1877. In words of one syl. Abr. and ad. by I. F. M. (i.e., W.) NY: McLoughlin. il. 4. [Same as #10393.] [NY]
†10424. 1877. [same as #10391] The S. f. R.; or, the advent of a shipwrecked family on an uninhabited island near New Guinea. A new and unabr. tr. from the orig. by Mrs. H. H. B. Paull. With orig. il. L: Warne. xiii;562p. 18cm. [BM]
["In this tr.--which is made entirely from the orig. Ger.--the incidents and events are faithfully preserved unaltered with one or two necessary but slight exceptions...(and) with the additions made by the Baroness Montolieu in the more modern Ger. eds." Not my idea of faithful preservation. --41 chaps.]

WYSS--Swiss family Robinson
10425. 1877. The S. f. R.; being the advent. of a family shipwrecked on a desert island. New ed. il. partly in col. L: Groombridge. x; 266p. 18cm. [42 chaps. Rewritten from #10379 or its offspring.] [BM]
10426. 1877. The S. f. R. From the German of J. Bonnett. With numerous ils. (Col. front.) L: M.Ward. 395p. 18cm. [BM]
[21 chaps. Much rewritten.]
10427. 1878. The S. f. R.: an account of the advent. of a Swiss pastor and his family on an uninhabited island. Tr. from the best orig. eds. by H. Frith. Col. pict. and nearly 200 engr. L: Ward, Lock. viii;556p. 21cm. [BM]
[58 chaps. "At once the most complete and the most correct issue of the S. f. R."]
10428. 1878. [same] 18cm. [BM]
[Identical with the foregoing except in size.]
10429. 1879. The S. f. R.: a new tr. from the orig. Ger. Ed. W: H. G. Kingston. 95 ils. on wood. L;NY: Routledge. x;566p. 18cm. [BM]
[18 chaps. Tr. by the editor's family, with some omissions and alterations.]
10430. 1879. [same] [Identical with the foregoing, but with col. plates.] [BM]
10431. 1879. [same] Ed. Kingston. L: Routledge. 142p. il. 19cm. [BM]
[Prtd. in double columns. with fine type.]
10432. 1879. Tr. anon. L;Guildford (printed). 8. (B45)
10433. 1880. Tr. anon. L: Nelson. 12. [EC]
10434. 1881. Kingston's tr. L: Routledge. [EC]
10435. 1881. [same as #10426?] New ed. L: Ward. il. 8. [EC]
10436. 1881. [same as #10424?] New ed. L: Warne. Incident and advent. lib. 8. (B45)
10437. 1882. [same tr. as #10396] Springfield, O. Farm & fireside co. 272p. 12. [LCO]
10438. 1882. [same tr. as #10429] New tr. ed. by Kingston. NY: Routledge. 323p. il. 21cm. [LC]
10439. 1882. [same tr. as #10429] (40) Il. by Sir J: Gilbert et al. L;NY: Routledge. Sixpenny series. 64p. 28cm. [BM]
10440. 1883(1882). [same] L: Routledge. 190p. il. col. front. 17cm. [Fine type ed.] [BM]
10441. 1883 (1882). [same as #10429] 95 ils. on wood. 566p. 18cm. [BM]
10442. 1884. Tr. anon. NY: Lovell. 383p. 16. [Paging suggests #10379.] [LCO]
10443. 1885. Ed. for schools by J. H. Stickney. Bost: Ginn, Heath. 364p. il. 18cm. [LC]
[38 chaps. Based on #10391, which it follows rather closely; but it is really "edited."]
10444. 1885. Tr. anon. L: Routledge. Books of travel and advent. 500 ils. 64p. 28cm. [Same text as #10439.] [BM]
10445. 1886. Ed. (from Montolieu) with...notes...for...schools by Alfonzo Gardiner. Manchester;L: Heywood. 254p. 17cm. [BM]
[35 chaps. Bears strong verbal resemblance to #10371.]
10446. 1887. [same] 95p. 21cm. [BM]
[Same text as the foregoing, different format.]
10447. 1888. [same as #10391] L: Warne. col. il. 8. [EC]
10448. 1889. [same as #10397?] Unabr. tr. from the French. New ed. NY: Nelson. [AC]
10449. 1889 (1888). [same as #10429] L: Routledge. 95 ils. on wood. x;566p. col. pl. 19cm. [BM]
10450. 1889. Tr. anon. L: Nisbet. New ed. 12. (B45)
10451. 1889. Tr. anon. L: Ward, L. [Cf. #10454 and #10427.] [AC]
10452. 1890. Tr. anon. L: Nelson. Story-book readers. 256p. il. 17cm. [56 lessons. Edited from #10397.] [BM]

WYSS--Swiss family Robinson
10453. 1890. [same as #10391] L: Warne. Chandos classics. xii;562p. il. 18cm. [BM]
10454. 1890. [same as #10427] L: Ward, L. il. 12. [AC]
10455. 1891 (1890). Kingston ed. L: Routledge. 489p. 95 ils. on wood. col. pl. 21cm. [Evidently the same ils. as in #10429.] [BM]
10456. 1890. [same as #10429] L: Routledge. 576p. 8. [EC]
10457. 1891. [same as #10466?] In words of one syl. NY: Cassell. 94p. sm. 4. [LCO]
10458. 1891. Tr. anon. New ed. Gall. 8. [EC]
10459. 1891. Kingston ed. L: Routledge. 8. (B45)
10460. 1892. Tr. anon. New ed. L: Hodder & S. x;266p. il. 18cm. [BM] [Slightly revised from Lovell's tr. #10396.]
10461. 1892. Kingston ed. L: Routledge. 8. (B45)
10462. 1893. Kingston ed. L: Scott. viii;292p. no il. 19cm. [BM]
10463. 1893. [same as #10445] New tr. ed. by A. Gardiner. Manchester: Heywood. 238p. il. 18cm. [BM]
[Identical with #10445 except for omission of the notes.]
10464. 1894. Kingston ed. L: King. 8. [EC]
10465. 1895. [same] [EC]
10466. 1895. In words of one syl. Cassell. 96p. sm. 4. [LCO]
[Cut down from #10393.]
10467. 1895. Kingston ed. New ed. L: Routledge. il. 8. [EC]
10468. 1895. Tr. anon. L: Chambers. il. 12. [EC]
10469. 1896. Tr. anon. Phil: Altemus. 202p. il. 16cm. [LC]
[Based on #10391.]
10470. 1897. Kingston ed. L: Routledge. x;566p. il. 21cm. [BM]
[42 chaps.]
10471. 1896. [same as #10425] 8 il. R: Mather. L: Bliss & Sands. 302p. 8. [BM]
*10472. 1896. New tr. by E: A. B. Hodgetts. 100 il. J. Finnemore. L: Newnes. 391p. 24cm. [BM]
[25 chaps. Tr. directly from the German, with cuts.]
10473. 1897. [same] Chic: Smith & Simon. 391p. 26cm. [LC]
10474. 1897. [same as #10471] [BM]
10475. 1898. Ed. for young readers. NY;Bost: Univ. pub. 127p. il. 12. [40 brief chaps. Revision based on Kingston ed.] [LC]
10476. 1899. [same as #10392?] In words of one syl. by Ma. Godolphin. Phil: Altemus. 161p. il. 12. [31 chaps.] [LC]
10477. 1899. Kingston ed. Il. H. Kley. L: Nister; NY: Dutton. 291p. 23 x 18cm. [BM,LC]
10478. 1899. [same as #10471] L: Bliss & Sands. 302p. 8. [EC]
10479. 1899. Retold in Engl. and abr. for schools. L: Bell. 160p. il. 17cm. [BM]
10480. 1899. Kingston ed. NY: Crowell. 399p. 19cm. [LC]
10481. 1900. Tr. anon. Bost: Caldwell. Juvenile classics. D. [AC]
10482. 1900. Tr. anon. NY: Burt. One syl. series. il. 4. [AC]
10483. 1903. Kingston ed. L: Nimmo. 300p. 8. [EC]
10484. 1903. Tr. anon. L: Blackie. 264p. 8. [EC]
10485. 1904. Tr. anon. New ed. Il. H. M. Brock. Pearson. 350p. 8. [EC]
10486. 1904. [same?] L: Partridge. 350p. il. 18cm. [BM]
[50 chaps. Rewritten.]
10487. 1904. In words of one syl. NY;L: Cassell. 95p. col. ils. 17cm. [Cut down from #10393.] [BM]
10488. 1905. Tr. anon. Chic: Conkey. il. D. [AC]
10489. 1905. Tr. anon. New ed. Gall & I. 326p. 8. [EC]
[Cf. #10458 and #10389.]
10490. 1906. Tr. anon. Culley. 382p. 8. [EC]
10491. 1906. Tr. anon. L: Collins. 360p. 8. [EC]
10492. 1906. Tr. anon. L: Milner. 8. [EC]

WYSS--Swiss family Robinson
10493. 1906. Tr. anon. L;NY: Nelson. 64p. col. front. and pl. 26cm. [Much abr.] [BM]
10494. 1907. Retold for Amer. boys and girls. Anon. Il. E. M. Bendovna. NY: Barnes. 110p. 19cm. [LC]
[Principally based on Kingston's ed.]
10495. 1907. Ed. G. E. Mitton. (12 col.) il. Harry Rountree. L: Black. xi;307p. 21cm. [BM]
[33 chaps. Considerably pruned. AC has: Phil: Lippincott 1907.]
10496. 1907. The S. f. R. reading leaflets. L: Charles & Dible. 19cm.[12 leaflets, 4p. each.] [BM]
10498. 1908. Tr. anon. NY: Bowman. il. D. [AC]
10499. 1908. Tr. anon. L: King. 296p. 8. [EC]
[Probably Kingston's ed. Cf. #10464.]
10500. 1909. Mrs. Paull's tr. Introd. W: D. Howells. Il. from sketches made in the tropics by L: Rhead. NY;L: Harper. xvii;602p. 23cm. [LC]
10501. 1909. Retold for little folks by Edith Robarts. L: Blackie. 8. [EC]
10502. 1909. Lovell's tr. L;NY: Cassell. 372p. 18cm. [45 chaps.][BM]
10503. 1909. Kingston ed. L: S. S. U. 292p. il. 18cm. [BM]
[EC dates this 1910.]
10504. 1910. [same as #10495] Phil: Lippincott. il. 8. [AC]
10505. 1910. [same as #10495] Il. in col. and in black and white by C: Folkard. L: Dent; NY: Dutton. 454p. 20cm. [59 chaps.] [BM]
10506. 1910. Kingston ed. Ed. with introd. by Wl. Jerrold. Il. (4 in col.) by Ern. Prater. L: Nister; NY: Dutton. 371p. 19cm. [BM]
10507. 1910. [same as #10501] Il. J: Hassall. L: Blackie. unp. 26cm. [8 chaps.] [BM]
10508. 1910. [same as #10397] L;NY: Nelson. xvi;565p. col. ils. 18cm. [13 chaps.] [BM]
10509. 1910. [same as #10378] L: Dent; NY: Dutton. Everyman's lib. 498p. il. 17cm. [57 chaps.] [BM.LC]
10510. 1910. [same as #10502] 4 il. Gordon Browne. L;NY: Cassell. 372p. 19cm. [45 chaps.] [BM]
10511. 1912. In words of one syl. NY: Cassell. il. [Cf. #10487.][AC]
10512. 1912. Tr. anon. Il. J: Hassall. Bost: Caldwell. Q. [AC]
[Cf. #10507.]
10513. 1913. Tr. anon. Il. T. H. Robinson. NY: Doran. 431p. O. [AC]
10514. 1913. [same?] Il. T. H. Robinson. L: Frowde. 442p. 8. [EC]
10515. 1913. Tr. anon. Gardner. 302p. 8. [EC]
10516. 1914. Paull's tr. Il. Elenore P. Abbott. Phil: Jacobs. 569p. il. 20cm. [LC]
10517. 1914. Retold for young children by Ma. Godolphin. Bost;NY: Dutton. 181p. il. 19cm. [32 chaps. Revised from #10476.] [LC]
10518. 1914. Tr. anon. Baldwin. 12. [EC]
10519. 1914. [same as #10495] L: Black. 320p. il. 8. [EC]
10520. 1914. [same?] Ed. G. E. Mitton. Il. Harry Rountree. NY: Macmillan. 307p. O. [AC]
10521. 1914. [same as #10510] 4 il. G. Browne. Cassell. 372p. 19cm. [45 chaps.] [BM]
10522. 1914. Kingston ed. L: Routledge; NY: Dutton. 566p. 20cm. [BM]
[18 chaps. Many new ils., some in col.]
10523. 1915. [same as #10443] Il. C: Copeland. Bost; NY: Ginn. viii; 417p. 18cm. [LC.BM]
10524. 1916. Kingston ed. Il. Milo Winter. Chic: Rand, McNally. 441p. 8. [18 chaps.] [LC]
10525. 1916. Tr. anon. NY: Crowell. [AC]
10526. 1916. In Lindsay, Ethel. "David Copperfield, etc." L: Partridge. Told to the little ones series. [EC]

WYSS--Swiss family Robinson
10527. 1916. Tr. anon. L: Seeley, S. 351p. Cr. 8. [EC]
[Cf. paging of #10485.]
10528. 1917. [same as #10508] Reissue. Nelson. x;565p. 15cm. [BM]
10529. 1919. [same as #10379] L: Oxford press. 256p. col. il. 19cm. [52 chaps.] [BM]
10530. 1920. [same as #10495] Ed. Geraldine E. Mitton. Il. Harry Rountree. L: Black. xi;307p. 21cm. [LC]
10531. 1922. Tr. Owen Wister. Il. F. Nichols. NY: Duffield. 25p. 26cm. [First pub. 1882, says LC card.] [LC]
10532. 1923. [same as #10500] NY;L: Harper. xvii;602p. 23cm. [BM]
[Howells' statement that this is the most popular Engl. tr. is not confirmed by my lists.]
10533. 1924. Tr. anon. Il. F. Brundage. Chic;Akron, O: Saalfield. 250p. 24cm. [LC]
10534. 1924. [same as #10530] 18cm. [BM]
10535. 1925. Retold in words of one syl. by Mrs. Gorham. NY: Burt. il. O. [AC]
10536. 1926. [same as #10530] 19cm. [LC]
10537. 1926? Col. il. C: Folkard. L: Dent; NY: Dutton. 128p. 18cm. [12 chaps. From #10379.] [BM]
10538. 1926. Abr. by J. C. Allen (from #10427). L;NY: Longmans. 170p. 19cm. [BM]
10539. 1926? Tr. anon. NY: Sears. Amer. home classics. Juvenile classics. [AC]
10540. 1926. [Reissue of #10505.] [BM]
10541. 1926. Kingston's ed. Photoplay title: Perils of the wild. Il. ...from photoplay. NY: Grosset. 371p. D. [AC]
[Cf. paging of #10521.]
10542. 1926. [same?] New ed. NY: Grosset. [AC]
10543. 1927. Tr. anon. L: Gardner. [EC]
10544. 1927. Tr. anon. Il. Arnold Hall. Minton. vi;408p. O. [AC]
10545. 1927? Tr. anon. Advent. on a desert island. Girard, Kan: Haldeman-Julius n.d. Little blue books. 64p. 12cm. [BQM]

WYSS, J: Rd.
10546. The treasure: a Swiss legend. The bitter wedding: a Swiss story. Tr. G: G. Cunningham. 1829. In C80.

ZACHARIAE, Jt. F: W: 1726-77.
10547. Tabby in Elysium: a mock poem (in five cantos and in prose). Tr. R. E. Raspe. L: Prtd. for the tr. by H. Goldney 1781. 24p. 24cm. [BM]

ZACHER, ---, (Regierungsassessor.)
10548. (Die rote Internationale.) The red international. Author. tr. from 3d Ger. ed. by E. M. and C. F. S. Geldart. L: Sonnenschein 1885. 167p. 8. [Copy missing.] [BM]

ZAHN, Ern. 1867- .
10549. (Herrgottsfäden.) Golden threads. Tr. Muriel R. Trollope. L: Hutchinson 1908. 324p. 8. [BM]
*10550. (Stefan der Schmied.) Stephen the smith. Tr. Kath. Royce. 1913-15. In C154(19).
[Rather disappointing: many fine points blurred or blunted.]

ZECH, Pl. 1881- . Sel. in C95.

ZEDLITZ, Js. Cn. Freiherr v. 1790-1862. Sel. in C17;50;141;144;152;219;295-6;309;366;372;380;393;397;437;448.
10551. (Totenkränze.) Poems. Tr. Lavinia Dick. L: Cunningham 1843. 17cm. [BM]
[Tr. is very free; occasionally one or more sonnets are condensed into one.]

ZEDLITZ-TRUETSCHLER, (K: Kst. F: E:) Rb. Graf v. 1863- .
10552. Twelve years at the imperial Ger. court. Tr. Af. Kalisch. L: Nisbet; NY: Doran. 1924. xxi;306p. 23cm. [LC]

ZEHNI, ---. Sel. in C486.

ZEISBERGER, D: 1721-1808.
10553. Diary. Tr. 1916. In C19.
*10554. Diary of D: Z--, a Morav. missionary among the Indians of Ohio. Tr. Eugene F. Bliss. Cincin: Clarke 1885. 2v. 464;535p. 24cm. [Seems to be faithful tr.] [LC.BM]
10555. The diaries of Z-- relating to the first missions in the Ohio basin, 1767-9. Tr. anon. "Ohio arch. and hist. quart.," vol. 12 (1912), pp. 1-125.
10556. D: Z--'s hist. of the north Amer. Indians. Tr. W: Nathaniel Schwarze. In "Ohio arch. and hist. quart.," vol. 19(1910), pp. 1-189.

ZEISE, H: 1822-1914. Sel. in C167;301.

ZEISS, ---. Sel. in C152.

"ZELL, F." (i.e., Camillo Walzel) and R: Genée.
*10557. (Apajune, der Wassermann.) Apajune, the water sprite: operetta in 3 acts by C. Millöcker. Tr. Sydney Rosenfeld. Libr. Engl. NY: Woodward 1885. 39p. 16. [LCM]
[Very good and spirited. No dialog.]
§10558. (Boccaccio.) B--; or, the Prince of Palermo. Opera comique in 3 acts by Fz. v. Suppé. Tr. anon. Libr. Engl. NY: Rullman 1879. 37p. with music. 8. [LCM]
[Fairly close, but with deviations; partly rhymed.]
§10559. do. 1880. [same] Libr. Engl. Phil: H. B. Mahn (copyright). 36p. 8. [No music in this copy.] [LCM]
10560. do. 1880. [same?] Libr. Engl. NY: Theatre ticket office. 38p. 8. [LCO]
§10561. do. 1880. B--; or, the Prince of Palermo. Tr. and ad. Dexter Smith. Vocal score. Bost: Ditson. 246p. 4. [Much adapted.] [LCM]
§10562. do. 1880. [same] The Prince of Palermo; or, the students of Florence. Ad. D. Smith. Libr. Bost: Ditson. 30p. [Not complete] [LCM]
†10563. do. 1882. B--. Tr. Frank W. Green. Vocal score. Engl. L: Cramer. 244p. 27cm. [BMM]
[Quite freely adapted; e.g., the husband has become the father.]
†10564. do. 1882. B--. Engl. ad. by H. B. Farnie and R. Reece. Vocal score. L: Boosey; NY: Pond. 216p. 27cm. [BMM]
[An even freer adaptation.]
§10565. do. 1908. [same as #10561] Bost: Ditson. [LCM]
§10566. do. 1908. [same tr.] Libr. Bost: Ditson. 64p. [LCM]
*10567. (Der Bettelstudent.) The beggar student: comic opera by C. Millöcker. Tr. W. Beattie Kingston. Vocal score. L: Chappell n.d. 183p. 27cm. [BMM.LCM]
[Very good and clever. Tr.'s name is really Beatty-Kingston.]
*10568. do. 1883. The beggar student. Engl. tr. and ad. of words to music by Emil Schwab. Libr. Bost;Chic: White, Smith. 42p. 16. [LCM]
[Very good.]
*10569. do. 1883. [same tr.] Vocal score. Bost: White, Smith. 182p. 4. [LCM]
§10570. do. 1884. Tr. and ad. F. F. Hagen. New rev. ed. Vocal score. n.i. 182p. 4. [Close, but without rhyme.] [LCM]
10571. (Der lustige Krieg.) The merry war: comic operetta in 3 acts by J: Strauss. Tr. anon. Libr. NY: Bartsch 1882. 38p. 12. [LCO]
*10572. do. 1882. Tr. and ad. L: C. Elson. Piano score. Bost;Chic: White, Smith. 55p. 4. [LCO]
10573. do. 1882. Tr. I. W. Norcross. NY: Grau. 28p. 8. [LCO]
*10574. do. 1884. [Elson's tr.] Libr. Engl. B: White, Smith. 34p [LCM]

ZELL and Genée.--Der lustige Krieg.
*10575. do. 1884. [same] Vocal score. Engl. 206p. 4. [LCM]
†10576. (Der Seekadet.) The naval cadets: comic opera in 3 acts by R: Genée. Tr. H. B. Farnie. Vocal score. L: Cramer 1800. 187p. 27cm. [Very freely adapted.] [BMM]
†10577. do. 1880. [same tr.] Libr. Engl. L: Cramer. 36p. 17cm. [BM]
10578. (Der Vizeadmiral.) The vice-admiral: opera in 3 acts by C. Millöcker. Tr. J: P. Jackson. Libr. NY: Pusey 1887. 8 unp. leaves. 8. [LCO]
10579. do. 1887. Tr. and ad. L: C. Elson. Vocal score. Bost: White, Smith. 34p. fol. [LCM]
*10582. (Eine Nacht in Venedig.) A night in Venice: comic opera in 3 acts by J: Strauss. Tr. and ad. L: C. Elson. Vocal score. Ger; Engl. Bost;Chic: White, Smith 1884. 143p. 4. [LCM]
*10583. do. 1884. [same tr.] Libr. Bost;Chic: White, Smith. 35p. 16. [LCM]
10584. (Fatinitza.) Fatinitza: comic opera by Fz. v. Suppé. Ad. H: S. Leigh. Libr. Engl. L: Co-op. print co. 1878. 49p. 18cm. [BM]
§10585. do. 1879. Tr. Td. T. Barker. Dialog tr. Sylvester Baxter. Vocal score. Ger;Ital;Engl. Bost: Ditson. 223p. 4. [LCM] [Not very good.]
§10586. do. 1879. [same tr.] Libr. Bost: Ditson. 41p. il. 24cm. [LCM]
§10587. do. 1887. Libr. rev. by Oscar Weil. Bost: Mudge. 69p. 8. [LCM] [Better than Barker, but still not very good.]
§10588. do. 1908. [reissue of #10585.] [LCM]
*10589. (Gasparone.) Gasparone: romantic comic opera in 3 acts by C. Millöcker. Ad. Sydney Rosenfeld. Libr. NY: Bartsch 1885. 23p. 8. [Much of it very cleverly tr.] [LCO]
*10590. (Gräfin Dubarry.) Countess D--: operetta in 3 acts by C. Millöcker. Tr. anon. Libr. Engl. NY: Bartsch 1883. 53p. 12. [LCO] [Very good and clever.]
*10591. (Nanon.) Nanon, the hostess of the Golden Lamb: opera comique in 3 acts by R: Genée. Tr. Sydney Rosenfeld. Libr. Engl. NY: Bartsch 1885. 23p. 8. [LCO] [Very good, not as close as Elson's tr.]
*10592. do. 1885. Tr. and ad. by L: C. Elson. Vocal score. Ger;Engl. Bost;Chic: White, Smith. 150p. 4. [Very good tr.] [LCM]
*10593. do. 1885. [same tr.] Libr. Bost;Chic: White,Smith. 56p. 16. [LCO]
*10594. do. 1886. Tr. and ad. El. August. Bost: Standard libretto co. 16p. 12. [Also very good.] [LCO]

ZELLER, Cn. H: 1779-1860. Sel. in C229.

ZELLER, E: 1814-1908.
*10595. (Aristoteles und die alten Peripatetiker.) Aristotle and the earlier Peripatetics. Tr. B: F. Costelloe and J: H: Muirhead. L; NY: Longmans 1897. 2v. 20cm. [BM.LC] [From "Die Philosophie der Griechen," part 2, section 2. The tr. take some doubtful liberties.]
**10596. (D: F: Strauss in seinem Leben und seinen Schriften geschildert.) D: F: S-- in his life and writings. Tr. anon. L: Smith, Elder 1874. 160p. port. 21cm. [Reads like an orig. work.] [BM.LCO]
*10597. (Die griechische Philosophie im 3. und 2. Jahrhundert v. C. Stoizismus, Epikureismus, Skepsis.) The Stoics, Epicureans, and Sceptics. Tr. by Rev. O. J. Reichel. L: Longmans 1870. 548p. 19cm. [BM.LC] [From "Die Philosophie der Griechen," part 3, section 1. Clear and accurate.]
*10598. do. 1880. [same] New and rev. ed. Longmans. xvi;585p. [BM] [Some obscurities removed.]

ZELLER, E:--Die griechische Philosophie
*10599. do. 1890. [same] [BM]
*10600. do. 1892. [same] xvi;585p. [BM]
*10601. (Die Philosophie der Griechen.) Hist. of Greek philos. from the earliest period to the time of Socrates. Tr. Sa. F. Alleyne. L: Longmans 1881. 2v. xi;642;541p. 19cm. [BM.LC]
[Tr. is quite literal.]
*10602. (Eklektizismus.) Hist. of eclecticism in Greek philos. Tr. Sa. F. Alleyne. L: Longmans 1883. viii;383p. 19cm. [BM]
[From "Die Philosophie der Griechen," part 3, section 1.]
*10603. (Grundriss der Geschichte der griechischen Philosophie.) Outlines of the hist. of Greek philos. Tr. Sa. F. Alleyne and Evelyn Abbott. L: Longmans 1886. xv;363p. 19cm. [BM]
[Alleyne is a better tr. than Abbott.]
10604. do. 1890. [same] [EC]
*10605. do. 1892. [same] 2d rev. ed. [BM]
*10606. (Plato und die alte Akademie.) Plato and the older academy. Tr. Sa. F. Alleyne and Af. Goodwin. L: Longmans 1876. xiii;629p. 19cm. [From "Die Philosophie der Griechen," part 2, section 2.] [BM]
*10607. do. 1888. [same] New ed. [LC]
*10608. (Sokrates und die Sokratiker.) S-- and the Socratic schools. Tr. by Rev. O. J. Reichel. L: Longmans 1868. xiv;350p. 8. [BM]
[Excellent tr. The tr. "aims at reproducing the meaning, whilst reducing the sentences." From "Die Philosophie der Griechen," part 2, section 2.]
*10609. do. 1877. [same] 2d ed. [BM]
*10610. do. 1885. [same] 3d rev. ed. Longmans. xii;410p. 19cm. [BM]
*10611. (Strauss und Renan.) S-- and R--. An essay. Tr. anon. L: Trübner 1866. 20cm. [BM.LCO]
[Tr. has expansive tendency. 25p. of introd.]
10612. Theory of cognition. Tr. Max Eberhardt. 1879. In C300(9).

ZELLER, Igs. 1842- .
10613. Conversion of two Lutheran ministers to the Roman Cath. church in 1863. Tr. Js. P. Brentano. NY: J. Schaefer 1918. 79p. 17cm. [LC]

ZELLER, Frau Lu. 1823-89. See "Lu. Pichler."

ZELTER, K: F: 1758-1832. Sel. in C12.
10614. Letters. In Goethe, Letters to Zelter, #3037.

ZERBONI, ---. Sel. in C36.

ZERKLAERE, Thomasin v. See Thomasin.

ZIEGLER, B. Sel. in C425.

ZIEGLER, F: W: 1761-1827. Sel. in C12.

ZIEGLER, Ka. 1844-1909.
10615. (Flirten?) Playing with fire. Elab. by Js. H: Neebe. Chic: 1910. Tw. [LC]

ZIEGLER, Tb. 1846-1921.
*10616. (Sittliches Sein und sittliches Werden.) Social ethics: outlines of a doctrine of morals. Tr. H. H. S. L: Williams & N. 1891. xii;140p. 19cm. [BM]
[Popular addresses. Tr. endeavors to preserve the style of oral discourse.]

ZIEHRER, K: Ml. 1843- . The kiss waltz: operetta. See "Bodanzky, Rd."

ZIEMSSEN, L: 1823-95.
10617. J: Sb. Bach. Tr. G: P. Upton. Chic: McClurg 1905. 133p. il. 17cm. [LC]

ZIETHE, W:
10618. (Anna Lavater. Ein christliches Lebensbild.) Anna L--: a pict. of Swiss pastoral life. Tr. Cath. E. Hurst. Cincin: Hitchcock & W. 1870. 16. [AC]

ZIHN, J: F: 1650-1719. Sel. in C232;272;276;489;489a.

ZIMMERMANN, El.
*10619. (Das deutsche Kaiserreich Mittelafrikas als Grundlage einer neuen deutschen Weltpolitik.) The Ger. empire of central Africa. Tr. anon. Introd. Edwyn Bevan. L: Longmans, Green 1918. lxiv;63p. 21cm. [BM]

ZIMMERMANN, J: G: Ritter v. 1728-95. Sel. in C42;173.
10620.[Sel.] Reflections on men and things. Tr. from a French MS found among the papers of a general officer of the old government of France, who lately died. Anon. L: Symonds 1799. 233p. 21cm. [BM.LC]
10621.[Sel.] 1800. Aphorisms and reflections on men, morals, and things. Tr. anon. L: Vernor & Hood. 356p. 19cm. [BM.LCO]
[Different from the foregoing. Said to be tr. from Ger. orig. Front. is port. by W. Ridley dated 1797.]
10622.[Sel.] 1804. Beauties of Z--, with a memoir of his life and writings. [Mentioned by Herzfeld in "Herrigs Archiv" 105:32.]
10623. [Sel.] 1806. Gleanings from Z-- on solitude...By Mrs. Rayfield. Lindsell. See "Anti-Jacobin R." 23(1806):431. (B26)
10624. The excellency of the knowledge of Jesus Christ. Tr. Moses Browne. L: Dilly 1772? See "Crit. R." 34(1772):148. (B26)
§10625. (Fragmente über F: den Grossen.) Select views of the life, reign, and character of F: the Gt., king of Prussia. Tr. Maj. Neumann. L: Hookham, Carpenter, Newbery 1792. 2v. 258;270p. 18cm. [BM.LC]
[Tr. omits quite freely, but can translate well when he chooses.]

ÜBER DIE EINSAMKEIT

*10626. 1791. Solitude considered with respect to its influence on the mind and the heart. Tr. from the French of J. B. Mercier. Anon. L: C.Dilly. vii;380p. 21cm. [BM]
[Mercier's title is: "La solitude considérée relativement à l'esprit et au coeur." Mercier reduces the bulk of the orig. considerably. He mistranslates noch as if it were nicht, and the Engl. follows. Excellent tr. of the French. A comparative table of contents is as follows:
Ger. 1. Cap. Einleitung und Plan.
Fr. Chap. 1. Introd. (very brief)
Engl. Chap. the first. Introd.
G. 9. Cap. Allgemeine Vorteile der Einsamkeit.
F. Chap. 2. Avantages généraux de la solitude.
E. The general advantages of solitude.
G. 10. Cap. Vorteile der Einsamkeit für den Geist.
F. Chap. 3. Avantages de la solitude pour l'esprit.
E. The influence of solitude upon the mind.
G. 11. Cap. Forteile der Einsamkeit für das Herz.
F. Chap. 4. Avantages de la solitude pour le coeur.
E. The influence of solitude upon the heart.
10627. 1792. [same] 2d ed. L: Dilly. x;420p. 21cm. [BM]
[Pref. is somewhat revised. Front. Kolloway after Singleton.]
10628. 1793. [same] [reprint] Phil: Prtd. for J. Crukshank, etc. vii; 328p. 12. (B6a) [Available: AAS.JCB.]
10629. 1793-1800. [same] 1st NY. ed. Prtd. for Duykinck, etc. 328p. 12. (B48)
10630. 1795. [same] 4th ed. [Identical with #10627.] [BM]
10631. 1796. [same] Albany (NY). Prtd. by Barber & Southwick. 280p. 8. [LC]

ZIMMERMANN, J: G:
10632. 1796. [same] NY: Prtd. by Mott & Lyon n.d. 12. (B6a)
10633. 1797. [same] Wilmington (Del.): Prtd. by Johnson & Preston. 298p. 12. [Available: AAS.JCB.NYPL.WIPL] (B6a)
10634. 1797. Solitude; or, the effect of occasional retirement... written orig. by J. G. Z--. To which are added, The life of the author; notes...and six beautiful engr. by W. Ridley (after Kirk). L: Vernor & H. lii;309p. index. 17cm. [BM]
[Chap. 2 of prev. eds. is now chap. 4, The general advantages of retirement. Chaps. 5-7 are added. Chap. 1 is rewritten, includ. more of Z--'s matter, freely handled.]
10635. 1798. [same] Solitude, written orig, by J. G. Z--. To which are added...and seven beautiful engr. L: Vernor & H. lii;309p. index. 21cm. [BM.LC]
[Front. and engr. t.p. both bear date 1797. T.p. reads: Solitude, or the effect of occasional retirement, etc. The front. is Z--'s port. This is really the foregoing, on larger paper and with a new t.p. The 7th engr. is probably the t.p. of the foregoing.]
§10636. 1798. Solitude consid. with respect to its dangerous influence upon the mind and heart. Sel. and tr. from the orig. German of M. Zimmerman [sic]. Being a sequel to the former Engl. tr. L: Dilly. 316p. 21cm. [BM]
[6 chaps. Tr. complains that Mercier omitted everything derogatory in solitude, thus distorting his author. "It has been (his aim) so to reduce the dimensions...that while it embraced every thing important to the full developement of the real sentiments and views of the author, it might not become burthensome to the patience of the reader." --Of the general inducements to society. On the love of solitude. The mischievous influence of solitude in particular instances. The ill effects of solitude on the imagination. The ill effects of solitude on the passions. Retrospect and conclusion. --Tr. is not very good.]
10637. 1799. L: Vernor & Hood. 2v. xlviii;310p., index, 338p. index. 17cm. [BM]
[Vol. 1 is not so designated. Vol. 2 repeats prtd. t.p. (as in #10635) but says: 4 engr. by Ridley. --This contains 8 chaps., as in #10635, plus two more: Introd. of the motives to solitude. The disadvantages of solitude. The influence of solitude on the imagination. The effects of solitude on a melancholy mind. The influence of solitude on the passions. Of the danger of idleness in solitude. The conclusion. The heading of p. 1 reads: Solitude or the pernicious influence of a total seclusion from society upon the mind and the heart. Text appears to be rewritten from #10635.]
10638. 1799. [same as #10627] 8th ed. x;420p. viiip. index.21cm.[BM]
10639. 1800. [same as #10637] 17cm. [BM.LC]
[Engr. front. and t.p. as in #10635, vol. 1 not so designated.]
10640. 1803? [same as #10635?] NY. 8. (B48)
10641. 1804. [same as #10631] Bost: Bumstead. 307p. 16. [LC]
10642. 1804. [reissue of #10637] [BM]
10643. 1805. 6th ed. L: Vernor & H. 2v. xxv;332; 372p. indices. 14cm. [This ed. has the same text as #10637. It omits engr. t.p. but still announces 7 engr. by Ridley. T.p. of vol. 2. also has: "seven beautiful engr." In fact this vol. contains four in addition to those of vol. 1.] [BM]
10644. 1808. S-- by M. Zimmerman [sic]. Engr. t.p. adds: L: Prtd. for J. Walker and J. Harris. Prtd. t.p. reads: Solitude: written orig. by J. G. Zimmerman. To which is added, The life of the author (abr.). xvi;403p. 13cm. [BM]
[7 plus 8 chaps. front. and t.p. by Noble after T. Uwins.]

ZIMMERMANN, J: G:--Ueber die Einsamkeit
10645. 1808. [same ad #10637?] New ed. L: Vernor. 2v. [EC]
10646. 1808. Engr. after Smirke. L: Suttaby. [EC]
10647. 1808. New London, Ct: Thomas & Whipple. (B48)
10648. 1809. L: Cundee. 2v. 8. [EC]
10649. 1811. 8th ed. Cupar-Fife. Prtd. by J. Arnot for T. Martin in L. 2v. xiv;276; 304p. indices. 15cm. [BM]
[Text is that of #10644. Vol. 2. has one pl. by Thurston.]
10650. 1813. Brooklyn (NY): Spooner. 296p. 16. (B48).
10651. 1813. [same as #10635] NY: Huntington. 402p. 13cm. [LC]
10652. 1819. NY. 24. (B48)
10653. 1819. [same text as #10644] Solitude; or, the effect of occasional retirement. L: J.Walker, etc. xvi;368p. 13cm. [BM]
[Front. and engr. t.p. by W. Findon after T. Uwins, not the same as in #10644.]
10654. 1824. Solitude; or, the influence of retirement on the mind and heart. With the life of the author. L: J:Bumpus. xix;444p. front. (port.) 15cm. [BM]
[Front. engr. by Freeman. Same text as the foregoing, in two parts. No indices.]
10655. 1824. Designs by Stothard. L: Griffiths. 12. [EC]
10656. 1825. [same?] Solitude: on the mind and heart. L: Griffiths. 344p. il. 17cm. [LC]
10657. 1827. Solitude; or, the effects, etc. With notes. New ed. rev. and corr. from the author's last ed. Embellished with numerous engr. L: T:Tegg. xxxi;399p. 23cm. [BM]
[Longer biog., other matter as in previous 2-vol. eds., without indices.]
10658. [before 1852] On solitude. Phil: Leary & Getz n.d. 18. [AC]
10659. 1872-6. On solitude. Phil: Sower, Potts n.d. 18. [AC]
10660. (Ueber F: den Grossen und meine Unterredungen mit ihm kurz vor seinem Tode.) Dr. Z--'s conversations with the late king (F: II) of Prussia, when he attended him in his last illness...To which are added several curious particulars...of that extraordinary prince. Tr. from last ed. anon. L: Prtd. for C. Forster 1791. 151p. 18cm. [BM]
[Not complete, but fairly close and correct.]
*10661. (Vom Nationalstolze.) An essay on national pride. Tr. anon. L: J. Wilkie & C. Heydinger 1771. 306p. 16cm. [BM]
[Front. J. Collyer from an engr. by S. H. Grimm on the t.p. of the Ger. ed.]
10662. do. 1778. Strictures on national pride. Tr. anon. Phil: R. Bell. 274p. 20cm. [LC]
§10663. do. 1797. To which are added memoirs of the author's life and writings. Tr. S: H. Wilcocke. L: Dilly. xl;260p. index. 22cm. [BM]
§10664. do. 1799. [same] NY: Caritat. 300p. 8. [BM]
§10665. do. 1806. [same] New ed. L: Cundee. 8. [BM]
10667. (Zerstreute Blätter vermischten Inhalts.) Reflections on the perfectibility of man, etc. Tr. anon. L: Hamilton 1799. See "New Lond. R." 1(1799):193. (B26)

ZIMMERMANN, K: 1803-77.
10668. (Geographische Analyse...des Kriegstheaters gegen China.) Memoir on the countries about the Caspian seas...Tr. Capt. W: Morier. L: Madden 1840. 75p. 23cm. [LC]

ZIMMERMANN, O: 1873- .
10669. (Warum Schuld und Schmerz?) The problem of evil and human destiny. Tr. J: S. Zybura. Introd. by Js. Schrembs. St.L: Herder 1924. xiv,135p. 19cm. [LC.BM]

ZIMMERMANN, W: 1807-78.
10670. (15) Poems from...W. Z-- by "Alethes," pseud. L: Hamilton, Adams 1841. viii;62p. 21cm. [BM]
10671. A popular hist. of Germany. Tr. Hugh Craig. NY: Johnson 1877. 4v. 600 ils. 29cm. [LC]

ZINZENDORF, Cn. Rs. v. 1727-52. Sel. in C269.

ZINZENDORF, Edme. Do. v. 1700-56. Sel. in C269.

ZINZENDORF, N: L: Graf v. 1700-60. Sel. in C230-1;235;240;269*;271; 273;276;486;489;570. See Spangenberg, A:, Life of..., #8819.]

ZINZERLING, Jt. ca. 1580-ca. 1620. Sel. in C483.

ZIRNDORF, H:, of Cincinnati.
10673. Some Jewish women. Tr. anon. Phil: Jewish publ. soc. 1892. viii;280p. 18cm. [BM]

ZITELMANN, Ern. 1852-1923. Sel. in C563.

ZOBELTITZ, Fedor K: Ma. Hm. A: v. 1857-1918. ("Hanns von Spielberg")
10674. Invisible hands: a novel. Tr. Sa. E. Boggs. NY: Bonner 1894. 372p. il. 19cm. [LC]
10675. The king's recruits. Tr. Sa. M. S. Clarke. L: Nisbet 1896 (1895). x;402p. 8. [BM]

ZOELLNER, ---. Sel. in C157.

ZOELLNER, Adalbert.
10675a. (Das Buch vom Porzellan.) The book of porcelain. Tr. by M. M. Morrow. Methuen 1927. 204p. 8. [EC]

ZOLLIKOFER, G: Jm. 1730-88. Sel. in C157.
10676. Exercises of piety; or, meditations...Abr. by Thaddeus M. Harris. 2d ed. Worcester, Mass: Thomas 1807. 191p. 12. [LCO]

ZORN, C: Manthey, 1846- .
10677. (Eunike: Väterliche Briefe.) Eunice: letters of a fatherly friend to a young Christian mother. Ad. from the German. anon. St.L: Concordia 1921. 98p. il. 19cm. [LC]

ZSCHOKKE, El. 1808-89.
10678. Memoirs of Fd. Rd. Hassler. Tr. Mrs. R. L. (Hassler) Norris. Nice: Prtd. by V. E. Gauthier 1882. 56lp. 18cm. [LC]

ZSCHOKKE, (J:) H: (Dn.) 1771-1848. Sel. in C98;142;155;190;194*;422; 469.
10679. [Coll.] n.d. Christmas stories. Tr. anon. Phil: Coates. (B13)
10680. [Coll.] 1839. The Swiss confederation; Wilhelm Tell. Tr. J. D. Haas. In C183.
§10681. [Coll.] 1844. Incidents of a social life amid the European Alps (Der Flüchtling im Jura). Tr. L: Strack. NY;Phil: Appleton. 373p. 19cm. [Great liberties taken.] [LC]
10682. [Coll.] 1845. The fool of the 19th cent. ("Ein Narr des 19. Jahrhunderts") and other tales. Tr. L: Strack. NY;Phil: Appleton. 373p. 18cm. [A reissue of the foregoing.]. [LC]
§10683. [Coll.] 1845. Tales by H: Z--. Tr. Parke Godwin and W: P. Prentice. NY: Putnam. (Ariel booklets.) 24. [UW]
[Advent. of a new year's eve ("Das Abenteuer der Neujahrsnacht"); The broken pitcher ("Der zerbrochene Krug"); Jonathan Frock (do.) Walpurgis night ("Die Walpurgisnacht"). The last tr. by Prentice, the others by Godwin. Tr. is not close enough.]
10684. [Coll.] 1846. Tales from...H: Zschökke [sic]. By Parke Godwin. L: Wiley & Putnam. x;214p. 19cm. [BM]
[The fool of the 19th cent. ("Ein Narr..."); Harmonius, tr. C. P. Cranch; Jack Steam ("Hans Dampf in allen Gassen"); Floretta, or the first love of H: IV ("Florette, erste Liebe H:s des IV");

ZSCHOKKE, H:
Advent. of a new year's eve ("Das Abenteuer..."). Godwin acted mainly as editor, apparently.]
10685. [Coll.] 1846. Tales...Zschökke (sic). Tr. Parke Godwin. 2d series. L: Wiley & Putnam. 238p. 19cm. [BM]
[Illuminations, or the sleep-waker ("Die Verklärungen"), tr. by F. B. and P. G. The broken cup ("Der zerbrochene Krug"), tr. by P. G. Jonathan Frock (do.), tr. by H. The involuntary journey, tr. by F. B. G. Leaves from the journal of a poor vicar in Wiltshire ("Blätter aus dem Tagebuch des armen Pfarr-Vikars"), tr. anon. Cf. the following entry.]
*10686. [Coll.] 1856. The Walpurgis-night ("Die Walpurgisnacht"); Leaves from the journal of a poor vicar in Wiltshire ("Blätter..."); The bean ("Die Bohne"). Tr. W. H. Furness. In "Julius and other tales from the German." Phil: Parry & McMillan. 303p. 18cm. [LC.BM]
["Julius" is by Rodolphe Toepffer; probably Furness had a German ed. of his stories.]
*10687. [Coll.] 1867. The princess of Brunswick-Wolfenbüttel ("Die Prinzessin v. Wolfenbüttel") and other tales. Tr. M. A. Faber. Lpz: Tauchnitz; L: Low. 323p. 16cm. [BM.LC]
[Also, A new year's eve advent. ("Das Abenteuer..."); The inn at Cransac ("Das Wirtshaus zu C--"). Excellent tr.]
§10688. [Coll.] 1890. [same as #10683] Putnam. Knickerbocker nuggets. 283p. 14cm. [Has also: About the author.] [BM]
10689. [Coll.] 1903. [same] Putnam. Ariel booklets. 18. [EC]
10690. (Abällino der grosse Bandit.) Abaellino, the great bandit: a dram. romance. Tr...and ad. to the NY. stage by W: Dunlap. NY: 1792. 82p. 12. (B6a)
10691. do. 1802. [same] NY: Longworth. 82p. 14cm. [LC]
[Prose, much adapted.]
10692. do. 1804. The bravo of Venice. Tr. M. G. Lewis. L: Hughes. See "Brit. Crit." 25(1804):201. (B26)
10693. do. 1805. [same] Hughes. viii;299p. 17cm. [BM]
10694. do. 1805. The Venetian outlaw: a drama in 3 acts [prose]. Tr. (from the French version) and ad. to the Engl. stage by R. W. Elliston. L: Baldwin. 60p. 14cm. [BM]
[Very free ad. Bandit is here named Vivaldi.]
10695. do. 1806. [same] reprint. NY: Longworth. 60p. 14cm. [BM]
10696. do. 1807. [same as #10693] 5th ed. Hughes. 17cm. [BM]
10697. do. 1809. [same] 6th ed. 299p. [BM]
10698. do. 1809. [same] reprint. Abaellino, the bravo of Venice. 1st Amer. from 5th L: ed. Balto: Warner & Hanna. 299p. 12. (B48)
10699. do. 1809. [same; reprint] Bost: Greenleaf. 299p. 18. (B48)
10700. do. 1814. [same as #10690] NY: Longworth. 60p. 16cm. [LC]
10701. do. 1820. [same] 4th ed. NY: Longworth. 66p. 15cm. [LC.BM]
[Abaellino on cover and in heading, thereafter Abaellino.]
10702. do. 1820. Rugantino; or, the bravo of Venice. A melodrama by M. G. Lewis. L: Simpkin & Marshall. 30p. 18cm. [BM.LC]
[In Vol. 9 of W: Oxberry's "The new Engl. drama." A dramatization of #10642.]
10703. do. 1830. [same as #10692] L: W:Mason. 246p. 19cm. [BM]
10704. do. 1856. [same] (With Walpole's "Castle of Otranto.") L: Ward & Lock. pp. 1-110. 16cm. [BM]
10705. do. 1857. [same] In "Clarke's home lib." L: 75p. no pref. 17cm. [BM]
10706. do. 1857. [same] (With Irving's "Rip van Winkle.") L: Vickers. pp. 1-85. 14cm. [BM]
10707. (Alamontade, der Galeerensklave.) Alamontade. Tr. C. A. Feiling. 1844. In C442.
§10708. do. 1845. The galley slave. Tr. from 45th Ger. ed.J: T. S. Sullivan. Phil: Joy. 230p. 19cm. ["Edited."] [LC]

ZSCHOKKE, H:--Alamontade, der Galeerensklave
§10709. do. 1882. Alamontada, the galley-slave. Tr. Ira G. Mosher. NY: Bennett. 194p. 19cm. [Style inadequate.] [LC]
10710. (Blätter aus dem Tagebuch des armen Pfarr-Vikars.) Leaves from the journal of a poor vicar in Wiltshire. Tr. W: H: Furness. In The Gift. Phil: Carey & Hart 1845. ["The Gift" was an annual. This number also contained poetry from Goethe.]
10711. do. 1845. Journal of a poor vicar, The Walpurgis-night, and other stories. Phil. 12. [LCO]
[This vol. was missing; possibly a first ed. of #10686.]
10712. do. 1852. Journal of a poor vicar. NY: Taylor. 8. [AC]
10712a. do. 1852. [same?] Journal of a poor vicar. Tr. anon. Il. by Toni Johannot. Lpz;Stuttgart: Winter. 47p. 8. [EC (Heinsius)]
10713. (Das Abenteuer der Neujahrsnacht.) Sylvester eve: the advent. of a watchman. Tr. Tobias Watkins. In "Tales of the tripod; or, a Delphian evening." By Pertinax Peculiar. Balto: Lucas 1821. 162p. 16. (B48)
10714. do. 1835. The advent. of a night. Tr. anon. In C472.
*10715. do. 1868. Advent. of a new year's eve. Tr. anon. In C130.
*10716. do. 1879. [same] In C168.
*10717. do. 1882. A new year's eve advent. Tr. anon. NY: Munro. Seaside lib. 24p. 32cm. [LC]
10718. do. 1884. A Sylvester night's advent. Tr. M. B. W. Cincin: Clarke. 119p. 19cm. [LC]
10719. do. 1898. Advent. of a new year's eve. Tr. anon. In C509.
10720. do. 1912-17. New year's eve. Student's literal tr. Translation pub. n.d. 15cm. [AC]
§10721. (Das Goldmacherdorf.) Goldenthal: a tale. Tr. anon. L: Whittaker 1833. xii;131p. 14cm. [BM]
§10722. do. 1845. Goldmaker's village. L: Burns. vi;177p. 17cm. [BM]
[Tr. makes rather free with the orig.]
10723. do. n.d. [same? same title] NY: Appleton. (before 1852) [AC]
10724. (Der Creole.) The creole. Tr. anon. NY: Colyer 1836. 8. [AC]
10725. (Der Flüchtling im Jura.) Refugee in the mountains of Jura. Tr. Parke Godwin. NY: Winchester 1844. 71p. (B12) [NY]
§10726. (Der Freihof v. Aarau.) Veronica; or, the free court of Aarau. Tr. S: Spring. NY: Harper 1845. 111p. 23cm. [LC]
[Tr. pads and omits, but is otherwise good.]
*10727. do. 1847. Tr. anon. In "The parlour novelist," vol. 14. Belfast. Simms & McIntyre; L: Orr. 376p. 16cm. [BM]
§10728. do. 1876. [same as #10726] [LC]
10729. (Der Millionär.) The two millionaires. Tr. Sa. Fry. In "Tait's Ed. Mag." 14(1847):163, 305. [Retold.] [BM]
10730. (Der tote Gast.) The dead guest. Tr. anon. 1835. In C472, pp. 1-178.
§10731. do. 1848. The lover's stratagem. Tr. anon. In C376.
[Tr. is quite good, but not strictly faithful.]
10732. do. 1869. The dead guest; and, The eccentric. Tr. G. C. McWhorter. NY: Appleton, 109p. il. 8. [NY]
10733. do. 1872-6. [same title] NY: Raddeen.d. [AC]
10734. do. 1878. [same title] Chic: Donnelley, Lloyd. Lakeside lib. 4. [LCO]
§10735. do. 1880. [same title] NY: Munro. Seaside lib. 32cm. [LC]
[Poor tr.]
10736. (Der zerbrochene Krug.) The broken cup. Tr. anon. 1847. In C20. Cf. C21.
10737. do. 1856. The broken cup. Tr. anon. In C454.
10738. do. 1888. The broken pitcher. Tr. anon. Sever. 12. [AC]
§10739. do. 1907. The broken cup. Tr. P(arke) G(odwin). 1907. In C447. [Errors.]

ZSCHOKKE, H:--Der zerbrochene Krug
10740. do. 1912-17. The broken pitcher. Tr. anon. Student's literal tr. Transl. pub. n.d. 15cm. [AC]
10741. do. 1915. [same as #10687] In C179.
10742. do. 1927. The broken pitcher. Tr. P. Godwin. In C367.
§10743. (Des Schweizerlands Geschichten für das Schweizervolk.) Z--'s popular hist. of Switzerland. With the author's subsequent alterations of the orig. work. Tr. W. Howard Howe. Frankfort o. M: Prtd. for J: D: Sauerländer 1833. 658p. 17cm. [Deviations in both style and matter. Sold in L. by Ackermann.] [BM]
§10744. do. 1834. [same] The hist. of Switzerland...from its earliest origin to the present time...L: E.Wilson. 395p. 17cm. [Caption title reads: Z--'s popular hist. of Switzerland. EC dates this 1833.] [BM.LC]
*10745. do. 1855. The hist. of Switzerland for the Swiss people. By H: Z-- with a contin. to the year 1848 by El. Zschokke. Tr. Fis. G: Shaw. NY: Francis; L: Low. 405p. front. 18cm. [LC] [Tr. from the 9th Ger. ed. Tr. is correct, does not follow Z--'s style.]
10746. do. 1872-6. [same?] NY: Mason n.d. [AC]
10747. (Die Branntweinpest. Eine Trauergeschichte zur Warnung.) The rum plague: a narr. for the admonition of both old and young. Tr. anon. NY: Taylor 1853. 18. [AC]
§10748. (Die Irrfahrt des Philhellenen.) Wanderings of a Phil-Hellene. Tr. Gustaf C. Hebbe. NY: Daggers 1845. 43p. 23cm. [LC] [Poor, errors.]
*10749. (Die Nacht in Brzwezmcisl.) The advent. of a night. Tr. anon. 1835. In C472, vol. 3, p. 95 sq.
§10750. (Die Prinzessin v. Wolfenbüttel.) Christina; or, memoirs of a Ger. princess. Tr. anon (from the French: "La Princesse de W--" of Baroness de Montolieu). L: Colburn 1808. 2v. in one. 208; 272p. 15cm. [Good, but suffers from the double transfer.] [BM]
§10751. do. 1809. [same] [BM]
*10752. do. 1881. [same tr. as #10687] NY: Munro. Seaside lib. 39p. 32cm. [LC]
*10753. (Die Rose v. Disentis.) The rose of D--: a novel. Tr. Jas. J. D. Trevor. NY: Sheldon 1873. 284p. 19cm. [LC] [From his "Aehrenlese."]
10754. (Die Verklärungen.) Hortensia. Tr. anon. NY: Winchester n.d. (before 1852). [AC]
*10755. do. 1868. [same?] Hortensia; or, the transfiguration. In Davis, A. J., "Memoranda of persons, etc." Bost: White. 19cm. pp. 345-464. [Not excellent.] [LCO.BM]
10756. (Florette, oder die erste Liebe H:s IV.) Floretta; or, the first love of H: IV. Tr. anon. In "The Parlour Novelist," vol. 7. Belfast: Simms & McIntyre; L: Orr 1846. 16cm. [BM]
10757. do. 1899. [Ad.] Floretta: opera in 2 acts by Eleanor Farjeon. Founded on...Libr. (verse) 31p. 20cm. [Performed July 17, 1899.] [BM]
§10758. (Geschichte vom Kampf und Untergang der...Berg- und Waldkantone.) Hist. of the invasion of Switzerland by the French, and the destruction of the democratical republics of Schwitz, Uri, and Unterwalden. Tr. anon. from the French of J. B. Briatte. Pref. and supplement by the tr. L: Longman & Rees 1803. vii;365p. 22cm. [Either the French or the Engl. tr. has not been overly faithful, though the general sense is correctly given.] [BM.LC]
10759. (Geschichtliche Darstellung von der Ausbreitung des Christentums auf dem Erdball.) Present state of Christianity...in all parts of the world. Ad. by F: Shoberl. L: Hurst, Chance 1828. xiv;440p. 18cm. [Founded on Z--'s work, not really a tr. of it] [BM]

ZSCHOKKE, H:
*10760. (Jonathan Frock.) J-- F--. Also, Floretta, etc. (see #10756) Tr. anon. In "The Parlour novelist," vol. 7. Belfast: Simms & McIntyre; L: Orr 1846. 16cm. pp. 273-376. [BM]
*10761. (Meister Jordan, oder Handwerk hat goldenen Boden.) Labour stands on golden feet; or, the life of a foreign workman. A holiday story. Tr. J: Yeats. L: Groombridge 1852. viii;162p. front. 15cm. [BM]
10762. do. 1855. [same] New ed. L: Groombridge. [EC]
10763. do. 1870. [same] 3d rev. ed. L;NY: Cassell. vi;162p. 16cm.[BM] [Diff. front. from #10711, and one pl.]
10764. do. 1870. [same?] NY: Dodd & Mead. [AC]
10765. do. 187- . [same] 4th rev. ed. L;Paris;NY: Cassell, Petter & Galpin. 162p. il. 17cm. [LC]
10766. do. 1887. [same?] A holiday story. 4th ed. Philip. 8. [EC]
10767. The prime minister. Tr. anon. NY: Winchester n.d. (before 1852) [AC]
10768. (Selbstschau.) Autobiog. Tr. anon. L: Chapman & Hall 1845. viii;220p. 21cm. [From part one of the orig.] [BM.LCO]
10769. do. 1847. [same] [EC]
10770. The sleepwaker. Tr. anon. Bost: Munroe 1842. iv;224p. 18.[LC]

STUNDEN DER ANDACHT

*10771. 1830. Hours of devotion. Tr. by Rev. E. T. (i.e., J.) Burrow. L: Rivington, xvii;574p. 22cm. [BM]
[He tr. 5 from each of the 8 vols. of the orig.]
§10772. 1834. Hours of devotion. Tr. anon. Bliss & Wadsworth; Phil: Kay; Pittsburg: Kay. 251p. 12. [LC]
[Tr..was Morris Mattson, according to Goedeke (B8), who dates this 1835. Tr. is quite free; Sel. derive largely from vol. 1 of the orig.]
10773. 1838? Burrow's tr. L. (B8)
§10774. 1843. Hours of meditation and devotional reflection...Tr. Jas. D. Haas. L: Chapman & Hall. xvi;356p. 17cm. [Pretty good.][BM]
10775. 1844. [same] Hours of meditation and reflection. NY: Redfield. [Goedeke (B8) says this was the tr. of Haas.] [AC]
*10776. 1845. Stray leaves from the German; or, select essays from Z--. Tr. W. B. Flower and E. F. S. L: Simpkin & Marshall. 168p. 22cm. [BM.LCO]
[Includes: Sketch of his life from his autobiog., pp. 1-29.]
10777. 1847. [same as #10774] 2d ed. L: Chapman & Hall. 356p. [LCO]
*10778. 1862. Meditations on death and eternity. Tr. Frederica Rowan. L: Trübner. vi;385p. 22cm. [BM]
[Sel. made by Queen Victoria on the death of Albert, with whom the work had been a favorite, and tr. for her.]
10779. 1863. [same as #10774] L: (B8)
*10780. 1863. [reissue of #10778] The hand-book of family devotion. L: Simpkin, Marshall. vi;368p. 21cm. [Four meditations added.][BM]
*10781. 1863. Meditations on life and its religious duties. Tr. Frederica Rowan. L: Trübner; Bost: Ticknor & F. 337p. 19cm. [LCO]
*10782. 1863. Meditations on death and eternity. Tr. Frederica Rowan. Bost: Ticknor & F. 414p. 19cm. [LC]
[A companion vol. to the foregoing, with a different selection.]
*10783. 1864. [same] [LC]
*10784. 1883. Meditations on life, death, and eternity. Tr. F. Rowan. Bost: Houghton. viii;678p. 20cm. [BM]
[This unites #10731 and #10732.]
*10785. 1884. [same] NY: Phillips & Hunt; Cincin: Cranston & Stowe. 2v. 16cm. [LC]

ZUCKERMANN, Hg. 1881-1915. Sel. in C423.

ZUR MUEHLEN, Herminia, 1883- .
10786. Fairy tales for workers' children. Tr. Ida Dailes. Il. Lydia Gibson. Chic: Daily worker 1925. 66p. 29cm. [LC]
[The rose-bush; The sparrow; The little grey dog; Why?]

ZURNOW, C:
10787. The maiden mother: or, Eugenia the guiltless. Secrets in the lives of prominent personages of Louisiana. (In Engl. or Ger.) Barclay n.d. (1872-6) 8. [AC]
[Not certain that this is a tr. from the German.]

ZWEIG, Arnold, 1887- .
10787a. (Der Streit um den Sergeanten Grischa.) Case of Sergeant G--. Tr. Eric Sutton. Viking; Secker 1927. vi;449p. O. [AC]

ZWEIG, Stefan, 1881- . Sel. in C28.
10788. [Coll.] Passion and pain. Tr. Eden and Cedar Paul. L: Chapman & Hall 1924. vii;266p. 19cm. [BM.LC]
[Letter from an unknown woman ("Brief einer Unbekannten"); The runaway; Transfiguration; The fowler snared; Compulsion ("Der Zwang"); The governess; Virata, or the eyes of the undying brother.]
10789. [Coll.] 1925. [same] NY: Richards. 273p. [AC]
10790. (Brennendes Geheimnis.) The burning secret. Tr. anon. L: Allen & Unwin 1921. 175p. 19cm. [BM]
10791. (Die unsichtbare Sammlung.) The invisible collection. Tr. anon. Il. Js. Malay. NY: Pynson, printers, 1926. 36p. 21cm. [LC]
[Tr. was made for "The living age," Aug. 1, 1925.]
§10792. (Jeremias.) Jeremiah: a drama in 9 scenes [prose]. Tr. from the author's rev. text by Eden and Cedar Paul. NY: Seltzer 1922. 336p. 24cm. [Rather poor; style and diction gone, also errors.] [LC]
*10793. (Verwirrung der Gefühle.) Conflicts. Tr. Eden and Cedar Paul. NY: Viking 1927. 297p. 19cm. [LC.BM]
[Four-and-twenty hours in a woman's life; A failing heart; Episode in the early life of privy councillor D.]

ZWICK, H: A:
*10794. (Reise von Sarepta...) Calmuc Tartary: a journey... Tr. anon. L: Holdsworth & Ball 1831. 262p. 19cm. [BM.LC]

ZWICK, J:s, d. 1542. Sel. in C231-2;273;287;489.

ZWINGLI, U: (or Huldreich), 1484-1531. Sel. in C469;486.
10795. The Christian educ. of youth. Tr. from reprint of orig. Swiss ed. by A. Reichenbach. Collegeville, Pa: Thompson 1909. 100p. il. 18. [LC]
*10796. The Latin works and the corr...together with select. from his Ger. works. Tr. H. Preble (Latin treatises), Wa. Lichtenstein, and L. A. McLouth. General editor, S: M. Jackson. NY: Putnam 1912- . 23cm. [LC]
[Revision of Myconius's life of Z-- by Preble. No more published.]
10797. (U: Zwingli, eine Auswahl aus seinen Schriften.) Sel. works. Tr. by L. A. McLouth (Ger.), H: Preble (Latin), and G: W. Gilmore (Latin). Ed. by S: M. Jackson. Phil: U. of Penn. 1901. 258p. 18cm. [LC.BM]
See Christoffel, R., Z--, or the rise of the reformation in Switzerland, #1128.
See Grob, J:, Life..., #3507.
See Hottinger, J:, Life and times..., #4602.

LIST A. ANONYMA

[Note. In revising this list, I have identified many anonymous publications; these are included here, with a reference to the name of the author. All "collections" have been transferred to List C; such titles have mostly been omitted here.]

A1. A., M. The war of 1870-71. Tr. Capt. C. H. F. Ellis. L: Bumpus 1873. 448p. 19cm. [M. A. is "a Prussian artillery officer."] [BM]
A2. AGNES de Lilien: a novel. 1801. See K:e Wolzogen.
A3. ALSACE. Village tales from Alsatia. Tr. Sir A. C. Duff Gordon. L: Cundall 1848. 247p. 18cm. [LC]
[LC ascribes these to Ax. (orig., Abraham) Weill, 1811-99. They are from the same orig. as the following.]
A4. ALSACE. (11) Tales from Alsace; or, scenes and port. from life in the days of the Reformation, as drawn from old chronicles. Tr. from the German, with introd. appended to the French ed. by the French tr., E. R. Saint-Hilaire. L: Nisbet 1868. xix;395p. front. 18cm. [Stories by an Alsatian lady, sometimes referred to as the "Strassburg tracts."] [BM]
A5. do. 1870. [same] New ed. 8. [EC]
A6. AMBER WITCH, THE. See Meinhold, J: W:
A7. AMIS, Pfaffe. Sel. Tr. anon. 1906. In C190.
A8. ANALYSIS OF NOBILITY, THE. From the German. Tr. anon. In "Scots Mag." 16(1754):552. (B26)
A9. ANGELION; or, the wizard in Elis. A romance. Tr. Ma. Geisweiler. L: Sherwood, Neely & Jones 1816. 3v. 18cm. [BM]
A10. ANDRONICUS. See Titus, A549.
A11. ANNA; or, the little runaway. Tr. anon. L: Hamilton 1875. 12. [EC]
A12. ANNA. Also, Meta Frantz; or, a Sunday at Lucerne. Tr. E. J. S. L: Hodder & S. 1886. 112p. il. 17cm. [BM]
A13. ANTHONY TRAUGOTT, the potter musician. Tr. anon. L: Darton 1848. 18. [EC]
A14. ARNOLD OF WINKELRIED: a drama. See Winkelried, A579.
A15. ART TREASURES OF GERMANY. See Goerling, Ad.
A16. AUS DEM CHEDER: pict. of Jewish life. See Biesenthal, J. H. R.
A17. B., A. v. The Lebanon. Herder 1916. See Berlichingen, A. v.
A18. B., E. R. A victim of the Falk laws. See Victim, A561.
A19. B., H. v. Tale of the swallow. 1884. See Buelow, Ma. He. v.
A20. B., Mrs. 'Vater unser.' 1844. See Vater, A560.
A21. BAERENBURG, Midsummer holidays at Castle B--. See Wildermuth, Ote. v.
A22. BARON OF MANSTOW, THE: a novel from the German. Tr. anon. L: Lane 1790. 2v. 236; 166p. 16cm. [BM]
A23. BASKET-MAKER. The little basket-maker, and other tales: a story book for holiday hours. Tr. anon. L: Cundall 1845. 87p. 4 (col.) ils. 17cm. [Title-story and "The two doves" are tr. from the Ger. of a lady writer.] [BM]
A24. BELLE and Lily. Tr. from Ger? NY: O'Shea n.d. (1872-6) il. 16. [AC]
A25. BERLICHINGEN. See Gottfried of the iron hand, A216.
A26. BERLIN. The romance of a court; or, Berlin and Sanssouci. 1866. See Muehlbach, Lu.
A27. BERNE. The prisoner of Berne; or, a brand from the burning. Tr. Mda. Wrench. L: Wertheim, Macintosh & Hunt 1859. 24p. 13cm. [BM]
A28. BETHLEHEMITES. Tr. Julie Sutter. L: Partridge 1886. 96p. il. 18cm. [BM]
A29. BIRD. Little bird red and little bird blue; a tale of the woods (in verse). Tr. Mda. B. B. Edwards. Il. by T. R. Macquoid. L: Low 1861. 48p. 18cm. [BM]
["Ad. with some alterations from...an unknown author."]

BIRD.
A30. do. 1862? [same] NY: Jas. Gregory. 48p. 17cm. [BM]
A31. do. 1883. [same] L;NY: Routledge. 21 x 17cm. [BM]
A32. BIRD. The bird's nest and other tales. 1843. See Schmid, J. C. v.
A33. BIRD. The bird's nest; or, the keeping of a promise rewarded. 1872. See Schmid, J. C. v.
A33a. The BLIND fisherman and his three sons. Tr. Mme. de Chatelain. Lpz: 1859. 25p. il. 4. [EC (Heinsius)]
A34. BOKUM, Hm., tr. The testimony of a refugee from East Tennessee ("Das Zeugnis eines Flüchtlings von Ost-Tennessee"). Phil: Prtd. for gratuitous distribution. 1863. 24p. 22cm. [BM]
A35. BREUGHEL bros., an art romance. 1854. See Ungern-Sternberg, Ax. v.
A36. BRUNO. Clever Bruno: a tale. Ad. from the German. L: S.P.C.K. 1879. 46p. front. il. 14cm. [BM]
A37. C., J. F. The Christmas tree: a parable--from the German. L: Wertheim 1863. 32p. 13cm. [BM]
A38. C., M. A. The Christmas tree: a story (in verse) founded on "Der Tannenbaum." 2d ed. L: Beer 1877. 15p. 15cm. [BM]
A39. do. 1886. [same] 3d ed. 15p. 16cm. [BM]
A40. CARL, Handschuhsheimer. 1868. See Karl.
A41. CARL'S SECRET: a story of life in Vienna. (Tr. from the German?) L: Relig. tract soc. 1887. 80p. il. 13cm. [BM]
A42. CHRISTIAN and Leah, and other Ghetto stories. 1895. See Kompert, Lp.
A43. CHRISTMAS. (Weihnachten.) Cantata by Fz. Abt. Tr. anon. Vocal score. L: Augener; NY: Schirmer 1884. 33p. 27cm. [BMM]
A44. CHRISTMAS. A Christmas present for children. Tr. anon. L: J.Masters 1856. 82p. 14cm. [BM]
A45. CHRISTMAS. The three Christmas trees. Tr. anon. L: S.P.C.K. 1864. 24p. il. 12cm. [BM]
A46. CHRISTMAS. The Christmas tree: a story for young and old. Tr. anon. L: J:Morgan 1864. 128p. col. front. 14cm. [BM]
A47. CHRISTMAS. The Christmas tree: a tale for children. Founded on facts. Tr. anon. L: Jarrold 1862. 20p. 16cm. [BM]
A48. CHRISTMAS. Why do we keep Christmas? Altered from the German. Anon. L: Hamilton, Adams 1862. 15p. 9cm. [BM]
CHRISTMAS. See also C., J. F. and C., M. A., this list.
A49. CLIMBING the glacier. 1865. See Hoffmann, Fz.
A50. COLOURED FRENCH TROOPS ON THE RHINE. Tr. anon. Lpz: Hartmann 1923. 4th rev. and extended ed. 60p. il. 21cm. [LC]
[Put out by the "Rheinische Frauenliga."]
A51. COMICAL CREATURES FROM WURTEMBURG. See Wurtemburg.
A52. CONFESSOR AT COURT; or, the martyrdom of St. John Nepomucene. Ad. from the Ger. by L. A: Rendter. Soc. of the divine word 1913. 208p. D. [AC]
A53. CONVERTED JEW. See Jew.
A54. CROSS. The stony cross in the Demon's Valley: an Austrian story. (Translation?) In Twelve nights' entertainments. Burns' Fireside lib. 1845. [BM]
A55. DANCE OF DEATH, THE: a story from the German. Tr. anon. "Blackwoods Mag." 31(1832):328. (B26)
A56. DAVENPORT, Mrs. W., tr. Land of glory. L: Wertheim 1847. 12. [EC]
A57. DAY IN CAPERNAUM, A. 1887. See Delitzsch, Fz.
A58. DEUTSCHE LIEBE. German love. See Mueller, F. Max.
A59. DOMESTIC SCENES. 1806. See Hildebrandt, J: A. C.
A60. DORN, OSWALD. 1857. See van der Velde, K: Fz.
A61. DOROTHEA TRUDEL; or, the prayer of faith. From the German. Anon. L: Morgan 1872. 12. [EC]
A62. DUNLOP, W: Peter the Great; or, the Russian mother. See Peter.

A63. ECCENTRIC TALES FROM THE GERMAN. Robins 1829. 12. [EC]
[These tales were really by C: Rb. Forrester, not a tr.]
A64. ELIZA; or, the pattern of women. 1802. See Wobeser, W:e K:e v.
A65. EMIN PASHA. African expedition. See Peters, K:
†A66. EMS. Bath Ems and its environs. (Bad Ems und seine Umgebungen.) A guide to travellers and visiters [sic]. Tr. anon. Il. J: Poppel, F. Abresch, and E. Willmann. Darmstadt;Wiesbaden: G. G. Lange 1803. 16p. 3pl. 22cm. [BM]
[Tr. evidently by a German, and quite grotesquely awkward.]
A67. ERL-KING'S DAUGHTER, THE. Tr. anon. 1823. In C456.
A68. ERNA; or, the forest princess. 1855. See Nieritz, Gst.
A69. EUGENIA: a German story. Tr. anon. 1845. See Fouqué, de La Motte-.

TILL EULENSPIEGEL

A70. [Sel.] 1826. Howleglas, the merry jester. Tr. T: Roscoe. In C477.
A71. [Sel.] 1834. Tr. W: J. Thoms. In C537.
A72. [Sel.] 1906. Tr. anon. In C190.
A73. [Sel.] 1926. E-- and the merchant. Tr. T: Roscoe. In C68.
A74. [Sel.] 1926. Tr. anon. In C405a.
A75. [Sel.] 1927. Tr. T: Roscoe. In C367.
A76. 1528? Here beginneth a merye Jest of a man that was called Howleglas, and of many marueylous thinges and Jestes that he dyd in his lyfe, in Eastlande and in many other places. Tr. anon. L: Wyllyam Copland. ff. A-Miv. 17cm. [Defective copy. Woodcuts.] [BM]
A77. 1530? [same text and paging] ...meruaylous thynges...Eastland. [This copy more defective than the foregoing. A different set-up, ending supplied in MS. Herford (B18) says this version was based on an undated Antwerp ed. ca. 1520-30, which contains about half of the orig. Ouvry thinks this date and the preceding one are both too early, as Copland did his printing on Fleet Street up to 1557, and later moved to the "Vintry on the 3 craned wharf," as in the colophon of these eds. Probably 1560 more nearly correct.] [BM]
A78. 1709. The Ger. rogue; or, the life and merry advent...of Till Eulespiegel...Made Engl. from the high Dutch. Anon. L: (B18)
†A79. 1720. The Ger. rogue; or, the life and merry advent., cheats, stratagems, and contrivances of Tiel Eulespiegle. Tr. anon. L: n.i. 111p. 18cm. [Tr. is negligible.] [BM]
§A80. 1860. The marvellous advent. and rare conceits of Master Tyll Owlglass. Newly coll., chronicled, and set forth in our Engl. tongue by K. R. H. Mackenzie. Il. (partly in col.) by Af. Crowquill. L: Trübner; Bost: Ticknor & F. xxxi;255p. 18cm. [BM.LCO]
[Uses Low German version of 1515; tr. 111 advent. into archaic Engl.]
A81. 1860. [same?] Tyl Owlglass, diverting and cunning devices. 2d ed. L: Trübner. il. 8. [Cf. 1923 ed.] [EC]
A82. 1867. [reprint of A76] Howleglas. Ed. by Frederic Ouvry. L: Priv. prt. viii;95p. 21cm. [BM.HCL]
§A83. 1880. [same tr. as A80] Cited in A86.
§A84. 1890. [same] New ed. L: Trübner. Lotos series. xxxv;319p. 16cm. [BM]
A85. 1899. Till Owlglass' funny pranks. Done in Engl. for the young folks, by Julia I. Bull. Il. E. Klimsch. Bost: Lothrop. 48p. 8. [LC]
§A86. 1923. [same as A84] L: Routledge; NY: Dutton. (Broadway tr.) xxxv;319p. il. 19cm. [BM.LC]
[This ed. cites as previous dates of issue: 1859(1860), 1880, 1890.]

A87. EVERY beginning is easy. Tr. from the Ger. anon. Bost: Phillips Sampson n.d. (1855-8) 4. [AC]
A88. EXILE of Idria: a German tale. 1833. Not a translation.
A89. EYE-WITNESS. A faithful account of the riot in Vienna, 13th April 1798, occasioned by the French ambassador's (Gen. Bernadotte) hoisting in that city the national flag of France. By an eye-witness. Tr. from the German. anon. L: J.Wright 1798. 29p. 20cm. [BM]
A90. EYE-WITNESS. The fall of Underwald. By an eye-witness. Tr. from the German. anon. L: J.Wright 1798. 20p. 20cm. [BM]
A91. FAIRY BALLADS, from the German. 1856. See Wolf, J: W:
A92. FAIRY BELLS, and what they tolled us. 1867. See List C, under Lander, S. W.
A93. FAIRY BOOK, the diamond. 1897. See C126.
A94. FAIRY FANCIES. 1870. See List C, under Eden, L. S.
A95. FALKENBOURG, The castle of, and other tales. 1843. See Schmid, J. C. v.
A96. FALKENBURGH, a tale of the Rhine. 1851. Not a tr.
A97. FALSELY ACCUSED: a criminal trial in Nürnberg, 1790. Tr. anon. In "Tales from Blackwood," new series, vol. 3, 1878, pp.65-107. [BM] [From "Der neue Pitaval," by Hitzig and Häring (W. Alexis).]
A98. FANCY TALES from the German. 1860. See List C, under Laurie, J. S.
A99. FATHERLAND SERIES. Tr. from the Ger. Phil: Lutheran pub. n.d. (1872-6) il. 17cm. [AC]
I find the following books listed for this series:
Anne du Bourg. (Unable to trace it.)
Anton the fisherman. See Hoffmann, Fz., #4443.
Buried in the snow. See Hoffmann, Fz., #4466.
Christmas. See Hoffmann, Fz., #4496.
Cottage by the lake. See Claudius, Mt., #1130.
A day in Capernaum. See Delitzsch, Fz., #1187.
Dominic. See Hoffmann, Fz., #4433.
The emerald. See Redenbacher, W., #7370.
Faithful unto death. See Nieritz, Gst., #6784.
Fritz; or, filial obedience. See Hoffmann, Fz., #4455.
Geyer Wälty. See Hoffmann, Fz., #4460.
Gottlieb Frey. See Nieritz, Gst., #6789.
Greek slave; or, filial love. See Hoffmann, Fz., #4472.
Gustavus Vasa. See Nieritz, Gst., #6791.
Hans Egede. See Nieritz, Gst., #6794a.
Herdsman of Dambach. See Koerber, Ph., #5119.
Hop blossoms. See Schmid, Cph., #8381.
In the midst of the North Sea. See Roskowska, Me., #7585.
Iron age of Germany. See Hoffmann, Fz., #4428.
Iron head. See Hoffmann, Fz., #4437.
Knight and peasant. See Hoffmann, Fz., #4491.
Leonhard, the runaway. See Horn, W., #4595.
Little cloister ruin. See Redenbacher, W., #7371.
Little Madelon; or, maternal love. See Hoffmann, Fz., #4483.
Olaf Thorlaksen. See Horn, W., #4598.
Rene the little Savoyard. See Hoffmann, Fz., #4487.
Rich man and the poor man. See Nieritz, Gst., #6806.
Salzburger exodus. See Nieritz, Gst., #6778a.
Schoolmaster and his son. See Caspari, K: H:, #1065.
Self will. See Hoffmann, Fz., #4451.
Seppeli, the Swiss boy. See A518.
The story of Father Miller. See Hoffmann, Fz., #4436.
The story of the old schoolmaster. See Hoffmann, Fz., #4449.
Three bank notes. See Hoffmann, Fz., #4447.

FATHERLAND SERIES
Three kings. See Nieritz, Gst., #6812.
Treasure of the Inca. See Hoffmann, Fz., #4441.
Under the earth. See Hoffmann, Fz., #4495.
Valley Mill. See Wild, F:, #10179.
Wolfgang, prince of Anhalt. See Hoffmann, Fz., #4458.

FAUST[1]

A100. [Sel.] 1926. Doctor F-- and the usurer. Tr. T: Roscoe. 1926. In C68.

A101. [Sel.] 1927. Dr. F-- arranges a marriage. Tr. T: Roscoe. In C367.

A102. 1592. The historie of the damnable life, and deserued death of Doctor Iohn Faustus, Newly imprinted, and in conuenient places imperfect matter amended: according to the true Copie printed at Franckfort, and tr. into Engl. by P. F. Gent. Seene and allowed. Imprinted at Lond. by T: Orwin, and are to be solde by E: White, dwelling at the little North doore of Paules, at the signe of the Gun. 80p. 18cm. [BM]
[Heading reads: A discourse of the most famous Doctor John Faustus of Wittenberg in Germanie, etc. This version follows in arrangement and matter the "Historia v. D. Johann Fausten" prtd. at Frankfurt by J: Spiess, 1587. 63 chaps. as against 69 of the orig. Very free tr., with additions by the tr.]

A103. (Ander Theil D. Johann Fausti Historien...) 1594. Second report of Doctor J: Faustus, containing his appearances, and the deeds of Wagner. Written by an Engl. gentleman student in Wittenberg an university of Germany in Saxony. Pub. for the delight of all those which desire novelties, by a friend of the same gentleman. L: Prtd. by Abell Jeffes, for Cuthbert Burby... 1594. 4. [This version of the so-called "Wagnerbuch" is cited by Thoms in A143.]

A104. 1608. [same as A102] L: Prtd. by I. Windet for E: White. ff. A-K3. 18cm. [BM]
[New t.p. but same reading as above. No table. 63 chaps. Engr. on copper of Mephostophiles and Ioan (sic) Faustus by Carl van Sichem pasted into vol.]

A105. 1620? The hist. of the damnable life and deserved death, etc. Anon. L: Prtd. for M. Hotham. 40 leaves. sm. 4. (B19a)
[Probably the same as A102; cf. A107.]

A106. 1636. [same title] Tr. P. R. (i.e., F.) Gent. L: prtd. for W: Whitwood, at the sign of the Bell in Duck Lane near Smithfield. 38ff. 4. [No pagination. Signatures A2 + B-K in fours.] [BM]

A107. 1648. The historie of the damnable life, etc. L: Prtd. for E: Wright. ff. A-K. 19cm. [BM]
[Same as A102. 63 chaps., no table. Tr. is called P. R. Spelling Frankford is used. T.p. has woodcut of Faust as necromancer.]

A108. 1650? [same] L: Prtd. for W: Whitwood. ff. A-K. 19cm. [BM]
[T.p. as in the foregoing. Spelling Frankford; also, "impertinent" for "imperfect."]

A109. 1664. The hist. of Dr. J: Faustus; compiled in verse, very pleasant and delightfull. L: Prtd. by E. Cotes and...sold by C: Tyns. ff. A-B. 13cm. [BM]
[7 chaps., ending with funeral oration. Woodcut as in A107.]

A110. 1680. (Wagnerbuch.) The second report, of Doctor J: Faustus. Declaring how he was amongst the Infernal Spirits, and how he used to appear again upon the Earth, and what strange things he did; Also very wonderful apparitions of the Infernal King and his followers. And likewise strange exploits of Wagner and his three

[1]Marlowe's Faustus is not included.

FAUST

familiars. L: Prtd. for Ralph Smith. ff. A-H. 18cm. [28 chaps. Woodcut on t.p. Orig. is the so-called Wagnerbuch, pub. 1593.][BM]

A111. 1696. [same as A109] The hist. of Dr. J: Faustus, compyled in verse, very pleasant and delightful. Prtd. in the year 1696. 24p. 12cm. [7 chaps. Small cut on t.p.] [BM]

A112. 1696. [same as A108] L: Prtd. by W. O. for J. Back. ff. A-K. 20cm. [62 chaps. Woodcut as in A107. Errors: P. R., impertinent, Frankford.] [BM]

A113. 1700? The hist. of the wicked life and miserable end of Dr. J: Faustus, etc. Tr. from the orig. copy printed at Frankford. Tr. P. F. Gent. L: Prtd. by W. O. for J. Back. 44p. 14cm. [BM] [7 chaps., retold.]

A114. 1700? [same as A112] L: Prtd. by C. Brown for M. Hotham. ff. A-K. 19cm. [BM] [62 chaps. Woodcut as in A107. Errors: P. R., impertinent, Frankford.]

A115. 1727. The surprising life and death of Doctor J: Faustus. To which is now added, The necromancer, or, Harlequin, Doctor Faustus ...Likewise, The whole life of Fryar Bacon...Truly tr. from the orig. copies. L: Prtd. and sold by the booksellers. 167p. 14cm. [BM] ["Faust," 46 chaps. (pp. 1-88), ending with funeral oration; "Necromancer," pp. 89-97. Woodcut as in A107. Text same as A102.]

A116. 1740? [same] L: Prtd. for A. Bettesworth and C. Hitch, etc. 14cm. ["Faust," pp. 1-79; "Necromancer," pp. 80-88.] [BM]

A117. 1750? The hist. of Dr. J: Faustus. Shewing, how he sold himself to the devil...for 24 years...how the devil came for him, and tore him to pieces. Prtd. and sold in Aldermary church yard, Bow Lane, L. 24p. 15cm. [Chapbook. 12 chaps.] [BM]

A118. 1777. The hist. of the wicked life and horrid death, etc. (as in foregoing). Chapbook. Glasgow: Prtd. for the company of flying stationers. 16p. 15cm. [14 chaps., no il.] [BM]

A119. 1780? [same] Chapbook. Newcastle: Prtd. in this present year. 24p. 15cm. [14 chaps. Woodcut as in A107.] [BM]

A120. 1780? [same as A117] Chapbook. Prtd. and sold in L. 24p. 16cm. [12 chaps. 11 cuts.] [BM]

A121. 1793. The famous hist. of Dr. J: Faustus, the noted conjurer and necromancer; wherein is contained many very strange things that himself had seen and done in the earth and air; with his bringing up, travels, and last end. Truly tr. from the orig. copy. Prtd. and sold at Exeter, New-Hampshire. 40p. 19cm. [LC] [46 chaps., somewhat abr. from the Engl. chap book as given in Thoms' Early Engl. prose romances (A135). This copy has newspaper covers, dated 1809.]

A122. 1795. [same as A115] The surprising life and death of Dr. J: Faustus, D. D. Commonly called the hist. of the devil and Dr. Faustus. Also, The necromancer, etc. Truly tr. etc. Prtd. at Worcester (Mass.). 144p. 14cm. [BM] [47 chaps. of "Faust," pp. 1-117; "Necromancer," pp. 118-29. No cuts. B6a says this ed. has a front.; copies available in AAS and NYPL.]

A123. 1796? The surprizing and damnable life, and deserv'd death of doctor J: Faustus. (Also, Fryar Bacon, etc.) Truly tr. L: Prtd. by L. Nisbet. ff. A-G5. 14cm. [BM] [46 chaps.; cf. A115. Woodcut on t.p. as in A107.]

A123a. 1798. Hist. of Dr. J: Faustus, the famous conjurer, and necromancer (and said to be the first inventor of printing). Truly tr. Bost: Bible and Heart. 51p. 8. [AAS]

A124. 1800? The hist. of the wicked life and horrid death, etc. Chapbook. n.i. 24p. 15cm.[14 chaps.,as in A119. Woodcut as in A107.][BM]

FAUST

A125. 1807. The devil and Doctor Faustus. Containing the hist. of the wicked life and horrid death, etc. Montpelier (Vt.): Prtd. by Carlos Darling. 12p. 19cm. [14 chaps., as in Engl. chapbooks.][LC]

A126. 1810? Hist. of Dr. Faustus. Shewing his wicked life, etc. Chapbook. Glasgow: Prtd. for the booksellers. 24p. sm. 8. (B19a)

A127. 1815? The hist. of the wicked life and horrid death, etc. Chapbook. Glasgow: Prtd. for J. Lumsden. 24p. 16cm. [BM] [14 chaps. Woodcut on t.p. shows Faust in robe, with book under arm.]

A128. 1818. Hist. of the wicked life and horrid death, etc. Chapbook Ed: Prtd. for the booksellers. 24p. 16cm. [14 chaps. No cuts.][BM]

A129. 1820. [same?] The hist. of the wicked life and horrid death, etc. Chapbook. Kilmarnock: H. Crawford. 24p. 16cm. [BM] [14 chaps. No cuts.]

A130. 1820? The hist. of the wicked life and horrid death, etc. Chapbook. Stirling: M. Randall. 24p. 15cm. [BM] [14 chaps. Small cut of Mephisto on t.p.]

A131. 1825. Faustus, his life, death, etc. L: Simpkin. 8. [EC]

A132. 1825. Faustus: a romantic drama in 3 acts [prose and verse] by G: Soane. L: J:Miller. 59p. 22cm. [Performed May 16, 1825.][BM]

A133. 1826. Hist. of that renowned arch-sorcerer, Dr. J: Faust. Tr. T: Roscoe. In C477, pp. 270-413. [Text from "Des durch die ganze Welt berufenen Erzschwarzkünstlers und Zauberers Dr. J. Fausts mit dem Teufel aufgerichtetes Bündnis." Pub. at Köln a. Rh. und Nürnberg. BM has a copy with part of the same title, pub. Braunschweig 1727. 8.]

A134. 1827. [reprint of A106] Hist. of the life and death of Dr. J: Faustus. L: W:Pickering. viii;138p. 19cm. [BM]

A135. 1828. Thoms, W: J. Early Engl. prose romances. L: 3v? [This is cited as the first ed. in A143.]

A136. 1829. The remarkable life of Dr. Faustus...Chapbook. L: Prtd. for Allman. 24p. 8. [Has one col. copperplate.] (B19a)

A137. 1830. [same?] The remarkable life of Dr. Faustus, a Ger. astrologer and enchanter, etc. Chapbook. Derby: T: Richardson;L: Hurst, Chance. 24p. 18cm. [Has a wonderful col. front., 18 x 22cm. Same text as in later chapbooks, but revised and without chapter divisions.] [BM]

A138. 1830? The remarkable life, etc. Chapbook. L: W.Mason n.d. 36p. 8. [Same text as in A135. One col. plate.] (B19a)

A139. n.d. [same?] Fairburn's ed. of the whole remarkable life of Dr. Faustus...L: J. Fairburn. 36p. one col. pl. 8. (B19a)

A140. 1847. Faust, a phantasia. Ed. by C. Simrock and tr. D. J. P. Drakeford. L: Bentley. 94p. 17cm. [Taken from the Puppenspiel.][BM]

A141. 1850. Hist. of Dr. Faustus. Shewing his wicked life and horrid death, etc. Chapbook. Glasgow: Prtd. for the booksellers. 24p. 15cm. [14 chaps., as in A127. Same title as A126. Woodcut of Faust on t.p.] [BM]

A142. 1850? Johnson's ed. of the life and death of Dr. Faustus. Chapbook. L: W. S. Johnson. 24p. 2 woodcuts. 8. (B19a)

A143. 1858. [same as A135] 2d ed. L: Nattali & Bond. [BM] [Vol. 3 has reprint of A114, pp. 163-300; also reprint of A110, pp. 301-414.]

A144. 1861. The famed book of fortune of Dr. Faustus. Tr. from the orig. ancient MS in the museum of Gottenburgh. With a key for... his matrimonial chart, and hieroglyphic of fate...L: H.Elliot. 16p. 18cm. [Col. front. Dr. Faustus's matrimonial chart, 16 x 23cm. No relation to the "Volksbuch."] [BM]

A145. 1863. [same as A137] Derby;L: T:Richardson. 24p. 18cm. [BM] [No front. in this copy.]

FAUST

A146. 1884. [reprint of A114] A discourse of the most famous Dr. J: Faustus, etc. In Mediaeval tales. H: Morley's universal lib. L: Routledge. pp. 177-287. 19cm. [BM]

*A147. 1887. (Faust Puppenspiel.) The old Ger. puppet play of Doctor Faust, turned into Engl...T: C: H. Hedderwick. L: Paul. xlviii; 207p. il. 20cm. [BM.LC]
[Tr. of version preserved in Wilhelm Hamm's transcript of the MS belonging to the puppet-player Guido Bonneschky, pub. at Leipzig in 1850. Front. of Faust after Rembrandt.]

*A148. 1893. do. Dr. Johannes Faustus. Puppet play (as played by the Kasperle co.). Now first done into Engl. In 4 acts. L: Nutt. 63p. 17cm. [BM]

A149. 1900. The Engl. Faust-book of 1592. Ed...H. Logemann. Gand: Engelcke; Amsterdam: Schröder. 175p. 25cm.[Reissue of A102.][BM.LC]

A150. 1916. Faust: a play in 4 acts [prose and verse]. Anon. n.p. Prtd. by G: E. Jackson co. 19p. double cols. 21cm. [BM]
[Copyright held by E. L. Viets, who is probably the author.]

A151. 1925. The hist. of the damnable life and deserved death...The second report of Faustus...both modernized and ed. by W: Rose. 24 ils. chiefly from woodcuts. L: Routledge; NY: Dutton. xvl;327p. 18cm. [Reprint of A102 and A110. Introd. extends to p. 58.][BM.LC]

[Note. For other German treatments of the Faust story, see Bernard, J. C., Goethe, and Klinger, F. M.]

*A152. FELDJAEGER. (Der junge Feldjäger in französischen und englischen Diensten.) Adventures of a young rifleman in the French and English armies, during the war in Spain and in Portugal from 1806 to 1816. Written by himself. 2d ed. (With a pref. by Goethe.) Tr. anon. L: H.Colburn 1826. viii;363p. 19cm. [BM]
[From vols. 1 and 2 of the orig.]

§A153. do. The young rifleman's comrade: a narrative, etc. Tr. anon. L: H.Colburn 1826. xxiv;310p. 19cm. [BM]
["Des jungen Feldjägers Kriegskamerad" forms vol. 3 of the orig. work. This vol. also contains Goethe's pref.]

A154. FEMALE CHARACTERS OF GOETHE. 1868. See Goethe gallery, #2451.

A155. FEUDAL TYRANTS; or, the counts of Carlsheim and Sargans. A romance. Taken from the Ger. by M. G. Lewis. L: Hughes 1806. 4v. 17cm. [BM]

A156. do. 1807. [same] 2d ed. Hughes. 4v. 18 x 10cm. [LC]

A157. FIDES; or, the beauty of Mayence. Tr. Lascelles Wraxall. L: Hurst & B. 1865. 3v. 19cm. [BM]

A158. FLIBUSTIER, THE: a tale from the German. Tr. by Herr Zander (Ger. lecturer at Dublin U.). In "Dublin univ. mag." 2(1833): 179. (B26)

A159. FOLK-LORE and legends. 1889. See T., C. J., this list.

A160. FORESTER of Altenhain. Tr. Shoberl. 1852. See Mueller, O:, #6528.

FORTUNATUS

A161. 1600. The pleasant comedy of old F--. Tr. T: Decker. L: Prtd. by S. S. for W. Aspley. 4. (B18)

A162. 1650? The hist. of F--. L? 92p. 18cm. [BM]
[42 chaps. 16 cuts, 2 of them repeated. Seems to be freely tr. from the Volksbuch. Herford (B18) says the orig. was a Frankfort ed. of 1550.]

A163. 1676. The right, pleasant, and variable tragical hist. of F--, whereby a young man may learn how to behave himself in all worldly affairs and casual chances. First penned in the (High?) Dutch tongue. There-hence abstracted, and now first of all pub. in

FORTUNATUS
Engl. By T. C. L: Prtd. by A. Purstow for G: Saubridge. 184p. 14cm. [BM]
[48 chaps. One more cut than in the foregoing, one of them repeated twice. Somewhat fuller text. Also has: To the reader: The sum and argument of this book (in verse). Tr. is probably T: Churchyard.]

A164. 1682. [same] ...trachical...Prt. by T. B. for Hanna Sawbridge. 159p. 14cm. [46 chaps. Cuts.] [BM]

A165. 1700? The famous and delightful hist. of F--, and his two sons. In 2 pts. 7th ed. L: Prtd. by and for T. Norris, at the Looking-glass on Lond. Bridge. il. 162p. 12. [BM]
[Same text as A162. Some new cuts; repetitions of old ones. Pt. 1 has 27 chaps., pt. 2 has 16.]

A166. 1740. The right, pleasant, and diverting hist. of F-- and his two sons. 11th ed. Il. with a variety of new pict. and new. add. L: J.Osborne, etc. 168p. 15cm. [BM]
[Text as in A163. 57 chaps. Most of the cuts are the same.]

A167. 1750? The hist. of F--, containing various surprising advent.. a purse that could not be emptied. Chapbook. Prtd. and sold in Aldermary Church-yard, Bow Lane, L. 24p. 14 cuts. 15cm. [BM]
[10 (i.e., 9) chaps.]

A168. 1779. The right pleasant and delightful hist. of F-- and his two sons, in two parts, etc. 14th ed. L: Prtd. for S. Crowder. 168p. cuts. 15cm. [48 chaps.] [BM]

A169. 1780? The pleasant and delightful hist. Chapbook. Worcester: Prtd. for S. Gamidge. 24p. 16cm. [9 chaps.] [BM]

A170. 1780? The most excellent and delightful hist. of F--. To which is added the lives and advent. of Ampedo and Andolocia, his two sons. Chapbook. Newcastle: Prtd. this present year. 24p. 15cm. [BM]
[6 chaps. A different telling of the story from the other chapbooks.]

A171. 1790. The hist. of F--, setting forth his birth, life, travels, etc. Chapbook. Glasgow: Robertson. 23p. 15cm.[9 chaps.] [BM]

A172. 1800? The hist. of F-- and his two sons. Tr. from the Greek [sic]. 6th ed. L: Sabine. iv;120p. 17cm. [BM]
[42 chaps. Same text as A163.]

A173. 1805? The most excellent and delightful hist. of F--. Chapbook. Newcastle: G: Angus. 24p. 2 cuts. 15cm. [BM]
[6 chaps. Same text as A170.]

A174. 1810? The hist. of F--, containing various surprising advent. Chapbook. Warrington: Prtd. for the travelling stationers. 24p. 13 cuts. 15cm. [9 chaps.] [BM]

A175. 1814. Reprint of A161. In Old Engl. plays, vol. 3. 8. [BM]

A176. 1815? The hist. of F--. Chapbook. Glasgow: R. Hutchinson. 24p. 16cm. [9 chaps.] [BM]

A177. 1816? The hist. of F--. Embellished with 4 elegant copper-plates. A new and corr. ed. Chapbook. L: Prtd. for the booksellers. 27p. (New juvenile lib.) 12cm. [BM]
[A new narr. without chapter divisions.]

A178. 1820? The hist. of F--. To which are added, The lives and advent. of Ampedo and Andolocia, his two sons. Chapbook. Ed: Prtd. for the booksellers. 24p. 16cm.[6 chaps., pp. 1-21. One cut on t.p.] [BM]

A179. 1830? The hist. of F--. Chapbook. Coventry: J. Turner. 16cm. [Last page missing. 9 chaps. 7 cuts, some old.] [BM]

A180. 1904. Old F--. Play by T: Dekker. L: Dent. Temple dramatists. [BM]

A181. FREIBERG, the young carpenters of. 1880. See Nieritz, Gst., #6775.
A182. FREIBURG in the Breisgau, and its vicinity. Tr. W. H. Johnston. Freiburg: Sommer bros. 1880. 63p. il. 17cm. [BM]
§A183. FREIER. (Die drei Freier; oder gleich und gleich gesellt sich gern.) The three suitors; or, like loves like. A musical farce. Tr. anon. Libr. Ger;Engl. L: Vogel 1805. 47p. 17cm. [BM]
[Prose very good; verse tr. line for line, without rhyme.]
A 84. FREY. True and authentic account of Andrew Frey. Tr. from German. Pub. by Robinson. See "Monthly R." 9(1753):393. (B26)
A185. FRIEDEMANN BACH; or, the fortunes of an idealist. 1875. See Brachvogel, A. E.
A186. FRITZ; or, the struggles of a young life. Tr. by the author of "Max." L: Jas. Nisbet 1872. 182p. il. 15cm. [BM]
A187. DER FREISCHUTZ; or, the mysteries of the wolf's glen. On cover: The legend of the wolf's glen, and the Bohemian forresters. Der Freischutz; or, ring of enchanted skulls. Abounding in supernatural mystery and terror. L: Bailey & Hunt 1820? 26p. col. front. 18cm. [BM]
[See also J: A: Apel and F: Kind for legend and opera.]
A188. FUNNY PICTURE BOOK, THE. 1875. See Picture, this list.
G., H. J. M. See Goetz, this list.
A189. GABRIEL; or, the Jews in Prague. 1869. See Kohn, Sl.
A190. GENIUS. The little genius: comic opera in 2 acts by Eg. v. Taund. Ad. from the Ger. by Sir A: Harris and Art. Sturgess. Libr. Engl. L: Ascherberg 1896. 31p. 21cm. [BM]
A191. do. 1896. [same] Vocal score. Engl. With add. numbers by L. Ronald and J. M. Glover. L: Ascherberg. 112p. fol. [BMM.LCM]
A192. do. 1896. [same] Vocal score. Engl. NY: Schuberth. 167p. 31cm. [LCM.BMM]
A193. GERMAN DESERTER'S WAR EXPERIENCE, A. Tr. anon. L: G.Richards 1917. 254p. 19cm. [Tr. is Jl. Koettgen.] [BM.LC]
A194. do. 1917. [same] NY: Huebsch. 192p. 19cm. [LC.BM]
[BM says: tr. from the "New Yorker Volkszeitung."]
A195. GERMAN DRUMMER BOY, THE; or, the horrors of war. Ad. Mrs. Campbell Overend. Ed: W: Oliphant 1870. viii;214p. 16cm. [BM]
A196. GERMAN EPIC TALES: Nibelungen, Walther and Hildegund. L: Whittaker 1888. 12.[Perhaps this is a school ed. of the German texts.] [EC]
A197. GERMAN GEMS in an Engl. setting. 1879. See List C, under Mulley, Jane.
A198. GERMAN LETTERS, tr. into Engl. by Cath. Selden: A novel. Cork. J. Connor 1804. 153p. 16cm. [BM]
A199. GERMAN SPECTACLES, THROUGH: an account of the Huns as they pictured themselves in their own press. Tr. anon. L: Nisbet 1917. 120p. 18cm. [Reprtd. from the "Daily Express."] [BM]
A200. GERMAN STORIES, tales and trad. 1855. See List C, under Cunningham, G: G.
A201. GERMANY and Italy. Tr. anon. 2d enl. ed. L: Hardwicke 1859. 30p. 21cm. [BM]
A202. GERMANY. The groans of Germany; or, the enquiry of a protestant Ger. into the original causes of the present distractions of the empire. Tr. from the orig. lately pub. at the Hague. anon. 3d ed. L: J.Huggonson 1741. 30p. 20cm. [LC]
A203. GERMANY. do. 1741. [same] 6th ed. L: [BM.LC]
A204. GERMANY. Lachrymae Germaniae; or, the teares of Germany. Unfolding her woefull distresse...In a sermon...Noremberg. Tr. out of the high Dutch coppy. L: Prtd. by I. Okes and...sold by H. Overson and J: Rothwell 1638. 3 leaves. 72p. 16cm. [BM]
A205. GERMANY. A present from Germany; or, the Christmas-tree. 1840. See List C, under Perry, E.

A206. GERMANY. Romantic and picturesque Germany. Saxon Switzerland. 1838. See Tromlitz, A.
A207. GERMANY unmasked; or, facts and coincidences explan. of her real views in seeking to wrest Schleswig from Denmark, with an append. containing remarks of the "Memoir on Schleswig and Holstein" presented to Viscount Palmerston by the Chevalier Bunsen. L: Richardson 1848. xlvi;90p. 19cm. [BM]
["Germany and Scandinavia," pp. 1-69, tr. from a Ger. work pub. in 1846, entitled "Our present and future."]
A208. GERMANY. (Wer ist schuld am Kriege zwischen Dänemark und Deutschland?) Who is to blame for the war between Denmark and Germany? Tr. anon. L: E.Wilson 1849. 32p. 20cm. [BM]
A209. GIANT MOUNTAINS, the spirit of the. 1864. See R., M. C., this list.
A210. GIPSEY, THE: a tale from the Ger. Tr. anon. Chapple 1826. 12. [EC]
A211. GIPSY. (Die Zigeunerfürstin.) The gipsy princess: a musical play in 3 acts by E. Kálmán. Book by Art. Miller. Vocal score. L: Chappell 1921. 120p. 27cm. [BMM]
A212. GOETZ JÄGER'S SON. (Tr?) By H. J. M. G. L: S.P.C.K. 1885. 80p. 17cm. [BM]
A213. GOLDEN MILL, THE: a tale of filial piety. Tr. anon. L: S.S.U; NY: Nelson 1872. 115p. 18cm. [BM.BPL]
A214. do. 1886. [same] L: S.S.U. 8. [EC]
A215. GOLDEN SANDS from the Ger. ocean of thought. (Tr?) L: Scott 1884. 64. [EC]
A216. GOTTFRIED of the iron hand: a tale of Ger. chivalry. Ed: Johnstone, Hunter; L: Hamilton, Adams 1865. 96p. 16. [BM]
[Contains consid. portions of the autobiog. of Götz v. Berlichingen, and of other contemp. tales. Appar. not a tr., but a renarration of Götz's life.]
A217. GREAT NAME, THE: operetta in 3 acts by R. Stolz. See Feld, Leo, and V: Leon.
A218. GREEN MANTLE OF VENICE, THE: a true story from the German. Tr. anon. In "Repository of arts" (II) 12(1821):31, etc. (B26)
A219. GRETCHEN; or, the chapel of Winkelried. (Tr?) NY: O'Shea 1864. 22p. 15cm. [Has Ger. names and setting.] [BM]
A220. GRETCHEN. Little G--, the peacemaker. (Tr?) L: Relig. tract soc. 1872. pp. 1-74. col. front. 14cm. [Names and scene are German.] [BM]
*A221. GRUND, Fis. J. (Die Aristokratie in Amerika, aus dem Tagebuch eines deutschen Edelmannes.) Aristocracy in America; from the sketchbook of a Ger. nobleman. Ed. by F. J. G--. L: Bentley 1839. 2v. xii;319; 321p. ports. 19cm. [BM]

GUDRUN

A222. [Sel.] Tr. Mme. Davésiès de Pontès. 1858. In C88.
A223. [Sel.] 1879. Tr. Bayard Taylor. In C530.
A224. [Sel.] 1906. Tr. anon. In C190.
A225. 1863. G--: a story of the North Sea; from the medieval Ger. by Emma Letherbrow. Ed: Edmonston & Douglas. lxvi;214p. front. 18cm. [BM.LC]
[Wholly rearranged and divided into 23 chaps; text is freely handled (in prose), but spirited and vivid. See Sandbach, B35.]
A226. 1864. do. [same] New ed. L: Hamilton. [EC]
A227. 1870. Tr. C. E. O. In "Translations, etc." L: Hunt. pp. 16-93. [A prose condensation from Simrock's version.] [BM]
A228. 1877. [same as A225] King Hetel's daughter; or, the fair Gudrun. A tale of the North Sea. Compiled by Emma Letherbrow. L: Warne. 220p. il. 16cm. [No. introd.] [BM]

GUDRUN

A229. 1881. G-- and other stories from the epics of the middle ages. By J: Gibb. L: Marshall & J. il. 8. [EC]
[Story is told for young people, but is almost a condensed tr., save that the three parts are arr. in the reverse of the usual order. See Sandbach, B35.]

A230. 1883. do. [same] 2d ed. G--, Beowulf, and Roland, with other medieval tales. L: Unwin. 8. [EC]

*A231. 1889. G--: a medieval epic tr. from MHG (Bartsch ed.) by Ma. P. Nichols. Bost;NY: Houghton. 363p. 22cm. xv;363p. [LC.BM]
[Excellent tr.] See also Fd. Schmidt, Gudrun.

A232. GUSTAVUS ADOLPHUS in Germany. Tr. Loui Lalk Weinstein. Burlington, Ia: Ger. lit. bd. 1907. 125p. 18cm. [LC]
[Adapted from anon. newspaper article.]

A233. GUTENBERG, the noble printer and his adopted daughter. 1873. See Nieritz, Gst.

A233a. do. J: G--, first master printer. See Dingelstedt, Fz.

A234. HAMLET. A tragedy of fratricide punished; or, prince Hamlet of Denmark. (As performed by English players in Germany ca. 1600.) Tr. Miss G. Archer. 1865. In C70.

A235. HANS IN LUCK and other favorite fairy tales. Ed;L: Nelson 1891. 8. [EC]
[Probably includes some of the Grimms' tales: "Hans in luck" is almost certainly by them.]

A236. HARDMAN, F: The great unknown: a jest from the German. Tr. F: Hardmann [sic]. In "Tales from Blackwood," new series, vol. 9, 1879, pp. 39-79. [BM]

A237. HAROLD. Fritz Harold; or, the temptation. Altered and enl... by Sa. A. Myers. NY: Carter 1855. 228p. il. 17cm. [BM]

A238. HARZ (7) Legends of the Harz. Tr. anon. L: Whitfield, Green 1866. 30p. 16cm. [Perhaps from Buesching's collection.] [BM]

A239. HARZ. Legends of the Harz Mts. By Toofie Lauder. L: Hodder & S. 1881. xi;259p. 19cm. [BM.LC]
[Evidently tr. from Ger. sources, though none are assigned. Authoress knows little German.]

A240. HE LOVES ME more than his life; or, Ludwig, Clara, and Randolph. A tale from the German. Tr. anon. "The minor novelist," no. 2. Bost;Troy, NY: Wright, Goodenow & Stockwell 1808. (B48)

A241. HEERFORT AND CLARA. (H-- und Klärchen.) Tr. anon. L: Robinsons 1789. 3v. See "Analytical R." 5(1789):487. (B26)

A242. HEINRICH AND BLANCA. 1845. See "H: Clauren," #1134; and cf. #8304.

A243. HELEN. St. Helena; or, the finding of the holy cross. A drama for girls in 3 acts [prose]. Tr. and rearr. I. A. Bergrath. Balto: Kelly, Piet 1872. 43p. 18cm. [BM]

A244. HELIAND. Sel. Tr. Bayard Taylor. 1879. In C530.

A245. HELL UPON EARTH: a novel. 1804(1803). See Gruber, J: G.

A246. HELLAS, or the home hist. of the Greeks. 1855. See Jacobs, F:

A247. HENRY. In what manner little Henry came to the knowledge of God. 1841. See Schmid, Cph. v.

A248. HENRY of Eichenfels, and Christmas eve. 1848. See Schmid, Cph. v.

A249. HERMIT OF THE ALPS, THE. Tr. from the Ger...with a few alterations. anon. Jones 1802. See "Anti-Jacobin R." 14(1803):188. (B26)

A250. HIDDEN CHAINS. Tr. C. Td. Benze. Erie, Pa: Erie press 1910. 394p. 19cm. [LC.BM]

A250a. HIDDEN TREASURES; or, the heir of Hohenberg. Ed. (i.e., tr.) F: Hardman. L: Grant & Griffith n.d. il. 12. See "Court Journal" 1852, p. 854. (B15a)

A251. HILDEBRANDSLIED. Tr. H: Weber (in prose). 1814. In C557.
A252. do. 1828. Tr. W: Taylor (prose). In C533.
A253. do. 1845. Tr. H: Weber. In C373.
A254. do. 1858. Tr. Mme. Davésiès de Pontès. In C88.
A255. do. 1879. Tr. Bayard Taylor. In C530.
A256. do. 1906. Tr. anon. In C190.
A257. do. 1909. Tr. F. B. Gummere. In "The oldest Engl. epic." NY: Macmillan. 203p. 19cm. [LC]
*A258. do. 1914. Tr. into Engl. allit. verse by Fis. A. Wood. Chic: U. of C. press. 11p. 18cm. [LC]
A259. do. 1926. Tr. W: Taylor. In C68.
*A260. HINDENBURG. (H--'s Einmarsch in London. Von einem deutschen Dichter.) H--'s march into London. Tr. anon. Ed. with pref. by L. G. Redmond-Howard. L: 1916. 253p. 18cm. [BM.LC]
*A261. do. 1916. [same] Phil: Winston. 220p. 19cm. [LC]
A262. HOLLY AND MISTLETOE. 1860. See Koch, Rle.
A263. HOUSEHOLD tales and fairy stories. Il. Sir J: Gilbert et al. L: Routledge 1892. 8. [EC]
[Probably wholly or largely from Grimms' "Märchen."]
A264. HUBER, J. C. German minstrelsy; or, gathering of choice flowers. L: Nutt 1862. 12. [EC]
[Possibly only an ed. of the Ger. texts; this was the case with C128-9 of my first ed.]
A265. HUGDIETRICH. [Sel.] Tr. H: Weber. 1814. In C557.
A266. HYMNS of Ter Steegen, etc. 1894. See List C, under Hymns, Bevan, Fes.
A267. I ACCUSE! 1915. See Grelling, R:
A268. IDA KLEINVOGEL. (Tr?) Phil: Claxton 1865. 18. [AC]
A269. ILSE, PRINCESS. See Petersen, Marie.
A270. IN EXILE. See St., W. v., this list.
A271. INNER LIFE OF THE PRUSSIAN CADET. 1914. See Szczepanski.
A272. J'ACCUSE! 1915. See Grelling, R:
A272a. JANNASCH, Lilli, ed. (Untaten des preussisch-deutschen Militarismus.) Ger. militarism at work: documents and notes. Introd. Frederic de Marwicz. Tr. J: Pollock. Cayme pr. 1926. 116p. 8. [EC]
A273. JEW. The converted Jew: a Ger. tale. Tr. Mrs. Ann Rolfe. In "Ladies pocket mag." 13(1830):54, etc. (B26)
A274. JEWS. Witty Jews and Jewish wits. NY: Amer. news 1879. il. 16. [Tr? Pub. in Ger. in same year.] [AC]
A275. JULIUS; and other tales from the German. 1856. See Zschokke, H:
A276. JULIUS AND HIPPOLITA...Containing part of Shakespeare's "Two gentlemen of Verona." Tr. Miss G. Archer. 1865. In C70.
A277. K., M. The fatal consequences of the unscriptural doctrine of predestination and reprobation; with a caution against it. Written in High Dutch by M. K. and tr. on desire. Germantown (Pa.): Christopher Sower 1753. 14p. 16 x 9cm. [LC]
A278. KAINER; or, the usurer's doom. Tr. F. R. Ribbans. L: Washbourne 1881. 64p. 8. [BM]
A279. KARL, HANDSCHUHSHEIMER. Who conquered at last? Or, H-- K--. Tr. by the author of "Advent. of Master Redtail." L: S.P.C.K. 1868. 64p. il. 12cm. [BM]
A280. KASEM THE MISER and other tales. 1872-6. See Moritz, A:
A281. KATHERINE; and, The moment of fortune. Tr. Lady Wallace. 1857. See Hackländer.
A282. KATHERINE PARR; or, the court of H: VIII. 1862. See Muehlbach, Lu., #6437.
A283. KING OF THE SWANS and other tales. See List C, under T., S.
A284. KING NUTCRACKER. See Hoffmann, H:
A285. KLAGE, DIE. [Sel.] Tr. H: Weber. 1814. In C557.

A286. KORTZ, J: tr. Interesting memoirs of four Ger. gentlemen, particularly distinguished for their advent. among the fair sex, with an appropriate appendix. NY: Marks 1819. 226p. 17cm. [LC]
A287. KRONER, ANTONY. Christmas eve; or, Antony Kroner, the orphan wanderer. 1849. See Schmid, Cph. v.
A288. KRUPP. A century's hist. of the K-- works, 1812-1912. Tr. anon. from commem. vol. Essen-Ruhr: 1912. 325p. 30cm. [LC]
A289. L., C., tr. Orphan boy; or, from peasant to prince. L: Ward & L. 1874. 152p. front. 14cm. [BM]
A290. L., M. S. The merry wedding (in verse). Dedicated without permission to the brides of England. Tr. anon. L: 1857. unp. 22 x 27cm. [BM]
A291. LACHRYMAE GERMANIAE. See Germany, A204.
A292. LAND OF GLORY. See Mrs. W. Davenport, tr., A56.
A293. LANDER, Sa. W. Fairy bells, and what they tolled us. See List C, under Lander.
A294. LAUDER, Toofie. Legends of the Harz Mts. See Harz, A239.
A296. LAURA: or, the influence of a kiss. By A. H. Gezner [sic]. 1796. See Meltzer, Ad. H.
A297. LAURIN. [Sel.] Tr. H: Weber. 1814. In C557.
A298. do. [Sel.] 1825. Tr. E. Taylor. In C532.
A299. do. [Sel.] 1845. Tr. anon. In C373.
A300. do. [Sel.] 1906. Tr. anon. In C190.
A301. LERMONT, L. My play is study. 1852. See C319.
A302. LETTERS. (Briefe aus dem Himmel.) Letters from Heaven. Tr. anon. from 4th Ger. ed. L: Hodder & S. 1886. 269p. 20cm. [BM]
A303. LEWIS, M. G. The monk, a romance. See C323 sq.
A304. do. Anaconda. Tr. from the Ger. (B31)
A305. do. Mistrust; or, Blanche and Osbright. Tr. from the Ger. (B31)
A306. do. My uncle's garret window. Tr. from the Ger. (B31)
A307. LIBER VAGATORUM. The book of vagabonds and beggars, with a vocab. of their lang. Ed. Mn. Luther in 1528. Tr. J: C. Hotten. L: Hotten 1860. 64p. il. 19 x 15cm. [BM.LC]
A308. LICHTENSTEINERS, THE: a tale. Tr. anon. In "Dublin Univ. Mag." 45(1855):51, 146. (B27) See van der Velde, K: Fz.
A309. LILIEN, AGNES DE. See Wolzogen, K:e v.
A310. LITTLE BIRD RED and little bird blue. See Bird, A29.
A311. LITTLE DON QUIXOTE, a story for youth. See Quixote.
A312. LITTLE DWARF'S MIRROR and the children's prayer. 1878. See Wildermuth, Ote. v.
A313. LITTLE GENIUS. See Genius, A190.
A314. LONG, HELENA. Three Indian tales from the German. See C370a.
A315. LOUISA v. PLETTENHAUS, the journal of a poor young lady. 1857. See Nathusius, Frau Ma.
A316. LUDWIGSLIED. Tr. Mme. Davésiès de Pontès. 1858. In C88.
A317. do. 1879. Tr. Bayard Taylor. In C530.
A318. LYRA GERMANICA. See List C, Hymns, Winkworth.
A319. MADDALENA, the Waldensian maiden and her people. Tr. Julie Sutter. L: Rel. tract soc. 1886. 320p. il. 18cm. [BM]
A320. MAMMA'S STORIES. 1872. See Kinkel, J:a.
A321. MANSTOW, the baron of. See Baron, A22.
A322. MANY A LITTLE makes a mickle. See Trauermantel, C545.
A322a. MARNA (Marna, Von C. J., Verfasserin von. "Aus Schutzengels Tagebuch.") and the Christmas tree: two tales for the young. From the Ger. by a lady. Berlin: 1862. 12. [EC (Appendix)] [Not in Heinsius.]
A323. MASSIE, E: Sacred odes. 1866-8. See C401.
A324. MAX'S AMBITION. See O., J. C.
A325. MILL, THE: a Moravian tale (in verse). Founded on fact. (Tr?) L: Bentley 1826. 23p. 18cm. [BM]

A327. MIRROR OF NATURE. 1849. See Schubert, G. H.
A328. MISTLETOE. A Ger. tale of Christmas. (Tr?) L: Allman 1846. 12. [EC]
A329. MODERN GERMANY in relation to the great war. 1916. See C563.
A330. MOLLY AND KITTY; or, peasant life in Ireland. Tr. anon. from the Ger. Bost: Crosby & N. 1855. 16. [AC]
A331. MONICA, mother of St. Augustine. Tr. Rebecca Schively. Ref. church pub. n.d. (1872-6) 16. [AC]
A332. MORAVIANS. Hist. of the M--. Tr. from Ger. anon. L: Robinson. 1754? See "Monthly Rev." 19(1754):79. (B26)
A333. MOTHER GOOSE from Germany. Tr? Phil: Leypoldt 1864. il. sm. 4. [AC]
A334. MUSPILLI. Tr. E. H. Dewar. 1845. In C96.
A335. do. 1906. Tr. anon. In C190.
A336. MY PLAY IS STUDY. See C319.
A337. N., C., translator. The blind children. L: S.P.C.K. 1865. 48p. 14cm. [BM]
A338. NANNIE'S JEWEL CASE. See "Trauermantel," C546.
A339. NATALIA. Cousin N--'s tales. See C426.
A340. NAUMBURG. The weaver of N--. See Nieritz, Gst. #6777.
A341. NEW CHILDREN'S FRIEND, THE; or, pleasing incitements to wisdom and virtue. Tr. chiefly from the Ger. anon. 1798? See "Lady's monthly museum" 1(1798):67. (B26)
[Possibly tr. from C. F. Weisse's "Kinderfreund."]
A342. NEW YEAR'S EVE, or, St. Spindler's night. From the German. Tr. anon. L: Burns 1844. 18. [EC]
[Could this be a confusion with Spindler's "St. Sylvester's Night"? See #8895.]

NIBELUNGENLIED

A343. [Sel.] 1814. Tr. H: Weber. In C557 (much).
A344. [Sel.] 1825. Tr. E. Taylor. In C532.
A345. [Sel.] 1840. Tr. T: Carlyle. In C56.
A346. [Sel.] 1845. Tr. Jos. Gostwick. In C173.
§A347. [Sel.] 1845. Tr. anon. In C373.
A348. [Sel.] 1854. Tr. Js. Gostwick. In C172.
A349. [Sel.] 1879. Tr. Bayard Taylor. In C530.
A350. [Sel.] 1896. Tr. anon. In C366.
A351. [Sel.] 1899. Tr. anon. In C469.
A352. [Sel.] 1906. Tr. anon. In C190.
A353. [Sel.] 1923. Tr. G: Borrow. In C34.
A354. [Sel.] 1926. Tr. Marg. Armour. In C68.
§A355. ARMOUR, MARG. The fall of the Nibelungs; done into Engl. (prose). Il. W. B. MacDougall. L: Dent 1897. xi;259p. 8. [BM.LC]
[Sandbach (B35) says very faulty and full of errors. However, she gives the spirit of the poem quite well.]
§A356. do. 1908. [same] L: Dent; NY: Dutton. Everyman's lib. xviii; 235p. 17cm. [BM.LC]
A357. "AUBER FORESTIER." Echoes from mist-land; or, the Nibelungen lay, revealed (in prose) to lovers of romance and chivalry. Chic: Griggs; L: Trübner 1877. 218p. 12. [LC.BM]
A358. do. 1889. [same] New ed. [EC]
§A359. BIRCH, J. Das Nibelungenlied; or, the lay of the last Nibelungen. Tr...after Lachmann's ...text. Berlin: Duncker 1848. 266p. 8. [BM.NY]
§A360. do. 1887. [same] 3d ed. Munich: Ackermann. 220p. [NY]
§A361. COBB, J: S. The Nibelungenlied. Bost: Small, Maynard 1906. 640p. 22cm. [Stilted; verse very boring.] [LC]
§A362. COX, J: H. Siegfried. Tr. and ad. (in prose) from the MHG. Chic;NY: Row, Peterson 1915. 193p. 18cm. [LC]
[Condensed narr., but keeping something of the spirit.]

NIBELUNGENLIED

†A363. FOSTER-BARHAM, A. G. The Nibelungenlied, lay of the Nibelung. L;NY: Macmillan 1887. xv;442p. 18cm. [BM.LC]

†A364. do. 1893. [same] L: Routledge.. 371p. 19cm. [BM.LC]

*A365. HORTON, ALICE. The lay of the Nibelungs. Metr. tr. from the old Ger. text. L: Bell 1898. lxxi;411p. 18cm. [BM.LC]
[Sandbach (B35) praises this very highly; I have not seen it.]

*A366. LETTSOM, W: N. The fall of the Nibelungers; otherwise, the book of Kriemhild. L: Williams & N. 1850. xxxii;447p. 19cm.[BM.LC]
[Has notes on the poem.]

*A367. do. 1874. [same] 2d ed. [BM]

*A368. do. 1901. [same] Rev. ed. NY: Colonial press. 8. [LC]

*A369. do. 1903. [same] 4th ed. NY: Scribner. 20cm. [LC]

*A370. NEEDLER, G: H: The Nibelungenlied. Tr. into rhymed Engl. verse in the metre of the orig. NY: Holt 1904. 349p. 20cm. [LC]

§A371. SHUMWAY, D. B. The Nibelungenlied. Bost;NY: Houghton 1909. 339p. 21cm. [Prose; should be more archaic.] [LC]

§A372. WAY, A. S. The lay of the Nibelung men. Cambridge: Univ. press 1911. xxi;325p. 22cm. [BM.LC]
[Spirited verse, smooth-flowing; but unmercifully padded.]

A373. [Ad.] 1823. The hoard of the Nibelungen. Anon. In C456.

A374. [Ad.] 1848. The heroic life and exploits of Siegfried the dragon slayer. Anon. Il. W: Kaulbach. L: Cundall 1848 (1847). 118p. 21cm. [BM]

A375. [Ad.] 1856. Siegfried the dragon-slayer. Anon. In C83, pp. 39-157. [Same as the foregoing.]

A376. [Ad.] 1880(1879). Golden threads from an ancient loom. "Das Nibelungenlied" ad. to the use of young readers by Lydia Hands. Il. w. 14 wood engr. by Schnorr v. Carolsfeld. L: Griffith & Farran; NY: Dutton. xi;75p. 27cm. [BM]
[9 chaps., 6 covering the story through Siegfried's death.]

A377. [Ad.] 1904. Teutonic legends in the "Nibelungenlied" and the "Nibelungen Ring" (of R: Wagner). By W. C. Sawyer (from W: Wägner's "Nibelungenlied"). Phil;L: Lippincott. 19cm. [BM]
[Introd. essay, by Fritz Schultze, to p. 48. Tr. of Wägner's prose, pp. 51-308.]

A378. [Ad.] 1906. The Nibelungs. By Fd. Schmidt. Tr. G: P. Upton. See Schmidt.

A379. [Ad.] 1907. The linden leaf; or, the story of Siegfried. Retold from the "Nibelungenlied," anon. L;NY: Nelson. 160p. col. il. 16cm.
[20 chaps. to death of S--.] [BM]

A380. [Ad.] 1911. Siegfried and Kriemhild: a story of passion and revenge. Anon. Il. F. C. Papé. L;NY: Nelson. The world's romances. 96p. 22cm. [BM]

A380a. NINFA, a tale from the German. Tr. Louisa Keir Grant. See "Athenaeum" 21(1848):267. (B15a)

A381. NORA: a novel. 1877. See Brackel, Fde.

A382. NORICA; or, tales of Nürnberg from the olden time. See Hagen, Ern. A:

A383. NUTCRACKER and mouseking. See Hoffmann, E. T. A.

A384. O., J. C., tr. Max's ambition. L: Gall & Inglis 1897. 115p. il. 18cm. [BM]

†A385. OBERAMMERGAU. Passion Play. The English words of the "Passion Play" (or rather, the words of the hymns in the interludes, from the Ger. of F. Schoeberl) by Mrs. E: (Fes. C.) Childe. 2d ed. L: Js. Master 1871. 36p. 16cm. [Attempts to reproduce the spirit, but certainly does not give the sense.] [BM]

†A386. do. 1880. [same] 3d ed. 40p. 18cm. [BM]
[This ed. adds four pages of information.]

OBERAMMERGAU

*A387. do. 1881. The great atonement at Golgotha: the passion play of O--. The complete text tr. for the first time by Ma. Fes. Drew. L: Burns & Oates. 116p. 19cm. [BM]
[The dram. action without the choruses. Pretty good tr.]

*A388. do. 1890. Choruses of the...Passion Play in rhyme and rhythm. Tr. Ma. Fes. Drew. An appendix to the whole text (i.e., A387). L: Burns & Cates. 45p. 15cm. [BM]

§A389. do. 1890. The passion play at O--, with the whole drama tr. into Engl., and the songs of the chorus, in Ger. and Engl. Tr. Maria Trench. (5th thous.) L;Calcutta: Allen. xiii;128p. 21 x 17cm. [Correct, but fails in poet. passages, which are, however, bad in the orig. 32 pages introd. on the play and place.] [BM.LC]

§*A390. do. 1891. The story that transformed the world; or, the passion play at O-- in 1890. By W: T: Stead. Ger;Engl. L: Review of Reviews; NY: C: E. Merrill. 160p. il. 26cm. [BM]
[Engl. tr. adds description of the acting. Prose tr. is excellent, verse only good.]

A391. do. 1900. Passion play. Tr. Jas. Fis. Dickie. Berlin: Steinitz. 169p. il. D. [UW]

A392. do. 1900. Passion play, 1900. Complete Ger. text. with Engl. tr. L: 'Rev. of Revs.' office. 318p. il. w. photos. 8. [EC]
[Probably same as A390.]

§A393. do. 1900. The passion play at Ober-Ammergau. Tr. into Engl. and the songs of the chorus in Ger. and Engl. by Maria Trench. L: K.Paul. xv;96p. 21 x 17cm. [Cf. A389.] [BM]

§A394. do. 1900. [same] [Ident. with the foregoing, but has 32p. introd. on the play and place, as in A389.] [BM]

*A395. do. 1900. The passion play of Ober-Ammergau. The complete text tr. for the first time from the Ger. in 1881. By Ma. Fes. Drew. With the addition of the choruses. L: Burns & Oates; NY: Benziger. xiv;132p. 18cm. [BM]

§A396. do. 1909. Tr. Montrose J. Moses. NY: Duffield. 218p. 20cm. [Rather poor tr.] [LC]

§A397. do. 1910. [same] The passion play of O--. Tr. with hist. introd. by M. J. Moses. L: Siegle, Hill. xviii;218p. port. of A. Lang. 20cm. [BM]

*A398. do. 1910. [same as A395][Has different t.p.;otherwise ident.][BM]

*§A399. do. 1910? [same as A390] The passion play at Ober Ammergau [sic], 1910. The complete official Ger. text...with Engl. tr. by W: T: Stead. Copiously il. Munich: Seyfried; L: Stead's pub. house. 384p. 18cm. [Mainly a reprint of A390.] [BM.LC]

§A400. do. 1910. [same as A393] L: Paul, T. & T. xv;96p. 21 x 17cm. [BM.LC]

§A401. do. 1911. Passion play. Tr. Esse Esto Maplestone. NY: B'way pub. 226p. 20cm. [Same comment as on A389.] [LC]

A402. OLD STORY-TELLER. See Bechstein, L:

A403. ORACLE, THE. Opera. See Huber, Fz. X.

A404. ORPHAN BOY, THE; or, from peasant to prince. See L., C., A289.

A405. ORTNIT. [Sel.] 1814. Tr. H: Weber. In C557.

A406. do. [Sel.] 1845. Tr. anon. In C373.

A407. do. [Sel.] 1858. Tr. Mme. Davésiès de Pontès. In C88.

A408. OTHELLO: a story. See Weigl, J. F.

A409. OTTO, THE MINER'S CHILD. 1861. 1863. See Nieritz, Gst., #6803.

A410. OUR FUTURE LIES ON THE WATER (Unsere Zukunft liegt auf dem Wasser). By a Prussian officer. Tr. M. Jebb Scott. L: Field & Queen 1915. 80p. 18cm. [BM]

A411. OUR MOTHER: a life picture by M. K. See Krummacher, M.

A412. P., memoirs of the count of. (Geschichte des Grafen P.) See Pfeil, J: G.

A413. PASTOR'S WIDOW AND HER SON, THE: a story for the young. Tr. from the Ger. anon. L: Houlston 1889. 72p. front. 15cm. [BM]
A414. PATZ AND PUTZ: a story for young children. 1869. 1876. See Gerstäcker, F:
A415. PAULINA: a tale from the German. Tr. anon. Ed;L: Houlston 1870. 18. [EC]
A416. do. 1871. [same] Ed: Gall & Inglis. 138p. front. 14cm. [BM]
A417. PAULINE, the foundress of an infant school. Tr. from the Ger. anon. L: Darton 1850. 18. [EC]
A418. PET LAMB: a tale by the author of the "Basket of flowers." See Schmid, Cph. v., #8365.
A419. PETER. P: the Gt; or, the Russian mother. A play in 5 acts. Altered from the Ger. by W: Dunlap. NY: Longworth 1814. 56p. 12. (B48)
A420. PETER SCHLEMIHL. See Chamisso, Adt. v.
A421. PHILOSOPHER, THE: a trag. in 5 acts. Tr. H: M. Milner. L: Chapple 1819. 58p. 8. [Wrongly attributed to G.E. Lessing.] [NY]
A422. PICTURE. The funny pict. book or 25 funny little lessons. A free tr. from...Der kleine A.-B.-C.- Schütz. Frankfort o. M: 1875. unp. col. il. 4. [Moral stanzas.] [BM]
A423. PICTURES AND RHYMES FOR CHILDREN. (Tr?) Ger;Engl. L: Bogue 1845. square. [EC]
A424. PICTURES OF MY BARRACK life. By a Ger. soldier. Tr. anon. In "Colburn's new monthly mag." 94(1852):50, etc. (B27)
A425. POEMS AND BALLADS for penny readings. 1883. See C2.
A426. POETRY OF OTHER LANDS: collections of translations into English verse. Phil: 1883. 12. [EC]
A427. POPULAR ACCOUNT OF THE FRANCO-GERMAN WAR, 1870-71. Tr. by Twyford. Pt. 1. Tarrant 1873. 8. [EC]
A428. POPULAR TALES of the Germans. See Musäus, J: K: A:
A429. POSTMASTER OF PRENZLAU. Tales from the German. L: S.P.C.K. 1875. 1878. 8. [EC]
A430. PRESENT FROM GERMANY; or, the Christmas tree. 1840. See C449.
A431. PRUSSIAN CADET, INNER LIFE OF THE. See Szczepanski, Pl. v.
A432. QUARRELSOME DOG. Tr. "Leopold Wray." Myers 1857. obl. 12. [EC]
A433. QUIXOTE, LITTLE DON; a story for youth. Tr. Raymond. Syracuse. 1855. [EC]
A434. R., M. C. tr. The spirit of the Giant Mts: a series of fairy tales. L: Murray 1864. 231p. 16cm. [BM]
A435. RACHEL, the little captive maid. Tr. Julie Sutter. L: Partridge 1886. 96p. il. 18cm. [BM]
A436. RED AND WHITE ROSES, and other tales from the Ger. See Schmid, Cph. v.

REINEKE FUCHS [1]

A437. [Sel.] 1840. Tr. T: Carlyle. In C56.
A438. [Sel.] 1906. Tr. anon. In C190.
A439. [Sel.] 1926. Bruin the bear and Reynard the fox. Tr. T: Roscoe. In C68.
A440. 1481. Hyer begynneth thystorye of reynard the foxe...Here endeth the historye of Reynard the foxe, etc. Tr. W: Caxton.

[1] In my first edition I omitted Caxton's tr. of the old epic, thinking it to be without connection with German literature. Further study has caused me to view the matter differently. In French versions of the story, Reynard is outwitted by the raven, the cat, and the sparrow; in Germanic ones, the wolf and his injuries occupy the centre of interest, and this agrees with the Latin. Caxton's tale is at all events Germanic, and while the story of Reynard lies somewhat to one side, I think it not improper to include it.--For another treatment of the story, See Goethe's "Reineke Fuchs."

REINEKE FUCHS
Westminster. no t.p. no pag. 29 x 20cm. [Tr. from Dutch orig. of 1479.] [BM]
A441. 1550. [same] Here beginneth the booke of Raynarde the foxe, etc. Imprinted in London in Saint Martens by T: Gaultier. ff. A-T. 14cm. [43 chaps.] [BM]
A442. 1629. The most delectable hist. of Reynard the fox. Newly corr. and purged from all grossenesse, in phrase and matter. As also augmented and inlarged, with sundry excellent morals and expos. upon every severall chapter. L: Prtd. by Eliz. All-de. ff. A-V. 18cm. [BM]
[25 chaps. Many woodcuts. Taken from an earlier ed. of 1620, not in BM. Here the Lion is at Sanden (Caxton has: Stade); the Hound is Curtise (C: Curtoys); the castle is Malepardus (Maleperduys); other names are Grimbard (Grimbert), Chauntecleere (Chantecler), Bruine (Bruyn).]
A443. 1639. Abr. version, from Caxton. L. (B8)
A444. 1656. [same as A442] L: J.Bell. 18cm. [BM]
[Same cuts as in A442, with some added at the end.]
A445. 1667. Abr. version, from Caxton. L. (B8)
A446. 1671. Abr. version, from Caxton. L. (B8)
A447. 1681. The most delightfull hist. of R. the fox in heroic verse. Tr. J: Shurley. L: Prtd. for Passinger. 114p. 18 x 15cm. [BM]
[23 chaps., corresponding to those of prose ed. of 1650. Sanden and Malepardus, as in A442.]
A448. 1684. Abr. version, from Caxton. L. (B8)
A449. 1694. The most delectable hist. of R. the fox. Newly corr. and purged, etc. L: Prtd. by T: James for E: Brewster. ff. A-V. 20cm. [Same text as in A442, but newly type-set. Same cuts.] [BM]
A450. 1700? The hist. of R. the fox and Reynardine his son. In two parts. With morals to each chapter. Written by an eminent statesman of the Ger. empire, and since done into Engl., Dutch, etc. Tr. anon. Pref. by D. P. Prtd. for the booksellers of L. and Westminster. 13cm. [BM]
[8 chaps., pp. 1-117. Reynardine in 9 chaps., to p. 166. Sanden, Malepardus, as in A442; also, some of the cuts used in that ed., reduced.]
A451. 1701. 1681. 1684. The most delectable hist., etc. (as in A442). To which may now be added a second part of the said hist., As also the shifts of Reynardine the son of R. the fox. L: Prtd. by T. Ilive for E: Brewster. ff. A-U. 19cm. --Sep. t.p. The most pleasant and delightful hist. of R. the fox. The second part. Containing much matter of pleasure and content. L: Prtd. by A. M. and R. R. for E: Brewster 1681. ff. A-O. (This part uses the old woodcuts. 32 chaps.)--Sep. t.p. The shifts of Reynardine, the son of R. the fox, or a pleasant hist. of his life and death. L: Prtd. by T. J. for E: Brewster and T: Passenger 1684. 160p. (33 chaps.)[BM]
A452. 1706. The crafty courtier; or, the fable of Reinard the fox. New done into Engl. verse from antient Latin Iambics of Hartm. Schopperus. L: J:Nutt. 311p. 19cm. [BM]
[4 books; 38, 9, 14, 11 chaps. Names differ, but the general course of the story is the same as in A442.]
A453. 1708. Abr. version, from Caxton. L. (B8)
A454. 1723. The most pleasing and delightful hist., etc. To which is added, The hist. of Cawwood the rook. 5th ed. L: T.Norris 1723. 141p. 15cm. [Reynard in 8 chaps., as in A450, with the old cuts, to p. 99; then Reynardine. Cawwood is sep. paged, 18p.] [BM]
A455. 1735. [same] 6th ed. Pref. by P.D. L: Prtd. for A. Bettesworth and C. Hitch. (81); (129); 154p. woodcuts. 15cm. [BM]
A456. 1750. The hist. of R. the fox. Chapbook. L: Prtd. and sold in Aldermary church yard. 24p. 15cm. [BM]
[10 chaps. Some of the old woodcuts (A442), one on t.p. Sanden, Malepardus.]

REINEKE FUCHS

A457. 1756. The hist. of R. the fox, Bruin the bear, etc. L: G.Smith. 160p. 16cm. [27 chaps. This begins like other Engl. versions, then breaks loose and goes off into quite different matter.] [BM]

A458. 1775? The hist. of R. the fox. Prtd. and sold in L. [BM] [Same as A456, but defective.]

A459. 1780? The most pleasant hist. of R. the fox, giving an account of the many cruelties committed by him, etc. Chapbook. Newcastle: Prtd. in this present year. 24p. 15cm. [BM] [12 chaps., a different abridgment. No cuts except one on t.p. Sanden, Malepardus.]

A460. 1826. The pleasant hist. of R. the fox. Tr. T: Roscoe. In C477, pp. 1-140. [Abr. from A449, with occasional abridgment of the Low Saxon version of 1498 pub. in Lübeck.]

A461. 1826. R. the fox: a burlesque poem of the 15th cent. Tr. from the Low-Ger. orig. by D. W. Soltan. Hamburg. Priv. prt. xi;170p. 21cm. [BM] [Doggerel verse. Changes names and transfers action to England.]

A462. 1844. The most delectable hist. of R. the fox, and of his son Reynardine. A rev. version of an old romance. L: Parker 1844. xv; 102p. 17cm. [BM] [Part 1 has 14 chaps., slightly revised from A442. Sanden, Malepardus.]

A463. 1844. The hist. of R. the fox from the ed. prtd. by Caxton in 1481. With notes and an introd. sketch of the lit. hist. of the romance by W: J. Thoms. L: Percy soc. ci;194p. 19cm. [BM]

A464. 1844. R. the fox, a renowned apologue of the middle age, reproduced in rhyme (by S: Naylor?). L: Longmans. 55; cclip. 20cm. [LC] ["The Low-Ger. ed...is that from which I have worked: 'hovering... between tr. and paraphrase.'" Pref. signed S: Naylor.]

A465. 1851. The story of R. the fox. In "The comical creatures from Wurtemberg," pp. 61-96. See A585.

†A466. 1852. R. the fox. A poem in 12 cantos. Tr. E. W. Holloway. Lpz: Payne. 81p. il. 4. [LC.BM] [Tr. from Lübeck ed. of 1548. Very free and much expanded.]

A467. 1853. The story of Reineke the fox for beginners...for the use of schools. Sel. by A. Kokemüller. Hannover: C. Rümpler. 35p. 16cm. [12 chaps. Apparently condensed from the German. Malepartus; new names.] [BM]

A468. 1853. The story of R. the fox: a new version by D: Vedder. Il. Gst. Canton. L: Orr. 76p. 26 x 20cm. engr. t.p. [BM] [18 chaps. Retold with modern epilog. from A452.]

A469. 1854. The story of R. the fox. L: D.Bogue. Comical story books. 20 x 17cm. [BM] [Pp. 63-96. Col. ils. No divisions. Abridgment. Malepardus.]

A470. 1856. [same as A468] L: Bogue; Ed: Menzies. 76p. [LC]

A471. 1857? [same] L: Orr; Ed: Menzies. 76p. il. 27 x 22cm. [BM]

A472. 1857. [same] L: Bogue. [BM]

A473. 1865. R. the fox: a burlesque poem from the Low-Ger. orig. Bost: De Vries, Ibarra; NY: Scribner. 202p. 18cm. [LC] [Pref. signed V. D. Paraphrase of orig. ascribed to N: Baumann. Very good verse. Done by J: L. Forrest; see A490.]

A474. 1871. R. the fox. L: Routledge. 6p. col. ils. 26 x 23cm. [BM] [Abr. from Caxton or A442.]

A475. 1872. The rare romance of R. the fox, the crafty courtier; together with the shifts of his son Reynardine. In words of one syl. by S: P. Day. L;NY: Cassell, Petter & Galpin. 221p. col. ils. 17cm. [17; 4 chaps. Sanden, Malepardus.] [BM]

REINEKE FUCHS

A476. 1873. The pleasant hist. of R. the fox. Tr. T: Roscoe. Nearly 100 designs by A. T. Elwes and J: Jellicoe. L: Low. 136p. 20 x 15cm. [23 chaps. Sanden.] [BM]

A477. 1878. The hist. of R. the fox. Tr. and prt. by W: Caxton. Ed. by E: Arber. L: Southgate. xvi;120p. 19cm. [BM]

A478. 1880. [same] Ltd. lib. ed. xi;120p. 21cm. [BM]

A479. 1885. R. the fox, an old story retold by Mme. De Sanctis. L: Sonnenschein. 168p. 24cm. [Engr. t.p. says: new told, and has date 1884. 12 chaps. Malepartus.] [BM]

A480. 1884. The hist. of R. the fox. Tr. and prt. W: Caxton. Ed. Edm. Goldsmid. Ed: Priv. prt. Biblioteca curiosa. 2v. 99; 120p. 22cm. [BM]

A481. 1887. [same as A475] L;NY: Routledge. [BM]

A482. 1892. The hist. of R. the foxe, by W: Caxton. Reprtd. by W: Morris. L: Kelmscott press. 159p. 29cm. [BM]

A483. 1894. The hist. of R. the fox, his friends and his enemies, his crimes, hair-breadth escapes and final triumph. A metrical version of the old Engl. tr. with glossarial notes in verse by F. S. Ellis. Il. Wl. Crane. L: Nutt. x;346p. 22cm. [BM] [45 chaps. He follows Caxton.]

A484. 1895. The most delectable hist. of R. the fox. Ed. with introd. and notes by Js. Jacobs. Il. W. Frank Calderon. L;NY: Macmillan. xxxvii;260p. 18cm. [BM] ["In the main...a resuscitation of 'Felix Summerley's' version." I have not traced a version by "Fx. Summerly," (i.e., Sir H: Cole).]

A485. 1897. [same as A483] L: Nutt. xi;289p. 19cm. [BM]

A486. 1901. [same as A473] Il. J. J. Mora. Bost: Estes. xi;186p. 25cm. [LC]

A487. 1903. R. the fox. Ad. by E. Louise Smythe. NY: Amer. book co. 122p. 18cm. [The matter is mainly Germanic, but in the end R. is killed.] [BM]

A488. 1908. R. the fox. Ed. (from Caxton) by T: Cartwright. Il. in col. Patten Wilson after Kaulbach. L: Heinemann. 120p. 16cm. [BM] [18 chaps.]

A489. 1919. The most delectable hist. of R. the fox. Ed. for schools by H. A. Treble. Il. W. F. Calderon. L: Macmillan. 117p. 17cm. [BM] [23 chaps. Sanden, Malepardus.]

A490. 1920. King Lion and R. the fox, retold by J: L. Forrest. Il. J. J. Mora. Chic: Whitman. xi;186p. 23cm. [LC] [This is the same as A473.]

A491. 1924. Hist. of R. the fox, tr. by W: Caxton, modernized by W: S. Stallybrass. In "The epic of the beast." With introd. by W: Rose and Kaulbach's famous ils. L: Routledge; NY: Dutton. Broadway translations. xxxviii;278p. 19cm. [BM.LC]

A492. 1925. The hist. of R. the fox. Ed. (from Caxton) J: Drinkwater. Sr. L;Glasgow: Collins. 112p. 20cm. [28 chaps.] [BM]

A493. 1925. [same as A475] NY: Burt. il. O. [AC]

A494. RINALDO RINALDINI, capt. of banditti. See Vulpius, Cn. A:

A495. RING, THE; or, the merry wives of Madrid. Tr. B: Thompson. L: Vernor & Hood 1799. See "Brit. Crit." 14(1799):549. (B26)

A496. RIPPOLDSAU. The Swedes at R--. See Scheffel, Js. V: v.

A497. ROLANDSLIED. [Sel.] Tr. Mme. Davésiès de Pontès. 1858. In C88.

A498. ROMEO AND JULIET, tragedy of. (As performed by Engl. players in Germany, ca. 1600.) Tr. Lothar Bucher. Ger. and Engl. 1865. In C70.

A499. ROSENGARTEN. [Sel.] 1814. Tr. H: Weber. In C557.

A500. do. 1845. Tr. anon. In C373.

ROSENGARTEN.
A501. do. 1858. Tr. Mme. Davésiès de Pontès. In C88.
A502. do. 1876. Tr. anon. In C372.
A503. do. 1906. Tr. anon. In C190.
A504. RÜGEN. A tour through the island of R-- in the Baltic during the year 1805, in a series of letters. By a temporary inhabitant. Tr. anon. L: Phillips 1807. "Coll. of mod. voyages," vol. 3. 64p. 21cm. [BM]
A505. Rumpelstiltskin. 1883. 1889. See Grimms Märchen.
A506. RUSSIA. Recoll. of R-- during 33 years' residence. By a Ger. nobleman. Rev. and tr. by Lascelles Wraxall. Ed: Constable; L: Hamilton, Adams 1855. 328p. 18cm. [BM]
A507. SACRED HYMNS from the German, with tr. by F. E. Cox. See C231.
A508. ST. HELENA: a drama for girls. See Helen, A243.
A509. SANTINE, X. B. A French writer, Saintine.
A510. SAPPHO: a drama. See Grillparzer, Fz.
A511. SCHINDERHANNES, the robber of the Rhine. See #8249a.
A512. SCHIVELY, REBECCA H. In olden days beyond the sea. See C491.
*A513. SCHOLEHOUS. (Der Bösen Weiber Zuchtschul.) The vertuous Scholehous of ungracious women. Tr. anon. n.i. 1600? ff. A-N. 13cm. [BM]
A514. SCHOOL AND HOLIDAYS: a description of Ger. upper-class life for girls. Tr. anon. L: S.P.C.K. 1872. 173p. il. 16cm. [BM]
A515.(SCHULE DES LEBENS, DIE.) Won: not wooed. A drama in 5 acts [verse]. Ad. from the Ger. 2d rev. ed. L: Wyman 1877. 67p. 18cm. [This may be a tr. from Ernst Raupach, whose play so entitled appeared in 1846.] [BM]
A516. SCOTT, M. JEBB. See Our future, A410.
A517. SEL. from Ger. poets, with translations. See C496.
A518. SEPPELI, the Swiss boy. Tr. A. H. Lochman. Phil: Lutheran bd. 1870. 123p. 18. [LCO]
A519. SEPPELI. Little Swiss S--; or, confidence in God rewarded. A true story. Tr. anon. L: Harvey & D. 1829. 81p. 3 pl. 14cm. [BM]
A520. SETMA, The Turkish captive. See Barth, Cn.
A521. SHADOWLESS MAN, Undine, and Liesli. 1845. See C494.
A522. SIBYLIA. 1888. See Vollmar, Ag.
A523. SIDONIA the sorceress. See Meinhold, J: W:
A524. SIEGE OF BUDA, THE: a tale from the Ger. Tr. anon. L: Longmans 1855. 12. [EC]
A525. SIEGE OF VIENNA, THE: a romance. Tr. anon. L: Smith & Elder 1837. 12. [EC]
A526. SIEGE OF VIENNA, THE: a story of the Turkish war in 1683. Tr. J. Latchmore, Jr. Ed: Oliphant 1880. 192p. il. 17cm. [BM] [EC has: L: Hamilton 1879.]
A527. SIEGFRIED. See Nibelungenlied.
A528. SKETCHES FROM THE DIARY of Queen Natalia of Servia. See Buettner, H:
A529. SKETCHES OF GER. LIFE. Tr. Lady Duff Gordon. See Varnhagen v. Ense.
A530. SLEEPING BEAUTY of the wood. 1843. See Grimms Märchen.
A531. SNOW KING'S TRUMPETER, THE. 1884. See "Horn, W. O. v."
A532. SONGS OF BIRD LIFE, from the Ger. by Josephine Pollard. Il. Giacomelli. NY: White, Stokes & Allen 1885. 56p. il. 31cm. [LC]
A533. ST., W. v. In exile. Tr. anon. Phil: Lippincott 1871. 480p. 18cm. [LC]
A534. STICK TO THY LAST and other stories. Ad. from the Ger. anon. L: S.P.C.K. 1883. 8. [EC]
A535. STORIES from Germany, tr. Annie Harwood. See C189.
A536. STORIES, tales, and trad., from the Ger. 1856. See C82.
A537. STORY OF FRITHIOF. Tr. J. Henderson. 1873. [EC]
[This is probably from Tegnér's Frithiofs Saga.]

A538. STORY OF SOLDIER FRITZ. Tr. J. C. Pickard. Chic: Interstate pub. 1886. 43p. 18cm. [LC]
A539. STORY WITHOUT AN END. See Carové, F: W:
A540. STRUWEL (Struwwel) PETER. See Hoffmann, H:
A541. SWISS FAMILY ROBINSON. See Wyss, J:
A542. T., C. J. Folk-lore and legends. Germany, Scotland, Ireland, Oriental. L: Gibbings 1889. 4v. 8. [BM]
A543. TALE WITHOUT AN END: an old friend with a new face. See Carové, F: W:
A544. TALES FOR THE YOUNG, by Nieritz and others. 1854. See C524.
A545. TALES FROM ALSACE. See Alsace, A3.
A546. TALES FROM THE GER. Tr. E. K. E. See C110.
A547. TARTAN PRINCESS, THE: a tale from the Ger. Tr. anon. In "Dublin Univ. mag." 4(1834):369. (B26)
A548. TESTIMONY OF A REFUGEE, etc. See Bokum, Hm., A34.
A549. TITUS ANDRONICUS: a drama in 8 acts. (Acted in Germany ca. 1600 by the Engl. players.) Tr. Mz. Lippner. 1865. In C70.
A550. TRAUGOTT, ANTHONY, the potter musician; or, the triumph of genius and virtue. Tr. Jas. D. Haas. Oxf: Trash; L: Darton 1849. x;163p. 14cm. [EC dates this 1848.] [BM]
A551. "TRAUERMANTEL." See C544 sqq.
A552. TRUE RELATION OF THE TAKING OF ALBA REGALIS, in the Ger. tongue called Stullweissenburgh, the chiefe cittie in Nether Hungarie...Truely tr. out of the Ger. tongue...1601. (B46)
A553. TWO BROTHERS: a romance from the German. See Raven, Frau Mde.
A554. TWO FRIENDS; or, rich and poor. Tr. B. Hitjer. L: S.S.U. 1885. 64p. front. 15cm. [Cf. #4489.] [BM]
A555. TYROL. The heroine of the T--; or, 'Tis time! A scene in the Tyrolese war. Tr. J. D. Haas.1839. In C183, pp. 357-71.
A556. UNDERWALD, THE FALL OF. See Eye-witness, A90.
A557. UNTERWALDEN, the wrongs of. Tr. by Rev. Weeden Butler. L: Cawthorn 1799. 50 (i.e., 54)p. 20cm. [BM]
[Seems to be from the German.]
A558. UTTERSON, SA. H. Tales of the dead. See C552.
A559. VAGABONDS. See Liber vagatorum, A307.
A560. VATER UNSER: a tale for children, il. of the Lord's prayer. Tr. freely by a lady (Mrs. B.). L: Whittaker 1844. 48p. 14cm. [BM]
A561. VICTIM OF THE FALK LAWS, the advent. of a Ger. priest in prison and in exile. Told by the victim. Tr. E. R. B. L: Bentley 1879. 178p. 17cm. [BM]
A562. VIELLIEBCHEN, THE; or, the double-almond. A story. Tr. Mrs. (Isabella F.?) Romer. In "Bentley's miscellany" 27(1850):255. (B27)
A563. VIENNA, RIOT IN, 1798. See Eye-witness, A89.
A564. VIENNA, SIEGE OF. See Siege, A524-5.
A565. VILLAGE astronomer. From the German. Anon. L: Wertheim 1852. 12. [EC]
A566. VIRGINS. (Das Spiel von den zehn Jungfrauen.) The mystery play of the ten virgins. Tr. anon. With a pref. by the Archbishop of Dublin (R. C. Trench). L: Masters 1879. 27p. 19cm. [BM]
[Suppressed because its performance in 1322, at Eisenach, so affected F: the Joyful that he fell into melancholy, and died soon after. The tr. differs from the orig. before me, and is apparently done rather freely, but in good style and spirit.]
A567. VISIT TO THE SEAT OF WAR IN THE NORTH. From the German by (Lascelles?) Wraxall. L: Chapman & Hall 1854. 12. [EC]
A568. VOICES FROM THE GREENWOOD: tales ad. from the Ger. orig. by Lady Wallace. L: Bell & D. 1857. 74p. il. 18cm. [BM]
[4 tales (by the same hand?): The poppy's tale; The fir-tree's tale; The tale of the mountain stream; The tale of the stone.]
A569. VOLKMANN, MARG. H. Text-book to the il. of the hist. of art. See Springer, An.

A570. WALLENSTEIN; or, the Swedes in Prague. See Pichler, K:e.
A571. WALTHARILIED. [Sel.] 1858. Tr. Mme. Davésiès de Pontès. In C88.
A572. do. 1906. [Sel.] Tr. anon. In C190. [Cf. Ekkehard, main list.]
A573. WARTBURG, THE: a monument of Ger. hist. and art, etc. See C555.
A574. WELL BEGUN IS HALF DONE; or, the young painter. Tr. anon. Bost: Crosby, N. n.d. (1855-8) 16. [AC]
A575. WERNIGERODE, COUNTESS. A story of our own times. See Wellmer, Arn.
A576. WILL AND A WAY, A. See "Trauermantel," C549.
A577. WILL-O'-THE-WISP: a fable. See Petersen, Me.
A578. WIND SPIRIT AND THE RAIN GODDESS. Tr. anon. Bost: Crosby, N. n.d. (1855-8) [AC]
A579. WINKELRIED, ARNOLD OF. A drama by M(ark) L(emon). L: Miller 1834. 119p. 21cm. [BM]
[He says: "I have borrowed many of the incidents, and, in one or two instances, the lang. of this drama from a period. publication called the 'Story Teller.'" The names are all German, and the action centers around the hist. fig. of Arn. Strutthan v. W--. Cf. #9550.]
A580. do. n.d. [same] Ed. from a prompt book. L: J.Duncombe. 49p. 14cm. [Vol. 22 of a series begun in 1825. First scene omitted, and some other alterations.] [BM]
A581. WINSBEKE. WINSBEKIN. [Sel.] Tr. Eg. Oswald. 1869. In C440.
A582. WINSBEKIN. [Sel.] Tr. A. E. Kroeger. 1873. In C310.
A583. WOLFDIETRICH. [Sel.] Tr. H: Weber. 1814. In C557.
A584. do. [Sel.] 1845. Tr. anon. In C373.
A585. WURTEMBURG, the comical creatures from. Tr. anon. NY: Putnam 1851. sq. 12. [AC]
*A586. YOUNG girl's diary, A. Pref. with a letter by S. Freud. Tr. Eden and Cedar Paul. L: Allen & U;NY: T. Seltzer 1921. 284p. 24cm. [Tr. seems to be excellent. Ger. pub. of later date: <u>Das Tagebuch eines halbwüchsigen Mädchens.</u>] [BM.LC]
A587. ZIMMERN, HELEN AND ALICE. Stories from foreign novelists. See C577.

LIST B. BIBLIOGRAPHIES [1]

B1. BAUMANN, LINA. <u>Die englischen Uebersetzungen von Goethes Faust.</u> Halle 1907. [Contains very extensive critical judgments, with copious extracts. A model study.] [BM.LC]
B2. BLUMENHAGEN, K: <u>Sir Walter Scott als Uebersetzer.</u> Diss. Rostock 1900. 75p. [UW]
B3. CARRÉ, JEAN MARIE. <u>Bibliographie de Goethe en Angleterre.</u> Paris 1920. 176p. 22cm. [Contains no critical judgments.] [LC.BM]
B4. COLBY, ELBRIDGE. T: Holcroft, translator of plays."Philol. Quart." 3:228. [Not found in BM.] [LC]
B5. CREIGHTON, J. E. Philos. of Kant in America."Kantstudien," Vol. 2. [LC.BM]
B6. DUNCAN, G: M. English translations of Kant's writings. "Kantstudien," Vol. 2. [Gives critical evaluations, seemingly reliable.]
B6a. EVANS, C: Amer. bibliography. A chronological dictionary of all books...prtd. in the U. S. A. 1639-1820. Chic: Priv. prt. 1904. [Probably in BM. In progress. Promises to say the last word in its field.] [LC]
B7. FAUST, Ab. B. Charles Sealsfield, <u>Carl Post, der Dichter beider Hemisphären, sein Leben und seine Werke.</u> Weimar; 1897. 295p. [No critical evaluations.] [LC.BM]
B8. GOEDEKE, K: <u>Grundriss zur Geschichte der deutschen Dichtung.</u> Hannover und Dresden. 1857- . [LC.BM]
[The volume on Goethe I found especially useful.]

[1] This list includes only those articles and books which I have consulted.

B9. GOETHE-JAHRBUCH. Bibliog. of Engl. and Amer. publications, prepared by Rd. Tombo, Jr., and Horatio S. White. [LC.BM]
B10. GOODNIGHT, SCOTT H. Ger. lit. in Amer. Mag. prior to 1846. Diss. Bulletin of U. of Wis. 1909. 264p. [LC.BM]
[Has no critical judgments on translations.]
B11. GREG, WL. W. English translations of "Lenore." "Mod. Quart. of Lang. and lit.," vol. 2, no. 5. [LC.BM]
[Contains trenchant critical comment.]
B12. GRIMM, MINERVA E. Translations of foreign novels. Bost. book co. 1917. 84p. 8. [Not found in BM. Uncritical.] [LC]
B12a. HAERTEL, MN. H: Ger. lit. in Amer. Mag., 1846-80. Diss. Bulletin of U. of Wis. 1908. 188p. [Uncritical.] [LC.BM]
B13. HANDSCHIN, C: H. A bibliog. of Engl. translations of Ger. novels. "Monatshefte für deutsche Sprache und Pädagogik," vol. 9 (1908). [Not found in BM. A compilation including only the better names, often with very incomplete data. Uncritical.] [LC]
B14. HANEY, J: L: Ger. lit. in England before 1790. NY: Ger. histor. soc. 1902. 25p. 26cm. [LC.BM]
B15. HARRIS, W: J. The first printed translations into Engl. of the great foreign classics. L: Routledge; NY: Dutton 1909. 209p. 17cm. [To be used with great caution; data frequently incomplete.] [BM.LC]
B15a. HATHAWAY, Lillie V. Ger. lit. of the mid-nineteenth cent. in Engl. and America as reflected in the journals 1840-1914. Diss. Bost: Chapman & Grimes 1935. 341p. 20cm. [LC]
B16. HAUHART, W: F: Reception of Goethe's Faust in England in the first half of the 19th cent. Diss. Columbia U. 1909. 149p. [LC.BM]
B17. HEINEMANN, W: Bibliog. list of the Engl. tr. of Goethe's Faust. "Bibliographer" 2(1882):79, 100. [BM.LC]
B18. HERFORD, C: H. Studies in the lit. relations of England and Germany in the 16th cent. Cambridge U. Press 1886. 426p. 8. [UW]
[Not found in BM. Small uncritical bibliog.]
B19. HINZ, Stella M. Goethe's poems in Engl. tr. after 1860. Diss. U. of Wis. Studies 1928. 303p. [Has extended critical discussion.] [LC.BM]
B19a. KIPPENBERG, Catalog der Sammlung. 2d ed. Lpz: 1928.
[I saw this at the Deutsche Bücherei in Leipzig. It is devoted exclusively to Goetheana. Uncritical.]
B20. KUEBLER, TD. Histor. notes to the "Lyra Germanica" (cf. C276 sq.):...brief memoirs of the authors of the hymns...notices of the hymn-writers...in Engl. collections. L: Longman 1865. xvi; 356p. 16cm. [BM]
B21. KURRELMEYER, W. Engl. translations of Wieland. "Mod. Lang. Notes" 32(1917):225. [BM.LC]
B22. L., C. F. Deutsche Dichtungen in englischen Uebersetzungen. "Grenzboten," vol. 28. (1869). [LC.BM]
B23. LIEDER, F: W. C. Bayard Taylor's adaptation of Schiller's Don Carlos. JEGPh., vol. 16(1917). [LC.BM]
[Has remarks on other Engl. versions.]
B24. do. Goethe in England and America. JEGPh., vol. 10(1911): 535. [LC.BM]
B25. LONG, ORIE W. Engl. translations of Goethe's Werther. JEGPh., vol. 14(1915). [Contains excellent critical remarks.] [LC.BM]
B26. MIX, MORTON. Ger. lit. in British mags., 1750-1835. Diss. U. of Wis. [Unpublished.]
B27. NICOLAI, MARTHA. Ger. lit. in Brit. mags., 1836-60. Diss. U. of Wis. [Unpublished.]
B28. OSWALD, Eg. Goethe in England and America. L: Nutt 1899. 50p. 23cm. [BM.LC]
--2d ed. rev. and enl. Lina and Ella Oswald. L: Moring 1909. 75p. 23cm. [BM.LC]

B29. PARRY, ELLWOOD COMLY. F: Schiller in America. Phil. "Americana Germ.," 1905. 116p. 25cm. [LC.BM]
B30. PRICE, LAWRENCE M. Review of this Bibliography, JEGPh., 23 (1924):114. [LC.BM]
B31. RAILO, EINO. The haunted castle: a study of the elements of Engl. romanticism. L: Routledge; NY: Dutton 1927. [BM.LC]
B32. REA, T. Schiller's dramas and poems in England. L: Unwin 1906. 155p. 12. [BM.LC]
[Has extensive critical comments; on careful examination, however, I find them unreliable, and have substituted my own wherever possible. E. g., the translator of Schiller's Fiesco (#8063) clearly knows little German and deviates willfully; yet Rea says, "It bears evidence of great care...its only defect is that it is too literal."]
B33. ROSCHER, HS. F. G. Die Wallensteinübersetzung von S. T. Coleridge. Diss. Tübingen. Borna-Leipzig 1905. 170p. O. [UW]
[Very thorough discussion.]
B34. SACHS, H: B. Heine in America. Phil. "Americana Germ.," no. 23 (1916). [LC.BM]
[Estimates of critics and translators must be accepted with caution; generally too ready to praise, he has severe strictures on F: H: Hedge as a translator--whom I regard very highly--almost indicating some personal animus.]
B35. SANDBACH, FIS. E. The Nibelungenlied and Gudrun in England and America. L: Nutt 1903. 200p. 8. [BM.LC]
[He passes judgment on several versions, but his lists are incomplete.]
B36. SCHAIBLE, K: H: Geschichte der Deutschen in England. Strassburg: Trübner 1885. 483p. 20cm. [An extensive account of the principal German travelers and settlers in England.] [LC]
B37. SCHNEIDER, FZ. Ger. novelistic and belletristic prose writers in Engl. translation, 1917-28. "The Spokesman," U. of Calif. 1929. 23p. 23cm. [Not in BM.] [LC]
B38. SCHOLZ, K: Bibliog. of Engl. renditions of mod. Ger. dramas. "Ger.-Amer. annals," vol. 15(1917). [LC.BM]
[Extensive list, including much MS and some probably unpub. material.]
B39. do. The art of translation, with special ref. to the prose dramas of Hauptmann and Sudermann. "Ger.-Amer. annals," vol. 20 (1918):3-70.
B40. SEIDENSTICKER, O. English and German lit. in the 18th and 19th century. "Poet-Lore," vol. 2 (1890): 57, 169. [LC]
B41. SELLIER, Wl. Kotzebue in England. Lpz: O. Schmidt 1901. 95p. 23cm. [LC.BM]
B42. SIMMONS, LUCRETIA v. T. Engl. Translations of Goethe's lyrics prior to 1860. Diss. Univ. of Wis. Studies, 1918. 202p. [LC.BM]
[Has critical comments.]
B43. STOKOE, F. W. Ger. influence in the Engl. romantic period. Cambridge U. press 1926. 202p. 22cm. [BM.LC]
B44. TODT, W: Lessing in England, 1767-1850. Diss. Heidelberg 1912. 38p. [BM]
B45. ULLRICH, HM. Robinson und Robinsonaden. Bibliog., Gesch., Kritik. Lit.-histor. Forschungen, 7. Heft (1898). [LC.BM]
[Lists Engl. eds. of the "Swiss family Robinson," and of Campe's "New Robinson Crusoe."]
B46. WATERHOUSE, GILBERT. The lit. relations of England and Germany in the 17th cent. Cambridge U. press 1914. 190p. 8. [BM.LC]
B47. WATT, RB. Bibliotheca brit. Ed: Constable; L: Longmans. 1824. [BM]
B48. WILKENS, F: H. Early influence of Ger. lit. in America. "Americana Germ.," vol. 3 (1899). [A rather complete list of Ger. works printed in America before 1826; Evans has found more.]

B49. WILLOUGHBY, L. A. Engl. tr. and ad. of Schiller's Robbers. "Mod. Lang. Rev." 16(1921):297.
B50. WORDEN, J. P. Bibliog. of all known versions (of Schiller's "Lied von der Glocke") in English. 1900. In #7949. [Has critical comments.]

LIST C. COLLECTIONS

This list, besides containing an increase of more than 300 over its predecessor, shows also a radical innovation in its technique: I have hoped to earn the gratitude of future bibliographers, compilers, and students, by registering the contents of all the volumes to which I could gain access. Many of the indices to these volumes are lacking in accuracy of ascription or spelling, so that these data cannot be guaranteed, the less so that my own transcriptions of these flocks of names and initials are subject to error in both writing and subsequent reading. However, I have thought it worthwhile to assume that risk. It seems to me not only that these name-lists may have some value for specialists but that they are not uninteresting from the point of view of their selection and distribution. My earliest plan, that of listing all the individual poems involved, I gave up as inhumanly difficult of execution, but not until some 11000 cards had been made out (taken only from the books available on this side of the Atlantic). Such studies may some time be attempted for individual authors (as has been done for Goethe at Wisconsin); then the analyses here presented should prove useful as a starting point for further research.

The preparation of these indices suggested one inquiry that could be pursued with relative ease, namely as to the frequency of occurrence of the various poets in these collections. No value attaches to the appended sequences; but I find them interesting, and possibly others may agree. I have set up two sequences, in fact: one based on the range of the poet, i.e., the number of separate volumes in which selections from him are printed; the other based on a rough computation of the aggregate amount of such selections (counting either a poem or a page as one). The figures in parentheses are hundreds; they indicate that in both frequency and range Goethe far outstrips all others, and that Schiller, Heine, and Uhland stand with Goethe in a group by themselves. It was not possible to distinguish between prose and verse in these computations; hence the relatively high frequency of Lessing, Luther, Richter, Tieck, Kant, etc. Tersteegen and Gerhardt owe their position to the large number of hymnals, as well as to other volumes which stress religious poetry. Interesting is the high rank of Walther von der Vogelweide, who easily leads the Minnesingers, followed at a long distance by Ulrich von Lichtenstein and Heinrich von Morungen. Of more modern poets, Dehmel leads, followed by Liliencron and Hofmannsthal; but none of these achieved the minimum of 10 necessary for inclusion in the range-sequence.

Frequency	Range
1. Goethe (21.7)	1. Goethe (1.7)
2. Schiller (12.9)	2. Schiller (1.4)
3. Heine (9.4)	3. Uhland (1.2)
4. Uhland (7)	4. Heine (1.1)
5. Rückert (3)	5. Rückert (.8)
6. Freiligrath (2.3)	6. Freiligrath (.6)
7. Geibel (2.1)	7. Körner
8. Lessing (2)	8. Bürger
9. Luther (1.8)	9. Chamisso (.5)
10. Körner (1.8)	10. Herder
11. Bürger (1.7)	11. Geibel
12. Wieland (1.7)	12. Klopstock
13. Müller (1.6)	13. Luther
14. Walther v. d. Vogelweide	14. Müller
15. Richter	15. Kerner
16. Herder (1.5)	16. Arndt
17. Chamisso	17. Claudius
18. Tersteegen (1.3)	18. Grün
19. Gerhardt (1.2)	19. Salis
20. Klopstock	20. Gellert (.3)
21. Novalis	21. Eichendorff
22. Grün (1.1)	22. Platen
23. Lenau	23. Lenau
24. Platen (.9)	24. Novalis
25. Kerner (.8)	25. Matthisson
26. Eichendorff	26. Lessing
27. Hölty (.7)	27. Gerhardt
28. Schlegels	28. Hölty
29. Zinzendorf	29. Stolbergs
30. Arndt	30. Fouqué
31. Claudius	31. Richter
32. Tieck	32. Gleim
33. Matthisson	33. Tieck (.2)
34. Herwegh (.6)	34. Herwegh
35. Schopenhauer	35. Angelus S.
36. Salis	36. Hoffmann v. F.
37. Fouqué	37. Tersteegen
38. Kant	38. Spitta
39. Spitta	39. Wieland
40. Gellert	40. Mörike
41. Auerbach (.5)	41. Walther v. d. V.
42. Fichte	42. Schlegels
43. Stolbergs	43. Reinick
44. Bodenstedt	44. Zedlitz
45. Scheffel	45. Dach
46. Angelus S. (.4)	46. Voss
47. Hoffmann v. F.	47. Bodenstedt (.1)
48. Gleim	48. Krummacher
49. Dehmel	49. Simrock
50. Vogl	50. Zinzendorf
51. Hoffmann	51. Heermann
52. Sachs	52. Sturm
53. Heermann	53. Neander
54. Krummacher	54. Mosen
55. Schmolck (.3)	55. Halm
56. Lavater	56. Nicolai
57. Liliencron	57. Vogl
58. Sturm	58. Schmolck

Frequency	Range
59. Ulrich v. L.	59. Lingg
60. Mörike	60. Schwab
61. Reinick	61. Seidl
62. Lingg (.2)	62. Mahlmann
63. Ebers	63. Kotzebue
64. Heinrich v. Mor.	64. Schubart
65. Neander	65. Scheffel
66. Hauff	66. Sachs
67. Heyse	67. Lavater
68. Rist	68. Rist
69. Gerok	69. Hebbel
70. Hebbel	70. Freylinghausen
71. Zedlitz	71. Hauff
72. Dietmar	72. Gerok
73. Dach	73. Dingelstedt
74. Voss	74. Hölderlin
75. Hofmannsthal	75. Pfeffel
76. Mosen	76. Schenkendorf
77. Simrock	
78. Dingelstedt	
79. Halm	
80. Nicolai	
81. Schwab	
82. Seidl	
83. Hölderlin	
84. Pfeffel	
85. Mahlmann	
86. Freylinghausen (.1)	
87. Kotzebue	
88. Schubart	
89. Hartmann v. A.	
90. Schenkendorf	

COLLECTIONS

§C1. A., C. Words for German melodies. Tr. by C. A. Oxf: E. W. Morris for priv. circ. 1885. 7p. 23cm. [BM]
[Not very good, and certainly not suited to music. --Heine (4), Hoffmann v. Fallersleben, Uhland, U: v. Lichtenstein.]

§C2. "AGRA." Poems and ballads for penny readings. L: Wyman 1883. 125p. 17cm. [Fair versions, but meter altered. --Bürger, Goethe (5), Trinius, Uhland (7).] [BM]

*C3. AIKMAN, C: MORTON. Poems from the German. L: Sonnenschein 1892. Ger;Engl. 97p. 8. [BM]
[Some tr. very good, some rather feeble. --Chamisso, Ferrand, Freiligrath (2), Geibel (2), Goethe (4), Hamerling, Heine (3), Herwegh (3), Keller, W: Müller, Rückert, Scheffel (3), Schiller, Sturm, Uhland (2).]

C4. ALGER, W: ROUNSEVILLE. The poetry of the east. 1856.
[I have not seen this.]

§C5. do. 1865. The poetry of the orient. Bost: Roberts. 337p. 17cm.
[Many of the Oriental poems through tr. of Herder and Rückert; a supplement adds misc. poems, some from the German. --L: Feuerbach (epigrams), Freiligrath (2), Grün, Herder (22), Hölderlin, Lenau, (20), Lessing, Rückert (27), Tholuck.] [LC,BM]

§C6. do. 1874. [same] Roberts. 371p. [BM]
[Adds: A. Feuerbach (2), Grün, Heine, Lavater, Als. Schreiber.]

C7. ANSTER, J: Ger. lit. at the close of the last cent. and the commencement of the present. In his Lect. on Lit. and Art. L: Bell & Daldy 1864. pp. 153-95. [BM]
[Probably most of the tr. cited are by other hands. --Bürger, "Lenore" (by W: Taylor); Stolberg, "Ode to a mt. torrent" (by Coleridge); Schiller, "Wallenstein" (2 pass. by Coleridge), 5 other sel.; Goethe, Mahomets Gesang.]

†C8. do. 1819. Poems; w. some tr. from the Ger. Edinb. 12. [BM]
[Goethe (3), Haller, Klopstock, Körner (2), v. Sassen, Schiller (2).]

†C9. do. 1837. Xeniola: poems. Dublin: Milliken. 174p. 16. [BM.LCO]
[Goethe, Körner, v. Sassen, Schiller; also scenes from "The pilgrimage," a drama, by Fouqué (49p.).]

†C10. ASTLEY, FIS. DUKINFIELD. Poems, and tr. L: Priv. prt. 1819. 198p. 16cm. [Bürger, Matthisson, Salis.] [LC]

*C11. A(TTWELL), H: A book of thoughts. Sel. from the writings of Engl., Fr., and Ger. authors. L: Cambr. 1865. 16. [BM]
[Short pithy sayings quoted in the original and tr. in a special section.]

§C12. AUSTIN, MRS. SA. (TAYLOR). Fragments from Ger. prose writers. NY: Appleton 1841. xii;353p. 19cm. [LC.BM]
[Very short extracts. --Arndt, Babo, Bna. Arnim, C. A. Brandis, Fichte, Fouqué, F: II, F: Gentz, Goethe, Jk. Grimm, Hahn-Hahn, Heine, Heinzelmann, Herder, Humboldt, I. Iselin, F: H: Jacobi, F: C. W: Jacobs, Kant, Knebel, Lessing, Königin Luise, Luther, Merkel, Möser, J:s v. Müller, K? O. Müller, Niebuhr, Novalis, Oehlenschläger, Pestalozzi, R. Varnhagen, Richter, Rumohr, Savigny, Schelling, Schiller, Schlegels, Schleiermacher, J:a Schopenhauer, H. P. Sturz, Tieck, Ferd. Walter, Weber, Zelter, F: W: Ziegler.]

§C13. AYTOUN, W: EDMONSTONE. Poems. L: Milford 1921. 509p. 18cm. [BM]
[Goethe (38), Uhland (7).]

C14. B., O. S. Christmas legends. Tr. from the Ger. by O. S. B. L: Washbourne 1890 (1889). 128p. 16cm. [BM]
[7 legends. No author named.]

§C15. BANCROFT, G: Lit. and hist. miscellanies. NY: Harper 1855. 517p. 23cm. [LC.BM]
[Undistinguished tr. --Goethe (8), Herder, Rist, Rückert, Schiller (5 plus epigrams).]

C16. BARTEN, J: A sel. coll. of Engl. and Ger. proverbs...w. tr. Hamburg: C. Kloss 1896. 323p. 8. [BM]
[4182 proverbs in Engl., not quite half of them tr. from Ger. Nos. 4183-8239 are in German, many tr. from Engl.]

*C17. BASKERVILLE, AF. The poetry of Germany. Lpz: Mayer; L: Wms. & N;NY: Garrigue 1853. Ger;Engl. 332 (i.e., 663)p. 8. [LC.BM]
--14th ed. Phil: Schaefer & Konradi 1886. [LC]
[Seldom in error, often stilted; does Schiller well, folksong poorly. --Arndt (7p.), Arnim (2), Beck (3), Brentano (3), Bürger (7), Chamisso (10), Claudius (2), Dingelstedt, Droste, Eichendorff (4), Freiligrath (3), Gaudy, Geibel (4), Gellert (2), Gleim (3), Goethe (12), Grün (5), Hagedorn, Mz. Hartmann (2), Heine (7), Herder, Herwegh (3), Hoffmann v. Fallersleben (4), Hölderlin, Hölty (2), Immermann, Jacobi (2), Kerner, Kinkel, E. Kleist, Klopstock (10), Kopisch, Körner (5), Eli. Kulmann (2), Lenau (3), Lessing, Lichtwer, Matthisson, Af. Meissner, Mörike, Mosen, W: Müller (2), Wfg. Müller, Novalis, Pfarrius, Rückert (6), Salis, Sallet, Schefer, Schenkendorf, Schiller (40), Schlegels (2), Schubart (3), Ern. Schulze, Schwab (2), Seume, Simrock, F: Stolberg (2), Stolterfoth, Strachwitz, Tieck (4), Tiedge (2), Uhland (9), Voss, Weisse, Wieland (6), Zedlitz (2).]

C18. BATES, AF. The drama; its hist., lit., and influence on civilization. L: Athenian soc. 1903. 20v. il. 24cm. [LC]
[Ger. drama, vols. 10-12. Selections and a few complete plays, largely reprinted. --V. 10: H. Sachs, "Raising the devil" (complete), tr. (prose) W. H. H. Chambers; Lessing, "Nathan" (lengthy excerpts), "Minna," tr. Ernest Bell; Schiller, "Wallenstein" (sel.), tr. Coleridge; "Camp of Wallenstein," tr. J. Churchill; Z. Werner, "Twenty-fourth of Feb," tr. W. H. H. Chambers. --V. 11: Goethe, "Faust" (sel.) "Iphigenia" (complete), both tr. Swanwick; Iffland, "Conscience," tr. B: Thompson; Kotzebue, "Egotist and pseudo-critic," tr. W. H. H. Chambers; Benedix, "Obstinacy," tr. Chambers. --V. 12: Babo, "Dagobert, king of the Franks" (complete), tr. B: Thompson; Z. Werner, "Sons of the valley" (lengthy sel.), tr. Mrs. Eliz. Lewis (?); Goethe, "Stella" (complete), tr. B: Thompson; Hauptmann, "Hannele" (complete), tr. W: Archer; Schnitzler, "Questioning the irrevocable" (from "Anatol"), tr. W. H. H. Chambers.]

C19. BEAUCHAMP, W: MN., Moravian journals relating to central N.Y., 1745-66. Onondaga hist. ass'n, Syracuse, NY: 1916. 242p. 24cm.
[Diaries of A. G. Spangenberg, Br. Cammerhoff, D: Zeisberger, Gf. Rundt, H: Frey. Tr. Ca. Frueauff, Rb. Rau, A. H. Leibert.] [LC]

C20. BEAUTIES of German lit. Sel. from various authors, w...biog. notices. L: Burns 1847. 66; 10; 68; 24; 212p. 17cm. [BM.NY]
[Pichler, "J:s Schoreel"; Richter, "The death of an angel"; Zschökke [sic], "The broken cup"; Tieck, "Camoens, or, the death of the poet"; Hoffmann, "Master Martin and his workmen."]

C21. do. 1877. [same] Ger. lit. as exemplified by the works of Pichler, Richter, Zschökke, and Tieck. L: Warne. Chandos classics. 376p. 8. [BPL]--L: Warne; NY: Scribner. [BM]
[Same as C20, exc. that Hoffmann is omitted, and Pichler's "Quentin Matsys" is added.]

†C22. BERESFORD, B: German Erato: a coll. of favorite songs tr. Berl. Falk; L: Boosey 1798. 31p. 4. [LC]
[Bürger (5), Claudius, Gleim, Goethe (5), Hölty, Jacobi, E. Kleist, Klopstock, Matthisson, Salis, Schiller, Stolberg, Voss, Weisse.]

C22a. do. 1798. 2d ed. Berl: sold by G. C. Nauk. 31p. 4. (B19a)
[This copy has MS dedication by tr. to Prof. Roy Nolte.]

†C23. do. 1800. [same] A coll. of Ger. ballads and songs. 2d ed. Berl: Fröhlich. 32p. 4. (B42)

C24. do. 1798. The German songster. A coll. of favorite airs. Berl: Falk. 27p. 4.--2d ed. Berl: Fröhlich 1800. (B42)

†C25. do. 1801. Tr. of Ger. poems...from...mus. pub...Berl: Fröhlich. Ger;Engl. viii;199p. 16cm. [BM]
[Contents appar. derived from C22 and C24. Kayser lists two vols., but BM has only one. Possibly confusion with C22 and C24? -- Bürger (5), Claudius, Gleim, Goethe (5), Hölty (2), Jacobi, Kleist, Klopstock, Matthisson (2), Müller, Salis, Schiller (2), Stolberg (3), Voss (3), Weisse.]

§C26. BERESFORD, B: and MELLISH, JOS. C: Specimens of the Ger. lyric poets: consisting of tr. in verse... L: Boosey 1822. 152p. il. 21cm. [LC]--2d ed. L: Blackwood 1823. [BM]--3d ed. L: Blackwood 1823. --4th ed. L: Longmans 1828. (B42)
[Advt. announced 1st ed. in 1821, but 1822 is actual date. Tr. taken largely or wholly from C22, C24, and C411. --Bürger (7), Claudius (2), Gleim (2), Goethe (6), Hölty (3), Jacobi, Kleist, Klopstock, Kotzebue (2), Matthisson (3), Müchler, Müller, Neubeck, Nostiz, Overbeck (2), Salis, Sander, Schiller (9), Schubart, Siegfried, Stolberg (3), Voss (3), Weisse (2).]

BEVAN, E. F. Songs of eternal life. See "Hymnals."

*C27. BITHELL, JETHRO. The minnesingers. Vol. 1. Translations. L;NY: Longmans 1909. 24cm. [BM.LC]
[Excellent style and spirit; takes liberties with the form. --Abr. v. Rapperschwyl, Abr. v. Johannsdorf (4), Der wilde Alexander (3), Bligger v. Steinach, Burggrafen v. Lüenz, Regensburg (3), Rietenburg (3), Burkhard v. Hohenfels (2), Cn. v. Hamle, Cn. v. Lupin, Der v. Sachsendorf, Der v. Suneck, Dietmar (12), Dürner, F: v. Hausen (6), F: v. Leiningen, Geltar, Gf. v. Neifen (3), Der Guter, Hartmann v. Aue (7), Hartwig v. Raute, Hadlaub (3), H: v. Anhalt, H: v. Breslau, H: v. Frauenberg, H: Hetzbold v. Weissensee, H: v. Meissen (3), H: Markgraf v. Meissen, H: v. Morungen (10), H: v. Mueglin, H: v. Rugge (2), H: v. Veldeke (7), Herrand v. Wildonje, Hildbold v. Schwangau (2), Hg. v. Montfort, Hg. v. Werbenwag, Herzog J: v. Brabant, Der v. Kolmas, Kd. v. Würzburg (2), Konradin, Kraft v. Toggenburg, Kürenberg (12), Markgraf O: v. Brandenburg (3), Markgraf v. Hohenburg, Meinloh (10), Neidhart (9), Oswald v. Wolkenstein (9), O: v. Botenlauben (2), Reinmar v. Hagenau (9), Reinmar v. Zweter (14), Rubin, Rd. v. Rotenburg, Spervogel I (8), Spervogel II (4), Steinmar (3), Der Taler, Tannhäuser (2), Truchsess v. St. Gallen (2), Der tugenhafte Schreiber, U: v. Lichtenstein (5), U. v. Winterstetten, Wachsmut v. Mülnhausen, Wl. v. d. Vogelweide (58), König Wenzel v. Böhmen, Wolfram v. Eschenbach (4), also some folksongs and anon. poems and one mastersong.]

*C28. do. 1909. Contemp. Ger. poetry. Sel. and tr. by J-- B--. L;NY: Scott. 191p. 14cm. [BM.LC]
[F: Adler, P. Baum (2), Hs. Benzmann (2), Hs. Bethge, O: Bierbaum (10), E. Bodmann (5), C: Busse (3), G: Busse-Palma, Mx. Dauthendey (10), R: Dehmel (22), "Dolorosa," Gst. Falke (8), Art. Fitger, C. Flaischlen (5), I. Forbes-Mosse (5), A. Geiger (7), Fx. Ginzkey (4), E. Hardt, O: Hartleben (5), K: Henckell (2), P: Hille (5), Hofmannsthal (6), A. Holz (5), R:a Huch (2), H. Lachmann (4), E. Lasker-Schüler (9), Liliencron (15), "Me. Madeleine" (4), A. Miegel (13), A. Mombert (15), C. Morgenstern, Eli. Paulsen (4), Rilke (9), A. Roffhack (2), R: Schaukal (15), Schoenaich-Carolath (3), C: Spitteler, M. v. Stern (3), Mge. Susman, F. Wedekind (2), P. Wertheimer (2), S. Zweig (2).]

§C29. BLACKIE, J: STUART. War songs of the Germans. Ed: Edmonston & Douglas 1870. 152p. 16cm. [BM.LC]
[Arndt (3), N. Becker, Claudius, Follen, Körner (4), Schenkendorf (2), Schneckenburger.]

§C30. BOHN, H: G: A polyglott of for. proverbs...w. Engl. tr. L: Bohn 1847. German, pp. 133-92. 17cm. [BM]

†C31. BOKUM, HM. Tr. in poetry and prose from celebrated Ger. writers. Bost: Munroe 1836. 146p. 16cm. [LC]
[Largely eclectic. --Bürger (4), Fouqué, Gleim, Goethe (9), Herder, Jacobi, Klopstock (4), Körner (6), Krummacher (2), Overbeck, Richter, Rückert (2), Schiller (8), Schmidt v. Lübeck, Schultze (3), Stolberg, Uhland.]

§C32. BOOTH, MRS. MA. H. C. Wayside blossoms from Ger. gardens. Heidelberg: Bangel und Schmitt; Milwaukee, S. C. West 1864. 190p. 14 x 11cm. [LC.BM]
[Tr. fair to poor. --M. F. Anneke (4), J. G. Fischer, Grün (2), Hebbel, Heine (4), Herwegh (4), Uhland (18).]

C33. BORROW, G: Ballads of all nations, tr. by G: B--. Sel. ed. by R. B. Johnson, from the texts of H. Wright. L: Rivers 1927. 366p. 8. [Sel. from "Nibelungenlied"; Goethe, "Erl-king"; W. Bornemann.] [BM]

*C34. do. 1923. Songs from the Ger. In his "Works," vol. 8, pp. 382-404. L: Constable; NY: Wells. 22cm. [BM]

BORROW, G:
[Good to very good tr. --Sel. from "Nibelungenlied"; Bürger, "Lenore" (good, though rhyme-scheme is altered); Goethe, 2 poems and fragments from "Faust."]

§C35. BOSANQUET, HELEN and BERNARD. Zoar, a book of verse. Oxf: Blackwell 1919. 19cm. [BM]
[Tr. by B. B., pp. 11-39; some good. --Goethe (15), Schiller.]

†C36. BOYD, A. German ballads and poems. L: Houlston 1859. Ger;Engl. 271p. 8. [Goethe, Heine (3), Klesheim (2), Lenau, Lutrow, Mosenthal (2), Seidl, Uhland (3), Vogl (23), Zerboni.] [BM]

†C37. BOYD, PERCY. A book of ballads from the Ger. Dublin: McGlashan 1848. 128p. il. 22cm. [LC]
[Negligible tr. --Freiligrath (2), Goethe, Heine (4), Körner, Müller, Schiller (8), Uhland (3); miscellany.]

§C38. BROICHER, DAISY. Ger. lyrics and ballads done into Engl. verse. L: Mathews 1912. 79p. 17cm. [BM.LC]
[Some very bad. --Brentano (6), Eichendorff (7), Hebbel (8), Hölderlin (6), Lenau (5), Meyer (9), Mörike (3), Platen (4), Storm (7).]

§C39. do. 1909. Ger. lyrists of today. L: Mathews. Vigo cabinet series. 68p. 12. [BM]
[Andrian-Werburg (3), G: Edward, George (30), Gundolf, Hardt (2), Hofmannsthal (5), Perls, Vollmoeller (3), Wolfskehl (2).]

†C40. BROMWELL, H. PELHAM. Translations. From poems of Schiller, Schlegel, etc. Denver, Col: Priv. prt. 1919. 81p. 19cm. [LC.BM]
[25 copies prt. --Butz (2), Chamisso, Freiligrath, Grün (8), Kerner, Rückert, Schiller (6), Schlegel, Schneckenburger, Schwab, Uhland.]

*C41. BROOKS, C: Ger. lyrics. Bost: Ticknor, R. & F. 1853. 237p. 19cm. [LC.BM]
[Brooks does the humorous best; fluent, easy; general spirit excellently caught; not always sure of the German. --Alexis, Chamisso (3), Claudius (2), Freiligrath, Geibel (3), Gellert (3), Grün (8), Gruppe, Herwegh, Kerner (2), Kopisch, Langbein, Laufenberg, Leitner, Lenau, Mörike, C. W. Müller, W. Müller (4), Nathusius (2), Nicolai, Platen (2), Plönnies, Rückert (7), Schnetzler, Schottel, Seidl (3), Stolle, Stolterfoth, Tiedge, Uhland (4), Würkert.]

*C42. do. 1885. Poems, orig. and tr. Sel. and ed. W. P. Andrews. Bost: Roberts. xiv;235p. 18cm. [LC.BM]
[Falk, Gellert, Goethe, Grün, Heine, Jäger, Kerner (2), Kinkel, Körner (2), Langbein, Mohr, Platen, Rückert (7), Salis, Schiller, Uhland (4), Zimmermann.]

*C43. do. 1847. Schiller's homage of the arts, and other translations. Bost: Munroe. viii;151p. 16. [LC.BM]
--NY: Miller 1864. [LC]--NY: Miller 1870. [HCL.BM]
[Bürger, Freiligrath (9), Gleim, Herwegh (2), Jacobi (4), Körner, Krummacher (2), Lieber (4), Luther, Rückert (16), Schiller (2), Schulze, Uhland (4), Wülfler.]

*C44. do. Songs and ballads from Uhland, Körner, Bürger, and other Ger. poets. Bost: Hilliard, Gray 1838. Ripley's specimens of for. standard lit. 400p. 8. [BM]--Bost: Munroe 1842. 400p. 20cm. [LC]
--Title; Ger. lyric poetry. A coll. of songs and ballads. Phil: Hazard 1863. xix;400p. 17cm. [LC.BM]
[Some of these tr. by Cranch, Dwight, Frothingham, Longfellow, Sa. Whitman. --Arndt, Brunn (2), Bürger (6), Claudius (2), Collin, A. Follen (2), Gellert, Gleim (2), Goethe (6), Herder (2), Hölty (6), Kerner (3), Kleist, Klopstock (3), Körner (18), Kosegarten (3), Kotzebue, Krummacher (2), Langbein (2), Mahlmann, Mellin, Miller, Novalis (2), Pfeffel (3), Poeschmann, Richter, Rosemann, Rückert (5), Salis, Schiller (10), Schmidt (2), Stolberg (3), Tieck, Uhland (27)]

C45. BRYANT, W: CULLEN, ed. Lib. of poetry and song. NY: Ford 1871. 789p. il. 24cm. [LC]
[A few tr. from the Ger., eclectic. Many subsequent editions. -- Altenburg, Freiligrath, Gerhardt, Goethe, Heine (2), Hölty, Körner (3), Krummacher (2), Luther (2), W: Müller, Pfeffel, Uhland.]

C46. do. A new lib. of poetry and song. NY: 1876, 1877. 1880. lxxvii;950p. [BM]
[Altenburg, Claudius, Freiligrath (2), Gerhardt, Gluck, Goethe (3), Holty [sic], Körner (3), Krummacher (2), Luther (2), W. Müller, Pfeffel, Uhland (2).]

§C47. do. 1872. 1873. Poems. NY: Appleton. 390p. 17cm. [LC.BM]
[Four tr.: Chamisso, N. Müller, Uhland.]

C48. BULFINCH, S. G. Poems. Charleston, S. C. J. S. Burges 1834. 108p. 16cm. [Körner (2), Schiller.] [BM]

C49. BURKHARDT, C: B. Fairy tales and legends of many nations. NY: Miller 187- . il. 16. [AC]

†C50. BURT, MA. ANNE. Spec. of the choicest lyr. prod. of the most celebrated Ger. poets. Lpz;L: Chapman & Hall 1854. 504p. 8. (B42) --2d ed. Lpz: Michelsen 1855. 503p. 20cm. [LC]
[Bürger (3), Dingelstedt (2), Freiligrath (3), Goethe (26), Grün (3), Heine (6), Hölty (5), Klopstock (4), L: I. v. Bayern (8), Marggraff (3), Mäurer (16), Platen (3), Prutz (3), Rückert (4), Salis (4), Schiller (18), Uhland (5), Zedlitz (3).]

C50a. do. 1853. The German Parnassus: specimens of the most celebrated Ger. poets, tr., etc. Vol. 1. Chur: Hitz. 126p. 16. [EC (Heinsius)]

C50b. do. 1853. Specimens of the choicest lyrical productions of the most celebrated Ger. poets. From Klopstock to the present time. Klopstock, Schiller, Goethe, Hölty, Bürger, etc., with biogr. and lit. notes. 1st ed. Zürich 2v. 268p. gr. 16. [Heinsius]

C51. C., MRS. L. T. Songs under his shadow. Orig., and tr. from the Ger. L: Partridge 1880. 111p. 18cm. [BM]
[Tr. embrace pp. 59-110, chiefly hymns. --Enslin, Gerhardt (2), K. Gerok (7), P. Gerok, Mahlmann (2), Schmolcke (2), Spitta, Strachwitz.]

*C52. CALDWELL, W. W. Poems, orig. and tr. Bost: Munroe 1857. 275p. 18cm. [Tr. from Geibel very well done. --Geibel (47), Hebel (7), Hoffmann v. Fallersleben (7).]

C53. CALVERLEY, C: STUART. Complete works. L: Bell 1910. 514p. 19cm. [Castelli (2), Heine.] [LC.BM]

†C54. CAMPBELL, J: J. The song of the bell and other poems from the Ger. Ed: Blackwood; L: Cadell 1836. xi;259p. 16cm. [BM]
[Negligible. --Bürger (17), Goethe (15), Matthisson (6), Salis (4), Schiller (21).]

†C55. CAPUCINER (i.e., a tr. of the friar's speech in Schiller, "Wallensteins Lager"). NY: Radde 1839. 23p. 12. [NY.BM]
[Also: Goethe (2), Hölty, Salis.]

*C56. CARLYLE, T: Crit. and misc. essays coll. and repub. 2d ed. L: Jas. Fraser 1840. 5v. 12. [BM]
[Prose from Fichte, Goethe, C. G. Heyne, Novalis, Richter, Schiller, Tieck, V. v. Ense, Z. Werner. Poetry: Goethe, "Helena" (13p.); Grillparzer, "Ottokar"; Klingemann, "Faust" (5p.); "Luther's Psalm," Schiller, "Robbers" (3p.); "Maid of Orleans" (2p.); "Nibelungenlied" (4p.); Stricker, Boner, "Reinecke Fuchs."]

*C57. do. [same] NY: Carey & Hart 1846. 8. [AC]
-- Mod. Brit. essayists, vol. 5. 1850. 568p. --NY: 1867. 4v. [UW]
--Also in his coll. "Works."

*C58. do. Ger. romance: spec. of its chief authors, w. biog. and crit. notices. Ed;L: Tait 1827. 4v. 16. [BM]
[Engr. t.ps. by W. H. Lizars after W. Heath. --V. 1. Musaeus, "Dumb love," "Libussa," "Melechsala"; Fouqué, "Aslauga's knight." --V. 2. Tieck, "The fair-haired Eckbert," "The trusty Eckart,"

CARLYLE, T:
"The Runenberg," "The elves," "The goblet"; Hoffmann, "The golden pot."--V. 3. Richter, "Army-chaplain Schmelzle's journey to Flätz," "Life of Quintus Fixlein."--V. 4. Goethe, "W: Meister's travels; or, the renunciants."]

*C59. do. 1841. [same] Bost: Munroe. 2v. 19cm. [LC]
[V. 1. Musäus, Fouqué, Tieck.--V. 2. Hoffmann, Richter. No. Goethe.]

*C60. do. [same] 1874. 1898. 1901. Tales by Musaeus, Tieck, Richter (and Fouqué and Hoffmann). NY: Scribner. 2v. 17cm. [LC]
[Identical with foregoing, exc. for prefatory matter.]

*C61. do. [same] 1858. Translations from the German. Musaeus, Tieck, Richter. L: Chapman & Hall. 389p. 18cm. [BM]
[Reprinted portions of C58, without C.'s introductions.]

C62. do. [same?] Translations from the German. L: Chapman & Hall 1871. 3v. 8. [LCO]

C63. CARPENTER, E: Ioläus. Anthology of friendship. L: Sonnenschein; NY: Doran 1902. 2d ed. Sonnenschein 1907. 3d ed. Unwin 1915. 235p.
[First ed. has: Goethe, Platen (2), K. H. Ulrichs (2).--2d ed. has: L: Frey (2), F: II (2), Herder, E. v. Kupffer, L: I. v. Bayern, Platen (3), Rückert, Schiller, Ulrichs, Wagner (2).][BM.LC]

*C64. CARUS, PL. Goethe's and Schiller's Xenions. Chic;L: Open court. 1896. 162p. 13 x 19cm.[LC.BM]--2d ed. 1915. 179p. 16cm.[LC]

*C65. CAWEIN, M. J. The white snake, and other poems tr. from the Ger. Louisville, Ky: Morton 1895. 79p. 21cm. [LC.BM]
[Excellent versions.--(Bodenstedt (7), Geibel (9), Goethe ("Faust II"), Heine (4), Uhland (10).]

§C66. CHARLTON, W. H. Poems and plays. L: Longmans 1868. 455p. 16.
[Halm, "The gladiator of Ravenna," "The son of the wilderness"; four poems by Bürger, Grün, Heine.] [BM.LC]

§C67. CHAWNER, E: Gleanings from the Ger. and Fr. poets. L: Ward, Lock 1879. 391p. 17cm. [BM.LC]
[Solid, correct; poor hexameters.--Arndt (7), Beck, Becker, F. Bucher, Bürger, Eichendorff, Feuchtersleben, Fink, Freiligrath (4), Geibel, Gleim (3), Goethe (87), Gottschall, Hauff, Heine (12), Herder, Herlossohn, Hertz, Hoefer, Kalm, Kerner (3), A. Kaufmann, Klopstock, Körner (12), Kotzebue, Lenau, Lessing, Mahlmann (2), Moltke, Mosen, W. Müller, Rittershaus, Rückert (5), Schenkendorf, Schiller (7), Schultze, Seidel, Stolterfoth, Sturm, Tensen (Jensen?), Uhland (30), Witzel.]

CHRISTMAS roses and other tales. See T., S.

C68. CLARK, B. H. and M. LIEBER. Great short stories of the world. L: Heinemann 1926. xv;1072p. 21cm. [BM]
[Germany, pp. 222-288.--"The lay of Hildebrand," tr. W: Taylor (C533); "Siegfried and Kriemhild," tr. Marg. Armour from the "Nibelungenlied" (A355); "The coming of Gandin," tr. Jessie L. Weston from "Tristan" (#3063); "Bruin the bear and Reynard the fox," tr. T. Roscoe (C477); "Eulenspiegel and the merchant," tr. Roscoe (C477); "Doctor Faust and the usurer," tr. Roscoe (C477); Gellert, "The sick wife," Tr. Clark for this vol.; Grimm, "Little briar-rose," tr. anon.; Hoffmann, "The story of Serapion," tr. Ax. Ewing (#4407); Keller, "A legend of the dance," tr. M. Wyness (#4905); Heyse, "The fury," tr. anon. (#4312); Schnitzler, "The triple warning," tr. Clark for this vol; Sudermann, "A new year's eve confession," tr. Colbron (#9261).]

§C69. CLARKE, J. F. and LILIAN. Exotics: attempts to domesticate them. Bost: Osgood 1875. 141p. 16. [LC]
[Mediocre or poor.--Bürger, Dingelstedt, Geibel (15), Gerok, Goethe (5), Heine (12), Herder (2), Körner, Mosen, Osterwald, Rückert (5), Schiller, Tholuck (3). Uhland.]

*C70. COHN, ALBERT. Shakespeare in Germany in the 16th and 17th centuries: an account of the Engl. actors in Germany and the Netherlands, and of the plays performed by them during the same period. L;Berl: 1865. 2 pts. 4. [BM]
[Ayrer, "Comedy of the beautiful Sidonia" (verse), "Comedy of the beautiful Sidonia" (verse), "Comedy of the beautiful Phaenicia" (verse, abridged), Tr. T: Solly; "Tragedy of Julius and Hyppolita" (prose), tr. Georgina Archer; "Tragedy of Titus Andronicus" (prose), tr. M. Lippner; "Tragedy of Prince Hamlet of Denmark" (verse), tr. Archer; "Tragedy of Romeo and Juliet" (prose), tr. L. Bucher.--All tr. appear to be excellent.]

C71. COLMAN, MISS. Wild flowers: a coll. of gems from the best authors. Bost: S. Colman 1846. 126p. 48. (B29)
[Two poems by Schiller, some by Goethe.]

C72. CONTINENTAL DRAMA. NY: Collier 1910. Harvard classics. 474p. 22cm. [Schiller, "W: Tell," tr. Martin; Lessing, "Minna von Barnhelm," tr. Bell.] [LC]

§C73. COWDREY, CECIL. Lyr. tr. of Ger. songs, tr. and ad. to the singing voice. NY: Alexander press 1915. 18p. 19cm. [LC]
[Some excellent. Poets not named. --Eichendorff, Gleim, Geibel, Goethe, Heine (8), Mörike, Rückert, Schmidt v. Lübeck, Uhland.]

COX, FES. ELIZ. See Hymnals, this list.

C74. COX, G: W: and E. H. JONES. Tales of the Teutonic lands. L: Longmans 1872. 394p. 19cm. [BM.LC]
[Free narratives of "Volsunga saga," "Nibelungen," "Heldenbuch," etc.]

§C75. CRAIGMYLE, ELIZ. Ger. ballads. L;NY: W. Scott 1892. 287p. 24. [Bürger (3), Freiligrath (2), Goethe (3), Heine (7), Herder (2), Platen (4), Rückert (3), Schiller (12), Uhland (10), miscellany.] [BM.LC]

C76. do. 1886. Poems and tr. Aberdeen. Edmond and Spark. 134p. 17cm. [Goethe (2), Heine (16), Schiller (5).] [BM]

§C77. CRAWFORD, AX. W: C. LINDSAY, EARL OF. Ballads, songs, and poems, tr. from the Ger. Wigan: Priv. prt. Simms 1841. 159p. 32 x 25cm. [Chamisso, Freiligrath, Goethe (6), Heine, Herder (2), Kerner, Platen, Schiller (7), Uhland (18).] [BM.LC]

†C78. CRONHELM, F: W: Poems, w. an hexametrical tr. of part of the 2d. book of Klopstock's "Messiah." L: Longmans et al. 1820? 200p. 17cm. [BM]
[Some notes. Klopstock, pp. 155-200, impossible. Also, "The nun," a tale imitated from the Ger.]

*C79. CROSSTHWAITE, G. F. Stories from the Ger. L: Ryde 1842. 220p. 8. [BM]
[Tr. appears to be well done.--J. Mosen. "Ishmael," "The Italian novel," "Helena Vallisneriana," "The picture of the mermaid"; Tieck, "Precipitation."]

C80. CUNNINGHAM, G: G. For. tales and trad., chiefly sel. from the fugitive lit. of Germany, Glasgow: Blackie, Fullarton 1829. (LC has 1830.) 2v. il. 18cm. [BM.LC]
[Rather freely treated. -- V. 1. F:a Lohmann, "The mill of the vale"; J. R. Wyss, "The treasure," "The bitter wedding"; Fouqué, "The modern Regulus"; C. Weisflog, "Measure for measure"; C:e Pichler, "The count of Barcelona"; Gottschalk, "The ring of matrimonial fidelity." --V. 2. Tieck, "The pictures"; F:a Lohmann, "The pilgrim"; K:e Fouqué, "The Castle on the beach"; Fouqué, "A story of Number Nip"; Körner, "Goldner"; Klusen, "My grandmother"; J. Baumann, "The rose of Jericho"; Lohmann, "The night on the mountain"; Apel, "The piper of Neisse." Also, a few of the Grimm fairy tales and other legends and myths.]

C81. do. [same] 1854. New ed. Ed: Fullarton. viii;407p. il. 18cm.
[Most of vol. 2 not included. This ed. contains all the items listed in vol. 1 of foregoing.] [BM]

CUNNINGHAM, G: G.
C82. do. [same] 1855. Ger. stories, being tales and trad. chiefly sel. from the lit. of Germany. Ed: Fullarton. 2d ed. 415p. 17cm. [BM]
[EC has: Fullarton 1856. Contents include vol. 2 of C80; also, Grimm, "Thornrose," "Tom Thumb," "Hans in luck," "Rumpelstilzchen"; Apel, "Der Freischutz" (from Laun's "Gespensterbuch"), "Legends of the Kyffhäuser," from Büsching's trad. of the Harz.]
C83. CURIOUS STORIES about fairies. Bost: Ticknor & F. 1856. il. Billings. 303p. 17cm. [LC.BM]
["Siegfried the dragon-slayer"; Carové, "The story without an end," tr. Austin.]
C84. CUST, RB. N. Poems of many years and many places, 1836-87, by a lifelong thinker and wanderer. 2d ser. Hertford. S: Austin 1897. 279p. 18cm. [BM]
[Bürger, L: Pfroepfer of Ratisbon (2), one song.]
C85. DANA, C: A. Christmas eve and other stories. Bost: Crosby & N. 1852. 48p. il. 15cm. [LC]
[No authors named. --Title; The cockerel and the hens; The dear mother in heaven; The horse's footprint; The crocodile.]
C86. do. The household book of poetry. NY: Appleton 1859. 798p. 25cm. [LC.BM]--11th rev. and enl. ed. 1867. 816p. --New ed. 1883. 862p. --1903. [LC]
[Tr. by various hands, fewer in 1903 ed. --First ed. has: Claudius, Freiligrath, Goethe, Heine (3), Luther (2), Müller, Salis, Schiller, Tersteegen, Uhland (2).]
C87. do. 1849. Nut-cracker and sugar-dolly, and other stories and legends for children. Ill. w. woodcuts after L: Richter. L: Cundall 1849. 151p. 16cm. [BM]
[Probably from the German, but no authors are named.]
§C88. DAVÉSIÈS DE PONTÈS, MME LUCIEN. Poets and poetry of Germany. L: Chapman & H. 1858. 2v. 19cm. [BM.LC]
[Some good tr. --V. 1. Gellert (2), Gleim, Hagedorn, Haller, H: VI, U: v. Hutten, Jk. v. d. Warte (2), E. Kleist (3), Konradin, U: v. Lichtenstein (14), Ramler (3), Sachs (2), Walther v. d. Vogelweide (4), Wernher v. Tegernsee. Also many extracts from epics and longer poems. --V. 2. Arndt, Bürger (6), Chamisso (3), Fouqué (2), Hölderlin, Hölty (4), Klopstock (5), Körner (4), Matthisson, Novalis (2), Salis (2), Schubert (7), Schulze (3), Stolberg, Tieck (2), Wieland.]
†C89. DE CRESPIGNY, CARO. My souvenir, or poems...w. tr. L: Longmans; Heidelberg: Hoffmeister 1844. xxiv;296p. 17cm. [BM]
[Some tr. by another unnamed hand, no better than hers. --Chamisso, Diefenbach (10), Freiligrath (2), Goethe ("Faust," 3; "Tasso," (2), R: Morning, Schiller (5), Uhland (3).]
†C90. do. 1848. A vision of great men...and tr. from the poetesses of Germany. L: Newby; Heidelberg; Groos. xii;211p. 16cm. [BM]
[Ackere, Assing, Bonar, Brachmann (2), Chezy (2), Droste (6), Freiligrath, Gunderode (3), Hahn-Hahn, Heine (2), Hohenhausen, Karschin (2), Kerner, Klenke, Lenau (2), Platen (2), Ploennies (4), Schiller (2).]
C91. DE STAËL, MME. Germany. L: J: Murray 1813. 3v. 21cm. --NY: 1871. 2v. 8. [BM]
[All tr. in prose. --Goethe ("Egmont," "Faust"), Klopstock (2), Richter, Schiller ("Stuart," "Jungfrau," "Tell"), A. W. Schlegel (2).]
§C92. DES VOEUX, C: Torquato Tasso. With other Ger. poetry. L: Longmans 1827. vi;307p. 8. [BM]
["Tasso" seems to me very well done, despite the sharp criticism of B22; lyrics much poorer. --Biernacky [sic], Bürger (4),

DES VOEUX, C:
Eichendorff (2), Goethe (17), Hölty, Schiller (6), Uhland (5).]
§C93. do. 1833. [same] 2d ed. rev. and cor. w. add. Weimar. viii; 298p. 8. [BM]
[Biernacky, Eichendorff (2), Goethe (13), Grillparzer, Heine, Hölty, Müchler, Schiller (9), Uhland, Uz, Werner.]
§C94. do. 1836. [same] L: Longmans. 307p. 8. [NY] --L: 1856. 8. (B8)
§C95. DEUTSCH, BABETTE, and A. YARMOLINSKY. Contemp. Ger. poetry. NY: Harcourt, Brace 1923. xxvii;201p. 19cm. [LC.BM]
[Attractive volume, readable verse; command of Ger. not wholly adequate. --J:s Becker, Gf. Benn (3), Brod, Däubler, Dauthendey (9), Dehmel (8), Ehrenstein (4), George (8), Goll (4), Hatzfeld (2), Heym (3), Heynicke (4), Holz (9), Hermann-Neisse, Klabund (4), Klemm (3), Lasker-Schüler (6), Leonhardt, Af. Lichtenstein, Liliencron (9), P. Mayer (3), Mombert (5), Morgenstern (11), Rilke (13), Schickele, Stadler, Studer-Goll, Trakl, Vagts, Wegner, Zech.]
*C96. DEWAR, E: H. Spec. of the early Ger. Christ. poetry of the 8th and 9th centuries...A literal tr. w...notes. L: J.Burns 1845. iv;31p. 23cm. [BM]
[Seems to be well done. --"Muspilli," "Wessobrunner Gebet," Otfrids "Krist."]
†C97. DEXTER, C: Versions and verses. Cambridge: Sever & Francis 1865. vii;156p. 17cm. [LC.BM]
[Arndt, Brachmann, Bürger (3), Eichendorff (3), Ferrand, Fischer, Freiligrath, Gaudy, Geibel (2), Goethe (2), Grün (8), Heine (6), Hölty, Lenau, Meissner, Mörike, W. Müller (6), Reinick, Schiller, Schwab, Sternau, Stöber, Uhland (5), Wackernagel.]
C98. THE DIADEM FOR MDCCCXLVI: a present for all seasons. Tr. from Goethe, Schiller, Uhland, Richter, and Zschokke. Phil: Carey & Hunt 1846. 95p. (B42)
†C99. DICKINSON, GIDEON. Poems...and tr. from the Ger. Bost: Williams 1883. 225p. 19cm. [LC]
[Chamisso, Goethe (2), Hiemer, Schiller, Uhland (3).]
C100. DICKINSON, T: H. Chief contemp. dramatists; twenty plays, etc. Bost;NY: Houghton Mifflin 1915. 676p. 21cm. [LC.BM]
[Hauptmann, "The weavers," tr. Ma. Morison; Sudermann, "The vale of content," tr. W. E. Leonard.]
C100a. do. 1921. [same] 2d series. 18 plays...Bost;NY: Houghton M. vi;734p. 21cm. [LC.BM]
[Bahr, "The concert," tr. B. Q. Morgan; Schnitzler, "Living hours," tr. G. I. Colbron; Thoma, "Moral," tr. C. Recht.]
†C101. DODD, C: E: An autumn near the Rhine...2d ed. To which are now added tr. etc. L: Murray 1821. 602p. 22cm. [LC]
[Mediocre tr. --Goethe (2), Körner, Schiller (3), A. W. Schlegel.]
*C102. DOHME, RB. ed. The early Teutonic, Italian, and French masters. Tr. (abr.) and ed. A: H. Keane. L: Chatto & Windus 1880. 559p. il. 28cm. [BM]
[Articles on single artists taken from "Kunst und Künstler des Mittelalters und der Neuzeit"; tr. rather freely, but with essential fidelity. --A. Schultz, W. Schmidt, A. Rosenberg, A. Woltmann, O. Eisenmann, K. Lemcke, K. Woermann, H. Lucke, D. Janitschek, R. Vischer, C. Regnet.]
C103. DOWNES, MRS. MINNA. Ger. wit and humor; a coll. Phil: Jacobs 1903. 299p. 16cm. [Anecdotes and jokes, very brief.] [LC]
*C104. DOWNES, R. P. Hours with the immortals. L: Kelley 1906. 1914. 307p. 19cm. [One essay, ea. on Goethe and Schiller, with many extracts, not all tr. by the author. Blank verse very good; rhymed verse less successful.] [BM]
DRAMATIC pieces from the Ger. 1792. See Mackenzie, H:
§C105. DUESSELDORF ARTISTS-ALBUM. L: Trübner 1854. 2v. col. front. and pl. 27cm. [Ger. poems tr. Mrs. Ma. Howitt. --Bruck, Geibel, Güll, Hübner, Hoffmann v. Fallersleben, Kugler, F. Meyer, V. Precht, Simrock, Vogl (2).] [LC]

*C106. DULCKEN, H: W: The book of Ger. songs: from the 16th to the 19th cent. L: Ward, Lock 1856. 324p. il. 18cm. [BM.LC]
[The orig. is mostly given. Many excellent tr. --Alexis, Arndt (5), W. Becker (2), Bürger, Chamisso (2), Claudius, Eberhard, Eichendorff (2), G. Fink, Fouqué, Gleim, Goethe (4), Grübel, G. v. Halem, Hartmann, Heine (10), Herklots, Herlossohn, Hinckel, Hoffmann v. Fallersleben, Hölty, Kerner (3), Kinkel, Kopisch, Körner (2), Kotzebue, Langbein, Luther (2), Mahlmann (2), C. Meister, Methfessel, A. Metzger, Müller (2), Neumark, Osiander, Reinick (5), Rochlitz, Rückert (4), Schenkendorf, Schiller (6), Schreiber, Simrock (2), E. Starke, Uhland (8), Usteri, Weisse.]

C107. DURAND, LADY. Imitations...of Spitta and Tersteegen. L: H:King 1873. xiv;152p. 8. [BM]
[Sel. from Spitta's "Psalter und Harfe" and Tersteegen's "Geistliches Blumengärtlein."

§C108. DUVALL, LINDA M. Song waifs. Delaware, O. F. T. Evans 1888. 33p. il. 20 x 16cm. [LC]
[Tr. are fair to poor. --Fischer, Halm, Heine (2), Scheurlin, Schiller.]

*C109. DWIGHT, J: S. ed. Sel. minor poems...of Goethe and Schiller, w. notes. Bost: Hilliard, Gray 1839. G. Ripley's Spec. of for. standard lit. 439p. 12. [LC.BM]
[197p. of Goethe, tr. by Bancroft (5), Channing, J. F. Clarke (3), Frothingham (2), M. Fuller (2), Hedge, Haven (2), the rest by Dwight; 156p. Schiller, tr. Bancroft, Brooks (3), Channing (6), Clarke, Cranch, Frothingham (5), Hedge, the rest presumably by Dwight.]

*C110.E., E. K. Tales from the Ger. L: Emily Faithfull 1863. 126p. 16cm. [Gertrude and Corona; Two sisters. Authors not named.] [BM]

§C111. ECHOES OF FOREIGN SONG. By the author of "A month in the camp before Sebastopol." L: Longmans, Green 1877. xiv;94p. 17cm. [BM]
["Paraphrased," i.e., rather closely tr. in excellent verse. Some French poetry included.--A. Buchhein, Claudius, Cronegk, Eichendorff, Freiligrath, Goethe (4), Grün, Halm, Hebbel, Heine (9), Herwegh, Hoffmann v. Fallersleben, Körner, W. Müller (3), H. Neumann, Pfeffel, Rückert, Salis, Schiller, Seidl (2), Uhland, Voss.]

§C112. ECHOES. Engl. echoes of Ger. song. Tr. R. E. Wallis, J. D. Morrell, and F. D'Anvers. Ed. Nancy D'Anvers. L: Ward 1877. 134p. il. 23cm. [LC]
[Bodenstedt (2), Eichendorff (2), Freiligrath (2), Geibel (8), Grün (3), J. Hammer (2), Hartmann (2), Hebbel (3), Heine (3), Herwegh (2), Lenau (4), Lingg (2), Prutz (2), Reinick (2), E. Rittershaus (2), Roquette (2), Rückert (3), Salis (2), Schiller (3), A: Silberstein (2), Storm (2), J. Sturm (4), A. Traeger (2), Uhland (5).]

§C113. EDEN, LIZZIE S. Fairy fancies, from the Ger. L: Hurst & Blackett 1870. 323p. il. 19cm. [BM.LCO]
[Il. by the Marchioness of Hastings. --Petersen, "The wandering lights," "Princess Ilse." Schmid, "Forget me not." --Tr. rather free, but good.]

C114. EDINBURGH TALES, THE. Conducted by Mrs. Johnstone. Ed: Tait; L: Chapman & H. 1845-6. 3v. 25cm. [BM]
[V. 1. Tieck, "The elves." V. 2. Hoffmann, "The golden pot." Both tr. Carlyle.]

EGESTORFF, G: Sel. of Ger. poetry. See Schiller, #7880.

ELLESMERE, earl of, see Gower, this list.

§C115. ELSON, LOUIS C: Ger. songs and song writers. B: Perry 1882. 34p. 23cm. [Four good translations from Heine.] [LC]

†C116. "ENIS." Gathered leaves. L: K.Paul, Trench 1885. 108p. 19cm.
[Much from French. --Freiligrath (2), Halm, P. Heuse [sic], P. Heyse, Reinick, J. Rodenburg [sic], Scheurlin, Uhland.] [BM]

C117. AN ESSAY OF THREE TALES...from the Ger. Ghent: W: de Busscher 1820. viii;106p. 18cm. [BM]
[Tr. by a Dutchman? Cf. #1665. --Fouqué, "The cypress crown"; K:e Fouqué, "The turn coat, a vision"; Gottwalt, "Christmas."]

*C118. ESSAYS OF FRENCH, GER., AND ITAL. ESSAYISTS. Rev. ed. Colonial press 1900. 466p. 24cm. [LC]
[Sel. largely from Hedge's prose writers, C194. --Goethe, Heine, Herder, Lavater, Lessing, Schiller, Schopenhauer, Wieland.]

C119. ESSAYS. Lit. and philos. essays, Fr., Ger., and Ital. NY: Collier 1910. Harvard classics. 419p. front. ports. 22cm. [LC]
[Lessing, "Ed. of the human race," tr. F. W. Robertson; Schiller, "Letters upon the aesthetic ed. of man" (#8158); Kant, "Fundamental principles of the metaphysic of morals," tr. T: K. Abbott.]

§C120. EVERETT, AX. HILL. Crit. and misc. essays. Bost; Munroe 1845. [Undistinguished tr. --Bürger, Goethe, Schiller.] [LC.BM]

§C121. do. 1845. Poems. Bost: Munroe. 105p. 19cm. [LC.BM]
[Bürger, Goethe ("Faust," pp. 41-56), H. Harring, Schiller.]

C122. F., A. Echoes of many voices from many lands. L: Macmillan 1865. xii;216p. 15cm. [BM]
[Tr. eclectic, some in prose. --Gellert, Hoffmann, Richter, Spitta]

†C123. F., C. K. A sel. of ballads, tr. chiefly from Ger. authors. L: priv. prt. 1873. vii;203p. 26cm. [BM.LC]
[Negligible. --N. Becker, Brachmann, Bürger (5), Chamisso (4), Freiligrath, Gellert (2), Goethe (2), Grün, Heine (3), Herder, Kerner (2), Körner, Lenau, Lessing, W. Müller (2), Platen, Reinecke, Sallet, Scherenberg, Schiller (7), Schmidt v. Lübeck, Schubart, Simrock (2), F: Stolberg, Uhland (8).]

C124. F., W. B. Little stories for little children. L: Jos. Masters 1848. 32p. 10cm. [BM]
[Gessner, Grimm, Hölder, Krümmacher (sic), Schmid (4).]

†C125. FABLES AND PARABLES...Lessing, Herder, etc. L: J.Burns 1845. 72p. 16cm. [BM]
[All tr. in prose, very poor. Introd. to p. 15. --Demme, Gellert (3), Herder (5), Krummacher (17), Lessing (73), Meissner (5), Pfeffel (3), Schmid, Schreiber (2), Willamow (2).]

FAIRIES, CURIOUS STORIES ABOUT. See Curious, this list.

§C126. FAIRY. The diamond fairy book. 83 il. H. R. Millar. L: Hutchinson 1897. 310p. 20cm. [BM]
[Brentano, "Wittysplinter"; Godin, "The magician and his pupil"; Hauff, "The advent. of Said"; Leander, "The story of the invis. kingdom"; Schanz, "The strawberry thief."]

C127. FAIRY. The silver fairy book. Il. Norman Little (in col.) and H. R. Millar. L: Hutchinson 1922. 312p. 20cm. [BM]
[Three from Ger. --"The iron casket"; "Fatma" by W: Hauf (sic); "The ship that could sail over land and sea."]

C128. FAIRY. Wonderworld: a coll. of fairy tales, old and new. Woodcuts by L: Richter, Oscar Pletsch, et al., 4 col. il. L: Bell 1875. viii;263p. 17cm. [BM]
[Possibly eclectic; I recognize some of the tr. from Grimm. --Bechstein (4), Buchmann, Grimm (9), Kletke, Lausch, Leander (3), Muldener.]

C129. FAMOUS GERMAN POEMS. Ed. w. introd. and notes Marg. Muensterberg. Girard, Kan: Haldeman-Julius 1925. 64p. 12cm. [BQM]
[Eclectic volume. --Chamisso (6), Claudius, Eichendorff (3), Gellert, Gerhardt, Goethe (8), Hartmann v. Aue (2), Heine (10), Herder, Hölty, Klopstock, Kerner, Körner (2), Luther (2), Matthisson, W. Müller, Novalis, Platen, Rückert (2), Schiller (3), Uhland (6), Walter v. d. V. (2).]

C130. FAMOUS STORIES. B: DeWolfe, Fiske 1868? 431p. 12. [LC]
[Contents in part the same as "Good stories," C168.]

C131. FIELD, EUGENE. Poems, complete. NY: Scribner 1910. 553p. 21cm. [Clever ad. from Heine, Körner, Luther, Uhland.] [LC.BM]

*C132. FLOWERS FROM THE FATHERLAND, by §J. P. Trotter, *G. Coltman, *A. M. Adam, and J: Pitcairn. L: 1870. 8. [BM]
[Arndt, Bürger (10), Claudius, Goethe, Heine (10), Körner (6), Kotzebue, Schiller (5), Uhland (58), Vogl, Voss.]

§C133. FLUEGEL, J: Gf. Flowers of Ger. poetry. Ger;Engl. Lpz: J. Klinkhardt 1835. 314p. 8. [BM]
[Mostly quite poor. --Bürger (4), Burmann, Claudius (2), Fouqué, Gleim, Goethe (7), Gotter, Herder, Hölty (3), Kleist, Klopstock, Körner (5), Kotzebue, Matthisson, Müchler, Müller, Novalis, Overbeck, Salis (2), Schikaneder, Schiller (12), A. Schlegel, Schubart, Stolberg (2), Suabe, Uhland.]

C134. FOLK-LORE AND LEGENDS. GERMANY. L: Gibbings 1889. xv;184p. 17cm. [Introd. signed C. J. T. 28 stories, some from Grimm, but no ascriptions.] [BM]

C135. FOLK SONGS tr. from the Ger. and prt. for the fair in and of the Mass. infant asylum. Bost: Wilson 1875. 32p. 8. [LCO]

C136. FOLLEN, ELIZA. Ger. fairy tales. 2 ser. Bost: Munroe 18- .[AC]

C137. FOX, S. H. Poems, orig. and tr. by S. H. F(ox). Il. E. G. F(ox). L: Longman et al. 1863. 189p. 16cm. [BM]
[Tr. pp. 113-46. --Lenau (2), Pfizer, Schenkendorf, Seidl (2).]

*C137a. FOX-STRANGWAYS, A. H. and STEUART WILSON. Schubert's songs. L: Milford 1924. xii;257p. 19cm. [BM]
[Excellent singing versions, some very good as poetry. 120 songs, tr. by various hands, including: P. England, Miss G. Faulding, A. Gray, Mrs. E. Lockwood, A. Shadwell, F. Simpson, Una Taylor, Lucia Young. --Castelli, Claudius (4), Collin, Goethe (22), Heine (6), Hölty (2), Jacobi, Kenner, Lappe (2), Leitner, Matthisson, Mayrhofer (6), Reil, Rellstab (2), Rochlitz, Rückert (4), Schiller (4), Schlechta, Schmidt v. L., Schober (2), Schubart, Seidl (3), Uhland; also, W. Müller, "Die schöne Müllerin," "Die Winterreise," 44 songs in all.]

*C138. FRANK, HELENA C. Tr. in verse. L;Bungay. R: Clay for the auth. 1911. vi;101p. 18cm. [BM]
[For priv. circ. only. Tr. from the Ger. pp. 29-43, good to very good. --Gerok (3), Goëthe (sic)(2), Heyse (2), Mayer, Strachwitz, Storm (2).]

C139. FRANKE, F., ed. One hundred fables w. il. (Hundert Fabeln in Wort und Bild. Cent fables illustrées.) Neue Ausgabe in 3 Sprachen. Engl. by J. H. Hedley. Fr. by Ad. Dupuy. Lpz: G: Wigand; L: Ackermann; Wien: C: Gerold 1891. ff. 100. 25cm. [BM]
[Diff. to determine the original, but I take it to be a Ger. publication.]

§C140. FRASER, RB. Poet. remains. Cupar. Tullis 1839. xxvi;208p. 8. [Fouqué (5), Goethe (6), Lessing (2), Schlegel.] [BM]

*C141. FROTHINGHAM, N. L. Metrical pieces, tr. and orig. Bost: Crosby & N. 1855. 362p. 19cm. [LC.BM]
[Many excellent. --Goethe (2), Grün (2), Herder, Rückert (18), Schiller (7), Uhland, Zedlitz.]

*C142. FUNCK, FRIEDRICH. A guide to Ger. lit...w. interlin. and free tr. etc. Frankfort a. M: C. Jugel 1853. 592p. 18cm. [BM]
[All tr. excellent except the most difficult lyrics, "Faust," etc., and even these very good. --Prose from B. Arnim, Goethe, Menzel, Pückler, Schiller, Wieland, Zschokke. --Dram. sel. from Halm, "Griselda"; Goethe, "Faust"; Schiller, "Braut," "Carlos," "Tell," "Wallenstein."--Verse by N. Becker, Bürger (2), Chamisso, Fouqué, Freiligrath, Goethe (3), Grün, Heine, Körner, Novalis, Salis, Schiller (6), Schlegel, Simrock, Stolberg, Uhland (2).]

§C143. FURNESS, W: H: Schiller's song of the bell. A new tr. by W. H. F. With poems and ballads tr. F: H: Hedge. Phil: Hazard & Mitchell 1850. 48p. 17cm. [By Hedge: Goethe (4), Körner, Schiller, Uhland.] [LC]

§C144. do. 1853. [same] Phil: Hazard. 70p. 18cm. [BM]
[Also has title: "Gems of Ger. verse," cf. C145. Includes Retzsch's "Outlines" as appendix. Two tr. by Frothingham, 3 by Furness, some anon., remainder by Hedge. --Chamisso (3), Goethe (4), Grün, Heine, Körner, Schiller, Uhland (4), Zedlitz.]

§C145. do. 1853. [same?] Gems of Ger. verse. Phil: Hazard. 150p. 16. --1860. [NY]

§C146. do. 1886: Verses, tr. from the Ger. and hymns. Bost;NY: Houghton Mifflin. 88p. 17cm. [LC.BM]
[A few excellent. --Chamisso (10), Gerok, Heine (2), Schiller, Uhland (11).]

C147. G., A. L. "The little dwarf's mirror" (by O. v. Wildermuth) and "The children's prayer." Ad. from the Ger. L: S.P.C.K; NY: Pott, Young 1878. 94p. 3 pl. 15cm. [BM]

C148. G., H. J. M. Stick to thy last and other stories. Ad. L: S.P.C.K. 1883. 76p. 17cm. [BM]
[Title: "Ch. F: of Baden"; "Admiral van Ruyter"; "Hor. Vernet and the young archer"; "The archbishop of Treves and the young Savoyard."]

§C149. GALLETLY, H. C. Ger. lyr. and other poems; isometrical tr. L: Wms. & N. 1897. 186p. 8. [BM]
[Arndt, Buchheim, Bürger (2), Eichendorff, Fischer, Freiligrath, Geibel (2), Goethe (26), Grün, Halm, Hartmann, Hauff, Hebbel, Heine (13), Herwegh (2), Kerner, Körner, Lingg, Matthisson (2), Meissner, Mosen, Müller (3), Neumann, Platen (2), Rückert (2), Sallet, Schiller (18), Uhland (7).]

C150. GALLOP, G. T. Poems from the Ger. 1823. (B15)
[Some by Schiller.]

*C151. GARNETT, R: Poems from the Ger. L: Bell & Daldy 1862. vi; 119p. 17cm. [BM.LC]
[Many exc. tr. --Brentano (3), Deutsch (2), Freiligrath, Goethe (2), Hebbel (2), Heine (7), Hölderlin, Lenau (3), Lingg (4), Platen (6), Rückert (8), Schefer (3), Uhland (5).]

*C152. GEIKIE, JAS. Songs and lyr. by Heine and other Ger. poets. Ed: J. Thin 1887. xvi;188p. 19cm. [BM]
[Very good to exc. --Heine to p. 112. Bürger, Chamisso, Dräxler-Manfred, Eichendorff, Ferrand, Geibel (4), Goethe (2), Hauff, Kerner (2), Kotzebue, Lenau, Lingg, Mahlmann, Müchler, W. Müller (2), Wfg. Müller, Reinick (2), Roquette (2), Rückert (2), Sallet, Schnetzler, Schulze, Strachwitz (3), Traeger, Uhland (5), Wegener, Zedlitz, Zeise.]

§C153. GER. BALLADS, SONGS, etc. L: Lumley 1845. 201p. il. 17cm.
[Tr. by S. M. and H. T. --Becker, Bürger (3), Chamisso, Fouqué (6), Freiligrath, Goethe (2), Körner (3), Schiller (9), Schmid, Stolterfoth, Uhland (4).] [BM.LC]

*C154. GER. CLASSICS OF THE 19TH AND 20TH CENTURIES, THE. Ed. Kuno Francke and W: G. Howard. NY: Ger. pub. soc. 1913-15. 20v. il. 8.
[A high standard of excellence maintained in this important coll., which is also noteworthy for the intelligence with which its material was selected. Contents noted and mostly rated under authors' names.] [LC]

C155. GERMAN LIFE, LIGHTS AND SHADOWS OF. L: Bull 1832? 2v. See "Athenaeum" 5(1832):803. (B26)
[Tales from Pichler, Spindler, Stahl, and Zschokke.]

C156. GERMAN LOVE TALES. Phil: Jacobs 189- . 295p. 24. [NY]

C157. THE GERMAN MUSEUM; or, monthly repos. of the lit. of Ger. L: for Geisweiler 1800-1. 3v. 22cm. [LC.BM]
[Numerous prose sel.; tr. not named, but many are signed P. W. (i.e., P: Will?) Others perhaps by Ma. Geisweiler.]
C158. GERMAN PROSE WRITERS. A sel...w. a double tr. for...the Hamiltonian system. L: Hunt & Clarke 1828. 63; 164; 95p. 22cm.[BM]
[Brief sel. with a lit. and a flowing tr. Textbook, very interesting. --Fichte, Fouqué, Goethe (12), Heyne, Jacobs, Krummacher, J. v. Müller (4), Raumer, Richter (2), Schiller (2), Tieck (2), Wieland.]
C159. GERMAN TREASURE-BOX, THE OLD. L: S.P.C.K. 1878. 95p. front. 14cm. [BM]
[Prob. tr., but no authors named. --"The wishing ring." "The king of Anacronia." "The little birdie." "Seth in search of a wife." "The little humpbacked girl." "The organ-builder"; "The invisible kingdom" (these two by Leander?). "Heins in the will-o'-the-wisp marsh." "Goldine." "Evergreen mill."
*C160. GERMANY, THE DISCLOSURES FROM. NY: Amer. assoc. for internat. concil. 1918. 266p. 20cm. [BM]
[Tr. w. introd. and notes Munroe Smith. --The Lichnowsky memorandum. Reply of Herr v. Jagow. Memoranda and letters of Dr. Muehlon.]
C161. GERMANY'S WAR MANIA. A coll. of speeches and writings by the Ger. Emperor and Crown Prince et al. L: Shaw 1914. 272p. 18cm.[BM]
--2d ed. 1914. [BM.LC]--NY: Dodd 1915. 18cm. [LC]
[Short extracts from many sources.]
C162. GILDEHAUS, C: In rhyme and time. St.L: Boland 1895. 132p. 12. [Unable to locate it.] [LC]
C163. GILDER, JEANETTE L. Masterpieces of the world's best lit. NY: Christ. Herald 1905. 8v. 15cm. --NY: Harris 1910. [LC]
[Eclectic, sources not usually given. --Ebers, Fouqué, Goethe, Grimm, Heine, Lessing, Richter, Schiller.]
§C164. GILLIES, RB. P. Ger. stories, etc. Ed: Blackwood 1826. 3v. 18cm. [BM.LC]
[Hoffmann, "Rolandsitten," "Mlle de Scuderi"; K:e Fouqué, "Scharfenstein castle"; H: Kruse, "The crystal dagger," "Oath and conscience"; Pichler, "G: Selding." Others unascribed.]
§C165. GLADSTONE, W. E. and LYTTELTON, G: W: Tr. by L. and G. L: Quaritch 1861. 151p. 20cm.[LC.BM]--2d ed. 1863. [BM]
[Book catalogued under L. --Schiller, "Count of Hapsburgh," Kind, "Freischütz" (extr.), both by Gladstone. Meter altered; no fem. rhyme.]
§C166. GOLDSCHMIDT, H. E. Ger. poetry, w. the Engl. versions of the best tr. ed. H. E. G. L: Wms. & N. 1869. 479p. 18cm. [BM.LC]
[Eclectic, some tr. very good. --Arndt, Becker, Bürger (2), Chamisso (2), Claudius, Dach, Fouqué, Freiligrath (9), Geibel, Gellert, Gerhardt, Gerok (3), Goethe (10, also sel. from "Faust"), Grün, Heine (15), Kerner, Körner (6), Kunth, Luther, Leander, Platen, Rückert (2), Salis, Scheffler, Schiller (9, also sel. from dramas), A. Schlegel, Spitta (3), Uhland (13).]
†C166a. GOMME, SIR W: Poems and trs. from the Ger. L: 1821. (B50)
[Contains Schiller's "Song of the Bell," said to be poorly done.]
C167. GOODFELLOW, J: Tr. from the Ger. Paisley. Ax. Gardner 1904. 46p. 18 x 8cm. [Bürger, "Lenôré" (very badly done), Friedländer, Rodenberg, Rückert, Simrock, Spitta, Zeise.] [BM]
C168. Good stories. Bost: Ticknor & F. 1879? 3 pts. [LC]
[Heyse, "Count Ernest's home"; Zschokke, "Advent. of a new year's eve."]
§C169. GOODWIN, MRS. ALICE H. Rhymes from the Rhineland. Bost: Sherman, French 1913. 102p. il. 19cm. [LC]

GOODWIN, MRS. ALICE H.
[Rather heterogeneous sel., tr. rather free. --Arndt, Bandelin, Bechstein, Blaul, Bodenstedt, Claudius, Crojan, Eiffer, Enslin, Förster, Gensichen, Goethe (2), Grün (2), Güll, Hebel (2), Heine, Hey (3), A. Klopisch (Kopisch?), Leitenberger, Mundlich, Reichmann, Reinick (3), Rückert (4), Sophie Traut, Uhland, H. Wild.]

C170. GORDON, GEORGINA, Sketches of for. novelists. L: Hogg 1861. 392p. 20cm. [BM.LC]
[Summaries, not tr. --Mühlbach, "A royal marriage"; Auerbach, "Cinderella of the Black Forest"; L. (sic) Mügge, "A peasant prince"]

†C171. GOSTWICK, JOS. (orig., Gostick). Ger. lit. Ed;Phil: Lippincott 1854. 324p. 23cm. [LC.BM]
[Numerous extracts, very bad. --Arndt, Eichendorff, Freiligrath, Grün, Klopstock, Konrad v. Kirchberg, Matthisson, Platen, Reinmar v. Zweter, Rückert, Schefer, Schubart, Uhland, Walther v. d. Vogelweide (3). Also numerous bits of prose and verse from epics and dramas.]

†C172. do. 1874. Ger. poets: a series of memoirs and tr. NY: Stroefer & K. 265p. il. 23cm. [LC.BM]
[The chapter headings indicate range of translated matter: Poets of the Hohenstaufen time; Master-singers, Klopstock, Wieland, Lessing, Herder, Goethe, Schiller, Jean Paul, Körner, Chamisso, Rückert, Uhland, Heine.]

†C173. do. 1845. The spirit of Ger. poetry: a series of tr. from the Ger. poets. L: W.Smith. 140p. 23cm. [BM.LC]
[Running comment and biog. remarks. --Brachmann (2), Chamisso (5), Deeg (2), Eichendorff (2), Freiligrath (20), Geibel (17), Gleim (2), Goethe (3, also sel. from "H. u. D.," "Tasso"), Grün (11), Halirsch (2), Heine (3), Lenau (4), Pfitzer (2), Platen (17), Rückert (4), Schiller (9), Uhland (8).]

†C174. GOSTWICK, JOS. and RB. HARRISON. Outlines of Ger. lit. L: Wms. & N. 1873. 588p. 19cm. [BM.LC]
[Wholly different from C171, with largely new tr.]

†C175. do. 1883. [same] 2d ed. rev. and extended. L: Wms. & N. 642p. 18cm.
["Tr. from Ger. poetry--none borrowed--have been increased."] [BM]

C176. GOULD, HANNAH F. The diosma, a perennial. Bost: Phillips, Sampson 1851. 287p. 16. (B29)
[Has Schiller, "Das Mädchen aus der Fremde," in Bulwer's tr.]

†C177. GOWER, LORD FIS., afterward EARL OF ELLESMERE. Tr. from the Ger., and orig. poems. L: Murray 1824. 153p. 22cm. [LC]
L: 1855. 8. [Bürger, Goethe, Körner (3), Salis, Schiller(7).] [BM]

§C178. GRAY, M. Lyrics and epigrams after Goethe and other Ger. authors. Ed: D: Douglas 1890. xi;120p. 19cm. [BM]
[28 poems from Goethe, also 71 "Xenien," epigrams, etc. Arndt, Bauernfeld, Chamisso, Ebert, Eichendorff, Ferrand, Feuchtersleben, Heine (3), Herder, Hoffmann, Jacobi, Platen, Rückert, Schiller (5). --Some quite good.]

C179. GREATEST SHORT STORIES, THE. NY: Collier 1915. 8v. 20cm. [LC]
[V. 5. Nordau, "Deliverance," tr. E. Johnson; Riehl, "Castle Neideck," tr. A. M. Reiner; Baumbach, "Fountain of youth," tr. Minnie Hudson. --V. 6. Heyse, "The young girl of Treppi"; Sacher-Masoch, "Thou shalt not kill," tr. Harriet Cohen; Sudermann, "A new year's eve confession," tr. Grace Colbron; Reuter, "Bric-a-brac and destinies," tr. Grace Colbron. --V. 7. Schnitzler, "The dead are silent," tr. C. Young; Zschokke, "The broken cup," tr. P(arke) G(odwin?). --V. 8. Eschstruth, "The gray nun," tr. L. Strachey; Niese, "The story of the little mamsell," tr. Miss E. Emerson; Wildenbruch, "Good blood" (same as #10182).]

§C180. GRIBBLE, JAS. D. B. Borrowed plumes; tr. from the Ger. poets. Dresden and Lpz; L: Trübner 1888. 241p. 8. [BM]

GRIBBLE, JAS. D. B.
[Pref. states that book was pub. anon. in India, 1874-5. Fair tr. --Bodenstedt*(6p.), Eichendorff, Freiligrath, Geibel (2), Goethe (2), Heine (44), Heyse (2), Schiller (3), Sturm, Walling (13).]

C181. GRIMM'S FAIRY TALES and other pop. stories (i.e., Hauff, "The caravan" w. Urdu tr. Engl. and Urdu. Allahabad: Ram Narain Lal 1904. ii;472p. 18cm. [BM]
[28 stories from Grimm; same tr. as C209.]

C181a. GRUNER, F., ed. Select specimens of Ger. lit. tr. into Engl. by M. Thomas. vol. 1. Stuttgart. Ebner & Seubert 1852. viii;198p. 8. [EC (Heinsius)]

§C182. H., M. A. Torquato Tasso and other poems, tr. and orig. L: Longmans 1855. 366p. 12. [BM]--2d ed. 1856. (B42)
[Rather poor, stilted diction. --Körner (5), Kosegarten (2), Matthisson, Schiller (3), Stolterfoth, Uhland (19).]

C183. HAAS, JAS. D. Gleanings from Germany; or, sel. spec. of Ger. romance and hist. L: Hodson 1839. 399p. 19cm. [BM.LC]
[Clauren, "Liesli, the maid of Solothurn," or "the cemetery of Schwytz"; J. Pichler, "The Swedes in Prague," or "the signal-rocket"; Deinhardstein, "Salvator Rosa," or "the portrait of Danae," a comedy; Weber, "A scene in the life of a musician," "The discordant harmonist"; Heinse, "Ardinghello," or "an artist's rambles in Sicily"; Castelli, "The castle of Cleves," or "the witness-hand"; Kohlrausch, "The character of Charlemagne"; Börne, "Goethe as a patriot"; Zschokke, "The Swiss confederation," "Wilhelm Tell"; Müchler, "Personal anecdotes of F: the great."]

†C184. HALLER, MRS. ADELA. Metrical tr. from the Ger...Hamburg; L: Wms. & N. 1852. 167p. 8. [BM]
[Example: "Happy the spirit that loves is alone." --Chamisso, Goethe (25), Heine (13), Körner, Langbein, Novalis, Pfarrius, Platen (4), Rückert (3), Schiller (5), Uhland (18).]

C185. HARBAUGH, H: Poems. Phil: Lindsay & B. 1860. 285p. 17cm.
[Claudius, Klopstock, anon.] [LC.BM]

*C186. HARVARD CLASSICS. Shelf of fiction. NY: Collier 1917. 462p. 20cm. [Seemingly excellent tr. --Goethe, "The sorrows of Werther," tr. Bayard Taylor (i.e., R. D. Boylan, #2576); Keller, "The banner of the upright seven," tr. M. Almon; Storm, "The rider on the white horse," tr. M. Münsterberg; Fontane, "Trials and tribulations," tr. K. Royce.] [LC]

§C187. HARVEY, ELLA L. Lays and legends of Germany. Tr...w. other poems. L: J.How 1846. 223p. 16cm. [BM]
[Not very good. No poets named. I recognized offhand: Brentano, Eichendorff, Goethe (6), Heine, Matthisson.]

C188. do. 1866. Songs of the twilight and some ballads and tr. Richmond. Priv. prt. 68p. 8. [One tr. from German, unnamed.] [BM]

C189. HARWOOD, ANNIE. Stories from Germany. L: Hodder & S. 1868. 205p. 18cm. [Hoffmann, "Gold-seekers and bread-winners"; Nieritz, "The cobbler, the clerk, and the lawyer of Liebstein."] [BM]

C190. HAWTHORNE, JULIAN, ed. The masterpieces and the hist. of lit. NY: Hamilton 1906. 10v. --Also 1898, w. title: The lit. of all nations and all ages. [UW]
[Probably most of the tr. are borrowed. Prose comment, various. --V. 1. Early Ger. lit., "Muspilli," "Song of Hildebrand," "Weissenbrunner Prayer," "Waltar Strong-Hand," Lamprecht's "Alexander," Conrad v. Kirchberg, Walther v. d. Vogelweide (2), Wolfram (2, sel. from "Parcival"), Hartmann v. Aue, "The garden of roses," "Laurin the dwarf-king," "The dwarf-king's court."--V. 2. "Nibelungenlied" (6p.), "Gudrun" (3p.).--V. 3. Tannhäuser, Hugo v. Trimberg, "Reynard the Fox" (prose), "Trial of Parson Amis," "Tyll Eulenspiegel," Sachs, "St. Peter and the goat."

HAWTHORNE, JULIAN
--V. 6. Brant, Hutten, Luther (8p.), Dach, Grimmelshausen, Ger. drama, Hrotsvit, "The lost child" (28p.). --V. 8. Hagedorn (2), Gellert (3), Gleim (3), Klopstock (3), Lessing (9), M. Mendelssohn, Wieland, Voss, The Stormsters (sic), Bürger, Goethe (9 plus 4 sel. from "Faust"), Schiller (8), 144p. total. --V. 9. Richter, Novalis (2), Tieck, Zschokke, Grimm (2), Fouqué (2), 42p. --V. 10. Lyrists of the war of liberation (4), The Suabian poets (2), Heine (8), Scheffel (2), 34p.]

C191. HAYWARD, A. Biog. and crit. essays. L: Longmans 1858. 2v. 21cm. --1873. 3v. [F: v. Gentz, Hahn-Hahn.] [BM]

*C192. HEATH, ELLA. Songs and poems from the Ger. NY: Putnam 1881. 109p. 18cm. [Chamisso, Heine (11), Körner, Reinick, Rückert (12), Uhland (18), Wieland.] [LC]

C193. HEDGE, F: H: Hours with the Ger. classics. B: Roberts 1886. 531p. [LC]
[Lectures on Ger. lit., w. brief sel. in tr. Among the more important: Gellert, Goethe, Heine, Herder, Hoffmann, Klopstock, Lessing, Luther, Mendelssohn, Nicolai, Novalis, Richter, Schiller, Schlegels, Tieck, Wieland.]

*C194. do. Prose writers of Germany. Phil: Carey & Hart 1849. 567p. 24cm. [LC.BM]
--New ed. Rev. and enl. Phil: Porter & Coates 1870. 580p. 25cm[LC]
[Tr. mainly by Hedge. --Abraham a Sa. Clara (4p.), J. Boehme (8), Chamisso (20), Claudius (4), Fichte (20), Goethe (94), Hamann (6), Hegel (11), Heine (12), Herder (26), Hoffmann (21), F: Jacobi (21), Kant (17), Lavater (14), Lessing (13), Luther (25), Mendelssohn (16), Möser (4), Musäus (23), Novalis (6), Richter (15), Schelling (10), Schiller (10), A. Schlegel (16), F. Schlegel (15), Schleiermacher (4), Tieck (7), Wieland (23), Zschokke (12).]

*C195. HEDGE, F: H: and MRS. A. L. WISTER. Metrical tr. and poems. Bost;NY: Houghton 1888. 127p. 16. [LC.BM]
[Bube (Wister), Chamisso (3,W), Eichendorff (W), Elze (W), J. Fischer (W), Fouqué (H), Freiligrath (W), Geibel (W), Goethe (14 plus 6 sel. from Faust, H), Gottschalk (W), Heine (H,W), Kerner (2,W), Körner (H), Lenau (4,W), Luther (H), A. Meissner (W), Mörike (W), W. Müller (2,W), G: v. Oertzen (W), Platen (W), Reinick (W), Rittershaus (W), Rodenberg (W), Roquette (W), Rückert (2,W), Scherenberg (W), Schiller (3,H), Strachwitz (W), Sturm (2,W), Uhland (3 H, 3 W).]

*C196. HEDLEY, F. H. Masterpieces of Ger. poetry, tr in the measure of the orig. Il. Louis Wanke. L: Trübner 1876. viii;119p. 18cm[BM]
[Not excellent, but very good. --Bodenstedt, Bürger, Chamisso, Curtius, Freiligrath, Geibel (2), Goethe (2), Grillparzer, Grün (2), Halm, Hamerling (2), Heine, Herwegh, Lenau (2), Lingg (2), Scheffel, Schiller, Seidl, F. Strauss, Uhland (3).]

C196a. HEINRICH, MAX, 1853- . (Ed.) Classic song album; fifty sel. songs of old and modern masters. Tr. Alice Mattullath. Fischer 1914. 232p. F. [AC]

C197. HENRY, E. L. Songs of the twilight and some ballads and tr. Richmond. Priv. prt. 1866. 68p. 16cm. [One from the German.] [BM]

§C198. HERBERT, W: Tr. from the German, Danish, etc. L: for T. Reynolds 1804. 82p. 20cm. [BM.LC]
[1806 ed. is duplicate w. new t.p. --Bürger, Gessner (4). 2d part has sel. (11 p.) from Schiller's "Jungfrau."]

C198a. HERFORD, C. H. (Ed. and tr.) Case of Ger. south Tyrol against Italy. Pref. and introd. Allen 1927. 96p. 8. [EC]

*C199. HEXAMETER TR. FROM SCHILLER, Goethe, Homer, etc. By J. C. Hare, J. Herschel, W. Whewell. L: Murray 1847. 277p. 14 x 21cm.
[Schiller: "The walk" (Herschel); "The dance," "The sexes" (W);

HEXAMETER
epigrams (2 by W., 26 by Hare). Goethe: "H. und D." (W), "Metam. d. Pflanzen" (W); (2) poet. epistles, "Alexis und Dora" (Hare). Some of the originals printed.] [BM.NY]

C200. Historians' hist. of the world. Ed. H: S. Williams. L.;NY: History assoc. 1907. 25v. [LC.BM]
[Contains copious extracts from Ger. historians listed under authors]

C201. HIST. OF ALL NATIONS, THE. Ed. J: H: Wright. Phil: Lea 1902. 24v. 28cm. [LC.BM]--1905. [BM]
[Vols. 1-19 are a carefully edited, slightly condensed tr. of "Allgemeine Weltgeschichte," with some paragraphs added by the editor, especially in the earlier volumes.]

†C202. HODGES, C: Orig. poems, etc. Munich: J. Bayer 1836. 240p. 18cm. [No attempt to preserve meter or rhyme.--Schiller, "Demetrius"; Scenes from the "Bride of Messina" (pp. 133-208); Goethe, scenes from "Faust" (pp. 211-40, Night, Wood and cave, Dungeon).] [BM]

§C203. HOLCRAFT, R: Tales from the Ger. L: Longmans; Ed: Oliver & Boyd; Glasgow: Robertson & Atkinson 1826. 304p. 16. [BM]--Tales of humour and romance. L: Longmans 1829. [LCO]--NY: Francis 1829[LCO]
[Hoffmann, "MMe (sic) de Scuderi"; Schiller, "The dishonoured irreclaimable"; Richter, "The death of an angel," "The moon"; Langbein, "The bridgroom's probation," "The broken leg"; Lafontaine, "The haunted castle"; Körner, "Woldemar," "The harp."]

C204. HOLCROFT, T: The theatrical recorder. L: Mercier 1805-6. 2v. 22cm. [BM]
[V. 1. Gellert, "The tender sisters" (tr. T. Holcroft?); Lessing, "Emilia Galotti," tr. Fanny Holcroft. J. J. Engel, "The affectionate son," tr. T: H.; Lessing, "Minna," tr. F. H; C. F. Weisse, "Rosamond," tr. F. H.]

§C205. HOOLE, C: H. Poems and tr. Oxford: Scrimpton; L: Simpkin & M. 1875. lv;120p. 19cm. [BM]
[Goethe, Prison scene from "Faust" done in rhymed verse; Heine(2).]

§C206. do. 1882. [same] New ed. Oxford;L: Parker. 264p. 17cm. [BM]
[Tr. revised for this ed.--2 add. poems by Heine.]

C207. HOOPER, LUCY H. Poems, w. tr. from the Ger. of Geibel and others. Phil: Leypoldt 1864. 96p. (B19)

C207a. do. 1871. [same?] Phil: Lippincott. 196p. 8. [BM]
[Geibel (14), Goethe (3), Hebbel, Scherenberg.]

§C208. HOSMER, JAS. K. Short hist. of Ger. lit. St.L: 1878. 2d ed. 1879. Rev. ed. 1891, 1906, 1910. 605p. [LC.BM]
[Some of the tr. by Hosmer. Freiligrath, Goethe, Heine (5), Luther (2), Rückert, Sachs, Schiller, Uhland.]

§C209. HOUSEHOLD TALES and pop. stories, sel. and tr. from...Grimm, W. Hauff, etc. Il. "Bertall" (C. A. d'Arnoux). L: Ward, Lock 1862. vi;312p. 17cm. [BM]
[Good, not excellent. 45 stories, including Hauff, "The caravan."]

*C210. HOWITT, MA. Ballads, and other poems. L: Longmans 1847. 394p. 21cm. [Freiligrath (3), Heine.] [BM]

C211. do. 1861. The golden casket: a treas. of tales for young people. Il. J: Palmer. L: Jas. Hogg. 415p. 17cm. [BM]
[Schmid, "The boy and the man"; Wildermuth, "The holidays at Bärenburg castle."]

C212. do. 1870. A treas. of old and favourite tales, etc. Ed: Gall & Inglis. 347p. 17cm. [BM]
[Campe, "New Robinson Crusoe" (abr.); passages from "Baron Munchausen."]

§C213. HOWITT, W: Ger. experiences. L: Longmans 1844. 352p. 17cm[BM]
[Chap. 8, "The living polit. poets of Germany," contains tr.--Dalei (3), Freiligrath, Grün (3), Herwegh (3), Hoffmann v. Fallersleben (3), Ortlepp.]

HOWITT, W:
§C214. do. 1843. The rural and domestic life of Germany. Frankfort o/M. C. Jugel. 422p. 14cm. [BM]
[Has various bits of verse, nursery rhymes, a fragment of "Hermann und Dorothea," a scene from Kotzebue, etc.]
*C215. do. 1841. The student-life of Germany. From the unpub. MS of "Dr. Cornelius." Containing nearly forty of the most famous student songs with the orig. music, etc. L: Longmans. xviii;484p. il. 22cm. [BM]
[Ger. and engl. Many texts unascribed. Some tr. very good.--Arndt, A. Binzer, Claudius, Hauff, Hinkel, Kerner, Kopisch, Körner (2), Rochlitz, K. Schall, Schiller, Schwab, Uhland (2). --Some of these names identified by the "Kommersbuch."]
§C216. HUBNER, C: W. Wild flowers. NY: Author's pub. co. 1877. 183p. 19cm. [A few poor translations. --Heine, Meissner, Sallet, Schultze, Uhland, Wieland.] [LC]
§C218. HUMPHREY, LUCY H. The poetic old world: a little book for tourists. NY: Holt 1908. 513p. L: Bell 1909. 538p. [BM]
[Similar volume to C372, quite well done. One fair tr. by editor, others appar. all eclectic. --Arndt, Geibel, Goethe, Heine (4), Schiller (2).]
§C219. HUNT, N. CLEMMONS. Poetry of other lands. Phil: Porter & Coates 1883. 445p. 21cm. [Wholly eclectic; mostly the versions are good. --Abraham a S. Clara, Arndt, Bürger, Chamisso, Freiligrath, Gerhardt, Gleim (3), Goethe (10), Grün (4), Heine (6), Hölty (2), Kerner, Körner, Kosegarten, Lenau, Matthisson (2), Pfeffel, Ramler, Salis (3), Schiller (10), Schnezler, Stolberg, Tieck, Uhland (6), Zedlitz.] [LC.BM]

HYMNS

C220. ALFORD, H: Dean of Canterbury. The year of praise. L: Strahan 1867. 216p. sm. 8. [BPL]
[Some Ger. hymns, largely or wholly eclectic.]
C221. BEVAN, EMMA F. Hymns of Tersteegen, Suso, and others. L: Nisbet 1895. 159p. 8.--Pickering & Inglis 1920. [BM]
[Suso (12), Tauler (2), Ter Steegen (38); others cited by initials, e.g. P(aul) G(erhardt?) (5); others of frequent occurrence are C.P.C. (9), T.S.M. (3), T.P. (11).]
C222. do. 1920. [same] 2d ser. L: Pickering. 158p. 8. [BM]
[Freylinghausen, Heerman, Gertrud of Hellfde (2), Mechtild of Hellfde (16), Kunth, Meyfarth, Neumeister, C. Richter, Rothe, Rolle (4), Spitta, Tauler, Tersteegen (46), Winkler; also C.P.C. (8), P. G(erhardt?) (2), T.S.M. (4), et al.]
C223. do. Songs of eternal life, tr. from the Ger. L: Hodgson 1858. 79p. 4. [BM]
[Allendorf, G. Arnold, J. Falckner, J: Freylinghausen, Gerhardt, Heerman, Kunth, F: Lampe, Laurenti, Meyfart, Neumeister, Nicolai, C. Richter (2), Rothe, Rumi, Spitta, Tersteegen (6), Winkler.]
C224. do. 1887. Three friends of God: records from the lives of J: Tauler, Nicholas of Basle, H: Suso. L: Nisbet. xv;388p. 8. [BM]
[Sermons and extracts from Ger. biog., comp. and tr.]
§C225. BORTHWICK, JANE and SARAH (BORTHWICK) FINDLATER. Hymns from the land of Luther. Ed: W: P. Kennedy; L: Hamilton 1854. 72p. 14cm. [BM]
[This was the first series. "A few of the following poems may be considered as rather imitations than tr." For contents see below. These tr. used the initials "H. L. L." for some of their subsequent translations, e.g., #4256.]
C226. do. 1855. [same] 2d ser. 75p. 13cm. [BM]
C227. do. 1859. [same] 3d ser. 64p. 14cm. [BM]

C228. do. 1862. [same] New ser., being the 4th. 96p. 14cm. [BM]

C229. do. 1862. [same] Ed: Kennedy; L: Hamilton, Adams. 348p. 16cm. [This ed. includes all four series. Other eds. are recorded by AC: NY: Randolph ca. 1855-8. 32mo. New and enl. ed. NY: Randolph 1858-60. 24mo. 15th thous. NY: Nelson 1884. EC lists also an ed. in 1867, probably complete. "...some cannot be called very literal tr., but rather aim at conveying the general idea or spirit." Many names are misspelled in index, seemingly not proofread at all.--C. Agte, Angelus, Arndt, C. A. Bernstein, Bianovsky, Bogatzki (sic), Dach, Fouqué, Freylinghausen, Garve (3), C. Gellert, Pl. Gellert, Gerhardt (4), Gotter, Häuser or Heusser (4), Hey, J: Höfel, Gf. Hoffmann, Ingolsteller (i.e. -stetter), Klopstock, Knorr v. Rosenroth, Koitsch, Krummacher, Langbecker, Lange (7), Laurenti (3), E. Liebich, Moraht, Möwes (8), Neander (3), Neumeister, Novalis, F. Sachse (2), Scheffler, Schmolck (5), Schubart, Schweinitz, Sperl, Spitta (14), Stier, Tersteegen (4), Woltersdorf, C. Zeller, Zinzendorf (4).] [BM]

C230. CONGREGATIONAL HYMN BOOK, The new. L: Jackson & Walford 1859. 1000 hymns, indices. 14cm. [BM] [Probably wholly eclectic.--Charlemagne, Decius, Gerhardt (4), Luther (3), Neumark, Nicolai, Rinckart, Ringwald, Sternhold, Tersteegen (2), Zinzendorf (3).]

§C231. COX, FES. E. Sacred hymns from the Ger. L: Pickering 1841. 231p. 15cm. [BM.BPL] [Prints orig. Some very good tr., truer to meter than to sense. --Angelus (3), Anton U:, Arndt, Bürde, Dach, Denicke, Edeling, Fouqué, Freylinghausen, Gellert (3), Gerhardt (2), Heermann (2), Herrmann, Lange, Lavater, Liebich, J. Löwe, Luther, M. Müller, Neander, Neumann, Neuss, Olearius, Oswald, Ritter, Sacer (2), Schenk, Schiebeler, Schmolck (2), Schröder, Stark, Tersteegen (2), Wegleiter, Wülffer, Zinzendorf, Zwick.]

§C232. do. 1864. Hymns from the Ger. 2d ed. rev. and enl. L: Rivingtons. 261p. 16cm.--L: S.P.C.K. 1890. 125p. 17cm. [BM] [1864 ed. has Ger. text, 1890 text has not; otherwise identical. Tr. are good to very good. --Angelus (4), Anton U: (2), Arndt, Bürde, Fouqué, Freylinghausen (2), Gellert (2), Gerhardt (8), Günther, Heermann (2), Lange, Lavater, Luise Hte., Luther, Meyfart, Neuss, Nicolai (2), Oswald, C. Richter, Rinckart, Rist (2), Sacer (2), Schenk, Schmolck (2), Schröder, Schuetz, Tersteegen (2), Wiesenmayer, Wülffer, Zihn, Zwick.]

§C233. DUNN, CATH. H. Hymns from the Ger. 2d ed. L: Hamilton, Adams 1861. 120p. 12cm. [BM] [Albinus, Gf. Arnold, H: Becker, Fabricius, Freylinghausen, Gellert, Gerhardt (8), Gryphius, Heermann (3), J: Hertzog, J: Koehler, Krummacher, Liscov, Ludaemilia Eli., Luther, Neumeister (2), Rist, J: Schade, Scheffler, Schmolck (2), Tersteegen (2).]

§C234. DUNN, R. P. In memoriam. Ed. by S: L. Caldwell. Priv. print n.d. 237p. 23cm. [LC] [Contains a sel. from his writings including some translations of German hymns. --Angelus (3), Eber, Gerhardt, Hiller, Luther (3), Nicolai, Sachs, Schmolke.]

C235. HYMNS ANCIENT AND MOD. for use in the...church, w...tunes. Histor. ed. L: Prt. for the proprietors by Clowes, 1909. 911p. 28 x 17cm. [BM.LC] [Claudius, J. Franck, Gellert, Gerhardt (2), Knapp, Luther, Meinhold, Neander, H: Oswald, Hrabanus Maurus (2), Rinckart, Ringwaldt, Scheffler, H: Schenk, Schütz, Tersteegen (2), Weisse, --Orig. ed. also had: P. Eber, Schmolck, Spitta, Zinzendorf.]

C236. HYMNS AND POEMS FOR LITTLE CHILDREN. Tr. from the Ger. (by a lady). L: Prt. by Gilbert & Rivington 1853. 2d ed. 102p. 17cm. [BM]
[First ed. pub. 1837. comprising pp. 1-40 of this ed. Pt. 2 completed by her daughters. No ascriptions.]
C237. JACOBI, J: CN. A coll. of divine hymns. L? 1720. (LC card) [15 hymns.]
§C238. do. 1722. Ger. psalmody: a spec. of divine hymns. L: H. Young. 144p. 8. [No ascriptions.] [BM]
§C239. do. 1732. Psalmodia germanica; or, the Ger. psalmody. Tr. from the High Dutch. 2d ed. cor. and enl. L: G.Smith. 212p. 17cm. [No ascriptions.] [LC]
§C240. do. 1765. [same] 3d ed. Ed. J: Haberkorn. L: J.Haberkorn. 210; 80p. 21cm. [BM]
[Supplement contains: Angelus (2), Breithaupt, Crasselius, H: Feld, A. Franck, Gerhardt (6), Helmbold, Herrnschmidt, Hogsenius, P. Lange, J. Lange, P. Misky, Neander (3), W. Petersen, F. Richter, J. Schade, Zinzendorf.]
C241. KNIGHT, ELLIS C. Tr. from the Ger. Windsor. Priv. prt. by E. Harding. 1812. 111p. il. 17cm. [BM.LC]
--Prayers and hymns. Reprint. L: Nicol 1832. 118p. [BM]
[Contains prayers by Seiler and 4 hymns, "some by Gellert."]
C242. MERCER, W: The church psalter and hymn book. L: Nisbet 1861. 376p. 20cm. [BM]
[This coll. adds 106 hymns to first ed. pub. 1854. "A large proportion" from "the protestant hymnology of Germany." Tr. by Miss Coxe (i.e., Cox? Cf. C231, C232), Rev. E. Jackson, Rev. H. G. Bunsen, and R. Massie. No ascriptions.]
C243. do. 1864. [same] New ed. Oxford. 266p. [BM]
[Appar. same contents in diff. arrangement.]
*C244. MILLS, H: Horae germanicae: a version of Ger. hymns. 2d ed. Auburn, NY: Miller, Orton & Mulligan 1856. 368p. 12. [LC]
--Ger. hymns tr. H: Mills. Newman & Co. (before 1852). [AC]
[Faithful to meter and sense; sometimes a trifle harsh.--Albinus, Allendorf, Angelus, Arnold, Aemilia Juliana, C. Barth, Bürde, P. Busch, Calisius, Dach, J. Dieterich (5), Flemming, Flessa, A. Franke, Freylinghausen, Frommann, Funk, Gedike, Gellert (6), Gerhardt (5), C. Goetz, Gregor, Grot, Gryphius, C. Gunther, Harms, Heeren, Heermann, Helmbolt, Hengstenberg, Herberger, Hermann, Hiller (5), Hopfensack (2), Jorgens, Lackmann, F. Lampe, Lehmus, Liebich, Liscov, Luise Hte., Luther (12), Magdeburg, Matthesius, Meinhold, Mentzer, J. Miller, Münter (4), Neander (2), Neumeister (2), Novalis, Pfefferkorn, Poliander (2), Rambach (3), Ramler, Reissner, Rinkart, Rodegast, Rothe, Sachs, Schalling, Schiebeler, J. Schlegel, J. Schmidt, Schmolke (4), J. Schoner, J. Schroeder (2), Spalding, Speratus (8), Sturm (3), Tafinger, E. Wagner, M. Weiss, J. Weissenborn, Witzstaedt, Woltersdorf.]
C245. MORAVIAN HYMNS. A coll. of hymns, etc. 1741. Cited in C269.
C246. do. 1742. A coll. of hymns, etc. 2d ed. Cited in C269.
C247. do. 1743, 1744. A coll. of hymns, w. several tr. from the hymn-book of the Moravian brethren. 2d ed. L: Jas. Hutton 1743. 310p. 12cm. Also, appendix, 1744, pp. 311-96, consisting chiefly of translations. [BM]
[No authors named. BM also has copy of 2d ed. without appendix.]
C248. do. 1746. [same] 3d ed. Hutton.[Page numbering corrected.][BM]
C249. do. 1746. Part II. pp. 397-818. L: Hutton. [BM]
C250. do. 1754. A coll. of hymns of the children of God in all ages ...L: At the brethren's chapels, 2 pts. 380;390p. 19cm. [BM]
[LC has 2d part. This coll. ed. by Bishop Gambold. 695; 460 full hymns and supplementary matter. No authors named.]

HYMNS--Moravian

C251. do. 1769. A coll. of hymns, chiefly extracted from the larger hymn-book...L: Sold at the brethren's chapels. 308p. [BM]
[257 hymns plus supplementary matter.]

C252. do. 1789. A coll. of hymns for the use of the prot. church of the united brethren. L: 276p. 20cm. [BM]
[This coll. ed. by J: Swertner, rev. cor., and newly arr. 886 hymns.]

C253. do. 1793. Liturgic hymns of the united brethren. rev. and enl. L: 168p. plus litanies. 17cm. [Tr. from the "Liturgische Gesänge."] [BM]

C254. do. 1801. A coll. of hymns...rev. and enl. Bath: Hazard et al. xxxii;312p. 19cm. [BM]
[1000 hymns, through p. 258; 200 additional hymns in supplement.]

C255. do. 1808. Supplement to hymn-book (i.e., C254). Manchester: Dean. pp. 255-312. 19cm. [Hymns 1001-1200.] [BM]

C256. do. 1809. A coll. of hymns...Manchester: Dean, et al. xxxiv; 258p. 21cm. [1000 hymns.] [BM]

C257. do. 1811. Liturgic hymns. 2d ed. rev. and enl. Manchester: Prt. by Nanfan & Davis. 147p. plus litanies. 17cm. [BM]

C258. do. 1823. Supplement, same as C255. Ashton-under-Lyme. Prt. by T: Cunningham. pp. 255-304. 21cm. [Hymns 1001-1200.] [BM]

C259. do. 1826. A coll. of hymns...New and rev. ed. Ashton-under-Lyme. Prt. by T: Cunningham. 326p. 18cm. [1200 hymns.] [BM]

C260. do. 1836. Hymns for the use...New ed. L: W.Mallalieu. xxxii; 326p. 14cm. [1200 hymns.] [BM]

C261. do. 1838. Liturgy and hymns...New ed. L: W.Mallalieu. xii;704p. 14cm. [1200 hymns.] [BM]

C262. do. 1844. Liturgy and hymns...New ed. L: W:Mallalieu. xxxii; unp. 14cm. [1200 hymns, double cols.] [BM]

C263. do. 1849. New hymns introduced in the hymn book...prtd. in 1849. L: W:Mallalieu. 44p. 14cm. [BM]

C264. do. 1854. Liturgy and hymns...New and rev. ed. L: W:Mallalieu. xxvi;unp. 14cm. [BM]
[1260 hymns. The old coll. thoroughly rev. by Jas. Montgomery and pub. in 1849, cf. foregoing. Some hymns omitted, many added, and the translations improved.]

C265. do. 1869. Liturgy and hymns...New and rev. ed. L: Mallalieu. [BM]
[This is identical with the foregoing.]

C266. do. 1876. An appendix of 82 hymns was added in this year to the coll. ed. by Montgomery (C264). See pref. to C269.

C267. do. 1886. Liturgy and hymns...
[New rev. of hymn-book; 1323 hymns. See pref. to C269.]

C268. do. 1911. Liturgy and hymns authorized for use in the Moravian church. L: Moravian pub. office. 42p., hymns unp. 14cm.
[851 hymns, the result of committee work since 1904. Complete re-arrangement and revision.] [BM]

C269. do. 1912. [same] 16cm.
[Larger type ed. Pref. gives brief hist. of Moravian hymnology; appendix gives list of authors and translators, mostly with dates. --Albert, Altenburg, Arnold, Bahnmayer, Bernstein, Bogatzky, Buchfelder, Claudius, Clausnitzer, Crasselius, Decius, Dessler, Dober, Drese, J. Falckner, Freylinghausen (3), Gellert, Gerhardt (12), Gersdorf, Gregor (13), Hayn (8), Heermann (2), Herrnschmidt (3), Homburg, Jacobi, Knorr v. Rosenroth, Koitsch, Jm. Lange, J: Lange, Laurentius, Lavater, Liscov, Luise Hte., Löwenstern, Luther (8), Mathesius, L. Mencken, Mensel, J. Miller, Mohr, M. Müller, Neander, Neumark, Neumeister, Nicolai (2), Nitschmann, Notker, Rambach (2), C. Richter (2), Ringwaldt, Rinkart, Rist, Roh, Rother, Schade, Scheffler (5), Schlicht, Schmolck, Schütz,

HYMNS--Moravian

Schwedler, Sengenberg (3), Spitta (3), Stegmann, Tersteegen (3), M. Weisse (3), G. Weissel, W: v. Sachsen-Weimar, J. Wolff, Zinzendorf (46), E. D. v. Zinzendorf (3), C. B. Zinzendorf (2).]

C270. PALMER, ROUNDELL. The book of praise, from the best Engl. hymn writers. L: Macmillan 1864. 502p. 22cm. [BM]
[A number of unassigned tr. from the Ger.]

C271. RUSSELL, ART. T. Psalms and hymns...for the...church of England. Camb: Deighton 1851. 24. [BM]
[E. Alber, H: Albert, Albinus (2), Behemb, C. Bienemann, Birken (2), Clausnitzer, Dessler, Flemming, S. Franck, J. Francke, Freylinghausen, Gellert (2), Gerhardt (6), Gesenius, C. Gunther (2), Heermann (6), Held, Helmbold, Herberger, N. Hermann (3), C. Hoier, Homburg, J: Kempff, Knophe (Knöpke?), Knorr v. Rosenroth (2), Lavater, Luise Hte., Luther (13), J. Magdeburg, Mentzler, Meyfarth, M. Moeller, J. Mühlmann, Nachtenhofer (2), Neumark, Neumeister, Neander, Nicolai, Olearius (2), Pappus, C. F. Richter, G. Richter, Rinckhart, Rist (5), Rodigast, Rothe, Schalling, Scheffler (3), Schein, Schenk, J. E. Schmidt, B. Schmolck (3), Schneegaz, Schneesing, Scriver, Selneccer, Spangenberg, Speratus, Thebesius, Thilo, S. Weingartner, M. Weiss (4), Wilhelm II von Sachsen-Weimar, Zinzendorf.]

C272. SACRED LYRICS FROM THE GERMAN. Phil: Presb. bd. 1859. 252p. 20cm. [Wholly eclectic, using C229, C244, C276, also miscellaneous and periodical sources.] [LC]

C273. SCHAFF, PHILIP. Christ in song: hymns...sel. from all ages. NY: Randolph 1869. 711p. 20cm.[LC] --L: Low 1870. 577p. 18cm. [BM]
[Largely eclectic; some editorial revision; also originals? Cf. also C489.--Angelus (2), Arndt (2), Asschenfeld, J. H. Boehmer (2), Claudius, Decius, Dessler (3), J. Franck (2), Gellert, Gerhardt (7), Greding, Gregor, Heermann (3), Held, Hensel, Heusser (5), Klopstock, Knapp, F. Krummacher, E. Lange, J. P. Lange, Laurentius, Lavater, Löwenstern, Luise Henriette, Luther (2), Moewes, Nicolai (3), Novalis (2), Rist, Rothe, Rückert (3), Sacer, Schalling, Schmolke (2), Schneesing, J. H. Schröder, Spitta (12), Tauler, Tersteegen (3), Uhland, Wegelin, Weiss (2), Weissel, Zinzendorf (2), Zwick.]

C274. SELECT HYMNS from Ger. psalmody. 1754. [Cited in C269.]

*C275. WINKWORTH, CATH. Chorale book for England. L: Longmans 1863. unp. 21cm. [BM]
[The hymns...tr. by Cath. Winkworth. Tunes...ed. W: S. Bennett and O: Goldschmidt. 200 hymns, plus 6 in appendix, with tunes. About one-third are new tr., many others revised to suit the music. No poets are named. Tr. seems to be excellent.]

§C276. do. 1855. "Lyra Germanica" (first series): hymns for the Sundays and chief festivals of the Christian year. L: Longman. xxii;258p. 17cm. [BM]
[Hymns mostly from Bunsen's "Versuch eines allgemeinen Gesang- und Gebetbuchs," 1733. --Albert, Albertini, Albinus, Allendorf, Altenburg, Angelus (5), Anton Ulrich (3), Arndt, G. Arnold, Bogatzky, Canitz, Claudius, Crasselius, Dach (2), Dessler (2), Drewes, Eber, Fouqué, J. Franck (3), S. Franck, A. H. Francke, Freylinghausen (2), Gerhardt (11), Gesenius, Gotter, Heermann (3), J. G. Hermann, N. Hermann (2), Hiller, Kunth, E. Lange, Laurentius, Lehr, Löwenstern, Luise Hte, Luther (6), Marperger, Mentzer, Neumann, Neumarck, Novalis (2), Raisner, C. F. Richter (2), Rist (4), Rosenroth, Sacer, Schenk, Schmolck (4), Schröder, Sinold, Tersteegen (4), Weissel, Winkler (2), Wulffer, Zihn, Zinzendorf.]

C277. do. 1856. [same] 2d ed. L: Longman. xxii;260p. 17cm. [BM]
[A few corr. made and additional verses of some hymns added.]

C277a. do. 1855. [same] NY: Worthington. 23 + 258p. [UW]

HYMNS--Lyra Germanica
C278. do. 1856. [same] NY: Stanford. xxiii;258p. 18cm. [LC]
[Probably reprint of first ed.]
C278a. do. 1858. [same] NY: Stanford & Delisser. xxiii;258p. [UW]
C278b. do. 1859. [same] [UW]
C279. do. 1861. [same] L: Longman. xix;272p. 22cm. [BM]
[With il. by and engr. under the superintendence of J: Leighton. EC dates this 1860.]
C280. do. 1862. [same] Bost: Dutton. [AC]
C281. do. 1867. [same] L: Longman. il. 4. [EC]
[I am uncertain whether these later editions listed only in AC or EC are of first or second series, or both.]
C281a. do. 1868. [same] 5th ed. L: Longman. xx;272p. [UW]
C282. do. 1875. [same?] L: Longman. New ed. 12. [EC]
C283. do. 1882. [same] Songs for the household: sacred poetry. NY: Worthington 1882. [LC]
C284. do. 1901. [same] L: Longmans. New ed. xxii;264p. 14cm. [BM]
C285. do. 1906. [same] L: Routledge; NY: Dutton. xx;235p. 15cm. [BM]
C286. do. 1912. [same?] Cheaper re-issue. L: Longmans. [EC]
C287. do. 1858. "Lyra germanica" (second series): the Christian life. L: Longmans. 239p. 16cm. [BM]
[Albinus, Angelus (2), Arndt, Arnold, Bahnmaier, Behemb (2), D: Böhme, J. H. Böhmer (2), Bürde, Clausnitzer, Dessler (2), Eber, Emilie Jle, Flemming, Fouqué (2), J. Franck (3), S. Francke, Gellert, Gerhardt (12), Greding, Gregor, Gross, L: Haym, Heermann (3), Hensel, Hey, Hojer, Josephson, Kern, Kiel, Knapp (3), F. Krummacher, Laurentius, Lindemann, Löwenstern, Meinhold, Mentzer, Meyfarth, L. Müller, Neander (3), Nicolai, Novalis, Pappus, Preiswerk, Puchta, Rambach (2), Rinckart, Rist (3), Rodigast, Rutilius, Sachs, Schade, Schalling, Schmolck (2), Schneesing, J. Schütz, Selnecker, Spangenberg, Spener, Spitta (3), Stegmann, V. Strauss, Tersteegen (7), Titius, J. Walther, Wegelin, M. Weiss, G: Werner, Winkelmann, Zwick.]
C288. do. 1865. [same] 6th ed. L: Longmans. 239p. 16cm. [LC]
C289. do. 1868. [same] L: Longmans. xvi;254p. 23cm.
[Il. J: Leighton, E. Armitage, and F. M. Brown. Companion vol. to C279.]
C290. do. 1858. "Lyra germanica" (both series). L: Longman. 12. [EC]
C291. do. 1867. [same] New ed. L: Longman. 2v. 12. [EC]
C292. do. 1907. [same] L: Newnes; NY: Scribner. 408p. 16 x 8cm. [LC]
[225 hymns, i.e., both series.]
C292a. do. 1859. Sel. from "Lyra germanica." L: Longman. x;94p. 14cm. [Pref. Ax. Ewing.] [BM]

C293. IDEALS AND OTHER POEMS. Tr. "Algernon." Phil: Perkins 1842. 102p. 12. [LC]
[Goethe ("Faust," Prolog in Heaven, "Tasso" II, 1, and one poem); Schiller.]
C294. ILLUSTRATED EUROPE. Zürich. O: Füssli 1884. il. 79 pts. 18cm. [BM]
[The following parts tr. from the German: Anon. The Arth-Rigi railway. 40p. 20 il. Baden-Baden. 40p. 21 il. J. Weber. Thun and the Lake of Thun. 40p. 23 il. G. Roux and Weber. Lucerne and its environs. 31p. 22 il. L. Mennet and Weber. Schaffhausen and the falls of the Rhine. 38p. 18 il. H. Metzger and Weber. Ragatz and the baths of Pfäffers, Switzerland. 32p. 9 il. Weber. Davos. 40p. 20 il. Weber. The St. Gothard railway. 68p. 43 il. Weber. Graz. 49p. 23 il. Weber. --H. A. Berlepsch. The Lucerne-Rigi railway at Vitznau. 40p. 22 il. Roux, Weber, and K. Corradi. --Ernst Buss. Canton Glarus and the Lake of Wallenstadt. 143p. 57 il. Weber. --W. Cubasch. The Bürgenstock. 40p. 10 il. Weber. --P. Dengler.

ILLUSTRATED EUROPE
The baths of Reinerz. 32p. 13 il. Weber.--B. Fricker, Baden in Switzerland. 40p. 26 il. by Weber.--Vicar Gerber. Interlaken. 46p. 20 il.--J. Hardmeyer. Milan. 64p. 16 il. Weber. The Lake of Lucerne. 62p. 40 il. Weber. The Black Forest railway. 104p. 53 il. Weber. Locarno and its valleys. 112p. 58 il. Weber.--J. Harfin. Zürich and its environs. 40p. 22 il. Weber.--E. Killias. Coire and its environs. 58p. 19 il. Weber.--L. Leiner. Constance and its environs. 40p. 22 il. Weber.--E. Mautner. Battaglia near Padua. 41p. 38 il. L. E. Petrovits and Weber.--Dr. May. The baths of Kreuth in the Bavarian Alps. 40p. 14 il. C. Bolze and Weber.--J. Neumann. Freiburg (Baden) and its environs. 40p. 31 il. Weber.--H. Noé. The southern railway of Austria. The line through Carynthia and the Pustertal. 111p. 52 il. Weber. From Germany to Italy. The Brenner railway. 112p. 52 il. Weber. From the Danube to the Adriatic. 111p. 61 il. Weber.--R. Ortmann. Görbersdorf. 56p. 26 woodcuts by Blätterbauer.--J. Pernisch. The Upper-Engadine. 40p. 21 il. Weber.--K. Pfaff. Heidelberg. 80p. 34 il. Weber. A. Rumpf. Thusis. 40p. 20 il. Weber.--E. Steinacker. Budapest. 108p. 49 il.]

†C295. IMPEY, ELIJAH B. Illustrations of German poetry. L: Simpkin, Marshall 1841. 2v. 17cm. [Alexis, Gellert, Goethe (4), Holtey, Kerner, Klopstock, Kotzebue, Körner, Langbein, Platen, Rückert, Schiller (7), A. v. Schlegel, Tieck, Uhland (5), Zedlitz.] [BM.LC]

§C296. INGLIS, H: Ballads from the German. Ed;L: Blackwood 1864. 172p. 17cm. [He abandons the original form and is too "poetical." --Arndt, Chamisso (2), Freiligrath (3), Geibel, Grün, Hartmann, Heine, Herder, Immanuel, Kerner, Körner (2), Lenau (3), Reinick, Rückert, Schiller (2), Schmidt-Phiseldeck, Schnezler, Schwab, Simrock, Trinius, Uhland, Zedlitz.] [BM]

C297. INTERESTING TALES, sel. and tr. from the German. L: Lane 1797. --1798. [Cited by B43. "Crit. Rev." for May 1798 doubts whether they are from the German. See B26.]

JACOBI, J: CN. See Hymns, C237ff.

C298. JAECK, EMMA G. Mme de Stael and the spread of Ger. lit. NY: Oxford 1915. 358p. 19cm. [A number of tr.; eclectic.] [BM.LC]

JAMIESON, ROBERT. Popular heroic and romantic ballads. Ed. 1814. 4. See Weber, H: Illustrations of Northern antiquities. C557.

§C299. JONES, ERNEST C. Corayda: a tale of faith and chivalry, and other poems. L: Kent 1860. 200p. 17cm. ["Transmarine," p. 166-200. --Freiligrath (3), Schiller (2), Uhland.] [BM]

C300. JOURNAL OF SPECULATIVE PHILOSOPHY, St.L: 1871 ff. [LC] [Early volumes contain many translations, most of which are included in my Main List.]

§C301. JOYNES, J. L. Songs of a revolutionary epoch. L: Foulger 1888. 176p. 21cm. [Some tr. quite good.--K: Beck, J: Becker, L. Derwinus, Freiligrath (23), A. Glassbrenner, Heine (9), Herwegh (17), Hoffmann v. Fallersleben (4), F. v. Holtzendorf, K: Pfau (3), H. Puttmann, Rückert, Scherr, A. Scheu, A Schults (2), M. Schwab, G: Weerth (5), L. Wittig, H: Zeise.] [BM]

C302. JUVENILE DRAMATIST, THE; or, a sel. of plays from the most celebrated writers upon education. Hamburgh: Bachmann & Gundermann 1801. 3v. 17cm. [BM]
[V. 1. J: J. Engel: "The page." F. Weisse: "The modish young lady"; "The birthday"; "Filial piety." V. 2. "The ill bred boy"; "The greyhound"; "Nature's magic," or, "a bad conscience"; "The grateful son." V. 3. "The young gamesters"; "The generous offender"; "The little family-dispute"; "The young archers."]

C303. KAINES, JOS. Love poems of all nations. L: Montagu, Pickering 1870. xvi;326p. 17cm. [BM]

KAINES, JOS.
[Eclectic. --Goethe (10, much from "Tasso"), Hoffmann, Klopstock, Ludwig I von Bayern.]
C304. KEANE, H. G. Verses, tr. and orig. L: Allen n.d. (B19)
*C305. KELLY, WALTER K. Proverbs of all nations, compared, explained, and il. 3d ed. L: Kent 1870. 238p. 17cm. [BM]
[Many from the German, well translated.]
§C306. KENDRICK, A. C. Echoes; or, leisure hours with the Ger. poets. Rochester, NY: Sage; NY: Evans & Dickerson 1855. 148p. 18cm. [LC]
[Correct, undistinguished. --Goethe (3), Herder, Jacobi, Körner (6), Salis, Schiller (10), Uhland (3).]
†C307. KENEALY, E: V. Poems and translations. New ed. L: Reeves Turner 1865. 460p. 12. [BM.LC]
[Mediocre or poor tr. --Goethe, Luther, Uhland, Voss.]
C308. KEYSERLING, H. A., Ed. Book of marriage; a new interpretation by 24 leaders of contemp. thought. ("Das Ehebuch.") NY: Harcourt 1926. 511p. 23cm. [LC.BM]
[Tr. by Therese Duerr, Paul Fohr, W: A. Drake et al. A. Adler, "Marriage as a task"; L. Baeck, "M. as mystery and command"; J. Bernhard, "M. as a sacrament"; P. Dahlke, "M. as a fetter"; P. Ernst, "M. and proletarianism"; L. Frobenius, "M. and Matriarchy"; H. v. Hattingberg, "M. as an analytical situation"; R:a Huch, "Romantic m."; C. Jung, "M. as a psychol. relationship"; Ma. Karlweis, "M. and the changing woman"; M. v. Kemnitz, "M. as a fulfilment"; Keyserling, "The correct statement of the marriage problem," "M. as an eternal problem," "The proper choice of partners"; E. Kretschmer, "Physical and spiritual harmony in m."; M. Lichnowsky, "M. as a work of art"; A. Maeder, "M. and self-development"; T: Mann, "M. in transition"; P. Thun-Hohenstein, "The m. of convention in Europe"; L. Ungern-Sternberg, "The m. of the future"; J. Wassermann, "Bourgeois m."; R: Wilhelm, "The Chinese conception of m."]
C308a. do. 1927. [same] Cape. 522p. 9 x 6. [EC]
KNIGHT, Ellis C. Translations, etc. See Hymns, C241.
C309. KNORTZ, K: Representative German poems, ballad and lyrical; orig. texts with Engl. versions by various translators. NY;Bost: Holt 1885. xix;352 (i.e., 693) p. 22cm. [LC.BM]
[Arndt (2), Bodenstedt (5), Brentano, Bürger (7), J. Burow, Chamisso (12), Claudius (5), Dach, Dahn, Dietmar, Dingelstedt, Eichendorff (7), J. Fischer, Freiligrath (7), Gaudy, Geibel (6), Gleim (2), Goethe (27), Grün (3), Güll, Haller, Halm, Hartmann, Hauff (2), Hebbel (2), Hebel (2), Heine (22), Herder (3), Herlossohn, Herwegh, Hoffmann v. Fallersleben (3), Hölderlin (2), Hölty (5), Jacobi, Körner (5), Kosegarten, Lenau (4), Lessing (2), Lingg (2), Lorm, Löwe, Matthisson, Mayer, Meissner (2), Methfessel, Mörike (2), Mosen (4), N. Müller, W. Müller (8), W. Müller v. Königswinter, Opitz, Paoli, Pfarrius, Pfeffel, Pfizer, Platen (5), Redwitz (3), Reinick (2), Rittershaus, Rodenberg (2), Rollett (3), Rückert (8), Salis (2), Sallet, Scheffel (4), Scheurlin, Schiller (16), Schneckenburger, Schubart, Schwab (2), Seidl, K: Siebel, Simrock (2), Spitta, Stolberg, Strachwitz, Tieck (2), Tiédge, Träger, Uhland (23), Vogl, Voss, Walther v. d. Vogelweide (6), Wieland, O. Wolff, Zedlitz (3).]
†C310. KROEGER, A. E. The minnesingers of Germany. NY: Hurd & H. 1873. 284p. 18cm. [LC.BM]
[Commendable faithfulness to difficult forms; troubled by rhymes, and does not escape the bizarre and grotesque. --Cn. v. Hamle, Düring, Gf. v. Neifen, Gf. v. Strassburg (incl. two long extracts from Tristan), Hadlaub, H: v. Meissen (2), Hohenburg, Marner, Meisner, Mulnhusen, Neidhart (2), Regenbogen, Tannhäuser, U: v.

KROEGER, A. E.
Lichtenstein (5), U: v. Winterstetten (3), Walther v. d. Vogelweide (27), Winli, Die Winsbeckin, Wolfram v. Eschenbach.]

*C311. KROEKER, KÄTHE F. A century of German lyrics. L: Heinemann 1894. xiv;225p. 17cm. [BM.LC]
[Arnim, K: Beck, Chamisso, Dahn (2), Droste (2), Eichendorff (3), Freiligrath (15), Geibel, Goethe (7), Grillparzer, Groth (8), Hamerling, Hartmann, Heine (46), Heyse, Keller (4), Lenau (4), Lingg, Mörike (2), Mosen, Müller (24), Platen (4), Rittershaus (2), Rückert (4), Scheffel, Uhland (3), Vierordt (2).]

C312. do. 1880. Alice and other fairy plays for children. 2 series. L: Sonnenschein. 8.[German fairy tales dramatized in English.][BM]

"LA MARA." See Lipsius, Marie.

§C313. LAMBERT, C: R. Poems and translations... L: Whittaker 1850. 224p. 17cm. [BM.LC]
[Correct, undistinguished. --Chamisso (4), Goethe (8), Heine (5), Platen, Rückert (4), Schiller (9), Uhland (4).]

C314. LANDER, SARAH W. Fairy bells, and what they tolled us. Bost: Fuller 1868. 204p. il. 17cm. [BM]
[AC has: 1867. --17 stories, no authors named--The palace of egg-shells. The strange play-fellow. The grateful mouse. The naughty children. The mittens. The fisherman's tom thumb. The money-box of little Max. The little gray man. The comforting angel. The Christmas tree. The May-beetle. The little tormentor. The giant's daughter. The flowers. The two little fishes. The inheritance. The rose of vulture mountain.]

†C315. LAURIE, JAS. S. Fancy tales from the German. Il. H. Sanderson. L: Low 1861. 125p. 17cm. [BM]
[EC has: 1860. --Arndt, "The three towers," "The gnome's cap," "Paiwai and Paiwuzzo." Bechstein, "The seven piebald mice" (really by Arndt), "The dog's distress," "Strong Godfrey, or the Christmas-box," "Lilly and Bessy." Strapolola, "The golden mermaid," "The green man."

§C316. LEA, H: C. Translations and other rhymes. Phil: Priv. prt. 1882. 114p. 19 x 15cm. [LC.BM]
[Dach, Heine (4), Herder, Goethe (3), Schiller (2), Uhland (2).]

*C317. LEGGE, JAS. G. Rhyme and revolution in Germany. L: Constable 1918. xxiv;584p. 22cm. [BM.LC]
[Many prose selections, letters, speeches, etc. Also verse fragments and complete poems. Trans. appear to be excellent. --Arndt (Prose 1, Verse 2), Beck (V), A. Binzer (V), F. Chemnitz (V), Eichendorff (V), L. Franzl (V), Freiligrath (V 4), C. Follen (P 2), Geibel (V), Gilm (P), Glassbrenner (P 1, V 2), Gottschall (P), Grillparzer (P8, V 2), Grün (P 3, V 3), Heine (P 3, V 3), Herwegh (P 2, V 8), C. Heinzen (P), Hoffmann v. Fallersleben (V 7), Keller (V 2), Kerner (V 2), Kleist (P 2), Lenau (V 4), Ludwig I (V 3), Pfizer (V), Platen (V 3), Prutz (V 3), Rückert (V), Sauerwein (V), L. Seeger (P), G. Sulzer (V), Uhland (P 1, V 3), Varnhagen v. Ense (P).]

§C318. LELAND, C: G. The poetry and mystery of dreams. Phil: Butler 1855. 270p. 19cm. [LC]
[Sel. from various literatures, il. the interpretation of dream visions. --Chamisso, Crescentius, Fouqué (3), Goethe, Heine (2), Hallberg, Planché, C. Reinhold, Schlippenbach, Simrock, Uhland (6).]

C319. LERMONT, L. My play is study. (Mein Spielen ist Lernen.) A book for children. Phil: Simon 1852. 110p. sq. 12. [LC] S
--Phil: Moore 1855. 111p. col. ils. 19 x 15cm. [BM]
[Sel. are mostly unascribed. Contains some of Krummacher's and of Lessing's fables, also extr. from Goethe and A. Schreiber.]

C320. LETTERS OF PASSION. L: Humphreys 1911. 68p. 14cm. [BM]
[Bismarck to Frln.v. Puttkamer (2), Heine to Camille Selden (2), Wagner to Mathilde Wesendonck (3).]

C321. LETTERS ON THE WAR BETWEEN GERMANY AND FRANCE. L: Trübner 1871. 130p. 19cm. [D. F. Strauss, Td. Mommsen (2).] [BM]

C322. LEWIS, M. G. Life and correspondence, with many pieces... never before pub. L: Colburn 1839. 2v. 22cm. [BM]
[V. 2. has 3 tr. from German, one from Goethe.]

C323. do. The monk: a romance. L: J.Bell. 1796. 3v. 19cm. [BM]
[This copy contains Lewis's corrections for the revised ed. Contains the tradition of the "Bleeding Nun," then widely current in Germany; also tr. of Goethe's "Fischer" and of "Der Wassermann" from Herder's "Volkslieder."]

C324. do. 1796. [same] Waterford. J. Saunders. 3v. 18cm. [BM]
[Has port. of author.]

C325. do. 1796. [same] 2d ed. L: Bell. 3v. 17cm. [BM]

C325a. do. 1798. Ambrosio; or, the monk. 4th ed. with considerable additions and alterations. L: Bell. 3v. 18cm. [BM]
[This ed. adds tr. of Goethe's "Erlkönig," "The Erl-King."]

C325b. do. 1799. Ambrosio; or, the monk. 2d Amer. from 4th Brit. ed. Bost: Thomas & Andrews. 2v. 258p. 12. [AAS]

C326. do. 1807. [same] The monk. New ed. w. plates. Paris: T. Barrois. 3v. 17cm. [BM]
[3 fronts. by L'Epine after Lafitte. This ed. does not contain "Erlkönig."]

C327. do. 1808. [same] The monk. Dublin: Prt. by J. Charles for the proprietor. 2v. 17cm. [Does not contain "Erlkönig."] [BM]

C328. do. 1820? [same] The monk. L: Prt. for the booksellers. 3v. 18cm. [BM]

C329. do. 1826. [same] The monk: a romance of the most intense interest. The orig. ed. embellished with superior engravings. L: J:Williams. 525p. 21cm. [Text is that of 4th ed. with "Erl-King." 5 plates listed, but only four in this copy.] [BM]

C330. do. 1906. [same] The monk. L: Gibbings. 3v. 18cm. [BM]
["This ed. is printed from the first, the author's corrections... excepted, with all the additions...of the fourth." Excellent unsigned introduction, xlvii pages, on Lewis and his book. Etchings by R. C. Armour.]

C331. do. 1907. [same] The monk. Ed. E. A. Baker. L: Routledge; NY: Dutton. xvi;356p. 20cm. [Reprinted from first editions.] [BM]

C332. do. 1924. [same] L: Brentano's. 3v. in one. 18cm. [BM]
[Reprint of 1906 ed. Port. of Lewis as front. Same introd. and etchings.]

C333. do. Romantic tales. L: Longman 1808. 4v. 17cm. [BM]
[6 items from the German: "Mistrust," "from a tragedy," "The anaconda," "My uncle's garret window," "Amorassan," "Bertrand and Mary-Belle," "The lord of Falkenstein" (the two last from ballads).]

C334. do. 1809. [same] NY: Ward. 2v. 12. (B48)[Reprint of foregoing.]

C335. do. Tales of terror. (verse). L: Prt. by Bulmer for J. Bell 1801. 149p. 19cm. [BM]
[Engr. t.p. Rare. --The only one definitely called German is "Albert of Werdendorff, or the midnight embrace." Some others are assigned to Scandinavian sources.]

C356. do. 1808. [same] 2d ed. L: R. Faulder et al. 155p. 17cm. [BM]

C357. do. 1801. (60) Tales of wonder (in verse). L: Prt. by W. Bulmer for the author; sold by J. Bell. 2v. (236); 482p. 23cm.[BM]
[Bürger, "Lenora," "The wild huntsmen," both tr. by Scott; Goethe, "The erl-king," "The fisherman," tr. Lewis; Goethe, "Frederick and Alice," tr. by Scott from "Claudina von Villa Bella"; "Sir Hengist," tr. by Lewis from Herder's "Volkslieder."]

LEWIS, M. G.--Tales of Wonder

C358. do. 1801. [same] 2d ed. L: Prt. by Bulmer for Bell. 251p. 18cm. [Only 32 tales, includ. all the German matter. Front. (port. of Lewis) by H. Meyer after Pickersgill.] [BM]

C359. do. 1801. [same] Dublin: Prt. by N. Kelly for P. Wogan et al. 2v. 220; 224p. 21cm. [60 tales.] [BM]

C360. do. 1869. [same] L: Groombridge. 136p. 10cm. [BM] [23 tales; contains all German matter but "Lenora." Front.]

C361. do. 1801. Tales of terror and wonder. L: Prt. for author, sold by Bell. 2v. 25cm. [Combines C335 and C358.] [BM.LC]

C362. do. 1887. [same] L;NY: Routledge. 283p. 18cm. [BM.LC] [Reprint of foregoing. Introd. H: Morley.]

C362a. do. 1926. [same] Ed. Lloyd E. Smith. Girard, Kan: Haldeman-Julius. 63p. 12cm. [11 tales, including "Albert of Werdendorff."][BQM]

C363. LEWISOHN, L: ed. Great modern German stories. NY: Boni and L. 1919. [AC]

C364. LIBRARY OF GERMAN STORIES FOR YOUNG PEOPLE. Anon. Bost: Crosby, Nichols n.d. (1855-8) 10v. [AC]

C365. LIBRARY OF ROMANCE. A coll. of traditions, poetical legends, and short standard tales of all nations. Anon. L: 1836. (B42)

*C366. LIBRARY OF THE WORLD'S BEST LITERATURE, ancient and modern. Ed. C: D. Warner. NY: Peale & Hill 1896-7. 30v. 24cm. --Teachers' ed. NY: Hill 1902. 31v. --New and rev. (2d) ed. NY: Warner lib. co. 1917-18. 30v. [LC]
[Biogr. sketches and translated poems or extracts, many done for this work. The general level of the tr. is high. -- Rev. ed. adds a number of more recent names. The following list refers to that ed. Arndt (6p.), Auerbach (37), Beethoven (14), Bismarck (30), Bodenstedt (12), Bodmer (5), Brant (8), Brentano (5), Bürger (11), Chamisso (10), Claudius (6), Curtius (10), Dahn (11), Dehmel (4), Dingelstedt (7), Ebers (10), Eichendorff (13), Fichte (13), K. Fischer (11), Fleming (5), Fouqué (14), Freiligrath (8), Frenssen (13), Freytag (11), Froebel (13), Geibel (5), Goethe (70, with much from "Faust"), Gottschall (8), Grillparzer (9), Grimm (12), Haeckel (13), Hauff (11), Hauptmann (36), Hegel (24), Heine (36), Herder (18), Heyse (12), Hoffmann (13), Hofmannsthal (8), Hölty (8), A. v. Humboldt (9), Immermann (9), Kant (20), Keller (11), Kleist (26), Klopstock (16), Körner (10), Lessing (20), Liliencron (6), Luther (29), Marx (20), Meinhold (14), F. Mendelssohn (14), Meyer (12), "Minnesingers" (under Walther in v. 25, same as tr. of Edgar Taylor, C532), Mommsen (11), Mörike (5), Müller (11), "Nibelungenlied" (30), Niebuhr (7), Nietzsche (24), Novalis (8), Platen (6), Ranke (20), Reuter (11), Richter (18), Rückert (14), Sachs (25), Scheffel (28), Schiller (34), A. and W. Schlegel (16), Schnitzler (14), Schopenhauer (34), Spielhagen (13), Storm (12), D. Strauss (11), Sudermann (34), Carmen Sylva (7), Tieck (18), Uhland (14), Wagner (18), Walther (2), Wieland (14), W:e v. Bayreuth (14). Also, in vol. "Songs, hymns, and lyrics": Bürger, Goethe, Grün, Hebel, Heine, Herwegh, Hölderlin, Kerner, U: v. Lichtenstein, H: v. Morungen, Opitz, Pfizer, Rückert, Salis, Scheffel, Schneckenburger, Sturm, Zedlitz.]

*C367. LIEBER, MAXIM and BLANCHE C. WILLIAMS, eds. Great stories of all nations: 158 complete short stories from all periods and countries. L: Harrap; NY: Brentano's 1927. xii;1121p. 22cm. [BM]
[Germany, pp. 458-521. Stories are all short, but good, and most of the tr. are very good.--Anon, "Eulenspiegel carries off the parson's horse," tr. Roscoe (cf. C477); "Dr. Faust arranges a marriage," tr. Roscoe; Grimm, "Rumpelstiltskin"; Keller, "The virgin and the nun," tr. M. Wyness (cf. #4916); T: Mann, "A railway accident," tr. Winifred Katzin for this ed.; Richter,

LIEBER, MAXIM and BLANCHE C. WILLIAMS
"The new-year's night of an unhappy man," tr. A. Kenney (cf. #7431); Schnitzler, "Flowers"; Sudermann, "The victim," tr. L. Lewisohn (cf. #9243); Tieck, "The friends," (from #9376); Wassermann, "The beast," tr. for this ed.; Zschokke, "The broken pitcher," tr. P. Godwin (cf. #10683).]

§C369. LIPSIUS, MARIE ("La Mara"). Thoughts of great musicians. (Musikalische Gedanken-Polyphonie.) Tr. C. P. S. L: Augener 1886. 71p. 18cm. [513 extracts, rather freely but not badly translated. Most of the great Ger. composers are represented.] [BM]

C370. LITERARY AND PHILOSOPHICAL ESSAYS, French, German, Italian. NY: Collier 1910. Harvard classics. front. ports. 419p. 22cm. [LC] [Kant, "Fundamental principles of the metaphysic of morals," tr. T: K. Abbott; Lessing, "Education of the human race," tr. F. W. Robertson; Schiller, "Letters upon the aesthetic education of man" (same tr. as #7771).]

C370a. LONG, HELENA. Three Indian tales from the German. St.L: Herder 1897. 12. [AC--Also ABP 1912.]
[A. Huonder, "Father René's last journey"; A. Baumgaertner, "Namameha and Watonilka"; A. v. B(erlichingen), "Tahko."]

*C371. LONGFELLOW, H: W. Poetical works. Bost;NY: Houghton 1886. 6v. 12. [LC.BM]
[Very superior translations. Dach (2), Goethe (2), Heine, Logau (13 aphorisms), Müller (2), Opitz, Platen, Mahlmann, Matthisson, Mosen (2), Salis, Stockmann, Tiedge, Uhland (4).]

*C372. do. 1876-9. Poems of places. Bost: Osgood. 31v. 15cm. [LC.BM]
[Tr. by various hands. --Alexis, V. 18, Arndt, V. 17 (2), 18, Becker, V. 18, Brentano, V. 14, Bürger, V. 18 (2), Chamisso, V. 9, 18, Claudius, V. 18, Dach, V. 18, Dingelstedt, V. 18, Eichendorff, V. 18, Freiligrath, V. 8, 15, 17 (5), 18 (5), 21, 22, 24 (8), 25, Geibel, V. 17 (2), 18, Gerhardt, V. 21, Gerok, V. 17, Gleim, V. 18, Goethe, V. 11, 13, 16, 17 (6), 18, 20 (2), 21, 22 (2), 23, Grün, V. 10 (2), 12, 14, 15 (4), 16 (3), 17 (3), 29, Heine, V. 9, 14, 17 (8), 18 (5), 22, 23 (2), Herder, V. 8, Herwegh, V. 18 (2), A. Hoffmann, V. 18, Immermann, V. 16, Kerner, V. 18 (4), E. Kleist, V. 8, Klopstock, V. 16, 17, Kobell, V. 17, Körner, V. 17 (4), 18 (2) Kopisch, V. 17, Krummacher, V. 16, H. v. Laufenberg, V. 16, Lenau, V. 18, Mahlmann, V. 21, Matthisson, V. 17, Matzerath, V. 18, Mörike, V. 16, Mosen, V. 11, 20, K. W. Müller, V. 17, W. Müller, V. 16, 17, 18 (4), Musäus, V. 19, 22, L: Nicolay, V. 23, Platen, V. 11, 14, Rapp, V. 17, Reinick, V. 18, Richter, V. 31, Rückert, V. 17 (3), 18 (2), 20, Scheffel, V. 17, 18, Schiller, V. 9, 10, 11, 13, 16 (4), 17, 18 (2), 19 (3), 22, 23, 24 (2), 25, 31, G. Schmidt, V. 17, Schneckenburger, V. 18, Schnezler, V. 18, A. Schreiber, V. 17, Schubart, V. 18, Schwab, V. 16, Seidl, V. 8, Simrock, V. 18, Stolterfoth, V. 18, Uhland, V. 1, 14 (3), 16 (2), 17 (2), 18, Vogl, V. 17, Voss, V. 17, Walther v. d. Vogelweide, V. 18, Zedlitz, V. 10.]

*C373. LONGFELLOW, H: W., ed. The poets and poetry of Europe. Phil: Porter & C.; L: Chapman 1845. 916p. 8. [BM.LC]--1855. [BM]
[Very good or excellent tr. Abraham a S. Clara, Arndt (2), Bodmer, Boner, Bürger (2), Chamisso, Claudius (4), Dalei (2), Dach (2), Dingelstedt (2), A. Follen, Freiligrath (11), Gellert, Gessner, Gleim (3), Goethe (12), Grabbe, Grün (5), Hagedorn, Haller, Hebel, Heine (7), Herder (6), Herwegh (4), Hoffmann v. Fallersleben (3), Hölty (5), J. Jacobi, E. Kleist, Klopstock (5), Knaust, Knebel (2), Körner (4), Kosegarten (2), Kotzebue (2), Lessing (2), Luther, Matthisson (3), Mosen (2), W. Müller (2), Neubeck, Pfeffel, Pfizer, Platen, Ramler (2), Rückert (5), Salis (4), Schiller (11), Schulze (4), Simrock, C. Stolberg, L. Stolberg (6), Tieck (2), Tiedge (2), Uhland (11), Voss (2), V. Weber, Wieland. Also, "Song of old

LONGFELLOW, H: W.
Hildebrand," tr. H: Weber; "Song of L: III," tr. W: Taylor; "Song of St. Anno," tr. by the same; "Minnesingers," some by Weber, mostly by Taylor; "Heldenbuch" and "Nibelungenlied," tr. Weber.]

§C374. LONGFELLOW, S: W. and T: W. Higginson. Bost: Ticknor & F. 1853. 206p. 19cm. [LC.BM]
[Tr. are not ascribed. --Freiligrath, Goethe, Heine (4), W. Müller, Rückert, Schiller, Stolberg.]

†C375. LOSCH, H: Poems. Phil: Internat. print. co. 1913. il. 19cm.
[Vol. 2., 194p., contains wholly negligible tr. --Dräxler-Manfred, Eichendorff, J. Evers, G. Fechner, L. Frankl, Geibel, Gerok (2), Goethe (8), O. Gruppe, Hebbel, Heine, Heusser-Schweizer (3), Herder (2), Kerner, Klopstock, Körner, Kosegarten, Lessing ("Nathan"), F. Loewe, Rückert (3), Schiller (8), Seidl, Spitta (4), A. Stoeber, Uhland.] [LC.BM]

§C376. THE LOVER'S STRATAGEM and other tales. L: Darling 1848. 332p. 24cm. [BM.LC]
[Orig. paper cover has: 1849. 100 il. Linton. Tr. is quite good, but not strictly faithful.--Zschokke, "The lover's stratagem" ("Der tote Gast"); Fouqué, "The crown of victory" ("Der Siegeskranz").]

C377. LOWELL, MRS. ANNA CABOT. Gleanings from the poets. Bost: Crosby & N. 1850. 430p. 12. [BPL]--New ed. 1854. [LCO]
[Contains three tr. from the German.]

§C378. LOWNDES, H: Poems and translations. L: K.Paul 1879. 245p. 19cm. [BM]
[Not very good tr. --Bürger, Gaudy, Goethe, Halm, Hebbel, Heine (6), Hoffmann v. Fallersleben, Kerner, Lenau, W. Müller, Neumann, Prutz, Rückert (3), Schiller, F: Stolberg, Uhland (5).]

C379. LUBLIN, ISABEL T. Primer of Ger. lit. L: Sonnenschein 1888. [BM]
267p. 18cm. [Based on F: Kluge. A few brief extracts in translation.]

§C380. LUCAS, ALICE (MRS. H:). Translations from the Ger. poets of the 18th and 19th centuries. L: King 1876. xii;198p. 17cm. [BM]
["In the following tr. the principal object has been to preserve strict fidelity." Quite good; much feminine rhyme abandoned. Some tr. done by J. O. L.--Arndt, Brentano (2), Chamisso (2), Claudius (3), Droste, Eichendorff (3), Feuchtersleben, Geibel (3), Goethe (11), Grün, Heine (12), Herder (2), Hölty, Hoffmann v. Fallersleben (2), J: Jacobi, Kerner, G. Kinkel, Körner (3), Lenau (2), Matthisson (2), W. Müller, Rückert, Salis, Schiller (8), Schmidt v. Lübeck, L. Stolberg, Tieck (2), Uhland (7), W: Wackernagel, Zedlitz.]

C381. LYRICAL GEMS. A sel. of...poetry. (Tr., sel., and orig.) Glasgow: Griffin 1825. xiii;468p. 14cm. [BM]
[Mostly English, the tr. doubtless eclectic. --Korner (sic), Schiller, Stolberg.]

LYRA DOMESTICA. See Spitta, K:, #8904.

LYRA GERMANICA. See Hymnals, Winkworth, C276.

LYTTELTON, G: W: See Gladstone, W. E., C165.

§C382. MAC CARTHY, JUSTIN. Con amore; or, critical chapters. L: Tinsley 1868. 360p. 12. [BM.LC]
[Severe criticism of #2395; some poems of Freiligrath.]

*C383. MACDONALD, G: Exotics. L: Strahan 1876. xv;177p. 17cm. [BM]
[Nearly all good; some very good. --Claudius (2); Goethe (3); Heine (4); Luther (16); Novalis, "Spiritual songs" (pp. 3-37); Salis (2); Schiller (11); Uhland (2).]

C384. do. 1871. Good words. --Duffy 1884. 2v. 24. [EC]
[Cited by B. Pick in #6965; has tr. from Novalis.]

*C385. do. 1897. Rampolli. Growths from a long-planted root. Tr. new and old, chiefly from the German. L: Longmans. 303p. 19cm. [BM]

MACDONALD, G:--Exotics
[Claudius (2), Goethe (3), Heine (8), "Luther's song book" (pp. 113-78), Novalis, "Hymns to night," "Spiritual songs," "A parable," Salis (2), Schiller (14), Uhland (2).]

C386. MACKENZIE, H: Dramatic pieces from the German. Anon. Ed: Prt. for W: Creech. L: Prt. for T. Cadell, 1792. 218p. 21cm. [LC]
[For ascription to Mackenzie, see R: Chambers, "Lives of eminent Scotchmen." --Ayrenhoff, "The set of horses" ("Der Postzug"); Gessner, "Conversation of a father with his children" (tr. from Diderot); Goethe, "The sister" ("Die Geschwister").]

§C387. MACRAY, J: Stray leaves, including tr. from the lyric poets of Germany. L: Treuttel; Ed: Clark 1827. 165p. 8. [BM]
[Indifferent versions. --Arndt, Claudius, Gleim (2), Goethe (3), Gramberg, Herder (4), Hölty, Langbein, Lessing, Mahlmann, Matthisson (10), Overbeck, Salis (3), Schiller (5), F. Stolberg (5), Uhland (2), Voss.]

§C388. do. 1836. Translations from the lyric poets of Germany. L: Blackwoods. 8. (B42).
[Arndt, Claudius (2), Gleim (2), Goethe (5), Gramberg, Heine (2), Herder (4), Langbein (2), Lessing, Kerner (4), L: I v. Bayern, Mahlmann, Marschner, Matthisson (9), Novalis (2), Ortlepp, Overbeck, Salis (3), Schenkendorf, Schiller (4), Schubart, Schwab, v. Spiegel, F. Stolberg, L. Stolberg (3), Tieck (2), Tollens, Uhland (10), Voss.]

§C389. do. 1838. [same] Oxford: Parker; L: Black & Armstrong. xvi; 144p. 17cm. [BM]
[Contents same as foregoing, except: Hölty, Mahlmann (2), Ramler.]

C390. MCSPADDEN, JOS. W. Stories from great operas. NY: Crowell 1925. vii;393p. col. ils. 20cm. [BM]
[Beethoven, "Fidelio"; Flotow, "Martha"; Humperdinck, "Hansel and Gretel," "The king's children"; Wagner, "Lohengrin," "Parsifal," "The ring of the Nibelungen," "Tannhauser" (sic); Weber, "Der Freishchütz (sic)".]

§C391. MANGAN, JAS. C. <u>Anthologia germanica</u>: German anthology: a series of tr. from the most popular of the Ger. poets. Dublin: Curry 1845. 2v. 17cm. [BM.LC]
[Able poet, but he takes unwarranted liberties with both form and sense. --Arndt, Bürger (5), B. Dunker, Ebert, Follen, Fouqué (3), Freiligrath (10), Geibler (sic), Gleim, Goethe (14), Herder (3), F. Heyden, Hölty (4), Immermann, Kerner (11), Klopstock (3), Körner, Kotzebue, A: Kuhn, Lamey, Mahlmann, Matthisson (3), J: Miller, Mörike, Mosen, Müller (3), Richter, Rückert (5), O. Runge, Salis (2), Schenkendorf, Schiller (19), J. Schlegel, Schnezler (2), A. Schreiber, Simrock, Stolberg (2), Tieck (4), Tiedge (2), Uhland (9), Wetzel (3).]

C392. do. Irish and other poems, with sel. from translations. Dublin: Gill 1886. 144p. 12. [BM]--L: Simpkin 1886. [EC]

§C393. do. Poems. NY: Haverty 1859. 460p. 19cm. [LC.BM]--1870. [LC]
[Biogr. introd. by J: Mitchel. German anthol., pp. 31-338. Adds a few poems to those in C391. --1870 ed. has: Arndt, Bürger (4), Ebert, Eichendorff, Follen, Fouqué (3), Freiligrath (11), Geibler (sic), Gleim, Goethe (14), Herder (3), Herwegh, Heyden, Hölty (4), Immermann, Kerner (12), Klopstock (3), Körner (2), Kotzebue, Kuhn, Lamey, Mahlmann, Rückert (6), Runge, Salis (2), Schenkendorf, Schiller (18), J. Schlegel, Schnezler (2), Schreiber, Simrock, Stolberg (2), Tieck (4), Tiedge (2), Uhland (9), Wetzel (3), Zedlitz.]

§C394. do. 1903. [same] Dublin: O'Donoghue; L: Bullen. 332p. 12.
[This ed. adds the following: Castelli, Gaudy, Heine, Kerner, Kopisch, Rückert (2), Salis, Schubart, Tieck, Wetzel (2). However, the total collection is much smaller.] [BM.LC]

§C395. MANNERS, LADY J: Gems of Ger. poetry. Ed: L: Blackwood 1865. 87p. 19cm. [BM]
[EC has: 1864. Tr. are on the whole fairly good. --Dingelstedt, Fontane, Freiligrath, Geibel (6), Goethe (3), Gottschall, Halm (5), Heine (2), Herder, Hoffmann v. F., Kerner, Lenau, A. Meissner, Molkte (sic), W. Müller (2), Novalis, Prutz, Redwitz (2), Reinick, Rückert (2), Ruperti (2), Scherenberg, Schiller, Stolterfoth, Sturm (6), Uhland (4).]

§C396. MARTIN, TD. Poems, orig. and tr. L: Priv. prt. 1863. 350p. 19cm. [Good versions; no feminine rhymes. --Goethe, pp. 2-212, mostly from "Faust," W. Müller (4), Rückhert (sic), Schiller, pp. 213-264, Uhland, pp. 265-96.] [BM.LCO]

§C397. do. 1889. Song of the bell and other tr. Ed: Blackwood. viii; 301p. 19cm. [BM]
[Cf. note to #7924. --Freiligrath (2), Goethe (2), G. Hartwig (2), Lingg (4), W. Müller (4), Rückert, Schiller (19), Uhland (15), Zedlitz.]

C398. MARVIN, F: ROWLAND. A book of quatrains, orig. and tr. Bost: Sherman, French 1909. 101p. 18cm. [LC]
[Angelus (4), Goethe (5), Lessing.]

§C399. do. 1902. Flowers of song from many lands. Troy, NY: Pafraets 132p. 26 x 18cm. [LC.BM]
[Angelus, Eichendorff, Goethe (18), Heine (5), Herder, Kinkel, Kulmann, Lessing, Luther, Matthisson, Rückert, Schiller (2).]

§C400. do. 1907. Poems and tr. Troy, NY: Pafraets. xiii;164p. 12. [LC.BM] --Bost: Sherman, French 1914. 250p. 12. [LC.BM]
[Includes C397 and C398. --Angelus (9 epigrams), Eichendorff, Goethe (19), Heine (5), Herder, Kinkel, Kulmann, Lessing, Luther, Matthisson, Rückert, Schiller (2).]

C401. MASSIE, E: Sacred odes, orig. and tr., on divers subjects. L: Hunt 1866. 143p. 16cm. ["Many of the tr. will be recognized at once...others are rather paraphrases or imitations." No authors named.] [BM]

C402. do. 1868. [same] Vol. II. L: Hunt. xv;224p. 16cm. [BM]
["In the tr. my thought has been rather to preserve the thought and spirit of the orig. than to render word for word." No authors named.]

C403. MASTERPIECES OF FOREIGN LIT. L: Griffin 1866. 339p. il. 24cm.
[Goethe, "Faust I," tr. Filmore; Schiller, "Piccolomini" and "Death of Wallenstein," tr. Coleridge.] [BM.LC]

*C404. MASTERPIECES OF GER. FICTION. Anon. Chic: Laird & Lee 1890. 649p. 19cm. [LC]
[Paged separately. Tr. seem to be very good. --Eckstein, "Against the stream," "The boarding-school girls," "The visit to the lock-up"; Heyse, "L'Arrabbiata," "Beppe, the star-gazer,""Maria Francisca"; Hopfen, "The fortunes and fate of little Spangle," "Trudel's ball"; Lewald, "The aristocratic world," "The maid of Oyas"; Lindau, "Hans the dreamer," "All in vain," "First love"; Wilbrandt,""The pilot captain."

C405. do. 1895. [same] 635p. [LC]
[Omits Lewald, "The maid of Oyas"; otherwise identical.]

C405a. MASTERPIECES OF GER. HUMOR. anon. Ed. (G: S. Viereck.) Girard, Kan: Haldeman-Julius 1926. 64p. 12cm. [BQM]
[Short selections, prose and verse. --W: Busch (V), Claudius (V), Eulenspiegel (2), Fulda (P), Goethe ("Faust"), Heine (V4, P2), Lessing (P5, V8), W. Müller (V), E: Pötzl (P), Raabe (P), Schiller (V), Stinde (P), G: S. Viereck (P).]

C406. MATHESON, ANNIE. Sel. poems old and new. L: Frowde 1899. 152p. 8. [BM]

MATHESON, ANNIE
C407. do. 1918. [same] Title: Roses, loaves, and old rhymes. L: Milford xxxviii;152p. 8. [BM]
[New ed. of foregoing. Contains one each of Goethe, Halm, Rückert.]
C408. MATHEWS, JAS. BRANDER. The chief European dramatists: 21 plays. Bost;NY: Houghton 1916. 786p. 21cm. [LC]
[Goethe, "Götz," tr. Scott; Lessing, "Minna," tr. Bell; Schiller, "Tell," tr. Martin.]
C409. do. 1901. Great plays. NY: Appleton. 504p. 8. [LC]
[Lessing, "Minna," tr. Bell; Schiller, "Tell," tr. Martin.]
†C410. MAURER, G: PH. A coll. of select pieces of poetry: containing ...some characteristic poems of the most eminent German bards. Darmstadt: Lang; L: Black & A. 1840. xx;141p. 19cm. [BM]
--NY: Lange 1848. 141p. il. 16. [LCO]
[German orig. given. He knows no English. Introd. (in German) G. B. Sternau.--Bürger ("Leonora"), Claudius, Goethe (2), Hölty, Klopstock, Matthisson, Salis, Schiller ("The lay of the bell," 7 others), Uhland.]
C411. MELLISH, JOS. C. Gedichte. Hamburg: Perthes & Besser 1818.[BM]
[Tr. from German, pp. 85-116. Bürger, Goethe (3), Hölty (2), Matthisson, Neubeck, Schiller (7).]
*C412. MERIVALE, J: H. Poems orig. and tr. L: Pickering 1844. 3v. 18cm. [BM.LC]
[Vols. 2 and 3 contain tr., some by other hands; at his best he is unsurpassed in translating Schiller. --V. 2: Prince Albert, Chamisso, Gleim, Goethe (5), Kerner, Raupach, Salis, Scheffer, Tieck, Uhland (6). V. 3: Schiller, 416p., incl. copious notes; 148 poems, among them "Bell," "Diver," "Glove," "Walk," etc.]
C413. MONTCLAIR, J: W: Gems of German poetry. NY: 1868? (B19)
*C414. do. 1865. Real and ideal. Phil: Leypoldt et al. L: Trübner 1865. x;119p. 19cm. [BM]
[Poems and translations, fairly good. --Chamisso (2), Grün, Heine (4), Rückert, Schwab, Storm, Vogl (2).]
*C415. do. 1867. Themes and translations. NY: Priv. prt. xi;167p. 20cm. [2d ed. of foregoing. --Chamisso (3), Heine (4), Rückert (3), Schreiber, Schwab, Storm, Vogl, Wysz.] [BM]
C416. MORGAN, BAYARD Q. Nature in M. H. G. lyrics. Göttingen: Vandenhoek & Rupprecht; Balto: Johns Hopkins 1912. 220p. 24cm. [LC.BM]
[Albrecht v. Rapperschwyl, der wilde Alexander, Burkhard v. Hohenfels, Cn. v. Hamle, Gf. v. Neifen, H: v. Meissen, H: v. Pressela, H: v. Rugge (2), H: v. Veldeke (2), Hildbold v. Schwangau, J: v. Brabant (2), der Kanzler, Kd. v. Würzburg (4), Kraft v. Toggenburg, Neidhart (6), O: v. Botenlauben, O: zum Turme (2), Rd. v. Fenis, der Schenk v. Limburg, Süsskind v. Trimberg, U: v. Lichtenstein, Wl. v. d. V. (6).]
C417. MORGAN, MA. ("Gowan Lea") Poems and translations. Montreal: Robinson 1887. 195p. 16cm. (B19)
[Fair tr.-- Geibel, Gleim, J. N. Götz, Gottschalk, Halm, Hebbel (2), Heine (3), Kerner, Körner, Lenau, Feodor Löwe, Sallet (2), Scherer, Schultze, Stöber, Uhland (3); also Max Müller's "German Love" (pp. 127-67) and two other prose sel.]
C418. do. 1888. Woodnotes in the gloaming: poems and tr. Cupples & H. sq. 16. [AC]
*C419. MORLEY, H: The dream of the lilybell...with translations. L: Sherwood, Gilbert, & Piper 1845. 16cm. [BM]
[Tr. fill pp. 121-64. --Blumauer (2); Herder; Lessing (2); Novalis, (6) "Hymns to night"; Richter, "The death of an angel."]
C420. MORRISON, J. H. Great poets as religious teachers. NY: Harper 1885. (B42)
C420a. MOSES, MONTROSE J. Representative continental drama, revolutionary and transitional. Little 1924. xiv;688p. 21cm. [LC]

MOSES, MONTROSE J.
[Contains: Schnitzler, "The lonely way"; Sudermann, "Fires of St. John"; Hauptmann, "The sunken bell."]
C420b. do. Represent. one-act plays by continental authors. Little 1923. xvi;463p. 21cm. [LC]
[Contains: Schnitzler, "Countess Mizzie"; Hofmannsthal, "Death and the fool"; Sudermann, "Teias"; Wedekind, "The court singer."]
§C421. MUELLER, F. Max. Chips from a German workshop. L: Longmans 1867-75. 4v. 22cm. [BM.LC]--1894-5. [BM]
[Vol. 3. has lectures on lit. with tr. --Dietmar, Groth (10), Kürenberg, W. Müller (3), Reinmar.]
*C422. MÜLLER-CASENOV, HANS. The humour of Germany. With introd. and biograph. index. Il. C. E. Brock. L: Scott 1892. xvi;437p. 20cm. [BM]--L: Scott; NY: Scribner 1909. [LC]
[Largely brief prose extracts, very well done; a few poems by other hands. --H. Arnold, Fr. Brentano, Chamisso, Eckstein, B. Golz, Grimmelshausen, Hackländer, Hauff (3), Heine (5), Hg. v. Trimberg, H. v. Kahlenberg, Keller (2), E. Kossak, Kotzebue, Leander (2), P. Lindau, Mörike, E. Pötzl, Raabe, Reuter (5), Richter (3), Riehl, Rosegger, Sachs, M. Saphir, H. Schaumberger, Scheffel (4), J. Scherr, A. Schlippenbach, Schönthan, J. Stettenheim, Stinde, Tieck (2), F. Vischer, Wildenbruch, Zschokke.]
§C423. MUENSTERBERG, MARG. A harvest of German verse. NY: Appleton 1916. 242p. 17cm. [LC.BM]
[Some excellent, some quite bad. --Angelus, Arndt, Bierbaum, Bodenstedt, Chamisso (2), Claudius, Decius, Dehmel (7), Droste, Eichendorff (4), Falke (2), Feuchtersleben, Fontane (2), Freiligrath, Fulda, Geibel (2), Gellert, George (2), Gerhardt (2), Goethe (16), Gryphius, Hauff, Heine (9), Hensel, Hesse (2), Hey, Heymel, Hoffmann v. F., Hofmannsthal, Holz, Huch, Jensen, Keller (3), Klopstock, Körner, Kürenberg, Kurz, Lenau (2), Leuthold, Liliencron (3), Luther (2), Meyer (5), Miegel, Mörike, Müller, Münchhausen (3), Neander, Novalis, Platen, S. Reinhold, Rilke (12), Rinckart, Rückert (2), Saar, Scheffel, Schenkendorf, Schiller, Schönaich-C., Spervogel, Spitteler, Storm (5), Strauss u. T., Terberg, Uhland (7), Vogl, Walther v. d. V. (6), Widmann (2), H. Zuckermann.]
C424. MULLEY, JANE. Ger. gems in Engl. setting. Reefe 1879. 12. [EC]
C425. MURDER OF K: LIEBKNECHT AND ROSA LUXEMBURG, THE. (<u>Der Meuchelmord an K: L-- und R-- L--.</u>) L: 1924. 72p. Ports. 21cm. [BM]
[M. Barthel, Freiligrath, H. Heine, E. Hoernle, Liebknecht. E. Mumbel, G. Rottenburger, B. Ziegler.]
C426. NATALIA, COUSIN. Cousin N--'s tales. By the tr. of "Little Henry." Il. Fanny Corbaux. L: Cundall 1841. 158p. 14cm. [BM]
[Houwald, "The goldsmith," "The new year's wish"; Schmid, "The little wooden crucifix."]
*C427. NICHOLSON, FRANK C. Old Ger. love songs. Tr. from the minnesingers of the 12th to the 14th cent. L: Unwin 1907. 196p. 20cm. [BM.LC]
[Abr. v. Johannsdorf, Abr. v. Rapperschwyl, der wilde Alexander (2), Bernger v. Horheim, Bligger v. Steinach, Boppe (2), Burggraf v. Lüenz, Burggraf v. Rietenburg, Burkhard v. Hohenfels, Cn. v. Hamle, Cn. v. Lupin, Dietmar (3), F: v. Hausen (5), Gf. v. Neifen (2), der Guter, Hadlaub (2), Hartmann v. Aue (5), Hartwig v. Raute, Hardegger (2), H: v. Breslau, H: v. Meissen (2), H: v. Morungen (8), H: v. Müglin, H: v. Rugge, H: v. Veldeke (6), Hildbold v. Schwangau, Hohenburg, J: v. Brabant, der v. Kolmas, Konrad der junge, Kürenberg (7), Graf v. Leiningen, Marner (2), Meinloh (2), Neidhart (7), Regenbogen, Reinmar v. B. (2), Reinmar v. H. (8), Reinmar v. Z. (10), Rubin (2), Rd. v. Fenis, Spervogel I (5), Spervogel II (3), Steinmar, v. Suneck, Tannhäuser (3), Truchsess

NICHOLSON, FRANK C.
v. St. Gallen, U: v. Lichtenstein (3), U: v. Winterstetten, Wachsmuth v. Mühlhausen, Wl. v. d. V. (17), Wl. v. Metz, Wenzel v. Böhman, Wildonje, Wolfram (3).]

†C428. NIND, W: The Ger. lyrist; or, metrical versions from the... lyric poets. Camb: Macmillan 1856. xvi;160p. 19cm. [BM]
[Very bad. --Bürger (5), Fouqué (2), Freiligrath (2), Geibel (10), Goethe (10), Klopstock (4), Körner (3), Schenkendorf, Schiller (11), Uhland (6).]

*C429. NOHL, L: ed. Letters of distinguished musicians. Tr. Lady Wallace. L: Longmans 1867. xviii;467p. 20cm. [BM.LC]
[Letters of P. E. Bach, Gluck, Haydn, Mendelssohn, Weber.]

C430. NOVELLIST, THE GERMAN: a choice coll. of novels. Tr. Miss Eliza C--. Görlitz: Anton. 1800? 8.
[Cited in catalog of the Easter Fair at Leipzig, 1800, reprinted in C157(2). --Huber, "Female experience"; Lafontaine, "Maria."]

C431. NOYES, MINNA B. Twilight stories. Tr. and ad. from the Ger. New and enl. ed. Hartford, Conn: Spencer 1898. 216p. il. 12. [LC]--4th ed. 1904. [AC]
[28 stories, retold for children, but not all from German; some fairy tales from Grimm, also some legends (Barbarossa, W: Tell, etc.)]

C433. do. 1917. [same] NY: Simmons. 154p. il. 19cm. [LC]

§C434. NUSKE, J: A. Free tr. from... Gellert and other poets. L: Whittaker; Farnham: Surrey. (Pref. dated 1850.) 64p. 24cm. [BM]
[Contents chiefly from Gellert's fables. Rather good; not closely rendered.]

C435. ODD VOLUME, THE. 1st ser. 2d ed. Ed: Lizars; L: Whittaker 1826. 376p. 19cm. [BM.LC]
[Tr. by the Misses Corbett, see C528. --Fouqué, "The mysterious invalid," "The lantern in the castle yard," "The vow." "Legends of Number-Nip" (not Musäus); "The devil's own" (from the "Taschenbuch für väterlandische (sic) Märchen").]

C436. do. 1827. [same] 2d ser. L: Longman et al. 381p. il. 19cm.
[L. Brachmann, "The three sons"; Musäus, "The elopement."][BM.LC]

C437. ODD VOLUME, THE, i.e., Cruikshank (I.R.) at home: a new family album. L: Bohn 1845. 4v. in 2. il. 17cm. [BM.LC]
[V. 3. has poem by Zedlitz, said to be tr. from the Hungarian; V. 4 has one item from the German.]

*C438. OLD STORIES OF SWITZERLAND; sel. and tr. from...Ger. and Swiss poets. By a lady. Berne; Haller 186-? 304p. 16cm. [LC]
[Mostly little known poets; excellent versions. --A. v. Arx, N. Camenisch, A. v. Flugi (3), A. Follen, A. Froehlich, Herder (2), A. Keller (2), Kerner, F. Otte, J. Reithard (16), Schiller, C. v. Schmid, A. Schults (2), Schwab (5), Simrock (3), A: Stoeber, Uhland (2), J. Usteri (6), Wagner v. Laufenburg, K. Witte.]

§C439. OSSOLI, SA. Life without and life within. Bost: Brown, Taggard & Chase; NY: Sheldon; Phil: Lippincott; L: Sampson 1859. 424p. 12. [Mediocre tr. --Goethe (5), Körner, Schiller. [LCO.BM]

*C440. OSWALD, EUGENE. Early Ger. courtesy books. L: Trübner 1869. Early Engl. text soc. Extra ser. 8, pt. 2. [BM]
[Competent tr. of extensive extracts, pp. 77-147. --"Tannhäuser," "Thomasin v. Zirclaria," "Knight and lady of Winsbeke."]

*C441. OXENFORD, J: and C. A. FEILING. Tales from the German. NY: Harper 1844. 110p. 24cm. [LC]
[Hauff, "The cold heart," "Nose the dwarf"; Immermann, "The wonders in the Spessart"; Kleist, "Michael Kohlhaas"; Musäus, "Libussa"; Schiller, "The criminal from lost honour"; Van der Velde, "Axel, a tale of the thirty years' war." --See the following entry.]

OXENFORD, J: and C. A. FEILING
C442. do. 1844. Tales from the German comprising specimens from the most celebrated authors. L: Chapman & Hall 1844. 446p. 8. [BM]
[Goethe, "The new Paris" (O); Hauff, "The cold heart" (F), "Nose, the dwarf" (F), "The severed hand" (F); Hoffmann, "The elementary spirit" (O), "The Jesuits' church in G--" (O), "The sandman" (O); Immermann, "The wonders in the Spessart" (O); Kleist, "Michael Kohlhaas" (O), "St. Cecilia, or the power of music" (O); Musäus, "Libussa" (O); A. Oehlenschlager, "Ali and Gulhyndi" (F); Richter, "The moon" (O); Schiller, "The criminal from lost honour" (O); Tieck, "The Klausenburg" (F); Van der Velde, "Axel" (F); Zschokke, "Alamontade" (F).]

§C443. P., W. Fables in verse, and other poems. Tr. from Ger. and French by a father and daughter, W. P. and E. I. S. P. L: S. P. C. K. 1874. 103p. vignettes. 15cm. [BM]
[Quite freely done, with moralizing intent. --N. Becker; Gellert (4); Gerhardt; Goethe; Hebel von Bothe (?); Herder; Kerner, i.e., Körner (3); Lichtwer; Michaelis (2); Overbeck; Pfeffel (5); Rudolphi; Schiller (3); Tiedge (2); O. Wolff.]

C444. PABKE, MARIE and MARGERY DEANE PITMAN. Wonder-world stories from Chinese, French, German, etc. NY: Putnam 1877. 292p. il. 19cm. [BM.LCO]
[*Musäus, "Reinald, the wonder-child; or, the chronicles of the three sisters"; B. Paul, "The flower monster."]

C445. PAGE, F: Employment. Poems from the German of Schiller and Goethe. Bath: Upham 1828. 40p. 8. [Goethe (3).] [BM]

§C446. PARKER, TD. Life and corr., by J: Weiss. NY: Appleton 1864. 2v. 23cm. [LC.BM]
[V. 2, Chap. XVI has tr. --Geibel, Heine (8), Mohnike, Opitz, Rückert. Biographer says he made some tr. from Dach, Geibel Gerhardt, Heine, "des Knaben Wunderhorn," Körner, Rückert, Schwab.]

C447. PATTEN, W: Short story classics (foreign). NY: Collier 1907. 5v. 21cm. [LC]
[V. 3. German. --Baumbach, "The fountain of youth," tr. Minnie B. Hudson; Fulda, "The fur coat," tr. Mrs. J. M. Lancaster; Heyse, "The young girl of Treppi"; Nordau, "Deliverance"; Riehl, "Castle Neideck," tr. A. M. Reiner; G. Reuter, "Bric-a-brac and destinies," tr. G. I. Colbron; Saar, "The stonebreakers," tr. A. M. Reiner; Sacher-Masoch, "Thou shalt not kill," tr. H. L. Cohen; Schnitzler, "The dead are silent," tr. C. H. Young; Sudermann, "A new year's eve confession," tr. G. I. Colbron; Viebig, "Margret's pilgrimage," tr. G. I. Colbron; Wildenbruch, "Good blood"; Zschokke, "The broken cup," tr. P(arke) G(odwin?). Cf. C179, which includes a number of the same stories.]

§C448. PEARSON, E: S. Tr. from the Ger. poets. Dresden: E. Pierson; L: S.Low et al. 1879. 272p. 8. [BM]
[Mostly mediocre versions. --L: Bauer (4), Beck, Bodenstedt (3), Bürger, Chamisso (2), Comtesse de la Corrée, Dahn, Dingelstedt (2), Droste, Eichendorff (3), Feuchtersleben, J. Fischer, Freiligrath (2), Fouqué (3), Geibel (4), Gerok, Goethe (9), Gottschall, Grün (2), Halm, Hamerling, Hammer, Hauff, Hebbel, Heine (6), Hoffmann v. F., Hopfen, Kerner, Kinkel, Körner (2), Leonhardt-Pierson (5), Lingg, Lenau (2), Mörike (4), Mosen, Müller (3), Platen, Plönnies, Prutz, Reinick (2), Rodenberg, Roquette (2), Rückert (8), Scheffel (2), Schiller (14), Schönbach, Storm, Strachwitz, Sturm (2), Traeger, Uhland (7), Weitbrecht, Zedlitz (2).]

C449. PERRY, EMILY. A present from Germany; or, the Christmas tree. L: C:Fox 1840. 152p. 13cm. [BM]
[12 stories, no author named. One of them is by A: Moritz, "Kasem the miser."]
C449a. PEWNELL, H.C. Muses of Mayfair. Sel. from "Vers de Societé" of the 19th cent. L: Chatto & Windus 1874. 382p. [LC]
[Four tr. from the German: Chamisso, Herlossohn, Uhland, Wegener; these done by Ethel Grey.]
§C450. PHILLIPS, H: Jr. German lyrics. Phil: Priv. prt. by MacCalla. 1892. 141p. 25cm. [LC]
[Tr. mostly mediocre. --Bodenstedt (7), Dahn (4), Fontane (7), Geibel (2), Greiff (3), Güll (2), Halm (2), Hartmann (4), M. Haushofer (2), Herwegh (2), Heyse (2), Kerner (3), K: Knortz (7), Kopisch (2), Lingg (4), Loewe (2), Lorm (9), K: Mayer (2), A. Meissner (3), Osterwald (2), L.v. Plönnies (2), Redwitz (2), Scheurlin (2), K: Siebel (2), Spitta (2), Storm (5), Strachwitz (2), Sturm (5), Uhland (6), L: Wucke (2).]
§C45.. do. 1878. Poems tr. from the Ger. and Spanish. Phil: Priv. prt. 36p. 16. [NY]
[Chamisso (3), Geibel (7), Gleim, Hartmann, Heine (3), Herder (2), Kerner (2), Neumann, M. v. Oer, Ploennies, Reinicke (3), Uhland (7), Zedlitz (10).]
*C452. PIERCE, F: E. and C. F. Schreiber. Fiction and fantasy of Ger. romance. Sel. from Ger. romantic authors, 1790-1830. NY: Oxford 1927. 392p. 8. [LC.BM]
[Excellent translations. --Arnim, "Isabella of Egypt," tr. (and condensed) Schreiber; Eichendorff, "The marble statue," tr. Pierce; Hölderlin, "Hyperion" (extracts), tr. Schreiber; Kleist, "Kaethchen of Heilbronn," tr. Pierce; Tieck, "The runenberg," tr. Carlyle; Wackenroder, 2 prose sel. tr. Pierce. Also poems: Chamisso (2), Hölderlin (3), Novalis, Uhland (9).]
C453. PIERCE, J: A. Masterpieces of modern drama. Garden City, NY: Doubleday, Page 1915. 2v. 21cm. [LC]
[V. 2 has Ger. drama. --Hauptmann, "The weavers," tr. Ma. Morison; Sudermann, "John the baptist," probably the same tr. as #9284. Résumé of the plots, with sections in translation.]
C454. PLEASANT HOURS IN FOREIGN LANDS: short romances. L: Lumley 1856. 249p. front. 16cm. [BM.LC]
[Hoffman, "Master Martin the cooper and his workman" (sic); Zschökke (sic), "The broken cup." Cf. C20.]
*C455. POLLAK, GUSTAV. Internat. perspective in criticism. NY: Dodd Mead 1914. 312p. 21cm. [LC]
[21 passages from Goethe's critical judgments; 22 from Grillparzer.]
C456. POPULAR TALES AND ROMANCES OF THE NORTHERN NATIONS. Anon. L: Prt. for Simpkin & Marshall 1823. 3v. 18cm. [LC]
[Anon. "The fatal marksman" (by Apel), "The tale" (by Goethe), "The hoard of the Nibelungen," "The erl-king's daughter," all in V. 3; Fouqué, "The bottle-imp" (V.1), "The magic dollar," "The collier's family," "Kibitz," "The victim of priestcraft" (V.2); Musäus, "The treasure-seeker" (V.1), "The spectre barber" (V.2); Tieck, "The sorcerers," "The enchanted castle," "Wake not the dead," "Auburn Egbert" (V.1), "The field of terror" (really by Fouqué), "Elfin-land" (V.2).]
C457. POPULAR TALES... The juvenile Englishman's library. Rugeley: J: T: Walkers; L: Burns 1844. 169p. il. 15cm. [BM]
[Fouqué, "Red mantle"; Hauff, "The cold heart"; Spindler, "St. Sylvester's night."]
C458. PROSE AND POETRY OF EUROPE AND AMERICA. Compiled by G. P. Morris and N. P. Willis. Consisting of literary gems and curiosities. NY: Leavitt, Trowbridge 1847. 598p. 27cm. [LC]

PROSE AND POETRY OF EUROPE AND AMERICA
--7th ed. 1848. [BM]
[Has one paraphrase from Goethe, and Hauff, "The beggar-girl of the Pont des arts." The Engl. sel. are peculiar: Barry Cornwall has 31p., C: Dibdin 12, E: C. Pinkney 9, T: Moore 94!]

†C459. R., M. C. (a lady). Fragments, orig. and tr. L: Nutt 1857. vi;54p. 18cm. [Bone, Chamisso, Heine, Schiller.] [BM]

†C460. RAAD, NEONE. Poems, with tr. from Germany's greatest poets. L: Digby, L. 1906. 160p. front. (port.) 18cm. [BM]
[Arnim, Chamisso (3), Freiligrath, Goethe (3), Grillparzer, J. Hammer, Heine (7), Hoffmann v. F., Lenau (2), Mörike, Platen, Rückert, Schiller (2), Uhland (5), Vogl.]

§C460a. RAINER FAMILY. The words in Ger. and Engl. of the Tyrolese melodies as sung by the Tyrolese minstrels, the Rainer family. Pub. by the R. F. L: 1830? 54p. 16cm. [BM]

§C461. RAMAGE, CRAUFURD TAIT. Beautiful thoughts from Ger. and Span. authors. Liverpool: E: Howell 1868. 559p. 17cm. [BM]
[Passages in the orig., with fair Engl. prose tr. beneath. --Arndt, Arnim, Bürger, Dinter, J. Engel, F. Ewald, Fichte (6p.), Flemming, J: Forster (15p.), Gellert, Gessner (5p.), Gleim, Goethe (125p.), Grün, Gryphius, Hagedorn, Haller, Halm, Heine, Herder (10p.), Hippel, Hofmannswaldau, Hölderlin, Hölty (3p.), W: Humboldt (45p.), Kant, Klopstock (16p.), F. Krummacher, Kulmann, Lessing (8p.), Lichtwer, Noleschott, Michaelis, Moeser, Müllner, Novalis (2p.), Opitz, Richter (78p.), Rist, Salis, Schefer, Schiller (73p.), Schlegel, Schleiermacher (9p.), Schopenhauer (17p.), Schubart, Seume, Stolberg, Sturz, Tieck (4p.), Tscherning, Weisse, Wieland (12p.).]

C462. READE, J: E. Lyrical poems from the German. L: Longmans 1856. (B42) [5 from Goethe.]

*C463. REARDEN, TIMOTHY H. Petrarch and other essays. San Francisco: Doxey 1893. 201p. 19cm. [LC.BM]
[Some tr. of Klaus Groth and Fritz Reuter.]

§C464. REEVE, H: and J: E. TAYLOR. Translations from the German. Prose and verse. L: Murray 1842. 78p. 17cm. [BM]
[Versions mostly fair. --Goethe, Tasso (12p., very good), Novalis (prose), Richter (3 prose sel.), Rückert (4), Uhland (4).]

C465. RETZSCH'S ILLUSTRATIONS of Shakespeare, Goethe, and Schiller. L: Tilt 1835. obl. 4. [EC]
[I assume that this has some text, but have not seen it.]

*C466. REUMONT, ALFRED v. Ruins of the Rhine, their times and traditions. Ed. by C: White. Aix-la-Chapelle: Kohnen 1838. 356p. il. 19cm. [BM.LC]
[40 of the 50 legends contained in Reumont's "Rheinlandssagen," tr. by several hands and very little edited. 8 engr. after orig. designs by painters of the Düsseldorf school, Aix, and Cologne. Individ. authors and tr. not named; identifications made by comparison with orig. --A. Beer (2), M. Friedheim, A. Grimm, A. Reumont (26), A. Schreiber, Schröder, F. Steinmann, N. Vogt, W. Weitz, E. Weyden (2).]

†C467. RICHARDSON, W: "Alma mater" and other poems. Glasgow: Hadden 1881. 302p. 16cm. [BM]
[Negligible versions. He likes to add a poem of his own to continue a tr. So he annuls the minstrel's curse that Uhland hurled. --Arndt, Bürger, Freiligrath, Goethe (4), Heine, Hoff-v. F., Körner, Müller, Rückert, Schiller (4), Uhland (4).]

C468. RICORD, F: W. English songs from foreign tongues. NY: 1879. [Cited in C309.]

C469. RIDPATH, J. C. Library of universal literature. NY: Globe 1899. 25v. 8. [UW]

RIDPATH, J. C.
[Alphabetically arranged. Very short selections, with biog. sketch of each writer. Tr. not ascribed, probably mostly eclectic. --F. Adler, Arndt, Auerbach, H. Barth, Bismarck, Bodenstedt, Bodmer, Boehme, Brant, Brentano, Bunsen, Bürger, Chamisso, Dahn, Dingelstedt, Ebers, Edersheim, Eginhardus, Eichendorff, Feuerbach, Fichte, K. Fischer, F: u. K:e Fouqué, Freiligrath, Freytag, Froebel, Geibel, Gellert, Gerhardt, Gessner, Goethe, Gottschall, H. Grimm, J. and W. Grimm, Grün, Gützlaff, Hackländer, Haeckel, Hahnemann, Hahn-Hahn, Hauff, Hauptmann, Heeren, Heermann, Hegel, Heine, Helmholtz, Herder, Herwegh, Heyse, A: Hoffmann, E. T. A. Hoffmann, Hölty, Hrotsvit, A. Humboldt, W: Humboldt, Hutten, Immermann, F. Jacobi, Kant, Keller, Klopstock, Körner, Kosegarten, Krummacher, Lessing, Luther, U: Megerle, Melanchthon, M. Mendelssohn, "Minnesingers," Mommsen, Mosen, Möser, Mühlbach, M. Müller, W. Müller, Münchhausen, Musäus, Neander, Neubeck, "Nibelungenlied," Niebuhr, Nordau, Novalis, Pestalozzi, Ranke, Reuter, Richter, Rückert, Sachs, Salis, Sallet, Schefer, Scheffel, Schelling, Scherer, Schiller, A. and F. Schlegel, Schleiermacher, Schliemann, Schopenhauer, Sealsfield, Simrock, Spielhagen, Steffens, Stolberg, D: Strauss, Sudermann, Tholuck, Tieck, Uhland, Voss, Wagner, E. Werner, Z. Werner, Wieland, Wyss, Zschokke, Zwingli.]

*C470. ROBINSON, E. Poems of 1848 and earlier days. L; Manchester: Sherratt & Hughes 1904. 199p. 19cm. [BM]
[A large number of favorite song texts included; tr. are mostly excellent, especially the songs. --Bodenstedt, Chamisso, Eichendorff, Gellert, Goethe (3), Heine (15), Kühnen, Matthisson (2), Mörike, W. Müller (6), Otto v. Botenlauben, Rellstab, Rückert (4), Schmidt v. Lübeck, Tannhäuser, Uhland, Walther v.d. V. (8).]

C471. ROBINSON, RB. Specimens of the Ger. lyric poets. L: Longman 1828. 110p. 8. [BM]
[Goethe (7), Körner (2), Matthisson (3), Richter, Salis (2), Schiller (17).]

C472. ROMANCES OF MANY LANDS. L: R:Bentley 1835. 3v. 19cm. [BM]
[No authors named. --"The dead guest" and "The adventures of a night" are by Zschokke; "Jacob never-sober" and "The white roses" are also from the German.]

C473. ROMANTIC FICTION: sel. tales...Anon. L: Burns 1843. 16cm.[BM]
[Stories are sep. paged. --Chamisso, "Peter Schlemihl, the shadowless man"; Fouqué, "The victor's wreath," "The unknown patient," "The prince's sword," "The eagle and the lion," "Rose," "The privy-councillor," "Headmaster Rhenfried"; Tieck, "The faithful Eckart," "The mysterious cup," "The runenberg."]

C474. do. 185-? [same?] 327p. 16. [NY]

C475. do. 1875. [same?] New ed. L: Routledge. 24. [EC]

C476. do. 187-? [same?] NY: Routledge. il. 16. [AC]

§C477. ROSCOE, T: The Ger. novelists...from the earliest period. L: Colburn 1826. 4v. 20cm. [BM.LC]
[Anon. "The pleasant history of Reynard the Fox" (numerous authors and eds. of R. F.); "Howleglass, the merry jester"; "Doctor Faustus"; all in vol. 1; popular traditions coll. and narr. by "Othmar," Gottschalck, Eberhardt, Büsching, Grimms, in vol. 2; M.(i.e., J: Jk.) Engel, "The anti-speculator," "Toby Witt," "Lady Eliz. Hill," vol. 4; Fouqué, "The field of terror," "The mandrake," vol. 2; Langbein, "Marianne Richards, or, memoirs of an actress," "Seven marriages and never a husband," "The irreconcilable man," "Albert Limbach," "An hour's instruction in political economy," "The lady's palfrey" (a tale of the court), vol. 3; Lothar, "The arch rogue," "Castle Christburg"; Musäus,

ROSCOE, T:
"The dumb lover," vol. 3; Schiller, "The apparitionist, a fragment," "The sport of destiny," "The criminal, or martyr to lost honor, a true story," "Fraternal magnanimity," "A walk among the linden-trees," vol. 3; Tieck, "Love magic," "The faithful Eckart and the Tannenhäuser," "The Tannenhäuser, or the lord of the fir woods," "Auburn Egbert," vol. 4.]

§C478. do. 1880. [same] L: Warne. xv;623p. 18cm. [BM]
[Reissue of the foregoing, but adds: Fouqué, "Head master Rhenfried and his family."]

C479. ROTHENSTEINER, J: E. Catholic hymns from the Ger. coll. of Mohr, Hellebusch, Dreves, and Rhode, tr. by J-- R--. St.L: 1922. 31p. 21cm. [LC]

C480. do. 1921. Garland of praise; a booklet of spir. songs. 2d ed. St.L: Herder 1923. xv;259p. --[LC has: 1921. 14cm.] [AC]

C481. ROUND TABLE OF THE REPRESENTATIVE GER. CATHOLIC NOVELISTS, A. NY;Cinc: Benziger 1902. 235p. il. 20cm. [LC]
[Bolanden, "King Ratbodo"; Brackel, "Just a simple story"; Domanig, "The postillion of Schoenberg"; Giehrl, "Children of Mary"; Haupt, "Nicholas Cusanus"; Hansjakob, "From the story of an unhappy life"; Herbert, "Tinsel"; Jüngst, "Sister Angela"; Kerner, "The good dean Ensfried"; Pütz, "Sacrifice"; Schaching, "Afra"; Spillmann, "Long Philip."]

C482. RUDWIN, M. J. Devil stories: an anthology. NY: Knopf 1921. xix;332p. 19cm. [LC]
[Hauff, "From the memoirs of Satan"; F. Mann, "The devil in a nunnery."]

C483. RYE, W: B. England as seen by foreigners in the days of Elizabeth and Jas. I...translations. L: J: R. Smith 1865. 300p. 20cm. [Arithmaeus, F: duke of Wirtemberg (pp. 1-53), Grasser, Hentzner, J: Ern. duke of Saxe-Weimar, Kiechel, L: prince of Anhalt, L: F: prince of Wirtemberg, O: prince of Hesse, Turler, Zinzerling.] [BM]

C484. ST. CLAIR, H: Tales of terror...tr. from the Chinese, Turkish, and German. Compiled by H. St. C--. Phil: Harding 1848. 2v. in one. 18cm. [LC]
[No authors named, but German names and scenes indicate origin. --"The magic dice, an awful narrative"; "The gored huntsman"; "Der Freischutz," or "The magic balls"(from Apel); "The boarwolf"; "The cavern of death"; "The astrologer of the 19th century."]

C485. do. 1856. Evening tales for the winter...NY: Marsh. 3v. in one. 19cm. [Same as the foregoing, with an added volume.] [LC]

C486. SAUNDERS, F: Evenings with the sacred poets. NY: Randolph 1870. 495p. 20cm. [LC]
[Apparently wholly eclectic. --Arndt (2), Bogatzky, Breithaupt, Canitz, Dach (3), Francke, Gellert, Gerhardt (2), Gleim, Goethe, Heermann, Princess Henriette, Heusser-S., Hermann, Hofel, F. Klopstock, Körner, Langbecker, Lange, Lindemann, Löwenstern, Luther (5), Marpurger, Melanchthon, Neander (3), Neumark, Nicolai, Niebuhr, Novalis, Rambach, Ringwaldt, Rosengarten, Rothe, Rückert, Schiller, Schmolke, Seidl, Selnecker, Spitta, Tersteegen, Trotznou, Uhland, Herzog Ulrich, Wallenstein, Weissel, Wetzel, Wülffer, Zehni, Zinzendorf, Zwingli.]

C487. do. 1885. [same] Rev. and enl. 574p. [LC]
--NY: Whittaker 1899. 574p. il. 20cm. [LC.BM]
[This ed. omits: Princess Henriette, Marpurger, Niebuhr, Rosengarten, Trotznou, Wallenstein, Zehni, and adds: Flemming, Speratus, Wette.]

C488. SAUNDERS, F: and MINNIE K. DAVIS. One thousand gems of genius in poetry and art. St.L; Phil: 1889. 743p. il. 22cm. [LC] [Goethe, "Wisdom," i.e., short prose epigrams; Heine, "Plagiarism," likewise; Schiller, "Poetry of life," tr. Bulwer.]
C489. SCHAFF, PH. and ARTHUR GILMAN. A lib. of relig. poetry. L: Low 1881. xxxi;1004p. il. 8. [BM]
[Tr. by various hands and uneven in quality. --Albrecht, Markgraf of Brandenburg-Culmbach, Anton U: Asschenfeldt, Bahnmaier, Böhmer, Dach, Dessler (2), Edeling, Fabricius, Fouqué, J. Frank (3), Freiligrath, Gerhardt (12), Gellert, Gerok, Goethe (8), Graeter, Gregor, Harms, F: Hartmann, L. Haym, Heine (2), Herder (3), Heusser (6), Immermann, Jacobi, G. Kern, E. Kleist, Klopstock (2), A. Knapp (2), Körner (2), Kosegarten, Langbecker, J. Lange (3), Laurentius, Lavater, Liebich, Luise Hte., Luther (10), Meyfahrt, Mosen, Neander (2), Neumark, Nicolai (2), Novalis, A. Reinecke, C. Richter, Ringwaldt, Rodigast, Rückert (5), Schefer, Scheffler (4), Schiller, Schmolke (4), Schröder, Seume, Spervogel, Spitta (6), Sturm, Tauler, Tersteegen (2), Uhland (4), M. Weisse, Weissel, Wette, Wülffer, Zihn, Zinzendorf (3), Zwick.]
C490. SCHIVELY, REBECCA H. Holy-day stories. Phil: Ref. church pub. 1869. 112p. il. 16. [No names or sources given.] [LCO]
C491. do. 1890. In olden days beyond the sea. With introd. and conclud. chaps. by the tr. Phil: Ref. church pub. 306p. il. 18cm. [Blaul, "True to their faith, a tale of the Walloons in the Palatinate"; Ebrard, "The siege of a Huguenot town," tr. C. G. Zipf.] [LC]
§C492. PETER SCHLEMIHL...L;NY: Cassell 1889. 133p. 13cm. [BM] [Same tr. as #1093; vol. includes: Carode (sic), "Story without an end"; Novalis, "Hymns to night."]
§C493. do. 1913. The marvellous hist. of the shadowless man (Peter Schlemihl)...Introd. A. S. Rappoport. Il. Forster Robson. L: Holden & H. xiv;93; 74p. 25cm. [BM]
[Same tr. as #1093; vol. includes: Hauff, "The cold heart."]
C494. do. 1845. The shadowless man (Peter Schlemihl)...Tales. L: Burns. 12. [Vol. includes: Clauren, "Liesli"; Fouqué, "Undine."] [EC]
C495. SEIDL, FZ. X. Spring and love. 100 Ger. poems tr. into Engl. Minden i. Westfalen: 1895. 104p. (B42)
C496. SELECTIONS FROM GER. POETS, with tr. L: Wms. & N. 1854. Sq. 8. [EC]
§C497. SMITH, LUELLA D. Flowers from for. fields. Buffalo: Peter Paul bk. co. 1895. 72p. 15cm. [LC]
[Fair versions. --Bodenstedt (2), Böttger, Detjen, Ebert, Freiligrath, Geibel (5), Gerok (2), Gieseler, Goethe, Grün (3), Hallermünde, Hartmann (2), Heine, Hensel, Herder, Hertz, Kayser-Langenhanss, Kerner, Körner, Lamerdin, Lavater, Lenau, Reineck (sic), Reuss, Roquette, Rückert (5), Schnauffer (2), Seidl, Stengel, Sturm (2), Traeger, Vogl.]
C498. SOANE, G: Specimens of Ger. romance, sel. and tr. from various authors. L: Prt. for Whittaker 1826. 3v. 12. [BM.LCO] [Hoffmann, "Master flea," vol. 2; Naubert, "The mantle," vol. 3; Schulze, "The blind passenger," vol. 3; Van der Velde, "The patricians," vol. 1.]
C499. SONDERLAND, J. B. Designs and border il. to poems...With tr. and orig. L: Senior 1841. 50p. 44 x 34cm. [BM.LC]
[Eclectic, mostly mediocre. --Bürger (2), Chamisso, Freiligrath (2), Goethe (2), Körner (2), Immermann, Kopisch, Langbein, Salis, Schiller (2), Uhland (3), Voss.]
§C500. SONGS OF LIFE, LOVE AND NATURE, from the Ger. L: Lingham 1840? ff. A-I. 13cm. [BM]
[Tr. fairly good. Authors unnamed. I recognized: Bürger, Goethe, Kerner, Körner, Richter, Rückert, Schiller, Schmidt v. L., Uhland.]

§C501. SPALDING, J: L. Songs chiefly from the Ger. Chic: McClurg 1896. 215p. 18cm. [LC]
[Negligible. --Blomberg, A. Christen, Claudius, Dahn, Eckstein, Eichendorff, Falkland, Fischer (4), Fouqué, Frankle (sic), Franzos, Freiligrath (4), Friedman, Geibel (28), Goethe (5), Gottschall (2), Greif (2), Grisebach, Groth, Grün, Haushofer, Heine (15), Herwegh (2), Holtz, Heyse, Hoffmann v. F., Hölderlin, Holstein, Jensen (2), Kerner (2), Kletke, Klopstock, Körner, Kuh, Laurillard, Lenau (2), Leuthold, Lingg, Lorm (2), Milow, Möricke (sic), Niondorf, Platen (2), Plonnies (sic), Reinick, Rodenberg, Rollett, Roquette, Rückert (5), Salis (2), Sallet, Schefer, Schiller (4), Siebel (2), Seidle (sic), Stolberg, Storm (3), Sturm, Strauss, Tiedge, Traeger, Uhland (3), Vogl, Volkmann.]

C502. SPECIMENS OF THE NOVELISTS AND ROMANCERS, with crit. and biogr. notices. 2d ed. Glasgow: R: Griffin 1826. 424p. 12. [BM]
[Goethe, "The minstrel and Mignon," tr. Carlyle, "The only unexceptionable passage, of moderate length, which could be sel. from W: Meister's Apprenticeship." Also, Hoffmann, "The Irishman", from "The devil's elixer" (sic), tr. Gillies.]

C503. STARRETT, LEWIS F: Poems and tr. Bost: Rand Avery 1887. 219p. (B19) [6 by Goethe; see B19.]

†C504. STIGAND, W: ANTHEA. Poems and tr...chiefly from...Heine, with sketch of his life (and notes). L: K.Paul 1907. xvi;384p. 19cm. [BM.NY]
[Heine, pp. 261-341; also: Bodenstedt, Claudius, Freiligrath, Goethe (3), Pfeffel, Rückert, Uhland (3).]

†C505. do. 1860. A vision of Barbarossa and other poems by W: Stigant (sic). L: Chapman & H. 267p. 17cm. [BM]
[Tr. pp. 231-end. --Claudius, Daumer (3), Freiligrath, Goethe (2), Heine (4), Pfeffel, Rückert, Uhland (4).]

C506. STOCK, COLLARD J. Tr. in verse from French...Ger...L: E.Stock 1891. 64p. 16cm. [Boddien, Heyse, Uhland.] [BM]

§C507. STOCK, J: S. Poems chiefly tr. from the Ger. L: Longmans 1892. viii;101p. 21cm. [BM]
[Ger. and Engl. Tr. not very good. --Burger (sic), Goethe (5), Schiller (4), Tieck. Also, "The legend of the Wartburg," containing 2 lyrics each from Goethe and Schiller.]

C508. STORIES AND LEGENDS OF THE RHINE BETWEEN WORMS AND COLOGNE. Heidelberg: Groos 1870. 138p. 16. [BPL]
[Apparently a tr. and ad. of Ger. orig.; a few poems.]

C509. STORIES BY FOR. AUTHORS. NY: Scribner 1898. 2v. 17cm. [LC]
[Largely or wholly eclectic. --Auerbach, "Cn. Gellert's last Christmas"; Baumbach, "The Egyptian fire-eater"; Chamisso, "P: Schlemihl"; Hauff, "The severed hand"; Heyse, "The fury"; Hoffmann, "The Cremona violin"; Kompert, "A ghetto violet"; Lindau, "The philosopher's pendulum"; Sacher-Masoch, "The bookbinder of Hort"; Zschokke, "Advent. of a new Year's eve."]

C510. STORR, F. and R. "Maria Wuz" (by Richter) and "Lorenz Stark" (by Engel); or, Engl. prints (i.e., tr.) of two Ger. orig. L: Longman 1881. 194p. 17cm. [BM]

*C511. STORY, JAS. A. "Carmina silvulae." Poems orig. and tr. L: Authors' co-op. pub. 1890. 131p. 18cm. [BM]
[Goethe, Körner, J: Schmidt (6), Others unassigned.]

§C512. STORY, W: W. Poems. Bost: 1847. 2v. 17cm. [LC]
[My first ed. says: A few very good tr. Can find no tr. in 1856 or 1886 ed. and have not been able to verify for first ed.]

C513. STRANG, J: Tales of humour and romance from the Ger. of Hoffmann, Langbein, Lafontaine, etc. Before 1836. (B29)

C514. STRETTELL, ALMA. Lullabies of many lands...into Engl. verse. 77 il. Emily J. Harding. L: Allen 1894. ff. A-R. 21cm. [BM]
[2 from Germany.]

*C515. SWANWICK, ANNA. Sel. from the dramas of Goethe and Schiller, with introd. remarks. L: Murray 1843. xvi;289p. 21cm. [BM]
--Also 1846. (B27)
[Goethe, "Iphigenia," "Tasso," Acts I, II, 1; Schiller, "Maid of Orleans," not complete.]

C516. SWAYNE, G: C. Specimens from Schiller and Uhland, Oxford: Macpherson; L: Pickering 1848. (B27)
[See "Athenaeum" for 1848, p. 195. Note also the following.]

C517. SWAYNE, G: C. and MARG. S. SWAYNE. Poems. Darmstadt: Prt. by C. F. Winter 1869. 95p. 17cm. [BM]
[His tr. excellent; hers adaptations. --Geibel (3), Uhland (3).]

C518. T., C. J. The best terrible tales from the Ger. L: Reeves 1912. 193p. 16cm. [BM]
[No authors named. I recognized: "The crazy half-heller" (Fouqué, das Galgenmännlein); "The goldsmith of the Rue Nicaise (Hoffmann, "das Frln. v. Scudery"); "The host of 'the sun'" (Schiller, "Der Verbrecher..."). Also: "The crystal dagger," "A strange bride.]

*C519. T., S. "The Christmas roses" and other tales. Chiefly tr. from the Ger. L: Cundall 1845. 256p. il. 14cm. [Tr. Sa. Taylor? --A. Grimm, "The Christmas roses"; "The water fairy's gifts," "Lina," "The hedgehog," "Tony, the miller's son," "The gleaner"; Hauff, "Story of a manikin, related by Muley, a Turkish merchant"; Houwald, "The Christian and the Mahometan" (excellent tr.); Rudolphi, "The tales of the stork, fox, and magpie"; "The labyrinth."] [BM]

C520. (T., S.) Fairy tales, tr. from the Ger. Salford: J: Wilson 1843. 176p. il. 14cm. [BM]
[Pref. signed S. T. (a lady): Sa. Taylor? --A Grimm, "Philemon and Baucis," "Duller," "The wicked nobody, or the golden egg"; Hauff, "Mahrchen (sic), i.e., preface to his "Märchen," "The dwarf nose," "The false prince" (same tr. as C521); Rudolphi, "The king of the swans"; "The children's spring."]

C521. T., S. King of the swans and other tales. L: Cundall 1846. 87p. 16cm. [BM]
["I have taken the liberty of freely selecting, varying, and adapting them to suit Engl. taste." --A. Grimm, "Tony, the miller's son" (same as C519), "The gleaner (do.); Hauff, "The false prince" (same as C520); Rudolphi, "The king of the swans" (same as C520); "The children's spring" (do.).]

C522. T., S. Stories of the head and heart for the young. From the Ger. L: Darton & Clark 1842. 107p. 14cm. [BM]
[Retold, chiefly from Schmid's "Kurze Erzählungen."]

C523. TALES FOR LITTLE ONES. Tr. from the Ger. L: S.P.C.K. 1864. 67p. front. 14cm. [BM]
[No authors named. --"The little storm-man," "The three cherries," "The gold fish," "The snowdrop," "The proud ranunculuses," "The lady-bird on his travels," "Spring."]

C524. TALES FOR THE YOUNG, by Gustave (sic) Nieritz, etc. Ed: Paton & Ritchie; L: Hamilton, Adams 1855. 424p. il. 14cm. [BM]
[Shekla (sic) v. Gumpert, "Life's sunbeams, or songs, birds, and flowers"; Nieritz, "The foundling, or the school of life"; "The siege of Magdeburg, a tale of 1631." Also, two stories by Frances Brown.]

C525. TALES FROM BLACKWOOD. 3 ser. Ed;L: Blackwood. [BM.LC]
[See entries under Alexis, Kinkel, Lindau, Sealsfield.]

C526. TALES FROM THE GER. By a lady. L: Anderson 1827? (B26)
[See "Imperial Mag." 9(1827):473.]

C527. TALES OF YORE. Ed. W: Taylor or Norwich. L: Mawman 1810. 3v. 17cm. [Stories from Gräter, Meissner (2), Wieland (2).] [BM]

C528. TALES AND LEGENDS. By the authors of the Odd Volume. (Misses M. and --- Corbett. BM cat.) Ed: 1828. 3v. 8. [BM]
[V. 1. Döring, "The rescue." V. 2. "Aloyse" from the Ger. of Döring and the Danish of A. F. Elmquist; "A legend of Number Nip" (Musäus?).]

*C529. TAYLOR, BAYARD, Crit. essays and lit. notes. NY: Putnam 1880. viii;382p. 8. [BM.LC]
[Ed. by M. Hansen-Taylor. Has an essay on "The German Burns," i.e., Hebel, with excellent dialect translations; also an essay on Rückert (3).]

*C530. do. Studies in Ger. lit. NY: Putnam; L: Low 1879. viii;418p. 8. [LC.BM]
[Tr. bits of "Gudrun," "Hildebrandslied," "Heliand," "Ludwigslied," "Nibelungenlied"; also from Birken, Dach, Dietmar, Flemming, Goethe's "Faust," Gottfried's "Tristan," Hartmann's "Erec," H: v. Meissen, H: v. Morungen, Klopstock, Konrad v. Würzburg, Lessing, Logau, Luther, Marner, Opitz, Otfrid, Sachs, Schiller, Tannhauser, U: v. Winterstetten, Walther v. d. V., Wieland, Wolfram's "Parzival," "Titurel."]

*C531. TAYLOR, BAYARD and LILLIAN KILIANI. A sheaf of poems. Bost: Badger 1911. 134p.12. [LC]
[Chamisso, Dietmar, Ebert, Eichendorff (4), Flemming (2), Freiligrath, Geibel (4), Goethe (13), Greif, Gottfried's "Tristan," Hebel (5), Heine (4), Konrad v. W., Matthisson, H: v. Morungen, Opitz, Platen, Rückert (2), Schiller (7), Sachs, Schneckenburger, Uhland (5), Walther v. d. V. (4).]

†C532. TAYLOR, EDGAR. Lays of the minnesingers, etc. L: Longman 1825. 326p.il. 20cm. [BM.LC]
[Both meter and sense astray. --Abr. v. Rapperschwyl, Burkhart v. Hohenfels, Buewenburg, Cn. v. Hamle, Cn. v. Lupin, Dietmar (2), Düring, Goesli v. Ebenheim, Gf. v. Neifen, Hadlaub (2), Kaiser H:, H: v. Anhalt, H: v. Breslau, H: v. Morungen (3), Kd. v. Kilchberg, Kd. v. Würzburg (2), Kraft v. Toggenburg, "Laurin," Lütolt v. Saven, Marner, Margraf O: v. Brandenburg, "Nibelungenlied," Rd. v. Rothenberg, Steinmar, Tugendhafte Schreiber, U: v. Lichtenstein, Walther v. d. V. (9), Wenzel v. Böhmen, Wolfram v. E. Also 4 mastersongs.]

§C533. TAYLOR, W: (of Norwich). Histor. survey of Ger. poetry. L: Treuttel 1828-30. 3v. 22cm. [BM.LC]
[Lyric tr. mostly very poor; prose and blank verse in part very fine; he knows his German, but is no poet. --V. 1. "Annolied" (sel.), Gellert, Gessner (2 idyls), Gleim, Gryphius, Hadlaub, Hagedorn, Haller,(Doris), "Hildebrandslied" (prose), E. Kleist, Klopstock (8 sel., some in prose, also from "Messiah" and "Battle of Hermann"), Lessing (25 epigrams, 5 fables, "Nathan, complete"), Otfrid (3 sel.), Pope Joan, canonization of (sel.). --V. 2. Blumauer, Bürger (6), Claudius (2), J. Jacobi, Matthisson, Pfranger, "Monk of Libanon" (complete!), Stolberg, Voss (1 poem, sel. from "Luise"), Wieland, "Golden mirror" (sel.), "Geron the courteous," "Wintermärchen" (40p.), "Oberon" (40 st.) "Dialogues of the dead" (48p.), "Rosamond" (2p.). -- V. 3. Gerstenberg, Ariadne on Naxos (5p.), Goethe ("Iphigenia," complete, 10 poems, some prose, sel. from other works), Herder (varia), Körner, "Zriny" (sel.), Kotzebue (sel. from dramas), C. Sander, Schiller (3 poems, sel. from dramas), Schulze (4 sel.). Also Oehlenschläger, "Correggio" (sel.).]

C534. THOMSON, AX. Ger. miscellany. Perth: Morison 1796. Prt. for Mitchel, Ed. and Vernor & H., L: 282p. 17cm. [BM]
[Kotzebue, "The Indians in England"; Meissner, "The Nutshell, a tale," "A genuine dialogue," "Bianca Capello, a dram. narr.," "The hist. of Lamberg," "The Ger. theatre at Venice, a true anecdote," "In what lang. should an author write?]

§C535. THOMSON, B: The Ger. theatre. L: Vernor & H. 1801. 6v. il. 21cm. [BM.LC]
[Sep. t.p. and date for each play. Il. various hands. T. was not certain of the Ger. and did not care for strict fidelity; yet

THOMSON, B:
some tr. are quite good. Did he perhaps have some assistant who knew German? --Babo, "O: of Wittelsbach, or the choleric count," "Dagobert, king of the Franks," vol. 4; Goethe, "Stella," vol. 6; Iffland, "Conscience," vol. 4; Kotzebue, "The stranger," "Rolla, or the virgin of the sun," "Pizarro, or the death of Rolla," vol. 1; "Lovers' vows, or the natural son," "Adelaide of Wulfingen," "Count Benyowsky, or the conspiracy of Kamtschatka," vol. 2; "Deaf and dumb, or the orphan," "The Indian exiles," "False delicacy," "The happy family," vol. 3; Lessing, "Emilia Galotti," vol. 6; Reitzenstein, "Count Koenigsmark," vol. 6; Schiller, "The robbers," "Don Carlos," vol. 6; Schroeder, "The ensign," vol. 6.]

*C536. THOMSON, JAS. Poetical works. 1895. [BM.LC]
[Tr. are good, not excellent. --Goethe (2), Heine (31).]

C537. THOMS, W: J. Lays and legends of Germany. L: Cowie 1834. x; 274p. il. 16cm. [BM.NY]
[Notes give the sources of these tales and sketches, mostly very short; they are freely retold. --Büsching (6), "Eulenspiegel," Grimm (15), Grimm's "Deutsche Sagen" (10), Herder's "Volkslieder" (4), "Knaben Wunderhorn," "Otmar" (3), Pfeffel; also, 8 legends of Rübezahl from Büsching from Praetorius.]

*C538. THRING, E: Poems and tr. L: Unwin 1887. 150p. 17cm. [BM]
[Two samples excellent. --Claudius, Droysen, Geibel, Gerhard, Goethe, Grimmelshausen, Hölty, Luther, Müller, Rist (2), Rückert, Schiller, Uhland.]

§C539. TILNEY, ROBT. Gleanings from poetic fields. Phil: Winston 1898. 139p. 12. [LCO]
[Some bad tr. --Chamisso (2), Geibel, Goethe (3), Heine (2), Kerner, Körner (2), Matthisson, Prutz, Rückert, Schiller, Schwab, Uhland (20), Wyss.]

§C540. TILTON, TD. Complete poetic works. L: Unwin 1897. 802p. 22cm. [4 good tr.] [LC]

C541. do. 1882. Swabian stories (in verse). NY: Worthington. 297p. 19cm. [Old tales and trad. of the Swabian land. Notes give histor. data and some sources.] [BM]

*C542. TRACY, T: Miniature romances from the Ger., with other prolusions of light lit. Bost: Little-Brown 1841. 324p. 21cm. [LC]
[Fouqué, "Undine," "The vial-genie and mad farthing," "The collier-family, or red-mantle and the merchant." Also, Table-talk notices of Phantasmion, including the "Fortunes of Fairylore" by W: Hauff.]

C543. TRANSLATIONS IN VERSE, FROM VARIOUS GER. AUTHORS. Anon. L: Harrison 1848. 64p. 21 x 16cm. [BM]
[Ad. rather than tr. Done by a lady, who died before 1848. --Bouterwek, Ebert (7), Franz, Gittermann, Goethe (4), Herder (8), Hohlfeldt, Klopstock (2), Köhler, Mahlmann, Müllner, Nicolai, Novalis, Richter, Rückert, Schiller (3), Tieck, Uhland (3).

C544. TRAUERMANTEL, pseud. Hurrah for the holidays; or, the pleasures and pains of freedom. Bost: Crosby, Nichols; Cinc: Blanchard 1857. 220p. il. 17cm. [BM]
[R. Koch, "The faithful dog," "The generous enemy"; A. Stein, "Schoolboys abroad and at home," "Anna's vacation," "Julian's experience."]

C545. do. 1860. Many a little makes a mickle: tales from the Ger. Bost: Crosby. 229p. il. 16. [Not found.] [LCO]

C546. do. 1858. Nannie's jewel-case; or, true stories and false. Tales...from...Julie Ruhkopf and A: Moritz. Bost: Crosby, Nichols. 223p. il. 12. [LCO]
[Moritz, "The hymn-book," "Kasem the miser," "W: the little chimney-sweeper."]

C547. do. 1857. The pearls and other tales. Bost: Crosby, Nichols; Cinc: Blanchard. 249p. 17cm. [LCO.BM]
[Eschenbach, "The pearls"; Franz, "The rivals," "The friends," "The best dowry"; Trauermantel, "The blind grandfather."]

C548. do. 1859. Seedtime and harvest: tales...from...Rosalie Koch and Maria Burg. Bost: Crosby & N. 291p. il. 16. [LCO]
[Koch, "Country cousins," "The little ragman," "The picture"; Burg, "The inquisitive boy."

C548a. do. 1867. [same] NY: O'Shea. [LC]

C549. do. 1859. A will and a way: tales from F. Michel and A: Moritz. Bost: Crosby & N. 213p. il. 16. [LCO]
[Michel, "Tailor and fiddler"; Moritz, "The benefactor's portrait," "The gardener's daughter," "Patience removes mountains," "The ways of providence."]

C550. TURNER, REV. C. Sonnets, lyrics, and tr. L: King 1873? (B19)
[See "Athenaeum" for 1873, p. 202.]

§C551. TYRRELL, G. Versions and perversions of Heine and others. L: Elkin Matthews 1909. 64p. 8. [BM]
[More per than ver. --Gottschall, Halm, M. Hartmann, Heine (17), Neumann, Rückert, Stolberg.]

C552. UTTERSON, SA. H. Tales of the dead. Principally tr. from the French. L: White, Cochrane 1813. viii;248p. 20cm. [BM.LC]
[All but one imitated from "Phantasmagoriana...traduit de l'allemand," par J. B. B. Eyriès. Paris 1812. --"The family portraits"; "The fated hour," "The death's head," "The death-bride," "The spectre-barber."]

C553. VARIETIES OF LITERATURE FROM FOREIGN LITERARY JOURNALS AND ORIGINAL MSS. By W: Tooke. L: Debrett 1795. 2v. 552;574p. 21cm. [Bahrdt, Meissner, Tiedemann are named; also: Wieland, "An excursion to the realms below," (2) "Olympic dialogues," "Phaon," vol. 1; "On the liberty of reasoning on matters of belief," (2) "Olympic dialogues," "On the liberty and licentiousness of the press," vol. 2.] [BM]

+C554. WARD, J. H. Ballads of life. Salt Lake City: Parry 1886. 202p. il. 12. [LC.BM]
[Chamisso, Goethe, Freiligrath, A.Müller, K. Rittermann, Schiller, Uhland.]

C555. THE WARTBURG[1]...monographs, etc. Ed. Max Baumgärtel. Tr. G. A. Greene. Berl: Baumgärtel 1907. xix;741p. 54pl. 706 il. 53 x 43 x 10cm. [Baumgärtel, "Prelim. to the restoration of the W--"; "The restor. of the W--"; C: Ax. of Saxe-Weimar-Eisenach, "Reminisc. of the restor. of the W--"; E. Martin, "The minnesingers in Thuringia and the contest of the singers in the W--"; Oncken, "M. Luther in the W--," "The Burschenschaft and the W-- festival"; Trinius, "The W-- in legend and poetry," "Modern life in the W--"; R: Voss, "A walk through the W--"; P. Weber, "Architect. hist. of the W--," "Old and new works of art in the W--"; K: Wenck, "Earliest hist. of the W--," "St. Eliz.," "Hist. of the landgraves and of the W-- as a princely seat, 13th-15th cent.] [BM]

§C556. WEBB, PH. G. L. Trans. from Heine and Goethe. L: Fifield 1912. 95p. 12. [Rather poor. --Goethe, "Song of the Fates" from "Iphigenia"; "Faust II," Act 5 (sel.); Heine, "Pilgrimage to Kevlaar," "Mountain Idylls" from the "Harzreise," sel. from "Heimkehr," "Lyrisches Intermezzo," "Romancero," pp. 7-72.] [BM]

C557. WEBER, H: Illustrations of northern antiquities...from the earlier Teutonic and Scand. romances...with notes and dissertations. Ed: J. Ballantyne, for Longman et al. L: 1814. ix;522p. 30cm. [BM]

[1] This is, if not the weightiest, certainly the heaviest book I ever handled: it weighs 55 lbs. without the case. The attendant at the B. M. assures me that the library has a still heavier volume.

WEBER, H:
[Sel. from "Heldenbuch," "Otnit and Elberich," "Hug-" and "Wolfdietrich," both "Rosengarten," "Laurin," "Nibelungenlied" (32p.), "Klage," "Hildebrandslied." The 2d part contains some folk ballads tr. by R. Jamieson.]

C559. WEIRD TALES FROM THE GER. Ed: Paterson; L: Dent 1895? 256p. 14cm. [BM.LC]
[Probably wholly eclectic. --Goethe, "The evil conscience" (Cf. #2617); Hauff, "The severed hand"; Hoffmann, "The elementary spirit"; Schiller, "The ghost-seer"; Scott, "The fortunes of Martin Waldeck" (based on a Ger. tale); Tieck, "The bracelet," "The Klausenburg," tr. by C. A. F(eiling?).]

C560. WEISS, J. L. H. Moral and relig. sel. from...Jacobi, Shubart (sic), Schiller, Ewald, Richter, Gellert, Haug, and others. Bost: Peabody 1841. 52p. 24. (B29)

C561. WESTALL, W. Tales and legends of Saxony and Lusatia. Il. H. W. Petherick. L: Griffith & Farran 1877. 311p. 17cm. [BM]
[Based on, or tr. from: Th. Grüsse's "Sagenbuch des Königreich Sachsens"; "Hauptsagenbuch der Lausitz"; "Sagen und Märchen aus der Oberlausitz." 14 stories.]

§†C562. WHEWELL, W: Verse tr. from the Ger. L: Murray 1847. 87p. 8. [Bürger, †"Lenore," Goethe (3), Schiller (10 poems, 41p.).] [BM]

*C563. WHITELOCK, W: W. Modern Germany in relation to the great war. NY: Kennerley 1916. 628p. 20cm. [LC.BM]
[Tr. of "Deutschland und der Weltkrieg." Rather free, but no errors noted. --Essays by C. Becker, P. Darmstädter, H. Delbrück, O: Francke, K: Hampe, O: Hintze, H. Luther, E. Marcks, F: Meinecke, H. Oncken, G. Schmoller, W. Schoenborn, H. Schumacher, W: Solf, F: Tezner, E. Troeltsch, H. Uebersberger, O. Weber, E. Zitelmann.]

§C564. WHITMAN, SA. H. Hours of life and other poems. Providence, R.I: Whitney 1853. 227p. 12. [LC.BM]
[Mediocre tr. --Bürger, Gleim, Goethe, Uhland.]

§C565. do. 1879. Poems. Bost: Houghton, Osgood. xiii;261p. 18cm. [LC.BM]
[Has the same tr.]

*C566. WILBERFORCE, E: Dante's inferno and other tr. NY;L: Macmillan 1903. 284p. 20cm. [BM.LC]
[Bodenstedt, Goethe ("Faust"), Heine, Lingg, Schiller.]

C567. MAX WILD THE MERCHANT'S SON, and other stories for the young. L;Ed: Nimmo 1874. 224p. 16cm. [BM]
[F. Hoffmann, title story; Nathusius, "Christfrid's first journey."]

C568. WILKINSON, W: C. Classic Ger. Course in Engl. NY: Chautauqua press 1887. 327p. 20cm. [LC]
[Chapters on main figures with eclectic translations.]

C569. WILLIAMS, MRS. SYDNEY. Memoirs of Felix Neff, J: F. Oberlin and B: Overberg. Bristol: Wright & Albright; L: Hamilton, Adams 1840. 94p. 24cm. [BM]
[Oberlin and Overberg both by G. H. Schubert, the former well translated, the latter much more freely.]

WINKWORTH, CATH. See Hymnals, this list.

§C570. WINKWORTH, CATH. Christian singers of Germany. L: Macmillan 1869. xiii;346p. 19cm. [BM.LC]
[Albertini, J: Andrea, Angelus, Anton U:, G. Arnold (3), Blaurer, Bogatzky, G: Brandenburg, Cramer, Dach, Dessler, Eber (2), Flemming (2), Freylinghausen, J. Franck, Gellert, Gerhardt (3), Gryphius (2), Hartmann v. Aue, Heermann (7), H: v. Meissen (2), Helmboldt, Hermann, Hiller (2), U: v. Hutten, Klopstock (3), H: v. Laufenburg (2), Logau (6), Luise Hte., Luther (5), Matthesius, Neander, Nicolai, Opitz, Otfrid, Konrad v. Queinfurt,

WINKWORTH, CATH.
Reinmar v. H., Ringwaldt, Rinkart, Rist (2), Roberthin, Rückert (2), Sachs (2), Selnecker (2), Spee, Spener, Spervogel (3), Tauler (3), Tersteegen (7), Walther v. d. V. (7), Weingartner, Wolfram, "Parzival" (sel.) Zinzendorf (2).]
§C571. WIREMAN, H: D. Gems of Ger. lyrics. Phil: Claxton. R. & H. 1869. 371p. 18cm. [LC]
[Ger. and Engl. Average tr. --Allmers, Bauernfeld, Boettger, Brentano, Burow, Chamisso (2), Dach, Dahm, Dräxler-Manfred, Eichendorff, Ernst, Ferrand, J. Fischer (2), Freiligrath (2), Halm, Hartmann, Hebbel, Hoeppl, Kerner (2), Lenau (25), Lingg, F. Löwe, Mosen, W. Müller (2), Mund, Platen, Prutz, Reinick, Roquette, Rückert (4), Sallet, Seidl, Siebel (2), Spitta, Stolle, Stolterfoth, Sturm, Traeger (3), Uhland, Vogl (2), Wegener.]
C572. WISTER, MRS. A. L. Seaside and fireside fairies. Phil: Ashmead & Evans 1864. 292p. il. 18cm. [LC]
--Phil: Duffield Ashmead 1867. [BM]
[15 stories, four of them by L: Wahl, woven into a series of tales by "Father Tobias." Something also by G: Blum.]
C573. WITZEL, C: Gems of Ger. poetry. Coll. of choicest Ger. songs and ballads tr. into Engl. by most eminent authors. Dresden: Köhler 1896. 118p. (B42, B19) [Has 9 by Goethe; see B19.]
C574. WORLD'S GREATEST BOOKS. Ed. Lorth Northcliffe and S. S. McClure. NY: McKinlay, Stone, and Mackenzie 1910. 20v. 12. [LC]
[Vol. 1. Auerbach, "On the height," 15p. --Vol. 2. Chamisso, "Peter Schlemihl," 11p. --Vol. 5. Ebers, "An Egyptian princess," 12p.; Goethe, "Werther," 9p., "W: Meister," 11p. --Vol. 7. Richter, "Hesperus," 8p., "Titan," 12p.; Rosegger, "Papers of the forest school-master," 10p. --Vol. 9. Goethe, "Letters to Zelter," 7p., "Poetry and truth," 11p., "Conversations with Eckermann," 11p. --Vol. 10. Luther, "Table talk," 8p. --Vol. 11. Schliemann, "Troy and its remains," 11p., Mommsen, "Hist. of Rome," 13p. --Vol. 12. Ranke, "Hist. of the Popes," 11p. --Vol. 13, Hegel, "Philos. of relig.," 11p. --Vol. 14. Hegel, "Philos. of hist.," 12p., Kant, "Critique of pure reason," 9p., "Critique of pract. reason," 10p., Schopenhauer, "The world as will and idea," 9p., Marx, "Capital," 11p. Vol. 15. Haeckel, "Evolution of man," 12p., Humboldt, "Cosmos," 11p., Lavater, "Physiognomical fragments," 11p., Liebig, "Animal chemistry," 11p., Virchow, "Cellular pathology," 12p. --Vol. 16. Goethe, "Faust," 16p. --Vol. 17. Goethe, "Götz," 17p., "Iphigenia," 11p., Heine, "Atta Troll," 15p., Klopstock, "Messiah" (by Egestorff), 8p., Lessing, "Nathan," 14p. --Vol. 18. "Nibelungenlied," 9p., Schiller, "Tell," 17p., Wagner, "Nib. ring," 39p. --Vol. 20. Lessing, "Laocoon," 8p.]
*C575. ZIMMERN, HELEN AND ALICE. Half hours with for. novelists. L: Remington 1880. 2v. viii;348;363p. 19cm. [BM]
[With short notices of the...various authors. Assisted by E. A. Haughton.]
*C576. do. 1882. [same] 2d ed. Chatto & W. [BM]
*C577. do. 1884. [same] New and rev. ed. Title: Stories from for. novelists, with short notices, etc. L: Chatto. viii;314p. [BM]
[Tr. seem to be very well done. --Auerbach. "The axe"; Freytag, "The Ger. professor" (from "Die verlor. HS"); Hackländer, "The volunteer"; Heyse, "The huntsman"; Keller, "The funeral," "Clothes make men" (part); Marlitt, "The twelve apostles"; Sacher-Masoch, "The sledge-ride"; Spielhagen, "The storm" (from "Hammer und Amboss"); Stifter, "The balloon ascent," "The heath."]

INDEX OF TRANSLATORS

INDEX OF TRANSLATORS

Note. --This list serves in the main a double purpose. On the one hand it has its face value, so to speak; on the other, it will help to make up for deficiencies in the critical judgments of the main list. Thus if a book is translated by E. A. Bowring, for example, the reader can get an approximate idea of its quality by noting in this list the ratings assigned to other translations done by him.

LC cards give the dates of translators as far as they are known, and I have followed that practice here; BM, however, prints no dates, and many could not be found. In order to give some idea of the translator's period, the publication date of the earliest translation recorded in this book is inserted in parentheses after the name, with A, E, or G prefixed, to indicate publication in America, England, or Germany, respectively.

The numbers, of course, refer to the main list, and to lists A (p.551), and C (p.577), and are assigned mostly the same diacritical marks as are given in these lists. Occasionally a double mark is given here, to indicate varying quality of the translator's work, as determined by examination of particular selections.

Abbreviations include those of the AC (A: for Augustus, B: for Benjamin, etc., as in those of German names), those which can be used for both English and German (Ab. for Albert, Tb. for Theobald, Pl. for Paul, etc.), and a few others easily recognizable: e.g., Cath. for Catherine, Eli. for Elizabeth, Fes. for Frances, Fis. for Francis, Sa. for Sarah. In a few cases certain abbreviations are given in my bibliographical sources; I cannot always be certain what these stand for.

A., C. (E1885)
§C1
ABBOTT, ALICE ASBURY (A1892)
†9307
ABBOTT, EVELYN, 1843-1901
*1280-1, *10603
ABBOTT, MABEL (A1924)
8952, §8953
ABBOTT, T: KINGSMILL, 1829-
*4790, 4816, *4836, C119, C370
ABBOTT, W. H.(E1914)
†4054
ACHURCH, JANET (A1900)
†3842
"ACKERLOS, J:"; see "Smith, J: S."
ADAM, A. MERCER (E1859)
*9547, *C132
ADAMS, ANNIE ELI., d. 1926
*744
ADAMS, J: QUINCY, 1767-1848.
2155
ADAMS, SA. HOLLAND, 1824-
§3129, 3130, *3131, §3132, †6224, 8645
ADAMS, W: H: DAVENPORT, 1828-91
10397
ADDISON, LOUISA (E1841)
§485, 9976
ADLER, G: J., 1821-68
§2909
"AGRA" (E1883)
§C2
AIKIN, LUCY, 1781-1864; see "GODOLPHIN, Ma."
AIKMAN, C: MORTON (E1892)
*C3
AINSLIE, (A.) DOUGLAS, 1865-
§2940
AINSLIE, DR. (E1799)
5302
ALBRECHT, ADALBERT (A1914)
*5166
ALEXANDER, ARCHIBALD (A1855-)
†9293
ALEXANDER, Jas. WADDELL, d. 1859
**Hymn in 2170
ALEXANDER, W: F. (E1894)
§6203
ALFORD, H: Dean of Canterbury, 1810-71
†C220
ALGER, ABBY LANGDON, 1850-
966, *1806, *7392, *9915
ALGER, W: ROUNSEVILLE, 1822-1905
C4, §C5, C6
"ALGERNON" (A1842)
C293
ALLEN, L. H. (E1914)
*3922
ALLEN, L. J. (G1910) 612

BARNETT, CA. F. (A1913)
8765
BARNETT, LIONEL D:, 1871-
5098, 9113, 9316
BARNETT, MORRIS, 1800-56
8121
BARON, MRS. (E1903)
446
BARRETT, C: J. (E1895)
2423a
BARRETT, FIS. (E1801)
9469
BARRETT, H: (E1796)
3661
BARRETT, J. (E1876)
§4429
BARRETT, R. G. L. (G1922)
*7499
BARRETT, Timothy (E1895)
2423a
BARRETT, W. A. (E1879)
7420
BARRETT-LENNARD, MRS. C: E: (E1907)
*5, §1263, 7405, 7504
BARROWS, SA. TRACY (A1916)
3653, *3839, *3903
BARTEN, J: (G1896)
C16
BARTER, C: St. LEGER, 1857-
*6266
BARTHOLOMEW, W. (A1872)
*2126, 2130, 2629
BARTLEY, SIR G: CHRISTOPHER TROUT, 1842-
*9122
BARWELL, ANNA (E1924)
3697, 4227, 5814, *9544
BARWICK, G: F:, 1853-
8911
BARWICK, MRS. JANET MA. EDNA (VIVERS), 1864-
8911
BASHFORD, NORAH (E1910)
5116
BASKERVILLE, Af. (A1853)
§859, *C17
BATES, Af. (E1903)
C18
BATKA, R: (A1913)
242
BATT, MAX, 1875-
§4550
BAUER, JULIETTE (E1852)
*5030, *7432
BAUKHAGE, HILMAR R., 1889-
§9264
BAUMAN, NELLY M. (A1902)
*9283
BAX, CLIFFORD (A1909)
9077
BAX, ERNEST BELFORT, 1854-1926
*4840, 8567
BAXTER, SYLVESTER (A1879)
§10585
BEALBY, J. T., 1858-
4378? §4381
BEASLEY, E. C. (E1853)
*5684, 5687, 5736
BEATRICE, H. R. H. (E1890)
5437
BEATTY, HERB. MACARTNEY (E1909)
†1492
BEATTY-KINGSTON, W:, 1837-1900
*947
BEAUCHAMP, W. MN. (A1916)
C19
BEAZLEY, J: DAVIDSON, 1885-
7160
BECK, JESSIE (E1893)
*7706
BECKFORD, W:, 1759-1844
*6623
BECKH, GUSTAV F. (E1911)
1535
BEDACHT, MAX (A1925)
1476
BEDELL, GREGORY TOWNSEND, 1793-1834
8342
BEECH, G: (E1821)
5270
BEER, MAX (A1906)
1231
BEESON, ERNEST (E1915)
§3345
BEHR, M. (E1850)
2910, *9937
BEHRINGER, Rev. G: F. (A1883)
7380
BELL, Mrs. Art., née NANCY MEUGENS D'ANVERS; see D'ANVERS, NANCY
BELL, C. W. (E1910)
§2217, *9190
BELL, Ca. Courtenay (Poynter), 1834-
*136, 1286, 1291, §1295, *1302, 1304, *1310, *1318, *1338, *1348, *1356, §1359, 1362, *1363, 1403, *1408, *1414, §1416, 3607, §4335, 4345, *4349, *5151, §6226, 6267, *6275, 8658, *8898, 9119, §10176, *10345
BELL, E:, 1844-
2365, *3031, C18
BELL, MRS. E: Hamilton (A1890)
1411, §1285
BELL, ELI. F. (E1850)
6781
BELL, ERN., 1851- 5761

BITTLE, BERCHMANS (A1925)
1553
BJÖRKMAN, EDWIN A:, 1866-
*8468
BLACK, D: (E1848)
*2185
BLACK, J:, 1783-1855
§817, 2171, *2359, *4644, *8253
BLACK, JOSEPHINE (E1887)
4209, 4212
BLACK, W: (A1882)
†4279
BLACKIE, J: STUART, 1809-95
§2424, †2699, §C29
BLACKSTONE, Rev. F. C. (E1856)
759
BLADES, W:, 1824-90
§7505
BLAKE, Ag. A. E. (E1893)
§709, *1859, 4994, §7339, 7592, 9099
BLAKEMORE, TREVOR (E1914)
†4565
BLAQUIÈRE, Capt. W: (E1799)
§8103
BLEICHMANN, Rd. (E1904)
*3724, 6236
BLES, ART. (A1906)
§9981
BLIND, MATHILDE, 1841-96
2962, *9204
BLISS, EUGENE F:, 1836-
*10554
BLOCH, STELLA (AE1914)
§478
BLOCK, L: Jas., 1851-
5941
BLOCK, OSCAR (A1894)
4909
BLOCK, T: J. (A1915)
1862
BLOOMFIELD, LEONARD, 1887-
*3904
BLOW, SUSAN Eli., 1843-1916
844, 2081, 2362
BLUM, EMIL (A1892)
6921
BLUMENTHAL, C: E. (E1851)
*6691
BLUNDEN, H. (E1654)
529, 550, 554
BLÜCHER v. WAHLSTATT, GEBHARD LEBRECHT, Fürst zu, 1865-
*7390
BOAS, Mrs. HARRIET BETTY (LEVISEUR) (A1916) 4563
BOESCHE, Ab. W: (1913)
*9961
BOGGS, Mrs. Sa. Eli. (Siegrist), 1843-
1233, 3605, §4193, 9342, 10674
BOHN, H: G:, 1796-1884
2380, 7769, 7779, *7963, *8035, *8064, *8110, §C30
BOHN, W: E:, 1877-
4871
BOILEAU, Dl. (E1795)
§7964
BOKUM, Hm., 1807-78
7472, 9226, A34, †C31
BOLDEY, ELLA (A1890)
†3200
BOLL. HELENE H. (A1913)
8927a, 8934, 8997
BOLTON, Td. (A1923) *1114
BOLTZ, Os. H. (A1927)
9107a
BONER, Chas., 1815-70
C372
BONNER, M. B. (A1888)
6918
BONZENTA, COUNT (A19-)
9280
BOOKSTAVER, Mrs. Ma. ANDREWS LEONARD, 1843-
†8617
BOOTH, Miss A. E. (E1794)
§6678
BOOTH, Mrs. Ma. H. C., 1831-65
§C32
BOOTH, MEYRICK, 1883-
*1512, §1524, *1644
BOOTT, Fis., 1813-1904
*2605
BORING, M. (E1927)
345a
BORROW, G: H:, 1803-81
§861, 2630, §5041, C33, *C34
BORTHWICK, JANE (E1854)
§C225, §4253, C166
BOSANQUET, BERNARD, 1848-1923
3971, *5893, §C35
BOSANQUET, HELEN (DENDY), Mrs. BERNARD, 1860-1925
§C35
BOTHMER, Countess AF. v. (A1914)
6978
BOTTENS, J. P. I. de, see MONTOLIEU
BOUTELL, ROGER S. G. (A1901)
9571
BOVILL, C. H. (A1912)
§735
BOWEN, C: Hartpole (E1878)
†2701
BOWEN, J: Eliot, 1858-90
*1020
BOWEN-WEDGWOOD, E. (E1922)
*9053

BOWER, H. M. (E1926)
2343a
BOWRING, EDGAR ALFRED, 1826-1911
2365, 2372, 2388, §2400, *2513, 2596, §2872, *2987, §4070, 4098, 7772, 7779, 7780, 7819, §7870
BOWRING, Sir J:, 1792-1878
*1087
BOYCE, S: (E1762)
2263
BOYD, A. (E1859)
†C36
BOYD, ERNEST (A1921)
§6002
BOYD, PERCY, d. 1876
†C37
BOYESEN, HJALMAR HJORTH, 1848-95
2425, 7772
BOYLAN, R. DILLON (E1854)
2365, 2367, §2481, 2511, §2934, 2986, *3003, 3008, 3013, 5683, 5686, *5722, 7769, 7770, 7779, *8075, *C186
BOYSE, S: (E1762)
2263
BOZMAN, M. M. (E1925)
*343, *9883, 10002
BRACKETT, ANNA CALLENDER, 1836-1911
*7565, 7576
BRADE, W. R. V. (E1922)
1531, 1536
BRADFORD, GAMALIEL, Jr., 1863-
*9317
BRADFORD, G: (A1849)
C194
BRAININ, SALOMEA NEUMARK (A1926)
§415
BRAMSEN, J: i.e., JENS ANDR. (E1820)
†3110
BRANDEIS, MRS. ALICE (GOLDMARK) (A1927)
3056a
BRANDON, VIVIAN (E1913)
§2878
BRANDOW, MELVIN (AE1907)
4354
BRAUN, F: A: (A1910)
2427
BRAUNFELS, ALPHONCE (A1845)
8885
BRAUNFELS, LUDWIG, 1810-85
8208, 8209
BRAUNHOLTZ, HM. JT. (E1923)
9241
BRECK, E:, 1861-
*10349
BRENNAN, R: (A1881)
821
BRENTANO, Js. P. (A1918)
10613
BRETT, HARRY (A1900)
9975
BRIDGES, C: (E1836)
715
BRIGGS, H. B. (E1888)
§4074
BRILL, ABRAHAM ARDEN, 1874-
1885, *1894, 1897, 1900, *1905, 1907, *1914, 1916
BRINTON, W:, 1823-67?
*862
BRITON, MARK (E1881)
§9182
BROADHOUSE, J: (E1882)
7, §9354
BROCKMEYER, (Brokmeyer), H: Cd., 1826-1906
3978
BRODBECK, Ad., 1853-
*804
BRODERIP, Fis. (E1871)
3762
BRODFÜHRER, J. C. (A1870)
4472
BROICHER, DAISY (E1892)
§C38, C39
BROMEHEAD, W. C. (E1885?)
863
BROMWELL, H: PELHAM HOLMES, 1823-1903
†C40
BROOKE OF ASSH, J: (E1579)
6182
BROOKS, C: TIMOTHY, 1813-83
*115, 140, 147, 154, 161, *864, 921, *960, *967, 973, §2702, *1587, *7454, *7459, 7475, *7476, *7613, *7693, *7701, 8211, *C41-*C44, C109
BROOKS, CYRUS HARRY, 1890-
9298
BROOKS, LOUISE (A1885)
8913, 8938, 8956, 9002, 9005
BROOKSBANK, T: (E1904)
*4077
BROSE, H: L. (E1922)
6363, 10114a
BROSSART, Rev. Fd. (A1909)
1192
BROUGH, LOUISA (E1889)
*9503
BROWN, Carroll N. (A1918)
*1226
BROWN, CYRIL (A1926)
600
BROWN, F. L. RUDSTON (E1925)
508
BROWN, HELEN KERR (E1879)
*10064

BROWN, HORATIO (AE1895)
2428
BROWN, J. E. A.(E1869)
*2127
BROWN, P. HUME, 1849-1918
§2429
BROWNE, EDGAR GORDON, 1871-
3830
BROWNE, F. W. STELLA(E1924)
§760
BROWNE, MARMADUKE E. (G1905)
§1140, 10119
BROWNE, MOSES (E1772)
10624
BROWNE, W: HAND, 1828-1912
*1548, §8836
BROWNELL, S. E.(A1849)
§2879
BROWNING, Eli. BARRETT, 1806-61
4055
BRUCE, C. (E1865)
*4231
BRUCE, J: W. (G1837)
*8076
BRUCH, Rev. R: (E1621)
2165, 2167
BRUMBAUGH, MN. GROVE, 1862-
1244
BRÜNNOW, Mrs. Fis. (E1877)
§7704, §7705
BRUSASQUE, Eli. ANNABELLA de
(E1806)
9299
BRYAN, Mrs. (A1906)
9193
BRYAN, DOUGLAS (E1927)
9
BRYAN, G: SANDS, 1879-
§3888
BRYANS, CLEMENT (E1888)
6284
BRYANT, HANNAH (E1907)
§733, §8684
BRYANT, W: CULLEN, 1794-1878
C45, C46, §C47
BRYANT, W: McKENDREE, 1843-
3982, 3985
BUCHANAN, A. M. (E1910)
9918
BUCHANAN, Sir G: (E1908)
§2705
BUCHER, LOTHAR, 1817-92
A498, *C70
BUCHHEIM, C. Adolphus, 1828-1900
*5943, 5950
BUCHHEIM, EMMA SO. (E1887)
*1327
BUCHNER, E: FRANKLIN, 1868-
*4848
BUCK, C: F. (A1875)
725
BUCKLEY, ADELAIDE S. (A1888)
7310
BUEHRLE, MARIE C. (A1914)
9936
BUELOW, GOTTFRIED V., 1831-
*9969
BULFINCH, St. GREENLEAF, 1809-70
C48
BULL, JULIA ISABEL (A1899)
A85
BULL, ROGER (E1739)
†1179
BULLOCK, ART. BRODRICK, 1860-
*8581
BULWER-LYTTON, see LYTTON
BUNNETT, FANNY Eli., 1832-75
116, 123, 1663, *1696, *3127,
*5927, *5929, 7600, 10341
BUNSEN, Rev. H. G. (E1861)
C242
BURDETTE, AMELIA (A1889) 4048
BURETTE, MME. (E1845) *9381
BURKE, KENNETH (A1925)
*5911, 6004
BURKHARDT, C: B. (A1845)
†1072, †4976, C49
BURKITT, C: GRAY (A1903)
10001
BURLINGAME, E: LIVERMORE, 1848-
1922
*9623
BURNAND, Sir Fis. Cowley, 1836-
1917
497, 3430
BURNHAM, LAFAYETTE (A1857)
4377
BURNS, C. D. (E1910)
*1264
BURNS, Jas., 1808-71
§1091? *1662? 1694, §1725
BURNS, Jas., DRUMMOND, 1823-64
Hymns in C269
BURRELL, Jas. L. A. (A1923)
7509
BURROW, Rev. E: J:, 1785-1861
*10771
BURROWS, HELEN (E1856)
*7097
BURT, B: CHAPMAN, 1852-
*1482
BURT, Ma. ANNE (E1854) †C50
BUSCH, MARIE (E1927)
*8678, 8685
BUSSE, ADOLF, 1873-
*65
BUTCHER, M. P. (A1882)
4463, 4471, 7246, 7247
BUTLER, Art. J:, 1844-1910
459, *7336
BUTLER, F:, 1849-
§2912

CHAMBERS, Art. (E1921)
103a, *3766
CHAMBERS, W. H. H. (A1903)
359, †7644, §8489, 10094, C18
CHAMOT, A. E. (A1925)
4536
CHAMPAGNAC, J. B. J. (A1873)
6780
CHANNING, EVA (A1885)
7077
CHANNING, W: H. (A1839)
C109
CHAPELLE, MAX (A1903)
§6232
CHAPMAN, H: GRAFTON (A1906)
*9864
CHAPMAN, J: (E1878)
†5137
CHARLES, Mrs. Eli. probably CHARLES. Mrs. ELIZABETH (RUNDLE), 1826-96
*6692
CHARLES, M. (E1907)
2841
CHARLTON, Ma. (E1802)
5544
CHARLTON, W: H:, 1814-
§867, 3667, 3670, §C66
CHARY, PAULINE de (E1922)
*5009, *7221
CHATELAIN, Mme. de, i.e., CLARA (de PONTIGNY) de, 1807-76
178, 1227, 2085, 4601, §6630, A33a, A432
CHATTERTON, GEORGIANA, Lady, probably HENRIETTA GEORGIANA MARCIA LASCELLES (IREMONGER), Lady, 1806-76
7434
CHATTERTON-HILL, GEORGE, 1883-
§7416, *9023
CHAUDRON, Mrs. ADELAIDE de VENDEL (A1883)
6361, 6428, §6465
CHAWNER, E: (E1866)
§868, §2404, §C67
CHAYTOR, J. H. (A1909)
409
CHEPMELL, HAVILLAND LE MESURIER, 1810 or 1811-1887
6719
CHESTER, Mrs. Hta. M. (EA1881)
5592
CHETWYND, KATH. (E1890)
†1936
CHILDE, Mrs. E: (Fes. C.) (E1871)
†A385
CHISHOLM, H: (i.e. G:) GOUDIE, 1850-
3530
CHITTENDEN, R: Handy, 1836-
7376
CHORLEY, H: FOTHERGILL, 1808-72
5036
CHORLEY, J. R.
Tr. in C372
CHORLEY, W. B. (E1834)
5132, *C373
CHRISTIAN, J. Rob. (E1870)
§869
CHRISTIAN, Princess. See "Princess"
*1969, §4581, 8766.
CHRISTIE, A. M. (E1896)
*4733, *5044
CHRISTMAS, H:, afterward Noel-Fearn, 1811-68
§10141
CHRYSTAL, G: W:, 1880-
*6151
CHURCHILL, Jas. (i.e., Janus) (E1870)
7769, 7779, †8170, C18
CHURCHILL, T. O. (E1800)
*4221
CHURCHYARD, T:, 1520?-1604
A163
CHURTON, ANNETTE (E1899)
*4847
CLAPAM, D: (E1545)
25
CLAPP, AMANDA R. (A1894)
2435
CLARE, LILLIAN A. (E1923)
1858
CLARK, BARRETT HARPER, 1890-
†348, †349, 2146, 8488, C68
CLARK, Fis. E. (A1898)
9324
CLARK, G. (E1901)
†7822, †7873
CLARK, H. (A1863)
§9180
CLARK, L. Pierce (A1927)
1901a
CLARK. T. E. (A1913)
*9018
CLARKE, Miss (A1898)
8865
CLARKE, Mrs. (A1858)
2338
CLARKE, C: Humphrey, 1870-
*1081, *6900
CLARKE, F: (AE1894)
*4570
CLARKE, HELEN ARCHIBALD, d. 1926
*10180
CLARKE, HUGH ARCHIBALD, 1839-1927
*10195

CLARKE, J. B. (E1824)
8122
CLARKE, Jas. Freeman, 1810-88
10111, §C69, C109
CLARKE, Js. THACHER, d. 1920
*7364, *7365
CLARKE, LILIAN REBECCA (A1875)
3088, §C69
CLARKE, Ma. E. (E1923)
*9471
CLARKE, Marg. L. (E1909)
§513, *9541
CLARKE, Sa. M. S. (E1892)
6897, 10675
CLARKE, W: BARNARD (G1865)
†2707
CLAUDY, FRANK, 1844-1919
2633, †2708
CLAXTON, Philander Priestley, 1862-
3233, 6177
CLAYTON, Fis. TREADWAY (A1924)
8983
CLEATHER, ALICE Leighton (E1903)
9690
CLIFTON, SYDNEY (A1888)
4688
CLOUGH, Mrs. A(rt.?) H(ugh?) (E1873)
*930
COBB, H: (A1862)
4582
COBB, J: STORER (E1899)
2387, *2948, §A361
COBBETT, SUSAN (E1860)
8613
COCHRAN, J: (E1858)
*1128
COCHRANE, Jas. (E1852)
1284, §2881, §9568
COCKE, (J.) Zitella, 1848?-
4176
COCKLE, J: (E1888)
*6538
CODMAN, ANNA KNEELAND (CRAFTS), "Mrs. RUSSELL CODMAN," (A1917)
1657
COFFIN, AMORY (A1867)
6423
COHEN, Rev. A. (E1927)
*5724
COHEN, Gst. (E1891)
*3691
COHEN, HARRIET L. (A1891)
*7635, 7637, 7640, C179, C447
COHN, PAUL V: (E1910)
*1648, 5803, 6816
COKE, C. R. (E1823)
*10154
COLBORNE, RHODA E. (E1877)
§4174
COLBRON, GRACE ISABEL (A1908)
*380, 736, *1256, 3511-3515, *3550, 7415, 8469, 8509, 8511, 9543, 10348, C68, C100a, C179, C447
COLE, CARTER STANDARD (i.e., Stanard), 1862-
§10186
COLE, H: (E1823) ("Summerly, Fx.") 1808-82
5958, *6709
COLEMAN, Alexis Irénée du Pont (A1913) 528, *1383, 4250, 4314, 7718, *8517
COLEMAN, CHAPMAN (A1868)
6444, 1453
COLEMAN, Mrs. Chapman, 1813-91
6391, 6409, 6413, 6419, *6526
COLERIDGE, Art. DUKE, 1830-1913
*1243, 2365, *2607, *3037, 3907, *5440, *6311, †C166
COLERIDGE, MARY Eli. d. 1907
3037
COLERIDGE, S: TAYLOR, 1772-1834
*8174-7, C7, C18
COLLES, J: MAYNE (E1893)
7188
COLLET-SANDERS, W. (E1926)
7564a
COLLIER, J. PAYNE, 1789-1883
*7955, *7972
COLLINGWOOD, J. F: (E1864)
*830
COLLINS, ADRIAN (E1910)
6816, §6880
COLLINS, SEWELL, 1876-
8549
COLLISON, HARRY (E1910)
9041, 9044, 9046, 9058, 9060, *9071, 9074, 9079, 9090, 9094, 9106
COLLYER, Js., d. 1776
†822, †5045, 5573
COLLYER, Mrs. Ma.(MITCHELL), d. 1763
†5045
COLMAN, Miss (A1846)
C71
COLOMB, Col. G. H. (E1877)
§870, §7874
COLQUHOUN, W. H. (E1878)
†2709
COLTMAN, G. (E1870)
C132
COLVIN, SIDNEY, 1845-1927
*10345
COLVIN, SOPHY G. (E1896)
*7618
COMMON, T: (E1899)
6815, 6816, 6829, *6836, *6838, 6842, *6852

COMYN, A. (E1898)
610
CONANT, Mrs. Hanna O'Brien (Chaplin), 1809-65
6749, 6779, 6782, 6799, 6805
CONDER, E. V. (A1889)
1303, 4047
CONDUIT, E. W. (A1888)
*10062
CONRAD, Mrs. H. C. (i.e., D.) (A1883)
4446
CONRIED, H: (A1888)
10318
CONWAY, Baron (E1874)
4591
CONWAY, Rev. Jas. (A1892)
§1073
CONWAY, W: Mn., 1856-
*1278
CONYBEARE, F: CORNWALLIS, 1856-1924
*5888
CONYBEARE, Mrs. F: CORNWALLIS (E1886)
*5888, *7732
CONYNGHAM, Lord A. (E1835)
*8884
COOK, ELLEN (E1864)
§2131
COOKE, ANNA B. (A1864)
6997, 10225, 10228
COOKE, CARRIE Adelaide (A1885)
2436
COOKE, REGINALD BANCROFT, 1887-
§7197
COOKE, R. H. (E1859)
*3940
COOKE, T: (E1826)
7743, 10162
COOKSON, G. M. (E1927)
§2710
COOLEY, W: DESBOROUGH, d. 1883
*1485, *7031
COOPER, Cte. FENIMORE (E1852)
*7129
COOPER, J. GILBERT (E1786)
1975
COOPER, W: ALPHA (1905)
*437, *1651
C(OOPER), W(ILLIAM) (E1673)
2336
COPELAND, CONSTANCE STEWART (A1894)
§4275
COPELAND, FANNY S. (G1914)
9639
COPPÉE, ---(A1893)
2437
CORBET, MILES (E1890)
1861
CORBET, Mrs. R. (E1902)
6498
CORBETT, E. K. (A1883)
*5784
CORBETT, Misses (E1828)
1252-3, 6643, 6645(?), C435, C528
CORBIN, ROYAL (A1904)
871
CORDER, F:, 1852-
*9504, 9636, *9644, *9676, *9730, *9748, *9774, *9802, *9822, *9865
CORDER, HARRIET
9639, *9676, *§9730, *9748, *9774, *9802, *9822, *9865
CORKRAN, SUTTON FRASER, (E1867)
3910a, *3911
CORNELL, J: H:, 1828-94
58, 4163, 5570, *6316, *10360
CORSON, CARO. ROLLIN, d. 1901
1501, 9181
CORSON, HIRAM, 1828-1911
Tr. from Heine in 4065
COSTELLOE, B: Fis. Conn, 1855-99
*10595
COTTON, W. C. (E1872)
§970
COTTRELL, C: HERBERT (E1846)
*5678, §8078
COULTHARD, Js., Jr. (E1844)
*4697
COUMBE, CLEMENT W. (A1926)
8931, 8986, 8987, §8992, 9004
COUPER, CATH. M. A. (E1849)
*4688
COUPLAND, W: CHATTERTON, 1838-1915
*3727 .
COURTNEY, W: LEONARD, 1850-
†1818
COVERDALE, MYLES (E1541)
912, 915
COWDERY, Miss E. (E1882)
*7315
COWDREY, CECIL (A1915)
§C73
COX, E: (E1838)
2356
COX, E. M. (E1863)
2595
COX, Fes. Eli. (E1841)
§5969, §C231, §C232, C242?
COX, Fis. F. (E1912)
440, 6661, 6662
COX, G: VALENTINE, 1766-1875
6689
COX, G: W:, 1827-1902
C74
COX, J: HARRINGTON, 1863-
§A362

DANA, C: Anderson, 1819-97
2487, C85, C86, C87
DANDRIDGE, Miss (A1889)
6207
DANFORD, C. G. (E1889)
*7609
DANNREUTHER, E:, 1844-1905
8559, *9628, §9638
DANTON, ANNINA PERIAM, 1878-
*3099, C154
DANTON, G: H:, 1880-
*3099, C154
"D'ANVERS, F.," see D'ANVERS, NANCY
D'ANVERS, NANCY (1876)
§C112, 6261, *7056, *7192, 8531
DANZIGER, Gst. ADOLPHE, 1863-
9576
D'ARCY, H: I. (A1881)
3731
DARE, Ern. (E1886)
3730
DAVENEY, Mrs. BURTON (E1878)
*5130
DAVENPORT, AMBROSE (A1891)
10315
DAVENPORT, Mrs. W. (E1847)
A56
DAVÉSIÈS DE PONTÈS, Mme. LUCIEN (E1850)
*5123, §7355, A222, A254, A316, §C88
DAVIDSON, Norman Jas. (E1904)
§3254
DAVIDSON, RALPH (AE1905)
*10332
DAVIDSON, S. C. (E1844)
*1064
DAVIDSON, T:, 1840-1900
5652, 5653, 7573, 7580, 7725, 7728, 9466, 10276
DAVIES of KIDWELLY, J:, 1627?-93
5997, *6987
DAVIES, WARBURTON (E1834)
†2711
d'AVIGDOR, Countess (E1848)
*5809
DAVIS, Mrs. J. W. (A1888)
*1196, 3733, 4009, 4011, 4019, 4030, 4033, 4037, 4043
DAVIS, Jas. (A1869)
§142
DAVIS, J: Fis. (E1887)
*5096
DAVIS, MATILDA Louisa (E1855)
§3142
DAVIS, MINNIE K. (A1889)
C488
DAVISON, D. (E1843)
*8301
DAWES, RUFUS, 1803-59
7800
DAWSON, E. M. TREVENEN (E1898)
*7381
DAY, H: NOBLE, 1808-90
5452
DAY, Willard Gibson, 1834-
§4196
DEANE, A. M. (E1898)
§7107
DE BENHAM-YACOBY, JULIUS (E1853)
†2314
DE BILLE, TORBEN (A1916)
*9429
DECKER, T: (E1600)
A161
DE GARMO, C:, 1849-
10303
DEIBEL, Mrs. Eli. C. (Hawley) (E1914)
*9482
DEICHMANN, Baroness (E1890)
*9009
de KAY, C:, 1848-
1451
DE LEON, Dl., 1852-1914
300, 4870, 4872, 4889, 4894, §5583, 6109
DELF, H. E. (A1904)
1024
DELFFS, SOFIE (E1872)
*7299, §7709, §7714
DELMER, F: SEFTON, 1865-
§1878
DELONEY, T:, 1543-1600
§2125
DE MILLE, H: CHURCHILL, 1850-93
2095
DEMMLER, Fz. K: F: (E1848)
§3567, *7329, *9532, *9534
DENIO, Eli. Harriet, 1844-1922
*5081
DENNIS, G. Ravenscroft (E1909)
7327
DENVIR, K. (A1915)
7679
DENT, E: Js., 1876-
7753, 9639, §9646
DE PEYSTER, J: WATTS, 1821-1907
1550
DE QUINCEY, T:, 1785-1859
4818, *7432, 7435
DERBY, HASKET (1900)
4040a
DESPARD, Mrs. MATILDA (PRATT) (A1874)
4507
DES VOEUX, Chas. (E1827)
*2980, 8215, §C92

DEUTSCH, BABETTE (A1923)
§C95
DE VERE, Prof. Mx. SCHELE, 1820-98
8833, §8834, §8839
DE VERE, META (A1893)
4363
DE VERICOUR, Prof. (1859)
†3666
DEWAR, E: H. (E1845)
7000, A334, *C96
DE WILDE, L. F. (E1902)
*7161
DEXTER, Art. (A1893)
*4157
DEXTER, C: (E1865)
†C97
DEYMANN, CLEMENTINUS (A1886)
4735
DIBDIN, T: J:, 1771-1841
5347, 5354, 5545
DICK, LAVINIA (E1843)
10551
DICKENS, C:, Jr.
2607a
DICKES, E. W. (E1926)
*9125
DICKEY, Kath. S. (A1882)
4035
DICKIE, Jas. Fis. (G1900)
§A391
DICKINS, Ma. (E1908)
§4390
DICKINSON, GIDEON (A1883)
†C99
DICKINSON, T: H. (A1915)
C100
DICKS, J. (E1885)
8039
DICKSON, W: Purdie, 1823-1901
*6280, 6293
DIGBY, Mrs. J. D. WINGFIELD (1857)
5538
DIGBY, Sir Kenelm (E1654)
40
DINGEE, GERTRUDE P. (A1902)
*9283
DIPPOLD, G: Theo. (A1879)
*2127, 9685
DIRCKS, Mrs. R. (E1897)
*8560
DISOSWAY, ELLA TAYLOR, 1840-95
4453, 7669
DITRICHSTEIN, LEO, 1865-
179, 495, 5590, 8550
DIXON, EDITH (E1872)
*5632
DOBSON, W:, 1809-67
8283
DODD, C: E: (E1821)
†C101
DODEL, F: W. (A1891)
1245
DODGSON, CAMPBELL, 1867-
*5084, *5087, *5089
DOHERTY, D: JESSUP (A1900)
*499
DOLE, HELEN James (Bennett) (A1888)
§263, 275, 8921, 8927-8, 8935, *8958, 8982, 8984-5, *8996, 8998-9, 9000, 9008, 9500
DOLE, NATHAN HASKELL, 1852-
6998, *9306, *9555, 10354
DOLE, Mrs. N. H. (A1914)
782
DOMVILE, Capt. BARRY (E1919)
*8826
DONAT, K: v. (E1912)
*396
DONAUER, CHRISTOPH (E1732)
282
DONELAN, Jas. (E1892)
51
DONNELLY, ELIZA A. (A1888)
5186
DONNER, Hm. MONTAGU (A1913-15)
Tr. from Koerner in C154
DOREMUS, Mrs. C: A. (A1915)
6501
DORNFORD, JOSIAH, 1764-97
*7264
DOUGHERTY, Ma. (E1913)
*7548
DOUGLAS, Mrs. M. (E1805)
§2143
DOWDEN, E:. 1843-1913
2439, *2988, 3628-9
DOWDEN, Mrs. Dickinson (West) (E1906)
*2913
DOWNES, Mrs. MINNA So. Mie. (BAUMANN), 1858-
C103
DOWNES, Rb. P. (E1906)
*C104
DOWNEY, HELEN M. (A1917)
*1892
DOWSON, Ern. CHRISTOPHER, 1867-1900
§6658
DRAKE, W: A. (A1927)
8523, *10008, C308
DRAKEFORD, D. J. P. (E1847)
A140
DRESEN, H. G. (A1885)
6336
DREW, Ma. Fes. (E1881)
*A387
DRINKWATER-BETHUNE, J: Eliot (E1835)
*8014, 8015

DROPPERS, GARRETT, 1860-
*8561
DRUCKER, A. (E1897)
*4715
DRUERY, C: T. (EA1913)
*1855
DRUGULIN, W: E:, 1822-79
8326, §8378
DUCKETT, Sir G: FLOYD, 1811-1902
§2634
DUDLEY, MARION V. (A1887)
2440
DUERR, THERESE (A1926)
C308
DUGDALE, Mrs. BLANCHE (A1899)
*929, *9429
DUKES, ASHLEY, 1885-
*4783, *9414
DULCKEN, H: W:, 1832-94
133, *134, *170, 949, 1144,
*4255, 6798, *7089, *7126,
*7134, *C106
DULZO, ROSE (A1915)
1223
DUNBAR, NEWELL (A1892)
2441, 4116
DUNCAN, G: Mn., 1857-
*1920, *5637
DUNCAN, Jas. MARRIOTT (E1828)
§8105
DUNCAN, W: CARY, 1874-
738
DUNDAS, LILIAN (E1919)
*5512
DUNLAP, W:, 1766-1839
4708, 5227, §5253, 5294, 5319,
5349, 8080, 10690, A62
DUNLOP, GEOFFREY (EA1927)
*834
DUNN, Cath. H. (A1861)
§C233
DUNN, ROBINSON POTTER, 1825-67
§C234
DURAND, E. A. (E1874)
9347
DURAND, Lady (E1873)
C107
DURBAN, Miss (E1923)
*9471
DURHAM, LILLA (E1901)
*6329
DUTHIE, W. (E1869)
3005, *3105
DUTTON, MAUDE BARROWS (A1904)
†9980
DUTTON, T:, fl. 1770-1815
†5300, *6702
DUVALL, LINDA M. (A1888)
§C108
DWIGHT, FANNIE E. (A1906)
2083
DWIGHT, J: SULLIVAN, 1813-93
2487, *C44, *C109
DYDE, S: WALTERS, 1862-
*3976
DYKERS, KATE (A1894)
4010, 4028
DYRSEN, Pl. (A1878)
†2405
E., E. K. (E1863)
C110
E., M. C. (E1890)
8861, 8876
E., M. A. C. (E1883)
*1161
EARLE, J: ROLLESTON (E1919)
532
EASSON, HELENA (EA1911)
*7713
EAST, Sir Cecil Jas., 1837-
101
EASTLAKE, Sir Chas. LOCK, 1793-
1865
*2618
EASTLAKE, Lady Eli. (Rigby),
1809-93
5504, 9590
EASTON, Rev. M. G. (E1869)
*5476
EASTWICK, E: BACKHOUSE, 1814-83
*8095
EATON, Dl. Cady, 1837-
§1964
EATON, W: D. (A1878)
7564
EATON, W: WELLS
C201
EBEN, K: Td., 1836-
6250
EBERHARDT, MAX (A1876)
5892, 10612
ECKHARDT, CARL CONRAD (EA1912)
*8252
ECKOFF, W: Jl., 1853-
†4807
EDEN, LIZZIE SELINA (A1870)
7093, 8373, §C113
EDEN, RYCHARDE, 1521?-76
6606
EDER, M. D. (E1914)
*1909
EDERSHEIM, ---
*Hymn in C269
EDERSHEIM, Rev. Af., 1825-89
*1075
EDWARDES, MARIAN (E1901)
*598, *3240, §9025
EDWARDS, H: SUTHERLAND, 1828-
1906
1035, *9345

EDWARDS, Mda. B. B. (E1861)
A29
EGAN, T: SELBY (E1867)
*4078, *4137, §8081
EGERTON, Lord Fis., afterwards Earl of ELLESMERE; see ELLESMERE
EGERTON, SEYMOUR (G1881)
*4538
EGESTORFF, GEORG HEINRICH Cph. (E1810)
5017, §5051, §5061, †7880, §8016
EGGERS, W. J. (G1922)
4964
EICHHORN, C: (E1811)
*2255
EICKMANN, WALTHER, 1872-
8624
EIFEL, ALOYSIUS J. (A1909)
4756
EISEMANN, F: (A1913)
§8470, 9956
EISLER, Mrs. LENA (A1900)
845
ELBING, RAY (A1896)
*2636, 2843
"ELEANOR" (E1800)
*5263
ELGARD, Mrs. (A1872)
6074, 6077, 105?
"ELIOT, G:" (MARIAN EVANS, afterward CROSS), 1819-80
*1570, 4056, 9216
ELIOT, Mrs. HENRIETTA ROBINS (MACK), 1845- 2801
ELIOT, S: Atkins, 1798-1862
6179, 7854, §7881
ELIOT, S: A., Jr., 1893-
9957, §9958, *9959
ELIOT, W. G. C. (E1856)
*6622
ELISCU, FERNANDA (A1906)
9291
ELKIN, ROSIE HELEN, 1865-
*5879, 8615
ELKIND, LOUIS (G1904)
*10246
ELLESMERE, Earl of
§330
ELLET, Mrs. Eli. FRIES (LUMMIS), 1818-87
§7801, 7802
ELLIOT, HUGH S: ROGER, 1881-
3619
ELLIOTT, Rev. Wl., 1842-1928
9336
ELLIS, A. J. (E1873) 4182
ELLIS, Capt. C. H. FAIRFAX (E1873)
A1
ELLIS, F: STARTRIDGE, 1830-1901
A483
ELLIS, HAVELOCK, 1859-
†4117
ELLIS, PHILLIS MARION (E1883)
§2914
ELLIS, VIVIEN (E1917)
†5113
ELLIS, W: ASHTON, d. 1919
*2333, *9624, 9625, §9883, *9902, *10359
ELLISTON, Rob. W:, 1774-1831
10694
ELLISTONE, J:, d. 1652
529, 546, 550, 556
ELRINGTON, J: BATERSBY (E1804)
10149
ELSON, L: C., 1848-1920
*699, §2153, *10572, *10582, *10592, §C115
ELWANG, W: WILSON (1906)
§7039
ELY, TALFOURD (A1904)
*1471
EMERSON, Miss E. C. (A1915)
6814, C179
ENDE, Mrs. AMELIA (Kremper) von, 1856-
3838, 7684, 10130, *10131
ENDEAN, Mrs. J. RUSSELL (E1874)
4591
ENDLICH, EMMA A. (A1896)
†4742, 9028
ENGELS, F: (E1888)
*6120
ENGLAND, PAUL (E1895)
*9230
"ENIS" (E1885)
†C116
von ERDBERG, AMY WESSELHOEFT (E1927)
*4947
ERDMANN, C: (A1794)
4191a
ESDAILE, ARUNDELL (E1913)
§965
ETCHISON, GEORGIA A. (EA1899)
3695
EVANS, C. DE B. (E1924)
*1397
EVANS, E: PAYSON, 1831-1917
*9014
EVANS, EDWIN, 1844-1923
5852b, §9631, §9633
"EVANS, Kath. W." (i.e., Emily VANDERBILT SLOANE) (A1895)
10187
EVANS, P. C. (E1887)
*5096
EVANS, T: WILTBERGER, 1823-97
§4156
EVANSON, W: A. (E1827)
791
EVE, Mrs. H. W. (E1873)
4182, §4320

EVERARD, T: (E1617)
43
EVERETT, Ax. Hill, 1792-1847
§874, §C120, §C121
EVERILL, G: (E1837)
§5901, *5903
EWING, Maj. Ax., 1830-
*4404, *7441, C68
EXNER, A. H. (E1912)
1019, 1038
EYRE, Rev. W. H. (E1898)
4211
EYRICK, G: C. (A1878)
1869a
F., A. (E1865)
C122
F., C. K. (E1873)
†7860, †7888, †C123
F., E. F. (E1842)
*5259
F., J. (E1651)
35, 7030
F., W. B. (E1848)
C124
F., P. (E1592)
A102, A107, A113
FABER, Mrs. M. A. (E1867)
3545, *3675, *3773, *3775, 4450, *10687
FADIMAN, Clifton P. (A1927)
5189, *6858, *10008
FAIRBAIRN, M. DOUGLASS (Miss or Mrs.) (E1896)
3087
FAIRBANKS, Art., 1864-
*7492
FAIRFAX, T. H. (A1870)
1195, 6191
FANE, JULIAN (H: C:), 1827-70
*4079, 7847
FARDELY, W: (E1807)
4613
FARIE, Rb. (E1849)
*2932, 2954, *3919
FARNEWORTH, ELLIS, d. 1763
*1987
FARNIE, H. B. (E1800)
10576
FARQUHARSON, AGNES CRUM (E1908)
§1743, *1751
FARR, Prof. (A1909)
10312
FARRER, W: (E1850)
8293
FAY, SIDNEY BRADSHAW, 1876-
*2094
FEBECK, Baron (E1831)
7823
FECHTER, O. A. (E1903)
6485
FEILING, C. A. (E1844)
*C441, C442, C559
FELKIN, Mrs. Rb. W: (E1888)
*1453
FELLOWES, Rb. (E1806)
2315
FELTON, CORNELIUS CONWAY, 1807-1862
*6209
FENN, F: (E1912)
6985
FERGUSON, Rev. J: W. (E1838)
5454
FERRIER, J: TURING (E1856)
*7383
FIELD, CLAUD Herb. ALWYN, 1863-
§1398, *7297
FIELD, EUGENE, 1850-95
C131
FIELD, LILIAN (E1885)
4764
FIELDING, Mrs. E. (E1889)
*3031
FILMORE, LEWIS, 1315-90
†2712, §8017
FINCK, H: T. (A1903)
§9717, §9733, §9803
FINDLATER, Sa. (Mrs. Eric) (E1854)
§C225
FINLAY, T: A., 1848-
*9154
FIRTH, Mrs. JULIA (E1886)
§3069
FISCHER, H: W. HUBERT, 1856-
6267, *6275
FISHER, I. I. G. (E1817)
*6511
FISHER, W. J. (E1893)
6349
FITCH, CLYDE, 1865-1909
1456, 10192
FITZGERALD, J. (A1873)
9205
FLEETWOOD, E: (E1652)
30
FLEISHMAN, Ca. S. (A1886)
§5829
FLEISHMAN, S. L. (A1876)
†4118, *4131, *C309
FLETCHER, C: Rob. LESLIE, 1857-
†3833
FLIGHT, W. (E1873)
4182
FLINT, F. S. (EA1927)
*2092, *2093
FLORER, WARREN WASHBURN, 1869-
4309
FLORY, Sa. A. (A1875)
5119

FULLER, FANNY (A1864)
*7234, *7387
FULLER, Sa. MARG., afterward OSSOLI, 1810-50
95, *96, §2981, 3039, 3533, C109, §C439
FUNCK, F: (G1853)
*C142
FURLY, B. (E1711)
1175
FURNESS, ANNIS LEE: see WISTER
4527
FURNESS, HELEN KATE (ROGERS), Mrs. HORACE HOWARD, 1837-83
*C309
FURNESS, W: H:, 1802-96
8662b, *10686, 10710, §C143, §C144
FUSSELI, H:, 1741-1825
†10277
FYNES, RANDLE (E1913)
9796
G., A. L. (E1878)
C147
G., E. M. (A1877)
4464, 6771
G., H. (E1721)
23
G., H. J. (E1871)
*6029
G., H. J. M. (E1883)
4585, A212, C148
G., W. A. (E1843)
52
GABE, JULIUS (E1911)
*3699
GAGE, W: LEONARD, 1832-89
3618, *5553, 6449, *9021
GALANTIÈRE, LEWIS (A1927)
9919
GALLETLY, H. CAMPBELL (E1897)
§C149
GALLINGER, Herb. PERCIVAL, 1869-
*5988
GALLOP, G. T. (E1823)
C150, 7814, †7825
GALTON, MARY (A1871)
2027
GALVAN, J: (E1860)
†2718
GAMERRA, SIGNOR (E1811)
†7740
GANDELL, S. M. K. (19-)
9062
GANNETT, LEWIS STILES (A1916)
§1961
GANS, J. (E1826)
1464
GARAHAN, ISABEL (A1926)
5439a, 7620, 7621
GARDINER, J. R. (E1856)
*9359
GARDNER, PETER (E1869)
C166
GARDNER, W: ATKINSON (E1845)
*8691
GARNETT, R:, 1835-1906
3933a, *C151, *C166
GARNHAM, L. W. (G1868)
†4959
GARVEY, MICHAEL ANGELO, d. 1877
307
GASKELL, G: (E1850)
*7193
GASPEY, T:, 1788-1871
*1465
GATH, T. C. (E1905)
3799
GATTY, C: T. (E1894)
9791
GAUSS, CHRISTIAN F:, 1878-
*10237
GAUSS, ERNEST F. L., 1842-1907
7163
GEDEN, Af. Shenington, 1857-
1202
GEDNEY, J. S. (A1885)
3987
GEIKIE, J. (E1887)
C152
GEISER, K: F: (A1927)
1470
GEISWEILER, CONSTANTIN (E1801)
8298a
GEISWEILER, MARIA, wife of CONSTANTIN G--, pub. (E1800)
*4709, *5203, *5265, 9583, A9, C157
GELDART, C. F. S. (E1885)
10548
GELDART, Ed. Mn. (E1885)
10548
GENESTE, Rev. Mx. (E1840)
§6503
GENUNG, C: H. (A1908)
8516, *10349, C366
GERBER, Adolf (A1927)
8710a
GETTELMAN, V: F. (A1924)
1157
GIBB, Prof. J:, 1835-1915
*5982, A229
GIBBERD, J. E. (E1912)
2443
GIBBS, Af. SEYMOUR, 1830-79
*3053
GIBSON, G. G. (A1867)
*2030
GIBSON, JAS. YOUNG, 1859-
*517

GORDON, S: (E1899)
*5125
GORDON, T: (E1840)
§6209a
GORDY, J: PANCOAST, 1851-1908
*1628
GOSSE, EDMUND W:, 1849-1928
*1804
GOSTWICK, Js. 1814-87
†C171, †C174
GOTWALD, W: H. (A1875)
*6795, 6806
GOTZBERG, F: (E1802)
2543
GOUGH, Af. Bradly, 1872-
*1971
GOULD, Kath. (E1892)
1248
GOWA, JULIETTE (BAUER?) (E1848)
*7445
GOWANS, ADAM LUKE (E1914)
†8484, *9430
GOWER, Lord Fis. L. (E1823)
2719, 3713, §8126, §C177
§8249
GRAETER, Fis.
C309
GRAHAM, HARRY, 1874-
4728
GRAHAM, M. E. W.(E1884)
§8367
GRANDE, JULIAN, 1874-
*7522
GRANT, Art. Jas., 1862-
1427
GRANT, Lieut.-Col. F. (E1872)
*6976
GRANT, J: (G1856)
§755
GRANT, J: WYNNIAT (E1865)
†877, †2638, †2721, 7862,
†7901
GRANT, LOUISA KEIR (1848)
A380a
GRANVILLE, PAULINA B. (E1873)
*5625
"GRAPHEUS" (E1875)
723
GRAVES, ALICE A. (A1892)
909
GRAVES, R: (E1779)
†2515
GRAY, Ax., 1882-
3094, *3095, *3096, *6890,
C177a
GRAY, Eli. C:e (Johnstone), Mrs.
Hamilton G--, 1810-87
6521
GRAY, J: (E1898)
*2959, 6815
GRAY, L: HERB., 1875-
*1612, §3030
GRAY, Ma. RICHARDS (A1899)
5496, 8857, 8859, 8863, 8868,
8869, 8881
GREEN, Mrs. (E1812)
5543
GREEN, FRANK W. (E1882)
10563
GREEN, PAULA (A1914)
†3931, §5920
GREENBANK, PERCY, 1878- (A1926)
4866
GREENE, G: Art., 1853-
§6658, C555
GREENE, NATHANIEL, 1797-1877
*5807, 6396, 6403, 6473, *9521
GREENWOOD, F: L. (A1883)
5578
GRÉTOR, W: (G1907)
509
GREY, Ethel (E1874)
C449a
GRIBBLE, Jas. DUNNING BAKER, d.
1906
185, §C180
GRIBBLE, R. T. (E1925)
§182
GRIFFIN (G1873)
§819
GRIGNON, R. S. (A1910)
5950
GRIMM, Rev. EUGENE (A1884)
365
GROS, Eli. (E1807)
3516?
GROVE, ELEANORE (E1870)
†1323, *3009, 3015
GRUMMANN, PAUL H., 1872-
§7586, *3647, §3649
GRUND, Fis. J., 1805-63
*A221
GRUNDY, SYDNEY, 1848-1914
6347
GRUSSI, ALPHONSE M. (A1898)
8432
GSCHWIND, F. (E1922)
*7144
GUERNSEY, Af. HUDSON, 1825-
9340
GUERNSEY, ETHEL (A1890)
9580
GUITERMAN, Art., 1871-
714
GÜLCHER, EDITH (E1913)
§475
GULLIVER, JULIA Hta., 1856-
*10363
GUMMERE, Fis. BARTON, 1855-
A257

GUNLOGSEN, ALBERT (HÖGNI) STAFANSSON, 1839-1918
*3010
GURNEY, ARCHER Thompson, 1820-87
†2722
GURNEY, Js. J:, 1788-1847
C272
GURNEY, MARIE DOROTHEA (E1896)
*8656
GUTHRIE, W: NORMAN, 1868-
2407
GYSI, MAX (E1912)
9056, 9073, 9087, 9097, 9103
H., A. (E1848)
*4505, *7463
H., E. E. (A1869)
7291, 7295
H., E. S. (1874)
†5780
H., J. G. (E1871)
*6029
H., M. (E1870)
10127.
H., M. A. (E1855)
§2982, §C182
H., R. (E1572)
5622
H., S. (A1884)
7311
H., S., "GENT." (E1887)
500
H., T. (E1860)
§2115
H., W. (E1878)
2089
H., Mrs. W. (E1843)
8626
HAAS, J: B. (A1926)
4374
HAAS, Jas. D. (previously J. D. ROSENTHAL) (E1826)
609, 1070, §1132, §1183, 4162, 5168, 6369, *7178, 9406, 9943, *10346c, 10680, §10774, A550, C183
HABERKORN, J:
C269
HADOW, GRACE ELEANOR, 1875-
*5854, *10365
HAGEDORN, HERMAN, 1882-
*5029
HAGELÜKEN, Fz. (E1876)
§7913
HAGEMAN, MAURICE (A1897)
5589
HAGEN, F. F. (EA1884)
§10570
HAGUE, C. (E1902)
*775
HAIRE, NORMAN, 1892-
254
HALDANE, Eli. SANDERSON, 1862-
*3994
HALDANE, R: BURTON, 1857-
*8584
HALE, Mrs. Sa. J. (A1854)
7803
HALES, R: C. (E1859)
§8410
HALFORD, J. (E1866)
2844
HALIBURTON, Marg. WINIFRED (A1900)
3233
HALL, Mrs. ANGUS W. (E1885)
6898
HALL, C: H: (E1820)
4579
HALL, GRANVILLE STANLEY, 1846-1924
7579, 7582-4
HALL, Mrs. Jas. (AE1849)
7804
HALL, M. (E1884)
6239
HALL, Mrs. Sa. J. (A1849)
8331
HALLECK, FITZ-GREENE, 1790-1867
C373
HALLER, Mrs. ADELE (G1852)
†C184
HALLIDAY, J. G. (E1876)
*3934
HALLING, Sl. (A1810)
5050
HAMDON, Mrs. (E1906)
2915
HAMER, S. H. (AE 1907)
9694
HAMILTON, Eli. (E1885)
*5889
HAMILTON, Mrs. Gustavus W. (1907)
*3090, *3092, *3093
HAMILTON, H. (E1893)
6352
HAMILTON, Kath. (A1884)
1217
HAMILTON, L: (EA1923)
611, 4561, 4568
HAMILTON, Mrs. Ma. AGNES (ADAMSON), 1883-
§1877, §6926
HAMILTON, Sa. (E1826)
§1992
HANCOCK, E. (E1883)
163
HANDS, LYDIA (A1880)
A376
HANDSCHIN, C: HART, 1873-
§4917

HANSEN, HARRY, 1884-
*9928
HANSTEIN, J. T. (1857)
*6633-5, *9525
HARBAUGH, H:, 1817-67
4496, C185
HARDER, C. Armin (A1903)
*457
HARDIE, MARTIN, 1875-
5852a
HARDING, J: (E1661)
9515
HARDING, WYNDHAM (E1923)
†9244
HARDMAN, F: 1814-74 (Sometimes falsely called "Francis.")
*4746, *4995, 8728-9, 8735-8, 8740, 8741a, 8742, A236, A250a
HARDY, Ern. G:, 1852-
*8526
HARE, Jl. C., 1795-1855
§1723, *6727, 9374, †9376, *C199
HARK, Js. Mx. (A1887)
5872
HARNED, Ma. (A1898)
*1266, §3837, §3859, §3875, §3901, 7587, *9282, *9292
HARNED, W. H. (A1899)
*9282
HARPER, S. B. A. (A1876)
708
HARRINGTON, E., see STANHOPE, Eli.
HARRINGTON, Eli. STILL (E1875)
§3796
HARRIS, Sir A: (E1896)
A190
HARRIS, J: (E1705)
5999
HARRIS, Jas. RENDEL, 1852-
§5672
HARRIS, Jk. B. (A1899)
†2892
HARRISON, Mrs. M. B. (E1879)
1220
HARRISON, Rb., 1820-97
*7402, †C174
HART, Cte. I. (E1883)
*7095
HART, Eva Freeman (A1895)
10022, 10042
HART, Jas. MORGAN, 1839-
*1234
HART, LORENZ M. (A1917)
102
HARTLEY, C. (A1864)
10386
HARTMANN, Fx., d. 1912 (E1887)
7020
HARTMANN, JACOB WITTMER, 1881-
§6137
HARTSHORNE, GRACE (A1899)
2444
HARTWIG, G: Ludwig, 1813-80
§2916
HARVEY, Ax. 1868-
§6871
HARVEY, BENNET, Jr., 1829-94
C269
HARVEY, EDITH C. (1909)
§403, 7241
HARVEY, ELLA LOUISA (E1846)
§C187, C188
HARVEY, Jas. CLARENCE, 1859-1917
1551
HARVEY, J: WILFRED (E1924)
§7005
HARVEY, Rb. (E1799)
§5751
HARVEY, W. F. (AE1907)
*6955
HARWOOD, ANNIE, i.e., Mrs. ANNE (HARWOOD) HOLMDEN (E1863)
4439, 6756, 6765, C189
HARWOOD, E: (E1776)
5574
HASELL, E: J.
2845
HASSE, EVELYN RENATUS, 1855-
C269
HASTIE, W., 1842-1903
3970, 4778, §4794, *4797, 4800, *4815, *6960, *7263, *7614, *8282
HATFIELD, Jas. TAFT, 1862-
2434, 4696, C154
HAUSSMANN, W: A. (E1899)
6815, 6816
HAVELOCK, H. (E1905)
*433
HAVEN, G: WALLIS (A1836)
*4154, C109
HAVERFIELD, F. (E1909)
*6295
HAWKER, C. E. (E1847)
§2357
HAWKINS, LAETITIA MATILDA, 1760-1835
*6248
HAWTHORNE, JULIAN (A1906)
C190
HAWTREY, Sir C: H:, 1858-1923
6335
HAWTREY, EMILY (1887)
9934a
HAY, Ag. Blanche Marie, 1873-
10263
HAY, C: A:, 1821-93
6695

HAY, C: Ebert, 1851-
5109, 6695
HAYLEY, Hm. Wadsworth, 1867-99
7248, C201
HAYNES, JESSIE (E1895)
*511, *3058, *6944
HAYWARD, ABRAHAM, 1801-84
2379, 2445, 2639, §2723, C191
HAYWARD, H: (E1890)
463-4
HAYWARD, W: STEPHENS (E1825)
68, 70?
HAYWOOD, Fis., 1796-1858
792, †4819
HAZELIUS, Ern. Lewis, 1777-1853
4766
HAZLITT, W:, 1811-93
*5990, *7114
"HEAD, Miss" (Catharine) (E1826)
§5064
HEAD, Mrs. H: (E1921)
1653
HEADLEY, JOEL TYLER, 1813-97
*8754
HEAGLE, D: (A1924)
423
HEARD, J: Jr. (A1913)
§3707, §4551, §4553, 6132, C154
HEARTMAN, C: F. (A1915)
7140
HEATH, E. P. (A1914)
10256
HEATH, ELLA (A1881)
*C192
HEATH, IRMA ANN (A1902)
*9185
HEATON, Mrs. C. (E1870)
*1276
HEBBE, GUSTAF CLEMENS, 1804-93
*8748, §10748
HECHT, DORA E. (E1899)
*1228
HECKETHORN, C: W: (E1889)
†781
HEDDERWICK, T: C: HUNTER, 1850-
*A147
HEDGE, F: H:, 1805-90
*1095, 1107, 1112, 1598, 2640, 5643, C109, §C144, C193, *C194, *C195, C300
HEDLEY, F. H. (E1876)
*878, *C196
HEDLEY, J. H. (E1891)
C139
HEIDEGGER, J: Jas., 1659?-1748
4626
HEIN, Gst. (E1879)
§6509
HEINEMANN, H: El. O: 1864-
*1941
HEISCH, P. J. (E1842)
2248
HELD, Fx. El., 1880-
61
"HELIODORA" (G1843)
§8406
HELLER, O:, 1863-
*5765, *10195
HELLMANN, Mrs. Fes. (A1893)
*4082, *4996
HELM, Jas. I. (A1882)
9031
HELME, Eli. (E1799)
§984, 988, 993
HEMANS, FELICIA DOROTHEA (BROWNE), Mrs. ALFRED H., 1793-1835
2974
HEMET, J:? (E1799)
5398, 5524
HEMPEL, C: JULIUS, 1811-79
7769
HENDERSON, Ern. Flagg, 1861-
§1925
HENDERSON, G: F. R., 1854-1903
*9111
HENDERSON, J: (E1870)
4886, 4494, 4584, 4597, A537
HENDERSON, W: Jas.,1855-
§9704, §9871
HENDRICK, WELLAND (A1888)
358
HENDRICKS, H.
8543
HENDY, F: Jas. Rb., 1858-
6284
HENEAGE, C: (E1875)
*9356
HENKEL, LILY (A1895)
*9258
HENNINGSEN, Miss (E1838)
9476
HENRY, Ag. (E1890)
§3781
HENRY, E. L. (E1866)
C197
HEPNER, ADOLPH (A1897)
2641
HERBERT, Js. W. (A1908)
§1258, 10270, §4736
HERBERT, Ma. Eli. Lady (E1874)
3642, *4619
HERBERT, MARY Eli. (1875)
3710
HERBERT, MAY (E1888)
§8683, §8686
HERBERT, W: dean of Manchester, 1778-1847
§C198
HERFORD, C. H. (E1927)
C198a

HERFORD, OLIVER, 1863-
1458
HERFORD, W: H: (E1902)
3771
HERMS, Ma. (A1892)
*6265, 6269
HERON, R: (E1799)
5303
HERON, Rb., 1764-1807
6735
HERRICK, Ma. E. (A1921)
§510
HERRIES, J: C:, 1778-1855
*2158
HERRING, G. (E1907)
*3083
HERSCHEL, Sir J: F: W:, 1792-1871
†879, *7979, *C199
HERSHEY, AMOS SHARTLE, 1867-
*6893
HERTER-NORTON, M. D. (E1927)
*344
HERZBERGER, F: W., 1859-
4780
HERZL, HANS (E1926)
*8456
HESS, F. (A1903)
4316
HESSE, E. H. (A1867)
2030
HESSE-WARTEGG, Ernst v., 1851-
§5904
HESTER, J:, d. 1593
7018-9, 7025
HEWETSON, W. B. (E1809)
8851
HEYDINGER, C. (E1874)
*9012
HEYKING, Eli., 1861-
§4261-2
HEYSER, K. E. (A1884)
7189
HICK, R. (E1855)
*1011
HICKSON, S: (E1849)
§7826, §7905
HIGGINSON, T: W. (A1853)
§C374
HIGHT, G: AINSLEE, 1851-
§1082
HILL, EMILY (E1875)
*1445, §6901
HILL, J. (E1887)
*5150, *6990
HILLEBRAND, Mme. K: (E1889)
*8562
HILLIER, Art. CECIL (E1895)
§6658
HILLIS, W. B. (EA1925)
7525
HILLS, J: (E1839)
§2746
HINCKLEY, J:, d. 1814
*5849
HINCKLEY, T. (E1800)
9584
HINTON, A. W. (A1874)
§4283
HIPSLEY, W. (E1886)
1798
HIRSCHFELD, P. C. (E1838)
5479, 5951-2
HITJER, B. (E1885)
A554
HOARE, WALTER, Prince, 1755-1834
§5205
HODDAM, -(A1860)
3073
HODGES, C: (E1836)
†2642, †C202
HODGES, E:, 1796-1867
§7612
HODGETTS, E: Art. BRAYLEY, 1859-
*10472
HOERNLÉ, AG. WINIFRED (TUCKER) (EA1916)
9058
HOERNLÉ, Rld. F: Af. (EA 1916)
9058
HOFSTETTER, J: (G1847)
5290a, 5719a, 5735
HOLCRAFT, R: (E1826)
§4388, 5139, 5529, 5561, 7447, 7449, §C203
HOLCROFT, FANNY, d. 1844
†5714, †5752, †10000, C204
HOLCROFT, T:, 1745-1809
§745, †1462, *1974, §2135, 2150, §2865, †2893, *9159, 9435, 9509, C204
HOLE, E. S. (E1922)
4239
HOLLAND, LUCY E. (E1894)
*7079
HOLLANDER, LEE Milton, 1880-
*9131
HOLLENIUS, L. J. (A1874)
5830
HOLLOWAY, E. W. (G1852)
†A466
HOLLS, F: W:, 1857-1903
*3126
HOLLYBUSH, J. (E1561)
764
HOLMAN, Js. G:, 1764-1817
8062
HOLMES, E:, 1797-1859
§6364
HOLMES, G. B. (E1877)
§7906

HOLMES, J: BECK, 1767-1843
C269
HOLMES, Sa. Eli. (A1891)
§3723, *5994
HOLMES, T. (AE1906)
*9308
HOLROYD, J. J. (E1838)
§5681, 5695, 5699
HOLT, EDWIN BISSELL, 1873-
§6611
HOLT, F: APPLEBY, 1888-
*3766, *4355, 10248
HOLZ, Marg. (A1915)
*9254
HOOD, BASIL C: WILLETT, 1864-1917
10268c
HOOLE, C: H. (E1875)
§C205
HOOPER, Mrs. LUCY HAMILTON (Jones), 1835-93
2128, C207
HOOPER, SUSAN T. (A1888)
5940
HOOPER, W:, 1770-1810
†2319
HOPE, ASCOTT R., i.e., ASCOTT Rb. HOPE MONCRIEFF, 1846-1927
*4413
HOPE, F. (E1838)
§10147
HOPE, M. J. (E1891)
*6961
HOPER, Miss M. W. (E1905)
*5, 7405, 7504
HOPKINS, EMMA STELTER, 1870-
8918
HOPKINS, J. H. (A1846)
2487
HOPKIRK, EDITH (A1901)
1026, †1027
HOPPIN, B:, 1851-1923
*6712, 7806
HOPPNER, R: BELGRAVE (E1813)
*5484
HORINE, Ca. (A1923)
§4084
HORNE, C: J: (E1905)
†3848
HORNE, T: (E1808)
†1463, *2345, §8098
HORNER, JOANNA B., fl. -1873
5103, *5673
HORNER, LEONORA (E1847)
*5673
HORNING, LEWIS EMERSON, 1858-
§10300
HORNSTEIN, J. G. (EA1912)
§3828
HORROCKS, Mrs. G: (E1848)
*6211
HORTON, ALICE (E1898)
*A365
HORWITZ, CARRIE NORRIS (A1891)
§3821
HOSMER, Jas. K. (A1878)
§C208
HOTHAM, C. (E1654)
559
HOTTEN, J: CAMDEN, 1832-73
A307
HOUGH, WILLISTON S:, 1860-
*1480, §1518, *1629, 1631
HOUGHTON, Mrs. LOUISE (SEYMOUR), 1838-
4452
HOUSE, ROY TEMPLE, 1878-
1384, 1924, *3839, 3843, 3895, *4543
HOVEY, ALVAH (A1854)
*7066
HOVEY, R:, 1864-1900
*3549
HOWARD, A. (A1890)
7304
HOWARD, Af. (E1834)
§5198
HOWARD, BLANCHE WILLIS, i.e., TEUFFEL, BLANCHE W. H. von (A1903)
3517
HOWARD, EMILY S. (A1892)
1505, 7167
HOWARD, W: GUILD, 1868-
*6225, 6227, 9540, C154
HOWE, W. HOWARD (E1833)
*§10743
HOWELL, Jas., 1594-1666
7023, 7024
HOWITT, Mrs. MARY (BOTHAM), 1799-1888
148?, 150, 1012, *3565, §4254. 5094a, *7011, 8370, *9127, 9153, §10222, §C105, *C210, C211, C212
HOWITT, W:, 1792-1879
§1090, §1092, 1096, *1478, 4571, §C213, §C214, *C215
HOWLAND, Art. C., 1869-
6290
HOWORTH, Mrs. J. (E1794)
†3663
HOWSE, Ma. C. (E1902)
907
HUBBACK, Miss C. J. M. (E1922)
*1902
HUBBARD, W. L. (A1888)
9570
HUBER, J. C. D. (E1856)
A264
HUBNER, C: W:, 1835-
§C216
HUCKEL, OLIVER, 1864-
9670, 9712, 9729. 9738, 9767

KING, C:, 1844-
§10181
KING, Fes. H. (A1913)
3036, *3924, 4699, 5027, 7474, C154
KING, H: C. (A1895)
5891
KING, Jas. (E1877)
4468
KING, J: (E1800)
§906
KING, MAUDE EGERTON (HINE), 1867-
*7549
KINGSLEY, E. H. (E1857)
§4263
KINGSTON, W. BEATTIE; see BEATTY-KINGSTON
KINGSTON, W: H. Giles, 1814-80
10429
KINMONT, ELEANOR (A1872)
10218
KIRBY, MAURICE BROWN (A1909)
186
KIRBY, W. F: (E1889)
*2483, 8628
KLEIMENHAGEN, MAURICE (E1911)
*8281
KLINGEMANN, Carl, d. 1862
*4198
KLINGEMANN, So. (G1867)
*4257
KNIGHT, (ELLIS) CORNELIA, 1757-1837
C241
KNORTZ, K:, 1841-
§C309
KNOX, Capt. (E1847)
†2749
KOBBÉ, GUSTAV, 1857-1918
*9901
KOCOUREK, Ab. (A1913)
*6213
KOELBING, Art. (G1919)
4375
KOENIGS, Jl. J. (1884)
*2123
KOETTGEN, Jl. 1877-
A193
KONODY, PAUL G., 1872-
*7034, *7165
KOPLOWITZ, ISIDORE (A1898)
7168
KORTSCHAK, A. (E1927)
*344
KORTZ, J: (A1818)
9409, A286
KRAFFT, HELEN (A1911)
2099
KRAMER, O. (E1905)
9693
KRASINSKI, WALER S. (E1834)
805
KRAUTH, C: PORTERFIELD, 1823-83
*9501
KRAUTH, H. R. (A1881)
10201
KRAUTKRAEMER, Ed. (A1927)
4861a
KREHBIEL, H: E:, 1854-
*337, *6366, *6956, 8465, 8807, *§9785
KRIEHN, G:, 1868-
*6660, *C154(2)
KROEGER, ADOLPH ERNST, 1837-82
1591, 1603, *1604, 1608, *1609, 1614, 4218, 4806, 4826, 4846, 5642, 5647, 5651, 6088, §C310
KROEKER, KATE FREILIGRATH, 1845-1904
785, *788, *4087, *4898, *C311, C312, §7507
KROTEL, GOTTLOB F:, 1826-1907
5631, 9497
KRUEGER, J: FRITZ, 1881-
424
KRUEGER, LUDMILLA (A1898)
8541, 10175
KRUEGLER, ANTHONY B. (A1923)
9116
KUHN, H: (A1924)
*6107
KULLMANN, ELLEN (E1910)
§9557
KUNZ, EDITH F. (A1906)
§8916
KUTTNER, Af. BOOTH, 1886-
801, *1914
L., A. H. (A1894)
8661
L., C. (E1874)
A289
L., C: R. (E1844)
7911
L., H. (E1799)
§6247
L., H. L., see JANE BORTHWICK
§4253
L., J. S. (A1872)
10017
L., M. S. (E1857)
A290
LACROIX, J: Power, d. 1879
*10366
LADD, G: TRUMBULL, 1842-
5881, *5882, *5883, 5884, 5886
LAIRD, J. L. (E1875)
§8832
LAIRD-CLOWES, W. (E1879)
10295

LAKE, Mrs. Eli. COOTE (E1920)
*6533
LAKE, HILDA AMELIA (E1920)
*6533
LALOR, J: Js., d. 1899
*4710, §6902, 6910
LAMB, ANTHONY (A1857)
*527
LAMBERT, C: R. (E1850)
§C313
LAMBERT, Jas. FRANKLIN, 1863-
*5971
LAMBERT, R: S. (E1923)
4608
LAMOND, E. M. (E1913)
*3506
LANCASTER, Mrs. J. M. (A1907)
2101, C447
LANDER, Sa. West (A1861)
4895, 7232, A293, C314
LANDER, W: (E1846)
*3804
LANDMANN, D. (E1891)
§6620
LANDSTONE, HETTY (E1927)
*8521
LANE, PAULINE C. (EA1887)
5627a
LANE, Mrs. J: (née ANNA EICHBERG)
(AE1906)
8655
LANG, ELSIE M. (E1926)
8471
LANGENAU, Baroness (E1886)
6047
LANGLEY, Af. GIDEON (EA1879)
5648
LANGLEY, P: (A1868)
§6385
LANKESTER, EDWIN RAY, 1847-
3608
LANSDALE, Ma. GOWEN (A1903)
*1166
LAPE, ESTHER EVERETT (A1911)
§1881
LASSELL, Caro. (E1873)
*810
LASSELL, Jane (E1873)
*810
LATCHMORE, J. (E1881)
4594, §6775
LATHAM, Ab. G:, 1864-
†2750, *8216
LATHROP, Ca. M. (A1906)
2215
LATHROP, ELISE L. (A1890)
385, 387, 978, 1503, 1507,
1511, 4016, 4022, 4038, *8644,
8648
LATROBE, B. H. (E1788)
§1975?
LA TROBE, CHRISTIAN IGNATIUS,
1758-1836
*5873, C269
LATIMER, E. W. (1878)
5841b
LATTA, Rb., 1865-
*5638
LAUDER, TOOFIE, i.e., Mrs.
MARIA ELISE TURNER (E1881)
A239
LAUER, M. Baroness v. (E1886)
10189
LAUGNER, RUTH (A1926)
10007, §10010
LAURIE, Jas. S. (E1860)
84, 304, 9199, †C315
LAW, Rev. W:, 1686-1761
573
LAWRENCE, Miss EVERETTE (E1885)
6351
LAWRENCE, J. (A1800)
*5295
LAWRENCE, ROSE (D'AGUILAR)
(E1799) *2851
LAWSON, J: PARKER, d. 1852
5989
LAWSON, Robert M. (A1920)
1443a
LAWSON, Sa. J. I. (A1927) 4569
LAWSON, WALTER E. (E1880)
*3687
LAWTON, W: CRANSTON, 1853-
*3698, *3702
LAZARUS, EMMA, 1849-87
4057, 4058, *4089
LAZELL, LOUISE T. (A1914)
4240
LEA, H: C:, 1825-1909
§C316
LEDERER, ALISON M., 1879-
9252
LEADREYT, M. C. (A1870) §2000
LEAKE, R. (E1901)
§2408
LEARNED, MARION DEXTER, 1857-
1917
*8846
LEDIARD, T:, 1685-1743
*6131
LEE, Mrs. ELIZA BUCKMINSTER,
1794-1864
§131, §3113, §7458, §7479
LEE, Eli., fl. 1890-
§1461, *6946, 7543
LEE-HAMILTON, EUGENE (E1878)
*2449
LEEDS, W: H:, 1786-1866
6263
LEES, J: (AE1911)
§1078
LEESON, N. (E1917) 1396

LEFEVRE, Ab. (AE1902)
*7045
LEFEVRE, Sir G: W:, 1798-1846
†2754
LEFTLEY, C:, d. 1814
*2473
LE GALLIENNE, R:, 1866-
*9879
LEGGE, Jas. GRANVILLE, 1861-
*C317
LEGGE, ROBIN HUMPHREY, 1862-
*1432
LEIBERT, A. H. (A1916)
C19
LEIGHTON, W:, 1833-1911
§7641
LEINSTEIN, Mme. (E1845)
3424
LEITCH, J: (E1844)
*6522, *6524
LELAND, C: GODFREY, 1824-1903
*1437, *1452, *4050, *4090,
4092, 4127, *4130, 4132, 4134,
4135, *4141, *7717, 8459,
C154, §C318
LEMCKE, H. J. K. (A1870)
4483
LEMON, MARK, 1809-70
§6639, 6646
LEMONT, JESSIE (A1919)
7498
LENTAIGNE, Lady (E1884)
6810
LEONARD, FLORENCE (A1913)
†6257
LEONARD, OSCAR (A1907)
2103, 3528
LEONARD, W: ELLERY, 1876-
*2450, 9245, C100
LEPPINGTON, C. H. d'E. (E1899)
1271
LERMONT, LORENTZ (A1852)
5463, A301, C319
LESLIE, HERBERT (A1904)
†1923
LETHERBROW, EMMA (E1863)
A225
LETTSOM, W: NANSON, 1796-1865
*A366
LEVY, CLIFTON HARLEY (AE1927)
1539
LEVY, Rb. (E1914)
*4095
LEWENZ, MARIE ADÈLE, 1876-
*837, 6920
LEWES, C: Lee, 1843-91
53, *191, *5721, §7406
LEWES, G: H:, 1817-78
2451, §2452
LEWIS, AUSTIN (A1903)
*1475, 4884
LEWIS, CHARLTON T:, 1834-1904
*456, §1869, 6483
LEWIS, Mrs. Eli. ALICIA MARIA (E1886)
§10095, *10096, C18
LEWIS, Sir G: Cornewall, 1806-63
§525, *6520
LEWIS, Mrs. L. P. (A1891)
§1869
LEWIS, MATTHEW GREGORY, 1775-1818
§880, 2456, 7777, 8040,
†8111, 10692, A155, C322, C333,
C335, C357
LEWISOHN, Mrs. ADÈLE GUGGENHEIMER, 1876-
4237, §4249
LEWISOHN, LUDWIG, 1884-
*243, 1540, *1565, *3839,
4358, *5585, 7196, §9243,
9268, *9922, 9929, C363,
*C367
LIBBEY, J: Dan., 1830-92
C269
LICHTENSTEIN, Walter, 1880-
*10796
LIEBE, JULIE (E1888)
*10233
LIEBER, MAXIM (E1927)
C68
LIEBLING, LEONARD (A1908)
*818
LIECHTENSTEIN, Mie. Hte. NORBERTE, Prinzessin von, 1843-
728
LINBERG, HENNING GOTFRIED (A1832)
1571
LIND, J: E. (E1921)
*18
LINDSAY, T: Mn., 1843-
*9489
LIPPNER, MORITZ (E1865)
*C70
LIVERMORE, EDITH (A1908)
§6698
LIVESEY, T. J. (E1876)
§7913
LLOYD, E. M. (E1842)
188
LLOYD, Fis. (E1875)
*5025
LLOYD, HANNIBAL EVANS, 1771-1847
1084, §4704, *6087, *6994,
*7252, *7346, 7348, *8907,
*9589, 10124, 10334
LLOYD, Rb. (E1763)
§5067

LOBSCHEID, Rev. W: (E1861)
8640
LOCHMAN, A: H. (A1870)
7370, A518
LOCKE, (Jas. DEWITT) CLINTON, 1829-1904
10374
LOCKHART, C: G. N. (E1887)
§8188
LOCKHART, J: GIBSON, 1794-1854
6519, *8261
LOCKWOOD, E. H. (A1898)
§8646
LOCOCK, Fes. (E1870)
*1283
LODGE, ADAM (E1841)
7769, 7770, 7779, †8000, 8001, 8157
LODGE, GILES H:, 1805-88
9505, *10279
LODGE, R:, 1855-
*501
LOEWE, Jas. H. (AE1900)
4576
LOEWENBERG, Jacob (A1913)
3972, *3977
LOEWY, Rev. A. (E1857)
5190
LOGAN, W. McGregor (E1824)
*4968
LONG, HELENA (A1895)
279, 369, 371, 4700, 8856, 8862, 8872, C370
LONGFELLOW, H: W., 1807-82
*C44, *C371, *C372, *C373
LONGFELLOW, S: W. (A1853)
§374
LONGWELL, SUE A. (A1875)
3981
LONSDALE, F:, 1881-
4728, 7690
LOOS, Ax. (A1873)
833
LOOS, I. K. (A1883)
*3507
LORD, EMILY (A1885)
§2078
LORD, Hta. Fes (A1885)
§2078
LORD, J: KING, 1848-
4233, 4234, 7533, C200
LORE, LILY (A1926)
§7069
LORENZ, T. (E1908)
*7038
LORIMER, LOUISE (E1893)
*7706
LOSCH, H:, 1823-
†C375
LOSSING, P: (E1831)
103
LOTHROP, HARRIET E. (A1902)
*6112
LOUIS, S. (G1845)
3610b
LOVELL, J: (A1872)
10396
LOVELL, Mrs. MARIA Anne (Lacy), 1803-77
†3669
LOVING, PIERRE, 1893-
†4370, §8472, 8505, †8518
LOW, BARBARA (E1923)
*7141, *7144
LOWDELL, Js. LANGRIDGE (E1869)
§146
LOWE, C:, 1848-
*8780
LOWE, HELEN (A1841)
§6968
LOWE, W. D. (AE1910)
*9320, *10183
LOWE-PORTER, H. T. (EA1924)
1855a, 6005, *9360
LOWELL, Mrs. ANNA CABOT (Jackson), 1819-74
C377
LOWNDES, H: (E1879)
§C378
LOWREY, Mrs. D. M. (A1889)
4013, 10040
LOWRIE, Rev. S: T. (A1886)
§1147
LOWRIE, WALTER (A1914)
8712
LOY, M. (A1869)
1617
LUBLIN, ISABEL T. (E1888)
C379
LUCAS, ALICE (Mrs. H:)
§C380
LUCAS, E: VERRALL, 1868-
9146
LUCAS, Mrs. EDGAR (E1900)
*3234
LUCAS, NEWTON IVORY (E1841)
†8018
LUDGER (i.e. Luedger), ca. 1848-
*4705, *5344, *5417
LUDOVICI, ANTHONY MARIO (E1909)
§1647, 1649, 6816, §6879
"LUIGI" (E1882)
8792
LUKENS, C: J. (A1870)
*848
LUKENS, H: CLAY, 1838-
881
LUNN, BRIAN (EA1925)
§942
LUSHINGTON, A. M. (E1868)
6140

MacLUSH, J: (pseud?) (E1872)
§951
MacMILLAN, Ax., 1818-96
4087
McMURRY, C: Ax., 1857-
8217
McSORLEY, J., 1874-
4938-41
McPHERSON, W: LENHART, 1865-
*6476
MACRAN, H: Stewart (A1912)
*3969
MACRAY, J: (E1827)
§C387, §C388, §C389
McSPADDEN, Js. W. (A1925)
C390
McWHORTER, G: Cumming (A1869)
10732
MAERKER-BRANDEN, A. Pl. (A1927)
1896
MAGNUS, LAURIE A., 1872-
*1971, *§3060, *5802
MAGNUS, MAURICE, 1876-1920
9263
MAHAFFY, J: PENTLAND, 1839-1919
*1627, *4839
MAITLAND, J: Ax. FULLER, 1856-
*8898
MAKEPEACE, T. W. (E1912)
§183
MALCOLM, Mrs. GEORGIANA (E1858)
*1918, *1928, *1938, *1939,
*1944, *5972
MALLON, Mrs. B. (A1873)
9108
MAN, J: (E1563)
6653
MANCHESTER, Art. LIVINGSTON,
1832-
1433
MANDEL, FRANK (A1911)
2099
MANDELBROTE, H. J. (1921)
6208
MANDERSON, Mrs. M. A. (A1871)
4437, 4443, 4455, 4460, 4466,
6784
MANGAN, Rev. Cosby Stopford (E1858)
*7384
MANGAN, Jas. CLARENCE, 1803-49
883, *7922, §C391, C392, §C393,
§C394
MANN, CHRISTOPHER WHARTON (E1842)
†8041
MANN, Mrs. HORACE (née Ma. TYLER
PEABODY), 1806-87
6015
MANN, Jas. SAUMAREZ, 1851-
*8526
MANN, W: Jl., 1819-92
8434
MANNERS, J. HARTLEY, 1870-
8548, 9034
MANNERS, Lady J: (E1864)
§C395, §C166
MANNHEIMER, H. (E1877)
4194
MANNHEIMER, Mrs. LOUISE (A1895)
*7398
MANNING, Wl. S. (G1900)
*1225
MAPLESTONE, ESSE ESTO (A1911)
§A401
MAR, CECIL (EA1910)
§7305
MARBURG, BLANCO (A1909)
10172
MARBURG, GUIDO (A1909)
10172
MARCKWORT, Fd. (GE1837)
†9395
MARKS, F. A. (A1927)
5501b
MARLOW, G: (A1867)
5720
MARQUAND, ALLAN, 1853-1924
1060
MARSDEN, J. (G1881)
*8828
MARSEILLE, F. H. (E1901)
*3715
MARSH, CAROLINE (CRANE), Mrs.
G: PERKINS, 1816-1901
*444
MARSH, Jas., 1794-1842
*4224
"MARSHALL"= (T: HOLCROFT)
MARSHALL, BEATRICE (E1884)
*3235, *9248, §9271, §9284
MARSHALL, CHRISTABEL ("CHRISTO-
PHER ST. JOHN") (E1923)
4605
MARSHALL, Mrs. F. E. (E1879)
*5016
MARTENS, F: HERMAN, 1874-
*1142, §1262, 1637a, 4745,
10310
MARTIN, EVA M. (E1910)
§7615
MARTIN, Jas. (E1855)
8106, *9363
MARTIN, RENIRA H. A. (E1849)
†7923
MARTIN, Sir Td., 1816-1909
2387, 2388, §2394, 2643,
†2759, 2958, 3668, §4096,
4098, 7769, 7779, §8189,
*8218, §C396, §C397
MARTINEAU, RUSSELL, 1831-98
3084
MARTINEZ, ISIDORA (A1913)
*7648

MARVIN, F: ROWLAND, 1847-1918
C398, §C399, §C400
MARWICZ, Fred. de (E1926)
A272a
MARX, F. (E1859)
1488
MARZ, Olga (A1915)
*9254
MASON, C: T. (G1909)
†4557, †10352
MASON, G: (E1807)
79
MASSEY, C: CARLETON (E1889)
*1282
MASSIE, E: (E1866)
†8224, C401-2
MASSIE, R. (E1854)
§5967, §5969, §8900, C242, C243
MATHESON, ANNIE, 1853-
C406-7
MATHESON, D. (A1904)
4229c
MATHESON, PERCY EWING, 1859-
*6301
MATHEWS, Jas. B. (1916)
C408-9
MATTHEWS, EDITH V. B. (A1897)
8454
MATT, Js. (A1916)
*7138
MATTOS, AX. TEIXEIRA L: de, 1865-
*7549, 9997
MATTSON, MORRIS (A1834)
§10772
MATTULLATH, ALICE (A1913)
3061, C196a
MATY, MATTHEW, 1718-76
*9012
MATY, Rev. P: H:, 1745-87
7495
MAUDSLAY, Ma. P. (E1875)
7235, §7236
MAURER, GEORGE PHILIPP (G1840)
†884, †C410
MAXSE, FITZHARDINGE (EA1878)
*454
MAXWELL, Ma. (A1886)
*8650
MAXWELL, PATRICK, 1826-1906
§5758, §5792, §8020, §8225
MAYER, HARRIET W. (A1923)
*9932
MAYHEW, RUTH (G1896)
*4998
MAYNE, ETHEL COLBURN (EA1912)
*592, *5915
MAYO, Marg., 1882-
8534
MEAD, EDWIN DOAK, 1849-
3992, 3998, C300
MEDLEY, GUIDO (E1738)
5174
MEEKE, Mrs. Mary, d. 1818
5053
MEESON, H: A. (E1846)
7926
MEIKLEJOHN, J: MILLER DOW,
1830-1902
*4822
MELCON, H. A. (A1901)
§8961
MELLISH, Js. C:, 1768-1823
2895, *2939, 7769, 7770,
7775, 7777, 7779, 8131?
*8132, §C26, C411
MELTZER, C: H:, 1853-
*3839, §3860, *4549, 7588,
9736, *9761, §9787, *9831,
*9880, *10266
MENCKEN, H: L:, 1880-
6831, 6844
MENDEL, S. (E1886)
3780, *3819, 5012
MENDEL, VERA (E1926)
*9417
MENDES, F: de SOLA, 1850-
4236
MENGE, Rev. J. P. (E1862)
7720
MENZIES, ALLAN, 1845-1916
*7153
MENZIES, Rb. (E1849)
*207, *214, 221, 3072
MERCER, W: (E1861)
C242
MERCIER, Lewis Page (E1874)
5177
MERCUR, LILLIE A. (A1882)
*4740
MEREDITH, Mrs. CHRISTABEL Marg.
(ILES), 1876-
*6687
MEREDITH, Jas. Creed (E1911)
§4834
MERIVALE, (G:) C:, 1808-93
4
MERIVALE, J: HERMAN, 1779-1844
*7838, 7928, *C412
MERRICK, J: MUDGE (A1874)
§4059
MERSCH, Prof. C: F: (A1844)
8730-1
MERTENS, F. C. (G1789)
1000-2
METAXA, G. (E1922)
*9074, 9081
METCALFE, Rev. F:, 1815-85
311, *317, 9545
MEYER, Miss (E1901)
7318

MEYER, MAX Friedrich, 1873-
*4322
MEYRICK, A. S. (E1880)
8706
MEZ, J: R:, 1886-
402, 1957, 1960
MIALL, BERNARD (A1921)
404, *461, 1229, *1499, 5095, 10240
MICHAELIS, EMILIE (A1886)
*2067
MICHAELIS, J: D: see SCHLICHTEGROLL, Ad.
MICHAELIS, KATE WOODBRIDGE (A1888)
6744
MICHAELIS, OTHO Ern., 1843-90
6744
MICHELS, Mrs. M. L. (A1879)
§7510
MIDDLEMORE, S. G. C. (A1878)
*934
MIDDLETON, EDDA (A1858)
†3115
MILLAR, Jas. (E1910)
*9175, *9178, *9179, *9192, *9194
MILLER, HETTIE E. (A1889)
366, 1216, 2025, 4020, 4039, 4045, 6024, 6048, 6071, 7501, †9255, 9421, 9577, 9594, 10033, §10052
MILLER, J. (A1836)
8427
MILLER, Theo. A:, 1885-
§3104
MILLINGTON, ELLEN J. (E1849)
§8259
MILLS, Art. (E1876)
7839
MILLS, H: (A1856)
*C244
MILMAN, Art., 1829-
*5172
MILNER, H: M. (E1819)
A421
MILNES, R: MONCKTON, 1809-85
C67
MILTON, J:, 1608-74
815
MINSHULL, J. (AE1881)
*5014
MIRSKI, Prince C. C. (AE1927)
977
MITCHELL, C: AINSWORTH, 1867-
4366
MITCHELL, Ma. A. (A1888)
729, 1023, *4733
MITCHELL, RUTH COMFORT (afterward YOUNG) (A1915)
5580, 9578
MOENS, S. B. (E1817)
5875
MOFFATT, Jas. (AE1904)
*3718
MOIR, G:, 1800-70
7758, *8099, *8190
MOLINE, ANNA (E1844)
1059
MOLLE, J: (E1621)
980
MOLTHER, Philip H:, 1714-80
C269
MONAHAN, M. (A1923)
4060
MONCRIEFF, W: T:, 1794-1857
5370
MONTAGU, M. (E1839)
†7931
"MONTCLAIR, J. W.," i.e., WEIDEMEYER, J: W:, 1819-96
C413, *C414, *C415
MONTGOMERY, G: REDINGTON, 1870-
5639
MONTGOMERY, W:, 1871-
8716, 8719, *8897, *9472
MONTOLIEU, Mrs. ISABELLE, i.e., Eli. JEANNE PAULINE POLIER DE, 1751-1832
5062, 5538
MOORE, Mrs. ANNIE AUBERTINE (WOODWARD); see "AUBER FORESTIER"
MOORE, G: GREVILLE (E1881)
3390, †5619
MOORE, H: KEATLEY (E1889)
*2067
MOORE, S: (E1887)
*6095, *6117
MORELL, J: Dl., 1816-91
3909, *4853, 1588, §C112
MORELL, J. R. (E1886)
§9333, 9344
MORGAN, BAYARD QUINCY, 1883-
65a-b, 180, 241, 2408a, 3071a, 3839, 3850, 3879, 3898, 3926a, 4152, 4546, 4555, 4902, 4906, 4912, 4920, 4948, 5923a, 6013, 7642a-b, 8512, 9364, C100a, C154, C416
MORGAN, Mrs. ELLA S. (A1882)
3711, 7724, 7721, 7726, 7727, 7729, 10275, C300
MORGAN, Mrs. JANNA A. (A1860)
2616
MORGAN, Mrs. J: PAUL, née VIRGINIA WOODS (G1891)
*9852

"NATALIA, Cousin" (E1841)
C426
NAYLOR, E: Woodall, 1867-
436
NAYLOR, S: (E1839)
§2644, 2951
NEDELLA, W: R. (A1921)
*9089
NEEBE, Js. H. (A1910)
7654, 10615
NEEDHAM, J:, Layland, 1841-
*7622
NEEDLER, G: H: (A1904)
*A370
NEOPER, PAUL W. (A1926)
8450
NESBITT, H: Art. (AE1904)
*1181, 4777
NESS, BERTHA (E1878)
3077, *10020, 10054
NEUENDORFF, Ad. (A1877)
5577, 5579, 7560
NEUMANN, Maj. H: (E1792)
*5244, §10625
NEWCOMBE, Rev. T: (E1763)
2265
NEVINSON, H: Woodd, 1856-
*7809
NEWMAN, Ern., 1869-
*8720, 9639, *9661, *9684, *9722, *9737, *9788, *9808, *9853, *9985
NEWMAN, Fis. W. (E1843)
4614
NEWMARCH, Mrs. ROSA HARRIET (JEAFFRESON), 1857-
*1184
NEWTON, W: (E1875)
*5025, C366
NICHOLL, Mrs. CORNELIA; see "McFADDEN, CORNELIA"
NICHOLS, Ma. PICKERING (E1889)
*A231
NICHOLSON, E. (E1882)
§164
NICHOLSON, FRANK CARR, 1875-
*C427
NILES, M. E. (A1867)
*3732
NIND, W:, 1809-1856
§5079, †C428
NISBET, C: (E1883)
260, 2365, §2470, 2499
NISBET, J:, 1853-1914
§3791
NOA, Lp. (A1876)
2373, §2957, 3580
NOBBE, W: (A1909)
3706, *10193
NOEHDEN, G: H:, d. 1826
*2468, 7777, †8066, §8082
NOEL, E: H: (E1845)
*7437
NOEL-FEARN, see CHRISTMAS, H.
NOEL, Rb. R. (E1840)
*5154, *9593
NOETHEN, Rev. Theo. (A1872)
703
NORCROSS, J. W. (A1882)
10573
NORDLINGER, Ca. (E1897)
*840
NORMAN, Ma. (E1849)
*7394, 9126
NORRIS, Mrs. R. L. (HASSLER) (1882)
10678
NORRIS, Sa. (E1880)
*4133
NORTON, C: ELIOT, 1827-1908
*3029
"NOTLAG, RYAM," see GALTON, MARY
NOVRA, LEWIS (E1879)
1061, 1063, 1840, §3108
NOYES, MINNA B. (A1898)
C431, C433
NUGENT, T: (E1870)
*9422
NUSKE, J: A. (E1850)
§2136, §C434
O., J. C. (E1897)
A384
O'BRIEN, E: Js. HARRINGTON, 1890-
9197, 9198
O'BRIEN, HELEN (E1927)
*4858
O'CALLAGHAN, Ma. (E1886)
*5627
O'CONNER, H: (A1884)
5956
O'CONNOR, Mrs. EVANGELINE Maria (Johnson) (A1876)
8662
O'CONOR, NORREYS J. (A1909)
10105
ODDIE, J. W. (E1896)
†4099
OGDEN, C: KAY (AE1914)
1267, *9512
OGDEN, Rb. MORRIS, 1877-
*4322
OKELY, Fis. (E1772)
1858, 6213a, C269
OKELY, W:, 1762-1824
C269
OLGIN, MOISSAYE Js., 1874-
*1472
OLIPHANT, T:, 1799-1873
8794, §8795
OLIVE, HARRIOTT S. (A1901)
†10170

OLLIVANT, Js. Earle (E1867)
*5179
OMAN, J: Wood, 1860-
*8291
ORAGE, A. R. (E1907)
6832
"ORCHELLE, R. L.," i.e., SCHEFFAUER, HERMAN G:, 1878-1927
6506
ORDYNSKI, R: (A1917)
§4562
O'REILLY, C: W: (E1849)
*10013
OSGOOD, G: LAURIE, 1844-
*1071, 3078
OSMUN, T. EMBLEY, 1826?-1902
4065
OSGOOD, Miss L. (A1846)
7453
OSGOOD, S:, 1812-80
10108
OSMASTON, Fis. PLUMPTRE BERESFORD, 1857-
3988
OSMOND, Miss D. S. (AE19--)
9062, *9075
OSSOLI, Sa. Marg. (FULLER) see Fuller
OSWALD, EUGENE (E1869)
*C440
OSWALD, Fx. Lp., 1845-1906
2177, 7426
OSWALD, Rev. J. (A1871)
7371
OTTÉ, ELISE C. (E1850)
*4638, *4653, *7035
OULTON, WALLEY CHAMBERLAIN (E1800)
2302, †5193
OUVRY, H: Aimé, 1813-99
§1561
OVERBECK, BERTHA (A1891)
§9272
OVEREND, CAMPBELL (E1873)
6794
OVEREND, Mrs. CAMPBELL (E1870)
A195
OWEN, Js. (1820)
§8453
OWEN, OCTAVIUS FREIRE, 1816?-73
5654
OXENFORD, E: (AE1900)
1846
OXENFORD, J:, 1812-77
†886, §1626, 2364, 2365, 2383, 2482, *3041, 4393, 4399, 4463, 4723, *4726, 4983, 5021, 5024, 6648, 7448, 9640, §9762, *C441, *C442
P., A. B. I. (E1847)
§7010
P., C. (A1864)
4167
P., D. M. (E1873)
*10003
P., E. I. S. (E1874)
§C443
P., M. (E1890)
9029
P., R. (1555)
6657
P., W. (E1874)
§C443
PABKE, MARIE, Mrs. Ax. (A1877)
*6641, C444
PACKARD, L. R. (A1880)
*710
PACKE, CHRISTOPHER (E1689)
2334
PAGE, F: (E1827)
7849, 7850, 7851? 7852? †7935, 7939? 7940, C445
PAGE, GREGORY A. (E1913)
808, *3027, *7941
PALM, J: (G1852)
*7755
PALMER, Fis. P. (E1855)
3408
PALMER, G. H. (AE1905)
*7372
PALMER, ROUNDELL (E1864)
C270
"PALMER, W. SCOTT," i.e., Ma. EMILY DOWSON, 1848-
541
PAPENDICK, G: (E1798)
*5396
PARKER, Mrs. (E1878)
*10019
PARKER, L: Napoleon, 1852-
2100, 9281, 9796
PARKER, Td., 1810-60
§C446
PARKHURST, F. (E1653)
7029
PARRISH, FERDINANDA CONSTANCE De C. (E1907)
*9636
PARRY, EMMA L. (A1883)
4465
PARSONS, Ab. ROSS, 1847-
*9626
PARTINGTON, T. C. (AE1921)
328
PATRICK, MAUD LYALL (E1913)
§5490
PATRICK, T: WHITE, 1857-
§5490
PATTEE, LOUEEN (A1909)
*3923

PATTEN, W: (A1907)
C447
PATTERSON, Mrs. ANTOINETTE (de COURCEY) (A1914)
1825
PAUL, B: HORATIO (E1849)
*4653
PAUL, C: KEGAN, 1828-1902
†2768
PAUL, EDEN, 1865-
477
PAUL, EDEN and CEDAR (Mrs. EDEN P--)
253, 5910, *5913, 6107a, *6130, §6174, *6252, 6975a, 7142, *7335, §8477, *9426, 10309, 10311, 10788, §10792, *A586
PAUL, Rb. BATEMAN, 1798-1877
7269, 7273, 9163
PAULL, Mrs. H: H. B. (E1868)
†3150, 10391, †10424
PAYNE, C: ROCKWELL, 1880-
*7143, *7144
PAYNE, J: HOWARD, 1791-1852
5226, 8114
PAYNE, J:, 1842-1916
§4100
PEABODY, Fis. GREENWOOD, 1847-
4353
PEACH, MABEL (E1902)
6498
PEARSON, E: STANHOPE (G1879)
2608, †8138, 8194, †8226, †8022, §C448
PEARSON, PHILIPPA M. (E1885)
§7244
PECK, ETHEL (E1908)
1643, *9110
PENNY, Mrs. ANNE Christian, 1731-84
2318
PERCIVAL, E: LOCKWOOD, d. 1844
†8002, †8139
PERCIVALE, W: (E1703)
7275
"PERCIVAL, J. M."; see SAFFORD, Ma. J.
PEREIRA, Sa. M. S. (E1885)
9357
PERETT, W. (A1923)
1443b
PERKINS, C: Callahan, 1823-86
*1547
PERKINS, F: Beecher, 1828-99
7351
PERRIN, Marshall Livingston, 1855-
*9317
PERRY, E: DELAVAN, 1854-
*7048
PERRY, EMILY (E1840)
C449
PETER, CARL (A1880)
1874
PETER, W:, 1788-1853
†8023, †8140, †8227
PETERS, J: PUNNETT, 1852-
6531
PETRE, MAUD DOMINICA MARY, 1863-
6816, §6821
PEWNELL, H. C. (E1874)
C449a
PHELPS, EMMA M. (A1893)
7639
PHELPS, G: T. (A1904)
§9789
PHELPS, MOSES STUART (A1880)
1525
PHILIP, G:, Jr. (E1888)
4999
PHILIP, Mrs. HERMAN (E1859)
§6667
PHILIPS, J: (E1887)
4273
PHILLIMORE, Sir Rb. Js.,1810-85
†5738
PHILLIPS, Af. R. (E1886)
2846
PHILLIPS, H:, Jr., 1838-95
*1086, §7530, §C450, §C451
PHILLIPS, S:, 1814-54
*3636
PHILLIPS, Sa. (E1878)
10031
PHILLIPS, STEPHEN, 1868-1915
†2847
PHILLIPS, Wl. Alison, 1864-
*9912
PHILLIPSON, Pl. Hm. (A1915)
7529
PICK, Rev. Bh., 1842-
§2170, 5968
PICKARD, J. C. (A1885)
1046, A538
PIERCE, F: E. (A1927)
*C452
PIERCE, H: NILES, 1820-99
6439
PIERCE, J: A. (A1915)
C453
PIERSON, H: Hg. (AEG1860)
§8687
PILLSBURY, WALTER BOWERS, 1872-
5491
PILTER, Rev. W: T. (E1905)
*5110
PINKERTON, Percy E. (1879)
*1274, §3816, *6529, 7780, *10265

PULSZKY, FERENCZ AURELIUS, 1814-97
9621
PURCELL, LYNDSEY (E1849)
*8280
PYE, H: Jas., 1745-1813
†887, 892
QUELCH, H. (E1906)
*6094
QUINIUS, J: G. (A190-)
7298
R., C. W. (E1855)
*8403
R., F. E. (E1873)
3552
R., H. E. (E1873)
3552
R., M. C. (E1857)
A434, †C459
R., W. (A1903)
416
R., W. S. (E16-)
8693
RAAD, NEONE (E1906)
†C460
RAAHAUGE, H. (E1908)
*5939, *9542
RABB, KATE M. (A1900)
6743
RADFORD, Ern: (E1882)
†4101
RADFORD, THÉRÈSE J. (A1868)
721, §6621
RADIN, P. (E1924)
17
RAE, Julia E. St. QUINTIN (E1899)
§7341
RAFFLES, T:, 1788-1863
5055
RAFTER, J. (G1864)
4731
RAHLSON, KURT JULIAN, 1878-
*3928
RAHN, CARL LEO, 1881-
7164
RAINY, Cte. ADA (E1896)
539
RALEIGH, J. (E1890)
*5628
RALEIGH, K. A. (E1892)
7108
RAM, HELEN (E1874)
8457
RAMAGE, CRAUFURD TATE, 1803-78
§C461
RAMSDEN, HERMIONE Ctte., 1867-
3692, §3694
RAND, B:, 1856-
1625
RANDOLPH, S. E. (A1880)
7337
RANKIN, Jas. REGINALD LEA, 1871-
9689
RANSOME, Art. (A1891)
*4235
RAPHAEL, H: (A1885)
§10050
RAPPOPORT, Dr. ANGELO S., 1871-
*10174
RASPE, Rd. Er., 1737-94
*1555, †5770, 5799, 6595,
10547
RAUSCH, EMIL H. (A1917)
7400
RAVEN, ANNA L. von (A1927)
1477
RAWSON, GRAHAM (A1926)
§7067
RAYFIELD, Mrs. (E1806)
10623
"RAYMOND" (1855)
A433
READ, Eli. FISHER (AE1911)
§1881
READE, J: EDMUND (E1840)
†2459, C462
REARDEN, TIMOTHY H:, 1839-92
*C463
RECHT, C: (A1916)
§9366, C100a
REDLICH, MARION A. (A1910)
†3880
REDMOND-HOWARD, LOUIS G., 1884-
†8790
REECE, J: HOLROYD (1925)
*4950, *6150, 6152, *6153
REED, H:, 1846-
1324
REEKS, Marg. (AE1911)
2460
REEVE, H:, 1813-95
2977, §C464
REHDER, C: Ad. (E1890)
4356
REICH, Dr. ADOLPHUS (E1860)
§5774
REICH, El. (E1892)
7686
REICHEL, Rev. Os. Js., 1840-
*10597, *10608
REICHENBACH, ALCIDE (A1899)
10795
REICHMANN, CARL, 1859-
*5825
REILLY, Sir Fis. SAVAGE, 1825-
83
*5917
REINBECK, Dr. (1824)
†8068
REINER, A. M. (A1907)
§7493, §7633, C179, C447

ROSENFELD, SYDNEY, 1855-
†347, *2152, 2355, *10319, *10557, *10591
ROSENGARTEN, Js. G:, 1835-1921
†10, §1420
ROSENTHAL, Hm., 1843-
2118
ROSENTHAL, J. D.; see HAAS (E1828)
*7178
ROSENTHAL, SYDNEY, 1855-
6348
ROSIER, F. W. (A1883)
*7512
"ROSS, ADRIAN," i.e., Art. REED ROPES, 1851-1916
3656, 10268, 10268d, 10273
ROSS, J. ELLIOT (A1922)
*7049
ROSS, R. S. (E1879)
7716
ROSS, THOMASINA (E1847)
*4670, §9479
ROSS, W. (E1836)
*5734
ROSSETTI, DANTE GABRIEL, 1828-82
†888, 3725
ROSSY, MARJORIE (A1925)
§1443
ROST, A. B. D. (E1888)
447
ROTHENSTEINER, J: ERNEST, 1860-
C479, C480
ROTHSTEIN, Td. (A1906)
1231
ROTHWELL, J. S. S. (E1873)
9474, cf. 956
ROUILLON, EMILIE de (E1838)
1089
ROUTLEDGE, EDMUND, 1843-
2238
ROWAN, FREDERICA Maclean, 1814-82
*1232, *8292, *10778, *10781, *10782, 10784
ROYCE, Mrs. Kath. Head, 1858-
*1652, *3926, 4934, §5489, *7810, *10550, *C186, C154
RUDELIUS, R. (A1880)
6350
RUDWIN, Mx. Js., 1885-
3832, C482
RUGE, FRANCISKA
4087
RUMSEY, Ma. C. (E1854)
§9394
RUNKLE, Cath. Bird (A1906)
1210
RUSSELL, Rev. --(E1847)
8334
RUSSELL, Art. TOZER, 1806-74
*5969, C271
RUSSELL, C: W: (E1850)
5655
RUSSELL, Gert. (E1893)
*9341
RUSSELL, Lord J: (E1889)
7777
RUSSELL, T: C. (A1927)
5572a
RYAN, DESMOND (E1856)
3056
RYCE, RYCHARD (E1548)
6655
RYE, W: B. (E1865)
C483
RYLAND, JONATHAN EDWARDS, 1798-1866
§215, 233, 6694, *9361
S., A. (E1876)
4910
S., A. (A1891)
1404
S., A. M. (E1850)
1254
S., B. (E1827)
769
S., C. P. (AE1879)
*9118
S., E. F. (E1845)
*10776
S., E. J. (E1886)
A12
S., G. (E1904)
9622
S., H. (E1847)
§7010
S., H. H. (E1891)
*10616
S., H. N. (E1844)
*3631
S., J. B. (E1845)
§3625
S., M. (A1872)
1194, 1198, 1200, 1219, *4332, 4339, 5664, 8850, 9596
S., M. (E1905)
2462
S., V. (AE1866)
§6527
SABBA, SIMON (1821)
8083
SABINE, Mrs. Eli. JULIANA (LEEVES), 1807-79
*4634, *4651
SABINE, G: HOLLAND (A1922)
*5433
SACHS, ROSA (A1878)
4179
SADLER, E. (E1889)
†3833
SADLER, M. T. H. (AE1918)
9135

SADLIER, AGNES, 1860-
4205, 4206, 4213, 4215
SADLIER, ANNA THERESA, 1854-
6780
SADLIER, Mrs. J. (E1890)
4210
SAFFORD, Ma. JOANNA, d. 1916
*1159, 1215, *1289, *1290, 1297, *1301, 1316, 1317, 1321, 1335, 1337, 1345, 1346, 1351, *1354, 1355, 1401, 1412, 1413, 1508, *1853, 3059, 3644, *3684, 3908, 3913, 4193, *4288, §4330, §4346, 4580, 6397, 6923, 6934, *6945, 6954, 7601, 8657, 8727, 8829, 9535, 9202, 9510, §9556, 9573, 9579, 9595, *9909, 9910, §10016, 10028, 10072, *10178
SAGORSKI, A. (E1845)
*6629
St. A., J. H. (E1866)
8359
ST. CLAIR, H: (A1848)
C484, C485
"ST. JOHN, CHRISTOPHER," i.e., CHRISTABEL MARSHALL, q. v.
St. Simon, Mrs. (A1848)
134a, 147a
SALTER, EMMA GURNEY, 1875-
593
SALVIN, Rev. HUGH, 1773-1852
*7757, *8024, *8142
SAMUEL, HORACE Barnett (E1910)
6816, 8473, 8483, *8487, 8492
SAMUEL, MAURICE, 1895-
4952
SANBORN, FRANKLIN B:, 1831-1917
2463
SANDARS, T: COLLETT, 1825-94
3974
SANDARS, W: COLLET (E1869)
7564a, §9493
SANDERS, C: F. (A1910)
4748a
SANDERSON, Miss J. Burdon (E1895)
*4004
SANDWITH, M. T. E. (E1904)
*439, *809
SANFORD, Jas. (E1569)
26
SANTFORD, Fes.; see VAN SANTFORD
8455
SARGENT, J: Osborne, 1811-91
*3526
SAUNDERS, F: (A1870)
C486-8
SAUNDERS, J: B. (E1840)
*7421
SAUNDERS, T: BAILEY, 1860-
§2963, 3713, *3716, 3721, 8565, 8572, *8576, 8587, 8590, *8591, 8601, *8606
SAVILLE, W: (E1881) *7513
SAWYER, Mrs. Caro. MEHETABEL (FISHER), 1812-94
*4217, *4593
SAWYER, W. C. (AE1904)
8670, 9692, A377
SAXTON, Mrs. IDA LOUISE, i.e., WILCOX (AE1898) 8791
SAYER, Js. (E1748)
7287
SCHAEFFER, C. W. (A1876)
666
SCHAEFFER, S: (A1846)
§4775
SCHAFER, Js., 1867-
†8204
SCHAFF, Ph., 1819-93
C273, C489, C489a
SCHAFFER, AARON, 1894-
5635
SCHEER, F. (E1849)
9552
SCHEFFAUER, Hm. G:, 1878-1927
*4125, *4782, *5005, *5006, *6008, 6142, 6506, 6816
SCHERZER, K: Ritter v., 1821-1903
*7737
SCHIERBRAND, WOLF. v., 1851-1920
450, †4900, *10245
SCHIMMELFENNIG, BERTHA M. (A1902)
*9184
SCHINK, A. (E1798)
§5393
SCHINNERER, O: Pl., 1890-
*9926
SCHIVELY, REBECCA H. (A1869)
473, 1130, 1389, 4428, 4433, 4447, 4495, 5033, 6812, A331, C490, C491
SCHLEUSSNER, ELLIE (AE1915)
§5895
SCHLICHT, Ern. LUDOLF, 1714-69
C269
SCHMIDT, FRIDA (E1882)
*1624
SCHMIDT, J. F. A. (E1858)
9173
SCHMITZ, L. DORA (E1877)
§9141, 2365, 3035, 3610, 7779, *8300
SCHMITZ, LEONHARD, 1807-90
6716, 6717, 6718, 6720, 6725
SCHODDE, Rev. G: H:, 1854-
*1187
SCHOMBURGK, Sir Rb. HM., 1804-65
*13
SCHÖNBERG, J. (E1850)
724, 6323
SCHOTTENFELS, Gert. RUTH (A1909)
5624

SCHRADER, F: FRANKLIN, 1857-
§10268e
SCHREIBER, CARL F. (1927)
100, 780, 4369, *C452
SCHUETZE, MARTIN, 1866-
2098
SCHUMM, G: (A1891)
*5994
SCHWAB, EMIL (A1884)
*10099, *10568
SCHWAB, F: A. (A1887)
*1127
SCHWARTZ, A. H. (A1914)
2102, *9296
SCHWARZE, W: NATHANIEL (A1910)
10556
SCHWETZKY, Prof. O: H: L:(A1905)
4530
SCOGGIN, GILBERT CAMPBELL(A1903)
10001
SCOLOKER, ANTHONY, fl. 1604-48
7645
SCOONES, W: DALTON (E1879)
†2769
SCOTT, M. JEBB (E1915)
A410
SCOTT, Sir WALTER, 1771-1832
†852, 2472, †2853, C357
SCOTT-GATTY, Af. (E1895)
3450
SCUDDER, JARED WATERBURY (A1917)
2117
SEELEY, J: Rb., 1834-95
§82
SEELYE, Jl. HAWLEY, 1824-95
*8694
SEIDL, Fz. X: (G1895)
C495
SELIGMANN, ALICE BENEDICT (AE1914)
§5634
SELLAR, ELEANOR C. (E1897)
*9896
SELLERS, EUGENIE, i.e., E-- S--
STRONG, Mrs. S. A. S-- (E1895)
2111, 10118
SELTZER, ADÈLE SZOLD (Mrs. T:),
1876-
§712, †3840, 5439, †5586, 9242
SELTZER, T: (A1909)
3599, †3840, †3851, *9246
SEMPLE, J: W., d. 1842
§4808, †4811
SENONOYS, IHÕ VERON (E1551)
917
SERNAU, MORITZ (E1853)
2245
SEVERANCE, J. (A1906)
5878
SEYDEWITZ, Marg. v. (AE1913)
1522
SEYMOUR, Mrs. (E1792)
§982
SHACKFORD, C: CHAUNCY (A1869)
*109, §143, 5511
SHADWELL, J: EMILIUS LANCELOT,
1843-
3523
SHAND, PHILIP MORTON (AE1914)
*8514
SHARMAN, K. B. (E1901)
7436
SHARP, Mrs. W: (née Eli. AMELIA
SHARP), 1856-
†4121, §4139
SHARP, W: (E1888)
4061
SHAW, Fes. A. (A1874)
10030, 10053, *10057, §10091
SHAW, Fis. G:, 1809-82
*10745
SHEARS, LAMBERT ARMOUR, 1890-
6003
SHEDLOCK, J: SOUTH, 1843-
*334, §335, §9897
SHEELEIGH, Rev. MATTHIAS, 1821-
1900
§4598
SHEIP, LEVI C. (A1874)
*4267, 4438
SHELDON, E: (1914)
9253
SHELLEY, PERCY Bysshe, 1792-
1822
2623, *2646, *C166
SHEPARD, Wl. Jas., 1876-
*5433
SHEPHERD, ELIZA (G1824)
*7075
SHERIDAN, R: BRINSLEY BUTCHER,
1751-1816
5305
SHERMAN, P. (A1891)
*789
SHIELDS, C: WOODRUFF, 1825-1904
C272
SHIELDS, Mrs. Eli. DOUGLAS
(AE1910)
*9100
SHIELL, ANTHONY G: (E1914)
*2647
SHIPLEY, Art. E. (E1889)
*9993
SHIRLEY, G. E.
C372
SHOBER, Gb., 1756-1838
4774
SHOBERL, F:, 1775-1853
1620, 2293, *2295, *5008,
5057, *5458, *6155, *6249,
6528, A160

SHRYOCK, Mrs. M. A.
6672
SHUCKARD, W: E:, 1802-68
9408
SHUMWAY, Dl. BUSSIER, 1868-
§A371
SHUMWAY, EDGAR SOLOMON, 1856-
5863
SHURLEY, J: (E1681)
A447
SHUTTLEWORTH, Janet; see Kay-S.
SIBER, J. C. (E1801)
*5258
SIBREE, J: (E1857)
*3995
SIEG, W. M. (E1871)
*3682
SIGMANN, A. (A1912)
64
SIGMUND, Js. A. (A1868)
4762, 6189
SILBER, W. M. S. (A1903)
267
SILL, E: Rowland, 1841-87
7340
SIME, Jas. (A1882)
*7811
SIMMONDS, FLORENCE (E1897)
512, *6151
SIMON, D: WORTHINGTON, 1830-
*9011
SIMON, R: L. (A1926)
*8510
SIMON, Rb. A. (A1925)
§8503
SIMON, Mrs. St. (A1853)
*4412
SIMONS, A. M. (A1909)
4876, 4879
SIMONS, MAY WOOD (A1899)
601, 4879, 4882
SIMPSON, AGNES & CARNEGIE (G1894)
*10358
SIMPSON, EDMUND K. (E1903)
422
SIMPSON, HAROLD (E1911)
10268a
SIMPSON, J: Palgrave, 1807-87
4614, 9946
SIMPSON, LEONARD (E1849)
§8241
SIMPSON, NELLIE HAMPSON (E1886)
9109
SIMSON, Fes. H. (E1892)
*3994
SINNETT, JANE (Mrs. Percy) (E1846)
§1595, §5162, *6255, 7122, *7508,
8710
SINNHOLD, W: (A1889)
5588
SIRMIS, A. (E1918)
5822
SKAE, HILDA (E1905)
8848
SKEAT, WALTER W:, 1835-1912
*9494
SKEETE, Mrs. BRATHWAITE (E1892)
§7096
SKINNER, Fes. E. (AE1901)
*7539, §7540, §7542
SKRINE, H: DUNCAN (E1870)
†7945
SLADE, BLANCHE E. (E1883)
§6041
SLADE, E. C. (A1923)
†8495
SLATE, HELEN T. (A1896)
1299, 4041, 4046
SLEE, JANE MARY (E1837)
§5865
SLOANE, EMILY VANDERBILT; see
"EVANS, Kath. W."
SLOMAN, H. (E1855)
3967
SMALL, WILLARD, 1830-1904
362
SMIETON, J. G. (E1882)
1189
SMITH, Ab. (E1870)
§889
SMITH, B: ELI., 1857-1913
8701
SMITH, C:, 1768-1808
5192, 5242, 5255, 5287, 5388,
5391, *5418
SMITH, C: ADAM, 1809-79
4432, 4451, 7294
SMITH, Mrs. C. A. (A1873)
4479
SMITH, C: FORSTER, 1852-
4232, C200
SMITH, D: MURRAY (E1868)
7117
SMITH, DEXTER, 1842-
§10561
SMITH, E. GOODRICH (E1852)
4323, *9496
SMITH, EDGAR (A1911)
505, 9035, 10270
SMITH, Eli., 1776-1806
§5069
SMITH, Mrs. F. H. (A1883)
8336
SMITH, GERARD W. (A1881)
*6219
SMITH, GESSNER HARRISON (A1846)
§5991, 6022, 10025, *10029
SMITH, HARRY BACHE, 1860-
737, 1255, *5667, 9038,
§10258, 10268b

STANWELL, H. B. (A1908)
6738
STANYON, J. Sandys (E1895)
4229a
STAPHORST, N: (E1693)
*7360
STARKE, Mrs. Mariana, 1762-1838
9412
STARRETT, LEWIS F: (A1887)
C309, C503
STEAD, W: T:, 1849-
§*A390
STEBBING, Dr. (E1849)
4689
STEELE, Dr. J.
C166
STEIGER, ISABELLE de (E1896)
1393
STEIN, ADOLPH (A1880)
7559
STEINER, Lewis H:, 1827-92
4436, 4449, 4497, 8394
STEINER, Rev. Pl. (E1901)
*7321
STEINESTEL, EMILY R. (A1875)
4868, 7629
STEINHAEUSSER, Fr. (G1855)
7738a
STEINITZ, Fis. (E1849)
*3657
STENHOUSE, N. (E1825)
1832
STENNING, H. J. (E1919)
261, *323, 328, 4877, 4880, §4883, 4885, 4892, *6093, 6362, *9239, 9240
STEPHANY, HILMAR (A1881)
6332
STEPHEN, Sir LESLIE, 1832-1904
*367
STEPHENS, J. M. (E1853)
2245
STEPHENSON, Ag. (E1876)
*9582
STEPHENSON, EMILY (E1876)
*9582
STEPHENSON, Ma. L. (A1916)
3836, *8480
STEPHENSON, S. E. A. H. (E1877)
*8845
STERLING, Eli. (E1890)
8769
STERLING, G: (A1917)
§4562
STERN, Mrs. META LILIENTHAL, 1875-
*301
STERN, SIMON ADLER, 1838-1904
§119, 122, 126, 169, §4124
STERNBERG, LEVI (A1891)
§8831
STERRETT, Jas. MACBRIDE, 1847-
*3966, 4003, C300
STEVENS, H.
2434
STEVENSON, G. S. (E1924)
*1121
STEWART, Ax. (E1886)
*7153
STEWART, GRANT (A1911)
§3527
STEWART, R. W. (A1904)
4229b-c
STEWART, W: J. (E1857)
†1947
STIGAND, ISOBELLA, S. E. (AE1894)
*9914
STIGAND, W:, 1825-1915
†4062, †C504, †C505
STIGELL, Prof. (E1854)
7271
STILKE, G: (G1915)
4170
STIRLING, Eli. (E1887)
§2106
STIRLING, Jas. Hutchinson, 1820-1909
*4825, *8695
STOCK, COLLARD J. (E1891)
C506
STOCK, J: SHAPLAND (E1862)
§C507
STOCKWOOD, Rev. J: (E1572)
910
STODART, Mrs. J: RIDDLE (E1851)
*7694, *7695
STODDARD, J: L. (E1924)
1552
STODDART, Sir J:, 1773-1856
7777, †8066, §8082
STODDART, JANE T. (E1886)
7598
STONE, NAHUM I:, 1873-
*6092, *6128
STONE, W: LEETE, 1835-1908
*1421, *7490
STORK, C: WHARTON, 1881-
*4560
STORK, ELI. PAUSINGER (A1915)
4178, 8923, 8929, 8932, 8936, 8937, §8962, 8988, §8991, 8994, 9007
STORR, Fis., 1839-
*1466, §4145, 7462, C510
STORR, RAYNER, 1835-1917
*1466, 7462, C510
STORRS, Mrs. CATHARINE H. (A1888)
1293

TAYLOR, EDGAR, 1793-1839
§3133, †C532
TAYLOR, E:, 1642-1729
535
TAYLOR, E: FAIRFAX (E1880)
§1392, *9549
TAYLOR, FLORENCE C. (A1916)
10307
TAYLOR, HORACE (E1914)
*2110
TAYLOR, J: E:, printer, of London, fl. 1840-55
*13, *167, †3135, §3920, 3921, 8296, §C464
TAYLOR, META (E1846)
*107, 155, 157?
TAYLOR, OLIVER ALDEN, 1801-51
*7382
TAYLOR, R:, 1781-1858
*7531
TAYLOR, SOPHIA (E1843)
*190, 2108, 2109
TAYLOR, W:, of Norwich, 1765-1836
484, §898, 893, 2508, 2615, *2923, 5142, 5689, §5771, 7159, 9569, 10135, 10136, 10150, §10153, C7, §C533
TEESDALE, MARMADUKE J. (E1874)
§2897
TELFER, Commander J: BUCHAN, d. 1907
*8248
TEMPLE, Js. (E1861)
*10362
TEN BROOK, ANDREW, 1814-99
*2331
TERRY, C: SANFORD (AE1920)
*1655
TERRY, EDITH (A1912)
§3877
TESCHEMACHER, E: (E1914)
§9790
TEUTHOLD, P: (E1794)
1634
THACKER, ARTHUR GORDON (E1909)
3619
THEIS, O. F. (A1922)
§8474
THESIGER, SYBIL (E1905)
3826
THIEME, CAREL (AE1916)
9137
THILLY, F., 1865-
§7039, 7040, *7046
THIRLWALL, CONNOP, 1797-1875
*6727, 8287, 10166
THOMAS, CALVIN, 1854-1919
2465, *7812
THOMAS, ERNEST CHESTER, 1850-92
*5564
THOMAS, LOWELL JACKSON, 1892-
5897
THOMAS, M. (G1852)
C181a
THOMAS, PAUL BERNARD (A1913)
*134, 3933, 4906, 4912, §8273, *9382, C154
THOMAS, W: GRASSETT (A1859)
†2409
THOMPSON, Miss (E1869)
6665
THOMPSON, Ax. M. 1861-
383, 9567
THOMPSON, B:, 1776?-1816
173, 175, §2970, 4701, 5194, §5200, *5222, §5249, 5268, §5278, *5288, *5293, §5376, *5380, §5387, §5399, †5713, 7393, 8044, †8086, 8625, A495, C18, §C535
THOMPSON, C. (E1903)
9567
THOMPSON, Cte., 1843-
496
THOMPSON, F: (E1923)
3656
THOMPSON, GRACE (E1927)
599
THOMPSON, H:, 1797-1878
§8239, †8029
THOMPSON, J: ARTHUR, 1861-
7008, 9995
THOMPSON, Marg. R. (E1907)
*774, 7008, 9995
THOMPSON, W: (A1904)
§428
THOMSON, Ax., 1763-1803
§5274, 6176, C534
THOMS, W: J. (E1834)
7002, C537
THOMSON, Jas., 1834-82
*4063, *C536
THOMSON (Thompson?) Marg. R. (E1896)
*774
THOMSON, W: M. (E1896)
8593
THORNTHWAITE, W: (E1882)
*1126
THORNTON, E: (G1854)
†8195
THRASHER, J: S. (E1856)
*4643
THRING, E: (E1887)
*C538
THURSTAN, F. W. (E1879)
*3102
THURSTON, HERBERT, 1856-
*8466

TURNBULL, MONICA PEVERIL, 1879-1901
§4107
TURNER, Rev. C. (E1873)
C550
TURNER, CORA LOUISE (A1889)
1509
TURNER, E. J. (E1882)
*2652
TURNER, E. S. (E1842)
*8030
TURNER, Fes. C. (E1894)
*7079
TURNER, F. J. (E1842)
*8030
TURNER, Rb., fl. 1654-65
36, 7014, §7015, 7191
TURNER, S: E. (A1880)
1425
TURNER, W: WADDEN, 1810-59
*7345
TURNER, WYLIAM, Dean of Wells (E1537)
7417
TUSKA, W. J. (A1867)
§3547
TUTHILL, Mrs. LOUISA C:e (HUGGINS), 1798-1879
7059
TWISS, TRAVERS, 1809-97
6729
TWYFORD, -- (A1873)
A427
TYNDALE, J: W: WARRE, 1811-
†902
TYNDALL, J:, 1820-93
4182
TYRRELL, CHRISTINA (E1879)
4034, 6740, *9524, 10034, *10048, 10066, *10074, 10080, 10085, *10087
TYRRELL, G. (E1909)
§C551
TYSON, M. (E1886)
1483
TYTLER, Ax. FRASER, Lord WOODHOUSELEE, 1747-1813
§8046
U. (E1846)
8824
UNDERHILL, Mrs. ZOE DANA (A1887)
1358, 3556
UNDERWOOD, EDNA WORTHLEY (A1921)
7551
UNTERMANN, ERNEST (A1901)
*292, 603, 1230, 5824, *6101
UNTERMEYER, LOUIS, 1885-
*4108, *9418
UPTON, G: PUTNAM, 1834-
310, *1816, 4195, 4364, 4365, 4475, 4476, 4482, 4596, 4936, 5485, 5486, 6215a, *6487, 6906, 6907, 6911, 7205, 7597, 8439-8445, 8616, *9188, 10361, 10617, A378
UTTERSON, SARAH Eli. BROWN, 1782-1851
C552
"V." (E1886)
*4172
VALE, LIONEL (A1902)
4315
VANCE, LOUISA
*7388
VANDAM, Ab. DRESDEN, 1843-1903
*7674
VAN DER SMISSEN, W. H., 1844-
*2828
VAN DOREN, CARL Clinton, 1885-
*3930
VAN EYNDHOVEN, J: W:, 1874-
4238
VAN GERPEN, E. (A1895)
10022, 10042
VAN PRANGH, LIONEL
3838a
VAN RENSSELAER, MARIANA (GRISWOLD), Mrs. SCHUYLER VAN R--, 1851-
9513
VAN SANTFORD, Fes. A. (A1894)
§4281, §4287, §4295, §4318, 8455
VAN STRAALEN, S: (E1899)
§1958
VARENNE, VIVIA de (G1914)
1136
VAUGHAN, -- (E1823)
5959
VAUGHAN, A. G. (E1866)
6390
VEDDER, D:, 1790-1854
A468
VEITCH, SOPHIE F. J. (E1876)
*1170, *1405
VERAGUTH, Mrs. Gert. (AE1926)
9905
VERAGUTH, O: (E1897)
9904
VERE, GUARTERICK (E1872)
3067
VESEY, CONSTANCE (E1922)
*8527
VICKROY, T: RHYS, 1833-
2362
VIERECK, G: SYLVESTER, 1884-
8032
VILLING, Lawrence (AE1906)
*1554
VOCKE, W:, 1839-1907
§7516
VOIGT, ANDREW G:, 1859
8821

VOLKMANN, Mrs. Marg. HICKS (A1883)
8910
VOLZ, J:a (E1903)
*6875
VOLZ, RAYMOND (A1917)
*1193
W., A. M. (E1913)
*9048
W., C. L. (A1870)
7631
W., E. (E1847)
*8612
W., E. F. R. (E1889)
3444
W., J. (E1671)
9519
W., M. B. (A1884)
10718
WACE, H:, 1836-1924
*5943
WADDILOVE, W. (G1835)
*8668
WADDINGTON, R: (E1851)
*519
WADDINGTON, S: FERRAND (E1806)
3055
WADE, T:, 1805-75
C499
WAITE, Art. E: (1893)
9517
WAKEMAN, T. B. (A1911)
3576
WALKER, E. K. (E1926)
*597
WALKER, Kath. KENT (CHILD) (A1865)
4430
WALKER, Rb. Fis. (E1843)
*5660
WALKER, W: (E1615)
55
WALKER, W: R. (A1875)
7581
WALKINGTON, W. R. (E1862)
§8196
WALL, ANNIE (1877)
*346
WALLACE, GRACE (STEIN) DON, Lady, d. 1878
§159, *333, 3124, §3559, §3568, 3569, *4336, *6199, *6365, 6408, *6912, *7012, *7098, *7231, 9944, A281, *C429
WALLACE, W:, 1844-97
*3962, *3964, *3965, §10350
WALLER, HANNAH (E1927)
*2339
WALLIS, J. E. (E1856)
*4110
WALLIS, Rb. Ern. (E1877)
§C112
WALLON, J. (E1855)
3967
WALLY, HAYA (A1912)
*2104
WALSH, MARIE (A1906)
9573
WALTER, Eli. (A1915)
§4545, §4552
WALTER, F. A. (E1827)
*6726
WALTER, W. Js. (E1811)
7740
WALTHER, H. B. ADAMS (A1885)
*294
WAPLER, LEWIS (G1825)
†7994
WARD, Sir ADOLPHUS W:, 1837-1924
*1149
WARD, ANNE WILLISTON (A1896)
§10181
WARD, Rev. Art. (E1891)
8464
WARD, J. H. (A1886)
†C554
WARD, Marg. May (A1908)
*1882
WARD, S: GRAY (A1845)
§2363
WARNECKE, Jn. An. F: (E1765)
*6258, 6259
WARRE, Marg. (E1890)
*1246
WASHBURN, Marg. FLOY, 1871-
*10363
WATERMAN, M. D. (or P.)(A1890)
4026, 6053a
WATERS, W: EVERETT, 1856-1924
1972
WATERS, W. G. (E1927)
§4111
WATTY (WATHY), Miss Ma. W. (i.e., F.) 1894-
*802
WATKINS, F: B. (E1874)
2870, †2900
WATKINS, HEZEKIAH (A1873)
§971
WATKINS, J: WESTROP (G1881)
§4187, *9358
WATKINS, SHIRLEY (A1925)
†8969
WATKINS, TOBIAS, 1780-1855
10713
WATSON, A. L. (E1896)
9686
WATSON, J:, 1847-
*4802, 4837

WATSON, T: (E1517)
749
WATT, Ax. P. (E1890)
8674
WAUGH, Mrs. ELLEN (A1893)
*1379, 3910, §4741, 8660, *9149
WAY, Art. SANDERS, 1847-
§A372
WEBB, GRACE H. (AE1898)
8791
WEBB, Phil. G: LANCELOT, 1856-
4112, §C556
WEBB, T: EBENEZER, 1827-
†2829
WEBBER, AMHURST (E1894)
9791
WEBER, Fis. (E1893)
§1448
WEBER, H: (E1814)
A285, C557
WEEDON, LUCY L. (E1898)
†3228, †3808, †3827
WEIL, Oc. (A1887)
§10587
WEILL, Ralph A. (A1893)
491, 10316
WEINSTEIN, LOUI LALK (A1907)
A232
WEIR, Eli. P. (E1883)
5149
WEISBERG, C: (A1925)
6833
WEISS, J: (L. H.), 1818-79
*2990, 7760, §7763, 8242, C560
WEITBRECHT, Mrs. Ma. (E1872)
7050
WELBY, Fes. ALICE (E1902)
*2020, *5114
WELDEN, C. F. (A1882)
10202
WELLS, Fis. BALLARD, 1810/11-88
§8415
WELLS, M. C. E. (E1890)
8861
WELLS, S. RUSSELL (E1915)
1450
WENCKSTERN, O: von (E1853)
*3043, *8295
WENDEBORN, GEBHARD F: A:, 1742-1811
6613
WENDHEIM, M. V. (G1885)
6222
WENNINGTON, W: (E1800)
19, 5522
WENTZEL, GRACE B. v. (E1906)
*6235
WENZEL, G. A. (A1881)
10212, 10213
WERNAER, Rb. Mx., 1865-
§10198
WERNER, ALICE, 1859-
*10114
WERNER, F: (E1859)
7813
WERNER-SPANHOOFD, A. (A1913)
*8764
WESLEY, C:, 1707-88
C235
WESLEY, J:, 1703-91
C235
WESSELHOEFT, Mrs. MINNA (A1842)
95, *96, 3533
WEST, LEWIS RENATUS, 1753-1826
C269
WESTALL, W., 1835-1903
C561
WESTMACOTT, A. B. (E1879)
953, 969, 972, 974
WESTON, JESSIE LAIDLAW (E1894)
*10338, C68
WETHERILL, H. M. (A1874)
6507
WEYER, O: W. (A1897)
*9632
WEYSZ, HANS (A1910)
§8482
WHARTON, EDITH NEWBOLD (JONES), 1862-
§9269
WHATELEY, STEPHEN (E1738)
7225
WHATELY, Eli. JANE, 1822-93
230a
WHEATLEY, LEONARD ABERCROMBY, 1835-95
†3207, 5924
WHEELER, C. E. (A1900)
†3831, 8479
WHEELER, G. C. (E1927)
*3534
WHEELOCK, LUCY, 1859-
8912, 8981, †9001
WHEWELL, W:, 1794-1866
†903, 2868, †2901, *C199, †C562
WHITBY, H: JAMES (A1908)
*7007
WHITE, Art. Cn. (E1859)
8210
WHITE, C: (G1838)
C466
WHITE, HELENE SCHIMMELFENNIG (A1901)
276, §6229, *6370, *6372, §8970
WHITE, JANE HUTCHINS (A1910)
§8763
WHITE, L. (E1882)
§8145

WINSLOW, W. H: (A1890)
10329, †10330, *10331
WINSTANLEY, LILIAN, 1875-
§1875
WINTER, ELLA (AE1924)
*760, 5107
WINTER, LILLIE (A1913)
*1270, 6971, §9383, C154
WINTER, M. (E1850)
§2906
WINTER, W:, 1836-1917
4317
WINTERSTED, Mr. (E1871)
§10145
WINTERTON, Ralph (E1640)
2166
WINTOUR, CAROLINE (E1858)
§1237
WIREMAN, H: D. (A1853)
§904, 7845, §C571
WIRGMANN, T. (E1871)
†8197
WIRTZ, Marg. CURME (A1909)
§10188
WISCHNEWETSKY, FLORENCE KELLEY, 1859-
6108
WISDOM, J. H. (E1914)
*8501
WISLIZENUS, F: A. (A1912)
*10298
WISTER, Mrs. ANNIS LEE (FURNESS), 1830-1908
*1378, *1438, 2341, 3557, 3703, 3734, 4014, 4281a, 4340, 4527, 4759, 5808, 6014, *6019, 6023, *6027, *6039, 6044, 6049, *6057, 6063, 6068, 6073, 6080, 6999, 7307, 7312, 7374, 8524, *8647, *8651, *8654, 9232, 9233, 9235, 9237, 9558, 10026, 10047, 10063, 10067, 10115, *C195, C572
WITTMANN, SIDNEY A. (E1879)
*3102, 6331, 6333, §6342
WITWORTH, I. M. (E1926)
4734a
WITZEL, C: (G1896)
C573
WODEHOUSE, P. G. (E1926)
3081
WOLCOTT, HARRY RIGGS (A1895)
*1630
WOLFE, Walter Béran (A1927)
18a
WOLFF, HELEN (E1891)
§4032
WOLFFSOHN, LILY (E1878)
*1160, *1162, *1168, §7229
WOLLSTONECRAFT, Ma. (E1790)
§7657
WOLTMANN, E. (E1879)
*3562
WOLZOGEN, Ernst v., 1858-
*10353
WOOD, ANDREW (E1873)
§5781, §7948, §8089
WOOD, ANNIE (E1875)
§6050, 6066, §6905
WOOD, Fis. ASBURY, 1859-
*A258
WOOD, SUSAN (E1887)
7470
WOODLEY, FRANK (E1846)
*3804
WOODS, Jas. Haughton, 1864-
1210
WOODWARD, Mt. (A1916)
-10270
WOOLRYCH, EDMUND (E1837)
*9597
WORDEN, J. PERRY, 1866-
*7949
WORDSWORTH, Eli., 1840-
C235
WORMELEY, Kath. P. (E1899)
†1119
WORSLEY, T:, 1797-1885
§2467, 2978
WORSTER, W. J. Ax. (E1919)
5445 .
WORTHINGTON, LILIAN B. (E1887)
*6206
WRANKMORE, W. C. (G1861)
§2354, §5753, §6056
WRAXALL, Sir F: C: LASCELLES, 1828-65
2207, *5157, *7514, 9619, A157, A567
"WRAY, LEOPOLD,"; see Mme. CLARA (DE PONTIGNY) DE CHATELAIN
WRENCH, GUY Td. (E1913)
6816
WRENCH, Mda. (E1859)
A27
"WRIGHT, ELLIS," i.e., Mrs. ELLEN WAUGH, q.v.
WRIGHT, H: (E1893)
*7429
WRIGHT, J: H:, 1852-1908
C201
WUNDERLI, OLGA (A1924)
8983
WYETH, C: A. (A1854)
8422
WYLIE, JEAN W. (A1889)
4007, 4023, 4229
WYLIE, LAURIE, (E1926)
3081
WYNEKEN, Rev. F. D. (A1917)
9974

WYNESS, Mn. (E1911)
4905, 4907, *4916, C68, *C367
WYNNE, -- (E1766)
7377
WYON, O. (E1927)
4006
WYTENBACH, -- (E1839)
†7950
YARMOLINSKY, AVRAHM, 1890-
§C95
YATES, M. T. (E1906)
3466
YBARRA, T: Russell, 1880-
10238
YEATS, J: (E1870)
*10761
YOUNG, BERTHA, (E1902)
*10191
YOUNG, COURTLAND H. (A1907)
§8494, C179, C447
YOUNG, G:, 1872-
*410, §1390
YOUNG, JESSIE
4442
YOUNG, Ma. J. (E1803)
6679
YOUNGHUSBAND, Fes. (A1883)
10301, 10304, 10306
ZANDER, Herr (E1833)
A158
ZEYDEL, Edwin Hm., 1893-
1182
ZICK, H: (A1905)
8246
ZIEGLER, Fis. Js., 1866-
9955, §9962, 9965, *9966
ZIMAND, SAVEL, 1891-
5820
ZIMMERMANN, Sa. (A1888)
466
ZIMMERMANN, T: CADWALLADER, 1838-
†7951
ZIMMERN, ALICE, 1855-
*480, *4371, *C575-7
ZIMMERN, HELEN, 1848-
1031, *5684, 5687, *5732, 5800, 6084, 6816, *6866, 7636, 9129, *C575-7
ZINKEISEN, FRANK E. (A1902)
7249, 7250, C201
ZIPF, C. G. (A1890)
C491
ZSCHALIG, H. (G1896)
*4998
ZYBURA, J: S. (A1924)
10669

A1